Tanzania

with Zanzibar, Pemba & Mafia

the Bradt Safari Guide

Philip Briggs

Updated by

Kim Wildman

edition
6

www

Bradt T
The Glo

D0235042

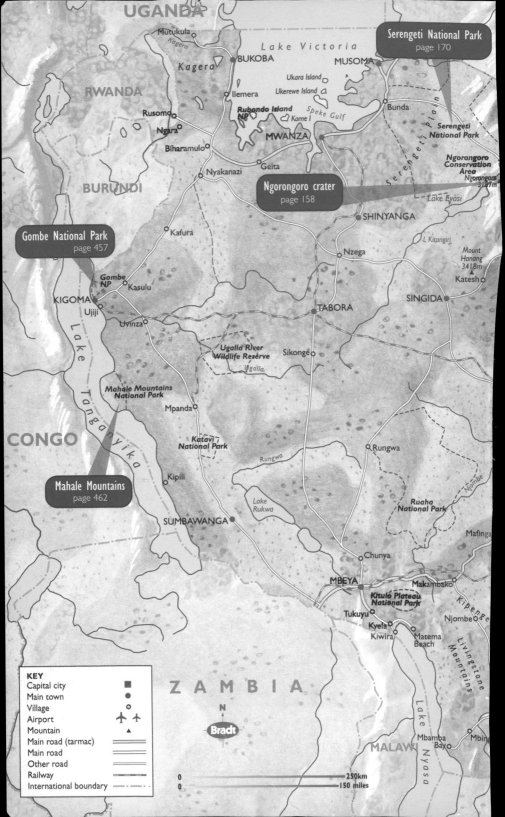

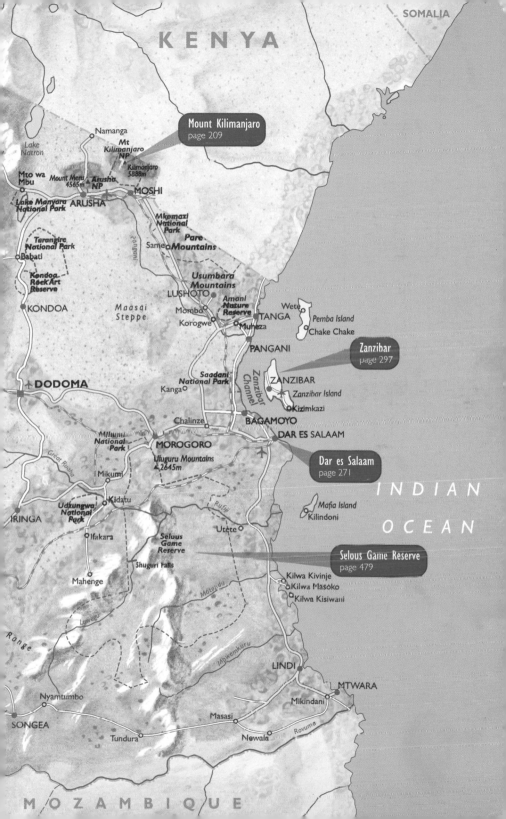

SOMALIA

K E N Y A

Lake Natron

Namanga

Mt Kilimanjaro NP

Kilimanjaro 5888m

Mount Kilimanjaro
page 209

Mto wa Mbu

Mount Meru 4565m

Arusha NP

MOSHI

Lake Manyara National Park

ARUSHA

Tarangire National Park

Babati

Kondoa Rock Art Reserve

Mkomazi National Park

Same

Pare Mountains

KONDOA

Maasai Steppe

Usumbara Mountains

LUSHOTO

Mombo

Amani Nature Reserve

Korogwe

Muheza

TANGA

Wete

Pemba Island

Chake Chake

PANGANI

DODOMA

Saadani National Park

Kanga

Zanzibar Channel

ZANZIBAR

Zanzibar Island

Kizimkazi

Zanzibar
page 297

Chalinze

BAGAMOYO

DAR ES SALAAM

Mikumi National Park

MOROGORO

Uluguru Mountains 2645m

Great Ruaha

Mikumi

Kidatu

Dar es Salaam
page 271

Udzungwa National Park

IRINGA

Ifakara

Rufiji

Utete

Mafia Island

Kilindoni

I N D I A N

Selous Game Reserve

O C E A N

Shuguri Falls

Mahenge

Matandu

Selous Game Reserve
page 479

Kilwa Kivinje

Kilwa Masoko

Kilwa Kisiwani

Luwegu

Range

Mbwemkuru

LINDI

MTWARA

Nyamtumbo

Mikindani

Masasi

Rovuma

SONGEA

Tundura

Newala

M O Z A M B I Q U E

Tanzania

Don't
miss...

Ngorongoro Crater
Its verdant floor is home
to some of Africa's densest
large mammal populations
(SE/MP/FLPA) page 158

Chimpanzee tracking
Chimpanzees in Gombe National
Park — where Jane Goodall
carried out her groundbreaking
research (GE/MP/FLPA) page 457

Mount Kilimanjaro
Reaching an altitude of 5,895m (19,340ft), Kilimanjaro is the highest mountain in Africa
(AVZ) page 209

Zanzibar
Children walking to school along Nungwi beach (EL) page 328

The southern safari circuit
Giraffes in Ruaha National Park – the largest of Tanzania's many national parks
(AVZ) page 506

Opposite

top left Swahili woman standing by a traditional door, Zanzibar (EL) page 297

top right Maasai warrior – every 15 years or so, a new generation of warriors or *Ilmoran* will be initiated (AVZ) page 136

right Tea picker at a tea estate near Tukuyu, the southern highlands (KW) page 525

bottom Tingatinga painter, Dar es Salaam (AVZ) page 289

This page

above Kilwa is home to a fishing community of around 300 people (EL) page 539

right Barabaig bride with circular eye tattoos, wearing a traditional cowhide dress (AVZ) page 406

below Women selling goods to passengers, Soni, Usambara Mountains (AVZ) page 231

above   A UNESCO World Heritage Site, the prehistoric rock art that adorns the Maasai Escarpment north of Kondoa is the most intriguing outdoor gallery of its sort in East Africa (AVZ) page 395

right   The tiny island of Mnemba, off the northeastern coast of Zanzibar, is one of Africa's ultimate beach retreats (EL) page 343

below   The Gereza on Kilwa Kisiwani was built by Omani Arabs in about 1800 (AVZ) page 545

bottom   A balloon safari over the Serengeti offers the chance to see the expansive plains from a new and thrilling angle (EL) page 176

AUTHOR

Philip Briggs is a travel writer specialising in Africa. Raised in South Africa, where he still lives, Philip first visited East Africa in 1986 and has since spent an average of six months annually exploring the highways and back roads of the continent. His first Bradt Travel Guide, to South Africa, was published in 1991; he has subsequently written Bradt's guides to Tanzania, Uganda, Ethiopia, Malawi, Mozambique, Ghana, and East and Southern Africa, and he recently co-authored the first travel guide to Rwanda. Philip has contributed sections to numerous other books about Africa and he contributes regularly to travel and wildlife magazines specialising in Africa.

AUTHOR'S STORY

We go back a bit, do Tanzania and I. Our first stilted encounter was back in 1986, when as a nervous novice traveller heading from Kenya to Zambia, I'd heard so much about the nightmarish black market, appalling public transport and obtuse officials that I decided to nip through Tanzania in less than a week, stopping only to catch my breath in the spectacularly rundown port of Dar es Salaam.

Two years later, I returned to Tanzania on a less intimidated footing, and followed a more adventurous route that incorporated side trips to somnambulant Tanga and the fabulous ferry ride down Lake Tanganyika. But I guess the real romance began in 1992, when I spend four unforgettable months bussing the length and breadth of Tanzania to research what would become the first dedicated guidebook to this extraordinarily diverse – and at the time vastly underrated – country.

Updating duties have recalled me to Tanzania regularly since then, and every time I'm struck afresh at how much it has blossomed over the course of our acquaintance. The Tanzania I first encountered in 1986 was seemingly stuck in inextricable economic decline, with every aspect of its infrastructure, from roads and public transport to electricity and water supplies, tottering on the verge of collapse. Meanwhile, manufacture had ground to a standstill – simply tracking down a warm beer in Dar was an exercise that could take on epic proportions.

Back then, tourist facilities, such as they existed, were barely functional. And an insane fixed exchange rate ensured that travel was dominated by a risky black market. Had anybody suggested that Tanzania might one-day rank as the most diverse, the most friendly, and arguably the best safari destination anywhere in Africa, I'd have thought they were insane.

And how wrong I'd have been… for today, almost 25 years on, that's exactly what Tanzania is!

Sixth edition August 2009
First published 1993
Bradt Travel Guides Ltd, 23 High Street, Chalfont St Peter, Bucks SL9 9QE, England
www.bradtguides.com
Published in the USA by The Globe Pequot Press Inc, 246 Goose Lane,
PO Box 480, Guilford, Connecticut 06475-0480

British Library Cataloguing in Publication Data
A catalogue record for this book is available from the British Library
ISBN-13: 978 1 84162 288 0

Photographs Ariadne Van Zandbergen (AVZ), Eric Lafforgue (EL), Frans Lanting/FLPA (FL/FLPA), Gerry Ellis/Minden Pictures/FLPA (GE/MP/FLPA), Kim Wildman (KW), Suzi Eszterhas/Minden Pictures/FLPA (SE/MP/FLPA)
Front cover Cheetah and cub (FL/FLPA)
Back cover Dhows (EL), Zebra (KW)
Title page Balloon over the serengeti (AVZ), Maasai woman (AVZ), Giraffe (KW)
Maps Alan Whitaker, Dave Priestley (colour map)
Illustrations Annabel Milne, Mike Unwin

Typeset from the authors' disk by Wakewing
Printed and bound in India by Nutech Print Services

UPDATER

Kim Wildman has spent the better part of the last ten years exploring the African continent from end to end as a guidebook author, travel writer and wannabe *National Geographic* wildlife photographer. During this time she co-authored 12 guidebooks including the fifth editions of Lonely Planet's *South Africa, Lesotho & Swaziland* and *West Africa* and Struik New Holland's *Offbeat South Africa*. Moving to Cape Town in 2003, she completed a Masters Degree in African Studies at the University of Cape Town. Her feature articles have appeared in *Travel Africa, abouTime, Planet Africa* and *Voyageur*. Visit her website at: www.wildwriting.com.au.

MAJOR CONTRIBUTORS

Ariadne Van Zandbergen, who took most of the photographs in this book and wrote the photographic tips, is a Belgian-born freelance photographer who first travelled through Africa from Morocco to South Africa in 1994–95 and is now resident in Johannesburg. She has visited more than 25 African countries and her photographs have appeared in numerous travel and wildlife guides, coffee-table books, magazines, newspapers, maps and pamphlets. Visit her website at: www.africaimagelibrary.com.

Chris McIntyre is co-author of Bradt's *Zanzibar*, which has been thoroughly revised and expanded for a new seventh edition. Chris started writing Bradt guides in 1990, and has since written all the successive Bradt guides on Namibia, Botswana and Zambia – as well as numerous articles. Chris now runs the specialist tour operator, Expert Africa, where he leads a team of dedicated Africa-addicts who provide impartial advice and great safaris to Africa, including Tanzania.

Susan McIntyre is co-author of Bradt's *Zanzibar: The Bradt Travel Guide*. Having joined the travel industry professionally in 1999, Susan sought a career focusing on African travel, the area about which she is most passionate. She has acted as a consultant for Expert Africa and has coordinated media campaigns for a number of southern Africa's finest independent safari camps and boutique hotels. She spends several months each year in Africa with Chris, and many more encouraging the press and public to visit.

Christine Osborne, who wrote the original chapter on Mafia Island, has travelled widely as a writer and photographer. Christine now runs the multi-faith and travel image libraries www.worldreligions.co.uk and www.copix.co.uk. She is a member of the British Guild of Travel Writers.

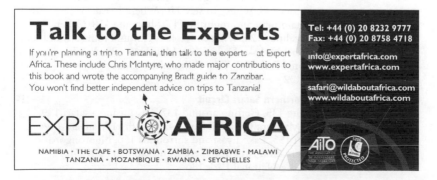

Contents

LIST OF MAPS

Acknowledgements

I've received an enormous amount of assistance from within the safari industry in the course of researching recent editions of this book as well as my Bradt *Safari Guide to Northern Tanzania*. I'd like to express my gratitude to the many safari companies and airlines that have helped ferry me around Tanzania, and to the myriad lodges, hotels and camps that have accommodated us over the years – this would be a poor guidebook indeed were it not for the support and hospitality that has made it possible for me to explore Tanzania so thoroughly over innumerable research trips.

I am also indebted to my wife, travel companion and photographic collaborator Ariadne Van Zandbergen; to Zanzibar experts Chris and Susan McIntyre for writing that section of the guide; to Kim Wildman for her sterling efforts in updating about half the content of this 6th edition; to my parents Roger and Kay Briggs for shuttling us to and from OR Tambo Airport so many times I've lost count; to Reggie Matemu of African Dream Safaris for his driving skills and enthusiasm over the long days on safari; and to various Bradt staffers past and present, notably Tricia Hayne, Adrian Phillips and Emma Thomson.

NOTE ABOUT MAPS

Several maps use grid lines to allow easy location of sites. Map grid references are listed in square brackets after listings in the text, with page number followed by grid number, eg: [156 C3].

TANZANIA UPDATES WEBSITE

For the latest travel news about Tanzania, please visit the new interactive Bradt Tanzania update website: http://updates.bradtguides.com/tanzania.

Administered by *Tanzania* author, Philip Briggs, this website will supplement the printed Bradt guidebook, providing a forum whereby the latest travel news can be publicised online with immediate effect.

This update website is a free service for readers of Bradt's *Tanzania* – and for anybody else who cares to drop by and browse – but its success will depend greatly on the input of those selfsame readers, whose collective experience of Tanzania's tourist attractions and facilities will always be more broad and divergent than those of any individual author.

So if you have any comments, queries, grumbles, insights, news or other feedback, you're invited to post them directly on the website, or to email them to Philip at philari@hixnet.co.za.

KEY TO SYMBOLS

— ·— ·— ·	International boundary	⌂	Hotel, inn, guesthouse etc	⚬⚬	Archaeological site
	National park	Å	Campsite	✚	Hospital/clinic
	Forest park/reserve	♦	Resthouse or hut	✚	Pharmacy
	Tarred roads (town plans)	$	Bank/ATM		Theatre/cinema
═══	Tarred roads (regional maps)	⌘	Bar	✿	Garden
───	Other roads (regional maps)	✕	Restaurant, etc	🏃	Stadium (track)
──────	Tracks/4x4 (regional maps)	☆	Nightclub/casino	♪	Telephone
	Railway	⊠	Post office	♔	Woodland feature
	Railway station	e	Internet access		Snorkel/scuba diving
	Urban market	✝	Church/cathedral	▲	Summit (heights in metres)
	Urban park		Hindu temple		Crater
✈	Airport	☾	Mosque		Glacier
	Airstrip/emergency airstrip	⊕	Sikh temple		Escarpment (rift valley)
	Pedestrian ferry & route		Museum		Footpath
	Bus station		Statue/monument	✕─✕	Barrier/gate
	Filling station/garage		Castle/fortification		Marsh
ℹ	Tourist information		Important/historic building		Coral
		■	Shopping mall/dept store		

Other map symbols are sometimes used. These are normally explained in separate keys on individual maps.

Introduction

It would be easy to reduce an introduction to Tanzania to a list of facts and figures. This vast East African country really is a statistician's dream: within its borders lie Africa's highest and fifth-highest mountains, the world's largest intact volcanic caldera, Africa's most famous national park and the world's largest game reserve, as well as portions of the three most expansive lakes on the continent, one of which is the second-largest freshwater body in the world, another the second-deepest.

When it comes to wildlife, Tanzania is practically without peer. An unprecedented 25% of the country is protected in national parks and other conservation areas. Together, these support an estimated 20% of Africa's large mammal population, and one of them plays host to the singular spectacle of an annual migration of some two million wildebeest, zebra and gazelle. Furthermore, Tanzania has recently overtaken Kenya as boasting Africa's second-longest bird checklist (after the Democratic Republic of Congo), with more than 1,130 bird species recorded, and new endemics being discovered all the time. And as if that were not enough, the three great lakes that lie along Tanzania's borders vie with each other for the honour of harbouring the world's greatest diversity of fish species.

The map of Tanzania may have statisticians salivating, but it will also touch the heart of any poet. It is a virtual litany of Africa's most evocative place names – Zanzibar, Kilimanjaro, Serengeti, Selous, Ngorongoro Crater, Olduvai Gorge, Gombe Stream, Dar es Salaam, Kilwa, Lake Victoria, Lake Tanganyika, Lake Malawi, the Rift Valley, the Maasai Steppe... In short, Tanzania is the Africa you have always dreamed about: vast plains teeming with wild animals; rainforests alive with cackling birds and monkeys; Kilimanjaro's snow-capped peak rising dramatically above the flat scrubland; colourful Maasai herding their cattle alongside herds of grazing wildebeest; perfect palm-lined beaches lapped by the clear warm waters of the Indian Ocean stretching as far as the eye can see.

You might expect a country that can be described in such superlative terms to be crawling with tourists. Yet, oddly enough, until recently Tanzania attracted a fraction of the tourism of countries such as Kenya, South Africa and Zimbabwe. When I first visited the country in 1986, it appeared to be in irreversible economic decline, and tourist arrivals were practically restricted to those backpackers who were crossing between Kenya and southern Africa and had no option but to pass through Tanzania. This dearth of tourism had several causes: an underfunded and underdeveloped tourist infrastructure, a reputation for corruption and bureaucracy, persistent food and fuel shortages, poor roads and grossly inefficient and uncomfortable public transport. Critically, too, Tanzania lacked international exposure – not because people hadn't heard of places such as Ngorongoro, Serengeti and Kilimanjaro, but because they tended to associate these archetypal East African reserves with Kenya.

Today, all this has changed. Modern Tanzania has an excellent tourist infrastructure, and the public transport along the main roads compares favourably with that of most African countries. What started off in the late 1980s as a trickle of tourism, lured across the Kenyan border to visit such big name attractions as the Serengeti, Ngorongoro Crater and Zanzibar, is threatening to become a veritable flood. However, practically all visitors to Tanzania follow the same well-defined tourist circuit, which combines some of Africa's finest game viewing with the historical old town and superb beaches of Zanzibar Island, and those who have two weeks or less in the country rarely stray much beyond it. This is not a criticism – I've visited most corners of Tanzania over the 18 months or so I've spent travelling there between 1986 and 2005, and I have to confess that were my time in the country limited to a couple of weeks, then my first priorities would undoubtedly be the Serengeti, Ngorongoro and Zanzibar. They are very special places.

The important implication of this is that the parts of Tanzania most frequently visited by tourists are also the most atypical in terms of tourist development. It is not improbable that the number of tourists who descend daily into the Ngorongoro Crater would be greater than the combined monthly total of visitors to all the reserves of southern and western Tanzania; just as probable that there are restaurants on Zanzibar whose average daily custom exceeds the number of tourists who make it to the splendid medieval ruins on Kilwa Kisiwani in any given year. In other words, while a few select spots in Tanzania are heavily touristed and well equipped to cater for this, Tanzania as a whole remains a surprisingly low-key tourist destination.

This is of interest to two classes of visitor, ironically lying at the extreme ends of the spectrum. For those seeking exclusivity at a price, the southern and western tourist circuit, which includes Mafia Island, Selous Game Reserve and Udzungwa, Ruaha, Mikumi, Mahale, Gombe Stream, Katavi and Rubondo Island national parks, has generally retained a real wilderness atmosphere, offering quality lodge accommodation and (mostly) fly-in safari packages at a price comparable to an upmarket lodge safari on the more popular northern safari circuit. And make no mistake, these are wonderful reserves, forming a safari circuit that many African countries would kill for. Their relative obscurity is largely due to the fact that they lie in the same country as the renowned Serengeti ecosystem.

With the exception of Udzungwa National Park, the southern and western reserves are rather inaccessible to those on a tight budget, but adventurous travellers who are willing to learn a smattering of Swahili and prepared to put up with basic accommodation and slow transport will find Tanzania to be one of the most challenging, rewarding and fascinating countries in Africa. Virtually anywhere south of the Dar es Salaam–Mwanza railway line (the part of the country covered in Chapter 13 onwards) is miles from any beaten tourist track, and even in the more 'touristy' northeast there are plenty of attractive spots that see little tourism (check out Chapters 8 and 9).

Travel isn't simply about ticking off the sights. When you spend a long time in a country, your feelings towards it are determined more than anything by the mood created by its inhabitants. I have no hesitation in saying that, on this level, my affection for Tanzania is greater than for any other African country I have visited. It is an oasis of peace and egalitarian values in a continent stoked up with political and tribal tensions, and its social mood embodies all that I respect in African culture. As a generalisation, I've always found Tanzanians to be polite and courteous, yet also warm and sincere, both amongst themselves and in their dealings with foreigners.

The one thing I can say with near certainty is that you will enjoy Tanzania. Whether you decide to stick to the conventional tourist circuit, opt to carry a dusty backpack around the southern highlands or charter a plane to go chimp tracking in the rainforests of Mahale, you'll find that Tanzania is a wonderful country.

Part One

GENERAL INFORMATION

TANZANIA AT A GLANCE

Location East Africa, between 1° and 11°45'S, and 29°20' and 40°35'E

Size 945,166km²

Climate Tropical along coast; temperate in the highlands

Status Republic

Ruling party Chama Cha Mapinduzi (CCM)

President Jakaya Kikwete

Population 40,000,000 (2009 estimate)

Life expectancy at birth 50.71 years

Capital Dodoma

Largest city Dar es Salaam

Major exports Coffee, cotton, cashew nuts, sisal, tobacco, tea, diamonds, gold

Languages Official languages KiSwahili, English; about 120 local languages

Religion 30% Christian, 35% Muslim, 35% indigenous beliefs; Zanzibar 99% Muslim

Currency Tanzanian shilling (Tsh)

Exchange rate £1 = Tsh1,988, US$1 = Tsh1,335, €1 = Tsh1,770 (May 2009)

International telephone code +255

Time GMT +3 hours

Electrical voltage 230V 60Hz. Round or square three-pinned British-style plugs

Weights and measures Metric

Flag Blue and green, with diagonal black-and-yellow stripe

Public holidays 1 January, 12 January, 5 February, 26 April, 1 May, 7 July, 8 August, 14 October, 9 December, 25–26 December. See also page 74.

Background Information

GEOGRAPHY

The bulk of East Africa is made up of a vast, flat plateau rising from a narrow coastal belt to an average height of about 1,500m. This plateau is broken dramatically by the 20-million-year-old Great Rift Valley, which cuts a trough up to 2,000m deep through the African continent from the Dead Sea to Mozambique. The main branch of the Rift Valley bisects Tanzania. A western branch of the Rift Valley forms the Tanzania–Congo border. Lakes Natron, Manyara, Eyasi and Nyasa/Malawi are all in the main rift, Lake Tanganyika lies in the western branch and Lake Victoria lies on an elevated plateau between them.

East Africa's highest mountains (with the exception of the Ruwenzori Mountains in Uganda) are volcanic in origin, created by the same forces that caused the Rift Valley. Kilimanjaro is the most recent of these: it started to form about one million years ago, and was still growing as recently as 100,000 years ago. Mount Meru is older. Ngorongoro Crater is the collapsed caldera of a volcano that would once have been as high as Kilimanjaro is today. The only active volcano in Tanzania, Ol Doinyo Lengai, lies a short way north of Ngorongoro.

LOCATION The United Republic of Tanzania came into being in 1964 when Tanganyika on the African mainland united with the offshore state of Zanzibar, the latter comprised of the Indian Ocean islands of Unguja (Zanzibar) and Pemba. It lies on the East African coast between 1° and 11°45'S, and 29°20' and 40°35'E, and is bordered by Kenya and Uganda to the north, Rwanda, Burundi and the Democratic Republic of Congo to the west, and Zambia, Malawi and Mozambique to the south.

SIZE Tanzania covers an area of 945,166km² (364,929 square miles). It is one of the largest countries in sub Saharan Africa, covering a greater area than Kenya and Uganda combined. To place its size in a European context, Tanzania is more than four times the size of Britain, while in an American context, it's about 1.5 times the size of Texas.

CAPITAL Dodoma was earmarked as the future capital of Tanzania in 1973. It has subsequently displaced Dar es Salaam as the official national capital, and is also where all parliamentary sessions are held. Most government departments, however, are still based in Dar es Salaam, which remains the most important and largest city in the country, and is the site of the main international airport, most diplomatic missions to Tanzania, and most large businesses.

CLIMATE

Tanzania on the whole has a pleasant tropical climate, but there are large regional climatic variations across the country, influenced by several factors, most

3

DAR ES SALAAM	Jan	Feb	Mar	Apr	May	Jun	Jul	Aug	Sep	Oct	Nov	Dec
Max (°C)	32	32	33	30	29	28	27	28	29	30	31	31
Min (°C)	25	25	26	26	25	24	23	23	23	25	25	26
Rain (mm)	50	65	140	310	290	45	25	25	35	60	180	135

ZANZIBAR TOWN	Jan	Feb	Mar	Apr	May	Jun	Jul	Aug	Sep	Oct	Nov	Dec
Max (°C)	32	32	33	30	29	28	27	28	29	30	31	31
Min (°C)	25	25	26	26	25	24	23	23	23	25	25	26
Rain (mm)	50	65	140	310	290	45	25	25	35	60	180	135

ARUSHA	Jan	Feb	Mar	Apr	May	Jun	Jul	Aug	Sep	Oct	Nov	Dec
Max (°C)	29	29	28	25	22	21	20	22	25	27	28	28
Min (°C)	10	12	12	14	11	10	10	9	9	10	10	10
Rain (mm)	50	85	180	350	205	20	10	15	15	20	105	100

MOSHI	Jan	Feb	Mar	Apr	May	Jun	Jul	Aug	Sep	Oct	Nov	Dec
Max (°C)	36	35	34	30	29	29	28	30	31	32	34	34
Min (°C)	15	15	15	16	14	13	12	12	13	14	14	15
Rain (mm)	50	60	120	300	180	50	20	20	20	40	60	50

significantly elevation. The hottest and most humid part of the country is the coast, where daytime temperatures typically hit around 30°C on most days, and are often higher. The high level of humidity exaggerates the heat on the coast, and there is little natural relief at night except from sea breezes – for which reason town centres often feel a lot hotter than nearby beaches.

Low-lying areas such as the Rift Valley floor, in particular the Lake Nyasa and Lake Tanganyika areas, are also hot, but far less humid, and thus more comfortable. At elevations of 1,000m or higher, daytime temperatures are warm to hot, and above 2,000m moderate to warm. Most parts of the interior cool down significantly at night, and montane areas such as the rim of the Ngorongoro Crater or Marangu on the foothills of Kilimanjaro can be downright chilly after dark. Alpine conditions and sub-zero night-time temperatures are characteristic of the higher slopes of Mount Meru and especially Kilimanjaro.

Tanzania is too near the Equator to experience the sort of dramatic contrast between summer and winter experienced in much of Europe or North America. The months between October and April are marginally hotter than May to September. In Dar es Salaam, for instance, the hottest month is February (average maximum 32°C; average minimum 23°C), and the coolest month is July (28°C; 18°C). Insignificant as this difference might look on paper, the coast is far more pleasant in the cooler months, while highland towns are far chillier.

Virtually all of Tanzania's rain falls between November and May. The rainy season is generally split into the short rains or *mvuli*, over November and December, and the long rains or *masika* from late February to early May. This pattern of two rainy seasons is strongest in coastal areas and in the extreme north around Arusha, where there is relatively little rainfall in January and February. Even then, there are years when the rain falls more continuously from November to May than is indicated by average rainfall figures. In many other parts of the country, figures suggest that rain falls fairly consistently between mid-November and mid-April.

DODOMA	Jan	Feb	Mar	Apr	May	Jun	Jul	Aug	Sep	Oct	Nov	Dec
Max (°C)	29	28	29	28	28	29	27	27	28	30	31	30
Min (°C)	18	18	18	17	15	13	12	13	14	17	18	18
Rain (mm)	150	100	135	50	–	–	–	–	5	15	25	100

MBEYA	Jan	Feb	Mar	Apr	May	Jun	Jul	Aug	Sep	Oct	Nov	Dec
Max (°C)	23	24	23	22	21	21	20	22	24	26	26	23
Min (°C)	14	14	14	13	11	9	8	10	11	12	12	13
Rain (mm)	195	160	160	110	15	–	–	–	10	15	50	135

KIGOMA	Jan	Feb	Mar	Apr	May	Jun	Jul	Aug	Sep	Oct	Nov	Dec
Max (°C)	26	27	27	27	28	28	29	29	29	28	26	25
Min (°C)	20	19	19	20	20	18	17	18	20	20	19	19
Rain (mm)	110	115	130	120	45	10	5	10	25	50	130	120

MWANZA	Jan	Feb	Mar	Apr	May	Jun	Jul	Aug	Sep	Oct	Nov	Dec
Max (°C)	33	34	33	31	31	30	29	29	30	32	32	31
Min (°C)	15	16	16	16	14	13	12	13	15	16	15	15
Rain (mm)	105	110	165	160	100	20	15	25	30	45	105	120

HISTORY

Tanzania has a rich and fascinating history, but much of the detail is highly elusive. Specialist works often contradict each other to such an extent that it is difficult to tell where fact ends and speculation begins, while broader or more popular accounts are commonly riddled with obvious inaccuracies. This is partly because there are huge gaps in the known facts; partly because much of the available information is scattered in out-of-print or difficult-to-find books; and partly because once an inaccuracy gets into print it tends to spread like a virus through other written works. For whatever reason, there is not, so far as I am aware, one concise, comprehensive and reliable book about Tanzanian history in print.

The following account attempts to provide a reasonably comprehensive and readable overview of the country's history. It is, to the best of my knowledge, as accurate as the known facts will allow, but at times I have had to decide for myself the most probable truth amongst a mass of contradictions, and I have speculated freely where speculation seems to be the order of the day. My goals are to stimulate the visitor's interest in Tanzanian history, and to give easy access to information that would have enhanced my first trip to Tanzania greatly. Many of the subjects touched on in this general history are given more elaborate treatment elsewhere in the book, under regional history sections or in tint boxes.

PRE-HISTORY OF THE INTERIOR The part of the Rift Valley passing through Ethiopia, Kenya and northern Tanzania is almost certainly where modern human beings and their hominid ancestors evolved. Hominids are generally divided into two genera, called *Australopithecus* and *Homo*, the former extinct for at least a million years, and the latter now represented by only one species – *Homo sapiens* (modern man). The paucity of hominid fossils collected before the 1960s meant that for many years it was assumed the most common australopithecine fossil, *A. africanus*, had evolved directly into the genus *Homo* and was thus man's oldest identifiable ancestor.

The word 'tribe' has fallen out of vogue in recent years, and I must confess that for several years I rigorously avoided the use of it in my writing. It has, I feel, rather colonial connotations, something to which I'm perhaps overly sensitive having lived most of my life in South Africa. Some African intellectuals have argued that it is derogatory, too, in so far as it is typically applied in a belittling sense to non-European cultures, where words such as nation might be applied to their European equivalent.

All well and good to dispense with the word tribe, at least until you set about looking for a meaningful substitute. 'Nation', for instance, seems appropriate when applied in an historical sense to a large and cohesive centralised entity such as the Zulu or Hehe, but rather less so when you're talking about smaller and more loosely affiliated tribes. Furthermore, in any modern sense, Tanzania itself is a nation (and proud of it), just as are Britain or Germany, so that describing, for instance, the modern Chagga as a nation would feel as inaccurate and contrived as referring to, say, the Liverpudlian or Berliner nation.

It would be inaccurate, too, to refer to most African tribes in purely ethnic or cultural or linguistic terms. Any or all of these factors might come into play in shaping a tribal identity, without in any sense defining it. All modern tribes contain individuals with a diverse ethnic stock, simply through intermarriage. Most modern Ngoni, for instance, belong to that tribe through their ancestors having been assimilated into it, not because all or even any of their ancestors were necessarily members of the Ngoni band who migrated up from South Africa in the 19th century. And, for sure, when the original Bantu-speaking people moved into present-day Tanzania thousands of years ago, local people with an entirely different ethnic background would have been assimilated into the newly established communities. Likewise, the linguistic and cultural differences between two neighbouring tribes are often very slight, and may be no more significant than dialectic or other regional differences within either tribe. The Maasai and Samburu, for instance, share a long common history, are of essentially the same ethnic stock, speak the

This neat linear theory of human evolution became blurred when Richard and Mary Leakey, who were excavating Olduvai Gorge in northern Tanzania, discovered that at least two australopithecine species had existed. Carbon dating and the skeletal structure of the two species indicated that the older *A. robustus* had less in common with modern man than its more lightly built ancestor *A. africanus*, implying that the *Australopithecus* line was not ancestral to the *Homo* line at all. This hypothesis was confirmed in 1972 with the discovery of a two-million-year-old skull of a previously undescribed species *Homo habilis* at Lake Turkana in Kenya, providing conclusive evidence that *Australopithecus* and *Homo* species had lived alongside each other for at least one million years. As more fossils have come to light, including older examples of *Homo erectus* (the direct ancestor of modern humans), it has become clear that several different hominid species existed alongside each other in the Rift Valley until perhaps half a million years ago.

In 1974, Donald Johansen discovered an almost complete hominid skeleton in the Danakil region of northern Ethiopia. Named Lucy (the song *Lucy in the Sky with Diamonds* was playing in camp shortly after the discovery), this turned out to be the fossil of a 3.5-million-year-old australopithecine of an entirely new species dubbed *A. afarensis*. Lucy's anatomy demonstrated that bipedal hominids (or rather semi-bipedal, since the length of Lucy's arms suggested she would have been as comfortable swinging through the trees as she would have been on a morning jog) had evolved much earlier than previously assumed.

same language, and are culturally almost indistinguishable. Yet they perceive themselves to be distinct tribes, and are perceived as such by outsiders.

A few years ago, in mild desperation, I settled on the suitably nebulous term ethno-linguistic group as a substitute for tribe. Clumsy, ugly, and verging on the meaningless it might be, but it does sound impressively authoritative, without pinning itself exclusively on ethnicity, language or culture as a defining element, and it positively oozes political correctness. It's also, well, a little bit silly! Just how silly dawned on me during the four months I spent back in Tanzania in 2001 researching the fourth edition of this guide. Just as Tanzanians are unselfconscious about referring to themselves as black and to *wazungu* as white, so too do they talk about their tribe without batting an eyelid. For goodness sake, at every other local hotel in Tanzania, visitors are required to fill in the 'Tribe' column in the standard issue guesthouse visitors' book! And if it's good enough for Tanzanians, well, who am I to get precious about it?

More than that, it strikes me that even in an African nation as united as Tanzania certainly is, the role of tribe in shaping the identity of an individual has no real equivalent in most Western societies. We may love – or indeed loathe – our home town, we might fight to the death for our loved ones, we might shed tears when our football team loses or our favourite pop group disbands. But we have no equivalent to the African notion of tribe. True enough, tribalism is often cited as the scourge of modern Africa, and when taken to fanatical extremes that's a fair assessment, yet to damn it entirely would be rather like damning English football, or its supporters, because of the actions of a fanatical extreme. Tribalism is an integral part of African society, and pussyfooting around it through an overdeveloped sense of political correctness strikes me as more belittling than being open about it.

So, in case you hadn't gathered, Tanzania's 120 ethno-lingual-cultural groupings are tribes for this edition of the guide, a decision that will hold at least for so long as I'm expected to fill in my tribe – whatever that might be – every time I check into a Tanzanian guesthouse!

In the 1960s it was widely thought that humans and apes diverged around 20 million years ago. Recent DNA evidence has shown, however, that modern man and chimpanzees are far more closely related than previously assumed – to the extent that less biased observers might place us in the same genus. It is now thought that the hominid and chimpanzee evolutionary lines diverged from a common ancestor between four and six million years ago. In 2001, it was announced that the candidate for the so-called 'missing link' between humans and chimps had been discovered in northern Ethiopia: the fossilised remains of a 5.8-million-year-old hominid that has been assigned to new genus *Arpipithecus*, with clear affiliations to both chimpanzees and humans.

The immediate ancestor of modern man is *Homo erectus*, which appeared about 1.5 million years ago. *Homo erectus* was the first hominid to surmount the barrier of the Sahara and spread into Europe and Asia, and is credited with the discovery of fire and the first use of stone tools and recognisable speech. Although modern man, *Homo sapiens*, has been around for at least half a million years, only in the last 10,000 years have the African races recognised today more or less taken their modern form. Up until about 1000BC, East Africa was exclusively populated by hunter-gatherers, similar in physiology, culture and language to the Khoisan (or Bushmen) of southern Africa. Rock art accredited to these hunter-gatherers is found throughout East Africa, most notably in the Kondoa-Irangi region of central Tanzania.

The pastoralist and agricultural lifestyles that were pioneered in the Nile Delta in about 5000BC spread to parts of sub-Saharan Africa by 2000BC, most notably to the Cushitic-speaking people of the Ethiopian Highlands and the Bantu-speakers of west Africa. Cushitic-speakers first drifted into Tanzania in about 1000BC, closely followed by Bantu-speakers. Familiar with Iron Age technology, these migrants would have soon dominated the local hunter-gatherers. By AD1000, most of Tanzania was populated by Bantu-speakers, with Cushitic-speaking pockets in areas such as the Ngorongoro Highlands.

There is no detailed information about the Tanzanian interior prior to 1500, and even after that details are sketchy. Except for the Lake Victoria region, which supported large authoritarian kingdoms similar to those in Uganda, much of the Tanzanian interior is too dry to support large concentrations of people. In most of Tanzania, an informal system of *ntemi* chiefs emerged. The *ntemi* system, though structured, seems to have been flexible and benevolent. The chiefs were served by a council and performed a role that was as much advisory as it was authoritarian. By the 19th century there are estimated to have been more than 200 *ntemi* chiefs in western and central Tanzania, each with about 1,000 subjects.

The *ntemi* system was shattered when southern Tanzania was invaded by Ngoni exiles from what is now South Africa, refugees from the rampantly militaristic Zulu Kingdom moulded by Shaka in the early 19th century. The Ngoni entered southern Tanzania in about 1840, bringing with them the revolutionary Zulu military tactics based on horseshoe formations and a short stabbing-spear. The new arrivals attacked the resident tribes, destroying communities and leaving survivors no option but to turn to banditry. Their tactics were observed and adopted by the more astute *ntemi* chiefs, who needed to protect themselves, but had to forge larger kingdoms to do so. The situation was exacerbated by the growing presence of Arab slave traders. Tribes controlling the areas that caravan routes went through were able to extract taxes from the slavers and to find work with them as porters or organising slave raids. This situation was exploited by several chiefs, most notably Mirambo of Unyamwezi and Mkwawa of the Uhehe, charismatic leaders who dominated the interior in the late 19th century.

THE COAST TO 1800 There have been links between the Tanzanian coast and the rest of the world for millennia, but only the barest sketch is possible of events before AD1000. The ancient Egyptians believed their ancestors came from a southerly land called Punt. In about 2500BC an explorer called Sahare sailed off in search of this mysterious land. Sahare returned laden with ivory, ebony and myrrh, a booty that suggests he had landed somewhere on the East African coast. There is no suggestion that Egypt traded regularly with Punt, but they did visit it again. Interestingly, an engraving of the Queen of Punt, made after an expedition in 1493BC, shows her to have distinctly Khoisan features. The Phoenicians first explored the coast in about 600BC. According to the 1st-century *Periplus of the Ancient Sea* they traded with a town called Rhapta, which is thought to have lain upriver of a major estuary, possibly the Pangani mouth or Rufiji Delta.

Bantu-speakers arrived at the coast about 2,000 years ago. It seems likely they had trade links with the Roman Empire: Rhapta gets a name check in Ptolemy's 2nd-century *Geography*, and a few 4th-century Roman coins have been found at the coast. The fact that the Romans knew of Kilimanjaro, and of the great lakes of the interior, raises some interesting questions. One suggestion is that the coastal Bantu-speakers were running trade routes into the interior and that these collapsed at the same time as the Roman Empire, presumably as a result of the sudden dearth of trade partners. This notion is attractive and not implausible, but the evidence seems rather flimsy. The Romans could simply have gleaned the information from Bantu-speakers who had arrived at the coast recently enough to have some knowledge of the interior.

Historians have a clearer picture of events on the coast from about AD1000, by which time trade between the coast and the Persian Gulf was well established. The earliest known Islamic buildings on the coast, which stand on Manda Island off Kenya, have been dated to the 9th century AD. Items sold to Arab ships at this time included ivory, ebony and spices, while a variety of oriental and Arabic goods were imported for the use of wealthy traders. The dominant item of export, however, was gold, mined in the Great Zimbabwe region, transported to the coast at Sofala (in modern-day Mozambique) via the Zambezi Valley, then shipped by local traders to Mogadishu, where it was sold to the Arab boats. The common assumption that Swahili language and culture was a direct result of Arab traders mixing with local Bantu-speakers is probably inaccurate. KiSwahili is a Bantu language, and although it did spread along the coast in the 11th century, most of the Arabic words that have entered the language did so at a later date. The driving force behind a common coastal language and culture was almost certainly not the direct trade with Arabs, but rather the internal trade between Sofala and Mogadishu.

More than 30 Swahili city-states were sprung up along the East African coast between the 13th and 15th centuries, a large number of which were in modern-day Tanzania. This period is known as the Shirazi Era after the sultans who ruled these city-states, most of whom claimed descent from the Shiraz region of Persia. Each city-state had its own sultan; they rarely interfered in each other's business. The Islamic faith was widespread during this period, and many Arabic influences crept into coastal architecture. Cities were centred on a great mosque, normally constructed in rock and coral. It has long been assumed that the many Arabs who settled on the coast before and during the Shirazi Era controlled the trade locally, but this notion has been questioned in recent years. Contemporary descriptions of the city-states suggest that Africans formed the bulk of the population. It is possible that some African traders claimed Shirazi descent in order to boost their standing both locally and with Shirazi ships.

In the mid 13th century, probably due to improvements in Arab navigation and ship construction, the centre of the gold trade moved southward from Mogadishu to the small island of Kilwa. Kilwa represented the peak of the Shirazi period. It had a population of 10,000 and operated its own mint, the first in sub-equatorial Saharan Africa. The multi-domed mosque on Kilwa was the largest and most splendid anywhere on the coast, while another building, now known as Husuni Kubwa, was a gargantuan palace, complete with audience courts, several ornate balconies, and even a swimming pool.

Although Mombasa had possibly superseded Kilwa in importance by the end of the 15th century, coastal trade was still booming. It came to an abrupt halt in 1505, however, when the Portuguese captured Mombasa, and several other coastal towns, Kilwa included, were razed. Under Portuguese control the gold trade collapsed and the coastal economy stagnated. It was dealt a further blow in the late 16th century when a mysterious tribe of cannibals called the Zimba swept up the coast to ransack several cities and eat their inhabitants before being defeated by a mixed Portuguese and local army near Malindi in modern-day Kenya.

In 1698, an Arabic naval force under the Sultan of Oman captured Fort Jesus, the Portuguese stronghold in Mombasa, paving the way for the eventual Omani takeover of the coast north of modern-day Mtwara. Rivalries between the new Omani and the old Shirazi dynasties soon surfaced, and in 1728 a group of Shirazi sultans went so far as to conspire with their old oppressors, the Portuguese, to overthrow Fort Jesus. The Omani recaptured the fort a year later. For the next 100 years an uneasy peace gripped the coast, which was nominally under Omani rule, but dominated in economic terms by the Shirazi Sultan of Mombasa.

SLAVERY AND EXPLORATION IN THE 19TH CENTURY The 19th century was a period of rapid change in Tanzania, with stronger links established between the coast and the interior as well as between East Africa and Europe. Over the first half of the 19th century, the most important figure locally was Sultan Seyyid Said of Oman, who ruled from 1804 to 1854. Prior to 1804, England had signed a treaty with Oman, and relations between the two powers intensified in the wake of the Napoleonic Wars, since the English did not want to see the coast fall into French hands. In 1827, Said's small but efficient navy captured Mombasa and overthrew its Shirazi sultan, to finally assert unambiguous control over the whole coast, with strong English support.

Having captured Mombasa, Sultan Said chose Zanzibar as his East African base, partly because of its proximity to Bagamoyo (the terminus of a caravan route to Lake Tanganyika since 1823) and partly because it was more secure against attacks from the sea or the interior than any mainland port. Said's commercial involvement with Zanzibar began in 1827 when he set up a number of clove plantations there, with scant regard for the land claims of local inhabitants. Said and his fellow Arabs had come to totally dominate all aspects of commerce on the island by 1840, the year in which the sultan permanently relocated his personal capital from Oman to Zanzibar.

The extent of the East African slave trade prior to 1827 is unclear. It certainly existed, but was never as important as the gold or ivory trade. In part, this was because the traditional centre of slave trading had always been west Africa, which was far closer than the Indian Ocean to the main markets of the Americas. In the early 19th century, however, the British curbed the slave trade out of west Africa, leaving the way open for Said and his cronies. Come 1839, over 40,000 slaves were being sold from Zanzibar annually. These came from two sources: the central caravan route between Bagamoyo and the Lake Tanganyika region, and a southern route between Kilwa Kivinje and Lake Nyasa.

The effects of the slave trade on the interior were numerous. The Nyamwezi of the Tabora region and the Yua of Nyasa became very powerful by serving as porters

VOICES OF THE EXPLORERS

In many instances, the best or indeed only surviving accounts of places and cultures in their 19th-century incarnation are to be found in the original writings of the Victorian explorers. One of the pleasures of researching this guidebook has been wading through a few of these obscure or out-of-print works for contemporary descriptions. What I discovered was not the stuffy, self-aggrandising, judgemental twaddle one might expect, but some remarkably vivid and fresh passages, of their time, for sure, but far more riveting and instructive than many of the blatantly masturbatory exercises that pass for modern travelogue writing.

Extended quotes from these and other works are scattered throughout this guide, with the intent of fleshing out the dry bones of corresponding factual historical accounts. In many instances, space restrictions have necessitated some vigorous editing, and I make no apology for having omitted irrelevant chunks of text, or even having re-ordered scattered but associated sections from a long notebook to create a greater sense of cohesion. Because this is not an academic work, I have taken the liberty of changing obsolete place spellings in line with the contemporary ones used elsewhere in this guide (for instance, Quiloa to Kilwa). I've also converted imperial measurements to their rough metric equivalent, and all written numbers to digits (for example, five thousand to 5,000). All quotes are otherwise exactly as their author wrote them – and I hope you enjoy them as much as I have!

along the caravan routes and organising slave raids and ivory hunts. Weaker tribes were devastated. Villages were ransacked; the able-bodied men and women were taken away while the young and old were left to die. Hundreds of thousands of slaves were sold in the mid 19th century. Nobody knows how many more died of disease or exhaustion between being captured and reaching the coast. Another long-term effect of the slave trade was that it formed the driving force behind the second great expansion of KiSwahili, which became the *lingua franca* along caravan routes.

Europeans knew little about the African interior in 1850. The first Europeans to see Kilimanjaro (Rebmann in 1848) and Mount Kenya (Krapf in 1849) were ridiculed for their reports of snow on the Equator. The Arab traders must have had an intimate knowledge of many parts of the interior that intrigued Europeans, but, oddly, at least in hindsight, nobody seems to have thought to ask them. In 1855, a German missionary, James Erhardt, produced a map of Africa, based on third-hand Arab accounts, which showed a large slug-shaped lake in the heart of the continent. Known as the Slug Map, it was wildly inaccurate, yet it did serve to fan interest in a mystery that had tickled geographers since Roman times: the source of the Nile.

The men most responsible for opening up the East African interior to Europeans were David Livingstone, Richard Burton, John Speke and later Henry Stanley. Livingstone, who came from a poor Scots background and left school at the age of ten, educated himself to become a doctor and a missionary. He arrived in the Cape in 1841 to work in the Kuruman Mission, but, overcome by the enormity of the task of converting Africa to Christianity, he decided he would be of greater service opening up the continent so that other missionaries could follow. Livingstone was the first European to cross the Kalahari Desert, the first to cross Africa from west to east and the first to see Victoria Falls. In 1858, Livingstone stumbled across Africa's third-largest lake, Nyasa. Later in the same year, on a quest for the source of the Nile funded by the Royal Geographical Society, Burton and Speke were the first Europeans to see Lake Tanganyika, and Speke continued north to Lake Victoria. Speke returned to the northern shore of Lake Victoria in 1863 and concluded – correctly, though it would be many years before the theory gained wide acceptance – that Ripon Falls in modern-day Uganda formed the source of the Nile.

Livingstone had ample opportunity during his wanderings to witness the slave caravans at first hand. Sickened by what he saw – the human bondage, the destruction of entire villages, and the corpses abandoned by the traders – he became an outspoken critic of the trade. He believed the only way to curb it was to open up Africa to the three Cs: Christianity, Commerce and Civilisation. Though not an imperialist by nature, Livingstone had seen enough of the famine and misery caused by the slavers and the Ngoni in the Nyasa area to believe the only solution was for Britain to colonise eastern Africa. In 1867, Livingstone set off from Mikindani to spend the last six years of his life wandering between the great lakes, making notes on the slave trade and trying to settle the Nile debate. He believed the source of the Nile to be Lake Bangweulu (in northern Zambia), from which the mighty Lualaba River flowed. In 1872, while recovering from illness at Ujiji, Livingstone was met by Henry Stanley and became the recipient of perhaps the most famous words ever spoken in Africa: 'Dr Livingstone, I presume' (see box, *Ujiji, 10 November 1871*, in *Chapter 15*, pages 454–5). Livingstone died near Lake Bangweulu in 1873. His heart was removed and buried by his porters, who then carried his cured body over 1,500km via Tabora to Bagamoyo, a voyage as remarkable as any undertaken by the European explorers.

Livingstone's quest to end the slave trade met with little success during his lifetime, but his death and highly emotional funeral at Westminster Abbey seem to have acted as a catalyst. Missions were built in his name all over the Nyasa region, while industrialists such as William Mackinnon and the Muir brothers invested in schemes to open Africa to commerce (which Livingstone had always believed was the key to putting the slavers out of business). In the year Livingstone died, John Kirk was made the British Consul in Zanzibar. Kirk had travelled with Livingstone on his 1856–62 trip to Nyasa. Deeply affected by what he saw, he had since spent years on Zanzibar hoping to find a way to end the slave trade. In 1873, the British navy blockaded the island and Kirk offered Sultan Barghash full protection against foreign powers if he banned the slave trade. Barghash agreed. The slave market was closed and an Anglican church built over it. Within ten years of Livingstone's death, however, the volume of slaves was a fraction of what it had been in the 1860s. Caravans reverted to ivory as their principal trade, while many of the coastal traders started up rubber and sugar plantations, which turned out to be just as lucrative as their former trade. Nevertheless, a clandestine slave trade continued on the mainland for some years – 12,000 slaves were sold at Kilwa in 1875 – and even into the 20th century, only to be fully eradicated in 1918, when Britain took control of Tanganyika

THE PARTITIONING OF EAST AFRICA The so-called scramble for Africa was entered into with mixed motives, erratic enthusiasm and an almost total lack of premeditation by the powers involved. Britain, the major beneficiary of the scramble, already enjoyed a degree of influence on Zanzibar, one that arguably approached informal colonisation, and it was quite happy to maintain this mutually agreeable relationship unaltered. Furthermore, the British government at the time, led by Lord Salisbury, was broadly opposed to the taking of African colonies. The scramble was initiated by two events. The first, the decision of King Leopold of Belgium to colonise the Congo Basin, had little direct bearing on events in Tanzania. The partitioning of East Africa was a direct result of an about-face by the German premier, Bismarck, who had previously shown no enthusiasm for acquiring colonies and probably developed an interest in Africa in the hope of acquiring pawns to use in negotiations with Britain and France.

In 1884, a young German metaphysician called Carl Peters arrived inauspiciously in Zanzibar, then made his way to the mainland to sign a series of treaties with local chiefs. The authenticity of these treaties is questionable, but when Bismarck announced claims to a large area between the Pangani and Rufiji rivers, it was enough to set the British government into a mild panic. Britain had plans to expand the Sultanate of Zanzibar, its informal colony, to include the fertile lands around Kilimanjaro. Worse, large parts of the area claimed by Germany were already part of the sultanate. Not only was Britain morally bound to protect these, it also did not want to surrender control of Zanzibar's annual import/export turnover of two million pounds.

Despite pressure put on the British government by John Kirk, angry that his promises to Barghash would not be honoured, there was little option but to negotiate with Germany. A partition was agreed in 1886, identical to the modern border between Kenya and Tanzania. (You may read that Kilimanjaro was part of the British territory before Queen Victoria gave it to her cousin, the Kaiser, as a birthday present. This amusing story, possibly dreamed up by a Victorian satirist to reflect the arbitrariness of the scramble, is complete fabrication.) In April 1888, the Sultan of Zanzibar unwillingly agreed to lease Germany the coastal strip south of the Umba River. Germany mandated this area to Carl Peters' German East Africa Company (GEAC), which placed agencies at most of the coastal settlements north of Dar es Salaam. These agents demanded heavy taxes from traders and were encouraged to behave high-handedly in their dealings with locals.

The GEAC's honeymoon was short. Emil Zalewski, the Pangani agent, ordered the sultan's representative, the Wali, to report to him. When the Wali refused,

Zalewski had him arrested and sent away on a German war-boat. In September 1888, a sugar plantation owner called Abushiri Ibn Salim led an uprising against the GEAC. Except for Dar es Salaam and Bagamoyo, both protected by German war boats, the GEAC agents were either killed or driven away. A horde of 20,000 men gathered on the coast, including 6,000 Shambaa who refused to relinquish their right to claim tax from caravans passing the Usambara. In November, the mission at Dar es Salaam was attacked. Three priests were killed and the rest captured. The coast was in chaos until April 1889 when the Kaiser's troops invaded Abushiri's camp and forced him to surrender. The German government hanged Abushiri in Pangani; they withdrew the GEAC's mandate and banned Peters from ever setting foot in the area.

The 1886 agreement only created the single line of partition north of Kilimanjaro. By 1890, Germany had claimed an area north of Witu, including Lamu, and there was concern in Britain that they might try to claim the rich agricultural land around Lake Victoria, thereby surrounding Britain's territory. Undeterred by the debacle at Pangani (and with a nod and a wink from Bismarck), Carl Peters decided to force the issue. He slipped through Lamu and in May 1890, after a murderous jaunt across British territory, he signed a treaty with the King of Buganda entitling Germany to most of what is now southern Uganda. This time, however, Peters' plans were frustrated. Bismarck had resigned in March of the same year and his replacement, Von Kaprivi, wanted to maintain good relations with Salisbury's government. In any case, Henry Stanley had signed a similar treaty with the Baganda when he passed through the area in 1888 on his way from rescuing the Emin Pasha in Equatoria.

Germany had its eye on Heligoland, a small but strategic North Sea island that had been seized by Britain from Denmark in 1807. To some extent, German interest in Africa had always been related to the bargaining power it would give them in Europe. In 1890, Salisbury and Von Kaprivi knocked out the agreement that created the modern borders of mainland Tanzania (with the exception of modern-day Burundi and Rwanda, German territory until after World War I). In exchange for an island of less than 1km² in extent, Salisbury was guaranteed protectorateship over Zanzibar and handed the German block north of Witu, and Germany relinquished any claims it might have had to what are today Uganda and Malawi.

GERMAN EAST AFRICA The period of German rule was not a happy one. In 1891, Carl Peters was appointed governor. Peters had already proved himself an unsavoury and unsympathetic character: he boasted freely of enjoying killing Africans and, under the guise of the GEAC, his lack of diplomacy had already instigated one uprising. Furthermore, the 1890s were plagued by a series of natural disasters: a rinderpest epidemic at the start of the decade, followed by an outbreak of smallpox, and a destructive plague of locusts. A series of droughts brought famine and disease in their wake. Many previously settled areas reverted to bush, causing the spread of tsetse fly and sleeping sickness. The population of Tanganyika is thought to have decreased significantly between 1890 and 1914.

It took Peters a decade to gain full control of the colony. The main area of conflict was in the vast central plateau where, led by Mkwawa, the Hehe had become the dominant tribe. In 1891, the Hehe ambushed a German battalion led by Emil Zalewski. They killed or wounded more than half Zalewski's men, and made off with his armoury. Mkwawa fortified his capital near Iringa, but the Germans razed it in 1894. Mkwawa was forced to resort to guerrilla tactics, which he used with some success until 1898, when he shot himself rather than face capture by the Germans.

Germany was determined to make the colony self-sufficient. Sugar and rubber were well established on parts of the coast; coffee was planted in the Kilimanjaro region, a major base for settlers; and cotton grew well around Lake Victoria. The colony's leading crop export, sisal, was grown throughout the rest of the country. In 1902, Peters decided that the southeast should be given over to cotton plantations. This was an ill-considered move: the soils were not right for the crop and the scheme was bound to cause great hardship. It also led to the infamous and ultimately rather tragic Maji Maji rebellion, which proved to be perhaps the most decisive event in the colony during German rule (see box, below).

Carl Peters was fired from the colonial service in 1906. He believed his African mistress had slept with his manservant, so he had flogged her close to death then

THE MAJI MAJI REBELLION

The people of what is now the southeast of Tanzania suffered throughout the 19th century. They had been terrorised by the notoriously cruel Kilwa slavers and suffered regular raids by the Ngoni, and a misguided German cotton scheme, which created backbreaking work for little financial return, was the final straw. In 1905, a prophet called Kinjikitile discovered a spring that spouted out magic water. He claimed that bullets fired at anyone who had been sprinkled with this water would have no effect. His messengers carried the water to people throughout the region; by August 1905 the entire southeast was ready to rise against the Germans.

The Maji Maji (water water) rebellion began in Kinjikitile's village in the Mutumbi Hills near Kilwa. The house of the German agent in Kibatu was burnt down, as was a nearby Asian trading centre. Troops from the regional headquarters at Kilwa captured and hanged Kinjikitile, but the news of his magic water had already spread. A group of missionaries led by the Bishop of Dar es Salaam was speared to death when they passed through the region, several trading posts were burnt along with their occupants, and the entire staff of the Ifakara garrison was killed.

The first setback came when several thousand warriors attacked the Mahenge garrison. The commander had been warned of the attack and a bank of machine guns awaited its arrival. Although many warriors were killed, the garrison was pinned down until troops from Iringa forced the rest to retreat. The Iringa troops then continued to the Ngoni capital of Songea, which was brewing up for its own rebellion. The Ngoni were extremely dubious about the water's power, so when a few Ngoni were shot, the rest of them fled.

News of the water's ineffectiveness spread; the rebellion had lost much of its momentum by mid-October when Count Gotzen and 200 German troops arrived in the area. Gotzen decided the only way to flush out the ringleaders was to create a famine. Crops were burnt indiscriminately. Within months most of the leaders had been hanged. The ensuing famine virtually depopulated the area: over 250,000 people died of disease or starvation and the densely populated Mutumbi and Ungindo hills were reclaimed by miombo woodland and wild animals. They now form part of the Selous Game Reserve.

The Maji Maji rebellion was the most important and tragic event during German rule, but it did leave some good effects in its wake. It was the first time a group of disparate tribes had dropped their own disputes and united against European invaders. Many Tanzanians feel the rebellion paved the way for the non-tribal attitude of modern Tanzania and it certainly affected the strategies used against colonial powers throughout Africa. More immediately, the public outcry it caused forced Germany to rethink its approach to its colonies.

hanged them both. His successor introduced a series of laws protecting Africans from mistreatment. To the disgust of the settler community, he created an incentive-based scheme for African farmers. This made it worth their while to grow cash crops and allowed the colony's exports to triple in the period leading up to World War I. When war broke out in Europe, East Africa too became involved. In the early stages of the war, German troops entered southern Kenya to cut off the Uganda Railway. Britain responded with an abortive attempt to capture Tanga. The balance of power was roughly even until Jan Smuts led the Allied forces into German territory in 1916. By January 1918, the Allies had captured most of German East Africa and the German commander, Von Lettow, retreated into Mozambique. The war disrupted food production, and a serious famine ensued. This was particularly devastating in the Dodoma region. The country was taken over by the League of Nations. The Ruanda-Urundi District, now the states of Rwanda and Burundi, was mandated to Belgium. The rest of the country was renamed Tanganyika and mandated to Britain.

TANGANYIKA The period of British rule between the wars was largely uneventful. Tanganyika was never heavily settled by Europeans so the indigenous populace had more opportunity for self-reliance than it did in many colonies. Nevertheless, settlers were favoured in the agricultural field, as were Asians in commerce. The Land Ordinance Act of 1923 secured some land rights for Africans; otherwise they were repeatedly forced into grand but misconceived agricultural schemes. The most notorious of these, the Groundnut Scheme of 1947, was an attempt to convert the southeast of the country into a large-scale mechanised groundnut producer. The scheme failed through a complete lack of understanding of local conditions; it caused a great deal of hardship locally and cost British taxpayers millions of pounds. On a political level, a system of indirect rule based around local government encouraged African leaders to focus on local rivalries rather than national issues between the wars. A low-key national movement called the Tanganyika Africa Association (TAA) was formed in 1929, but it was as much a cultural as a political organisation.

Although it was not directly involved in World War II, Tanganyika was profoundly affected by it. The country benefited economically. It saw no combat so food production continued as normal, while international food prices rocketed. Tanganyika's trade revenue increased sixfold between 1939 and 1949. World War II was a major force in the rise of African nationalism. Almost 100,000 Tanganyikans fought for the Allies. The exposure to other countries and cultures made it difficult for them to return home as second-class citizens. They had fought for non-racism and democracy in Europe, yet were victims of racist and non-democratic policies in their own country.

The dominant figure in the post-war politics of Tanganyika/Tanzania was Julius Nyerere. Schooled at a mission near Lake Victoria, he went on to university in Uganda and gained a master's degree in Edinburgh. After returning to Tanzania in 1952, Nyerere became involved in the TAA. This evolved into the more political and nationalist Tanganyika African National Union (TANU) in 1954. Nyerere became the president of TANU at the age of 32. By supporting rural Africans on grass roots issues and advocating self-government as the answer to their grievances, TANU gained a strong national following. By the mid 1950s, Britain and the UN were looking at a way of moving Tanganyika towards greater self-government, though over a far longer time scale than TANU envisaged. The British governor, Sir Edward Twining, favoured a multi-racial system that would give equal representation to whites, blacks and Asians. TANU agreed to an election along these lines, albeit with major reservations. Twining created his own 'African party', the UTC.

In the 1958 election, there were three seats per constituency, one for each racial group. Electors could vote for all three seats, so in addition to putting forward candidates for the black seats, TANU indicated their preferred candidates in the white and Asian seats. Candidates backed by TANU won 67% of the vote; the UTC did not win a single seat. Twining's successor, Sir Richard Turnball, rewarded TANU by scrapping the multi-racial system in favour of open elections. In the democratic election of 1960, TANU won all but one seat. In May 1961, Tanganyika attained self-government and Nyerere was made prime minister. Tanganyika attained full independence on 9 December 1961. Not one life had been taken in the process. Britain granted Zanzibar full independence in December 1963. A month later the Arab government was toppled and in April 1964 the two countries combined to form Tanzania.

TANZANIA At the very core of Tanzania's post-independence achievements and failures lies the figure of Julius Nyerere, who ruled Tanzania until his retirement in 1985. In his own country, where he remains highly respected, Nyerere is called *Mwalimu* – the teacher. In the West, he is a controversial figure, often portrayed as a dangerous socialist who irreparably damaged his country. This image of Nyerere doesn't bear scrutiny. He made mistakes and was intolerant of criticism – at one point Tanzania had more political prisoners than South Africa – but he is also one of the few genuine statesmen to have emerged from Africa, a force for positive change both in his own country and in a wider African context.

In 1962, TANU came into power with little policy other than their attained goal of independence. Tanganyika was the poorest and least economically developed country in East Africa, and one of the poorest in the world. Nyerere's first concerns were to better the lot of rural Africans and to prevent the creation of a money-grabbing elite. The country was made a one-party state, but had an election system which, by African standards, was relatively democratic. Tanzania pursued a policy of non-alignment, but the government's socialist policies and Nyerere's outspoken views alienated most Western leaders. Close bonds were formed with socialist powers, most significantly China, who built the Tanzam Railway (completed in 1975).

Relations with Britain soured in 1965. Nyerere condemned the British government's tacit acceptance of the Unilateral Declaration of Independence (UDI) in Rhodesia. In return, Britain cut off all aid to Tanzania. Nyerere also gave considerable vocal support to disenfranchised Africans in South Africa, Mozambique and Angola. The ANC and Frelimo both operated from Tanzania in the 1960s.

Nyerere's international concerns were not confined to white supremacism. In 1975, Tanzania pulled out of an Organisation of African Unity (OAU) conference in Idi Amin's Uganda saying: 'The refusal to protest against African crimes against Africans is bad enough … but … by meeting in Kampala … the OAU are giving respectability to one of the most murderous regimes in Africa.' Tanzania gave refuge to several Ugandans, including the former president Milton Obote and the current president Yoweri Museveni. Amin occupied part of northwest Tanzania in October 1978, and bombed Bukoba and Musoma. In 1979, Tanzania retaliated by invading Uganda and toppling Amin. Other African leaders condemned Tanzania for this action, despite Amin having been the initial aggressor. Ousting Amin drained Tanzania's financial resources, but it never received any financial compensation, not from the West, nor from any other African country.

At the time of independence, most rural Tanzanians lived in scattered communities. This made it difficult for the government to provide such amenities as clinics and schools and to organise a productive agricultural scheme.

In 1967, Nyerere embarked on a policy he called villagisation. Rural people were encouraged to form *Ujamaa* (familyhood) villages and collective farms. The scheme met with some small-scale success in the mid 1970s, so in 1975 Nyerere decided to forcibly re-settle people who had not yet formed villages. By the end of the year 65% of rural Tanzanians lived in *Ujamaa* villages. In many areas, however, water supplies were inadequate to support a village. The resultant mess, exacerbated by one of Tanzania's regular droughts, ended further villagisation. *Ujamaa* is often considered to have been an unmitigated disaster. It did not achieve what it was meant to, but it did help the government improve education and health care. Most reliable sources claim it did little long-term damage to agricultural productivity.

By the late 1970s Tanzania's economy was a mess. There were several contributory factors: drought, *Ujamaa*, rising fuel prices, the border closure with Kenya (to prevent Kenyan operators from dominating the Tanzanian safari industry), lack of foreign aid, bureaucracy and corruption in state-run institutions, and the cost of the Uganda episode. After his re-election in 1980 Nyerere announced he would retire at the end of that five-year term. In 1985, Ali Hassan Mwinyi succeeded Nyerere as prime minister. Nyerere remained chairman of the Chama Cha Mapinduzi (CCM), the party formed when TANU merged with the Zanzibari ASP in 1975, until 1990.

Under President Mwinyi, Tanzania moved away from socialism. In June 1986, in alliance with the IMF, a three-year Economic Recovery Plan was implemented. This included freeing up the exchange rate and encouraging private enterprise. Since then Tanzania has achieved an annual growth rate of around 4% (in real terms). Many locals complain the only result they have seen is greater inflation. In 1990 attempts were made to rout corruption from the civil service, with surprisingly positive results. The first multi-party election took place in October 1995. The CCM was returned to power with a majority of around 75% under the leadership of Benjamin Mpaka, who stood down in December 2005 following the country's third multi-party election. This, once again, was won by the CCM, which polled more than 80% of the 11.3 million votes under its new leader, Jakaya Kikwete. The next election is scheduled for 2010, and it seems likely that Kikwete – who will turn 60 in the same year – will stand for a second term.

Now well into the fifth decade of the post-independence era, Africa as a whole still suffers from the tribal divisions it had had at the outset. Tanzania is a striking exception to this rule, and hindsight demonstrates that Nyerere's greatest achievement was the tremendous sense of national unity he created by making KiSwahili the national language, by banning tribal leaders, by forcing government officials to work away from the area in which they grew up, and by his own example. True, Tanzania remains one of the world's least-developed countries, but most sources agree that the economic situation of the average Tanzanian has improved greatly since independence, with unusually high growth shown over the past ten years, as have adult literacy rates and health care. Tanzania's remarkable political stability and its increasingly pragmatic economic policies form a positive basis for future growth.

GOVERNMENT

The ruling party of Tanzania since independence has been Chama Cha Mapinduzi (CCM). Up until 1995, Tanzania was a one-party state, under the presidency of Julius Nyerere and, after his retirement in 1985, Ali Hassan Mwinyi. Tanzania held its first multi-party election in late 1995, when the CCM was returned to power with an overwhelming majority under President Benjamin

Region	Capital	Population (millions)	Area	People per km²
Dar es Salaam	Dar es Salaam	2.6	1,393km²	1,870
Zanzibar & Pemba	Zanzibar	1.0	2,460km²	406
Mwanza	Mwanza	3.0	19,592km²	153
Kilimanjaro	Moshi	1.8	13,309km²	135
Mtwara	Mtwara	1.4	16,707km²	83
Mara	Musoma	1.5	19,566km²	76
Tanga	Tanga	2.0	26,808km²	75
Kagera	Bukoba	2.1	28,388km²	74
Shinyanga	Shinyanga	2.8	50,781km²	55
Dodoma	Dodoma	2.0	41,311km²	48
Mbeya	Mbeya	2.4	60,350km²	40
Kigoma	Kigoma	1.4	37,037km²	38
Iringa	Iringa	1.9	56,864km²	33
Pwani	Bagamoyo	1.0	32,407km²	31
Morogoro	Morogoro	1.9	70,799km²	29
Arusha	Arusha	2.1	82,306km²	25
Singida	Singida	1.2	49,341km²	24
Tabora	Tabora	1.7	76,151km²	22
Ruvuma	Songea	1.2	63,498km²	18
Rukwa	Sumbawanga	1.1	68,635km²	16
Lindi	Lindi	1.0	66,046km²	15

Mkapa, who remained the country's leader until the 2005 election, when he was succeeded by Jakaya Kikwete.

ADMINISTRATIVE REGIONS Tanzania is divided into 21 administrative regions, each with a local administrative capital. These are listed in the box above in descending order of population density, based on the 2002 national census.

ECONOMY

Immediately after independence, Tanzania became one of the most dedicated socialist states in Africa, and its economy suffered badly as a result of a sequence of well-intentioned but misconceived or poorly managed economic policies. By the mid 1980s, Tanzania ranked among the five poorest countries in the world. The subsequent swing towards a free market economy, making the country more attractive to investors, has resulted in dramatic improvement, and Tanzania today – while hardly wealthy – has managed to ascend out of the list of the world's 20 poorest countries. The mainstay of the economy is agriculture, and most rural Tanzanians are subsistence farmers who might also grow a few crops for sale. The country's major exports are traditionally coffee, cotton, cashew nuts, sisal, tobacco, tea and diamonds, but gold – Tanzania is now the third-largest gold producer in Africa after South Africa and Ghana – and a unique gem called tanzanite are of increasing importance to the export economy. Zanzibar and Pemba are important clove producers. The tourist industry that practically collapsed in the mid 1980s has grown steadily over the last decade. Over the past few years, more than 500,000 visitors annually have generated up to US$750 million annually in foreign revenue, a fivefold increase since 1990.

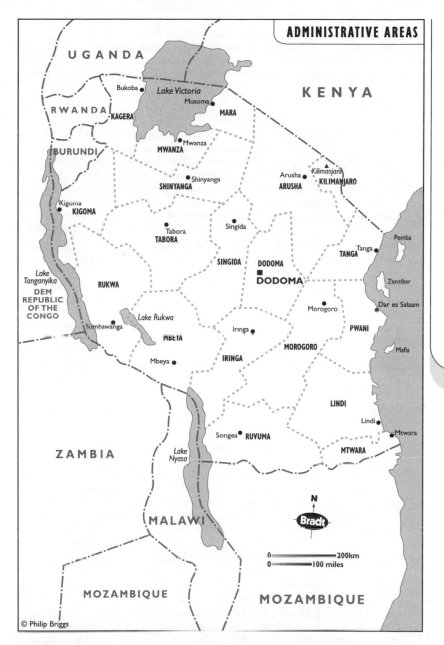

ADMINISTRATIVE AREAS

UGANDA

KENYA

RWANDA

Bukoba
Lake Victoria
Musoma

MARA

KAGERA

BURUNDI

Mwanza
MWANZA

Shinyanga
SHINYANGA

Arusha
ARUSHA

Kilimanjaro
KILIMANJARO

Kigoma
KIGOMA

Tabora
TABORA

Singida

Lake
Tanganyika

DEM
REPUBLIC
OF THE
CONGO

SINGIDA

DODOMA
■ DODOMA

TANGA

Tanga
Pemba

Zanzibar

RUKWA

Sumbawanga

Lake Rukwa

MBEYA

Mbeya

IRINGA

Iringa

MOROGORO

Morogoro

PWANI

Dar es Salaam

Mafia

LINDI

Songea
RUVUMA

Lindi
Mtwara

ZAMBIA

Lake
Nyasa

MTWARA

N

Bradt

0 ▬▬▬ 200km
0 ▬▬▬ 100 miles

MALAWI

MOZAMBIQUE

MOZAMBIQUE

© Philip Briggs

CURRENCY The unit of currency is the Tanzanian shilling (pronounced *shillingi*), which is in theory divided into 100 cents. The rate of exchange has deteriorated against all hard currencies over the last two decades. Between the publication of the third edition of this guide in 1999 and the fifth edition in 2006, the exchange rate against the US dollar slid from Tsh670 to around Tsh1,220, a drop of around 10% annually. It is reasonable to expect a similar trend will persist during the lifespan of this edition.

The total population of Tanzania was estimated at around 40 million in 2009. The most densely populated rural areas tend to be the highlands, especially those around Lake Nyasa and Kilimanjaro, and the coast. The country's largest city is

TRADITIONAL MUSICAL INSTRUMENTS

Tanzania's tribal diversity has meant that a vast array of very different – and, for that matter, very similar – traditional musical instruments are employed around the country under a bemusing number of local names. Broadly speaking, however, all but a handful of these variants can be placed in one of five distinct categories that conform to the classes of musical instrument used in Europe and the rest of the world.

The traditional music of many Tanzanian cultures is given its melodic drive by a **marimba** (also called a *mbira*), a type of instrument that is unique to Africa but could be regarded as a more percussive variant on the familiar keyboard instruments. The basic design of all marimbas consists of a number of metal or wooden keys whose sound is amplified by a hollow resonating box. Marimbas vary greatly in size from one region to the next. Popular with several pastoralist tribes of the Rift Valley and environs are small hand-held boxes with 6–10 metal keys that are plucked by the musician. In other areas, organ-sized instruments with 50 or more keys are placed on the ground and beaten with sticks like drums. The Gogo of the Dodoma region are famed for their marimba orchestras consisting of several instruments that beat out a complex interweave of melodies and rhythms.

The most purely melodic of Tanzanian instruments is the **zeze**, the local equivalent to the guitar or fiddle, used throughout the country under a variety of different names. The basic zeze design consists of between one and five strings running along a wooden neck that terminates in an open resonating gourd. The musician rubs a bow fiddle-like across the strings, while manipulating their tone with the fingers of his other hand, generally without any other instrumental accompaniment, but sometimes as part of an orchestra. Less widespread stringed instruments include the zither-like *enanga* of the Lake Tanganyika region and similar *bango* and *kinubi* of the coast, all of which are plucked like harps rather than stroked with a bow, to produce more defined melodic lines than the zeze.

The most important percussive instrument in African music is the **drum**, of which numerous local variations are found. Almost identical in structure and role to their European equivalent, most African drums are made by tightly stretching a membrane of animal hide across a section of hollowed tree trunk. A common and widespread type of drum, which is known in most areas as a *msondo* and is often reserved for important rituals, can be up to 1m tall and is held between the drummer's legs.

Percussive backing is also often provided by a variety of instruments known technically as **idiophones**. Traditionally, these might include the maraca-like *manyanga*, a shaker made by filling a gourd with dry seeds, as well as metal bells and bamboo scrapers. A modern variant on the above is the *chupa*: a glass cold drink bottle scraped with a piece of tin or a stick. Finally, in certain areas, horned instruments are also used, often to supply a fanfare at ceremonial occasions. These generally consist of a modified animal horn with a blowing hole cut into its side, through which the musician manipulates the pitch using different mouth movements.

Readers with an interest in traditional music are pointed towards an excellent but difficult-to-locate booklet, *The Traditional Musical Instruments of Tanzania*, written by Lewis and Makala (Music Conservatoire of Tanzania, 1990), and the primary source of this box.

SWAHILI NAMES

In KiSwahili, a member of a tribal group is given an m- prefix, the tribe itself gets a wa- prefix, the language gets a ki- prefix, and the traditional homeland gets a u- prefix. For example, a Mgogo person is a member of the Wagogo tribe who will speak Kigogo and live in Ugogo. The wa- prefix is commonly but erratically used in English books; the m- and ki- prefixes are rarely used, except in the case of KiSwahili, while the u- prefix is almost always used. There are no apparent standards; in many books the Swahili are referred to as just the Swahili while non-Swahili tribes get the wa- prefix. I have decided to drop most of these prefixes: it seems as illogical to refer to non-Swahili people by their KiSwahili name when you are writing in English as it would be to refer to the French by their English name in a German book. I have, however, referred to the Swahili language as KiSwahili on occasion. I also refer to tribal areas – as Tanzanians do – with the u- prefix, and readers can assume that any place name starting with U has this implication; in other words that Usukuma is the home of the Sukuma and Unyamwezi the home of the Nyamwezi.

Dar es Salaam, whose population, of some 2.5 million, exceeds that of the country's next ten largest towns combined. Other towns with a population estimated to exceed 100,000, in descending order of size, are Mwanza, Zanzibar Town, Morogoro, Mbeya, Tanga, Moshi, Dodoma, Arusha, Tabora, Iringa, Geita, Musoma, Songea, Kigoma, Shinyanga and Korogwe.

There are roughly 120 tribes in Tanzania, each speaking their own language, and none of which exceeds 10% of the country's total population. The most numerically significant tribes are the Sukuma of Lake Victoria, Haya of northwest Tanzania, Chagga of Kilimanjaro, Nyamwezi of Tabora, Makonde of the Mozambique border area, Hehe of Iringa and Gogo of Dodoma.

LANGUAGE

More than 100 different languages are spoken across Tanzania, but the official languages are KiSwahili and English. Until recently, very little English was spoken outside of the larger towns, but this is changing rapidly, and visitors can be confident that almost anybody involved in the tourist industry will speak passable English. KiSwahili, indigenous to the coast, spread through the region along the 19th-century caravan routes, and is today spoken as a second language by the vast majority of Tanzanians.

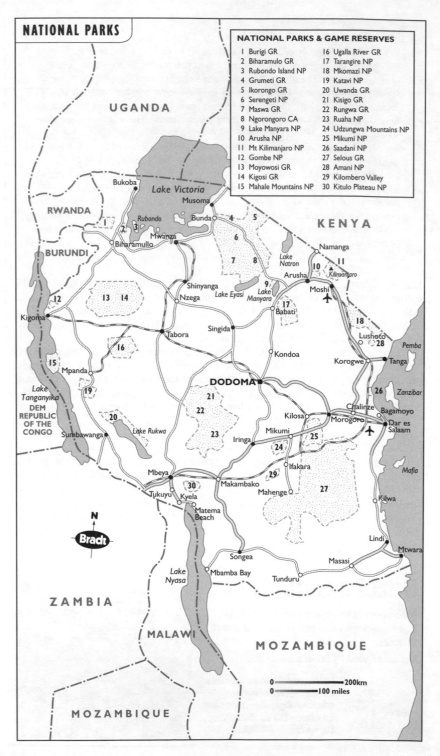

NATIONAL PARKS

NATIONAL PARKS & GAME RESERVES

1	Burigi GR	16	Ugalla River GR
2	Biharamulo GR	17	Tarangire NP
3	Rubondo Island NP	18	Mkomazi NP
4	Grumeti GR	19	Katavi NP
5	Ikorongo GR	20	Uwanda GR
6	Serengeti NP	21	Kisigo GR
7	Maswa GR	22	Rungwa GR
8	Ngorongoro CA	23	Ruaha NP
9	Lake Manyara NP	24	Udzungwa Mountains NP
10	Arusha NP	25	Mikumi NP
11	Mt Kilimanjaro NP	26	Saadani NP
12	Gombe NP	27	Selous GR
13	Moyowosi GR	28	Amani NP
14	Kigosi GR	29	Kilombero Valley
15	Mahale Mountains NP	30	Kitulo Plateau NP

2

Natural History

There are plenty of good reasons to visit Tanzania — the beautiful coastline, fascinating history and magnificent scenery – but for most people one attraction overwhelms all others, and that is the wildlife. Tanzania is Africa's prime game-viewing country, best known for the deservedly well-publicised Serengeti and Ngorongoro Crater, highlights in a mosaic of national parks and other conservation areas that cover almost 25% of the country and protect an estimated 20% of Africa's large mammals.

MAIN CONSERVATION AREAS

There are currently 12 national parks in Tanzania, with two more likely to be gazetted in the immediate future, and numerous other conservation areas gazetted, ranging from the vast Selous Game Reserve and Ngorongoro Conservation Area to several smaller forest reserves and even a couple of marine parks. All the national parks receive detailed coverage in the main part of the guide, as do any other conservation areas that are reasonably accessible, and several that are not. The following potted descriptions are intended to provide an introductory overview to the country's most significant and accessible conservation areas, not to replicate the more extended descriptions in, again, the main body of the guide. The listings start with the Serengeti in the north of the country and run roughly clockwise from there.

SERENGETI NATIONAL PARK This world-famous national park, notable for its million-strong migratory herds of wildebeest and zebra, is the linchpin of the popular northern safari circuit. It also harbours large numbers of predators; it is not unusual to see lion, leopard, cheetah, spotted hyena, bat-eared fox and a couple of jackal and mongoose species in the same day. The Serengeti is so vast that any sense of over-crowding in this popular park is restricted to the Seronera area in the southeast. The northern and western Serengeti have more of a wilderness feel, with surprisingly little tourist traffic around, except when the migration passes through them. Numerous lodges and campsites are dotted around the park.

NGORONGORO CONSERVATION AREA This dual-use conservation area – inhabited by the Maasai and their cattle as well as wildlife – protects a large part of Ngorongoro Highlands, including the magnificent Ngorongoro Crater, the largest intact caldera in the world. Ngorongoro Crater supports the world's densest population of lions and spotted hyena. It is the last place in Tanzania where black rhinoceros are reasonably easy to see, and is also notable for its magnificent old tuskers, a rare sight today elsewhere in Tanzania. The Ngorongoro Crater is heavily touristed, which does detract from many people's visit. A number of other remote natural landmarks in the Ngorongoro Highlands can be visited by vehicle or on foot. Numerous lodges and campsites are found on the crater rim.

LAKE MANYARA NATIONAL PARK The most low-key of the triad of reserves situated between Lake Victoria and the main Arusha–Dodoma road, Lake Manyara has a fabulous situation at the base of the Rift Valley and is a worthy addition to any itinerary taking in the Serengeti and Ngorongoro. The small park's once famous elephant population suffered badly at the hands of poachers in the 1980s, but it is well on the way to recovery today, and the elephants are perhaps the least jittery of anywhere in Tanzania. Manyara is also renowned for its tree-climbing lions, and the large flocks of flamingo that sometimes congregate on the lake. A recent development at Manyara is a number of adventure activities – canoeing, mountain biking, walking and abseiling – run out of the Serena Hotel. There is one lodge in the park, a lovely campsite at the gate, and accommodation to suit all budgets within 5km of the gate.

TARANGIRE NATIONAL PARK Lying to the east of Lake Manyara, this excellent national park is included on many northern circuit itineraries. It preserves a classic piece of dry African woodland studded with plentiful baobabs and transected by the perennial Tarangire River. Best known for the prodigious elephant herds that congregate along the river in the dry season, Tarangire also harbours a rich birdlife and such localised antelope species as fringe-eared oryx and gerenuk. Several lodges are to be found in and around the park.

ARUSHA NATIONAL PARK This underrated but eminently accessible park lies an hour's drive from Arusha town, the northern 'safari capital', and is best known perhaps for protecting Mount Meru, Africa's fifth-tallest peak. Other attractive features include the Momella Lakes, which host large concentrations of waterbirds including flamingos, and Ngurdoto Crater, a smaller version of Ngorongoro whose jungle-clad slopes harbour a variety of monkeys and forest birds. The park can be visited as a day trip from Arusha, but there is a remote lodge on the northern border and a budget campsite on the southern one.

MT KILIMANJARO NATIONAL PARK Encompassing the two peaks and higher slopes of Africa's highest mountain, Kilimanjaro is of all the country's national parks the least oriented towards game viewing. Thousands of tourists climb it every year, however, to stand on the snow-capped pinnacle of Africa, and to experience the haunting and somewhat otherworldly Afro-montane moorland habitat of the upper slopes. Accommodation within the park is limited to simple mountain huts and campsites, but several lodges lie outside the boundary.

MKOMAZI NATIONAL PARK The most obscure of Tanzania's northeastern conservation areas, Mkomazi is essentially a southern extension of Kenya's vast Tsavo East and West national parks. Wildlife is relatively skittish, and tourist development practically non-existent, but it's a definite possibility for travellers seeking to get away from the beaten track. Basic accommodation and campsites are available.

AMANI NATURE RESERVE This reserve in the Eastern Usambara Mountains, inland of Tanga, protects some of the most important montane forest in Tanzania and a wealth of rare and endemic birds, mammals, butterflies and other creatures. Comfortable and inexpensive accommodation is available within the nature reserve, and a good range of walking trails will keep hikers and birdwatchers busy for days. It's easily accessible on public transport, too.

SAADANI NATIONAL PARK This proposed national park (likely to be gazetted very soon) is the only savannah reserve in East Africa to be lapped by the waves of the

Indian Ocean. As things stand, it is more accurately characterised as a beach retreat with some wildlife around than as a full-blown safari destination. Boat and walking safaris are a bonus, peace and quiet a given, and the beach really is lovely. One excellent lodge lies on the beach.

JOZANI-CHWAKA BAY NATIONAL PARK The main stronghold for the rare Kirk's red colobus, endemic to Zanzibar Island, this small forested national park is well worth the slight effort required to reach it from Zanzibar Stone Town or the beach resorts of the island's east coast.

MAFIA MARINE NATIONAL PARK Protecting the extensive reefs that surround the Mafia archipelago, Tanzania's first marine park offers superlative snorkelling, diving and game fishing – as do the several upmarket lodges on Mafia Island.

SELOUS GAME RESERVE This is the largest game reserve in Africa, and the linchpin of Tanzania's under-utilised but utterly compelling southern safari circuit. Main attractions include the wetland scenery associated with the Rufiji River, the largest remaining population of the endangered African wild dog, large numbers of lion, elephant, hippo, buffalo, giraffe, and the other usual safari suspects. Several low-key upmarket lodges offer game walks, river trips and fly-camps, as well as the standard game drives.

MIKUMI NATIONAL PARK Transected by the main surfaced road through southern Tanzania, Mikumi is an underrated savannah reserve that forms a westerly extension of the much larger Selous. Game viewing can be excellent on the plains to the north of the main road, with substantial elephant and lion populations present, along with large herds of grazers. The lodges in this park are among the cheapest in Tanzania.

UDZUNGWA MOUNTAINS NATIONAL PARK Gazetted in 1992, this seldom-visited national park protects part of the Udzungwa Mountain chain, home to a host of endangered endemics including three primate and two bird species as well as numerous plants and invertebrates. Several hiking opportunities, easy access on public transport and affordable accommodation at the entrance gate add up to a good destination for backpackers.

KILOMBERO VALLEY This extensive floodplain ecosystem immediately west of the Selous Game Reserve is one of the most important wetlands in Africa, home to 70% of the continent's puku antelope, large herds of elephant, a high density of lions and three endemic bird species. Tourist development is minimal, but a recently established ecotourism project offers organised trips to the area, and backpackers have limited access from the Ifakara ferry.

RUAHA NATIONAL PARK Tanzania's second-largest national park protects a variety of woodland, grassland and riverine habitats, as well as the full gamut of large predators (including African wild dog), huge elephant herds and localised antelope such as sable, roan and greater and lesser kudu. Game viewing is almost secondary to the untrammelled wilderness atmosphere that envelops this park, serviced by only two (top-notch) lodges.

KITULO PLATEAU NATIONAL PARK Another proposed national park, likely to be gazetted over the next year or two, Kitulo is the least conventional of Tanzania's main conservation areas. Little wildlife is to be seen in the area, but it's a hiker's

2

and botanist's paradise, especially during the rainy season when the prodigious wild flowers are in bloom.

KATAVI NATIONAL PARK The wildest and most underrated savannah reserve in East Africa, Katavi offers mind-boggling game viewing during the dry season, and you can explore the area for days without encountering another vehicle. If you're after an exclusive wilderness experience – and hang the expense – look no further. One very exclusive tented camp operates seasonally.

MAHALE MOUNTAINS NATIONAL PARK This large and scenic park runs from the lovely shores of Lake Tanganyika to forested peaks almost 2,000m above the lakeshore. It harbours the greatest variety of primates of any Tanzania national park, including 700–1,000 chimps, as well as several West African species that occur nowhere else in Tanzania. The main attraction is chimp tracking, which is normally excellent. Two upmarket tented camps lie on the lakeshore, and inexpensive *bandas* (freestanding huts) are available too.

GOMBE NATIONAL PARK Also situated on the shores of Lake Tanganyika, Gombe is where Jane Goodall undertook her famous research into chimp behaviour in the 1960s. Although smaller than Mahale Mountain, and less scenically majestic, Gombe also offers great chimp tracking, and it is very accessible on public transport. It can also be visited (at a cost) as a day trip from the main lake port of Kigoma. Inexpensive *banda* accommodation is available.

RUBONDO ISLAND NATIONAL PARK This immensely peaceful national park protects a forested island in Lake Victoria, and is well suited for those who want to explore on foot or by boat. The indigenous fauna includes the sitatunga antelope and spotted-necked otter – both surprisingly easily observed – and introduced elephant, giraffe and chimps can also be seen. The island offers good birdwatching and game fishing. An upmarket lodge and national park *bandas* are found on the island.

HABITATS AND VEGETATION

The bulk of Tanzania is covered in open grassland, savannah (lightly wooded grassland) and woodland. The Serengeti Plains are an archetypal African savannah: grassland interspersed with trees of the acacia family – which are typically quite short, lightly foliated, and thorny. Many have a flat-topped appearance. An atypical acacia, the yellow fever tree, is one of Africa's most striking trees. It is relatively large, has yellow bark, and is often associated with water. Combretum is another family of trees typical of many savannah habitats. The dry savannah of central Tanzania can be so barren during the dry season that it resembles semi-desert.

Woodland differs from forest in lacking an interlocking canopy. The most extensive woodland in Tanzania is in the *miombo* belt, which stretches from southern and western Tanzania to Zimbabwe. *Miombo* woodland typically grows on infertile soil, and is dominated by broad-leafed *brachystegia* trees. You may come across the term 'mixed woodland': this refers to woodland with a mix of *brachystegia*, acacia and other species. Many woodland habitats are characterised by an abundance of baobab trees.

True forests cover less than 1% of Tanzania's surface area, but are the most diverse habitat ecologically. The forests of the Usambara, for instance, contain more than 2,000 plant species. Most of the forest in Tanzania is montane, associated with the Eastern Arc Mountains, Crater Highlands, Kilimanjaro and other tall mountains. The lowland forests found in the extreme west of the country have strong affinities with the rainforests of Congo. Three national parks contain extensive lowland forests: Gombe Stream, Rubondo Island and Mahale Mountains.

Other interesting but localised vegetation types are mangrove swamps (common along the coast, particularly around Kilwa) and the heath and moorland found on the higher slopes of Kilimanjaro and Meru.

ANIMALS

MAMMALS Over 80 large mammal species live in Tanzania. On an organised safari your guide will normally be able to identify all the mammals you see. For serious identification purposes (or a better understanding of an animal's lifestyle and habits) it is worth investing in a decent field guide or a book on animal behaviour. Such books are too generalised to give much detail on distribution in any one country, so the section that follows is best seen as a Tanzania-specific supplement to a field guide. A number of field guides are available (see *Appendix 3*) and are best bought before you get to Tanzania.

In the listings below, an animal's scientific name is given in parentheses after its English name, followed by the Swahili (Sw) name. The Swahili for animal is *mnyama* (plural *wanyama*); to find out what animal you are seeing, ask *'mnyama gani?'*.

Cats, dogs and hyenas
Lion (*Panthera leo*) Sw: *simba*. Shoulder height: 100–120cm; weight: 150–220kg. Africa's largest predator, the lion is the one animal that everybody hopes to see on safari. It is a sociable creature, living in prides of five to ten animals and defending a territory of between 20 and 200km². Lions hunt at night, and their favoured prey is large or medium antelope such as wildebeest and impala. Most of the hunting is done by females, but dominant males normally feed first after a kill. Rivalry between males is intense, and battles to take over a pride are frequently fought to the death, for which reason two or more males often form a coalition. Young males are forced out of their home pride at three years of age, and male cubs are usually killed after a successful takeover. When not feeding or fighting, lions are remarkably indolent – they spend up to 23 hours of any given day at rest – so the anticipation of a lion sighting is often more exciting than the real thing. Lions naturally occur in any habitat but desert and rainforest, and once ranged across much of the Old World, but these days they are all but restricted to the larger conservation areas in sub-Saharan Africa (one remnant population exists in India). They are reasonably common in most savannah and woodland reserves in Tanzania, notably Selous, Katavi and Ruaha. The Serengeti and Ngorongoro Crater are arguably the best places in Africa for regular lion sightings.

Leopard (*Panthera pardus*) Sw: *chui*. Shoulder height: 70cm; weight: 60–80kg. The powerful leopard is the most solitary and secretive of Africa's large cat species. It hunts using stealth and power, often getting to within 5m of its intended prey before pouncing, and it habitually stores its kill in a tree to keep it from hyenas and lions. The leopard can be distinguished from the superficially similar cheetah by its rosette-like spots, lack of black 'tear marks' and more compact, powerful build. Leopards occur in all habitats, favouring areas with plenty of cover such as riverine woodland and rocky slopes. There are many records of individuals living in proximity to humans for years without being detected. The leopard is the most common of Africa's large felines, found throughout Tanzania, yet a good sighting must be considered a stroke of extreme fortune. Relatively reliable spots for leopard sightings are the Seronera Valley in the Serengeti and the riverine bush in Ruaha National Park. An endemic race of leopard occurs on Zanzibar, though recent research suggests that it is probably extinct on the island, and that the handful of local reports of leopard sightings were probably the result of confusion with the African civet and introduced Java civet.

Cheetah (*Acynonix jubatus*) Sw: *duma*. Shoulder height: 70–80cm; weight: 50–60kg. This remarkable spotted cat has a greyhound-like build, and is capable of running

at 70km/h in bursts, making it the world's fastest land animal. It is often seen pacing the plains restlessly, either on its own or in a small family group comprised of a mother and her offspring. A diurnal hunter, favouring the cooler hours of the day, the cheetah's habits have been adversely affected in areas where there are high tourist concentrations and off-road driving is permitted. Males are territorial, and generally solitary, though in the Serengeti they commonly defend their territory in pairs or trios. Despite superficial similarities, you can easily tell a cheetah from a leopard by its simple spots,

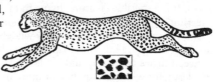

disproportionately small head, streamlined build, diagnostic black tear marks, and preference for relatively open habitats. Widespread, but thinly distributed and increasingly rare outside of conservation areas, the cheetah is most likely to be seen in savannah and arid habitats such as the Serengeti Plains (where sightings are regular on the road to Seronera) and the floor of the Ngorongoro Crater.

Similar species The **serval** (*Felis serval*) is smaller than a cheetah (shoulder height: 55cm) but has a similar build and black-on-gold spots giving way to streaking near the head. Seldom seen, it is widespread and quite common in moist grassland, reed beds and riverine habitats.

Caracal (*Felis caracal*) Sw: *simbamangu*. Shoulder height: 40cm; weight: 15–20kg. The caracal resembles the European lynx with its uniform tan coat and tufted ears. It is a solitary hunter, feeding on birds, small antelope and livestock, and ranges throughout the country favouring relatively arid savannah habitats. It is nocturnal and rarely seen.

Similar species The smaller **African wild cat** (*Felis sylvestris*) ranges from the Mediterranean to the Cape of Good Hope, and is similar in appearance to the domestic tabby cat. Like the caracal, it is common, but nocturnal, and infrequently seen.

African wild dog (*Lycaon pictus*) Sw: *mbwa mwitu*. Shoulder height: 70cm; weight: 25kg. Also known as the African hunting dog or painted dog, the wild dog is distinguished from other African canids by its large size and cryptic black, brown and cream coat. Highly sociable, living in packs of

up to 20 animals, the hunting dog is a ferocious hunter that literally tears apart its prey on the run. Threatened with extinction as a result of its susceptibility to diseases spread by domestic dogs, it is extinct in several areas where it was formerly abundant, for instance in the Serengeti and most other reserves in northern Tanzania. The global population of around 4,000 wild dogs is spread across much of eastern and southern Africa, but the Selous Game Reserve is the most important stronghold (estimated population 1,300) and Ruaha National Park also hosts a viable population. The only place in northern Tanzania where hunting dogs can reliably be observed is the Mkomazi Game Reserve, where a recently re-introduced population is reportedly thriving. A few recent scattered sightings in Tarangire and Lake Manyara national parks provide some hope that this endangered creature might yet re-colonise this area.

Black-backed jackal (*Canis mesomelas*) Sw: *mbweha*. Shoulder height: 35–45cm; weight: 8–12kg. The black-backed (or silver-backed) jackal is an opportunistic feeder capable of adapting to most habitats. Most often seen singly or in pairs at dusk or dawn, it is ochre in colour with a prominent black saddle flecked by a varying amount of white or gold. It is probably the most frequently observed small predator in Africa south of the Zambezi, and its eerie call is a characteristic sound of the bush at night. It is the commonest jackal in most Tanzanian reserves.

Similar species The **side-striped jackal** (*Canis adustus*) is more cryptic in colour, and has an indistinct pale vertical stripe on each flank and a white-tipped tail. Nowhere very common, it is distributed throughout Tanzania, and most likely to be seen in the southern reserves. The **common jackal** (*Canis aureus*), also known as the Eurasian or golden jackal, is a cryptically coloured North African jackal, relatively pale and with a black tail tip. Its range extends as far south as the Serengeti and Ngorongoro Crater, and it is probably more readily seen than the black-backed jackal on the crater floor, since it is more diurnal in its habits.

Bat-eared fox (*Otocyon megalotis*) Shoulder height: 30–35cm; weight: 35kg. This small, silver-grey insectivore, unmistakable with its huge ears and black eye-mask, is most often seen in pairs or small family groups during the cooler hours of the day. Associated with dry open country, the bat-eared fox is quite common in the Serengeti and likely to be encountered at least once in the course of a few days' safari, particularly during the denning season (November and December).

Spotted hyena (*Crocuta crocuta*) Sw: *fisi*. Shoulder height: 85cm; weight: 70kg. Hyenas are characterised by their bulky build, sloping back, brownish coat, powerful jaws and dog-like expression. Despite looking superficially canine, they are more closely related to mongooses and bears than to cats or dogs. Contrary to popular myth, hyenas are not exclusively scavengers: the spotted hyena in particular is an adept hunter capable of killing an animal as large as a wildebeest. Nor are they hermaphroditic, an ancient belief that stems from the false scrotum and penis covering the female hyena's vagina. Sociable animals, and fascinating to observe, hyenas live in loosely structured clans of about ten animals, led by females who are stronger and larger than males. The spotted hyena is the largest hyena, distinguished by its blotchily spotted coat, and it is probably the most common large predator in eastern and southern Africa. It is most frequently seen at dusk and dawn in the vicinity of game reserve lodges, campsites and refuse dumps, and is likely to be encountered on a daily basis in the Serengeti and Ngorongoro Crater.

Similar species The North African **striped hyena** (*Hyaena hyaena*) is pale brown with several dark vertical streaks and an off-black mane. It occurs alongside the spotted hyena in dry parts of Tanzania, but is scarce and secretive. The equally secretive **aardwolf** (*Proteles cristatus*) is an insectivorous striped hyena, not much bigger than a jackal, occurring in low numbers in northern Tanzania.

African civet (*Civettictus civetta*) Sw: *fungo*. Shoulder height: 40cm; weight: 10–15kg. This bulky, long-haired, rather feline creature of the African night is primarily carnivorous, feeding on small animals and  carrion, but will also eat fruit. It has a similarly coloured coat to a leopard or cheetah, and this is densely blotched with large black spots becoming stripes towards the head. Civets are widespread and common in many habitats, but very rarely seen.

Similar species The smaller, more slender **tree civet** (*Nandinia binotata*) is an arboreal forest animal with a dark-brown coat marked with black spots. The **small-spotted genet** (*Genetta genetta*) and **large-spotted genet** (*Genetta tigrina*) are the most widespread members of a group of similar small predators, all of which are very slender and rather feline in appearance, with a grey to golden brown coat marked with black spots and an exceptionally long ringed tail. Most likely to be seen on nocturnal game drives or scavenging around game reserve lodges, the large-spotted genet is golden brown with very large spots and a black-tipped tail, whereas the small-spotted genet is greyer with rather small spots and a pale tip to the tail.

Banded mongoose (*Mungos mungo*) Shoulder height: 20cm; weight: around 1kg. The banded mongoose is probably the most commonly observed member of a group of small, slender, terrestrial carnivores. Uniform dark brown except for a dozen black stripes across its back, it is a diurnal mongoose occurring in family groups in most wooded habitats and savannah.

Similar species Several other mongoose species occur in Tanzania, though some are too scarce and nocturnal to be seen by casual visitors. The **marsh mongoose** (*Atilax paludinosus*) is large, normally solitary and has a very scruffy brown coat. It's widespread in the eastern side of Africa where it is often seen in the vicinity of water. The **white-tailed ichneumon** (*Ichneumia albicauda*) is another widespread, solitary, large brown mongoose, easily identified by its bushy white tail. The **slender mongoose** (*Galerella sanguinea*) is as widespread and also solitary, but it is very much smaller (shoulder height: 10cm) and has a uniform brown coat and black tail tip. The **dwarf mongoose** (*Helogate parvula*) is a diminutive (shoulder height: 7cm) and highly sociable light-brown mongoose often seen in the vicinity of termite mounds, particularly in Tarangire National Park.

Ratel (*Mellivora capensis*) Sw: *nyegere*. Shoulder height: 30cm; weight: 12kg. Also known as the honey badger, the ratel is black with a puppyish face and grey-to-white back. It is an opportunistic feeder best known for its symbiotic relationship with a bird called the honeyguide which leads it to a bee hive, waits for it to tear the nest open, then feeds on the scraps. The ratel is among the most widespread of African carnivores, but it is thinly distributed and rarely seen.

Similar species Several other mustelids occur in the region, including the **striped polecat** (*Ictonyx striatus*), a common but rarely seen nocturnal creature with black underparts and bushy white back, and the similar but much more scarce **striped weasel** (*Poecilogale albincha*). The **Cape clawless otter** (*Aonyx capensis*) is a brown freshwater mustelid with a white collar, while the smaller **spotted-necked otter** (*Lutra maculicollis*) is darker with white spots on its throat.

Primates

Chimpanzee (*Pan troglodytes*) Sw: *sokwe-mtu*. Standing height: 100cm; weight: up to 55kg. This distinctive black-coated ape is, along with the bonobo (*Pan paniscus*) of the southern Congo, more closely related to man than to any other living creature. The chimpanzee lives in large troops based around a core of related males dominated by an alpha male. Females aren't firmly bonded to their core group, so emigration between communities is normal. Primarily frugivorous (fruit-eating), chimpanzees eat meat on occasion, and though most kills are  opportunistic, stalking of prey is not unusual. The first recorded instance of a chimp using a tool was at Gombe Stream in Tanzania, where modified sticks were used to 'fish' in termite mounds. In west Africa, chimps have been observed cracking open nuts with a stone and anvil. In the USA, captive chimps have successfully been taught Sign Language and have created compound words such as 'rock-berry' to describe a nut. A widespread and common rainforest resident, the chimpanzee is thought to number 200,000 in the wild. In East Africa, chimps occur in western Uganda and on the Tanzanian shore of Lake Tanganyika, where they can be seen at the research centre founded by primatologist Jane Goodall in Tanzania's Gombe Stream, as well as at Mahale Mountains and on Rubondo Island.

Common baboon (*Papio cynocaphalus*) Sw: *nyani*. Shoulder height: 50–75cm; weight: 25–45kg. This powerful terrestrial primate, distinguished from any other monkey by its much larger size, inverted U-shaped tail and distinctive doglike head, is fascinating to watch from a behavioural perspective. It lives in large troops that boast a complex, rigid social structure characterised by matriarchal lineages

and plenty of inter-troop movement by males seeking social dominance. Omnivorous and at home in almost any habitat, the baboon is the most widespread primate in Africa, frequently seen in most Tanzanian game reserves. There are several races of baboon in Africa, regarded by some authorities to be full species. In Tanzania, the yellow baboon (*P. c. cynocephalus*) is the light yellow-brown race occurring in the south and east of the country, while the olive or anubis baboon (*P. c. anubis*) is the darker and hairier green-brown baboon found in the northern reserves.

Vervet monkey (*Cercopithecus aethiops*) Sw: *tumbili*. Length (excluding tail): 40–55cm; weight: 4–6kg. Also known as the green or grivet monkey, the vervet is probably the world's most numerous monkey and certainly the most common and widespread representative of the *Cercopithecus* guenons, a taxonomically controversial genus associated with African forests. An atypical guenon in that it inhabits savannah and woodland rather than true forest, the vervet spends a high proportion of its time on the ground and in most of its range could be confused only with the much larger and heavier baboon. However, the vervet's light-grey coat, black face and white forehead band should be diagnostic – as should the male's garish blue genitals. The vervet is abundant in Tanzania, and might be seen just about anywhere, not only in reserves.

Similar species The terrestrial **patas monkey** (*Erythrocebus patas*), larger and more spindly than the vervet, has an orange-tinged coat and black forehead stripe. Essentially a monkey of the dry northwestern savannah, the patas occurs in low numbers in the northern Serengeti.

Blue monkey (*Cercopithecus mitis*) Sw: *kima*. Length (excluding tail): 50–60cm; weight: 5–8kg. This most variable of African monkeys is also known as the samango, golden, silver or Syke's monkey, or the diademed or white-throated guenon. Several dozen races are recognised, divided by some authorities into more than one species. Taxonomic confusion notwithstanding, *C. mitis* is the most common forest guenon in eastern Africa, with one or other race occurring in just about any suitable habitat. Unlikely to be confused with another species in Tanzania, the blue monkey has a uniformly dark blue-grey coat broken by a white throat which in some races extends all down the chest and in others around the collar. It lives in troops of up to ten animals and associates with other primates where their ranges overlap. It is common in Arusha and Lake Manyara national parks and in many forest reserves.

Similar species The **red-tailed monkey** (*Cercopithecus ascanius*) is a small brown guenon with white whiskers, a red tail and distinctive white heart on its nose. In Tanzania, it is restricted to forested parts of the Lake Tanganyika shore, such as Mahale Mountains and Gombe Stream. The **crested mangabey** (*Cercocebus*

galeritus) is a yellowish west African monkey, two isolated populations of which occur in East Africa, one in Tanzania's Udzungwa Mountains and another along Kenya's Tana River. Both are classified as full species by most authorities.

Black-and-white colobus (*Colobus guereza*) Sw: *mbega mweupe*. Length (excluding tail): 65cm; weight: 12kg. This beautiful jet-black monkey has bold white facial markings, a long white tail and in some races white sides and shoulders. Almost exclusively arboreal, it is capable of jumping up to 30m, a spectacular sight with white tail streaming behind. Several races have been described, and most authorities recognise more than one species. The black-and-white colobus is a common resident of forests in Tanzania, often seen in the forest zone of Kilimanjaro and in Arusha National Park.

Similar species The **Angola colobus** (*Colobus angolensis*) is very similar in appearance to the black-and-white colobus, and both species are subdivided further into a number of races. Some controversy surrounds the breakdown of the various races and species, but three Tanzanian races, those of the Eastern Arc, southern highlands, and Lake Tanganyika forests, are now generally assigned to *C. Angolensis*.

Red colobus (*Procolobus badius*) Length (excluding tail): 60cm; weight: 10kg. The status of this variable monkey is again controversial, with between one and ten species recognised by different authorities. Most populations have black on the upper back, red on the lower back, a pale tufted crown and a long-limbed appearance unlike that of any guenon or mangabey. Four populations are known in East Africa, of which two live in isolated pockets in Tanzania, and are regarded by some authorities to be full species. The first of these is Kirk's red colobus *P. kirkii*, which is restricted to Zanzibar Island. Only 1,500 of these animals remain in the wild, but they are easily seen in the Jozani Forest on eastern Zanzibar. The Uhehe red colobus *P. gordonorum* is a fairly common and conspicuous resident of the Udzungwa Mountains in southern Tanzania.

Lesser bushbaby (*Galago senegalensis*) Sw: *komba*. Length (without tail): 17cm; weight: 150g. The lesser bushbaby is the most widespread and common member of a group of small and generally indistinguishable nocturnal primates, distantly related to the lemurs of Madagascar. More often heard than seen, the lesser bushbaby can sometimes be picked out by tracing a cry to a tree and shining a torch into its eyes.

Similar species The most easily identified bushbaby due to its size, the **greater bushbaby** (*Galago crassicaudatus*) occurs throughout the eastern side of Africa as far south as East London. It produces a terrifying scream, which you'd think was emitted by a chimpanzee or gorilla. Recent studies in Tanzania have determined that the smaller bushbabies are far more specifically diverse than was previously realised.

Large antelope

Roan antelope (*Hippotragus equinus*) Sw: *korongo*.
Shoulder height: 120–150cm; weight: 250–300kg.
This handsome equine antelope is uniform fawn-
grey with a pale belly, short de-curved horns and a
light mane. It could be mistaken for the female sable
antelope, but this has a well-defined white belly, and
lacks the roan's distinctive black-and-white facial markings.
The roan is widespread but thinly distributed in most
reserves in southern Tanzania, and it is very rare in the
Serengeti.

Sable antelope (*Hippotragus niger*) Sw: *pala hala*. Shoulder
height: 135cm; weight: 230kg. The striking male sable
is jet black with a distinct white face, underbelly and
rump, and long de-curved horns. The female is
chestnut brown and has shorter horns. The main
stronghold for Africa's sable population is the *miombo*
woodland of southern Tanzania, where a population of
30,000 is concentrated in Ruaha National
Park and Selous Game Reserve. The sable is
absent from most reserves in northern
Tanzania.

Oryx (*Oryx gazella*) Sw: *choroa*. Shoulder height: 120cm; weight:
230kg. This regal, dry-country antelope is unmistakable with
its ash-grey coat, bold black facial marks and flank strip, and
unique long, straight horns. The fringe-eared oryx is the only
race found in Tanzania, where it is most common in Tarangire
National Park, though present in small numbers in the northern
Serengeti and Mkomazi Game Reserve.

Waterbuck (*Kobus ellipsiprymnus*) Sw: *kuro*. Shoulder
height: 130cm; weight: 250–270kg. The waterbuck is
easily recognised by its shaggy brown coat and the
male's large lyre-shaped horns. The Defassa race of the
Rift Valley and areas further west has a full white rump,
while the eastern race has a white U on its rump. The
waterbuck is frequently seen in small family groups grazing
near water in all but the most arid of game reserves in
Tanzania.

Blue wildebeest (*Connochaetes taurinus*) Sw:
nyumbu. Shoulder height: 130–150cm;
weight: 180–250kg. This rather ungainly
antelope, also called the brindled gnu, is
easily recognised by its dark coat and bovine
appearance. The superficially similar buffalo
is far more heavily built. Immense herds of
blue wildebeest occur on the Serengeti Plains,
where the annual migration of more than a million
heading into Kenya's Maasai Mara forms one of
Africa's great natural spectacles. There are also

significant wildebeest populations in the Ngorongoro Crater, Tarangire and in most reserves in southern Tanzania.

Hartebeest (*Alcelaphus buselaphus*) Shoulder height: 125cm; weight: 120–150kg. Hartebeests are ungainly antelopes, readily identified by the combination of large shoulders, a sloping back, red-brown or yellow-brown coat and smallish horns in both sexes. Numerous races are recognised, all of which are generally seen in small family groups in reasonably open country. The race found in northern Tanzania, Coke's hartebeest or kongoni, is common in open parts of the Serengeti and Ngorongoro. In southern Tanzania, it is replaced by Liechtenstein's hartebeest, which is regarded by some authorities to be a full species.

Similar species The **topi** or **tsessebe** (*Damaliscus lunatus*) is basically a darker version of the hartebeest with striking yellow lower legs. Widespread but thinly and patchily distributed, the topi occurs alongside the much paler kongoni in the Serengeti National Park, where it is common.

Common eland (*Taurotragus oryx*) Sw: *pofu*. Shoulder height: 150–175cm; weight: 450–900kg. Africa's largest antelope, the common eland is light brown in colour, sometimes with a few faint white vertical stripes. It has a somewhat bovine appearance, accentuated by the relatively short horns and large dewlap. It is widely distributed in east and southern Africa, and small herds may be seen almost anywhere in grassland or light woodland. The eland is fairly common in the Serengeti and Mikumi national parks, but difficult to approach closely.

Greater kudu (*Tragelaphus strepsericos*) Sw: *tandala*. Shoulder height: 140–155cm; weight: 180–250kg. In many parts of Africa, the greater kudu is the most readily observed member of the genus *Tragelaphus*, a group of medium to large antelopes characterised by the male's large spiralling horns and a dark coat generally marked with several vertical white stripes. The greater kudu is very large, with a grey-brown coat and up to ten stripes on each side, and the male has magnificent double-spiralled horns. A widespread animal occurring in most wooded habitats except for true forest, the greater kudu is rare in northern Tanzania, but more common in the southern reserves, where it is most often seen in mixed- or single-sex herds of up to ten animals.

Similar species The thinly distributed and skittish **lesser kudu** (*Tragelaphus imberbis*) is an East African species largely restricted to arid woodland. In Tanzania, it often occurs alongside the greater kudu, from which it can be distinguished by its smaller size (shoulder height: 100cm), two white throat patches and greater number of stripes (at least eleven). Nowhere common, it is most likely to be encountered in Tarangire and Ruaha national parks. The semi-aquatic **sitatunga** (*Tragelaphus spekei*) is a widespread but infrequently observed inhabitant of west and central African swamps from the Okovango in Botswana to the Sudd in Sudan. Tanzania's Rubondo Island is one of the few places where it is readily observed. The male, with a shoulder height of up to 125cm and a shaggy fawn coat, is unmistakable in its habitat. The smaller female might be mistaken for a bushbuck (see below) but is much drabber.

Medium and small antelope

Bushbuck (*Tragelaphus scriptus*) Sw: *pongo*. Shoulder height: 70–80cm; weight: 30–45kg. This attractive antelope, a member of the same genus as the kudu and sitatunga, shows great regional variation in colouring. The male is dark brown, chestnut or, in parts of Ethiopia, black, while the much smaller female is generally pale red-brown. The male has relatively small, straight horns for a *tragelaphus* antelope. Both sexes have similar throat patches to the lesser kudu, and are marked with white spots and sometimes stripes. One of the most widespread antelope species in Africa, the bushbuck occurs in forest and riverine woodland throughout Tanzania, where it is normally seen singly or in pairs. It tends to be secretive and skittish except where it is used to people, so it is not as easily seen as you might expect of a common antelope.

Thomson's gazelle (*Gazella thomsoni*) Shoulder height: 60cm; weight: 20–25kg. Gazelles are graceful, relatively small antelopes that generally occur in large herds in open country, and have fawn-brown upper parts and a white belly. Thomson's gazelle is characteristic of the East African plains, where it is the only gazelle to have a black horizontal stripe. It is common to abundant in the Serengeti and surrounds.

Similar species Occurring alongside Thomson's gazelle in many parts of East Africa, the larger **Grant's gazelle** (*Gazella granti*) lacks a black side stripe and has comparatively large horns. An uncharacteristic gazelle, the **gerenuk** (*Litocranius walleri*), is a solitary, arid country species of Ethiopia, Kenya and northern Tanzania, similar in general colour to an impala but readily identified by its very long neck and singular habit of feeding from trees standing on its hind legs. Good places to see it include Mkomazi, Tarangire and the Loliondo area.

Impala (*Aepeceros melampus*) Sw: *swala pala*. Shoulder height: 90cm; weight: 45kg. This slender, handsome antelope is superficially similar to some gazelles, but in fact belongs to a separate family. Chestnut in colour, the impala has diagnostic black and white stripes running down its rump and tail, and the male has large lyre-shaped horns. One of the most widespread antelope species in sub-equatorial Africa, the impala is normally seen in large herds in wooded savannah habitats, and it is one of the most common antelope in many Tanzanian reserves.

Reedbucks (*Redunca spp*) Sw: *tohe*. Shoulder height: 65–90cm; weight: 30–65kg. The three species of reedbuck are all rather nondescript fawn-grey antelopes generally seen in open grassland near water. The mountain reedbuck (*Redunca fulvorufula*) is the smallest and most distinctive, with a clear white belly, tiny horns, and an overall grey appearance. It has a broken distribution, occurring in mountainous parts of eastern South Africa, northern Tanzania, Kenya and southern Ethiopia. The Bohor reedbuck is found in northern Tanzania, whereas the southern reedbuck occurs in southern Tanzania.

Similar species The golden brown **puku** (*Kobus vardoni*), similar in appearance to the kob of Uganda, lives in marsh and moist grassland from Lake Rukwa in Tanzania to the Okovango in Botswana. Its main stronghold is the Kilombero Valley in southeast Tanzania.

Klipspringer (*Oreotragus oreotragus*) Sw: *mbuze mawe*. Shoulder height: 60cm; weight: 13kg. The klipspringer is a goat-like antelope, normally seen in pairs, and easily identified by its dark, bristly grey-yellow coat, slightly speckled appearance and unique habitat preference. Klipspringer means 'rockjumper' in Afrikaans, an apt name for an antelope that occurs exclusively in mountainous areas and rocky outcrops. It is found throughout Tanzania, and is often seen around the Lobo Hills in the Serengeti and the Maji Moto area in Lake Manyara.

Steenbok (*Raphicerus cempestris*) Sw: *tondoro*. Shoulder height: 50cm; weight: 11kg. This rather nondescript small antelope has red-brown upper parts and clear white underparts, and the male has short straight horns. It is probably the most commonly observed small antelope in Africa, though it has a broken range, and is absent from southern Tanzania despite being common in the north of the country and in areas further south. Like most other antelopes of its size, the steenbok is normally encountered singly or in pairs and tends to 'freeze' when disturbed.

Similar species The **oribi** (*Ourebia ourebi*) is a widespread but uncommon grassland antelope which looks much like a steenbok but stands about 10cm higher at the shoulder and has an altogether more upright bearing. **Kirk's dik-dik** (*Madoqua kirki*), smaller than the steenbok and easily identified by its large white eye circle, is restricted primarily to Tanzania and Kenya, and it is particularly common in Arusha National Park.

Red duiker (*Cephalophus natalensis*) Sw: *pofu*. Shoulder height: 45cm; weight: 14kg. This is the most likely of Africa's 12 to 20 'forest duikers' to be seen by tourists. It is deep chestnut in colour with a white tail and, in the case of the East African race *C. n. harveyi* (sometimes considered to be a separate species), a black face. The red duiker occurs in most substantial forest patches along the eastern side of Africa, though it is less often seen than it is heard crashing through the undergrowth.

Similar species The **blue duiker** (*Cephalophus monticola*) is widespread in Africa and the only other forest duiker to occur in countries south of Tanzania, and it can easily be told from the red duiker by its greyer colouring and much smaller size (it is the smallest forest duiker, about the same size as a suni). **Abbott's duiker** (*Cephalophus spadix*) is a large duiker, as tall as a klipspringer, restricted to a handful of montane forests in Tanzania, including those on Kilimanjaro and the Usambara, Udzungwa and Poroto mountains. The endangered **Ader's duiker** (*Cephalophus adersi*) is presumably restricted to forested habitats on Zanzibar Island, where as few as 1,000 animals may survive, most of them in the Jozani Forest. Recent reports suggest that this duiker is extinct in the only other locality where it has been recorded, the Sokoke Forest in Kenya.

Common duiker (*Sylvicapra grimmia*) Sw: *nysa*. Shoulder height: 50cm; weight: 20kg. This anomalous duiker holds itself more like a steenbok and is the only member of its family to occur outside of forests. Generally grey in colour, the common duiker can most easily be separated from other small antelopes by the black tuft of hair that sticks up between its horns. It occurs throughout Tanzania, and tolerates most habitats except for true forest and very open country.

Other large herbivores
African elephant (*Loxodonta africana*) Sw: *tembe*. Shoulder height: 2.3–3.4m; weight: up to 6,000kg. The world's largest land animal, the African elephant is intelligent, social and often very entertaining to watch. Female elephants live in close-knit clans in which the eldest female plays matriarch over her sisters, daughters and granddaughters. Mother–daughter bonds are strong and may last for up to 50 years. Males generally leave the family group at around 12 years to roam singly or form bachelor herds. Under normal circumstances, elephants will range widely in search of food and water, but when concentrated populations are forced to live in conservation areas, their habit of uprooting trees can cause serious environmental damage. Elephants are widespread and common in habitats ranging from desert to rainforest and, despite heavy poaching, they are likely to be seen on a daily basis in most of the country's larger national parks, the exception being the Serengeti where they are common only in the Lobo region.

Black rhinoceros (*Diceros bicornis*) Sw: *faru*. Shoulder height: 160cm; weight: 1,000kg. This is the more widespread of Africa's two rhino species, an imposing, sometimes rather aggressive creature that has been poached to extinction in most of its former range. It occurs in many southern African reserves, but is now very localised in East Africa, where it is most likely to be seen in Tanzania's Ngorongoro Crater. The most substantial Tanzania population is in the Selous Game Reserve, but sightings here are infrequent.

Hippopotamus (*Hippopotamus amphibius*) Sw: *kiboko*. Shoulder height: 150cm; weight: 2,000kg. Characteristic of Africa's large rivers and lakes, this large, lumbering animal spends most of the day submerged, but emerges at night to graze. Strongly territorial, herds of ten or more animals are presided over by a dominant male who will readily defend his patriarchy to the death. Hippos are abundant in most protected rivers and water bodies, and they are still quite common outside of reserves, where they kill more people than any other African mammal.

African buffalo (*Syncerus caffer*) Sw: *nyati*. Shoulder height: 140cm; weight: 700kg. Frequently and erroneously referred to as a water buffalo (an Asian species), the African buffalo is a distinctive ox-like animal that lives in large herds on the savannah and occurs in smaller herds in forested areas. Common and widespread in sub-Saharan Africa, herds of buffalo are likely to be encountered in most Tanzanian reserves and national parks. The best place to see large buffalo herds is on the Ngorongoro Crater floor or in Katavi National Park.

Giraffe (*Giraffa camelopardis*) Sw: *twiga*. Shoulder height: 250–350cm; weight: 1,000–1,400kg. The world's tallest and longest-necked land animal, a fully grown giraffe can measure up to 5.5m high. Quite unmistakable, the giraffe lives in loosely structured herds of up to 15, though herd members often disperse and are seen singly or in smaller groups. Formerly distributed throughout east and southern Africa, the giraffe is now more or less restricted to conservation areas, where it is generally common and easily seen. Two places in Tanzania where there are no giraffe are the part of the Selous south of the Rufiji and the Ngorongoro Crater floor.

Common zebra (*Equus burchelli*) Sw: *punda milia*. Shoulder height: 130cm; weight: 300–340kg. This attractive striped horse is common and widespread throughout most of east and southern Africa, where it is often seen in large herds alongside wildebeest. The common zebra is the only wild equine to occur in Tanzania, and is common in most conservation areas, especially the Serengeti.

Warthog (*Phacochoerus africanus*) Sw: *ngiri*. Shoulder height: 60–70cm; weight: up to 100kg. This widespread and often conspicuously abundant resident of the African savannah is grey in colour with a thin covering of hairs, wartlike bumps on its face, and rather large upward curving tusks. Africa's only diurnal swine, the warthog is often seen in family groups, trotting off briskly with its tail raised stiffly (a diagnostic trait) and a determinedly nonchalant air.

Similar species Bulkier, hairier and browner, the **bushpig** (*Potomochoerus larvatus*) is as widespread as the warthog, but infrequently seen due to its nocturnal habits and preference for dense vegetation. Larger still, weighing up to 250kg, the **giant forest hog** (*Hylochoerus meinertzhageni*) is primarily a species of the west African rainforest. It does occur in certain highland forests in northern Tanzania, but the chance of a sighting is practically non-existent.

Small mammals
Aardvark (*Orycteropus afer*) Shoulder height: 60cm; weight: up to 70kg. This singularly bizarre nocturnal insectivore is unmistakable with its long snout and huge ears. It occurs practically throughout the region, but sightings are extremely rare.

Similar species Not so much similar to an aardvark as equally dissimilar to anything else, **pangolins** are rare nocturnal insectivores with distinctive armour plating and a tendency to roll up in a ball when disturbed. Most likely to be seen in Tanzania is Temminck's pangolin (*Manis temmincki*). Also nocturnal, but spiky rather than armoured, several **hedgehog** and **porcupine** species occur in the region, the former generally no larger than a guinea pig, the latter generally 60–100cm long.

Rock hyrax (*Procavia capensis*) Sw: *pimbi*. Shoulder height: 35–30cm; weight: 4kg. Rodent-like in appearance, hyraxes are more closely related to elephants. The rock hyrax and similar bush hyrax (*Heterohyrax brucei*) are often seen sunning in rocky habitats and become tame when used to people, for instance at Seronera and Lobo lodges in the Serengeti. The less common tree hyrax (*Dendrohyrax arboreus*) is a nocturnal forest creature, often announcing its presence with an unforgettable shrieking call.

Similar species The **elephant shrews** (Sw: *sange*) are rodents that look like miniature kangaroos with absurdly elongated noses. A number of species are recognised, but they are mostly secretive and nocturnal, so rarely seen. The smaller species are generally associated with savannah habitats, but the much larger chequered elephant shrew is a resident of Eastern Arc forests – I've only ever seen it in Amani and Udzungwa.

Scrub hare (*Lepus saxatilis*) This is the largest and commonest African hare or rabbit. In some areas a short walk at dusk or after nightfall might reveal three or four scrub hares. They tend to freeze when disturbed.

Unstriped ground squirrel (*Xerus rutilus*) An endearing terrestrial animal of arid savannah, the unstriped ground squirrel is grey to grey-brown with a prominent white eye ring and silvery black tail. It spends much time on its hind legs, and has the characteristic squirrel mannerism of holding food in its forepaws. In Tanzania, it is most likely to be seen in the Serengeti.

Bush squirrel (*Paraxerus cepapi*) This is the typical squirrel of the eastern and southern savannah, rusty brown in colour with a silvery black back and white eye rings. A great many other arboreal or semi-arboreal squirrels occur in the region, but most are difficult to tell apart in the field.

BIRDS Tanzania is a birdwatcher's dream, and it is impossible to do justice to its rich avifauna in the confines of a short introduction. Casual visitors will be stunned at the abundance of birdlife: the brilliantly coloured lilac-breasted rollers and superb starlings, the numerous birds of prey, the giant ostrich, the faintly comic hornbills, the magnificent crowned crane – the list could go on forever. And for more dedicated birdwatchers, Tanzania ranks with the top handful of birding destinations in Africa, with 1,130 species included on a working checklist compiled by Neil and Liz Baker of the Tanzania Bird Atlas Project, the second most varied avifauna of any African country.

Virtually anywhere in Tanzania offers good birding, and species of special interest are noted under the relevant site throughout the main body of this guide.

The weavers of the family Ploceidae are a quintessential part of Africa's natural landscape, common in virtually every habitat from rainforest to desert. The name of the family derives from the intricate and elaborate nests built by the dextrous males of most species, typically a roughly oval ball of dried grass, reeds and twigs.

It can be fascinating to watch a male weaver at work. First, a nest site is chosen, usually at the end of a thin hanging branch, which is stripped of leaves to protect against snakes. The weaver carries building material back and forth to the site, blade by blade in its heavy beak, using a few thick strands to create the skeletal framework, then completing the structure by interweaving thinner blades. Once complete, the nest is inspected by the female, who will tear it apart if the result is unsatisfactory.

All but 12 of the 113 described weaver species are resident on the African mainland or associated islands, with at least 45 represented within Tanzania alone. A full 20 of these Tanzanian species are placed in the genus *Ploceus* (true weavers), which are typically slightly larger than a sparrow, and display strong sexual dimorphism. Females tend to be drab olive-brown with some streaking on the back and perhaps a hint of yellow on the belly, while many male *Ploceus* weavers conform to the basic colour pattern of the 'masked weaver' – predominantly yellow with a distinct black facial mask, often bordered orange. Seven Tanzanian weaver species fit this masked weaver prototype more or less absolutely, and a similar number approximate it rather less exactly, for instance by having a chestnut-brown mask, or a full black head, or a black back, or being more chestnut than yellow on the belly. Identification of the masked weavers can be tricky without experience – useful clues are the exact shape of the mask, the presence and extent of the fringing orange, and the colour of the eye and the back. Among the more conspicuous *Ploceus* species in northern Tanzania are the Baglafecht, spectacled, vitelline masked, lesser masked and black-headed weavers – for the most part gregarious breeders forming single or mixed species colonies of hundreds, sometimes thousands, of pairs, often in reed beds and waterside vegetation.

While most of Tanzania's *Ploceus* weavers are common, three are of global conservation concern: the Taveta palm weaver (restricted to the plains immediately below Kilimanjaro) and the Usambara and Kilombero weavers (both endemic to a limited number of sites in eastern Tanzania).

Most of the colonial weavers build relatively plain nests with a roughly oval shape and an unadorned entrance hole. The nests of more solitary weavers are often more elaborate. Several species protect their nests from egg-eating invaders by building tubular entrance tunnels, sometimes twice as long as the nest itself. The grosbeak weaver, a peculiar brown-and-white weaver of reed beds, placed in the monospecific genus *Amblyospiza*, constructs a distinctive domed nest, which is supported by a pair of reeds, and woven as precisely as the finest basketwork.

By contrast, the scruffiest nests are built by the various species of sparrow- and buffalo-weaver, relatively drab but highly gregarious dry-country birds that occur throughout northern Tanzania. The most striking bird in the group is the white-headed buffalo weaver, which despite its name is most easily identified by its unique bright red rump. The endemic rufous-tailed weaver, a close relative the buffalo-weavers, is a common resident of Tarangire, Serengeti and the Ngorongoro Conservation Area.

ENDEMICS Full list of confirmed and probable species confined to Tanzania:

Grey-breasted spurfowl (*Pternistes rufopictus*) Serengeti and vicinity; common in scattered woodland around Seronera.

Udzungwa forest partridge (*Xenoperdix udzungwensis*) Discovered 1991 in Udzungwa. Estimated population 3,500–4,000.

Rubeho forest partridge (*Xenoperdix obscurata*) Discovered Rubeho Highlands 2003, proposed as new species 2005. Population may be < 1000.

Pemba Green Pigeon (*Treron pembaensis*) Confined to Pemba Island, greyer underneath than the mainland equivalent, but unmistakable in its limited range.

Fischer's lovebird (*Agapornis fischeri*) Feral population exists in Kenya. Serengeti and vicinity, where common.

Yellow-collared lovebird (*Agapornis personatus*) Feral population exists in Kenya. Common in Tarangire and semi-arid parts of central Tanzania.

Tanzanian red-billed hornbill (*Tockus ruahae*) Recently described, range centred on Ruaha National Park, where common.

Pemba scops-owl (*Otus pembae*) Very rare. Confined to Pemba Island.

Nduk Usambara eagle-owl (*Bubo vosseleri*) Eastern Arc forests including Usambara, Uluguru and Udzungwa.

Usambara nightjar (*Caprimulgus guttifer*) Recent debatable split from mountain nightjar. Usambara Mountains and possibly other Eastern Arc ranges.

Beesley's lark (*Chersomanes beesleyi*) Recent split from the spike-heeled lark. Population < 1,000 in short grasslands west of Kilimanjaro.

Neumann's mountain greenbul (*Andropadus neumanni*) Recent split from mountain greenbul. Uluguru forests.

Yellow-throated mountain greenbul (*Andropadus chlorigula*) Recent split from mountain greenbul. Forests of Udzungwa, Ukaguru and Nguru.

Usambara thrush (*Turdus roehli*) Recent split from olive thrush. Usambara and Pare forests.

Usambara Akalat (*Sheppardia montana*) Forests of Western Usambara.

Iringa Akalat (*Sheppardia lowei*) Udzungwa and other Eastern Arc ranges.

Rubeho Akalat (*Sheppardia sp*) Recently discovered in Rubeho Mountains.

Ruaha chat (*Myrmecocichola ruahae*) Proposed new species. Present Ruaha and Katavi.

Mrs Moreau's Winifred's warbler (*Bathmocercus winifredae*) Udzungwa, Rubeho, Uluguru and some other Eastern Arc ranges.

Usambara hyliota (*Hyliota usambarae*) East Usambara.

Kilombero cisticola (*Cisticola sp*) Recently discovered and undescribed. Kilombero Valley.

White-tailed cisticola (*Cisticola sp*) Recently discovered and undescribed. Kilombero Valley.

Reichenow's batis (*Batis reichenow*) Eastern Arc forest canopies.

Banded Green sunbird (*Anthreptes rubritorques*) Udzungwa, Nguru, Uluguru and Usambara.

Rufous-winged sunbird (*Cinnyris rufipennis*) Discovered in 1981. Udzungwa Mountains.

Rubeho sunbird (*Cinnyris sp*) Recently discovered in Rubeho Mountains.

Moreau's sunbird (*Cinnyris moreaui*) East Usambara, Udzungwa and other Eastern Arc ranges.

Loveridge's sunbird (*Cinnyris loveridgei*) Uluguru Mountains.

Usambara double-collared sunbird (*Cinnyris usambararicus*) Usambara and Pare Mountains.

Pemba sunbird (*Cinnyris pembae*) Confined to Pemba Island.

Pemba white-eye (*Zosterops vaughani*) Confined to Pemba Island.

South Pare white-eye (*Zosterops winifredae*) Controversial split from mountain white-eye. South Pare Mountains.

Uhehe fiscal (*Lanius marwitzi*) Confined to highlands around Iringa.

Uluguru bush shrike (*Malaconotus alius*) Rare. Forest canopies in Uluguru.

Ashy starling (*Cosmopsarus unicolor*) Central plains. Common in Tarangire and Ruaha.

Rufous-tailed weaver (*Histurgops ruficauda*) Serengeti, Ngorongoro and Tarangire national parks.

Kilombero weaver (*Ploceus burnieri*) Recently described. Kilombero Valley.

Usambara weaver (*Ploceus nicolli*) West Usambara, Uluguru and Udzungwa mountains.

Kipengere seedeater (*Serinus melanochrous*) Southern highlands.

NEAR ENDEMICS Several species have a range confined to Tanzania and one neighbouring country:

Fischer's turaco (*Tauraco fischeri*) Coastal Tanzania and Kenya.

Sokoke scops-owl (*Otus Ireneae*) Eastern Usambara and one locale in Kenya.

Red-faced barbet (*Lybius rubrifacies*) Kagera Region, nudging into Uganda and possibly Rwanda.

Friedmann's lark (*Mirafra pulpa*) Grassland at base of Kilimanjaro, Tanzania and Kenya.

Athi short-toed lark (*Calendrella athensis*) Grassland in Tanzania–Kenya border between Rift Valley and Lake Victoria.

Sokoke pipit (*Anthus sokokensis*) Coastal forest; Kenya and northern Tanzania.

Red-throated tit (*Parus fringillinus*) Serengeti–Mara ecosystem.

Dappled mountain robin (*Modulatrix orostruthus*) Udzungwa, East Usambara and one locale in Mozambique.

Spot-throat (*Modulatrix orostruthus*) Eastern Arc, nudging into Malawi.

Stripe-faced greenbul (*Andropadus strifacies*) Eastern Arc, nudging into Kenya.

Sharpe's akalat (*Sheppardia sharpie*) Eastern Arc, nudging into Malawi.

Swynnerton's robin (*Swynnertonia Swynnertoni*) Montane forests of Eastern Arc and Zimbabwe.

Schalow's wheatear (*Oenanthe schalowi*) Rocky grassland, southern Kenya and northern Tanzania.

Black-lored cisticola (*Cisticola nigriloris*) Southern highlands, extending into Malawi.

Kungwe apalis (*Apalis argentea*) Albertine Rift endemic; isolated and racially discrete population in Mahale Mountains.

Karamoja apalis (*Apalis karamojae* Serengeti Plains and northeast Uganda.

Moreau's tailorbird (*Artisornis moreaui*) Eastern Usambara and one locale in Mozambique.

African tailorbird (*Artisornis metopias*) Eastern Arc through to north Mozambique.

Fulleborne's black boubou (*Laniarius fuelleborni*) Eastern Tanzania, nudging into Malawi.

Grey-crested helmet-shrike (*Priniops poliolophus*) Serengeti-Mara ecosystem, into Kenya.

Hildebrandt's starling (*Lamprotornis hildebrandti*) South Kenya and north Tanzania.

Abbott's starling (*Pholia femoralis*) Pare Mountains, other forested locales in Kenya.

Kenrick's starling (*Poeoptera kenricki*) Montane forests in Tanzania and Kenya.

Amani sunbird (*Hedydipna pallidigaster*) Coastal forests, Tanzania and Kenya.

Taveta weaver (*Ploceus castaneiceps*) North Tanzania and south Kenya.

Tanzania masked weaver (*Ploceus taeniopterus*) Swamps in Tanzania–Zambia border region.

Montane marsh widowbird (*Euplectes psammocromius*) Southern highlands, extending into Malawi.

In many areas a reasonably competent novice to East African birds could hope to see between 50 and 100 species in a day. Any of the northern reserves are recommended: Arusha and Lake Manyara National Park are both good for forest and waterbirds; the Serengeti and Tarangire are good for raptors and acacia and grassland species. *Miombo*-associated species can be seen in the southern reserves: the Selous, with the advantage of the many birds that live along the Rufiji River, is particularly recommended. Western reserves such as Gombe Stream and Rubondo Island offer a combination of water and forest habitats, with the possibility of glimpsing one or two west African specials.

Recent new discoveries now place Tanzania second to South Africa for its wealth of endemic birds – species that are unique to the country. At present, at least 30 endemic species should probably be recognised, including a few controversial splits, three species discovered and described in the 1990s, and four that still await formal description. Five of the national endemics are readily observed on the northern safari circuit, but a greater number are restricted to the Eastern Arc Mountains, together with about 20 eastern forest and woodland species whose core range lies within Tanzania. A comprehensive and regularly updated checklist of Tanzania's birds, together with atlas maps for a growing number of species, is posted on the Tanzania Bird Atlas Project website: www.tanzaniabirdatlas.com.

REPTILES

Nile crocodile The order Crocodilia dates back at least 150 million years, and fossil forms that lived contemporaneously with dinosaurs are remarkably unchanged from their modern ancestors, of which the Nile crocodile is the largest living reptile, growing to 6m long. Widespread in Africa, the Nile crocodile has been exterminated in many areas over the past century – hunted professionally for its skin as well as by vengeful local villagers. It feeds mostly on fish where densities are sufficient, but will also prey opportunistically on drinking or swimming mammals, dragging its victim underwater until it drowns. A large crocodile is capable of killing a lion or wildebeest, or an adult human for that matter, and in certain areas such as the Mara or Grumeti rivers in the Serengeti, large mammals do form their main prey. Today, large crocodiles are mostly confined to protected areas within Tanzania.

Snakes A wide variety of snakes are found in Tanzania, but they are typically very shy and unlikely to be noticed unless actively sought. Often seen on safari is Africa's largest snake, the rock python, which has a gold-on-black mottled skin and regularly grows to lengths exceeding 5m. Non-venomous, pythons kill their prey by strangulation, wrapping their muscular bodies around it until it cannot breathe. Pythons feed mainly on small antelopes, large rodents and similar, and are harmless to adult humans, but could conceivably kill a child.

One of the more commonly encountered venomous snakes is the puff adder, a large, thick resident of savannah and rocky habitats. Although it feeds mainly on rodents, the puff adder is rightly considered the most dangerous of African snakes, not because it is especially venomous or aggressive, but because its sluggish disposition means it is more likely to be often disturbed. Several cobra species, including the spitting cobra, are present, but they are all seldom seen. The widespread black mamba is the largest venomous snake in Africa, measuring up to 3.5m long. Theoretically, the most toxic of Africa's snakes is the arboreal boomslang – literally 'tree-snake' – but it is back-fanged and very non-aggressive, and only represents a threat to snake-handlers.

Most snakes are in fact non-venomous and harmless to any living creature larger than a rat. One of the more non-venomous snakes in the region is the green tree-

Arguably the most intriguing of African reptiles, true chameleons are confined to the Old World, with the most important centre of speciation being Madagascar, to which about half of the world's 130 described species are endemic. Another two species of chameleon occur in each of Asia and Europe, while the remainder live in mainland Africa, where Tanzania boasts the greatest national diversity of 26 species, including 11 endemics (for an annotated list of endemics, visit our website, http://bradttanzania.wordpress.com).

Chameleons are renowned for their capacity to change colour, a trait that's been exaggerated in popular literature, and is generally influenced by mood more than the colour of the background. Most African chameleons are green in colour but take on a browner hue when they descend from the foliage, and some change colour more dramatically when threatened or confronted by a rival. Species vary greatly in size, with the largest being Oustalet's chameleon of Madagascar, known to reach a length of almost 80cm.

A remarkable physiological feature of chameleons is their protuberant round eyes, which offer 180° vision on both sides and can swivel independently of each other. Only when one eye isolates a suitably juicy-looking insect will both focus in the same direction as the chameleon stalks forward to unleash the other unique weapon in its armoury: a sticky-tipped, body-length tongue that uncoils in a blink-and-you'll-miss-it flash to zap a selected item of prey. Many chameleons are adorned with an array of facial casques, flaps, horns and crests that enhance their somewhat fearsome prehistoric appearance.

In Tanzania, you're most likely to come across a chameleon when it crosses a road, in which case it should be easy to take a closer look, since most species move painfully slowly and deliberately. Chameleons are also often seen on night game drives, when their ghostly nocturnal colouring shows up clearly under a spotlight –making it pretty clear why these strange creatures are feared in many African cultures.

The flap-necked chameleon *Chamaeleo delepis*, probably the most regularly observed species of savannah and woodland habitats, is generally around 15cm long and bright green in colour with few distinctive markings, but individuals might be up to 30cm in length and will turn tan or brown under the right conditions. Another closely related and widespread species is the similar graceful chameleon *C. gracilis*, which often has a white horizontal stripe along its flanks.

Characteristic of East African montane forests, the horned chameleons form a closely allied species cluster of some taxonomic uncertainty. Typically darker than the savannah chameleons and around 20cm in length, the males of all taxa within this cluster are distinguished by up to three nasal horns that project forward from their face. The most widespread of Tanzania's horned chameleons is the giant one-horned chameleon *C. melleri*, a dark-green creature associated with the Eastern Arc forests and coastal woodland. Distinguished by its yellow stripes and small solitary horn, this is also the largest chameleon indigenous to the African mainland, measuring up to 55cm long, and it supplements a diet of insects with more substantial fare such as small lizards and snakes.

snake, which feeds mostly on amphibians. The mole snake is a common and widespread grey-brown savannah resident that grows up to 2m long, and feeds on moles and other rodents. The remarkable egg-eating snake lives exclusively on bird eggs, dislocating its jaws to swallow the egg whole, then eventually regurgitating the crushed shell in a neat little package. Many snakes take eggs opportunistically, and large-scale agitation among birds in a tree is often a good indication that a snake (or small bird of prey) is around.

Lizards All African lizards are harmless to humans, with the arguable exception of the two species of monitor lizard, which grow up to 2.2m long and could inflict a nasty bite if cornered. These versatile predators feed on anything from bird eggs to smaller reptiles and mammals, but will also eat carrion opportunistically. Of smaller species, look out for the common house gecko, an endearing bug-eyed, translucent white lizard that scampers up lodge walls and upside-down on ceilings in pursuit of pesky insects attracted to the lights. Also very common in some lodge grounds are various agama species, distinguished from other common lizards by their relatively large size of around 20–25cm, basking habits, and almost plastic looking scaling – depending on the species, a combination of blue, purple, orange or red, with the flattened head generally a different colour to the torso.

Tortoises and terrapins These peculiar reptiles are protected by a prototypal suit of armour formed by their heavy exoskeleton. The most common terrestrial species, often seen motoring in the slow lane of game reserve roads, the leopard tortoise is named after its gold-and-black mottled shell, weighs up to 30kg, and can live for more than 50 years. Four species of terrapin – essentially the freshwater equivalent of turtles – are resident in East Africa, all somewhat flatter in shape than the tortoises, and generally with a plainer brown shell. They might be seen sunning on rocks close to water or peering out from roadside puddles. The largest is the Nile soft-shelled terrapin, which occasionally reaches a length of almost 1m.

MARINE TURTLES

Tricia Hayne
Marine turtles live in seawater, coming ashore only to nest, and unlike their landlubber cousins are unable to retract either their heads or flippers into their shell for protection. The world's eight marine turtle species are all protected under the Convention on International Trade in Endangered Species (CITES). Five have been recorded off Tanzania. Most common is the green turtle *Chelonia mydas*, so called because its fat is a greenish colour. Also present is the hawksbill turtle *Eretmochelys imbricata*, whose exquisite shell is the source of traditional 'tortoiseshell', an important trade item along the coast since ancient Egyptian times, but now outlawed by CITES. The loggerhead turtle *Caretta caretta*, named for its unusually large head, and the leatherback *Dermchelys coriacea*, which can reach a length of over 2m, are both present off the shores of Tanzania but do not nest on its beaches. The olive ridley turtle *Lepidochelys olivacea* was first recorded breeding in Tanzania in 1974.

Turtles do not nest until they are at least 25 years old, when they lay their eggs deep in the sand. The eggs take around 60 days to hatch, at which time the hatchlings make their way towards the sea, attracted by the play of moonlight on the waves. The green turtle lays 300–540 eggs per season, nesting every three or four years, with the eggs hatching from May to September. In their first year, the hatchlings grow up to 2.7kg, and they can be expected to weigh up to 24kg by the time they are three or four. Green turtles may live to be centuries old, and can weigh in excess of 200kg. Turtles are cold-blooded animals, requiring warm water to survive. Water temperature affects the sex of the hatchlings – at 28°C a balance between male and female is to be expected; cooler than that and males will dominate; hotter and there will be a predominance of females.

3

Practical Information

WHEN TO VISIT

You can visit Tanzania at any time of year. Each season has different advantages, and unless you have strong reasons to travel in a certain season, we would tend to let the timing of your visit be dictated by your schedule at home rather than seasons in Tanzania. For those with the option, there is much to be said for trying to avoid peak tourist seasons, as the parks and other main tourist attractions will be less crowded, and you can often negotiate camping safaris at prices that wouldn't be offered in season. Broadly speaking, tourism arrivals are highest during the northern hemisphere winter, while the low season runs from the end of the Easter weekend until the end of September, though this is distorted by a surge of tourism over June and July, when the wildebeest migration is on in the Serengeti.

The rainy season between November and April is a good time to visit the Serengeti; it is when the countryside is greenest, and it offers the best birdwatching, with resident species supplemented by a number of Palaearctic and intra-African migrants. The rainy season is hotter than the period May to October, but in most parts of the country this will only be by a matter of a couple of degrees. The seasonal difference in temperature is most noticeable along the humid coast, which can be rather uncomfortable in the hotter months. The wettest months are March and April, when parts of the country may experience storms virtually on a daily basis.

The dry season, in particular March and September, offers the best trekking conditions on Mount Kilimanjaro and Meru. The dry season is the best time for hiking generally, and for travelling in parts of the country with poor roads. Temperatures at the coast tend to be more bearable during the dry season, which is also considerably safer than the wet season in terms of malaria and other mosquito-borne diseases.

SUGGESTED ITINERARIES

Tanzania has a well-defined tourist circuit. It would be no exaggeration to say that as many as 90% of visitors probably divide their time in the country between the two main tourist attractions, which are the game reserves of the northern safari circuit and the island of Zanzibar. If this is what you plan on doing, then any tour operator or safari company in Arusha will be able to put together a package to meet your requirements. A 10–14 day trip is ideal for the Zanzibar-safari combination. You might want to read the section on organising a safari (see page 139) before making contact with a tour operator. With Zanzibar, the main decision you need to make in advance is whether you want to be based at a hotel in the old Stone Town, or out on one of the beaches, or a combination of the two. For a short trip to Tanzania, it is advisable to fly between Arusha (the springboard for safaris in northern Tanzania) and Zanzibar. If you are really tight for time, you'll get more out of your safari by flying between lodges. A fly-in safari will also be less tiring than the more normal drive-in safari.

For those with budgetary restrictions, it will probably work out cheaper to make your travel arrangements once you are in Tanzania. It is easier to get a cheap camping safari in Arusha on the spot, and you will be able to stay at cheaper guesthouses and hotels than those favoured by tour operators. The disadvantage of doing this is that you will lose time making arrangements once you are in the country, and will probably need two days to travel overland and by sea from Arusha to Zanzibar. If you plan on arranging things as you go along, I would advise against trying to squeeze a safari and a visit to Zanzibar into a trip of less than 14 days.

After the northern safari circuit and Zanzibar, Tanzania's main tourist attraction is Kilimanjaro, which can be climbed over five or six days. A Kilimanjaro climb is one of those things that you either do or don't want to undertake: for a significant minority of travellers, climbing Kilimanjaro is the main reason for visiting Tanzania, but for the majority it is of little interest. If you want to do a Kili climb, it can be organised in advance through any number of tour operators and safari companies, and there is a lot to be said for arranging the climb through the same operator who organises your safari. As with safaris, it is generally possible to get cheaper prices on the spot. To combine a Kili climb with a few days on safari and a visit to Zanzibar, you would need an absolute minimum of two weeks in the country on an organised package, and even that would be very tight, allowing for no more than two nights on Zanzibar. Bank on at least three weeks in the country if you are travelling independently.

Beyond the above, it is difficult to recommend any particular itinerary. The southern circuit of game reserves is slowly catching on with tourists, most normally combined with a visit to Mafia or Zanzibar Island, but it is not a cheap option. Few would claim that the southern reserves offer a game-viewing spectacle to compare with the Serengeti or Ngorongoro in northern Tanzania, but they are fine reserves by any standard, and the relative exclusivity of tourist facilities in the south means that the reserves have retained more of a wilderness character. Other reserves that are of great interest to fly-in tourists are Gombe Stream, Mahale Mountains and Rubondo Island National Parks, all of which support substantial patches of rainforest habitats and offer the opportunity to see chimpanzees in the wild. Accessibility, however, is a problem and short of chartering a direct flight you would need to set aside the best part of a week to visit any of them.

For budget travellers with sufficient time, a visit to the Usambara or Pare Mountains, or to the historical seaports of Tanga, Bagamoyo and Pangani, can easily be appended to the overland trip between Arusha and Zanzibar. With yet more time, and a sense of adventure, the southern and western parts of Tanzania are rich in off-the-beaten-track possibilities, ranging from the Shirazi ruins on Kilwa Kisiwani to the fantastic hiking country around Tukuyu and the memorable steamer ride down Lake Tanganyika. The most sensible advice we can give to adventurous travellers is to allocate their time generously, or they are likely to spend a disproportionate amount of time on public transport.

To give some idea, if you wanted to visit Rubondo Island overland, you would be looking at a 10–14 day round trip from Dar es Salaam, and even Gombe Stream would be a week's round trip. The south coast could be explored comfortably over seven to ten days, the Udzungwa Mountains would be a good four to five day trip, the southern highlands and Lake Nyasa would be good for anything over a week, and the Selous is normally visited on a four to five day safari.

Independent travellers who have a longer period of time could do one of a few loops. You could, for instance, catch a train to Mbeya, spend a few days exploring around Tukuyu, cross to Mtwara via Lake Nyasa and Songea and then work your way up the south coast, a trip that will open your eyes to just how 'untouristy' even a popular tourist destination such as Tanzania can be. Another possibility from Mbeya is to work your way up to Mwanza via Lake Tanganyika taking in some of the western national parks on the way, then catch a bus across the Serengeti to Arusha and return to Dar es Salaam from there. For either of these trips, you would need at least a month.

i TOURIST INFORMATION

The Tanzania Tourist Board (*TTB; http://tanzaniatouristboard.com*) has improved greatly over recent years, and their offices in London, New York, Stockholm, Milan and Frankfurt may be able to supply you with an information pack and leaflets about the country.

Head office PO Box 2485, Dar es Salaam; ✆ 022 211 1244; f 022 211 6420; e safari@ud.co.tz

UK Tanzania Tourist Office, Tanzania House, 3 Stratford Place, London W1C 1AS; ✆ 020 7569 1470; e tanzarep@tanzania-online.gov.uk

IN TANZANIA There are helpful Tanzania Tourist Board offices in Dar es Salaam and in Arusha. The TTB office in Arusha is a good source of information about the cultural tourism programmes, and it holds a list of blacklisted safari companies.

TOUR OPERATORS

UK

Abercrombie & Kent ✆ 0845 618 2200; e info@ abercrombiekent.co.uk; www.abercrombiekent.co.uk. Tailored safaris.
Africa-in-Focus (UK) ✆ 01803 770956; e info@ africa-in-focus.com; www.africa-in-focus.com. Comfortable mobile camping safaris targeting wildlife enthusiasts, photographers & families.
Africa Select ✆ 01670 787646; e pg@ africaselect.com; www.africaselect.com. Tailor-made itineraries, including tours to safari & mountain destinations.
Africa Travel ✆ 0845 450 1520; e info@ africatravel.co.uk; www.africatravel.co.uk
Aim 4 Africa ✆ 0114 255 2533; e enquiries@ aim4africa.com; www.aim4africa.com
Alpha Travel ✆ 020 8423 0220; e alpha@ alphauk.co.uk; www.arpsafaris.com. Arranges tours with Ranger Safaris in Tanzania.
Baobab – Alternative Roots to Travel ✆ 0121 314 6011; f 0121 314 6012; e enquiries@ baobabtravel.com; www.baobabtravel.com. An ethical tour operator specialising in ecotourism in Africa.
Cazenove & Loyd Safaris ✆ 020 7384 2332; e experts@cazloyd.com; www.caz-loyd.com
Crusader Travel ✆ 020 8744 0474; e info@ crusadertravel.com; www.crusadertravel.com

Explore Worldwide ✆ 0845 013 1537; e hello@ explore.co.uk; www.exploreworldwide.com
Footloose ✆ 01943 604030; e info@ footlooseadventure.co.uk; www.footlooseadventure.co.uk. Tailor-made tours, safaris & treks throughout Tanzania, & including Zanzibar.
Gane & Marshall ✆ 01822 600 600; e holidays@ ganeandmarshall.co.uk; www.ganeandmarshall.co.uk.
Hartley's Safaris ✆ 01673 861600; e info@ hartleys-safaris.co.uk; www.hartleys-safaris.co.uk. Safaris to east & southern Africa, as well as diving & island holidays in the region.
Journeys by Design ✆ 01273 623 790; e info@ journeysbydesign.co.uk; www.journeysbydesign.co.uk
Okavango Tours & Safaris ✆ 020 8347 4030; e info@okavango.com; www.okavango.com. Individually tailored holidays to east & southern Africa.
Rainbow Tours ✆ 020 7226 1004; e info@ rainbowtours.co.uk; www.rainbowtours.co.uk
Safari Drive ✆ 01488 71140; e info@ safaridrive.com; www.safaridrive.com. Self-drive & tailor-made safaris.
Sherpa Expeditions ✆ 020 8577 2717; e sales@ sherpa-walking-holidays.co.uk; www.sherpaexpeditions.com
Steppes Africa ✆ 01285 880 980; e safaris@ steppesafrica.co.uk; www.steppesafrica.co.uk

Sunvil Africa ↘ 020 8568 4499; e africa@
sunvil.co.uk; www.sunvil.co.uk
Tanzania Odyssey ↘ 020 7471 8780 or US +1 866
356 4691; e info@
tanzaniaodyssey.com; www.tanzaniaodyssey.com. Tailor-
made tours throughout Tanzania.

Tribes Travel ↘ 01728 685971; e bradtanz@
tribes.co.uk; www.tribes.co.uk
Wildlife Worldwide ↘ 0845 130 6982; e sales@
wildlifeworldwide.com; www.wildlifeworldwide.com
World Odyssey ↘ 01905 731373; e info@
world-odyssey.com; www.world-odyssey.com. Tailor-
made safaris.

US
Aardvark Safaris ↘ 1 888 776 0888; e info@
aardvarksafaris.com; www.aardvarksafaris.com. Tailored
trips to southern & northern Tanzania, including
walking safaris.
Abercrombie & Kent ↘ 1 800 554 7016;
www.abercrombiekent.com. A leader in luxury
adventure travel.
Adventure Center ↘ 1 800 228 8747;
www.adventurecenter.com. Provides safaris, treks,
expeditions & active vacations worldwide, with a
focus on value. Represents Explore Worldwide.
Big Five Tours & Expeditions ↘ 1 800 244 3483;
e info@bigfive.com; www.bigfive.com. Family-owned
safari company.
Eco-resorts ↘ 1 866 326 7376; e info@
eco-resorts.com; www.eco-resorts.com. Offers a variety
of safaris. A percentage of the booking fee is used
to support local communities & the environment.
Ker & Downey USA ↘ 1 800 423 4236;
e safari@kerdowney.com; www.kerdowney.com

Micato Safaris ↘ 1 800 642 2861; e inquiries@
micato.com; www.micato.com. Family company, based
in Nairobi but with an office in New York.
Naipenda Safaris ↘ 1 888 404 4499 or Tanzania
+255 27 250 3565; e jo@
naipendasafaris; www.naipendasafaris.com
Next Adventure ↘ 1 800 562 7298; e safari@
nextadventure.com; www.nextadventure.com. California-
based company with strong ties to Tanzania.
International Expeditions ↘ 1 800 633 4734;
e nature@ietravel.com.com; www.ietravel.com
Thomson Safaris ↘ 1 800 235 0289; e info@
thomsonsafaris.com; www.thomsonsafaris.com.
Specialising in Tanzania for 20 years, Thomson
operates innovative safaris throughout the country,
including walking tours & adventure camps.
Remote River Expeditions ↘ + 261 20 95 52347
(Madagascar); e info@remoterivers.com;
www.remoterivers.com
United Travel Group ↘ 1 800 223 6486; e info@
unitedtravelgroup.com; www.unitedtravelgroup.com.
One of the oldest safari companies in Africa.

SOUTH AFRICA
Pulse Africa ↘ +27 11 325 2290; f +27 11 325
2226; e info@pulseafrica.com; www.pulseafrica.com

Safari specialists in Tanzania are found under their various regions in *Part Two, The Guide*.

RED TAPE

Check well in advance that you have a valid **passport** and that it won't expire within six months of the date on which you intend to *leave* Tanzania. Should your passport be lost or stolen, it will generally be easier to get a replacement if you have a photocopy of the important pages.

If there is any possibility you'll want to drive or hire a vehicle while you're in the country, do organise an **international driving licence**, which you may be asked to produce together with your original licence. Any AA office in a country in which you're licensed to drive will do this for a nominal fee. You may sometimes be asked at the border or international airport for an **international health certificate** showing you've had a yellow fever shot.

For security reasons, it's advisable to detail all your important information on one sheet of paper, photocopy it, and distribute a few copies in your luggage, your money-belt, and amongst relatives or friends at home. The sort of things you want to include are your travellers' cheque numbers and refund information, travel insurance policy details and 24-hour emergency contact number, passport number, details of relatives or friends to be contacted in an emergency, bank and credit card details, camera and lens serial numbers etc.

VISAS Visas are required by most visitors to Tanzania, including UK and USA passport holders, and cost between US$30 and US$60, depending on your nationality. These can be obtained on arrival at any international airport in Tanzania, or at any border post. This is a straightforward procedure: no photographs or other documents are required, but the visa must be paid for in hard currency. The visa is normally valid for three months after arriving in the country, and it allows for multiple crossings into Uganda and Kenya during that period (but not from neighbouring countries). For current information about visa requirements, visit http://tanzaniatouristboard.com/pages/ttb_visa.php. This page links to a full list of Tanzanian embassies and high commissions abroad.

Ⓔ EMBASSIES AND DIPLOMATIC MISSIONS

Major embassies and high commissions in Dar es Salaam are listed below. Most are open mornings only and not at all at weekends. Typical hours are 09.00–12.30, but this varies considerably.

Algeria 34 Ali Hassan Mwinyi Rd; ✆ 022 211 7619; f 022 211 7620; www.mae.dz

Belgium 5 Ocean Rd, Upanga; ✆ 022 211 2688/2503; f 022 211 7621; www.diplomatie.be/dar-es-salaam

Burundi Lugalo Rd, Upanga; ✆ 022 212 6827; f 022 211 5923; e burundemb@raha.com

Canada 38 Mirambo St; ✆ 022 216 3300; f 022 211 6897; www.canadainternational.gc.ca

China 2 Kajifcheni St; ✆ 022 266 7475/105; f 022 266 6353; http://tz.china-embassy.org

Denmark Ghana Av; ✆ 022 211 3887/8; f 022 211 6433; www.ambdaressalaam.um.dk

Egypt 24 Ghana Av; ✆ 022 211 3591; f 022 211 2543; e egypt.emb.tz@Cats-net.com

Finland Cnr Mirambo St & Garden Av; ✆ 022 219 6565; f 022 219 6573; www.finland.or.tz

France Ali Hassan Mwinyi Rd; ✆ 022 266 6021/3; f 022 266 8434; www.ambafrance-tz.org

Germany Cnr Mirambo St & Garden Av; ✆ 022 211 7409/15; f 022 211 2944; www.daressalam.diplo.de

Greece 64 Upanga Rd; ✆ 022 211 5895; f 022 260 0151

Hungary 204 Chake Chake Rd, Oyster Bay; ✆ 022 266 8573; f 022 266 7214

India Haile Selassie Rd, Masiki; ✆ 022 260 0714/6; f 022 260 0697; www.hcindiatz.org

Ireland 353 Toure Dr; ✆ 022 260 2355; f 022 260 2362; e daressalaamembassy@dfa.ie

Italy 316 Lugalo Rd; ✆ 022 211 5935/6; f 022 211 5938; www.ambdaressalaam.esteri.it

Japan 1081 Ali Hassan Mwinyi Rd; ✆ 022 211 5827/9; f 022 211 5830; www.tz.emb-japan.go.jp

Kenya Old Bagamoyo Rd; ✆ 022 266 8285/6; f 022 266 8213; www.kenyahighcomtz.org

Malawi Zambia Hse, Ohio/Sokoine Rd; ✆ 022 213 6951; f 022 213 6951

Mozambique 25 Garden Av; ✆ 022 211 6502; f 022 211 6502

Netherlands Cnr Mirambo St & Garden Av; ✆ 022 211 0000; f 022 211 0044; www.netherlands-embassy.go.tz

Norway Cnr Mirambo St & Garden Av; ✆ 022 211 3366/3610; f 022 211 6564; www.norway.go.tz

Pakistan 149 Malik Rd; ✆ 022 211 7630; f 022 211 3205

Poland 63 Ali Kahn Rd; ✆ 022 211 5271; f 022 211 5812

Romania 11 Ocean Rd, Upanga; ✆ 022 211 5899; f 022 211 3866

Russia 73 Ali Hassan Mwinyi Rd; ✆ 022 266 6005/6; f 022 266 6818; www.russianembassy.net

Rwanda 32 Ali Hassan Mwinyi Rd; ✆ 022 213 0119; f 022 211 5888

South Africa Mwaya Rd, Msasani; ✆ 022 260 1800; f 022 260 1684; e ntombelal@foreign.gov.za

Spain 99B Kinondoni Rd; ✆ 022 266 6936/6018; f 022 266 6938; e embesptz@mail.mae.es

Sudan 64 Ali Mwinyi Rd; ✆ 022 211 7641; f 022 211 5811

Sweden Cnr Mirambo St & Garden Av; ✆ 022 211 0101; f 022 211 0102; www.swedenabroad.com

Switzerland Kinondoni Rd; ➘ 022 266 6008/9;
f 022 266 6736; www.eda.admin.ch/daressalaam
Uganda Extelcom Bldg, Samora Machel Av; ➘ 022
266 7391; f 022 266 7224
UK Cnr Mirambo St & Garden Av; ➘ 022 211 0101;
f 022 211 0102; http://ukintanzania.fco.gov.uk

USA 686 Old Bagamoyo Rd; ➘ 022 266 8001;
f 022 266 8238; http://tanzania.usembassy.gov
Zambia Cnr Ohio Rd & Sokoine Dr; ➘ 022 211
2977; f 022 211 2977

GETTING THERE AND AWAY

✈ **BY AIR** The following airlines fly to Tanzania from Europe or the United Kingdom:

Air Tanzania www.airtanzania.com
British Airways www.britishairways.com
KLM www.klm.com

Lufthansa www.lufthansa.com
Swissair www.swiss.com

African airlines which fly to Tanzania from elsewhere in Africa include

Air Tanzania www.airtanzania.com
Ethiopian Airlines www.ethiopianairlines.com
Kenya Airways www.kenya-airways.com

South African Airways www.flysaa.com
Zambia Airways www.zambianairways.com

There are two international airports on the Tanzanian mainland. Julius Nyerere International Airport in Dar es Salaam is the normal point of entry for international airlines, which is generally convenient for business travellers, but for tourists Dar es Salaam is usually no more than a point of entry, and many people transfer directly on to flights to elsewhere in the country. Kilimanjaro International Airport, which lies midway between Moshi and Arusha, is the more useful point of entry for tourists, and following recent privatisation this airport is likely to catch on with more international airlines. For the meantime, however, the only prominent airlines that run direct flights to Kilimanjaro from outside of Africa are the national carrier Air Tanzania and KLM, which flies there daily from Europe. Quite a number of international flights land at Zanzibar, and many tourists fly into East Africa at Nairobi and transfer from there to Arusha by road or local flight. Once in Tanzania, a good network of domestic flights connects Kilimanjaro, Dar es Salaam and Zanzibar, as well as other less visited towns. You will generally get a better price (and will definitely save yourself a lot of hassle) by booking all your international and domestic flights as a package from home.

Budget travellers looking for flights to East Africa may well find it cheapest to use an airline that takes an indirect route. London is the best place to pick up a cheap ticket; many continental travellers buy their tickets there. It is generally cheaper to fly to Nairobi than to Dar es Salaam, and getting from Nairobi to Arusha by shuttle bus is cheap, simple and quick. Be warned, however, that a high proportion of travellers is robbed in Nairobi, so it isn't the greatest introduction to the continent. Nairobi is the best place to pick up cheap tickets out of East Africa. For short stays in East Africa, some of the best deals are charter flights to Mombasa (Kenya), a few hours' bus ride from Tanga, or an overnight train ride from Nairobi.

Getting a flight that lets you feel as if you've got a good deal is becoming more daunting as local flight specialists fight with global flight consolidators. Put everybody on the internet, and the competition just gets hotter. Below is a list of operators who give good service at a reasonable price. Getting the cheapest price will require several calls and may result in some rather complicated re-routing.

Flight specialists
From the UK

Flight Centre 13 The Broadway, Wimbledon SW19 1PS; ✆ 020 8296 8181; f 020 8296 0808; www.flightcentre.co.uk. An independent flight provider with over 450 outlets worldwide. They also have offices in Australia, New Zealand, South Africa & Canada.

Quest Travel Stoneham Hse, 17 Scarbrook Rd Croydon, Surrey CR0 1SQ; ✆ 0845 263 6963; f 020 8406 7255; www.questtravel.com. An independent agent that has been in operation for a decade offering competitive prices specialising in long-haul flights.

STA Travel 52 Grosvenor Gardens, Victoria, London SW1W 0AG; ✆ 0871 468 0649 f 020 7881 1299; e enquiries@statravel.co.uk; www.statravel.co.uk. STA has 10 branches in London & 30 or so around the country & at various university sites. STA also has several branches & associate organisations around the world.

Trailfinders Main office: 194 Kensington High St, London W8 7RG; ✆ 020 7938 3939; f 020 7938 3305; www.trailfinders.com. With origins in the discount flight market, Trailfinders now provides a one-stop travel service including visa & passport service, travel clinic & foreign exchange.

Travel Bag Main office: 2–3 High St, Alton, Hants GU34 1TL; ✆ 020 7810 6831; f 01420 82133. London office: 373–75 The Strand, London WC2R 0JE; ✆ 0844 880 4436; f 020 7497 2923; www.travelbag.co.uk. Provides tailor-made flight schedules & holidays for destinations throughout the world.

Travel Mood 24 Islington Green, London N1 8DU; ✆ 0844 815 9560; f 0844 815 9561; e sales@travelmood.com; www.travelmood.com. Provides flights & tailor-made holidays.

WEXAS 45–49 Brompton Rd, Knightsbridge, London SW3 1DE; ✆ 020 7589 3315; f 020 7589 8418; e mship@wexas.com; www.wexas.com. More of a club than a travel agent. Membership is around £40 a year, but for frequent fliers the benefits are many.

From the USA

Airtech ✆ 212 219 7000; e fly@airtech.com, www.airtech.com. Standby seat broker that also deals in consolidator fares, courier flights & a host of other travel-related services.

Net Fare ✆ 1 800 766 3601; e admin@netfare.net; www.netfare.net. Provides fares for destinations throughout the world.

Council on International Educational Exchange ✆ 207 553 4000; f 207 553 4299; e contact@ciee.org; www.ciee.org. Although the Council focuses on work exchange trips, it also has a large travel department.

STA Travel ✆ 1 800 781 4040; e go@statravel.com; www.statravel.com. Has several branches around the country.

Worldtek Travel ✆ 1 800 243 1723; e info@worldtek.com; www.worldtek.com. Operates a network of rapidly growing travel agencies.

From Canada

Flight Centre ✆ freephone: 1 877 967 5302; www.flightcentre.ca. Has a network of branches around the country.

Travel CUTS ✆ 1 866 246 9762; www.travelcuts.com. A Canadian student-based travel organisation with 60 offices throughout Canada.

From Australia

Flight Centre ✆ freephone 133 133; www.flightcentre.com.au. An independent flight operator with offices around the country. They also have offices in the UK, New Zealand, South Africa & Canada.

STA Travel ✆ 134 782; www.statravel.com.au. A student travel specialist with a network of branches around Australia.

From New Zealand

Flight Centre ✆ 0800 2435 44; www.flightcentre.co.nz. A good starting point for cheap airfares.

From South Africa

Flight Centre ✆ 0860 400 727; www.flightcentre.co.za. Part of the international chain with a number of branches around the country.

Student Flights ✆ 0860 400 700; www.studentflights.co.za. This outfit is linked to the Flight Centre network.

Wild Frontiers ✆ 11 702 2035; f 11 468 1655; e wildfront@icon.co.za; www.wildfrontiers.com. This excellent Johannesburg-based tour operator has years of experience arranging general & ornithological safaris to East Africa, as well as reasonably priced air tickets.

🚐 **OVERLAND** The viability of the established overland routes between Europe and East Africa depends on the current political situation. In recent years, it has usually been possible to reach East Africa via Egypt, Sudan and Ethiopia. However, it's not easy to predict the local political situation in advance, and many people get stuck in the Sudan and either have to turn back or else fly from Khartoum to Ethiopia or Kenya. As for the so-called 'Nile Route', a variant on the above passing through southern Sudan to Uganda, the south of Sudan has been closed to tourists for almost two decades. Recent events in southern Sudan are cause for slight optimism that this may change in the near future, bearing in mind that much of northern Uganda is also highly unstable.

A route via the Sahara and west Africa used to be favoured by several overland truck companies. Unfortunately, it has been impassable since the mid 1990s, at first due to banditry, then after a major bridge collapsed in what was then Zaire, and then due to the civil war in the Democratic Republic of the Congo. This route has always been tough going for independent travellers, whether or not they have a vehicle, and in the present climate of instability we would advise anybody who is considering travelling this way to think seriously about going with an overland truck company. However you plan to travel, it would be advisable to contact a couple of overland truck companies for current advice about safety.

With the end of apartheid, the Cape to Nairobi route has become the backpackers' standard in Africa. Some people start this trip in East Africa, others start in South Africa – there's not a lot in it. The advantage of starting in the south is that you can adapt to African conditions in the more organised environment of South Africa before you hit the relative chaos of East Africa. The disadvantage is that you will have to put up with the most trying travel conditions of the trip towards the end, after the novelty of being in Africa has worn off. These days Johannesburg is almost as good as Nairobi for cheap air tickets, so that is not a factor.

There is a proliferation of overland truck companies which run regular trips between southern Africa (normally Johannesburg or Cape Town) and East Africa. A few of these are:

Acacia Expeditions Ltd ✆ 020 7706 4700; f 020 7706 4686; e info@acacia-africa.com; www.acacia-africa.com
Dragoman ✆ 01728 861133; f 01728 861127; e info@dragoman.co.uk; www.dragoman.co.uk
Exodus ✆ 0845 863 9600; f 020 8673 0779; e sales@exodus.co.uk

Kumuka ✆ 0800 3892328; 020 7937 8855; f 020 7937 6664; e adventuretours@kumuka.com; www.kumuka.com
Tana Travel ✆ 01789 414200; f 01789 414420; e info@tanatravel.com; www.tanatravel.com

The advantages of travelling on an overland truck are that it will visit remote areas that you would be unlikely to reach otherwise, and that you will see far more than you would by travelling independently for the same period of time. The disadvantages are that you will be in the company of the same ten to 20 other people for the duration of the trip, and that the truck will cut you off from everyday African life. Most of the people we've spoken to say that their main reason for travelling on a truck is that it seems to be safer than travelling alone. It's worth noting, therefore, that this is, by and large, a safe and well-travelled region (something that cannot be said for the overland truck route between Europe and Nairobi via west Africa) and that you will meet plenty of other single travellers. If you feel you would prefer to travel independently, don't let fear swing you in the opposite direction.

Border crossings Tanzania borders eight countries. A brief outline of frequently used border crossings follows:

To/from Kenya The most popular crossing is between Nairobi and Arusha via Namanga. Several reasonably priced shuttle bus services run along this route daily in both directions; see *Chapter 6, Arusha* for further details. You can travel between Nairobi and Arusha more cheaply in stages, catching a minibus between Nairobi and Namanga (these leave Nairobi from Ronald Ngala Road), crossing the border on foot, and then catching a shared taxi to Arusha. Expect this to take around six hours.

Provided that your papers are in order, Namanga is a very straightforward border crossing. There is a bank where you can change money during normal banking hours. At other times, you'll have to change money with private individuals – don't change more than you need, as there are several con artists about.

An increasingly popular route between Kenya and Tanzania is from Mombasa to Tanga (three to four hours) or Dar es Salaam. Again, this is straightforward enough, and a couple of buses do the run every day. Another route is between Kisumu and Mwanza on Lake Victoria. There are several buses daily along this route, leaving in the early morning and taking around 12 hours.

Several airlines run daily flights between Nairobi and Kilimanjaro International Airport.

To/from Uganda The best way to cross from Uganda to Tanzania depends on which part of Tanzania you want to visit. The weekly ferry service between Port Bell and Mwanza was suspended after the MV *Bukoba* sank in 1996. However, it is possible to arrange passage to Port Bell on a cargo ship from Mwanza's main port for a negotiable fee. Otherwise, the popular alternative is to travel by road from Masaka to Bukoba, by ferry from Bukoba to Mwanza and then by train to Dar es Salaam on the coast or Kigoma on Lake Tanganyika. If you are in Uganda and want to get to Arusha or Moshi, it will be quicker, cheaper and more comfortable to travel via Kenya.

The direct route between Masaka and Bukoba passes through the Mutukula border post. If all goes well, you can get from Masaka to Mutukula in a couple of hours. Regular minibuses go as far as Kyotera, where you won't have to wait long to find a pick-up truck going through to Mutukula. If you arrive at Mutukula in the late afternoon and don't think you are going to get as far as Bukoba, you may want to stay at the basic guesthouse on the Ugandan side of the border and cross into Tanzania the following morning. The road between Mutukula and Bukoba is fairly rough, but a couple of 4x4 vehicles travel up and down it every day with the express purpose of transporting passengers. These take ages to fill up, so it's also worth seeing if you can get a lift with a truck. If you can get a lift as far as Kyaka, there's more transport to Bukoba from there. For details of ferries between Bukoba and Mwanza, see page 414.

To/from Rwanda The only route between Kigali and Mwanza is by road, through the Rusumu border post. Plenty of minibuses zoom along the road between Kigali, the capital of Rwanda, and the border. From there, you'll need to catch a bus to Mwanza over a few days. For further details see the website http://bradttanzania.wordpress.com.

To/from Burundi The straightforward option is the Lake Tanganyika ferry (see *Chapter 15*). The trip can also be done in steps. Minibuses go from Bujumbura to the immigration office at Nyanza Lac and on to the border. At Kagunga, a 20-minute walk past the border, lake taxis run to Gombe Stream and Kalalangabo, 3km from Kigoma. Burundi is another country with a troubled history, and if the Lake Tanganyika Ferry isn't running there – as has been the case for the past few years – we would tend to assume it's for a good reason.

To/from the Congo Cargo boats between Kigoma and Kalemie might sometimes carry passengers, but don't rely on this. Most people used to go via Burundi, but this whole part of central Africa is too dangerous for travel to be recommended.

To/from Zambia Zambia, the main gateway between East and southern Africa, can be reached by boat, rail or road. Tazara trains run twice weekly from Dar es Salaam to Kapiri Mposhi, and are met by a bus to Lusaka (see box, *The Tazara Railway*, page 475). From western Tanzania, the easiest way to get to Zambia is on the Lake Tanganyika ferry (see box, *The MV Liemba*, page 456).

To/from Malawi The turn-off to the Malawi border at Songo is 5km from Kyela, on the Mbeya road. Several buses depart weekly from Mbeya leaving in the afternoon and arriving in to Lilongwe the next day. Otherwise, you can catch one of the Coastal minibuses that run daily from Mbeya to Kyela and continue on to the border. The bus stand at the border is a few minutes walk from the border post. In Malawi, a bus to Karonga arrives at the border at 19.00 and leaves at 06.00, but provided that you arrive at the border before late afternoon, you should have no difficulty picking up a ride on a pick-up truck to Karonga. There is now a very good guesthouse on the Tanzanian side of the border if you arrive there late in the day.

To/from Mozambique The only viable border crossing from Tanzania to Mozambique is at Kilamba, which lies on the Rovuma River between Mtwara and Palma. This used to be a difficult route, but there is now a regular motorboat across the river at high tide, and a fair amount of transport on to Palma. A bridge is likely to be constructed during the lifespan of this edition.

SAFETY

Crime exists in Tanzania as it does practically everywhere in the world. There has been a marked increase in crime in Tanzania over recent years, and tourists are inevitably at risk, because they are far richer than most locals, and are conspicuous in their dress, behaviour and (with obvious exceptions) skin colour. For all that, Tanzania remains a lower crime risk than many countries, and the social taboo on theft is such that even a petty criminal is likely to be beaten to death should they be caught in the act. With a bit of care, you would have to be unlucky to suffer from more serious crime while you are in Tanzania.

MUGGING There is nowhere in Tanzania where mugging is as commonplace as it is in, say, Nairobi or Johannesburg, but there are areas where walking around alone at night would place you at some risk. Mugging is generally an urban problem, with the main areas of risk being Dar es Salaam, Arusha, Tanga and Zanzibar Town, as well as the beach at Pangani, and anywhere in the vicinity of Bagamoyo or Kanduchi Beach. Ask for local advice at your hotel, since the staff there will generally know of any recent incidents in the immediate vicinity.

The best way to ensure that any potential mugging remains an unpleasant incident rather than a complete disaster is to carry as little as you need on your person. If you are mugged in Tanzania, the personal threat is minimal provided that you promptly hand over what is asked for.

CASUAL THEFT The bulk of crime in Tanzania consists of casual theft such as bag-snatching or pickpocketing. This sort of thing is not particularly aimed at tourists (and as a consequence it is not limited to tourist areas), but tourists will be considered fair game. The key to not being pickpocketed is not having anything of value in your pockets; the key to avoiding having things snatched is to avoid having valuables in a place where they could easily be snatched. Most of the following points will be obvious to experienced travellers, but they are worth making:

- Many casual thieves operate in bus stations and markets. Keep a close watch on your belongings, and avoid having loose valuables in your pocket or daypack.
- Keep all valuables in a moneybelt, ideally one you can hide under your clothes.
- Never carry day-to-day spending money in your moneybelt. A normal wallet is fine provided it contains only a moderate sum of money. Better still is a wallet you can hang around your neck.
- Many people prefer to carry their moneybelt on their person at all times. We believe it is generally safer to leave it hidden in your hotel room, depending to some extent on circumstances, because pickpocketing and mugging are more commonplace than theft from hotel rooms. Note however that some travellers' cheque companies won't issue refunds on cheques stolen from a hotel room.
- Leave any valuable jewellery at home.
- If you can afford it, catch a taxi to your hotel when you first arrive in a large town. If you arrive after dark, catch a taxi to your hotel even if you can't afford it.
- If you are robbed, think twice before you chase the thief, especially if the stolen items are of no great value. An identified thief is likely to be descended on by a mob and quite possibly beaten to death.

DOCUMENTATION The best insurance against complete disaster is to keep things well documented. If you carry a photocopy of the main page of your passport, you will be issued a new one more promptly. In addition, keep details of your bank, credit card (if you have one), travel insurance policy and camera equipment (including serial numbers).

Keep copies of your travellers' cheque numbers and *a record of which ones you have cashed*, as well as the international refund assistance telephone number and local agent. If all this information fits on one piece of paper, you can keep photocopies on you and with a friend at home. You will have to report to the police the theft of any item against which you wish to claim insurance.

SECURITY Tanzania is very secure and has a strong record of internal stability since independence. Tanzania shares a western border with the troubled countries of the Congo, Rwanda and Burundi, an area that sees very little tourism. Border areas have been overrun with refugees at several points over recent years, a situation that is of concern to locals, officials and international aid workers, but has had no effect on parts of Tanzania likely to be visited by tourists.

WOMEN TRAVELLERS Women travellers in Tanzania have little to fear on a gender-specific level. Over the years, we've met several women travelling alone in Tanzania, and none had any serious problems in their interactions with locals, aside from the hostility that can be generated by dressing skimpily. Otherwise, an element of flirtation is about the sum of it, perhaps the odd direct proposition, but nothing that cannot be defused by a firm no. And nothing, for that matter, that you wouldn't expect in any Western country, or – probably with a far greater degree of persistence – from many male travellers.

It would be prudent to pay some attention to how you dress in Tanzania, particularly in the more conservative parts of the Swahili coast. In areas where people are used to tourists, they are unlikely to be deeply offended by women travellers wearing shorts or other outfits that might be seen to be provocative. Nevertheless, it still pays to allow for local sensibilities, and under certain circumstances revealing clothes may be perceived to make a statement that's not intended from your side.

More mundanely, tampons are not readily available in smaller towns, though you can easily locate them in Dar es Salaam and Arusha, and in game lodge and hotel gift shops. When travelling in out-of-the-way places, carry enough tampons to see you through to the next time you'll be in a large city, bearing in mind that travelling in the tropics can sometimes cause heavier or more regular periods than normal. Sanitary pads are available in most towns of any size.

WHAT TO TAKE

There are two simple rules to bear in mind when you decide what to take with you to Tanzania, particularly for those using public transport. Rule one is to bring with you *everything* that you could possibly need and that mightn't be readily available when you need it. Rule two is to carry as little as possible. Somewhat contradictory rules, you might think, and you'd be right – so the key is finding the right balance, something that probably depends on personal experience as much as anything. Worth stressing is that most genuine necessities are surprisingly easy to get hold of in the main centres in Tanzania, and that most of the ingenious gadgets you can

Gordon Rattray

It's a good indication of the quality of Tanzania's wildlife, but not an encouraging sign for disabled travellers, that it is still easier to stumble upon a big-cat kill in a game park than to find accessible accommodation in the nearby lodge. Yes, level-entry flat-floored showers, ramps and grab handles do exist, but only in a few luxury hotels and resorts. Most travellers will need to be able to cope with standard facilities. This is even more applicable to those who venture out of the game-park circuit and want to explore more of the country, where conditions are often a challenge for the hardiest of able-bodied travellers. On a positive note, because Africans – helpful by nature – are used to dealing with problems, you will have no shortage of assistance and useful advice.

BUSES AND TRAINS There is no effective legislation in Tanzania to facilitate disabled travellers' journeys by public transport. If you cannot walk at all then both of these options are going to be difficult, requiring help from people to lift you in and out of your seat.

AIR TRAVEL At international airports the necessary equipment and staff to assist non-ambulant travellers will be present, but in practice things may not go as you're used to and will almost certainly take longer than you expected. Domestic airports can offer even less of a guarantee of efficient service, and there may be no aisle chair present so be prepared to be manually lifted from your seat to your wheelchair.

VEHICLE TRANSFERS Vehicles in Tanzania are often four-wheel drive and are therefore higher than normal cars, making wheelchair transfers more difficult. Drivers/guides are normally happy to help, but are not trained in this skill, so you must thoroughly explain your needs and always stay in control of the situation.

SEATING Distances are large and roads are often bumpy, so if you are prone to skin damage you need to take extra care. Place your own pressure-relieving cushion on top of (or instead of) the original car seat and if necessary, pad around knees and elbows.

BATHROOMS Occasionally (more by accident than through design), showers and toilets are wheelchair accessible. Where this is not the case, be prepared to be carried again, or do your ablutions in the bedroom.

HEALTH Doctors will know about 'everyday' illnesses, but you must understand and be able to explain your own particular medical requirements. African hospitals are often basic so, if possible, take all necessary medication and equipment with you. It is advisable to pack this in your hand luggage during flights in case your main luggage gets lost.

SECURITY It is worthwhile remembering that, as a disabled person, you are more vulnerable. Stay aware of who is around you and where your bags are, especially during car transfers and similar. These activities often draw a crowd, and the confusion creates easy pickings for an opportunist thief.

In summary, for anybody, a visit to Tanzania is often an adventure in itself, which requires preparation and patience. This applies even more to people with physical disabilities. However, with enough effort anywhere is within reach and the rewards of getting there are just as great, perhaps even greater.

Practical Information **WHAT TO TAKE**

3

buy in camping shops are unlikely to amount to much more than deadweight on the road. If it came to it, you could easily travel in Tanzania with little more than a change of clothes, a few basic toiletries and a medical kit.

CARRYING YOUR LUGGAGE Visitors who are unlikely to be carrying their luggage for any significant distance will probably want to pack most of it in a conventional suitcase. Make sure it is tough and durable, and that it seals well, so that its contents will survive bumpy drives to the game reserves. A lock is a good idea, not only for flights, but for when you leave your case in a hotel room – in our experience, any theft from upmarket hotels in Africa is likely to be casual, and a locked suitcase is unlikely to be tampered with. A daypack will be useful when on safari, and you should be able to pack your luggage in such a manner than any breakable goods can be carried separately in the body of the vehicle and on your lap when necessary – anything like an MP3 player or camera will suffer heavily from vibrations on rutted roads.

If you are likely to use public transport, then a backpack is the most practical way to carry your luggage. Once again, ensure your pack is durable, that the seams and zips are properly sewn, and that it has several pockets. If you intend doing a lot of hiking, you definitely want a backpack designed for this purpose. On the other hand, if you'll be staying at places where it might be a good idea to shake off the sometimes negative image attached to backpackers, then there would be obvious advantages in using a suitcase that converts into a backpack.

A more practical solution is a robust 35-litre daypack. The advantages of keeping luggage as light and compact as possible are manifold. For starters, you can rest it on your lap on bus trips, avoiding complications such as extra charges for luggage, arguments about where your bag should be stored, and the slight but real risk of theft if your luggage ends up on the roof. A compact bag also makes for greater mobility, whether you're hiking or looking for a hotel in town. The sacrifice? Leave behind camping equipment and a sleeping bag. Do this, and it's quite possible to fit everything you truly need into a 35-litre daypack, and possibly even a few luxuries such as binoculars and a bird field guide. Frankly, it puzzles us as to what the many backpackers who wander around with an enormous pack and absolutely no camping equipment actually carry around with them!

If your luggage won't squeeze into a daypack, a sensible compromise is to carry a large daypack in your rucksack. That way, you can carry a tent and other camping equipment when you need it, but at other times reduce your luggage to fit into a daypack and leave what you're not using in storage.

Travellers carrying a lot of valuable items should look for a pack that can easily be padlocked. A locked bag can, of course, be slashed open, but in Tanzania you are still most likely to encounter casual theft of the sort to which a lock would be real deterrent.

CAMPING EQUIPMENT If you go on a budget safari or do an organised Kilimanjaro climb, camping equipment will be provided by the company you travel with. Taken together with the limited opportunities for camping outside of the safari circuit, this means that for most travellers a tent and sleeping bag will be dead weight in Tanzania. Nevertheless, it is advisable to carry a tent if you plan to travel or hike in remote areas.

If you decide to carry camping equipment, the key is to look for the lightest available gear. It is now possible to buy a lightweight tent weighing little more than 2kg, but make sure that the one you buy is mosquito-proof. Other essentials for camping include a sleeping bag and a roll-mat, which will serve as both insulation and padding. You might want to carry a stove for occasions when no firewood is available, as is the case in many montane national parks where the collection of firewood is forbidden, or for cooking in a tropical storm. If you do carry a stove, it's worth knowing that Camping Gaz cylinders are not readily available in Tanzania. A box of firelighter blocks will get a fire going in the most unpromising conditions. It would also be advisable to carry a pot, plate, cup and cutlery.

CLOTHES Assuming that you have the space, you ought to carry at least one change of shirt and underwear for every day you will spend on safari. Organising laundry along the way is a pain in the neck, and the dusty conditions will practically enforce a daily change of clothes. It's a good idea to keep separate one or two shirts for evening use only.

Otherwise, and especially if you are travelling with everything on your back, try to keep your clothes to a minimum, bearing in mind that you can easily and cheaply replace worn items in markets. In our opinion, the minimum you need is one or possibly two pairs of trousers and/or skirts, one pair of shorts, three shirts or T-shirts, one light sweater, maybe a light waterproof wind-breaker during the rainy season, enough socks and underwear to last five to seven days, one solid pair of shoes or boots for walking, and one pair of sandals, thongs or other light shoes.

When you select your clothes, remember that jeans are heavy to carry, hot to wear, and slow to dry. Far better to bring light cotton trousers and, if you intend spending a while in montane regions, tracksuit bottoms, which will provide extra cover on chilly nights. Skirts are best made of a light natural fabric such as cotton. T-shirts are lighter and less bulky than proper shirts, though the top pocket of a shirt (particularly if it buttons up) is a good place to carry spending money in markets and bus stations, since it's easier to keep an eye on than trouser pockets. One sweater or sweatshirt will be adequate in most parts of the country, though you will need serious alpine gear for Kilimanjaro and to a lesser degree Mount Meru.

Socks and underwear *must* be made from natural fabrics. Bear in mind that re-using sweaty undergarments will encourage fungal infections such as athlete's foot, as well as prickly heat in the groin region. Socks and underpants are light and compact enough that it's worth bringing a week's supply. As for footwear, genuine hiking boots are worth considering only if you're a serious off-road hiker, since they are very heavy whether on your feet or in your pack. A good pair of walking shoes, preferably made of leather and with good ankle support, is a good compromise. It's also useful to carry sandals, thongs or other light shoes.

Another factor in deciding what clothes to bring is the sensibilities of Tanzania's large Muslim population, which finds it offensive for a woman to expose her knees or shoulders. It is difficult to make hard and fast rules about what to wear, but some generalisations may help. Shorts are fine at most beach resorts, in game reserves, and possibly in Dar es Salaam, Zanzibar Town or Arusha where people are used to tourists. Elsewhere, we wouldn't wear shorts. For women, trousers are frowned upon in some quarters. The ideal thing to wear is a skirt that covers your knees. A shoulderless T-shirt that exposes your bra – or worse – is unlikely to go down well.

Men, too, should be conscious of what they wear. Shorts seem to be acceptable, but few Tanzanian men wear them and it is considered more respectable to wear trousers. Walking around in a public place without a shirt is totally unacceptable.

Many Tanzanians think it is insulting for Westerners to wear scruffy or dirty clothes. Quite accurately, they feel you wouldn't dress like that at home. It is difficult to explain that at home you also wouldn't spend three successive days in crowded buses on dusty roads with a limited amount of clothing crumpled up in a backpack. If you are travelling rough, you are bound to look a mess at times, but it is worth trying to look as spruce as possible.

OTHER USEFUL ITEMS Your **toilet bag** should at the very minimum include soap (secured in a plastic bag or soap holder unless you enjoy a soapy toothbrush!), shampoo, toothbrush and toothpaste. This sort of stuff is easy to replace as you go along, so there's no need to bring family-sized packs. Boys will probably want a **razor**. Girls should carry enough **tampons** and/or **sanitary pads** to see them through at least one heavy period, since these items may not always be immediately available. Nobody should forget to bring a **towel**, or to keep handy a roll of **loo paper** which, although widely available at shops and kiosks, cannot always be relied upon to be present where it's most urgently needed.

Other essentials include a **torch**, a **penknife** and a compact **alarm clock** for those early morning starts. You should carry a small **medical kit**, the contents of which are discussed in *Chapter 4, Health*, as are **mosquito nets**. If you wear **contact lenses**, bring all the fluids you need, since they are not available in Tanzania. You might also want to bring a pair of **glasses** to wear on long bus rides, and on safari – many lens wearers suffer badly in dusty conditions. In general, since many people find the intense sun and dry climate irritates their eyes, you might consider reverting to glasses.

Binoculars are essential if you want to get a good look at birds, or to watch distant mammals in game reserves. For most purposes, 7x21 compact binoculars will be fine, though some might prefer 7x35 traditional binoculars for their larger field of vision. Serious birdwatchers will find a 10x magnification more useful, and should definitely carry a good field guide.

$ MONEY

The unit of currency is the Tanzanian shilling, divided into 100 cents. The banknotes come in Tsh10,000, 5,000, 1,000, 500 and 200 denominations. It is often very difficult to find change for larger denomination notes, so keep a spread of notes available. At the time of writing the exchange rate of roughly US$1 = Tsh1,335, UK£1 = Tsh1,988 and €1 = Tsh1,770 was reasonably stable.

Most upmarket hotels and safari companies in Tanzania quote rates in US dollars. Some will also demand payment in this or another prominent hard currency, though other hotels and lodges actually prefer payment in local currency. The situation with national parks and other conservation areas is variable, but if you expect to pay fees directly rather than through an operator, then you'll need enough hard currency to cover the full amount (see box, *Paying park fees*, opposite).

The above exceptions noted, most things in Tanzania are best paid for in local currency, including restaurant bills, goods bought at a market or shop, mid-range and budget accommodation, public transport and most other casual purchases. Indeed, most service providers geared towards the local economy will have no facility for accepting any currency other than the Tanzanian shilling.

ORGANISING YOUR FINANCES There are three ways of carrying money: hard currency cash, travellers' cheques or a credit card. Our advice is to bring at least as much as you think you'll need in the combination of cash and travellers' cheques, but if possible to also carry a credit card to draw on in an emergency. US dollars, followed closely by euros, are the preferred form of foreign currency.

From the point of view of security, it's advisable to bring the bulk of your money in the form of travellers' cheques, which can be refunded if they are lost or stolen. It's best to use a widely recognised type of travellers' cheque such as American Express or Thomas Cook, and to keep your proof of purchase discrete from the cheques, as well as noting which cheques you have used, in order to facilitate a swift refund should you require one. Buy your travellers' cheques in a healthy mix of denominations, since you may sometimes need to change a small sum only, for instance when you're about to cross into another country. On the other hand, you don't want an impossibly thick wad of cheques. Currency regulations and other

Prior to October 2007, entrance, camping and other fees for all national parks, game reserves and other conservation areas were payable in hard currency cash or travellers' cheques (ideally US dollars). However, in order to combat staff pilfering, Tanzania National Parks (Tanapa) has now installed electronic payment systems at all entrance gates and other revenue collection centres in the major national parks in the northern safari circuit, ie: Serengeti, Lake Manyara, Tarangire, Kilimanjaro and Arusha National Parks. The electronic systems accept fee payment by international MasterCard and Tanapa Card only. No other cards are accepted, nor are travellers' cheques or Tanzania shillings, and in order to discourage hard currency cash payments, Tanapa now also charges a 50% penalty on these – in other words, if you arrive at the Serengeti wanting to pay your daily US$50 entrance fee in US dollar cash, you'll be charged an additional US$25 per day.

This isn't an issue for travellers on organised safaris, as their operator will pay the fees and will most likely have a Tanapa card that operates much like a credit card. Independent travellers, however, must either pay by MasterCard or must arrive at the gate with sufficient funds in the form of prepaid Tanapa Cards, which can be bought at any branch of the Exim Bank. There are two such banks in Arusha: the main branch on Sokoine Avenue near the Clocktower (⊕ 09.00–15.00 Mon–Fri; 09.00–12.30 Sat) and the subsidiary branch in the TFA (Shoprite) Centre at the other end of Sokoine Avenue (⊕ 09.00–16.30 Mon–Fri; 09.00–14.30 Sat). The cards cannot be bought outside these banking hours nor on Sundays.

Prepaid Tanapa Cards come in denominations of US$500, US$250, US$100, US$70 and US$50. They are not refundable, so you ideally want to buy exactly the right amount to cover your total stay in all parks that use the electronic system. The tellers who sell the cards aren't so hot when it comes to this sort of calculation, so try to work out the best combination of cards yourself (a couple spending three days in the Serengeti and one each in Tarangire and Manyara but not camping would need prepaid cards to the value of US$440, ie: one US$250 card, one US$50 and two US$70). You can pay for these Tanapa cards with a MasterCard (not much point, though, as this card would be accepted at the entrance gate anyway), but otherwise your *only* option is hard currency cash – neither local currency cash nor hard currency travellers' cheques are accepted, and Exim Bank doesn't have the facility to accept other international cards such as Visa or American Express. It's all monumentally user-unfriendly, and injury is added to insult by the levying of a service fee of US$1 per prepaid card (so the example above would cost US$444).

It is important to note that as things stand this system applies only to the five parks listed above. Other national parks covered in this guidebook still operate as before, taking hard currency cash or travellers' cheques, though this could change during the lifespan of this edition (check www.tanzaniaparks.com for news). Fees for Ngorongoro Conservation Area are also still payable in hard currency cash or travellers' cheques. This payment is treated as a foreign exchange transaction, which means that if you don't have the exact amount in US dollar notes or travellers' cheques, you will have to exchange a larger denomination and will receive the change in local currency at a poor exchange rate.

complications make it practically impossible to break down a large denomination travellers' cheque into smaller ones in most African countries, so don't bring travellers' cheques in denominations larger than US$100.

In addition to travellers' cheques, you should definitely bring a proportion of your money in hard currency cash, say around US$200 to US$300, since you are bound to hit situations where travellers' cheques won't be accepted, and cash gets a better exchange rate than travellers' cheques, especially large denomination banknotes. This would not be much consolation were all your money to be stolen, so we'd strongly advise against bringing cash only, but would suggest that you save what cash you do bring for situations where it will buy you a real advantage. Note that US dollar notes printed before 2002, particularly larger denominations such as US$100 and US$50, may be refused by banks and foreign exchange (forex) bureaux. Also, larger denomination notes get a better exchange rate than smaller ones.

Carry your hard currency and travellers' cheques as well as your passport and other important documentation in a money belt that can be hidden beneath your clothing. Your money belt should be made of cotton or another natural fabric, and everything inside the belt should be wrapped in plastic to protect it against sweat.

Credit cards are widely accepted in upmarket tourist-oriented shops and facilities in Arusha, Dar es Salaam and Zanzibar, as well as at most game lodges and upper range hotels. They can also be used to draw cash directly from ATMs in Dar es Salaam, Arusha, Mwanza and most major towns. Otherwise, they are of limited use. No matter how long you are travelling, do make sure that you are set up in such a way that you won't need to have money transferred or drafted across to Tanzania.

FOREIGN EXCHANGE Foreign currencies can be changed into Tanzanian shillings at any bank or bureau de change (known locally as forex bureaux). All banks are open from 08.30 to 12.30 on weekdays and in many larger towns they stay open until 15.00. They open from 08.30 to 11.30 on Saturdays. Most private forex bureaux stay open until 16.00 or later. You can normally change money at any time of day at Dar es Salaam's international airport. Most private forex bureaux deal in cash only (sometimes US dollars only), for which reason you'll probably be forced to change your travellers' cheques at a bank. The rate for this is often slightly lower than the cash rate and a small commission is also charged.

Generally, private forex bureaux offer a better rate of exchange than banks, but these can vary greatly so it's worth shopping around before a major transaction. The private bureaux are almost always far quicker for cash transactions than the banks, which might be a more important consideration than a minor discrepancy in the rate they offer. Before you change a large amount of money, check the bank or forex bureau has enough high denomination banknotes, or you'll need a briefcase to carry your local currency.

The legalisation of private forex bureaux has killed off the black market that previously thrived in Tanzania. Private individuals may give you a slightly better rate than the banks, but the official rate is so favourable it seems unfair to exploit this. In Dar es Salaam or Arusha you will be offered exceptionally good rates on the street, but if you are stupid or greedy enough to accept these, you can expect to be ripped off. There are plenty of forged US$100 notes floating around Tanzania, and anyone who suggests a deal involving a US$100 note is likely to be trying to unload a forgery.

CREDIT CARDS Most major international credit cards (especially Visa but to a lesser extent MasterCard and American Express) are accepted by the safari operators, upmarket hotels and some smarter restaurants in Dar es Salaam, Arusha, Moshi and Zanzibar Town. They are also accepted in many but certainly not all game lodges and upmarket beach resorts, and in a handful of city hotels elsewhere in the country. Increasingly, carrying a credit card is a viable alternative to cash or travellers' cheques, since it can be used to draw up to Tsh400,000 (about US$400) daily at 24-hour ATMs (auto-tellers) outside selected banks in most major towns.

Having said that, there are still many lodges and beach resorts that accept payment only in cash or travellers' cheques, and you are not permitted to pay park fees and the like with a card. Budget travellers can safely assume that hotels and other facilities within their reach cannot process credit card payments. Although things are changing, and surprisingly rapidly, we would still recommend that you carry most of the money you're likely to need in cash or travellers' cheques, and carry a credit card primarily as a backup for emergencies. Tourists on pre-booked holidays will not of course need to carry a vast amount of cash, and can check with their tour operator whether the lodges they are booked into will accept credit card payments for extras.

BUDGETING Any budget for a holiday in a country such as Tanzania will depend so greatly on how and where you travel that it is almost impossible to give sensible advice in a general travel guide. At one end of the spectrum, a fly-around safari staying at the very best lodges might set you back US$500 per person per day, while at the other end a budget traveller could probably get by on US$10 per person per day in some parts of southern Tanzania.

As a rule, readers who are travelling at the middle to upper end of the price range will have pre-booked most of their trip, which means that they will have a good

CHANGING MONEY AT OVERLAND BORDERS

There is nowhere to change money formally at most overland borders, so if you need some local currency to pay for a bus ride to the next town and a room when you get there, you'll need to deal with a private moneychanger. This is usually a fairly open procedure and there is no real risk of running into trouble with the authorities, but the exchange rate is generally poorer than elsewhere, and con artists often thrive in these situations.

One way around this is to try to locate some Tanzanian money in advance, for instance by asking travellers coming from Tanzania if they have anything left over to swap. Otherwise, rather than exchange hard currency at overland borders, carry a small surplus of the currency of the country you are leaving (the equivalent of about US$10) then exchange it for the other currency after you've crossed the border, ideally forearmed with a rough idea of the proper exchange rate. Don't be unduly worried about being offered a slightly lower rate than this, but be wary of allowing a quick-talking moneychanger to exploit the decimal shifts that are often involved in such African currency transactions.

Try to carry whatever banknotes you intend to change separately from your main stash of foreign currency. If you are mobbed by moneychangers, pick one and tell him that you'll discuss rates only when his pals back off. Having agreed a rate, take the local currency and count it before you hand over, or expose the location of, your own money. If the amount is incorrect, it is almost certainly phase one of an elaborate con trick, so safest to hand it back and refuse to have anything further to do with the moneychanger. Alternatively, recount the money after he hands it back to you and keep doing so until you have the correct amount in your hand (some moneychangers have such sleight of hand that they can seemingly add notes to a wad while actually removing others). Only when you are sure you have the right amount should you hand over your money.

Bogus passengers and staff on public transport between Nairobi and Namanga routinely try to persuade travellers that if they arrive at the border without local currency they will be in trouble, then offer to change money with the concerned traveller at a laughable exchange rate. Assume that anybody who approaches you with this sort of story on public transport heading towards any border is a con artist, and ignore them!

idea of what the holiday will cost them before they set foot in Tanzania. Prebooked packages do vary in terms of what is included in the price, and you are advised to check the exact conditions in advance. Generally, however, the price quoted will cover everything but drinks, tips and perhaps some meals (safari lodge accommodation is normally on a full-board basis, but city hotels are typically bed and breakfast only, though some packages may include other meals). Another variable, assuming that you are visiting Zanzibar, is whether the package does or doesn't include the cost of a spice tour and other day trips. To give some idea of what 'extras' might entail on a typical package tour, a meal in a top-notch restaurant will cost around US$10–15, a beer in a lodge or upmarket hotel around US$3, a bottle of wine US$15–20, and a soda US$1. Tips are at the discretion of the individual traveller, but you should be looking at around US$10 per day for your safari driver.

For budget travellers, Tanzania can be very cheap, though day-to-day costs are now higher than in countries such as Malawi and Ethiopia, and most recognised tourist activities are relatively expensive. Day-to-day costs vary regionally, and are highest in major tourist centres such as Arusha, Moshi, Dar es Salaam and Zanzibar. Throughout the country, a soft drink will cost less than US$0.50 and a beer less than US$1 in a local bar, but two to three times that price in a hotel or restaurant that caters primarily to Westerners. A meal in a local restaurant will cost US$2–3, while a meal in a proper restaurant might cost US$5–10. Basic local guesthouses typically cost around US$3–4, though you can expect to pay double this amount in towns which see a lot of tourist traffic. Self-contained rooms in moderate hotels start at around US$10, while you might pay anything up from US$200 to US$1000 for a double room in a game lodge. Public transport costs will vary on how far and how regularly you travel, but buses aren't expensive. Taking the above figures into account budget travellers could get by in most parts of Tanzania on around US$20 per day for one person or US$30 per day for two. Double this amount, and within reason you could eat and stay where you like.

The above calculations don't allow for more expensive one-off activities, such as climbing Mount Kilimanjaro, going on safari or catching the ferry between Dar and Zanzibar. If you want to keep to a particular budget and plan on undertaking such activities, you would be well advised to treat your day-to-day budget separately from what you are likely to spend on safari. Set aside at least US$150 for each day you plan to spend on safari (bearing in mind additional costs such as tips and drinks) and perhaps US$200 for each day you plan to spend on Kilimanjaro, again allowing for tips.

GETTING AROUND

✈ **BY AIR** There has been a tremendous improvement in the network of domestic flights within Tanzania over recent years, especially between major tourist centres. In addition to the national carrier, Air Tanzania, several private airlines now run scheduled flights covering most parts of the country. Contact details are as follows:

Air Tanzania ☎ 022 211 0245; e commercial@airtanzania.com; www.airtanzania.com
Coastal Travel ☎ 022 211 7959/60; e safari@coastal.cc; www.coastal.cc
Precision Air ☎ 027 250 6903/2818/7319; e information@precisionairtz.com; www.precisionairtz.com

Safari Airlink ☎/f 022 550 4384; e flightops@safariaviation.info or flights@safariaviation.info; www.safariaviation.info
ZanAir ☎ 024 223 3670; e reservations@zanair.com; www.zanair.com
Regional Air Services ☎ 027 250 2541/4077; e resvns@regional.co.tz; www.regionaltanzania.com

BY RAIL There are two main railway lines in Tanzania. The central line connects Dar es Salaam to Tabora, Kigoma, Mwanza and Mpanda (see box, *The Central Railway*, in *Chapter 13*, page 393), while the Tazara line connects Dar es Salaam to Ifakara, Mbeya and Kapiri Mposhi in Zambia (see box, *The Tazara Railway*, in *Chapter 16*, page 475).

BY BOAT There are several useful ferry services on Tanzania's oceans and lakes. The most important to travellers are the several boats daily that connect Dar es Salaam to Zanzibar Island, some of which continue on to Pemba. For further details, see the *Getting there and away* section in *Chapter 11, Zanzibar*, pages 299–302. The ferry services run by the Tanzania Railway Corporation on all three of Tanzania's great lakes are covered in *Chapter 14, Lake Victoria; Chapter 15, Lake Tanganyika;* and *Chapter 17, The Southern Highlands and Lake Nyasa*.

BY ROAD Buses are the main mode of road transport for independent travellers. In recent years, there has been a gradual improvement in Tanzania's major roads and also in the standard of vehicles. Bus and coach services along major routes through Tanzania are now reasonably efficient. Good express coach services, typically covering in excess of 60km per hour, connect Arusha, Moshi, Lushoto, Tanga and Dar es Salaam. Bus services along the Tanzam Highway running south from Dar es Salaam to Morogoro, Iringa and Mbeya are also reasonably quick and reliable, as are services between Mbeya and Kyela, and between Dar es Salaam and Dodoma.

For long trips on major routes, ensure that you use an 'express bus', which should travel directly between towns, stopping only at a few prescribed places, rather than stopping wherever and whenever a potential passenger is sighted or an existing passenger wants to disembark. Be warned that so far as most touts are concerned, any bus that will give them commission is an express bus, so you are likely to be pressured into getting in the bus they want you to get in. The best way to counter this is to go to the bus station on the day before you want to travel, and make your enquiries and bookings in advance, when you will be put under less pressure and won't have to worry about keeping an eye on your luggage. Despite a now ageing fleet and some cutbacks to scheduling, Scandinavia Express remains the most reliable and comfortable coach company, approaching if not quite attaining Greyhound-type standards, with at least one daily service on each of the country's two most important routes, ie: Dar es Salaam to Arusha and Dar Es Salaam to Mbeya. Hood and Sumry High Class are also recommended.

The alternative to buses on most routes, and the only means of transport on more obscure routes, are *dala-dalas* – a generic name that seems to encompass practically any public transport vehicle other than a bus. This can be a minibus, a covered 4x4 or a pick-up truck. On the whole, *dala-dalas* are overcrowded by comparison with buses, more likely to try to overcharge tourists, and driven by maniacs, resulting in regular fatal accidents.

On busy routes and relatively short hauls, say up to 200km, buses tend not to operate to any fixed schedule, but instead simply set off when they are full. There is no need to book for such bus services, but be warned that long waits for a bus to fill up are commonplace. On long hauls and quieter routes, buses more normally leave at a fixed time, so it is advisable to book a seat a day in advance. Locally, we have often been given wildly inaccurate information about bus schedules, so we would recommend that you ask a few people and don't take the word of the first person you speak to. In the main part of the guide we have given the current situation regarding frequency of buses and indicated where booking is necessary. Things change, however, so you should make your own enquiries.

When you check bus times, be conscious of the difference between Western time and Swahili time. Many Tanzanians will translate the Swahili time to English without making the six-hour conversion – in other words, you might be told that a bus leaves at 11.00 when it actually leaves at 05.00. The best way to get around this area of potential misunderstanding is to confirm the time you are quoted in Swahili – for instance ask '*saa moja?*' if you are told a bus leaves at 13.00. See *Swahili time* in *Appendix 1, Language*, for more details.

Car hire Self-drive car hire isn't a popular or particularly attractive option in Tanzania, as it is generally more straightforward to visit game reserves on an organised safari. If you are going to drive, though, you'll need both your home driver's licence and an International Driving Permit. In Dar es Salaam, you can hire a 2WD from around US$35 per day. Outside of the city, the majority of companies will only hire 4x4s and in most cases only with a driver. Rates for a 4x4 average around US$55–75 per day including fuel, driver, and driver's daily allowance.

Hitching There is little scope for hitching in Tanzania. On routes where there is no public transport you may have to hitch, but generally this will be on the back of a truck and you will have to pay. Hitching is an option on the Arusha–Dar es Salaam–Mbeya road.

 # ACCOMMODATION

The volume of hotels in Tanzania's towns, and particularly in major tourist centres such as Arusha and Dar es Salaam, is quite remarkable. So, too, is the variety in standard and price, which embraces hundreds of simple local guesthouses charging a couple of US dollars a night, as well as fantastic exclusive beach resorts and lodges charging upwards of US$500 per person – and everything in between.

All accommodation entries throughout the guide have been placed in one of six categories: exclusive, upmarket, moderate, budget, shoestring and camping. The purpose of this categorisation is twofold: to break up long hotel listings that span a wide price range, and to help readers isolate the range of hotels that will best suit their budget and taste. The application of categories is not rigid. Aside from an inevitable element of subjectivity, we have categorised hotels on their feel as much as their rates (the prices are quoted anyway), and this might be influenced by what other accommodation is available in any given town. It should also be noted that assessments relating to the value for money represented by any given hotel are to be read in the context of the individual town and the stated category. In other words, a hotel that seems to be good value in one town might not be such a bargain were it situated in another town where rates are generally cheaper. Likewise, a hotel that we regard to be good value in the upmarket category will almost certainly seem to be madly expensive to a traveller using budget hotels.

Before going into more detail about the different accommodation categories, it's worth noting a few potentially misleading quirks in local hotel-speak. In Swahili, the word *hoteli* refers to a restaurant while what we call a hotel is generally called a lodging, guesthouse or *gesti* – so if you ask a Tanzanian to show you a hotel you might well be taken to an eatery (see *Appendix 1, Language*). Another local quirk is that most Tanzanian hotels in all ranges refer to a room with an en-suite shower and toilet as being self-contained, a term that is used widely in this guide. Finally, at most hotels in the moderate category or below, a single room will as often as not be one with a three-quarter or double bed, while a double room will be what we call a twin, with two single or double beds.

EXCLUSIVE This category does not generally embrace conventional international-style hotels, but rather small and atmospheric beach resorts and game lodges catering to the most exclusive end of the market. Lodges in this category typically consist of no more than 20 accommodation units built and decorated in a style that complements the surrounding environment. The management will generally place a high priority on personalised service and quality food and wine, with the main idea being that guests are exposed to a holistic 24-hour bush or beach experience, rather than just a hotel room and restaurant in a bush/beach location. In several instances, lodges that fall into the exclusive category might be less conventionally luxurious, in terms of air conditioning and the like, than their competitors in the upmarket category. It is the bush experience, not the range of facilities, that lend lodges in this category a quality of exclusivity. Rates are typically upwards of US$250 per person all-inclusive, with substantial discounts offered to operators. This is the category to look at if you want authentic, atmospheric bush or beach accommodation and have few financial restrictions.

UPMARKET This category includes most hotels, lodges and resorts that cater almost entirely to the international tourist or business travel market. Hotels in this range would typically be accorded a two- to four-star ranking internationally, and they offer smart accommodation with en-suite facilities, mosquito netting, air conditioning or fans depending on the local climate, and satellite television in cities and some beach resorts. Hotels in this bracket might charge anything from under US$100 to upwards of US$300 for a double room, dependent on quality and location. As a rule, upmarket hotels in areas that see few foreign visitors are far cheaper than equivalent hotels in or around urban tourist centres such as Dar es Salaam or Arusha, which are in turn cheaper than beach hotels and lodges in national parks and game reserves. Room rates for city and beach hotels invariably include breakfast, while at game lodges they will also normally include lunch and dinner. Most package tours and privately booked safaris use accommodation in this range.

MODERATE In Tanzania, there is often a wide gap in price and standard between the cheapest hotels geared primarily towards tourists and the best hotels geared towards local travellers and budget travellers. For this reason, the moderate bracket is rather more nebulous than other accommodation categories, essentially consisting of hotels which, for one or other reason, couldn't really be classified as upmarket, but equally are too expensive or of too high quality to be considered budget lodgings. Many places listed in this range are superior local hotels that will suffice in lieu of any genuinely upmarket accommodation in a town that sees relatively few tourists. The category also embraces decent lodges or hotels in recognised tourist areas that charge considerably lower rates than their upmarket competitors, but are clearly a notch or two above the budget category. Hotels in this range normally offer comfortable accommodation in self-contained rooms with hot water, fan and possibly satellite television, and they will have decent restaurants and employ a high proportion of English-speaking staff. Prices for moderate city and beach hotels are generally in the US$30–60 range, more in some game reserves. This is the category to look at if you are travelling privately on a limited or low budget and expect a reasonably high but not luxurious standard of accommodation.

BUDGET Hotels in this category are aimed largely at the local market and definitely don't approach international standards, but are still reasonably clean and comfortable, and a definite cut above the basic guesthouses that proliferate in most towns. Hotels in this bracket will more often than not have a decent restaurant attached, English-speaking staff, and comfortable rooms with en-suite facilities, running cold or possibly hot water, fans (but not air conditioning) and good

3

mosquito netting. Hotels in this category typically charge around US$15–30 for an en-suite double, but they may charge less in relatively out-of-the-way places and more in major tourist centres. This is the category to look at if you are on a limited budget, but want to avoid total squalor!

SHOESTRING This category is aimed at travellers who want the cheapest possible accommodation irrespective of quality. In most Tanzanian towns, this will amount to a choice of dozens of small private guesthouses, which are almost exclusively used by locals, are remarkably uniform in design, and generally charge below US$10 for an uncluttered room. The typical guesthouse consists of around ten cell-like rooms forming three walls around a central courtyard, with a reception area or restaurant at the front. Toilets are more often than not long-drops. Washing facilities often amount to nothing more than a lockable room and a bucket of water, though an increasing number of guesthouses do have proper showers, and a few have hot water. Tanzanian guesthouses may be basic, and in many cases they double as brothels, but the majority are reasonably clean and pleasant, and are good value when compared with similar establishments in some neighbouring countries. We have found that guesthouses run by women or with a strong female presence are generally cleaner and more hospitable than those run by men. There is a strong town-to-town variation in guesthouse quality and price: in some towns a clean, freshly painted room with mosquito nets and a fan is standard; in others – Iringa and Bukoba leap to mind – three-quarters of the places we looked at were total dumps. In most medium-sized towns there are a couple of dozen guesthouses, usually clustered around the bus station and often with little to choose between them. In such cases we have avoided making individual recommendations. There are several cheap church-run guesthouses and hostels in Tanzania, and these are normally also included under the shoestring listings.

CAMPING There are surprisingly few campsites in Tanzania, and those that do exist tend to be in national parks, where camping costs US$20–30 per person. Along the coast north of Dar es Salaam and in Moshi and Arusha, several private sites cater to backpackers and overland trucks. If you ask at moderate hotels in out-of-the-way places, you may sometimes be allowed to camp in their grounds for a small fee.

If you are hiking in areas off the beaten track, a tent will be a distinct asset. You should, however, be discreet; either set up well away from villages or else ask permission from the village headman before you pitch a tent. We've not met many people who have camped rough in Tanzania, but it's hard to imagine there would be a significant risk attached to camping in rural areas, provided you didn't flaunt your presence or leave your tent unguarded for a lengthy period.

✗ EATING AND DRINKING

EATING Most tourists will eat 90% of their meals at game lodges or tourist-class hotels, whose kitchens range in standard from adequate to excellent. Game lodges tend to offer a daily set menu with a limited selection of choices, so it is advisable to have your tour operator specify in advance if you are a vegetarian or have other specific dietary requirements. First-time visitors to Africa might take note that most game lodges in and around the national parks have isolated locations, and driving within the parks is neither permitted nor advisable after dark, so that there is no realistic alternative to eating at your lodge. You will rarely be disappointed.

Most game lodges offer the option of a packaged breakfast and/or lunch box, so that their guests can eat on the trot rather than having to base their game-viewing hours around set meal times. The standard of the packed lunches is rather variable (and in some cases pretty awful) but if your first priority is to see wildlife, then taking a breakfast box in particular allows you to be out during the prime game-viewing hours immediately after sunrise. Packed meals must be ordered the night before you need them.

When you are staying in larger towns such as Dar es Salaam, Mwanza, Morogoro, Arusha and Moshi, there is a fair selection of eating-out options. Indian eateries are particularly numerous in most towns, thanks to the high resident Indian population, and good continental restaurants and pizzerias are also well represented. Seafood is excellent on the coast. A selection of the better restaurants in each town are listed in the main part of the guide.

In smaller towns, numerous local restaurants, called *hotelis*, serve unimaginative but filling meals for around US$2. Most *hoteli* food is based around a stew eaten with one of four staples: rice, *chapati*, *ugali* or *batoke*. *Chapati* is a type of dry pancake-shaped fried bread similar to Indian breads. *Ugali* is a stiff maize porridge eaten throughout sub-Saharan Africa. *Batoke* or *matoke* is cooked plantain, served boiled or in a mushy heap. In the Lake Victoria region, *batoke* replaces *ugali* as the staple food. The most common stews are chicken, beef, goat and beans. In coastal towns and around the great lakes, whole fried fish is a welcome change.

Mandaazi, the local equivalent of doughnuts, are tasty when freshly cooked. They are served at *hotelis* and sold at markets. You can eat cheaply at stalls around markets and bus stations. Goat kebabs, fried chicken, grilled groundnuts and potato chips are often freshly cooked and sold in these places. While the central markets in most towns offer a reasonable variety of fruits, you can also buy vegetables, pulses and beans, depending on the season. The most common fruits are mangoes, oranges, bananas, pineapples, papaya and coconuts. Fresh fruit is dirt cheap in Tanzania.

Note: Swahili names for various foods are given in *Appendix 1, Language*.

DRINKING The most widely drunk beverage is *chai*, a sweet tea where all ingredients are boiled together in a pot. Along the coast *chai* is often flavoured with spices such as ginger. In some places *chai* is served *ya rangi* or black; in others *maziwa* or milky. Sodas such as Coke, Pepsi, Sprite and Fanta are widely available, and normally cost less than US$0.50. In large towns you can often get fresh fruit juice. On the coast and in some parts of the interior, the most refreshing, healthy and inexpensive drink is coconut milk, sold by street vendors, who will decapitate the young coconut of your choice to create a natural cup, from which the juice can be sipped.

Tap water in Tanzania is often dodgy, and most travellers try to stick to mineral water, which is available in most tourist centres, coming in 1.5-litre bottles that cost around US$1. We've been told that in some countries it is common practice to fill mineral water bottles with tap water, but we've not heard of this happening in Tanzania, and wouldn't be concerned about it provided that the bottle is sealed.

The two main alcoholic drinks are beer and *konyagi*. *Konyagi* is a spirit made from sugarcane. It tastes a bit strange on its own, but it mixes well and is very cheap. The local Safari lager used to be appalling, but since the national brewery was taken over by South African Breweries a few years ago there has been a dramatic improvement not only in the quality of Safari, but also in the selection of other brands available. Around ten different lager beers are now available, of which Castle, Kilimanjaro and Serengeti seem to be the most popular. All beers come in 500ml bottles and cost anything from US$1 at a local bar to US$5 at the most upmarket hotels.

A variety of imported spirits is available in larger towns. South African wines are widely available at lodges and hotels, and they are generally of a high standard and reasonably priced by international standards.

3

PUBLIC HOLIDAYS

Banks, forex bureaux and government offices close on public holidays. In addition to Good Friday, Easter Monday, Idd-ul-Fitr, Islamic New Year and the Prophet's Birthday, which fall on different dates every year, the following public holidays are taken:

1 January	New Year's Day
12 January	Zanzibar Revolution Day
5 February	CCM Day
26 April	Union Day (anniversary of union between Tanganyika and Zanzibar)
1 May	International Workers' Day
7 July	Saba Saba (Peasants') Day
8 August	Nane Nane (Farmers') Day
14 October	Nyerere Memorial Day
9 December	Independence Day
25 December	Christmas Day
26 December	Boxing Day

SHOPPING

Until a few years ago it was difficult to buy anything much in Tanzania. Thankfully, things have improved greatly in recent years. In Dar es Salaam and most other large towns a fair range of imported goods is available, though prices are often inflated. If you have any very specific needs – unusual medications or slide film, for instance – bring them with you.

Toilet rolls, soap, toothpaste, pens, batteries and locally produced food are widely available. *Dukas*, the stalls you see around markets or lining roads, are cheaper than proper shops and are open seven days a week. Even in Dar es Salaam, we were rarely overcharged simply because we were tourists.

Shopping hours normally are between 08.30 and 16.30, with a lunch break between 13.00 and 14.00.

CURIOS A variety of items specifically aimed at tourists is available: Makonde carvings (see box in *Chapter 18*, page 565), Tingatinga paintings (see box in *Chapter 10*, page 289), batiks, musical instruments, wooden spoons, and various soapstone and malachite knick-knacks. The curio shops near the Clocktower in Arusha are the best place to shop for curios. Prices are competitive and the quality is good. Prices in shops are fixed, but you may be able to negotiate a discount. At curio stalls, haggling is necessary. Unless you are good at this, expect to pay more than you would in a shop.

If you have an interest in African music, a good range of tapes is available at stalls in Dar es Salaam city centre. Most are of Congolese groups popular in East Africa: Loketa, Kanda Bongoman, Bossi Bossiana and the like.

The colourful *vitenge* (the singular of this is *kitenge*) worn by most Tanzanian women can be picked up cheaply at any market in the country. I've been told Mwanza is a particularly good place to shop for these and other clothes.

MEDIA AND COMMUNICATIONS

NEWSPAPERS The English-language *Daily News* (*www.dailynews-tsn.com*), *Daily Guardian* (*www.ippmedia.com*) and *The Citizen* (*www.thecitizen.co.tz*) are available in

Dar es Salaam and other major towns. They don't carry much international news, but the local news can make interesting reading and the international coverage seems to be steadily improving. The Kenyan *Daily Nation* (*www.nation.co.ke*), available in Dar es Salaam, Arusha and Mwanza, is slightly better. The excellent *East African* (*www.theeastafrican.co.ke*) is a weekly newspaper published in Kenya but distributed throughout the three countries to which it dedicates roughly equal coverage, ie: Kenya, Tanzania and Uganda. Stalls in Uhuru Avenue, Dar es Salaam, sell *Time* and *Newsweek*, as well as a variety of European, British and American papers. You can sometimes buy the same from vendors around the Clocktower in Arusha.

PHONE CALLS If you want to make an international phone call or send a fax, you can do so at one of the many private telephone centres which can be found in, next to or near the post office or Tanzania Telecom (*TTCL; www.ttcl.co.tz*) offices in most large towns. Calls are cheap by international standards, and some centres will receive as well as send faxes. Otherwise you can buy a pre-paid *Rafiki* calling card from a TTCL office which can be used at any of the public phone booths around the country. A costlier but more convenient alternative is to phone directly from your lodge or hotel.

If you are carrying a mobile phone, network coverage is excellent in and around towns and extends into several (but not all) of the national parks and game reserves. Rather than paying the expensive international rates that apply to calls made from Tanzania to elsewhere on a non-Tanzanian mobile phone, it might be worth buying a local SIM card. Starter packages, which cost around US$2, can be purchased from any Vodacom or Celtel. Using local pay-as-you-go cards, US$1 will buy you something like 20 international text messages, and international phone calls are also very affordable.

Note that all Tanzanian mobile phone companies have changed their prefixes since the last edition of this guide. The changes are as follows: 0741 is now 0713; 0748 is now 0784; 0745 is now 0755; and 0747 is now 0777 or 0774. If you are dialling from outside of Tanzania – no matter whether you are calling a mobile or a land line – the leading zero must be dropped and the international code +255 added (eg: 0741 555555 becomes 00255 741 555555 if dialled from the UK), while three zeros must be prefixed to any non-domestic number dialled from within Tanzania. Testament to the efficiency of satellite links over land links is the remarkable estimate that mobiles now comprise around 95% of all phones in Tanzania, by comparison to just 5% in the late 1990s.

INTERNET AND EMAIL The spread of internet use in Africa has been remarkable over the last half-decade, and the existence of email represents a real communications revolution on a continent where international lines tend to be unreliable and expensive. Internet and email have caught on particularly quickly in Tanzania, where internet cafés are more prolific and affordable than in any other African country we've visited recently. Numerous internet cafés are dotted around major urban tourist centres such as Dar es Salaam, Arusha, Mwanza and Moshi, the servers are generally pretty fast, and rates are very affordable, typically around US$1–1.50 per hour. Internet access is not available in most game reserves and national parks, and the few game lodges that do offer browsing or email services tend to charge very high rates.

If you're travelling with your own computer, many of the upmarket hotels in Dar es Salaam, Arusha and Mwanza offer ADSL (plug in) connectivity in the rooms, requiring only the phone connection jack for your modem. Some, like the Dar es Salaam Southern Sun, also have wireless (Wi-Fi) hotspots in their public spaces and have wireless cards available for guests.

3

CULTURAL ETIQUETTE

Tanzania has perhaps the most egalitarian and tolerant mood of any African country that we've visited. As a generalisation, Tanzanians tend to treat visitors with a dignified reserve, something that many Westerners mistake for a stand-offish attitude, but in my opinion is more indicative of a respect both for our culture and their own. Granted, dignified probably won't be the adjective that leaps to mind if your first interaction with Tanzanians comes from the pestilence of touts that hang around bus stations in Arusha or Moshi, or somewhere similar. But then in most poor countries, you'll find that people who make a living on the fringe of the tourist industry tend to be pushy and occasionally confrontational in their dealings – from their perspective, they probably have to be in order to make a living. But anybody who spends time travelling in Tanzania will recognise the behaviour of touts to be wholly unrepresentative of what is essentially a conservative, unhurried and undemonstrative society.

PHOTOGRAPHIC TIPS
Ariadne Van Zandbergen

EQUIPMENT Although with some thought and an eye for composition you can take reasonable photos with a 'point and shoot' camera, you need an SLR camera with one or more lenses if you are at all serious about photography. The most important component in a digital SLR is the sensor. There are two types of sensor: DX and FX. The FX is a full size sensor identical to the old film size (36mm). The DX sensor is half size and produces less quality. Your choice of lenses will be determined by whether you have a DX or FX sensor in your camera as the DX sensor introduces an additional 0.5x multiplication to the focal length. So a 300mm lens becomes in effect a 450mm lens. FX ('full frame') sensors are the future, so I will further refer to focal lengths appropriate to the FX sensor.

Always buy the best lens you can afford. Fixed fast lenses are ideal, but very costly. Zoom lenses are easier to change composition without changing lenses the whole time. If you carry only one lens a 24–70mm or similar zoom should be ideal. For a second lens, a lightweight 80–200mm or 70–300mm or similar will be excellent for candid shots and varying your composition. Wildlife photography will be very frustrating if you don't have at least a 300mm lens. For a small loss of quality, teleconverters are a cheap and compact way to increase magnification: a 300 lens with a 1.4x converter becomes 420mm, and with a 2x it becomes 600mm. NB 1.4x and 2x teleconverters reduce the speed of your lens by 1.4 and 2 stops respectively.

The resolution of digital cameras is improving all the time. For ordinary prints a six-megapixel camera is fine. For better results and the possibility to enlarge images and for professional reproduction, higher resolution is available, up to 21 megapixels.

It is important to have enough memory space when photographing on your holiday. The number of pictures you can fit on a card depends on the quality you choose. You should calculate how many pictures you can fit on a card and either take enough cards or take a storage drive on to which you can download the cards' content. You can obviously take a laptop which gives the advantage that you can see your pictures properly at the end of each day and edit and delete rejects. If you don't want the extra bulk and weight you can buy a storage device which can read memory cards. These drives come in a variety of different capacities.

Keep in mind that digital camera batteries, computers and other storage devices need charging. Make sure you have all the chargers, cables and converters with you. Most hotels/lodges have charging points, but it will be best to enquire about this in advance. When camping you might have to rely on charging from the car battery.

On the whole, you would have to do something pretty outrageous to commit a serious *faux pas* in Tanzania. But, like any country, Tanzania does have its rules of etiquette, and while allowances will always be made for tourists, there is some value in ensuring that they are not made too frequently!

GENERAL CONDUCT Perhaps the most important single point of etiquette to be grasped by visitors to Tanzania is the social importance of formal greetings. Tanzanians tend to greet each other elaborately, and if you want to make a good impression on somebody who speaks English, whether they be a waiter or a shop assistant (and especially if they work in a government department), you would do well to follow suit. When you need to ask somebody directions, it is rude to blunder straight into interrogative mode without first exchanging greetings. With Tanzanians who don't speak English, the greeting '*Jambo*' delivered with a smile and a nod of the head will be adequate.

In Tanzania, a tourist isn't normally greeted with a shrieked '*Mzungu*' (or whatever local term is used for a white person) or a 'give me money', something

DUST AND HEAT Dust and heat are often a problem. Keep your equipment in a sealed bag, and avoid exposing equipment to the sun when possible. Digital cameras are prone to collecting dust particles on the sensor, which results in spots on the image. The dirt mostly enters the camera when changing lenses, so you should be careful when doing this. To some extent photos can be 'cleaned up' afterwards using Photoshop, but this is time-consuming. You can have your camera sensor professionally cleaned, or you can do this yourself with special brushes and swabs made for this purpose, but note that touching the sensor might cause damage and should only be done with the greatest care.

LIGHT The most striking outdoor photographs are often taken during the hour or two of 'golden light' after dawn and before sunset. Shooting in low light may enforce the use of very low shutter speeds, in which case a tripod/beanbag will be required to avoid camera shake. The most advanced digital SLRs have very little loss of quality on higher ISO settings, which allows you to shoot at lower light conditions. It is still recommended not to increase the ISO unless necessary.

With careful handling, side lighting and back lighting can produce stunning effects, especially in soft light and at sunrise or sunset. Generally, however, it is best to shoot with the sun behind you. When photographing animals or people in the harsh midday sun, images taken in light but even shade are likely to look nicer than those taken in direct sunlight or patchy shade, since the latter conditions create too much contrast.

PROTOCOL In some countries, it is unacceptable to photograph local people without permission, and many people will refuse to pose or will ask for a donation. In such circumstances, don't try to sneak photographs as you might get yourself into trouble. Even the most willing subject will often pose stiffly when a camera is pointed at them; relax them by making a joke, and take a few shots in quick succession to improve the odds of capturing a natural pose.

Ariadne Van Zandbergen is a professional travel and wildlife photographer specialising in Africa. She runs The Africa Image Library. For photo requests, visit the website www.africaimagelibrary.co.za or contact her directly at ariadne@hixnet.co.za.

that you become accustomed to in some African countries. On the contrary, in Tanzania adults will normally greet tourists with a cheerful '*Jambo*', and children will offer a subdued '*Shikamu*' (a greeting reserved for elders). We find this to be a very charming quality in Tanzanian society, one that is worth reinforcing by learning a few simple Swahili greetings.

Among Tanzanians, it is considered poor taste to display certain emotions publicly. Affection is one such emotion: it is frowned upon for members of the opposite sex to hold hands publicly, and kissing or embracing would be seriously offensive. Oddly, it is quite normal for friends of the same sex to walk around hand-in-hand. A male traveller who gets into a long discussion with a male Tanzanian shouldn't be surprised if that person clasps them by the hand and retains a firm grip for several minutes. This is a warm gesture, one particularly appropriate when the person wants to make a point with which you might disagree. On the subject of intra-gender relations, homosexuality is as good as taboo in Tanzania, to the extent that it would require some pretty overt behaviour for it to occur to anybody to take offence.

It is also considered bad form to show anger publicly. It is difficult to know where to draw the line here, because many touts positively invite an aggressive response, and we doubt that many people who travel independently in Tanzania will get by without the occasional display of impatience. Frankly, we doubt that many bystanders would take umbrage if you responded to a pushy tout with a display of anger, if only because the tout's behaviour itself goes against the grain of Tanzanian society. By contrast, losing your temper will almost certainly be counterproductive when dealing with obtuse officials, dopey waiters and hotel employees, or unco-operative safari drivers.

MUSLIM CUSTOMS Visitors should be aware of the strong Muslim element in Tanzania, particularly along the coast. In Muslim society, it is insulting to use your left hand to pass or receive something or when shaking hands. If you eat with your fingers, it is also customary to use the right hand only. Even those of us who are naturally right-handed will occasionally need to remind ourselves of this (it may happen, for instance, that you are carrying something in your right hand and so hand money to a shopkeeper with your left). For left-handed travellers, it will require a constant effort. In traditional Muslim societies it is offensive for women to expose their knees or shoulders, a custom that ought to be taken on board by female travellers, especially on parts of the coast where tourists remain a relative novelty.

TIPPING AND GUIDES The question of when and when not to tip can be difficult in a foreign country. In Tanzania, it is customary to tip your guide at the end of a safari and/or a Kilimanjaro climb, as well as any cook and porter who accompanies you. A figure of roughly US$5–10 per day is accepted as the benchmark, though it is advisable to check this with your safari company in advance. We see no reason why you shouldn't give a bigger or smaller tip based on the quality of service. Bear in mind, however, that most guides, cooks and porters receive nominal salaries, which means that they are largely dependent on tips for their income. It would be mean not to leave a reasonable tip in any but the most exceptional of circumstances.

In some African countries, it is difficult to travel anywhere without being latched on to by a self-appointed guide, who will often expect a tip over and above any agreed fee. This sort of thing is comparatively unusual in Tanzania, but if you do take on a freelance guide, then it is advisable to clarify in advance that whatever price you agree is final and inclusive of a tip. By contrast, any guide who is given to you by a company should most definitely be tipped, as tips will probably be their main source of income. In Zanzibar and Arusha, a freelance guide may insist upon helping you find a hotel room, in which case they will be given a commission by the hotel, so there is no reason for you to provide an additional tip. In any case, from the guide's point of view, finding you a room is merely the first step in trying to hook you for a safari or a spice tour, or something else that will earn a larger commission.

It is not customary to tip for service in local bars and *hotelis*, though you may sometimes *want* to leave a tip (in fact, given the difficulty of finding change in Tanzania, you may practically be forced into doing this in some circumstances). A tip of 5% would be very acceptable and 10% generous. Generally any restaurant that caters primarily to tourists and to wealthy Tanzania residents will automatically add a service charge to the bill. Since the government claims the lion's share of any formal service charge, it would still be reasonable to reward good service with a genuine tip.

BARGAINING Tourists to Tanzania will sometimes need to bargain over prices, but generally this need exists only in reasonably predictable circumstances, for instance when chartering a private taxi, organising a guide, agreeing a price for a safari or mountain trek, or buying curios and to a lesser extent other market produce. Prices in hotels, restaurants and shops are generally fixed, and overcharging in such places is too unusual for it to be worth challenging a price unless it is blatantly ridiculous.

You may well be overcharged at some point in Tanzania, but it is important to keep this in perspective. After a couple of bad experiences, some travellers start to haggle with everybody from hotel owners to old women selling fruit by the side of the road, often accompanying their negotiations with aggressive accusations of dishonesty. Unfortunately, it is sometimes necessary to fall back on aggressive posturing in order to determine a fair price, but such behaviour is also very unfair on those people who are forthright and honest in their dealings with tourists. It's a question of finding the right balance, or better still looking for other ways of dealing with the problem.

The main instance where bargaining is essential is when buying curios. What should be understood, however, is that the fact a curio seller is open to negotiation does not mean that you were initially being overcharged or ripped off. Curio sellers will generally quote a price knowing full well that you are going to bargain it down (they'd probably be startled if you didn't) and it is not necessary to respond aggressively or in an accusatory manner. It is impossible to say by how much you should bargain the initial price down. Some people say that you should offer half the asking price and be prepared to settle at around two-thirds, but my experience is that curio sellers are far more whimsical than such advice allows for. The sensible approach, if you want to get a feel for prices, is to ask the price of similar items at a few different stalls before you actually contemplate buying anything.

In fruit and vegetable markets and stalls, bargaining is the norm, even between locals, and the most healthy approach to this sort of haggling is to view it as an enjoyable part of the African experience. There will normally be an accepted price band for any particular commodity. To find out what it is, listen to what other people pay and try a few stalls. A ludicrously inflated price will always drop the moment you walk away. When buying fruit and vegetables, a good way to feel out the situation is to ask for a bulk discount or a few extra items thrown in. And bear in mind that when somebody is reluctant to bargain, it may be because they asked a fair price in the first place.

It appears that the conductors on bus services connecting Arusha, Moshi, Tanga and Dar es Salaam (but not elsewhere in the country) routinely overcharge tourists. One reader who spent three months in northern Tanzania and travelled regularly between towns reckons that overcharging *wazungu* is almost customary on long-haul bus rides in this part of the country, but not on shorter trips. This agrees with our experience: we have never been quoted the wrong fare on minibuses within Arusha, or when travelling between Arusha and Moshi, yet we've had to argue to get the correct fare on the last three occasions when we travelled between Moshi and Tanga. The best way to avoid being overcharged is to check the correct ticket price in advance with an impartial party, and to book your ticket a day in advance of when you want to travel. Failing that, you will have to judge for yourself whether the price is right, and if you have reason to think it isn't, then question the conductor. In such circumstances, it can be difficult to find the right balance between standing up for rights and becoming overtly obnoxious.

A final point to consider on the subject of overcharging and bargaining is that it is the fact of being overcharged that annoys; the amount itself is generally of little consequence in the wider context of a trip to Tanzania. Without for a moment wanting to suggest that travellers should routinely allow themselves to be overcharged, we do feel there are occasions when we should pause to look at the bigger picture. Backpackers in particular tend to forget that, no matter how tight for cash they are, it is their choice to travel on a minimal budget, and most Tanzanians are much poorer than they will ever be. If you find yourself quibbling over a pittance with an old lady selling a few piles of fruit by the roadside, you might perhaps bear in mind that the notion of a fixed price is a very Western one. When somebody is desperate enough for money, or afraid that their perishable goods might not last another day, it may well be possible to push them down to a lower price than they would normally accept. In such circumstances, we see nothing wrong with erring on the side of generosity.

BRIBERY Bribery is not much of an issue. There is said to be plenty of corruption in Tanzanian business circles, but it is unlikely to affect tourists. We have never been in a situation where we felt a bribe was being hinted at, nor have we heard of one from another traveller.

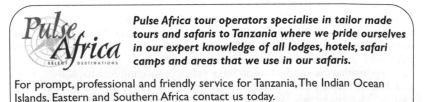

4

Health

with Dr Felicity Nicholson

PREPARATIONS

Preparations to ensure a healthy trip to Tanzania require checks on your immunisation status: it is wise to be up to date on tetanus, polio and diphtheria (now given as an all-in-one vaccine, Revaxis, that lasts for ten years), and hepatitis A. Immunisations against meningococcus and rabies may also be recommended. Proof of vaccination against yellow fever is needed for entry into Tanzania if you are coming from another yellow fever endemic area and this includes travelling from Tanzania to Zanzibar. There is much debate as to whether yellow fever vaccine is actually needed for Tanzania as there hasn't been a case since 1992. Whether the vaccine is given should be discussed on an individual basis with a doctor who is used to conducting such an assessment. If the vaccine is not suitable for you then an exemption certificate will be needed to cross borders. This can be obtained from your GP or a travel clinic. Immunisation against cholera is no longer required for Tanzania.

Hepatitis A vaccine (Havrix Monodose or Avaxim) comprises two injections given about a year apart. The course costs about £100, but may be available on the NHS; it protects for 25 years and can be administered even close to the time of departure. Hepatitis B vaccination should be considered for longer trips (two months or more) or for those working with children or in situations where contact with blood is likely. Three injections are needed for the best protection and can be given over a three-week period if time is short. Longer schedules give more sustained protection and are therefore preferred if time allows. Hepatitis A vaccine can also be given as a combination with hepatitis B as 'Twinrix', though two doses are needed at least seven days apart to be effective for the hepatitis A component, and three doses are needed for the hepatitis B.

The newer injectable typhoid vaccines (eg: Typhim Vi) last for three years and are about 85% effective. Oral capsules (Vivotif) are currently available in the US (and soon in the UK); if four capsules are taken over seven days it will last for five years. They should be encouraged unless the traveller is leaving within a few days for a trip of a week or less, when the vaccine would not be effective in time. Meningitis vaccine (ideally containing strains A, C, W and Y, but if this is not available then A+C vaccine is better than nothing) is recommended for all travellers, especially for trips of more than four weeks (see *Meningitis*, page 92). Vaccinations for rabies are ideally advised for everyone, but are especially important for travellers visiting more remote areas, especially if you are more than 24 hours from medical help and definitely if you will be working with animals (see *Rabies*, page 92).

Experts differ over whether a BCG vaccination against tuberculosis (TB) is useful in adults: discuss this with your travel clinic.

In addition to the various vaccinations recommended above, it is important that travellers should be properly protected against malaria. For detailed advice, see page 82.

Ideally you should visit your own doctor or a specialist travel clinic (see pages 84–6) to discuss your requirements, if possible at least eight weeks before you plan to travel.

PROTECTION FROM THE SUN Give some thought to packing suncream. The incidence of skin cancer is rocketing as Caucasians are travelling more and spending more time in the sun. Keep out of the sun during the middle of the day and, if you must be exposed, build up gradually from 20 minutes per day. Be especially careful of sun reflected off water and wear a T-shirt and lots of waterproof SPF15 suncream when swimming; snorkelling often leads to scorched backs of the thighs so wear Bermuda shorts. Sun exposure ages the skin and makes people prematurely wrinkly; cover up with long, loose clothes and wear a hat when you can. The glare and the dust can be hard on the eyes, too, so bring UV-protecting sunglasses and, perhaps, a soothing eyebath.

MALARIA PREVENTION There is no vaccine against malaria, but there are other ways to avoid it; since most of Africa is very high risk for malaria, travellers must plan their malaria protection properly. Seek current advice on the best antimalarials to take: usually mefloquine, Malarone or doxycycline. If mefloquine (Lariam) is suggested, start this 2½ weeks (three doses) before departure to check that it suits you; stop it immediately if it seems to cause depression or anxiety, visual or hearing disturbances, severe headaches, fits or changes in heart rhythm. Side effects such as nightmares or

LONG-HAUL FLIGHTS

Long-haul air travel increases the risk of deep vein thrombosis. Although recent research has suggested that many of us develop clots when immobilised, most of these resolve without us ever having been aware of them. In certain susceptible individuals, though, clots form on clots and when large ones break away and lodge in the lungs this is dangerous. Fortunately this happens in a tiny minority of passengers.

Studies have shown that flights of over 5½ hours are significant, and that people who take lots of shorter flights over a short space of time can also form clots. People at highest risk are:

- Those who have had a clot before – unless they are now taking warfarin
- People over 80 years of age
- Anyone who has recently undergone a major operation or surgery for varicose veins
- Someone who has had a hip or knee replacement in the last three months
- Cancer sufferers
- Those who have ever had a stroke
- People with heart disease
- Those with a close blood relative who has had a clot.

Those with a slightly increased risk are:

- People over 40
- Women who are pregnant or have had a baby in the last couple of weeks
- People taking female hormones, the combined contraceptive pill or other oestrogen therapy
- Heavy smokers
- Those who have very severe varicose veins
- The very obese
- People who are very tall (over 6ft/1.8m) or short (under 5ft/1.5m).

dizziness are not medical reasons for stopping unless they are sufficiently debilitating or annoying. Anyone who has been or is being treated for depression or psychiatric problems, has diabetes controlled by oral therapy or who is epileptic (or who has suffered fits in the past) or has a close blood relative who is epileptic, should avoid mefloquine. In the past doctors were nervous about prescribing mefloquine to pregnant women, but experience has shown that it is relatively safe and certainly safer than the risk of malaria. That said, there are other issues, so if you are travelling to Tanzania whilst pregnant, seek expert advice before departure.

Malarone (proguanil and atovaquone) is as effective as mefloquine. It has the advantage of having few side effects and need only be continued for one week after returning. However, it is expensive and because of this tends to be reserved for shorter trips although it is generally accepted that it can be taken for three months. Malarone may not be suitable for everybody so advice should be taken from a doctor. Paediatric Malarone for children over 11kg and under 40kg is now available in the UK and is given based on weight.

The antibiotic doxycycline (100mg daily) is a viable alternative when neither mefloquine nor Malarone are considered suitable for whatever reason. Like Malarone it can be started one or two days before arrival. Unlike mefloquine, it may also be used in travellers with epilepsy, although certain anti-epileptic medication may make it less effective. Users must be warned about the possibility of allergic skin reactions developing in sunlight, which can occur in about 1–3% of people. The drug should be stopped if this happens. Women using the oral contraceptive should use

A deep vein thrombosis (DVT) is a blood clot that forms in the deep leg veins. This is very different from irritating but harmless superficial phlebitis. DVT causes swelling and redness of one leg, usually with heat and pain in one calf and sometimes the thigh. A DVT is only dangerous if a clot breaks away and travels to the lungs (pulmonary embolus). Symptoms of a pulmonary embolus (PE) include chest pain that is worse on breathing in deeply, shortness of breath, and sometimes coughing up small amounts of blood. The symptoms commonly start three to ten days after a long flight. Anyone who thinks that they might have a DVT needs to see a doctor immediately who will arrange a scan. Warfarin tablets (to thin the blood) are then taken for at least six months.

PREVENTION OF DVT Several conditions make the problem more likely. Immobility is the key, and factors like reduced oxygen in cabin air and dehydration may also contribute. To reduce the risk of thrombosis on a long journey:

• Exercise before and after the flight
• Keep mobile before and during the flight; move around every couple of hours
• Drink plenty of water or juices during the flight
• Avoid taking sleeping pills and excessive tea, coffee or alcohol
• Perform exercises that mimic walking and tense the calf muscles
• Consider wearing flight socks or support stockings (see www.legshealth.com)
• Ideally take a meal each week of oily fish (mackerel, trout, salmon, sardines etc) ahead of your departure. This reduces the blood's ability to clot and thus DVT risk. It may even be worth just taking a meal of oily fish 24 hours before departure if this is more practical.

If you think you are at increased risk of a clot, ask your doctor if it is safe to travel.

an additional method of protection for the first four weeks when using doxycycline. It is also unsuitable in pregnancy and breast feeding or for children under 12 years.

Chloroquine and proguanil are no longer considered to be very effective for Tanzania. However, they may still be recommended if no other regime is suitable.

All prophylactic agents should be taken with or after the evening meal, washed down with plenty of fluid and with the exception of Malarone (see above) continued for four weeks after leaving.

Travellers to remote parts would probably be wise to carry a course of treatment to cure malaria. Experts differ on the costs and benefits of self-treatment, but agree that it leads to over-treatment and to many people taking drugs they do not need; yet treatment may save your life. Discuss your trip with a specialist to determine your particular needs and risks, and be sure you understand when and how to take the cure. If you are somewhere remote in a malarial region you probably have to assume that any high fever (over 38°C) for more than a few hours is due to malaria (regardless of any other symptoms) and that you should seek treatment. Diagnosing malaria is not easy, which is why consulting a doctor is sensible: there are other dangerous causes of fever in Africa, which require different treatments. Presently Malarone or Co-artemether are the favoured regimes, but check for up-to-date advice on the current recommended treatment. And remember malaria may occur anything from seven days into the trip to up to six months or even one year if you have taken prophylactic medication after leaving Africa. The risk of malaria above 1,800m above sea level is low.

In addition to antimalarial medication, it is important to avoid mosquito bites between dusk and dawn. Pack an insect repellent containing around 50–55% DEET, such as Repel or Expedition Plus. You may also need either a permethrin-impregnated bednet or a permethrin spray so that you can 'treat' bednets in hotels, unless you are staying in five-star accommodation with air conditioning. Always check the details before you go. Putting on long clothes at dusk means you can reduce the amount of repellent you need to put on your skin, but be aware that malaria mosquitoes hunt at ankle level and will bite through socks, so apply repellent under socks too. Travel clinics usually sell a good range of nets, treatment kits and repellents.

TRAVEL CLINICS AND HEALTH INFORMATION A full list of current travel clinic websites worldwide is available on www.istm.org/. For other journey preparation information, consult www.nathnac.org/ds/map_world.aspx. Information about various medications may be found on www.netdoctor.co.uk/travel.

UK

Berkeley Travel Clinic 32 Berkeley St, London W1J 8EL (near Green Park tube station); ℡ 020 7629 6233; ⏲ 10.00–18.00 Mon–Fri, 10.00–15.00 Sat.
Cambridge Travel Clinic 41 Hills Rd, Cambridge CB2 1NT; ℡ 01223 367362; f 01223 368021; e enquiries@travelcliniccambridge.co.uk; www.travelcliniccambridge.co.uk; ⏲ 10.00–16.00 Mon, closed Tue, 12.00–19.00 Wed–Thu, 11.00–18.00 Fri, 10.00–16.00 Sat.
Edinburgh Travel Health Clinic 14 East Preston St, Newington, Edinburgh EH8 9QA; ℡ 0131 667 1030; www.edinburghtravelhealthclinic.co.uk; ⏲ 09.00–19.00 Mon–Wed, 9.00–18.00 Thu & Fri. Travel vaccinations & advice on all aspects of malaria prevention. All current UK prescribed anti-malaria tablets in stock.

Fleet Street Travel Clinic 29 Fleet St, London EC4Y 1AA; ℡ 020 7353 5678; www.fleetstreetclinic.com; ⏲ 08.45–17.30 Mon–Fri. Injections, travel products & latest advice.
Hospital for Tropical Diseases Travel Clinic Mortimer Market Centre, 2nd Flr, Capper St (off Tottenham Court Rd), London WC1E 6AU; ℡ 020 7388 9600; www.thehtd.org. Offers consultations & advice, & is able to provide all necessary drugs & vaccines for travellers. Runs a healthline (℡ 020 7950 7799) for country-specific information & health hazards. Also stocks nets, water purification equipment & personal protection measures.
MASTA (Medical Advisory Service for Travellers Abroad), at the London School of Hygiene &

Tropical Medicine, Keppel St, London WC1 7HT; ✆ 09068 224100; www.masta-travel-health.com. This is a premium-line number, charged at 60p per minute. For a fee, they will provide an individually tailored health brief, with up-to-date information on how to stay healthy, inoculations & what to take. **MASTA pre-travel clinics** ✆ 01276 685040. Call for the nearest; there are currently 30 in Britain. They also sell malaria prophylaxis memory cards, treatment kits, bednets, net treatment kits etc. **NHS travel website** www.fitfortravel.scot.nhs.uk. Provides country-by-country advice on immunisation & malaria prevention, plus details of recent developments, & a list of relevant health organisations. **Nomad Travel Store** 3–4 Wellington Terrace, Turnpike Lane, London N8 0PX; ✆ 020 8889 7014; f 020 8889 9528; e turnpike@nomadtravel.co.uk; www.nomadtravel.co.uk; walk in or appointments, ⏰ 09.15–17.00 daily, late night Thu. 6 stores

countrywide. As well as dispensing health advice, Nomad stocks mosquito nets & other anti-bug devices, & an excellent range of adventure travel gear. **InterHealth Travel Clinic** 157 Waterloo Rd, London SE1 8US; ✆ 020 7902 9000; e askus@interhealth.org.uk; www.interhealth.org.uk; ⏰ 09.00–17.00 Mon–Fri. Competitively priced, one-stop travel health service by appointment only. **Trailfinders Immunisation Centre** 194 Kensington High St, London W8 7RG; ✆ 020 7938 3999; www.trailfinders.com/travelessentials/travelclinic.htm; ⏰ 09.00–17.00 Mon, Tue, Wed & Fri, 09.00–18.00 Thu, 10.00–17.15 Sat. No appointment necessary **Travelpharm** www.travelpharm.com.The Travelpharm website offers up-to-date guidance on travel-related health & has a range of medications available through their online mini-pharmacy.

Irish Republic
Tropical Medical Bureau Grafton St Medical Centre, Grafton Buildings, 34 Grafton St, Dublin 2; ✆ 1 671 9200. Has a useful website specific to tropical destinations: www.tmb.ie.

USA
Centers for Disease Control 1600 Clifton Rd, Atlanta, GA 30333; ✆ 404 498 1515 or 1 800 311 3435; e cdcinfo@cdc.gov; www.cdc.gov/travel. The central source of travel information in the USA. Each summer they publish the invaluable *Health Information for International Travel*.

IAMAT (International Association for Medical Assistance to Travelers) 1623 Military Rd, #279, Niagara Falls, NY 14304-1745; ✆ 716 754 4883; e info@iamat.org; www.iamat.org. A non-profit organisation with free membership that provides lists of English-speaking doctors abroad.

Canada
IAMAT (International Association for Medical Assistance to Travellers) Suite 1, 1287 St Clair Av W, Toronto, Ontario M6E 1B8; ✆ 416 652 0137; www.iamat.org

TMVC Suite 314, 1030 W Georgia St, Vancouver, BC V6E 2Y3; ✆ 905 648 1112; www.tmvc.com. One-stop medical clinic for all your international travel medicine & vaccination needs.

Australia, New Zealand and Thailand
TMVC (Travel Doctors Group) ✆ 1300 65 88 44; www.tmvc.com.au. 22 clinics in Australia, New Zealand & Thailand, including: *Auckland* Canterbury Arcade, 170 Queen St, Auckland; ✆ 9 373 3531; *Brisbane* Dr Deborah Mills, Qantas Domestic Building, 6th Flr, 247 Adelaide St, Brisbane QLD 4000; ✆ 7 3221 9066; f 7 3321 7076;

Melbourne Dr Sonny Lau, 393 Little Bourke St, 2nd floor, Melbourne, VIC 3000; ✆ 3 9602 5788; f 3 9670 8394; *Sydney* Dr Mandy Hu, Dymocks Building, 7th Flr, 428 George St, Sydney, NSW 2000; ✆ 2 221 7133; f 2 221 8401 **IAMAT** PO Box 5049, Christchurch 5, New Zealand; www.iamat.org

South Africa
SAA-Netcare Travel Clinics e travelinfo@netcare.co.za; www.travelclinic.co.za or www.malaria.co.za. 12 clinics throughout South Africa.

TMVC NHC Health Centre, corner Beyers Naude & Waugh Northcliff; ✆ 0 11 214 9030; www.traveldoctor.co.za. Consult the website for details of clinics.

Private clinics, hospitals and pharmacies can be found in most large towns, and doctors generally speak fair to fluent English. Consultations and laboratory tests are remarkably inexpensive when compared with most Western countries, so if you do fall sick it would be absurd to let financial considerations dissuade you from seeking medical help. Commonly required medicines such as broad-spectrum antibiotics are widely available and cheap throughout the region, as are malaria cures and prophylactics. It is advisable to carry all malaria-related tablets with you, and only rely on their availability locally if you need to restock your supplies. If you are on any medication prior to departure, or you have specific needs relating to a known medical condition (for instance if you are allergic to bee stings or you are prone to attacks of asthma), then you are strongly advised to bring any related drugs and devices with you.

Switzerland
IAMAT 57 Chemin des Voirets, 1212 Grand-Lancy, Geneva; e info@iamat.org; www.iamat.org

PERSONAL FIRST-AID KIT A minimal kit contains:

- A good drying antiseptic, eg: iodine or potassium permanganate (don't take antiseptic cream)
- A few small dressings (plasters or Band-Aids)
- Suncream
- Insect repellent; anti-malarial tablets; impregnated bed-net or permethrin spray
- Aspirin or paracetamol
- Antifungal cream (eg: Canesten)
- Ciprofloxacin or norfloxacin, for severe diarrhoea
- Tinidazole for giardia or amoebic dysentery (see below for regime)
- Antibiotic eye drops for sore, 'gritty', stuck-together eyes (conjunctivitis)
- A pair of fine pointed tweezers (to remove hairy caterpillar hairs, thorns, splinters, coral etc)
- Alcohol-based hand rub or bar of soap in plastic box
- Condoms or femidoms
- Digital thermometer (for those going to remote areas).

MAJOR HAZARDS
People new to exotic travel often worry about tropical diseases, but it is accidents that are most likely to carry you off. Road accidents are very common in many parts of Tanzania, so be aware and do what you can to reduce risks: try to travel during daylight hours and refuse to be driven by a drunk. Listen to local advice about areas where violent crime is rife, too.

COMMON MEDICAL PROBLEMS
TRAVELLERS' DIARRHOEA Travelling in Tanzania carries a fairly high risk of getting a dose of travellers' diarrhoea; perhaps half of all visitors will suffer and the newer you are to exotic travel, the more likely you will be to suffer. By taking precautions against travellers' diarrhoea you will also avoid typhoid, cholera, hepatitis,

dysentery, worms etc. Travellers' diarrhoea and the other faecal-oral diseases come from getting other peoples' faeces in your mouth. This most often happens from cooks not washing their hands after a trip to the toilet, but even if the restaurant cook does not understand basic hygiene you will be safe if your food has been properly cooked and arrives piping hot. The maxim to remind you what you can safely eat is:

PEEL IT, BOIL IT, COOK IT OR FORGET IT.

This means that fruit you have washed and peeled yourself, and hot foods, should be safe, but raw foods, cold cooked foods, salads, fruit salads which have been prepared by others, ice cream and ice are all risky. And foods kept lukewarm in hotel buffets are often dangerous. If you are struck, see the box below for treatment.

WATER STERILISATION It is much rarer to get sick from drinking contaminated water but it happens, so try to drink from safe sources.

Water should have been brought to the boil (even at altitude it only needs to be brought to the boil), or passed through a good bacteriological filter or purified with iodine; chlorine tablets (eg: Puritabs) are also adequate although theoretically less effective and they taste nastier. Mineral water has been found to be contaminated in Tanzania but should be safer than contaminated tap water.

MALARIA Whether or not you are taking malaria tablets, it is important to protect yourself from mosquito bites (see box, *Malaria in Tanzania*, pages 88–9, and *Malaria prevention*, pages 82–4), so keep your repellent stick or roll-on to hand at all times. Be aware that no prophylactic is 100% protective but those on prophylactics who

TREATING TRAVELLERS' DIARRHOEA

It is dehydration that makes you feel awful during a bout of diarrhoea and the most important part of treatment is drinking lots of clear fluids. Sachets of oral rehydration salts give the perfect biochemical mix to replace all that is pouring out of your bottom but other recipes taste nicer. Any dilute mixture of sugar and salt in water will do you good: try Coke or orange squash with a three-finger pinch of salt added to each glass (if you are salt-depleted you won't taste the salt). Otherwise make a solution of a four-finger scoop of sugar with a three-finger pinch of salt in a 500ml glass. Or add eight level teaspoons of sugar (18g) and one level teaspoon of salt (3g) to one litre (five cups) of safe water. A squeeze of lemon or orange juice improves the taste and adds potassium, which is also lost in diarrhoea. Drink two large glasses after every bowel action, and more if you are thirsty. These solutions are still absorbed well if you are vomiting, but you will need to take sips at a time. If you are not eating you need to drink three litres a day plus whatever is pouring into the toilet. If you feel like eating, take a bland, high carbohydrate diet. Heavy greasy foods will probably give you cramps.

If the diarrhoea is bad, or you are passing blood or slime, or you have a fever, you will probably need antibiotics in addition to fluid replacement. A dose of norfloxacin or ciprofloxacin repeated twice a day until better may be appropriate (if you are planning to take an antibiotic with you, note that both norfloxacin and ciprofloxacin are available only on prescription in the UK). If the diarrhoea is greasy and bulky and is accompanied by sulphurous (eggy) burps, one likely cause is giardia. This is best treated with tinidazole (four x 500mg in one dose, repeated seven days later if symptoms persist).

are unlucky enough to catch malaria are less likely to get rapidly into serious trouble. It is easy and inexpensive to arrange a malaria blood test.

DENGUE FEVER This mosquito-borne disease may mimic malaria but there is no prophylactic medication available to deal with it. The mosquitoes that carry this virus bite during the daytime, so it is worth applying repellent if you see any mosquitoes around. Symptoms include strong headaches, rashes, excruciating joint and muscle pains and high fever. Dengue fever lasts only for a week or so and is not usually fatal. Complete rest and paracetamol are the usual treatment; plenty of fluids also help. Some patients are given an intravenous drip to prevent dehydration. It is especially important to protect yourself if you have had dengue fever before, since a second infection with a different strain can result in the potentially fatal dengue haemorrhagic fever.

INSECT BITES It is crucial to avoid mosquito bites between dusk and dawn; as the sun is going down, don long clothes and apply repellent on any exposed flesh. This will protect you from malaria, elephantiasis and a range of nasty insect-borne

MALARIA IN TANZANIA

Along with road accidents, malaria poses the single biggest serious threat to the health of travellers in most parts of tropical Africa, Tanzania included. The Anopheles mosquito which transmits the parasite is most abundant near marshes and still water, where it breeds, and the parasite is most prolific at low elevations. Parts of Tanzania lying at an elevation of 2,000m or higher (a category that includes the Ngorongoro Crater rim, Mount Kilimanjaro and Meru, and parts of the Eastern Arc Mountains) are regarded as free of malaria. In mid-elevation locations, malaria is largely but not entirely seasonal, with the highest risk of transmission occurring during the rainy season. Moist and low-lying areas such as the Indian Ocean coast and the hinterland of lakes Tanganyika, Victoria and Nyasa are high risk throughout the year, but the danger is greatest during the rainy season. This localised breakdown might influence what foreigners working in Tanzania do about malaria prevention, but all travellers to Tanzania must assume that they will be exposed to malaria and should take precautions throughout their trip (see page 82 for advice on prophylactic drugs and avoiding mosquito bites).

Even those who take their malaria tablets meticulously and do everything possible to avoid mosquito bites may contract a strain of malaria that is resistant to prophylactic drugs. Untreated malaria is likely to be fatal, but even strains resistant to prophylaxis respond well to prompt treatment. Because of this, your immediate priority upon displaying possible malaria symptoms – which might include any combination of a headache, flu-like aches and pains, a rapid rise in temperature, a general sense of disorientation, and possibly even nausea and diarrhoea – is to establish whether you have malaria.

The blood test for malaria takes ten minutes to produce a result and costs about US$1 in Tanzania. A positive result means that you have malaria. A negative result suggests that you don't have malaria, but bear in mind that the parasite doesn't always show up on a test, particularly when the level of infection is mild or is 'cloaked' by partially effective prophylactics. For this reason, even if you test negative, it would be wise to stay within reach of a laboratory until the symptoms clear up, and to test again after a day or two if they don't. It's worth noting that if you have a fever and the malaria test is negative, you may have typhoid, which should also receive immediate treatment. Where typhoid testing is unavailable, a routine blood test can give a strong indication of this disease.

It is preferable not to attempt self-diagnosis or to start treatment for malaria before you have tested. There are, however, many places in Tanzania where you will be unable viruses. Otherwise retire to an air conditioned room or burn mosquito coils (which are widely available and cheap in Tanzania) or sleep under a fan. Coils and fans reduce rather than eliminate bites. During the day it is wise to wear long, loose (preferably 100% cotton) clothes if you are pushing through scrubby country; this will keep ticks off and also tsetse and day-biting Aedes mosquitoes which may spread dengue and yellow fever. Tsetse flies hurt when they bite and are attracted to the colour blue; locals will advise on where they are a problem and where they transmit sleeping sickness.

Minute pestilential biting blackflies spread river blindness in some parts of Africa between 90°N and 170°S; the disease is caught close to fast-flowing rivers since flies breed there and the larvae live in rapids. The flies bite during the day but long trousers tucked into socks will help keep them off. Citronella-based natural repellents do not work against them.

Mosquitoes and many other insects are attracted to light. If you are camping, never put a lamp near the opening of your tent, or you will have a swarm of biters waiting to join you when you retire. In hotel rooms, be aware that the longer your light is on, the greater the number of insects will be sharing your accommodation.

to test for malaria, for instance in the game reserves and in most of the popular hiking areas. With malaria, it is normal enough to go from feeling healthy to having a high fever in the space of a few hours (and it is possible to die from falciparum malaria within 24 hours of the first symptoms). In such circumstances, assume that you have malaria and act accordingly – whatever risks are attached to taking an unnecessary cure are outweighed by the dangers of untreated malaria.

It is imperative to treat malaria promptly. The sooner you take a cure, the less likely you are to become critically ill, and the more ill you become the greater the chance you'll have difficulty holding down the tablets. There is some division about the best treatment for malaria. Currently Malarone or Co-artemether are considered the best standby treatments, but other regimes such as a quinine/doxycycline course are usually effective. Alternatively quinine and fansidar can be used if doxycycline is unavailable. And if there is no quinine either then fansidar alone can be used. The latter is widely available in Tanzania. One cure that you should avoid is Halfan, which is dangerous, particularly if you are using Lariam as a prophylactic.

In severe cases of malaria, the victim will be unable to hold down medication, at which point they are likely to die unless they are hospitalised immediately and put on a drip. If you or a travelling companion start vomiting after taking your malaria medication, get to a hospital or clinic quickly, ideally a private one. Whatever concerns you might have about African hospitals, they are used to dealing with malaria, and the alternative to hospitalisation is far worse.

Malaria typically takes around two weeks to incubate (minimum time seven days), but it can take much longer, so you should always complete the prophylaxis as recommended after returning home. If you display possible malaria symptoms up to a year later, then get to a doctor immediately and ensure that they are aware you have been exposed to malaria.

Every so often we run into travellers who prefer to acquire resistance to malaria rather than take preventative tablets, or who witter on about homoeopathic cures for this killer disease. That's their prerogative, but they have no place expounding their ill-informed views to others. Travellers to Africa cannot acquire any effective resistance to malaria, and those who don't make use of prophylactic drugs risk their life in a manner that is both foolish and unnecessary.

Ticks in Africa are not the rampant disease transmitters they are in the Americas, but they may spread tickbite fever and a few dangerous rarities in Tanzania. Tickbite fever is a flu-like illness that can easily be treated with doxycycline, but as there can be some serious complications it is important to visit a doctor.

Ticks should ideally be removed as soon as possible as leaving them on the body increases the chance of infection. They should be removed with special tick tweezers that can be bought in good travel shops. Failing that you can use your finger nails: grasp the tick as close to your body as possible and pull steadily and firmly away at right angles to your skin. The tick will then come away complete, as long as you do not jerk or twist. If possible douse the wound with alcohol (any spirit will do) or iodine. Irritants (eg: Olbas oil) or lit cigarettes are to be discouraged since they can cause the ticks to regurgitate and therefore increase the risk of disease. It is best to get a travelling companion to check you for ticks; if you are travelling with small children, remember to check their heads, and particularly behind the ears.

Spreading redness around the bite and/or fever and/or aching joints after a tick bite imply that you have an infection that requires antibiotic treatment, so seek advice.

Tumbu flies or putsi are a problem where the climate is hot and humid. The adult fly lays her eggs on the soil or on drying laundry and when the eggs come in contact with human flesh (when you put on clothes or lie on a bed) they hatch and bury themselves under the skin. Here they form a crop of 'boils', each of which hatches a grub after about eight days, when the inflammation will settle down. In putsi areas either dry your clothes and sheets within a screened house, or dry them in direct sunshine until they are crisp, or iron them.

Jiggers or sandfleas are another flesh-feaster. They latch on if you walk barefoot in contaminated places, and set up home under the skin of the foot, usually at the side of a toenail where they cause a painful, boil-like swelling. They need picking out by a local expert; if the distended flea bursts during eviction the wound should be doused in spirit, alcohol or kerosene, otherwise more jiggers will infest you.

BILHARZIA OR SCHISTOSOMIASIS *With thanks to Dr Vaughan Southgate of the Natural History Museum, London, and Dr Dick Stockley, The Surgery, Kampala*

Bilharzia or schistosomiasis is a disease that commonly afflicts the rural poor of the tropics. Two types exist in sub-Saharan Africa – Schistosoma mansoni and Schistosoma haematobium. It is an unpleasant problem that is worth avoiding, though it can be treated if you do get it. This parasite is common in almost all water sources in Tanzania, even places advertised as 'bilharzia free'. The most risky shores will be close to places where infected people use water, wash clothes etc.

It is easier to understand how to diagnose it, treat it and prevent it if you know a little about the life cycle. Contaminated faeces are washed into the lake, the eggs hatch and the larva infects certain species of snail. The snails then produce about 10,000 cercariae a day for the rest of their lives. The parasites can digest their way through your skin when you wade or bathe in infested fresh water.

Winds disperse the snails and cercariae. The snails in particular can drift a long way, especially on windblown weed, so nowhere is really safe. However, deep water and running water are safer, while shallow water presents the greatest risk. The cercariae penetrate intact skin, and find their way to the liver. There male and female meet and spend the rest of their lives in permanent copulation. No wonder you feel tired! Most finish up in the wall of the lower bowel, but others can get lost and can cause damage to many different organs. *Schistosoma haematobium* goes mostly to the bladder.

Although the adults do not cause any harm in themselves, after about 4–6 weeks they start to lay eggs, which cause an intense but usually ineffective immune reaction, including fever, cough, abdominal pain, and a fleeting, itching rash called 'safari itch'. The absence of early symptoms does not necessarily mean there is no infection. Later symptoms can be more localised and more severe, but the general symptoms settle down fairly quickly and eventually you are just tired. 'Tired all the time' is one of the most common symptoms among expats in Africa, and bilharzia, giardia, amoeba and intestinal yeast are the most common culprits.

Although bilharzia is difficult to diagnose, it can be tested at specialist travel clinics. Ideally tests need to be done at least six weeks after likely exposure and will determine whether you need treatment. Fortunately it is easy to treat at present.

Avoiding bilharzia If you are bathing, swimming, paddling or wading in fresh water which you think may carry a bilharzia risk, try to get out of the water within ten minutes.

- Avoid bathing or paddling on shores within 200m of villages or places where people use the water a great deal, especially reedy shores or where there is lots of water weed.
- Dry off thoroughly with a towel; rub vigorously.
- If your bathing water comes from a risky source try to ensure that the water is taken from the lake in the early morning and stored snail-free, otherwise it should be filtered, or Dettol or Cresol added.
- Bathing early in the morning is safer than bathing in the last half of the day.
- Cover yourself with DEET insect repellent before swimming: it may offer some protection.

SKIN INFECTIONS Any mosquito bite or small nick in the skin gives an opportunity for bacteria to foil the body's usually excellent defences; it will surprise many travellers how quickly skin infections start in warm humid climates and it is essential to clean and cover even the slightest wound. Creams are not as effective as a good drying antiseptic such as dilute iodine, potassium permanganate (a few crystals in half a cup of water) or crystal (or gentian) violet. One of these should be available in most towns. If the wound starts to throb, or becomes red and the redness starts to spread, or the wound oozes, and especially if you develop a fever, antibiotics will probably be needed: flucloxacillin (250mg four times a day) or cloxacillin (500mg four times a day). For those allergic to penicillin, erythromycin (500mg twice a day) for five days should help. See a doctor if the symptoms do not start to improve in 48 hours.

Fungal infections also get a hold easily in hot moist climates so wear 100% cotton socks and underwear and shower frequently. An itchy rash in the groin or flaking between the toes is likely to be a fungal infection. This needs treatment with an antifungal cream such as Canesten (clotrimazole); if this is not available try Whitfield's ointment (compound benzoic acid ointment) or crystal violet (although this will turn you purple!).

EYE PROBLEMS Bacterial conjunctivitis (pink eye) is a common infection in Africa; people who wear contact lenses are most open to this irritating problem. The eyes feel sore and gritty and they will often be stuck closed in the mornings. They will need treatment with antibiotic drops or ointment. Lesser eye irritation should settle with bathing in salt water and keeping the eyes shaded. If an insect flies into

Most established tourist beaches in Tanzania can be assumed to be safe for swimming. Elsewhere along the coast, it would be wise to ask local advice before plunging into the water, and to err on the side of caution if no sensible advice is forthcoming, since there is always a possibility of being swept away by strong currents or undertows that cannot be detected until you are actually in the water.

Snorkellers and divers should wear something on their feet to avoid treading on coral reefs, and should never touch the reefs with their bare hands – coral itself can give nasty cuts, and there is a danger of touching a venomous creature camouflaged against the reef. On beaches, never walk barefoot on exposed coral. Even on sandy beaches, people who walk barefoot risk getting coral or urchin spines in their soles or venomous fish spines in their feet.

If you do tread on a venomous fish, soak the foot in hot (but not scalding) water until some time after the pain subsides; this may be for 20–30 minutes in all. Take the foot out of the water to top up; otherwise you may scald it. If the pain returns, re-immerse the foot. Once the venom has been heat-inactivated, get a doctor to check and remove any bits of fish spine in the wound.

your eye, extract it with great care, ensuring you do not crush or damage it; otherwise you may get a nastily inflamed eye from toxins secreted by the creature.

PRICKLY HEAT A fine pimply rash on the trunk is likely to be heat rash; cool showers, dabbing dry, and talc will help. Treat the problem by slowing down to a relaxed schedule, wearing only loose, baggy, 100% cotton clothes and sleeping naked under a fan; if it's bad you may need to check into an air conditioned hotel room for a while.

MENINGITIS This is a particularly nasty disease as it can kill within hours of the first symptoms appearing. The telltale symptoms are a combination of a blinding headache (light sensitivity), a blotchy rash and a high fever. Immunisation protects against the most serious bacterial form of meningitis and the tetravalent vaccine ACWY is recommended for Tanzania. Other forms of meningitis exist (usually viral) but there are no vaccines for these. Local papers normally report localised outbreaks. A severe headache and fever should make you run to a doctor immediately. There are also other causes of headache and fever; one of which is typhoid, which occurs in travellers to Tanzania. Seek medical help if you are ill for more than a few days.

SAFE SEX Travel is a time when we might enjoy sexual adventures, especially when alcohol reduces inhibitions. Remember that the risks of sexually transmitted infection are high, whether you sleep with fellow travellers or locals. About 80% of HIV infections in British heterosexuals are acquired abroad. Use condoms or femidoms to help reduce the risk of transmission. If you notice any genital ulcers or discharge, get treatment promptly since these increase the risk of acquiring HIV. If you do have unprotected sex, visit a clinic as soon as possible; this should be within 24 hours, or no later than 72 hours, for post-exposure prophylaxis.

RABIES Rabies can be carried by all mammals (beware the village dogs and small monkeys that are used to being fed in the parks) and is passed on to humans through a bite, scratch or a lick of an open wound. You must always assume any animal is rabid (unless personally known to you) and seek medical help as soon as possible. Meanwhile scrub the wound with soap under a running tap or while pouring water from a jug. Find a reasonably clear-looking source of water (but at this stage the quality of the water is not important), then pour on a strong iodine or alcohol solution of gin, whisky or rum. This helps stop the rabies virus entering the body and will guard against wound infections, including tetanus.

If you intend to have contact with animals and/or are likely to be more than 24 hours away from medical help, then pre-exposure vaccination is advised. Ideally three doses should be taken over a minimum of three weeks. Contrary to popular belief, these vaccinations are relatively painless!

If you are exposed as described, treatment should be given as soon as possible, but it is never too late to seek help as the incubation period for rabies can be very long. Those who have not been immunised will need a full course of injections together with rabies immunoglobulin (RIG), but this product is expensive (around US$800) and may be hard to come by. This is another reason why pre-exposure vaccination should be encouraged in travellers who are planning to visit more remote areas!

Tell the doctor if you have had pre-exposure vaccine, as this will change the treatment you receive. And remember that, if you do contract rabies, mortality is 100% and death from rabies is probably one of the worst ways to go!

SNAKES Snakes rarely attack unless provoked, and bites in travellers are unusual. You are less likely to get bitten if you wear stout shoes and long trousers when in the bush. Most snakes are harmless and even venomous species will dispense venom in only about half of their bites. If bitten, then, you are unlikely to have received venom; keeping this fact in mind may help you to stay calm. Many so-called first-aid techniques do more harm than good: cutting into the wound is harmful; tourniquets are dangerous; suction and electrical inactivation devices do not work. The only treatment is antivenom. In the event of a bite which you fear may have been from a venomous snake:

- Try to keep calm – it is likely that no venom has been dispensed.
- Prevent movement of the bitten limb by applying a splint.
- Keep the bitten limb BELOW heart height to slow the spread of any venom.
- If you have a crêpe bandage, bind up as much of the bitten limb as you can, but release the bandage every half-hour.
- Evacuate to a hospital which has antivenom.

And remember:

- NEVER give aspirin; you may offer paracetamol, which is safe.
- NEVER cut or suck the wound.
- DO NOT apply ice packs.
- DO NOT apply potassium permanganate.
- If the offending snake can be captured without risk of someone else being bitten, take this to show the doctor – but beware since even a decapitated head is able to bite.

HOOPOE SAFARIS

In July, 2004, Hoopoe Safaris was awarded the "Best Ecotourism Company in the World" by the respected Condé Nast Traveler magazine (USA). This award caps a number of other awards and accolades. The company is dedicated to being a responsible operator and helping in conservation efforts. At the same time it offers its guests the highest standards and the most satisfying safari experience.

Hoopoe Safaris is an East African company, with offices in the UK and USA, offering a range of luxury safaris, mountain climbs, beach holidays and special interest safaris across East Africa. We also arrange tailor-made walking safaris throughout Tanzania with our dedicated sister company Tropical Trekking, and we are the marketing agents for Kirurumu Tented Camps & Lodges. We are renowned for being flexible and innovative in tailor-making personalised itineraries to accommodate individual budgets and time restrictions. In addition to the wide range of lodge accommodation available, we specialise in luxurious mobile tented safaris both in the National Parks and in our own private wilderness concessions.

We invite you to experience the best that East Africa has to offer with East Africans who know the land intimately…

For further information, contacts, or to enquire about an agent in your area please visit

www.hoopoe.com

Part Two

THE GUIDE

5

Arusha

Situated in the fertile southern foothills of Mount Meru, less than 100km from the Kenyan border as the crow flies, the bustling town of Arusha is Tanzania's so-called 'safari capital', the most popular and convenient springboard from which to explore the legendary northern game-viewing circuit. The town is also an important gateway into Tanzania, the first town visited by travellers coming across the border from Nairobi, and the entry point for a growing number of fly-in tourists thanks to the daily KLM flights that link Europe to the nearby Kilimanjaro International Airport.

First impressions of Arusha are that practically *everything* there revolves around the safari industry, a perception that is only reinforced by more prolonged exposure. Wander around the old town centre or backroads north of the stadium, and it can feel like every second person you pass has something to sell, be it a safari, a batik or last week's edition of some or other foreign newspaper, while every other vehicle sports a safari company logo.

In reality, Arusha's rare economic vitality is buoyed by several contributory factors, not the least of which is its location in the bountiful Mount Meru foothills, whose drizzly sub-montane microclimate nurtures the rich volcanic soil to agricultural profligacy. There is also the proximity of the Mererani Hills, the only known source of the increasingly popular gemstone tanzanite, while a more ephemeral economic boost has been provided by the presence of UN and other NGO personnel linked to the Rwandan War Crimes Tribunal, which took up residence in the Arusha International Conference Centre some years back and shows no signs of leaving any time soon. For all this, however, one suspects that the lure of the tourist dollar has been the driving force behind Arusha's steady rise from ninth-largest town in Tanzania in 1978 to second-largest today, with a population of 270,000 according to the 2002 census.

Situated at an elevation of around 1,500m in the rainshadow of Mount Meru, Arusha makes for a climatically temperate – and, during the rainy season, often downright soggy – introduction to tropical Africa. The town itself is a pleasant enough place to hang out, and these days it boasts a growing number of trendy bars, restaurants and cafés catering to expatriates, tourists and wealthier locals. Away from these few select spots, however, Arusha remains something of an African everytown, where low-rise colonial-era buildings rub shoulders with a small but gradually increasing number of more modern structures. Indeed, it could be argued that the wealth generated by the safari industry serves to accentuate the vast economic gulf between the haves and have-nots and the spectrum of cultural influences that play havoc with those visitors seeking to pigeonhole the 'real Africa'. Which is it, then: the colourfully dressed Maasai and Arusha women who sell traditional beadwork on the pavement, the suited businessmen who scurry in and out of the International Conference Centre, or the swaggering, sunglass-shrouded wide-boys who scurry about offering cheap safaris, change money, marijuana...?

If nothing else, Arusha is an attractively green town, with its northern skyline – weather permitting – dominated by the imposing hulk of Africa's fifth-highest mountain. And for those who prefer not to stay in the town centre, there are plenty of more rustic options in the immediate area. The 4,556m Mount Meru is the dominant geographical feature in Arusha National Park which, despite its proximity to Arusha and manifold points of interest, attracts little more than a trickle of tourism. Also of interest in the immediate vicinity of Arusha is Lake Duluti, an attractive forest-fringed crater lake that lies immediately south of the Moshi road, and a cluster of attractive farms set on the coffee plantations and forested hills between Arusha and Usa River – many of which offer views to Meru *and* Kilimanjaro on a clear day.

HISTORY

Little is known about the Arusha area prior to the 17th century, when the Bantu-speaking Meru people – migrants from the west with strong linguistic and cultural affinities to the Chagga of Kilimanjaro – settled and farmed the fertile and well-watered northern foothills of Mount Meru. In 1830 or thereabouts, the southern slopes of the mountain verging on the Maasai Steppes were settled by the Arusha, a Maasai subgroup who lost their cattle and territory in one of the internecine battles characteristic of this turbulent period in Maasailand. The Arusha people speak the same Maa language as the plains Maasai and share a similar social structure based around initiated age-sets, but when they settled in the Mount Meru area they forsook their pastoralist roots, turning instead to agriculture as a primary source of subsistence.

The Arusha economy was boosted by the trade in agricultural produce – in particular tobacco – with the closely affiliated Maasai of the plains. The Arusha also became known as reliable providers of food and other provisions for the Arab slave caravans that headed inland from the Pangani and Tanga area towards modern-day Kenya and Lake Victoria. Invigorated by this regular trade, the Arusha had, by 1880, cleared the forested slopes of Mount Meru to an elevation of around 1,600m to make way for cultivation. As their territory expanded, however, the Arusha people increasingly came into contact with their northern neighbours, the Meru, resulting in several territorial skirmishes and frequent cattle raids between the two tribes.

In 1881, prompted by the need to defend their combined territories against the Maasai and other potential attackers, the incumbent warrior age-sets of the Arusha and Meru united to form a formidable military force. Since they were settled on the well-watered slopes of Mount Meru, and their subsistence was not primarily dependent on livestock, the Arusha and Meru people were less affected than the plains pastoralists by the devastating series of droughts and rinderpest epidemics of the 1880s and early 1890s. As a result, the combined army, known as the Talala – the Expansionists – was able to exert considerable influence over neighbouring Maasai and Chagga territories.

The Talala staunchly resisted German attempts to settle in their territory, killing the first missionaries to arrive there and repelling an initial punitive attack by the colonial army. In October 1896, however, the Arusha and Meru were soundly defeated by a military expedition out of Moshi led by Karl Johannes and consisting of 100 German troopers supported by some 5,000 Chagga warriors. In the aftermath of this defeat, the Germans drove home the point by razing hundreds of Arusha and Meru smallholdings, killing the men, confiscating the cattle and repatriating women of Chagga origin to the Kilimanjaro area.

In 1889, the Germans established a permanent settlement – modern-day Arusha town – on the border of Arusha and Maasai territories, and used forced Arusha and Maasai labour to construct the Boma that can still be seen on the north end of Boma Road. Relations between the colonisers and their unwilling subjects remained tense, to say the least. During the construction of the fort, a minor dispute led to some 300 labourers being massacred while marching peacefully along present-day Boma Road, and several local chiefs from outlying areas were arbitrarily arrested and taken to Moshi to be hanged in the street.

Following the construction of the Boma, Arusha quickly developed into a significant trading and administrative centre, with about two dozen Indian and Arab shops clustered along what is today Boma Road. John Boyes, who visited Arusha in 1903, somewhat fancifully compared the Boma to 'an Aladdin's Palace transported from some fairyland and dropped down in the heart of the tropics'. The town, he wrote, was 'a real oasis in the wilderness' and 'spotlessly clean', while 'the streets [were] laid out with fine sidewalks, separated by the road from a stream of clear water flowing down a cemented gully'.

At the outbreak of World War I, the small German garrison town was of some significance as a local agricultural and trade centre, but it remained something of a backwater by comparison with Moshi, which lay a week's ox-wagon trek distant at the railhead of the Tanga line. Much of the area around Arusha was, however, settled by German farmers, who had forcibly displaced the original Arusha and Meru smallholders. In 1916, British troops captured Arusha and expelled the German farmers, resulting in some resettlement by indigenous farmers, but the German farmland was eventually re-allocated to British and Greek settlers. The British also set aside large tracts of land around Arusha for sisal plantations, which meant that by 1920, less than 20% of the land around Mount Meru was available to local farmers, most of it on dry foothills unsuited to cultivating the local staple of bananas.

Arusha grew steadily between the wars. The settler economy was boosted by the introduction of coffee, sisal and other export crops, and trade links were improved with the construction of road links to Moshi and Nairobi and the opening of the railway line to Moshi and the coast in 1929. Yet the land issues continued to simmer, eventually coming to a head after World War II, with the eviction of thousands of Meru farmers from north of Mount Meru to make way for a peanut production project overseen by 13 white farmers. The peanut project, aside from being a dismal and costly failure, resulted in the pivotal Meru Land Case, which not only caused great embarrassment to the UN Trusteeship Council, but also proved to be an important catalyst to the politicisation of the anti-colonial movement in Tanganyika.

Prior to independence, Arusha remained a relatively small town whose primary role was to service the surrounding agricultural lands. The official census of 1952 placed the urban population at fewer than 8,000 people, of which more than half were of Asian or European stock. The town has, however, grown markedly since independence, attracting large numbers of domestic migrants from surrounding rural areas and beyond. This can be attributed to a number of factors: the town's short-lived but prestigious role as capital of the East African community in the 1960s, the tanzanite mining boom, and perhaps most of all its strategic location as the springboard for the northern safari circuit. The permanent population of Arusha is estimated at around 300,000 in 2009, with a similar number of tourists passing through annually!

GETTING THERE AND AWAY

BY AIR The main local point of entry is Kilimanjaro International Airport (KIA), which lies roughly two-thirds along the 80km asphalt road that runs eastward from Arusha to Moshi. KIA is connected to Europe by daily KLM flights, eliminating the need to travel to northern Tanzania via Nairobi or Dar es Salaam. Other international carriers that fly to KIA are Kenya Airways, Ethiopian Airlines and South African Airways, while Air Tanzania operates connecting flights there from

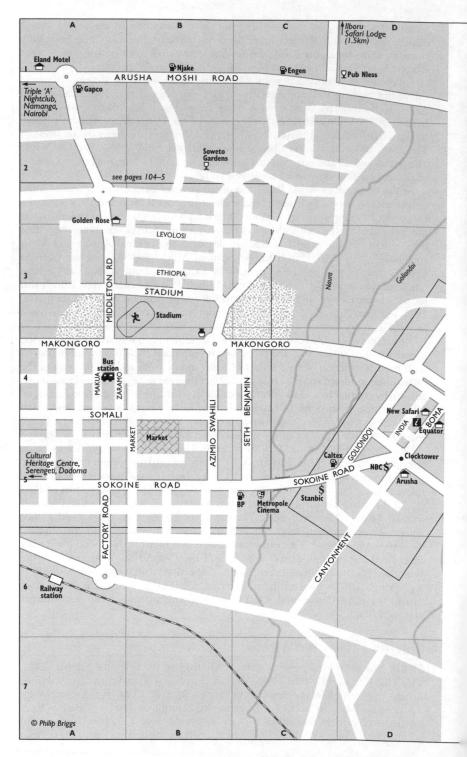

Eland Motel

Njake

Engen

Ilboru
Safari Lodge
(1.5km)

Pub Nless

ARUSHA   MOSHI   ROAD

Triple 'A'
Nightclub,
Namanga,
Nairobi

Gapco

Soweto
Gardens

see pages 104–5

Golden Rose

LEVOLOSI

MIDDLETON RD

ETHIOPIA

STADIUM

Naura

Goliondoi

Stadium

MAKONGORO

MAKONGORO

Bus
station

MAKUA

ZARAMO

SOMALI

MARKET

Market

AZIMIO SWAHILI

SETH BENJAMIN

New Safari

INDIA

BOMA

Equator

Clocktower

Caltex

GOLIONDOI

NBC

Cultural
Heritage Centre,
Serengeti, Dodoma

SOKOINE   ROAD

SOKOINE ROAD

Arusha

FACTORY ROAD

BP

Metropole
Cinema

Stanbic

CANTONMENT

Railway
station

© Philip Briggs

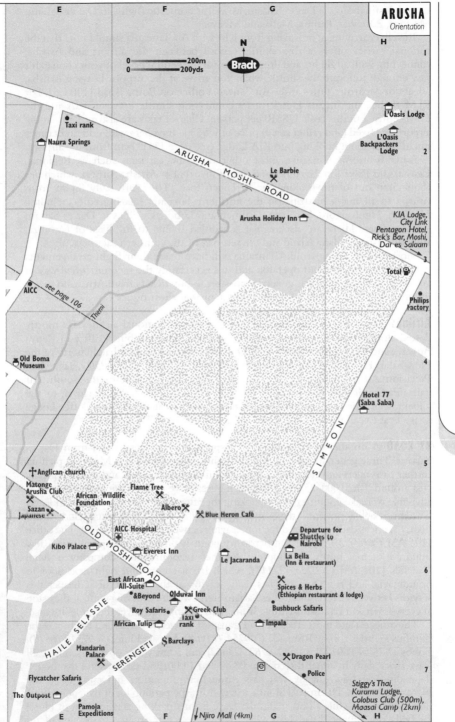

ARUSHA
Orientation

N

0 ————— 200m
0 ————— 200yds

Bradt

Taxi rank

Naura Springs

ARUSHA MOSHI ROAD

Le Barbie

L'Oasis Lodge

L'Oasis
Backpackers
Lodge

Arusha Holiday Inn

KIA Lodge,
City Link
Pentagon Hotel,
Rick's Bar, Moshi,
Dar es Salaam

Total

Philips
factory

AICC   *see page 106*

Themi

Old Boma
Museum

Hotel 77
(Saba Saba)

SIMEON

Anglican church

Matonge
Arusha Club

African Wildlife
Foundation

Flame Tree

Albero

Blue Heron Café

Departure for
Shuttles to
Nairobi

Sazan
Japanese

AICC Hospital

La Bella
(Inn & restaurant)

Kibo Palace

Everest Inn

Le Jacaranda

OLD MOSHI ROAD

East African
All-Suite

&Beyond

Olduvai Inn

Spices & Herbs
(Ethiopian restaurant & lodge)

Bushbuck Safaris

Roy Safaris

Greek Club

Taxi
rank

African Tulip

Impala

HAILE SELASSIE

Mandarin
Palace

Barclays

SERENGETI

Dragon Pearl

Police

Flycatcher Safaris

The Outpost

Pamoja
Expeditions

Njiro Mall (4km)

Stiggy's Thai,
Kurama Lodge,
Colobus Club (500m),
Maasai Camp (2km)

several destinations via Dar es Salaam, as well as domestic flights to Dar es Salaam, Mwanza, Zanzibar, Pemba, Mafia and Mbeya.

Travellers arriving at or leaving from KIA with Air Tanzania should note that the national carrier offers a free shuttle service between the airport and Arusha, connecting with all flights and dropping you at the central hotel of your choice. It's easy enough to locate the shuttle when you arrive at the airport. Leaving Arusha, ask about departure times at the Air Tanzania office on Boma Road [106 C5]. For KLM flights, the Impala Hotel runs a connecting shuttle between KIA and the town centre, but this costs US$10 per person. Charter taxis are also available at the airport, at a fixed (and rather steep) price of US$50. Travellers with odd flight times might think about booking into KIA Lodge (see page 111), 1km from the airport.

Aside from Air Tanzania, most other domestic carriers, such as Regional, Coastal and Precision Air, fly in and out of the smaller Arusha Airport, which lies about 5km out of town along the Serengeti road. There are daily flights from Arusha to all major airstrips on the northern Tanzania safari circuit, including Manyara, Ngorongoro, Seronera, Grumeti and Lobo, as well as to Dar es Salaam and Zanzibar. There are also regular scheduled flights to the likes of Mwanza, Rubondo Island, Mafia Island and the reserves of the southern safari circuit.

Most tourists flying around Tanzania will have made their flight arrangements in advance through a tour operator, and this is certainly the recommended way of going about things, but it is generally possible to buy tickets from Arusha to major destinations such as Dar es Salaam and Zanzibar at short notice.

Airlines The offices of the main domestic and international airlines are mostly dotted along Boma Road in the old town centre. The combined office of Kenya Airways and KLM [106 C4] (✆ 027 254 8062) is situated immediately north of the New Safari Hotel, as is that of Ethiopian Airlines [106 C4] (✆ 027 250 7512), while Precision Air [106 C4] (✆ 027 250 3261; ⊕ daily) is just to the south. Air Tanzania/South African Airways [106 C5] (✆ 027 250 3201) is closer to the Clocktower. The Regional Air office is out of town near the Arusha Coffee Lodge so it's best to call them (✆ 027 250 4164/254 8536; m 0753 500300).

BY ROAD A number of companies run express bus services to and from Dar es Salaam. These generally take around ten hours, stopping only at Moshi to pick up further passengers and at Korogwe for a 20-minute lunch break, and tickets typically cost around Tsh20,000–25,000. Most such buses leave early in the morning, so it is advisable to make enquiries and a booking the afternoon before you want to leave. The best coach at present is the Scandinavia Express, which runs three standard and luxury services daily in either direction, leaving between 07.30 and 08.30. The office [104 A5] (✆ 027 250 0153) and departure point is on Makao Mapya Road, a few hundred metres north of Shoprite. Another recommended company is Mtei Coaches [104 A5] (✆ 0755 717117), which has a compound right next door to Scandinavia, and runs two coaches daily, leaving at the same time. Cheaper bus services between Arusha and Dar es Salaam aren't worth bothering with, as they stop at every town and can take anything from 12 to 15 hours to cover the same distance.

The quickest and most efficient road transport between Arusha and Nairobi is the minibus shuttles run by Riverside (✆ 0754 474968), Impala Hotel (✆ 0754 678678), Bobby (✆ 0754 960122), Osa (✆ 0762 773662) and a few other operators. These all leave twice daily in either direction at 08.00 and 14.00, and take around five hours, depending on how quickly you pass through immigration and customs at the Namanga border. The Impala Shuttle leaves from the parking lot of the eponymous hotel [101 G7], while all other shuttles leave from a parking area in front of Hotel La Bella on Simeon Road [101 G6], though you can arrange to be picked up elsewhere (it is unclear whether these shuttles will return to their old terminus in the parking lot of the former Mount Meru Novotel when it eventually reopens as the Arusha Holiday Inn). Tickets officially cost US$20–25 for non-residents, but more often than not walk-in customers will be permitted to pay the cheaper resident's rate. Tickets for the Impala Shuttle can be bought directly from the Impala Hotel, while those for the other shuttles can be bought at kiosks in the foyer of the La Bella, by calling the company directly, or through any safari operator in Arusha. Another option is to travel to Nairobi with Scandinavia Express (see above), which runs two buses daily, leaving at around 15.30 and costing Tsh25,000.

A steady stream of minibuses and buses connect Moshi and Arusha. I would avoid using minibuses along this route due to the higher incidence of accidents, but they are generally quicker than buses. This trip usually takes between one and two hours. There are also regular buses to other relatively local destinations such as Mto wa Mbu, Karatu, Mbulu, Babati and Kondoa; the best company servicing these routes is Mtei Coaches (see above). Most other buses and minibuses leave from the main bus station near the football stadium [100 B3 & 105 F3].

ORIENTATION

Unlike Dar es Salaam or Zanzibar's labyrinthine Stone Town, Arusha is not a difficult town to familiarise yourself with. Its most significant geographical features are the Naura and Goliondoi rivers, which run parallel to each other through the town centre, cutting it into two distinct parts. To the east of the rivers lies the 'old' town centre, a relatively smart area whose main north–south thoroughfares – Boma, India and Goliondoi roads – are lined with upmarket hotels, tourist-friendly restaurants, safari companies, curio shops, banks, bookshops and tourist offices. Major landmarks in this part of town include the Clocktower [100 D5 & 106 C5], the Old Boma (now a museum) [101 E4 & 106 C2] and the Arusha International Conference Centre (AICC) [106 B1].

Connected to the old town centre by Sokoine Road in the south and Makongoro Road in the north, the more bustling modern town centre consists of a tight grid of roads west of the rivers, centred on the market and bus station south of the stadium. This area is well equipped with small budget hotels and Indian restaurants, but it boasts few facilities that approach international standards. Similar in feel, though more residential and less commercially orientated, is the suburb of Kaloleni immediately north of the stadium and main bus station.

Another important suburb is Kijenge, which lies to the southeast of the old town centre, and is reached by following Sokoine Road across a bridge over the Themi River to become the Old Moshi Road. Kijenge has a spacious, leafy character and it is dotted with relatively upmarket hotels (notably the Impala) and restaurants, as well as an increasing number of safari company offices.

GETTING AROUND

TAXIS There are plenty of taxis in Arusha. Good places to pick them up include the market and bus station, the filling station on the junction of Goliondoi Road and the Old Moshi Road, and the open area at the north end of Boma and India roads. A taxi ride within the town centre should cost roughly Tsh3,000–4,000, though tourists are normally asked a slightly higher price. A taxi ride to somewhere outside the town centre will cost more.

PUBLIC TRANSPORT A good network of minibus *dala-dalas* service Arusha. A steady flow of these vehicles runs along the length of Sokoine Road, some of which

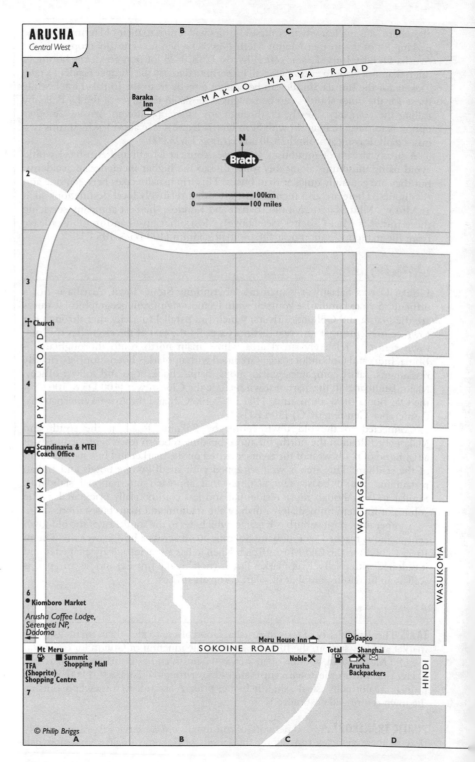

ARUSHA
Central West

A　B　C　D

1

MAKAO MAPYA ROAD

Baraka
Inn

N

Bradt

0 ━━━━━ 100km
0 ━━━━━ 100 miles

2

3

✝ Church

MAKAO MAPYA ROAD

4

🚌 Scandinavia & MTEI
Coach Office

5

WACHAGGA

WASUKOMA

6
● Kiomboro Market

Arusha Coffee Lodge,
Serengeti NP,
Dodoma
←

Meru House Inn 🏠

🏤 Gapco

Mt Meru
SOKOINE ROAD
Total　Shanghai

■ 🏧　■ Summit
TFA　　Shopping Mall
(Shoprite)
Shopping Centre

Noble ✕

🏧 ⌂✕⌧
Arusha
Backpackers

HINDI

7

© Philip Briggs

A　B　C　D

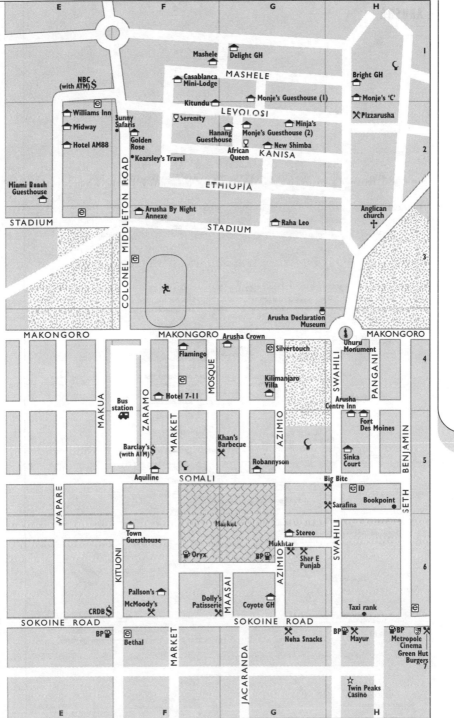

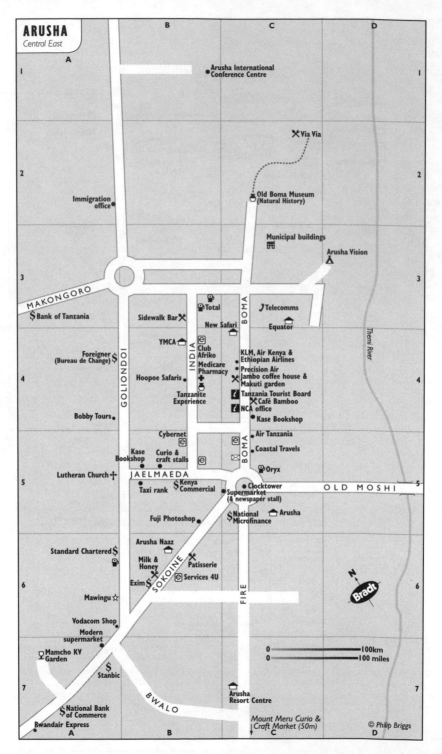

ARUSHA
Central East

A   B   C   D

1

Arusha International
Conference Centre

✕ Via Via

2

Immigration
office

Old Boma Museum
(Natural History)

Municipal buildings

Arusha Vision

3

MAKONGORO

💲 Bank of Tanzania

Sidewalk Bar ✕

Total

♪ Telecomms

New Safari

Equator

YMCA

Club
Afriko

KLM, Air Kenya &
Ethiopian Airlines

GOLIONDOI

Foreigner
(Bureau de Change) 💲

Medicare
Pharmacy

Precision Air

4

Hoopoe Safaris

✕ Jambo coffee house &
Makuti garden

INDIA

Tanzanite
Experience

Tanzania Tourist Board

✕ Café Bamboo

NCA office

Bobby Tours

Kase Bookshop

Cybernet

Air Tanzania

Kase
Bookshop

Curio &
craft stalls

Coastal Travels

Lutheran Church ✝

JAELMAEDA

Oryx

5

Taxi rank

Kenya
Commercial

Clocktower

OLD MOSHI 5

Supermarket
(& newspaper stall)

Fuji Photoshop

National
Microfinance

Arusha

Standard Chartered 💲

Arusha Naaz

Milk &
Honey

Patisserie

SOKOINE

Exim

Services 4U

FIRE

6

Mawingu ☆

Vodacom Shop

Modern
supermarket

Mamcho KV
Garden

N

Bradt

0   100km
0   100 miles

Stanbic

BWALO

7

National Bank
of Commerce

Rwandair Express

Arusha
Resort Centre

Mount Meru Curio &
Craft Market (50m)

© Philip Briggs

A   B   C   D

Them River

BOMA

BOMA

continue west out of town past the Tanganyika Farmers Association (TFA) centre, while others run east of the clock tower to the Impala Hotel and beyond. There are also regular *dala-dalas* between the town centre and the main Nairobi-Moshi bypass. Fares are nominal, and it's easy enough to hop on or off any passing *dala-dala* heading in your direction.

TOURIST INFORMATION

The **Tanzania Tourist Board** (TTB) office on Boma Road [106 C4] (✆ *027 250 3842; www.tanzaniatouristboard.com*) is refreshingly helpful and well informed. It stocks a useful colour road map of Tanzania as well as a great street plan of Arusha, both given free of charge to tourists, though this doesn't stop the book vendors out on the street from trying to sell the same maps at a very silly price. If you want to check out a safari company, the TTB office keeps a regularly updated list of all registered safari and trekking companies, as well as those that are blacklisted.

The TTB has been actively involved in the development of cultural tourism programmes in Ng'iresi, Mulala, Mkuru, Longido, Mto wa Mbu, Usambara, North Pare and South Pare, as well as several projects further afield. The Arusha office stocks informative pamphlets about these programmes, and can help out with information on prices and access. Details are also available at the **Cultural Tourism Programme** office in the Old Boma (✆ *027 250 0025;* f *027 250 8216;* e *culturaltourism@habari.co.tz*).

> ### SAFETY
>
> Arusha can be a daunting prospect on first contact, particularly if you arrive by bus. Competition between budget safari companies is fierce, and 'flycatchers' – the street touts who solicit custom for these companies – know that their best tactic is to hook travellers who don't have a pre-booked safari when they arrive. As a consequence, when you arrive in Arusha by bus you're likely to spend your first few minutes dodging the attention of a dozen yelling touts, all of whom will claim to be able to offer you the cheapest safari and room in town. In most cases, the touts probably will show you to a decent room, but allowing this to happen does open the door to your sense of obligation being exploited later in your stay.
>
> Fortunately, once you've run the bus station gauntlet, things do calm down somewhat, though the flock of flycatchers, newspaper vendors and curio sellers who hang around the old town centre can be a nuisance. Unlike in some other parts of Africa, however, it is unusual for such an exchange to descend into something truly unpleasant: most touts here seem capable of taking a good-humoured 'no' for an answer, especially one spoken in Swahili, and they will usually back down at any show of genuine irritation. As for the dodgy moneychangers that sometimes hang around with the touts, don't let the offer of a superior rate sucker you in – changing money on the street in Arusha as elsewhere in Tanzania is a definite no-no!
>
> Such annoyances aside, Arusha is not an especially threatening city, though it is certainly not unheard of for tourists to be mugged after dark. The usual commonsense rules apply: avoid walking around solo or in pairs at night, especially on unlit roads and parks, and avoid carrying valuables on your person or taking out significantly more money than you need for the evening. After dark, the dodgiest part of town for muggings is probably the area east of the Themi River, in particular the quiet, unlit roads between the Arusha Hotel, and Impala Hotel, and Arusha Holiday Inn. On the whole, Arusha is very safe by day, but do be wary of bag-snatchers and pickpockets in and around the central market.

The head office of **Tanzania National Parks** (TANAPA; *PO Box 3134, Arusha;* ℡ *027 250 1930/4;* f *027 250 8216;* e *tanapa@habari.co.tz; www.tanzaniaparks.com*) recently moved to the new Mwalimu J K Nyerere Conservation Centre, about 3km out of town along the Serengeti road, roughly opposite the Cultural Heritage Centre.

The **Ngorongoro Conservation Authority** [106 C4] (NCA; ℡ *027 254 4625; www.ngorongorocrater.org*) has recently opened an information office on Boma Road close to the Tourist Board office. In addition to some worthwhile displays on the conservation area, it sells a good range of books and booklets about the northern circuit.

The **Immigration Office** [106 A2] (*Simeon Rd;* ℡ *027 250 6565*) will normally extend visas on the spot.

SAFARI OPERATORS

The list below is by no means definitive, but it provides a good cross-section of the sort of services that are on offer, and except where otherwise noted, it sticks to companies that have maintained high standards over several years. The listed companies generally specialise in northern circuit safaris, but most can also set up Kilimanjaro and Meru climbs, fly-in safaris on the southern safari circuit, and excursions to Zanzibar.

Africa Dream Safaris m 0752 225551/4 or US toll free ℡ 877 572 3274; e inquiries@ africadreamsafaris.com; www.africadreamsafaris.com. Emerging as one of the leading upmarket operators in Tanzania, this award-winning outfit specialises in customised safaris aimed at serious wildlife enthusiasts & photographers. The emphasis is on maximising wildlife encounters through early morning & full-day game drives with enthusiastic & knowledgeable driver-guides, avoiding circuits that tend to suffer from overcrowding, taking advantage of seasonal wildlife concentrations, & using intimate tented camps rather than large lodges. It won the 2008 Tanzania Tour Operator Conservation Award, presented by the Tanzania Tourist Board, for its work with the Serengeti Lion Project, & was selected Best Safari Outfitter by National Geographic Adventure in 2009. It also won the TTB's 2009 Humanitarian Award for its work with the Foundation for African Medicine & Education. The website is helpful for anyone planning a safari in Tanzania.
Asilia ℡ 027 250 4118/9; e enquiries@ sokwe.com; www.sokwe.com. Founded in 1989 under the name Sokwe & affiliated to the eponymous chain of exclusive tented camps, Asilia specialises in top-end safaris in the traditional East African style using luxury mobile tented camps. The standard of driver-guides is among the very highest in Tanzania, vehicles are well outfitted, & itineraries place high emphasis on escaping standard tour circuits for more untrammelled areas.

Auram Safaris m 0732 972 459; e info@ auramsafaris.com; www.auramsafaris.com. Based in Arusha, this Tanzanian-run company offers safari, trekking and mountaineering holidays.
Bushbuck Safaris [101 G6] ℡ 027 250 7779, 254 4186 or 254 8924; f 027 254 8293/2954; e bushbuck@yako.habari.co.tz; www.bushbuckltd.com. This reliable company specialises in lodge safaris. It has a large fleet of new & competently maintained 4x4 vehicles, & employs articulate drivers & guides. Prices & service are relatively upmarket, but not extortionate.
Easy Travel & Tours ℡ 027 250 3929/7322; m 0754 400141/0784 400141; e gm@easytravel.co.tz; www.easytravel.co.tz
Great African Safaris ℡ 027 254 8163; m 0784 493606; f 027 254 4563; e info@ greatafricansafaris.com; www.greatafricansafaris.com. This new Tanzanian-run company offers the usual mid-range safari options as well as Kili climbs using all routes, & an exciting selection of cultural tourism itineraries to Maasailand, the Usambara Mountains & Marangu.
Green Footprint Adventures ℡ 027 254 4635; m 0784 203000; e info@greenfootprint.co.tz; www.greenfootprint.co.tz. This environmentally minded safari company specialises in top-end safaris that pass over more mainstream circuits in favour of wilderness areas & low impact tented camps. The owner runs a renowned guide training school outside Arusha & as such the standard of guiding is exceptional. It also runs canoeing trips in Arusha

National Park, Lake Duluti & Lake Manyara. Specialist excursions include 4–5 day walking safaris in southern Tarangire, 3 day visits to the Hadza & 2–5 day walking safaris in the Serengeti. **Hoopoe Safaris** [106 B4] ✆ 027 250 7011; f 027 254 8226; e information@hoopoe.com; www.hoopoe.com. One of the most highly regarded safari companies in Arusha, Hoopoe specialises in personalised luxury camping & lodge safaris. It owns tented camps outside of Lake Manyara & Tarangire national parks, as well as a superb private camp in West Kilimanjaro. It is also one of the best companies to contact with regard to trekking & walking safaris in Natron, the Ngorongoro Highlands, & the game-rich Maasai Plains to the east of the Serengeti. It was voted the Best Ecotourism Operator in the World by *Condé Nast Traveller* for 2004.

Kamakura Safaris & Tours ✆ 0732 978956; m 0773 616671; f 0732 978901; e info@kamakurasafaris.co.tz ; www.kamakurasafaris.co.tz

Leopard Tours ✆ 027 250 3603/8441/3; f 027 250 8219; e leopard@yako.habari.co.tz; www.leopard-tours.com. One of the largest operators out of Arusha, Leopard Tours specialises in mid-range safaris concentrating on the larger lodges & more established game-viewing areas, & offers a highly reliable service to those who want to stick firmly to the beaten track.

Nature Discovery m 0732 971 859; e info@naturediscovery.com; www.naturediscovery.com. This eco-friendly operator is widely praised for its high-quality, top-end Kilimanjaro climbs, & it also arranges standard northern circuit safaris as well as trekking expeditions in the Ngorongoro Highlands & elsewhere.

Oreteti Cultural Discovery ✆ 027 250 4961; m 0755 744 992; f 027 250 4962; e info@oreteti.com; www.oreteti.com. This small, Arusha-based, family company is run by an English woman & her Maasai husband. They offer personalised cultural & educational programmes, combining academic lectures & seminars in anthropology with a range of walking tours, safaris or volunteer work camps. Other activities on offer include visits to Maasai & Chagga villages, short courses in Maasai beadwork, drumming, dance, cookery & Swahili hip-hop. They also visit the Kondoa Rock Paintings, the Hadza near Lake Eyasi, & Rangi agro-pastoralist communities in Dodoma Region. 10% of profits are donated to community-based organisations.

Roy Safaris [101 F6] ✆ 027 250 7940/2115; f 027 254 8092; e roysafaris@intafrica.com; www.roysafaris.com. Founded in the late 1980s, this dynamic & efficient company has established itself as a leading operator when it comes to high quality but reasonably priced budget & mid-range camping safaris. Vehicles are always in excellent condition & the drivers are usually competent & knowledgeable. It also offers reasonably priced semi-luxury camping safaris & lodge safaris.

Safari Makers ✆ 027 254 4446; m 0744 300817/318520; e safarimakers@habari.co.tz; www.safarimakers.com. Owned & managed by a dynamic hands-on American–Tanzanian couple, Safari Makers runs competitively priced camping & lodge safaris, & is one of the few companies in Arusha committed to promoting the cultural programmes in communities outside Arusha – a recommended first contact at the budget to mid-range level, & notable for its flexible & responsive management.

Sunny Safaris [105 F2] ✆ 027 250 7145/8184/8037; e info@sunnysafaris.com; www.sunnysafaris.com. This established company has long offered the cheapest reliable camping safaris in Arusha, though rates vary depending on season & group size. Their cheapest safaris won't involve camping in national parks, & you might find your driver inflexible about doing any excursion that puts extra kilometres on the clock, but otherwise you will get a thoroughly reliable service, with good vehicles & drivers. They also organise more upmarket camping safaris & lodge-based safaris at reasonable rates. The office is opposite the Golden Rose Hotel.

Tanzania Adventure m 0732 975210; e info@tanzania-adventure.com; www.tanzania-adventure.com. Dynamic new joint German–Tanzanian company offering a wide selection of safaris, including an extensive walking programme in the Ngorongoro Highlands & Serengeti border areas. Especially recommended for German-speakers.

Tropical Trails ✆ 027 250 0358; f 027 250 5578; e info@tropicaltrails.com; www.tropicaltrails.com Based at Maasai Camp, this is a genuinely eco-friendly company which arranges standard lodge-based & camping safaris for all budgets, as well as walking excursions on the fringes of the main national parks, & Kili climbs along the Machame & Shira routes. Tropical Trails is especially worth contacting if you have unusual requirements, or you want to get really off the beaten track. They also have some experience in arranging special one-off charity or group events.

TrueAfrica m 0784 999 738; e info@trueafrica.com; www.trueafrica.com. This is a new Dutch–Tanzanian run company that specialises in exclusive upmarket safaris using small tented camps & lodges. Personalised tailor-made itineraries include interaction with Maasai communities that are only visited a couple of times per month, & game drives in relatively off-the-beaten-track areas. It can also arrange mountain climbs, beach extensions, & gorilla & chimpanzee treks.

Wild Frontiers ☎ 027 250 2668; e bookings.wildfrontiers@habari.co.tz; www.wildfrontiers.com. Founded in South Africa but now with its own ground operation in Arusha, this well-established & flexible company offers a varied range of motorised, walking & combination safaris using standard lodges or its own excellent tented camps in the Serengeti & NCA, depending on taste & budget. Recommended to those seeking a relatively unpackaged safari at a reasonable price. It's good for Kili climbs too.

&Beyond [101 F6] ☎ 027 254 8549/8038 or South Africa +27 11 809 4447; e inboundsales@andbeyond.com; www.andbeyond.com. Formerly known as CCAfrica, this organisation is lauded throughout Africa for its commitment to genuine ecotourism & superlative lodges, which include top-end units in Serengeti, NCA & Lake Manyara. It arranges fly-in, drive-in & mixed safaris throughout northern Tanzania, as well as mobile safaris using seasonal camps in the 'Under Canvas' brand. &Beyond makes no bones about its commitment to high-cost, low-impact tourism, & its Tanzanian properties are notable for their fine attention to detail, informal & personalised service, well-trained guides & rangers, & general air of exclusivity.

WHERE TO STAY

This section concentrates on accommodation located within the city limits. It also includes a handful of individual hotels situated along the Old Moshi and Serengeti roads within 5km of the town centre, but excludes the ever-growing assortment of lodges that flank the Moshi road east of the Arusha Holiday Inn. Hotels in the latter category are covered in the *Cultural tours around Arusha* section, but it is worth noting that most of these would make a perfectly viable – and, on the whole, more aesthetically pleasing – alternative to staying in the town itself.

EXCLUSIVE (ABOVE US$200)

The Arusha Hotel [100 D5 & 106 C5] (65 rooms) ☎ 027 250 7777/8870; f 027 250 8889; e marketing@thearushahotel.com; www.thearushahotel.com. Giving Arusha Coffee Lodge a close run for its money is the newly renovated & reopened Arusha Hotel (formerly the New Arusha), which – situated right opposite the Clocktower – now offers the only 5-star accommodation in central Arusha. Situated in large wooded grounds running down towards the Themi River, this stately hotel has an Edwardian feel about the décor, befitting its status as the oldest hostelry in Arusha, & the spacious rooms all come with satellite TV, netting, in-room internet access, smoke detector, electronic safes & tea- & coffee-making facilities. AC & non-smoking rooms available. Facilities include 24hr room service, business centre, several curio shops, 24hr satellite internet access, a heated swimming pool, 3 bars, 2 restaurants & airport shuttle service. *Executive rooms US$200/240 sgl/dbl B&B; suites US$400/440.*

Arusha Coffee Lodge (18 rooms) ☎ 027 254 0630/9; f 027 254 8245; e info@elewana.com; www.elewana.com. Justifiably billed as 'the first truly 5-star hotel in Arusha' when it opened in 2002, the immaculate Arusha Coffee Lodge lays even stronger claims to that accolade following its acquisition by Elewana Lodges, & subsequent renovations. It is situated about 5km out of town along the Serengeti road, close to Arusha Airport, on what is reputedly the largest coffee estate in Tanzania, with a good view of Mount Meru. Accommodation is in stand-alone split-level chalets distinguished by their elegant Victorian décor, hardwood floors, huge balconies & stunning fireplaces, & in-room percolators to provide the true aroma of the coffee estate. Designed around the original plantation houses, the excellent restaurant serves a spit-roasted lunchtime grill & a sumptuous à la carte dinner. Facilities include a swimming pool. *US$190/370 sgl/dbl B&B, US$260/450 Jan–Feb & Jun–Oct, US$150/300 Apr & May.*

Arusha Holiday Inn [101 G3] (168 rooms) ☎ South Africa +27 11 442 0488; e pacro@africansunhotels.com; www.africansunhotels.com. Formerly the government owned & French-managed Mount Meru Novotel, this high-rise hotel set in large landscaped gardens overlooking the golf course was closed for renovations at the time of writing, but was set to reopen in late 2009.

Onsea House (4 rooms) m 0784 833207; e info@onseahouse.com; www.onseahouse.com. Situated on the slopes of Namasi Hill less than 10

THE ARUSHA HOTEL

Symbolic of Arusha's growing significance in the 1920s was the opening of the New Arusha Hotel in lushly wooded grounds formerly occupied by the small town's only hostelry, the small boarding house operated by the Bloom family since the late 1890s. A 1929 government brochure eulogised the newly opened establishment as having 'hot and cold water in all bedrooms, modern sanitation, teak dancing floor, electric light and really excellent food, as well as golf, tennis, big game and bird shooting' Less complimentary was the description included in Evelyn Waugh's amusingly acerbic travelogue A Tourist in Africa in 1960: it 'seeks to attract by the claim to be exactly midway between Cape Town and Cairo... I did not see any African or Indian customers. Dogs howled and scuffled under the window at night. Can I say anything pleasant about this hotel? Yes, it stands in a cool place in a well-kept garden and it stocks some potable South African wines in good conditions.' The New Arusha continued its slide, hosting the likes of John Wayne along the way, until finally it closed for overdue renovations a few years back, to reopen in 2004 as the Arusha Hotel, the only five-star establishment in the city centre.

mins' drive from central Arusha (along the Moshi Rd), this attractive & intimate boutique hotel has drawn praise from all quarters since it opened in Jul 2006. The large green gardens contain a swimming pool & the restaurant, managed by a Michelin trained Belgian chef, serves superb Afro-European fusion cuisine. Low season rates are US$145/170 sgl/dbl B&B or US$220/320 FB; whole high season rates are US$175/210 B&B & US$250/360 FB.

UPMARKET (US$90–200)

⌂ **Moivaro Coffee Plantation Lodge** (20 units) ☎ 027 255 3243; e reservations@moivaro.com; www.moivaro.com. This elegantly rustic lodge, set on a 40-acre coffee estate 7km from central Arusha & 1.5km from the Moshi Rd, has received consistently good reports from travellers & tour operators since it opened in the late 1990s. The self-contained bungalows are set in a circular arrangement around a clean swimming pool & flowering lawns. The main dining & reception building has a large patio facing Mount Meru. Facilities include walking & jogging paths, internet & a massage room. US$185/250 sgl/dbl B&B or US$230/340 FB, discounted Mar–Jun & Sep–21 Dec.

⌂ **KIA Lodge** (20 units) ☎ 027 255 3243; e reservations@kialodge.com; www.kialodge.com. Under the same management as Moivaro Lodge, & similar in feel & quality, the recently opened KIA Lodge is recommended to visitors with unusual or inconvenient flight times, as it lies just 1km from Kilimanjaro International Airport, & the staff are used to monitoring flight arrivals & departures for guests. It's an attractive set-up, with a good makuti restaurant & hilltop swimming pool, plenty of birdlife in the surrounding acacia scrub, & great views towards Kilimanjaro (the mountain, that is), but the noise from overhead flights makes it less than ideal

for an extended stay. Self-contained bungalows US$168/264 sgl/dbl B&B or US$213/489 FB, US$143/214 or US$188/414 Mar, Jun, Sept–Dec & US$114/171 or US$159/358 Apr & May.

⌂ **Kigongoni Lodge** (20 units) ☎ 027 255 3087; e assistant.managers@kigongoni.net; www.kigongoni.net. Set on a forested hilltop in a 70ha coffee plantation about 10km from Arusha along the Moshi Rd, this superb new lodge consists of 20 large, airy & organic en-suite chalets, all with private balcony, 2 dbl beds with netting, hot shower & bath, & log fire. The countrified atmosphere of the accommodation is complemented by superb food & a good wine list, while other attractions include a swimming pool & plenty of monkeys & birds in the grounds. A significant portion of the profits is used to support Sibusiso, a home for disabled Tanzanian children situated on the same coffee estate. US$165/230 sgl/dbl B&B or US$195/330 FB; discounted Mar–Jun & Sep.

⌂ **Kibo Palace Hotel** [101 E6] (65 rooms) ☎ 027 254 4472; e info@kibopalacehotel.com; www.kibopalacehotel.com. Also situated on the Old Moshi Rd, this smart new 5-storey hotel has an unusual design, centred on a circular lobby with a tall sky roof above the 5th floor. Comfortable but undistinguished, the rooms have a linoleum faux-wood floor, AC, satellite TV, safe, coffee/tea-making facilities & en-suite combination tub/shower. Facilities include a restaurant, & swimming pool surrounded by wrought iron outdoor furniture. Pleasant enough in its rather sterile manner, it seems a touch overpriced. *US$150/170/180 sgl/dbl/suite.*

⌂ **East African All-Suite Hotel** [101 F6] (40 rooms) ℡ 027 205 0075; m 0757 600110; reservations@eastafricanhotel.com; www.eastafricanhotel.com. This slick new hotel on the Old Moshi Rd doesn't exactly evoke a safari atmosphere, but the accommodation is to a very high standard, consisting of large suites with varied facilities, including flat screen satellite TV, king-size bed, safe, kitchen with stove & fridge, large bathroom with combination tub/shower, AC, & rather bombastic leather furnishing that creates a slightly cluttered effect. The restaurant serves an imaginative selection of contemporary dishes in the Tsh6,000–12,000 range & there's a swimming pool & cigar bar. Good value. *US$145 dbl suite or US$180 presidential suite with 2 bedrooms.*

⌂ **The African Tulip** [101 F7] (29 rooms) ℡ 027 254 3004/5; e info@theafricantulip.com; www.theafricantulip.com. This chic new boutique hotel is set in an attractive suburban garden with a swimming pool, along the same road as The Outpost. The rooms are large & attractively decorated with Zanzibar-style wooden furnishing, & good facilities including a safe, minibar, WiFi, satellite TV & large en-suite bathroom with a choice of tub or shower. There's a well-stocked gift shop on the ground floor, along with the aptly named Zanzibar Bar & promising Baobab Restaurant. *US$135/170 sgl/dbl B&B, US$290 suite.*

⌂ **Naura Springs Hotel** [101 E2] (124 rooms) ℡ 027 205 0001/8; e naura@ nauraspringshotel.com; www.nauraspringshotel.com. Spanning 12 storeys & sporting a scary reflective blue exterior, this extrovertly modernistic hotel to the north of the AICC might politely be described as a prominent landmark. The large rooms are more attractive, with wooden floors & décor, 2 double beds, flat screen satellite TV, & en-suite shower & jacuzzi, & there's a pleasant swimming pool area, but other public areas are lacking in charm or character. One to avoid. *US$120 dbl.*

⌂ **Ilboru Safari Lodge** (30 rooms) m 0754 270357 or 0784 270357; e reservations@ ilborusafarilodge.com; www.ilborusafarilodge.com. Situated in large, leafy grounds among the banana plantations that swathe the Mount Meru foothills some 2.5km north of the town centre, this highly

regarded lodge has been offering good-value accommodation for some years, & despite a recent change of ownership, it remains a very pleasant & peaceful retreat, centred on a large swimming pool. Accommodation in comfortable thatched bungalows is very reasonably priced. *US$83/99 sgl/dbl B&B or US$109/151 FB.*

⌂ **Impala Hotel** [101 G7] (150 rooms) ℡ 027 254 3082/7; m 0754 678678/008448; f 027 254 3088/9; e impala@impalahotel.com; www.impalahotel.com. The recently expanded & renovated Impala Hotel, situated in Kijenge about a 10min walk from the town centre, is justifiably rated by many tour operators as the best-value hotel in its range in the immediate vicinity of Arusha, & it's certainly one of the largest, busiest, smoothest running & most reasonably priced, though somewhat deficient in character. Facilities include 4 restaurants variously specialising in Indian, Italian, Chinese & continental cuisine (the Indian is among the best in town), an internet café, a forex bureau offering good rates, a swimming pool, a gift shop, an inexpensive shuttle service to Nairobi as well as to KIA, & an in-house safari operator. The rooms are comfortable & attractively decorated, & have satellite TV, hot showers & fridge. *US$90/110/155 sgl/dbl/trpl B&B; HB & FB rates additional US$12 pp per meal. Executive rooms/suites US$150/230.*

⌂ **Karama Lodge & Spa** (23 rooms) m 0754 475188; e info@karama-lodge.com; www.karama-lodge.com. Aptly named after the Swahili word for 'blessing', this fabulous eco-lodge, constructed by Tropical Trails, is remarkable for possessing a genuine bush atmosphere, despite being situated only 3km from central Arusha along the Old Moshi Rd. Perched on the small but densely wooded Suye Hill, the lodge consists of 22 stilted wood-&-*makuti* units with Zanzibar-style beds draped in netting, en-suite shower & toilet, & private balcony facing Kilimanjaro. The *brachystegia* woodland in the lodge grounds & adjacent forest reserve harbours a wide range of birds (the localised brown-throated barbet prominent among them) as well as small nocturnal mammals such as bushbaby, genet & civet. The restaurant serves tasty snacks & meals, & offers views to Kilimanjaro & Meru on a clear day. A recently opened spa currently offers massage only, but sauna, yoga & other treatments will soon be available. Overall, it's highly recommended as an antidote to the bland city hotels that otherwise characterise Arusha in this price range, though the sloping grounds would make it a particularly poor choice for disabled & elderly travellers. *US$87/118 sgl/dbl B&B.*

⌂ **New Safari Hotel** [100 D4 & 106 C4] (48 rooms)
☎ 027 250 3261/2; e newsafarihotel@habari.co.tz;
www.thenewsafarihotel.com. Recently reopened after
protracted renovations, this long-serving hotel, once
popular with the hunting fraternity, now seems more
geared towards business travellers, with its convenient
– though potentially noisy – central location a few
minutes from the AICC & a number of government
offices & restaurants. Facilities include a ground-floor
internet café & a good restaurant. The large tiled en-
suite rooms with digital satellite TV have a modern
feel, & seem fair value. *US$85/105 sgl/dbl.*

⌂ **Hotel Equator** [100 D4 & 106 C3] (40 rooms)
☎ 027 250 8409/3727/3127; e Equator@ars.bol.tz.
This recently refurbished old hotel on Boma Rd has
spacious & well kept rooms with fridge & TV, but – as
with so many former government hotels – the fixtures
are as outmoded as the atmosphere is bland &
institutional. Still, it's not bad value, especially if you are
looking for a central location. *US$80/100 sgl/dbl B&B.*

MODERATE (US$50–90)

⌂ **Arusha Crown Hotel** [105 G4] (38 rooms)
☎ 027 254 4161; e info@arushacrownhotel.com;
www.arushacrownhotel.com. This gleaming new multi-
storey hotel looks decidedly misplaced in the seedy
backroads between the bus station & football stadium,
a location that might well feel mildly intimidating to
the more timid traveller. If you can get past that, it's
not a bad option, albeit with zero ambience, & the
functional & airy en-suite rooms with tiled floor,
digital satellite TV & modern décor seem fair value.
The cafeteria-style restaurant on the ground floor has
meals for around Tsh6,000. *US$65/75 sgl/dbl.*

⌂ **Golden Rose Hotel** [100 A2 & 105 F2] (40 rooms)
☎ 027 250 7959/8862; m 0713 510696;
e goldenrose@habari.co.tz;
www.goldenrosehoteltz.com. This well-known landmark
on the western side of town, the most central
departure point for the Riverside Shuttle to Nairobi,
used to be regarded as one of the top hotels in
Arusha. Today, however, the small en-suite rooms with
TV, fan, net & balcony feel rather timeworn & gloomy,
& are indifferent value. *US$40/60 sgl/dbl B&B/HB old
wing; US$50/70 new wing.*

⌂ **The Outpost** [101 E7] (23 rooms) ☎ 027 250
8405; e outpost@bol.co.tz;
www.outposttanzania.com. Probably the pick in this
range, the welcoming & homely Outpost, set in a
suburban garden at 37A Serengeti St, has proved to
be consistently popular with travellers seeking the
combination of affordability & comfort. Cheap & tasty
lunches & dinners are available. To get here from the

⌂ **L'Oasis Lodge** [101 H2] (22 rooms) ☎ 027 250
7089; m 0755 749945; f 027 250 7089;
e s.broadbent@edi-africa.com; www.loasislodge.com.
Set in large green grounds about 500m north of the
Moshi Rd, along a side road signposted opposite the
soon-to-reopen Arusha Holiday Inn, this pleasant
lodge has recently undergone some major
renovations & expansions but it retains the rustic
feel that made it popular in the first place & is
easily one of the best value options in its range in
the Arusha area. A variety of comfortable en-suite
rooms is available, including some attractive stilted
bungalows, while other facilities include a restaurant,
a large bar alongside the swimming pool, & the
wonderful Lounge at Oasis, whose funky but earthy
décor is complemented by a cosmopolitan menu of
light snacks, salads, wraps & full meals.
*US$79/97/127 sgl/dbl/trpl B&B or
US$115/189/235 FB.*

Clocktower, head out in the direction of the Impala
Hotel for about 1km, then follow a signposted right
turn into Serengeti Rd, passing the Roy Safaris office,
& you'll reach it after another 300m or so. *En-suite
rooms with TV US$48/66 sgl/dbl.*

⌂ **Hotel Le Jacaranda** [101 G6] (9 rooms) ☎ 027
254 4624; e jacaranda@tz2000.com;
www.chez.com/jacaranda. Situated in the garden
suburbs immediately east of the town centre, not far
from the Outpost, this converted colonial-era
homestead ranks among the most characterful hotels
in Arusha, & it's also exceptionally good value. It lies
in prettily overgrown grounds with a mini-golf
course & shady, highly rated restaurant/bar area. The
large en-suite rooms all have 4-poster beds with
netting & hot water. *US$45/50 sgl/dbl.*

⌂ **Klub Afriko Hotel** (7 rooms) ☎ 027 250 9205;
m 0744 369475; e info@klubafriko.com;
www.klubafriko.com. The intimate & stylish Klub
Afriko is a newly opened lodge set in compact, neat
grounds on the Moshi Rd about 3km out of Arusha.
The 6 self-contained chalets have a traditional
African appearance with a bright & airy interior,
while the spacious dining area is decorated in a
more classical style. The accommodation is excellent
value, while 3-course set lunches & dinners cost
Tsh8,000 & Tsh9,000 respectively. *US$40/60 sgl/dbl
B&B; suites sleeping up to 4 people US$80.*

⌂ **La Bella Inn** [101 G6] (12 rooms) m 0732
978013l; e mbegatouristcamp@yahoo.com. Recently
acquired by the Mbega lodge group, this homely

hotel lies in large gardens close to the Impala Hotel, & is very convenient for early departures & late arrivals with the Riverside, Bobby & Osa Shuttles from Nairobi, all of which depart from the parking lot. There's a good Italian garden restaurant, & live African music 19.00–20.00 Fri–Sun. The neat tiled rooms with net, TV, fan & en-suite hot shower seem good value too. *US$40/50 sgl/dbl.*

⌂ **Everest Inn** [101 F6] (7 rooms) ✆ 027 250 8419; m 0784 255277; e everesttzus@ yahoo.com; www.everest-inn.com. This homely guesthouse is attached to an excellent Chinese restaurant set in an old colonial house in a lush garden on the Old Moshi Rd. The small but clean & comfortable en-suite rooms come with TV, hot water & nets, & there's 24hr free internet & Skype. Rooms in the main house are nicer than those out the back. The restaurant serves authentic Chinese food in the Tsh7,000–10,000 range. *US$40/50 sgl/dbl.*

⌂ **Sinka Court Hotel** [105 H5] (29 rooms) ✆ 027 250 4961; e sinkacourthotel@hotmail.com. The new multi-storey hotel in the backroads between the market & the Naura River has cramped but clean en-suite rooms with satellite TV. *US$40/50 sgl/dbl; more spacious executive rooms US$60 dbl.*

⌂ **Hotel Seventy Seven** [101 H4] (120 rooms) ✆ 027 254 3800; m 0744 381047; e hotel77@ tz2000.com; www.seventysevenhotel.netfirms.com. It once billed itself as 'the largest tourist village in East Africa', more recently as the 'Geneva of Africa', yet one could be forgiven for thinking the true architectural inspiration of this hotel lay somewhere in Soviet-era Siberia. The 'Saba Saba' was closed for renovations in early 2009, but unless these are truly radical, it is likely to remain an aesthetically confrontational introduction to a Tanzanian safari.

⌂ **Songota Falls Lodge** (5 rooms) m 0744 095576/688806; e joice_kimaro@yahoo.com; www.songotafallslodge.com. Situated along a monumentally bad 1.5km dirt road that runs northward from the Moshi Rd 2km east of Club Afriko, Songota Lodge currently consists of a few unfussy but clean en-suite bungalows overlooking the large green valley below the Songota Waterfall – to which guided walks are offered when underfoot conditions are reasonably dry. It's a refreshingly unpretentious set-up, owned & managed by a friendly Tanzanian woman with years of experience in the hotel trade, & likely to expand its facilities in due course, but as things stand it feels slightly overpriced for what you get. *US$38/45/68 sgl/dbl/trpl B&B or US$60/89/134 FB.*

⌂ **Arusha Naaz Hotel** [106 B6] (21 rooms) ✆ 027 250 2087; m 0754 282799; e arushanaaz@ yahoo.com; www.arushaneez.net. Situated on Sokoine Rd close to the Clocktower, this clean, convenient & secure hotel, once a favourite with budget travellers, now slots more into the moderate category following extensive renovations. The en-suite rooms with net, fan, hot water & satellite TV are on the cramped side, & can't exactly be described as a bargain, though the hotel remains a good compromise between price & comfort in the town centre. There is a good, inexpensive Indian restaurant on the ground floor & an internet café & car hire firm on the premises. *US$30/45 sgl/dbl occupancy.*

BUDGET (US$25–45)

⌂ **City Link Pentagon Hotel** (53 rooms) ✆ 027 254 4444; e reservations@hotelcitylink.com; www.hotelcitylink.com. This eccentrically shaped high-rise hotel is rather characterless & has an indifferent location on the Moshi Rd about 2km past the Arusha Holiday Inn, but otherwise it seems like very good value. The large tiled rooms come with satellite TV, writing desk & en-suite hot shower, & there's a pleasant beer garden serving *nyama choma* & other food. *US$45 twin or dbl.*

⌂ **Arusha Resort Centre** [106 C7] (30 rooms) ✆ 027 250 8333; m 0787 830495; e aruahsresort@habari.co.tz. Situated on a quiet back road only 2min walk from the central Clocktower, this is a comfortable & safe, albeit rather institutional, double-storey hotel offering clean & good value accommodation with discounts for long-stay visitors. *US$35/45 en-suite sgl/dbl or US$50 self-catering apt.*

⌂ **Hotel Pallson's** [105 F6] (28 rooms) ✆ 027 254 8483; m 0754 400747; e hotel_pallsons@ yahoo.com. This long-serving multi-storey hotel is centrally located on Sokoine Rd a short walk south of the bus station. The rather timeworn en-suite rooms, with satellite TV, fan & hot shower, are adequate value. *US$33/43 sgl/dbl B&B.*

⌂ **Stereo Hotel** [105 G6] (33 rooms) ✆ 027 250 3995; e aaronm@hotmail.com; www.stereohotel.com. The smart new 4-storey hotel near the central market has spotless spacious tiled rooms with queen or twin beds, phone, satellite TV & nets, & seems excellent value compared with most other places in this range. *Tsh35,000/40,000 sgl/dbl.*

⌂ **Olduvai Inn** [101 F6] (15 rooms) ✆ 027 254 3044; m 0732 975362; e magiesaria@yahoo.com. Set in a large garden on the junction of Serengeti & Old

Moshi roads, this is a great little guesthouse offering clean & very reasonably priced en-suite accommodation with nets, TV & hot shower. There's internet access on site & plenty of choice of restaurants within a few hundred metres. *US$25/30 sgl/dbl B&B.*

⌂ **Williams Inn** [105 E2] (30 rooms) ☎ 027 250 3578. Part of a cluster of hotels situated along Corner Rd northwest of the stadium, this charges for a clean but spartan dbl with en-suite hot shower & TV, in which 'women of immoral turpitude are strictly not allowed'. *US$25 dbl.*

⌂ **Hotel Fort Des Moines** [105 H5] (20 rooms) ☎ 027 250 0277; e bimel@cybernet.co.tz; www.bimel.co.tz. Pretentious name aside, this clean &

reasonably smart new hotel near the market & bus station seems decent enough value. *US$20/25 sgl/dbl.*

⌂ **L'Oasis Backpackers Lodge** [101 H2] (12 rooms) contact details as for L'Oasis, page 113. Situated opposite L'Oasis Lodge & under the same management, this offers newcomers to East Africa a comfortable & reasonably affordable suburban retreat. The small tree house-like rooms with wooden floors & screened windows aren't cheap, & the hot showers & toilets are shared, but this is a good, safe choice, & the price includes access to all hotel facilities & restaurant at the main lodge. *US$20 pp inc a full b/fast.*

SHOESTRING AND CAMPING (UNDER US$25)

⌂ **Bakara Inn** [104 B1] m 0732 978274; e bakarainn@gmail.com. Remote from the main cluster of budget accommodation, this new guesthouse is conveniently located for early departures on the Mtei & Scandinavia buses. The tiled en-suite rooms with fan, TV, hot shower & tea/coffee-making facilities are good value too. *Tsh25,000 dbl.*

⌂ **Hotel Flamingo** [105 F4] (9 rooms) ☎ 027 254 8812; m 0744 260309; e flamingoarusha@yahoo.com. Sensibly priced & conveniently close to the central bus station, this small guesthouse has clean twin rooms with netting, en-suite hot shower & toilet. *Tsh20,000/25,000 sgl/dbl.*

⌂ **Arusha By Night Annex** [105 F3] m 0713 485237. For a long time dauntingly overpriced thanks to its inflated non-resident rates, this stalwart of the Arusha accommodation scene now evidently operates on a one-price-for-all-comers policy. As a result, the slightly faded but spacious rooms with twin or dbl bed, TV, fan, writing desk & en-suite hot shower actually feel like one of the best deals in this range. *Tsh16,000 dbl or twin.*

⌂ **Casablanca Mini-lodge** [105 F1] ☎ 027 250 3419. Also one of the better lodges in the area north of the stadium, this has 12 small but clean rooms with en-suite hot shower. *Tsh15,000.*

⌂ **Monje's Guesthouse** [105 G1, 105 G2 & 105 H1] ☎ 027 250 3060. Narrowly the pick of a cluster of bottom-of-the-range guesthouses in the backroads north of the stadium, this quiet, family-run affair actually consists of 4 guesthouses running along the same road. All 4 places have clean rooms, friendly staff, hot showers & a vigorously enforced anti-flycatcher policy! *Tsh12,000–20,000.*

⌂ **YMCA** [106 B4] ☎ 027 272 2544. This Arusha institution is looking pretty run-down these days,

but it has a conveniently central location on India Rd, & room rates that haven't changed in years mean it is now relatively good value. *Tsh11,500/14,500 sgl/dbl.*

⌂ **Arusha Backpackers Hotel** [104 D7] (34 rooms) ☎ 027 2504474; m 0773 377795; e info@arushabackpackers.co.tz; www.arushabackpackers.co.tz. Affiliated to the long-serving Kindoroko hotel in Moshi, this new shoestring hotel lies on Sokoine Rd within easy walking distance of the central bus station. It's a safe & reliable set-up, & has quickly established itself as a favourite rendezvous for budget-conscious travellers. The small but clean rooms have desk & fan, & use common hot showers & toilets. Kindoroko Tours on the ground floor is a reliable bet for budget camping safaris & Kilimanjaro climbs. *US$10/16 sgl/dbl B&B or US$6 dorm bed; with lunch & dinner an additional US$7 pp.*

Å **Masai Camp** m 0744 507131/898800; e masaicamp@africamail.com; http://masaicamp.tripod.com. About 2km out of town along the Old Moshi Rd, Masai Camp is one of the best campsites in Tanzania, & it also offers simple accommodation in huts. Facilities include an ablution block with hot water, a pool table, volleyball & lively 24hr bar, & an excellent safari company called Tropical Trails is on site. The restaurant is well known for its pizzas, which cost around Tsh4,000. If you're without transport, you can get a taxi here for around Tsh2,000. *Camping US$5 pp, rooms US$10 pp.*

⌂ **Kilimanjaro Villa** [105 G4] ☎ 027 250 8109; m 0713 510696. A backpacker standby close to the market & bus station, the Kilimanjaro Villa is nothing special but it's friendly, clean & reasonably priced. *US$7/10 sgl/dbl, common showers.*

✕ WHERE TO EAT

Many good restaurants are dotted around Arusha, with a wide range of international cuisines represented and most budgets catered for by a number of places. The following is an alphabetical selection of some long-standing favourites and interesting recent additions, but new places open and close frequently, so don't be afraid to try restaurants that aren't listed.

✕ **Albero Restaurant** [101 F5] Haile Selassie Rd; ☎ 027 254 8987; ⊕ lunch & dinner daily. This new open-air Italian restaurant has a pleasant setting in leafy suburbia & serves a varied selection of pasta dishes & pizzas in the Tsh8,000–10,000 range, while seafood & grills cost Tsh12,000–16,000.

✕ **Arusha Naaz Hotel** [106 B6] Sokoine Rd; ☎ 027 250 2087; ⊕ lunch & dinner daily. The ground-floor restaurant at this popular central hotel offers a great all-you-can-eat Indian buffet lunch at US$7. No alcohol.

✕ **Big Bite** [105 H5] Cnr Swahili & Somali rds; ⊕ dinner only, daily except Tues. This misleadingly named & rather low-key eatery near the market isn't a fast food outlet but one of the oldest & best north Indian restaurants in Arusha. Mains in the Tsh8,000–12,000 range.

✕ **Blue Heron Coffee & Gift Shop** [101 F5] Haile Selassie Rd; ☎ 0784 505555; ⊕ 09.00–17.00. Combining classic colonial architecture with contemporary décor, this new coffee shop is a great spot for a relaxed open-air lunch, with seating on the veranda & in the green garden. Pasta dishes & salads cost around Tsh6,000 & it serves cheaper sandwiches, cakes & coffee.

✕ **Café Bamboo Restaurant** [106 C4] Boma Rd; ☎ 027 250 6451; ⊕ 07.00–21.00 Mon–Sat. This homely restaurant serves decent coffee, fruit juices, sandwiches, pancakes & snacks, & full meals for around Tsh4,000–6,000. The lunch of the day is usually a bargain. It's justifiably packed at lunchtime, but quiet later.

✕ **Chocolate Temptation** [104 A7] TFA Centre, Sokoine Rd; ☎ 0754 696993; ⊕ 09.30–18.00 Mon–Sat. An oasis for the sweet toothed, this has indoor & outdoor seating, a wide range of yummy cakes & ice creams, & strong filter coffee.

✕ **Dolly's Patisserie** [105 F6] Sokoine Rd; ☎ 027 254 4013; ⊕ 09.00–18.00 Mon–Sat. The highly rated bakery sells fresh bread & cakes, along with tasty pastries & sandwiches to take away.

✕ **Everest Inn Chinese Restaurant** [101 F6] Old Moshi Rd; ☎ 0744 377299; ⊕ lunch & dinner. The best Chinese food in Arusha is served at this suburban family-run restaurant, which also caters to

vegetarians & charges around Tsh7,000–10,000 for a main course.

✕ **Flame Tree** [101 F5] Haile Selassie Rd; ☎ 0744 377299; ⊕ 12.00–14.00 & 19.00–22.00 Mon–Sat. This is a popular upmarket eatery serving a varied selection of continental fare with Asian & African influences. Main dishes are in the Tsh7,000–12,000 range & a 4-course set menu costs Tsh20,000.

✕ **Greek Club** [101 F6] Old Moshi Rd; ☎ 0754 652747; ⊕ 12.00–14.00 & 17.30–late daily except Mon & Thu. Converted from a stately colonial homestead set in large green gardens, this popular expat hangout has live sports on TV, a busy bar, free WiFi, a wide veranda & a great children's playground. The tasty Greek cuisine is complemented by a selection of sandwiches, salads & baked potatoes, with most meals around Tsh8,000.

✕ **Green Hut House of Burgers** [105 H7] Sokoine Rd. Excellent & inexpensive burgers & other greasy fast food staples & light meals. No alcohol.

✕ **Impala Hotel** [101 G7] Old Moshi Rd; ☎ 027 254 3082/7; www.impalahotel.com. The Indian restaurant in this large hotel is justifiably rated as one of the best in Arusha – & there are 3 other specialist restaurants to choose from if Indian isn't your thing.

✕ **Jambo Coffee House & Makuti Garden** [106 C4] Boma Rd; ⊕ 08.00–22.00. The coffee house serves decent coffee, cooked b/fasts & light snacks. The adjacent Makuti Garden, set in a green courtyard, is one of the best places in the town centre for evening meals – curries & grills in Tsh7,000–10,000 range.

✕ **Khan's Barbecue** [105 G5] Mosque St; ☎ 0754 652747; ⊕ 18.00–21.00. This eatery near the market is a motor spares shop by day & street barbecue in the evening. A mixed grill including beef, chicken & mutton kebabs, with a huge selection of salads, naan bread & the like, costs Tsh7,000. No alcohol.

✕ **McMoody's** [105 C6] Sokoine Rd; ☎ 027 254 4013; ⊕ 10.00–22.00 Tue–Sun. This McDonald's clone serves burgers for around Tsh3,000–4,000 – the plastic décor, like the food, is designed to make fast-food junkies feel at home, & there's a fast internet café attached.

✕ **Milk & Honey Restaurant** [106 B3] Sokoine Rd; ☎ 027 250 2087; ⊕ lunch Mon–Sat. This popular local lunch venue serves a variety of Tanzanian, Indian & Western dishes from Tsh2,500 to Tsh4,000.

✗ **Patisserie** [106 B6] Sokoine Rd; m 0754 302174; ⏰ 08.30–18.00 Mon–Sat, closes 14.00 Sun. This popular backpacker & volunteer hangout near the Clocktower serves freshly baked loaves, rolls & pastries, adequate light meals & fruit juice, & dismal coffee. Fast internet café attached.

✗ **Pizzarusha Restaurant** [105 H2] Off Mashele Rd; m 0754 366292. Recently relocated to Monje's 'C' Guesthouse, this backpacker stalwart serves a range of pizzas, curries & grills in the Tsh4,000–5,000 range & sandwiches for around Tsh2,000. Lacks the atmosphere of the old venue, but still one of the best-value eateries in town!

✗ **Sapporo Restaurant** [104 A7] TFA Centre, Sokoine Rd; m 0787 225224; ⏰ 12.00–14.30 & 19.00–22.00 daily. This superb upmarket restaurant serves sushi & other Japanese mains for around Tsh8,000–10,000, or lavish set menus for Tsh22,000–32,000 per person.

✗ **Sazan Japanese Restaurant** [101 E5] Old Moshi Rd; ⏰ lunch & dinner daily. This quirky eatery serves platters of sushi, cooked seafood & other rather greasy Japanese food for around Tsh5,000.

✗ **Sidewalk Bar** [106 B3] India Rd; ⏰ lunch only Mon–Fri. This cramped but clean eatery specialises in filled pita bread, sandwiches, burgers & fruit juices. For vegetarians, there's a lunchtime salad buffet Tue & Thu.

✗ **Spices & Herbs Restaurant** [101 G6] Simeon Rd; m 0754 313163; ⏰ lunch & dinner daily. The oldest & best Ethiopian restaurant in Arusha lies close to the Impala Hotel & serves the distinctive Ethiopian staples such as *kai wat* (a spicy meat or

vegetarian stew) served with *injera* (flat round sour bread). There's occasional live music, & an internet café on site. Most meals are around Tsh6,000–8,000.

✗ **Stiggy's Thai Restaurant** [101 H7] Old Moshi Rd; m 0754 375535; ⏰ 12.00–late daily except Mon. This has a relaxed informality matched by the Australian–Thai owner-manager's golden touch behind the stove. The Thai & continental cuisine isn't cheap (around Tsh16,000 or more for a main course), but quality & presentation are up to international standards. The bar has a pool table & is a pleasant place to hang out.

✗ **Stiggybucks** [104 A7] TFA Centre, Sokoine Rd; m 0754 375535; ⏰ 09.00–17.00 Mon–Sat. Under the same ownership as Stiggy's, this is an excellent coffee shop that also serves a tempting selection of cakes, bagels, salads, sandwiches & light meals in the Tsh4,000–7,000 range.

✗ **Vama Restaurant** [104 A7] TFA Centre, Sokoine Rd; m 0784 326325; ⏰ 12.00–14.30 & 19.00–22.00 daily. Arusha's top Indian restaurant has a varied selection of meat & vegetarian dishes in the Tsh8,000–10,000 range.

✗ **Via Via Restaurant** [106 C2] Boma Rd; m 0754 384922; http://users.telenet.be/tanzania/via_via_arusha.html; ⏰ 09.30–22.00 Mon–Thu, later Fri & Sat, closed Sun. This Belgian-owned garden restaurant-cum-bar tucked away behind the Old Boma has a relaxing suburban atmosphere, & the most eclectic selection of music in Arusha. It's a nice spot for a drink or sandwich, but cooked meals are unexceptional & portions seem mean for the asking price of around Tsh7,000–10,000. It hosts regular film evenings & cultural events involving artistes from all of Africa, & live music Thu night.

ENTERTAINMENT AND NIGHTLIFE

BARS AND NIGHTSPOTS There has been a notable increase in nightspots around Arusha in recent years. The liveliest at the time of writing is **Colobus Club** [101 H7], which reopened in revamped form in October 2008 after a period of closure. It lies on the Old Moshi Road about 500m past the Impala Hotel, and doubles as disco, snack bar, boozer and pool hall – it keeps going all night over weekends. Another popular venue is the **Boogaloo Nightclub** [101 F7] in the basement of Njiro Mall.

Opposite the Colobus Club, the more sedate **Stiggy's Thai Restaurant** [101 H7] is a popular drinking spot with expatriates. Popular sports bars, all with large screen TVs, well stocked bars and pub grub, are the **Greek Club** [101 F6] on Old Moshi Road, **Pirate's Cove** in the Njiro Mall [101 F7] and **Empire Sports Bar** in the TFA Centre [104 A7].

There are several decent bars in the same area as the cluster of guesthouses behind the Golden Rose Hotel. The best place to drink in this part of town is **Soweto Gardens** [100 B2], a relaxed but atmospheric garden bar that often hosts live bands over the weekends. Other good spots for live Tanzanian music include the outdoor restaurant of the **La Bella Hotel** [101 G6] (Friday–Sunday night), **Via Via** [106 C2] (Thursday night) and **Rick's Bar** [101 H3] on the Moshi Road.

CINEMA The best cinema is the Arusha Cinemax [101 F7] (**m** *0732 102221; www.pigadeal.com/cinemax/nowplaying.php*) in the out-of-town Njiro Mall, whose three screens show a varied selection of reasonably current Hollywood and Bollywood fare. Seats start at Tsh6,000.

SHOPPING

BOOKSHOPS Your best bet is one of two branches of Kase Book Shop, which lie on Boma Road next to Café Bamboo [106 C4] and on Jael Marda Road opposite the

---

ALL THAT GLISTERS...

In 1962, local legend goes, a Maasai cattle herder called Ali Juyawatu was walking through the Mererani Hills after a bush fire, and noticed some unusual blue crystals lying on the ground. Ali picked up the beautiful stones, and took them to the nearby town of Arusha, from where they somehow made their way to the New York gemstone dealer Tiffany & Co, which had never seen anything like them before. In 1967, Tiffany launched the newly discovered gem on the market, naming it tanzanite in honour of its country of origin.

Tanzanite is by any standards a remarkable stone. A copper brown variety of zoisite, it is rather dull in its natural condition, but responds to gentle heating, transforming into a richly saturated dark-blue gem, with purple and violet undertones that have been compared to, among other things, the, um, eyes of Elizabeth Taylor! The stone is known only from Tanzania's Mererani Hills – rumours of a second deposit in Usangi, 75km from Arusha, have yet to be confirmed – and it is on the order of a thousand times rarer than diamonds. Despite its upstart status in the jewellery world, tanzanite has rocketed in popularity since its discovery. By 1997, 30 years after its launch, it had become the second most popular gemstone in the North American market, second to sapphires and ahead of rubies and emeralds, generating an annual trade worth US$300 million in the USA alone.

Remarkable, too, is the degree of controversy that the tanzanite trade has attracted in recent years. In the late 1990s the Tanzanian government, comparing international tanzanite trade figures against their documented exports, realised that as much as 90% of the tanzanite sold in the USA was being smuggled out of Tanzania, resulting in a huge loss of potential government revenue in taxes and royalties. The ease with which the stones were being smuggled was clearly linked to the unregulated nature of the workings at Mererani, which consisted of more than 300 small claims operating in what has been described by more than one observer as a Wild West atmosphere. For the small-claim holders, rather than distributing the stones they collected through legitimate sources, it was more profitable – and considerably more straightforward – to sell them for cash to illicit cross-border traders.

The lack of regulations at Mererani, or at least the lack of a body to enforce what regulations do exist, is also largely to blame for a series of tragedies that has dogged the workings in recent years. The greatest single catastrophe occurred during the El Niño rains of 1998, when one of the shafts at Block D flooded and at least 100 miners drowned. But it has been estimated that a similar number of miners died underground subsequent to this mass tragedy, as a result of suffocation, inept dynamite blasting or periodic outbreaks of violent fighting over disputed claims. Aside from such accidents, it has long been rumoured that miners who are down on their luck will kidnap and sacrifice children from neighbouring villages, in the hope it will bring them good fortune and prosperity.

Kenya Commercial Bank [106 B5]. Both stock a good range of books about Tanzania and a more limited selection of contemporary bestsellers and novels.

A few vendors usually hang around the Clocktower selling the maps and national park booklets at highly inflated prices, and most of the upmarket hotels also sell a limited selection of reading matter in their curio shops.

To buy or exchange secondhand novels, there are a couple of stalls dotted around town, one in the alley connecting Boma and India roads and several along Sokoine Road west of the market.

CRAFT AND CURIO SHOPS Arusha is one of the best places in East Africa to buy Makonde carvings, Tingatinga paintings, batiks, Maasai jewellery and other souvenirs. The curio shops are far cheaper than those in Dar es Salaam and their quality and

In 1999, the Tanzanian government put out to tender a lease on Block C, the largest of the four mining blocks, accounting for about 75% of the known tanzanite deposit. The rights were acquired by a South African company – with a 25% Tanzanian stake – called African Gem Resources (AFGEM), which reputedly pumped US$20 million into establishing the mine with the intention of going online in early 2000. This goal proved to be highly optimistic, as local miners and stakeholders, understandably hostile to the corporate intrusion on their turf, not to mention the threat it posed to the illicit tanzanite trade, attempted to disrupt the new project and persuade AFGEM to withdraw.

The long-simmering tensions erupted in April 2001, when a bomb was set off in the new mining plant, killing nobody but causing large-scale material damage. Later in the same month, AFGEM security guards opened fire on a group of 300 irate miners who had invaded the plant, killing one trespasser and causing serious injury to nine. When the Minister for Energy and Minerals visited the scene a few days later, the trespassers claimed to have been protesting against AFGEM's alleged complicity in the alleged death of 20 miners who were buried alive. AFGEM refuted the claims as pure fabrication, part of a smear campaign designed to discredit them and protect the illicit tanzanite trade. The result of the official investigation into the incident has yet to be released.

The tanzanite plot took a new and wholly unexpected twist in late December 2001, when press reports linked four of the men convicted on charges relating to the 1998 US embassy bombings in Nairobi and Dar es Salaam with the illicit tanzanite trade. Amid wild speculation that the underground tanzanite trade was funding Osama bin Laden and his Al-Qaeda organisation, three major US jewellery dealers announced a total boycott on the purchase or sale of the gem. Among them, ironically, was the retailer that had first placed it in the spotlight back in 1967. Tiffany & Co publicly conceded a lack of hard evidence supporting the bin Laden link, but announced that it 'troubled' them regardless. By the end of January 2002, the price of tanzanite had fallen from around US$300 per gram to below US$100.

The Tanzanian government elected to suspend operations at Mererani until the claims were fully investigated. At a Tucson trade fair in February 2002, the American Gem Trade Association and the Tanzanian Minister of Energy and Minerals signed a protocol that placed several significant new controls on local access to the tanzanite mines. After the protocol was signed, the US State Department praised Tanzania for having 'done everything in its power to assist us in the war against terrorism' and declared it had 'seen no evidence that... any terrorist group is currently using tanzanite sales to finance its efforts or launder money.' Sales of the gem have since boomed, and many specialist stores line the streets of Arusha, while the recent opening of a museum called the Tanzanite Experience (see page 121) seems likely to raise the gems profile even higher.

variety are excellent. Most of the curio shops are clustered between the Clocktower and India Road, though be warned that the outdoor stalls can be full of hassle.

Two places stand out. The Cultural Heritage Centre [100 A5], about 3km out of town on the road towards the Serengeti, stocks the vastest collection of Tanzanian and other African crafts, ranging from towering carvings to colourful batiks and jewellery and a useful selection of books about Tanzania. It's where the likes of King Harald of Norway and former presidents Thabo Mbeki (South Africa) and Bill Clinton (USA) did their curio shopping in Arusha, and an on-site branch of DHL can arrange shipping to anywhere in the world. It can be visited on the way back from a safari, or as a short taxi trip from Arusha.

Altogether different in atmosphere is Mount Meru Craft & Curio Market [100 D5 & 106 C5] – more informally known as the Maasai Market – on Fire Road about 200m south of the Clocktower. Here, 50-plus stalls sell Maasai beadwork, Tingatinga and other local paintings, batiks, jewellery and pretty much any other ethno-artefact you might be interested in. Prices are lower than the Cultural Heritage Centre, and very negotiable, but the downside is that there is a bit more hassle, generally of a friendly rather than intimidating nature.

SHOPPING MALLS AND SUPERMARKETS The biggest and best shopping mall is TFA Centre on the west end of Sokoine Road. It is also often referred to as the **Shoprite Centre** [104 A7], after the eponymous supermarket, a warehouse-sized representative of a major South African chain that stocks a huge range of imported and local goods (including South African wines at a third the price the hotels charge) and is an excellent place to stock up with whatever goodies you need before you head out on safari. Also in the TFA Centre are half a dozen upmarket restaurants and coffee shops, several safari outfitters, and a good selection of other clothing and craft shops, hairdressers, banks with ATMs, internet cafés etc.

The more out-of-town **Njiro Mall** [101 F7], 4km south of the Impala Hotel, also boasts several eateries, and Arusha's best cinema, but the selection of shops is limited.

OTHER PRACTICALITIES

FOREIGN EXCHANGE Various private and bank-related bureaux de change are dotted all around Arusha, and it is worth shopping around to find the best rate for US dollar cash. Many bureaux de change won't accept less widely used international currencies or travellers' cheques, but the National Bank of Commerce on Sokoine Road [106 A7] will, as will the bureau de change at the Impala Hotel [101 G7]. Whatever else you do, don't change money on the streets of Arusha, as you are sure to be ripped off. If you are desperate for local currency outside banking hours, Foreigners Bureau de Change on Goliondoi Road [106 A4] is open seven days a week from 07.00 to 18.30; later than that you will probably have to ask a safari company or hotel to help you out with a small transaction.

There are now numerous ATMs where around US$200 in local currency can be drawn against selected credit cards. For Visa, Maestro and Cirrus card holders, the ATMs at the Standard Chartered Bank on Goliondoi Road [106 A6] and the Barclays Bank on Serengeti Road [101 F7] offer a 24-hour withdrawal service, and there are also ATMs offering similar facilities in the Njiro Mall and TFA Centre on Sokoine Road. By contrast, the ATMs at the two branches of the Exim Bank, one on the junction of Goliondoi and Sokoine roads [106 B6] and the other in the TFA Centre [104 A7], accept MasterCard only. American Express is represented by Rickshaw Travels on Sokoine Road near McMoody's. Travellers heading off on safari should be aware that Arusha will offer the first and last chance to reliably draw money against a credit card.

INTERNET AND EMAIL There are numerous internet cafés dotted all over Arusha, generally asking around Tsh500–1,500 per hour, depending largely on the speed of the server. One of the best – not least because so few people seem to know about it or use it, so access is generally very fast – is the Telecom-run internet café on the first floor of the Post Office building on Boma Road [106 C5]. Also good are the Cybernet Centre on India Road [106 B5], The Patisserie on the east end of Sokoine Road [106 B6], and McMoody's [105 F6] on the west end of the same road. Many hotels also offer internet access but at an inflated rate. The Greek Club on Old Moshi Road [101 F6] offers free WiFi to clients who eat or drink there.

MEDICAL The AICC Hospital [101 F6] (*Old Moshi Rd;* ⟍ *027 250 2329*) is generally regarded as the best in Arusha, while the nearby Trinity Clinic (*Engira Rd;* ⟍ *027 254 4392*) can be recommended for malaria and other tests. For further information, consult your hotel reception or safari company.

NEWSPAPERS A selection of local newspapers is available on the day of publication, as is the *Kenya Nation*, which is generally stronger on international news. You won't need to look for these newspapers, because the vendors who sell them will find you quickly enough. The excellent *East African*, a weekly newspaper, is available at several newspaper kiosks. The American weeklies *Time* and *Newsweek* are widely available in Arusha.

POST AND TELEPHONE The main post office is on Boma Road facing the Clocktower [106 C5]. The telecommunications centre further along Boma Road [106 C3] is a good place to make international phone calls and faxes. If you want to buy a local SIM card for your mobile phone, the best place to do so is the Vodacom Shop at the junction of Sokoine and Goliondoi roads [106 A6] – it should cost around Tsh300, though you'll need to buy some pay-as-you-go airtime (Tsh1,000–5,000) to activate it.

SWIMMING The swimming pools at the Ilboru Lodge [100 D1] and Impala Hotel [101 G7] are open to non-residents for a small daily fee.

WHAT TO SEE

Arusha town is better known as a base for safaris and other excursions than as a sightseeing destination in its own right. However, a trio of museums dot central Arusha, none of which could be described as a 'must see', but all worth a passing look if you're in the area.

NATURAL HISTORY MUSEUM [106 C2] (*Boma Rd;* ⟍ *027 250 7540;* ◷ *09.00–17.00; Tsh4,400*) Housed in the old German Boma, this might more accurately be renamed the Archaeological or Palaeontological Museum. The limited displays – you can walk around the museum in one minute – include a selection of animal and hominid fossils unearthed at Olduvai and Laetoli in the Ngorongoro Conservation Area, as well as life-size models of Australopithecus hunter gatherers at play.

ARUSHA DECLARATION MUSEUM [105 G4] (*Uhuru Monument Circle;* ◷ *08.30–17.30; Tsh1,000*) Dedicated primarily to 20th century developments in Tanzania, this has some interesting displays on the colonial and post-independence Nyerere era. It also contains a few decent ethnographic displays.

THE TANZANITE EXPERIENCE [106 B5] (*3rd floor, Blue Plaza Bldg, India Rd;* ⟍ *027 250 5101;* ◷ *09.00–16.00 Mon–Fri, 09.00–13.00 Sat; no entrance fee*). This recently opened museum, operated by TanzaniteOne, the world's largest tanzanite mining company, provides a fascinating overview of the discovery and extraction of this exquisite blue gem, which occurs in Tanzania only. Imaginative multimedia displays and enthusiastic staff are complemented by many examples of rough and cut tanzanite (and other striking locally sourced rocks) and there's a coffee shop and buying room attached.

CULTURAL TOURS AROUND ARUSHA

A number of widely praised and increasingly popular cultural tourism programmes have been implemented around Arusha in recent years with the assistance of the Dutch agency SNV. Any one of these programmes makes for an excellent half- or full-day trip out of Arusha, offering tourists the opportunity to experience something of rural Africa away from the slick lodges and main safari circuit. You can ask your safari company to tag a visit to one of the cultural programmes on to your main safari, or can arrange a stand-alone day trip once you arrive in Arusha. Several of the programmes also offer the opportunity to spend a night locally, though it should be stressed that accommodation is not up to accepted tourist-class standards. Of the various programmes, the one at Longido can easily be visited on public transport, but the rest are only realistically visited in a private vehicle. Details of recommended safari operators can be found on pages 108–10. The TTB office on Boma Road and Cultural Tourism Office in the Old Boma, both in Arusha (see page 107), stock useful pamphlets about all the cultural programmes, and can advise you about current costs and accessibility.

MKURU CAMEL SAFARI This most successful of the cultural tourism programmes around Arusha is based at Mkuru at the northern base of Mount Meru. It's a very well organised set-up, offering a selection of facilities and activities that seems to increase with every passing year, though these days it's pitched more at the mid-range market than at budget travellers. The main attraction here is organised camelback trips, which range in duration from day outings (*US$45 pp*) and overnight trips into the wildlife-rich plains towards Longido (*US$220 pp*) to a week-long trek to Ol Doinyo Lengai and Lake Natron (*US$995 pp*). In addition to camel rides, it offers a variety of day walks – a bird walk on the plain, a hike to the top of Ol Doinyo Landare, cultural visits to local healers and women's craft groups – for around US$20 per person. All activities are slightly cheaper as group sizes increase.

Activities operate out of the down-to-earth Mkuru Camel Camp, which is situated near the pyramidal Ol Doinyo Landare (literally 'Mountain of Goats') and Ngare Nanyuki (on the northern border of Arusha National Park) and offers great views of Kilimanjaro and Meru. This solar-powered camp has comfortable accommodation in furnished standing tents set on wooden platforms (*US$28 pp bed only or US$$45 FB*), simple ground tents with beds, sleeping bags, sheets and towels (*US$17 pp bed only or US$35 FB*), or you can pitch your own tent (*US$13 pp bed only or US$31 FB*). For further details contact Mkuru Camel Safari (m *0784 724498/472475*; e *info@mkurucamelsafari.com; www.mkurucamelsafari.com*).

LONGIDO The cultural tourism project run out of the overgrown village of Longido is one of the most accessible in the region for independent travellers, and it is an excellent place to visit for those who want to spend time among the Maasai. The original programme co-ordinator was a local Maasai who studied abroad as a sociologist before he was paralysed in a serious accident, and his successor can tell you anything you want to know about Maasai culture. Three different walking modules are on offer to tourists. On all modules, you can expect to see a variety of birds (including several colourful finches and barbets), and there is a fair amount of large game left in the area, notably gerenuk, lesser kudu, giraffe, Thomson's gazelle and black-backed jackal. It is worth trying to be in Longido on Wednesday, when a hectic cattle market is held on the outskirts of the village.

The first module is a half-day bird walk through the Maasai Plains, which also includes a visit to a rural Maasai *boma* (homestead), and a meal cooked by the local women's group. There is a full-day tour which follows the same route as the bird walk does, before climbing to the top of the 2,637m Longido Mountain, an ascent of roughly 400m, offering views to Mount Meru and Kilimanjaro on a clear day, as well as over the Maasai Plains to Kenya. The two-day module follows the same route as the one-day walk, but involves camping out overnight in the green Kimokouwa Valley, before visiting a dense rainforest that still harbours a number of buffaloes as well as the usual birds and monkeys.

Longido straddles the main Namanga road roughly 100km from Arusha, so any of the regular minibuses and taxis that run between Arusha and Namanga can drop you there – these usually leave Arusha from the north end of the bus station opposite the stadium. The tourist project maintains a neat and inexpensive guesthouse about 100m from the main road, or you can arrange to pitch a tent at a Maasai *boma* for a small fee. A limited selection of cheap Tanzanian fare is available from one or two small restaurants that lie along the main road, and a couple of local bars (with pool table) serve cold beers and soft drinks. For further details contact Longido Cultural Tourism (✆ 027 250 9209; m 0787 855185; e touryman@yahoo.com).

NG'IRESI VILLAGE Set on the slopes of Mount Meru some 7km from Arusha town, this cultural tourism programme based in the traditional Wa-Arusha village of Ng'iresi offers many insights into the local culture and agricultural practices. There are also some lovely walks in the surrounding Mount Meru foothills, an area characterised by fast-flowing streams, waterfalls and remnant forest patches. From Ng'iresi, it is possible to walk to Lekimana Hill, from where there are good views over the Maasai Steppes and on a clear day to Kilimanjaro. Another walk takes you to Kivesi Hill, an extinct volcano whose forested slopes support a variety of birds and small mammals.

Three different modules are available at Ng'iresi, all inclusive of meals prepared by the Juhudu Women's Group and guided activities, while the overnight module includes a night's camping in the garden of Mzee Loti. There is no public transport to Ng'iresi, so you must either set up a visit through a safari company or make arrangements with a private vehicle.

MULALA VILLAGE This cultural tourism programme is situated in a village on the footslopes of Mount Meru. Mulala lies at an elevation of 1,450m, some 30km from Arusha, in a fertile agricultural area, which produces coffee, bananas and other fruit, and vegetables. Several short walks can be undertaken in the surrounding hills, including one to the forested Marisha River, home to a variety of birds and primates, and to Mazungu Lake, where it is said that a *mazungu* was once lured to his death by a demon. Another local place of interest is Mama Anna's dairy, which supplies cheese to several upmarket hotels in Arusha. The tourist programme here is run in conjunction with the Agape Women's Group, which provides most of the guides as well as snacks and camping facilities.

MONDULI JUU The settlement of Monduli Juu ('Upper Monduli') is situated some 50km west of Arusha in the Monduli Hills, a forested range that rises from the Rift Valley floor to an elevation of 2,660m, offering some superb views to other larger mountains including Kilimanjaro, Meru and Ol Doinyo Lengai. Monduli Juu consists of a cluster of four Maasai villages, namely Emairete, Enguiki, Eluwai and Mfereji, the first of which is set alongside a spectacular crater that betrays the mountains' volcanic origins and is still held sacred by locals.

The cultural programme at Monduli Juu offers several programmes, ranging from a few hours to several days in duration. For nature lovers, a recommended option is the hike to Monduli Peak, passing through patches of montane forest that support a large variety of monkeys, antelope, birds and butterflies as well as relic populations of elephant and buffalo – an armed ranger is mandatory. Other attractions include visits to a traditional healer and to the Naramatu bead factory, and general cultural programmes including a Maasai *boma* visit and a meat market.

A few local families in Monduli Juu offer camping sites, only one of which, Esserian Maasai Camp, has running water. Meals – traditional or Western, as you like – can be prepared with a bit of notice. A useful contact for setting up trips to this area is Tanzania Adventure (see under *Safari Operators*, page 109).

LAKE DULUTI

The small but attractive Lake Duluti lies roughly 10km east of Arusha and only 2km from the Moshi road near the busy little market town of Tenguru. Some 62ha in extent, 15m deep and fed by subterranean springs, the lake is nestled within an extinct volcanic crater whose formation was linked to that of Mount Meru. Although much of the surrounding area is cultivated and settled, the steep walls of the crater support a fringing gallery of riparian forest, while the lake itself is lined with beds of papyrus. The lake is of particular interest to birdwatchers, as it supports numerous diving and shore birds, as well as seven kingfisher species and breeding colonies of various weavers. An added attraction is the good views of Mount Meru and Kilimanjaro from the lakeshore on clear days.

The relatively developed northern lakeshore is open to the public, but the southern, eastern and western shores are now protected in the 19ha **Lake Duluti Forest Reserve** (❨ 027 250 9522; e *cmisutu@yahoo.co.uk; US$12 pp inc guided walk; additional photography, camping, fishing & canoeing fees of US$12 pp per activity*). A 60–90 minute walking trail has been established in the reserve, offering the opportunity to see some of the 50-odd tree species, wildlife such as blue monkey, vervet monkey and monitor lizard, and an interesting selection of forest birds including Hartlaub's turaco, crowned and silvery-cheeked hornbills, Narina trogon, brown-breasted and white-eared barbets, Africa broadbill, little greenbul, black-throated wattle-eye, paradise flycatcher, white-starred robin and black-breasted apalis. Canoe trips on the crater lake are operated by Green Footprint Adventures (❨ 027

254 4635; m *0784 203000;* e *info@greenfootprint.co.tz; www.greenfootprint.co.tz*) out of the nearby Serena Mountain Village Lodge.

GETTING THERE AND AWAY Lake Duluti lies about 2km south of the Arusha–Moshi road, and the side roads to Serena Mountain Village Lodge and the Duluti Club, both on the lakeshore, are signposted. On public transport, any vehicle heading from Arusha towards Moshi can drop you at the junction – hop off when you see a large carved wooden giraffe to your left coming from Arusha. The turn-off to Duluti Club is signposted to the right opposite this statue, and the turn-off to Serena Mountain Village Lodge is another 200m or so towards Moshi. It's about 20 minutes' walk from the main road to the campsite. Entrance to the Lake Duluti Forest Reserve, on foot only, is via a manned entrance gate that lies along a rough road 1km east of the Duluti Club and 500m south of Serena Mountain Village Lodge.

WHERE TO STAY
Upmarket
Serena Mountain Village Lodge ⬛ 027 255 3313/4/5; e reservations@serenahotels.com; www.serenahotels.com. With expansive green lawns verging on the northern shore of the gorgeous Lake Duluti, & fabulous views across to Mount Meru & Kilimanjaro, Serena Mountain Village Lodge is easily one of the most attractive upmarket lodges in the greater Arusha area. The main building is a converted thatched farmhouse dating to the colonial era, & accommodation is in comfortable self-contained chalets. Subsequent to the lodge being taken over by the excellent Serena chain, the quality of service, meals & décor have all been upgraded to match the atmospheric setting. *US$195/245 sgl/dbl B&B, US$125/185 Apr–May; additional US$30 pp FB.*

Camping
Ⓧ **Duluti Club** m 0754 373977. The lovely & surprisingly little-used campsite at the Duluti Club is slightly run-down, but the lakeshore setting is fabulous. Facilities include an ablution block with hot showers & a cafeteria serving basic, reasonably priced meals & chilled drinks. *Camping US$6 pp.*

USA RIVER
The small and rather amorphous village of Usa River flanks the Moshi road about 20km east of Arusha near the turn-off to Arusha National Park. It is of interest to tourists primarily for a cluster of upmarket hotels, several of which rank as among the most attractive in the Arusha area, as well as being conveniently located for day safaris into the national park. If you're staying in the area, there are several good boutiques and adequate eateries in and around the Usa Mall, which also has an internet café and banking facilities.

WHERE TO STAY
Upmarket
Dik Dik Hotel (21 rooms) ⬛ 027 255 3499; e dikdik@habari.co.tz; www.dikdik.ch. Owned & managed by the same Swiss family since it opened back in 1990, this attractive small hotel with comfortable, well-equipped en-suite chalets lies about 1km north of Kilala, a small village on the Arusha–Moshi road a few hundred metres west of Usa River. The thickly wooded 10ha grounds are bisected by an energetic stream, & contain a swimming pool, a small dam, a viewing tower & offering clear views to Kilimanjaro, & a restaurant rated as one of the best in the Arusha area. Rooms 19 & 20 are particularly recommended for their view on to a riverine gallery forest inhabited by monkeys & numerous bird species. *US$150/200 sgl/dbl B&B or US$200/300 FB.*
Mount Meru Game Sanctuary (17 rooms) ⬛ 027 255 3643, f 027 255 3730; e reservations@intimate-places.com; www.mountmerugamelodge.com. Established in 1959,

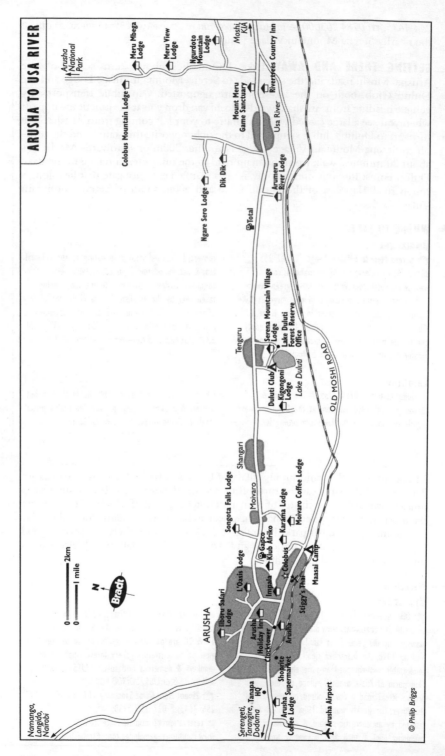

ARUSHA TO USA RIVER

Namanga,
Longido,
Nairobi

Serengeti,
Tarangire, Tanapa
HQ
Dodoma

Arusha
Coffee Lodge
Supermarket

Arusha Airport

Arusha

Shoprite

Clocktower

Arusha

Holiday Inn

Impala

L'Oasis Lodge

Iliboru Safari
Lodge

Gapco
Klub Afriko

Colobus

Stiggy's Thai

Maasai Camp

Karama Lodge

Moivaro Coffee Lodge

Songota Falls Lodge

Moivaro

Shangari

Duluti Club

Kigongoni
Lodge

Lake Duluti

Tenguru

Lake Duluti
Forest Reserve
Office

Serena Mountain Village
Lodge

OLD MOSHI ROAD

Ngare Sero Lodge

Total

Dik Dik

Arumeru
River Lodge

Mount Meru
Game Sanctuary

Usa River

Colobus Mountain Lodge

Arusha
National
Park

Meru Mbega
Lodge

Meru View
Lodge

Ngurdoto
Mountain
Lodge

Moshi,
KIA

Rivertrees Country Inn

0   2km
0   1 mile

N

Bradt

© Philip Briggs

126

about 1km east of Usa River immediately before the turn-off to Arusha National Park, this long-serving & highly recommended lodge has something of an *Out of Africa* ambience, consisting of a main stone building & a few semi-detached wooden cabins surrounded by bougainvillaea-draped gardens. A large open enclosure in front of rooms 1 & 2 is stocked with various antelope, while naturally occurring blue monkeys make mischief on the lawn, nicely setting the tone for your safari, & it is also the site of a papyrus heronry where hundreds of cattle egrets roost at dusk, alongside saddle-billed & yellow-billed storks. Rooms are stylishly decorated in classic Edwardian safari style. *US$150/205 sgl/dbl B&B or US$186/277 FB, huge low-season discount Apr–Jun.*

⌂ **Ngare Sero Lodge** (12 rooms) ⍠ 027 250 3638; m 0713 560055; e Reservations@Ngare-Sero-Lodge.com; www.Ngare-Sero-Lodge.com. One of the nicest places to stay in the Arusha area is this small, exclusive country-style lodge set on a forested 25ha estate dating to the German colonial era, & accessible along the same dirt road as the Dik Dik Hotel. As is implicit in the name Ngare Sero (Maasai for 'dappled water'), the owner-managed estate is fed by several streams flowing from the higher slopes of Mount Meru, & a crystal clear reservoir below the lodge is stocked with barbel & trout, while also driving the turbine that generates the lodge's electricity. The forest & lake support an incredibly varied selection of birds & butterflies, while blue monkey & black-and-white colobus are both resident on the grounds. A superb range of activities & facilities includes horseback excursions, coffee farm tours, boat rides on the lake, cultural visits to a nearby village, a swimming pool, internet access, yoga & meditation classes, & massages. The rooms, though attractively decorated, are set out in a rather cramped row opposite the main building, but overall this is an excellent option for those who enjoy outdoor pursuits. *US$175/250 pp FB.*

⌂ **Rivertrees Country Inn** (12 rooms) ⍠ 027 255 3894; m 0713 339873; e rivertrees@habari.co.tz; www.rivertrees.com. Situated 300m from the main Moshi road facing the Mount Meru Game Sanctuary, this highly regarded owner-managed lodge is set in magnificently shady green gardens on an old family estate offering great views to Mount Meru & Kilimanjaro, & bounded by a forest-fringed stretch of the Usa River. Centred on a rambling old farmhouse, the inn offers comfortable accommodation in spacious en-suite rooms with large wooden 4-poster beds, as well as a more exclusive river cottage & a stunning river house with 2 dbl bedrooms (the latter used by the German head of state on a recent visit to Tanzania). Facilities include a TV room (with digital satellite TV), internet access, a swimming pool & a highly rated restaurant serving hearty country food, while activities on offer include horseback excursions, village tours & bird walks. *Std rooms US$155/195 sgl/dbl B&B; river cottage US$280 dbl; river house US$1,280 for up to 4 people.*

⌂ **Arumeru River Lodge** (20 rooms) ⍠ 027 255 3573; m 0784 459639; e info@ arumerulodge.com; www.arumerulodge.com. The newest lodge in the Usa River area, having opened in Apr 2005, German-owned Arumeru consists of 10 2-room thatch chalets set on a 6ha plot bounded by 2 rivers. A stunning open-sided thatch common area overlooks the heated swimming pool, & the restaurant, complete with French chef, serves top-notch continental cuisine. The gardens currently feel a little underdeveloped, but you won't notice this if you ask for one of the rooms facing the river & associated swampland – home to 3 monkey species & a wide variety of birds – & there is also talk of introducing some antelope into the undeveloped 'bush' part of the property. The en-suite semi-detached rooms have a pleasing airy organic feel, & seem good value. *US$117/174/234 sgl/dbl/trpl B&B or US$160/260/360 FB; discounted Apr & May.*

ARUSHA NATIONAL PARK

Only 45 minutes from Arusha town, this is the most accessible of northern Tanzania's national parks, but – after the remote Rubondo Island and recently created Mkomazi – it is also the one that has been most neglected by the safari industry, largely because it offers limited possibilities to see the so-called Big Five. And yet, this one perceived failing aside, Arusha National Park is a quite extraordinary conservation area, and thoroughly worth a visit. Recently extended from 137km² to 542km², the park boasts a habitat diversity that spans everything from montane rainforest to moist savannah to alpine moorland, and its prodigious fauna includes some 400 bird and several unusual mammal species.

The most prominent landmark is Mount Meru, Africa's fifth-highest massif and a popular goal for dedicated hikers. The park also has much to offer non-hikers, including a cluster of attractive lakes, a spectacular extinct volcanic crater, and stirring views of Kilimanjaro looming large on the eastern skyline, all of which can be seen in the course of a day trip out of Arusha town or Usa River. A recently introduced and highly attractive alternative to game drives are the canoe trips run by Green Footprint Adventures (❜ *027 254 4635;* m *0784 203000;* e *info@greenfootprint.co.tz; www.greenfootprint.co.tz*).

A detailed booklet, *Arusha National Park*, containing detailed information on every aspect of the park's ecology and wildlife, is widely available in Arusha town, as is Giovanni Tombazzi's excellent map, which has useful details of the ascent of Mount Meru on the flip. The park entrance fee of US$35 per person per 24 hours should be paid by MasterCard or Tanapa Card (issued at any Exim Bank). No other cards are accepted, nor are travellers' cheques, and cash payments attract a 50% penalty.

GETTING THERE AND AWAY From Arusha, follow the surfaced Moshi road for about 20km to Usa River, then take the turn-off to the left signposted for Arusha National Park. After about 8km, this dirt road enters the park boundary, where park entrance fees are paid at the new main gate. The road reaches Hatari! and Momella Lodges after another 15km or so, immediately outside the northern national park boundary. This road is in fair condition and can normally be driven in an ordinary saloon car, though a 4x4 may be necessary after rain.

Any safari company can arrange an overnight trip to the park or a day trip out of Arusha. Most companies can also organise a three-day climb up Meru. If you want to organise your own climb or spend some time exploring the park on foot, you will have to find your own way there. You could hire a taxi in Arusha, but it is cheaper to catch a bus or *dala-dala* along the Moshi road as far as the turn-off, from where 4x4 vehicles serve as *dala-dalas* to the village of Ngare Nanyuki about 3km past the northern boundary of the park, passing through the main entrance gate (where fees must be paid) *en route*.

⌂ WHERE TO STAY
Exclusive
⌂ **Hatari!** (8 rooms) ❜/f 027 255 3456; e marlies@theafricanembassy.com; www.hatarilodge.com. This characterful owner-managed lodge, situated in a patch of moist yellow fever woodland just outside the Momella Gate, is named after the 1961 film *Hatari!* (*Danger!*), & stands on a property formerly owned by Hardy Kruger, one of the film's co-stars. Accommodation is in large en-suite dbl chalets with king-size beds & tall *makuti* ceilings, while the individualistic décor is an imaginative, colourful blend of a classic African bush feel & a more 'retro' look dating back to the era of the film. The common areas — littered with *Hatari!* memorabilia — overlook a swampy area inhabited by buffalo, waterbuck, crowned crane & various other waterbirds. The food is excellent, the service is highly personalised, & there are also stirring views across to nearby Kilimanjaro & Meru. Activities on offer include game drives & walks, canoeing on the Momella Lakes & birdwatching excursions. *Rates on application.*

Upmarket
⌂ **Ngurdoto Mountain Lodge** (188 rooms) ❜ 027 255 5217/26; f 027 255 5227/8; e Ngurdoto@ thengurdotomountainlodge.com; www.thengurdotomountainlodge.com. Situated on a lush 70ha coffee plantation alongside the road between Usa River & Arusha National Park, this impressive new tourist village, affiliated to the Impala Hotel in Arusha, has some of the best facilities of any lodge or hotel in the Arusha area, including a 9-hole golf course, a gym, a 600-seat conference centre, a large swimming pool, 24hr internet access, 2 restaurants & 2 bars. Given the

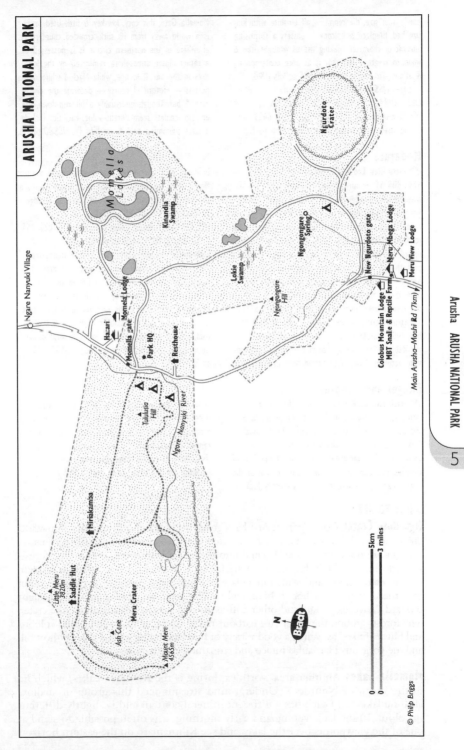

Momella Lakes

Ngare Nanyuki Village

Kinandia Swamp

Ngurdoto Crater

Ngongongare Spring

Lokie Swamp

Ngongongare Hill

Momella Lodge

Hazari

Momella gate

Park HQ

Resthouse

New Ngurdoto gate

Colobus Mountain Lodge
MBT Snake & Reptile Farm

Meru Mbega Lodge

Meru View Lodge

Main Arusha–Moshi Rd (7km)

Ngare Nanyuki River

Tululusia Hill

Ngare Nanyuki River

Hiriakamba

Little Meru 3820m
Saddle Hut

Meru Crater

Ash Cone

Mount Meru 4565m

5km

3 miles

© Philip Briggs

hotel's vast size, the rooms – all en-suite with king-size bed, fireplace & balcony – possess a surprising amount of character, making use of wrought iron & wood to create a feel that is at once contemporary & ethnic. *Std rooms US$135/175 sgl/dbl B&B; cottages US$160/200; executive rooms US$200/240, additional meals US$15 pp.*

⌂ **Momella Lodge** (55 rooms) 057 250 6423. Set in the shadow of Mount Meru about 3km past

Moderate

⌂ **Meru View Lodge** (15 rooms) m 0784 41 9232/805259; e africanview@habari.co.tz; www.meru-view-lodge.de. This small & very friendly German-owned lodge lies on the eastern side of the road from Usa River, about 1km south of where the road enters the national park. The en-suite rooms, dotted around flowering gardens & a large swimming pool, though very comfortable, aren't quite the bargain they once were. *US$90/110 sgl/dbl B&B; other meals additional US$10–15 pp.*

⌂ **Meru Mbega Lodge** (12 rooms) m 0713 897911; info@mt-meru.com; www.mt-meru.com. Opened in mid 2008, this latest addition to the chain of affordable lodges run by Mbega has comfortable en-suite accommodation with netted beds in 2-storey

Budget and camping

⌂ **National Park Resthouse** This self-catering resthouse 2km from Momella Gate sleeps up to 5. You can book it in advance through the National Parks office outside Arusha. *US$20 pp.*

⋏ **National Park campsites** 3 sites lie at the foot of Tululusia Hill, 2km from Momella Gate, & one in the forest near Ngurdoto Gate. All are scenically located

Momella Gate, this cosy, low-key & little-used lodge is a world away from its slick, crowded counterparts elsewhere in the northern circuit. It is possessed of a rather alpine atmosphere, reinforced by the log fires in the bar & lounge, while black-&-white movie posters – *Hatari!* of course – decorate the dining area & bar. Though undeniably a bit run-down, the en-suite chalets seem decent value. Facilities include a large swimming pool & satellite TV. *US$80 pp FB.*

buildings that offer views over a small pond towards Mount Meru. An attractive *makuti* structure serves as the bar & restaurant. It's a good place to arrange Meru climbs. *US$80/90 sgl/dbl.*

⌂ **Colobus Mountain Lodge** (18 rooms) ⍐ 027 255 3632; info@colobusmountainlodge.com; www.colobusmountainlodge.com. Clearly signposted 200m from the public road between Usa River & Ngare Nanyuki, this rustic lodge lies in the shadow of Mount Meru immediately outside the southern boundary of the park. The centrepiece of the site is an open-sided bar & restaurant with a tall *makuti* roof, serving sensibly priced Western & local dishes. *Spacious semi-detached chalet rooms US$75/80 sgl/dbl B&B.*

close to a stream, have drop toilets & firewood. Note, however, that you may not walk between the campsites & the entrance gates without an armed ranger. *US$20 pp.*

⋏ **Colobus Mountain Lodge.** See *Moderate* above. Camping on the large, green lawn. *US$5 pp.*

WHAT TO SEE

Ngurdoto Crater Coming from Arusha, a good first goal is this fully intact 3km-wide, 400m-deep volcanic caldera, which has often been described as a mini-Ngorongoro. Tourists are not permitted to descend into the crater, but the views from the forest-fringed rim over the lush crater floor are fantastic. A large herd of buffalo is resident on the crater floor, and with binoculars it is normally possible to pick up other mammals, such as warthog, baboon and various antelope. Look out, too, for augur buzzard, Verreaux's eagle and other cliff-associated raptors soaring above the crater. The forests around the crater rim harbour many troops of black-and-white colobus and blue monkey, as well as a good variety of birds including several types of hornbill and the gorgeous Hartlaub's turaco and cinnamon-chested bee-eater.

Momella Lakes Another area worth exploring is the Momella Lakes, which lie to the north of Ngurdoto. Underground streams feed this group of shallow alkaline lakes, and each has a different mineral content and is slightly different in colour. In the late evening and early morning, it is often possible to stand at one of the viewpoints over the lakes and see Kilimanjaro on the eastern horizon and Mount Meru to the west. It is on these lakes that Green Footprint Adventures (see page 108) undertakes canoe safaris, a very tranquil way to enjoy the birdlife and scenery.

Momella is one of the best places in Tanzania for waterbirds: flamingo, pelican, little grebe and a variety of herons, ducks and waders are common. Among the more common mammals around the lakes are hippo, buffalo and waterbuck – the waterbuck population evidently intermediate to the Defassa and common waterbuck races. You should also come across a few pairs of Kirk's dik-dik, an attractively marked small antelope that seems to be less skittish here than it is elsewhere in the country. Other large mammals likely to be seen in Arusha National Park include giraffe, zebra and vervet monkey. Elephants are present but seldom seen, since they tend to stick to the forest zone of Mount Meru, while the only large predators are leopard and spotted hyena.

MBT Snake and Reptile Farm Signposted a short distance from the entrance to Arusha National Park, this long-serving private park has a good collection of reptiles and offers an intelligent guided tour. Creatures in residence include Nile crocodile, various chameleon species and other lizards, and a fearsome collection of snakes, including spitting cobras, mambas, puff adders, Gabon viper, water snakes and some hefty pythons. It lies outside the national park so no park fees are payable but an entrance ticket inclusive of guided tour costs Tsh3,000.

Mount Meru Arusha National Park's tallest landmark and most publicised attraction is Mount Meru, whose upper slopes and 4,566m peak lie within its boundaries. The product of the same volcanic activity that formed the Great Rift Valley 15 to 20 million years ago, Mount Meru attained a height similar to that of Kilimanjaro until 250,000 years ago, when a massive eruption tore out its eastern wall. Meru is regarded as a dormant volcano, since lava flowed from it as recently as 100 years ago, but there is no reason to suppose it will do anything dramatic in the foreseeable future. The Arusha and Meru people deify Mount Meru as a rain god, but it is unlikely that any local person actually reached the peak prior to Fritz Jaeger's pioneering ascent in 1904.

Often overlooked by tourists because it is 'only' the fifth-highest mountain in Africa, Meru is no substitute for Kilimanjaro for achievement-orientated travellers. On the other hand, those who climb both mountains invariably enjoy Meru more. Also going in its favour, Meru is less crowded than Kilimanjaro, considerably less expensive, and – although steeper and almost as cold – less likely to engender the health problems associated with Kilimanjaro's greater elevation. Meru is just as interesting as Kilimanjaro from a biological point of view and, because comparatively few people climb it, you are more likely to see forest animals and plains game on the lower slopes.

Meru can technically be climbed in two days, but three days is normal, allowing time to explore Meru Crater and to look at wildlife and plants. Most people arrange a climb through a safari company in Arusha. The going rate for a three-day hike is around US$300 per person. You can make direct arrangements with park officials at the gate, but you won't save much money by doing this, and should check hut availability at the Tanapa office in Arusha in advance. The compulsory armed ranger/guide costs US$20 per day (US$10 park fee and US$10 salary), hut fees are US$20 per night, and there is the usual park entrance fee of US$30 per day. A rescue fee of US$20 per person covers the entire climb. The minimum cost for a three-day climb is therefore US$165 per person, with an additional US$60 to be divided between the climbers. Food and transport must be added to this, and porters cost an additional US$5 per day each.

Meru is very cold at night, and you will need to bring clothing adequate for alpine conditions. In the rainy season, mountain boots are necessary. At other times, good walking shoes will probably be adequate. The best time to climb is from October to February.

Day 1 The trail starts at Momella Gate (1,500m). From there it is a relatively gentle three-hour ascent to Miriakamba Hut (2,600m). On the way you pass through well-developed woodland where there is a good chance of seeing large animals such as giraffe. At an elevation of about 2,000m you enter the forest zone. If you leave Momella early, there will be ample time to explore Meru Crater in the afternoon. The 1,500m cliff rising to Meru Peak overlooks the crater. The 3,667m-high ash cone in the crater is an hour from Miriakamba Hut, and can be climbed.

Day 2 It is three hours to Saddle Hut (3,600m), a bit steeper than the previous day's walk. You initially pass through forest, where there is a good chance of seeing black-and-white colobus, then at about 3,000m you will enter a moorland zone similar to that on Kilimanjaro. It is not unusual to see Kilimanjaro peeking above the clouds from Saddle Hut. If you feel energetic, you can climb Little Meru (3,820m) in the afternoon. It takes about an hour each way from Saddle Hut.

Day 3 You will need to rise very early to ascend the 4,566m peak, probably at around 02.00. This ascent takes four to five hours. It is then an eight- to nine-hour walk back down the mountain to Momella Gate.

Note: Some people prefer to climb from Miriakamba Hut to Saddle Hut and do the round trip from Saddle Hut to Meru Peak on the second day (11 hours altogether), leaving only a five-hour walk to Momella on the third. Others climb all the way up to Saddle Hut on the first day (six hours), do the round trip to the peak on the second (eight hours), and return to Momella from the Saddle Hut on the third (five hours).

WEST KILIMANJARO CONSERVATION AREA

Wedged between the northwestern base of Kilimanjaro and Kenya's Amboseli National Park, some two to three hours' drive northeast of Arusha, West Kilimanjaro consists of six contiguous blocks of Maasai communal land that are currently in the process of amalgamating as a formal Wildlife Management Area. Although the main attractions here are the superb close-up views of Kilimanjaro and a well-protected elephant population noted for the even temperament and immense tusks of its bulls, this southern extension of Amboseli also retains a genuine wilderness feel, since only one of the six land blocks is currently open to tourists, run as an exclusive concession by Kirurumu Under Canvas.

Much of West Kilimanjaro is comprised of very flat land whose fine volcanic soil once formed the bed of Lake Amboseli – then twice as big as present-day Lake Manyara – before it started to dry up some 10,000–15,000 years ago. As the lake dried it left calcareous deposits that were later mined by the Germans in order to make the famous Meerschaum tobacco pipes. The abandoned pits left behind by the open-cast mines are now an important part of the ecosystem, since they trap rainwater to provide drinking for the Maasai cattle as well as the wildlife at the driest times of the year.

West Kilimanjaro supports a near-pristine cover of lightly wooded acacia savannah where Maasai herdsmen coexist with a remarkable variety of wildlife, including wildebeest, zebra, eland, impala, Grant's gazelle, hartebeest and yellow baboon, as well as one of the few Tanzanian populations of the remarkable stretch-necked gerenuk.

The area also forms part of a migration corridor used by elephants to cross between Amboseli and the forested slopes of Kilimanjaro. Many impressive bulls are resident throughout the year, but numbers peak in June–July, after the rains, when the smaller family groups merge to form 100-strong herds. This also is when mating takes place, and irascible bulls follow the family herds accompanied by a fanfare of trumpeting.

WHERE TO STAY

Hemingway's Camp (5 rooms) ☎ 027 250 7011; info@kirurumu.com; www.kirurumu.com. This upmarket mobile-style camp consists of 5 double tents with solar lighting & en-suite showers set out in a stand of mature *Acacia tortilis* trees at the base of an extinct volcanic cone offering views to Kilimanjaro & Meru, as well as the more distant mountains at Longido & Namanga. In addition to standard game drives, which can offer superb opportunities to track & photograph giant tuskers in the shadow of Kilimanjaro, the camp can arrange night drives & bush walks led by local Maasai guides. It is normally booked out to one party at a time, though more than one party can share it by arrangement, & a minimum booking of 2 nights is mandatory. *US$540/640 sgl/dbl FB or US$810/1,020 inc activities, around 20% less in shoulder season; plus conservancy fee of US$70 pp per night.*

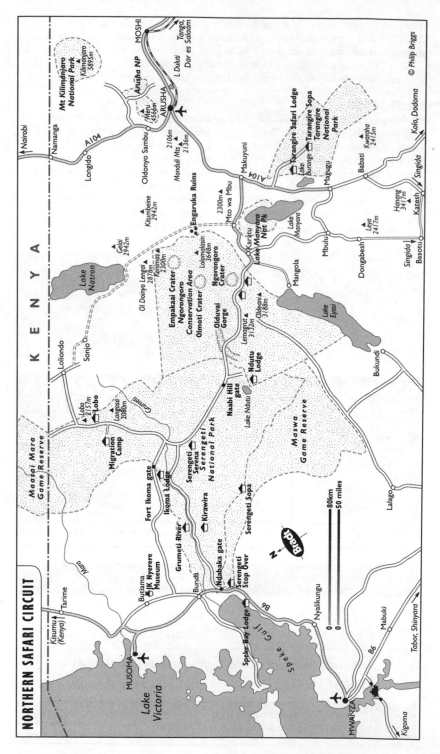

NORTHERN SAFARI CIRCUIT

© Philip Briggs

K E N Y A

Mt Kilimanjaro National Park
Kilimanjaro 5895m

Arusha NP
Meru 4566m
ARUSHA
Nairobi
Namanga
Longido
A104
Oldonyo Sambu
Monduli Mts 2138m
2106m

MOSHI
L Duluti
Tanga, Dar es Salaam

Makuyuni
Tarangire Safari Lodge
Burunge Tarangire Sopa
Lake Burunge
Tarangire National Park
Magugu
Babati
Kwaraha 2415m
Kolo, Dodoma
Singida

Kitumbeine 2942m
Engaruka Ruins
2300m
Mto wa Mbu
Karatu
Lake Manyara Npt Pk
Lake Manyara
Mbulu
Dongabesh
Hanang 3417m
Leya 2417m
Katesh
Singida
Basotu

Gelai 2942m
Lake Natron
Ol Doinyo Lengai 2878m
Kerimasi 2300m
Empakaai Crater
Ngorongoro Conservation Area
Olmoti Crater
Lolmalasin 3648m
Ngorongoro Crater
Olduvai Gorge
Olkeani 3188m
Mangola
Lake Eyasi

Loliondo
Sonjo
(Grumeti)
Lobo 2157m
Lobo
Longosa 2080m

Lemagrut 3132m
Ndutu Lodge
Naabi Hill gate
Lake Ndutu
Bukundi

Maasai Mara Game Reserve
Migration Camp
Ikoma Lodge
Fort Ikoma gate
Kirawira
Serengeti Serena
Serengeti National Park
Serengeti Sopa
Maswa Game Reserve
Lalago

Grumeti River
Butiama
JK Nyerere Museum
Bunda
Ndabaka gate
Serengeti Stop Over
Nyalikungu
B8
Tabora, Shinyara
B6
Mabuki

Ksumu (Kenya)
Tarime
Mara
MUSOMA
Speke Bay Lodge
Speke Gulf
Lake Victoria
MWANZA
Kigoma

N
Baobab

0   80km
0   50 miles

6

The Northern Safari Circuit

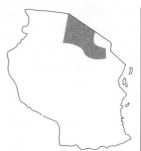

The cluster of national parks, game reserves and other conservation areas that runs southwest from Arusha town through to the eastern shore of Lake Victoria forms one of the most extensive safari circuits in Africa, and arguably the finest. The Serengeti National Park and adjacent Ngorongoro Conservation Area, the latter dominated by the Ngorongoro Crater, are possibly the most publicised game reserves in the world. And justifiably so: the Serengeti Plains host Africa's greatest wildlife spectacle, the annual migration of more than a million wildebeest and zebra, while also supporting remarkably dense populations of predators such as lion, cheetah, leopard and spotted hyena. The floor of the spectacular Ngorongoro Crater is if anything even more densely packed with large mammals, and the best place in East Africa to see the endangered black rhino. Less celebrated components of this safari circuit include Lake Manyara and Tarangire national parks, the former protecting a shallow but expansive lake on the Rift Valley floor, the latter a tract of dry acacia woodland notable for its innumerable ancient baobabs and dense elephant population.

The main reserves in northern Tanzania are covered fully in this chapter, as is the process of organising a safari to these reserves. Although Arusha National Park (covered in *Chapter 5*) can be appended to the northern safari circuit, it lies in a different direction from Arusha, and is most often visited as a self-standing trip out of Arusha. Those travellers who want to climb Mount Meru (in Arusha National Park) or Kilimanjaro (100km east of Arusha) will almost certainly treat this climb separately from their safari, and might well want to deal directly with a company that specialises in trekking rather than a standard safari company.

CLIMATE

The northern safari circuit as a whole is far cooler than many visitors expect. Lying at an elevation of roughly 2,300m, the Ngorongoro Crater rim in particular tends to be chilly at night and misty in the morning, and it also receives a sufficiently high annual rainfall to support a belt of montane rainforest. The crater floor and Serengeti Plains are warmer but, since they lie above the Rift Valley escarpment at elevations of well over 1,000m, they are far from being oppressively hot. Tarangire and Lake Manyara national parks lie at lower elevations and are considerably warmer, with Tarangire in particular sometimes becoming seriously hot in the afternoon. Both areas cool down after dusk, however, and most visitors to Manyara will sleep at one of the lodges on the cool, breezy escarpment.

The main rainy seasons fall over November and December and from March to May, though this can often vary considerably from one year to the next. Game viewing in the Ngorongoro Crater and Lake Manyara is not strongly affected by season, and tends to be good at any time of year. The southern Serengeti, the part of the park visited by most tourists, hosts the greatest concentration of animals between December and March, while the northern and western Serengeti are normally best over May to July and late October to November, when the migration passes through. That said, game viewing in the Serengeti is pretty good at any time of year, and the more remote northern and western areas have the big advantage of being practically bereft of tourists outside of the migration periods. Tarangire National Park has the most seasonal game viewing on the northern circuit, with animal concentrations generally peaking between July and the start of the rains in November or early December.

THE MAASAI

The northern safari circuit is the homeland of the Nilotic-speaking Maasai, whose reputation as fearsome warriors ensured that the 19th-century slave caravans studiously avoided their territory, which was one of the last parts of East Africa ventured into by Europeans. The Maasai today remain the most familiar of African people to outsiders, a reputation that rests as much on their continued adherence to a traditional lifestyle as on past exploits. Instantly identifiable, Maasai men drape themselves in toga-like red blankets, carry long wooden poles, and often dye their hair with red ochre and style it in a manner that has been compared to a Roman helmet. And while the women dress similarly to many other Tanzanian women, their extensive use of beaded jewellery is highly distinctive too.

The Maasai are often regarded to be the archetypal East African pastoralists, but are in fact relatively recent arrivals to the area. Their language Maa (Maasai literally means 'Maa-speakers') is affiliated to those spoken by the Nuer of southwest Ethiopia and the Bari of southern Sudan, and oral traditions suggest that the proto-Maasai started to migrate southward from the lower Nile area in the 15th century. They arrived in their present territory in the 17th or 18th century, forcefully displacing earlier inhabitants such as the Datoga and Chagga, who respectively migrated south to the Hanang area and east to the Kilimanjaro foothills. The Maasai territory reached its greatest extent in the mid 19th century, when it covered most of the Rift Valley from Marsabit (Kenya) south to Dodoma. Over the 1880s/90s, the Maasai were hit by a series of disasters linked to the arrival of Europeans – rinderpest and smallpox epidemics exacerbated by a severe drought and a bloody secession dispute – and much of their former territory was re-colonised by tribes whom they had displaced a century earlier. During the colonial era, a further 50% of their land was lost to game reserves and settler farms. These territorial incursions notwithstanding, the Maasai today have one of the most extensive territories of any Tanzanian tribe, ranging across the vast Maasai Steppes to the Ngorongoro Highlands and Serengeti Plains.

The Maasai are monotheists whose belief in a single deity with a dualistic nature – the benevolent Engai Narok (Black God) and vengeful Engai Nanyokie (Red God) – has some overtones of the Judaic faith. They believe that Engai, who resides in the volcano Ol Doinyo Lengai, made them the rightful owners of all the cattle in the world, a view that has occasionally made life difficult for neighbouring herders. Traditionally, this arrogance does not merely extend to cattle: agriculturist and fish-eating peoples are scorned, while Europeans' uptight style of clothing earned them the Maasai name Iloredaa Enjekat – Fart Smotherers! Today, the Maasai co-exist peacefully with their non-Maasai compatriots, but while their tolerance for their neighbours' idiosyncrasies has increased in recent decades, they show little interest in changing their own lifestyle.

The Maasai measure a man's wealth in terms of cattle and children rather than money – a herd of about 50 cattle is respectable, the more children the better, and a man who has plenty of one but not the other is regarded as poor. Traditionally, the

Access to the Serengeti, Ngorongoro and Manyara is via the B142, the road which runs northwest from the junction village of Makuyuni on the main Dodoma road about 80km southwest of Arusha. The Dodoma road as far as Makayuni is surfaced and in good condition, and it can easily be covered in one hour from Arusha. The B142 northwest of Makayuni bypasses Lake Manyara at Mto wa Mbu village after 37km, then ascends the Rift escarpment before passing through cultivated highlands for about 25km to reach the busy market town of Karatu, about 15km

Maasai will not hunt or eat vegetable matter or fish, but feed almost exclusively off their cattle. The main diet is a blend of cow's milk and blood, the latter drained – it is said painlessly – from a strategic nick in the animal's jugular vein. Because the cows are more valuable to them alive than dead, they are generally slaughtered only on special occasions. Meat and milk are never eaten on the same day, because it is insulting to the cattle to feed off the living and the dead at the same time. Despite the apparent hardship of their chosen lifestyle, many Maasai are wealthy by any standards. On one safari, our driver pointed out a not unusually large herd of cattle that would fetch the market equivalent of three new Land Rovers.

The central unit of Maasai society is the age-set. Every 15 years or so, a new and individually named generation of warriors or Ilmoran will be initiated, consisting of all the young men who have reached puberty and are not part of a previous age-set – most boys aged between 12 and 25. Every boy must undergo the Emorata (circumcision ceremony) before he is accepted as a warrior. If he cries out during the five-minute operation, which is performed without any anaesthetic, the post-circumcision ceremony will be cancelled, the parents are spat on for raising a coward, and the initiate will be taunted by his peers for several years before he is forgiven. When a new generation of warriors is initiated, the existing Ilmoran will graduate to become junior elders, who are responsible for all political and legislative decisions until they in turn graduate to become senior elders. All political decisions are made democratically, and the role of the chief elder or Laibon is essentially that of a spiritual and moral leader.

Maasai girls are permitted to marry as soon as they have been initiated, but warriors must wait until their age-set has graduated to elder status, which will be 15 years later, when a fresh warrior age-set has been initiated. This arrangement ties in with the polygamous nature of Maasai society: in days past, most elders would typically have acquired between three and ten wives by the time they reached old age. Marriages are generally arranged, sometimes even before the female party is born, as a man may 'book' the next daughter produced by a friend to be his son's wife. Marriage is evidently viewed as a straightforward child-producing business arrangement: it is normal for married men and women to have sleeping partners other than their spouse, provided that those partners are of an appropriate age-set. Should a woman become pregnant by another lover, the prestige attached to having many children outweighs any minor concerns about infidelity, and the husband will still bring up the child as his own. By contrast, although sex before marriage is condoned, an unmarried girl who falls pregnant brings disgrace on her family, and in former times would have been fed to the hyenas.

For further details about Maasai society and beliefs, get hold of the coffee-table book *Maasai*, by the photographer Carol Beckwith and Maasai historian Tepilit Ole Saitoti (Harry N Abrams, New York, reprinted 1993).

before the main eastern entrance gate to the Ngorongoro Conservation Area. From the crater, the B142 descends to the Serengeti Plains, passing through the park headquarters in the Seronera Valley before reaching Bunda on the main Musoma–Mwanza road. Seronera lies about halfway along the 300km stretch of road between the crater and Bunda. Unlike the other northern reserves, Tarangire National Park lies to the east of the Dodoma road, about 30km south of the junction with the B142.

Some stretches of the 80km road between Makayuni and the Ngorongoro entrance gate are legendarily poor and rutted, and the road has closed down completely at least once in recent years through flooding. This entire 80km stretch was in the process of being surfaced in 2002, and roadworks are scheduled for completion during the lifespan of this edition. The improved road will cut the driving time from Arusha to the Ngorongoro Crater from a long three hours to perhaps two hours, meaning that it will just about lie within realistic day tripping distance of Arusha, which could place further environmental strain on this already over-touristed reserve. On the plus side, it will cut down the proportion of unproductive driving time associated with northern safaris – not to mention the wear on safari vehicles and their passengers' spines – though some argue that arriving at Ngorongoro on a pristine surfaced road will dilute the romance of the safari experience!

The most viable ways of exploring this area are in a private 4x4 or on an organised safari out of Arusha, Moshi or another major town (see *Organising a safari*, opposite). People driving themselves through the region should note that the higher entrance fees charged to all foreign-registered vehicles mean that it may

THE NORTHERN SAFARI CIRCUIT ON PUBLIC TRANSPORT

The combination of steep national park entrance and camping fees, and the expense of running 4x4 vehicles in northern Tanzania, places the northern safari circuit pretty much out of bounds for travellers on a very tight budget. It is possible, however, to see parts of the circuit relatively cheaply by using public transport and/or hiring vehicles locally.

The most affordable way of traversing the Serengeti National Park is on one of the buses and Land Rovers that run daily along the B142 between Arusha and Mwanza. This route passes through conservation areas for a total of about 250km, first the Serengeti's Western Corridor and Seronera Plains, then the plains of the western Ngorongoro Conservation Area and over the Ngorongoro Crater rim. You'd get a good feel of the scenery and landscapes from a bus window, and between November and July you should see plenty of game, including large predators, but of course the vehicle cannot be expected to stop for special sightings. The trip will entail paying US$60 in park entrance fees, over and above the bus fare. In theory, it is possible to make advance arrangements for one of these buses to drop you off at Seronera, and to pick you up at a later stage, but it's difficult to see any reason why anybody would want to do this.

A more satisfying option for travellers who specifically want to see the Serengeti, have time on their hands, and cannot afford a safari of several days' duration, is to approach the park from the western side. This cuts out the long drive and overnight stops coming from Arusha, allowing you to get within 1km of the entrance gate on public transport and to visit the park as a day or overnight trip rather than as part of a longer safari. The best place to set something like this up would be Safari Stopover, a private campsite situated right next to the entrance gate to the Serengeti's Western Corridor and alongside the main road between the Lake Victoria ports of Mwanza and Musoma. The Western Corridor itself generally offers good game viewing, particularly when the migration passes through between May and July, and the game-rich Seronera Plains and Campsite are only actually work out more cheaply to join an organised safari. The options for backpackers with limited financial resources are laid out in the box *The northern safari circuit on public transport*, below.

ORGANISING A SAFARI

Arusha is the most popular and convenient base from which to organise a safari to Tanzania's northern reserves, though a small proportion of tourists do organise safaris out of Moshi, Dar es Salaam or even Mwanza. With literally hundreds of safari companies operating out of Arusha, competition for custom is fierce, particularly at the bottom end of the price scale where there are several unscrupulous and incompetent companies willing to cut any corner and promise anything in order to keep down costs and attract budget travellers.

There are, in essence, **four types of safari package** on offer: budget camping safaris, standard lodge-based safaris, upmarket camping safaris and fly-in safaris. In all categories of safari, the price you are quoted should include the vehicle and driver/guide, fuel, accommodation or camping equipment and fees, meals and park entrance fees. You are expected to tip the driver and cook. Around US$5 per day per party seems to be par, but you should check this with the company. Drivers and cooks are poorly paid; if they have done a good job, be generous.

BUDGET CAMPING SAFARIS These are generally designed to keep costs to a minimum, so they will make use of the cheapest camping options, often outside the national parks, and clients are normally expected to set up their own tents.

about two hours' drive from the western entrance gate. Serengeti Stop Over charges US$130 per day for a vehicle that can carry up to five people into the park, which means that a day trip would work out at around US$120 per person for two people including park fees, and about US$85 per person for four people. For further details, see *Between Mwanza and the Kenyan Border* in Chapter 14, page 423.

On the eastern side of the northern safari circuit, affordable local buses run daily from Arusha to Karatu, stopping at the village of Mto wa Mbu near the entrance of Lake Manyara National Park. The Ngorongoro Safari Resort in Karatu rents out 4x4 vehicles seating up to four people, or five at a push, for US$110/120 for a half-/full-day visit to Lake Manyara National Park or the Ngorongoro Crater. Once again, this would work out to be reasonably affordable, at US$90–100 per person for two people or around US$65 per person for four people, for a day trip to either of these reserves. Should you want to make advance arrangements, the resort's contact details are included under the accommodation listings for Karatu (see page 156). It's worth noting, too, that safari vehicles are found in abundance in Mto wa Mbu and Karatu, so there's every chance you could make cheaper private arrangements to hire a vehicle for a day. Were you to do something like this, you should be very clear about what the deal covers and how long you will spend in the game reserve – ambiguities at the negotiating stage often result in frayed tempers later in the day.

Hitching into most of the reserves covered in this chapter is pretty much out of the question. Relatively few private vehicles pass this way, and most safari companies forbid their drivers to pick up hitchhikers. In any case, people who have paid for a safari, or who are in a private vehicle loaded with supplies, are unlikely to want to carry freeloaders. Even if you were to catch a lift, you may well get stuck in the Serengeti or Ngorongoro and although you will see little game from a campsite or lodge, you will still have to pay park fees.

Most backpackers and volunteers working in Tanzania go on budget camping safaris, though even with these there is a gap between the real shoestring operators, who'll skimp on everything, and those operators who offer a sensible compromise between affordability and adequate service.

LODGE SAFARIS Most fly-in tourists go on a standard lodge-based safari, which will generally cost around double the price of a similar budget camping safari. For the extra outlay, you get a roof over your head at night, restaurant food, and a far higher degree of luxury and comfort. If you decide to go on a lodge safari, the probability is that the operator will decide which lodges you stay at. If you have the choice, however, it's worth noting that the former government 'Wildlife Lodge' chain generally has the best natural settings, but the rooms are relatively basic. The Sopa Lodges are far more luxurious and slightly more expensive, but only the Ngorongoro Sopa Lodge has a setting to compare with the equivalent 'Wildlife Lodge'. The lodges in the Serena chain are generally the best of the mainstream chain lodges, with modern facilities, good locations and attractive décor.

The above chain lodges are all of the institutionalised 'hotel in the bush' variety, but there are also a number of smaller lodges scattered around the circuit, offering accommodation in standing tents and a more intimate bush atmosphere. Many of these, though absolutely superlative, are considerably more expensive than the larger chain lodges – well worth it if you can afford it, but not within everybody's means. Fortunately, there are also a number of tented camps offering a bush atmosphere at rates comparable to the chain lodges – Tarangire Safari Lodge, Kirurumu Tented Camp and Ndutu Safari Lodge stand out – and these are highly recommended to those seeking a bush experience at a package price.

UPMARKET CAMPING SAFARIS Camping isn't necessarily a cost-reducing device. Sleeping under canvas and eating under the stars will unquestionably make you feel more integrated into the bush environment than staying in a lodge, and this is where upmarket camping safaris come into play. At the top end of the range, you can organise safaris using private or so-called 'special' campsites, as well as tented lodges, and these will be as luxurious as any lodge safari, with top-quality food, a full team of staff, large tents, portable showers and the like. The cost of a safari like this will depend on your exact requirements, but it will probably cost at least as much as a similar lodge safari. What you are paying for is exclusivity and a real bush experience.

FLY-IN SAFARIS Regular scheduled flights connect all the main reserves in northern Tanzania, and an increasingly high proportion of safari-goers choose to fly around rather than bump along the long, dusty roads that separate the parks. Flying around will be particularly attractive to those who have bad backs or who tire easily, but it is more expensive and does dilute the sense of magic attached to driving through the vast spaces that characterise this region. Fly-in safaris allow you to see far more wildlife in a shorter space of time, because you don't lose hours on the road.

GROUP SIZE One factor that all visitors should consider is the size of the group doing the safari. It is almost invariably cheaper to go on safari as part of a group, but it can also ruin things if the people in that group are not compatible. A group safari will be highly frustrating to those who have a special interest such as birding or serious photography. And, frankly, we think it is unfair to impose this sort of interest on other passengers, who will have little interest in identifying every raptor you drive past, or in waiting for two hours at a lion kill to get the perfect shot. Another consideration is that non-stretch Land Rovers can feel rather cramped with four people in the back, especially when the luggage is in the vehicle, and jostling for headroom out of the roof can be a nightmare when four cameras are vying for the best position.

A small proportion of companies – generally the large package tour operators – use minibuses as opposed to conventional 4x4s. In our opinion, minibuses have several disadvantages, notably that the larger group size (typically around eight people) creates more of a package tour atmosphere, and that it is difficult for a large group to take proper advantage of the pop-up roofs which are usually found on safari vehicles. In any event, bouncing around rutted roads in a Land Rover is an integral part of the safari experience – it just wouldn't be the same in a minibus.

Finally, there is the question of aesthetics. Without wishing to wax too lyrical, the thrill of being on safari doesn't derive merely from the animals you see. There is an altogether more elusive and arguably spiritual quality attached to simply being in a place as wild and vast and wonderful as the Serengeti, one that is most easily absorbed in silence, whether you travel on your own or with somebody with whom you feel totally relaxed. It isn't the same when one has to make small talk to new acquaintances, crack the rote jokes about who should be put out of the vehicle to make the lion move, decide democratically when to move on, listen to the driver's educational monotones, and observe social niceties that seem at odds with the surrounding wilderness.

ITINERARY Your itinerary will depend on how much time and money you have, and also the time of year. There are endless options, and most safari companies will put together the package you ask for. They know the ground well and can advise you on what is possible, but may tend to assume you will want to cover as many reserves as possible. This is not always the best approach.

A typical five- or six-day safari takes in Ngorongoro, Serengeti, Manyara and Tarangire. A typical three-day trip takes in all these reserves except for the Serengeti. In the dry season (July to October) there is little game in the Serengeti; most safari companies will suggest you spend more time in Tarangire.

The distances between these reserves are considerable and the roads are poor; you will have a more relaxed trip if you visit fewer reserves. On a five-day safari, we would drop either the Serengeti or Tarangire. To visit all four reserves, six days is just about adequate, seven or more days would be better.

Three days isn't long enough to get a good feel for Tarangire, Manyara and Ngorongoro; four or even five days would be better. The combination of Ngorongoro and Tarangire would make an unhurried three-day safari. If you are limited to two days, you could either visit Tarangire on its own or do a combined trip to Manyara and Ngorongoro. If your budget is really limited, Tarangire can be visited as a day trip from Arusha; it is less than two hours' drive each way.

At the other end of the time scale, there is enough to see and do in the area to warrant a safari of two weeks in duration, or even longer. You could easily spend a few days exploring the Serengeti alone. In a two-week package, you could also visit Lake Natron and Ol Doinyo Lengai, the Kondoa-Irangi rock art and/or the Lake Eyasi area.

MISCELLANEOUS WARNINGS Malaria is present in most parts of the region, with the notable exception of the Ngorongoro Crater rim, and the normal precautions should be taken. Aside from malaria, there are no serious health risks attached to visiting this area. Tsetse flies are seasonally abundant in well-wooded areas such as Tarangire and the Western Corridor of the Serengeti. Sleeping sickness is not cause for serious concern, but the flies are sufficiently aggravating that it is worth applying insect repellent to your arms and legs before game drives (though this doesn't always deter tsetse flies) and avoiding the dark clothing that tends to attract them.

Tarangire can be reached via a good tar road, as can Lake Manyara and the eastern gate to the Ngorongoro Conservation Area. The **roads** within the Ngorongoro Conservation Area through to the Serengeti are very rough, for which reason safari-goers with serious back problems or a low tolerance for bumping around in the back of a vehicle might want to consider flying between the reserves. If one member of a safari party has a particular need to avoid being bumped around, they will be best off in the front passenger seat or the central row of seats – the seats above the rear axle tend to soak up the most punishment.

The combination of **dust and glare** may create problems for those with sensitive eyes. Sunglasses afford some protection against glare and dust, and if you anticipate problems of this sort, then don't forget to pack eye drops. Many people who wear contact lenses suffer in these dusty conditions, so it is a good idea to wear glasses on long drives, assuming that you have a pair. Dust and heat can damage sensitive camera equipment and film, so read over the precautions mentioned in the box, *Photographic tips*, pages 76–7.

As is standard practice in many countries, safari drivers earn a commission when their clients buy something from one of the many **curio stalls** in Mto wa Mbu and elsewhere in the region. There's nothing inherently wrong with this arrangement, but you might find that your safari driver is very keen to stop at a few stalls along the way. If this isn't what you want, then the onus is on you to make this clear the first time it happens – there's no need to be rude or confrontational, just explain gently that this isn't why you're on safari. Even if you do want to buy curios, don't fall into the obvious trap of assuming that you'll get a better deal buying locally. Many of the curios you see in places like Mto wa Mbu probably found their way there from outside, and they will generally be cheaper in Arusha than they will be at roadside stalls dealing exclusively with tourists.

Travellers on a budget camping safari who want to keep down their extra costs should be aware that **drinks**, although available at all game lodges, are very expensive. A beer at a lodge will typically cost around US$3–4, as opposed to less than US$1 in a shop or local bar, and prices of sodas are similarly inflated. It is definitely worth stocking up on mineral water in Arusha (at least one 1.5-litre bottle per person per day), since this will be a lot more expensive on the road. Once in the game reserves, some travellers might feel that it's worth spending the extra money to enjoy the occasional chilled beer or soda at a lodge. Those travellers who don't should ask their driver where to buy drinks to bring back to the campsite – there are bars aimed at drivers near to all the budget safaris' campsites, and the prices are only slightly higher than in Arusha.

Finally, and at risk of stating the obvious, it is both illegal and foolhardy to get out of your safari vehicle in the presence of any wild animal, and especially buffalo, elephant, hippo or lion.

LAKE MANYARA NATIONAL PARK

Lake Manyara is a shallow, alkaline lake set at the base of a sheer stretch of the Western Rift Valley escarpment. The northwestern part of the lake and its immediate hinterland are protected in a scenic 330km² national park whose diversity of terrestrial habitats – grassy floodplain, rocky escarpment, acacia woodland and lush groundwater forest – seems all the more remarkable given that up to two-thirds of the surface area comprises water. And this habitat diversity is reflected in Manyara's varied mammalian fauna, with buffalo, giraffe, olive baboon, blue monkey and various antelopes likely to be seen in the course of any game drive.

A notable feature of Lake Manyara is its prolific elephants, as immortalised by Iain Douglas-Hamilton in his 1970s book *Amongst the Elephants*. Although the elephant population suffered a subsequent decline due to poaching, this was not as severe as in many larger parks in southern Tanzania, and numbers are now fully recovered. The elephants in Manyara are generally very relaxed around vehicles by comparison with their counterparts in Tarangire and the southern reserves, which makes for great elephant watching – especially as there are still some serious tuskers around.

Manyara, despite its small size, is a *great* birding reserve, with almost 400 species recorded. As Duncan Butchart, writing in the CCAfrica *Ecological Journal*, noted, 'If a first-time birdwatcher to Africa had the time to visit only a single reserve in Tanzania, then Manyara must surely be it.' It's perfectly feasible for a casual birder to see 100 species here in a day, ranging from a variety of colourful bee-eaters, barbets, kingfishers and rollers to the gigantic ground hornbill and white-backed pelican. Substantial flocks of flamingo are also present when the water level is suitable. A remarkable 51 diurnal raptor species are known from the park, of which 28 are resident or regular. In addition, six species of owl are regularly recorded.

Manyara's well-defined game-viewing circuit kicks off a high proportion of safaris through northern Tanzania. And the park is a valuable addition to a safari of several days' duration, offering the opportunity to see several species that are less common or shyer elsewhere on the northern circuit. Those on shorter safaris, however, might reasonably elect to forsake Manyara's more subtle attractions for an additional day on the predator-rich plains of the Serengeti.

The booklet *Lake Manyara National Park*, published by Tanzania National Parks, gives detailed coverage of the park's flora and fauna, as does the newer booklet *Lake Manyara*, published by the African Publishing House in association with TANAPA. The park entrance fee of US$35 per person per 24 hours should ideally be paid by MasterCard or Tanapa Card (issued at any Exim Bank). No other cards are accepted, nor are travellers' cheques, and cash payments attract a 50% penalty.

GETTING THERE AND AWAY The only entrance gate to Lake Manyara lies at the northern end of the park on the outskirts of the village of Mto wa Mbu. The 120km drive from Arusha takes less than two hours following the completion of the new surfaced road from Makuyuni.

WHERE TO STAY AND EAT There is only one lodge situated within the park boundaries, the new Lake Manyara Tree Lodge. There is, however, plenty of accommodation bordering the park. Most of the tourist-class lodges are situated on the Rift Valley escarpment overlooking Lake Manyara, while the budget accommodation and campsites are dotted around the small village of Mto wa Mbu outside the main entrance gate.

Exclusive

Lake Manyara Tree Lodge (10 rooms) 027 754 8549/8038 or South Africa +27 11 809 4447; e inboundsales@andbeyond.com; www.andbeyond.com. Opened in 2003 as a replacement for the defunct Maji Moto Lodge, Lake Manyara Tree Camp is a small luxurious tented camp operated by &Beyond (formerly CCAfrica) deep in a mahogany forest about 20mins' drive south of the hot springs at Maji Moto. Like other &Beyond lodges, Lake Manyara Tree Lodge offers the ultimate in exclusive bush luxury, consisting of 10 stilted en-suite tree houses built with wood & *makuti*, & with private decks offering great views of the escarpment. Exciting walking routes run from the lodge to the lakeshore through the forest, while other facilities include a swimming pool & personal butler service. US$950 pp FB, US$625 Mar, May, Nov & early Dec, Inc all meals, drinks & activities. Closed Apr.

6

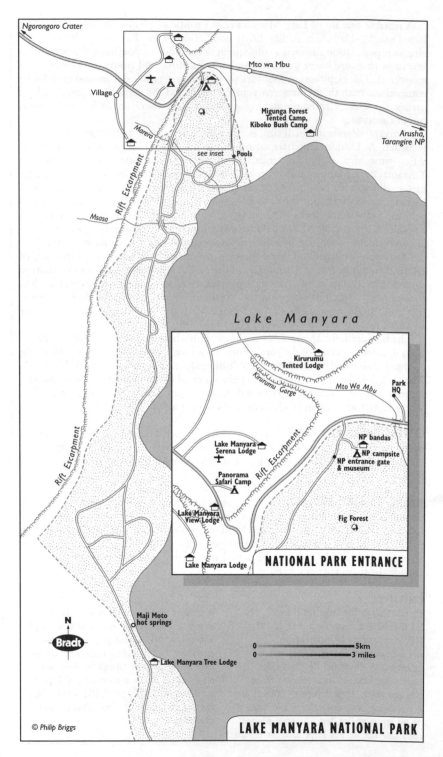

Ngorongoro Crater

Mto wa Mbu

Village

Marera

Migunga Forest
Tented Camp,
Kiboko Bush Camp

Arusha,
Tarangire NP

Rift Escarpment

Msasa

see inset   Pools

Lake Manyara

Kirurumu
Tented Lodge

Kirurumu Gorge

Mto Wa Mbu

Park
HQ

Rift Escarpment

Lake Manyara
Serena Lodge

NP bandas

NP campsite

NP entrance gate
& museum

Panorama
Safari Camp

Lake Manyara
View Lodge

Fig Forest

Lake Manyara Lodge

NATIONAL PARK ENTRANCE

Rift Escarpment

Maji Moto
hot springs

N

Bradt

0   5km
0   3 miles

Lake Manyara Tree Lodge

© Philip Briggs

LAKE MANYARA NATIONAL PARK

Upmarket

⌂ **Lake Manyara Serena Lodge** (54 rooms) ☎ 028 262 1507; **f** 028 262 1520; **e** reservations@serena.co.tz; www.serenahotels.com. This smart & popular upmarket lodge is situated on the edge of the escarpment overlooking the lake & its environs. Like other lodges in the Serena chain, it is a very appealing set-up, run through by a small wooded stream that attracts a wide range of birds including chattering flocks of breeding weavers. Adventure activities such as abseiling & mountain biking are offered by Serena Active, a company based in the lodge. Accommodation is in attractively furnished, ethnic-looking rondawels with private balconies. The buffet food is generally very good. US$375/550 sgl/dbl FB, US$225/335 Apr–Jun.

⌂ **Kirurumu Tented Lodge** (20 rooms) ☎ 027 250 7011/7541; **f** 027 254 8226; **e** info@kirirumu.net; www.kirurumu.net. Owned & managed by Hoopoe Adventure Tours, this popular tented lodge is perched on the rift escarpment to the north of the Serena, from where it offers a grand view across the plains of the Rift Valley to the north of Lake Manyara. The unpretentious rustic bush atmosphere that characterises Kirurumu contrasts strongly with that of the other more built-up lodges on the Rift escarpment, & it will be far more attractive to people who want to feel like they are sleeping in the bush rather than in a large hotel. There's plenty of small wildlife around too, ranging from bush

Moderate

⌂ **Migunga Forest Camp** (19 rooms) ☎ 027 255 3243/250 6315; **e** migunga@moivaro.com; www.moivaro.com. This well-established but little-known tented camp, recently taken over by Moivaro Lodge, shares many assets with Kirurumu, but it is considerably more downmarket in feel, & priced accordingly. Migunga has a winning location in a yellow fever forest about 2km by road from Mto wa Mbu. When the lake is high, the camp lies close to the northeast lakeshore & can be reached by a short walking trail, but at the time of writing the distance to the lake was around 5km. Reedbuck, bushbuck & buffalo sometimes pass through, while a troop of vervet monkeys is more or less resident & the lesser bushbaby is often seen at night. Roughly 70 acacia-associated bird species have been recorded within the camp. Accommodation is in comfortable dbl standing tents with en-suite hot showers. Price-wise, it's an excellent compromise between the smarter but more expensive lodges & the relatively utilitarian accommodation in Mto wa

squirrels to foot-long yellow-speckled plated lizards by day to hedgehogs & bushbabies by night – plus a wide variety of birds. The food is good & the service friendly & efficient. Accommodation is in comfortable & secluded en-suite dbl tents, each of which has a private veranda. US$176/249 sgl/dbl B&B or US$238/386 FB high season, US$105 pp FB low season.

⌂ **Lake Manyara Lodge** (100 rooms) ☎ 027 254 4595; **f** 027 254 8633; **e** res@hotelsandlodges-tanzania.com; www.hotelsandlodges-tanzania.com. The oldest & most spectacularly located of the lodges that line the escarpment above Lake Manyara, this former government property fell into a terribly run-down state in the 1990s, & it remains somewhat architecturally confrontational. That said, the new private management embarked on an ambitious facelift during 2008, & the renovated & redecorated common areas & en-suite rooms are now in line with other similarly priced lodges on the northern safari circuit. A definite attraction of this lodge is the attractively wooded grounds centred upon a large swimming pool, but its single best feature remains the peerless view over Manyara's groundwater forest & lake, with the Rift Valley hills fading to the horizon. With binoculars, you should be able to pick out elephants, giraffes & buffaloes on the Rift Valley floor; closer to home, there is good birding within the lodge grounds. Rates on application.

Mbu. US$206/257 sgl/dbl FB, low-season discount Apr & May.

⌂ **Kiboko Bush Camp** (12 rooms) ☎ 027 253 9152; **e** kibokotz@yahoo.co.uk; www.equatorialsafaris.com. Situated a few hundred metres away from Migunga, & similar in price & standard, though with a more nondescript setting, this new camp provides comfortable accommodation in en-suite standing tents, each with 2 three-quarter beds & set on a stilted wooden platform with a small private veranda. Once again, it's good value. US$100 pp FB. Camping US$5 pp.

⌂ **Lake Manyara View Lodge** (10 rooms) ☎ 027 250 1329; **m** 0732 978474; reservations@lakemanyaraview.com; www.lakemanyaraview.com. This recently constructed lodge rises above the Rift Valley escarpment alongside the main asphalt road between Mto wa Mbu & Karatu. In common with other lodges along the escarpment, it offers stunning views over Lake Manyara & Rift Valley floor, but its enormous potential is totally undermined by the unfinished look of the common areas (including an empty swimming pool) & general aura of operating with all lights dimmed. Nothing wrong with the en-suite rooms, however, & the ambience & service must surely improve once the lodge becomes more settled. *US$60/100 to US$150/170 sgl/dbl B&B, depending on season & room type; FB US$30 pp more.*

Budget and camping

🏠 **Njake Jambo Lodge & Campsite** (16 rooms) ➲ 027 250 1329; e info@njake.com; www.njake.com. Following extensive renovations over recent years, this once rather low-key campsite in the heart of Mto wa Mbu is now a top quality budget lodge, offering accommodation in 4 double-storey blocks, each containing 4 smart en-suite rooms with 2 four-poster beds with netting, satellite TV, fridge, telephone & tiled bathroom with hot shower. The large green gardens also host a restaurant, bar & large swimming pool area, as well as a shady campsite. It lacks the bush atmosphere of pricier lodges, but still seems excellent value. *Rooms US$60/90 sgl/dbl B&B, US$50/60 low season; camping US$7.*

🏠 **Twiga Campsite & Lodge** m 0754 288430; e twigacampsite@yahoo.com; www.twigacampsite.com. Once the pick of several locally run lodges in Mto wa Mbu, Twiga lies in neatly cropped gardens in the heart of town. It consists of a spacious campsite, popular with budget safari operators, & a block of large self-contained dbl rooms with hot water & nets. There is a 'wild video show' in the lounge every evening, a good restaurant, & a recently constructed swimming pool to flop around in by day. It remains a likeable set-up, but it's not as smart or well managed as Njake Jambo, & overall it seems like poor value by comparison. *Camping US$10 pp, dbl US$70 (old wing) to US$110 (new wing).*

🏠 **National Park Bandas & Campsite** ➲ 027 250 3471/4082; f 027 250 8216; e info@ tanzaniaparks.com; www.tanzaniaparks.com. Situated in a lovely forest glade immediately outside the national park entrance gate, this is easily the most inherently attractive place to stay in this price category, & comparatively good value too. Clean self-contained brick *bandas* have hot water but no net – the latter a serious omission in Mto wa Mbu. Facilities include a kitchen & dining area, & an elevated tree house looking into the forest canopy. *US$30 pp camping or US$20 pp banda accommodation for non-residents.*

🏕 **Migunga Campsite** ➲ 027 255 3243 or 250 6315; e migunga@moivaro.com; www.moivaro.com. Situated alongside the eponymous tented camp & under the same management, this campsite boasts a stunning setting amid the yellow fever trees, & facilities include hot showers – highly recommended. *US$5 pp.*

🏕 **Panorama Safari Camp** m 0755 118514. Boasting a prime location on the escarpment overlooking the lake, this relatively new campsite set only 500m from the main asphalt road towards Karatu forms an attractively located alternative to the more mundane cheapies in town. There's a clean shower & toilet block with running hot water, & other facilities include a bar & restaurant, though the swimming pool that was due to be constructed a few years back has yet to materialise. *Large standing tent with bedding & towel Tsh7,000 pp; camping in your own tent Tsh4,000.*

WHAT TO SEE AND DO

Game drives For logistical reasons, most safari operators visit the national park in the afternoon. But there's much to be said for doing an additional morning game drive, starting as soon as possible after the entrance gate opens at 06.30. Manyara is wonderfully and unexpectedly peaceful in the morning, and you'll probably see fewer other vehicles over two or three hours than you would in five minutes in the late afternoon. By being the first car through the gate, you also stand a chance of disturbing one of the park's profuse but skittish leopards before it vanishes into the thickets for the day.

All game drives start at the entrance gate, which lies on the northern boundary near Mto wa Mbu. From the entrance gate, the main road winds for several kilometres through a cool, lush, mature groundwater forest dominated by large ficus trees and a tangle of green epiphytes. With appropriate jungle noises supplied by outsized silvery-cheeked hornbills, this is one part of the northern safari circuit that might conjure up images of Tarzan swinging into view. It's a good place to see olive baboons (Manyara supports a density of 2,500 baboons per 100km^2), which plonk themselves down alongside the road, sometimes in the company of the smaller and more beautiful blue monkey. The shy bushbuck might also be encountered here, but otherwise the main point of faunal interest is the diversity of birds and butterflies.

The road emerges from the forest on to the northern floodplain, where a series of small pools on the Mto wa Mbu River supports a wide variety of birds, notably giant kingfisher and African and painted snipe. This is a lovely spot, too, with the Rift Valley escarpment rising to the west, and the sparsely vegetated floodplain of Lake Manyara stretching to the south. Giraffes are common in this area, many of them so dark in colour that they appear to be almost melanistic. The nearby hippo pool was submerged for several years following the El Niño floods of 1997–8, causing the hippos to relocate to the main lake, but it has since re-emerged and harbours several dozen soaking, yawning hippos, as well as an impressive selection of waterbirds. An ongoing relic of the El Niño floods is the ghost forest of dead tree stumps lining the floodplain between the fig forest and the lakeshore.

For large mammals, the best road runs inland of the lake to the Maji Moto (literally 'Hot Water') springs in the south. The tangled acacia woodland here offers views across the floodplain, where you should see large herds of zebra and wildebeest, and the occasional warthog, impala, Kirk's dik-dik and giraffe. The acacia woodland is the place to look out for the famous tree-climbing lions of Manyara (see box, pages 148–9) – though on an afternoon game drive, the safari driver grapevine is bound to ensure that you know about any arboreal lions long before you encounter them. The marshy area around the hot springs reliably harbours waterbuck and plenty of buffaloes, while several pairs of klipspringer are resident on the rocky escarpment base towards the southern end of the park.

Other activities An exciting aspect of Lake Manyara is a varied selection of mild adventure activities operated exclusively by Green Footprint Adventures for Serena Active, which is based out of the Manyara Serena Lodge, but takes on guests staying

6

MTO WA MBU

This village, which lies close to the Lake Manyara entrance gate, sees a large volume of tourist traffic and is said locally to be the only place in Tanzania where representatives of 120 Tanzanian tribes are resident. Mto wa Mbu is the normal base for budget safaris visiting Lake Manyara, and even if you aren't staying in the village or visiting Lake Manyara, your safari driver will probably stop at the huge curio market in the hope of picking up a commission. Mto wa Mbu (pronounced as one word) means River of Mosquitoes, and if you do spend the night here, you'll be in no doubt about how it got its name. By day, the curio dealers who will swarm around you the moment you leave your vehicle might draw an obvious analogy.

A clutch of inexpensive walking tours out of Mto wa Mbu have been set up as part of a cultural tourism programme with the assistance of SNV. One of the most interesting of these walks is the papyrus lake tour, which takes you to the Miwaleni waterfall, as well as to a papyrus lake where Rangi people collect basket- and mat-weaving material, and to the homesteads of Sandawe hunter-gatherers. Other tours take you to Balaa Hill, which boasts excellent views over the village and lake, and to Chagga farms and Maasai bomas. The tourism programme is run out of the Red Banana Restaurant in the centre of the village, where you must pay your fees, arrange a guide and (if you like) rent a bicycle, as well as paying the mandatory village development fee.

at other lodges in the area. These activities offer safari-goers tired of bouncing around dusty roads within the confines of a vehicle the opperty to stretch their legs or arms in natural surrounds. No experience is required for any of the activities, and all equipment is supplied at no extra cost. On-the-spot enquiries are welcomed, but bookings can be made through any safari operator or directly through Serena Active (✆ 027 254 4635; m 0784 203 0000; e info@greenfootprint.co.tz; www.serenahotels.com/serena-active.htm or www.greenfootprint.co.tz).

The most popular of these activities is mountain biking down the Rift Valley escarpment, with a variety of itineraries available. Also offered are an afternoon walk through the groundwater forest in the Kirurumu Gorge outside the national park entrance, and a village walk with a local guide through agricultural areas around Mto wa Mbu. For more hardcore adventurers, there is the option of abseiling down the rift escarpment above the lake with a qualified instructor. Canoeing on Lake Manyara may one day be resumed if the water level is sufficiently high. Most of these activities cost around US$50–70 per person. A more recent – and costly – addition to the programme is a microlight flight over the lake or (if you like) as far north as Natron.

THE TREE-CLIMBING LIONS OF MANYARA

Lake Manyara National Park is famous for its tree-climbing lions, which, unlike conventional lions, habitually rest up in the branches for most of the day, to the excitement of those lucky tourists who chance upon them. But while the tree-climbing phenomenon is well documented, the explanation behind it remains largely a matter of conjecture.

In the 1960s, Stephen Makacha undertook research into lion behaviour at Manyara to compare with similar studies being conducted by George Schaller in the Serengeti. In Schaller's book, *The Serengeti Lion: A Study of Predator–Prey Relations*, he noted that:

> The lions in the Lake Manyara National Park climbed trees far more often than those in the Serengeti. They were resting in trees on two-thirds of the occasions on which we encountered them during the day… The reason why Manyara lions rest in trees so often is unknown. Fosbrooke noted that lions in the Ngorongoro Crater ascended trees during an epidemic of biting flies, but this is an unusual situation… and the vegetation in the various parks is in many respects so similar that no correlation between it and tree climbing is evident. The Manyara lions sometimes escaped from buffalo and elephant by climbing trees, but there would seem to be no reason for lions to remain in them all day because of the remote chance that they might have to climb one. I think that the behaviour represents a habit, one that may have been initiated by, for example, a prolonged fly epidemic, and has since been transmitted culturally.

Schaller's suggestion that the lions were climbing trees to avoid flies made the most sense to me, but I had also heard that the lions climbed to enjoy the cool breezes that came off the lake, and to keep a lookout for prey and threats. So I decided to make notes whenever I saw the lions in order to explore these theories. For every sighting I noted whether flies were present on the ground or in the trees; the temperature and breeze conditions; whether buffalo or elephant were in the vicinity; how high up the tree the lions were and the view it afforded; and the species of tree.

In the 1960s, Iain Douglas-Hamilton noted that on 80% of the occasions when tree-climbing lions were observed, they were in one of just 17 individual trees. These favoured trees were so well known to park guides at the time that they were given

The vast majority of Serengeti safaris head directly west from Manyara along the new asphalt road that climbs the Rift Valley escarpment into the Ngorongoro Highlands, and then return to Arusha exactly the same way. An offbeat alternative to this well-trodden route, one that will transform your safari itinerary into a genuine loop, is the spine-jarring 265km road that connects Mto wa Mbu to the northern Serengeti via the parched stretch of the Rift Valley abutting the border with Kenya. This is not, it should be stressed, a route that should instil any great enthusiasm in anybody who nurses a dodgy back or chronic agoraphobia, or who has limited tolerance for simple travel conditions. But equally this half-forgotten corner of northern Tanzania also possesses some genuinely alluring off-the-beaten-track landmarks in the form of the ruined city of Engaruka, the malevolent Lake Natron, and above all perhaps the fiery volcanic majesty of Ol Doinyo Lengai.

Most experienced safari operators can arrange trips to the northern Rift Valley, taking Lake Natron as their focal point, but many will also discourage you from visiting the area as it is rough on vehicles and has been prone to outbursts of banditry in the past. Technically, it is possible to travel between Mto wa Mbu and

particular names and – to protect them from debarking and destruction by elephants – wrapped in coils of wire mesh. My observations indicated a similar pattern. Lions were found to be resting in trees on about half of the times they were sighted, and although six different tree species were used, three – Acacia tortilis, Kigelia africana and Balanites aegyptiaca – accounted for 90% of sightings. Specific trees were usually favoured, and the lions often moved a considerable distance to reach them.

In most cases the lions were seen to be resting during the heat of the day, and they would usually come down at dusk. Only 5% of sightings coincided with hot weather and breezy conditions, and at most sightings there was no significant breeze, so it seems unlikely that the lions climb to escape the heat. Although buffalo have been documented killing lions at Manyara, there was never any sign of the lions taking to trees to avoid harassment. Most of the time the lions were found to be resting approximately 5–6m above the ground, which afforded them a better view of their surroundings, but since the trees were normally in densely vegetated areas, it would have been difficult for them to observe any potential prey or threat.

My conclusions were similar to those of Makacha and Schaller. Although lions that I found resting on the ground were apparently not greatly concerned by biting flies, lions observed in trees were surrounded by flies in only 10% of cases, when flies were present on the ground below them about 60% of the time. Because the lions generally rested above 5m and flies were seldom encountered at this height, it seems likely that the behaviour was originally initiated during a fly epidemic, and it has since been passed on culturally. I observed the cubs of the Maji pride begin their attempts to climb up to the adults when they were about seven or eight months old. It seemed definitely to be a case of 'lion see lion do', as there was no apparent reason why they should have climbed. Once they had mastered climbing, they too spent a lot of time playing and climbing up and down the trees. More thorough research would be required to fully understand the reasons for this unusual and fascinating behaviour.

Edited from *Notes on Tree-climbing Lions of Manyara* by Kevin Pretorius, a former manager of Maji Moto Lodge, as originally published in the *CCAfrica Ecological Journal*, volume 2:79–81 (2000). The journal can be ordered online at www.wildwatch.com.

the northern Serengeti via Natron in nine to ten hours of flat driving, but it would make for a very long day and would rather defeat the point of the exercise. More realistic is to split the drive over two days, stopping for a night at the lakeshore village of Ngare Sero, or two nights if you intend to climb Ol Doinyo Lengai or undertake any other exploration of the region. It is common practice to tag this area on to the end of a safari, but there is a strong case for slotting it in between the Tarangire/Manyara and Ngorongoro/Serengeti legs of your itinerary, if for no other reason than it would break up the vehicle-bound regime of game drives with a decent leg-stretch – whether you opt for a gentle stroll around the Engaruka Ruins or the southern shore of Natron, the slightly more demanding hike to the Ngare Sero Waterfall in the escarpment west of Natron, or the decidedly challenging nocturnal ascent of Ol Doinyo Lengai.

If you visit this area in your own vehicle, treat it as you would any wilderness trip: carry adequate supplies of food, water and fuel. If you go with a safari company, avoid those at the lower end of the price scale, or you risk getting stuck in the middle of nowhere in a battered vehicle. Note that the scenic 160km road between Natron and Klein's Gate suffered a spate of unrest in 1998–99, instigated by Somali exiles from Kenya. The insurgents killed at least one police officer and several local Maasai, and a tourist vehicle was attacked near Loliondo, fortunately without any fatalities. The situation has been stable for a few years now, but still you are advised to make enquiries with a specialised operator.

ENGARUKA RUINS Situated below the Rift Valley escarpment about 65km north of Manyara, Engaruka is the Maasai name for the extensive ruins of a mysterious terraced city and irrigation system constructed at least 500 years ago by a late Iron Age culture in the eastern foothills of Mount Empakaai. Nobody knows for sure who built the city: some say it was the Mbulu, who inhabited the area immediately before the Maasai arrived there; others that it was built by Datoga settlers from the north. Locally, the city is said to have been home to forebears of the Sukuma, whose greeting 'mwanga lukwa' was later bastardised to Engaruka by the Maasai – more likely, however, that the name of this well-watered spot has roots in the Maasai word ngare (water).

The discovery of the ruins by outsiders is generally credited to Dr Fischer, who followed the base of the Rift Valley through Maasailand in 1883, and wrote how 'peculiar masses of stone became suddenly apparent, rising from the plain to heights up to ten feet. Partly they looked like mouldering tree trunks, partly like the tumbled down walls of ancient castles.' An older reference to Engaruka can be found on the so-called Slug Map drawn up by the missionaries Krapf and Erhardt in 1855. The first person to excavate the site was Hans Reck in the early 20th century, followed by the legendary Louis Leakey, who reckoned it consisted of seven large villages containing roughly 1,000 homes apiece and thought the total population must have exceeded 30,000.

The ruined villages overlook a complex stone-block irrigation system that extends over some 25km² and is fed by the perennial Engaruka River. This highly specialised and integrated agricultural community was abandoned in the 18th century, probably due to a combination of changes in the local hydrology and the immigration of more militaristic pastoralist tribes from the north. Yet Engaruka is unique only in scale, since a number of smaller deserted sites in the vicinity form part of the same cultural and agricultural complex, and recent radiocarbon dating suggests it might be older than has been assumed in the past – possibly as old as the 4th century AD, which would make it a likely precursor to the great centralised empires that thrived in pre-colonial Uganda and Rwanda.

Guided tours of the ruins can be arranged easily in Engaruka village – the Engaruka Ruins Campsite is as good a place to ask around as any. Without a local guide, it's debatable whether the ruins would convey anything much to the average passing tourist. The floor plan of the main village is still quite clear, and a few of the circular stone houses remain more or less intact to around waist level, their floors strewn with shards of broken earthenware. Substantial sections of the irrigation canal are still in place, as are some old burial mounds that might or might not be related to the war with the Maasai that caused the village to be abandoned.

Getting there and away The ruins can be reached by forking westward at the modern village of Engaruka, which is almost exactly halfway along the 120km road between Mto wa Mbu and Ngare Sero, and takes about 90 minutes to reach coming in either direction. From the junction, continue through the semi-urban sprawl of Engaruka for about 5km until you reach the Jerusalem Campsite, from where it is a ten-minute walk to the nearest ruined village. No entrance fee is charged, but the local guides will expect to be paid around US$5 per party to show you around. At least one bus daily connects Arusha to Engaruka, leaving Arusha from opposite the Shoprite at 10.00 and passing through Mto wa Mbu at around 14.00 before dropping passengers at the station next to the Engaruka Ruins Campsite at around 18.00.

Where to stay

Å **Engaruka Ruins Campsite** 077 253 9103 or 0455 507939; e engaruka@yahoo.com. Set in compact green grounds next to the bus station, this friendly campsite has the best facilities in town, including hot running water, electricity, flush toilets, a bar & a restaurant. The staff can arrange guided tours of the ruins for a nominal fee, as well as visits to local Maasai bomas & traditional dancing displays. Guided ascents of Ol Doinyo Lengai arranged through the campsite work out at around US$50 pp, & the camp can also lay on 4x4 transport to/from the base of the mountain for US$120 one-way for up to 4 or 5 people. US$7 pp.

Å **Jerusalem Campsite** Set in a pretty grove close to the ruins, this site has no facilities other than toilets, making it more suitable for groups than for independent travellers. US$5 pp.

LAKE NATRON There are but a handful of places where the Rift Valley evokes its geologically violent origins with graphic immediacy. Ethiopia's Danakil Desert is one such spot; the volcanic Virunga Range in the Albertine Rift is another. And so too is the most northerly landmark in the Tanzanian Rift Valley, the low-lying Lake Natron, a shallow sliver of exceptionally alkaline water that extends southward from the Kenya border near Mount Shompole for 58km. The Natron skyline is dominated by the textbook volcanic silhouette of Ol Doinyo Lengai, which rises more than 2,000m above the Rift Valley floor, its harsh black contours softened by an icing of white ash that glistens brightly below the sun, as if in parody of Kilimanjaro's snows. Then there is the lake itself, a thrillingly primordial phenomenon whose caustic waters are enclosed by a crust of sodden grey volcanic ash and desiccated salt, punctuated by isolated patches of steamy, reed-lined swamp where the hot springs that sustain the lake bubble to the surface.

Thought to be about 1.5 million years old, Natron is a product of the same tectonic activity that formed the Ngorongoro Highlands and Mount Gelai, the latter being an extinct volcano that rises from the eastern lakeshore. Nowhere more than 50cm deep, it has changed shape significantly since that time, largely as a result of volcanic activity associated with the creation of Ol Doinyo Lengai to its immediate south. It lies at an elevation of 610m in an unusually arid stretch of the rift floor, receiving an average of 400mm of rainfall annually, and it would have probably dried out centuries ago were it not also fed by the freshwater Ewaso

6

Ngiro River, which has its catchment in the central Kenyan Highlands, and the hot springs that rise below its floor. The alkaline level has also increased drastically over the millennia, partially because of the high salinity of ash and lava deposits from Lengai, partially because the lake's only known outlet is evaporation. Today, depending on recent rainfall, the viscous water has an average pH of 9–11, making it almost as caustic as ammonia when the level is very low, and it can reach a temperature of up to 60°C in extreme circumstances.

Natron's hyper-salinity makes it incapable of sustaining any but the most specialised life forms. The only resident vertebrate is the endemic white-lipped tilapia *Oreochromis alcalica*, a 10cm-long fish that congregates near hot spring inlets where the water temperature is around 36–40°C. The microbiology of the lake is dominated by halophytic (salt-loving) organisms such as Spirulina, a form of blue-green algae whose red pigments make the salt-encrusted flats in the centre of the lake look bright red when seen from the air. Natron is also the only known breeding ground for East Africa's 2.5 million lesser flamingoes, which usually congregate there between August and October, feeding on the abundant algae (whose pigments are responsible for the birds' trademark pink hue). The breeding ground's inhospitality to potential predators makes it an ideal flamingo nursery, but it also makes it difficult to access for human visitors – situated in the centre of the lake, it was discovered as recently as the 1950s and it can only be seen from the air today. In addition to the flamingoes, Natron attracts up to 100,000 migrant waterbirds during the European winter, and its hinterland supports a thin population of large mammals typical of the Rift Valley, including wildebeest, zebra, fringe-eared oryx, Grant's and Thomson's gazelle, and even the odd lion and cheetah.

Getting there and away The centre of tourist activity on Natron is the small lakeshore village of Ngare Sero, bisected by the wooded freshwater stream from which its Maasai name is derived ('black water', 'clear water', 'dappled water' or 'forest of water', depending on who's doing the translating). The village lies about 120km north of Mto wa Mbu along a very rough road – bank on a four-hour drive, though this might improve if and when bridges are built across the larger watercourses north of Engaruka. The village is about 160km from Klein's Gate in the northern Serengeti, a drive that takes five to six hours without stops, and involves a spectacular ascent (or descent) of the Rift escarpment to the west of the lake. There is no public transport to Ngare Sero, but buses do run twice daily as far as Engaruka, where you can hire a 4x4 to Natron and/or Lengai from the Engaruka Ruins Campsite.

Where to stay

Lake Natron Camp (9 rooms) ❜ 027 255 3243/ 250 6315; e reservations@moivaro.com; www.moivaro.com. Established in Ngare Sero in 1989, this low-key camp has a spectacular setting alongside a stream some 4km from the southern lakeshore, & offers great views across the floodplain to Mount Gerai, an extinct volcano less impressive in outline but actually marginally taller than nearby Lengai. Though it has a decidedly no-frills feel in keeping with the austere surrounds, the camp does have a welcoming swimming pool, & there's a pleasant restaurant & bar area. Accommodation is in en-suite tents with hot water. Inexpensive organised guided climbs of nearby Ol Doinyo Lengai are offered too. *US$240/300 sgl/dbl FB; low-season*

discount Apr & May, premium charged over Christmas period.

Riverside Campsite (5 rooms) ❜ 027 250 7145; f 027 250 8035; e info@sunnysafaris.com or sunny@arusha.com. This new campsite is run by a local Maasai elder & set alongside the river running through Ngare Sero. *US$50 pp FB bed in basic en-suite twin standing tent with netting; US$10 pp to pitch a tent on the lawn.*

Waterfall Campsite Situated a kilometre or two out of town close to the starting point for the walk to Ngare Sero Waterfall, this basic campsite has a great location but it seems very overpriced. *US$10 pp to pitch a tent.*

What to see

Southern lakeshore To reach the southern lakeshore from Ngare Sero, you need to drive for around 5km to an unofficial parking spot about 1km from the water's edge, then walk for about ten minutes across salt-encrusted flats to a series of pockmarked black volcanic protrusions that serve as vantage points over the water. It's a lovely spot, with Lengai looming in the background, and it hosts a profusion of waterbirds, most visibly large flocks of the pink-tinged lesser flamingo, but also various pelicans, egrets, herons and waders. Wildebeest and zebra are also often seen in the area. If your driver doesn't know the way to the lakeshore – it's a rather obscure track – then ask for a local guide at one of the campsites. Whatever else you do, don't let the driver take the vehicle beyond the tracks left behind by his predecessors, or you run a serious risk of getting stuck in the treacherously thin saline crust that surrounds the lake.

Ngare Sero Waterfall The Ngare Sero River forms a series of pretty waterfalls as it descends from the Nguruman Escarpment west of Lake Natron. The lowest two falls can be reached by driving out to Waterfall Campsite, then following the river upstream on foot for 45–60 minutes, through the gorge it has carved into the escarpment wall. If you are not already sufficiently doused by the time you reach the second waterfall, there's a chilly natural swimming pool below it. There is no clear footpath through the gorge: you will need to wade across the river several times (potentially dangerous after heavy rain) and can also expect to do a fair bit of clambering along ledges and rocks. This walk can only be recommended to reasonably fit and agile travellers, and it's advisable to take somebody who knows the way to help you navigate a couple of tricky stretches – a guide can be arranged at any of the camps listed above.

Ol Doinyo Lengai Estimated to be around 350,000–400,000 years old, Ol Doinyo Lengai – the Maasai 'Mountain of God' – is one of the youngest volcanoes in East Africa and possibly the most active. Its crater is known to have experienced almost continuous low-key activity since 1883, when Dr Fischer, the first European to pass through this part of Maasailand, observed smoke rising from the summit and was told secondhand that the mountain regularly emitted rumbling noises. At least a dozen minor or major eruptions have occurred since then. An interesting feature of Lengai is that it is the only active volcano known to emit carbonate lava, a form of molten rock that contains almost no silicon, is about 50% cooler than other forms of lava at around 500°C, and is also exceptionally fluid, with a viscosity comparable to water.

During one recent eruption, in 2004, plumes in the crater could be seen from as far away as Ngare Sero and many local Maasai herdsmen moved their livestock out of the area. The mountain once again experienced a high level of volcanic activity between July 2007 and June 2008. On 18 July 2007, tremors emanating from the mountain measured 6.0 on the Richter scale and were felt as far away as Nairobi city. It erupted spectacularly on 4 September, creating an ashen steamy plume stretching almost 20km downwind and sending fresh lava flows along the north and west flanks. Eruptions continued intermittently into mid 2008, with further eruptions occurring in March and April. It has quietened down since then, but further eruptions during the lifespan of this edition are more than likely.

An increasingly popular option with adventurous travellers is the ascent of Lengai, which passes through some magnificently arid scenery and offers spectacular views back towards the Rift Valley, before leading to the bleakly visceral lunar landscape of the crater, studded with ash cones, lava pools, steam vents and other evidence of volcanic activity. Suitable only for reasonably fit and agile travellers, the track to the top of Lengai is very steep, climbing in elevation from

The most impressive eruption of Ol Doinyo Lengai in recorded history occurred in the latter part of 1966, when ashfall was reported as far away as Seronera, more than 100km to the west, as well as at Loliondo and Shombole, both some 70km further north. It is believed that the otherwise inexplicable death of large numbers of game around Empakaai Crater in that year was a result of an ashfall that coated the grass up to 2cm deep, though it is unclear whether the animals starved to death or succumbed to a toxin within the ash. The effect on Maasai livestock was also devastating, according to Tepilit Ole Saitoti, who recalled the incident as follows in his excellent book, *Worlds of a Maasai Warrior*:

In the year 1966, God, who my people believe dwells in this holy mountain, unleashed Her fury unsparingly. The mountain thunder shook the earth, and the volcanic flame, which came from deep down in the earth's crust, was like a continuous flash of lightning. During days when the eruption was most powerful, clouds of smoke and steam appeared. Many cattle died and still more would die. Poisonous volcanic ash spewed all over the land as far as 100 miles away, completely covering the pastures and the leaves of trees. Cattle swallowed ash each time they tried to graze and were weakened. They could not wake up without human assistance. We had to carry long wooden staffs to put under the fallen animals to lift them up. There must have been more than enough reason for God to have unleashed Her anger on us, and all we could do was pray for mercy. My pastoral people stubbornly braved the gusting warm winds as they approached the flaming mountain to pray. Women and men dressed in their best walked in stately lines towards God, singing. The mountain was unappeased and cattle died in the thousands. Just before the people started dying too, my father decided to move; as he put it: 'We must move while we still have children, or else we will all lose them.

around 800m to over 2,878m, while the descent can be very tough on knees and ankles. The climb normally takes five to six hours along slopes practically bereft of shade, for which reason many locals recommend leaving at midnight to avoid the intense heat and to reach the crater rim in time for sunrise. If you ascend by day, a 05.00 start is advised, and precautions should be taken against dehydration and sunstroke. Either way, the descent takes about two hours.

Most adventure safari operators in Arusha offer guided Lengai climbs, but it is also possible to arrange a one-day climb locally for around US$50 per person. The best place to pick up a reliable guide is either at Engaruka Ruins Campsite or at one of the camps dotted around Ngare Sero. The mountain lies outside any conservation area, so no park fees are charged, but you may be required to pay a daily fee of around US$20 per person. If you are thinking of sleeping on the mountain, then it is strongly recommended that you set up camp in the inactive south crater rather than the active north crater – not only is it far more pleasant to camp in the south crater, but you also don't run the risk of your camp being engulfed by an unexpected lava flow or bombarded by eruptive rocks. All hikers should be aware that the cones on the crater floor can easily collapse under pressure and they often cover deadly lava lakes. Under no circumstances should you climb on a cone, or walk inside a partially collapsed cone. It is inadvisable to climb the mountain altogether during periods of high activity.

For further information on the Ol Doinyo Lengai, check out the excellent websites www.mtsu.edu/~fbelton/lengai.html (good practical information) and http://it.stlawu.edu/~cnya/ (with detailed geological background).

KARATU

This small, dusty town straddling the main road between Manyara and Ngorongoro may not look like much when you pass through coming from Arusha, but it is probably the most populous settlement anywhere along the 400km length of the B142 between Arusha and Mwanza. Tourists on a lodge-based safari typically pass through Karatu in the blink of an eye *en route* to Ngorongoro or the Serengeti, but the town does boast a fair selection of tourist facilities, including several restaurants, guesthouses, filling stations and shops. The Ngorongoro Camp & Lodge in the town centre has the most affordable internet connection in the region, and the nearby National Bank of Commerce offers good foreign exchange facilities and an ATM where local currency can be drawn against Visa cards.

Nicknamed 'safari junction', Karatu and its environs form a popular stopover for budget camping safaris, since camping is a lot cheaper here than in the Ngorongoro Conservation Area (NCA), but it's also a useful base for day trips into Ngorongoro Crater. The farmland west of Karatu also hosts an ever-growing number of more exclusive lodges built to supplement the limited bed space in the NCA, and these too are routinely used as bases for crater game drives. Note, however, that sleeping outside the NCA precludes the sort of very early start that allows you to get the most from a trip into Ngorongoro Crater. Another worthwhile overnight trip (or, at a push, day trip) out of Karatu is to Lake Eyasi and one of the Hadza settlements in the surrounding area (see box, *The last hunter-gatherers*, pages 158–9).

GETTING THERE AND AWAY Karatu is now connected to Mto wa Mbu and Arusha by a good asphalt road and the drive from Mto wa Mbu takes about one hour. Regular buses connect Karatu to Arusha via Mto wa Mbu, and the Ngorongoro Camp & Lodge in Karatu rents 4x4 vehicles for day safaris to Ngorongoro and Manyara.

WHERE TO STAY
Exclusive

Gibb's Farm (18 rooms) ☎ 027 250 8930; f 027 250 8930; e reservations@gibbsfarm.net; www.gibbsfarm.net. This small boutique hotel, once a rather low-key & idiosyncratic farm retreat on the eastern border of the NCA, has blossomed into one of the most sumptuously exclusive lodges anywhere in northern Tanzania following radical renovations in 2008. It lies 6km from Karatu along a rough dirt road, on an active coffee estate bordering an extensive patch of indigenous forest on the Ngorongoro footslopes. The main building, a converted 1920s farmhouse, retains a strong period feel with its red polished cement floor, tall bay windows, hearty home-style 4-course meals, & leather & wood furnishing, & its colonial ambience is far removed

from the relative uniformity that characterises so many upmarket lodges in northern Tanzania. The exquisite suites combine a more contemporary feel with farmhouse rusticity, & are seriously spacious, with 2 dbl beds in each bedroom, varnished wood floors, comfy armchairs, lovely views from the balcony, & the choice of indoor or outdoor shower. The lodge is a popular base for day trips into the Ngorongoro Crater (though it does have the disadvantage of lying away from the spectacular crater rim) & other activities include bird walks with the resident naturalist, cultural & farm excursions, a 2hr hike to a waterfall & cave made by elephants on the forested slopes of the crater, & a spa & massage room. There is no TV or swimming pool. *US$514/744 sgl/dbl FB.*

Upmarket

Ngorongoro Farm House (50 rooms) ☎ 027 254 4556; m 0784 207727; f 027 250 8937; e twc-reservations@habari.co.tz; www.tanganyikawildernesscamps.com. Situated on a

large coffee farm about halfway between Karatu & the NCA, this stylish new lodge offers luxurious en-suite accommodation in 3 separate camps of large semi-detached thatched cottages with views across what will eventually be a 9-hole golf course to the forested slopes of Ngorongoro. There's a very pleasant swimming pool area & the restaurant serves good country-style cooking. In terms of location, it doesn't quite match up to the lodges on the crater rim, but it's much smaller & has a less packaged feel than most lodges set within the NCA. Guided nature walks, mountain biking & other leg stretching activities are on offer too. *US$300/400 sgl/dbl FB.*

⌂ **Tloma Mountain Lodge** (20 rooms) ✆ 027 254 4556; m 0784 207727; f 027 250 8937; e twc-reservations@habari.co.tz; www.tanganyikawildernesscamps.com. Situated about 1km from Gibb's Farm & sharing a similarly lovely view over the forested Ngorongoro footslopes, this attractive new lodge is set in spacious grounds that lead down to a wooden deck enclosing a large swimming pool. Accommodation is in large, cosy earth-coloured cottages with colonial-style green

corrugated iron roofs, screte floors, wood ceilings, fireplaces, 4-poster king-size or twin beds, & a large bathroom with shower. The food is excellent, & facilities include birdwatching tours, massage, village walks, internet, coffee plantation demonstrations & the obligatory day tours to Ngorongoro Crater. *US$300/400 sgl/dbl FB.*

⌂ **Plantation Lodge** (16 rooms) ✆ 027 253 4364/5; m 0744 393180; e info@plantation-lodge.com; www.plantation-lodge.com. This popular German-owned lodge is set in flowering grounds only 2km from the Ngorongoro road a few kilometres out of Karatu. It has a classic whitewash & thatch exterior, complemented by the stylish décor of the spacious self-contained rooms, making for a refreshingly individualistic contrast to the chain lodges that characterise the northern circuit, while also forming a good base for day trips to Ngorongoro Crater. *US$270/390 sgl/dbl FB.*

Moderate

⌂ **Bougainvillea Lodge** (24 rooms) ✆ 027 253 4063; f 027 253 4600; e bougainvillea@ habari.co.tz; www.bougainvillealodge.net. Owned & managed by the highly regarded Tanzanian chef Reggie Bayo, this comfortable new lodge lies in large but characterless gardens about 300m from the main road towards NCA just outside Karatu. For budget conscious tourists it's a decent compromise between quality & cost, offering unpretentious

accommodation in neat & comfortably decorated tiled cottages set in a circle around the swimming pool area. All cottages have twin or king-size beds with netting, a fan, a fireplace, a sitting area with cane furniture & a private balcony facing the pool. The lodge serves good meals & has a gift shop specialising in local Iraqw beadwork, & it's a useful base for excursions to Eyasi & Ngorongoro. Good value. *US$109/201 sgl/dbl FB.*

Budget and camping

⌂ **Kudu Lodge & Campsite** (15 rooms) ✆ 025 253 4055; m 0744 474792; f 025 453 4268; e kuducamp-lodge@kuducamp.com; www.kuducamp.com. The best of a few campsites in the Karatu area catering primarily to budget camping safaris, Kudu Lodge lies on a small farm just outside town in the direction of Ngorongoro. It offers a good selection of activities ranging from day trips to the crater to local village walks. In addition to camping, it also now offers a range of en-suite rooms catering more to the mid-range market than budget safarigoers. *Camping on the neat lawn US$15 pp; rooms US$150/158 to US$237/274 sgl/dbl B&B.*

⌂ **Ngorongoro Safari Resort** (32 rooms) ✆ 025 253 4287/90; f 025 253 4288; e info@ngorongorocampandlodge.net; www.ngorongorocampandlodge.net. This smart & modern complex in Karatu offers accommodation in clean, comfortable self-contained rooms, as well as camping in a neat well-maintained site. The attached supermarket, though not cheap, is the best in Karatu, & the restaurant serves a good range of tasty Indian & continental dishes at around Tsh8,000 per main course. Other facilities include an internet café (Tsh1,000 per 15min), a filling station, a large bar with satellite TV, & 4x4 rental. *US$79/128 sgl/dbl B&B; camping US$5 pp.*

LAKE EYASI AND SURROUNDS

The vast Lake Eyasi verges on the remote southern border of the Ngorongoro Conservation Area, and lies at the base of the 800m Eyasi Escarpment, part of the Western Rift Valley wall. In years of plentiful rain, this shallow soda lake can extend for 80km from north to south, but in drier periods it sometimes dries out altogether to form an expansive white crust. Most of the time, it falls somewhere between the two extremes: an eerily bleak and windswept body of water surrounded by a white muddy crust and tangled dry acacia scrub. When we visited in the middle of the day, the lake had a rather desolate appearance, but we imagine that it might be very beautiful in the early morning or late afternoon. There is little resident wildlife in the area, aside from dik-dik and baboons, but depending on the water level, the lake is an important source of fish for Arusha and it often supports hundreds of thousands of flamingoes as well as a variety of other waterbirds.

Lake Eyasi is primarily of interest to tourists as the home of the Hadza (see box, *The last hunter-gatherers*, pages 158–9), and it is now reasonably straightforward to visit a Hadza encampment and go hunting with its male inhabitants. These visits must be arranged through one of three appointed guides based in the largest village in the region, which is called Mang'ola but sometimes referred to as Lake Eyasi (misleadingly, since it actually lies about 10km from the lakeshore). In addition to the entrance fee of US$2 per person charged by the Council of Mang'ola, fees of around US$10 and US$15 per party must be paid respectively to the guide and to the Hadza encampment visited.

We felt our visit to a Hadza encampment highly worthwhile. The people struck us as being very warm and unaffected, and going on an actual hunt was a primal and exciting experience – even if the waiting wives were mildly disappointed when their men returned to camp with only two mice and one bird to show for their efforts. Other travellers we've spoken to were luckier, though do be warned that a temporary conversion to vegetarianism might be in order should you come back from the hunt with a baboon or another large mammal – as a guest, you'll be offered the greatest delicacy, which is the raw liver. It could be argued that regular exposure to tourists might erode the traditional lifestyle of certain Hadza bands, but we saw no sign of this, and it should be borne in mind that the Hadza have chosen their nomadic lifestyle despite repeated attempts to settle them by successive governments. So far as we can ascertain, the guides ensure that no one band is visited more than once or twice a week, and the fee paid to the community is used to buy metal for spears and beads for decoration, but not food. And, incidentally, if you're the sort of daft person who wanders around African villages armed with piles of sweets or pens or whatever to hand out, then either don't visit the Hadza, or if you do, please leave the bag of goodies in Karatu.

GETTING THERE AND AWAY Mang'ola lies about one hour's drive from Karatu, and can be reached by following the Ngorongoro road out of town for about 5km, then taking a left turn towards the lake. Once at Mang'ola, it's easy enough to locate the guides and arrange a visit to a Hadza encampment. The full excursion can be completed as a half-day trip out of Karatu with private transport, and can easily be appended to a standard northern circuit safari.

WHERE TO STAY
Upmarket
Kisima Ngeda (6 rooms) 027 254 8715; m 0782 101150; f 027 250 2283; e reservations@kisimangeda.com; www.kisimangeda.com. This remote owner-managed tented camp is set in a shady grove of doum palms near the eastern shore of Lake Eyasi, with magnificent views across to the kilometre-tall western Rift Valley escarpment, the Ngorongoro

Highlands & the Oldeani Mountains. It makes an excellent base for visiting a Hadza encampment or exploring the arid lake hinterland. The accommodation is comfortable but simple, rather than luxurious, & the structures around the en-suite tents are made entirely from organic local materials. The excellent food includes tilapia caught fresh from the lake. *US$287/540 sgl/dbl FB.*

6

Camping

▲ **Council Campsite** Mang'ola Council operates a lovely but basic campsite, set about 4km from the town on the road towards the lake, in a glade of acacias surrounding a hot spring. There are few facilities.

NGORONGORO CONSERVATION AREA

An eastern annexe to Serengeti National Park, the 8,292km² Ngorongoro Conservation Area (NCA) is named after Ngorongoro Crater, the world's largest intact volcanic caldera, and a shoo-in contender for any global shortlist of natural wonders – not only for its inherent geological magnificence, but also because its verdant floor serves as a quite extraordinary natural sanctuary for some of Africa's densest large mammal populations. The rest of the NCA can be divided into two broad ecological zones. In the east lie the Crater Highlands, a sprawling volcanic massif studded with craggy peaks (notably the 3,648m-high Lolomalasin, the

THE LAST HUNTER-GATHERERS

The Hadza (or Hadzabe) of the Lake Eyasi hinterland, which lies to the east of Karatu, represent a unique – and increasingly fragile – link between modern East Africa and the most ancient of the region's human lifestyles and languages. Numbering at most 2,000 individuals, the Hadza are Tanzania's only remaining tribe of true hunter-gatherers, and their Hadzame language is one of only two in the country to be classified in the Khoisan family, a group of click-based tongues that also includes the San (Bushmen) of southern Africa.

The Hadza live in nomadic family bands, typically numbering about 20 adults and a coterie of children. Their rudimentary encampments of light grass shelters are erected in the space of a couple of hours, and might be used as a base for anything from ten days to one month before the inhabitants move on. These movements, though often rather whimsical, might be influenced by changes in the weather or local game distribution, and a band will also often relocate close to a fresh kill that is sufficiently large to sustain them for several days. The Hadza are fairly indiscriminate about what meat they eat – anything from mice to giraffe are fair game, and we once saw a family roasting a feral cat, fur and all, on their campfire – but baboons are regarded as the ultimate delicacy and reptiles are generally avoided. Hunting with poisoned arrows and honey gathering are generally male activities, while women and children collect roots, seeds, tubers and fruit – vegetarian fodder actually accounts for about 80% of the food intake.

The Hadza have a reputation for living for the present and they care little for conserving food resources, probably because their lifestyle inherently places very little stress on the environment. This philosophy is epitomised in a popular game of chance, which Hadza men will often play – and gamble valuable possessions on – to while away a quiet afternoon. A large master disc is made from baobab bark, and each participant makes a smaller personal disc, with all discs possessing distinct rough and smooth faces. The discs are stacked and thrown in the air, an action that is repeated until only one of the small discs lands with the same face up as the large disc, deciding the winner.

Many Hadza people still dress in the traditional attire of animal skins – women favour impala hide, men the furry coat of a small predator or baboon – which are often decorated with shells and beads. Hadza social groupings are neither permanent nor strongly hierarchical: individuals and couples are free to move between bands, and there is no concept of territorial possession. In order to be eligible for marriage, a Hadza man must kill five baboons to prove his worth. Once married, a couple might stay together for several decades or a lifetime, but there is no taboo against separation and either partner can terminate the union at any time by physically abandoning the other partner.

third-highest mountain in Tanzania after Kilimanjaro and Meru) and more than a dozen calderas, among them Ngorongoro itself. By contrast, the sparsely wooded western plains of the NCA are essentially a continuation of the Serengeti ecosystem, supporting a cover of short grass that attracts immense concentrations of grazers during the rainy season.

Coming from the direction of Arusha, the approach road to the Ngorongoro Crater rim is a sensational scene setter, winding up the extinct volcano's densely forested outer slopes to Heroes Point, where most visitors will catch their first breathtaking view over the 260km² crater floor lying 600m below. Even at this distance, it is possible to pick out ant-like formations chomping their way across the crater floor – in fact, thousand-strong herds of wildebeest, zebra and buffalo – and with binoculars you might even see a few of the elephants that haunt the fringes of Lerai Forest. The drive along the crater rim to your lodge will be equally riveting: patches of forest interspersed with sweeping views back across the Rift

The Hadza might reasonably be regarded as the sociological and anthropological equivalent of a living fossil, since they are one of the very few remaining adherents to the hunter-gatherer lifestyle that sustained the entire human population of the planet for 98% of its history. In both the colonial and post-independence eras, the Hadza have resolutely refused to allow the government to coerce them into following a more settled agricultural or pastoral way of life. The last concerted attempt to modernise Hadza society took place in the 1960s under the Nyerere government, when a settlement of brick houses with piped water, schools and a clinic was constructed for them alongside an agricultural scheme. Within ten years, the model settlement had been all but abandoned as the Hadza returned to their preferred lifestyle of hunting and gathering. The government, admirably, has since tacitly accepted the right of the Hadza to lead the life of their choice; a large tract of communal land fringing Lake Eyasi has been set aside for their use and they remain the only people in Tanzania automatically exempt from taxes!

The Khoisan language spoken by the Hadza is also something of a relic, belonging to a linguistic family that would almost certainly have dominated eastern and southern Africa until perhaps 3,000 years ago. As Bantu-speaking agriculturists and pastoralists swept into the region from the northwest, however, the Khoisan-speaking hunter-gatherer communities were either killed, assimilated into Bantu-speaking communities or forced to retreat into arid and montane territories ill-suited to herding and cultivation. This slow but steady marginalising process has continued into historical times: it has been estimated that of around 100 documented Khoisan languages only 30 are still in use today, and that the total Khoisan-speaking population of Africa now stands at less than 200,000.

That most Khoisan languages, if not already extinct, are headed that way, takes on an added poignancy if, as a minority of linguists have suggested throughout the 20th century, the unique click sounds are a preserved element of the very earliest human language. In order to investigate this possibility, the anthropological geneticists Alec Knight and Joanna Mountain recently analysed the chromosome content of samples taken from the geographically diverse San and Hadza, and concluded that they 'are as genetically distant from one another as two populations could be'. Discounting the somewhat improbable scenario that the clicking noises of the Hadza and San languages arose independently, this wide genetic gulf would imply a very ancient common linguistic root indeed. Several linguists dispute Knight and Mountain's conclusion, but if it is correct, then Hadzame, along with Africa's other dying Khoisan languages, might represent one last fading echo of the first human voices to have carried across the African savannah.

For more information visit www.hadzabe.com.

Valley, and the possibility of encountering buffalo, zebra, bushbuck, elephant and even the occasional leopard.

The Ngorongoro Crater is the main focal point of tourist activity in the NCA. But those who have the time can explore any number of less publicised natural features further afield. Olduvai Gorge, for instance, is the site of some of Africa's most important hominid fossil finds, and can easily be visited en route from the crater rim to the Serengeti. Other highlights include the Empakaai and to a lesser extent Olmoti Craters in the northern NCA, while the crater rim is highly rewarding for montane forest birds.

An excellent 84-page booklet, Ngorongoro Conservation Area, similar in style to the national park booklets, is readily available in Arusha and has good information on the crater and Olduvai Gorge. It is especially worth buying if you plan to visit some of the off-the-beaten-track parts of the conservation area. For a more detailed overview of the national park, Veronica Roodt's excellent Tourist Travel & Field Guide to the Ngorongoro Conservation Area is widely available at hotel gift shops and craft shops in Arusha and elsewhere in northern Tanzania.

The NCA entrance fee of US$50 per person per 24 hours is payable by all, even those in quick transit to or from Serengeti National Park. An additional Crater Fee of US$200 per vehicle is levied for each and every visit to the crater floor during the course of a stay in the NCA. In order to curb congestion, the fee is now valid for half a day only. Unlike the surrounding national parks, all fees for the NCA are payable in hard currency cash or travellers' cheques (ideally US dollars); no credit card of any form is accepted, nor is local currency. Note, too, that the crater rim gets very cold at night, and is often blanketed in mist in the early morning, so you will need a jumper or two, and possibly a windbreaker if you are camping.

GEOLOGY AND HISTORY With an altitudinal range of 1,230–3,648m above sea level, the NCA is among the most geologically spectacular reserves anywhere in Africa, comprising flat short-grass plains in the southwest and low rocky mountains in the northwest, while the west is dominated by the so-called Crater Highlands, a tall breezy plateau studded with stand-alone mountains. The mountains of the NCA date from two periods. The Gol Range, to the north of the main road to the Serengeti, is an exposed granite block that formed some 500 million years ago. Somewhat less antiquated, at least in geological terms, the Crater Highlands and associated free-standing mountains of the eastern NCA are volcanic in origin, their formation linked to the same fracturing process that created the Rift Valley 15 to 20 million years ago.

Ngorongoro Crater itself is the relic of an immense volcanic mountain that attained a similar height to that of Kilimanjaro before it imploded violently some two to three million years ago. It is the world's sixth largest caldera, and the largest with an unbroken wall. Eight smaller craters in the NCA, most notably Olmoti and Empakaai, are the product of similar eruptions. The Crater Highlands are no longer volcanically active, but the free-standing Ol Doinyo Lengai immediately northeast of the main highland block is among the world's most active volcanoes, having last erupted during 2007–08.

Based on fossil evidence unearthed at Olduvai Gorge in the western NCA, it is known that various species of hominid have occupied this area for at least three million years. It was the domain of hunter-gatherers until a few thousand years ago, when pastoralists moved in. The fate of these early pastoralists is unknown, because a succession of immigrants replaced them: the ancestors of the Cushitic-speaking Mbulu some 2,000 years ago and those of the Nilotic-speaking Datoga about 300 years ago. A century later the militaristic Maasai drove both of these groups out of what is now the NCA: the Datoga to the Eyasi Basin and the Mbulu to the highlands near Manyara. Most place names in the area are Maasai, and

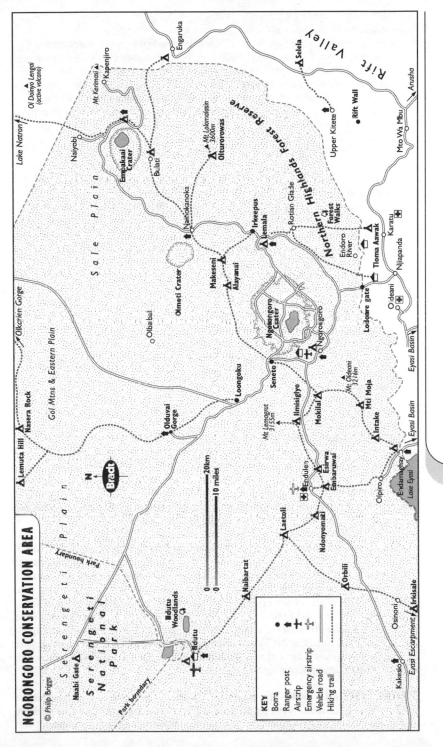

NGORONGORO CONSERVATION AREA

© Philip Briggs

KEY
• Borra
⬤▲⛪ Ranger post
✈ Airstrip
✈ Emergency airstrip
— Vehicle road
⋯ Hiking trail

A regular criticism of the Ngorongoro Crater, one that in my opinion is desperately misguided, is that it is 'like a zoo'. Aside from being yawningly unoriginal – I must hear this phrase two dozen times in the course of researching any given edition of this book – this allegation is as facile as it is nonsensical. The wildlife in the crater is not caged, nor is it artificially fed, surely the defining qualities of a zoo, but is instead free to come and go as it pleases. Yes, the crater's animals are generally very relaxed around vehicles, but that doesn't make them tame, merely habituated – no different, really, to the mountain gorillas of Rwanda or the chimps at Mahale.

The point that many visitors to Ngorongoro miss is that, for all the elitism attached to Africa's more remote game reserves, it is only in places where the wildlife is almost totally habituated that casual visitors can watch the animals behave much as they would were no human observers present. And, trust me, this is an infinitely more satisfying experience than travelling through a reserve where the wildlife is so skittish that most sightings amount to little more than a rump disappearing into the bush.

I suspect that the notion of Ngorongoro as a glorified zoo stems from something else entirely. This is the high volume of tourist traffic, which admittedly robs the crater floor of some of its atmosphere, and has some potential to cause environmental degradation, but is of questionable impact on the animals. On the contrary, the wildlife of Ngorongoro is apparently far less affected by the presence of vehicles than, say, the elephants and giraffes in the Selous, which regularly display clear signs of distress at the approach of a vehicle.

The problem, basically, is that the high volume of other tourists in the relatively small and open confines of the crater jars against our sense of aesthetics – especially when game spotting entails looking for a group of vehicles clustered together in the distance rather than looking for an actual animal! Personally, I feel that the scenery and abundance of animals more than makes up for the mild congestion, but if crowds put you off, then there are other places to visit in Tanzania. Instead of adding to the tourist traffic, then moaning about it, why not give the crater a miss? Or, better still, make the effort to be in the crater first thing in the morning when, for a brief hour or two before the post-breakfast crowds descend, it really does live up to every expectation of untrammelled beauty.

---

although several explanations for the name Ngorongoro are floating around, the most credible is that it is named after a type of Maasai bowl.

Europeans settled in the NCA around the turn of the 20th century. Two German brothers farmed on the crater floor until the outbreak of World War I. One of their old farmhouses is still used by researchers, and a few sisal plants dating to this time can be seen in the northeast of the crater. Tourism began in the 1930s when the original Ngorongoro Crater Lodge was built on the crater rim. The NCA formed part of the original Serengeti National Park as gazetted in 1951, but Maasai protests at being denied access to such a huge tract of their grazing land led to it being split off from the national park in 1959 and downgraded to a multi-use conservation area. The NCA was inscribed as a UNESCO World Heritage Site in 1979, and two years later it was declared an International Biosphere Reserve, together with the neighbouring Serengeti.

GETTING THERE AND AWAY The road from Arusha to the eastern entrance gate of the NCA via Makuyuni, Mto wa Mbu and Karatu is now surfaced in its entirety and it can be covered comfortably in less than three hours, with another 30–60 minutes required to get to any of the lodges on the crater rim. All roads within the NCA are unsurfaced, and a decent 4x4 is required to reach the crater floor. Most tourists visit Ngorongoro as part of a longer safari, but those with time or budgetary restrictions could think about visiting the crater as a self-contained one-night safari out of Arusha.

WHERE TO STAY AND EAT No accommodation or camping facilities exist within Ngorongoro Crater, but four upmarket lodges are perched on the rim, all offering superb views to the crater floor, as does the public campsite there. The crater can be (and often is) visited as a day trip from one of the mid-range to upmarket lodges that lie along the road between the NCA and Karatu, while budget-conscious travellers have a choice of more basic accommodation in Karatu itself (see page 155 for details of lodges in and around Karatu), though this does mean missing out on the dusk view over the crater and dawn game drives on the crater floor. The anomalous Ndutu Safari Lodge, which lies just within the western border of the NCA, is not a realistic base from which to explore the Ngorongoro Highlands and ecologically it really feels like part of the Serengeti, so it is covered in that section.

Exclusive

Ngorongoro Crater Lodge (40 rooms) ☎ 027 254 8549/8038 or South Africa +2711 809 4447; e inboundsales@andbeyond.com; www.andbeyond.com. This top-of-the-range lodge was originally built in 1934 as a private hunting lodge with a commanding view over the crater, & was converted to a hotel shortly after independence in 1961. The property was bought by &Beyond (formerly CCAfrica) in 1995 & rebuilt from scratch with the stated aim of creating 'the finest safari lodge in Africa'. Architecturally, the lodge is literally fantastic. Each individual suite consists of 2 adjoining round structures, similar to African huts but distorted in an almost Dadaist style. The large interiors boast a décor as ostentatious as it is eclectic, combining elements of baroque, classical, African, colonial & much more besides in a manner the management describes as 'Maasai meets Versailles'. The entire lodge has been designed in such a way that the crater is almost constantly in sight (even the baths & toilets have views!), & the food, service & ambience are all world class. Whether or not &Beyond has succeeded in creating Africa's finest safari lodge is a matter of taste & opinion – certainly, the decidedly non-'bush' atmosphere might offend some purists but it is difficult to fault in

terms of ambition & originality. The fact that it was commended in *Condé Nast Traveller's* prestigious 1998 end-of-year listings says enough. *US$1,280 pp, US$1,450 Jul–Aug, US$655 Mar–May, Nov & early Dec, inc meals, most drinks & game drives. No sgl supplement.*

Lemala Camp (9 tents) ☎ 027 254 8966; f 027 254 8937; e info@lemalacamp.com; www.lemalacamp.com. Opened in Dec 2007, this is the only semi-permanent luxury tented camp on the crater rim, situated in a wonderful stand of lichen-stained flat-topped red-thorn acacias immediately inside the Lemala Gate (the start of the same road used to descend into & ascend from the crater rim from Ngorongoro Sopa Lodge). The views from the camp are great, it has an outdoor atmosphere lacking from all other camps on the rim, & it also has a peerless location for early morning game drives into the crater itself. The tents are very spacious & decorated in classic safari style, with a wooden floor & canvas top, & all have twin or king-size beds, solar powered lighting & hot water. It's not cheap, but must rank as the first choice of accommodation for anybody seeking to experience Ngorongoro in a real bush atmosphere. Closed Oct–Nov, Apr & May. *US$710/960 sgl/dbl FB*

Upmarket

Ngorongoro Wilderness Camp (10 rooms) ☎ 027 250 2668; e serecamp.wildfrontiers@habari.co.tz; www.wildfrontiers.com. This comfortable mobile camp provides a more down-to-earth bush alternative to the large bland lodges that otherwise occupy the crater rim. It moves location every 3–6 months in

line with NCA policy, but locations usually offer great views over the crater floor & the camp offers a varied programme of game drives into the crater & guided walks elsewhere in the NCA. The en-suite tents have solar lighting, eco-friendly toilets, & warm duvets & hot water bottles to protect against chilly

6

highland nights. Closes mid-Apr to May. US$450/680 FB.

🏠 **Ngorongoro Serena Lodge** (75 rooms) ➘ 027 253 7050/2/3/5; f 027 253 7056; e reservations@serena.co.tz; www.serenahotels.com. Meeting the usual high Serena standards, this is arguably the pick of the more conventional lodges on the crater rim, receiving consistent praise from tourists & from within the safari industry. It lies on the western crater rim along the road towards Seronera, several kilometres past the park headquarters & Crater Lodge. It is the closest of the lodges to the main descent road into the crater, a decided advantage for those who want to get to the crater floor as early as possible. The setting is a secluded wooded valley rustling with birdlife & offering a good view over the crater. Serena Active, which operates out of the lodge, offers a good range of afternoon & full-day walks ranging from a gentle stroll through the grassy highlands to a rather more challenging ascent of Olmoti Crater. The facilities, food & service are all of a high standard, & rooms are centrally heated. US$375/550 sgl/dbl FB, US$225/335 Apr–Jun.

🏠 **Ngorongoro Sopa Lodge** (96 rooms) ➘ 027 250 0630/9; f 027 250 8245; e info@sopalodges.com; www.sopalodges.com. Situated on the forested eastern edge of the crater rim some 20km distant from the headquarters & main cluster of lodges, this attractive modern hotel is similar in standard to the Serena & arguably nudges ahead of it on the basis of location. Accommodation is in vast semi-detached suites, each with 2 dbl beds, a heater, a large bathroom, a fridge, & a wide bay window facing the crater & Ol Mokarot Mountain. There is a swimming pool in front of the bar, & the food & service are excellent. One thing that stands out about this lodge is the large, forested grounds, a good place to look for characteristic montane forest birds, with sunbirds (tacazze, golden-winged & eastern double-collared) well represented & a variety of weavers, seedeaters & robins present. Another is that it lies close to what, in effect, is a private road that can be used both to ascend from & descend into the crater, which greatly reduces the driving time either side of game drives – particularly useful for an early morning start. US$320/550 sgl/dbl FB, US$265/450 Mar, Nov & early Dec, US$100/200 Apr & May.

🏠 **Ngorongoro Wildlife Lodge** (72 rooms) ➘ 027 254 4595; f 027 254 8633; e res@hotelsandlodges-tanzania.com; www.hotelsandlodges-tanzania.com. Situated roughly 2km away from Ngorongoro Crater Lodge, this former government hotel is one of the oldest on the crater rim & it shows its antiquity in the rather monolithic architecture. Until recently, fittings & furnishings also carried a rather timeworn sheen, but as with other hotels in this chain, it has received a real facelift in 2008, though service & food remain a little substandard. This is compensated for by the finest location of all the crater rim lodges, directly above the yellow fevers of Lerai Forest – it truly defies superlatives. Following renovations, the rooms are comfortable & pleasantly furnished, with piping hot baths & windows facing the crater. You can pick out animals on the crater floor using a telescope fixed on the patio, & the grounds support a fair range of forest birds. Rates on application.

Moderate

🏠 **Rhino Lodge** (24 rooms) m 0762 359055; e rhino@ngorongoro.cc; www.ngorongoro.cc. Formerly the home of the first conservator of NCA & later managed as a guesthouse by the conservation authorities, this modest low-rise lodge had been closed for the best part of a decade prior to being leased to the Dar es Salaam-based operator Coastal Aviation, who undertook extensive renovations prior to reopening it in 2007. It is far & away the most affordable lodge on the crater rim, & though it lacks a direct crater view, the surrounding mist-swathed forest has a charm of its own, & the location is very convenient for game drives. Accommodation is in simple but comfortable ground-floor rooms with twin or dbl beds & en-suite hot shower, & rates include good buffet meals in the cosy dining room, which comes complete with log fire. It's superb value. US$125/220 sgl/dbl FB.

Budget and camping

Å **Simba Campsite** Situated about 2km from the park headquarters, this is the only place where you can pitch a tent on the crater rim, & it's hardly great value, given that facilities are limited to basic latrines, a cold shower & rubbish pit. Still, the wonderful view makes it a preferable option to camping in Karatu, assuming you place a greater priority on the experience than creature comforts. The village near the headquarters has a few basic bars & shops, & there is nothing preventing you from dropping into nearby Ngorongoro Wildlife Lodge for a drink or snack. US$30 pp.

Ngorongoro Crater has always been noted for its density of black rhinos. Back in 1892, Dr Oscar Baumann, the first European to visit the area, remarked on the large numbers of rhino, particularly around Lerai Forest – and he shot seven of the unfortunate beasts to prove his point. More recently, the biologist John Goddard estimated the resident population at greater than 100 in 1964. By 1992, poaching had reduced the crater's rhino population to no more than ten individuals, although this number had increased to 18 by 1998, including a mother and calf relocated from South Africa's Addo National Park to boost the local genetic pool. Sadly, five of these rhinos died in the early part of the present decade, one taken by a lion and the remainder thought to be victims of a tick-borne disease linked to the low rainfall of 2000–01. Since then, numbers have gradually recovered and the population resident in the crater stood at around 20 individuals in 2008. The crater's rhinos all have a tracking device implanted in their horns, to discourage poachers and to enable the rangers to monitor movements.

Despite the overall decline in numbers over recent decades, Ngorongoro is today the only accessible part of the northern safari circuit where these endangered animals are seen with any regularity. For many visitors to the crater, therefore, rhino sightings are a very high priority, and fortunately the chances are pretty good. In the wet season, the rhinos are often seen in the vicinity of the Ngoitokitok Springs and the Sopa road. For most of the year, however, they range between the Lerai Forest by night and Lake Magadi by day. Early risers are very likely to encounter a pair on the road fringing the forest, since they tend to move towards the lake shortly after dawn.

The crater's rhinos display a couple of local quirks. The black rhino (unlike its 'white' cousin) is normally a diurnal browser, which makes it rather odd to see them spending most of the day in open grassland, but the story is that they mostly feed by night while they are in the forest. Baumann noted that the crater's rhinos were unusually pale in colour, a phenomenon that is still observed today, due to their predilection for bathing and rolling in the saline lake and fringing salt flats.

WHAT TO SEE

Ngorongoro Crater Floor The opportunity of spending a day on the crater floor is simply not to be missed. There are few places where you can so reliably see such large concentrations of wildlife all year round, and your game viewing (and photography) will only be enhanced by the striking backdrop of the 600m-high crater wall. The crater is also excellent Big Five territory: lion, elephant and buffalo are all but guaranteed, rhino are regularly seen, and a leopard is chanced upon from time to time. The official road down to the crater descends from Malanja Depression to the western shore of Lake Magadi, while the official road up starts near Lerai Forest and reaches the rim on the stretch of road between Wildlife and Crater lodges. There is a third road into the crater, which starts near the Sopa Lodge, and this can be used either to ascend or to descend.

There are several notable physical features within the crater. Lerai Forest consists almost entirely of yellow fever trees, large acacias noted for their jaundiced bark (it was once thought that this tree, which is often associated with marsh and lake fringes, the breeding ground for mosquitoes, was the cause of yellow fever and malaria). To the north of this forest, Lake Magadi is a shallow soda lake that varies greatly in extent depending on the season. Standing close to the lakeshore is a cluster of burial cairns that show some similarities with the tombs at the Engaruka Ruins further east, and are presumably a relic of the Datoga occupation of the

6

crater prior to the arrival of the Maasai. To the south and east of this, the Gorigor Swamp also varies in extent seasonally, but it generally supports some water. There is a permanent hippo pool at the Ngoitokitok Springs at the eastern end of the swamp. The northern half of the crater is generally drier, though it is bisected by the Munge River, which is lined by thickets and forms a seasonally substantial area of swamp to the immediate north of Lake Magadi.

The open grassland that covers most of the crater floor supports large concentrations of wildebeest and zebra (the population of these species is estimated at 10,000 and 5,000, respectively), and smaller numbers of buffalo, tsessebe, and Thomson's and Grant's gazelles. The vicinity of Lerai Forest is the best area in which to see waterbuck, bushbuck and eland. The forest and adjoining Gorigor Swamp are the main haunt of the crater's elephant population, which typically stands at around 70. All the elephants resident in the crater are old males (though females and families sometimes pass through the area), and you stand a good chance of seeing big tuskers of the sort that have been poached away elsewhere in East Africa. Two curious absentees from the crater floor are impala and giraffe, both of which are common in the surrounding plains. Some researchers attribute the absence of giraffe to a lack of suitable browsing fodder, others to their presumed inability to descend the steep crater walls. Quite why there are no impala in the crater is a mystery.

The crater floor reputedly supports the densest concentration of predators in Africa. The resident lion population has fluctuated greatly ever since records were maintained, partly as a result of migration in and out of the crater, but primarily because of the vulnerability of the concentrated and rather closed population to epidemics. Over the course of 1962, the lion population dropped from an estimated 90 to about 15 due to an outbreak of disease spread by biting flies, but it had recovered to about 70 within a decade. In recent years, the pattern of fluctuation saw the population estimated at 80 in 1995, 35 in 1998, and 55 divided into four main prides and a few nomadic males in 2000. The crater's lions might be encountered just about anywhere, and are generally very relaxed around vehicles.

The most populous large predator is the spotted hyena, the population of which is estimated at around 400. You won't spend long in the crater without seeing a hyena: they often rest up on the eastern shore of Lake Magadi during the day, sometimes trying – and mostly failing – to sneak up on the flamingoes in the hope of a quick snack. Until recently, no cheetahs were resident within the crater, which might seem surprising given that the open grassland is textbook cheetah habitat, but is probably due to the high rate of competition from other predators. At least two female cheetahs recently colonised the crater floor – one had four cubs in late 2001 – and sightings are now fairly regular. Leopards are resident, particularly in swampy areas, but they are not often seen. Other common predators are the golden and black-backed jackals, with the former being more frequently encountered due to its relatively diurnal habits.

The crater floor offers some great birding. Lake Magadi normally harbours large flocks of flamingo, giving its edges a pinkish tinge when seen from a distance. The pools at the Mandusi Swamp can be excellent for waterbirds, with all manner of waders, storks, ducks and herons present. The grassland is a good place to see a number of striking ground birds. One very common resident is the kori bustard, reputedly the world's heaviest flying bird, and spectacular if you catch it during a mating dance. Ostrich are also common, along with the gorgeously garish crowned crane, and (in the rainy season) huge flocks of migrant storks. Less prominent, but common, and of great interest to more dedicated birders, is the lovely rosy-throated longclaw. Two of the most striking and visible birds of prey are the augur

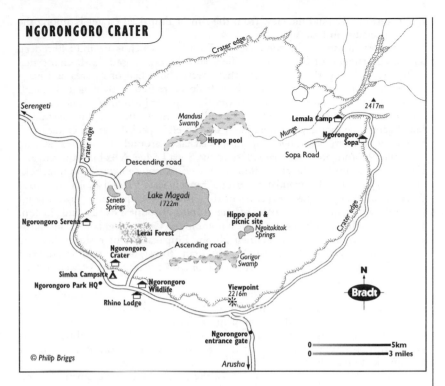

Crater edge

Serengeti

2417m

Mandusi
Swamp

Lemala Camp

Hippo pool

Munge

Ngorongoro
Sopa

Crater edge

Descending road

Sopa Road

Lake Magadi
1722m

Seneto
Springs

Hippo pool &
picnic site

Ngoitokitok
Springs

Ngorongoro Serena

Lerai Forest

Ascending road

Ngorongoro
Crater

Gorigor
Swamp

Crater edge

N

Simba Campsite

Ngorongoro Park HQ

Ngorongoro
Wildlife

Viewpoint
2216m

Bradt

Rhino Lodge

Ngorongoro
entrance gate

0 ▬▬▬▬▬ 5km
0 ▬▬▬▬▬ 3 miles

© Philip Briggs

Arusha

buzzard, sometimes seen here in its unusual melanistic form, and the foppish long-crested eagle. The localised Egyptian vulture – whose ability to crack open ostrich eggs by holding a stone in its beak makes it the only bird that arguably uses tools – is sometimes seen in the vicinity of Mungu Stream.

There are a few hippo pools in the crater, but the one most often visited is Ngoitokitok Springs, a popular picnic spot where lunch is enlivened by a flock of black kites which have become adept at swooping down on tourists and snatching the food from their hands.

The authorities rigidly forbid tourists from entering the crater before 07.00, and they must be out of the crater before 18.00. This is a frustrating ruling for photographers, since it means that you miss out on the best light of the day, and it has encouraged most safari drivers to suggest that their clients take breakfast before going on a game drive, and carry a picnic lunch. This programme is difficult to avoid if you are on a group safari, but for those on a private safari, it is well worth getting down to the crater as early as permitted. Photography aside, this is the one time in the day when you might have the crater to yourself, the one time, in other words, when you can really experience the Ngorongoro Crater of television documentary land. Note that it is forbidden to descend to the base of the crater after 16.00, and that a 'crater service fee' of US$200 per vehicle for a half-day visit is payable every time you enter the crater.

Empakaai and Olmoti Craters The NCA also protects two other major craters, both relics of the volcanic activity that shaped the breezy Crater Highlands over the past ten million years or so. Both are worth a visit, despite being dwarfed in size and reputation by the peerless Ngorongoro, as they offer welcome opportunity to break the regime of twice-daily game drives with a stiff steep walk in lovely mountain scenery. And the view from the rim of Empakaai Crater is among the most spectacular in East Africa.

The most alluring of the two craters is Empakaai, which is around 540m deep and has a diameter of almost 8km. The crater floor, enclosed by sheer forested cliffs, supports a sparkling soda lake that covers about half of its area and has a depth of around 60m. The emerald lake's shallows are frequently tinged pink with thousands of flamingoes, and a variety of other aquatic birds are common too. As for mammals, elephant and leopard are still present in the area, but bushbuck, buffalo and blue monkey are more likely to be seen, especially on the crater rim.

The drive from Ngorongoro to Empakaai takes around 90 minutes, leaving from the Ngorongoro Crater rim close to the Sopa Lodge. A 4x4 is required, and if you want to hike to the crater floor you need to stop *en route* at Nainokanoka village to pick up the mandatory armed ranger. Past Nainokanoka, the road descends to the open grassy expanses of the Embulbul Depression (lowest point 2,325m), which lies at the base of the 3,260m Mount Losirua and 3,648m Lolomalasin, the latter being the highest point in the Crater Highlands (and third-highest in Tanzania). The road then climbs Empakaai's outer slopes, passing through alpine moorland and lush Afro-montane forest, before reaching the rim and its fantastic views over the crater to Ol Doinyo Lengai and, on very clear days, Kilimanjaro and Lake Natron.

A road circles part of the forested rim, which reaches an elevation of 3,200m in the east. An excellent footpath to the crater floor was constructed in 2008 – a steep but wonderful walk that takes around 45 minutes each away and requires decent walking shoes. There is a campsite with rustic ablution facilities on the crater rim a few metres from the start of the footpath, but no other accommodation in the area.

If that walk hasn't sapped your energy, the smaller and less dramatic Olmoti Crater, a sunken caldera situated close to Nainokanoka, is worth a stop on the way back to Ngorongoro. A motorable track leads from Nainokanoka to a ranger post further west, from where the crater rim can only be reached on foot, following a recently upgraded footpath through montane forest that takes about 30 minutes up and 20 minutes back down. From the ranger post it is a half-hour walk to the rim. This is a shallow crater, covered in grass and bisected by a river valley, and it offers good grazing for Maasai cattle and also sometimes supports a few antelope. From the viewpoint at the rim, you're bound to see pairs of augur buzzard cartwheeling high in the sky, and might also catch a glimpse of the mighty cliff-loving Verreaux's eagle. On a clear day, the viewpoint also offers glimpses of the distant southern wall of Ngorongoro Crater, and you can follow a short footpath to the seasonal Munge Waterfall, where the eponymous river leaves the crater.

Olduvai Gorge Difficult to believe today perhaps, but for much of the past two million years the seasonally parched plains around Olduvai – or more correctly *ol-dupai*, the Maasai name for sisal – were submerged beneath a lake that formed an important watering hole for local animals and our hominid ancestors. This was a fluctuating body of water, at times expansive, at other times drying up altogether, creating a high level of stratification accentuated by sporadic deposits of fine ash from the volcanoes that surrounded it. Then, tens of thousands of years ago, volcanic activity associated with the rifting process caused the land to tilt, and a new lake formed to the east. The river that flowed out of this new lake gradually incised a gorge through the former lakebed, exposing layers of stratification up to 100m deep. Olduvai Gorge thus cuts through a chronological sequence of rock beds preserving a practically continuous archaeological and fossil record of life on the plains over the past two million years.

The significance of Olduvai Gorge was first recognised by the German entomologist Professor Katwinkle, who stumbled across it in 1911 while searching for insect specimens. Two years later, Katwinkle led an archaeological expedition to the gorge, and unearthed a number of animal fossils before the excavations were abandoned at the outbreak of World War I. In 1931, the palaeontologist Louis Leakey visited the long-abandoned diggings and realised that the site provided ideal conditions for following the hominid fossil record back to its beginnings. Leakey found ample evidence demonstrating that ancient hominids had occupied the site, but lacking for financial backing, his investigations went slowly and frustratingly refused to yield any truly ancient fossilised hominid remains.

The payoff for the long years of searching came in 1959 when Mary Leakey – Louis's wife, and a more than accomplished archaeologist in her own right – discovered a heavy fossilised jawbone that displayed unambiguous human affinities but was also clearly unlike any other hominid fossil documented at the time. Christened 'Nutcracker man' by the Leakeys in reference to its bulk, this jawbone proved to be that of an Australopithecine (now designated as *Australopithecus boisei*) that had lived and died on the ancient lakeshore some 1.75 million years ago. Subsequently superseded by more ancient fossils unearthed elsewhere in East Africa, this was nevertheless a critical landmark in the history of palaeontology: the first conclusive evidence that hominid evolution stretched back over more than a million years and had been enacted on the plains of East Africa.

This important breakthrough shot the Leakeys' work to international prominence, and with proper funding at their disposal, a series of exciting new discoveries followed, including the first fossilised remains of *Homo habilis*, a direct ancestor of modern man that would have dwelt on the lakeshore contemporaneously with *Australopithecus boisei*. After Louis's death in 1972, Mary Leakey continued working in the area until she retired in 1984. In 1976, at the nearby site of Laetoli, she discovered footprints created more than three million years ago by a party of early hominids which had walked through a bed of freshly deposited volcanic ash – still the most ancient hominid footprints ever found.

Olduvai Gorge lies within the conservation area about 3km north of the main road between Ngorongoro Crater and the Serengeti, and is a popular and worthwhile place to stop for a picnic lunch. The actual diggings may only be explored with a guide, and – since all fossils are immediately removed – they are probably of greater immediate interest for the geology than for the archaeology. Not so the excellent site museum, which displays replicas of some of the more interesting hominid fossils unearthed at the site as well as the Laetoli footprints. Also on display are genuine fossils of some of the extinct animals that used to roam the plains: pygmy and short-necked giraffes, giant swine, river elephant, various equines, and a bizarre antelope with long de-curved horns. Outside the museum, evolutionary diversity is represented by the variety of colourful – and very alive – dry-country birds that hop around the picnic area: red-and-yellow barbet, slaty-coloured boubou, rufous chatterer, speckle-fronted weaver and purple grenadier are practically guaranteed.

Lake Ndutu This alkaline lake lies south of the B142 on the Ngorongoro–Serengeti border. When it is full, Maasai use it to water their cattle. In the rainy season it supports large numbers of animals, so Ndutu Safari Lodge (see page 180) is a good base for game drives. The acacia woodland around the lake supports different birds to those in surrounding areas. The campsite on the lakeshore costs US$40 per person.

Because the NCA lies outside the national park system, it is permissible to walk and hike along a number of trails covering most main points of interest (but not the crater floor) in the company of an authorised guide. For those seeking a short morning or afternoon walk on the crater rim appended to a standard road safari, the best option is to take one of three short guided hikes offered by Serena Active, based in the Ngorongoro Serena Lodge. These walks can be pre-booked, but it's also fine just to pitch up at their booking desk (↘ 027 253 9160/1/2; f 027 253 9163; e serenaactive@serena.co.tz) spontaneously on the day, whether you're staying at the Serena or at another lodge on the crater rim.

You could in theory spend a fortnight exploring the NCA along a network of longer trails that connects Lake Eyasi in the south to Lake Natron in the north, as well as running west across the plains towards Laetoli and Lake Ndutu and northwest to Olduvai Gorge. Other possible targets for hikers include the Olmoti and Empakaai craters, the 3,600m Mount Lolmalasin (the third-highest in Tanzania), and the remote Gol Mountains. In theory, any safari operator can advise you about routes and arrange hikes with the NCA authorities, but I would strongly advise the traveller thinking of doing this to work through an operator with specialist trekking experience (see the Safari operator listings in Chapter 5, Arusha, pages 108–10).

It would also be possible to set up a trekking trip directly with the NCA, bussing to the crater rim from Arusha. Were you to attempt something like this, you would have to organise food yourself, clarify arrangements for a tent, sleeping bag and other equipment, and take warm clothes since parts of the NCA are very chilly at night. The best place to make initial enquiries and arrangements for a DIY trekking trip would be the NCA Information Centre (Boma Rd, Arusha; ↘ 027 254 4625; f 027 250 2603; www.ngorongorocrater.org). At least five different one-day hiking trails from the crater rim can be arranged at very short notice. Some of the longer hikes and trekking routes require 30 days' notice to set up, so you will need to make advance contact.

SERENGETI NATIONAL PARK

There is little to say about the Serengeti that hasn't been said already. It is Africa's most famous wildlife sanctuary, renowned for its dense predator population and annual wildebeest migration, and the sort of place that's been hyped so heavily you might reasonably brace yourself for disappointment when you actually get to visit it. But the Serengeti is all it is cracked up to be – arguably the finest game reserve anywhere in Africa, as notable for the sheer volume of wildlife that inhabits its vast plains as for the liberating sense of space attached to exploring them.

Serengeti National Park covers an area of almost 15,000km², but the Serengeti ecosystem – which includes a number of game reserves bordering the national park as well as Kenya's Maasai Mara National Reserve – is more than double that size. Most of the national park is open and grassy, broken by isolated granite hillocks or koppies (a Dutch or Afrikaans word literally meaning 'little heads') and patches of acacia woodland. There is little permanent water, so animal migration in the area is strongly linked to rainfall patterns.

Several guides to the park are available locally. They include the official 72 page booklet Serengeti National Park, with good maps and introductory information, and the newer and glossier Serengeti, published by African Publishing House. Far more detailed is Veronica Roodt's Tourist Travel & Field Guide to the Serengeti, which is strong on maps, photos and information.

Entrance costs US$50 per 24 hours and there is speculation it will increase in the not too distant future. The fee should ideally be paid by MasterCard or Tanapa Card (issued at any Exim Bank). No other cards are accepted, nor are travellers' cheques, and cash payments attract a 50% penalty.

HISTORY Prior to becoming a national park, the Serengeti was inhabited by the Maasai, who migrated into the area in the 17th century, when they forcefully displaced the Datoga pastoralists then in residence. The name Serengeti derives from the Maa word *serengit*, meaning 'endless plain', and it most properly refers to the short-grass plains of the southeast rather than the whole park. Partly because it lay within the territory of the then inhospitable Maasai, the Serengeti area was little known to outsiders until after World War I, when the first European hunters moved in to bag its plentiful wildlife.

AVOIDING THE CROWDS

Many visitors whose experience of the Serengeti is limited to the Seronera area complain that the park is uncomfortably crowded, and that any worthwhile sighting attracts a gaggle of safari vehicles within a few minutes. To some extent, this reputation is justified: Seronera is the most accessible part of the park coming from the direction of Arusha, and it boasts the highest concentration of camping and lodge facilities, so that game viewing roads within a 5–10km radius tend to carry an uncharacteristically high level of vehicular traffic.

This situation is exacerbated by the tendency of the budget safari companies that favour Seronera to impose heavy budgetary restrictions on drivers, discouraging them from burning excess fuel to explore further afield. Furthermore, the safari industry's obsession with the 'Big Five' and large predators has created a mindset where drivers tend to rely heavily on radio messages from other drivers to locate the animals they think their clients most want to see. As a result, all vehicles within radio earshot tend to congregate on any such sighting within minutes. Sadly, this all goes to create the common misperception that one of Africa's wildest and most wonderful parks is far more crowded with tourists than is actually the case.

What can you do about this? Well, for one, assuming that you can afford it, arrange your safari through a company that specialises in more offbeat areas of the park and whose budget incorporates unlimited mileage – see pages 108–10 for recommendations. If you work with a cheaper company, try to avoid being based at Seronera. True, this area does usually offer the best wildlife viewing in the park, but many other parts of the Serengeti are almost as good, whilst carrying a significantly lower tourist volume. Failing that, should your itinerary include Seronera, speak to the safari company about what if any fuel restrictions they impose on drivers, and try to reach an understanding in advance.

It's also worth bearing in mind that roads around Seronera tend to be busiest during peak game viewing hours of 07.30–10.00 and 14.00–16.30. So it's well worth asking for a packed breakfast and heading out as early as possible – game drives are permitted to drive from 06.00 onwards, and even if you ignore the crowding issue, that first hour of daylight is the best time to see predators on the move. Bearing in mind that drivers tend to place emphasis on seeking out big cats because they think it's what their clients want, travellers with different priorities should talk these through with the driver – more radically, ask him to switch off his radio, stop worrying about what everybody else might be seeing, and just enjoy what animals you happen to chance upon.

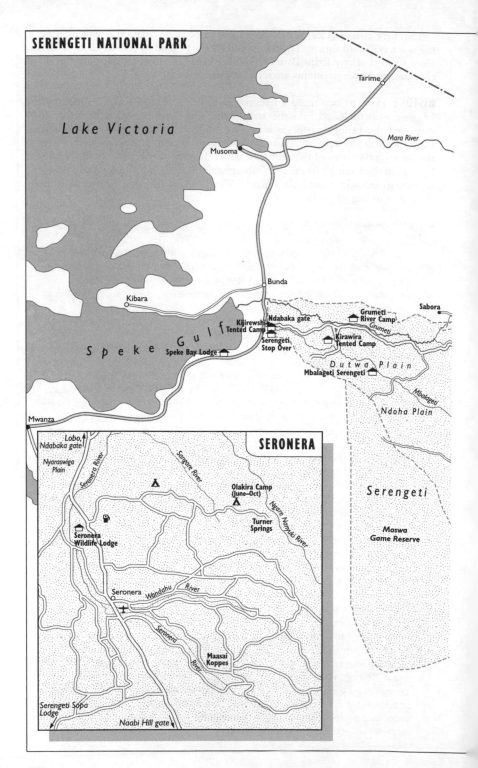

SERENGETI NATIONAL PARK

Lake Victoria

Tarime

Mara River

Musoma

Bunda

Kibara

Sabora

Grumeti
River Camp

Ndabaka gate

Kijirewshi
Tented Camp

S p e k e G u l f

Speke Bay Lodge

Serengeti
Stop Over

Kirawira
Tented Camp

Grumeti

D u t w a P l a i n

Mbalageti Serengeti

Mbalageti

Mwanza

Ndoha Plain

SERONERA

Lobo,
Ndabaka gate

Nyaraswiga
Plain

Serengeti

Songore River

Serengeti River

Olakira Camp
(June–Oct)

Ngare Namuki River

Turner
Springs

Maswa
Game Reserve

Seronera
Wildlife Lodge

Seronera

Wandahu River

Seronera River

Maasai
Koppes

Serengeti Sopa
Lodge

Naabi Hill gate

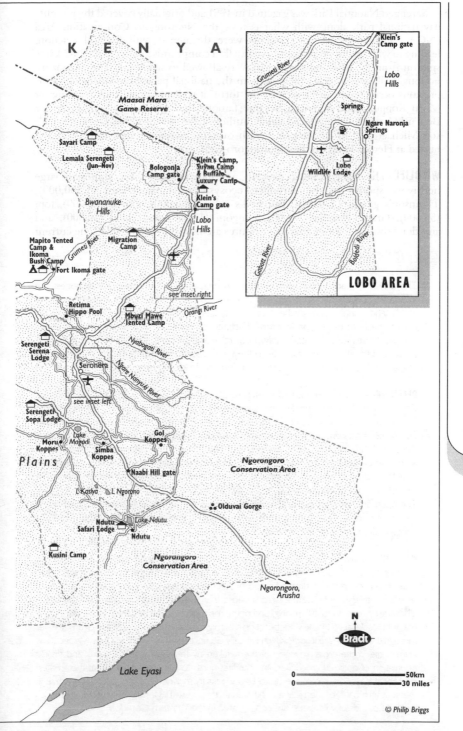

KENYA

Maasai Mara
Game Reserve

Sayari Camp

Lemala Serengeti
(Jun–Nov)

Bologonja
Camp gate

Klein's Camp,
Suyan Camp
& Buffalo
Luxury Camp

Klein's
Camp gate

Bwananuke
Hills

Lobo
Hills

Mapito Tented
Camp &
Ikoma
Bush Camp

Grumeti River

Migration
Camp

Fort Ikoma gate

see inset right

Orangi River

Retima
Hippo Pool

Mbuzi Mawe
Tented Camp

Nyabogati River

Serengeti
Serena
Lodge

Seronera

Ngare Nanyuki River

see inset left

Serengeti
Sopa Lodge

Lake
Magadi

Gol
Koppes

Moru
Koppes

Simba
Koppes

Plains

Naabi Hill gate

Ngorongoro
Conservation Area

L. Kasiya

L. Ngorano

Olduvai Gorge

Ndutu
Safari Lodge

Lake Ndutu

Ndutu

Kusini Camp

Ngorongoro
Conservation Area

Ngorongoro,
Arusha

Lake Eyasi

N

Bradt

0 ————— 50km
0 ————— 30 miles

© Philip Briggs

LOBO AREA

Klein's
Camp gate

Grumeti River

Lobo
Hills

Springs

Ngare Naronja
Springs

Lobo
Wildlife Lodge

Gabot River

Bolodi River

Serengeti National Park was gazetted in 1951 and originally covered the present-day national park along with what is now the Ngorongoro Conservation Area (NCA). The park's Maasai residents were threatened with forceful eviction, leading to widespread protests and eventually a compromise wherein the NCA was split off from the park and the Maasai were allowed to stay there. The Maasai are no longer allowed to graze their cattle in the national park, but evidence of their previous occupation can be seen in the form of well preserved rock paintings at Moru Koppies. The Serengeti became famous through the work of Professor Bernard Grzimek (pronounced *Jimek*), author of *Serengeti Shall Not Die*. Grzimek's son Michael died in an aeroplane crash over the Serengeti aged just 24, and is buried at Heroes Point on the Ngorongoro Crater rim.

WILDLIFE The most recent census figures indicate that the commonest large herbivore species in the Serengeti ecosystem are wildebeest (1,300,000), Thomson's gazelle (250,000), Burchell's zebra (200,000), impala (70,000), topi (50,000), Grant's gazelle (30,000), kongoni (15,000) and eland (10,000), and anecdotal sources indicate that these figures are now on the low side. The current

THE GREAT MIGRATION

The annual migration of at least two million ungulates – predominantly wildebeest but also large concentrations of zebra and lesser numbers of Thomson's gazelle, Grant's gazelle and eland – through the greater Serengeti ecosystem is indubitably the greatest extant spectacle of its type in Africa. Dictated by local rainfall patterns, the Serengeti migration does follow a reasonably predictable annual cycle, though there is also a fair amount of variation from one year to the next, dependent mainly on the precise timing of the rainy seasons. The cycle breaks up into the following main periods:

DECEMBER–APRIL The plains that stretch southeast from Seronera into the Ngorongoro Conservation Area form the Serengeti's main wildebeest calving grounds, centred on the Ndutu area of the NCA/Serengeti border. The wildebeest typically disperse into this area during the short rains, which fall in late November or early December, and stay put until the end of the long rains, generally in early May. These southeastern plains are the most accessible part of the park, particularly for those on a budget safari, and this is a fantastic time to be on safari in the Serengeti. True, you won't see the big herds on the move, but it's not uncommon to see herds of 10,000 animals, and the scenery is lush and green. The optimum time to visit this area is the peak calving season (late January into February) when hundreds, even thousands, of calves are dropped daily, and predator concentrations are also at their peak.

MAY–JULY Usually towards the end of April, the wildebeest and their entourage start to congregate on the southern plains in preparation for the 800km northward migration. The actual migration, regularly delayed in recent years due to late rain, might start any time from late April into early June, with a herd of more than a million migrating animals marching in a braying column up to 40km long, one of the most impressive spectacles in the world. The major obstacle faced by the wildebeest on this migration is the crossing of the Grumeti River through the Western Corridor, which typically occurs from June into early July. A great many animals die in the crossing, many of them taken by the Grumeti's ravenous and prolific population of outsized crocodiles, and the first herds to cross are generally at the greatest risk. For this reason, it can take up to two weeks from when the first wildebeest arrive at the southern bank of the river for the actual crossing to begin, by which time thousands upon thousands of wildebeest are congregated in the Western Corridor.

population of wildebeest may well be as high as two million, while the total number of zebra probably stands at around 500,000, with the two species often encountered together in immense mixed herds.

Other antelope species include Kirk's dik-dik, klipspringer, and small numbers of roan, oryx, oribi and waterbuck. There are significant numbers of buffalo, giraffe and warthog. Elephant are relatively scarce on the open plains, but can be very common in the north and west. The park's last resident herd of black rhinoceros – a mere seven individuals, as opposed to an estimated 700 in the mid 1970s – is restricted to the vicinity of the Moru Koppies in the far southeast, while another small population evidently ranges between Kenya's Maasai Mara National Reserve and the small wedge of the Serengeti that lies to the northwest of the Mara River. The most common and widespread diurnal primates are the olive baboon and vervet monkey, but an isolated and seldom seen population of patas monkey is resident in the west, and a few troops of black-and-white colobus haunt the riparian woodland along the Grumeti River through the Western Corridor.

Ultimately, the success of any safari lies in the number and quality of encounters with big cats. There is something infinitely compelling about these animals, a

AUGUST–NOVEMBER Following the great northward sweep across the Grumeti, the ungulates usually cross the Mara River in August, before dispersing across the plains of the northwest. Conventional wisdom has it that August–October is a bad time to visit the Serengeti, because the wildebeest have crossed the Kenya border into the Maasai Mara National Reserve. In reality, however, about half of the wildebeest stay in the northwest Serengeti over these months, and game viewing can be excellent, assuming that you can afford to base yourself at one of the exclusive tented camps in the Mara River area. Here, relatively small herds of wildebeest – typically between 500 and a few thousand – frequently move back and forth between the northern and southern banks of the Mara River in response to changes in the local rainfall pattern, a truly spectacular event. In October, sometimes earlier, the animals generally cross the Mara River one last time and start to plod back southward to the short-grass plains of the southeast, and there is a good chance of catching the southward migration in the Lobo area between late October and mid-November. The wildebeest usually reach the short-grass plains around Ndutu in late November, when the cycle starts all over again.

Whether it is worth planning your safari dates around the migration is a matter of choice. With the best will in the world, it would be practically impossible to ensure that a few days in the Serengeti will coincide with the exact date of a river crossing, which is the most spectacular event in the migration calendar, but impossible to predict to the day or even week. On the other hand, if you choose the right part of the Serengeti – the southeast from December to May, the Western Corridor over May–July, the Mara River area from July to October and the Lobo area over October–November – large herds of grazers should be easy enough to locate and there's a fair chance of witnessing a more spectacular migrational movement or river crossing.

On the other hand, bearing in mind that most predators and ungulate species other than zebra and wildebeest are strongly territorial and do not stray far from their core territory over the course of any given year, there is a lot to be said for avoiding the migration. Most of the lodges now charge considerably lower rates over April and May, with a knock-on effect on the rates offered by safari companies that suddenly become hungry for business. Furthermore, the safari circuit as a whole is far less crowded outside of peak seasons, and in our experience the Serengeti, irrespective of season, will still offer game viewing to equal that of any game reserve in Africa.

6

fascination that seems to affect even the most jaded of safari drivers – many of whom are leopard obsessive, content to drive up and down the Seronera Valley all day in the search for a telltale tail dangling from a tree. And when it comes to big cats, the Serengeti rarely disappoints. Lions are a practical certainty: the Tanzania side of the greater Serengeti ecosystem supports an estimated 2,500–3,000 individuals, which is probably the largest single population anywhere in Africa, and hundreds of resident lions stalk the plains around Seronera, with the main concentration centred on Simba, Moru and Gol Koppies close to the main Ngorongoro road. Here, it's normal to see two or three prides in the course of one game drive. Sociable, languid and deceptively pussycat-like, lions are most often seen lying low in the grass or basking on rocks. The challenge is to see a lion exert itself beyond a half-interested movement of the head when a vehicle stops nearby. Cheetahs, too, are very common: the park's estimated population of 500–600 is densest in the open grasslands around Seronera and further east towards Ndutu. In direct contrast to their more languid cousins, these streamlined, solitary creatures are most normally seen pacing the plains with the air of an agitated greyhound.

Of the other predators which can be seen in the Serengeti, spotted hyenas are very common, perhaps more numerous than lions. Golden jackals and bat-eared foxes appear to be the most abundant canid species on the plains around Seronera, while black-backed jackals are reasonably common in the thicker vegetation

SERENGETI BALLOON SAFARIS

Serengeti Balloon Safaris is – no prizes for guessing – the name of the company that runs balloon safaris from a launch site close to Seronera Lodge at 06.00 every morning. Although not cheap, a balloon safari is definitely worth the expense if you can afford it. Gliding serenely above the trees as the sun rises allows you to see the expansive plains from a new and quite thrilling angle. It also offers the chance to see secretive species such as bushbuck and reedbuck, and, because you leave so early in the morning, you are likely to spot a few nocturnal predators (we saw hyenas in abundance, civet twice and had a rare glimpse of an African wild cat). That said, any images you have of sweeping above innumerable wildebeest and zebra may prove a little removed from reality; you can be confident of seeing large herds of ungulates only if you're fortunate enough to be around during the exact week or two when animals concentrate immediately around Seronera.

The balloon safari culminates with a champagne breakfast in the bush, set up at a different site every day, depending on which way the balloons are blown. The meal is presented with some flourish: the immaculately uniformed waiters in particular conjure up images of the safaris of old. Our particular mad-hatters' breakfast party was enlivened by the arrival of three male lions, who strolled less than 100m from the table, apparently oblivious to the unusual apparition of 24 people eating scrambled eggs and sausages at a starched tablecloth in the bush. Presumably, this sort of thing doesn't happen every day, whether you're a lion or a human!

The package, which costs US$479 per person, includes the transfer to the balloon site, a flight of roughly one hour's duration, and the champagne breakfast. There is a booking desk at the Seronera Wildlife Lodge, as well as at the Serengeti Sopa and Serena Lodges. The other Serengeti lodges are too far from the launching site to get there in time (as things stand the transfer from Seronera leaves at 05.30 and from the other lodges at around 04.30!). If you want to be certain of a place, however, it is advisable to book in advance, particularly during high season. Reservations can be made through any safari company, or directly through Serengeti Balloon Safaris (❨ 027 254 8967; e info@balloonsafaris.com; www.info@balloonsafaris.com).

The Serengeti National Park, though popularly associated with grassland and open savannah, is in fact a reasonably ecologically varied entity. The western part of the national park consists of broken savannah, interspersed with impenetrable stands of whistling thorns and other acacias, and run through by the perennial Grumeti River and an attendant ribbon of riparian forest. The north, abutting Kenya's Maasai Mara Game Reserve, is unexpectedly hilly, particularly around Lobo, and it supports a variety of more or less wooded savannah habitats. So, while the actual Serengeti Plains in the southeast of the park do support the relatively limited avifauna one tends to associate with open grassland, the national park ranks with the best of them in terms of avian variety. A working Serengeti checklist compiled by Schmidt in the 1980s tallied 505 species, and at least 30 species have been added since 1990.

The Serengeti Mara ecosystem is one of Africa's Endemic Bird Areas, hosting five bird species found nowhere else, half of which are confined to the Tanzanian portion of the ecosystem. These 'Serengeti specials' are easy to locate and identify within their restricted range. The grey-throated spurfowl, a common roadside bird around the park headquarters at Seronera, is easily distinguished from the similar red-throated spurfowl by the white stripe below its red mask. In areas of woodland, parties of exquisite Fischer's lovebird draw attention to themselves by their incessant screeching and squawking as they flap energetically between trees. If the endemic spurfowl and lovebird are essentially local variations on a more widespread generic type, not so the rufous-tailed weaver, a fascinating bird placed in its own genus, but with nesting habits that indicate an affiliation to the sparrow-weavers. The rufous-tailed weaver is significantly larger and more sturdily built than most African ploceids, and its scaly feathering, pale eyes and habit of bouncing around boisterously in small flocks could lead to it being mistaken for a type of babbler – albeit one with an unusually large bill!

Of the two other Serengeti–Mara EBA endemics, the most visible and widespread is the Usambiro barbet, a close relative of the slightly smaller D'Arnaud's barbet, with which it is sometimes considered conspecific. Altogether more elusive is the grey-crested helmet-shrike, which strongly resembles the white helmet-shrike but is larger, has a more upright grey crest, and lacks an eye wattle. Although this striking bird indulges in typically conspicuous helmet-shrike behaviour, with small parties streaming noisily from one tree to the next, it is absent from the southern Serengeti, and thinly distributed in the north, where it is often associated with stands of whistling thorns.

Endemic chasing will be a priority of any serious birding visit to the Serengeti, but the mixed woodland and grassland of the north and west produce consistently good birdwatching including many species that will delight non-birders. The massive ostrich is common, as are other primarily terrestrial giants such as the kori bustard, secretary bird and southern ground hornbill. Perhaps the most distinctive of the smaller birds is the lilac-breasted roller, an exquisitely coloured gem often seen perched on trees alongside the road. Highlights are inevitably subjective, but recent memorable sightings included a breeding colony of Jackson's golden-backed weaver at Grumeti River Camp, a magnificent black eagle soaring above the cliffs at Lobo, and six different vulture species squabbling over a kill in the Western Corridor. And there is always the chance of an exciting 'first'. In 2001, close to Grumeti River Camp, we were fortunate enough to see (and photograph) the first golden pipit ever recorded in the national park. Recent additions to the Tanzanian bird list from Serengeti include European turtledove (1997), short-eared owl (1998), long-tailed nightjar, black-backed cisticola and swallow-tailed kite (2000), and Abyssinian roller and white-billed buffalo-weaver (2005).

towards Lobo. Driving at dusk or dawn, you stand the best chance of seeing nocturnal predators such as civet, serval, genet and African wildcat. The real rarity among the larger predators is the African wild dog, which was very common in the area until the 1970s, before the population dwindled to local extinction as a result of canid-borne diseases and persecution by farmers living on the park's periphery. Fortunately, wild dogs are very mobile and wide-ranging animals, and sightings have been reported with increased frequency over recent years, particularly in the far north and the adjacent Longido concessions.

SERONERA AND THE SOUTHERN PLAINS The short-grass plains stretching southeast from Seronera into the NCA might be termed the 'classic' Serengeti: a vast open expanse teeming with all manner of wild creatures ranging from the endearing bat-eared fox to the imperious lion, from flocks of habitually panicked ostrich to strutting pairs of secretary birds, and from the gigantic eland antelope to the diminutive mongoose. Densely populated with wildlife all year through, these southern plains are especially rewarding between December and May, when the rains act as a magnet to the migrant herds of wildebeest and zebra.

The main focal point of the region – indeed of the entire national park – is the park headquarters at Seronera, which is also the site of the oldest lodge in the Serengeti, as well as a cluster of public and special campsites, the staff village and various research projects. The recently opened visitors' information centre at Seronera is well worth a visit: facilities include a small site museum, as well as a picnic area and coffee shop, while an elevated wooden walkway leads through an informative open-air display.

The southern plains are interspersed with several clusters of rocky hills known as koppies, each of which forms a microhabitat inhabited by non-plains wildlife such as klipspringer, rock hyrax, leopard, rock agama, rock thrushes, mocking chat and various cliff-nesting raptors. As the name suggests, Simba Koppies, which straddles the main road between the NCA and Seronera, is particularly good for lion, while the grassland around the more easterly Gol Koppies is excellent for cheetah and lion. About 25km south of Seronera, the Moru Koppies area can also provide good lion and cheetah sightings, and it's home to the park's last resident black rhino, a herd of seven that evidently migrated across from the NCA in the mid 1990s.

A striking feature of this part of the Serengeti is the paucity of trees, which flourish only at the sides of koppies and along the riparian belts that follow the Mbalageti and Seronera rivers. The most likely explanation for this quirk is that the soil, which consists of volcanic deposits from an ancient eruption of Ngorongoro, is too hard for most roots to penetrate, except where it has been eroded by flowing water. Paradoxically, one consequence of this is that the thin strip of sausage trees and camelthorn acacias that follows the course of the Seronera River Valley ranks among the best places in Africa to search for leopards – there are simply too few tall trees for these normally elusive creatures to be as well hidden as they tend to be in dense woodland.

Aside from the two perennial rivers, both of which might be described as streams in another context, there is little permanent standing water in this part of the Serengeti. One exception is the small, saline Lake Magadi, which is fed by the Mbalageti River immediately northeast of Moru Koppies, and supports large numbers of aquatic birds, including thousands of flamingoes when the water level is suitable. A small hippo pool lies on the Seronera River about 5km south of Seronera along the road back towards the NCA. Far more impressive, however, is the Retima Hippo Pool, where up to 100 of these aquatic animals can be seen basking near the confluence of the Seronera and Grumeti rivers about 15km north of the park headquarters.

An unusual relic of the Serengeti's former Maasai inhabitants is to be found at Moru Koppies in the form of some well-preserved rock paintings of animals, shields and other traditional military regalia near the base of a small koppie. This is one of the few such sites associated with the Maasai, and the paintings, which are mostly red, black and white, may well have been inspired by the more ancient and more accomplished rock art of the Kondoa area – though it's anybody's guess whether they possess some sort of ritual significance, or are purely decorative. On another koppie not far from the rock paintings is an ancient rock gong thought to have been used by the Datoga predecessors of the Maasai – a short but steep scramble up a large boulder leads to the rock gong, which also makes for a good picnic spot.

The most central base for exploring this region is Seronera Wildlife Lodge, or one of the nearby campsites at the park headquarters. Two of the other three large lodges in the Serengeti – respectively part of the Serena and Sopa chains – are also well positioned for exploring the southern plains, and have far better facilities. Many safari companies also set up seasonal or semi-permanent tented camps at one or other of the myriad special campsites in the vicinity of Seronera. Of the smaller lodges in the national park, the underrated Ndutu Safari Lodge (which actually lies within the NCA; see page 180) and the wonderfully remote Kusini Camp (see below) are both well sited for exploring the southern plains, and remote from the perennially busy road circuit in the immediate vicinity of Seronera.

⌂ Where to stay
Exclusive
⌂ **Lemala Serengeti** (10 tents). This mobile tented camp, described on page 182, is set up about 5km from Ndutu Airstrip in Dec–Apr, when it is well positioned to catch the migration as it disperses in the southeast & during calving season. US$745/990 sgl/dbl FB.

⌂ **Olakira Camp** (6 tents) ☏ 027 250 4118/9; m 0784 763338; e info@asilialodges.com; www.asilialodges.com. This wonderful mobile camp moves seasonally between 2 different locations in the southern Serengeti to complement its more northerly sister camp Sayari. It is based at Ndutu for the wildebeest calving season, usually Nov–Mar. It closes Apr & May, then moves up to Turner Springs, a private special campsite a 20min drive from Seronera, in an area notable for its dense (& nocturnally vociferous) population of spotted hyena. The Turner Springs site is well placed to catch the migration as it passes through the area in Jun–Jul, & for balloon flight from Seronera Wildlife Lodge. It has a classic safari ambience & décor, consisting of 6 attractively furnished standing tents with king-size or twin beds, private veranda & en-suite flush toilet & hot shower. US$670/990 sgl/dbl FB or

US$730/1,110 full game package; low-season discount around 20%.

⌂ **Kusini Camp** (14 rooms) ☏ 027 250 9817; f 027 250 8273; e tanzania@sanctuarylodges.com; www.sanctuarylodges.com. With its fantastic location among a set of tall black boulders some 40km south of the Moru Koppies, this spaciously laid out camp is the most remote & exclusive place to stay in the southern Serengeti, especially in Mar when the area hosts immense herds of wildebeest & zebra. At other times of the year, elephant, giraffe & buffalo are quite common in the surrounding acacia woodland – indeed, some impressively hefty buffalo bulls are resident in camp – & lion & leopard are seen with some frequency. The best goal for game drives out of Kusini is Moru Koppies, where lion are plentiful & rhino present but seldom seen, & there are plenty of birds around, including the striking secretary bird for which the camp is named. US$470/640 FB inc drinks, or US$575/850 full game package; substantial discount Nov–mid-Dec & Jan–Mar. Closed Apr & May.

Upmarket

Serengeti Wilderness Camp (10 rooms) ⟍ 027 250 2668; e serecamp.wildfrontiers@habari.co.tz; www.wildfrontiers.com. This down-to-earth mobile tented camp, run by the highly regarded operator Wild Frontiers, moves location every few months as dictated by the movements of the wildebeest migration. The en-suite tents have solar lighting, eco-friendly toilets, & comfortable but unpretentious furnishings. It generally spends Nov–mid-Apr in the southern plains, relocating to the Western Corridor Jun–Jul & moving further north Aug–Oct. Closed mid-Apr–May. *US$450/680 FB.*

Serengeti Serena Lodge (66 rooms) ⟍ 028 262 1507; f 028 262 1520; e reservations@ serena.co.tz; www.serenahotels.com. Situated on a hilltop roughly 20km west of Seronera, this is probably the most comfortable of the larger lodges in this part of the Serengeti. Accommodation is in a village-like cluster of Maasai-style double-storey rondawels (round African-style huts), built with slate, wood & thatch to create a pleasing organic feel. The spacious self-contained rooms each have 1 sgl & 1 king-size bed, nets & fans, & hot showers. There is a swimming pool, & the buffet meals are far superior to those in most East African safari lodges. The one negative is that game viewing in the thick scrub around the lodge is poor except for when the migration passes through, & it's a good half-hour drive before you reach the main game-viewing circuit east of Seronera Lodge. *US$375/550 sgl/dbl FB, US$225/335 Apr–Jun.*

Serengeti Sopa Lodge (73 rooms) ⟍ 027 250 0630/9; f 027 250 8245; e info@sopalodges.com; www.sopalodges.com. This large ostentatious lodge lies about 30min drive south of Seronera, on the side of a hill near the Moru Koppies. The rooms here are practically suites: each has 2 dbl beds, a small sitting room, large bathroom complete with bidet, private balcony & large window giving a grandstand view over the plains below, perfectly appointed to catch the sunset. Following extensive renovations over 2005–6, the formerly rather ostentatious & jarring interior has been supplanted by a more attractive & distinctively African look. The food is excellent & facilities include a swimming pool & internet café. Game viewing in the surrounding area is generally very good, with a high chance of encountering tree-climbing lions on the road north to Seronera, & there's much less traffic in the immediate vicinity than there is around the park headquarters. *US$320/550 sgl/dbl FB, US$265/450 Mar, Nov & early Dec, US$100/200 Apr & May.*

Simiyu Mobile Camp (9 rooms) ⟍ 027 254 4556; m 0784 207727; f 027 250 8937; e twc-reservations@habari.co.tz; www.tanganyikawildernesscamps.com. This highly rated luxury mobile camp moves among 4 locations over the course of the year in order to stick close to the migration. Dates might change from one year to the next depending on the movement of the wildebeest, but usually it would be around Ndutu Dec–Mar, split between the Seronera area & the Western Corridor May–Aug & somewhere further north Aug–Nov. All tents are en-suite & comfortably furnished with king-size or twin bed, flush toilet & bucket shower inside. Dinner is usually served outside, weather permitting. Good value. *US$300/400 sgl/dbl FB.*

Serengeti Savannah Camps (12 rooms) ⟍ 027 254 7066 e bookings@serengetisavannahcamps.com; www.serengetisavannahcamps.com. This small mobile tented camp, one of the few in northern Tanzania that's not part of a chain, aims to offer safari-goers a genuine bush experience at a reasonable price. It moves between 2 locations, one in the Seronera area Jun–Nov & one near Ndutu Dec–Mar to catch the calving season. The tents are simply but comfortably furnished & all have a private veranda, chemical toilet & starlight shower. *US$280/460 sgl/dbl FB, hefty discounts for residents.*

Ndutu Safari Lodge (35 rooms) ⟍ 027 250 2829/6702; f 027 250 8310; e bookings@ ndutu.com; www.ndutu.com. Although it is actually situated just within the Ngorongoro Conservation Area on the southeast border with the Serengeti, Ndutu is most logically bracketed with the Seronera lodges, since the western plains of the conservation area essentially belong to the same seasonal ecosystem. A low-key & underrated retreat, Ndutu Safari Lodge is set in thick acacia woodland overlooking the seasonal Lake Ndutu, & it has a distinct 'bush' atmosphere lacking from other comparably priced lodges in the Serengeti ecosystem. The rooms are in small, unfussy stone chalets & have netting & hot water. The bar & restaurant are open-sided stone & thatch structures frequented by a legion of genets by night. This is an excellent place to stay if you want to avoid the crowds, & the surrounding plains offer good general game viewing, particularly during the wet season when they are teeming with wildebeest. Despite lying within the NCA, Ndutu isn't well positioned for visiting Ngorongoro Crater. It should also be noted that crossing into the Serengeti while staying at Ndutu would attract a separate national park entrance fee. *Self-contained bungalows US$249/385 sgl/dbl FB, US$199/302 May–Nov.*

⌂ **Seronera Wildlife Lodge** (100 rooms) ✆ 027 254 4595; f 027 254 8633; e res@ hotelsandlodges-tanzania.com; www.hotelsandlodges-tanzania.com. The most central lodge in the Serengeti, situated only a couple of kilometres from the park headquarters at Seronera, has an unbeatable location for game drives. It was built around a granite koppie in the early 1970s, & uses the natural features to create an individual & unmistakably African character. The bar, frequented by bats & rock hyraxes, is reached through a narrow corridor between 2 boulders, while the natural rock walls of the cavernous restaurant are decorated with traditionally styled paintings. In common with other former government lodges, the service, food & facilities have long lagged behind those of most newer lodges, & the outmoded fittings just feel rather tacky after 3 decades of service, but this should have changed following an extensive renovations & refurnishing programme initiated by the new private management in 2008. Rooms are compact but comfortable, with en-suite bathrooms & large windows facing the surrounding bush. The best reason to select this lodge is simply its brilliant location for game drives, at the heart of the superlative (but sometimes rather overcrowded – see page 171) Seronera game viewing circuit. *Rates on application.*

Budget and camping There is a simple resthouse at the Seronera park headquarters (*US$30 pp B&B*), as well as a hostel with bunk accommodation (*US$20 pp B&B*).

A cluster of seven campsites lies about 5km from Seronera Lodge (*camping US$30 pp*). Facilities are limited to long-drop toilets & a rubbish pit. You may be able to organise a shower and fill up water containers for a small fee at the lodge. There is a good chance of seeing nocturnal scavengers such as hyena and genet – even, rather disconcertingly, the occasional lion pride – pass through the campsites after dark.

LOBO AND THE NORTHERN SERENGETI Wildly beautiful, and refreshingly untrammelled coming after Seronera, the northern third of the Serengeti is characterised by green, rolling hills that undulate gently towards the Kenya border, capped by some spectacular granite outcrops, particularly in the vicinity of Lobo. A cover of dense acacia woodland is interspersed with tracts of more open grassland, bisected by the ribbons of lush riparian woodland that enclose the Grumeti and Mara rivers and their various tributaries. Partly due to the relatively dense foliage, the northern Serengeti doesn't generally match up to the south in terms of game viewing, but then nor is it anything like as overrun with tourist traffic as the road circuits around Seronera – it's still possible to do an entire game drive without seeing another vehicle in this part of the Serengeti.

If it is sheer volumes of wildlife you're after, Lobo and surrounds generally come into their own during September and October, when the wildebeest pass through on the southward migration from Kenya to the Serengeti Plains. But even at other times of year, there is plenty to hold your interest. The area supports most of the park's elephant population, and the base of the Lobo Hills in particular is noted for large prides of lions, as well as providing refuge to cheetah, leopard, spotted hyena, bat-eared fox and several pairs of the exquisite serval, a small spotted cat most often seen darting through open grassland shortly after sunrise.

The one part of the northern Serengeti to match the southern plains for general game viewing is the wedge of sloping grassland that divides the Mara River from the Kenya border. Sometimes referred to as the Mara Triangle, this southern extension of the legendary Maasai Mara National Reserve supports prodigious herds of eland, topi, gazelle, zebra, wildebeest, buffalo *et al.* throughout the year, and it can be little short of mind-boggling when the migration moves in over July to September. During this time of year, large herds of wildebeest frequently gather on one or other side of the river, sometimes milling around for hours, even days, before one brave or foolish individual initiates a sudden river crossing, often for no apparent reason – indeed, it's not unusual for the same group of wildebeest to cross back in the opposite direction within hours of the initial crossing, suggesting these rather slow-witted beasts adhere firmly to the maxim that the grass is always greener on the other side.

Prior to 2005, the Mara Triangle had been effectively closed to casual tourism for decades, partly due to its remoteness from any lodge, and partly due to problems with banditry and poaching. Today, the few visitors who make it up this far are still unlikely to see much other tourist traffic, but the area can be readily accessed from two seasonal tented camps, Sayari and Lemala Serengeti, both of which lie to the south of the Mara River near Kogatende Rangers Post, where a concrete causeway crosses the river.

Where to stay
Exclusive

Migration Camp (20 rooms) ☎ 027 254 0630/9; f 027 254 8245; e info@elewana.com; www.elewana.com. Set in the Ndasiata Hills about 20km from Lobo, this formerly rather run-down camp has undergone 2 major makeovers, most recently after it was acquired by Elewana in 2004. It now ranks as one of the most exclusive lodges within the Serengeti National Park. Accommodation is in spacious en-suite luxury 'tents' made of canvas & wood, complemented by stylish wooden décor evoking the Edwardian era, & with large balconies facing the perennial Grumeti River. The lushly wooded grounds are rustling with birds & lizards, & there is a hippo pool on the river, with larger mammals often passing through camp. The surrounding area supports resident populations of lion, leopard, elephant & buffalo, & is fantastic when the migration passes through. Facilities include a swimming pool, jacuzzi, cocktail bar, library & lounge. An unusual feature of the camp is that short, guided game walks can be undertaken along several trails leading out from it. *US$1,118/1,490 sgl/dbl FB, inc most drinks, laundry, transfer to/from Lobo airstrip; US$1,020/1,360 Mar, Nov & early Dec, US$945 /1,260 Apr & May. Full game package inc driver additional US$100 pp.*

Sayari Camp (6 rooms) ☎ 027 250 2799; m 0784 763338; e info@asilialodges.com; www.asilialodges.com. Established in 2005, this wonderful remote tented camp lies close to the south bank of the Mara River, offering ready access to what is arguably the best-kept game-viewing secret in all of northern Tanzania: the superb Mara Triangle. This untrammelled wedge of open grassland supports some of the densest grazer populations in East Africa, as well as all the Big Five (rhino sometimes cross from Kenya's Maasai Mara) & a great many birds. The accommodation is as upmarket as you might hope for in a semi-permanent camp, consisting of 6 stylishly decorated walk-in tents with private balconies & en-suite toilets & hot showers, & the food is both imaginative & classy. But the main attraction of Sayari is the genuine wilderness atmosphere & remoteness from other lodges. *US$775/1,160 sgl/dbl FB or US$830/1,290 full game package; low-season discount around 20%.*

Lemala Serengeti (10 tents) ☎ 027 254 8966; f 027 254 8937; e info@lemalacamp.com; www.lemalacamp.com. Established in 2007, this semi-permanent luxury tented camp spends Dec–Apr in the Ndutu area, then relocates to the north early Jun–mid-Nov. The northern location lies on a boulder-strewn slope close to the main Lobo road about 25km south of the Kogatende Rangers Post & causeway offering access to the Mara Triangle. The impressive koppies between Lemala & Kogatende have long hosted a resident pride of large lions, which are often seen sprawled out on the rocks. The tents are very spacious & decorated in classic safari style, with a wooden floor & canvas top, & all have twin or king-size beds, solar powered lighting & hot water. *US$775/1,150 sgl/dbl FB; substantial discount Jun & Nov.*

Klein's Camp ☎ 027 254 8549/8038 or (South Africa) +27 11 809 4447; e inboundsales@andbeyond.com; www.andbeyond.com. This excellent &Beyond lodge lies just outside the eastern border of the national park, on a private conservancy leased from the local Maasai, & it effectively functions as an exclusive private game reserve, since camp residents have sole use of the concession. Because Klein's Camp lies outside the national park, there are no restrictions prohibiting night drives & guided game walks, both of which add an extra dimension to a safari. The camp has a stunning location on the side of a hill offering panoramic views in all directions, & game viewing in the region is generally good, particularly along the Grumeti

River, with a similar range of species as found in the Lobo area. The camp consists of 10 self-contained *bandas*, each with hot shower, nets, & private balcony with view. *US$950 pp FB, US$625 Mar, May, Nov & early Dec, inc all meals, drinks & activities. Closed Apr.*

⌂ **Suyan Camp** (6 rooms) ☎ 027 250 2799; m 0784 763338; e info@asilialodges.com; www.asilialodges.com. Situated about 2km outside Klein's Gate, this wonderful luxury tented camp lies along a stretch of lush riverine forest in the vast Loliondo Game Controlled Area, which is bounded by Serengeti National Park to the west, Lake Natron to the east & the NCA to the south. A good base for game drives in the Lobo area or Serengeti National Park, & within day-tripping distance of the Mara River, the camp also offer guided game walks with a Maasai guide, & night drives in the concession, which

supports a similar range of species to the neighbouring national park. A significant portion of proceeds is paid to the local Maasai community from whom the land is leased. *US$730/1,110 full game package; low-season discount around 20%.*

⌂ **Buffalo Luxury Camp** (20 rooms) ☎ 027 255 3858; e info@buffaloluxurycamp.com; www.buffaloluxurycamp.com. Situated within the Loliondo Game Controlled Area, on a 30ha titled plot near Klein's Gate, this promising new luxury tented camp offers the opportunity to undertake game drives in the game-rich Lobo Hills of the northern Serengeti as well as other activities such as guided walks & night drives. Large en-suite standing tents have an elevated sleeping area, a sitting room, electricity, running water & flush toilets. *US$625 pp FB, US$560 Apr–May, inc unlimited day & night game drives, walking safaris, Maasai cultural*

Upmarket

⌂ **Lobo Wildlife Lodge** (75 rooms) ☎ 027 254 4595; f 027 254 8633; e sales@hotelsandlodges-tanzania.com; www.hotelsandlodges-tanzania.com. As with the other former government hotels in this chain, Lobo boasts an inalienable asset in the form of a stunning location, but one that was long let down by the poor standard of service & maintenance, though is soon to change following the initiation of an extensive programme of renovations in late 2008. The lodge was built over 1968–70, at which time the majority of tourism to the Serengeti came directly from Kenya, & it has waned in popularity now that visitors to the Serengeti come through Arusha. This is a shame, because it is an amazing construction. Like Seronera, it's built around a koppie, but the design is even more impressive & imaginative than that of the more southerly lodge, spanning 4 floors & with a fantastic view over the surrounding plains. The surrounding hills can offer some wonderful game viewing (a pride of 20 lions

is resident in the immediate vicinity of the lodge), & the grounds are crawling with hyraxes & colourful agama lizards. Lobo is relatively good value. *Rates on application.*

⌂ **Mbuzi Mawe Tented Camp** (16 rooms) ☎ 027 250 4058; f 027 250 8282; e reservations@serena.co.tz; www.serenahotels.com. This new tented camp is set among a group of ancient granite koppies overlooking the Tagora Plains roughly 45km northeast of Seronera & 30km southwest of Lobo. The lodge's central location makes it a useful base from which to explore most of the key game-viewing areas in the Serengeti, & there is quite a bit of wildlife resident in the immediate vicinity (including the rock-dwelling klipspringer for which it is named), supplemented by the migration as it heads southwards in Nov or Dec. Accommodation is in large, earthily decorated en-suite standing tents, each with 2 dbl beds & a private stone patio with a view towards the rocks. A swimming pool is planned. *US$375/550 sgl/dbl FB, US$225/335 Apr–Jun.*

Camping The campsite (*US$30 pp*) immediately outside the Lobo Wildlife Lodge is little used by comparison with those at Seronera. Facilities are limited to a toilet and rubbish pit. You can pop into the neighbouring lodge for a drink or meal if you like.

THE WESTERN CORRIDOR The relatively narrow arm of the Serengeti that stretches westward from Seronera almost as far as the shore of Lake Victoria is generally flatter than the more northerly parts of the park, but moister and more densely vegetated than the southern plains. Aside from a few small isolated mountain ranges, the dominant geographic feature of the Western Corridor is a pair of rivers, the Grumeti and Mbalageti, whose near-parallel west-flowing courses, which run less than 20km apart, support tall ribbons of riparian forest before eventually exiting

6

the national park to empty into Lake Victoria. The characteristic vegetation of the Western Corridor is park-like woodland, interspersed with areas of open grassland and dense stands of the ghostly grey 'whistling thorn', *Acacia drepanolobrium*.

Tourist traffic in this part of the park is relatively low: few camping safaris make it this far south, and accommodation is limited to a handful of smallish camps. Game viewing is pretty good throughout the year: the broken savannah to the south of the Grumeti River supports substantial resident populations of lion, giraffe, wildebeest, zebra and most other typical plains animals, while the riverine forest harbours a few troops of the exquisite black-and-white colobus monkey, and the little-visited vistas of open grassland north of the river are especially good for cheetah. Between May and July, the migration usually passes through the Western Corridor, though it may stick further east in years of heavy rain. The crossing of the Grumeti, usually in June or July, is one of the most dramatic sequences in the annual wildebeest migration, and a positive bonanza for a dense population of gargantuan crocodiles.

Where to stay
Exclusive

Singita Grumeti Reserves (24 rooms across 3 lodges) ✆ (South Africa) +27 (0)21 683 3424; e singita@singita.com; www.singita.com. The legendary South African lodge operator Singita recently acquired exclusive traversing rights across the 1,400km² Grumeti Game Reserve, a northern extension of the Western Corridor, where it now operates a trio of luxury upmarket lodges aimed at seriously affluent travellers seeking an exclusive safari experience. The flagship Sasakwa Lodge on the eponymous hill offers dramatic elevated views across the verdant plains of the Western Corridor, while Faru Faru Lodge lies in a wooded area noted for its high mammal & bird diversity. The more earthy Sabora Camp is a tented camp set in the open plains. The wildlife in this formerly undeveloped corner of the greater Serengeti is similar to other parts of the vast ecosystem, but notable population increases have been recorded since 2003, & plans to translocate 48 black rhino from South Africa are underway. The enterprise employs 600 people, mostly from surrounding communities, & it offers cultural visits to nearby villages. Although wildlife viewing is good all year through, it peaks during Jul–Sep, when the migration is in the area. *US$1,250/1,990 sgl/dbl for Sabora or Faru Faru, or US$2,000/3,200 sgl/dbl for Sasakwa. Rates inc all meals, drinks & activities.*

Kirawira Tented Camp (25 rooms) ✆ 027 250 4058; f 027 250 8282; e reservations@ serena.co.tz; www.serenahotels.com. Part of the Serena chain, this is another very upmarket tented camp, set on a small acacia-covered hill offering sweeping views over the Western Corridor. The Edwardian décor of the communal areas creates something of an *Out of Africa* feel, & while the atmosphere is neither as intimate nor as 'bush' as at Grumeti, Kirawira does have a

definite charm – & it will probably appeal more to safari-goers who don't find the thought of having hippo & buffalo chomping around their tent a major draw. Accommodation consists of 25 standing tents, each set on its own raised platform & comfortably decorated with a netted king-size bed & en-suite shower & toilet. There is a large swimming pool, the service is immaculate, & the food is probably the best in the Serengeti. *US$950/1,450 sgl/dbl, US$435/755 Apr–May, inc all meals, drinks, game drives & walks.*

Grumeti River Camp (10 rooms) ✆ 027 254 8549/8038 or (South Africa) +2711 809 4447; e inboundsales@andbeyond.com; www.andbeyond.com. Overlooking a small pool near the Grumeti River, this archetypal bush camp easily ranks as our favourite lodge anywhere in the Serengeti. The mood here is pure in-your-face Africa: the pool in front of the bar supports a resident pod of hippos & attracts a steady stream of other large mammals coming to drink, while birdlife is prolific both at the water's edge & in the surrounding thickets. At night, the place comes alive with a steady chorus of insects & frogs, & hippos & buffaloes grazing noisily around the tents. This place isn't for the faint-hearted, & you shouldn't even think about walking around at night without an armed escort, as the buffaloes have been known to charge. Facilities include an outdoor *boma*, where evening meals are served (except when it rains), & a small circular swimming pool from where you can watch hippos bathing while you do the same thing. Accommodation consists of 10 stylish tents, each of which has a netted king-size bed & en-suite toilet & showers. The atmosphere is very informal, & the service is excellent without ever becoming impersonal. *US$950 pp FB, US$625 pp Mar, May, Nov & early Dec, inc all meals, drinks & activities. Closed Apr.*

Upmarket

🏠 **Mbalageti Serengeti** (40 rooms) ☎ 028 262 2387; e mbalageti@bol.co.tz; www.mbalageti.com. Located in the Western Corridor, Mbalageti is perched on the northwestern slopes of Mwamnevi Hill, which lies 16km south of the main road through the Western Corridor, crossing the game-rich seasonal Dutwa floodplain & the Mbalageti River en route. Accommodation is in stunning thatch, wood, stone & canvas cottages, all of which are secluded in the evergreen woodland running along the ridge of the hill, & come with large wooden decks offering a superb view over the river to the Dutwa Plains from the outdoor bath. The dining area & bar are centred on a swimming pool, also offering panoramic views, & the food — different theme buffets every night — is excellent. Overall, it's a very comfortable & relatively affordable alternative to the more established lodges in the Western Corridor. *US$340/420 std sgl/dbl, US$350/645 tented chalet; US$260/395 & US$330/585 most of Dec–Mar, Sep & Oct, US$200/290 & US$250/370 Apr & May, inc all meals & most drinks.*

Moderate

🏠 **Ikoma Bush Camp** (17 rooms) ☎ 027 255 3243/250 6315; e reservations@moivaro.com; www.moivaro.com. This refreshingly unpretentious camp is situated on a concession immediately outside of the national park, roughly 3km from Ikoma Gate by road, & about 40km northwest of Seronera. The concession has been granted to the lodge by the nearby village of Robanda, which is paid a fee (used to fund the local school, water pump & clinic) in exchange for use of the land & assistance with anti-poaching patrols. Set in a glade of acacias, accommodation is in old-style no-frills dbl & twin tents with en-suite showers & small verandas facing out towards the bush. Because it lies outside the park, guided game walks are on offer, as are night drives, which come with a chance of encountering the likes of leopard, genet & more occasionally the secretive aardvark. It's a great base at any time of year, but especially Jun when the migration passes through, & still quite reasonably priced. *US$286/357 sgl/dbl FB, US$251/314 Mar, Jun, Sep–mid-Dec, US$176/220 Apr & May.*

🏠 **Mapito Tented Camp** (10 rooms) m 0732 975210; f 0784 864626; info@mapito-tented-camp.com; www.mapito-tented-camp.com. Similar in style & feel to Ikoma Bush Camp & situated outside the same entrance gate, this is a very likeable & reasonably priced tented camp with a real bush feel, plenty of avian & mammal activity in the immediate vicinity, & a variety of activities on offer, including guided walks & night drives. Set on stone platforms, the standing tents come with twin or king-size beds, & are furnished with a strong African touch, & have a private veranda & en-suite toilets & showers. The solar-lit mess tent serves hearty home-style meals. *US$259/428 sgl/dbl FB, US$248/408 Sep–mid-Dec. Closed Apr & May.*

🏠 **Kijireshi Tented Camp** ☎ 028 262 1231; e tilapia@mwanza.com; www.kijireshi.com. Under the same ownership as the Tilapia Hotel in Mwanza, this little-known camp lies close to Bunda on the western border of the Serengeti. It offers comfortable accommodation in furnished tents, & has a bar & restaurant. *US$100/150 FB self-contained dbl.*

Budget and camping

🏠 **Serengeti Stop Over** (10 rooms) ☎ 028 262 273; m 0784 406996/422359; f 028 250 0388; e info@serengetistopover.com; www.serengetistopover.com. This excellent budget lodge lies along the eastern side of the main Mwanza–Musoma road, in an area where quite a bit of game can be present, about 1km south of the Ndaraka Entrance Gate to Serengeti National Park & 18km south of Bunda. The lodge consists of 10 *bandas* & a campsite with hot showers & cooking shades. A great advantage of staying here for motorised travellers coming from Kenya or Mwanza is that park fees are only payable once you enter the park. The lodge can arrange safaris to Serengeti National Park, which will work out more cheaply than a safari out of Arusha, if only because the lodge is a mere 1km from the entrance gate & 135km from Seronera, so that an overnight or day trip is a realistic possibility. The cost of a vehicle to carry up to 5 people for a day trip into the park is US$130. Other activities include a walking safari to Lake Victoria at US$18 per trip, traditional & game fishing trips, a visit to the Nyerere Museum, & dancing & other cultural activities. *Camping US$10, tent hire plus US$5 pp; banda accommodation US$30/55 sgl/dbl B&B.*

TARANGIRE NATIONAL PARK

The 2,850km² Tarangire National Park lies at the core of a much more expansive ecosystem, one that also comprises the 585km² Tarangire Conservation Area (TCA) and some 5,000km² of unprotected land extending across the Maasai Steppes. In general, the Tarangire region is drier than the Serengeti, but also more densely vegetated, covered primarily in a tangle of semi-arid acacia and mixed woodland. The park's dominant geographic feature is the Tarangire River, which is flanked by a cover of dense elephant grass and a sporadic ribbon of riparian woodland dotted with the occasional palm tree. A memorable feature of the park is its immense baobab trees, which are abundant throughout.

As with the Serengeti, there is a great deal of migratory movement within the greater Tarangire ecosystem. During the wet season, most of the wildlife disperses from the park on to the Maasai Steppes, while the wildebeest and zebra move northwest to the Rift Valley floor between lakes Natron and Manyara. In direct contrast to the Serengeti, Tarangire comes into its own during the dry season, between July and November, when the large herds of game attracted to the permanent waters of the Tarangire River make this reserve as alluring as any in Tanzania.

Abutting the northeastern border of the national park, the TCA consists of four contiguous tracts of land that were used for trophy hunting until ownership was restored to their traditional Maasai inhabitants in the late 1990s. The TCA now functions as a buffer conservation area to the national park, encompassing the main watershed for the Tarangire River, the wetlands around Gosuwa Swamp, and the migration routes used by wildebeest and zebra to reach their breeding grounds near Lolkisale Mountain. The Maasai communities in the area earn revenue from levies raised by tourist lodges such as Tarangire Treetops, Boundary Hill and Naitolia. An important difference between these lodges and their counterparts within the national park is that game walks and night drives are permitted.

A detailed booklet, *Tarangire National Park*, is available from the National Parks office in Arusha. The park entrance fee of US$35 per person per 24 hours should ideally be paid by MasterCard or Tanapa Card (issued at any Exim Bank). No other cards are accepted, nor are travellers' cheques, and cash payments attract a 50% penalty.

GETTING THERE AND AWAY Tarangire lies about 7km off the main Arusha–Dodoma road. Coming from Arusha, this road is tarred as far as the turn-off to the park, which is clearly signposted about 100km south of Arusha and 20km past Makuyuni (the junction for Manyara and the Serengeti). Most people tag a visit to Tarangire on to a longer safari, but if your time or money is limited, a one- or two-day stand-alone safari would be a viable option.

WHERE TO STAY
Exclusive

↑ **Tarangire Treetops Lodge** (20 rooms) ☏ 027 254 0630/9; f 027 254 8245; e info@elewana.com; www.elewana.com. Situated to the northeast of the national park within the Tarangire Conservation Area, this architecturally innovative lodge consists of 20 spacious & luxurious en-suite tree houses, each with a floor area of 65m², perched up in the branches of a stand of massive baobab trees – so atmospheric & comfortable it almost seems a shame to leave

them to go on a game drive! Because the lodge lies on private land, activities such as game walks, birding walks along a nearby watercourse, night drives & mountain biking excursions supplement the usual diurnal game drives. The quality of game viewing in the immediate vicinity varies seasonally, but it's only 45min by road to Boundary Hill Gate, the main road circuit in northern Tarangire. Ideal for honeymooners, this lodge is also a wonderful

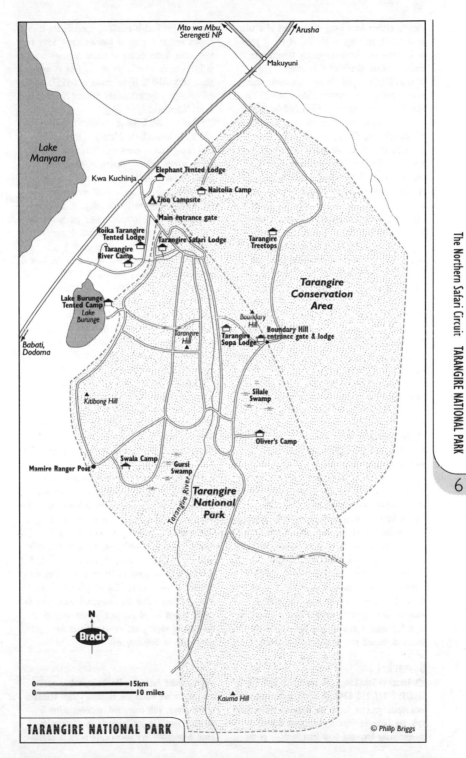

Lake
Manyara

Mto wa Mbu,
Serengeti NP

Arusha

Makuyuni

Elephant Tented Lodge

Kwa Kuchinja

Naitolia Camp

Zion Campsite

Main entrance gate

Roika Tarangire
Tented Lodge

Tarangire Safari Lodge

Tarangire
Treetops

Tarangire
River Camp

Tarangire
Conservation
Area

Lake Burunge
Tented Camp

Lake
Burunge

Boundary
Hill

Babati,
Dodoma

Tarangire
Hill

Tarangire
Sopa Lodge

Boundary Hill
entrance gate & lodge

Kitibong Hill

Silale
Swamp

Oliver's Camp

Swala Camp

Gursi
Swamp

Mamire Ranger Post

Tarangire River

Tarangire
National
Park

N

Bradt

0 ———————— 15km
0 ———————— 10 miles

Kauma Hill

TARANGIRE NATIONAL PARK

© Philip Briggs

place to recover from jetlag at the start of a safari, or to stretch your legs at the end of one. A portion of the room rate funds community projects such as the construction of schools & boreholes. US$1,118/1,490 sgl/dbl FB, inc most drinks, laundry, transfer to/from Kuro airstrip; US$1,020/1,360 in Mar, Nov & early Dec; US$945 /1,260 Apr & May. Full game package inc drives additional US$100 pp.
⌂ **Oliver's Camp** (5 rooms) ☎ 027 250 4118; m 0784 763338; e info@asilialodges.com; www.asilialodges.com. This excellent bush camp is located near the Silale Swamp within the park boundaries, but far away from the busy northern section of the park so that activities can usually be undertaken without seeing other tourists. It caters both for 2-night stays incorporated into more wide-ranging safaris as well as for extended stays of 3 days or more, in which visitors explore the area on foot (it is the only location where walking safaris can be undertaken inside Tarangire) & by vehicle, as well as spending one or more nights at a mobile fly-camp. The lodge itself is unpretentious & comfortable rather than opulently luxurious, the guides are unusually personable & knowledgeable, & a superb library of natural-history books underscores the emphasis on substance over style – strongly recommended to anybody seeking a genuinely holistic bush experience. US$620/890 sgl/dbl FB or US$730/1,110 full game package; low-season discount around 20%.
⌂ **Swala Camp** (9 rooms) ☎ 027 250 9817; f 027 250 8273; e tanzania@sanctuarylodges.com; www.sanctuarylodges.com. Situated in the southern half of the park, this classic luxury tented camp stands in a grove of tall acacia trees overlooking the remote Gurusi Swamp, where it is wonderfully isolated from any other lodge or the more popular game-viewing circuits. The camp itself is something of a magnet for wildlife: the *swala* (antelope) for which it is named are much in evidence, especially a resident herd of impala, accompanied by a noisy entourage of vervet monkeys, guineafowl & various plovers, buffalo-weavers & starlings. The small waterhole in front of the camp attracts elephants in Jul & Aug, while a near-resident lion pride & the occasional leopard pass through with surprising

regularity. The food is excellent, especially the bush dinners held in a grove of baobabs about 5min drive from camp, & the quality of tented accommodation is in line with the best lodges of this type in southern Africa. US$470/640 FB inc drinks, or US$575/850 full game package; substantial discount Nov–mid-Dec & Jan-Mar. Closed Apr & May.
⌂ **Boundary Hill Lodge** (8 rooms) m 0787 293727; e simon@eastafricansafari.info; www.tarangireconservation.com. Situated on a hilltop in the private Lolkisale concession, outside the Boundary Hill entrance gate, this new lodge is the first in Tanzania to have a local community shareholding, with the Maasai village of Lolkisale owning 50%. The 8 spacious suites, set among the rocky cliffs, are individually designed & lavishly decorated, & have private sitting areas & wide balconies offering spectacular views over the Silale & Gosuwa Swamps, where elephant & buffalo are resident, & en-suite facilities include cast-iron baths. In addition to daytime game drives into the national park, the lodge offers guided game walks with the local Maasai & night drives. The concession lies on a migration route & is particularly busy with wildlife over Nov–Mar. US$390/480 sgl/dbl FB, or US$550 pp for a full game package.
⌂ **Naitolia Camp** (5 rooms) m 0787 293727; e simon@eastafricansafari.info; www.tarangireconservation.com. Under the same management as Boundary Hill, this excellent bush camp is set in an exclusive 55km² tract of Maasailand on the northern border of the park. The main camp consists of attractively furnished huts made entirely of canvas & local materials such as stone, wood & thatch, each with a king-size bed with walk-in netting & a private balcony, shower & toilet with a view. Because the camp lies on communal land, guided game walks can be undertaken, with a good chance of spotting giraffe, elephant, zebra & a variety of antelope & birds, & it is possible to be taken to Maasai *bomas* that don't normally receive tourists. Also on offer are overnight walking safaris within the community area, using fly-camps. It was leased out to a private operator at the time of writing, but expect rates to be comparable to Boundary Hill.

Upmarket
⌂ **Tarangire Sopa Lodge** (75 rooms) ☎ 027 250 0630/9; f 027 250 8245; e info@sopalodges.com; www.sopalodges.com. Set in the heart of the national park, the Tarangire Sopa is the largest & most conventionally luxurious – & least 'bush' – of the

lodges around Tarangire. The facilities & accommodation match the customary high standards of this chain, with smart self-contained suites & excellent food. The indifferent location, alongside a small & normally dry watercourse below a baobab-studded slope, is compensated for by the superb game viewing in the surrounding area – the roads between here & Tarangire Safari Lodge are far & away the most rewarding in the park. *US$320/550 sgl/dbl FB, US$265/450 Mar, Nov & early Dec,US$100/200 Apr & May.*

🏠 **Lake Burunge Tented Camp** (16 rooms) ℄ 027 254 1556; m 0784 207727; f 027 250 8937; e twc-reservations@habari.co.tz; www.tanganyikawildernesscamps.com. Overlooking the seasonal Lake Burunge, this intimate new lodge lies a 10min drive outside the park boundary, some distance south of the main Tarangire tourist circuit, in an area of dense bush known for its populations of dry country antelope such as lesser kudu & gerenuk. Accommodation is in spacious & attractively rustic en-suite twin & dbl tents built on stilted platforms & shaded by makuti roofs. The camp is well positioned for game drives, & also offers guided nature walks, along with canoe trips when the lake holds water. Comparable in feel & style to several places in the exclusive category, this underutilised camp is good value. *US$300/400 sgl/dbl FB.*

🏠 **Tarangire River Camp** (20 rooms) ℄ 027 254 7007; m 0787 532785; e zina@mbalimbali.com; www.mbalimbali.com. Just 3.5km outside the main gate as the crow flies (but more like 15km by road) this relatively new tented camp lies within a 250km² concession, set aside for conservation by the Maasai community of Minjingu, along the northwest boundary of the national park. The camp is set below a massive old baobab on a cliff overlooking the (normally dry) Minjingu River, a tributary of the Tarangire, & wildlife can be quite prolific in the vicinity seasonally, even though it is not in the park. The lodge is centred on a vast stilted thatch & timber structure comprised of a main lounge, a small library, & a dining & cocktail area, offering

sweeping views across the riverbed to the Maasai Steppes. The large en-suite tents with private balcony, 2 three-quarter beds & 24hr solar power are good value. *US$250/350 sgl/dbl FB.*

🏠 **Roika Tarangire Tented Lodge** (21 rooms) ℄ 027 250 9994; e info@roikatours.com; www.roikatours.com. Situated in a stand of tangled acacia scrub about 5km from the park entrance gate en route to Tarangire River Lodge, this recent addition to Tarangire's burgeoning selection of lodges offers accommodation in large en-suite standing tents set on stilted wooden platforms. Shaded by makuti roofs, the tents are very comfortable, with 2 dbl beds each, & decorated simply in safari style, though the rustic mood undermined somewhat by the tackily sculpted animal-shaped baths. The main building is thatched with open sides & overlooks a large swimming pool. Good value. *US$125 pp FB.*

🏠 **Tarangire Safari Lodge** (40 rooms) ℄ 027 253 1447; m 0784 202777; f 027 254 4752; e bookings@tarangiresafarilodge.com; www.tarangiresafarilodge.com. This owner-managed lodge is the oldest in the park, with a sublime location on a tall bluff overlooking the Tarangire River. Game viewing from the veranda can be excellent, with large herds of hippo, giraffe & other animals coming down to the river to drink. The grounds are also highly attractive for birders, not only for the remarkably habituated hornbills, buffalo-weavers & starlings that parade around the common areas, but also for the host of smaller birds that are resident in the acacia scrub. Facilities include a swimming pool. This comfortable, unpretentious & well-managed lodge ranks as one of our favourites anywhere on the northern circuit. The accommodation in standing tents with en-suite toilets is outstanding value. *US$109/188 sgl/dbl B&B. Lunch US$16, dinner US$20, limited selection of snacks around US$5 each.*

Budget and camping

🅰 **Zion Campsite** This small private camp, formerly known as Kigongoni, lies a few kilometres outside the park entrance gate, & is used by many budget camping safaris to Tarangire. To get there, turn off

from the main Arusha–Dodoma road as if heading towards the entrance gate to Tarangire. After about 2km, you'll see the campsite immediately to your left. *Camping Tsh10,000 pp.*

For those on camping safaris, there are a couple of campsites within Tarangire. These are strong on bush atmosphere, but short on facilities, & rather costly (*US$20 pp*).

WHAT TO SEE Most people spend only one day in Tarangire and thus concentrate on the game-viewing roads along its well-developed northern circuit, which follows the river between the Tarangire Safari Lodge and Tarangire Sopa Lodge. And this is unambiguously the best game-viewing area, especially in the dry season when many of the greater Tarangire ecosystem's 25,000 wildebeest, 30,000 zebra, 6,000 buffalo, 2,700 giraffe, 5,500 eland, 30,000 impala and 2,000 warthog congregate along the river, the only source of water for many miles around.

Tarangire is justifiably famous for the prolific elephant herds that congregate along the river during the dry season. According to the most recent census, now several years old, the region supports a total population of around 3,000 elephants, but it's likely the population has grown significantly in the interim. Indeed, in peak times, it is no exaggeration to say that you might see 500 elephants over the course of a day here. Tarangire's elephants used to be a lot more skittish than their counterparts in Manyara and Ngorongoro, but these days they are quite relaxed.

The full range of large predators is present on the main tourist road circuit too, but the dense vegetation can make it relatively difficult to pick up the likes of lion and leopard, even though they are quite common. Two localised antelope that occur in Tarangire are the fringe-eared oryx and gerenuk, though neither is seen with great regularity. Of the smaller mammals, the colonial dwarf mongoose is characteristic of the park, and often seen on the termite hills where it breeds.

Tarangire is a great birdwatching site, with around 500 species recorded to date. A wide range of resident raptors includes bateleur, fish eagle and palmnut vulture, while the river supports saddle-billed and yellow-billed storks and several other waterbirds. Characteristic acacia birds are yellow-necked spurfowl, orange-bellied parrot, barefaced go-away bird, red-fronted barbet, and silverbird. A personal favourite is the red-and-yellow barbet, with its quaintly comical clockwork duet, typically performed on termite mounds.

Tarangire's location at the western limit of the Somali-Maasai biome means it harbours several dry-country bird species at the extremity of their range, among them vulturine guineafowl, Donaldson-Smith's nightjar, pink-breasted lark, northern pied babbler and mouse-coloured penduline tit. It is also the easiest place to observe a pair of bird species endemic to the dry heartland of central Tanzania: the lovely yellow-collared lovebird, and the somewhat drabber ashy starling, both of which are common locally.

For those with sufficient time to explore beyond the main tourist circuit, the Lake Burunge area offers the best chance of seeing bushbuck and lesser kudu, while the Kitibong Hill area is home to large herds of buffalo, and Lamarkau Swamp supports hippo and numerous waterbirds during the wet season. Further south, cheetahs favour the southern plains, while the Mkungero Pools is a good place to look for buffalo, waterbuck and gerenuk.

7

Moshi and Kilimanjaro

Kilimanjaro is Africa's highest mountain, and one of the most instantly recognisable landmarks on the continent. It is also the highest mountain anywhere that can be climbed by an ordinary tourist, and thousands of visitors to Tanzania attempt to reach its peak every year. Kilimanjaro straddles the border with Kenya, but because the peaks all lie within Tanzanian territory they can be climbed only from within Tanzania. There are several places on the lower slopes from where the mountain can be ascended, but most people use the Marangu or 'tourist' route (which begins at the village of Marangu), largely because it is the cheapest option and has the best facilities. The less heavily trampled Machame route, starting from the village of the same name, has grown in popularity in recent years. A number of more obscure routes can be used, though they are generally available only through specialist trekking companies. Prospective climbers can arrange their ascent of 'Kili' – as it is popularly called – at one of the hotels in Marangu, or in Arusha town, but the main cluster of trekking companies is to be found in the town of Moshi on the plains to the south of the mountain.

CLIMATE

The higher slopes of Kilimanjaro are cold at all times. Moshi is relatively low-lying and has a climate typical of this part of the African interior, hot by day and cool by night, though it is often more humid than you might expect. Kilimanjaro can be climbed at any time of year, but the hike is more difficult in the rainy months, especially between March and May.

GETTING AROUND

Moshi is an important public transport hub, connected by surfaced roads and regular express buses to Dar es Salaam, Tanga and Arusha. If you want to arrange your hike in Marangu, plenty of public transport runs there from Moshi. Most travellers prefer to make all arrangements for the climb in Moshi, and this includes transport to and from the trailhead.

MOSHI

Situated at the heart of a major coffee-growing region about 80km east of Arusha, the smaller but not insubstantial town of Moshi – population 250,000 – is a likeable if intrinsically unremarkable commercial centre salvaged from anonymity by its spectacular location. At dusk or dawn, when the great white-helmeted dome of Kilimanjaro is most likely to emerge from its customary blanket of cloud, Moshi can boast a backdrop as imposing and dramatic as any in Africa. And yet, the teasing proximity of that iconic snow-capped silhouette notwithstanding, Moshi is not the

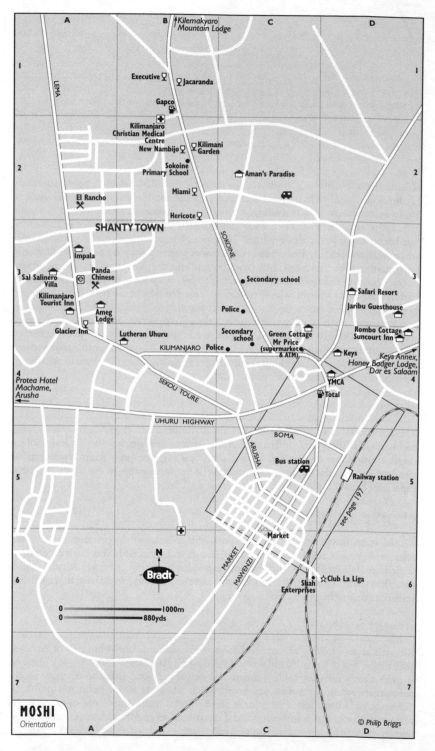

Kilemakyaro
Mountain Lodge

Executive ♀   ♀ Jacaranda

Gapco

Kilimanjaro
Christian Medical
Centre
New Nambijo ♀   ♀ Kilimani
Garden

Sokoine
Primary School

Miami ♀   Aman's Paradise

El Rancho

Hericote ♀

SHANTY TOWN

Impala

Panda
Chinese

Sal Salinero
Villa

Kilimanjaro
Tourist Inn
Ameg
Lodge

Glacier Inn

Lutheran Uhuru

KILIMANJARO Police

Secondary school

Police

Secondary
school

Green Cottage
Mr Price
(supermarket
& ATM)

Safari Resort

Jaribu Guesthouse

Rombo Cottage
Suncourt Inn

Keys

Keys Annex,
Honey Badger Lodge,
Dar es Salaam

YMCA

Total

Protea Hotel
Machame,
Arusha

SEKOU TOURE

UHURU HIGHWAY

BOMA

ARUSHA

Bus station

Railway station

see page 197

N

Bradt

MARKET

MAWENZI

Market

Shah
Enterprises

☆ Club La Liga

0 _____ 1000m
0 _____ 880yds

MOSHI
Orientation

© Philip Briggs

cool, breezy highland settlement you might expect it to be. Indeed, situated at an elevation of 810m, it is generally far hotter than Arusha, and not so drizzly, with a hint of stickiness in the air that recalls the coast.

Prior to the arrival of the Germans, Moshi was the capital of the area ruled by Rindi, who came into power in about 1860 and, largely through his diplomatic skills, became one of the most important chiefs in the area. By allying with the Maasai, Rindi extracted large taxes from passing caravans. He made a favourable impression on John Kirk, the British consul in Zanzibar, and signed a treaty with Carl Peters in 1885. When the first German colonial forces arrived at Kilimanjaro in 1891, Rindi assured them he ruled the whole area. At his insistence, they quelled his major rival, Sina of Kibosha.

Moshi is the Swahili word for smoke, but exactly when and why the town acquired that name is something of a mystery. Some sources suggest that it is because Moshi served as the terminus for the steam railway line from Tanga after 1911, but this seems unlikely given that the name pre-dates the arrival of the railway by many years. Equally improbable is the suggestion that the reference is due to the town lying at the base of a volcano, since Kilimanjaro hadn't displayed any significant activity for thousands of years when its present-day Bantu-speaking inhabitants arrived there.

Stirring views of Kilimanjaro aside, there is little to do or see in Moshi that you couldn't do or see in pretty much any similarly sized African market town. But it's a pleasant enough place to explore on foot, with an interesting central market area, and it comes across as far less tourist-oriented than Arusha, despite the inevitable attention paid to any visiting *mazungu* by a coterie of (mostly very affable) flycatchers offering relatively cheap'n'dodgy Kilimanjaro climbs.

In terms of facilities, Moshi boasts an immense selection of decent budget to mid-range hotels, as well as several commendable and affordable restaurants. An ever increasing selection of smarter hotels is concentrated in the attractively leafy and somewhat misleadingly named suburb of Shanty Town, a short walk north of the town centre and the Arusha Highway. There are also plenty of more upmarket options in the villages of Marangu and Machame at the foot of Kilimanjaro, and the area can also be explored from the lodges that run along the main road between Arusha and Usa River.

GETTING THERE AND AWAY Note that passenger trains between Moshi, Tanga and Dar es Salaam were suspended indefinitely several years ago, and are unlikely to resume.

By air Kilimanjaro International Airport (KIA) lies about 40km from Moshi town centre off the Arusha road. The national carrier Air Tanzania flies directly to KIA from some international destinations, and KLM operates a daily direct flight there from Europe. For domestic flights, Air Tanzania, Regional Airlines, Precision Air and several private airlines fly daily between KIA and Dar es Salaam or Zanzibar, while regular Air Tanzania flights also connect KIA to Mwanza and other major urban centres. A potential source of confusion to travellers booking their own flights is that flights to the parks on the northern safari circuit don't leave from KIA, but from Arusha Airport on the outskirts of Arusha town.

If you fly to KIA with Air Tanzania, note that all their flights tie in with a free shuttle service to Moshi, easily located at the airport. When you leave Moshi for the airport, the correct shuttle departure time can be checked in advance at the Air Tanzania office near the Clocktower [197 C3]. For flights operated by other airlines, you'll need to charter a taxi (a none-too-negotiable US$30 from the airport) or arrange to be met by a safari company.

Moshi central bus station has a justified reputation as one of the most hellish in Africa, and it is certainly the most chaotic and daunting in Tanzania, thanks to gaggles of persistent hustlers who will say anything to get a punter on to any bus, provided they can secure a commission. In my experience, when you've half a dozen hustlers yelling at you, punching each other and trying to grab your bags, the instinct for self-preservation tends to prevail, and you're likely to get on to any bus heading in the right direction before things turn ugly. One traveller who spent several weeks in Moshi wrote of how she was pushed into 'a couple of nightmarish journeys, sitting on a stationary bus for two hours after it was scheduled to leave, then stopping for half an hour at practically every settlement it passed'. This isn't such a problem for short trips, for instance to Arusha or Marangu, but for long trips you should use your judgement in boarding the first 'express bus' that is pointed out to you, and be aware that overcharging *wazungu* is commonplace. Bearing all this in mind, it's a good idea to visit the bus station the day before you're due to travel and book a seat in advance – that way, you don't have to deflect the hustlers while protecting your luggage at the same time. Better still, use one of the (generally superior) companies whose booking offices lie outside the main bus station.

By road The town centre runs southward from the main surfaced road to Dar es Salaam some 80km east of Arusha. The driving time from Arusha in a private vehicle is about 60–90 minutes, and from Dar es Salaam at least seven hours. It is possible to drive from Nairobi (Kenya) to Moshi via Namanga and Arusha in about five hours.

Express coaches between Dar es Salaam and Moshi take roughly seven hours, with a 20-minute lunch break in Korogwe or Mombo. Recommended services include Akamba [197 C6] (*next to Buffalo Hotel;* ✆ 027 275 3908; m 0744 057779), Dar Express [197 C2] (*Old Moshi Rd opposite NBC;* m 0744 286847), Royal Coach [197 C4] (*Aga Khan Rd;* ✆ 027 275 0940) and Scandinavia Express [197 C5] (*opposite Hindu Temple on Nyerere Rd;* ✆ 027 275 1387; m 0744 295245). Numerous cheaper and inferior bus services leave from the main bus station, mostly in the morning. There are also plenty of direct buses between Moshi and Tanga, which can drop you off at Same, Mombo, Muheza or other junction towns *en route*.

A steady flow of buses and *dala-dalas* runs between Arusha and Moshi, taking up to two hours, and to a lesser extent between Moshi and Marangu. There is no need to book ahead for these routes, as vehicles will leave when they fill up, but be warned that there is a high incidence of accidents, particularly with minibuses.

Most shuttle bus services between Nairobi and Arusha continue on to Moshi, or start there. The Impala Shuttle [197 C2] (*Kibo Rd next to Chrisburgers;* ✆ 027 275 1786; m 0754 293119; e impala@kilinet.co.tz) runs two services daily, as does the Riverside Shuttle [197 C3] (*THB bldg on Boma Rd;* ✆ 027 275 0093) and the Bobby Shuttle [197 C5] (✆ 027 250 3490; e shuttle@bobbytours.com; *www.bobbytours.com*), represented by Duma Expeditions, next to the Coffee Shop on Hill Street. These coaches generally leave Moshi at 06.30 and 12.00 and Nairobi at 08.00 and 14.00 daily, and take about six hours in either direction, but timings may change to fit in with departure and arrival times for Arusha.

TOURIST INFORMATION There's no tourist information office as such in Moshi, but if you are spending some time there it's worth getting hold of the *Moshi Guide*, compiled and sold by the people who run the Coffee Shop on Hill Street [197 B5]. Most of the tour operators in town can provide (not necessarily impartial) local travel information. Also worth a look is the website www.kiliweb.com.

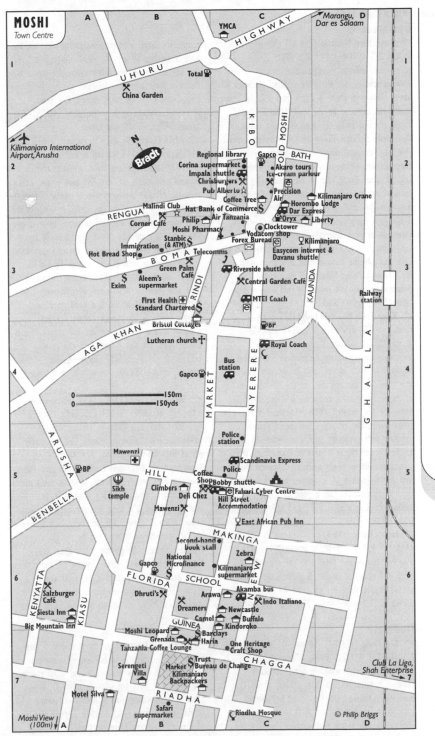

MOSHI
Town Centre

A   B   C   D

Marangu,
Dar es Salaam

YMCA

HIGHWAY

UHURU

Total

China Garden

KIBO

OLD MOSHI

BATH

Kilimanjaro International
Airport, Arusha

N
Bradt

Regional library   Gapco
Corina supermarket   Akaro tours
Impala shuttle   Ice-cream parlour
Chrisburgers
Pub Alberto   Precision
Coffee Tree   Air
Malindi Club   Horombo Lodge   Kilimanjaro Crane
Nat Bank of Commerce   Dar Express
Corner Café   Philip   Air Tanzania   Oryx   Liberty
Moshi Pharmacy   Clocktower
Stanbic   Vodacom shop
(& ATM)   Forex Bureau
Immigration   Kilimanjaro
Hot Bread Shop   Telecomms   Easycom internet &
  Davanu shuttle
Green Palm   Riverside shuttle
Café
Aleem's   Central Garden Café
supermarket
Exim   First Health
Standard Chartered   MTEI Coach
Railway
station
Bristol Cottages   BP
Lutheran church   Royal Coach
Bus
station
Gapco

RENGUA
BOMA
RINDI
KAUNDA
GHALLA
AGA KHAN
MARKET
NYERERE

0   150m
0   150yds

Police
station

ARUSHA
BENBELLA
KENYATTA
KIASU
HILL
GUINEA
FLORIDA
SCHOOL
MAKINGA
CHAGGA
RIADHA

Mawenzi
BP
Sikh
temple
Climbers
Deli Chez
Mawenzi

Scandinavia Express
Police
Coffee
Shop   Bobby shuttle
Fahari Cyber Centre
Hill Street
Accommodation
East African Pub Inn

Second-hand
book stall   Zebra
National
Microfinance
Gapco   Kilimanjaro
supermarket
Salzburger   Dhruti's   Arawa   Akamba bus
Café   Dreamers   Indo Italiano
Siesta Inn   Camel   Newcastle
Big Mountain Inn   Kindoroko
Moshi Leopard   Buffalo
Grenada   Barclays
Tanzania Coffee Lounge   Harta
One Heritage
Craft Shop
Serengeti   Trust
Villa   Market   Bureau de Change
Kilimanjaro
Backpackers
Motel Silva
Moshi View   Safari   Riadha Mosque
(100m)   supermarket

Club La Liga,
Shah Enterprise

© Philip Briggs

WHERE TO STAY
Upmarket

Protea Hotel Machame [194 A4] (30 rooms) 027 275 6941/8; f 027 275 6821; e proteaaishareservations@satconet.com; www.proteahotels.com. Along the surfaced Machame Rd about 12km from Moshi & 27km from KIA, this smart rural hotel, managed by the South Africa Protea Hotels group, is easily the most upmarket option in the vicinity of Moshi. The recently refurbished motel-style en-suite rooms aren't exactly bursting with character, but the property itself is lovely, with a large thatched dining room & bar area facing a patch of indigenous forest at the foot of the great mountain. The hotel specialises in Kilimanjaro climbs & has good equipment, but also offers a variety of excursions to more sedentary guests, ranging from local cultural tours & horseback trips to day visits to Lake Chala, Arusha National Park & a short walk to the 30m-high Makoa Waterfall & bat-infested Matangalima Cave. The swimming pool is solar heated. *US$115/145 sgl/dbl B&B.*

Kilemakyaro Mountain Lodge [194 B1] (20 rooms) 027 275 4925; m 0744 264845; e info@kilimanjarosafari.com; www.kilimanjarosafari.com. Wonderfully sited, on a hilltop 9km north of the town centre, this smart new hotel was formerly part of the Kifumbu Tea Estate, & the gracious reception & dining areas are housed in the restored 1880s homestead of the estate owner. The attractive landscaped gardens, complete with swimming pool, offer wonderful views to the forested slopes & peak of Kilimanjaro. The accommodation, in newly built self-contained chalets with digital satellite TV, is nothing special & is a touch overpriced, but still a good choice for atmosphere & location. *US$85/145 sgl/dbl B&B or US$110/190 FB.*

Impala Hotel [194 A3] (18 rooms) 027 275 3443/4; f 027 275 3440; e impala@kilinet.co.tz; www.impalahotel.com. Related to the eponymous hotel in Arusha but smaller & plusher, the recently opened Impala Hotel lies on Lema Rd in the leafy suburb of Shantytown about 2km from the town centre. The large wood-panelled rooms with fan, hot bath & satellite TV are fair value. Although it lacks the fine location of the Kilemakyaro, the rooms are better & there are more facilities, notably swimming pool, internet café & forex bureau, & a good restaurant specialising in Indian dishes. *US$80/100 sgl/dbl B&B, US$140 vast suites.*

AMEG Lodge [194 A3] (20 rooms) 027 275 0175/0185; m 0744 058268; f 027 275 0196; e info@ameglodge.com; www.ameglodge.com. This modern new lodge, set in a 2ha plot in the leafy northern suburbs of Shantytown, is probably now the smartest hotel within the city limits, & certainly the best value option in the mid to upper price range. The large, airy en-suite rooms are unusually stylish, combining an ethnic feel with a contemporary touch, & they all come with digital satellite TV, fan & private balcony. Other facilities include swimming pool with views of Kilimanjaro, gym, business centre with 24hr internet access, & a good restaurant serving Indian & continental cuisine. The only negative is that the gardens are still rather bare & undeveloped, but this is bound to change with time. *US$79 std dbl B&B, US$94 larger dbl with walk-in dressing area, US$110 suite with AC & unlimited internet.*

Sal Salinero Hotel [194 A3] (7 rooms, more scheduled for 2009) 027 275 2240; m 0784 683605; f 027 275 2240; e salinerohotel@yahoo.com; www.salinerohotel.com. This reasonably priced but rather pretentious new hotel in Shantytown has large smart rooms with tiled floors, king-size beds, wooden ceilings, huge changing rooms & excellent facilities, including satellite TV, tea/coffee-making facilities & a large en-suite bathroom with separate tub & shower. The otherwise high quality of the accommodation is let down by the rather bombastic décor. The gloomy public areas are similarly schizoid, with classy finishes set alongside some decidedly tacky touches. Far nicer are the restaurant & bar, with outdoor seating in a green garden. *US$75/95 std sgl/dbl B&B, US$130 suites.*

Moderate

Keys Hotel [194 D4] (30 rooms) 027 275 2250/1875; f 027 275 0073; e info@keys-hotel-tours.com; www.keys-hotel-tours.com. Situated in attractive suburban grounds about 1km from the Clocktower, the Keys Hotel has offered good value for several years, & it remains, with justification, one of the most popular hotels within its price range. Visitors have the choice of a room in the double-storey main building or a makuti-roofed cottage in the gardens behind it. All rooms are en-suite & have hot water, satellite TV & nets. There is a swimming pool & decent restaurant serving typical Tanzania hotel fare. Keys is also one of the more reliable places to organise climbs of

Kilimanjaro, & while rates are a little higher than at some other places, they include I night's HB accommodation at the hotel on either side of the climb. *Self-contained rooms US$55/65 sgl/dbl B&B, discounted by roughly 50% for Tanzanian residents. Camping US$5 pp.*

⌂ **Keys Annex** [194 D4] (48 rooms) Contact details as for Keys Hotel. Tucked away in an unsignposted location on Mbokomu Rd off the main Dar es Salaam highway, this larger annexe to the Keys Hotel is smarter & more modern than its elder sibling, but comparatively lacking in character. Smart tiled rooms in a large double-storey building have 2 beds & large bathrooms with combined tub/shower. Facilities include restaurant, bar & swimming pool. *US$55/65 sgl/dbl B&B, discounted by roughly 50% for Tanzanian residents.*

⌂ **Bristol Cottages** [197 B3] (17 rooms) ☎ 027 275 5083; f 027 275 3745; e info@ bristolcottages.com; www.bristolcottages.com. Located behind the Standard Chartered Bank close to the bus station, this neat lodge set in small, secure & peaceful manicured gardens is probably the pick in this range, as well as being very central. Accommodation is in spacious suites & cottages with AC & hot shower, satellite TV, nets, two beds & attractive modern décor. Facilities include secure parking, internet, email, fax & secretarial services. The clean open-sided restaurant serves a variety of Asian & continental dishes in the Tsh6,000–8,000 range. *New wing US$45/60 sgl/dbl B&B, suites & cottages US$66–140.*

⌂ **Moshi Leopard Hotel** [197 B7] (47 rooms) ☎ 027 275 0884/5134; f 027 275 1261; e leopardhotel@eoltz.com; www.leopardhotel.com. Among the most commodious options in the town centre, the recently extended multi-storey Leopard Hotel is clean, comfortable & thoroughly adequate without approaching the Kilimanjaro Crane Hotel in terms of quality or amenities. Smart tiled en-suite rooms have AC, fan, TV, dbl or twin bed with netting & hot shower. *US$40/50 sgl/dbl B&B.*

⌂ **Kilimanjaro Crane Hotel** [197 C2] (40 rooms) ☎ 027 275 1114; f 027 275 4876; e kilicrane@ kilionline.com; www.kilimanjarocranehotels.com. The smartest place in the town centre is this modern high-rise hotel, with en-suite rooms with large beds, digital satellite TV, private balcony, netting, fan & hot

bath. On Kaunda St, a block east of the Clocktower, the hotel has a compact but green garden, a welcome swimming pool, & the rooftop bar is a great spot for sundowners facing Kilimanjaro. A good restaurant serves pizzas as well as Chinese & Indian cuisine. The ground-floor souvenir shop stocks probably the most comprehensive selection of books in Moshi. Excellent value. *US$40/45 sgl/dbl B&B with fan; US$50 dbl with AC; US$90 suite.*

⌂ **Aman's Paradise Hotel** [194 C2] m 0754 919127; e liliantanz@hotmail.com. In a rambling green compound on a quiet back road in the Shantytown area, this cosy private house, run by a Swedish–Tanzanian family, is well suited to those seeking a more down-to-earth experience than is offered by any formal tourist hotel. It's a friendly set-up, orientated mainly towards long stays, & 5% of room rates go towards local NGOs. Facilities include satellite TV & internet, with a proper restaurant likely to be added following pending renovations. *En-suite rooms US$35–60, substantial discounts for longer stays.*

⌂ **Lutheran Uhuru Hostel** [194 B4] (60 rooms) ☎ 027 275 4084; m 0753 037216; f 027 275 3518; e uhuru@elct.com; www.uhuruhostel.org. Set in vast & pretty suburban gardens about 1.5km from the town centre on Shantytown's Sekou Toure Rd, this hostel used to be popular with tourists, but the recent boom in hotel construction in & around Moshi seems to have reduced its custom, & it feels somewhat overpriced for non-residents. It offers a variety of rooms, some self-contained with running hot water & private balconies, & some with TV. The attached Bamboo Restaurant serves decent meals, but smoking & drinking are strictly prohibited. The hostel is about 1.5km out of town. *US$30/40 sgl/dbl with common shower, US$40/50 en-suite sgl/dbl, US$45/55 en-suite with TV; about 30% cheaper for residents.*

⌂ **Kilimanjaro Tourist Inn** [194 A3] (8 rooms) ☎ 027 275 3252; f 027 275 2748; e kkkmarealle@yahoo.com; www.kiliweb.com/kti. This converted colonial house set in a large suburban garden has a friendly, homely atmosphere that will appeal to travellers who avoid more institutionalised hotels. It's good value, & all rooms come with large bed, net, fan & en-suite shower. *Tsh10,000/20,000 sgl/dbl.*

Budget

⌂ **Honey Badger Lodge** [194 D4] (8 rooms) ☎/f 0754 309980; e honeybadger@africamail.com; www.hbcc-campsites.com. 6km out of town along the Dar es Salaam road, this rustic, friendly lodge is a

refreshingly low-key alternative to the budget hotels in town. Basically a converted house set within a fenced green compound, it consists of 4 large en-suite dbl rooms in the main house & 4 newer luxury rooms, all with hot showers. Camping is also available in individual campsites with common hot shower. Local dishes are available by advance order, & there is a self-catering kitchen & well stocked outdoor *makuti* bar. Traditional drumming performances & lessons can be arranged. They also arrange performances of traditional Chagga *ngoma* (drums) with songs & acting depicting stories about marriage, harvesting time & initiation rites. Other cultural activities include traditional face painting, traditional fashion shows & culinary lessons, & they also arrange day hikes in the Kilimanjaro foothills. Internet is available at US$2/hr in high season (Jun–Oct). A swimming pool will be ready by late 2009. *US$30–50 pp B&B, camping US$5 pp.*

🏠 **Zebra Hotel** [197 C6] (72 rooms) ✆ 027 275 0611; f 027 275 0611; e zebhoteltz@yahoo.com; www.zebrahotelstz.com. This smart 7-storey hotel, which opened around the corner from the Kindoroko in 2005, is exceptional value for money, partly because lack of elevator access has made it difficult to market in the mid-range category where it otherwise belongs. Rooms are clean & spacious, & come with AC, fan, satellite TV & en-suite hot shower. A ground-floor restaurant is attached. *US$30 sgl, US$35 dbl or twin.*

🏠 **Horombo Lodge** [197 C2] (29 rooms) ✆ 027 275 0134; e horomboldge_2005@yahoo.co.uk. With a central location on Old Moshi Rd immediately north of the Clocktower, this neat new hotel is a good compromise between quality & cost, with compact but clean en-suite rooms with TV, fan, net, telephone & hot water. *From US$20/30 sgl/dbl.*

🏠 **Big Mountain Inn** [197 A6] (10 rooms) ✆ 027 275 1862; m 0754 376921; e pmtitos@hotmail.com. This new hotel on Kiusa St has large clean rooms with tiled floor, TV, fan & en-suite hot shower. The pleasant courtyard restaurant serves a good selection of mostly Indian dishes in the Tsh5,000–7,000 range. Fair value. *Tsh25,000/30,000 sgl/dbl.*

🏠 **Kindoroko Hotel** [197 C6] (30 rooms) ✆ 027 275 4054; m 0787 037263; f 027 275 4062; e info@kindorokohotels.com;

Shoestring

🏠 **YMCA Hostel** [194 D4 & 197 C1] (42 rooms) ✆ 027 275 1754/4240; f 027 275 1734. On the opposite side of town to the above hotels, the YMCA is a perennial favourite with travellers, offering clean secure accommodation in green grounds with a large swimming pool. *US$13/17small sgl/dbl B&B with communal showers.*

www.kindorokohotels.com. For some years the smartest of the cluster of popular budget hotels on & around Nyerere Rd a couple of blocks south of the bus station, the 4-storey Kindoroko has maintained high standards & reasonable prices over several years. Following a complete refurbishment, the small but very clean rooms come with hot shower, fan, netting & digital satellite TV. Facilities include lively courtyard bar, popular with travellers & locals alike, restaurant serving adequate meals, on-site internet café & massage centre. The hotel also arranges reliable Kilimanjaro climbs. *US$15/30/45 sgl/db/trpl B&B.*

🏠 **Camel Hotel** [197 C6] (6 rooms) ✆ 027 275 2029; m 0784 879050. Opened in 2007, this small central hotel seems very friendly & reasonably priced, & the clean rooms have tiled floors, satellite TV, & large bathrooms with hot shower. *Tsh18,000/23,000 sgl/dbl with fan, Tsh23,000/25,000 with AC.*

🏠 **Buffalo Hotel** [197 C6] (31 rooms) ✆ 027 275 0270; m 0754 018302; e buffalohotel2000@yahoo.com. This clean & perennially popular budget hotel behind the Kindoroko underwent major renovations in 2007, & the spacious rooms are now brightly tiled with en-suite hot showers throughout. The attached restaurant serves tasty & inexpensive Indian & Chinese meals. *Tsh15,000/20,000 sgl without/with fan, Tsh25,000 dbl with fan & TV, Tsh30,000 dbl with AC, fridge & TV, Tsh50,000 suite.*

🏠 **Hotel Newcastle** [197 C6] (40 rooms) ✆ 027 275 0853. A couple of doors down from the Kindoroko, this used to be similar in feel & standard but these days it's a lot more frayed at the edges. The run-down self-contained rooms have hot shower, fan & nets. The ground-floor restaurant/bar is sometimes very lively. Overpriced. *Tsh15,000/20,000 sgl/dbl.*

🏠 **Motel Silva** [197 A7] (11 rooms) ✆ 027 275 3122. Situated close to the market, this 3-storey hotel has been one of the better budget options in Moshi for longer than a decade. The small but clean & brightly painted en-suite rooms have fans, nets & hot showers, & there is an agreeable rooftop garden. *Tsh15,000/20,00 en-suite sgl/dbl, Tsh10,000 sgl with common shower.*

🏠 **Siesta Inn** [197 A6] (10 rooms) ✆ 027 275 0158. Alongside the Big Mountain Inn, this is another new hotel with large, clean but rather tatty rooms with en-suite hot showers & king-size beds. It's a friendly set-up, & reasonably priced. *Tsh18,000 dbl.*

🏠 **Hill Street Accommodation** [197 C5] (12 rooms) ✆ 027 275 3455. This friendly hotel on Hill St has a convenient location close to the bus station & several good eateries, & the recently renovated rooms all have tiled floors & en-suite hot showers, but no fan or netting. *Tsh15,000/20,000/30,000 sgl/dbl/trpl.*

🏠 **Kilimanjaro Backpackers Hotel** [197 B7] (16 rooms) 🕿 027 275 5189; e info@kilimanjarobackpacker.com; www.kilimanjarobackpacker.com. Situated one block south of the affiliated Kindoroko, the former Hotel Da Costa is deservedly the most popular cheapie in Moshi, offering accommodation in clean but no-frills tiled rooms & dormitories with net, fan & common shower with 24hr hot water. Good value. *US$7/12 sgl/dbl B&B, US$5 per dorm bed; lunch & dinner an additional US$4 pp.*

🏠 **Coffee Tree Hotel** [197 C2] (57 rooms) 🕿 027 275 1382. This long-standing cheapie really couldn't

be more centrally located, & the spacious rooms, though admittedly a bit run-down, are very good value. The restaurant isn't up to much, but it affords good views towards Kilimanjaro. *Tsh8,000/12,000 self-contained sgl/dbl with net, fan & cold water.*

🏠 **Harla Hotel** [197 B7] (8 rooms) m 0754 305453. Formerly a downmarket annexe to the Kindoroko Hotel opposite, this remains one of the best-value cheapies in Moshi, offering secure accommodation in large, clean rooms with tiled floors & nets. *Tsh8,000 twin with common shower, Tsh10,000 en-suite twin with hot shower.*

🏠 **Climbers Hotel** [197 B5] (8 rooms) 🕿 027 275 8025. Another decent & convenient cheapie along Hill St, with small but clean rooms. *Tsh8,000 dbl with common shower, Tsh10,000 en-suite.*

Camping Camping is permitted at the **Keys Hotel** [194 D4] for US$5 per person. Further out of town, the campsite at the **Honey Badger Lodge** [194 D4] is a far more homely option for campers.

✖ **WHERE TO EAT** Many of the places listed under *Where to stay* have restaurants. Of the costlier places, the one most likely to attract passing custom to its restaurant is the **Kilimanjaro Crane Hotel** [197 C2], which has a central location, good Indian food at around Tsh5,000–6,000, pizzas and a great view of Kilimanjaro from the rooftop bar. The restaurant at the **Kindoroko Hotel** [197 C6] is popular with budget travellers, and there's a lively bar attached. The majority of stand-alone restaurants are in the town centre but there are also several smarter options in the suburb of Shantytown to the north. The Shantytown restaurants are not accessible by public transport, so travellers staying more centrally will need to walk there and back (probably not a clever idea after dark) or arrange to be collected by taxi.

✖ **Central Garden Café** [197 C3]. Located opposite the Clocktower & close to the bus station, this is a convenient spot for a quick alfresco cold drink or greasy local meal. Meals & 'bitings' are in the Tsh1,000–3,000 range.

✖ **Chrisburgers** [197 C2] ⏰ 08.00–15.00 daily except Sun. Cheap daytime snacks like hamburgers, samosas & excellent fruit juice, opposite the Clocktower.

✖ **Corner Café** [197 B2]. Centrally located on Rengua Rd a block west of the Clocktower, this small café serves good toasted & cold sandwiches for around Tsh2,000, as well as salads, local dishes & coffee. Seating is inside or outdoors.

✖ **Deli Chez Restaurant** [197 B5] 🕿 027 275 1144; m 0784 786241; ⏰ lunch & dinner daily except Tue. This new deli on the corner of Hill & Market streets serves a great selection of Indian dishes, as well as a more limited selection of Chinese meals & fast food, & a sumptuous

selection of milkshakes, sundaes & other desserts. No alcohol served.

✖ **El Rancho** [194 A2] 🕿 027 275 5115; ⏰ lunch & dinner Tue–Sun. Top-notch Indian restaurant & bar in a converted old house & green garden close to the Impala Hotel in Shantytown. A broad selection of vegetarian meals is available at around Tsh4,000, while meat dishes are slightly more expensive. Highly recommended.

✖ **Indo-Italiano Restaurant** [197 C6] 🕿 027 275 2195; ⏰ 09.00–22.00 daily. This popular restaurant has a convenient location opposite the Buffalo Hotel & serves a wide range of Indian & Italian dishes – tandoori grills & pizzas particularly recommended – in the Tsh5,000–6,000 range. Meals can be served indoors or on the wide veranda.

✖ **Panda Chinese Restaurant** [194 A3] m 0754 838193/0784 875725; ⏰ lunch & dinner daily. This friendly & reliable Chinese eatery lies in pretty gardens just around the corner from the AMEG Lodge in Shantytown. It has the usual lengthy menu of meat, fish, chicken & vegetarian dishes, most at around Tsh7,000–8,000, though prawns are more expensive. Take-away available.

✕ **Salzburger Café** [197 A6] ☎ 027 275 0681; ⏲ 11.00–22.00 daily. Owned by a Tanzanian formerly resident in Austria, this unique restaurant on Kenyatta St is a real gem, decorated with mementoes of the old European city to create an atmosphere of full-on kitsch. If the décor doesn't do it for you, then the food certainly should – Tsh5,000–6,000 for a variety of very good steak, chicken & spaghetti dishes, with the unusual (for Tanzania) accompaniment of mashed potato & salads in addition to the conventional chips & rice.

✕ **Tanzania Coffee Lounge** [197 B7] ☎ 027 275 1006; www.toku-tanzania.com. Indisputably the tastiest caffeine fix in Moshi, with filter, espresso, latte & cappuccino available, this trendy little place on Chagga Rd also serves great waffles, & variable cakes & pastries. The tasty lunchtime salads will satisfy those desperate for some fresh greens. A bona fide 1950s jukebox beats out a selection of songs you probably haven't heard in years, & there's a high-speed internet café at the back.

✕ **The Coffee Shop** [197 B5] ☎ 027 275 2707; ⏲ 08.00–20.00 daily. Tucked away on Hill St between the bus station & market, this church-run institution used to be *the* place for a fix of real coffee. It has been superseded in this role by the newer Tanzania Coffee Lounge, but it's still worth visiting for the irresistible selection of homemade cakes, burgers, sandwiches, pies, snacks & light lunches, mostly at around Tsh2,000–3,000, served indoors or in a tranquil courtyard garden. It's also a good spot for b/fast.

NIGHTLIFE

☆ **Club La Liga** [194 D6] m 0767 770022/0715 750076; ⏲ 18.00–late daily except Mon; entry Tsh5,000 Fri, Tsh3,000 other nights, free for women Sun. Moshi's premier nightclub lies about 500m from the town centre, among a row of old warehouses that can be reached by following Chagga Rd eastward across the railway tracks, where it becomes Viwanda Rd. It usually has live music Thu; DJs play Bongo Flava (Tanzanian hip-hop) & other dance music on other nights.

🍷 **East African Pub Inn** [197 C5] Nyerere Rd, 2 blocks north of Kindoroko Hotel. This lively 2-storey bar has a wooden roof, TV & loud music, with cheap'n'cheerful drink prices aimed at a predominantly local clientele.

🍷 **Glacier Inn** [194 A4] m 0737 022764. Set in large jacaranda-shaded gardens on the corner of Lema & Kilimanjaro roads, this is a great spot for a few outdoor drinks in suburban Shantytown. It also serves a varied selection of grills, Indian & Italian dishes in the Tsh4,000–6,000 range, & cheaper pub grub. A satellite TV ensures its popularity during major international sporting events.

☆ **Pub Alberto** [197 C2] ⏲ 18.00–04.00 daily except Mon. This brightly decorated nightclub next to Chrisburgers is a good place for a last round.

SHOPPING

Books A good secondhand bookstall can be found on Nyerere Road, between the bus station and the Newcastle Hotel. For new books, particularly material relating specifically to Tanzania, the bookshop on the ground floor of the Kilimanjaro Crane Hotel [197 C2] is the best-stocked in town.

Crafts and souvenirs Although Moshi doesn't boast quite the proliferation of curio stalls and shops associated with Arusha, there are still plenty around, and prices tend to be a bit lower, as does the pushiness factor. The main concentration of craft shops in the town centre lies along Chagga Road close to the main cluster of budget hotels, and there's no better starting point here than the vast and hassle-free One Heritage Craft Shop [197 C7], which stocks a good selection of books and postcards alongside the usual carvings, paintings and other local crafts. Follow Chagga Road east across the railway tracks towards Club La Liga to visit Shah Enterprises [194 C6] (☎ *027 275 2414*), an excellent craft workshop specialising in leatherwork and staffed mainly by disabled Tanzanians. For paintings, the best selection is a cluster of perhaps a dozen stalls situated about 200m east of the main traffic circle along the Arusha–Dar es Salaam highway.

Supermarkets Aleem's supermarket on Boma Road (behind the post office) [197 B3] stocks a good range of imported goods and foods. The Carina supermarket next to Chrisburgers [197 C2] is also very well stocked. Opposite Aleem's, the Hot Bread Shop [197 B3] sells freshly baked bread as well as a selection of cakes and pies. There are also several good supermarkets on Nyerere Road between the bus station and the central market.

OTHER PRACTICALITIES

Foreign exchange and banks The National Bank of Commerce opposite the Clocktower [197 C2] changes cash and travellers' cheques at the usual rate and commission. Several forex bureaux are dotted around town, but while exchange rates are fairly good, you will generally get better in Arusha or Dar es Salaam. One exception, Trust Bureau de Change [197 B7] (© 09.00–18.00 Mon–Sat, 09.00–14.00 Sun), on Chagga Road diagonally opposite the Kindoroko Hotel, offers good rates on US dollar travellers' cheques or cash, and charges no commission.

There are now several 24-hour ATMs where up to Tsh200,000 cash can be drawn daily with certain credit or debit cards. The ATMs at the Standard Chartered Bank [197 B3], National Bank of Commerce [197 C2] and Barclays Bank [197 B7] accept Visa, the one at the Exim Bank [197 B3] accepts MasterCard, while the one at Stanbic [197 B3] accepts both Visa and MasterCard, as well as Maestro and Cirrus. Other cards such as American Express are not accepted anywhere in Moshi.

Hospitals and clinics The best place to head for in the case of a medical emergency is the Kilimanjaro Christian Medical Centre (KCMC) in Shantytown [194 B2] (\ 027 275 4378), about 5km north of the town centre. More central options include the First Health Hospital on Rindi Road alongside the Standard Chartered Bank [197 B3] (\ 027 275 4051) and Mawenzi Hospital [197 B5] next to the Hindu Temple on the junction of Hill and Benbella.

Immigration Situated in Kibo House on Boma Road, a few doors east of the Stanbic Bank, the immigration office [197 B3] (© 08.00–15.00 Mon–Fri) can process visa extensions on the spot.

Internet and email Numerous internet cafés are dotted around town. Most charge around Tsh500 per 15 or 30 minutes – the more expensive cafés generally provide a faster service – and are open around 08.00–20.00 daily, though some close on Sundays. In the Clocktower area, IBC Internet and Twiga Communications, set alongside each other on the Old Moshi Road near the Coffee Tree Hotel [197 C2], are speedy and helpful, as is Easycom in Twiga House on the main traffic circle [197 C3]. South of the bus station, Fahari Cyber Centre on Hill Street [197 C5] and the Tanzania Coffee Lounge on Chagga Road [197 B7] are both recommended, though the latter is a little pricier than average.

Swimming pool Use of the swimming pool at the YMCA [194 D4 & 197 C1] is free to hostel residents, but visitors must pay a daily entrance fee of Tsh3,000 per person. The Keys Hotel [194 D4] charges a similar price to casual swimmers, but the pool is smaller and further out of town. You could also try the pool at the Kilimanjaro Crane Hotel [197 C2].

Telephone phonecards These can be bought and used at the Tanzania Telecommunications Centre next to the post office near the Clocktower [197 C3]. This is also the best place to make international phone calls, and to send and receive faxes.

CULTURAL TOURS AROUND MOSHI

Several cultural tourism projects operate in the Kilimanjaro foothills in association with local communities. In addition to offering insights into Chagga culture and the opportunity to limber up before a full-on ascent of Kilimanjaro, these cultural tours allow non-climbers to get a good look at the scenic Kilimanjaro foothills, with a chance of a glimpse of the snow-capped peak itself. One operator in Moshi that specialises in setting up budget-friendly day trips to the cultural programmes, as well as running its own day hike in the Kilimanjaro foothills, is Akaro Tours (see page 220).

MACHAME CULTURAL TOURISM PROGRAMME This programme (✆ 027 275 7033) is based at the village of Kyalia, close to the Machame Gate of Mount Kilimanjaro National Park. A good day tour for those with a strong interest in scenery is the five-hour Sieny-Ngira Trail, which passes through the lush montane forest to a group of large sacred caves, a natural rock bridge over the Marire and Namwi rivers, and a nearby waterfall. For those with a greater interest in culture, the five-hour Nronga Tour, which visits a milk purification and processing co-operative run by women, is best done on Monday, market day in Kyalia village. Of similar duration, the Nkuu Tour focuses instead on agriculture, in particular coffee production. Longer excursions include the two-day Ng'uni Hike and three-day Lyamungo Tour. In a private vehicle, Kyalia can be reached by following the Arusha road out of Moshi for 12km, following the signposted turn-off for Machame Gate and driving for another 14km. The road to Kyalia is surfaced in its entirety, and regular *dala-dalas* run to Kyalia from the junction on the Moshi–Arusha road.

MARANGU CULTURAL TOURISM PROGRAMME Geared primarily towards travellers staying in Marangu prior to a Kilimanjaro climb, this programme offers a variety of half-day trips taking in various natural and cultural sites in the surrounding slopes. Popular goals include any of three waterfalls, as well as the first coffee tree planted in Tanzania more than a century ago, and a traditional conical Chagga homestead. Few prospective climbers will be unmoved by the grave of the legendary Yohanu Lauwo, who guided Hans Meyer to the summit of Kilimanjaro back in 1889, continued working as a guide into his 70s, and lived to the remarkable age of 124! Other walks lead to nearby Mamba and Makundi, known for their traditional Chagga blacksmiths and woodcarvers, and for the Laka Caves, where women and children were hidden during the frequent 19th-century clashes with the Maasai of the surrounding plains. Guided tours can be arranged through any of the hotels in and around Marangu.

MATERUNI AND KURINGE WATERFALL TOUR Operated exclusively by Akaro Tours, whose founder grew up in a nearby *shamba* (smallholding/subsistence farm), this rewarding half- or full-day tour starts at the village of Materuni on the foothills of Kilimanjaro, some 14km from Moshi. The walk follows sloping roads and footpaths through the surrounding mountainside to the Kuringe Waterfall, a 70m-high 'bridal veil' fall set at the head of a steep wooded gorge. One of the loveliest waterfalls I've seen anywhere in Africa, Kuringe is genuinely worth making an effort to visit, something I don't say lightly after having regularly hiked for miles in the line of duty to check out what, it transpired, was yet another unmemorable small cataract. On the full day, you continue from the waterfall, climbing steep cultivated slopes, to a Chagga homestead, where lunch and home-grown coffee are provided. From here, you can continue on to the Rua Forest, which harbours black-and-white colobus monkeys as well as most of the montane forest birds associated with Kilimanjaro. The full-day version can also incorporate a visit to a typical Chagga coffee and banana subsistence farm.

MARANGU

The village of Marangu, whose name derives from the local Chagga word meaning 'spring water', is situated on the lower slopes of Kilimanjaro about 40km from Moshi and 5km south of the main entrance gate to Mount Kilimanjaro National Park. Unlike lower-lying Moshi, Marangu has an appropriately alpine feel, surrounded as it is by lush vegetation and bisected by a babbling mountain stream, and it remains a popular springboard for Kilimanjaro ascents using the Marangu Route. For those who lack the time, inclination or money to climb Kilimanjaro, Marangu is a pleasant place to spend a night or a few days exploring the lower slopes of the great mountain, with several attractive waterfalls situated within easy striking distance.

GETTING THERE AND AWAY The 40km drive from Moshi shouldn't take much longer than 30 minutes in a private vehicle. To get there, first head out along the Dar es Salaam road, bearing left after 23km as if heading towards Taveta, then turning left again after another 4km at the junction village of Himo. Buses and *dala-dalas* between Moshi and Marangu leave in either direction when they are full, normally at least once an hour, and generally take from 45 minutes to an hour.

WHERE TO STAY AND EAT
Upmarket
Nakara Hotel (18 rooms) ✆ 027 275 6599; e nakaratz@africaonline.co.tz; www.nakara-hotels.com. Probably the smartest option in Marangu these days, this soulless but efficiently staffed high-rise hotel lies about 3km past Marangu & 2km before the eponymous entrance gate to Kilimanjaro NP. Compact but comfortable self-contained twin rooms might lack for character, but they are in far better shape than those at several rivals. Unfortunately, the rather cramped grounds lack the greenery & character of other options in this price range. *US$100/160 sgl/dbl B&B, plus US$25 pp for FB.*

Marangu Hotel (26 rooms) ✆ 027 275 6591; f 027 275 6594; e info@maranguhotel.com; www.maranguhotel.com. This comfortable, family-run hotel, along the Moshi Rd 5km before Marangu, has an unpretentiously rustic feel, all ivy-draped walls & neat hedges that might have been transported straight from the English countryside. It also has a long-standing reputation for organising reliable Kilimanjaro climbs, whether you're looking at the standard all-inclusive package or the 'hard way' package aimed at budget travellers. Accommodation is in self-contained rooms. The large green campsite behind the main hotel buildings has a hot shower & is probably the best value for campers in the Marangu area. *US$85/120 sgl/dbl FB; camping US$3 pp.*

Capricorn Hotel (70 rooms) ✆ 027 275 1309; m 0754 841981; f 027 275 2442; e capricorn@africaonline.co.tz; www.capricornhotel.com. Straggling over a steep hillside some 7km from Marangu along the road towards Kilimanjaro NP's Marangu entrance gate, this is one of the newer hotels in the Marangu area, but the en-suite rooms with satellite TV & minibar are rather variable in quality & the older ones are starting to look quite frayed at the edges. Set within the forest zone, the lushly wooded 2.5ha garden is teeming with birds. The restaurant has a mediocre reputation, but Kilimanjaro climbs arranged through the hotel are as reliable as it gets. *US$60/80 B&B sgl/dbl cottage in old wing, US$95/130 new wing, FB additional US$27 pp.*

Kibo Hotel (35 rooms) ✆/f 027 275 1308; e info@kibohotel.com or kibohotel@yahoo.com; www.kibohotel.com. The venerable Kibo Hotel stands in attractive flowering gardens roughly 1km from the village centre towards the park entrance gate. Formerly on a par with the Marangu Hotel, the Kibo has emphatically seen better days — incredibly, lest it escape your attention, former US President Jimmy Carter stayed here in 1988 — but it has retained a winning air of faded dignity epitomised by the liberal wood panelling & creaky old verandas. If nothing else, following a recent change of management & sensible cut in rates, the large, self-contained rooms are good value. Facilities include swimming pool, internet access, gift shop & a decent restaurant bursting with character. The hotel makes a great base for casual rambling in the Kilimanjaro foothills, & has been arranging reliable Kilimanjaro climbs for decades. *US$45/69/99 sgl/dbl/trpl B&B, US$71/117/160 FB; camping US$5 pp.*

Moderate

🏠 **Babylon Lodge** (22 rooms) ☎ 027 275 6355
f 027 275 6597; e babylon@africaonline.co.tz.
Situated 500m from Marangu post office along the
Mwika Rd, this former budget hotel has undergone a
series of facelifts over the past decade, the most
recent scheduled for completion in early 2009. The
en-suite rooms with combination tub/shower &
attractive ethnic décor are immaculately kept but a
touch on the cramped side. Overall, it's one of the
best value lodges in the Marangu area, especially
when it comes to cleanliness & quality of service. An
onsite internet café should be operational in 2009.
US$30/50 sgl/dbl B&B, plus US$10 pp for lunch or
dinner.

Budget and camping

🔺 **Coffee Tree Campsite** ☎ 027 275 6604;
e kilimanjaro@iwayafrica.com. Along the road to
the NP entrance, alongside the Nakara Hotel, this
neatly laid out site is also a good place to arrange
budget Kilimanjaro climbs. It's not exactly great
value, but you won't find cheaper in Marangu. The
camping seems a bit dear; even allowing for the
above-average facilities — fridge, bar, barbecue, sauna
& hot shower — the campsites at the Marangu &
Kibo hotels (see above) seem infinitely better value.
Tents & gas stoves are available for hire, various
cultural tours can be arranged, & there are on-site
email & internet facilities. If you don't fancy self-
catering, you could eat at the adjacent Nakara
Hotel. Dbl chalets US$15 pp, rondavel US$12 pp;
camping US$8 pp.

🔺 **Gilman's Camping Site** ☎ 027 275 6490; m 0744
299486; e gilmanscamp@yahoo.com. Near the
Moonjo Waterfall, about 1km past the Kibo Hotel,
where it is reached by a 200m dirt track, this
campsite charges a rather hefty price only partially
justified by its superior facilities, namely a clean
ablution block with hot showers, & access to a kitchen
& comfortable lounge. The tall, conical traditional
Chagga house behind the campsite is one of the last
in existence & well worth a look. Camping US$10 pp.

EXCURSIONS FROM MARANGU

Kinukamori Waterfall The most central tourist attraction in Marangu is the
Kinukamori ('Little Moon') Waterfall. About 20 minutes' walk from the town
centre, from where it is signposted, this approximately 15m-high waterfall lies in a
small park maintained by the district council (*US$1 entrance*) as an ecotourism
project in collaboration with two nearby villages. It's pretty enough without being
an essential side trip, though the wooded banks of the Unna River above the
waterfall harbour a variety of forest birds, and regularly attract troops of black-and-
white colobus in the rainy season. A legend associated with Kinukamori relates to
an unmarried girl called Makinuka, who discovered she was pregnant, a crime
punishable by death in strict Chagga society, and decided to take her own life by
jumping over the waterfall. When Makinuka arrived at the waterfall and looked
over the edge, she changed her mind and turned to go home to plead for mercy. As
she did so, however, she came face to face with a leopard and ran back screaming
in fear, forgetting about the gorge behind her, to plunge to an accidental death. A
statue of Makinuka and her nemesis stands above the waterfall. The waterfall can
be visited independently, or by arrangement with your hotel as part of a longer
sightseeing tour.

Kilasia Waterfall Clearly signposted to the left of the dirt road connecting the Kibo
Hotel and Kilimanjaro Mountain Resort lies the rather spectacular Kilasia Waterfall,
the centrepiece of a new ecotourist community that charges US$3 for a guided
nature walk. Approximately 30m high, the waterfall tumbles into the base of a
sheer-sided gorge before running through a set of violent rapids into a lovely pool
that's said to be safe for swimming. The waterfall is at its most powerful during the
rains, but it flows solidly throughout the year – the name Kilasia derives from a
Chagga word meaning 'without end', reputedly a reference to its reliable flow. The
path to the base of the falls, though no more than 500m long, is very steep and
potentially dangerous when wet. The rocky gorge below the waterfall is lined with

ferns and evergreen trees, and a troop of blue monkeys often passes through in the early morning and late afternoon. For further details, contact the community project manager (m *0755 041040/252893;* e *kilasiawaterfalls@yahoo.com*).

LAKE CHALA

Straddling the Kenyan border some 30km east of Moshi as the crow flies, this roughly circular crater lake, a full 3km wide yet invisible until you virtually topple over the rim, is one of northern Tanzania's true off-the-beaten-track scenic gems. The brilliant turquoise water, hemmed in by sheer cliffs draped in tropical greenery, is an arresting sight at any time, and utterly fantastic when Kilimanjaro emerges from the clouds to the immediate west. Not for the faint-hearted, a very steep footpath leads from the rim to the edge of the lake, its translucent waters plunging near-vertically to an undetermined depth from the rocky shore. Abundant birdlife aside, wildlife is in short supply, though Chala, in common with many other African crater lakes, is said locally to harbour its due quota of mysterious and malignant Nessie-like beasties. A more demonstrable cause for concern should you be nurturing any thoughts of dipping a toe in the water, however, is the presence of crocodiles, one of which savaged and drowned a British volunteer off the Kenyan shore in March 2002.

Recent attempts to attract tourism to Chala could hardly be deemed an unqualified success. A tourist lodge established in 1999 on the Kenyan rim closed down several years ago, and the Kilimanjaro Chala Lodge and Campsite on the Tanzanian side has been under construction since 2002 and looks unlikely to be completed any time soon. For the time being, the only practical way to reach Chala is as an organised day or overnight trip out of Moshi, or in a private 4x4 vehicle. If you're driving, follow the Dar es Salaam road out of Moshi for 25km until you reach the junction at Himo, where a left turn leads to the Kenyan border at Taveta. About 7km along the Taveta road, turn left on to the rough road signposted for Kilimanjaro Mountain Lodge, which you must follow for about 40 minutes to reach the lake.

MKOMAZI NATIONAL PARK

Gazetted as a game reserve in 1951 and upgraded to National Park status in 2008, Mkomazi is effectively a southern extension of Kenya's vast Tsavo National Park, covering an area of 3,234km² to the east of Kilimanjaro and immediately north of the Pare Mountains. Together with Tsavo, it forms part of one of East Africa's most important savannah ecosystems, characterised by the semi-arid climatic conditions of the Sahel Arc, and housing a great many dry-country species rare or absent elsewhere in Tanzania.

In 1992, the Tanzanian government invited the Royal Geographical Society to undertake a detailed ecological study of Mkomazi. Although mammal populations were very low, it was determined that most large mammal species present in Tsavo are either resident in Mkomazi or regularly migrate there from Kenya, including lion, cheetah, elephant, giraffe, buffalo, zebra, impala and Tanzania's most significant gerenuk population. African wild dogs were re-introduced into Mkomazi in the 1990s, as was a herd of black rhinos from South Africa, though neither is likely to be seen on an ordinary safari – for more details of these breeding projects see www.mkomazi.com.

Mkomazi is listed as an Important Bird Area, with more than 400 species recorded, including several northern dry-country endemics that were newly added to the Tanzania list by the RGS – for instance three-streaked tchagra, Shelley's starling, Somali long-billed crombec, yellow-vented eremomela and the extremely localised Friedmann's lark. It is the only place in Tanzania where the lovely vulturine guineafowl, notable for its bright cobalt chest, is likely to be seen. Other conspicuous large ground birds include common ostrich, secretary bird, southern ground hornbill, and various francolins and bustards.

Until recently, Mkomazi was practically undeveloped for tourism. It had also been subject to considerable pressure as the human population around its peripheries grew in number. As a result, wildlife is thinly distributed and skittish. This is likely to change, however, as animal populations benefit from the higher level of protection Mkomazi will be accorded as part of the national park system. It is also likely that the wildlife will become more habituated to safari vehicles following the recent construction of an exclusive tented camp within the park's boundaries.

Although Mkomazi doesn't offer game viewing to compare with other reserves in northern Tanzania, this is compensated for by the wild scenery – mountains rise in all direction, with Kilimanjaro often visible to the northwest at dawn and dusk – and the near certainty of not seeing another tourist. The best game viewing circuit runs for about 20km between Zange Entrance Gate and Dindera Dam, where topi, eland, giraffe, common zebra and gazelles are all quite likely to be seen. The thicker bush further east is a good place to see lesser kudu and gerenuk.

GETTING THERE AND AWAY Mkomazi is among the most accessible of Tanzania national parks. The gateway town is Same, a small but busy trading centre that straddles the main Dar es Salaam Highway about 105km southeast of Moshi. The drive from Moshi to Same shouldn't take longer than 90 minutes in a private vehicle, and any public transport heading from Moshi to places further south can drop you off there. From Same, a good 5km dirt road runs to the Zange Entrance Gate, where you need to pay the entrance fee of US$20 per person per 24-hour period.

Although Mkomazi is not often included on northern Tanzania safari itineraries, this is likely to change as wildlife viewing improves and its tented camp gains greater publicity, and there is no reason why any established safari operator couldn't append it to a longer safari. For budget travellers, the park could easily be visited as a day trip out of Same, where 4x4 and other vehicles are usually available for hire at a negotiable rate. Mkomazi is best avoided in the rainy season, due to the poor roads.

WHERE TO STAY AND EAT
Upmarket

Babu's Camp (5 rooms) \ 027 250 3094; e babuscamp@bol.co.tz; www.babuscamp.com. Established in 2006, this exclusive tented camp, some 13km inside the park coming from Zange Entrance Gate, is spaciously laid out within a grove of gigantic baobabs & acacias, & offers great views across the plains to the Pare Mountains & lower hills within the park. Spacious walk-in tents have their own balcony & a private open roof shower & toilet out the back, offering fabulous views of the sparkling African night sky. It is usefully based for game drives, a 45min drive from Dindera Dam. The birdlife around camp can be fabulous, & African wild dogs & other predators occasionally pass through. US$288/520 sgl/dbl B&B.

Budget

Elephant Motel (20 rooms) \ 027 275 8193; m 0754 839545; e manager@elephantmotel.com; www.elephantmotel.com. The smartest accommodation in the vicinity of Same is this recently refurbished motel, set in large green grounds about 1.5km south of the town centre along the B1 to Dar es Salaam. It offers clean en-suite rooms with netting, TV & hot running water; good Indian, Tanzanian & Western meals in the restaurant or garden cost around Tsh5,000–6,000. Booking ahead is highly recommended. US$20/28 sgl/dbl.

Shoestring

Amani Lutheran Centre On the main tar road through Same, about 200m uphill from the bus station, this clean & long-serving hostel consists of around a dozen rooms enclosing a small green courtyard. It's a friendly set-up, & facilities include internet café, canteen & safe parking. *Tsh7,000/10,000 en-suite sgl/dbl B&B, Tsh15,000 suite.*

MBAGA AND THE SOUTH PARE

The mountains that tower so impressively over Mkomazi's southeast horizon are the South Pare, a range separated from the Western Usambara (see *Chapter 8*) by the Mkomazi River Valley. Named for their Pare inhabitants, the mountains boast a wealth of low-key cultural sites and natural attractions, most of which are accessible through a cultural tourism programme that operates out of Hilltop Tona Lodge in Mbaga (or Manka).

Mbaga itself is an attractively wooded semi-urban sprawl that follows the main road along the northern slopes of the range. Its most striking feature, an oddly Bavarian apparition in these remote African hills, is the century-old church built by Jakob Dannholz. Further afield, the lodge can also arrange visits to a highly respected traditional healer (who also happens to be a Seventh-Day Adventist, so don't bother visiting on a Saturday), to the Mghimbi Caves (where the Pare hid from slave raiders in the 1860s), to Malameni Rock (where children were sacrificed to appease evil spirits until the practice was outlawed in the 1930s), to the forested Ronzi Dam and to the legendary 'Red Reservoir'.

Longer hikes include a three-day trip through Chome Forest Reserve, which lies on the slopes of the 2,462m Mount Shengena, and harbours various monkeys and birds including the endemic South Pare white-eye. Nominal guides fees must be paid for all activities.

GETTING THERE AND AWAY As with Mkomazi, the main springboard is Same on the Dar es Salaam road south of Moshi. With private transport, the most interesting route skirts the boundary of Mkomazi Game Reserve before passing through the small town of Kisiwani (an old slave-trading centre with a distinctly coastal feel and legendarily succulent mangoes) and ascending to Mbaga via a spectacular forest-fringed pass.

Using public transport, the 35km road from there to Mbaga is traversed by at least one bus and a couple of *dala-dalas* daily run along the 35km road connecting Same to Mbaga. Normally, all transport out of Mbaga leaves before 07.00, and begins the return trip from Same at around 11.00. Sometimes there's a second run back and forth in the afternoon, but this is the exception rather than the rule. If you need to overnight in Same, see *Where to stay* under *Mkomazi National Park*, opposite, for details.

⌂ WHERE TO STAY AND EAT

⌂ **Hilltop Tona Lodge** (11 rooms) m 0754 852010; e tona_lodge@hotmail.com; http://tonalodge.org. This hub of tourist activity in South Pare consists of several en-suite cottages in a wonderful jungle setting with great views over the Mkomazi Plains. There is a natural swimming pool in the river below the lodge, & a restaurant serves cheap meals & cold drinks. *Tsh10,000 pp; camping Tsh6,000 pp.*

MOUNT KILIMANJARO NATIONAL PARK

Reaching an elevation of 5,895m (19,340ft), Kilimanjaro is the highest mountain in Africa, and on the rare occasions when it is not veiled in clouds, its distinctive silhouette and snow-capped peak form one of the most breathtaking sights on the continent. There are, of course, higher peaks on other continents, but Kilimanjaro is effectively the world's largest single mountain, a free-standing entity that towers an incredible 5km above the surrounding plains. It is also the highest mountain anywhere that can be ascended by somebody without specialised mountaineering experience or equipment.

Kilimanjaro straddles the border with Kenya, but the peaks all fall within Tanzania and can only be climbed from within Tanzania. There are several places on the lower slopes from where the mountain can be ascended, but most people use the Marangu Route (which begins at the eponymous village) because it is the cheapest option and has the best facilities. The less heavily trampled Machame Route, starting from the village of the same name, has grown in popularity in recent years. A number of more obscure routes can be used, though they are generally only available through specialist trekking companies. Most prospective climbers arrange their ascent of 'Kili' – as it is popularly called – well in advance, through an overseas tour operator or online with a local operator, but you can also shop around on the spot using specialist trekking companies based in Moshi, Marangu or even Arusha. Kilimanjaro can be climbed at any time of year, but the hike is more difficult in the rainy months, especially between March and May.

GEOLOGY In geological terms, Kilimanjaro is a relatively young mountain. Like most other large mountains near the Rift Valley, it was formed by volcanic activity, first erupting about one million years ago. The 3,962m Shira Peak collapsed around half a million years ago, but the 5,895m Uhuru Peak on Mount Kibo and 5,149m Mawenzi Peak continued to grow until more recently. Shira plateau formed 360,000 years ago, when the caldera was filled by lava from Kibo after a

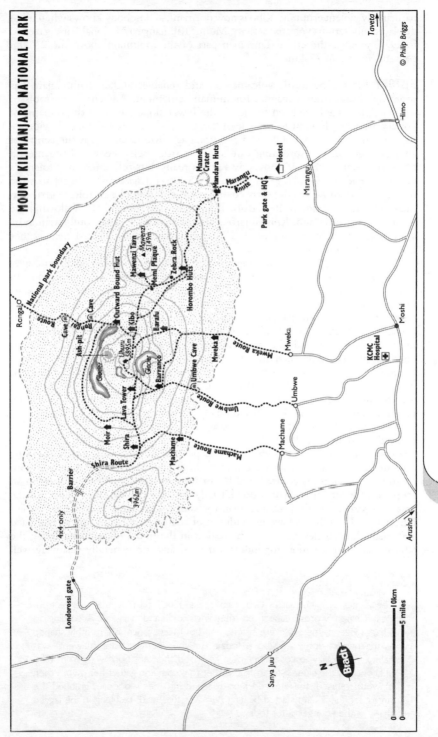

© Philip Briggs

Taveta

Himo

Hostel

Maundi
Crater

Mandara Huts

Marangu
Route

Park gate & HQ

Marangu

Mawenzi
5149m

Mawenzi Tarn

Meml Plaque

Zebra Rock

Outward Bound Hut

Horombo Huts

National park boundary

Rongai
Route

Cave

Cave

Cave

Ash pit

Uhuru
5895m

Gilman's

Kibo

Barafu

Glacier

Barranco

Umbwe Cave

Mweka

Mweka Route

Mweka

Moshi

KCMC
Hospital

Lava Tower

Moir

Shira

Umbwe Route

Umbwe

Umbwe

Shira Route

Machame

Machame Route

Machame

3962m

Barrier

4x4 only

Londorossi gate

Arusha

Sanya Juu

N

Bradt

10km

5 miles

0

0

particularly violent eruption. Kibo is now dormant, and nobody knows when it last displayed any serious volcanic activity. Mount Kilimanjaro National Park, gazetted in 1977, protects the entire Tanzanian part of the mountain above the 2,700m contour, an area of 756km².

HISTORY Blessed by fertile volcanic soil and reliable rainfall, Kilimanjaro has probably always been a magnet for human settlement. Ancient stone tools of indeterminate age have been found on the lower slopes, as have the remains of pottery artefacts thought to be at least 2,000 years old. Archaeological evidence suggests that, between 1,000 and 1,500 years ago, Kilimanjaro was the centre of an Iron Age culture spreading out to the coastal belt between Pangani and Mombasa. Before that, it's anybody's guess really, but references in Ptolemy's *Geography* and the *Periplus of the Erythraean Sea* (see *Chapter 1*) suggest that the mountain was known to the early coastal traders, and might even have served as the terminus of a trade route starting at modern-day Pangani and following the eponymous river inland. Kilimanjaro is also alluded to in an account written by a 12th-century Chinese trader, and by the 16th-century Spanish geographer Fernandes de Encisco.

These ancient allusions fired the curiosity of 19th-century geographers, who outdid each other in publishing wild speculations about the African interior. In 1848, locals told Johan Rebmann, a German missionary working in the Taita Hills, about a very large silver-capped mountain known to the Maasai as *Ol Doinyo Naibor* (White Mountain) and reputedly protected by evil spirits that froze anybody who tried to ascend it. When Rebmann visited the mountain, he immediately recognised the spirit-infested silver cap to be snow, but this observation, first published in 1849, was derided by European experts, who thought it ludicrous to claim there was snow so near the Equator. Only in 1861, when an experienced geologist, Von der Decken, saw and surveyed Kilimanjaro, was its existence and that of its snow-capped peaks accepted internationally. Oral tradition suggests that no local person had successfully climbed Kilimanjaro – or at least returned to tell the tale – before Hans Meyer and Ludwig Purtscheller reached the summit in 1889.

Kilimanjaro is home to the Chagga people, a group of Bantu-speaking agriculturists whose ancestors are said to have arrived in the area in the 15th century. This dating is contradicted by an intriguing local legend relating to an eruption of Kilimanjaro, which doesn't tally with the geological evidence for the past 500 years, so it's probable that the story was handed down by earlier inhabitants. The Chagga have no tradition of central leadership, and an estimated 100 small chieftaincies existed in the region in the mid 19th century. Today, the Chagga have a reputation for industriousness, and are generally relatively well

An unsubstantiated legend holds that Emperor Menelik I of Ethiopia, the illegitimate son of King Solomon and the Queen of Sheba, visited Kilimanjaro about 3,000 years ago while returning from a successful military campaign in East Africa. The emperor camped on the saddle for a night and then ascended Kibo, where he suddenly fell ill and died, possibly from exposure and/or altitude-related causes. Menelik's slaves buried the imperial corpse in the snowy crater, where it remains to this day, so the story goes, together with a royal cache of jewels, religious scrolls and other treasures. An extension of this legend prophesies that a descendant of Menelik I will one day ascend Kibo, find the frozen body and claim the seal ring of Solomon worn by it, endowing him with the wisdom of Solomon and heroic spirit of Menelik. Pure apocrypha, so far as I can ascertain, is the story that the ancient Ethiopian emperor's 19th-century successor and namesake Menelik II once climbed Kilimanjaro in an unsuccessful bid to fulfil this centuries-old prophecy.

educated, for which reason you'll find that a high proportion of salaried workers and safari guides come from the Kilimanjaro region.

VEGETATION AND BIOLOGY There are five vegetation zones on Kilimanjaro: the cultivated lower slopes, the forest, heath and moorland, alpine, and the barren arctic summit zone. Vegetation is sparse higher up due to lower temperatures and insufficient rainfall.

The **lower slopes** of the mountain were probably once forested, but are now mainly cultivated. The volcanic soils make them highly fertile and they support a dense human population. The most biologically interesting aspect of the lower slopes is the abundance of wildflowers, seen between Marangu and the park entrance gate.

The **montane forest zone** of the southern slopes lies between 1,800m and 3,000m elevation. Receiving up to 2,000mm of rainfall annually, this zone displays a high biological diversity, and still supports a fair amount of wildlife. The most frequently seen mammals are the black-and-white colobus and blue monkeys, while typical forest antelope include three duiker species and the beautifully marked bushbuck. Leopard, bushpig and porcupine are fairly common but seldom encountered by hikers, while eland, buffalo and elephant are present in small numbers. The forest is home to many varieties of butterfly, including four endemic species. The forests of Kilimanjaro are less rich in birds (particularly endemics) than the more ancient forests of the Eastern Arc Mountains, but some 40 species peculiar to Afro-montane forest have been recorded. Most forest birds are quite

Nobody is sure about the meaning of the name Kilimanjaro, or even whether it is Swahili, Maasai or Chagga in origin. That the term *kilima* is Swahili for 'little mountain' (a joke?) is not in doubt. But *njaro* could derive from the Chagga word for caravan (the mountain was an important landmark on the northern caravan route), or from the Maasai word *ngare*, meaning water (it is the source of most of the region's rivers), or from the name of a Swahili demon of cold. Another unrelated version of the name's origin is that it's a bastardisation of the phrase *kilema kyaro* ('impossible journey'), the initial Chagga response to European queries about trekking to the peak!

Emma Thomson

For decades the Chagga have been making use of the fertile soil that lies at the foot of Kilimanjaro. Originally, the land was divided into family allotments or shamba (usually 0.68ha) and passed from father to son. Later on land was seized by the state, and re-allocated depending on the size of the family. These lush plots are used to grow coffee, plantain, bananas and medicinal herbs and were unique in their ability to allow the Chagga to be self-sufficient. This cropping system remained stable for at least a century, and only recently has it come under pressure from rapid population growth, diminishing land resources, changes in dietary habits and economic pressures for improved housing and schooling. These pressing needs have forced the younger generations to travel into the towns in search of paid work. However, this migration of youngsters to urban areas not only leads to labour shortages on the farms but also disrupts the traditional transmission from one generation to the next of the knowledge and experience required for the successful management of the farms.

difficult to observe, but trekkers should at least hear the raucous silvery-cheeked hornbill and beautiful Hartlaub's turaco.

The semi-alpine **moorland zone**, which lies between 3,000m and 4,000m, is characterised by heath-like, vegetation and abundant wildflowers. As you climb into the moorland, two distinctive plants become common. These are *Lobelia deckenii*, which grows to 3m high, and the groundsel *Senecio kilimanjarin*, which grows up to 5m high and can be distinguished by a spike of yellow flowers. The moorland zone supports a low density of mammals, but pairs of klipspringer are quite common on rocky outcrops and several other species are recorded from time to time. Hill chat and scarlet-tufted malachite sunbird are two birds whose range is restricted to the moorland of large East African mountains. Other localised birds are lammergeyer and alpine swift. Because it is so open, the views from the moorland are stunning.

The **alpine zone** between 4,000 and 5,000m is classified as a semi-desert because it receives an annual rainfall of less than 250mm. The ground often freezes at night, but ground temperatures may soar to above 30°C by day. Few plants survive in these conditions; only 55 species are present, many of them lichens and grasses. Six species of moss are endemic to the higher reaches of Kilimanjaro. Large mammals have been recorded at this elevation, most commonly eland, but none is resident.

Approaching the summit, the **arctic zone** starts at an elevation of around 5,000m. This area receives virtually no rainfall, and supports little permanent life other than the odd lichen. Two remarkable records concern a frozen leopard discovered here in 1926, and a family of hunting dogs seen in 1962. The most notable natural features at the summit are the inner and outer craters of Kibo, surrounding a 120m-deep ash pit, and the Great Northern Glacier, which has retreated markedly since Hans Meyer first saw it in 1889.

CLIMBING KILIMANJARO As Africa's highest peak and most identifiable landmark, Kilimanjaro offers an irresistible challenge to many tourists. Dozens of visitors to Tanzania, ranging from teenagers to pensioners (a seven-year-old boy recently became the youngest person to reach the summit), set off for Uhuru Peak every day, and those who make it generally regard the achievement to be the highlight of their time in the country. A major part of Kilimanjaro's attraction is that any reasonably fit person stands a fair chance of reaching the top. The ascent requires no special climbing skills or experience; on the contrary, it basically amounts to a long uphill slog over four days, followed by a more rapid descent.

The relative ease of climbing Kilimanjaro should not lull travellers into thinking of the ascent as some sort of prolonged Sunday stroll. It is a seriously tough hike, with potentially fatal penalties for those who are inadequately prepared or who

PORTER TREATMENT GUIDELINES

These guidelines are produced by the Kilimanjaro Porters Assistance Project (KPAP), an initiative of the International Mountain Explorers Connection, a non-profit organisation based in the US.

1 Ensure your porters are adequately clothed with suitable footwear, socks, waterproof jackets and trousers, gloves, hats, sunglasses etc. Clothing for loan is available at the KPAP Office in Moshi (see below).

2 Fair wages should be paid. Mount Kilimanjaro National Park recommends Tsh6,000 daily on the Marangu Route and Tsh8,000 on other routes. Ask your company how much your porters are paid (and whether it includes food) to encourage fair treatment from operators and guides.

3 Porters should eat at least two meals a day and have access to water.

4 Check the weights of the loads. The recommended maximum of 25kg includes the porter's personal gear (assumed to be 5kg, so the load for the company should not exceed 20kg). If additional porters need to be hired make sure that the tour company is paying each porter their full wage when you return.

5 Count the number of porters every day: you are paying and tipping for them. Porters should not be sent down early as they will not receive their tips, and the other porters will then be overloaded.

6 Make sure your porters are provided with proper shelter. Where no shelter is available, porters need proper sleeping accommodation that includes tents and sleeping bags. Sleeping in the mess tent means that porters must wait outside for climbers to finish their meals.

7 Ensure that each porter receives the intended tip. If you give your tips to one individual you run the risk that they may not distribute the proper amount to the crew.

8 Take care of sick or injured porters. Porters deserve the same standard of treatment, care and rescue as their clients. Sick or injured porters need to be sent down with someone who speaks their language and understands the problem. If available, porters should also be provided insurance.

9 Get to know your porters. Some porters speak English and will appreciate any effort to speak with them. Free Swahili-language cards are available at the KPAP office. The word *pole* (which translates loosely as 'sorry') shows respect for porters after a long day carrying your bags. *Asante* means 'thank you'.

10 After your climb, report any instances of abuse or neglect, by emailing info@kiliporters.org or visiting the KPAP office.

Visit www.kiliporters.org for further information, or drop into the KPAP office (*below the Kilimanjaro Backpackers Hotel on Nyerere Rd, Moshi;* m *0754 817615*) to attend a 'porter briefing', obtain a free Swahili/English language card, purchase discounted maps, arrange for off-the-beaten-path trips and home-stays which directly support the local people, report any instances of porter abuse, or make a donation of clothing, money or volunteer help.

belittle the health risks attached to being at an elevation of above 4,000m. It should also be recognised that there is no such thing as a cheap Kilimanjaro climb. Indeed, following the fee increases of 2006 (when the main entrance fee rose from US$40 to US$60 per day), the full set of park fees (entrance, camping, guide, porter and rescue) amount to US$525 per person for a five-day hike (the minimum length) and an additional US$110 per person for every extra day. Realistically, it would be difficult for the most corner-cutting of local operators to put together a five-day Marangu climb at much under US$900 per person, and most budget operators now charge more than US$1000 for the same route, depending to some extent on group size. People using high quality operators and/or the more obscure route should be prepared to pay considerably more!

Marangu Route Starting at the Marangu Gate some 5km from the village of the same name, the so-called 'tourist route' is the most popular way to the top of Kilimanjaro, largely because it is less arduous than most of the alternatives, as well as having better facilities and being cheaper to climb. Marangu is also probably the safest route, due to the volume of other climbers and good rescue facilities relative to more obscure routes, and it offers a better chance of seeing some wildlife. It is the only route where you can sleep in proper huts throughout, with bathing water and bottled drinks normally available too. The main drawback of the Marangu route is that it is heavily trampled by comparison with other routes, for which reason many people complain that it can feel overcrowded.

Day 1: Marangu to Mandara Hut (12km, 4 hours) On an organised climb you will be dropped at the park entrance gate a few kilometres past Marangu. There is a high chance of rain in the afternoon, so it is wise to set off on this four-hour hike as early in the day as you can. Foot traffic is heavy along this stretch, which means that although you pass through thick forest, the shy animals that inhabit the forest are not likely to be seen. If your guide will go that way, use the parallel trail which meets the main trail halfway between the gate and the hut. Mandara Hut (2,700m) is an attractive collection of buildings with room for 200 people.

Day 2: Mandara Hut to Horombo Hut (15km, 6 hours) You continue through forest for a short time before reaching the heather and moorland zone, from where there are good views of the peaks and Moshi. The walk takes up to six hours. Horombo Hut (3,720m) sleeps up to 120 people. It is in a valley and surrounded by giant lobelia and groundsel. If you do a six-day hike, you will spend a day at Horombo to acclimatise.

Day 3: Horombo Hut to Kibo Hut (15km, 6–7 hours) The vegetation thins out as you enter the desert-like alpine zone, and when you cross the saddle Kibo Peak comes into view. This six- to seven-hour walk should be done slowly: many people start to feel the effects of altitude. Kibo Hut (4,703m) is a stone construction that sleeps up to 120 people. Water must be carried there from a stream above Horombo. You may find it difficult to sleep at this elevation, and as you will have to rise at around 01.00 the next morning, many people feel it is better not to bother trying.

Days 4 and 5: Kibo Hut to the summit to Marangu The best time to climb is during the night, as it is marginally easier to climb the scree slope to Gillman's Point on the crater rim when it is frozen. This 5km ascent typically takes about six hours, so you need to get going between midnight and 01.00 to stand a chance of reaching the summit in time to catch the sunrise. From Gillman's Point it is a further two-hour round trip along the crater's edge to Uhuru Peak, the highest point in Africa.

From the summit, it's a roughly seven-hour descent with a break at Kibo Hut to Horombo Hut, where you will spend your last night on the mountain. The final day's descent from Horombo to Marangu generally takes 7–8 hours, so you should arrive in Marangu in mid-afternoon.

Other routes Although the vast majority of trekkers stick to the Marangu Route, some prefer to ascend Kilimanjaro using one of five relatively off-the-beaten-track alternatives. While the merits and demerits of avoiding the Marangu Route are

MOUNTAIN HEALTH

Do not attempt to climb Kilimanjaro unless you are reasonably fit, or if you have heart or lung problems (although asthma sufferers should be all right). Bear in mind, however, that very fit people are more prone to altitude sickness because they ascend too fast.

Above 3,000m you may not feel hungry, but you should try to eat. Carbohydrates and fruit are recommended, whereas rich or fatty foods are harder to digest. You should drink plenty of liquids, at least three litres of water daily, and will need enough water bottles to carry this. Dehydration is one of the most common reasons for failing to complete the climb. If you dress in layers, you can take off clothes before you sweat too much, thereby reducing water loss.

Few people climb Kilimanjaro without feeling some of the symptoms of altitude sickness: headaches, nausea, fatigue, breathlessness, sleeplessness and swelling of the hands and feet. You can reduce these by allowing yourself time to acclimatise by taking an extra day over the ascent, eating and drinking properly, and trying not to push yourself. If you walk slowly and steadily, you will tire less quickly than if you try to rush each day's walk. Acetazolamide (Diamox) helps speed acclimatisation and many people find it useful; take 250mg twice a day for five days, starting two or three days before reaching 3,500m. However, the side effects from this drug may resemble altitude sickness and therefore it is advisable to try the medication for a couple of days about two weeks before the trip to see if it suits you.

Should symptoms become severe, and especially if they are clearly getting worse, then descend immediately. Even going down 500m is enough to start recovery. Sleeping high with significant symptoms is dangerous; if in doubt descend to sleep low.

Pulmonary and cerebral oedema are altitude-related problems that can be rapidly fatal if you do not descend. Symptoms of the former include shortness of breath when at rest, coughing up frothy spit or even blood, and undue breathlessness compared with accompanying friends. Symptoms of high-altitude cerebral oedema are headaches, poor co-ordination, staggering like a drunk, disorientation, poor judgement and even hallucinations. The danger is that the sufferer usually doesn't realise how sick he/she is and may argue against descending. The only treatment for altitude sickness is descent.

Hypothermia is a lowering of body temperature usually caused by a combination of cold and wet. Mild cases usually manifest themselves as uncontrollable shivering. Put on dry, warm clothes and get into a sleeping bag; this will normally raise your body temperature sufficiently. Severe hypothermia is potentially fatal: symptoms include disorientation, lethargy, mental confusion (including an inappropriate feeling of well-being and warmth!) and coma. In severe cases the rescue team should be summoned.

A US$20 rescue fee is paid by all climbers upon entering the national park. The rescue team ordinarily covers the Marangu Route only; if you use another route their services must be organised in advance.

hotly debated, there is no doubt about two things: first that you'll see few other tourists on the more obscure routes, and second that you'll pay considerably more for this privilege. Aesthetic and financial considerations aside, two unambiguous logistical disadvantages of the less-used routes are that they are generally tougher going (though only the Umbwe is markedly so) and that the huts – where they exist – are virtually derelict, which enforces camping.

Machame Route In recent years, the Machame Route has grown greatly in popularity. It is widely regarded as the most scenic viable ascent route, with great views across to Mount Meru, and on the whole it is relatively gradual, requiring at least six days for the full ascent and descent. Short sections are steeper and slightly more difficult than any part of the Marangu Route, but this is compensated for by the longer period for acclimatisation.

The route is named after the village of Machame, from where it is a two-hour walk to the park gate (1,950m). Most companies will provide transport as far as the gate (at least when the road is passable), and then it's a six- to eight-hour trek through thick forest to Machame Hut, which lies on the edge of the moorland zone at 2,890m. The Machame Hut is now a ruin, so camping is necessary, but water is available. The second day of this trail consists of a 9km, four- to six-hour hike through the moorland zone of Shira Plateau to Shira Hut (3,840m), which is near a stream. Once again, this hut has fallen into disuse, so the options are camping or sleeping in a nearby cave.

From Shira, a number of options exist: you could spend your third night at Lava Tower Hut (4,630m), four hours from Shira, but the ascent to the summit from there is tricky and only advisable if you are experienced and have good equipment. A less arduous option is to spend your third night at Barranco Campsite (3,950m), a tough 12km, six-hour hike from Shira, then to go on to Barafu Hut (4,600m) on the fourth day, a walk of approximately seven hours. From Barafu, it is normal to begin the steep seven- to eight-hour clamber to Stella Point (5,735m) at midnight, so that you arrive at sunrise, with the option of continuing on to Uhuru Peak, a two-hour round trip, before hiking back down to Mweka Hut via Barafu in the afternoon. This day can involve up to 16 hours of walking altogether. After spending your fifth night at Mweka Hut (3,100m), you will descend the mountain on the sixth day via the Mweka Route, a four- to six-hour walk.

Although the huts along this route are practically unusable, you still get to pay the US$40 'hut fee'. Any reliable operator will provide you with camping equipment and employ enough porters to carry the camp and set it up.

Mweka Route This is the steepest and fastest route to the summit. There are two huts along it – Mweka (3,100m) and Barafu (4,600m), uniports that sleep up to 16 people – though neither is reputedly habitable at the time of writing. There is water at Mweka but not at Barafu. This route starts at the Mweka Wildlife College, 12km from Moshi. From there it takes about eight hours to get to Mweka Hut, then a further eight hours to Barafu, from where it replicates the Machame Route. The Mweka Route is not recommended for ascending the mountain, since it is too short for proper acclimatisation, but is often used as a descent route by people climbing the Machame or Shira routes.

Shira Route Although this route could technically be covered in five days by driving to the high-elevation trailhead, this would allow one very little time to acclimatise, and greatly decrease the odds of reaching the summit. A minimum of six days is recommended, but better seven so that you can spend a full day at Shira Hut to acclimatise. The route starts at Londorossi Gate on the western side of the

ABBOTT'S DUIKER

An antelope occasionally encountered by hikers on Kilimanjaro is Abbott's duiker, *Cephalophus spadix*, a montane forest species that was formerly quite widespread in suitable East African habitats, but is today endemic to eastern Tanzania due to environmental loss and poaching elsewhere in its natural range. After Ader's duiker, a lowland species of the East African coastal belt, Abbott's is the most threatened of African duikers, categorised as Vulnerable in the International Union for Conservation of Nature (IUCN) Red Data list for 2000, but based on present trends is likely to decline to a status of Critically Endangered in the foreseeable future. Abbott's duiker is today confined to five forested montane 'islands' in eastern Tanzania, namely Kilimanjaro, Usambara, Udzungwa, Uluguru and Rungwe. The total population is unknown – a 1998 estimate of 2,500 based on limited data is not implausible – but Udzungwa probably harbours the most substantial and secure single population, followed by Kilimanjaro. Should you be lucky enough to stumble across this rare antelope, it has a glossy, unmarked off-black torso, a paler head and a distinctive red forehead tuft. Its size alone should, however, be diagnostic: the shoulder height of up to 75cm is the third-largest of any duiker species, and far exceeds that of other more diminutive duikers that occur in Tanzania.

mountain, from where a 19km track leads to the trailhead at around 3,500m. It is possible to motor to the trailhead in a 4x4, but for reasons already mentioned it would be advisable to walk, with an overnight stop to camp outside Simba Cave, which lies in an area of moorland where elephants and buffalo are regularly encountered. From the trailhead, it's a straightforward 4km to the campsite at the disused Shira Hut. If you opt to spend two nights at Shira in order to acclimatise, there are some worthwhile day walks in the vicinity. From Shira Hut, the route is identical to the Machame Route, and it is normal to return along the Mweka Route.

Rongai Route The only route ascending Kilimanjaro from the northeast, the recently reopened Rongai Route starts close to the Kenyan border and was closed for several years due to border sensitivity. In terms of gradients, it is probably less physically demanding than the Marangu Route, and the scenery, with views over the Tsavo Plains, is considered to be as beautiful. The Rongai Route can be covered over five days, with equally good if not better conditions for acclimatisation than the Marangu Route, though as with Marangu the odds of reaching the summit improve if you opt for an additional day.

The route starts at the village of Nale Moru (2,000m) near the Kenyan border, from where a footpath leads through cultivated fields and plantation forest before entering the montane forest zone, where black-and-white colobus monkeys are frequently encountered. The first campsite is reached after between three and five hours, and lies at about 2,700m on the frontier of the forest and moorland zone. On the five-day hike, the second day involves a gentle five- to six-hour ascent, through an area of moorland where elephants are sometimes seen, to Third Cave Campsite (3,500m). On the third day, it's a four- to five-hour walk to School Campsite (4,750m) at the base of Kibo, with the option of camping here or else continuing to the nearby Kibo Hut, which is more crowded but more commodious. The ascent from here is identical to the Marangu Route. A six-day variation on the above route involves spending the second night at Kikelewa Caves (3,600m, six to seven-hour walk), a night at Mawenzi Tarn near the eponymous peak (4,330m, four-hour walk), then crossing the saddle between Mawenzi and Kibo to rejoin the five-day route at School Campsite.

Umbwe Route This short, steep route, possibly the most scenic of the lot, is not recommended as an ascent route as it is very steep in parts and involves one short stretch of genuine rock climbing. It is occasionally used as a descent route, and can

KILIMANJARO: RECOMMENDED TOUR OPERATORS

The most popular base for organising a Kilimanjaro climb on the spot is Moshi, but most of the hotels at Marangu arrange reliable climbs, and many tourists who pre-book a climb prefer to work through a company based in Arusha. The following companies are all recommended.

MOSHI

Zara Tours Rindi Lane diagonally opposite Stanbic Bank; ☏ 027 275 0233 or toll-free USA +1 866 550 4447; m 0754 451000; e zara@zaratours.com; www.zaratours.com. Zara Tours has been one of the most prominent & reliable operators of Kili climbs for more than 20 years. Marangu Route ascents cost US$1,172 pp; 6-day climbs using other routes cost US$1,447.
Keys Hotel ☏ 027 275 2250/1870; f 027 275 0073; e keys-hotel@africaonline.co.tz; www.keys-hotels.com. Excellent & experienced operator based out of one of the town's best hotels, & very reasonably priced.
Akaro Tours ☏ 027 275 2986; m 0744 272124; f 027 275 2249; e safaris@akarotours.com; www.akarotours.com. Founded by a dynamic former Kilimanjaro guide with vast hands-on experience of the mountain, this small operator offers reliable no-frills climbs at a good price for Kili climbs, as well as a great range of cultural day tours out of Moshi.

MARANGU The family-run **Marangu Hotel** has been taking people up Kilimanjaro for decades, and they have an impeccable reputation. The standard packages aren't the cheapest available, but they are pretty good value, and the standard of service and equipment is very high. The self-catering 'hard-way' climbs organised by the Marangu Hotel are probably the cheapest reliable deals you'll find, working out at US$720 per person for five days, and US$135 per person each day thereafter, inclusive of park fees. Also reliable are the **Capricorn** and **Kibo** hotels and **Babylon Lodge**. Contact details for these hotels are found under *Where to stay* in the *Marangu* section, page 205.

ARUSHA Most safari companies in Arusha arrange Kilimanjaro climbs, but will generally work through a ground operator in Moshi or Marangu, which means that they have to charge slightly higher rates. Any of the Arusha-based safari companies listed in that section can be recommended, and short-stay visitors who are already going on safari with one of these companies will probably find that the ease and efficiency of arranging a Kilimanjaro climb through that company outweighs the minor additional expenditure.
There are a few companies that arrange their own Kili climbs out of Arusha. **Hoopoe Safaris** has a long track record of organising ascents along the lesser-known routes, and is well worth contacting should you want to do that sort of thing and you're prepared to pay a premium for top guides and equipment. So too is **Nature Discovery**, a highly regarded company that specialises in the more obscure routes up the mountain, and routinely sets up camp in the crater of Kibo, allowing you to explore the peaks area and ash cone at relative leisure. **Tropical Trails**, based at Maasai Camp on the outskirts of Arusha, has an excellent reputation for Kili climbs. **Roy Safaris** also arranges its own trekking and climbing on Kilimanjaro, Mount Meru and elsewhere. Contact details of all these companies are on pages 108–10.

be tied in with almost any of the ascent routes, though many operators understandably prefer not to take the risk, or charge a premium for using it. Umbwe Route descends from Barranco Hut, and comes out at the village of Umbwe. It is possible to sleep in two caves on the lower slopes along this route.

Arranging a climb The *only* sensible way to go about climbing Kilimanjaro is through a reliable operator that specialises in Kili climbs. Readers who pre-book a climb through a known tour operator in their own country can be confident that they will be going with a reputable ground operator in Tanzania. For readers who want to make their arrangements online or after they arrive in Tanzania, several trekking companies operate out of Moshi, Arusha and Marangu, and you should be able to negotiate a far better price by cutting out the middleman, but do be very circumspect about dealing with any company without a verifiable pedigree. A list of respected operators is included in the box opposite, and while such a list can never be comprehensive, it is reasonable to assume that anybody who can offer you a significantly cheaper package than the more budget-friendly companies on this list is not to be trusted.

In 2009, five-day Marangu climbs with a reliable operator start at an all-inclusive price of around US$1,000 per person for two people. You may be able to negotiate the starting price down slightly, especially for a larger group, but when you are paying this sort of money, it strikes me as sensible to shop around for the best quality of service rather than a fractional saving. A reputable operator will provide good food, experienced guides and porters, and reliable equipment – all of which go a long way to ensuring not only that you reach the top, but also that you come back down alive. You can assume that the cost of any package with a reputable operator will include a registered guide, two porters per person, park fees, food, and transport to and from the gate. It is, however, advisable to check exactly what you are paying for, and (especially for larger parties) to ensure that one porter is also registered as a guide, so that if somebody has to turn back, the rest of the group can still continue their climb. It might also be worth pointing out the potential risk attached to forming an impromptu group with strangers merely to cut 5% or so off the price. If you hike on your own or with people you know well, you can dictate your own pace and there is less danger of personality clashes developing mid-climb.

The standard duration of a climb on the Marangu Route is five days. Many people with repeated experience of Kilimanjaro recommend adding a sixth day to acclimatise at Horombo Hut. It is often said that this will improve the odds of reaching the summit by as much as 20%. Others feel that the extra day makes little difference except that it adds a similar figure to the cost of the climb. One person who owns a climbing company in Arusha kept records for three years and noted only a slightly increased success rate in people who take the extra day, and which he attributes to their extra determination to reach the top after having paid more money.

In this context, it is worth noting that the exhaustion felt by almost all hikers as they approach the peak is not merely a function of elevation. On the Marangu Route, for instance, most people hike for six to eight hours on day three, and then after a minimal dose of sleep (if any at all) rise at around midnight to start the final five- to six-hour ascent to the peak. In other words, when you reach the peak following the conventional five-day hike, you will have been walking for up to 14 of the last 20-odd hours, without any significant sleep – something that would tire out most people even if they weren't facing an altitudinal climb of around 2,000m. On that basis alone, an extra night along the way would have some value in pure recuperative terms. And certainly, my firm impression is that travellers who spend six days on the mountain enjoy the climb far more than those who take five days, whether or not they reach the peak. The choice is yours.

Of the less popular routes up Kilimanjaro, the one most frequently used by tourists is the Machame Route, which requires a minimum of six days. Most operators will charge at least 25% more for this route, because it requires far more outlay on their part. The huts along the Machame Route are in such poor condition that tents and camping equipment must be provided, along with a coterie of porters to carry and set up the makeshift camp. The same problem exists on all routes except Marangu, so that any off-the-beaten-track climb will be considerably more costly than the standard one. Should you decide to use a route other than Marangu, it is critical that you work through an operator with experience of that route.

The dubious alternative to using a reputable company is to take your chances with a small operator or private individual who approaches you in the street. These guys will offer climbs for around US$100 cheaper than an established operator, but the risks are greater and because they generally have no office, there is little accountability on their side. Many of these guides *are* genuine and reliable, but it's difficult to be certain unless you have a recommendation from somebody who has used the same person. A crucial point when comparing this situation with the similar one that surrounds arranging a safari out of Arusha is that you're not merely talking about losing a day through breakdown or something like that. With Kilimanjaro, you could literally die on the mountain. I've heard several stories of climbers being supplied with inadequate equipment and food, even of travellers being abandoned by their guide mid-climb. The very least you can do, if you make arrangements of this sort, is to verify that your guide is registered; he should have a small wallet-like document to prove it, though even this can be faked.

The reason why climbing Kilimanjaro is so expensive boils down to the high park fees. The daily entrance fee is US$60 per person, then there's a hut or camping fee of US$40 per person per night, and a one-off rescue fee of US$20 per person per climb. An additional daily entrance fee of US$10 is charged for the guide, along with a separate one-off rescue fee of US$20. To this must be added the cost of transport, food and cooking fuel, and the guide's and porters' salaries. Hikers are expected to tip their guides and porters; the company you go with can give you an idea of the going rate, but around US$5 per day per guide/porter per climbing party is fair.

Other preparations Two climatic factors must be considered when preparing to climb Kilimanjaro. The obvious one is the cold. Bring plenty of warm clothes, a windproof jacket, a pair of gloves, a balaclava, a warm sleeping bag and an insulation mat. During the rainy season, a waterproof jacket and trousers will come in useful. A less obvious factor is the sun, which is fierce at high elevations. Bring sunglasses, sunscreen and a hat.

Other essentials are water bottles, and solid shoes or preferably boots that have already been worn in. Most of these items can be hired in Moshi or at the park gate, or from the company you arrange to climb with. I've heard varying reports about the condition of locally hired items, but standards seem to be far higher than they were only a few years back.

A good medical kit is essential, especially if you are climbing with a cheap company. You'll go through plenty of plasters if you acquire a few blisters (assume that you will), and can also expect to want headache tablets.

You might want to buy biscuits, chocolate, sweets, glucose powder and other energy-rich snacks to take with you up the mountain. No companies supply this sort of thing, and although they are sometimes available at the huts, you'll pay through your nose for them.

Maps and further reading Trekkers are not permitted on the mountain without a registered guide, and all sensible trekkers will make arrangements through a reliable operator, which means that there is no real need for detailed route descriptions once you're on the mountain. Nevertheless, many trekkers will benefit from the detailed practical advice and overview of route possibilities provided in a few specialist Kilimanjaro guidebooks. The pick of these is undoubtedly the 336-page *Kilimanjaro: The Trekking Guide to Africa's Highest Mountain* by Henry Stedman (Trailblazer Guides), which can be bought locally or ordered in advance through online bookshops such as Amazon. Also recommended, *Kilimanjaro & East Africa: A Climbing and Trekking Guide* by Cameron M Burns, published in 2006 by Mountaineers Books, is especially useful for anybody planning to do serious rock climbing or to hike away from the main routes, or for those who also want to hike on Mount Kenya and the Rwenzori.

More concerned with the overall geology and natural history of Kilimanjaro, making it a more useful companion to trekkers on organised hikes, *Kilimanjaro: Africa's Beacon* is one of a series of glossy and informative pocket-sized guides published by the Zimbabwe-based African Publishing Group in association with TANAPA. It is widely available in Arusha and Moshi for around US$8. Its predecessor, the 60-page national park handbook *Kilimanjaro National Park*, is arguably more informative but less attractively put together, and is still widely available in Arusha and Moshi for around US$5.

Giovanni Tombazzi's *New Map of Kilimanjaro National Park*, sold all over Arusha and Moshi, is arguably the best map available, and certainly the most visually attractive. Current climbing tips are printed on the back of this map, along with a close-scale map of the final ascent to Kibo, and day-by-day contour 'graphs' for the Machame and Marangu routes.

Before you leave home – or as a memento when you get back – try to get hold of *Kilimanjaro* by John Reader (Elm Tree Books, London, 1982), which is long out of print but easily bought secondhand through the likes of Amazon. Although it is superficially a coffee-table book, it offers a well-written and absorbing overview of the mountain's history and various ecosystems. The photographs are good too.

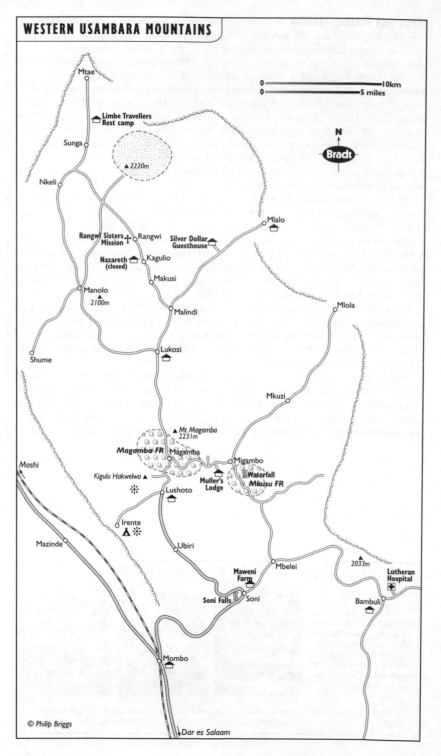

WESTERN USAMBARA MOUNTAINS

Mtae

Limbe Travellers
Rest camp

Sunga

▲2220m

Nkeli

0 ———————— 10km
0 ———————— 5 miles

N

Bradt

Mlalo

Rangwi Sisters
Mission ✝ Rangwi   Silver Dollar
Guesthouse

Nazareth
(closed)   Kagulio

Makusi

Manolo
▲
2100m

Malindi

Mlola

Shume

Lukozi

Mkuzi

▲ Mt Magamba
2231m

Magamba FR Magamba

Migambo

Moshi

Kigulu Hakwelwa ▲   Waterfall
Mkusu FR

Muller's
Lodge

※   Lushoto

Irente
▲※

Mazinde

Ubiri

Mbelei

▲
2033m

Lutheran
Hospital
✚

Maweni
Farm

Soni Falls   Soni

Bambuli

© Philip Briggs

↓Dar es Salaam

8

The Usambara Mountains

Rising east from the main road between Moshi and Tanga, a series of forested mountain ranges offers some of the most accessible, affordable and underpatronised opportunities for hiking and rambling anywhere in northern Tanzania. The largest of these ranges, and the most developed for tourism, is the Usambaras, a single geological entity split into discrete eastern and western components by a deeply incised river valley. The main tourist focus in this region, Lushoto in the Western Usambara, makes for a low-key but attractive extension to the busy northern safari circuit, and forms an excellent base for relaxed day or overnight forays deeper into the mountains. However, the more alluring goal for nature lovers and birdwatchers, reached via an entirely separate access road closer to Tanga, is the forested Amani Nature Reserve in the Eastern Usambara. Both form part of the Eastern Arc formation, a sequence of isolated mountain ranges known for its rich biodiversity and high levels of endemism (see box, *An African Galápagos?*, pages 234–5).

Online coverage of North Pare, Lake Jipe, Nyumba ya Mungu Reservoir and other places of interest in the area can be found at http://bradttanzania.wordpress.com/.

LUSHOTO

Set at an elevation of 1,400m, Lushoto is the principal town of the Western Usambara, the most densely populated and cultivated mountain range in northern Tanzania. The town peaked in significance during German colonial times, which may account for the slightly anachronistic aura that pervades it today. Many buildings on the main street date to the early 20th century, when Lushoto – then known as Wilhelmstal – provided weekend relief for German settlers farming the dry, dusty Maasai Steppes below. But if the main street dimly recalls an alpine village, the side roads of Lushoto are unambiguously African in architecture and spirit. So, too, is the vibrant market – busiest on Sunday and Thursday – where colourfully dressed Shambaa women sell fresh fruit and other agricultural produce grown on the surrounding slopes.

The vegetation around Lushoto is similarly schizoid. Broad-leafed papaya and banana trees subvert neat rows of exotic pines and eucalyptus, which in turn are interspersed by patches of lush indigenous forest alive with the raucous squawking of silvery-cheeked hornbills and the banter of monkeys. These scenic highlands form superb walking country, riddled with small footpaths and winding roads, and studded with spectacular viewpoints over the low-lying plains below.

Less than an hour's drive from the main road between Moshi and Dar es Salaam, Lushoto has developed into the focal point of a backpacker-dominated tourist industry that feels delightfully low-key by comparison to the hype, hustle and extravagant prices associated with the likes of Arusha and Zanzibar. Indeed, a plethora of guides, community tourism projects and jumped-up guesthouses aimed at independent travellers makes Lushoto reminiscent of parts of west Africa, for instance Dogon Country or the eastern highlands of Ghana. For those with the time, and an interest in experiencing something of Tanzania other than beach resorts and game reserves, Lushoto is well worth a diversion.

HISTORY The Shambaa of the Western Usambara are Bantu-speaking agriculturalists whose modern population totals around 200,000. Their origin is difficult to ascertain. Some clans claim they have always lived in the mountains, others that they moved there during times of drought, or in response to the 18th-century Maasai invasion of the plains. Quite possibly, these divergent accounts simply reflect divergent clan histories, since the ancestral Shambaa had a reputation for welcoming refugees, and the loosely structured political system that characterised the region until about 300 years ago would have encouraged the peaceful assimilation of newcomers. The notion that Shambaa identity was initially forged by physical proximity (rather than cultural affiliation or centralised leadership) is reinforced when one realises the their name derives from the geographical term used to describe the moister upper reaches of the mountains, ie: Shambaai ('where the banana trees thrive').

Prior to the 18th century, the social structure of Shambaai was similar to the *ntemi* chieftaincies of western Tanzania. Each clan lived in a clearly defined territory with its own petty leadership of elders. A regional council of elders had the authority to settle disputes between different clans, and to approve marriages that would help cement inter-clan unity. According to tradition, the move towards centralised power – probably a response to the threat posed by the Maasai – was led by an outsider called Mbegha, the first Simba Mwene (Lion King) of Shambaai.

That Mbegha is a genuine historical figure is not in doubt, and the oral traditions of neighbouring tribes support the local tradition that he moved to the mountains from the plains below and became king after resolving a major crisis in Shambaai. Quite how Mbegha achieved his leonine coup is open to question. An implausible local tradition has it that, as a hunter of renown, Mbegha was called upon by a delegation of elders to rid the mountains of the bushpigs that were destroying all their crops, and was so effective in his campaign that he was appointed ruler of all Shambaai.

Mbegha went on to forge regional unity by taking a wife from each major clan and placing their firstborn son in charge of it. The Shambaa invested Mbegha and the Kilindi dynasty of Lion Kings that succeeded him with supernatural powers, believing among other things that they were able to control the elements. The dynasty consolidated power under the rule of Mbegha's grandson Kinyashi, who adopted a militaristic policy with the aim of forging the most important state between the coast and the great lake region. This ambition was realised by Kinyashi's son and successor, Kimweri, the greatest Simba Mwene of them all. Towards the end of his reign, Kimweri was held in sufficient esteem outside his kingdom that the explorer Richard Burton undertook the trek inland from Pangani to visit the Shambaa capital of Fuga (now more often called Vuga), close to modern-day Bumbuli (see box, *Portrait of a Lion King*, page 228).

Kimweri's death, a few years after Burton's visit, was the catalyst for the first major rift in Shambaa. Vuga was too deep in the mountains to have attracted regular contact with the Kilimanjaro-bound caravans. Not so the Shambaa town of Mazinde, on what is now the main Moshi–Dar es Salaam road, whose chief Semboja exerted considerable influence over passing traders and was able to stockpile sufficient arms to overthrow Kimweri's successor at Vuga. This event split the Shambaa into several splinter groups, and although Semboja retained nominal leadership of Shambaa, he controlled a far smaller area than Kimweri had.

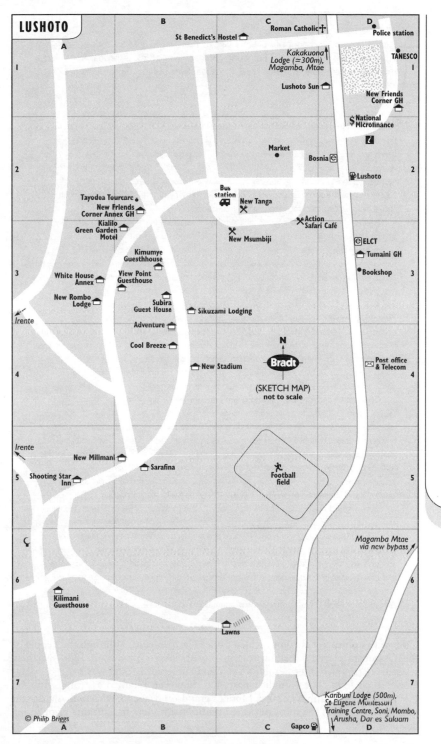

LUSHOTO

A · B · C · D

St Benedict's Hostel
Roman Catholic ✝
Police station

Kakakuona
Lodge (≈300m),
Magamba, Mtae
TANESCO

Lushoto Sun

New Friends
Corner GH

National
Microfinance

Market
Bosnia

Lushoto

Bus
station
New Tanga

Tayodea Tourcare
New Friends
Corner Annex GH
Kialilo
Green Garden
Motel
New Msumbiji
Action
Safari Café

ELCT
Tumaini GH

Kimumye
Guesthouse

White House
Annex
View Point
Guesthouse
Bookshop

New Rombo
Lodge
Subira
Guest House
Sikuzami Lodging

Irente
Adventure

Cool Breeze

N

Bradt

(SKETCH MAP)
not to scale

New Stadium
Post office
& Telecom

Irente

New Milimani
Sarafina

Shooting Star
Inn
Football
field

Magamba Mtae
via new bypass

Kilimani
Guesthouse

Lawns

Karibuni Lodge (500m),
St Eugene Montessori
Training Centre, Soni, Mombo,
Arusha, Dar es Salaam

Gapco

© Philip Briggs

A · B · C · D

Richard Burton's account of his 1857 visit to the Lion King of Shambaai, published in Volume 83 of Blackwell's Edinburgh Magazine in 1858, is probably the most revealing description of pre-colonial Shambaai ever printed. Some edited extracts follow:

Kimweri half rose from his cot as we entered, and motioned us to sit upon dwarf stools before him. He was an old, old man, emaciated by sickness. His head was shaved, his face beardless, and wrinkled like grandam's; his eyes were red, his jaws disfurnished, and his hands and feet were stained with leprous spots. The royal dress was a Surat cap, much the worse for wear, and a loinwrap as tattered. He was covered with a double cotton cloth, and he rested upon a Persian rug, apparently coeval with himself. The hut appeared that of a simple cultivator, but it was redolent of dignitaries, some fanning the Sultan, others chatting, and all holding long-stemmed pipes with small ebony bowls.

Kimweri, I was told, is the fourth of a dynasty ... originally from Nguru, a hilly region south of the river ... Kimweri, in youth a warrior of fame, ranked in the triumvirate of mountain kings above Bana Rongua of Chagga, and Bana Kizunga of the Wakuafy. In age he has lost ground [and] asserts kinghood but in one point: he has 300 wives, each surrounded by slaves, and portioned with a hut and a plantation. His little family amounts to between 80 and 90 sons, some of whom have Islamised, whilst their sire remains a 'pragmatical pagan'. The Lion [King]'s person is sacred; even a runaway slave saves life by touching royalty. Presently [Kimweri] will die, be wrapped up in matting, and placed sitting-wise under his deserted hut, a stick denoting the spot. Dogs will be slaughtered for the funeral-feast, and [Kimweri's son] Muigni Khatib will rule in his stead, and put to death all who dare, during the two months of mourning, to travel upon the king's highway.

Kimweri rules ... by selling his subjects – men, women, and children, young and old, gentle and simple, individually, or, when need lays down the law, by families and by villages .... Confiscation and sale are indigenous and frequent. None hold property without this despot's permission ... In a land where beads are small change, and sheeting and 'domestics' form the higher specie, revenue is thus collected. Cattle-breeders offer the first fruits of flocks and herds; elephant-hunters every second tusk; and traders a portion of their merchandise. Cultivators are rated annually at ten measures of grain ... The lion's share is reserved for the royal family; the crumbs are distributed to the councillors and [royal bodyguards].

Fuga, a heap of some 3000 souls, [is] defenceless, and composed of ... circular abodes [made with] frameworks of concentric wattles, wrapped with plantain-leaves ... fastened to little uprights, and plastered internally with mud ... The [people] ... file their teeth to points, and brand a circular beauty-spot in the mid-forehead; their heads are shaven, their feet bare, and, except talismans round the neck, wrists, and ankles, their only wear is a sheet over the shoulders, and a rag or hide round the loins. A knife is stuck in the waist-cord, and men walk abroad with pipe, bow, and quiverless arrows. The women are adorned with charm-bags; and collars of white beads – now in fashion throughout this region – from three to four pounds weight, encumber the shoulders of a 'distinguished person'. Their body-dress is the African sheet bound tightly under the arms, and falling to the ankles ...

Shambaa unity was further divided under German rule. Although the people of the Usambara played a leading role in the Abushiri Uprising of 1888–89, their resistance crumbled after Semboja's son and successor Mputa was hanged by the Germans in 1898. The Kilindi dynasty has, however, retained a strong symbolic role in modern Shambaa culture. Mputa's grandson Magogo, who took the throne in 1947, was one of the most respected traditional leaders in Tanzania prior to his death in 2000.

GETTING THERE AND AWAY Lushoto is connected to Mombo on the B1 by a surfaced 33km road that offers splendid views in all directions. In a private vehicle, the drive from Moshi normally takes about three hours and that from Tanga about two hours, with the actual ascent from Mombo taking 45 minutes or so. Coming from Tanga on public transport, the best way to get to Lushoto is to hop on one of the regular minibuses that connect the two towns via Muheza, Korogwe and Mombo, a three-hour trip. Coming from Arusha, Moshi or Dar es Salaam, it's better to take a bus heading through Mombo and asked to be dropped there to pick up one of the regular minibuses through to Lushoto.

TOURIST INFORMATION AND TOURS Prominently signposted opposite the park, the tourist office run by the TTB-endorsed **Friends of Usambara** (⤳ 027 264 0132; e usambaras2000@hotmail.com; ⏱ 07.30–12.00 & 13.00–18.00 daily) stocks plenty of useful brochures, and the staff – most of whom double as guides – can arrange any walk or activity around Lushoto. They are also willing to dispense advice without being pushy about paid services. The fee structure is rather complex, but most guided day trips work out at around Tsh20,000–30,000 per person, while the daily rate for overnight excursions is about double that. The tourist office also arranges bicycle, tent, sleeping bag and roll-mat hire. All profits go towards the development of community projects.

The rival **Tayodea Tour Care** [227 B2] (m 0784 861969; e youthall2000@ yahoo.com) is an offshoot of an NGO called the Tanga Youth Development Association. It offers a similar range of tours at similar prices, and also has a good reputation, unofficial status notwithstanding. Its Lushoto office, which opened in 2004, lies about 200m west of the bus station. You can expect to hear quite a bit of backbiting between the two tourist agencies, both of which regard the other as lacking professionalism, but this seems to be so much hot air – though do be circumspect about any guide who doesn't operate out of an office.

🏠 **WHERE TO STAY** The listings below are restricted to places within a 3km radius of Lushoto. A great many other – and for the most part arguably better – options are to be found elsewhere in the Western Usambara, as covered later in this chapter.

Moderate

🏠 **Lawns Hotel** [227 C6] (21 rooms) ⤳ 027 264 0005; m 0784 420252; e lawnstony@yahoo.com; www.lawnshotel.com. Centred around a German homestead built circa 1900, the venerable Lawns Hotel, set in large gardens on a low hill above the town centre, is the most characterful accommodation option in Lushoto, & has benefited greatly from renovations under new Greek management since 2005. The restaurant is the smartest in town. Mountain-bike hire & horseback excursions can be arranged through reception, & other facilities include an atmospheric bar, satellite TV, table tennis &

library. Comfortable en-suite rooms US$56 dbl; camping US$7 pp.

🏠 **St Eugene Montessori Training Centre** [227 D7] (14 rooms) ⤳ 027 264 0055; f 027 264 0267; e steugenes_hostel@yahoo.com. 2km from Lushoto town centre at Ubiri on the Soni road, this modern training centre run by the Usambara Sisters is known locally for producing good jam, cheese, & banana wine. Within the landscaped grounds stands a comfortable & well-maintained hostel & a good restaurant. US$20/36/42/45 en suite sgl/dbl/trpl/suite B&B.

Budget

🏠 **St Benedict's Hostel** [227 C1] (4 rooms) ⤳ 027 264 0101; m 0784 471690. Centrally located beside the associated Catholic Church, this pleasant hostel has large twin rooms with nets & en-suite hot shower, & a homely shared lounge. A good

choice though maybe overpriced. Tsh25,000 dbl B&B.

🏠 **Kakakuona Lodge** [227 D1] (9 rooms) ⤳ 027 264 0273; f 0714 006969; e kakakuonainfo@ yahoo.com. This smart new lodge at the north end of the town centre has comfortable modern en-suite accommodation with tiled floors, pine furniture, dbl beds with net & TV. An added attraction is the outdoor dining area, which overlooks a tree-fringed stream, serves a great range of western & Indian dishes in the Tsh4,000–5,000 bracket (preparation takes up to an hour), & is one of the few eateries in the town centre to serve alcohol. Great value. *Tsh20,000/25,000 sgl/dbl.*

🏠 **Kialilo Green Garden Motel** [227 B3] ☎ 027 264 3466; e kialilo24@yahoo.co.uk. On a slope about 200m west of the bus station, this new hotel has a homely atmosphere & comfortable en-suite rooms with hot water & TV. No food or alcohol served. *Tsh15,000/20,000 sgl/dbl.*

🏠 **Lushoto Sun Hotel** [227 D1] ☎ 027 264 0082. This established travellers' favourite has a usefully central location & welcoming atmosphere but the gloomy rooms feel a bit overpriced. Decent meals cost Tsh2,000–3,000. *Tsh12,000/15,000 en-suite sgl/dbl with hot shower.*

🏠 **Tumaini Guesthouse** [227 D3] (22 rooms) ☎ 027 264 0094; e tumaini@elct.org. This 2-storey church-run guesthouse on the main road may be too institutional for some tastes, but otherwise it's arguably the best choice in this range – clean, secure, friendly & very central. All rooms have nets, showers are hot, there's a good internet café next door & the restaurant serves tasty Western & Indian dishes (no alcohol). *Tsh8,000/14,000 sgl/dbl with shared facilities, Tsh13,000/17,000 en-suite rooms, Tsh25,000 suites.*

Shoestring

🏠 **White House Annex** [227 A3] (10 rooms) m 0784 427471; e whitehouse@raha.com. This friendly local hotel less than 5mins' walk from the bus station is a standing budget favourite, though the nocturnal noise from an adjoining bar can be a nuisance. Meals are excellent – a heaped plate of meat, roast potatoes & vegetables for Tsh2,500. Small en-suite rooms are fair value. *Tsh6,000/8,000 sgl/dbl.*

🏠 **Kilimani Guesthouse** [227 A6] ☎ 027 264 0014. This once popular backpackers' haunt has re-emerged from years in the doldrums following a change of ownership, & the freshly painted rooms are among the best deals in town. There's a garden bar to the left of the entrance, so try for a room on the other side of the main bldg. *Tsh3,000/5,000 sgl/dbl, Tsh10,000 en-suite dbl.*

✗ **WHERE TO EAT** Lushoto the town is surprisingly short on decent, affordable eateries. An exception is the **Tumaini Café** [227 D3] in the eponymous guesthouse, which serves a good selection of tasty pasta, seafood and curry dishes in the Tsh4,000–5,000 range, but no alcoholic beverages. Also very good, and only slightly pricier, is the outdoor restaurant at the **Kakakuona Lodge** [227 D1], which does serve alcohol. Slightly further afield, **Lawns Hotel** [227 C6] serves decent à la carte dishes for Tsh6,000–10,000 and three-course meals for Tsh12,000. Elsewhere, a few rather indifferent eateries serving the usual local fare are dotted around the bus station and market area. Better for local grub are the **White House Annex** [227 A3] and **Lushoto Sun Hotel** [227 D1].

PRACTICAL INFORMATION

Foreign exchange Foreign exchange is available at the National Microfinance Bank [227 D2], which also has the only ATM, though it doesn't accept foreign cards. The internet café at Tumaini Guesthouse [227 D3] can exchange small amounts of hard currency cash.

Internet services Your best option is the internet café in Tumaini Guesthouse [227 D3], but a few other cafés are scattered around town. The services here are all quite slow and unreliable.

AROUND LUSHOTO A number of day and overnight trips can be undertaken out of Lushoto. Popular goals within day tripping distance include Soni Falls, Irente Viewpoint and Magamba Forest. Worthwhile destinations further afield include Bumbuli, Mtae and Mlalo. All can be visited independently or with a guide provided by the tourist office in Lushoto.

Irente and Yoghoi viewpoints About 7km from Lushoto by road, Irente is the most popular goal for day trips in the Usambara. It lies at the edge of the Usambara massif and offers a fantastic, vast view across the Maasai Steppes 1,000m below. A second viewpoint at Yoghoi, about 1km further south, offers a very similar view encompassing the viewpoint at Irente. Either of the two viewpoints can be visited as a round trip from Lushoto, or you can loop between the two on foot. A popular option is to combine the walk with a picnic lunch of home-baked rye bread, homemade cheese, organic vegetables, fruit juice and other farm produce at Irente Farm (*contact details under Mkuyu Lodge below;* ⊕ *10.00–14.00 Mon–Sat*). The farm shop also sells an array of local produce such as cheese for consumption off the premises.

The road to Irente and Yoghoi leads eastward out of Lushoto from the Catholic Church. Once you're on it, there's no serious likelihood of getting lost. After about 3km, it passes through the village of Yoghoi and a large junction – keep going straight for Irente, or turn left for Yoghoi. By road, it's 4km from here to either viewpoint. There's no direct road between the viewpoints, but there is a clear footpath. It's perfectly possible to head out here alone, but most travellers arrange an official guide through the tourist office. The round trip takes around three hours.

🏠 *Where to stay and eat*

🏠 **Irente View Cliff Lodge & Campsite** (16 rooms) 📞 027 264 0026; 📱 0784 866877; e info@ irenteview.com; www.irenteview.com. Ostensibly the most upmarket option in the Western Usambara, this new lodge looks the part initially, with its impressive thatched roof, modern décor, nice restaurant & stunning clifftop location. The en-suite rooms are also quite comfortable, but let down a little by poor quality fittings. A clifftop campsite with hot shower is attached. Good value. *US$50/65 sgl/dbl B&B; camping Tsh5,000 pp.*

🏠 **Mkuyu Lodge** (6 rooms) 📞 027 264 0000; 📱 0784 502935; e murless@elct.org; www.elct.org. Irente Farm, run by the ELCT church since 1963, is an orphanage & school for the blind funded partially by profits from the excellent home produce sold in its shop, as well as proceeds from the recently opened Mkuyu Lodge. Rooms at this pleasant retreat have self-catering facilities, but picnic lunches & simple home-cooked meals in the Tsh3,000–4,000 range are provided. *Tsh12,000/20,000 sgl/dbl B&B; Tsh25,000/40,000/50,000 sgl/dbl/trpl cottage; camping Tsh4,000 pp.*

Soni Falls Straddling the surfaced road that connects Mombo to Lushoto, the small town of Soni is of interest primarily for the attractive but less than spectacular Soni Falls. This waterfall is visible from the main road to Lushoto, but to see it properly you need to stop in the town, from where a short, steep path leads to the rocky base. The drive between Lushoto and Soni takes no more than 30 minutes in either direction, using one of the regular minibuses that run back and forth to Mombo. If you visit Soni as a day trip, there is no reason to take a guide along. The tourist office in Lushoto organises a half-day tour out of Soni, taking in Kwa Mongo peak, known for its colourful butterflies, as well as the 300-year-old grave of the Shambaa King Mbegha and the so-called 'Growing Rock' at Magila.

🏠 *Where to stay and eat*
Moderate

🏠 **Maweni Hotel** (17 rooms) 📱 0784 297371. This rustic farm retreat lies 2km from Soni along a side road signposted from the Mombo–Lushoto road near the junction with the Bumbuli road. Set in pretty gardens below a tall granite cliff, the main building consists of a 1920 farmhouse, & there's a more modern but dingier annexe & standing tents too. *US$40/60 sgl/dbl HB; US$65/110 standing tent.*

🏠 **Soni Falls Resort** (4 rooms) 📱 0784 384603. One of the most attractive lodges in the Usambaras, this lovingly renovated & restored Bavarian-style double-storey German building is set in well-wooded hilltop grounds, signposted to the right as you enter the village of Soni coming from Mombo. *Tsh37,000 dbl with shared bathroom; Tsh65,000 family room with bath, toilet & separate children's room.*

Budget

⌂ **Old Soni Falls Hotel** (8 rooms) ☎ 0787 763378. Built in the 1930s, this small hotel overlooking the waterfall reopened in 2005 & retains plenty of period charm, though the partially restored rooms aren't as nice as the wood dominated lounge, bar & dining room. Good value. *Tsh15,000 en-suite dbl or twin.*

⌂ Shoestring

Kimalube Hotel This friendly, family-run place lies on the Mombo road about 1km from the centre of Soni. *Tsh6,000 dbl with common shower.*

Bumbuli

Bumbuli Locally renowned for its old Lutheran Mission and associated hospital, Bumbuli lies 23km from Soni near the eastern rim of the Western Usambara, where King Mbegha reputedly entered the mountains some 300 years ago. A small waterfall lies on the outskirts of the town, close to the Soni road, and the Saturday market is very colourful. The town lies in the shadow of Mazumbai Peak, whose upper slopes, covered in high montane forest, protect a variety of indigenous plants and rare birds. Bumbuli can be visited independently, but the tourist office in Lushoto also offers overnight hikes to the town and Mazumbai Forest, inclusive of guide, public transport and accommodation.

Getting there and away The 23km road between Soni and Bumbuli takes 45 minutes to cover in a private vehicle, passing through Mbelai, Kiboani and Kwahangara on the way. Using public transport, several buses daily connect Bumbuli directly to Korogwe, Mombo and Lushoto. All these buses pass through Soni, so if no direct bus is about to leave, you could always catch one of the more frequent minibuses along the Mombo–Lushoto road, and hop off at Soni to board the next Bumbuli-bound vehicle.

⌂ **Where to stay**

⌂ **Lutheran Hospital Guesthouse** (8 rooms) Set in the mission grounds a 10min walk uphill from the town centre, this atmospheric restored colonial building has neat rooms with common hot shower & bath, as well as a lounge & self-catering kitchen. Cheap meals are also available. *Tsh8,000/10,000 sgl/dbl.*

Magamba Forest Reserve

Magamba Forest Reserve Situated 15km from Lushoto, the most accessible indigenous forest in the Western Usambara covers the slopes of 2,230m Mt Magamba, the highest peak in the range. It is of great interest to birdwatchers, with the track to the old sawmill in particular offering a good chance of seeing Usambara weaver and Usambara akalat (both endemic to Western Usambara forests) and the localised red-capped forest warbler. A variety of mammals also live in this forest, though only black-and-white colobus and blue monkey are likely to be encountered by the casual visitor.

Guided day walks can be arranged through the tourist office in Lushoto, but it is possible to visit Magamba independently and explore it along a few self-guided trails. Any vehicle heading north from Lushoto to Mtae, Mlalo or Mlola can drop you at the Magamba junction, 7km from Lushoto. The road heading to the right at this junction leads through the heart of the forest, following the course of the lushly vegetated Mkusu River for 7km to Migambo village. You could walk the length of this road in about 90 minutes in either direction, and it is also covered by a daily bus between Lushoto and Mlola.

The most popular goal for day walks in the Magamba Forest is a small but pretty waterfall on the forest-fringed Mkuzu River about 2km from Migambo village. To reach this waterfall, take the right fork as you enter Migambo on the Magamba road. Follow this road downhill for about 20 minutes, passing a group of rocks in the river where local people wash their clothes, until you reach a bridge across the river. To your right, immediately after crossing the river, you'll see a signpost that reads 'Dr Kwangua's residence'. You need to turn to the left – opposite the signpost – to follow a rough track along the riverbank for about 10 minutes to the waterfall.

🏠 Where to stay and eat

🏠 **Muller's Mountain Lodge** ✆ 027 264 0204; e mullersmountainlodge@yahoo.com. This family-run 1930s farm cottage, set in flowering gardens within the Magamba Forest, is arguably the most attractive place to stay anywhere in the Western Usambara, & an excellent base for birdwatchers. Home-cooked meals are available in the small restaurant or the gardens. Several day trails lead from the lodge; maps & directions can be supplied. It lies about 6km past Magamba junction on the Migambo road. A free transfer to/from Lushoto is offered to parties of 2 or more. US$30/40 B&B en-suite sgl/dbl; camping Tsh5,000 pp.

⛺ **Sawmill Campsite** The campsite at the old sawmill lies in the heart of the forest, in an area known for its excellent birding. There's a toilet & running water. The best way to get here is to hire a car through the tourist office in Lushoto. Tsh2,000 pp.

The Mtae road The small but sprawling town of Mtae, 63km north of Lushoto by road, has perhaps the most spectacular location of any town in the Western Usambara. Boasting several fine examples of traditional Shambaa mud houses, it runs for about 2km along what is in effect a dry peninsula, jutting out to the north of the range, and with a drop of several hundred metres on either side. Mtae offers panoramic views across Lake Kalimawe and Mkomazi Game Reserve, and on clear mornings Mount Kilimanjaro, 250km distant, is often visible. The nearby Shagayu Mountain can be visited as a day hike, preferably with a guide, and its forested slopes support a rich birdlife as well as many species of colourful butterfly.

The name Mtae translates as 'Place of Counting', a reference to its strategic importance to the Shambaa people during the 19th-century Maasai wars, when it was the site of several battles won by the Shambaa, who were able to see and count any raiding Maasai war party from afar. The striking Lutheran church that stands in the middle of the town was built in the late 19th century on a site where, formerly, the most powerful ancestral spirits were believed to reside. The story is that the local chief showed this site to the missionaries, expecting them to flee in fear. Instead, the missionaries were unmoved, and the chief – concluding that they must be in touch with more powerful spirits – granted them permission to build a church there.

About six buses run directly from Lushoto to Mtae daily, originating in Arusha, Dar es Salaam or Tanga. These buses all pass through Lushoto in the early afternoon – between 13.00 and 15.00 – and arrive in Mtae about three hours later. The buses usually start the return trip out of Mtae at around 05.00; miss them and you'll likely be stuck in Mtae for another 24 hours. It is also possible to do the trip between Lushoto and Mtae in hops, stopping at settlements such as Lukozi, Kagulio and Rangwi on the way.

The best lodging in Mtae is the **Mwivano I Guesthouse**, which has a friendly owner, very inexpensive and basic rooms using a common cold shower, and an attached restaurant serving tasty, filling meals for next to nothing. *En route* from Lushoto, the substantial market town of **Lukozi**, 24km along the Mtae road, has a few basic lodgings, of which the oddly named **Watoto Wanyumbani** (literally 'Children in the Rooms') **Guesthouse** is about the best. The **Rangwi Catholic Mission**, 3km further towards Mtae, has the most comfortable accommodation in the area (*Tsh20,000/25,000 FB en-suite sgl/dbl*). Finally, the rather run-down **Fadhili Resthouse** (✆ 027 264 0231), also known as Limbe Historical & Cultural Centre, lies on a smallholding 6km before Mtae and 3km after the village of Sunga, and offers basic accommodation for around Tsh5,000 per person.

The phrase 'Eastern Arc' was coined by Dr Jon Lovett in the mid 1980s to describe a string of 13 physically isolated East African mountain ranges that share a very similar geomorphology and ecology. All but one of these crystalline ranges lies within Tanzania, forming a rough crescent that runs from Pare and Usambara in the north to Udzungwa and Mahenge in the south. Following a fault line that runs east of the more geologically recent Rift Valley, these are the oldest mountains in East Africa, having formed at least 100 million years ago, making them 50 times as old as Kilimanjaro.

For the past 30 million years, the Eastern Arc has supported a cover of montane forest, one that flourished even during the drier and colder climatic conditions that have periodically characterised the globe, thanks to a continuous westerly wind that blew in moisture from the Indian Ocean. It was during one such dry phase, 10 million years ago, that these became isolated from the lowland rainforest of western and central Africa. More recently, each of the individual forested ranges became a discrete geographical entity, transforming the Eastern Arc into an archipelago of forested islands jutting out from an ocean of low-lying savannah. And as with true islands, these isolated ancient forests became veritable evolutionary hotspots.

The Eastern Arc Mountains host an assemblage of endemic races, species and genera with few peers anywhere in the world. In the two Usambara ranges alone, more than 2,850 plant species have been identified, a list that includes 680 types of tree, a greater tally than that of North America and Europe combined. At least 16 plant genera and 75 vertebrate species are endemic to the Eastern Arc forests. Their invertebrate wealth can be gauged by the fact that 265 invertebrate species are thus far known from just one of the 13 different ranges – an average of 20 endemics per range. Little wonder that the Eastern Arc is classified among the world's 20 top biodiversity hotspots, and is frequently referred to as the Galápagos of Africa.

Eastern Arc endemics fall into two broad categories: old endemics are modern relics of an ancient evolutionary lineage, while new endemics represent very recently evolved lineages. A clear example of a 'living fossil' falling into the former category are the giant elephant shrews of the suborder Rhynchocyonidae, whose four extant species are almost identical in structure to more widespread 20-million-year-old ancestral fossils. In many cases, these older, more stable endemics are affiliated to extant west African species from which they have become isolated: Abbott's duiker and the endemic monkey species of Udzungwa are cases in point.

The origins of new endemics are more variable. Some, such as the African violets, probably evolved from an ancestral stock blown across the ocean from Madagascar in a freak cyclone. Others, including many birds and flying insects, are local variants on similar species found in neighbouring savannahs or in other forests in East Africa. The origin of several other Eastern Arc endemics is open to conjecture: four of the endemic birds show sufficient affiliations to Asian species to suggest they may have arrived there at a time when moister coastal vegetation formed a passage around the Arabian peninsula.

The forests of the Eastern Arc vary greatly in extent, biodiversity and the degree to which they have been studied and accorded official protection. A 1998 assessment by Newmark indicates that the Udzungwa range retains almost 2,000km^2 of natural forest, of which 20% has a closed canopy, while the forest cover on Kenya's Taita Hills is reduced to a mere 6km^2. The most significant forests in terms of biodiversity are probably

Mlalo This bizarre town sprawls over a large valley some 50km from Lushoto along a road that forks from the Mtae road at Malindi, 30km from Lushoto. Mlalo has an insular, almost otherworldly feel, epitomised by the unusual style of many of the buildings: two-storey mud houses whose intricately carved wooden balconies show German or Swahili influences.

Udzungwa, East Usambara and Uluguru. However, ranges such as Nguru and Rubeho remain little studied compared with the Usambara and Udzungwa, so they may host more endemics than is widely recognised.

The Eastern Arc forests are of great interest to birdwatchers as the core of the so-called Tanzania–Malawi Mountains Endemic Bird Area (EBA). This EBA includes roughly 30 forest pockets scattered across Malawi, Mozambique and Kenya, but these outlying forests cover a combined 500km^2 as compared with 7,200km^2 of qualifying forest in Tanzania. Of the 37 range-restricted bird species endemic to this EBA, all but five occur in Tanzania, and roughly half are confined to the country. In terms of avian diversity, the Udzungwa Mountains lead the pack with 23 regional endemics present, including several species found nowhere else or shared only with the inaccessible Rubeho Mountains. For first-time visitors, however, Amani Nature Reserve has the edge over Udzungwa in terms of ease of access to prime birding areas.

Distribution patterns of several range-restricted bird species within the EBA illuminate the mountains' pseudo-island ecology, with several species widespread on one particular range being absent from other apparently suitable ones. The Usambara akalat, for instance, is confined to the Western Usambara, while Loveridge's sunbird and the Uluguru bush-shrike are unique to the Uluguru. The most remarkable distribution pattern belongs to the long-billed tailorbird, a forest-fringe species confined to two ranges set an incredible 2,000km apart – the Eastern Usambara in northern Tanzania and Mount Namuli in central Mozambique. Stranger still is the case of the Udzungwa partridge: this evolutionary relic, discovered in 1991 and known only from Udzungwa and Rubeho, has stronger genetic affiliations to Asian hill partridges than to any other African bird!

The Eastern Arc has suffered extensive forest loss and fragmentation in the past century, primarily due to unprecedented land use pressure – the population of the Western Usambara, for instance, increased 20-fold in the 20th century. Of the 12 Eastern Arc ranges within Tanzania, only one – the inaccessible Rubeho massif – has retained more than half of its original forest cover, while five have lost between 75% and 90% of their forest in the last two centuries. Fortunately, none of Tanzania's Eastern Arc forests has yet approached the crisis point reached in Kenya's Taita Hills, where a mere 2% of the original forest remains.

Given that many Eastern Arc species are highly localised and that animal movement between forest patches is inhibited by fragmentation, it seems likely that 30% of Eastern Arc endemics have become extinct in the last century, or might well do so in the immediate future. True, the salvation of a few rare earthworm taxa might be dismissed as bunny-hugging esoterica, but the preservation of the Eastern Arc forests as water catchment areas is an issue of clear humanistic concern. Most of the extant Eastern Arc forests are now protected as forest reserves. The proclamation of a large part of the Udzungwa Mountains as a national park in 1992 is a further step in the right direction. Even more encouraging is the more recent creation of Amani Nature Reserve as part of a broader effort to introduce sustainable conservation and ecotourism with the involvement of local communities in the Eastern Usambara.

Anybody wishing to come to grips with the fascinating phenomenon of 'island' ecology in the Eastern Arc Mountains (and elsewhere on the African mainland) is pointed to Jonathon Kingdon's superb *Island Africa*.

Three buses run daily between Lushoto and Mlalo, leaving Lushoto in the early afternoon and Mlalo at around 07.00. The trip takes around two hours.

Where to stay Near the bus stop there are a few **guesthouses** in the US$2–3 range, of which the New Sambara Annex and Mlalo Motel are equally basic and charge

Tsh2,000–3,000 for a room. The smarter Silver Dollar Guesthouse (m *0784 736251*), about 10km out of town at Mwangoye, which lies 2km from the main road, charges Tsh3,000/5,000 for a clean single/double with net, fan and common showers.

AMANI AND THE EASTERN USAMBARA

The Eastern Usambara is one of the smallest of the Eastern Arc ranges, as well as one of the lowest, barely exceeding 1,500m in elevation. It is, however, one of the most important ecologically, receiving an annual rainfall of up to 2,000mm and covered in some of the most extensive and least degraded montane rainforest extant in Tanzania. In some places the indigenous vegetation has been replaced by tea plantations, while in others there has been more recent encroachment by subsistence farmers, but at least 400km² of natural forest remains. In common with the other montane forests of eastern Tanzania, the Eastern Usambara is cited as a biodiversity hotspot, characterised by a high level of endemism (see box, *An African Galápagos?*, pages 234–5). It is also a vital catchment area, providing fresh water to some 200,000 people, and the East Usambara Catchment Management Project (EUCAMP), funded by Finnish aid, has implemented a community-based conservation plan to protect the catchment forests.

The centrepiece of this project is the Amani Nature Reserve, which formally opened in 1997 and protects almost 10,000ha of relatively undisturbed forest. Amani must rank close to being the most underrated reserve anywhere in northern Tanzania, offering the combination of excellent walking, beautiful forest scenery and a wealth of animal life. Although the nature reserve is a recent creation, Amani was settled by Germany as an agricultural research station in 1902, at which time the surrounding area was set aside to form what is reputedly still the second-largest botanical garden in the world. Lying at an elevation of roughly 900m, Amani remains a biological research station of some note, as well as an important centre for medical research. Most of the buildings date to the German and British colonial eras, giving it the genteel appearance of an English country village transplanted to the African jungle.

The development of Amani for ecotourism, with the emphasis on walking and hiking, has been a high priority over recent years. Nine trails have been demarcated at Amani, ranging in length from 3km to 12km, and leaflets with trail descriptions are available to visitors. The directions in the leaflets are reportedly not 100% accurate, so it might be worth hiking with a trained guide, who will also help you to spot birds and monkeys. The rehabilitated German stationmaster's house at Sigi (aka Kisiwani), some 7km from Amani on the Muheza road, doubles as an entrance gate and information centre, with an adjoining resthouse offering visitors a second, lower-elevation site from which to explore the forest.

It is worth consulting with the reserve's guides about the trail most suited to your specific interest. The 10km Konkoro Trail, which can be covered on foot or in a vehicle, is good for African violets, and it cuts through several different forest types, as well as passing a viewpoint and terminating in an overnight campsite in the heart of the forest. The shorter Turaco and Mbamole Hill trails are recommended first options for birdwatchers. In addition to the prescribed walking trails, there is much to be seen along the roads and paths that lie within the research centre and botanical garden. Wandering around the forest-fringed village, you are likely to encounter a wide variety of birds, as well as black-and-white colobus and blue monkey – and you might even catch a glimpse of the bizarre and outsized Zanj elephant shrew.

Entrance for non-residents costs US$30 per person per day (US$5 for under-16s). Other fees include a US$5 daily vehicle entrance fee (US$30 if the vehicle is

Without doubt the most familiar of the thousands of taxa that are endemic to the Eastern Arc Mountains is a small flowering plant first collected in the Eastern Usambara in 1892 by the District Commissioner of Tanga, Baron Walter von Saint Paul Illaire. Subsequently described as *Saintpaulia ionantha* in honour of its discoverer, the African violet (as it is more commonly known) was made commercially available in 1927, when ten different blue-flowered strains were put on the market. It is today one of the world's most popular perennial pot plants, with thousands of cultivated strains generating a global trade worth tens of millions of US dollars, and yet few enthusiasts realise that the wildflower is threatened within its natural range.

Although they vary greatly in shape and colour, most cultivated strains of African violet are hybrids of the original seeds collected by Baron Saint Paul, which belonged to two highly malleable races, *S. i. ionantha.* and *S. i. grotei*. The specific taxonomy of the genus *Saintpaulia* is controversial: at one time more than 20 species were recognised but a 2006 study has reduced that number to six. The genus is unique to the Eastern Arc Mountains, and its main strongholds are the Eastern Usambara and Nguru Mountains.

Not affiliated to the true violets, *Saintpaulia* is a relatively recently evolved genus whose ancestral stock was most likely blown across from Madagascar in a cyclone (a flowering plant in the genus *Streptocarpus* has been cited as the probable ancestor). The wild *Saintpaulia* has probably never enjoyed a wide distribution or a high level of habitat tolerance. In the wild, as in the home, most species require continuous shade and humidity in order to flourish. Because it depends on surface rather than underground moisture, *Saintpaulia* has an unusually shallow root system. It typically grows in moist cracks in porous rocks close to streams running through closed-canopy forest – though some specimens do lead an epiphytic existence on cycad trunks or the shady branches of palms.

The main threat to the wild *Saintpaulia* is the logging of tall trees, which creates breaks in the closed canopy. Researchers in the Eastern Usambara have come across dead or dying plants at several established *Saintpaulia* sites where the canopy has been broken due to logging. One of the many positive effects of the gazetting of Amani Nature Reserve in 1997 is that it should help secure the future of the genus – or at least those species that are resident within the reserve. Local guides will be able to show you the wildflowers on several of the established walking and driving trails.

foreign registered), a photography fee of US$10 per day and an additional charge of US$20 per person for a guided walk.

GETTING THERE AND AWAY The springboard for visits to Amani is the small town of Muheza, 40km west of Tanga on the main surfaced road to Moshi. Buses between Moshi or Dar es Salaam and Tanga can drop you at Muheza, as can the minibuses that ply between Tanga and Lushoto. Liveliest on the local market days of Thursday and Sunday, Muheza boasts half a dozen small guesthouses should you need to spend a night.

From Muheza, the road to Amani is clearly signposted, and the drive should take about 90 minutes, passing through the entrance gate at Sigi after an hour. Driving times will depend on the condition of the road, in particular the spectacular but steep 7km stretch between Sigi and Amani. Three buses daily run between Muheza and Sigi, leaving Muheza at around 12.30 to arrive about two hours later.

Eastern Usambara takes second place to the Udzungwa as the most important avian site in the Eastern Arc Mountains, but it is still one of the most significant birding sites anywhere in East Africa. Amani in particular has several logistical advantages over the best birdwatching sites in the Udzungwa, namely relative ease of access, proximity to the established tourist circuit of northern Tanzania, and a superior tourist infrastructure and quality of guides. The Eastern Usambara's avifauna has received far more scientific attention than that of the other Eastern Arc ranges, dating from 1926 to 1948 when Amani was the home of the doyen of Tanzania ornithology, Reginald Moreau, credited with discovering and describing several new species including the long-billed tailorbird. This extensive study is reflected in a checklist of 340 bird species, including 12 that are globally threatened and 19 that are either endemic to the Eastern Arc Mountains or to the East African coastal biome.

The temptation on first arriving at Amani might be to rush off along one of the trails into the forest interior. In fact some of the most productive general birdwatching is to be had in the gardens and forest fringe around Amani village, slow exploration of which is likely to yield up to 50 forest-associated species including half a dozen genuine rarities. One of the more conspicuous and vocal residents around the resthouses is the green-headed oriole, a colourful bird that is restricted to a handful of montane forests between Tanzania and Mozambique. The flowering gardens are a good site for three of the four range-restricted sunbirds associated with the Eastern Usambara, ie: Amani, banded green and Uluguru violet-backed sunbird. The rare long-billed tailorbird has recently been discovered breeding at two sites within Amani village.

Having explored the resthouse area, the guided Turaco and Mbamole Hill trails are recommended for sighting further montane forest specials. Noteworthy birds resident in the forest around Amani include the Usambara eagle owl, southern banded snake eagle, silvery-cheeked hornbill, half-collared kingfisher, African green ibis, Fischer's turaco, African broadbill, East Coast akalat, white-chested alethe, Kenrick's and Waller's starlings, and several forest flycatchers. It is also worth noting that several of the more interesting Usambara specials are lowland forest species, more likely to be seen in and around Sigi than at Amani. Among the birds to look out for on the trails around Sigi are eastern green tinkerbird, African cuckoo-hawk, square-tailed drongo, bar-tailed trogon and chestnut-fronted helmet-shrike.

One bus continues up the steep road to Amani, arriving an hour later. The bus from Amani to Muheza leaves at 06.30 and passes through Sigi at about 07.00.

🏠 WHERE TO STAY AND EAT

🏠 **Amani Resthouse** ☎ 027 254 0313; e anr@ twiga.com. This well maintained & comfortable stone building set in the middle of the research village dates to the colonial era. There is a log fire in the lounge & meals can be provided. *Tsh10,000 pp; camping Tsh5,000 pp.*

🏠 **Sigi Resthouse** ☎ 027 254 0313; e anr@ twiga.com. The new resthouse at Sigi is similar in standard to the one at Amani, albeit with a rather more modern feel. Meals are available. *Tsh10,000 pp; camping Tsh5,000 pp.*

⚤ **Kamkoro Campsite** This little-used campsite lies in a stand of forest some 10km from Amani along the Kamkoro vehicle trail. *Camping Tsh5,000 pp.*

9

The North Coast

The coastline running southward from the Kenya border to Dar es Salaam, though more developed than the south coast, is eclipsed in reputation by the offshore island of Zanzibar. Bypassed by the main road between Moshi and Dar es Salaam, the north coast attracts surprisingly few tourists, but it does boast a wealth of little known travel possibilities to reward those with the time and initiative to explore. The principal town along the north coast is Tanga, a somewhat time-warped port that briefly served as the capital of German East Africa before this role was usurped by Dar es Salaam. Also of interest are the more traditional Swahili trading centres of Bagamoyo and Pangani, which lie between Dar es Salaam and Tanga, and are separated by the remote Saadani National Park.

The north coast has a typically sultry coastal climate, with hot and humid conditions throughout the year. Travel conditions are most pleasant over June–September and least so over the hotter and wetter months of November–May. The main access road to the north coast is an excellent 71km stretch of asphalt that runs east from Segera (on the B1 from Moshi to Dar es Salaam) to Tanga. There is also now a good surfaced road between Dar es Salaam and Bagamoyo. By contrast, the coastal road between Tanga and Bagamoyo is mostly unsurfaced and in poor condition. The stretch from Tanga to Pangani can usually be covered in any vehicle, but Pangani to Saadani may require 4x4 and Saadani to Bagamoyo has been impassable for decades due to a collapsed bridge. As a result, there is no public transport on this road, and Bagamoyo is most easily visited as a round trip out of Dar es Salaam, while Pangani works best as a round trip out of Tanga.

TANGA

Characterised by quiet, pot-holed avenues lined with timeworn pastel-shaded German and Asian buildings, Tanga's compact city centre has a somnambulant aura belying its status as Tanzania's second busiest port and seventh-largest town (population 180,000). Bypassed by the main northern highway, the city never attracted a great volume of travellers, and it practically dropped off the East African travel map following the termination of passenger train services to Moshi and Dar es Salaam in the 1990s. This, we feel, is a shame – Tanga's city centre certainly doesn't lack for atmosphere, it boasts a few intriguing architectural relicts, and it forms a relaxed base for exploring the likes of the limestone Amboni Caves and mediaeval Tongoni Ruins.

The air of semi-abandonment that hovers over central Tanga, reminiscent of much of Tanzania during its mid 1980s economic nadir, does reflect a real demise in commercial fortunes in recent decades. Indeed, it is some barometer of Tanga's descent into backwater status that it is the only Tanzanian town where fewer hotel rooms are available in the city centre today than was the case when the first edition

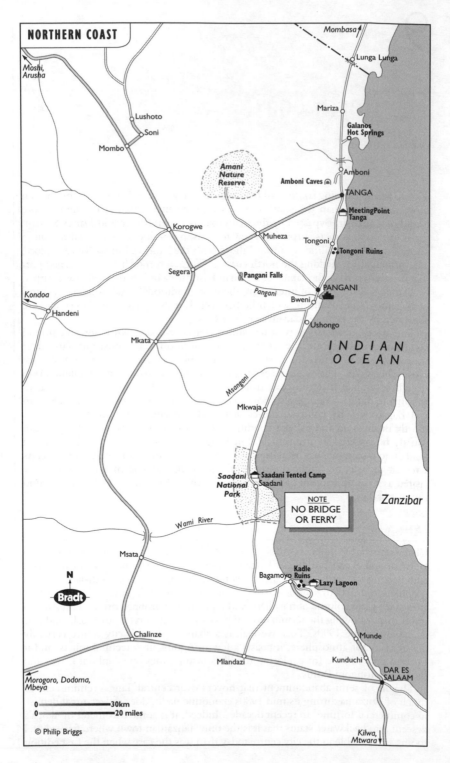

Mombasa

Lunga Lunga

Moshi,
Arusha

Lushoto

Soni

Mombo

Mariza

Galanos
Hot Springs

Amani
Nature
Reserve

Amboni Caves

Amboni

TANGA

MeetingPoint
Tanga

Korogwe

Muheza

Tongoni

Tongoni Ruins

Segera

Pangani Falls

Pangani

Kondoa

Handeni

Bweni

PANGANI

Mkata

Ushongo

INDIAN
OCEAN

Msangani

Mkwaja

Saadani
National
Park

Saadani Tented Camp

Saadani

NOTE
NO BRIDGE
OR FERRY

Zanzibar

Wami River

Msata

N

Bradt

Kadle
Ruins

Bagamoyo

Lazy Lagoon

Chalinze

Munde

Mlandazi

Kunduchi

DAR ES
SALAAM

Morogoro, Dodoma,
Mbeya

0 ————————30km
0 ————————20 miles

© Philip Briggs

Kilwa,
Mtwara

of this guide was researched. Another factor in Tanga's unusually sedate atmosphere is that the real hub of commercial activity has shifted outside the city centre. The grid of streets that surround the bus station and market seem far more colourful and crowded, and they positively bustle with low-key entrepreneurial activity. Ras Kazone Peninsula, northeast of the town centre, supports a quiet but well preserved residential area, complete with upmarket(ish) hotels and swimming beach.

HISTORY Tanga, despite its aura of faded prosperity, lacks the historical pedigree of smaller ports such as Pangani or Bagamoyo. The ruined mosques on Toten Island in Tanga Harbour indicate the presence of a small trading centre in the Omani and Shirazi eras, as do similar ruins within a 20km radius of the modern city. But while it can be assumed that some sort of fishing settlement has existed here for millennia, there's no written or archaeological evidence of a more substantial settlement prior to the early 19th century. The name Tanga – 'sail' in Swahili – is probably derived from Mtangani, the original name for Tongoni, and it could well be that the foundation of modern Tanga was linked to the decline and eventual abandonment of that nearby ruined city.

By the mid 19th century, Tanga was a substantial ivory trade centre, neither as renowned as Pangani, nor as architecturally distinguished, but sufficiently profitable to be governed by an agent of the Sultan of Zanzibar. When the Sultan of Zanzibar leased the coastal strip to Germany in 1887, few would have predicted that Tanga would rise to prominence. Yet only two years after establishing its first headquarters at Bagamoyo, Germany relocated its administration to the deeper and better protected natural harbour at Tanga. Thus did Tanga become Germany's *ipso facto* East African capital, and although it relinquished this status to Dar es Salaam in 1891, its excellent harbour ensured that it was earmarked for colonial development. The first school in German East Africa was built at Tanga in 1893, and several other impressive buildings on the modern waterfront – notably the Regional Headquarters and Cliff Block – date to the German era.

In 1911, the completion of a railway line to Moshi sealed Tanga's role as the country's second busiest seaport. No less significant was the introduction of sisal, which became Tanzania's most important agricultural export in the colonial era, and remains the most visible crop around Tanga to this day. Unfortunately, the city fell into economic decline following the collapse of the post-independence sisal boom and the widespread closure of local industries in the 1980s. It has been further sidelined in modern times by improvements to the national road

---

TANGA IN 1857

Richard Burton, who spent several days in Tanga in 1857, wrote that:

Tanga... is a patch of thatched pent-shaped huts, built upon a bank overlooking the sea, in a straggling grove of coconuts and calabash. The population numbers between 4,000 and 5,000...The citizens are a homely-looking race, chiefly occupied with commerce, and they send twice a-year, in June and November, after the great and little rains, trading parties to the Chagga and the Maasai countries. The imports are chiefly cotton-stuffs, brass and iron wires, and beads... The returns consist of camels and asses, a few slaves, and ivory, of which I was told 70,000lb passes through Tanga. The citizens also trade with the coast savages, and manufacture hardware from imported metal.... Of late years Tanga has been spared the mortification of the Maasai, who have hunted and harried in this vicinity many a herd. It is now, comparatively speaking, thickly inhabited.

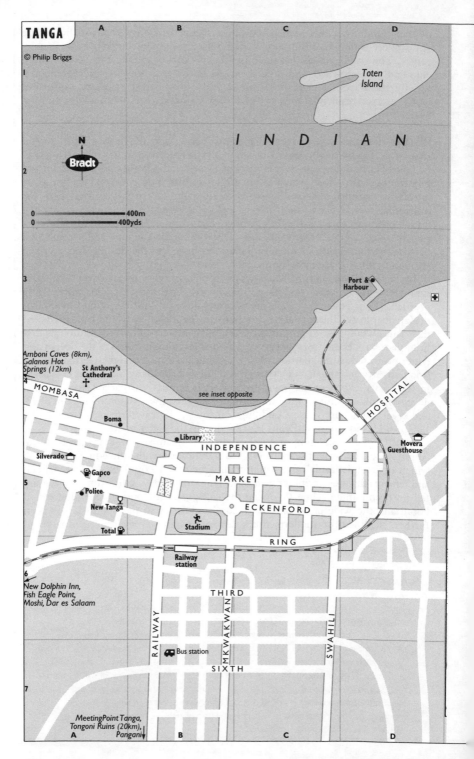

TANGA

© Philip Briggs

I

Toten
Island

N

Bradt

I N D I A N

2

0 _____ 400m
0 _____ 400yds

3

Port & ⚓
Harbour

✚

Amboni Caves (8km),
Galanos Hot
Springs (12km)

St Anthony's
Cathedral
✝

4

M O M B A S A

see inset opposite

H O S P I T A L

Boma ●

● Library

Movera
Guesthouse

I N D E P E N D E N C E

Silverado ⌂

🏪 Gapco

M A R K E T

5

● Police

E C K E N F O R D

New Tanga

Total 🏪

Stadium

R I N G

Railway
station

6

New Dolphin Inn,
Fish Eagle Point,
Moshi, Dar es Salaam

T H I R D

R A I L W A Y

M K W A K W A N

S W A H I L I

🚐 Bus station

S I X T H

7

MeetingPoint Tanga,
Tongoni Ruins (20km),
Pangani↓

A   B   C   D

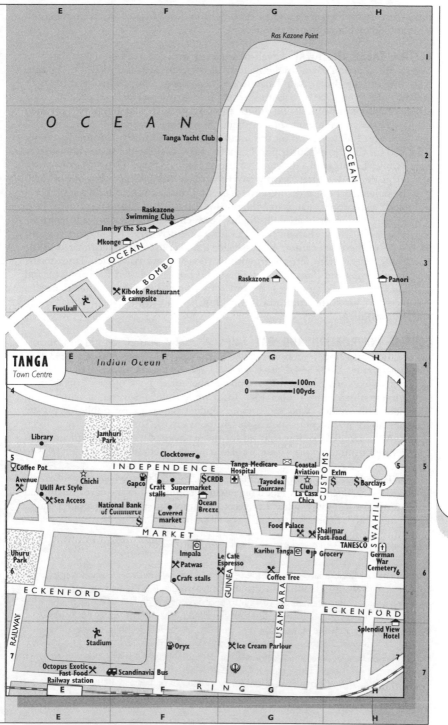

TANGA
Town Centre

Indian Ocean

0 ———— 100m
0 ———— 100yds

Places

Ras Kazone Point

OCEAN

Tanga Yacht Club

Raskazone
Swimming Club

Inn by the Sea

Mkonge

OCEAN

BOMBO

Kiboko Restaurant
& campsite

Football

Raskazone

Panori

Library

Jamhuri
Park

Clocktower

Coffee Pot

INDEPENDENCE

Tanga Medicare
Hospital

Coastal
Aviation

Exlm

Avenue

Chichi

Ukili Art Style

Gapco

Craft
stalls

Supermarket

SCRDB

Tayodea
Tourcare

Club

Barclays

Sea Access

National Bank
of Commerce

Ocean
Breeze

La Casa
Chica

Lovered
market

MARKET

Food Palace

Shalimar
Fast Food

TANESCO

Uhuru
Park

Impala

Karibu Tanga

JP Grocery

German
War
Cemetery

Patwas

Le Cafe
Espresso

Coffee Tree

Craft stalls

ECKENFORD

GUINEA

USAMBARA

ECKENFORD

RAILWAY

Stadium

Oryx

Ice Cream Parlour

Splendid View
Hotel

Octopus Exotic
Fast Food

Scandinavia Bus

Railway station

RING

SWAHILI

CUSTOMS

infrastructure and a corresponding decline in the significance of rail, leaving the harbour somewhat without purpose.

GETTING THERE AND AWAY A well-maintained surfaced road connects Tanga to Segera, the junction town on the main road between Arusha and Dar es Salaam. The total driving distance to Tanga from Arusha is 435km, from Lushoto about 200km, and from Dar es Salaam 352km. In a private vehicle, expect to cover around 80–100km per hour on any of these routes. Regular buses run between Tanga and the above towns, the best being Scandinavia Express [243 F2] (✆ 027 264 4337) on Railway Road on the south side of the football stadium. It charges Tsh4,000 for the three-hour trip to Lushoto, Tsh12,000 for the seven-hour trip to Arusha, and Tsh10,000 for the six-hour trip to Dar es Salaam. Other inferior buses also cover the same routes, leaving from the main bus station 500m out of town past the railway station, as do numerous faster but more dangerous *dala-dalas*. Local minibuses also connect Tanga to Muheza (for Amani) and Korogwe.

Coastal Aviation operates daily flights between Dar es Salaam and Tanga via Zanzibar and Pemba, charging US$130 for a one-way trip. The airport is about 3km west of the town centre. All passenger train services were terminated in the late 1990s. Intermittent ferry or motorboat services have connected Tanga to the islands of Pemba and Zanzibar in the past, but none has lasted for very long and nothing appears to be running at the time of writing. It may be possible to catch a fishing dhow between Tanga and Pemba, but it's dangerous, uncomfortable and (for tourists) illegal.

TOURIST INFORMATION AND DAY TRIPS A useful source of current tourist information and hotel recommendations, Tayodea Tourcare Tanzania [243 G5] (*Independence Av;* ✆ 027 264 4350; e info@tayodea.org; www.tayodea.org) operates out of a kiosk-like office diagonally opposite the main post office. Effectively a government-funded tour operator, Tourcare employs several articulate and knowledgeable guides, who can arrange budget day trips by public or private transport to local attractions such as the Amboni Caves, Tongoni Ruins and Toten Island. A flat fee of US$10 is charged for the services of a guide. Mountain bikes can be hired from the office. Tourcare also arranges all-inclusive overnight trips to Amani Nature Reserve.

The Tanga Heritage Centre (m 0713 467695/0715 307285; e urithitanga@yahoo.com; www.geocities.com/urithitanga) is a local organisation committed to the development and publicising of a variety of cultural projects and historical sites in and around Tanga. *Urithi*, the centre's quarterly newsletter, is well worth a look.

THE BATTLE FOR TANGA

In late 1914, German Tanga was the setting of a tragically farcical British naval raid. Suffering from seasickness after a long voyage from India, 8,000 Asian recruits were instructed to leap ashore at Tanga, only to become bogged down in the mangroves, then stumble into a swarm of ferocious bees, and finally trigger off German trip-wires. The raid was eventually aborted, but not before 800 British troops lay dead, and a further 500 were wounded. In the confusion, 455 rifles, 16 machine guns and 600,000 rounds of ammunition were left on the shore – a major boon to the Germans. This battle forms a pivotal scene in William Boyd's excellent novel *An Ice Cream War*. The Germans were eventually forced out of Tanga in 1916, when the British, better prepared this time, launched a land offensive from Moshi on the weakened German outpost.

WHERE TO STAY
Upmarket

Mkonge Hotel [243 F3] (49 rooms) ☎ 027 264 3440/4446; e mkongetanga@kaributanga.com. Built in the 1950s, this former government hotel is the smartest in Tanga, set in large attractive gardens overlooking the harbour & Toten Island on Ras Kazone Peninsula. It looked somewhat timeworn at the turn of the millennium, following a succession

of management changes, but has since been totally renovated & refurbished under dynamic Swiss–Indian owner-management. The characterful wooden floored en-suite rooms have AC, satellite TV & hot water, while facilities include a decent restaurant & a swimming pool. Good value. *US$60/70 sgl/dbl B&B, plus US$10 for sea view.*

Moderate

Panori Hotel [243 H3] (22 rooms) ☎ 027 264 6044; f 027 264 7425; e panori@africaonline.co.tz. An isolated location on Ras Kazone Peninsula, some distance from any beach, makes this inconvenient for travellers without private transport. In all other respects, it's probably the best deal in this range, offering the choice of large rooms with wooden floor, AC, TV & hot bath, or smaller scruffier rooms in the old wing. The *makuti*-style restaurant, widely regarded as the one of the best places to eat in Tanga, has a varied menu with most dishes around Tsh4,500. *Tsh32,000/42,000 sgl/dbl or Tsh25,000/29,000 in old wing.*

Silverado Hotel [242 A5] (9 rooms) ☎ 027 264 5259. This amenable hotel has been converted from an attractive old homestead on Chubageni St, a few blocks west of the city centre. Comfortable en-suite dbls have AC, fridge & DSTV, & the ground floor

restaurant serves good meals in the Tsh5,000–6,000 range. *Tsh40,000 dbl.*

New Dolphin Inn [242 A6] (27 rooms) ☎/f 027 264 6061; m 0784 505 750. This modern multi-story hotel with its gleaming white façade is rather inconveniently located in the Chuda area just east of the railway tracks, signposted off the Dar es Salaam road. There's a good restaurant on the ground floor. *Tsh25,000 en-suite dbl with AC; Tsh20,000 smaller sgl with TV & fan.*

Hotel Raskazone [243 G3] (17 rooms) ☎/f 027 264 3897; m 0713 670790. 5mins' walk from the Mkonge Hotel, this quiet, unassuming little hotel with its oddly landscaped front garden is a friendly mid-range choice. Recently spruced up, it's now good value, & an OK restaurant & bar are attached. *US$10/22 en-suite sgl/dbl with fan/AC. Camping US$5 pp.*

Budget

Inn by the Sea [243 F3] ☎ 027 264 4614. Situated alongside the Mkonge Hotel, this has long been the only place to offer inexpensive seafront accommodation away from the town centre. It could do with a facelift, but the en-suite dbls with AC are more than adequate. No alcohol, bland food – you might well find yourself gravitating towards the adjoining Mkonge Hotel or Ras Kazone Swimming Club at meal times. *Tsh20,000 dbl.*

Ocean Breeze Hotel [243 F5] ☎ 027 264 3441/4545; m 0744 844337. The best budget lodging in the town centre is this well maintained multi-storey block facing the main market square. Large clean rooms with net, fan, firm dbl bed, hot shower & balcony are great value. Some rooms have TV. An attached restaurant & beer garden serves reasonable Indian food for around Tsh5,000, as well as reliably cold beers & sodas. *Tsh10,000/15,000 without/with TV.*

Shoestring

Splendid View Hotel [243 H7]. It has no view, of course, nor any other aspect which anybody but its mother would be likely to describe as splendid. It is

also a tad overpriced. On the plus side, it's one of the few real budget options close to the centre. *Tsh8,000 for a scruffy en-suite dbl with net & fan.*

Camping

Kiboko Restaurant & Campsite [243 F3] m 0784 469292; e jda-kiboko@bluemail.ch. This popular restaurant on the Ras Kazone Peninsula has a clean ablution block with hot water, 24hr security, lock-up

store room, safety deposit boxes for hire, self-catering facilities, laundry service, bicycle rental & of course an excellent on-site restaurant. *US$4 pp, additional US$2 to rent 3-person tent.*

9

Out of town

MeetingPoint Tanga [242 B7] (20 rooms)
m 0783 164495/0762 013902;
e meetingpointtanga@gmail.com;
www.meetingpointtanga.net. Also known as the TICC,
this inspiring new community-integrated centre, located
12km from the town centre, is one of the best
discoveries of our latest research trip. Tucked away on
the mangrove-lined shores of Pemba Channel near
Mwahako village, it offers socially conscious travellers
something more than just your average beach
holiday. The focus is on the community experience:
all profits are reinvested into local projects (eg:
HIV/AIDS education) & guests are encouraged to
'make a difference' by sharing their knowledge &
skills during their stay. Accommodation currently
consists of 20 smart dbl rooms, mostly twins, which
have net, fan & writing desk, & use a common
shower, but 20 en-suite dbls are in the works for

2009. Other facilities include an excellent restaurant,
bar, local tours & boat trips. To get there from
Tanga, follow the Pangani road south for 8km, to a
turn-off on the left signposted TICC. It's then another
4km along a dirt road following the signs. By public
transport, catch a *dala-dala* from the town centre
marked 'Mwahako' (Tsh400). The bus turns at
Mwahako but you can ask the driver to take you
all the way to TICC by paying an extra fee
(negotiable). Alternatively, a taxi from city centre
costs around Tsh15,000. *US$35/50 sgl/dbl.*

Fish Eagle Point [242 A6] m 0784 346006;
e outthere@kaributanga.com. Under construction in
early 2009, this mid-range lodge lies along the
remote baobab-lined beach of Manza Bay, some 50km
north of Tanga along the Mombasa road. Snorkelling,
fishing & coastal birding are all on offer. Expect rates
comparable to the affiliated Outpost in Arusha.

✗ **WHERE TO EAT** If you have transport, the restaurant at **MeetingPoint Tanga** [242 B7] is well worth the trek. Set under a breezy thatched-roof terrace in the heart of the centre, it serves a combination of African, Chinese and continental dishes in the Tsh5,000–6,000 range. The fish fillet à la Seychelles is well-recommended.

In the town centre, the first choice for those who enjoy spicy cuisine is the **Food Palace** [243 G6] (*Market St;* ℩ *027 264 2816*). The extensive and sumptuous menu is dominated by Indian dishes, most of which cost around Tsh3,000 inclusive of chips, rice or naan bread, though prawns are more expensive. The outdoor barbecue, open in the evening only, is good for chicken tikka and *mishkaki* (beef kebabs). The restaurant is closed through the month of Ramadan; at other times of year, no alcohol is served, but the JP Grocery opposite sells wine and beer, which you are allowed to drink on the balcony. Around the corner, the smart new **Shalimar Fast Food** [243 G6], with its American style café set-up, also offers a lengthy menu of Indian dishes in the Tsh3,000–5,000 range.

Just south of the market, the venerable **Patwas Restaurant** [243 F6] has been serving great snacks and passion fruit juice for at least 15 years. A block east, **Le Café Espresso** [243 G6] offers a decent selection of curries and stews for around Tsh3,000, but the coffee is of the tinned variety.

Pricey but highly recommended is the **Kiboko Restaurant** [243 F3] (m *0784 469292*), set in a pretty garden on the Ras Kazone Peninsula about 300m from the Mkonge Hotel. This has a varied menu of seafood, Indian and continental dishes, and is well-known locally for its steaks, *mishkaki* and other grills. Generous portions of most main courses cost around Tsh6,000–10,000, and booking is sometimes necessary if you're eating later in the evening, when it is often full.

In the same part of town, the **Ras Kazone Swimming Club** [243 F3] next to the Inn by the Sea is a good spot for a beachfront meal. An entrance fee of Tsh500 is charged, but the restaurant itself is similar in price and standard to the better ones in town. Another nearby possibility is the **Tanga Yacht Club** [243 G2], which charges a Tsh2,000 daily membership fee, has a good swimming beach and serves a selection of tasty meals in the Tsh5,000–7,000 range.

Back in the centre, the long-standing **Club la Casa Chica** [243 G5], next to the Coastal Aviation office, is Tanga's top nightspot hosting regular discos ('ladies' are admitted for free, while 'gents' pay Tsh3,000). Other popular drinking holes include the **New Tanga Hotel** [242 A5] (despite the name, no rooms or meals available), **Coffee Tree Restaurant** [243 G6] (despite the name, more of a bar than an eatery or coffee house) and the garden bar at the **Ocean Breeze Hotel** [243 F5].

OTHER PRACTICALITIES

Football Home matches are played at the central Mkwakwani Stadium [243 E7], usually on Wednesday and Saturday during March–August, with kick-off at 16.30. Tickets cost from Tsh500 upwards.

Foreign exchange The National Bank of Commerce [243 F6] (*Market St*) offers full foreign exchange facilities for cash and travellers' cheques during normal banking hours. The normal 0.5% commission is charged to change travellers' cheques and they may ask to see proof of purchase, but are unlikely to insist on it. There is no private forex bureau in Tanga, which means that travellers who come from Kenya and expect to arrive in Tanga in the late afternoon or over the weekend ought to change sufficient cash into local currency at the border.

Internet Karibu Tanga [243 G6] (*Market St;* ⟍ *027 264 2230; www.kaributanga.com*), opposite the Food Palace, is very fast, keeps long hours, and charges Tsh1,000 per hour. Several other internet cafés are dotted around town.

Swimming There's no public swimming pool. If you fancy a dip in the ocean, try the small, sandy beach at the Ras Kazone Swimming Club next to the Inn by the Sea [243 F3] (*entrance Tsh500*). The Tanga Yacht Club [243 G2] (⟍ *027 264 4246; e tyctanga@gmail.com; www.tangayachtclub.com*) also has a swimming beach, and charges a daily entry fee of US$2 per person. Both places have shower, bar and restaurant. There's also a swimming beach on Toten Island.

WHAT TO SEE

Historical buildings A wealth of colonial-era buildings line the leafy avenues of the town centre, including numerous early 20th century two-storey residences that were built for Indian and Arabic merchants and would originally have doubled as shops. Notable for their intricately carved wooden balconies, thick pillars, large raised verandas, carved hardwood doors, small grilled windows and wooden shutters, these old residences are generally in a poor state of repair, but the Tanga Heritage Centre intends to restore some in the near future. The Tanga School, opposite the stadium on Eckenford Avenue, is the oldest school in the country, built in 1895 and currently used as a medical college. The current railway station on Ring Road was built by the British, but the older German station dating to 1896, can be found by following the railway line towards the port. The Usambara Courthouse on Usambara Street is a beautiful two-storey building that has recently been fully restored by the Tanga Heritage Centre.

The main concentration of German administrative buildings lies between Independence Avenue and the waterfront. The old German Boma [242 A4], complete with underground bunkers and passages to the sea, is now the police station, and stands close to the gracious whitewashed library [242 B5 & 243 E5] built during the British colonial era. Also along Independence Avenue you'll find the original Clocktower [243 F5], dating to 1901, and the courthouse, built as provisional German regional headquarters. Less centrally, the partially disused Cliff Block on Hospital Road was the country's first hospital, built in the 1890s. Good examples of British architecture include the Katani Building and Lead

Memorial Hall on Hospital Road, both dating to the early 1950s. There are two World War I cemeteries: the German Sakarani Cemetery on Swahili Street [243 H6], at the east end of Market Street, and the Commonwealth War Cemetery on Bombo Road. A British War Memorial in Usagara, near the Mkonge Hotel, consists of a plaque with illustrations and a brief history of the war.

Toten Island Tiny and uninhabited, Toten Island, protected within Tanga Harbour, is dotted with overgrown relics of earlier Islamic settlements. On the west of the island, a large ruined mosque established in the 14th or 15th century and renovated during the late 18th century has a large east-facing balcony, a staircase leading to the roof and a well-preserved ornamental *mihrab* (the interior niche indicating the direction of Mecca), while a nearby cemetery contains inscribed Islamic tombs. A smaller and more ruinous mosque stands on the southern shore, and many ceramic artefacts and household objects from the 15th–18th centuries have been unearthed. No trace remains of a third mosque depicted on a German era map, or the large rectangular fort described by Burton, who visited the island in 1857, some 30 years before it was abandoned. There is also a German war cemetery, and a small swimming beach. The northern shore is the site of a recently implemented mangrove conservation project.

Toten Island can be reached by boat as a three- to four-hour round-trip excursion from Tanga. The most straightforward way to visit is with Tourcare, which charges US$15/30 per person/group for a guide, and US$40 per person for the use of a motorised boat and US$25 per person to go by dhow. Alternatively, you can negotiate with local boatmen at the harbour for a cheaper price using a traditional dhow. Best visit at low tide, when it is easier to walk on the beaches.

Amboni Caves The labyrinth of subterranean passages that runs through the 250km^2 limestone bed to the east of Tanga is probably the most extensive cave system in East Africa. Caves 3a and 3b, known less prosaically as the Amboni Caves, have been open to the public for years, and offer a combined 750m of accessible passages. Another two caves, 7 and 8, were opened in October 2000. The total network of caves is often said to be more than 200km long, and a persistent rumour has it that one passage runs all the way to Fort Jesus in Mombasa. However, a comprehensive survey undertaken by a German–Turkish expedition in 1994 found the largest of ten caves studied to be less than 1km long.

The Amboni Caves make for a good day trip out of Tanga, even though their initial impact is diminished by the graffiti around the entrance – the handiwork of past visitors who couldn't resist the urge to paint their name for posterity. This unsightly roll call of buffoons doesn't extend far into the main cave, which opens into a magnificent 15m high chamber overhung with large rippled stalactites. From this first chamber, the route leads through a succession of narrow passages and larger caverns, past natural sculptures including the so-called Madonna and Statue of Liberty. The caves support thousands upon thousands of bats, which can be seen streaming out of the entrance at dusk, and whose droppings feed a variety of cockroaches and weird invertebrates.

The entrance to the main cave lies on the north bank of the Mkulimuzi River, a beautiful clear stream that rises in the Usambara Mountains and is also fed locally by freshwater springs. The river is fringed by palms, and runs through one of the largest extant patches of coastal forest in northern Tanzania. A variety of localised birds inhabit the forest near the caves, as does a resident and regularly observed troop of black-and-white colobus monkeys. This is also a good place to look for the African violet in a wild state, but note that it is forbidden to pick or damage this protected flower.

To reach the Amboni Caves from Tanga, follow the Mombasa road for 5km, then turn left on to a dirt road signposted for 'Mohamed Enterprises'. About 100m along this dirt road turn left again, then continue more or less straight along a rough road through the shambas of Kiomoni village for 1.5km to the signposted entrance to the caves. There is no public transport to the caves, but *dala-dalas* between Tanga and Amboni village, which lies 2km further along the Mombasa road, will drop passengers at the first junction, from where it's a 20–30 minute walk. It is also possible to charter a taxi from Tanga, or to cycle there – mountain bikes can be rented from the Tourcare office, and local bikes are available to rent on the main market square. The caves are open from 08.00 to 17.00 daily, and the entrance fee of Tsh3,000 includes the services of the English-speaking caretaker/guide and use of a good torch. Entering the caves without a guide would be extremely foolhardy, and there is a real danger of getting lost or being injured. No accommodation or camping facilities are available at the caves.

Galanos Hot Springs Named after a Greek sisal plantation owner, the Galanos Hot Springs lie 8km from the Amboni Caves, and the two can be visited in conjunction. The clear, green water, which forms a large pool before flowing into a stream caked with lime deposits, is reputed to cure rheumatism, arthritis and other ailments. Locals bathe in the pool, but the sulphuric odour doesn't make this a very attractive prospect. A Tsh2,000 entrance fee is reputedly charged, but there's seldom anybody there to collect it. To reach the springs from Amboni, follow the main Tanga–Mombasa road north for 2km, where the road passes through Amboni village immediately before crossing a bridge over the Sigi River (where crocodiles are sometimes seen). About 1km past the bridge, turn right at an unsignposted junction on to a dirt track. After another 1km, you'll come to a fork in front of a school building. The 2km track to the springs lies along the left fork. If you need to ask directions, the Swahili for hot springs is *maji moto*.

Tongoni Ruins Tongoni means 'Place of Ruins', and the village of that name, situated alongside the Pangani road 20km south of Tanga, stands adjacent to the remains of an abandoned Swahili town known contemporaneously as Mtangata. Little is known about the early history of this settlement, but it must have been founded before the late 14th century (one unverifiable local tradition relates that it was founded at the same time as Kilwa, and by the same family). During its 15th century commercial peak, Mtangata was the most prosperous trade centre for 100km in any direction.

Three Portuguese ships under the command of Vasco Da Gama ran aground at Mtangata in 1498, making it one of the first places in East Africa to be visited by Europeans. A year later, Da Gama spent two weeks at Mtangata, where he abandoned one of his ships due to a shortage of hands, and named the distant Usambara Mountains after São Raphael. Traditionally hostile to Mombasa, the rulers of Mtangata maintained a good relationship with the Portuguese, and the town evidently prospered until 1698, when the Portuguese were evicted from Mombasa. Thereafter Mtangata slid into obscurity, to be abandoned in about 1730. It enjoyed a minor 18th century revival when settled and renamed Sitahabu ('Better Here Than There') by refugees from Kilwa. The new settlers never renovated the larger structures, but they did leave offerings in the *mihrab* of the abandoned mosque, and also appropriated the old cemetery.

Mtangata was long deserted in 1857, when Richard Burton stopped by *en route* between Tanga and Pangani. Burton, clearly affected by the ruinous apparition, wrote that:

LEGENDS AND LOST DOG STORIES

The main Amboni Cave has long held a strong spiritual significance to the local Digo people, who refer to it as Mabavu. According to the caretaker, this translates as 'sacrifice', though most written sources suggest Mabavu is the name of a deity who lives within the cave. The chamber associated with this deity is called Mzimuni (Place of Spirits) and it contains a sacrificial altar that is normally scattered with bones, food and other gifts, left by pilgrims from all around East Africa. The cave's resident deity can reputedly alleviate all forms of illness and misfortune, but his speciality is making barren women fertile. The perceived powers of Amboni remain as strong today as ever – Tanga's football team reputedly slaughters a cow or goat at the altar before pivotal matches!

Amboni has attracted its fair share of modern legends. During the time of Kenya's Mau-Mau rebellion, the main cave formed a hideout for the brave freedom fighter (or heinous bandit, depending on who's telling the tale) Osale Otango and his Tanzania sidekick Paul Hamiso, at least until Otango was shot dead by the authorities in 1958. It is difficult to know what to make of another popular legend relating to two retired army officers who undertook a survey expedition of Amboni shortly after World War II. The men reputedly vanished without trace, but the dog that accompanied them into the caves turned up four months later at the entrance to another cave – on the lower slopes of distant Kilimanjaro!

Moonlight would have tempered the view; it was a grisly spectacle in the gay and glowing shine of the sun. Shattered walls, the remnants of homesteads in times gone by, rose, choked with the luxuriant growth of decay, and sheltering in their desert shade the bat and the nightjar... I was shown the grave of a wali or saint – his very name had perished – covered with a cadjan roof, floored with stamped earth, cleanly swept, and garnished with a red and white flag. Near a spacious mosque, well built with columns of cut coralline, and adorned with an elaborate prayer-niche, are several tall mausoleums of elegant construction, their dates denoting an antiquity of about two hundred years. Beyond the legend of the bay, none could give me information concerning the people that have passed away... [One particular engraved tile] was regarded with a superstitious reverence by the Swahili, who declared that Sultan Kimweri of Usambara had sent a party of bold men to bear it away; nineteen died mysterious deaths, and the tile was thereupon restored to its place.

Today, the ruins at Tongoni consist of one large mosque, several disused wells and walls, and a cemetery of 40 tombs. The ruined mosque, with a ground plan of 150m², is the only vaguely habitable structure, and aside from the ornate niche referred to by Burton, it is rather poorly preserved. However, the cemetery holds the largest known concentration of pillar tombs, a type of construction unique to the Swahili Coast. Most of the tombs have decorated borders and white plaster panels, and all except one has toppled over. Much of old Mtangata has been submerged through erosion, and it is feared that without adequate protection the cemetery may also eventually crumble into the ocean. In nearby Tongoni village stand the discrete ruins of a more recent mosque, dating from the Omani era. The surrounding area forms one of the successful mangrove conservation areas on the Tanga coast.

To reach the ruins from Tanga, follow the Pangani road south for 18km to Tongoni village, then turn left at the signposted junction and follow this motorable track for 1km. Any bus heading to Pangani can drop you at the junction, from where it is a ten-minute walk to the ruins. A return charter taxi from Tanga to Tongoni should cost around Tsh15,000–20,000. Entrance costs Tsh1,000.

Largely bypassed by 20th-century developments, Pangani was a pivotal trade centre in the 19th century, and it is endowed with a number of crumbling old buildings dating to that time. It retains the most traditional Swahili character of any north coast port, and has a lovely position on the north bank of the forest-fringed Pangani River mouth, from where a gorgeous beach stretches northward as far as the eye can see. And although Pangani itself remains little developed, the surrounding coast has witnessed an extraordinary mushrooming of beach resorts in recent years. The most accessible and affordable of these establishments line the Pangani–Tanga road, while a more attractive cluster of costlier resorts can be found some 12km south of Pangani at the attractive coastal village of Ushongo, whose fabulous and practically deserted beach ranks as one of the best-kept secrets on the Tanzanian coast.

Once settled into Pangani, there's plenty to keep you busy. The old town itself warrants a couple of hours' exploration, whether on a self-guided walking tour or with a guide from the recently established tourist office on the waterfront. There's a good beach in front of the Pangadeco Beach Hotel, but you're advised against taking valuables. Other activities include a boat trip up the forested Pangani River, a snorkelling excursion to Maziwe Island, an agricultural walking tour of the hinterland, and a trip to the Tongoni Ruins.

GETTING THERE AND AWAY Pangani is situated 53km south of Tanga. The dirt coastal road between the two is generally in reasonable condition, and can be covered in about 1.5 hours in a private vehicle. The beach resorts between Tanga and Pangani all lie within 1–2km of this road. Buses between Tanga and Pangani charge Tsh2,000 per person and take less than three hours. There are no minibuses along this route. Emayani Beach Lodge, Tulia, The Tides and Beach Crab Resort all lie to the south of the Pangani River. There is no bridge over the Pangani Mouth, but a motor ferry is permanently in place to carry vehicles and passengers across on demand. After being forced into dry-dock for several months in mid 2008 for repairs, the ageing ferry continues to slowly limp across the river. Rumour has it that a new (used) ferry purchased from Denmark will replace it sometime in early 2009. The crossing takes 5–10 minutes, and costs Tsh4,000 per vehicle plus Tsh500 per person. Small local boats can take passengers without a vehicle for marginally less.

From the south bank of the river, an erratic dirt road leads to Saadani village in the eponymous national park, an 80km drive that should take about two hours in dry conditions but might be impossible after heavy rain. The short, steep turn-off to Crab Beach Resort lies about 1km past the ferry along this road. The 5km turn-off to Ushongo, accessible in any weather, is signposted 10km along the Saadani road. There are no scheduled flights to Pangani. Either you'll need to charter a flight to Ushongo airstrip, 7km from The Tides and Emayani, or else fly into Tanga on the daily Coastal Aviation flight from Zanzibar and arrange road transport from there.

TOURIST INFORMATION AND TOURS A waterfront tourist information office (⊕ 8.30–16.00 Mon–Sat) alongside the post office is home to the helpful Pangani Coast Cultural Tourism Programme [253 B2] (m 0784 916494/868499; e sekibahaculturetours@yahoo.co.uk; www.infojep.com/culturaltours), an ecotourism project developed in association with the Dutch SNV agency. Independent travellers can arrange most of the activities listed below at the tourist office, which levies a development and administration fee of US$6 per person, and a guide fee of US$6 per group for all activities. Bicycles can be hired at around Tsh3,000 per day. Travellers staying at the smarter beach lodges to the north and south of town should be able to arrange the same activities through their hotel. The tourist office can also arrange overnight trips to Saadani National Park at around US$165 per person for groups of two or more.

🏠 WHERE TO STAY AND EAT
North of Pangani
Moderate

🏠 **Mkoma Bay Tented Lodge** [253 E1] (12 tents) ➊ 027 263 0000; m 0786 434001; e mkomabay@gmail.com; www.mkomabaycom. This smart & very reasonably priced tented camp run by a friendly Danish–American couple has a stunning location in large, landscaped grounds that sprawl down to a swimming pool on a low cliff overlooking the deserted beach at Mkoma Bay. It lies 1km off the main road, along a side-road signposted 49km from Tanga & 5km before Pangani. There are comfortable, attractive en-suite standing tents with fan & netting, 5 cosy en-suite dbl *bandas* & a rambling 4-bedroom 'Swahili House' (min 4 guests). The restaurant serves good continental meals & seafood. *Bandas US$50 B&B, tents US$80/150 sgl/dbl, Swahili House US$75 pp.*

🏠 **Capricorn Beach Cottages** [253 E1] (3 rooms) m 0784 632529; e annabel@satconet.net; www.capricornbeachcottages.com. This very welcoming owner-managed lodge, 33km south of Tanga off the Pangani road, lies in baobab-studded gardens sloping down to an attractive palm-lined beach.

Accommodation is in smart self-catering cottages with *makuti* roof, tiled floor, king-size bed with netting, fan, secluded balcony, well equipped kitchen & 24hr internet access. There's a small onsite deli where you can purchase delicious gourmet items such as smoked fish & home-baked bread; otherwise you can eat & drink at the neighbouring Peponi Beach Resort. Good value. *US$70/104 sgl/dbl B&B.*

🏠 **Tinga Tinga Lodge** [253 E1] (10 rooms) ➊ 027 263 0022; m 0784 879638; e info@tingalodge.com; www.tingatingalodge.com. Given a facelift under new management, this unpretentious lodge is signposted 500m past Mkoma Bay in the direction of Pangani. Set in large, green grounds with an attractive beachfront location, it comprises 10 spacious en-suite dbl *bandas*, all with TV, fridge, fan, net & hot showers. The breezy thatched roof restaurant & bar, set on a rise overlooking the ocean, serves delicious continental & Asian-inspired dishes in the US$4–5 range. Activities include river cruises, walking tours & day trips to Maziwe Island. *US$60/70/90 sgl/dbl/trpl B&B; camping US$5 pp.*

Budget

🏠 **Peponi Holiday Resort** [253 E1] m 0784 202962/0713 540139; e info@peponiresort.com; www.peponiresort.com. Owned & managed by long-term East Africa residents, this popular & friendly beachfront resort is clearly signposted a short distance off the Pangani road 30km south of Tanga. The rustic en-suite *makuti bandas* are good value at the special backpackers rate but the full price feels a little steep. Facilities include clean ablution blocks, laundry service, & an attractive bar & restaurant serving good Western meals & seafood dishes. Dependent on tides, the beach in front of the

resort is good for swimming & offers reasonable snorkelling. Local boats can be arranged for snorkelling or fishing excursions to the outer reefs or Maziwe Island. The owners are a reliable source of information about local tourist attractions. It's a very chilled spot, & readily accessible using public transport, or by charter taxi (approx Tsh25,000 from Pangani). *US$50 B&B, US$15 pp backpackers & students; camping under shelters US$4 pp.*

🏠 **Pangani Beach Resort** [253 E1] (10 rooms) ➊ 027 263 0088; m 0784 539989. Signposted 500m past the Tinga Tinga Resort, the Pangani

---

PILLAR OF STONE

In the early days of Pangani, there was an important annual celebration day on which it was forbidden to swim in the ocean. One wealthy Arab woman decided to ignore this taboo, and went in the ocean with her slave to wash her hair. When God saw this, he was so incensed that he punished both women by turning them into a stone, which stands in the water outside town to this day.

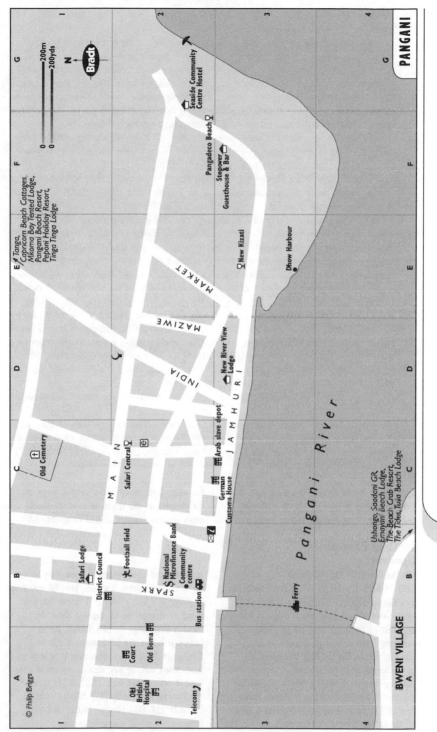

PANGANI

© Philip Briggs

0 ____ 200m
0 ____ 200yds

N

Bradt

E ✓ Tanga,
Capricorn Beach Cottages,
Mkoma Bay Tented Lodge,
Pangani Beach Resort,
Peponi Holiday Resort,
Tinga Tinga Lodge

Old Cemetery

Safari Lodge

District Council

Court

Old Boma

Old British Hospital

Telecom

Football field

National Microfinance Bank

Community centre

Bus station

S P A R K

Safari Central

Ferry

Seaside Community Centre Hostel

Pangadeco Beach

Stopover Guesthouse & Bar

New Kizati

Dhow Harbour

New River View Lodge

Arab slave depot

German Customs House

M A I N

I N D I A

J A M H U R I

M A Z I W E

M A R K E T

Pangani River

Ushongo, Saadani GR,
Emayani Beach Lodge,
The Beach Crab Resort,
The Tides, Tuia Beach Lodge

BWENI VILLAGE

253

Pangani has been cited by one historian as 'the Bagamoyo of the first eighteen centuries of the Christian era'. In a sense, this description is probably rather misleading. True, for much of the 19th century, Pangani was the main terminus for slave caravans heading to the Lake Victoria region, and probably the most important trading centre on the Tanzanian mainland after Bagamoyo and Kilwa Kivinje. But the town that now stands on the north bank of the Pangani River mouth is not particularly old, having been founded by Omani Arabs in the late 18th century and totally rebuilt in 1810 following a destructive flood.

It is possible, too, that the very name Pangani is of 19th century derivation – *panga* being a Swahili word for arrange, and Pangani the place where slaves from the interior were arranged into groups by their Arab captors. Other sources, however, suggest the name could be far older, alluding to the locally common *panga* shellfish or a type of boat known locally as *mtepe* but referred to by an English naval offer in 1608 as *pangaia*. Burton, meanwhile, translated Pangani as meaning 'in the hole'.

Pangani is a relatively modern settlement, possibly even a modern name, but it is equally true that the mouth and lower reaches of the Pangani River have played a major role in coastal trade for several centuries. Prior to the arrival of the Omani, the main settlement on the river mouth was Bweni, situated then, as it is now, on the southern bank facing the modern town. Prior to that, a larger trading post, Muhembo, was situated on Pangani Bay about 2km north of the present town. A local tradition dating Muhembo to the earliest Shirazi times is supported by the name of the oldest coconut plantation in the area, El Harth – also the name of the Arabic founding family who arrived at Pangani in AD900. Archaeological excavations at Muhembo suggest that, aside from its impressive ruined mosque, the town was less built up than, and probably politically subservient to, the contemporary town of Mtangata at modern-day Tongoni. Muhembo suffered heavily in 1588 at the hands of the cannibalistic Zimba, and was razed in a Portuguese punitive raid in 1635, after which it was evidently abandoned.

The most intriguing historical question surrounding the lower Pangani River is whether it was the site of the ancient trade settlement referred to in the 1st century *Periplus of the Erythraean Sea* and Ptolemy's 2nd-century *Geography* as Rhapta. The case for Pangani as Rhapta is compelling, if largely circumstantial. The anonymous author of the *Periplus* places Rhapta 'two days' sail' beyond a 'flat and wooded' island he calls Menouthesias,

---

Beach Resort exudes a faintly depressing aura of mildewed neglect. However, the beach is all you could ask for, & the spacious en-suite rooms with hot water & AC, though rather tatty & musty, are the cheapest on this stretch of coast. Inexpensive meals are also available. *US$20/40 sgl/dbl B&B.*

South of Pangani
Upmarket
⌂ **The Tides** [253 B4] (13 rooms) m 0784 225812/ 0713 325 812; e info@thetideslodge.com; www.thetideslodge.com. This popular beachfront lodge, owned by a friendly British couple, is among the finest on the north coast, set on a superb swimming beach in Ushongo, & noted for its excellent seafood. The laid-back atmosphere is complemented by a wide selection of activities including deep-sea & in-shore fishing (US$300 half day, max 4 people), snorkelling in Maziwe Marine Park (US$35 pp including fees, equipment & drinks), bicycle hire ($10 per day), kayaking in the mangrove-lined creeks nearby (a good place to see the localised mangrove kingfisher, beautiful malachite kingfisher & a host of waders & marine birds) & diving by arrangement for qualified divers. Rd transfers from Tanga, Pangani, Saadani, Dar es Salaam or Arusha can be arranged, as can boat transfers to Zanzibar. Accommodation is in large en-suite chalets with an airy, classical interior of stone floors & whitewashed walls. *US$238/262 pp HB/FB.*

⌂ **Emayani Beach Lodge** [253 B4] (12 rooms) \/f 027 254 4752 (Arusha) or 027 264 0755 (Pangani); e info@emayanilodge.com;

which itself lay 'slightly south of southwest after a voyage of two days and nights' from 'the Pyralaae Islands and the island called Diorux [the Channel]'. These vague directions lack any name that has survived into the modern era, and are open to interpretation, but they do seem to point to Menouthesias as either Pemba or Mafia Island, respectively making Pangani or the Rufiji Delta the most likely location of Rhapta.

Ptolemy's *Geography*, based on the firsthand and secondhand observations of three different sailors, talks of Rhapta as 'the metropolis of Barbaria, set back a little from the sea' on the river Rhapton, but – contradicting the *Periplus* – it places Menouthias Island (presumably the same as Menouthesias) as lying considerably further south. More intriguingly, based on information gathered by a Greek merchant called Diogenes, Ptolemy talks of two snow-capped peaks and two large lakes lying 25 days' trek up the river Rhapton. The Pangani River has its source near Moshi, at the base of snow-capped Kilimanjaro.

No trace of an appropriately ancient settlement has ever been found near Pangani, which would not be entirely surprising had Rhapta been situated upriver and lacked the permanent stone structures of later mediaeval ports. Several other possible locations for Rhapta have been suggested, including Ras Kimbiji near Dar es Salaam and more plausibly the Rufiji Delta, the latter so vast and labyrinthine that the remains of a 2,000-year-old settlement would be difficult to locate and might well be submerged. To further complicate the picture, many historians regard it as unlikely that Rhapta was the local name for a port, since it appears to derive from *ploiaria rhapta*, the Greek name for a type of boat which, coincidentally, was later referred to by an English navigator as *Pangaia*. Furthermore, given that these two ancient documents were written centuries apart, and appear to contradict each other on several details, there's every chance that the Rhapta of the *Periplus* is a totally different port to the Rhapta described by Ptolemy's sources.

Whatever the truth of the matter, it does seem certain that the Pangani River has long formed an important route for exploration of the interior, largely because it provides a reliable source of fresh water as far inland as Moshi. It almost certainly served as an important trade inland corridor for Mtangata and Muhembo in the Shirazi era, and could as easily have done so 2,000 years ago. Ptolemy's information about the Rhapton River and the African interior, flawed and confusing as it may have been, seems too close to the truth to be dismissed as mere coincidence.

www.emayanilodge.com. This intimate beachfront resort, constructed by the owners of Tarangire Safari Lodge, consists of a dozen airy chalets made entirely from organic material & spaced out along a long, deserted stretch of sandy beach at Ushongo. It's a great place just to chill out with a beach towel & novel, but with the well-run **Kasa Divers** (*www.kasadivers.com*) based at the lodge offering a range of activities from snorkelling, windsurfing, kayaking & fishing to PADI dive courses, there is plenty to keep more active visitors busy. The beach is good for swimming at high tide, while the exposed reefs & mudflats in front of the lodge offer decent snorkelling at low tide. Sea kayaks can be used to explore a mangrove-lined creek 1km north of the lodge, & wind-surfers & a catamaran are also available. Good value. *US$80 B&B, plus US$12 pp lunch or dinner.*

Moderate

⌂ **Tulia Beach Lodge** [253 B4] (15 rooms) \ 027 264 0680; e info@tuliabeachlodge.com; www.tuliabeachlodge.com. Formerly Ushonga Beach Resort, this is now under the same management as nearby Emayani. It's a comfortable, functional set-up with a great beachfront location, but the densely clustered buildings lack the ambience of its neighbour. The clean en-suite chalets with net & fan & small private veranda seem a little steeply priced too. The open-air restaurant serves decent grills & seafood starting at around US$6. All the same activities as Emanyani are offered through Kasa Divers. *US$45 pp B&B; camping US$10 pp.*

PANGANI IN 1857

The following edited extracts from Richard Burton's *Zanzibar and Two Months in East Africa*, originally published in 1858 in Blackwell's *Edinburgh Magazine* (vol 83), provide a vivid impression of Pangani in the mid 19th century, as well as its relationship with the kingdoms of the immediate interior:

Pangani… and its smaller neighbour Kumba, hug the left bank of the river, upon a strip of shore bounded by the sea, and a hill range 10 or 11 miles distant. Opposite are Bweni and Mzimo Pia, villages built under yellow sandstone bluffs, impenetrably covered with wild trees…. Pangani boasts of 19 or 20 stone houses. The remainder is a mass of cadjan huts, each with its wide mat-encircled yard, wherein all the business of life is transacted… Pangani, with the three other villages, may contain a total of 4,000 – Arabs, Muslim Swahili, and heathens. Of these, female slaves form a large proportion.

Pangani, I am told, exports annually 35,000lb of ivory, 1750lb of black rhinoceros horn, and 16lb of hippopotamus' teeth… Twenty Banyans manage the lucrative ivory trade… These merchants complain loudly of their pagazi, or porters, who receive 10 dollars for the journey, half paid down, the remainder upon return; and the proprietor congratulates himself if, after payment, only 15% run away. The Hindus' profits, however, must be enormous. I saw one man to whom 26,000 dollars were owed by the people. What part must interest and compound interest have played in making up such sum…? Their only drawback is the inveterate beggary of the people. Here the very princes are mendicants; and the Banyan dare not refuse the seventy or eighty savages who every evening besiege his door with cries for grain, butter, or a little oil…'

Coconuts… and plantains grow about the town. Around are gardens of paw-paws, betel, and jamlis; and somewhat further, lie extensive plantations of… maize… and other grains. The clove flourishes, and as elsewhere upon the coast a little cotton is cultivated for domestic use. Beasts are rare. Cows die after eating the grass; goats give no milk; and sheep are hardly procurable. But fish abounds. Poultry thrives, as it does all over Africa; and before the late feuds, clarified cow-butter, that 'one sauce' of the outer East, was cheap and well-flavoured…. The wells produce heavy and brackish drink; but who, as the people say, will take the trouble to fetch sweeter? The climate is said to be healthy in the dry season, but the long and severe rains are rich in fatal bilious remittents.'

The settlement is surrounded by a thorny jungle, which at times harbours a host of leopards. One of these beasts lately scaled the high terrace of our house, and seized upon a slave girl. Her master… who was sleeping by her side, gallantly caught up his sword, ran into the house, and bolted the door, heedless of the miserable cry, "Bwana, help me!" The wretch was carried to the jungle and devoured. The river is equally full of alligators [crocodiles], and whilst we were at Pangani a boy disappeared. When asked by strangers why they do not shoot their alligators, and burn their wood, the people reply that the former bring good-luck, and the latter is a fort to which they can fly in need.'

Pangani and Bweni, like all settlements upon this coast, belong, by a right of succession, to the [Sultan] of Zanzibar, who confirms and invests the governors and diwans. At Pangani, however, these officials are *par conge d'elire* selected by Kimweri [the king of Usambara], whose ancestors received tribute and allegiance from para to the seaboard. On the other hand, Bweni is in the territory of the Wazegura, a violent and turbulent heathen race, inveterate slave-dealers, and thoughtlessly allowed by the Arabs to lay up goodly stores of muskets, powder, and ball. Of course the two tribes [Usambara and Wazeregu] are deadly foes. Moreover, about a year ago, a violent intestine feud broke out amongst the Wazegura, who, at the time of our visit, were burning and murdering, kidnapping and slave-selling in all directions.

Budget

🏠 **The Beach Crab Resort** [253 B4] m 0784 543700; e info@thebeachcrab.com; www.thebeachcrab.com. The cheapest resort at Ushongo, this very laid-back spot is the kind of place you visit for a couple of days & end up staying for a couple of weeks – or at the very least try to come up with reasons to return. Around 1km past The Tides, it's the closest thing to a backpackers on the north coast. There are 6 permanent safari-style tents with shared showers, as well as more comfortable en-suite *bandas*. The large thatched-roof beachside bar & restaurant offers a set daily menu with most meals around US$4. There are also plenty of activities on offer including windsurfing, diving, snorkelling, mountain biking & beach volleyball. *En-suite bandas US$50/65 sgl/dbl B&B; safari tents US$16 B&B; camping US$3.50 pp.*

In Pangani
Budget

🏠 **Seaside Community Centre Hostel** [253 G2] (10 rooms) ☎ 027 630 318. Run by Catholic nuns, this new purpose-built hostel & conference centre surrounded by lovingly tended gardens is by far the best place to stay in Pangani. Despite its slightly institutional feel, it has clean, comfortable dbl rooms (all with twin beds, fans & nets), a campsite, & a huge thatched dining room with a fridge & basic cooking appliances for self-caterers. There's private access to a safe swimming beach. On the downside, it's located alongside the noisy Pangadeco nightclub. *Tsh20,000 dbl; camping Tsh5,000 per tent.*

Shoestring

🏠 **New River View Lodge** [252 D3] m 0784 530371. This long-serving guesthouse, set on the main waterfront road about 300m from where the buses stop, is the best of a dismal choice of cheap lodgings scattered around Pangani town. Though basic, it is quite clean with running water & electricity. A good variety of street food is available along the nearby waterfront in the evening. *Dbl with net Tsh4,000 with communal showers.*

🏠 **Stopover Guesthouse & Bar** [253 F3] (8 rooms) m 0712 999121. Across the road from the Pangadeco, this small guesthouse offers musty but clean en-suite dbls with nets & fan. It lies a 5–10min walk from the bus stop, but with the far more appealing & only slightly more expensive Seaside Community Centre Hostel just a stone's throw away, it's definitely a second choice. Basic meals are available at the bar which tends to get loud in the evenings, so try to get a room towards the back. *Tsh8,000 pp.*

OTHER PRACTICALITIES

Foreign exchange Cash and travellers' cheques can be exchanged at the National Microfinance Bank [252 B2], though a hefty commission is levied on the latter.

Internet A small internet café a block back from Safari Central Bar [252 C2] offers unreliable connections for Tsh500 per half hour.

ACTIVITIES AND EXCURSIONS FROM PANGANI

Pangani town tour Strongly Swahili in mood, Pangani has seen little development in recent decades, and several buildings dating to the 19th and early 20th century are still standing. Guided tours of the old town can be arranged through the tourist office, but it is equally possible to explore the town independently, following the walking tour described below.

The obvious place to start is the ferry jetty at the raised waterfront [252 B3], where an Omani trader erected a coral rag wall in 1810 after the town was destroyed by flooding. From here, walk a few metres up Spark Street, and to your left, surrounded by an open park-like area, stands the **Old Boma** [252 B2]. This rectangular two-storey building, the oldest in Pangani, was constructed in 1810 as the residence of the same wealthy Omani trader responsible for the waterfront wall. Legend has it that several slaves were buried alive under the pillars to ensure the building had strong foundations. The carved Zanzibar-style doors are

Pangani was the birthplace and home of Abushiri ibn Salim al-Harthi, the half-caste African–Arabic trader who masterminded the first and most successful indigenous uprising against German rule. On 20 September 1888, Abushiri's hastily assembled troops evicted the German East Africa Company from Pangani and several other minor German stations along the coast. On September 22, Abushiri personally led a force of 8,000 men in an assault on Bagamoyo, at that time the German capital, and days of intense fighting resulted in the destruction of much of the town before a German Marine detachment of 260 men deflected Abushiri's army. Nevertheless, by the end of the month, only Bagamoyo and Dar es Salaam remained fully under German control, while Kilwa Kivinje was under permanent siege.

In the face of this onslaught, the trading company appealed to its government for support. A ragbag army of 21 German officers, 40 NCOs and 1,000 African mercenaries assembled by the German commander Hermann von Wissmann recaptured a number of the ports following naval bombardments that drove the occupying forces away, but the spirit of revolt remained high. The naval force was able to further secure the coast by setting up a blockade preventing arms and equipment from reaching the rebels. In May 1889, the Germans attacked Abushiri's fort at Jahazi (also called Nzole), between Pangani and Bagamoyo. Using artillery fire, Wissmann drove the defenders back from the 2m-high fortifications, then led a charge in which more than 100 Arabs were killed and Jahazi was captured. Abushiri escaped, to launch a new series of mostly unsuccessful assaults assisted by Yao and Shambaa recruits.

Von Wissmann, realising he would not be able to wrest control of the hinterland while the revolution's leader remained at large, put a price of 10,000 rupees on Abushiri's head. This rich bounty persuaded a local chief who had been harbouring Abushiri to hand him over to the German commander. On 15 December 1889, Abushiri was taken to his hometown of Pangani, paraded through the streets clad in a skimpy loincloth, and hanged later the same day. The town bears no trace of the revolutionary's existence today.

thought to be the originals. The fortified roof is a later addition, dating to the early German era, when the building was appropriated to serve as an administrative centre (*boma*). The Old Boma has been maintained well: it was used as District Commissioner's Office in colonial times, and today houses an immigration office.

About 100m further west, behind the new telecommunications office, the **Former British Hospital** [252 A2] was built in 1918 as a 'native hospital' and subsequently served as a jail. A double-storey building with a creaky old balcony, it shows some Arabic influences in its architecture. It is currently a government office, but there is some talk of converting it to a resthouse. About 500m west of the hospital behind a football field stands several 17th-century **Portuguese graves** and 19th-century **German graves**, all quite difficult to locate in the dense bush.

Two significant adjacent buildings stand on the waterfront east of the ferry jetty. The older, built in the 1850s, is the castellated double-storey **Slave Depot** [252 C3], which supposedly opened into a subterranean tunnel through which slaves were taken to Bweni on the south bank. The building is derelict today, but the façade remains intact, and there is talk of restoring it as a tourist information centre and/or museum. The **German Customs House** [252 C3], constructed in the Hanseatic style with an impressive castellated front, is reminiscent of a fort or cathedral, though it served as the customs house since its construction in 1910 to the modern day. Inland of these buildings, **India Street**, the main shopping drag through Pangani, is lined with old Indian residences. Dating to the late 19th century, these are typically double-storey buildings with ornate iron balconies, and the ground floors are used as shops.

Bweni, on the south side of the Pangani River, predates the modern town by perhaps two centuries, though no significant historical relics can be seen there today. About 1km east of the ferry crossing at Bweni, however, stands the shell of a **German Fort** built in 1916 to repel British naval invasions. A further 1.5km along this stretch of coast, a tall **commemorative pillar** is dedicated to Christian Luutherborn, a Danish sisal estate director whose death in 1907 was probably linked to the Maji Maji Rebellion. Of greater antiquity is the Shirazi mosque at **Muhembo**, some 2km north of Pangani and accessible from the Tanga road. This mosque was larger than its counterpart in Mtangani, but is more poorly preserved possibly as a result of damage perpetrated in the Portuguese raid of 1635.

Pangani River Trip Boat trips up the forested Pangani River are of interest primarily for the scenery and birds such as the mangrove kingfisher, though some large mammals still occur in the area, most visibly vervet monkeys. In the wet season, you can boat upriver to the base of the Pangani Falls, now swallowed by a hydro-electric plant, though pools at the base harbour crocodiles and hippos. Boat trips can be arranged through any of the beach resorts at Ushongo. The tourist office in Pangani charges around US$80 (for one to four people) to arrange the boat, plus the guide and development fees.

Maziwe and Fungu Islands These two small offshore islands south of Pangani form the centrepieces of a recently proclaimed marine park. Maziwe was once regarded as the most important nesting site on the Tanzanian coast for sea turtles, but it has been abandoned since the 1980s due to erosion, which submerges the beach at high tide. Today, the main attraction is the snorkelling on the offshore reefs, where the usual host of colourful reef fish can be observed. It is important to time a visit so you arrive at low tide, when the snorkelling is best. Boat trips to the islands can be arranged through the resorts at Ushongo, which charge US$35 per person (US$120 for three or fewer people) to charter a large local dhow. The tourist office in Pangani arranges trips for TshUS$120 (one to six people) inclusive of gear but excluding the development fees of US$6 per person. A park entrance fee of Tsh1,000 is levied.

SAADANI NATIONAL PARK

Protected as a game reserve since 1969, Saadani is the only wildlife sanctuary in East Africa with an Indian Ocean beachfront, and – having been run by TANAPA since 2001 – was officially gazetted as a national park in 2006, when it was expanded from 200km² to its present area of 1,062km². Until recently, Saadani was among the most obscure conservation areas in East Africa, lacking for tourist facilities and heavily affected by poaching. However, a concerted clampdown on poaching and an attempt to integrate adjacent villages into the conservation effort, initiated by the Department of Wildlife with assistance from Germany's GTZ agency in 1998, has changed all that. Saadani cannot yet bear comparison to Tanzania's finest game reserves, but it is a thoroughly worthwhile retreat, offering the hedonistic pleasures of a perfect sandy beach with wildlife viewing activities such as guided bush walks, game drives, and boat trips up the Wami River. It is the closest game-viewing destination to Zanzibar, and the two are now connected by daily flights.

Industry and associated opportunities for formal employment are thin on the ground in Pangani, but the surrounding district is self-sufficient in food, thanks to its fertile soil and the rich bounty of the ocean. Cashew and sisal – the latter introduced by a German botanist in 1892 – form the region's main export crops, but Pangani is also known for its extensive coconut palm plantations. The coconut plantations around Pangani are significant employers (monthly salaries are equivalent to US$40), and also provide an estimated 50% of Tanzania's coconut yield!

Even on a casual stroll around Pangani, the ubiquity of coconuts is striking. Vendors selling young nuts provide travellers with a refreshing and nutritious alternative to bottled soft drinks. Near the harbour, you'll see large piles of drying husks, the debris of nuts shipped to other parts of the country. Women wander home from the market carrying their goods in palm fronds converted with a few deft strokes to disposable shopping baskets.

No part of the coconut palm goes unused. The flesh of the mature nut, harvested twice annually, is not only a popular snack, but also an important ingredient in Swahili cuisine, and a source of cooking oil. The fibrous husks surrounding the nut are twined to make rope and matting, or dried for fire fuel. Palm fronds form the basis of the makuti roofs characteristic of the Swahili coast, and are also used as brooms. The sap and flowers are brewed to make a popular local wine, and the timber is used for furniture. A multi-faceted resource indeed!

Set within the reserve, the fishing village of Saadani, with a population estimated at 1,000, briefly rivalled Bagamoyo in stature during the 19th century. Its growth was inhibited by a defensive wall, built to protect against the warring Wadoe and Wazigua clans, whose ongoing fighting also dissuaded caravans from passing through the Saadani hinterland. Saadani was briefly considered as a site for the London Missionary Society's first East African mission, but it was passed over in favour of Bagamoyo. A crumbling old German customs house and a clutch of late-19th-century German and British graves serve as reminders of those days.

FEES AND FURTHER INFORMATION Park entrance costs US$20 per person per 24 hours. The lodge – and effectively the park – is often forced to close over April and May when the black cotton soil roads tend to become waterlogged. Although dated, an excellent source of information about the park is *Saadani: An Introduction to Tanzania's Future 13th National Park* by Dr Rolf Baldus, Doreen Broska and Kirsten Röttcher. You can download it for free from www.wildlife-programme.gtz.de/wildlife/tourism_saadani.html.

GETTING THERE AND AWAY ZanAir (*www.zanair.com*) currently operates a daily flight between Zanzibar and the Saadani airstrip. Otherwise, air charters can be arranged through either of the lodges, as can road transfers from Dar es Salaam via Chalinze or boat transfers from Dar via Bagamoyo. For budget travellers, the best way to reach the park at present is the overnight package arranged by the tourist office in Pangani. This costs around US$185 per person all inclusive and involves overnighting at the TANAPA resthouse.

Coming from Dar es Salaam using a private vehicle or public transport, the shortest route (on paper) is the coastal road via Bagamoyo, but this has in fact been impassable for a decade, ever since the government ferry over the Wami River sank. There is some talk of a new ferry being installed, but until such time as that happens, the only viable route from the south is through Chalinze and Miono. This route, a drive of roughly four hours, entails following the main surfaced road towards Morogoro west out of Dar es Salaam for 105km to the junction town of Chalinze, then turning right along the Moshi road. After 50km, the Moshi road crosses a bridge over the Wami River, and 1.5km further a signpost to your right reads 'Tent With a View Safaris Saadani Game Reserve 58km'. Follow this road through Mandera, Miono (10km) and Mkange (27km), ignoring the signpost to your right for the WWF Forestry Centre (48km) and crossing a railway track (53km) until you reach the reserve entrance gate (58km). From the entrance gate, it's an 8km drive to Saadani village and a further 1km or so to the lodge. Parts of this road are *very* rough, and can only be attempted in a good 4x4. The road is sometimes impassable during April and May, so you are advised to ask about its current condition when you book. One very beat-up bus runs between Dar es Salaam's Ubungo station and Saadani daily (Tsh5,000). It would probably be a lot quicker to catch a fast bus heading in the direction of Moshi as far as the Miono junction, where you could hop on the Saadani bus or one of the occasional pick-up trucks that ply the route.

Coming from the north, the coastal road from Tanga through Pangani and Mkwaja is normally viable in a 4x4 vehicle, though it may become impassable after heavy rain. The drive from Pangani to Saadani generally takes about two hours. A daily bus connects Tanga to Mkwaja via Pangani (Tsh5,000), leaving Mkwaja at around 05.00 and Tanga at around 10.00, taking four hours in either direction. There is no public transport at all between Mkwaja and Saadani.

WHERE TO STAY
Upmarket
Saadani Safari Lodge (9 rooms) \/f 022 277 3294; m 0713 555678; e info@saadanilodge.com; www.saadanilodge.com. This small & intimate tented camp, which runs attractively along a palm-fringed beach about 1km north of Saadani village, has undergone a major facelift over the last couple of years, most notably with the addition of a swimming pool. Accommodation is in comfortable framed canvas tents with a *makuti* roof, en-suite facilities, solar electricity & twin or dbl bed, as well as a second netted bed on the balcony should you want to sleep outside. The open wooden bar & dining area is very peaceful, while a tree house overlooks a waterhole regularly visited by waterbuck, bushbuck, buffalo & various waterbirds – & very occasionally by lion & elephant. Activities include game drives, guided walks with a ranger, & boat trips on the river.

US$290/500 sgl/dbl FB inc 1 activity per day. Honeymoon rate US$300 pp (inc private candlelit dinner & wine).

Tent With A View (9 rooms) \ 022 211 0507; m 0713 323318; f 022 212 3812; e info@ saadani.com; www.saadani.com. This small camp lies along a pretty beach some 30km north of Saadani village near Mkwaja, an area regarded as the best in the park for elephant sightings. The camp consists of 9 standing tents on stilted wooden platforms spaced out in the coastal scrub immediately behind the beach. It offers a similar range of guided activities to Saadani Safari Lodge, while several short self-guided walking trails emanate from the camp, & you can canoe in the nearby Mafuwe Creek. US$275/390 sgl/dbl FB; US$385/590 full game package.

Budget
Saadani Resthouse (10 rooms) Though somewhat run-down, this government-run resthouse on the beach some 500m north of Saadani Safari Lodge is by far the most affordable option in the park. Bookings are seldom necessary & although camping is permitted, it costs the same as a room. US$30 pp.

Shoestring
Mwango Guesthouse Situated in the pretty & laid-back coastal village of Mkwaja, which lies off the Pangani road about 1km outside the national park boundary & 0km north of Tent With A View, this is a basic but clean guesthouse. Tsh2,000/3,000 sgl/dbl with net & fan.

WHAT TO SEE Inland of its 20km coastline, Saadani supports a park-like cover of open grassland interspersed with stands of acacia trees and knotted coastal thicket. Along the coast, palm-lined beaches are separated by extensive mangrove stands, while the major watercourses are fringed by lush riparian woodland. Game densities are highest in January–February and June–August, when the plains hold more water. At all times, you can be reasonably confident of encountering giraffe, buffalo, warthog, common waterbuck, reedbuck, hartebeest and wildebeest, along with troops of yellow baboon and vervet monkey. Something of a Saadani special, the red duiker is a diminutive and normally very shy antelope of coastal scrub and forest. Quite common, but less easily seen, are greater kudu and eland. Saadani also harbours a small population of Roosevelt's sable, an endangered race elsewhere found in the Selous Game Reserve and Kenya's Shimba Hills. The elephant population is on the increase, with herds of up to 30 being sighted with increasing frequency, and lion are also making a solid comeback. Leopard, spotted hyena and black-backed jackal are also around, along with the usual small nocturnal predators.

In addition to game drives, guided walks offer a good chance of seeing various antelope and representatives of Saadani's rich variety of woodland birds. Best of all are boat trips on the Wami River, which hosts several pods of hippo, as well as crocodiles and a good selection of marine and riverine birds including mangrove kingfisher, Pel's fishing owl and various herons, storks and waders. The beaches in and around Saadani form one of the last major breeding sites for green turtles on mainland Tanzania.

BAGAMOYO

Situated on a superb white beach some 70km north of Dar es Salaam, Bagamoyo ranks among the most historically compelling towns in East Africa, having flourished in the 19th century as the mainland terminus for the slave trade between Lake Tanganyika and Zanzibar. Despite its proximity to Dar es Salaam, Bagamoyo slid backwards in economic terms throughout most of the 20th century, and its beautiful setting and deep sense of history have never generated as much tourist interest as might be expected – incredibly, the only tourist accommodation here 15 years ago was the (now defunct) Badeco Beach Hotel.

Since them, a minor tourist boom has precipitated a flurry of beachfront hotel construction, and trade opportunities were further enhanced by the rehabilitation, *circa* 2002, of the once appalling road south to Dar es Salaam. Not only has this improved tourist access, but it has also led to Bagamoyo's emergence as a popular conference destination for businesses based in Dar es Salaam. Assuming that the long-mooted installation of a ferry on the Wami River ever goes ahead, this would also open up the coastal route north, ending Bagamoyo's current end-of-the-road status, with obvious advantages for locals and tourists alike. For the time being, however – although it probably offers little consolation to residents of the once prosperous town – the museum-like quality that makes Bagamoyo so absorbing is difficult to disentangle from its air of economic stagnation and physical disintegration.

HISTORY Bagamoyo Bay has long been an important centre of maritime trade. During the Shirazi era, the main centre of activity was Kaole, whose ruins lie 5km south of the modern town. Founded in the 12th century, Kaole enjoyed strong trade links with Kilwa, and prospered for the three centuries prior to the Portuguese occupation, when it fell into economic decline, eventually to be abandoned.

The modern town dates to the 18th century, and as the closest mainland port to Zanzibar, it formed the 19th-century coastal terminus for slave caravans from the Lake Tanganyika area. At the peak of the slave trade, approximately 50,000 captives arrived in Bagamoyo annually, chained neck-to-neck and hoarded in dingy dungeons before being shipped to Zanzibar. Ironically, Bagamoyo's trade links to the interior ensured that it became the springboard for the European exploration of the African interior, which in turn played a major role in ending the slave trade. Such Victorian luminaries as Burton, Speke, Grant, Stanley and Livingstone all passed through Bagamoyo at some point. Livingstone's graphic descriptions and outright condemnation of the trade he described as 'the open sore of the world' led to the Holy Ghost Fathers establishing Bagamoyo Mission in 1868. The newly founded mission ransomed as many slaves as it could afford to, and settled its purchases in a Christian Freedom Village on the outskirts of Bagamoyo. Fittingly, when Livingstone died in 1873, his preserved body was carried 1,600km by his porters to Bagamoyo Mission, before being shipped to Zanzibar (on the improbably named HMS *Vulture*) and eventually to England.

Between 1868 and 1873, the slave-based society of Bagamoyo town coexisted in uneasy proximity with the free society of the adjacent Catholic compound. This period was marked by a pair of disasters: first, the cholera epidemic of 1869, which claimed 25–30% of the townspeople's lives, then in 1872 a destructive hurricane that razed large parts of the town. In 1873, Bagamoyo suffered a third blow, when the Sultan of Zanzibar, reacting to British pressure, abolished the slave trade. Bagamoyo's main source of revenue was curtailed – or at least forced underground – and the already battered town entered a period of economic transition and physical reconstruction. Nevertheless, its established trade infrastructure and proximity to Zanzibar made Bagamoyo the obvious site for the first German headquarters in East Africa, established in 1888. Stanley, who returned to Bagamoyo in 1889 after three years' absence, was struck by how much the port town had grown in its first year of German occupation.

By 1890, Germany had realised Bagamoyo harbour was too shallow for long-term use, and opted to relocate the administration first to Tanga and then to Dar es Salaam. Bagamoyo remained an important regional centre for some years after this (the impressive State House was built in 1897) but its steady decline since 1900 is testified to by the near absence of large buildings in the town centre post-dating Omani and German times. In the 1890s, Bagamoyo's population was estimated at more than 10,000. By 1925, it had dropped below 5,000, and Bagamoyo had been reduced to little more than a glorified fishing village, with one of the highest unemployment rates in the country. Bagamoyo's fortunes have looked up somewhat over the last decade, propped up largely by a growth of tourism and in particular as a conference venue servicing nearby Dar es Salaam.

GETTING THERE AND AWAY The 70km road between Dar es Salaam and Bagamoyo is now surfaced in its entirety and the drive should take no longer than one hour, depending on how heavy the traffic is on the way out of Dar. Regular minibuses run between Mwenge, just north of Dar es Salaam on New Bagamoyo Road, and Bagamoyo taking around two hours and costing Tsh1,400. At present, no public transport or passable road of interest to tourists runs north from Bagamoyo.

TOURIST INFORMATION AND DAY TRIPS The helpful **Bagamoyo Institute of Tourism** [264 C6] (*Uhuru Rd;* ☏ 023 244 0155; m 0752 626541; ☉ 08.00–20.00 *daily*) arranges walking tours, trips to Kaole and other activities. All the beach resorts offer good advice and can also organise the same tours and activities. The Bagamoyo Friendship Society website (*www.bagamoyo.com*) is well worth a look.

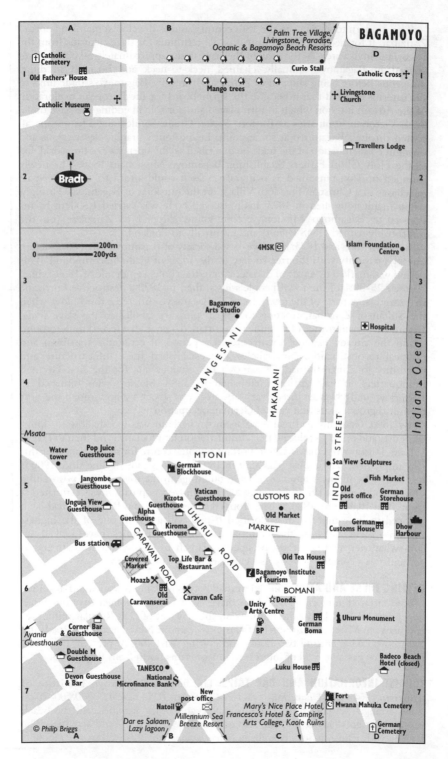

BAGAMOYO

Catholic Cemetery
Old Fathers' House
Catholic Museum

Palm Tree Village, Livingstone, Paradise, Oceanic & Bagamoyo Beach Resorts

Curio Stall
Mango trees

Catholic Cross
Livingstone Church

Travellers Lodge

Bradt

200m
200yds

4MSK

Islam Foundation Centre

Bagamoyo Arts Studio

Hospital

Indian Ocean

Msata

MANGESANI
MAKARANI
INDIA STREET

Water tower
Pop Juice Guesthouse
MTONI
German Blockhouse
Sea View Sculptures
Fish Market

Jangombe Guesthouse
Kizota Guesthouse
Vatican Guesthouse
CUSTOMS RD
Old post office
German Storehouse

Unguja View Guesthouse
Alpha Guesthouse
Old Market
Kiroma Guesthouse
MARKET
German Customs House
Dhow Harbour

Bus station
CARAVAN ROAD
UHURU ROAD

Covered Market
Top Life Bar & Restaurant
Old Tea House
Bagamoyo Institute of Tourism

Moazb
Old Caravanserai
Caravan Café
BOMANI
Donda
Unity Arts Centre
German Boma
Uhuru Monument

Ayania Guesthouse
Corner Bar & Guesthouse
BP

Double M Guesthouse

Badeco Beach Hotel (closed)

Devon Guesthouse & Bar
TANESCO
National Microfinance Bank
Luku House

New post office
Natoil
Fort
Mwana Mahuka Cemetery

© Philip Briggs
Dar es Salaam, Lazy lagoon
Millennium Sea Breeze Resort
Mary's Nice Place Hotel, Francesco's Hotel & Camping, Arts College, Kaole Ruins
German Cemetery

WHERE TO STAY AND EAT
Exclusive

Lazy Lagoon (10 rooms) \/f 022 286 2357;
UK 01452 862288; m 0784 237422;
e info@tanzaniasafaris.info;
www.tanzaniasafaris.info. This excellent resort, under
the same ownership as Ruaha River Lodge, is set on
the tip of a long spit on the Mbegani Lagoon
about 7km south of Bagamoyo. The beautiful,
isolated setting – it is to all intents & purposes an
island – is complemented by the uncluttered
accommodation, which consists of 10 en-suite
makuti beach chalets cut off from each other by
the thick coastal scrub. The seafood is excellent too,
with a speciality being beach dinners below a
sparkling night sky, & the lights of Bagamoyo
twinkling in the distance. The emphasis is very
much on chilling out at the beach or next to the
swimming pool, but there's decent snorkelling in the
coral shore close to the lodge & good walking
along the spit. Day trips to Bagamoyo, Kaole &
elsewhere can also be arranged. Coming from Dar
es Salaam, the turn-off to Lazy Lagoon lies about
7km before Bagamoyo & is signposted for the
Kasika Marine Camp. Follow the turn-off for about
2km to the fenced Mbegani Fisheries compound,
where you need to enter the gate & continue along
the road for another 500m to the landing jetty.
The boat transfer to the lodge takes about 20min
& should be arranged in advance. A more direct
7km road between the landing strip & Bagamoyo
runs close to the coast, passing through Kaole en
route. US$245/330 sgl/dbl FB, low-season discount
around 15%.

THE BURDEN OF BAGAMOYO

In a pattern repeated all along the East African coast, the modern town of Bagamoyo is essentially a 19th-century entity, constructed by Omani slave traders close to the ruins of a mediaeval Shirazi town (in this case Kaole) that fell into disuse during the Portuguese era. The name Bagamoyo, too, dates to the 19th century, and is clearly linked to the town's role in the iniquitous slave trade, though the precise meaning is debatable. A Victorian explorer claimed that Bagamoyo referred to the port's role as the gateway to the African interior. Today, it is more widely accepted to be a corruption of the phrase *bwaga moyo*, at least a dozen translations of which have been published, falling into two broad categories.

The first set of interpretations, variations on 'lose heart' or 'lay down my heart', would have the phrase as the refrain of a slave lament: although the captives were to be shipped from the African mainland, their hearts would be left behind, in Bagamoyo. The second is that the phrase translates as 'lay down the burden of your heart' or similar, and was coined by caravan porters for whom Bagamoyo afforded an opportunity to lay down their burden at the end of the arduous trek from the Lake Tanganyika hinterland. The traditional Swahili porter's song, displayed in the Catholic museum and loosely translated below, would certainly back up the second theory:

Be happy, my soul, release all cares, for we soon reach the place you yearn for
The town of palms, Bagamoyo!
When you were far away, how my heart ached when I thought of you, you pearl
You place of happiness, Bagamoyo!
The women wear their hair parted; you can drink palm wine all year through
In the gardens of love of Bagamoyo!
The dhows arrive with streaming sails to take aboard the treasures of Europe
In the harbour of Bagamoyo!
Oh, such delight to hear the drums and the lovely girls swaying in dance
All night through in Bagamoyo!
Be quiet, my heart, all cares are gone. Let the drumbeats rejoice:
We are reaching Bagamoyo!

Upmarket

Oceanic Beach Resort [264 D1] (98 rooms)
023 244 0181/3; m 0744 000197; f 023 244
0196; e info@oceanicbay.com; www.oceanicbay.com.
The newest resort in Bagamoyo, this conference-
oriented set-up consists of several 2-storey blocks
offering accommodation in large but rather bland
en-suite rooms with AC, DSTV, fridge & private
balcony. Facilities & services include 2 good
restaurants, a swimming pool, business centre, direct
beach access & AC shuttle to Dar es Salaam airport.
US$96/126/162 sgl/dbl/trpl B&B.

Livingstone Club [264 D1] (40 rooms) 023
2440059/80; f 023 2440104; e info@
livingstone.ws; www.livingstone.ws. Distinguished by the
imaginative & impressive use of traditional Swahili
elements in the architecture & décor, the Livingstone
Club is a top-quality beach hotel 600m north of the
town centre, past the turn-off to the old mission.
Centred around a great swimming pool area
overlooking the beach, the hotel has all the facilities
you would expect as well as an internet café &
Italian-style coffee bar. A good range of activities, also
on offer to non-residents, & generally with a minimum
group size of 4, includes snorkelling & diving
excursions, boat trips to the Ruvu Delta, guided town
walks & mountain bike excursions. *US$90/114/132
sgl/dbl/trpl B&B in spacious semi-suites.*

Paradise Holiday Resort [264 D1] (95 rooms)
023 244 0000/0030/0111; f 023 244 0142;
e reservations@paradiseresort.net;
www.paradiseresort.net. On the beach some 400m
past the junction to the old mission, the blandly
plush Paradise Holiday Resort has comfortable en-
suite rooms with large dbl beds, nets, satellite TV, AC
& private balcony. It has a great beach & swimming
pool area, a good seafood restaurant, & offers a
wide range of activities from table tennis & beach
volleyball to scuba diving & game fishing.
Characterless as its name would suggest, it is good
value & difficult to flaw, without being anything to
get excited about. *US$90/110 sgl/dbl.*

Millennium Sea Breeze Resort [264 B7] (32
rooms) 023 244 0201/3; f 023 244 0204;
e reservation@millennium.co.tz;
www.millennium.co.tz. This recently expanded lodge,
set on the beachfront south of the town centre, is
an attractive set-up from the outside, with a great
beach, swimming pool area & *makuti* restaurant.
The rooms come with the usual facilities – AC,
DSTV & fridge. Older rooms are rather cramped &
gloomy, & feel like poor value, but the spacious
newer rooms are much more appealing. *US$78/102
sgl/dbl B&B; US$72/96 for older rooms.*

Moderate

Travellers Lodge [264 D2] (26 rooms) 023
244 0077; m 0754 855485; f 023 244 0154;
e travellers@baganet.com; www.travellers-lodge.com.
A good choice in this range, the German-owned
Travellers Lodge is set in large green grounds that
sprawl down to an attractive beach on the edge of
the town centre. Accommodation is in spacious,
simply decorated en-suite cottages with large beds,
netting, AC & private balcony. A good restaurant &
bar are attached. *Garden cottage US$45/65 sgl/dbl
B&B; beach cottage US$60/80; camping US$8 pp.*

Palm Tree Village [264 D1] (43 rooms) 023
244 0245; m 0756 878695; f 023 244 0246;
e reservations@palmtreevillage.com;
www.palmtreevillage.com. Out of town about 200m
past the Livingstone Club, Palm Tree Village is a
decent, sensibly priced, somewhat characterless set-up
with the usual good beach & alluring swimming

pool. En-suite rooms in the whitewashed chalets; all
rooms have DSTV & AC. Good value. There are also
double en-suite flats in a newer & smarter (but to
my mind less attractive) 2-storey block. *US$40/55
sgl/dbl B&B; flats US$45/65.*

Bagamoyo Beach Resort [264 D1] (18 rooms)
023 2440083; m 0754 588969; f 023
2440154; e bbr@baganet.com. This refreshingly
unpretentious & perennially popular resort has en-
suite rooms with AC, & budget beach huts with
natural ventilation. It is situated on an attractive
beach between the junction for the old mission &
the Paradise Holiday Resort. The menu, with most
items at around US$5, reflects the nationality of its
French owners. A variety of watersport activities &
other excursions are on offer. *US$42/52/62
sgl/dbl/trpl B&B; beach huts US$12 pp.*

Budget

Mary's Nice Place Hotel [264 D7] 023 244
0133; m 0754 336229; e info@
maryniceplacehotel.com; www.maryniceplacehotel.com.

'Nice' is a little trumped up for the overpriced,
bland rooms on offer, but nonetheless this new hotel
in a converted old house just off the main road

Caravan trade in Bagamoyo was of little importance. The old caravanserai below the station has been evacuated; it will no longer be used, for hygienic reasons. A new location has been chosen to lodge the caravans, further above the station, within the palms. While slave trade in general can be regarded as suppressed, in singular cases, men deep-rooted in the slave trade try to catch free men and ship them from smaller coastal places in the vicinity of Bagamoyo. A certain Ibrahim, who has been arrested for slave trade last year, but who had succeeded in escaping from the prison, was again brought in by natives a few weeks ago, as, with a few aides, he had ambushed free men, killed some, captured the others and sold them as slaves. As his crimes were proven by numerous witness reports, he was hung on September 23rd.

Extracted from a report by the Deputy Commissioner of German East Africa, September 1890

past the Arts College is a friendly choice, & the clean en-suite rooms have fan, nets, AC & TV. Meals are available with notice. *Tsh25,000/30,000/35,000 sgl/dbl/trpl B&B.*
⌂ **Francesco's Hotel & Camping** [264 D7] (13 rooms) m 0784 819221; e mbese2001@gmail.com; www.francescoshotel.com.

Shoestring
⌂ **Double M Guesthouse** [264 A7] m 0762 186836. Among the best of a dozen or more generally squalid guesthouses scattered around Bagamoyo, the Double M lies about 500m from the bus station & has reasonably priced en-suite rooms with net, fan & three-quarter bed. The Devon Bar

About 50m past Mary's, this newly opened hotel-come-backpacker hostel is a much better budget option. Set on a large green compound just 3km from the Kaole Ruins, it has clean, no-frills en-suite dbls with net & fan, & camping with access to clean facilities. There's also a small restaurant & curio store. *US$15 dbl; camping US$5 pp.*

50m away is a good spot for a mellow drink below a *makuti* roof. *Tsh10,000/20,000 sgl/dbl.*
⌂ **Pop Juice Guesthouse** [264 A5] m 0784 595112. This clean & quiet guesthouse also stands out from the pack. *Tsh6,000 en-suite dbl, Tsh4,000 dbl with common shower.*

OTHER PRACTICALITIES
Foreign exchange Aside from the beach hotels, which will only change money for hotel residents, and then generally at poor rates, the only foreign exchange service is at the National Microfinance Bank on the Dar es Salaam road opposite the new post office [264 B7].

Internet The internet cafés at the Paradise Holiday Resort [264 D1] and Livingstone Club [264 D1] are open to all-comers, but the rates are high by local standards. Far cheaper is the MSK Internet Café near the junction of Mangesani and India streets [264 C3], or the Arts College [264 D7], but both are rather slow and sometimes attract long queues. There's also an internet café at the Bagamoyo Institute of Tourism [264 C6].

Swimming The entire waterfront of Bagamoyo amounts to one long swimming beach, though wandering around public parts of the beach in swimming trunks or bikini probably wouldn't be appreciated. Better to swim from one of the resorts.

ACTIVITIES AND EXCURSIONS
Town walking tour The old town of Bagamoyo warrants a good half-day's exploration. Local guides can be arranged at any of the beach hotels, or you can

wander around independently. A good first port of call is the **Holy Ghost Mission**, which lies on the outskirts of town, along a mango-lined avenue planted by the missionaries in 1871. Within the mission grounds, the superb **Catholic Museum** [264 A1] (⊕ *10.00–17.00; entrance Tsh1,500; camera/video fee Tsh1,000/ 5,000*) stands in the double-storey Sisters' House, built in 1876. The museum provides a good overview of the history of Bagamoyo and Kaole, and sells an extensive selection of books and booklets about Bagamoyo past and present.

Also within the mission grounds, the **original Holy Ghost Church**, built in 1872, is reputedly the oldest church on the East African mainland. Opposite, the wide-balconied three-storey **Old Fathers' House** [264 A1] is a fine though somewhat deteriorated example of a style of pre-colonial mission architecture more normally associated with west Africa. In front of it stands the **New Holy Ghost Church**, constructed shortly before World War I and more imposing than its predecessor. A few hundred metres past the main mission buildings is the **cemetery** [264 A1] where the early missionaries are buried, and a **grotto** built in 1876 by the emancipated slaves living in the mission grounds. Several of the exotic trees in the wooded grounds were the first of their type to be planted in Tanzania.

Returning to town from the mission, follow the mango-lined avenue to the junction with Ocean Road. The unimposing tin-roofed **Livingstone Church** [264 D1] on the right side of the intersection is where, in 1874, Livingstone's sun-dried body, after an initial night in the Holy Ghost Mission, was interred before it was shipped to Zanzibar. On the seafront, about 200m behind this church, a green marble monument and cross, erected in the 1870s and replanted in 1993, marks the spot where Father Horner landed in 1868 to establish the Holy Ghost Mission.

From the Anglican church, you can follow Ocean Road southwards until it becomes India Street, the main thoroughfare through **Dunda**, the old stone town of Bagamoyo. Dunda, which houses most of the town's old buildings and administrative offices, has changed little in shape since the late 19th century. It also retains a singularly Swahili atmosphere, and a tangible sense of community exists among its estimated 1,000 residents. At the junction of India Street and Customs Road, the **old post office** [264 D5] was the first to be established on the Tanzania mainland and it was used until as recently as 1995. Opposite the old post office is one of the oldest and most ornate of several carved **Zanzibar doors** that decorate the façades of India Street. From the intersection with India Street, Customs Road leads down to the main port, still dominated by the **German Customs House** [264 D5] built in 1895, opposite which stand the remains of a **German storehouse** [264 D5] built in 1888. The old beachfront **slave market** [264 D5] is today a fish market; the white sands in front of it are lined with picturesque fishing dhows and scuttled across by legions of ghostly white crabs at dusk.

Continuing south for a few hundred metres, India Street runs past a trio of noteworthy buildings. First up is the former **Bagamoyo Tea House** [264 C6], which possibly predates the German occupation, and has authentic carved Zanzibar doors. Next door, the dilapidated **German Boma** [264 C6], built in 1897 as the regional headquarters, is an impressive two-storey building with a fortified roof, but in urgent need of restoration. Opposite the Boma, in front of an abandoned bandstand, stands the **Uhuru Monument** [264 D6] celebrating Tanzania's independence in 1961, together with a plaque commemorating Burton and Speke's departure from Bagamoyo on their expedition to Lake Tanganyika and Victoria. The third building of note, **Luku House** [264 C7], is a pre-colonial two-storey construction appropriated to serve as Germany's first East Africa headquarters from 1888 to 1891 (see box, *The Emin Pasha's fall*, page 270).

A short distance south of this, at the junction for the Badeco Beach Hotel, stands the **Old Fort** [264 D7], which incorporates the oldest extant house in Bagamoyo.

The fort was built by an Arab trader in 1860 as a slave prison – a subterranean passage leads to a landing point where slaves were herded to dhows on the shore – and fortified by the Sultan of Zanzibar *circa* 1880. A fortified garrison in German times, and later a police post, it now houses the Department of Antiquities.

Nearby, in the grounds of the defunct Badeco Beach Hotel, a plaque identifies the **hanging tree** where the Germans dispatched any African considered insufficiently sympathetic to their rule. Immediately south of the Old Fort and Badeco Beach Hotel, the Muslim **Mwana Mahuka Cemetery** [264 D7] houses the oldest tomb in Bagamoyo, dating to 1793, while the **German Cemetery** [264 D7] is the last resting place for 20 German soldiers who died in the late 19th century. Further south, perhaps 100m along the Kaole Road, the **Bagamoyo College of Arts** or **Chuo Cha Sanaa** [264 D7] is a striking example of modern architecture constructed entirely from traditional materials. At weekends, students often stage local plays or put on a show of traditional music, dancing and mime.

Northwest of the Old Fort along Caravan Road, the relatively modern settlement of **Magomeni** is home to more than 95% of Bagamoyo's population. The bustling market and bus station are situated alongside each other here, as are numerous local guesthouses, but the only historical buildings are the **Old Caravanserai** [264 B6] and **German Blockhouse**. The Caravanserai, situated close to the modern bus station, is where caravan parties assembled and stocked up before trekking into the interior. In its prime, it comprised an open central courtyard surrounded by low-rise market stalls and shops – not dissimilar, in fact, from many modern bus terminals in Tanzania – and it is currently being restored as a museum and information centre. Far better preserved is the German Blockhouse (also known as Dunda Tower), a circular coral rag structure built by Von Wissman to protect Bagamoyo against the Abushiri rebellion of 1889.

Kaole Ruins On the outskirts of Kaole village, 5km south of Bagamoyo, stand the brooding ruins of the urban precursor to modern Bagamoyo, a relatively minor but wealthy trading settlement that peaked in prosperity at about the same time as Kilwa Kisiwani and Mtangata (Tongoni). The main ruins consist of one large mosque with a well preserved outer staircase and ornate engraved *mihrab*,

The North Coast BAGAMOYO

9

SECURITY IN BAGAMOYO

An unfortunate truism of travel in the developing world is that once a particular place has acquired a reputation for crime, no matter how flimsy or dated the basis, it tends to be stuck with the tag. Bagamoyo is a case in point. The town has never shaken off a reputation for armed muggings it acquired in the late 1980s, but this particular writer has heard of no specific incident in the last two decades to substantiate the legend. Back then, some local sources claimed that Bagamoyo's reputation stemmed from one isolated incident, the violent rape of a traveller, which has little or no bearing on safety in Bagamoyo today. Others – admittedly local guides, with a vested interest in propagating the legend – reckoned that walking without a guide along the avenue to the old mission or the road to Kaole was tantamount to inviting an attack.

Is Bagamoyo any more or less crime-ridden than, say, Tanga or Pangani? The honest answer: I have no idea! It has the reputation, for which reason I've always erred on the side of caution, and would advise readers to do the same. Should you disregard this advice, however, then do at least ensure you leave all valuables, cameras and extra money locked up safely at your hotel. Finally, whatever risks might be attached to wandering out of town, I've never heard anything to suggest a security problem in central Bagamoyo.

surrounded by a cemetery of 22 graves including four tall pillar tombs that stand up to 7m high. Close to the mosque stand a footbath and well, the latter still containing water. Some 300m away, a second mosque and a building of unknown purpose stand in total isolation.

Surprisingly little is known about mediaeval Kaole. No reference survives in the chronicles of the Shirazi or early Portuguese era, and it is highly unlikely it was called Kaole – or Bagamoyo, for that matter – in its commercial heyday. Even the dating of the ruins is controversial. The main mosque displays features consistent with 7th century construction, which would make it the oldest surviving mosque on the East African mainland, but the 12th or 13th century seems more probable. Based on its humpback topography and the absence of secular buildings, it has been suggested that Kaole was not a town but a religious retreat set on a holy offshore highland.

Kaole was abandoned in the 16th century, presumably due to the intervention of the Portuguese or the appetite of the Zimba. It enjoyed a revival as a military and administrative centre for the Sultan of Zanzibar in the late 18th century, though the actual ruins bear little trace of this resettlement. By the early 19th century, the main centre of trade had relocated to Bagamoyo, whose larger harbour could hold a greater number of ships, while Kaole's had become increasingly clogged by mangrove swamps.

While the major buildings at Kaole don't stand comparison to the splendid architecture of Kilwa – or even the Gedi Ruins in Kenya – the decorated tombs are perhaps the best preserved on the Swahili coast. A better reason to visit, perhaps, is the aura of mystery that surrounds the ruins: crumbling relics of an undocumented centre of international trade, one that must have flourished for three centuries or longer – a powerful physical reminder of Africa's forgotten past.

With a private vehicle, Kaole can be reached by following the coastal road south out of Bagamoyo, past the Art College, for 5km. In Kaole village, a signposted 600m turn-off leads to the ruins (⊕ *08.00–16.00 w/day, 08.00–17.00 w/end; entrance Tsh1,500*). Unfortunately, no *dala-dalas* head out this way, so the options are walking (about an hour each way), cycling (ask your hotel to arrange a bike) or hanging around the junction to wait for a lift with one of the very occasional pick-up trucks that run along this road. If you're walking or cycling, leave all valuables and extra cash behind.

THE EMIN PASHA'S FALL

In 1889, the renowned explorer Henry Stanley marched into Bagamoyo at the end of a three-year trek across Africa that had seen his original party of 700 reduced to less than 200. With him was the Emin Pasha, the German-born governor of Equatoria Province (then nominally part of Egypt, now part of southern Sudan), who against all odds had managed to defend his isolated territory against the Mahdist onslaught for three years following the fall of Khartoum in 1885. The German garrison at Bagamoyo, then at the height of the Abushiri Rebellion, must have embraced any excuse for a bit of festivity. Stanley and the Emin Pasha were welcomed with open arms – and a stockpile of open bottles – culminating in a wild party at the headquarters in present-day Luku House. The festivities ended in tragedy, as the Emin Pasha – presumably drunk at the time, and certainly short-sighted at the best of times – celebrated his safe return from the trials of Equatoria and a trans-Africa march with a fall from the balcony of Luku House to the street below. Scheduled to sail to Zanzibar with Stanley the next day, the Governor of Equatoria instead spent the next six weeks in the Holy Ghost Mission hospital recuperating from head injuries. The offending balcony, still present in 1992, appears to have been removed during the subsequent restoration of Luku House.

10

Dar es Salaam

Tanzania's largest city, Dar es Salaam is also the country's *ipso facto* commercial and social capital, a lively, bustling Indian Ocean port whose regional maritime significance is rivalled only by Mombasa (Kenya). Often abbreviated to 'Dar', this city of 2.5 million people has a relatively low tourist profile, thanks to the ease with which fly-in visitors can pass through its international airport without setting foot in the city itself. Whether or not this is a good thing is a matter of opinion. Dar es Salaam often draws extreme reactions from travellers, a real 'love it or hate it' kind of place, and many would regard a Dar-free itinerary to be a desirable state of affairs.

Others would characterise Dar as East Africa's most likeable city, with a distinct sense of place derived from the cultural mix of its people and buildings, and the torpid coastal humidity that permeates every aspect of daily life. Architecturally, elements of German, British, Asian and Arab influence are visible, but this is fundamentally a Swahili city, and beneath the superficial air of hustle, a laid-back and friendly place. Except in the vicinity of the New Africa Hotel (where a resident brigade of hissing money-changers froths into action every time a *mazungu* walks past), people are willing to pass away the time with idle chat and will readily help out strangers, yet tourists are rarely hassled.

HISTORY

Dar es Salaam is, by coastal standards, a modern city, founded in the 1860s by Sultan Majid of Zanzibar, close to a then insignificant fishing village called Mzizima (on the site of present-day Ocean Road Hospital). The city's name dates to Majid's tenancy and is usually cited as an abbreviation of Bandari Salaam (Haven of Peace), reflecting the sultan's great love of the site. More likely, however, that it is a corruption of Dari Salaam (House of Peace), the name Majid gave his palace in reference to nearby Mzizima, which means healthy or tranquil place in the local dialect.

BEFORE MAJID Prior to 1862, Mzizima was a typical coastal fishing village, ruled by small-time self-styled Sultans of the Shomvi and Pazi clans with a peripheral interest in the coastal trade. The only evidence of mediaeval maritime trade out of Dar es Salaam harbour is a quantity of 13th century Chinese pottery unearthed at Kivukoni, near the present-day ferry terminal. The absence of structural ruins or more modern artefacts indicates that this site was abandoned before the 14th century, when stone buildings became the vogue on the coast. Otherwise, the area's most important pre-1860s ports, respectively about 30km north and 15km south of the modern city, were Kunduchi and Mbwamaji, both of which house the remains of Shirazi mosques and Omani pillar tombs.

Modern writers sometimes treat it as an oversight on the part of the Shirazi and Portuguese that Dar es Salaam, with its fine harbour, stood alone among modern

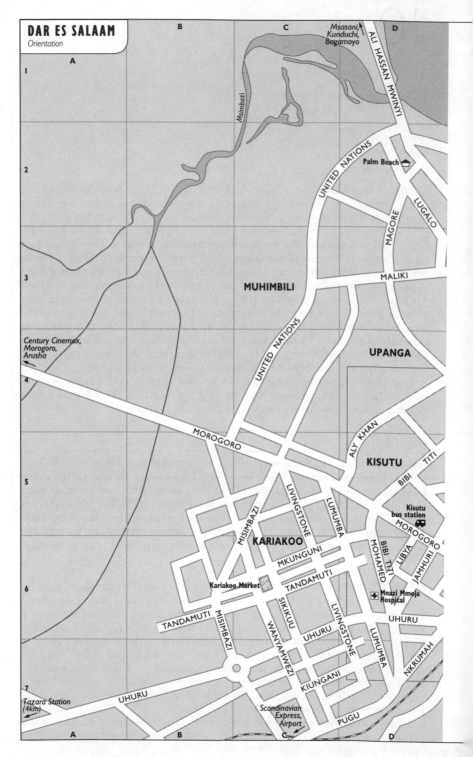

DAR ES SALAAM
Orientation

Msasani,
Kunduchi,
Bagamoyo

ALI HASSAN MWINYI

Msimbazi

Palm Beach

UNITED NATIONS

MAGORE

LUGALO

MALIKI

MUHIMBILI

UNITED NATIONS

UPANGA

Century Cinemax,
Morogoro,
Arusha

MOROGORO

ALY KHAN

KISUTU

TITI

BIBI

Kisutu
bus station

MOROGORO

MISIMBAZI

LIVINGSTONE

LUMUMBA

BIBI TITI
MOHAMED

LIBYA

JAMHURI

KARIAKOO

MKUNGUNI

TANDAMUTI

Kariakoo Market

Mnazi Mmoja
Hospital

UHURU

TANDAMUTI

MISIMBAZI

SIKIKUU

WANYAMWEZI

UHURU

LIVINGSTONE

LUMUMBA

NKRUMAH

KIUNGANI

Tazara Station
(4km)

UHURU

Scandinavian
Express,
Airport

PUGU

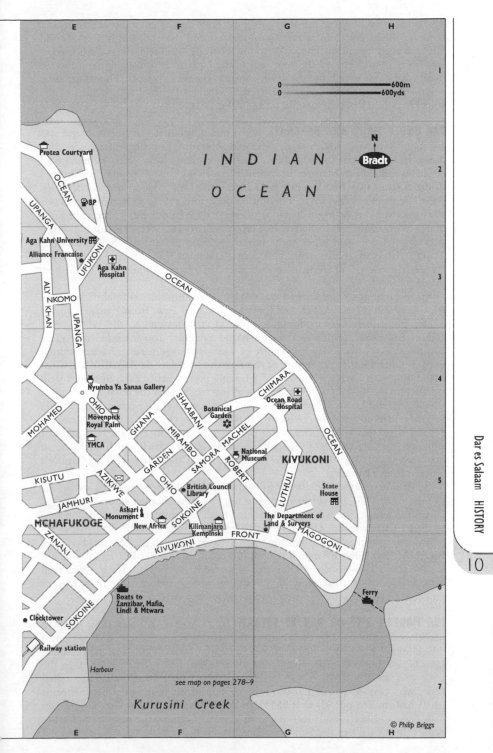

INDIAN

OCEAN

Protea Courtyard

OCEAN

UPANGA

BP

Aga Kahn University
Alliance Francaise

UFUKONI

Aga Kahn
Hospital

OCEAN

ALY KHAN

NKOMO

UPANGA

MOHAMED

Nyumba Ya Sanaa Gallery

OHIO

Mövenpick
Royal Palm

YMCA

GHANA

SHAABANI

MIRAMBO

GARDEN

Botanical
Garden

SAMORA MACHEL

CHIMARA

Ocean Road
Hospital

OCEAN

KISUTU

AZIKIWE

OHIO

ROBERT

National
Museum

KIVUKONI

LUTHULI

State
House

JAMHURI

Askari
Monument

SOKOINE

British Council
Library

MCHAFUKOGE

ZANAKI

New Africa

Kilimanjaro
Kempinski

FRONT

The Department of
Land & Surveys

MAGOGONI

KIVUKONI

SOKOINE

Clocktower

Railway station

Boats to
Zanzibar, Mafia,
Lindi & Mtwara

Ferry

Harbour

see map on pages 278–9

Kurusini Creek

© Philip Briggs

273

Tanzanian ports in being unused during the great eras of coastal trade. In reality, however, the harbour's main assets to modern ships – its depth and shelter – would not have been significant advantages to the relatively small seafaring vessels used in earlier eras. Furthermore, the approach to the harbour is unusually hazardous to small ships, as noted by the 19th-century explorer Joseph Thomson, who described it as 'a narrow, zigzag dangerous channel [where] a false turn of the wheel or a mistaken order would bring [a ship] to grief'.

DAR UNDER MAJID AND BARGHASH Local tradition has it that Sultan Majid was encouraged to visit Mzizima by Said bin Abdullah, the illegitimate son of a prominent Zanzibari merchant and a high-ranking local Pazi woman. Said originally sailed from Mzizima to Zanzibar to seek the sultan's counsel with regard to the unpunished murder of a local merchant's son. Majid, impressed by his guest's description, decided to join him on the return voyage to Mzizima, and was so enamoured that he immediately arranged to lease land there. Three years later, Majid returned with a small garrison and several artisans, and set about building a palace, hotel, fort and other stone buildings along present-day Sokoine Drive. Majid's new capital officially opened in September 1867, when the English, French, American and German consuls attended a large banquet held in the new palace.

Majid's relocation to Mzizima was not quite so whimsical as folklore suggests. It is likely that the sultan believed moving his capital away from Zanzibar would reduce his vulnerability to domestic political intrigues and to the influence of various European consuls sited there. Majid evidently also intended to replace Bagamoyo as the main mainland centre of trade opposite Zanzibar. A letter written in November 1866 by Dr Seward of the British Consulate on Zanzibar notes that Majid 'hopes to form the nucleus of a trading port, whence caravan routes shall radiate into the interior, and which bye and bye roads along the coast may connect with Kilwa and Lamu'. One factor in this decision might have been that Dar es Salaam's harbour was more suitable to large European ships than Bagamoyo. Seward noted that 'the capacity of this new port for shipping is of the best' and that although 'the narrowness of the leading channel is a drawback which only a steam tug can countervail... this want has been anticipated and a powerful tug has been ordered from Hamburg'.

We shall never know whether Majid would have realised his grand plans for Dar es Salaam. In 1870, the sultan slipped in his new palace, broke several bones and punctured a lung, and was hastily taken for medical treatment to Zanzibar, where he died a few days later. His successor Barghash decided to retain Zanzibar as his capital and to stick with the existing trade network through the mainland ports of Bagamoyo and Kilwa Kivinje. Barghash did retain an agent at Dar es Salaam, and his abode – a two-storey building that still stands on Sokoine Road – was well maintained, but the palace and other buildings were abandoned. By 1873, Majid's capital had become something approaching a ghost town.

THE MODERN RISE OF DAR ES SALAAM In 1877, the anti-slaver Sir William Mackinnon proposed Dar es Salaam as the starting point for the construction of 'Mackinnon's Road', intended to encourage legitimate trade between the coast and Lake Nyasa, but eventually abandoned after 112km had been completed. In the same year, a GEAC station was established there under an administrator called Leue, who penned a brief but vivid description of his posting: 'a town of ruins [that] had sunk as quickly as it had risen under Majid... Streets were overgrown with grass and bush [and] teeming with snakes, scorpions, centipedes and other pests... In the halls of the Sultan's palace lived bats... part of the palace was used as a gaol and... where once the harem ladies' tender feet had trodden, now clanked the prisoners' chains'.

Ironically, it would be the German colonists who revived and realised Majid's grand plans for Dar es Salaam. Four years after Leue first set foot there, the 'town of ruins' replaced Tanga as capital of German East Africa. Between 1893 and 1899 several departments of the colonial government were established there, along with a Roman Catholic cathedral in 1898. The arrival of the central railway consolidated Dar es Salaam's position; by 1914, when the line was completed, Dar was the country's most significant harbour and trading centre. After World War I, when German East Africa became Tanganyika, Dar es Salaam remained the capital, and its importance has never been challenged – although the national capital is now Dodoma, Dar remains the country's economic hub, with a population that has increased from about 1,000 people in 1867 to 20,000 in 1900, 270,000 in 1967, and 2.5 million today.

Along with the rest of Tanzania, Dar es Salaam slumped to an economic nadir during the socialist 1970s. By the early 1980s, its streets were acneous with pot-holes, shops had long given up the pretence of having anything to sell, water ran for about an hour on a good day, and 'tourist traffic' was limited to the occasional overland traveller crossing between eastern and southern Africa. Since then, the city has staged a remarkable recovery. True, many of its buildings could use a scrub and a whitewash, and poverty remains as rife as in any large African city. But the overall impression on visiting Dar today is that of a modern, vibrant city: smoothly surfaced streets, pavements spilling over with pedlars and colourful informal markets, well-stocked shops, an increasing number of smart high-rise buildings, and water and electricity supplies as reliable as you could hope for.

GETTING THERE AND AWAY

Dar es Salaam has good local and international transport links. Details of transport to other parts of the country are given throughout this guide, under the relevant town or area, but a brief overview follows.

BY AIR There are air links between Dar es Salaam and many African and European cities, and domestic flights to most large Tanzanian towns. For further details see the *Getting there and away* and *Getting around* sections in *Chapter 3, Practical information*. International and domestic airlines represented in Dar es Salaam are listed below.

The Julius K Nyerere International Airport lies 13km from the city centre, a 20–40 minute taxi ride that costs Tsh15,000–20,000, depending on how hard you bargain. Numerous *dala-dalas* ply the main road outside the airport travelling to and from the centre of town. The best is the one marked 'Posta' which stops at the main post office in the centre of town. However, you might think twice about exposing all your valuables in this way, as *dala-dalas* are notoriously overcrowded and have a reputation for pickpockets.

✈ **Air India** Opp Peugeot Hse, Ali H Mwinyi; ☏ 022 215 2642/3. To/from Mumbai 3 times weekly

✈ **Air Tanzania** [279 F3] ATC Bldg, Ohio St; ☏ 022 211 8411/2. To/from Johannesburg daily, to/from Entebbe 3 times weekly, to/from Nairobi 4 times weekly.

✈ **British Airways** [273 E4 & 279 E2] Mövenpick Royal Palm, Ohio St; ☏ 022 211 3820/2. To/from London 3 times weekly.

✈ **Egypt Air** [279 E2] Matasalamat Bldg, Samora Machel Av; ☏ 022 211 3333. No flights at present.

✈ **Ethiopian Air** [279 E2] TDFL Bldg, Ohio/Ali H Mwinyi; ☏ 022 211 7063/5. To/from Addis Ababa daily (with connections to Europe).

✈ **Kenya Airways** Peugeot Hse, Ali H Mwinyi; ☏ 022 211 9377. To/from Nairobi 7 times daily (with connections to Europe).

✈ **KLM** Peugeot Hse, Ali H Mwinyi; ☎ 022 216 3914/6. To/from Amsterdam via KIA daily.
✈ **South Africa Air** Raha Towers, Maktaba St; ☎ 022 211 7044/7. To/from Johannesburg daily.

✈ **Swiss International Air** Luther Hse, Sokoine Dr; ☎ 022 211 8870/3. To/from Zurich 3 times weekly.

BY BOAT Several boats run between Dar es Salaam and Zanzibar every day, with the more reliable services generally taking around two hours. There are also regular services to Pemba Island. All the commercial boat operators have kiosks near the harbour on Sokoine Drive, so it's easy enough to shop around for prices to Zanzibar – around US$25–40 depending on how fast the boat is – and to check departure dates for other destinations.

BY RAIL Trains on the central railway to Dodoma, Tabora, Mwanza and Kigoma leave from the Tanzanian Railways Corporation (☎ 022 211 7833; www.trctz.com) railway station on Sokoine Drive in the city centre [278 C6]. Bookings to these destinations should also be made at this station. For details of departure times, see box, *The Central Railway*, in *Chapter 13, Dodoma and the Central Rift Valley*, page 393. Trains to southern destinations such as Ifakara and Mbeya leave from the separate Tazara station [272 A7] (☎ 022 286 5187; www.tazara.co.tz), 5km from the city centre. The booking office for southbound trains is at Tazara station. Regular minibuses run between the central post office (*posta*) on Maktaba Road in the city centre [279 E3] and the Tazara station. Details of Tazara train services are under the heading *By rail* in the *Getting there and away* and *Getting around* sections of *Chapter 3, Practical information*.

BY BUS Almost all long-haul buses to destinations around the country arrive and depart from the Ubungo bus station, which is 8km out of town along the Morogoro road. Its distance from the city centre more or less enforces a special trip out of town to book tickets a day ahead of departure (strongly advised for most destinations). A taxi from the city centre to Ubungo will cost around Tsh5,000–7,000, depending on how receptive the driver is to negotiation.

Once regarded as Tanzania's most reliable and luxurious bus line, Scandinavia Express [272 A7] (☎ 022 218 4833; e info@scandinaviagroup.com; www.scandinaviagroup.com) has struggled in recent years. But, unlike most other cheaper companies, they do still run to a schedule and offer a relatively luxurious and reasonably affordable coach service. Services, which depart from their terminal on the corner of Msimbazi Street and Nyerere Road, connect Dar es Salaam to Arusha (twice daily), Nairobi (once daily), Mwanza (once daily), Dodoma (twice daily), Tanga (twice daily) Iringa (three times daily), Mbeya (twice daily) and Songea (twice daily), and several other towns along the way.

GETTING AROUND

PUBLIC TRANSPORT Shared minibus-taxis called *dala-dalas* cover almost every conceivable route through the city for a few hundred shillings per seat. The most important *dala-dala* station (called Posta) is outside the post office on Azikiwe Street [279 E3]. Other important stops are at the old post office on Sokoine Drive and the railway station near the Clocktower [278 C6]. The system is confusing for new arrivals; this, coupled with the high incidence of theft, probably makes it pointless to try to get to grips with things on a short visit to the city. The one exception is if you want to buy a ticket for the Tazara Railway to Zambia, in which case you can hop into a vehicle marked *Vigunguti* at the main post office.

Avoid using public transport when loaded down with luggage – aside from the crowding, petty theft is a real risk. When you first arrive in town (or at any other time when you are carrying luggage or valuables), use a taxi.

TAXIS There are taxis all over the place. A good place to find one is in front of the New Africa Hotel [273 F5 & 279 F4], though you are more likely to be overcharged there than elsewhere. The standard price for a ride within the city centre is around Tsh2,000, though you'll probably be asked slightly more at first, and should expect to pay more for trips further afield.

CAR RENTAL Most safari operators in Dar es Salaam can arrange car rental. A recommended specialist is Xpress Rent-A-Car [278 D3] (✆ 022 212 8356/7; m 0744 604958; e business@raha.com or tours@xpresstours.org; www.xpresstours.org), which owns a fleet of modern AC minibuses, 4x4s and saloon cars suitable both for safaris further afield and for travel in and around the city centre. Self-drive and chauffeur services are available. City tours and airport transfers can also be arranged. The office is in the central Haidery Plaza on the corner of Kisutu and Upanga streets.

TOURIST INFORMATION

The **Tanzania Tourist Board (TTB)** tourist information office [278 D5] (✆ 022 211 1244; e ttb-info@habari.co.tz; www.tanzaniatouristboard.com; ⏰ 08.00–16.00 Mon–Fri, 08.30–13.00 Sat) is on the ground floor of the IPS Building on Samora Machel Avenue.

Other useful sources of current information are the bi-monthly booklet Dar es Salaam Guide, published by East African Movies Ltd (e info@eastafricanmovies.com), and the monthly What's Happening In Dar es Salaam, published by Hakuna Matata Travels (e whatshappeningindar@hotmail.com). Both can be obtained at no charge from foyers or gift shops of upmarket hotels, embassies and other diplomatic missions, and branches of A Novel Idea bookshop. They are also stocked at Tanzanian embassies abroad.

A useful online source of current information about Dar es Salaam is www.tanzaniadirectory.info.

TOUR OPERATORS

Most tour operators in Dar es Salaam specialise in visits to the southern reserves. It is more normal to organise northern safaris in Arusha. It is also cheaper, as most tour operators in Dar es Salaam are in the middle to upper range. Some tour companies can do day trips to Bagamoyo. Safaris can usually be arranged through the owners of various camps in the Selous; see *Chapter 16, The Tanzam Highway and Southern Safari Circuit*, for details of these. Because few budget safaris run out of Dar es Salaam, there is no pirate safari industry similar to the one in Arusha, which means that you can be reasonably confident in your dealings with any tour company. The following companies are recommended.

Authentic Tanzania m 0786 019965/0784 825899; e info@authentictanzania.com; www.authentictanzania.com. Innovative private safaris in the south & west of Tanzania & Zanzibar, Pemba & Mafia.
Coastal Travel ✆ 022 211 7959/60; e safari@coastal.cc; www.coastal.cc. Highly regarded booking agent to numerous lodges & hotels, also

arranges personalised safaris throughout Tanzania & runs scheduled flights to the most popular reserves & resort areas countrywide.
Foxes African Safaris m 0784/754/713 237422; e fox@tanzaniasafaris.info; www.tanzaniasafaris.info. Upmarket southern safari specialist running several camps in the region as well as its own charter & scheduled flights to the major southern reserves.

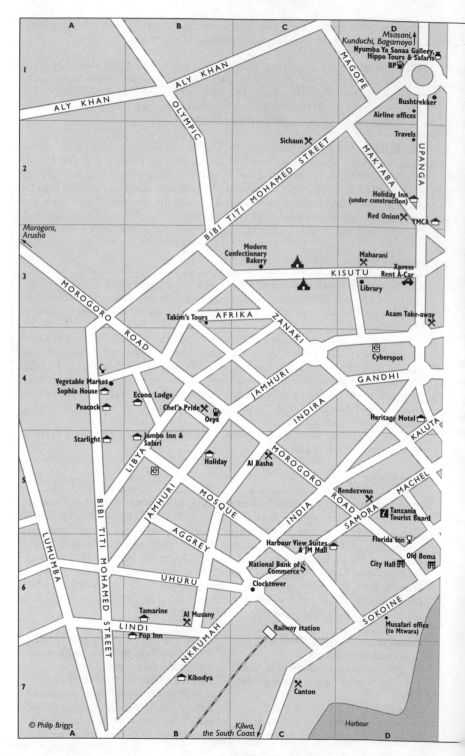

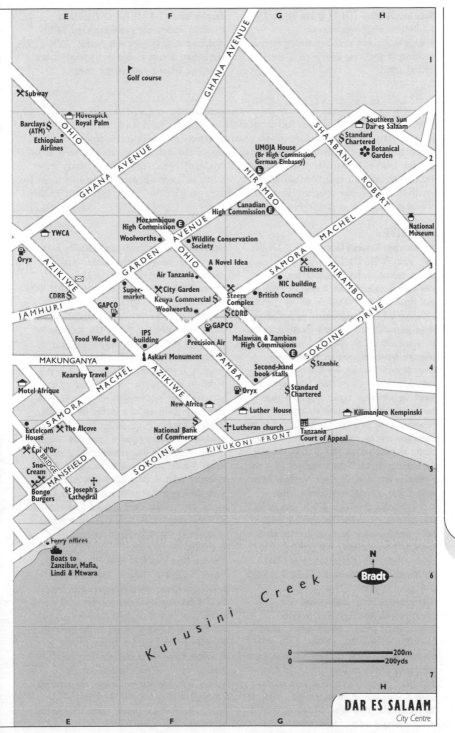

Golf course

✕ Subway

Barclays (ATM) $
Ethiopian Airlines

🏨 Mövenpick Royal Palm

OHIO

GHANA AVENUE

GHANA AVENUE

MIRAMBO

SHAABANI

ROBERT

Southern Sun
Dar es Salaam
Standard Chartered $
Botanical Garden

UMOJA House
(Br High Commission,
German Embassy) Ⓔ

Canadian
High Commission Ⓔ

MACHEL

MIRAMBO

National Museum

Mozambique Ⓔ
High Commission
Woolworths ●

🏠 YWCA

GARDEN AVENUE

OHIO

Wildlife Conservation
Society
● A Novel Idea

SAMORA

AZIKIWE

Oryx

Air Tanzania ●

Chinese ✕
● NIC building

SOKOINE DRIVE

CDRB $

JAMHURI

Super-
market

GAPCO

✕ City Garden
Kenya Commercial $
Woolworths ●

Steers
Complex ✕ ● British Council

$ CDRB

🅿 GAPCO

Food World ●

IPS
building

● Precision Air

Malawian & Zambian Ⓔ
High Commissions

MAKUNGANYA

Askari Monument

PAMBA

Second-hand
book stalls

$ Stanbic

Kearsley Travel

SAMORA

MACHEL

AZIKIWE

🏠 Motel Afrique

🅿 Oryx

$ Standard
Chartered

New Africa 🏠

🏠 Kilimanjaro Kempinski

Extelcom ✕ The Alcove
House

✕ Epi d'Or

BRIDGE

MANSFIELD

National Bank
of Commerce $

† Lutheran church

🏠 Luther House

Tanzania
Court of Appeal Ⓔ

Sno-
Cream ✕

✕ Bongo
Burgers

† St Joseph's
Cathedral

SOKOINE

KIVUKONI FRONT

Ferry offices

Boats to
Zanzibar, Mafia,
Lindi & Mtwara

K u r u s i n i   C r e e k

N

Bradt

0 ————— 200m
0 ————— 200yds

E   F   G   H

DAR ES SALAAM
City Centre

Hippo Tours & Safaris [273 E4 & 278 D1] \ 022 212 8663; e info@hippotours.com; www.hippotours.com. Another long-standing operator specialising in good value fly-in Selous & other southern safaris.

Kearsley Travel [279 E4] \ 022 2115026/30; e info@kearsleys.com; www.kearsleys.com. Well established safari company with dynamic management & years of experience arranging safaris throughout Tanzania, especially the south.

WHERE TO STAY

There are plenty of hotels in and around the city centre to suit all budgets, and new places seem to open at an ever-increasing pace. The section below covers all accommodation that lies within the confines of the city centre and as well as in greater Dar es Salaam north towards the Msasani Peninsula. The (mostly more attractive) accommodation along the stretches of coast immediately north and south of the city are covered later in this chapter under the headings *The coast north of Dar es Salaam* and *Beach resorts south of Dar*.

EXCLUSIVE

Kilimanjaro Kempinski Hotel [273 F5 & 279 H4] (180 rooms) \ 022 213 1111; e reservations.kilimanjaro@kempinski.com; www.kempinski-daressalaam.com. Built in the 1950s on what remains the finest location in the city centre, overlooking the main seafront above the harbour, this former government hotel – widely referred to as 'The Kili' – reopened in 2005 following 4 years of exhaustive renovations under the international Kempinski chain. Extending over 8 storeys, it now ranks as the most upmarket hotel in the city centre, though the ostentatious angular architecture glazed over by arctic AC recalls a Soviet-era airport in midwinter, making for a rather surreal contrast to the superb view over the tropical harbour. Still, if 5-star facilities are what you are after (& ideally somebody else is footing the bill), 5-star is what you get – the immense en-suite rooms come with broadband internet access, LCD TV with satellite & in-house movie channels, multilingual voicemail & 24hr room service, while other facilities include 20m wave-free swimming pool, gymnasium, health spa, casino, 7 restaurants & bars, & an internal shopping mall. *Dbls from US$320, executive rooms from US$400, suites from US$610.*

Mövenpick Royal Palm Hotel [273 E4 & 279 E2] (230 rooms) \ 022 211 2416. e hotel.daressalaam@movenpick.com; www.moevenpick-daressalaam.com. The former Sheraton, geared primarily towards business travellers, faces stiff competition from a growing horde of less luxurious but significantly cheaper chain hotels. Set in lush tropical grounds on Ohio St, the Royal Palm is characterised by excellent service & plush interiors. Rooms & suites have all the facilities you'd expect in this price bracket. There is a 24hr business centre & several meeting & business rooms. Other facilities include 2 restaurants, beauty salon, shopping arcade & gymnasium, sauna & outdoor swimming pool. *Std rooms US$270 B&B; suites available too.*

Sea Cliff Hotel [281 D1] (85 rooms) \ 022 260 0380/7; e information@hotelseacliff.com; www.hotelseacliff.com. Arguably the top hotel within Dar's greater city limits, the Sea Cliff was razed by fire in late 2007 but is set to reopen in early 2009. It has a fabulous seafront location on Msasani Peninsula, at the north end of Toure Dr, & is only 15mins by taxi from the city centre, making it attractive to business travellers who want to spend their leisure hours out of town. Post-fire upgrades include a franchise of the popular Alcove Restaurant, a remodelled swimming pool & gymnasium, redesigned executive floor complete with private lounge & butler service, new business centre & conference room. In the attached mall, you'll find a good travel agent, hair salon, massage studio & several book & curio shops. A casino & bowling alley also adjoin the hotel. *En-suite rooms with AC & satellite TV from US$170 std non-sea-facing dbl to US$400 executive suite.*

New Africa Hotel [273 F5 & 279 F4] (126 rooms) \ 022 211 7050/1; e reservations@ newafricahotel.com; www.newafricahotel.com. Reopened in 1998 following total renovation, this is the only central hotel to rival the Royal Palm, & stands on the corner of Azikiwe & Sokoine Dr, the site of the legendary Kaiserhof, the first hotel to open in Dar es Salaam, during the German era. It's a plush modern hotel, & all rooms have AC, satellite TV, minibar & WiFi; services include same-day laundry & car rental. Attached are 2 excellent but pricey restaurants, a bar & a popular casino. *US$170/180 std/superior dbl; US$250 suite.*

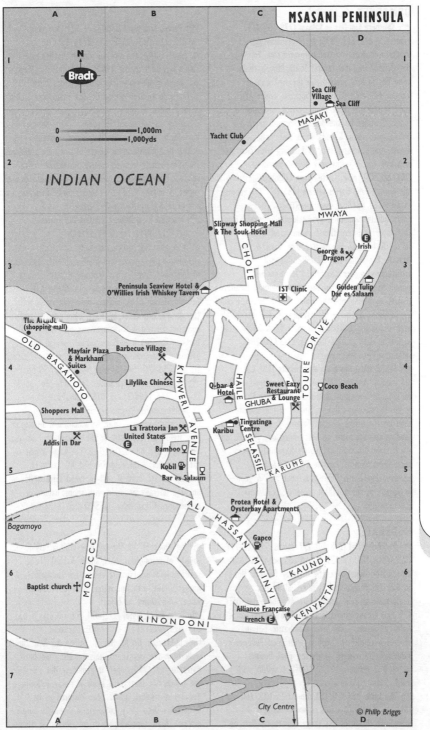

N

Bradt

0 —————— 1,000m
0 —————— 1,000yds

INDIAN OCEAN

Sea Cliff Village
Sea Cliff

MASAKI

Yacht Club

MWAYA

Slipway Shopping Mall
& The Souk Hotel

CHOLE

George & Dragon
Irish

Peninsula Seaview Hotel &
O'Willies Irish Whiskey Tavern

IST Clinic

Golden Tulip
Dar es Salaam

The Arcade
(shopping mall)

OLD BAGAMOYO

Mayfair Plaza
& Markham Suites

Barbecue Village

TOURE DRIVE

Lilylike Chinese

KIMWERI AVENUE

Q-bar & Hotel

HAILE

Sweet Eazy
Restaurant
& Lounge

Coco Beach

Shoppers Mall

GHUBA

Karibu

Tingatinga Centre

SELASSIE

Addis in Dar

La Trattoria Jan
United States

KARUME

Bamboo

Kobil

Bar es Salaam

ALI HASSAN

Protea Hotel &
Oysterbay Apartments

Bagamoyo

MWINYI

KAUNDA

Gapco

MOROCCO

KENYATTA

Baptist church

Alliance Française
French

KINONDONI

City Centre

© Philip Briggs

UPMARKET

⌂ **Southern Sun Dar es Salaam** [279 H2] (152 rooms) ☏ 022 213 7575; e reservations@southernsun.co.tz; www.southernsuntz.com. Formerly the Holiday Inn, this central South African chain hotel lies in lush grounds on the east end of Garden Av. Facilities include business centre, WiFi, 2 good restaurants, 16hr room service, non-smoking rooms, facilities for the disabled, on-site travel centre, good curio & book shop, swimming pool & fitness centre. Idiosyncratic & bristling with character it is not, but it seems very acceptable value. *US$180/200 sgl/dbl; suites from US$250.*

⌂ **Golden Tulip Dar es Salaam** [281 D3] (91 rooms) ☏ 022 260 0288; e enquiries@goldentuliptanzania.com; www.goldentuliptanzania.com. This superior international chain hotel lies on Toure Dr between the Oyster Bay Hotel & the Msasani Peninsula. The Swahili-influenced architecture & fine beachfront location are complemented by varied facilities including business centre, swimming pool overlooking the beach, travel agent, shops & choice of restaurants. The rooms all have sea-facing balconies, satellite TV & large bathroom with marble fixtures. *US$150/200 sgl/dbl; suites also available.*

⌂ **Protea Hotel Oysterbay Apartments** [281 C5] (24 rooms) ☏ 022 266 6665; e marketingprotea@dar.bol.co.tz; www.proteahotels.com/oysterbay. Also part of the Protea chain, this reasonably priced all-suite hotel on the corner of Haile Selassie & Ali Hassan is a good secure alternative to the nearby luxury hotels on the Msasani Peninsula. Attractively furnished modern suites come with AC, satellite TV, Wi-Fi & fully equipped kitchenette. There is a pool, gym & good restaurant on site. Excellent value. *US$130/160 dbl/studio apt.*

⌂ **Protea Courtyard Hotel** [273 E2] (52 rooms) ☏ 022 213 0130/0560; m 0784 555130; e courtyard@raha.com; www.proteahotels.com/courtyard. Built in the 1940s, the former Sea View is yet another adequate international chain hotel centrally located on Ocean Dr. The rooms are looking a little faded as things stand, but renovations — including an additional 18 rooms — are on the horizon. In the meantime, it remains reasonably priced by comparison to places of a similar standard. Facilities include business centre, restaurant, coffee shop, DSTV in all rooms, swimming pool, conference centre & library. *US$125/150 sgl/dbl B&B; deluxe rooms US$150/180 sgl/dbl B&B.*

⌂ **Harbour View Suites** [278 C6] (80 rooms) ☏ 022 212 4040; m 0784 564848; e reservations@harbourview-suites.com; www.harbourview-suites.com. Comfortably the best deal in this price range is this centrally located all-suite hotel above the JM Mall on Samora Machel Av. Accommodation is in spacious open-plan suites with cheerful modern décor, AC, DSTV, 24hr internet, well-equipped kitchen & stunning views over the city & harbour. Facilities include restaurant, cocktail bar, gymnasium, swimming pool & business centre. *US$110 std dbl, US$120 executive dbl; b/fast US$7.50 pp.*

⌂ **Markham Executive Suites** [281 A4] (26 rooms) ☏ 022 277 1800/2; m 0784 786298; e markhamsuites@cats-net.com or info@markhamsuites.co.tz; www.markhamsuites.co.tz. This stylish private hotel in the Mayfair Mall on the Old Bagamoyo Rd in Mikacheni has large bright self-catering suites with king-size bed, AC, cable TV, internet access, bath & well-equipped kitchenette in an area liberally endowed with shops, banks & restaurants. Great value. *US$90 dbl.*

MODERATE

⌂ **Peacock Hotel** [278 A4] (97 rooms) ☏ 022 211 4071; m 0782 112729; info@peacock-hotel.co.tz; www.peacock-hotel.co.tz. The 8-storey Peacock Hotel on Bibi Titi Muhammad St offers bland but comfortable en-suite rooms with AC, hot water, DSTV & fridge. Recent renovations & refurbishments come across as rather gaudy, even bombastic, but it remains a comfortable option, with good facilities including safe parking, swimming pool, business centre & 2 restaurants. *US$100/120 sgl/dbl, with small discount for residents.*

⌂ **The Souk** [281 C3] (20 rooms) ☏ 022 260 0893; e slipway@coastal.cc; www.coastal.cc. A convenient choice in this range, the studio flats on the top floor of the Slipway Mall offer access to a variety of restaurants, bars, shops & banks in a seafront location. En-suite rooms are comfortable & unpretentious, with hot water, AC & DSTV. Good value. *US$90 not inc b/fast.*

⌂ **Palm Beach Hotel** [272 D2] (32 rooms) ☏ 022 213 0985/212 2931; e info@pbhtz.com; www.pbhtz.com. On Ali Hassan Mwinyi Rd & a 20min walk from the city centre, this rambling old hotel dates to the 1950s, when it genuinely did overlook the beach, not that you'd know it today. Following decades of neglect, it has been restored to its former Art Deco glory, complete with bright purple exterior, & its time-warped charm elevates it above most other options in this range. A pleasant garden bar/restaurant serves good meals. Comfortable en-suite rooms have mini-safe, hot water, TV & internet. Good value. *US$85/110 sgl/dbl.*

🏠 **Sophia House Hotel** [278 A4] (20 rooms) ☎ 022 211 2521/2; e info@sophiahouse.com; www.sophiahouse.com. On Bibi Titi Muhammad St a few doors up from the Peacock, the standard rooms here have AC, DSTV, safe, hot bath & access to a swimming pool, & would be good value were it not for the confrontational furnishing. The executive dbl ranks as the scariest room we've seen in Africa in its own Barbie-goes-bordello-chic way. *US$70/80 sgl/dbl; US$100 executive dbl.*

🏠 **Heritage Motel** [278 D4] (50 rooms) ☎ 022 211 7471; e heritagemotel@heritagemotel.co.tz; www.heritagemotel.co.tz. This new centrally located hotel, just off Samora Machel on the corner of Bridge & Kaluta streets, is the most convenient mid-range option for anyone catching the ferry to Zanzibar. Catering mostly to business travellers, its

BUDGET

🏠 **Luther House** [279 G4] (16 rooms) ☎ 022 212 6247/0734; e luther@simbanet.net. Tucked away behind the waterfront Lutheran Church, this is another long-serving budget favourite, though not the bargain it used to be. On the plus side, it's quiet, clean & all rooms have TV & AC. *Tsh30,000/35,000/40,000 sgl/dbl/trpl with common showers.*

🏠 **Jambo Inn** [278 B5] (28 rooms) ☎ 022 211 0711/4293; e jamboinnhotel@yahoo.com; www.jamboinnhotel.com. This secure & sensibly priced guesthouse in Libya St has been deservedly popular with budget travellers for as long as we can remember, & remains a favoured central standby. There is a ground floor internet café & airy restaurant serving tasty & affordable Indian food, with 10% discount for hotel residents.

SHOESTRING

🏠 **YMCA** [278 D2] (27 rooms) ☎ 022 213 5457. The YMCA is around the corner from the superior & more affordable YWCA. *Tsh13,000/17,000 clean sgl/dbl with net but no fan.*

🏠 **Kibodya Hotel** [278 B7] ☎ 022 211 7856. One of the best compromises between quality & price in Dar. All rooms are clean with en-suite hot shower, fan & netting. *Tsh12,000/16,000 without/with TV, Tsh24,000 with AC.*

🏠 **YWCA** [279 E3] (25 rooms) ☎ 022 212 2439; m 0713 633707; e ywca.tanzania@africaonline.co.tz. Centrally located on Maktaba St, the

simply furnished en-suite rooms are spacious & clean. Not bad value. There's a decent restaurant attached & internet is available. *US$66/102/138 sgl/dbl/trpl B&B.*

🏠 **Starlight Hotel** [278 A5] (154 rooms) ☎ 022 213 9387/8; e starlight@ctvsatcom.net. Situated alongside the Peacock, this is more downmarket & less pretentious than its neighbour. En-suite rooms with AC, hot water, 8-channel satellite TV & fridge rank as very good value. *US$51/60 sgl/dbl.*

🏠 **Q-Bar & Guesthouse** [281 C4] (20 rooms) ☎ 022 260 2150; m 0744 282474; e qbar@hotmail.com. This smart but unpretentious guesthouse has budget rooms with shared baths, large self-contained suites, & backpacker accommodation in a 4-bed dorm. With the attached bar & restaurant a popular spot for watching international sporting events it can get very rowdy, so bring ear plugs if you don't plan on joining in the fun. *US$35/45 sgl/dbl, US$65/75 sgl/dbl (suite) B&B inc laundry; dorm US$12 pp.*

Tsh20,000/25,000 sgl/dbl en-suite with reliable hot water & fans; Tsh30,000 dbl with AC & TV.

🏠 **Econo Lodge** [278 B4] (61 rooms) ☎ 022 211 6048/9; e econolodge@raha.com. This relatively smart hotel boasts a convenient central location off Libya St, & offers outstanding value in its range. *Tsh18,000/24,000/30,000 en-suite sgl/dbl/trpl with fan, Tsh30,000/35,000/40,000 sgl/dbl/trpl with AC.*

🏠 **Safari Hotel** [278 B5] ☎ 022 211 9104; e safari-inn@lycos.com. A little less salubrious than the Jambo but just around the corner at the end of a cul de sac, this is another long-serving & popular budget lodge. *Tsh15,000/20,000 en-suite sgl/dbl with fan; Tsh17,500/22,500 with TV; Tsh30,000 dbl with AC & TV.*

YWCA has long been a favourite with couples & single women travelling on the cheap, but single men are not accommodated. Rooms are clean & a canteen serves inexpensive if unexciting meals for under Tsh2,000. *Rooms with fans & nets cost Tsh10,000 sgl, Tsh15,000 dbl (couple), Tsh20,000 dbl (2 women sharing), Tsh20,000/30,000 dbl/trpl en-suite flat.*

🏠 **Tamarine Hotel** [278 B6] ☎ 022 212 0233; e zelda@africaonline.co.tz. Although rather run-down, this is one of the better cheapies in central Dar, & very reasonably priced. *Tsh6,000/10,000 sgl/dbl with common showers; Tsh12,000 en-suite dbl.*

🏠 **Pop Inn Hotel** [278 B6] ☎ 022 260 1273. Across the road from the Tamarine, this decidedly shabby place is a last resort. *Tsh5,000/7,000 small,* *windowless sgl/dbl with shared showers, Tsh10,000 en-suite dbl.*

✖ WHERE TO EAT

Dar es Salaam has a good range of restaurants to suit all tastes & budgets, and the number of options seems to have grown exponentially every time we visit the city. Typically, restaurants open for lunch between 12.00 and 15.00 and for dinner between 18.00 and 23.00. Generally food is of a high standard and good value for money. It would be impossible to list every restaurant and *hoteli* in Dar es Salaam, so you might well want to adventure beyond the following recommendations.

CITY CENTRE

✖ **Al-Basha** [278 C5] Cnr Morogoro & Indira Sts; ☎ 022 212 6888; ⊕ daily for b/fast, lunch & dinner. This is one of the best value eateries in Dar es Salaam, with a wide range of Lebanese dishes at around Tsh3,000–6,000. There's a second outlet at the Mayfair Plaza near the US Embassy.

✖ **Bongo Burgers** [279 E5] ☎ 022 222 5659. Next door to Sno-Cream, this friendly little eatery is good for a quick bite while waiting for the ferry to Zanzibar. It serves burgers & light snacks for Tsh3,000–4,000.

✖ **Chef's Pride** [278 B4] ⊕ daily for lunch & dinner. Popular central café serving a good selection of inexpensive snacks & light meals, as well as tasty fruit juice.

✖ **City Garden** [279 F3] Garden Av; ☎ 022 212 4211; ⊕ 11.00–23.00 daily. This shady outdoor terraced restaurant is a popular central choice. An extensive à la carte menu features the ubiquitous chicken, fish & rice dishes as well as a reasonable selection of pizzas from Tsh6,500. The w/day buffet lunch costs Tsh11,000. No alcohol.

✖ **Épi d'Or** [279 E5] Samora Machel Av; ☎ 022 213 6006; ⊕ 07.00–17.00. This French bakery is great for breakfast – excellent coffee, & a good range of fresh croissants & pastries as well as sandwiches & pizzas. There's a second outlet at Sea Cliff Village.

✖ **Jambo Inn** [278 B5]. The reliable restaurant here boasts an extensive Indian menu with some Chinese & Western selections. Portions are generous & tasty, & excellent value at around Tsh3,000–5,000 for a main course with rice or naan bread. Meals are served throughout the day, & there's a tandoor barbecue in the evening. No alcohol, great fresh fruit juice.

✖ **Red Onion** [278 D2] 2nd floor Haidery Plaza Bldg, Maktaba St opp YMCA; ☎ 022 212 8368. This excellent Indian restaurant serves a wide selection of well-priced curries. There's a nice rooftop dining area.

✖ **Sawasdee Restaurant** [273 F5 & 279 F4] 9th floor, New Africa Hotel; ☎ 022 211 7050. With a grandstand view over the harbour, this superb Thai restaurant is one of the best places to eat anywhere in Dar, but relatively expensive – expect a bill of at least US$15 pp.

✖ **Serengeti Restaurant** [273 E4 & 279 E2] Ground floor, Mövenpick Royal Palm Hotel; ☎ 022 211 2416. The Serengeti Restaurant prepares sumptuous themed buffets – Mediterranean (Mon), Italian (Tue), Oriental (Wed), Seafood (Thu), Fondue (Fri), Mexican (Sat) or Indian (Sun). It's been described as 'the ultimate culinary experience in Dar' – & so it should be at Tsh30,000 pp.

✖ **Sno-Cream Parlour** [279 E5]. This Dar institution dates back to the days when the city's other ice cream parlours served nothing but orange juice spiced with flies. The extravagant interior & marvellous sundaes don't have quite the air of surrealism they did back then, but the sundaes are still the best in town.

✖ **Steers Complex** [279 G3] Cnr Ohio & Samora Machel Avs; ☎ 022 212 2855. Deprived fast-food junkies should make a beeline for this complex of South African fast food franchises – try Steers for burgers, steak rolls & such, Debonairs for pizzas, subs & wraps, or the attached patisserie for croissants, coffee & other b/fast staples.

✖ **Subway** [279 E1] ☎ 022 212 6258; ⊕ 09.00–18.00. This American franchise serves good baguettes with a wide selection of tasty hot & cold fillings for Tsh2,000 upwards.

✖ **The Alcove** [279 E5] Samora Machel Av; ☎ 022 213 7444; m 0713 324319; ⊕ 12.00–15.00 & 17.00–22.30 daily, closed Sun lunchtime. This long-standing & central restaurant serves top-notch Indian & Chinese food at around US$5–10 for main course & condiments – recommended! There's now a second outlet at the Sea Cliff Hotel.

SUBURBAN

✗ **Addis in Dar** [281 A5] Ursino St; m 0713 266299. This long-standing favourite in the Oyster Bay area near the US Embassy serves wonderfully spicy Ethiopian dishes from Tsh5,000. Closed Sundays.

✗ **Azuma Japanese Restaurant** [281 C3] ✆ 022 260 0893. Situated in the Slipway Shopping Mall, the Azuma is known for its excellent Japanese & Indian cuisine. Main courses are in the US$5–7 range.

✗ **Barbecue Village** [281 B4] ✆ 022 266 7927; m 0713 320736; ⊕ 18.30–23.30 daily except Mon. This relaxed & affordable restaurant, with rooftop & garden dining areas, serves seafood for around Tsh6,000, & Indian & Chinese dishes (good vegetarian choice) for Tsh4,000–5,000.

✗ **La Trattoria Jan** [281 B5] ✆ 022 266 8739; ⊕ 11.00–23.00 daily. Also known as Jan's Pizzeria, this busy restaurant in Namanga serves the best pizzas in town for Tsh5,000–7,000, as well as other Italian dishes & grills.

✗ **The Mashua Waterfront** [281 C3] ✆ 022 260 0908; ⊕ 09.00–23.00 daily. Good, moderately priced pizzeria & grill overlooking the Indian Ocean in the Slipway Shopping Mall.

✗ **The Pub** [281 C3] ✆ 022 260 0893. This English style pub has a decidedly non-English tropical beach setting in the Slipway shopping mall. Indoor & courtyard seating is available, along with draught beer, bar meals, & a Sunday lunchtime roast.

✗ **Q-Bar** [281 C4] ✆ 0754 282474; ⊕ 12.00–late. This popular drinking hole in the Oyster Bay area serves good bar grub & does an evening barbecue with mishkaki & chicken tikka, mostly for under Tsh5,000. Live music Fri nights.

✗ **Sweet Eazy Restaurant & Lounge** [281 C4] m 0755 754074. A popular bar & live music venue, this airy rooftop restaurant in Oyster Bay Shopping Mall serves a variety of Thai & African dishes from around Tsh5,000 upwards.

✗ **O'Willies Irish Whiskey Tavern** [281 B3] ✆ 022 260 1273. This popular bar, attached to the Peninsula Seaview Hotel, serves large helpings of traditional Irish pub grub for Tsh6,000–10,000 (the Irish Stew is particularly tasty), as well as pizzas, grills & an all-day b/fast. It has a good selection of import beers, a pleasant outdoor terrace, & live music & karaoke at w/ends.

✗ **George & Dragon** [281 D3] ✆ 0717 800001 Another expat favourite, this busy pub-restaurant, tucked away just off Haile Selassie, is the place for old-fashioned English pub fare, though dishes are on the expensive side at around Tsh11,500. Better value, the Sun roast lunch for Tsh14,500 comes complete with Yorkshire pudding.

ENTERTAINMENT AND NIGHTLIFE

BARS There is something of a dearth of decent bars in the centre of Dar, presumably due to the strong Muslim presence, and many hotels and restaurants don't serve alcohol. The **Florida Inn** [278 D6], a block from the ferry port, is one of the few genuine drinking holes in the city centre, with ice-cold beer on tap. Meanwhile, the **Level 8 Bar** at the Kilimanjaro Kempinski Hotel [273 F5 & 279 I I4], with its killer view and superb cocktail list, is the choice place to be at sunset. Further out of town, among the better places for a drink are **O'Willies Irish Whiskey Tavern** [281 B3], the **George and Dragon** [281 D4], **Sweet Eazy** [281 C4], **Q-Bar** [281 C4] and **The Pub** at the Slipway Mall [281 C3], all of which are mentioned in the restaurant listings and can only be reached by taxi or with private transport. The **Coco Beach Bar** [281 C4] at Oyster Bay is a good place to while away a day sipping cold beers and eating mishkaki kebabs.

CINEMA AND THEATRE Most cinemas in Dar es Salaam concentrate on Bollywood extravaganzas, kung-fu films and gung-ho American war fodder. The multiple screen **Century Cinemax** [272 A4] (Milimani City Mall, Sam Nujoma Rd, Ubongo; ✆ 022 277 3053; tickets Tsh7,000) shows more current Western movies, with up-to-date listings on www.tanzaniadirectory.info. The only theatre is the **Little Theatre** (m 0784 277388) near Oyster Bay. **Alliance Française** [281 C6] (✆ 022 213 1406; www.ambafrance.tz.org) on Ali Hassan Mwinyi Road holds weekly film screenings – movies are subtitled in English.

10

SHOPPING

In the city centre, local goods are cheapest at stalls such as those lining Maktaba Street. The well-stocked **City Supermarket** [279 F3] (↘ *022 212 2130*) on Samora Machel Avenue in the JM Mall is one of many so-called luxury shops, selling a variety of imported foodstuffs and toiletries at inflated prices. Several clothes shops and fruit stalls line Zanaki Street, but the most colourful place to buy this sort of thing is **Kariakoo Market** [272 C6] (described under *What to see and do*). Curio stalls in Dar es Salaam are very expensive when compared with those in Arusha.

The last few years have seen a proliferation of shopping malls constructed in suburban Dar es Salaam. The newest is Mlimani City on Sam Nujoma Road in Ubongo, which boasts the biggest supermarket in East Africa. Another popular choice is the Slipway on the Msasani Peninsula [281 C3], which has four restaurants, an excellent bookshop, a South African chain supermarket and a bank with an ATM. Also good are the Oyster Bay Shopping Centre [281 C4], The Arcade and Shoppers Paradise on the Old Bagamoyo Road [281 A4], and Sea Cliff Village adjacent to the Sea Cliff Hotel [281 D1].

BOOKS The best bookshop is **A Novel Idea** (↘ *022 260 1088; www.anovelideatanzania.com*), with branches in the Slipway Shopping Mall [281 C3], Sea Cliff Village [281 D1], Shopper's Plaza [281 A4] (*Old Bagamoyo Rd*) and next to the central Steers Complex [279 G3]. Branches stock a great selection of novels, field and travel guides, and local-interest books. Other bookshops in Dar es Salaam focus more on textbooks, but several stalls along Samora Machel Avenue sell secondhand novels and much else besides at negotiable prices. Shops or kiosks selling books in the foyers of most tourist class hotels tend to be very overpriced. You can sometimes buy recent European and American newspapers at the stalls on Samora Machel Avenue.

OTHER PRACTICALITIES

COMMUNICATIONS The central **post office** is on Azikiwe Street [279 E3]. Several kiosks outside sell postcards, envelopes and writing paper.

For **international phone calls and faxes**, the telecommunications centre, Extelcom House, is on Bridge Street [279 E5], close to the post office. Here you can buy phonecards, now more useful than coins when it comes to finding a phone box. A few private shops dotted around the city centre offer more efficient international phone and fax facilities at slightly inflated prices.

Internet cafés are dotted all over and generally charge around Tsh1,000 per hour. The fastest and most reliable café is Africaonline in the Steers Complex [279 G3] (*cnr Ohio & Samora Machel;* ⊕ *08.30–21.00 daily*), but it's a little pricey at Tsh1,000 per 30 minutes. There is, however, plenty of choice – several internet cafés are marked on the map – though most places are closed on Sundays.

HAIRDRESSERS There are unisex salons in most of the upmarket hotels, and in the YMCA building. Top Knots (↘ *022 260 0380*) at the Sea Cliff Hotel [281 D1] is well-recommended.

MAPS The Department of Lands and Surveys building is in Ardhi House on Kivukoni Front [283 G5]. The map sales office, tucked away behind a building on the block before this, stocks 1:50,000 maps covering practically the whole country, which are particularly useful for hiking in remote areas. The staff are helpful, and if the map you require is unavailable, a monochrome copy can be made – this takes anything from two to 24 hours.

MEDICAL The Aga Khan Hospital [273 E3] (*Ocean Rd;* ✆ *022 211 5151; www.agakhanhospitals.org*), Nordic Clinic (✆ *022 260 1650; 24hr hotline* m *0713 325569; www.nordic.or.tz*) and suburban International School of Tanzania (IST) Clinic [281 C3] (✆ *022 260 1307/8; 24hr hotline* m *0754 783393; www.istclinic.com*) are recommended for emergencies. For malaria and other blood tests, several clinics are dotted around town; try the Oyster Bay Medical Centre (✆ *022 266 7932*), Regency Medical Centre (✆ *022 215 0500; www.regencymedicalcentre.com*) or TAG Clinic (✆ *022 212 4394*). For dental emergencies, try the Swedish-run Three Crowns Dental Clinic [273 E4 & 279 E2] (*Mövenpick Royal Palm Hotel;* ✆ *022 213 6801*) or the Nordic Dental Clinic (✆ *022 213 6664*).

MONEY Numerous forex bureaux usually give marginally better rates than banks and keep longer hours. Rates vary considerably, so shop around before you change large sums. There are plenty of forex bureaux on Samora Machel Avenue and Zanaki Street. If you need to change money after the bureaux have closed, try the airport. Under no circumstance get involved with street dealers – there is no black market worth talking about here, only con artists.

Rickshaw Travel (✆ *022 1111003;* e *amex@rickshaw.africaonline.co.tz; www.rickshawtz.com;* ⊕ *08.00–17.00 Mon–Fri, 08.30–12.30 Sat*), with offices on Ali Hassan Mwinyi Road and in the Mövenpick Royal Palm Hotel [273 E4 & 279 E2], is the local representative of American Express, and can provide associated financial services. You can get cash with a credit card at Coastal Travel (see *Tour operators* on pages 277–80), though the exchange rate isn't brilliant.

Visa credit or debit cards can be used to draw up to Tsh400,000 of local currency daily at any of several ATMs (auto-tellers) in central Dar es Salaam. Some of the more convenient ATMs are at the Barclays Bank branches in the TDFL Building opposite the Mövenpick Royal Palm Hotel [279 E2] and in the Slipway [281 C3] (both of which also accept MasterCard), and the Standard Chartered Bank on Garden Avenue next to the Southern Sun [279 H2]. Unless the ATM is temporarily closed, money can be drawn 24 hours a day, seven days a week.

To change travellers' cheques, your best bet is any branch of the National Bank of Commerce (there are branches in the mall next to the Sea Cliff Hotel [281 D1] and in the city centre [279 H2]), since other banks generally refuse them or levy a commission. Some branches of the National Bank of Commerce may insist you produce proof of purchase.

SWAHILI COURSES Swahili & Culture Trainers [281 C3] (*KIU;* ✆ *022 285 1509;* e *kiu@swahilicourses.com; www.swahilicourses.com*) offers a variety of beginners and advanced courses, as well as cultural familiarisation courses, and translation and other linguistic services.

SWIMMING POOL The Missions to Seamen, on Bandari Road near the intersection with Kilwa Road, charges Tsh5,000 for use of its swimming pool. The Golden Tulip Hotel on Toure Drive [281 D3] charges Tsh10,000 daily.

WILDLIFE CONSERVATION SOCIETY The Wildlife Conservation Society of Tanzania [279 F3] (✆ *022 211 2518;* f *022 212 4572;* e *wcst@africaonline.co.tz; www.wcstarusha.org*) holds monthly talks at their headquarters on Garden Avenue.

WHAT TO SEE AND DO

Dar es Salaam offers little in the way of conventional sightseeing. The harbour area and back streets between Maktaba Road and the station house several old

German buildings, as does the area around the national museum and botanical gardens. If you have a couple of days to kill in Dar es Salaam, you might want to spend them at the beaches north or south of the city centre (covered later in this chapter) or around Bagamoyo (see *Chapter 9, The North Coast*). The beaches immediately north or south of Dar also form realistic goals for a day trip from the city centre.

HISTORICAL BUILDINGS Several relics of Dar es Salaam's early days are dotted around the city centre. The oldest is the **Old Boma** [278 D6] on the corner of Morogoro Road and Sokoine Drive. A plain, rather austere whitewashed monolith, built using coral rubble in the traditional coastal style, the Old Boma is easily recognised by its inscribed Zanzibari door. It was built in 1867 as a hotel to house visitors to the court of Sultan Majid, whose palace stood alongside it. Between 1870 and 1887, the building was the residence of the Sultan of Zanzibar's local agent, and it subsequently served as the GEAC's first administrative headquarters in Dar es Salaam, and the police charge office.

Several late-19th-century German buildings have survived into modern times. The **Ocean Road Hospital** [273 G4], which lies east of the city centre at the end of Samora Machel Avenue, was built in 1897, and is notable for its twin domed towers. The nearby **State House** [273 G5] also dates to a similar time, though it was heavily damaged in World War I, and the modern building, restored in 1922, bears little resemblance to photographs of the original.

The **Lutheran Church** [279 G5] on the corner of Sokoine Drive and Maktaba Road was built in 1898 in Bavarian style. Following the recent restoration of its exterior, it's a striking and attractive landmark, best viewed from the park on Sokoine Drive. A few blocks down on Sokoine Drive, the Gothically influenced **St Joseph's Cathedral** [279 E5] was built between 1897 and 1902. Other buildings dating from the German era include the **City Hall** [278 D6] (on Sokoine Road opposite the Old Boma), several ex-civil servants' residences around the botanical garden, and the buildings housing the Department of Lands and Surveys and Magistrate's Court on Kivukoni Front [273 G5].

KARIAKOO MARKET [272 C6] A huge variety of clothes, foodstuffs, spices and traditional medicines can be bought at this lively and colourful covered market which extends on to the surrounding streets in the form of a chaotic miscellany of stalls. The name *Kariakoo* derives from the British Carrier Corps, which was stationed in the area during World War II.

NATIONAL MUSEUM AND HOUSE OF CULTURE Located near the Botanical Gardens on Shaabani Robert Street, the National Museum and House of Culture [279 H3] (\ *022 211 7508;* e *houseofculture@museum.or.tz; www.museum.or.tz;* ⊕ *09.30–18.00 daily; entrance around US$5*) is one of the best in Africa. The section on early hominid development contains some of the world's most important fossils. The history displays upstairs have a good selection of exhibits dating back to the era of European exploration and German occupation. If you plan to visit Kilwa Kisiwani, don't miss the display of coins, pottery and other artefacts found during excavations there.

The area around the museum is notable for its pre-1914 German buildings, recognisable by their red-tiled roofs. The botanical garden, established in 1906, and now pretty run-down, is worth a look, as is the State House, built by the British in 1922. From State House, if you walk back to town along Kivukoni Front, you will be rewarded by good views of the city and harbour. You will also pass the 19th-century Lutheran Church, the oldest building in the city.

NYUMBA YA SANAA Founded in 1972 by a nun, this well-known gallery [273 E4 & 278 D1] (**m** *0754 264461; gallery & adjoining café* ① *8.30–18.00 w/days, 8.00–16.00 w/ends*) is today housed in an unusually designed building erected in 1983 and located next to the Mövenpick Royal Palm Hotel with the help of Norwegian funding. It exhibits arts and crafts made by handicapped people. A variety of carvings, batiks and pottery items can be bought. The standard of craftsmanship is generally regarded as high.

OYSTER BAY This is the closest swimming beach to the city centre. It is a reasonably attractive spot and very popular at weekends. Coco Beach bar [281 C4] is a pleasant spot to have a drink and catch an Indian Ocean sunset. No public transport goes directly to Oyster Bay, but if you take any *dala-dala* out of the city centre towards Msasani Peninsula, it can drop you at a junction near Q-Bar about 500m from the beach. A taxi from the city centre will cost around Tsh5,000–7,000.

TINGATINGA PAINTINGS

Visitors to the coast of Tanzania are bound to notice the brightly coloured paintings of fabulous creatures that line the streets of the country's main tourist centres. These are Tingatinga paintings, unique to Tanzania, and named after their originator Edward Tingatinga. The style arose in Dar es Salaam in the early 1960s, when Tingatinga fused the vibrant and popular work of Congolese immigrants with art traditions indigenous to his Makua homeland in the Mozambique border area (a region well known to aficionados of African art as the home of Makonde carving). When Tingatinga died in 1972, the accidental victim of a police shoot-out, his commercial success had already spawned a host of imitators, and shortly after that a formal Tingatinga art co-operative was formed with government backing.

In the early days, Tingatinga and his followers produced fairly simple paintings featuring a large, bold and often rather surreal two-dimensional image of one or other African creature on a monotone background. But as the paintings took off commercially, a greater variety of colours came into play, and a trend developed towards the more complex canvases you see today. Modern Tingatinga paintings typically depict a menagerie of stylised and imaginary birds, fish and mammals against a backdrop of a natural feature such as Kilimanjaro or an abstract panel of dots and whorls. An offshoot style, reputedly initiated by Tingatinga himself, can be seen in the larger, even more detailed canvases that depict a sequence of village or city scenes so busy you could look at them for a hour and still see something fresh.

Tingatinga painters have no pretensions to producing high art. On the contrary, the style has been commercially driven since its inception: even the largest canvases are produced over a matter of days and most painters work limited variations around favourite subjects. It would be missing the point altogether to talk of Tingatinga as traditional African art. With its bold, bright images – tending towards the anthropomorphic, often subtly humorous, always accessible and evocative – Tingatinga might more appropriately be tagged Africa's answer to Pop Art.

Labels aside, souvenir hunters will find Tingatinga paintings to be a lively, original and surprisingly affordable alternative to the identikit wooden animal carvings that are sold throughout East Africa (and, one suspects, left to gather dust in cupboards all over Europe). Take home a Tingatinga panel, and you'll have a quirky but enduring memento of your African trip, something to hang on your wall and derive pleasure from for years to come. The best place to buy Tingatinga painting is at the **Tingatinga Centre** [281 C5] (*Haile Selassie Rd, Oyster Bay;* ① *08.30–17.30 daily*).

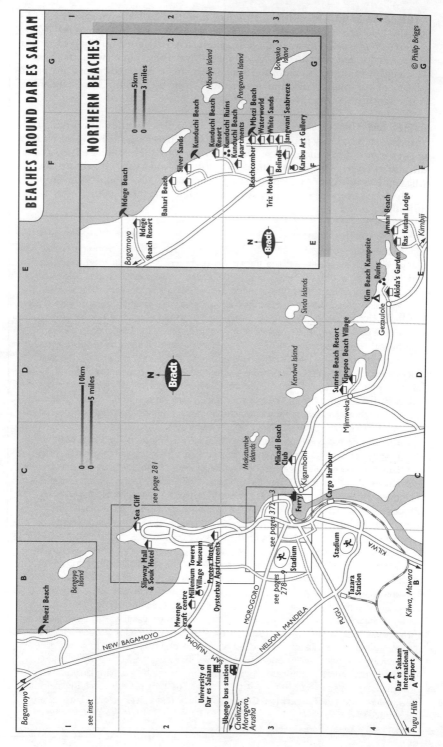

BEACHES AROUND DAR ES SALAAM

see inset

Bagamoyo

Mbezi Beach

Bongoyo Island

0 10km
0 5 miles

N
Bradt

NEW BAGAMOYO

Sea Cliff

see page 281

Slipway Mall & Souk Hotel

Mwenge craft centre

Millenium Towers
Village Museum

Protea Hotel
Oysterbay Apartments

University of Dar es Salaam

Ubongo bus station

Chalinze, Morogoro, Arusha

MOROGORO

NELSON MANDELA

PUGU

see pages 278–9

see pages 372–3

Ferry

Stadium

Stadium

Tazara Station

Kilwa, Mtwara

Dar es Salaam International Airport

Pugu Hills

Makatumbe Islands

Mikadi Beach Club

Kigamboni

Cargo Harbour

KILWA

Kendwa Island

Sinda Islands

Sunrise Beach Resort

Kipepeo Beach Village

Mjimweka

Gezaulole

Kim Beach Kampsite

Ruins

Akida's Garden

Amani Beach

Ras Kutani Lodge

Kimbiji

NORTHERN BEACHES

0 5km
0 3 miles

Bagamoyo

Ndege Beach

Ndege Beach Resort

Bahari Beach

Silver Sands

Kunduchi Beach

Mbudya Island

Kunduchi Beach Resort

Kunduchi Ruins

Kunduchi Beach Apartments

Pongwani Island

Mbezi Beach

Waterworld

White Sands

Jangwani Seabreeze

Karibu Art Gallery

Beachcomber

Belinda

Triz Motel

Bongoko Island

N
Bradt

© Philip Briggs

290

VILLAGE MUSEUM AND MWENGE MARKET The Village Museum [290 B22] (↘ 022 270 0437; e villagemuseum@museum.or.tz; www.museum.or.tz; ⏰ 09.30–18.00 daily; entrance US$5) consists of 16 life-size replicas of huts built in architectural styles from all over Tanzania. The best time to visit is between 14.00 and 16.00 on weekends and public holidays, when a traditional dance performance is held; an additional US$2 is charged to see the dance. The nearby Mwenge Market [290 B2] is a traditional Makonde carving community, and one of the best places to buy these unique sculptures (see box, *Makonde carvings*, in *Chapter 18*, page 565) – prices are negotiable.

Both are along the Bagamoyo road, 10km and 13km from the city centre respectively. If you want to get there on public transport, pick up a *dala-dala* from the post office to Makumbusha bus stand, which lies around the corner from the village museum.

BONGOYO ISLAND This small island lies within a marine reserve, and has a pretty beach where – unusually for Tanzania – swimming is possible at any time of day due to the absence of an offshore reef. A motorised dhow service runs between the island and the Msasani Slipway shopping mall [281 C3] four times daily, leaving Dar at 09.30, 11.30, 13.30 and 15.30, and leaving Bongoyo at 10.30, 12.30, 14.30 and 16.30. The return trip costs Tsh11,000 plus an additional US$5 for the park entrance fee.

PUGU HILLS FOREST RESERVE The main water catchment for Dar es Salaam, the forested Pugu Hills lie 25km southwest of the city centre, and receive a significantly higher rainfall due to their greater elevation. In 1954, a roughly 20km^2 tract of evergreen forest here was set aside as a forest reserve, much of which has since been destroyed or severely degraded due to a combination of commercial logging, planting of exotic eucalyptus trees, and local subsistence exploitation for charcoal, firewood and timber. Today, less than 5km^2 of pristine forest remains, supporting a surprisingly varied fauna. The reserve is crossed with trails and roads, making it one of the most accessible coastal forests in Tanzania.

Large mammals include vervet and blue monkey, bushpig, suni antelope, chequered elephant shrew and Rondo galago, while lion, spotted hyena and elephant pass through from time to time. A bird checklist of more than 100 species includes localised forest dwellers such as spotted ground thrush and east coast akalat, as well as crowned eagle and southern banded snake eagle. A wealth of butterflies can be seen, as with luck can chameleons. A site of particular interest is a large artificial cave in a disused limestone quarry that harbours around 100,000 bats – the whole flock streams out of the cave entrance at dusk, a quite spectacular phenomenon.

The base for visiting Pugu Hills is the small town of Kisarawe, which lies 25km from Dar es Salaam by road and is connected to it by regular *dala-dalas*. To reach Kisarawe, follow Nyerere Road out of Dar es Salaam, passing the airport, until about 20km from the city centre you reach a fork in the road opposite a filling station. Here, head straight along a dirt road (as opposed to forking left along a surfaced road). After about 1km, this dirt road passes through a corner of the forest reserve and perhaps 2km further it enters Kisarawe. At the second traffic circle in Kisarawe, a road to the left leads into the forest, and to the starting point of the 3km Mpugu Pugu walking trail. There is a forestry checkpoint at the junction where you must pay the entrance fee of Tsh5,000. The poor road into the forest is suitable for 4x4 vehicles only, and parts may be washed away during the rains. The bat cave lies about 3km from Kisarawe, on the right side of the road no more than 20m after it passes through a small tunnel.

10

Two major resort clusters lie along the coast immediately north of Dar es Salaam, the more established of which is Kunduchi Beach, about 35km from the city centre off the Bagamoyo road. Immediately south of Kunduchi, and divided from it by a large lagoon, Mbezi Beach has seen major tourist development over the last decade, and is now fringed by a compact string of upmarket and moderate resort hotels, generally of a higher quality than the older hotels at Kunduchi. While neither beach is as scenic as Tanzania's finest, both are likely to be a more attractive prospect to the average holidaymaker than staying in or around the city centre.

Both beaches are sandy and quite attractive, and good for swimming at high tide, though Kunduchi Beach is detracted from scenically by the series of concrete piles that were constructed along the waterfront to control erosion. At both beaches, tied to one or other hotel, there are diving, snorkelling, watersport and angling facilities, as well as motorboats for hire to visit one of the many small offshore islands dotted along the coastline. In all honesty, however, nothing along this stretch of coast matches Bagamoyo – only 50km further north and in the process of being linked to Dar by a zippy surfaced road – for scenery or for atmosphere.

A short walk from the Kunduchi Beach Hotel, the Kunduchi Ruins are well worth a visit. Little is known about their history, but at least one ruined building, a mosque, dates to the 16th century. The main point of interest, however, is an 18th-century graveyard set amongst a grove of baobab trees. The pillar tombs at Kunduchi, the most extensive such assemblage on the East Africa coast, are decorated with porcelain plates, and inscribed in a manner that is unique among Swahili graveyards of this period. Pottery collected at the site suggests the town was wealthy and had trade links with China and Britain.

GETTING THERE AND AWAY If you are driving, head out of Dar es Salaam along the Bagamoyo road until after about 35km you see the Karibu Art Gallery [290 F3] to your right. A short distance after this, the turn-off to Mbezi Beach and associated hotels – several of which are signposted – lies to the right. The beach and hotels are no more than 3km from the main road. For Kunduchi Beach, bypass this junction and continue towards Bagamoyo for about 2km, then turn right along the side road signposted for the various Kunduchi Beach resorts.

For day trippers, especially anyone on a budget, you can catch a *dala-dala* from outside the main post office in the centre of Dar es Salaam [279 E3] to Mwenge, then catch the 'Tegeta' *dala-dala* to Kunduchi or Mbezi village, from where you could walk to one of the hotels. This is not recommended if you are weighed down with luggage or carrying valuables, as thefts and mugging have been reported, but if you're just out for the day with a bit of cash, the risk of a problem is lessened. Otherwise, a taxi from the centre of town will cost Tsh15,000–20,000 one way.

WHERE TO STAY AND EAT
Upmarket
Kunduchi Beach Hotel & Resort [290 F2] (196 rooms) ☎ 022 265 0050/1; e reservations@kunduchiresort.com; www.kunduchiresort.com. After years of extensive renovations, this is the smartest hotel on the coast immediately north of Dar es Salaam, with excellent facilities including business centre & internet café, gymnasium & health centre, numerous watersport options, 5 restaurants & bars, 24hr room service & free access to the neighbouring Wet 'n' Wild Water Park (see box, opposite). The en-suite rooms are light & airy, with a king-size bed, AC, DSTV, sea-facing balconies, internet connectivity & minibar. The superb seafront location is on one of the best swimming beaches in the greater Dar es Salaam area, though the fussy pseudo-Arabian décor of the common areas & loud piped muzak might not suit all tastes. *US$150/170 sgl/dbl; US$300 executive suite.*

A particularly attractive feature of Kunduchi Beach for families – and children of all ages – is the Kunduchi Wet & Wild Water World complex, situated alongside the recently renovated Kunduchi Beach Hotel. Consisting of 22 water slides, the longest of which is 200m, as well as seven swimming pools, the complex also offers go-kart racing and watersports, and has a good selection of shops, video games and restaurants, as well as an internet café. A diving centre is planned, too. A day pass costs Tsh5,000. It is open daily, but only women are allowed in on Tuesday, a move geared towards the sensibilities of the local Muslim community. A similar but less elaborate water slide park called Waterworld can be found on Mbezi Beach, right next to the Beachcomber Hotel.

⌂ **White Sands Hotel** [290 F3] (124 rooms) ↘ 022 264 7620/6; e info@hotelwhitesands.com; www.hotelwhitesands.com. The largest hotel on Mbezi Beach, White Sands feels a bit like a city hotel transplanted to the beach, though the monolithic structure is redeemed by the attractive location & smart whitewashed exterior. The attached Sea Breeze Marine Diving School offers diving courses, dives & various other watersports. Rooms are en-suite with AC & satellite TV. Decent value; w/ender specials can be a bargain. *US$130/150 sgl/dbl.*

Moderate, budget and camping

⌂ **Belinda Ocean Resort** [290 F3] (62 room) ↘ 022 264 7551; f 022 264 7552; e info@ belindaresort.com; www.belindaresort.com. On a back road about 500m from the beach at Mbezi, this lodge seems too pricey to be a viable mid-range alternative to the smarter beachfront hotels, & too tacky & too far from the beach to offer them much competition on the aesthetic front. There's a pleasant swimming pool area. Ugly grounds & lack of direct beach access aside, the rooms, with AC, satellite TV & private balcony, are fair value. *US$65/90 sgl/dbl B&B.*

⌂ **Jangwani Seabreeze Resort** [290 F3] (32 rooms) ↘ 022 264 7215/7067; m 0713 320875; e gmjangwani@eclipsehotelsafrica; www.jangwani.org. This comfortable, tastefully decorated hotel, operated by the Eclipse Hotels group, straddles the main road along Mbezi Beach, dividing the accommodation, restaurant & reception area from the beach bar & swimming pool. It's renowned for w/end seafood buffets, & the long palm-lined beach is one of the most attractive around Dar. Facilities include tennis court, gym & go-kart track. Boat trips to the Islands are on offer, as are fishing, snorkelling & diving. The large, comfortable rooms have AC, fan, hot water, fridge,

⌂ **The Beachcomber Hotel & Resort** [290 F3] (35 rooms) ↘ 022 264 7772/4; e info@ beachcomber.co.tz; www.beachcomber.co.tz. This modern hotel at the north end of Mbezi Beach is marred slightly by the overuse of concrete & the garish blue & pink décor, but otherwise it's a very attractive set-up with a great beachfront swimming pool area facing Mbupi Island. Facilities include diving, health club & free airport transfers. Rooms have AC, satellite TV, fridge & private balcony. The seafood restaurant comes highly recommended. *US$104/122 en-suite sgl/dbl B&B, US$134/158 suites.*

safe & satellite TV. Great value, but expect prices to rise when it becomes part of the Holiday Inn chain in 2009. *US$59/83 sgl/dbl B&B.*

⌂ **Silver Sands Hotel, Campsite & Conference Centre** [290 F2] (37 rooms) ↘ 022 265 0567; e relax@ silversands.co.tz; www.silversandshotel.co.tz. Silver Sands has long provided an alternative to the main upmarket hotels for budget-conscious travellers wishing to spend time on the north coast beaches. Slightly run-down but pleasantly laid-back, it has a good beachfront location, a decent restaurant & bar, & offers a range of marine activities including snorkel hire & diving courses. There are en-suite 'deluxe' sea-facing dbl rooms with AC, standard dbls with no view & AC, dormitory accommodation & a campsite. *US$50/65 std/deluxe dbl B&B; US$15 pp dorm bed; US$5 pp camping plus US$2 per vehicle.*

⌂ **Bahari Beach Hotel** [290 F2] (40 rooms) ↘ 022 265 0352; e baharibeachhotel@yahoo.com. This former government hotel, constructed from coral rock & thatch in traditional Swahili style, lies in large, naturally vegetated grounds running down to arguably the finest stretch of beach on the north coast. The en-suite chalets evoke the 1970s motel-style rooms they undoubtedly started life as, but they are very comfortable nonetheless, with satellite TV, AC, & private sea-facing balconies. Other facilities include restaurant, internet café, swimming pool & watersport equipment. Good value. US$45/65/90 sgl/dbl/trpl. ⌂ **Triz Motel** [290 F3] ✆ 022 264 7414. Situated on the main Bagamoyo Rd about halfway between the junctions to Mbezi & Kunduchi beaches, this low-key & rather run-down local hotel feels overpriced & is miles from any beach. Tsh20,000 AC dbl. ⌂ **Visiwa Guesthouse** This bog-standard local guesthouse in Kunduchi has simple rooms with common showers. Tsh5,000/10,000 sgl/dbl.

BEACH RESORTS SOUTH OF DAR

Separated from central Dar es Salaam by the main harbour entrance – not bridged, but crossed by a regular motor ferry – the coast immediately south of Dar es Salaam seems worlds rather than a kilometre or two from the city centre. The suburban belt south of the harbour consists of the village of Kigamboni, a small cluster of shops and houses that sprawl for about 500m past the ferry terminal. Once past that, the road south passes through rustic fields barely touched by urban development, and overlooking a series of idyllic beaches pockmarked with large mushroom-shaped coral outcrops. A few years ago, these southern beaches were also practically bereft of tourist resorts. Today, however, the area is studded with a varied selection of resorts and lodges that – possibly because they are relatively new – seem to be far more geared towards the requirements of modern travellers of all budgets than are the generally somewhat outmoded monolithic hotels that characterise the northern beaches.

The best known accommodation on the southern beaches are the exclusive Ras Kutani Beach Resort and Amani Beach Hotel, which abut each other about 35km past the ferry, and vie with each other for the accolade of the best tourist lodge serving Dar es Salaam. For budget travellers, an increasingly popular goal is Kipepeo Beach Campsite, which lies about 7km south of the ferry at Mjimwema, and is the closest thing to a conventional backpacker hostel in the Dar es Salaam area. Another 5km south of this, the village of Gezaulole was formerly the site of a cultural tourist project, Akida's Garden, but at the time of writing this has closed.

GETTING THERE AND AWAY The Kivukoni Ferry leaves Dar es Salaam from the southeast of the city centre, where Kivukoni Front meets Ocean Road, every 15 minutes or so. The crossing takes about five minutes and costs Tsh1,000 per vehicle plus Tsh100 per person.

In a private vehicle, you can drive straight off the ferry and through Kigamboni on a good surfaced road for about 7km until you reach the Y-junction at Mjimwema. Kipepeo Lodge and other resorts around Mjimwema are signposted along a road leading east just before this Y-junction. To reach any coastal resort that lies south of Mjimwema, you need to turn along a dirt road that forms the left fork of the Y-junction. The surfaced right fork leads further southwest to the coastal villages of Kongowe and Mbajura, which are of little interest to travellers unless they happen to be trying to catch a dhow to Mafia Island.

Those using public transport will find plenty of dala-dalas lined up at Kigamboni to take ferry passengers to various villages further south. If you are heading to Kipepeo Lodge at Mjimwema, you shouldn't have to wait for more than a few minutes, since all vehicles heading south must pass through the village. Dala-dalas leave more erratically for Gezaulole, but several vehicles pass through the village daily en route to Gomvu or Kimbiji.

⌂ **WHERE TO STAY AND EAT**
Exclusive
⌂ **Ras Kutani** [290 E4] (13 rooms) ✆ 022 213 4802; f 022 211 2794; e reservations@selous.com; www.selous.com. Closer in spirit & feel to a bush retreat than a typical beach resort, this wonderful

small lodge lies on a wild isolated stretch of coast 35km south of Dar es Salaam. *Bandas* are constructed with organic materials (wood, bamboo & *makuti*) & set well apart in a patch of coastal woodland overlooking a mangrove-lined lagoon & wide sandy beach, to create a very soothing & relaxed atmosphere. Vervet & blue monkeys & prolific terrestrial birdlife are complemented by good snorkelling & fishing in the nearby reefs. Non-

motorised watersports are on offer, & there is a swimming pool, but diving facilities are not available. *US$305/365 sgl/dbl FB, plus US$55 pp high season supplement mid-July–Aug & Christmas/New Year.*

⌂ **Amani Beach Hotel** [290 E4] (10 rooms)
m 0754 410033/0755 775566; e reservations@amanibeach.com; www.amanibeach.com. The now French-owned Amani Beach Hotel is no less exclusive than Ras Kutani, but with a more cultivated, perhaps

DHOWS OF THE SWAHILI COAST

The word 'dhow', commonly applied by Europeans to any traditional seafaring vessel used off the coast of East Africa, is generally assumed to be Arabic in origin. There is, however, no historical evidence to back up this notion, nor does it appear to be an established Swahili name for any specific type of boat. Caroline Sassoon, writing in *Tanganyika Notes & Records* in 1970, suggests that the word is a corruption of *não*, used by the first Portuguese navigators in the Indian Ocean to refer to any small local seafaring vessel, or of the Swahili *kidau*, a specific type of small boat described below.

The largest traditional sailing vessel in wide use off the coast of East Africa is the *jahazi*, which measures up to 20m long and whose large billowing sails are a characteristic sight off Zanzibar and other traditional ports. With a capacity of about 100 passengers, the *jahazi* is mainly used for transporting cargo and passengers over relatively long distances or in open water, for instance between Dar es Salaam and Zanzibar. Minor modifications in the Portuguese and Omani eras notwithstanding, the design of the modern *jahazi* is pretty much identical to that of similar seafaring vessels used in mediaeval times and before. The name *jahazi* is generally applied to boats with cutaway bows and square sterns built on Zanzibar and nearby parts of the mainland. Similar boats built in Lamu and nearby ports in Kenya are called *jalbut* (possibly derived from the English 'jolly boat' or Indian 'gallevat') and have a vertical bow and wineglass-shaped stern. Smaller but essentially similar in design, the *mashua* measures up to 10m long, has a capacity of about 25 passengers, and is mostly used for fishing close to the shore or as local transport.

The most rudimentary and smallest type of boat used on the Swahili Coast is the *mtumbwi*, which is basically a dugout canoe made by hollowing out the trunk of a large tree – the mango tree is favoured today – and used for fishing in mangrove creeks and other still-water environments. The *mtumbwi* is certainly the oldest type of boat used in East Africa, and its simple design probably replicates that of the very first boats crafted by humans. A more elaborate and distinctive variation on the *mtumbwi* is the *ngalawa*, a 5–6m long dugout supported by a narrow outrigger on each side, making it sufficiently stable to be propelled by a sail. The *ngalawa* is generally used for fishing close to shore as well as for transporting passengers across protected channels such as the one between Mafia and Chole islands in the Mafia Archipelago.

The largest traditional boats of the Indian Ocean, the ocean-going dhows that were once used to transport cargo between East Africa, Asia and Arabia, have become increasingly scarce in recent decades due to the advent of foreign ships and other, faster modes of intercontinental transport. Several distinct types of ocean-going dhow are recognised, ranging from the 60-ton *sambuk* from Persia to 250-ton boats originating from India. Oddly, one of the larger of these vessels, the Indian *dengiya*, is thought to be the root of the English word dinghy. Although a few large dhows still ply the old maritime trade routes of the Indian Ocean, they are now powered almost exclusively with motors rather than by sails.

The village of Gezaulole, which lies on a fabulous sandy bay about 13km south of the Kivukoni ferry and Dar es Salaam, reputedly received its name many hundreds of years ago, when it was settled by a group of Zaramo fishermen. In the 16th century, Gezaulole became an Arabic trading post, and for reasons that sadly go unrecorded it was renamed Mbwamaji (literally 'Dog Water' or possibly a derivation of Mbu Maji, ie: 'Mosquito Water'!). The name Mbwamaji remained in use until the 1970s, when the village became one of the first Ujamaa villages established under the Nyerere administration, and the old Zaramo name – which means 'try and see' in the local dialect – took on a fresh resonance. The remains of a 16th-century mosque can still be seen at Mbwamaji, as can several 18th-century pillar tombs, all located close to the small local fishing harbour. Snorkelling excursions to the uninhabited Sinda Island in a local dhow are also possible.

even mildly pretentious feel. It consists of several whitewashed chalets with a traditional Swahili architectural influence, whose vast interiors are dominated by 4-poster Swahili beds. The cropped flowering lawns, crossed by neat footpaths, seem rather tepid compared with the wilder bush

atmosphere of Ras Kutani. Facilities for fishing & other watersports are available, & there is a lovely beachfront swimming pool & a tennis court in the grounds. US$290/520 sgl/dbl FB, 10% low-season discount.

Moderate

🏠 **Kipepeo Beach Village** [290 D4] (34 rooms) ❯ 022 212 2931; m 0732 920211; e info@ kipepeovillage.com; www.kipepeovillage.com. This started life as the closest thing around Dar es Salaam to a backpacker hostel, but now caters to a more affluent clientele, though budget accommodation & camping are still available. It lies on a lovely beach at Mjimwema, less than 1km along a side road signposted from the main surfaced road 7km south of the ferry terminal. Accommodation is simple beach *bandas* (no fan but a reliable sea breeze) or more comfortable en-suite rooms with net & fan. Facilities include beach volleyball & pool table. The food is good – snacks such as chicken in pita bread cost around US$2, full meals US$5–6. The camp has become a popular w/end hangout for young expatriates working in Dar, for which reason a small

entrance fee is charged to day visitors, refundable against drinks & food bought at the bar. US$15/25/35 sgl/dbl/trpl beach banda; US$55/75/105 en-suite rooms; camping US$5 pp.

🏠 **Sunrise Beach Resort** [290 D4] (30 rooms) ❯ 022 550 7038; m 0732 920205; f 022 218 0196; e info@sunrisebeachresort.co.tz; www.sunrisebeachresort.co.tz. Situated alongside Kipepeo, this lodge has an attractive beachfront location & good facilities include swimming pool, internet access, watersport equipment & beach bikes for hire, & free transfers for overnight guests from anywhere within the Dar es Salaam area. It's good value too. As with Kipepeo, a small entrance fee is charged to day visitors, refundable against drinks & food bought at the bar. US$30/36 en-suite sgl/dbl, US$60/80 with sea view; camping US$5 pp.

Budget, shoestring and camping

🏠 **Mikadi Beach Club** [290 C3] ❯ 022 282 0485; e mikadibeach@yahoo.com. Situated perhaps 2km south of the ferry terminal, this resort caters more to locals than to tourists, & can get rowdy at w/ends, making it of interest less as a place to stay than as somewhere for a few drinks away from the established expatriate hangouts. The simple beach *bandas* are poor value. Tsh15,000 dbl.

⚠ **Kim Beach Kampsite** [290 E4] Gezaulole. This basic campsite lies on a superb sandy beach, with the tankers in Dar es Salaam harbour visible in the distance & 2 large coral islands closer by. Facilities are limited to a long-drop toilet & bucket shower, food is not available (though drinks can be arranged) & there's little in the way of watersport facilities – but if these things don't worry you, this is a real stunner. Camping US$5 pp.

11

Zanzibar

Chris and Susan McIntyre

Zanzibar is one of those magical travel names, richly evocative even to the many Westerners who would have no idea where to start looking for it on a global map. Steeped in history, and blessed with a sultry tropical climate and a multitude of idyllic beaches, Zanzibar is also that rare travel destination which genuinely does live up to every expectation. Whether it's a quick cultural fix you're after, or scintillating diving, or just a palm-lined beach where you can laze away the day, a few days on Zanzibar is the perfect way to round off a dusty safari on the Tanzanian mainland.

A separate state within Tanzania, Zanzibar consists of two large islands, Unguja (Zanzibar Island) and Pemba, plus several smaller islets. Zanzibar Island is about 85km long and between 20km and 30km wide; Pemba is about 75km long and between 15km and 20km wide. Both are flat and low-lying, surrounded by coasts of rocky inlets or sandy beaches, with lagoons and mangrove swamps, and coral reefs beyond the shoreline. Farming and fishing are the main occupations, and most people live in small villages. Cloves are a major export, along with coconut products and other spices. The capital, and by far the largest settlement, is Zanzibar Town on the west coast.

Zanzibar used to be hard to reach, with a reputation for being expensive and unfriendly. Not any more! The island now positively welcomes tourists, and it offers facilities suitable to all tastes and budgets, though unrestricted development in some areas, especially around Nungwi, is becoming an issue.

For many, the highlight of a stay is the old Stone Town, with its traditional Swahili atmosphere and wealth of fascinating buildings. For others, it is the sea and the coral reefs, which offer diving, snorkelling and game fishing to compare with anywhere in East Africa. And then there are the clove and coconut plantations that cover the interior of the 'Spice Island'; the dolphins of Kizimkazi; the colobus monkeys of Jozani; and the giant sea turtles of Nungwi ... and above all, some will say, those seemingly endless tropical beaches.

For a dedicated guide to Zanzibar and Pemba, see our comprehensive *Zanzibar, Pemba & Mafia: The Bradt Travel Guide* (7th edition, 2009). An extensive range of literature about Zanzibar, mainly coffee-table style books, is stocked at The Gallery on Gizenga Road in Zanzibar Town (e *gallery@swahilicoast.com*). The Zanzibar Travel Network can be contacted at info@zanzibar.net (*www.zanzibar.net*).

HISTORY

Zanzibar has been trading with ships from Persia, Arabia and India for about 2,000 years. From about the 10th century AD, groups of immigrants from Shiraz (Persia) settled in Zanzibar and mingled with the local Swahili. The Portuguese established a trading station on the site of Zanzibar Town in the early 16th century. At the end of the 17th century, the Sultan of Oman's navy ousted the Portuguese from the island.

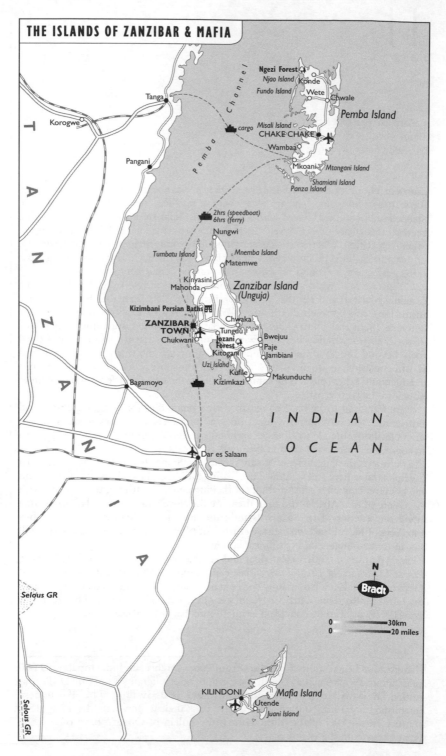

THE ISLANDS OF ZANZIBAR & MAFIA

Tanga

Korogwe

Pangani

Pemba Channel

Ngezi Forest
Njao Island Konde
Fundo Island Wete
Chwale
Pemba Island

cargo
Misali Island
CHAKE CHAKE
Wambaa

Mkoani Mtangani Island
Shamiani Island
Panza Island

T
A
N
Z
A
N
I
A

2hrs (speedboat)
6hrs (ferry)

Nungwi

Tumbatu Island
Mnemba Island
Matemwe

Kinyasini
Mahonda

Zanzibar Island
(Unguja)

Kizimbani Persian Baths
ZANZIBAR
TOWN
Chukwani

Chwaka
Tunguu
Jozani
Forest
Kitogani

Bwejuu
Paje
Jambiani

Uzi Island
Bagamoyo

Kufile
Kizimkazi
Makunduchi

Dar es Salaam

I N D I A N

O C E A N

Selous GR

N
Bradt

0 ———— 30km
0 ———— 20 miles

KILINDONI Mafia Island
Utende
Juani Island

Selous GR

298

In 1840, Sultan Said of Oman relocated his capital in Muscat to Zanzibar. Many Omani Arabs settled on Zanzibar as rulers and landowners, forming an elite group, while Indian settlers formed a merchant class. The island became an Arab state, an important centre of regional politics, and the focus of a booming slave trade. Britain had interests in Zanzibar throughout the 19th century; explorers such as Livingstone, Speke and Burton began their expeditions into the African interior from there. In 1890 Zanzibar became a British protectorate.

Zanzibar gained independence from Britain in December 1963. In 1964, the sultan was overthrown in a revolution, and nearly all Arabs and Indians were expelled. Later the same year, Zanzibar and Tanganyika combined to form the United Republic of Tanzania.

Today, the distinctions between Shirazi and Swahili are often blurred. The islanders fall into three groups: the Hadimu of southern and central Zanzibar, the Tumbatu of Tumbatu Island and northern Zanzibar, and the Pemba of Pemba Island. Many people of mainland origin live on Zanzibar, some the descendants of freed slaves, others more recent immigrants. Many of the Arab, Asian and Goan people expelled in 1964 have since returned.

CLIMATE

Zanzibar has a typical coastal climate, warm to hot all year round and often very humid. It receives more rainfall and is windier than the mainland.

GETTING THERE AND AWAY

BY AIR An ever-increasing number of airlines offer direct flights between Zanzibar and Dar es Salaam, a 30-minute trip that costs around US$80. There are also regular flights to Zanzibar from Kilimanjaro International Airport (between Moshi and Arusha), some of which are direct, taking roughly one hour, while others require a change of plane at Dar and might take three to four hours depending on your connection. The main established airlines covering these routes are Air Tanzania, Precision Air, ZanAir and Coastal Aviation, all of which offer a range of other domestic flights, while some also fly to Kenya, so the best choice will depend largely on your other travel plans. Any reliable tour operator will be able to advise you about this.

Airlines

✈ **Air Tanzania** [317 B7] Vuga Rd, near junction with Creek Rd, Zanzibar Town; ✆ 024 223 0213/0297; e bookings@airtanzania.com; www.airtanzania.com

✈ **Coastal Travel** [317 C8] Zanzibar Airport: ✆ 024 223 3112; m 0713 670815/0777 414201; Stone Town: Kelele Sq, Shangani (close to Serena Hotel); ✆ 024 2239664; e aviation@coastal.cc/ safari@coastal.cc; www.coastal.cc

✈ **Precision Air Flight Services** [305 C3] Kenyatta Rd (next to Mazsons Hotel), Zanzibar Town; ✆ 024 2234521; e pwznz@precisionairtz.com, contactcentre@precisionairtz.com; www.precisionairtz.com

✈ **Zan Air** [305 C2] Zanzibar Airport: ✆ 024 223 2993; m 0777 413240; Stone Town: Malawi Rd, Malindi; ✆ 024 223 3670/3788; e reservations@zanair.com; www.zanair.com

BY BOAT A number of hydrofoils and catamarans run daily between Dar es Salaam and Zanzibar, with prices determined largely by the efficiency and speed of the service. The booking kiosks for all these boats are clustered together at the ports on Zanzibar and in Dar. There's a lot to be said for asking around before you make any firm arrangements, or for using a tour operator to make your booking (this won't cost much more and saves a lot of hassle). Do be wary of the hustlers who

11

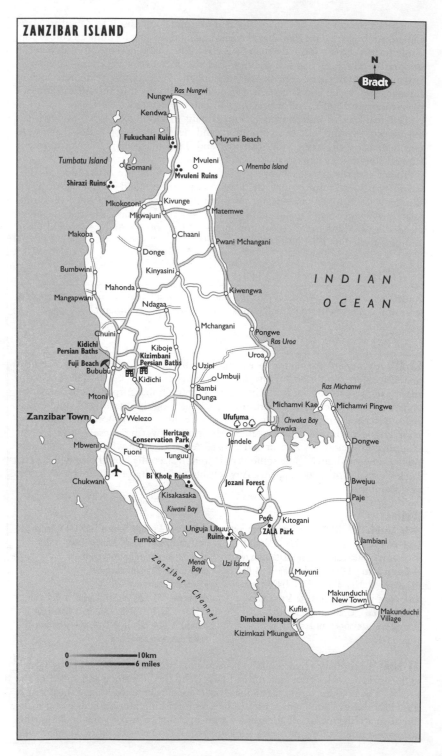

ZANZIBAR ISLAND

N
Bradt

Ras Nungwi
Nungwi
Kendwa
Fukuchani Ruins
Muyuni Beach
Tumbatu Island
Gomani
Mvuleni
Mnemba Island
Shirazi Ruins
Mvuleni Ruins
Mkokotoni
Kivunge
Mkwajuni
Matemwe
Makoba
Chaani
Pwani Mchangani
Donge
Bumbwini
Kinyasini
Mahonda
Kiwengwa
Mangapwani
Ndagaa
Chuini
Mchangani
Pongwe
Kidichi
Persian Baths
Kiboje
Ras Uroa
Fuji Beach
Kizimbani
Persian Baths
Uzini
Uroa
Bububu
Kidichi
Umbuji
Mtoni
Bambi
Dunga
Ras Michamvi
Michamvi Kae
Michamvi Pingwe
Zanzibar Town
Welezo
Ufufuma
Chwaka Bay
Jendele
Chwaka
Dongwe
Heritage
Conservation Park
Mbweni
Fuoni
Tunguu
Bwejuu
Chukwani
Bi Khole Ruins
Jozani Forest
Paje
Kisakasaka
Kiwani Bay
Pete
Kitogani
Unguja Ukuu
Ruins
ZALA Park
Jambiani
Fumba
Menai
Bay
Uzi Island
Muyuni
Zanzibar Channel
Makunduchi
New Town
Kufile
Makunduchi
Village
Dimbani Mosque
Kizimkazi Mkunguni

INDIAN
OCEAN

0 ⸻ 10km
0 ⸻ 6 miles

hang around both ports – many are con artists and some are thieves. Tickets must be paid for in hard currency, as must the port tax of US$5.

🚢 **Aziza I & Aziza II** These 2 ships sail daily between Dar & Zanzibar, leaving at the same times as the MV *Flying Horse*. Going the other way it's an overnight trip. The journey time is 5–8hr. *Dar–Zanzibar US$20, Zanzibar–Dar US$20, Zanzibar–Pemba US$20.*

🚢 **Flying Horse** African Shipping Corp; ℡ 022 212 4507 (Dar); m 0784 472497/606177 (Zanzibar); e asc@raha.com. This large catamaran, with a capacity of more than 400 passengers, operates from Dar to Zanzibar at 12.30 daily, arriving at 15.30. The return trip departs at 21.00, arriving in Dar at 06.00 the following morning, to avoid disembarkation during the night. Seating areas have AC & it's also possible to travel on deck. *US$20 pp inc mattress overnight.*

🚢 **Mapinduzi** Zanzibar Shipping Corp (ZSC); ℡ 024 223 0302/2857. The state-owned boat plies between Dar & Zanzibar, & also between Zanzibar & Pemba, & Dar & Mtwara on the southern coast of mainland Tanzania. Services are slow & cheap, but cabins are quite airy & comfortable. The official schedule follows a 2-week pattern, although it is notoriously unreliable. *Deck, around US$5; shared cabin US$10; private cabin US$12.*

🚢 **Sea Bus I & Sea Bus II** Azam Marine; ℡ 024 223 1655 (Zanzibar), 022 2123324 (Dar); m 0777 334347; e azam@cats-net.com; www.azam-marine.com. Highly recommended, these 2 large high-speed boats run once daily in either direction between Zanzibar & Dar, taking about 2hr on each leg. *Sea Bus I* departs Dar 10.30, returning from Zanzibar 13.00; *Sea Bus II* departs Zanzibar 10.00, returning from Dar 16.00. *1st class US$40; 2nd class US$35; children US$20.*

🚢 **Sea Express** Fast Ferries; ℡ 022 213 7049 (Dar); m 0754 278692 (Zanzibar); e fastferries@cats-net.com; www.fastferriestz.com. *Sea Express I* is a large, fairly steady hydrofoil linking Dar with Zanzibar once daily in each direction, & taking 2–2½hrs. Departures from Dar are at midday, & from Zanzibar at 16.00. The newer *Sea Express II* takes in a circuit between Dar, Zanzibar Island & Pemba. At the time of writing, departures from Zanzibar for Pemba were at 12.00 Mon, Wed & Sat, & from Dar to Zanzibar at 07.30 & 09.00. *Dar–Zanzibar US$40; Zanzibar–Pemba US$45; Dar–Pemba US$65, all one way.*

🚢 **Sea Star** ℡ 024 2234768; m 0777 411505. This large catamaran is one of the more efficient services between Dar & Zanzibar, departing Zanzibar daily for Dar at 07.00 for a 2hr crossing. *1st class US$40; 2nd class US$30.*

🚢 **Seagull** ℡ 024 223 6315. Another daily Dar connection, departing Dar 12.00 for the 3hr crossing to Zanzibar – though arrival time is usually nearer to 17.00–19.00. Like the *Flying Horse*, the return service leaves at 21.00, arriving 06.00 next morning. *US$20 pp.*

🚢 **Sepideh** Mega Speed Liners; m 0774 447 333, 0777 303308; e megaspeed@zanzinet.com. This nippy service between Dar & Zanzibar continues on to Pemba, taking around 2hr for each leg. Departures from Dar are 07.15 Mon, Thu & Sat, & from Zanzibar to Pemba 09.30. The return boat leaves Pemba at 12.30, & Zanzibar at 16.00. On Tue, Wed & Sun, the *Sepideh* departs Dar for Zanzibar at 07.30 & returns at 16.00; Pemba boats depart Zanzibar 10.00 & return 12.30 on these days. There is no service to Pemba on Fri or Sun. *Zanzibar–Dar US$35; Zanzibar–Pemba US$44*

It is both unsafe and illegal to travel between Zanzibar and the mainland by fishing dhow.

ORGANISED TOURS Most international tour operators (see pages 51–2) offering safaris to Tanzania can append a flight to Zanzibar (or a full travel package on the island) to your safari arrangements. Likewise, most safari companies based in Arusha are able to set up excursions to Zanzibar. If you are booking a safari in advance, there is probably a lot to be said for making all your travel arrangements in Tanzania through one company.

ARRIVAL AND DEPARTURE Zanzibar being a separate state from mainland Tanzania, all visitors were formerly required to complete an immigration card and to show their passport and visa (and sometimes their yellow fever certificate) upon arrival. Visitors who fly in to Zanzibar from elsewhere in Tanzania no longer need to complete an immigration card and show their passport and visa, but they may still be asked to show a yellow fever certificate. This documentation is, however, still required if you arrive at the port by ferry from the mainland.

Travellers flying into Zanzibar from outside of Tanzania can now buy a visa on arrival at the airport. A visa costs between US$20 and US$100 depending on your nationality and should be paid for in US dollar cash (travellers' cheques and local currency are not accepted, though either can be converted into cash at a bureau de change at a poor rate; and while cash in most other hard currencies is accepted, it will be at a highly unfavourable rate). The airport tax of US$20 for international flights out of Zanzibar is usually incorporated into the price of a ticket but, if not, it must be paid in US dollar cash (not by credit card or travellers' cheque). Flights within Tanzania attract a US$5 airport tax, payable in local currency.

If you lose your passport while on Zanzibar, you will need to have an Emergency Travel Document issued at the Ministry of the Interior. This will allow you to travel back to the mainland (where nationals of most countries will find diplomatic representation in Dar es Salaam) or directly to your home country.

GETTING AROUND

PUBLIC MINIBUSES AND *DALA-DALAS* Local minibuses and small converted trucks called *dala-dalas* cover many routes around Zanzibar Island. These are faster than buses, and fares are cheap: typically around US$0.50 around Zanzibar Town and a few dollars to cross the island.

Dala-dalas have standardised route numbers, destinations and frequencies. Buses and *dala-dalas* from outlying villages heading for Zanzibar Town tend to leave very early in the morning but, apart from that, most vehicles simply leave when they're full. Be aware that the last buses to some coastal villages will leave Zanzibar Town by mid afternoon.

There are three main terminals in Zanzibar Town: Darajani Bus Station on Creek Road (opposite the market), Mwembe Ladu and Mwana Kwerekwe. The latter two stations are a few kilometres from town and are best accessed by a short hop on a *dala-dala* from Darajani.

The most useful *dala-dala* routes and times are in the box opposite; the name in brackets is the destination as written on the front of the vehicle:

BUSES It is possible to reach many parts of Zanzibar Island by public bus, although most visitors use tourist minibuses or *dala-dalas*. All buses leave from Darajani Bus Station, on Creek Road in Zanzibar Town. Generally you can expect to pay only a few dollars to travel half the length of the island between Zanzibar Town and Bwejuu. Note, though, that journeys can be very slow.

On most routes, especially the longer ones, there is only one bus each day, leaving Zanzibar Town around midday, to reach their destination in the evening and return in time for the morning market. Always check that the bus is going to the destination you think it should be.

Some of the bus routes are also covered by public minibuses or *dala-dalas*. These are usually slightly more expensive than the buses, but also tend to be quicker.

The bus route numbers, destinations and frequencies are given in the box on page 304.

CAR HIRE To hire a car (in reality, probably a Suzuki 'jeep') or scooter, contact one of the island's tour operators (see pages 306–7). A jeep for a day will cost around US$50–60, and is unlikely to have much fuel in the tank when you hire it. Insurance cover is in theory comprehensive, but it is important to check this thoroughly. Note, too, that driving standards on Zanzibar are not good, and the roads are often poor, so think carefully before hiring a car. You should also be aware that, unlike on the mainland, you need an international driving licence to drive a vehicle in Zanzibar.

Petrol is available (usually, but not with total reliability) in Zanzibar Town, Kinyasini, Chwaka, on the road to Nungwi and at Kitogani, near the junction where the road turns off to Paje. Prices here, as in the rest of the world, are increasing.

TAXIS Taxis are fairly widely available. A short hop within Zanzibar Town costs just over US$3, while the trip to Mtoni costs around US$7–10 one way; to Jozani or

DALA-DALA ROUTES AND FREQUENCY

Dala-dala number	Departs	To	No per day	First	Last
AROUND ZNZ TOWN					
502	Darajani	Bububu, via Marahubi & Mtoni	Lots	06.00	21.00
505	Darajani	Airport (U/Ndege)	Lots	06.00	21.00
510	Darajani	Mwana Kwerekwe (m/Kwerekwe)	Lots	06.00	21.00
511	Darajani	Kidichi Spice (K/Spice), via Kidichi Persian baths	Lots	06.00	21.00
NORTH					
101	Creek Rd	Mkokotoni	15	05.30	21.00
102	Darajani	Bumbwini, via Mangapwani	5	10.00	16.00
116	Creek Rd	Nungwi	25	05.30	21.00
121	Darajani	Donge & Mahonda	5	10.00	18.00
NORTHEAST					
117	Creek Rd	Kiwengwa, some continue to Pwani Mchangani	9	06.00	19.00
118	Creek Rd	Matemwe	10	06.00	19.00
206	Darajani or	Chwaka, via Dunga Palace Mwembe Ladu	10	06.00	18.00
209	Mwembe Ladu	Pongwe	3	07.00	16.00
214	Mwembe Ladu	Uroa, via Dunga Palace	7	06.00	18.00
SOUTHEAST					
309	Darajani or Mwana Kwerekwe	Jambiani, via Jozani	5	07.30	16.00
310	Darajani	Makunduchi, via Jozani	10	06.30	21.00
324	Darajani	Bwejuu, via Jozani, Paje & Kae Michamvi	Lots	09.00	14.00
SOUTHWEST					
308	Mwembe Ladu or Mwana Kwerekwe	Unguja Ukuu	4	08.00	15.00
336	Darajani or Mwana Kwerekwe	Kibondeni	Lots	06.00	20.00
326	Darajani or Mwana Kwerekwe	Kizimkazi, via Zala Park	5	07.00	16.00

Route number	To	No per day	First	Last
NORTH				
1	Mkokotoni (occas continuing to Nungwi)	15	05.30	20.00
2	Bumbwini & Makoba, via Mangapwani	3	05.30	18.00
14	Nungwi, via Mahonda, Kinyasini & Chaani	7	07.00	18.00
NORTHEAST				
6	Chwaka (some continue to Uroa & Pongwe)	5	07.00	16.00
13	Uroa	5	08.00	16.00
15	Kiwengwa	5	08.00	18.00
16	Matemwe	6	07.00	18.00
SOUTHEAST				
9	Paje, sometimes to Bwejuu & Jambiani	7	06.00	17.00
10	Makunduchi, via Tunguu, Pete & Munyuni	4	07.00	16.00
SOUTHWEST				
7	Fumba, via Kombeni	4	06.00	16.00
8	Unguja Ukuu	4	06.00	16.00
CENTRAL				
3	Kidichi & Kizimbani, via Welezo	7	06.00	18.00
4	Mchangani, via Dunga, Bambi & Uzini	5	06.00	17.00
5	Ndagaa, via Kiboje	4	06.00	16.00
11	Fuoni, via Tungu & Binguni	10	07.00	18.00
12	Dunga, then north to Bambi	5	07.00	17.00

the east coast US$20–25 one way or US$30–35 return. The going rate for transfers between the airport and Zanzibar Town is US$10–15.

BICYCLE HIRE Most of the tour operators in Zanzibar Town can arrange bicycle hire. The going rate for a heavy Chinese bike is from US$10 per day, while mountain bikes go for around US$15.

ZANZIBAR TOWN

Zanzibar's old quarter, usually called the Stone Town, is a fascinating maze of narrow streets and alleyways which lead the visitor past numerous old houses and mosques, ornate palaces, and shops and bazaars. Many buildings in the Stone Town date from the 19th-century slave boom. Houses reflect their builder's wealth: Arab houses have plain outer walls and large front doors leading to an inner courtyard; Indian houses have a more open façade and large balconies decorated with railings and balustrades. Most are still occupied.

A striking feature of many houses is the brass-studded doors with their elaborately carved frames. The size of a door and intricacy of its design was an indication of the owner's wealth and status. The use of studs probably originated in Persia or India, where they helped prevent doors being knocked down by war-elephants. In Zanzibar, studs were purely decorative.

The area outside the Stone Town used to be called Ng'ambo (The Other Side), and is still often referred to as such, though its official name is actualy Michenzani

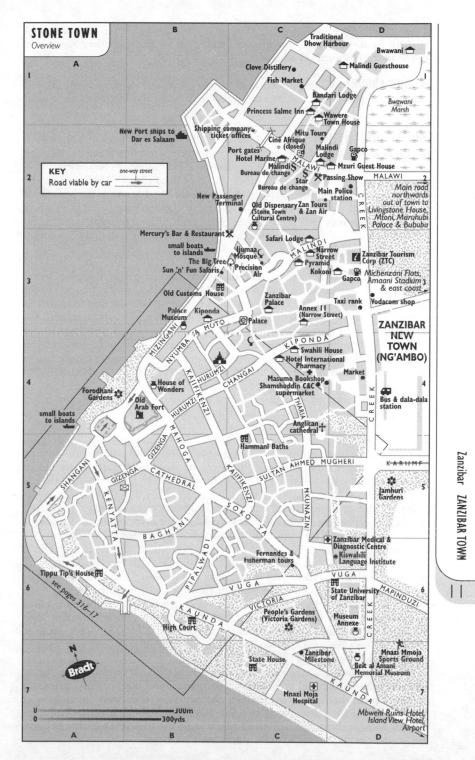

STONE TOWN
Overview

A

B

Traditional
Dhow Harbour

Bwawani

Clove Distillery

Malindi Guesthouse

Fish Market

Bandari Lodge

Bwawani
Marsh

Princess Salme Inn

Wawere
Town House

New Port ships to
Dar es Salaam

Shipping company
ticket offices

Mitu Tours

Ciné Afrique
(closed)

Malindi
Lodge

Gapco

Port gates

Hotel Marine

Malindi

Mzuri Guest House

Bureau de change

KEY

one-way street

Road viable by car

Star

Passing Show

MALAWI

New Passenger
Terminal

Bureau de change

Main Police
station

Main road
northwards
out of town to
Livingstone House,
Mtoni, Maruhubi
Palace & Bububu

Old Dispensary
(Stone Town
Cultural Centre)

Zan Tours
& Zan Air

Mercury's Bar & Restaurant

Safari Lodge

small boats
to islands

Ijumaa
Mosque

Narrow
Street

Zanzibar Tourism
Corp (ZTC)

The Big Tree

Pyramid

Sun 'n' Fun Safaris

Precision
Air

Kokoni

Gapco

Michenzani Flats,
Amaani Stadium
& east coast

Old Customs House

Vodacom shop

Palace
Museum

Kiponda

Zanzibar
Palace

Taxi rank

Palace

Annex 11
(Narrow Street)

**ZANZIBAR
NEW
TOWN
(NG'AMBO)**

Swahili House

Hotel International
Pharmacy

Forodhani
Gardens

House of
Wonders

Masumo Bookshop
Shamshuddin C&C
supermarket

Market

Old
Arab Fort

Bus & dala-dala
station

small boats
to islands

Anglican
cathedral

Hammani Baths

Jamhuri
Gardens

Tippu Tip's House

Fernandes &
Fisherman tours

Zanzibar Medical &
Diagnostic Centre

Kiswahili
Language Institute

State University
of Zanzibar

People's Gardens
(Victoria Gardens)

Museum
Annexe

High Court

Mnazi Mmoja
Sports Ground

State House

Zanzibar
Milestone

Beit al Amani
Memorial Museum

Mnazi Moja
Hospital

Mbweni Ruins Hotel,
Island View Hotel,
Airport

500m

300yds

N

Bradt

Zanzibar **ZANZIBAR TOWN**

11

(New City). Attempts have been made to modernise it: at the centre of Michenzani are some ugly apartment blocks, built by East German engineers as part of an international aid scheme.

GETTING AROUND Walking is the easiest way to get around Zanzibar Town. Buses, pick-up vans (*dala-dalas*) and taxis are available. You can also hire bikes and motor scooters.

TOURIST INFORMATION The head office of the Zanzibar Tourist Corporation (ZTC) in Livingstone House, about 1km from the town centre along the Bububu road, is the best place to make bookings for the ZTC bungalows on the east coast. For general information, the ZTC office on Creek Road [305 D3] will probably be more clued up and helpful. Alternatively, ask at your hotel or one of the better tour companies, such as Eco+Culture, Sama Tours or Gallery Tours. The information desk at the Arab Fort [305 B4 & 316 A4] has details of local musical, cultural and sporting events, and the noticeboard at the Fort's open-air restaurant is another good source of information.

TOUR OPERATORS A number of tour companies operate out of Zanzibar Town, offering the tours mentioned in *What to see and do*, page 315, as well as transfers to the east coast and Nungwi. The better companies can set up bespoke trips to anywhere on the island, as well as make hotel reservations and other travel arrangements. For straightforward day trips and transfers, there is no real need to make bookings before you arrive in Zanzibar, as they can easily be set up at the last minute. If, however, you want to have all your travel arrangements fixed in advance through one company, or you have severe time restrictions, then it would be sensible to make advance contact with one of the companies with good international connections.

While prices vary greatly depending on standard of service, season and group size, typical costs per person for the most popular outings are US$15–20 for a Stone Town tour, US$20–25 for a Prison Island tour, US$20–25 for a spice tour, US$20–25 for a trip to Jozani Forest and US$30–45 for a Kizimkazi dolphin tour. These are based on four to eight people sharing, and will be substantially higher for smaller groups. That said, prices are negotiable, particularly out of season, but do be wary of unregistered companies offering sub-standard trips at very low rates.

It's possible to arrange many of the standard tours more cheaply through taxi drivers or independent guides (nicknamed *papaasi* after a type of insect). With spice tours, this may often turn out to be a false economy, in that the guide will lack botanical knowledge and may cut the excursion short, rendering the whole exercise somewhat pointless. One taxi driver who has been consistently recommended by travellers over many years is Mr Mitu (✆ *024 223 4636*). His spice tours leave every morning from in front of the Ciné Afrique [305 C2], though these days they are so popular that you might find yourself joining a fleet of minibuses rather than hopping into Mr Mitu's own vehicle! It makes little difference if you use *papaasi* to set up trips to the islands, because specialist knowledge isn't required, and you can agree in advance how long you want to spend on any given island.

You can assume that any tour operator working through one of the upmarket hotels will be reliable and accountable, bearing in mind that they deal primarily with a captive, big-spending clientele, though their costs may be somewhat inflated. A list of a few recommended and well-established tour companies follows. Most of them offer a pretty similar selection of trips at reasonably uniform prices, and can also make flight, ferry and hotel bookings.

Eco&Culture Tours [316 C1] Hurumzi St; ℡ 024 223 3731; m 0777 410873/462665; e ecoculturetours@gmail.com; www.ecoculture-zanzibar.org. A respected, ethically minded operator offering slightly more expensive, but excellent, day trips for those who want to avoid the more established circuits & contribute to community development.

Sama Tours [316 C3] Gizenga St; m 0713 608576, 0777 430385; e samatours@zitec.org; www.samatours.com. Trips include 'special' spice tours with a knowledgeable local naturalist, plus boat trips & tailor-made tours, with guides who speak English, French, German or Italian.

Sun 'n' Fun Safaris [305 B3] ℡ 024 223 7381/7665; m 0713 600206; e zanzibarsun@hotmail.com.

From an office in Sea View Indian Restaurant, runs town & island tours, plus transfer services to the airport or east coast. Can also assist with visas, car & bike hire, boat trips & transport tickets.

Tropical Tours [317 D7] Kenyatta Rd; ℡ 024 223 0868; m 0777 413454; e tropicalts@hotmail.com. A straightforward & friendly budget company, recommended by several travellers, & offering the usual range of tours, plus car hire, & ticket reservations.

ZanTours [305 C2] ℡ 024 223 3042/3116; m 0777 417279; e zantoursinfo@zantours.com; www.zantours.com. Largest operator on Zanzibar, linked to ZanAir, with efficient staff, a fleet of clean vehicles & an impressive range of tours, transfers, excursions & safaris.

🏠 WHERE TO STAY

The last decade has seen a mushrooming of new hotels in Zanzibar Town, as well as around the island, and there are now numerous options at every level, from basic guesthouses to smart upmarket hotels. As a rule, room rates on Zanzibar are quoted in US dollars, and at the top end of the range the management will probably insist that you pay in hard currency. Hotels at the lower end of the price bracket generally accept local currency at an exchange rate similar to those given at forex bureaux.

Most prices include breakfast, though at budget hotels this may amount to little more than a slice of stale bread and a banana. The rates quoted in this guide are high season only; most upmarket hotels will offer a discount out of season. At the lower end of the price range, rates may be negotiable depending on how busy the hotel is and the intended duration of your stay. It is advisable to make an advance reservation for any upmarket or moderate hotel, particularly during peak seasons, but this shouldn't be necessary for cheaper lodgings.

Travellers who arrive on Zanzibar by boat can expect to be met by a group of hotel touts. Some are quite aggressive and likely to take you to whichever hotel gives them the largest commission, while others are friendly and will find you a suitable hotel if you tell them what you want. Either way, the service shouldn't cost you anything, since the tout will get a commission from the hotel, and it may save a lot of walking in the confusing alleys of the Stone Town. Given the difficulty of getting past the touts and the general aura of chaos around the ferry port, there is probably a lot to be said for taking the path of least resistance when you first arrive. Should you not like the place to which you are first directed, you can always look around yourself once your bags are securely locked away, and change hotel the next day.

However you arrive, many of the hotels in the Stone Town cannot be reached by taxi. You are liable to get lost if you strike out on foot without a guide, though we found that people were always very helpful when it came to being pointed in the right direction (bearing in mind that the right direction may change every few paces). Most taxi drivers will be prepared to walk you to the hotel of your choice, but they will expect a decent tip.

Upmarket

🏠 **Zanzibar Serena Inn** [317 B8] (51 rooms) ℡ 024 223 2306; e zserena@zanzinet.com; www.serenahotels.com. This large, impressive hotel, converted from 2 historic buildings, overlooks the sea in the Shangani area. The staff are excellent & the

hotel boasts all the in-room & public facilities that you would expect of an international-class establishment, including inviting pool, 2 excellent restaurants (or a porter escort to the public food market), coffee shop, AC, WiFi, satellite TV &

reasonably priced, in-house massage treatments. *US$475 dbl.*

⌂ **236 Hurumzi** [316 C2] (16 rooms) m 0777 423266; e 236hurumzibookings@zanlink.com; www.emerson-green.com. The former Emerson & Green Hotel sprawls across 2 restored buildings dating from 1840–70, decorated with antique Zanzibari furniture & carpets. Each room is different, but each, very deliberately, is without phone, TV or fridge. Some have AC, others natural cooling – shutters, shades, deep balconies & a sea breeze. The hotel's Tower Top Restaurant, the second-highest building in Zanzibar Town, has fine views, but standards at dinner (US$30 pp, reservations essential) are not always up to scratch. *US$185–250 dbl.*

⌂ **Africa House Hotel** [317 D8] (15 rooms) ↘ 0777 432340; e info@theafricahouse.com; www.theafricahouse-zanzibar.com. This sea-facing hotel ranks among the most popular places to stay in Zanzibar Town. It served as the English Club from 1888 until the end of the colonial era, but is perhaps best known for its expansive sunset bar (see page 311). The en-suite rooms, mixing stylish traditional décor with modern facilities, are cool, clean & functional, & a particularly good low-season deal. *High season US$160–215 dbl, low-season (Apr–Jun) US$90–160 dbl.*

⌂ **Beyt al Chai** [317 C7] (6 rooms) m 0777 444111; e reservations@stonetowninn.com; www.stonetowninn.com. With its thick walls & antique shuttered windows, the peaceful & friendly Beyt al Chai was a private home until 2005 & it continues to offer relaxed hospitality & home comforts. Large, en-suite rooms are full of character with authentic Zanzibari furniture & vibrant fabrics; the Princess room is the only one without a view over the

square. The restaurant is one of Zanzibar Town's culinary hotspots &, though relatively expensive, good value for money. *US$155–305 dbl.*

⌂ **Swahili House** [305 C4] (22 rooms) e reservations@moivaro.com; www.moivaro.com. The dilapidated Hotel International, in the Ukatani area, was acquired for regeneration by Moivaro Lodges in 2008. Given the high quality of their beach property, Fumba Beach Lodge (see page 351), this was an exciting development for the towering white townhouse built around its central roofed courtyard. Swahili House finally opened its doors in early 2009 to offer plush, traditionally styled bedrooms & open en-suite bathrooms, & is well worth checking out. *US$150–270 dbl.*

⌂ **Al Johari** [317 C7] (15 rooms) ↘ 024 223 6779; e info@al-johari.com; www.al-johari.com. Al Johari, meaning 'jewel' in Swahili, brings a touch of boutique bling to Stone Town's upmarket hotel scene, yet with a décor & ambience reminiscent of a bygone era. Rooms are tastefully furnished, & the lovely rooftop bar adjoins a fine-dining restaurant, Fusion. There is also a spa, run by a professional Indian therapist. *US$140–350 dbl.*

⌂ **Zanzibar Palace Hotel** [305 C3] (9 rooms) ↘ 024 223 2230; m 0773 079222/047370; e info@zanzibarpalacehotel.com; www.zanzibarpalacehotel.com. One of the best boutique hotels in Stone Town, this place has a distinctly Zanzibari feel, with steep staircases, handcrafted wooden furniture & antique Arab *objets d'art*, yet modern creature comforts abound: AC throughout, DVD library & in-room player, & WiFi. Helpful staff are on hand for travel tips, & the small bar serves cold drinks throughout the day. *US$135–315 dbl.*

Moderate

⌂ **Chavda Hotel** [317 D6] (41 rooms) Baghani St; ↘ 024 223 2115; e chavdahotel@zanlink.com; www.chavdahotel.co.tz. Situated in the Shangani area, Chavda is pretty soulless in spite of its antique-style Indian furniture & Persian carpets, & its generally spacious bedrooms are adequate, if uninspiring. The upstairs restaurant & very pleasant rooftop bar offer one of the best skyline views of St Joseph's Cathedral & the city beyond. There are free collections from the port or airport to pre-booked guests. *US$110 dbl.*

⌂ **Tembo Hotel** [317 A6] (36 rooms) Shangani Rd; ↘ 024 223 3005/2069; e tembo@zitec.org; www.tembohotel.com. In a great location just west of Forodhani Gardens, Tembo combines a grand old white house & a more recent extension, both quite Indian in

décor. Rooms are en suite, including mosaic bath, with heavily carved furniture, AC, fridge, phone & TV; most have a sea view or overlook the pool. There's a beachfront restaurant under a row of almond trees (non-residents welcome; no alcohol served). On the beach itself, expect a degree of hassle from touts, & note that swimming is not advisable. *US$100 dbl.*

⌂ **Mazson's Hotel** [317 D7] (35 rooms) Kenyatta Rd; ↘ 024 223 3062/3694, m 0713 340042; e mazons@zanlink.com; www.mazsonshotel.com. Built in the mid 19th century by Said bin Dhanin, who is thought to have settled here about the time that Sultan Said moved his court to Zanzibar, Mazson's has had a chequered history. Today, it is beginning to look a little tired. Its reception area, with heavily carved desk, chandeliers & plastic flowers, is dated, & the bedrooms are slightly soulless. There's a reasonable restaurant, Yungi Yungi, serving Swahili set menus, as well as a business centre & bureau de change. *US$90–120 dbl.*

🏠 **Dhow Palace Hotel** [317 D7] (28 rooms) 🤙 024 223 3012; e dhowpalace@zanlink.com; www.tembohotel.com/dhowpalace.html. This excellent hotel in the Shangani area is a renovated old house built around 2 central courtyards. Newer rooms have private balconies, while larger original rooms access a private section of shared balcony; all are en suite (complete with Persian baths), & are furnished with Zanzibari beds & antiques, plus mod cons including AC. The stylised Indian restaurant overlooks the city's rooftops (no alcohol served). All is spotlessly clean, the staff are friendly & the atmosphere tranquil. *US$90 dbl.*

🏠 **Zanzibar Coffee House** [316 D1] (8 rooms) 🤙 024 2239319; m 0773 061532; e coffeehouse@zanlink.com; www.riftvalley-zanzibar.com. Housed in an 1885 Arabic home, this unpretentious haven is above the excellent café of the same name. Most of the rooms, with traditional Zanzibari 4-poster beds & AC, are en suite, though a few share facilities. Gracious staff provide a friendly service, the tower-top terrace offers one of Stone Town's best b/fast views, & rates remain great value. *US$75–90 dbl.*

🏠 **Asmini Palace** [316 B1] (12 rooms) Forodhani Rd; m 0774 276464; e info@asminipalace.com; www.asminipalace.com. Located in the Kiponda area, the good-value Asmini is a new white building, constructed along traditional lines, with an arched entrance, central courtyard, carved timber doors, &

balconies from every bedroom. The staff are delightful & rooms are clean & uncluttered. There is a rooftop restaurant for lunch & dinner & a large b/fast area on the ground floor. Very unusually for Zanzibar, the hotel also has a lift: a real bonus for those with limited mobility or simply weary legs. *US$70–130 dbl.*

🏠 **Abuso Inn** [317 B6] (18 rooms) Shangani Rd; 🤙 024 223 5886; m 0777 425565. This central family-run hotel is much better than first impressions suggest, as its entrance & reception have a distinctly half-finished feel. Beyond, however, its spacious en-suite rooms are pretty good, with polished timber floors & sea views from some, making it one of the best deals in this range. A rooftop restaurant is planned for the future. *US$65 dbl; seaview supplement US$10.*

🏠 **Clove Hotel** [316 C2] (8 rooms) Hurumzi St; m 0777 484567; e clovehotel@zanlink.com; www.zanzibarhotel.nl. Service, reliability & fresh décor make this one of the best mid-range options in the city. Behind its white walls & green shutters, en-suite rooms boast coconut wood furniture & batik bedcovers beneath mosquito nets & fans. The shady, sea-view rooftop terrace is for guests only. *US$60 dbl.*

🏠 **Victoria House** [317 G6] (9 rooms) 🤙 024 2232861; e booking@victoriahotel-zanzibar.co.uk; www.victoriahotel-zanzibar.com. An excellent choice in the mid-range bracket, this 3-storey house features en-suite rooms that are simple, cool & thoughtfully furnished. Fans & mosquito nets are standard, & a few rooms also have AC; rooms on the first floor benefit from the breeze. The 2nd-floor balcony houses the Bustani Restaurant (🕐 12.00–21.00). *US$60 dbl.*

Budget Even the cheapest lodgings in Zanzibar are rather pricey, for which reason hotels charging US$50 or below for a double room are listed in the budget category, and the cut-off price for the shoestring category is around US$30 per double.

🏠 **Coco de Mer Hotel** [317 B5] (13 rooms) Off Kenyatta Rd; 🤙 024 223 0852; m 0777 433550; e cocodemer_znz@yahoo.com. Clean & friendly, this has en-suite rooms set around an airy courtyard in the Shangani area. Those downstairs are a bit dark, but upstairs they're bright & cheerful. All have ceiling fans & hot-water showers, & there are plans to add AC downstairs. The restaurant serves good-value food & there's an adjacent bar with a variety of snacks. Free transfers are available from the port/airport but be sure that you have a confirmed reservation as there have been rumours of people being taken to a less-salubrious annexe. *US$50 dbl.*

🏠 **Kiponda Hotel** [316 B1] (15 rooms) Nyumba ya Moto St; 🤙 024 2233052; m 0777 431665; e info@kiponda.com; www.kiponda.com. Formerly a sultan's harem, this quiet, friendly hotel has been renovated in local style & retains the original carved wooden door. Rooms are fastidiously clean, with simple furnishings & efficient fans. After b/fast, the airy restaurant with clear sea views mutates into a casual coffee bar, serving cold drinks & beer (🕐 11.00–18.00). *US$45 dbl.*

🏠 **Safari Lodge** [305 C3] (28 rooms) 🤙 024 223 6523; m 0784 606177; e asc@raha.com, info@safarilodgez.com; www.safarilodgez.com.

11

Relatively new in the Malindi quarter is this 3-storey building with impressive carved timber balconies spanning the width of its upper floors. Bright, spacious en-suite rooms are immaculately clean, though somewhat sterile. Each has a large Zanzibari bed or 2, AC & fan, safe & cable TV. With a convenient location for exploring the Old Town & a decent rooftop restaurant, it remains good value for money. US$45 dbl.

⌂ **Warere Town House** [305 C1] (12 rooms) ✆ 024 2233835; m 0773 272760; e warere_townhouse@hotmail.com. Situated in a leafy corner, this 3-storey lodge with a basic rooftop terrace has been popular for years with travellers on a tight budget. It is a simple, comfortable haunt, slightly tatty around the edges, with en-suite rooms offering traditional Zanzibari furnishings & *kanga* curtains; 4 rooms boast breezy balconies, albeit with an unattractive view. US$40 dbl.

⌂ **Malindi Guesthouse** [305 D1] (13 rooms) ✆ 024 223 0165; e malindi@zanzinet.com. Despite its location in an area of questionable security, Malindi is consistently popular with travellers. From the bustling port area, a gate leads into a calm, private courtyard where a homely feel prevails. Rooms are spotlessly clean with safes, ceiling fans & mosquito nets. Some are en suite with AC; others share bathrooms. Comfortable communal seating areas vie with the rooftop coffee house (☺ *all day Mon–Sat*), serving the usual seafood or meat with rice dishes & chilled drinks. After dark, do heed the warning signs on the gate & walk in the opposite direction to the port. US$40 dbl.

⌂ **Garden Lodge** [317 G6] (18 rooms) Kaunda Rd; ✆ 024 223 3298; e gardenlodge@zanlink.com. This bougainvillea-clad white house near Victoria Gardens is simple but very friendly, catering primarily to the over-40s. En-suite rooms all have dbl beds, fans, mosquito nets & reliable hot water. Those upstairs are brighter & airier; try to get one at the back away from traffic noise. Small balconies at the front of the hotel, a cool 1st-floor lounge & a rooftop terrace make this a good choice for the price. A few good restaurants lie within easy walking distance. US$40 dbl.

⌂ **Karibu Inn** [317 B5] (25 rooms) ✆ 024 223 3058; m 0777 417392; e karibuinnhotel@yahoo.com. On a narrow street parallel with Kenyatta Rd, this very simple, hostel-like place with its laissez-faire vibe caters mainly for young travellers, budget tour groups or people on overland expeditions. As well as clean but basic en-suite rooms there are dormitories sleeping 4–7 people each. The friendly management can set up budget tours. US$40 dbl, US$10 pp dorm.

Shoestring

⌂ **St Monica's Hostel** [316 F2] (11 rooms) Sultan Ahmed Mugheiri Rd; ✆ 024 223 5348; e monicaszanzibar@hotmail.com; www.stmonicahostelzanzibar.s5.com. Built in the 1890s to house workers at the UMCA mission, St Monica's now welcomes both church guests & younger backpackers. Cool thick walls, wide staircases & Arabesque arches form the backdrop for simple & very clean rooms with wide balconies overlooking the cathedral or gardens. The restaurant, run by the Mother's Union, offers fresh Swahili cuisine (no alcohol); there's also an art shop & an airy lounge area. US$25–30 dbl.

⌂ **Jambo Guesthouse** [316 F3] (8 rooms) ✆ 024 223 3779; m 0777 496571; e jamboguest@hotmail.com. In a quiet quarter of the Mkunazini area, near the Anglican Cathedral, this good-value place has been justifiably popular with backpackers for years. Its simple rooms, all sharing facilities, have mosquito nets & ceiling fans, & 2 have AC. Extras include free luggage store, free tea & coffee, & cheap internet access. With advance bookings it's possible to arrange free pick-up from the port or airport. The shady café opposite is a pleasant outdoor hang-out too. US$25–30 dbl.

⌂ **Pyramid Hotel** [305 C3] (11 rooms) Kokoni St; ✆ 024 223 3000; m 0777 461451/0784 255525; e pyramidhotel@yahoo.com. Between the Malindi & Kiponda areas, this old hotel is a short walk from the seafront. A budget travellers' favourite for many years, & deservedly so, it gets its name from the very steep & narrow staircases (almost ladders) that lead to the upper floors. Rooms have netting, fan & hot water, but some are large & bright, & others small & dark, so choose carefully. The manager & his staff are friendly, the rooftop restaurant does great b/fast, & there's a book-swap service. Free pick-up from the airport or port. US$30 dbl.

⌂ **Bandari Lodge** [305 C1] (10 rooms) ✆ 024 223 7969; m 0777 423638; e bandarilodge@hotmail.com. Just 100m north of the port, Bandari is one of a clutch of affordable hotels in Malindi. Good-value, no-frills accommodation is in clean, functional rooms with mosquito nets & fans; 2 are en suite. B/fast is served & a basic kitchen is available for guest use; there's also a book exchange. The friendly owner is on hand to help with advice & onward plans. US$15 pp.

above left	**Leopard** *Panthera pardus* (AVZ) page 27	*above right*	**Spotted hyena** *Crocuta crocuta* (AVZ) page 30
below left	**African wild dog** *Lycaon pictus* (AVZ) page 29	*below right*	**Lion** *Panthera leo* (AVZ) page 27

above left	**Hippopotamus** *Hippopotamus amphibius* (AVZ) page 38	*above right*	**Warthog** *Phacochoerus africanus* (AVZ) page 39
below left	**Giraffe** *Giraffa camelopardis* (AVZ) page 39	*below right*	**Burchell's zebra** *Equus burchelli* (AVZ) page 39

top left **Black rhino**
Diceros bicornis
(AVZ) page 38

top right **African buffalo**
Syncerus caffer
(AVZ) page 39

right **African elephant**
Loxodonta africana
(AVZ) page 38

below **Nile crocodile**
Crocodylus niloticus
(AVZ) page 44

above left **Yellow baboon**
Papio cynocephalus
(AVZ) page 32

above right **Greater galago (bushbaby)**
Galago crassicaudatus
(AVZ) page 33

right **Rock hyrax** *Procavia capensis*
(AVZ) page 269

below right **Dwarf mongoose** *Helogale*
parvula (AVZ) page 31

clockwise from top left

Greater flamingoes
Phoenicopterus ruber (AVZ)

Fischer's lovebird
Agapornis fischeri (AVZ)

Pearl-spotted owlet
Glaucidium perlatum (AVZ)

Lilac-breasted roller
Coracias caudata (AVZ)

White-fronted bee-eater
Merops bullockoides (AVZ)

Kori bustard
Ardeotis kori (AVZ)

Crowned crane
Balearica pavonina (AVZ)

D'Arnaud's barbet
Glaucidium perlatum (AVZ)

✖ WHERE TO EAT AND DRINK There are now dozens of restaurants catering specifically to tourists, and the following serves as an introduction only. Top-end options, with main courses averaging from US$10, include:

✖ Baharia [317 B8] Serena Hotel, Shangani Rd; ☎ 024 2233587. Less flamboyant than Kidude, the Baharia is nonetheless a good-quality place. The food is a mix of Asian, African & European. In the hotel's coffee shop & patisserie, snacks & light meals start from around US$5.

✖ Beyt al Chai [317 C7] Kelele Sq; m 0777 444111; www.stonetowninn.com. At one of Zanzibar Town's current culinary hot-spots, succulent prawn curries, grilled line fish & crisp vegetables are matched with a tempting wine list. Service is friendly & polite, if sometimes a little slow &, though prices are relatively high, the food & sophisticated atmosphere combine to make it good value for money & highly recommended.

✖ Fusion [317 C7] Al Johari Hotel; ☎ 024 223 6779; www.al-johari.com. Fusion serves an eclectic menu, with tastes from Italian to Indian equally well served. Delicious seafood starters are complemented with summer soups, pastas, marinated meats & totally tropical desserts, not to mention a lengthy wine & cocktail lists.

✖ Kidude [316 C1] 236 Hurumzi Hotel; Hurumzi St; ☎ 024 223 0171; m 0777 423266. During the day, light jazz plays in the background & you can enjoy great cakes & coffees, order Middle Eastern snacks (from around US$5) or take lunch (the US$12 daily set menu). In the evenings there's also a fixed menu (US$25), with a vast & impressive range of dishes, & a buffet (US$15) on Fri. With 30min notice, you can even order a take-away pizza.

There are numerous more affordable options, with main courses in the US$5–8 range. The following is just a selection; there are plenty more to choose from, and the level of competition for custom means that standards are generally reflected by prices. Quality is highly variable, and any one place can go up or down, so do ask reliable local sources for the current hot-spots.

✖ Africa House Hotel [317 D8] Shangani; m 0774 432340. No visit to Zanzibar is complete without a visit to the Sunset Bar at the Africa House Hotel. You can order snacks & meals (US$4–8) to enjoy on the veranda, or have something more formal upstairs in the Tradewinds Restaurant or Sunset Grill. Cocktails are de rigueur, & popular among locals & more adventurous visitors are the traditional pipes, also known as hubble-bubble pipes, water pipes or, correctly, shisha pipes. Sunset is usually around 18.30; get there in good time for the best terrace seats.

✖ Amore Mio [317 C8] Shangani Rd; ☎ 024 223 3666. As well as pasta & pizzas, this is a good bet for coffee & ice cream.

✖ Archipelago Restaurant [317 B5] Shangani Rd; ☎ 024 223 5668. Come here for curries, seafood & burgers.

✖ Livingstone Beach Restaurant [317 A5] m 0784 694803. Opposite Zawadi Chest, this is a good place for seafood & grills.

✖ Mercury's Bar & Restaurant [305 C3] Mizingani Rd; ☎ 024 2233076; m 0777 416666; ⏱ daily. Named after Zanzibar's most famous son, this has a fine setting on the bay & is perennially popular. The menu unashamedly cashes in on the former Queen singer's apparent dietary preferences – Freddie's

Favourite Salad (US$4) & Mercury's Special Pizza (US$6). Despite this corniness, the food is reliably good, & there's a baffling range of cocktails. Happy 'hour' is 17.00–20.00, & there's live music Fri–Sun nights (from 19.30).

✖ Monsoon Restaurant [317 A5] ☎ 0747 411362. Facing Forodhani Gardens, this is a good place for traditional Zanzibari & Mediterranean food, accompanied by live taarab music on Wed & Sat nights. Aside from its bar, & a shady terrace with tables, Monsoon is a place to lounge around, kasbah style. Thick walls & good ventilation mean it's always cool, & so are most of the clients. You can even enjoy a hubble-bubble pipe with your Arabic coffee or cocktail. Main courses from US$4; 4-course dinner US$8–10.

✖ Old Fort Restaurant [305 B4 & 316 A4] Mizingani Rd; m 0744 278737/0713 630206; ⏱ 08.00–20.00 lunch & dinner daily. Opposite the Forodhani Gardens, Zanzibar's old Arab Fort was renovated in the early 1990s & now incorporates a shady outdoor café-restaurant. There's a good selection of snacks for around US$2, local dishes such as chicken & ugali (maize meal) or octopus & chips for around US$3, plus coffees, beers & chilled wine. Every Tue, Thu & Sat, there's live entertainment & a BBQ (US$9); booking is advised.

✕ **Rendezvous Les Spices** [317 E7] Kenyatta Rd; m 0777 410707. With what is arguably the best Indian food on the island & some strikingly colourful murals, the restaurant buzzes most evenings & is reasonably priced too, with main courses such as crab masala, chicken tikka, lamb biriyani or various tandooris for US$5–6. Vegetarian dishes are available, & specials, such as prawn curry, are around US$8. No credit cards.

✕ **Sambusa Two Tables** [317 G6] Victoria St; ✆ 024 223 1979. This small place on the balcony of a private house really does have only 2 tables (although I seats about 8 people). It's a family affair, so phone or visit to book a table at least in the afternoon of the day to allow time for shopping & preparation. A full meal of spiced rice, curries & numerous local delicacies costs about US$10.

The cheapest place to eat in the Stone Town is at **Forodhani Gardens** [305 A4 & 316 A4], along the seafront, where dozens of vendors serve freshly grilled meat, chicken, fish, calamari and prawns with salad and chips or naan bread. This is far and away the best street food we've come across anywhere in southern and East Africa, and yet you'd have to be seriously hungry or prawn-obsessed not to come back with change from US$3. The stalls cater primarily to locals, but plenty of travellers eat here, and many return night after night.

At the time of writing, the gardens themselves are undergoing extensive renovations and the market has temporarily moved to the northern boundary wall of the Old Fort. It will eventually (probably end 2009) return to a purpose built hard-standing in the revamped gardens.

For coffee and/or light snacks and sandwiches, two places stand out. First up is the **Buni Café** [317 A5], which has a prime central location opposite the NBC, and a raised balcony that forms an excellent spot for a late breakfast or light lunch. Rather more difficult to find is the **Zanzibar Coffee House** [316 D1], a friendly new place on Mkunazini Street near the main market, which serves fresh juice, milkshakes and strong coffee as well as a delicious selection of cakes, pies, pastries, croissants and sandwiches.

ENTERTAINMENT AND NIGHTLIFE Most tourist restaurants serve beer and many of the larger hotels have separate bars. The rooftop bar at the Africa House Hotel [317 D8] is about the nearest things in Zanzibar to a pub, and has long been very popular for pre-dinner drinks, offering the tantalising combination of well-made cocktails and brilliant sunsets. There's also **Mercury's** [305 C3] (*Mizingani Rd*), noted for good sundowners and a happy hour that, out of high season, is a generous 17.00–20.00.

Cheaper beer is available at the rather sordid **New Happy Bar** [317 D7] in Shangani (a few doors down from the Africa House Hotel), which caters to a predominantly local clientele.

Currently, the favourite after-dinner hang-out for island expats and hip locals is the relatively new **Dharma Lounge** [317 G5] (*Vuga Rd;* ✆ *024 223 3626;* m *0747 416374/413031*), with a well-stocked cocktail bar and invariably lively dance-floor. If something more seedy appeals, there's the disco beneath the swimming pool at the **Bwawani Hotel** [305 D1], but a trip here is not for the faint-hearted.

There is live *taarab* music at the **Monsoon Restaurant** [317 A5] on Wednesday and Saturday nights. Otherwise, there is no one particular venue in Zanzibar Town for live music, but local artists – from traditional taarab to afro-pop and rap – often perform at bars such as **Mercury's** [305 C3]. The **Arab Fort** [305 B4 & 316 A4] is another good venue for live music – mostly traditional musicians and dancers, but sometimes contemporary performances, too. A couple of times each week a 'night at the fort' evening is organised, which includes at least two performances plus a barbecue dinner. To find out what's happening, call in at the fort during the day, and ask the staff. For an equally authentic location, Mtoni Palace Ruins (page 325) occasionally organise *taarab* orchestra concerts amid the crumbling palace pillars.

SHOPPING Zanzibar Town is something of an Aladdin's cave for shoppers, with a vast array of shops catering for the ever-growing tourist influx. Even die-hard deal-hunters will be hard pushed to visit them all, and there are bound to be even more by the time you visit. A selection of both favourites and perennials are listed here, though particularly worth checking out are those mentioned in the box, *Fair-trade fashion*, below; aside from their positive credentials, their products are some of the best quality and most original around.

In the larger tourist shops, prices are fixed and payable in Tanzanian shillings or US dollars, or by credit card (surcharges are usual), but in the market and at smaller, locally run outlets, cash is necessary and bargaining is part of the experience. There are no hard and fast rules to the latter, and sensible judgement is required, but a basic rule of thumb is to start negotiations at half the asking price; if you ultimately pay around 75% of the initial price, then it's likely that both parties will walk away happy.

One of the best places to start a shopping trip is the **Zanzibar Gallery** [317 B6] on Kenyatta Road. This shop sells an excellent range of carvings, paintings, jewellery, materials, maps, clothes, rugs, postcards, antiques and real pieces of art from all over Africa. You can also buy local spices, herbs, pickles and honey, and locally made oils. It also has a very good selection of books. The shop is run by local photographer and publisher Javed Jafferji, whose own books (signed) are sold here, plus illustrated diaries and address books featuring photos from Zanzibar and Tanzania.

Also on Kenyatta Road is **Memories of Zanzibar** [317 C6], opposite the post office, selling everything from beaded flip-flops and silver bracelets to carpets and gourd-lamps, as well as a good selection of books about Zanzibar, and African music CDs. At the seafront end of the same road is **Zawadi Chest** [317 A5]. A relative newcomer on the shopping scene, it has a particularly good display of *kikois*, metalwork from the Dar es Salaam charity Wonder Welders, and an excellent selection of swimwear.

Another place for good-quality crafts is **Hurumzi Art & Craft Gallery**, next to the 236 Hurumzi Hotel on Hurumzi Street [316 C2]. The same owner has another fine shop called **Kibriti** on Gizenga Street, near the post office, selling arts and crafts and a good selection of antiques and curios.

There are many more shops along these streets, and on Changa Bazaar Road. You'll also find pavement traders here offering carvings, paintings and beaded trinkets. Tingatinga paintings on canvas or wooden trays, assorted gold, silver and stone jewellery, packets of spices, and mobiles made from coconut shells in the shapes of dolphins, dhows or tropical fish are readily available at every turn.

FAIR-TRADE FASHION

There has been a welcome trend recently towards training members of the local community, especially women, to produce high-quality, well-designed clothing and accessories for sale to tourists. The women benefit from a new skill and a fair price for their efforts. The best of these projects and products currently available include **Moto** (Hurumzi St, & outside Jozani Forest; www.solarafrica.net/moto); **Malkia** (several hotel shops & Bwejuu village); **Sasik** (Gizenga St), and **Upendo** (next to Coco de Mer hotel; www.upendomeanslove.com).

Around Zanzibar Town several shops sell antiques from Arabia and India, dating from Omani and British colonial times. **Coast Antique Shop** on Gizenga Street has a particularly good selection of Zanzibar clocks. There are several more antique shops on the street between St Joseph's Cathedral and Soko Muhogo crossroads.

Other places to buy paintings and pieces of art include **Paul's Gallery** at St Monica's Hostel [316 F2] near the Anglican Cathedral (where you can also buy hand-painted T-shirts) and the **Tower Workshop** at the Old Fort [305 B4 & 316 A4], where the resident artists deliberately don't stock Tingatinga stuff, concentrating instead on watercolours and some beautiful batik-like works 'painted' with different-coloured candle wax. In the main part of the fort is another cluster of spice and craft shops, including **Namaan Art Gallery**, which has Tingatinga works, some watercolours and some superb oil paintings. Alternatively, for original, slightly more contemporary products, **Keramica**, in the shadow of the amphitheatre, is worth a look.

Outside the fort, **Forodhani Gardens** [305 A4 & 316 A4] – closed for renovations at the time of writing – boasted several more stalls selling carvings and jewellery, especially in the evening when nearby food stalls attracted the crowds. During the renovations, these stalls are more mobile, but will likely return to the new food market when Forodhani reopens. Nearby, beside the House of Wonders, Tingatinga painting salesmen hang their works on the railings, and you can also watch some of the artists (all men) working here. In the same area, local weavers (all women) make mats and baskets from grass and palm leaves. This area is also a good place to find colourful fabrics and clothing.

Local craftwork can also be found in the **Orphanage Shop**, on Mizingani Road near the fort, where blind craft-workers weave a good range of baskets, rugs and other items. The orphanage is a large building, with a tunnel passing right through the middle of it; the shop is on the side nearest the sea.

On Gizenga Street, the tailor at **Mnazi Boutique** can copy any shirt, skirt or trousers you like, from material you buy in the shop or elsewhere in town. Prices start at US$10, and go up to US$25 for a complicated dress. If you prefer traditional African clothing, consider a *kanga* or a *kikoi*. On Kenyatta Road, the smart **One Way** boutique specialises in T-shirts embroidered with giraffes and elephants or emblazoned with Kenyan and Tanzanian slogans and logos.

For postcards you can't go wrong at **Angi's Postcards & Maps**, on Mizingani Road, near the Big Tree; there's a truly massive selection here, all at good prices. Books – coffee-table, fact and fiction – can be purchased from the well-stocked **Gallery Bookshop** [317 C5] (*Gizenga St;* ✆ *09.00–19.00 Mon-Sat, 09.00–14.00 Sun*).

If a more precious purchase is what you're after, Eddy G at **Hassan Jewellers** (*Mkunazini St;* ✆ *027 223 1242*), close to the market, is reliable and reputable. He stocks a good range of tanzanite and is able to supply authentication certificates. Be aware that tanzanite is a soft stone which scratches easily; better to have it set as earrings or in a necklace than as a ring.

OTHER PRACTICALITIES

Banks and money changing A number of banks and forex bureaux are dotted around the Stone Town, offering similar exchange rates against cash to their mainland counterparts. The only place that exchanges travellers' cheques is the first-floor 'Foreign Trade Dept' at the National Bank of Commerce on Kenyatta Road [317 B5]. You can draw cash against Visa cards at the ATM outside the same bank, but the only place where you can draw against MasterCard is the ATM at Barclays Bank, a couple of kilometres out of town along the road towards the north coast. Most upmarket hotels accept major credit cards.

These days, there isn't much to choose between banks and private bureaux in terms of rates, but you'll generally find the transaction takes a minute or two at a private bureau whereas changing money at banks often involves long queues and plenty of paperwork. Good private bureaux de change include the **Shangani Bureau de Change** (at the northern end of Kenyatta Road, near the Tembo Hotel) and **Malindi Bureau de Change** [305 C2] (next to the ZanAir office, east of the port gates). Most large hotels will also change money, although some deal only with their own guests, and they often offer poor rates.

Communications The main **post office** lies outside the Stone Town towards the stadium, but the old post office on Kenyatta Road [317 C6] in the Shangani area is the most convenient for tourists, and is also the place to collect poste restante mail addressed to Zanzibar. A better place from which to make international phone calls lies next door at the **Tanzanian Telecommunications** office [317 C6]. Rates here are generally similar to those at some of the private bureaux around town, though it's as well to ask around.

Numerous **internet cafés** have sprung up in Zanzibar Town over the past few years, charging a fairly uniform US$0.50 per 30 minutes. These include Palace Internet [305 C3] (*Forodhani Rd*), Sanjay Internet Café (*off Gizenga St near House of Wonders*), Shangani Internet Café [317 C6] (*Kenyatta Rd*) and Too Short Internet Café [317 B5] (*Shangani St*).

Maps Aside from those in this book, the most accurate and attractive map of the Stone Town is Giovanni Tombazzi's *Map of Zanzibar Stone Town*, which also has a good map of the island on the flip side. Survey maps of the island are sold for around US$2 each at the map office in the Department of Lands and Surveys in the Ministry of Environment building, near the Old Arab Fort and the People's Bank of Zanzibar.

Medical facilities Zanzibar's private medical clinics, where staff speak English and drugs are more readily available, are usually a better option for visitors than the public Mnazi Mmoja General Hospital. There are pharmacies at the medical centres as well as in Stone Town.

✚ **Zanzibar Medical & Diagnostic Centre** [305 D6] Off Vuga Rd; ✆ 024 2231071, 24hr emergency m 0777 750040/413714. Recommended by most expatriates.
✚ **Zanzibar Medical Group** [317 F7] Kenyatta Rd; ✆ 024 223 3134. Another good-quality private clinic.
✚ **Afya Medical Hospital** [317 E7] Off Vuga Rd; ✆ 024 223 1228; m 0777 411934. Large & well

stocked, with friendly staff, & cheaper consultations than above.
✚ **Dr Mehta's Hospital** [317 F7] Vuga Rd; ✆ 024 223 0194; m 0713 612889
✚ **Fahand Health Centre** Nr St Joseph's Cathedral. A basic centre that offers cheap malaria tests & normally sells malarial cures such as Fansidar.

Swahili lessons The Institute of KiSwahili and Foreign Languages [305 D6] (*Vuga Rd; ✆ 024 223 0724/3337; e takiluki@zanlink.com; www.glcom.com/hassan/takiluki.html*) offers week-long courses for US$80.

Swimming pool The pool at the Dhow Palace Hotel [317 D7] is open to non-residents for Tsh3,000 per person. Out of town, there's the option to swim at Maruhubi Beach Villas for US$5 per day.

WHAT TO SEE AND DO
Spice tours and other excursions The one organised trip that practically all visitors to Zanzibar undertake is a 'spice tour', something that would be logistically

11

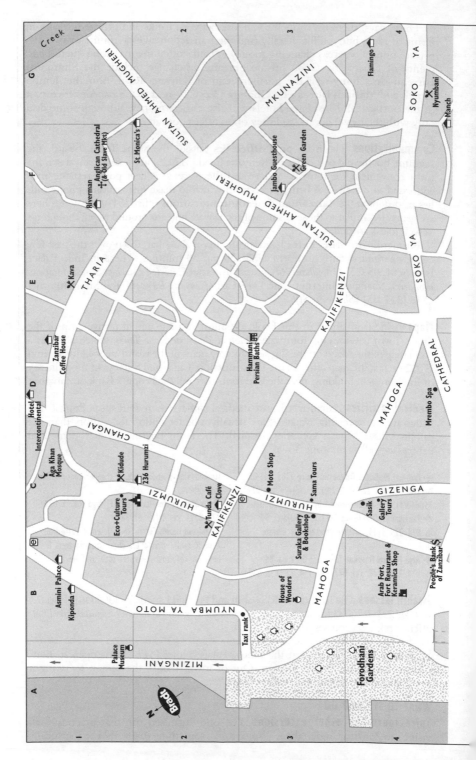

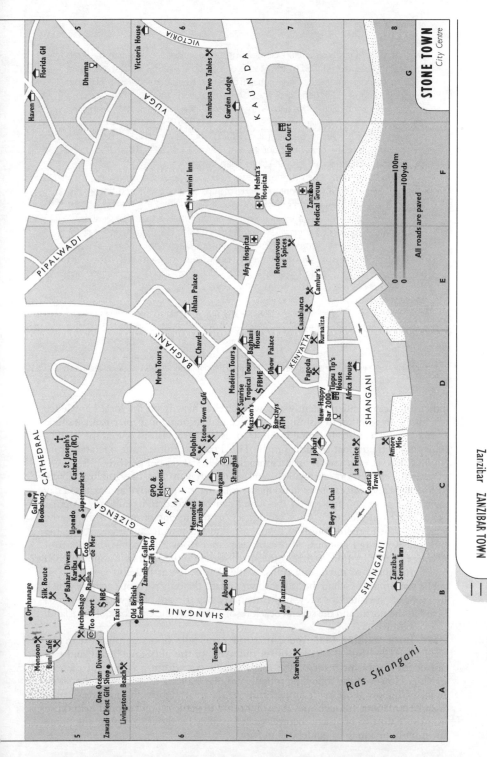

Zanzibar **ZANZIBAR TOWN** 11

STONE TOWN
City Centre

0 ___ 100m
0 ___ 100yds

All roads are paved

Ras Shangani

317

The Forodhani Gardens (Jamituri Gardens on some maps) are between the Arab Fort and the sea, overlooked by the House of Wonders. They were first laid out in 1936 to commemorate the Silver Jubilee of Sultan Khalifa (ruled 1911–60), and were called Jubilee Gardens until the 1964 revolution. In the centre stands a podium where the band of the sultan's army used to play for the public. Nearer the sea is a white concrete arabesque arch, built in 1956 for the visit of Princess Margaret (sister of Queen Elizabeth II of Britain), but never officially used as the princess arrived at the dhow harbour instead. She did visit the gardens, however, and planted a large tree, which can still be seen today.

Forodhani has long been a popular place for local people and visitors in the evenings, lured by the waterfront gathering of stalls serving drinks and hot snacks. Years of excessive overuse and poor maintenance has taken its toll, though, and for several years 'gardens' was a euphemism for an unattractive, parched wasteland. Fortunately, things are changing. On 17 January 2008, the Aga Khan Trust for Culture, with approval from the Zanzibar government, finally began a major rehabilitation of the park. Whilst few people locally seem to be aware of the exact redevelopment plans, scale models, architects drawings, artists' impressions and clear descriptions are freely displayed in the lobby area of the Palace Museum and are worth a look.

The project was due for completion in early 2009. While many believe this date is over-optimistic, almost everyone is agreed that the development will be a vast improvement, with a new sea wall of salvaged stone, an organised food court for the stallholders, a bandstand, a dhow-shaped adventure playground and tropical planting – as well as the introduction of wheelie bins, lighting and waste collections.

difficult to set up independently, and which relies heavily on the local knowledge of a guide. In addition to visiting a few spice plantations, most spice tours include a walk around a cultivated rural homestead, as well as a visit to one of the island's ruins and a traditional Swahili lunch. The Princess Salme tour operated from Mtoni Palace is a particularly good example at US$50–55 per person.

Several other short excursions can be undertaken out of Zanzibar Town. Although many visitors prefer to do their exploring in the form of an organised day tour, most places of interest on the island can be visited independently. Popular excursions from the Stone Town include a boat trip to one or more of the nearby islands, a visit to the dolphins at Kizimkazi, and a trip to Jozani Forest to see the endemic Kirk's red colobus. Also easily explored from Zanzibar is the 10km of coastline stretching northwards to the small seaside settlement of Bububu, which boasts a number of interesting ruins, while Fuji Beach at Bububu is the closest public swimming beach to the Stone Town. In fact, the only parts of Zanzibar which are more often visited for a few nights than as a day trip are Nungwi and Mnemba Island in the north, and the several beach resorts that line the east coast of the island.

Stone Town walking tour You can spend many idle hours getting lost in the fascinating labyrinth of narrow streets and alleys of the old Stone Town, and will almost inevitably hit most of the main landmarks within a couple of days of arriving. However, the following roughly circular walking tour through the Stone Town will allow those with limited time to do their sightseeing in a reasonably organised manner (though they are still bound to get lost), and should help those with more time to orientate themselves before they head out to explore the Stone Town without a map or guidebook in hand.

The obvious starting point for any exploration of Zanzibar Town is **Forodhani Gardens** [305 A4 & 316 A4] (see box, opposite), a small patch of greenery lying between Mizingani Road and the main sea wall. Laid out in 1936 to mark the silver jubilee of Sultan Khalifa, the gardens are a popular eating and meeting point in the evening, and the staircase rising from the gardens to the arched bridge to the south offers a good view over the old town.

Three of the most significant buildings in the Stone Town lie alongside each other overlooking the seafront behind the Forodhani Gardens. The **Palace Museum** [305 B4 & 316 A1] (⊕ 09.00–18.00 daily; admission US$3 pp) is the most northerly of these, a large white building with castellated battlements dating from the late 1890s. The palace was the official residence of the Sultan of Zanzibar from 1911 until the 1964 revolution, after which it was renamed the People's Palace. For many years after this, it served as a government office and was closed to the public. Since 1994, however, it has housed an excellent museum, with a variety of displays relating to the early days of the sultanate, including a room devoted to artefacts belonging to Princess Salme. The graves of all the early sultans of Zanzibar are in the palace garden.

Next to the Palace Museum, the **House of Wonders** [305 B4 & 316 B3] is a square, multi-storey building surrounded by tiers of impressive balconies and topped by a clocktower. It was built as a ceremonial palace in 1883, and was the first building on Zanzibar to have electric lights. Local people called it Beit el Ajaib, meaning the House of Wonders. Until recently it was the CCM party headquarters, and it has recently opened to tourists as the Museum of History and Culture (admission US$3), which in late 2005 housed about half of the eight planned permanent exhibitions (dedicated to the history of the Swahili Coast, and Zanzibar in particular). It's a pity to rush a visit here, so allow plenty of time.

Directly facing Forodhani Gardens, the **Old Arab Fort** [305 B4 & 316 A4] (admission free, donations welcome) is probably the oldest extant building in the Stone Town, built by Omani Arabs between 1698 and 1701 over the site of a Portuguese church constructed a century before that, remnants of which can still be seen in the inner wall. A large, squarish, brown building with castellated battlements, the fort ceased to serve any meaningful military role in the 19th century, since when it has served variously as prison, railway depot and women's tennis club. The interior of the fort is open to visitors, who can climb to the top of the battlements and enter some of the towers. There is a restaurant in the fort, serving cold drinks, and traditional dancing shows take place there at least three evenings every week.

Heading southwest from the fort, under an arched bridge, the fork to your right is Shangani Road, the site of notable important buildings. Just before following this fork, to your left, the **Upimaji Building** was the home of the German merchant Heinrich Ruete (later the husband of Princess Salme) in the 1860s. To the left of the fork is a block of government offices which served as the **British Consulate** [317 B6] from 1841 until 1874, and next to that the **Tembo Hotel** [317 A6], a restored 19th-century building. As you follow Shangani Road around a curve, you'll come out to a leafy green square, where the **Zanzibar Shipping Corporation Building**, dating to around 1850, stands to your left and the **Zanzibar Serena Inn** [317 B8], formerly Extelcomms House, to your right.

Perhaps 100m past the Serena Inn, to your left, you'll see the rear of **Tippu Tip's House** [305 A6 & 317 D7], a tall brown building which once served as the residence of Tippu Tip, the influential 19th-century slave trader who helped explorers such as Livingstone and Stanley with supplies and route planning. The building is privately owned and is closed to visitors, but if you follow the alley around the rear of the house, you can see its huge carved front door from the street, and the residents will sometimes show visitors around. From here, wander up another 50m past the New Happy Bar, and you'll pass the **Africa House Hotel** [317 D8], which served as the English Club from 1888 onwards, and is a good place to punctuate your walk with a cold drink on the attractively positioned balcony.

From the Africa House Hotel a small alley leads to Kenyatta Road, an important thoroughfare dotted with hotels, shops and restaurants, as well as a number of old buildings with traditional Zanzibari doors. Follow Kenyatta Avenue eastwards for about 300m, passing the somewhat unkempt **People's Gardens** [305 B6], originally laid out under Sultan Barghash for the use of his harem, until you reach the **Zanzibar Milestone** [305 C7]. This octagonal marble pillar shows the distance from Zanzibar Town to various settlements on the island and further afield.

Cross the gardens in front of the milestone to the distinctive **Beit el Amani (House of Peace) Memorial Museum** [305 D7] (⊕ *08.30–19.00 Mon–Fri, 08.30–15.00 Sat & Sun; small entrance charge*), which, despite its name, is now little more than a library; most of its exhibits have been shifted to the rapidly developing museum in the House of Wonders. The Zanzibari door at the back of the building is reputedly the oldest in existence.

From the museum, follow Creek Road northwards for about 400m, and to your left you'll easily pick out the imposing **Anglican Cathedral** [305 C4 & 316 F1] built by the Universities' Mission in Central Africa (UMCA) over the former slave market between 1873 and 1880. Tradition has it that the altar stands on the site of the market's whipping block, and the cellar of the nearby St Monica's Guesthouse

MREMBO TRADITIONAL SPA

Recently, a number of 'spas' have sprung up around Zanzibar as the Western craze for 'wellness' treatments has descended on the island. Many are little more than a massage table, some lemongrass oil and a friendly, if untrained, local masseuse; a few, in the larger hotels, are more sophisticated and professional. All can prove an enjoyable distraction, but the most engaging and original by far is Mrembo Traditional Spa (*Cathedral St;* ⤷ *0777 430117;* e *mrembozanzibar@yahoo.co.uk*).

In an old antique store close to St Joseph's Cathedral, Mrembo is a small, wonderfully unassuming place offering the finest traditional treatments from Zanzibar and Pemba. Their flagship treatment, Singo, is a natural exfoliating scrub traditionally used when preparing Zanzibari girls for marriage. Prepared by hand with a pestle and mortar (*kinu*), the fresh jasmine, ylang ylang, rose petals, *mpompia* (geranium), *mrehani* (sweet basil) and *liwa* (sandalwood) combine to create the most wonderfully aromatic blend. For men, the clove-based scrub Vidonge is said by Pembans to increase libido and stamina, and is even offered in souvenir packages. Hot sand massages, authentic henna painting and beauty treatments are available too, with all the herbal products coming from the owner's garden and skilfully prepared in front of you.

Although not its *raison d'être*, Mrembo is also an impressively inclusive community project. Two of the four local therapists are disabled: one deaf, Ali, and one blind, Asha. Trained in therapeutic massage by professional therapists from The African Touch (a Canadian-funded, community-based organisation in Kenya), they have both benefited enormously in confidence and social standing from their practical education and employment. Each has an able-bodied assistant at Mrembo to ease understanding, though Ali will cheerfully encourage you to try a little KiSwahili sign-language, using the alphabet poster for guidance.

For a lazy afternoon, or a simple massage or manicure whilst the sun's at its peak, Mrembo Traditional Spa is a great place. It is a true oasis of calm in the centre of Stone Town, and an experience not to be hurried.

[316 F2] is said to be the remains of a pit where slaves were kept before being sold. Sultan Barghash, who closed the slave market, is reputed to have asked Bishop Steere, leader of the mission, not to build the cathedral tower higher than the House of Wonders. When the bishop agreed, the sultan presented the cathedral with its clock. The foundation of the UMCA was inspired by Livingstone: a window is dedicated to his memory, and the church's crucifix is made from the tree under which his heart was buried in present-day Zambia. Several other missionaries are remembered on plaques around the cathedral wall, as are sailors killed fighting the slave trade and servicemen who died in action in East Africa during World War I. The cathedral is open to visitors for a nominal fee, which also covers entrance to the dungeon below the guesthouse.

A short distance further along Creek Road lies the **covered market** [305 D4], built at around the turn of the 20th century, and worth a visit even if you don't want to buy anything. It's a vibrant place where you can buy anything from fish and bread to sewing machines and secondhand car spares. Once you've taken a look around the market, follow Creek Road back southwards for 100m or so, passing the cathedral, then turn into the first wide road to your right. This is New Mkunazini Road, and if you follow it until its end, then turn right into Kajificheni Street and right again into Hammani Street, you'll come out at the **Hammani Baths** [305 C4 & 316 D3] – one of the most elaborate Persian baths on Zanzibar, built for Sultan Barghash; the caretaker will show you around for a small fee.

Barely 200m from the baths, on Cathedral Street, **St Joseph's Catholic Cathedral** [317 C5] is notable for its prominent twin spires, and was built between 1896 and 1898 by French missionaries and local converts. There are now few Catholics on Zanzibar, and the cathedral is infrequently used, but visitors are welcome when the doors are open. The best way to get here from the baths is to retrace your steps along Kajificheni Street, then turn right into the first alley (which boasts several good examples of traditional Zanzibari carved doors) until you reach an open area where several roads and alleys meet – Cathedral Street among them. If you're in this area, or indeed if you fancy some serious pampering, consider making an appointment at the nearby **Mrembo Traditional Spa** [316 D4] (see box, opposite).

From the cathedral, continue northwards along Cathedral Street for perhaps 50m, then turn right into Gizenga Street, a good place to check out the work of local Tingatinga artists and other curios at any of numerous small shops. If you follow Gizenga Street until you see the old Arab Fort to your left, you can conclude your walk by wandering back out to Forodhani Gardens. Alternatively, if you want to keep going, turn right opposite the fort into Harumzi Street and, after continuing straight for about 300m, you'll come to the open square close to the new **Africa Coffee House** (a good place to take a break for a tasty snack and a drink). A left turn as you enter this square takes you past the Jamat Khan Mosque and on to Jamatini Road, which after about 200m will bring you out at the seafront opposite the **Big Tree** [305 C3]. Known locally as Mtini, this well-known landmark was planted in 1911 by Sultan Khalifa and now provides shade for traditional dhow builders.

On Mizingani Road, next to the Big Tree, the **Old Customs House** [305 B3], a large, relatively plain building dating to the late 19th century, is where Sultan Hamoud was proclaimed sultan in 1896. Next to this is another large old building, formerly **Le Grand Hotel**, which is currently being renovated and is likely to reopen under its original name in the next couple of years.

From the open area next to the Big Tree, a left turn along Mizingani Road will take you back to the Arab Fort, passing the above-mentioned buildings. Turn right into

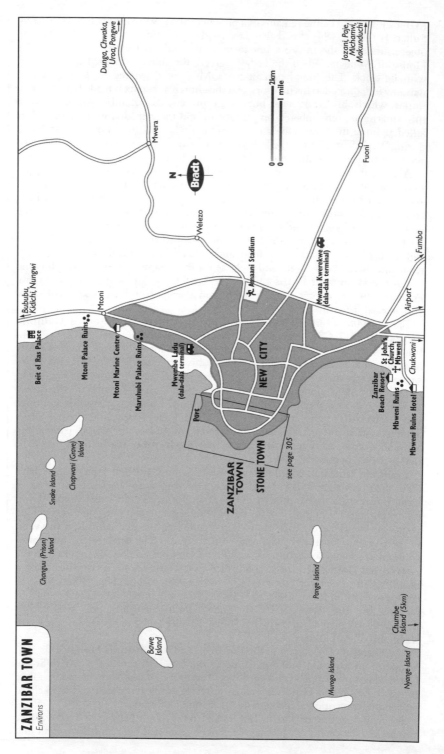

ZANZIBAR TOWN

Environs

Changu (Prison) Island

Snake Island

Chapwani (Grave) Island

Bawe Island

Murogo Island

Pange Island

Nyange Island

Chumbe Island (5km) →

ZANZIBAR TOWN

STONE TOWN

NEW CITY

see page 305

Port

Mwenbe Ladu (dala-dala terminal)

Maruhubi Palace Ruins

Mtoni Marine Centre

Mtoni Palace Ruins

Beit el Ras Palace

← Bububu, Kidichi, Nungwi

Mtoni

Welezo

Mwera

Fuoni

← Airport

Fumba →

Chukwani

Mbweni Ruins Hotel

Mbweni Ruins

Zanzibar Beach Resort

St John's Church, Mbweni

Mwana Kwerekwe (dala-dala terminal)

Amaani Stadium

N

Bradt

0 — 2km
0 — 1 mile

← Dunga, Chwaka, Uroa, Pongwe

Jozani, Paje, Michamvi, Makunduchi →

Mizingani Road, however, and after about 100m you'll pass the **Old Dispensary** [305 C2], an ornate three-storey building built in the 1890s. Restored to its former glory by the Aga Khan, the dispensary now also contains a small exhibition hall of old monochrome photographs of the Stone Town. You can continue for a few hundred metres further, past the port gates, to the **traditional dhow harbour** [305 C1], though based on our experience you are unlikely to be allowed inside.

If the above directions seem too complicated, or you want further insight into the historical buildings of the Stone Town, most tour operators can arrange a guided city tour for around US$15–20 (see pages 306–7 for tour operator listings).

AROUND ZANZIBAR TOWN

North of Zanzibar Town, the small town of **Bububu** served as the terminus for a 10km stretch of 36-inch gauge track to connect the north coast to the Arab Fort, constructed in 1904 and used until 1928. The springs outside Bububu supply most of Zanzibar Town's fresh water, and the name of the town presumably derives from the bubbling sound that they make. For most tourists, Bububu's main attraction is **Fuji Beach**, the closest swimming beach to town, no more than 500m to your left when you disembark from the *dala-dala* at the main crossroads at Bububu.

Of interest in Bububu is a small, centuries-old **mosque** about 200m from the main crossroads, along the road back towards Zanzibar Town. There is a little-known but large **double-storey ruin** on the beachfront about 500m north from where you arrive at the Fuji Beach. Complete with Arabic frescoes, this house must date to the early 19th century, and it could well have been the Bububu residence of Princess Salme in the 1850s, as described in her autobiography (see page 326).

Between Zanzibar Town and Bububu lie the ruined palaces of Maruhubi and Mtoni, and Bububu is also the closest substantial settlement to the Persian baths at Kidichi and Kizimbani.

GETTING AROUND Although some of the places mentioned below might be included in your spice tour, it is easy to visit most of them independently, using a combination of *dala-dala* No 502 (with frequent services to Bububu from the bus station on Creek Road) and your legs. Another possibility is to hire a motor scooter or bicycle from one of the tour operators (see pages 306–7).

WHERE TO STAY AND EAT
Upmarket
⌂ **Mbweni Ruins Hotel** (13 rooms) ☎ 024 223 5478/9; e hotel@mbweni.com; www.mbweni.com. This small hotel in the grounds of the Mbweni Ruins is rated as one of the best of its type in & around Zanzibar Town. Comfortable en-suite rooms with AC & private balconies are a short hop to the pool or beach. It's a relaxing spot, with a spa

(www.eternaldreamspa.com) & waterside bar, & a popular restaurant (lunch US$10–20; dinner US$10–35). The staff are keen naturalists, & can advise visitors on local natural history. There's a free shuttle service to & from town, & port/airport transfers cost US$15 for 4 people. *US$200–260 dbl.*

Moderate
⌂ **Imani Beach Villa** (9 rooms) ☎ 024 225 0050; m 0713 333731; e info@imani.it; www.imani.it. About 9km from Stone Town, clearly signposted off the main road, this delightful home from home is tucked away down a bumpy track by the sea. En-suite rooms, with enormous Zanzibari beds, offer a superb sea view, while in the tropical garden are an

Arab-style bar & restaurant, with meals (around US$20) taken seated on piles of cushions & Persian carpets at low tables. A change of management in 2008 is bringing a fresh approach & buckets of enthusiasm. Bikes are free for guest use. *US$100 dbl.*
⌂ **Maruhubi Beach Villas** (12 rooms) m 0777 451188; e maruhubi@zanlink.com;

11

Created by the team at Mtoni Palace Conservation Project (✆ 024 225 0140; m 0777 430117; e mtoni@zanzibar.cc; www.mtoni.com), this day trip combines a number of historical palaces and traditional ceremonies with an informative spice tour and delicious Swahili lunch. Escorted by a guide from the conservation project, small groups (approximately 4–6) are taken by boat from the evocative ruins of Mtoni Palace, Princess Salme's birthplace, to Bububu for a traditional coffee ceremony with tasty local treats (kashata – peanut brittle – and candy-like halua). After a short walk, perhaps into the grounds of Salme's cousin's home, visitors are transported by donkey and cart, Salme-style, to the Kidichi plantation area, where Mzee Yussuf guides a tour of his spice farm before his wife serves a deliciously fresh, homemade meal. Heading back down the hillside after lunch, there are great views towards the Indian Ocean and Stone Town before the cart arrives at the Persian Baths, originally built in 1850 for Sultan Said's second wife Scheherazade. From here, visitors are whisked back to Mtoni Marine by minibus for a chilled drink in the bar.

Departs Mtoni Marine 08.00, return 14.00; cost US$50 per person, plus US$5 per person supplement for fewer than three people, including entrance fees, lunch, & US$5 donation to Mtoni Palace Conservation Project. Reservations one day in advance essential.

www.maruhubibeachvillas.com, www.zanzibarmaruhubi.com. Some 3km north of Stone Town, close to the eponymous ruins, this attractive beachfront resort is clearly signposted off the main road. Spacious yet deceptively simple semi-detached bungalows, with en-suite bathrooms & AC, are set in beautiful tropical gardens or perched on the rock overlooking the sea. The huge thatched restaurant offers varied dishes, from vegetarian pancake (US$5) to calamari tempura (US$7) & beef kebab (US$10), & is licensed to serve alcohol. Non-residents (US$5/day) are welcome to indulge in the swimming pool above the beach. US$95–120 dbl.
🏠 **Mtoni Marine** (46 rooms) ✆ 024 2250140; m 0777 486214; f 024 2250496; e mtoni@

zanzibar.cc; www.mtoni.com. Between the palaces of Maruhubi & Mtoni, about 5min drive north of Zanzibar Town, this highly recommended, friendly hotel is set in tropical gardens overlooking the bay & a large sandy beach. Rooms are cool & comfortable with high ceilings & a raft of mod-cons. There's plenty of choice at mealtimes, with the Zansushibar on the beach particularly popular, as well as a casual bistro with sports TV & a candlelit restaurant. The hotel has a spa, swimming pool & a great playhouse/climbing frame for children. Sunset (US$15 pp) & all-day (US$40 pp) dhow cruises are offered, & tours can be arranged, including The Princess Salme tour (see box, above). US$80–120 dbl.

Budget

🏠 **Via Via** (5 rooms) m 0744 286369; e zanzibar.tanzania@viaviacafe.com. This affiliate of the well-known Belgian-run café in Arusha lies in shady green gardens about 7km from Stone Town towards Bububu, within 5min walk of Fuji Beach. It's a relaxed set-up, offering uncluttered accommodation in rustic 4-bed en-suite bungalows, with AC & fan, suitable for budget travellers & families. Facilities include free airport pick-ups & transport to & from Stone Town, as well as a home-cooked plat de jour for around US$5. US$40 dbl.

🏠 **Bububu Beach Guesthouses** (8 rooms) m 0777 422747; e kilupyomar@hotmail.com; www.bububu-zanzibar.com. A short walk from the dala-dala stop in Bububu village, these 2 simple guesthouses are clean, friendly & reasonably good value. Each sleeps up to 8 people in adequate en-suite rooms with nets, fans & AC. Although mainly geared to longer-stay visitors & family groups, rooms can be rented individually, with self-catering or FB options available. Meals are available at nearby Fuji Beach. US$30 dbl.

WHAT TO SEE AND DO Most people visit this area as a day trip from Zanzibar Town, but it is perfectly possible to explore using Bububu as a base.

Maruhubi Palace This palace (*admission US$0.30*) is probably the most impressive ruin on this part of the coast, built in 1882 for the concubines of Sultan Barghash. At one time he kept around 100 women here. The palace was destroyed by fire in 1899, and all that remain are the great pillars which supported the upper storey, and the Persian-style bath-house. You can also see the separate bathrooms for the women, the large bath used by the sultan, and the original water tanks, now overgrown with lilies. The palace is signposted about 200m from the Bububu road, roughly 3km from the Stone Town. Traditional dhow builders can be seen at work on the beach in front of the palace.

Mtoni Palace The ruins of Mtoni Palace lie a short way north of Maruhubi, and can be reached along the beach. The oldest palace on Zanzibar, Mtoni was built for Sultan Said in the 1840s. A book written by his daughter Salme describes the palace in the 1850s. At one end of the house was a large bathhouse, at the other the quarters where Said lived with his principal wife. Gazelles and peacocks wandered around the large courtyard until Mtoni was abandoned around 1885. Now, only the main walls, roof and bathhouses remain, but members of the resident Mtoni Palace Conservation Project are working hard to restore significant sections and offer interesting guided tours. The palace was used as a warehouse in World War I, with evidence of this alteration still visible.

Kidichi and Kizimbani Persian baths The Kidichi baths were built in 1850 for Said's wife, Binte Irich Mirza, the granddaughter of the Shah of Persia, and are decorated with Persian-style stucco. You can enter the bath-house and see the bathing pool and toilets, but there is mould growing on much of the stucco. The baths lie about 3km east of Bububu; from the main crossroads follow the road heading inland (ie: turn right coming from Zanzibar Town) and you'll see the baths to your right after a walk of around 30 minutes.

The Kizimbani baths are less attractive and less accessible on foot, lying a further 3km or so inland. The surrounding Kizimbani clove plantation, which is visited by many spice tours, was founded in the early 19th century by Saleh bin Haramil, the Arab trader who imported the first cloves to Zanzibar.

Mangapwani Slave Chamber Near the village of Mangapwani, some 10km north of Bububu, are a large natural cavern and a manmade slave chamber. This square cell cut into the coral was apparently built to hold slaves by one Muhammad bin Nassor Al-Alwi, an important slave trader. Boats from the mainland would unload their human cargo on the nearby beach, and the slaves would be kept here before being taken to Zanzibar Town for resale, or to plantations on the island. It is thought that some time after 1873, when slavery was officially abolished, the cave was used as a place to hide slaves, as an illicit trade continued for many years.

To get there from Zanzibar Town, take bus route 2 or a No 102 *dala-dala*. Coming by *dala-dala*, disembark at Mangapwani, where a road forks left towards the coast. About 2km past the village this road ends and a small track branches off to the right. Follow this for 1km to reach the slave chamber. About halfway between Mangapwani and the track to the slave chamber, a narrow track to the left leads to the cavern, which has a narrow entrance and a pool of fresh water at its lowest point.

ISLANDS CLOSE TO ZANZIBAR TOWN Several small islands lie between 2km and 6km offshore of Zanzibar, many of them within view of Zanzibar Town and easily visited from there as a day trip. Boat transport to Chumbe arranged with an

Princess Salme was born at Mtoni Palace, on the coast about 8km outside Zanzibar Town. The daughter of Seyyid Said, Sultan of Oman and Zanzibar, she had around 36 brothers and sisters, almost all of different mothers, and some of whom were old enough to be her grandparents. Her own mother, one of around 75 'wives' or *sarari*, owned by the sultan, was a Circassian by birth, but had been abducted by bandits as a child from her home near the Black Sea.

It was at Mtoni Palace that Salme spent her early years, playing with her brothers and sisters, floating toy boats on the river. Hers was an idyllic childhood, surrounded by love and attention, and wanting for nothing. Much of the palace social life was centred on the numerous bathing houses, where people would spend several hours each day, praying, working, reading or even taking their meals. In spite of the restrictions of traditional 19th-century Muslim society, members of the household had considerable freedom and Salme and her sisters were encouraged to be active. Twice a day, children over five years of age were given riding lessons. While the boys rode on horseback, the girls were given much-valued white donkeys. Unusually for a woman, Salme was also taught to read and write.

Salme's father had several properties on the island, many by the sea, some in the city and others on his 45 plantations. At the age of seven, Salme and her mother reluctantly moved with an elder brother into the town at Beit el Watoro. As her brothers Barghash and Majid grew older, petty jealousies surfaced, and at around the time of her father's death, when she was nine, such jealousies turned to intrigue and feuds. Three years later, after a cholera epidemic carried off Salme's mother, the princess became entangled in a web of conspiracy as Barghash, supported by Salme, sought to overthrow his brother. Although Majid defeated the rebellion, Salme claims that he continued to maintain a good relationship with his younger sister.

It was shortly after this that Salme found herself living next door to a young German who worked for a Hamburg mercantile firm. Although their friendship was known to Salme's family, the prospect of a Christian marriage would not have been acceptable, and the two planned their escape so that they could marry in a Christian church. With the help of the British vice-consul, Salme boarded a British man-of-war, the *Highflier*, and headed north to Aden. Here she was baptised, taking the name Emily, and shortly after this the two were married. They spent just three years together in Germany before Emily was widowed, left alone in a strange country with three young children. Nevertheless, she made her home in Germany, and later in London; it was 19 years before she was to set foot once again on Zanzibar soil.

Emily Ruete's Memoirs of an Arabian Princess *from Zanzibar is published by Markus Wiener.*

independent guide will cost around US$20, but you will pay more to go on an organised tour (see pages 306–7 for tour operators). To cut the individual cost, it is worth getting a group together. Despite their individual attractions, these islands are quiet yet close to main shipping routes, so are not ideal overnight stays for those in search of either total isolation or entertainment and nightlife. Note that crossing to or from Zanzibar Town in an unlit boat at night is dangerous.

Chumbe Island The coral island of Chumbe, along with several surrounding reefs, is gazetted as a nature reserve under the title of Chumbe Island Coral Park

(CHICOP). The area is in near-pristine condition because it served as a military base for many years and visitors were not permitted. Snorkelling here is as good as anywhere around Zanzibar, with more than 350 reef fishes recorded, as well as dolphins and turtles. A walking trail circumnavigates the island, passing rock pools haunted by starfish, and beaches marched upon by legions of hermit crabs. Look out, too, for the giant coconut crab, an endangered nocturnal creature that weighs up to 4kg. Some 60 species of bird have been recorded on the island, including breeding pairs of the rare roseate tern, and the localised Ader's duiker, hunted out in the 1950s, has been re-introduced. Of historical interest are an ancient Swahili mosque and a British lighthouse built in 1904.

Day trips to the island (*US$80 pp, inc transfers, guides, snorkelling equipment & lunch*) can be arranged only through reputable tour operators or from the Mbweni Ruins Hotel. Alternatively visitors can stay overnight.

Where to stay

Chumbe Island Lodge (7 rooms) ✆ 024 223 1040; m 0777 413 582; e chumbe@zitec.org; www.chumbeisland.com; closed mid-Apr–mid-Jun. Bungalows here are simple but clean, very comfortable & genuinely ecologically sensitive, with solar electricity, composting toilets & funnelled roofs designed to collect rainwater. Made mostly from local materials, each has 2 storeys, with an open fronted lounge-terrace & a bathroom below, & upstairs, a mattress laid on the floor, shrouded in a mosquito net, with a stunning view. An ingenious main *boma* houses the dining room (good seafood), education centre, snorkelling equipment room & lounge/bar. Chumbe makes no pretension to be a chill-out beach resort, but it is highly recommended to those with a strong interest in wildlife & conservation & has won numerous global awards for ecotourism. *US$500 dbl, inc FB, soft drinks, guides, transfers & all activities.*

Changuu (Prison) Island

Changuu was originally owned by a wealthy Arab, who used it as a detention centre for disobedient slaves. A prison was built there in 1893, but never used; today it houses a café, library and boutique. A path circles the island (about an hour's easy stroll). There is a small beach, a secluded hotel and a restaurant, and masks and fins can be hired for snorkelling. The island is home to several giant tortoises, probably brought from the Seychelles in the 18th century, which spend much of their time mating, a long and noisy process though numbers remain severely threatened. An entrance fee of US$5 per person must be paid in hard currency.

Where to stay

Changuu Private Island Paradise (27 rooms) m 0773 333241/2; e info.changuu@ privateislands-zanzibar.com; www.privateislands-zanzibar.com The restoration & conversion of many of the crumbling buildings on the island, & construction of individual beachfront cottages, has resulted in spacious & colourful rooms, the latter in the 'deluxe' category & with greater privacy. There is no mains electricity (& thus no AC), & it's worth taking a good torch for evening beach walks. The restaurant, in a restored 19th-century home, serves extensive 4-course dinners & a good, predominantly seafood, lunch menu. Facilities include swimming pool & floodlit tennis court, & there's a pleasant beach – though it's important to be careful when swimming as these are busy shipping waters. While guests have free run of the island, day visitors are confined to the ruins & tortoise sanctuary. *US$320–460 dbl HB.*

Chapwani (Grave) Island

This long, narrow and very pretty island has been the site of a Christian cemetery since 1879. Most of the graves belong to British sailors who were killed fighting Arab slave ships, while others date from World War I, when the British ship *Pegasus* was sunk in Zanzibar harbour. The island also has a small swimming beach – good at low and high tide – and faces Snake Island, where thousands of egrets roost overnight. The indigenous forest supports about 100 duikers, large numbers of fruit bats, and various coastal scrub birds. The giant coconut crab is often seen along the shore.

11

Where to stay

Chapwani Private Island (10 rooms) e info@
houseofwonders.com; www.chapwaniisland.com. Rooms in
5 small, semi-detached bungalows have recently opened
on the sandy beach. All are en suite with Zanzibari
beds, mosquito nets & a timber-decked terrace. Power
is by generator, so there's no AC, & don't forget a
torch. There's a nice pool tucked among the trees or,
for a more natural dip, a tidal outlet in a coral
crevasse on the northeast of the island makes a
pleasant place to swim at high tide. At low tide, the
exposed reef offers coral, starfish & barnacle-clad rock
pools to explore. *US$260 dbl HB; US$300 dbl FB.*

Bawe Island About 6km due west of Zanzibar Town, Bawe has broad sandy
beaches and a densely vegetated centre. In 1879, it was given to the Eastern
Telegraph Company by Sultan Barghash to be used as the operations station for the
underwater telegraphic cable linking Cape Town with Zanzibar, the Seychelles and
Aden in Yemen. A second line was run from Bawe Island to the External
Telecommunications building in the Shangani area of Zanzibar Town. The old
'Extelcoms' building has now been converted into the Serena Inn, but the original
phone line is largely redundant.

Lovely as the beach may be, it is firmly on the busy shipping route to Zanzibar
Town and isn't visited as frequently as Changuu. In theory, it's possible to combine
trips here with the tortoise excursions or simply arrange an out-and-back voyage
with a boat captain in Zanzibar Town, though access prices do tend to be higher
than those to Changuu.

Where to stay

Bawe Tropical Island (15 rooms) m 0773
333241/2; e info.bawe@privateislands-zanzibar.com;
www.privateislands-zanzibar.com. With the arrival of
this new lodge, sister to the one on Changuu Island,
visitors can retreat to this pretty beach spot from
the frenzy of Zanzibar Town. Thatched cottages, with
en-suite bathrooms & colourful interiors, line the
sand, just a stone's throw from the warm, shallow
sea – though a good awareness of the shipping
traffic is important if you plan to swim. Otherwise
there is little more to do than sit on the beach &
relax. *US$600–680 dbl, FB.*

NORTHERN ZANZIBAR

The large fishing village of Nungwi, situated on the northern end of the island, is
the centre of Zanzibar's traditional dhow-building industry. It has also emerged
over the last decade as probably the most popular tourist retreat on Zanzibar,
thanks to a lovely beach lined with palm and casuarina trees, good snorkelling and
diving in the surrounding waters, and a profusion of cheaper hotel options. That
said, recent years have seen almost unbridled tourist development in this area, with
a twofold increase in hotel beds in just two years, so it's important to choose your
accommodation carefully to avoid disappointment; many travellers find that the
bustling atmosphere that characterises Nungwi is not to their taste.

On the west coast, about 4km south of Nungwi, is the tiny village of Kendwa,
and a beautiful beach that doesn't suffer the vast tidal changes of the east coast. It
has seen plenty of tourist development since the mid 1990s, when it was the site of
a solitary backpacker lodge and campsite, but it remains relatively serene (most of
the time). The arrival of La Gemma dell'Est in 2005 heralded the first of a new
style of development, yet the main beach remains relatively peaceful, with some
well-spaced places to stay, a clutch of beach bars, and a dive school. Things do liven
up in the evenings, with bonfires, barbecues and full-moon beach parties, but apart
from these, it's a haven of peace. Let's hope it can stay this way.

GETTING THERE AND AWAY An erratic handful of *dala-dalas* connect Zanzibar Town
to Nungwi daily, while the local bus (No 14) operates from north to south between

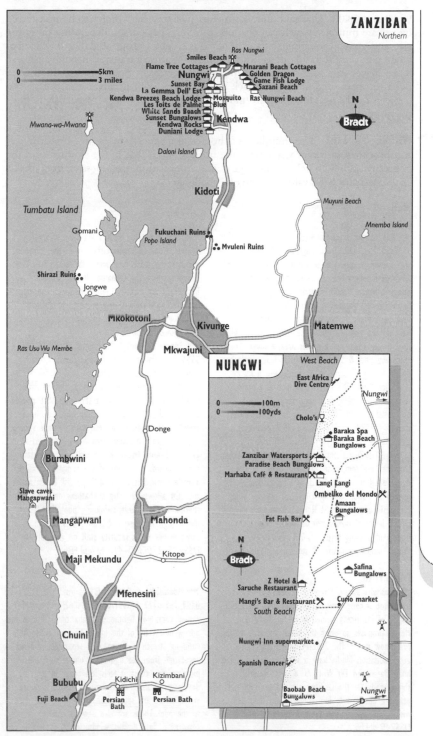

ZANZIBAR
Northern

0 ————— 5km
0 ————— 3 miles

Ras Nungwi

Mwana-wa-Mwana

Smiles Beach
Flame Tree Cottages
Nungwi
Sunset Bay
La Gemma Dell' Est
Kendwa Breezes Beach Lodge
Les Toits de Palme
White Sands Beach
Sunset Bungalows
Kendwa Rocks
Duniani Lodge
Mosquito
Blue
Kendwa

Mnarani Beach Cottages
Golden Dragon
Game Fish Lodge
Sazani Beach
Ras Nungwi Beach

N

Bradt

Daloni Island

Kidoti

Muyuni Beach

Tumbatu Island

Gomani
Popo Island
Fukuchani Ruins
Mvuleni Ruins

Mnemba Island

Shirazi Ruins
Jongwe

Mkokotoni
Kivunge
Matemwe

Ras Uso Wu Membe

Mkwajuni

NUNGWI

West Beach

East Africa
Dive Centre

Nungwi

Donge

0 ————— 100m
0 ————— 100yds

Cholo's

Baraka Spa
Baraka Beach
Bungalows

Bumbwini

Zanzibar Watersports
Paradise Beach Bungalows
Marhaba Café & Restaurant

Langi Langi

Ombeliko del Mondo

Amaan
Bungalows

Slave caves
Mangapwani

Fat Fish Bar

Mangapwani
Mahonda

N

Bradt

Maji Mekundu
Kitope

Safina
Bungalows

Z Hotel &
Saruche Restaurant

Mfenesini

Mangi's Bar & Restaurant
South Beach

Curio market

Chuini

Nungwi Inn supermarket

Spanish Dancer

Bububu
Kidichi
Kizimbani
Fuji Beach
Persian
Bath
Persian Bath

Baobab Beach
Bungalows

Nungwi

Zanzibar NORTHERN ZANZIBAR

11

329

07.00 and 18.00. That said, the vast majority of travellers prefer to be transferred by private minibus, which can cost up to US$15 per person depending on group size and your negotiating skills. The ideal is to get a group together in Zanzibar when you want to head out to Nungwi, then organise a transfer through a *papaasi*, a taxi driver or a tour company. Unless you have very rigid timings, there is no need to organise your transfer back to Zanzibar Town in advance, since several vehicles can be found waiting around for passengers in Nungwi, especially in mid-morning.

WHERE TO STAY The number of hotels and guesthouses in this area has mushroomed in recent years, with the busiest beach that to the southwest of the peninsula. While there's no shortage of accommodation, finding something that is both good and good value is more of a challenge.

Nungwi
Upmarket

Ras Nungwi Beach Hotel (32 rooms) ☎ 024 223 3767/2512; e info@rasnungwi.com; www.rasnungwi.com. This perennially popular choice for honeymooners lies at the southern end of Nungwi's beach. Rooms of various categories are set in well-tended gardens & include AC, safes & neatly tiled bathrooms, though those situated further back have no sea view. Alongside the central bar & split-level dining room are a games area, a small swimming pool & a spa. Activities include snorkelling, diving, fishing & kayaking, & there's also a highly professional spa. The exceptional food & a great wine list are highlights of any stay, with the occasional seafood BBQ featuring Swahili cuisine classics. *US$340–1,980 dbl, inc HB & activities.*

Z Hotel (35 rooms) m 0732 940303; e info@theZhotel.com, reservations@theZhotel.com; www.thezhotel.com; closed mid-Apr–end May. The new kid on the South Beach accommodation block opened in 2008, bringing a level of city-boy bling previously unseen around Nungwi. Rooms are divided into 6 levels of luxury, but all boast indulgences from iPod docking stations, AC & plasma TVs to White Company toiletries & stocked minibars. Every room has a balcony with a sea view, of varying degrees, from each one. Elsewhere in the compact complex, the stone pool above the beach is a fine hangout, whilst the Cinnamon Bar & Saruche Restaurant are already evening hotspots. The biggest issue for style-seekers may prove to be the less salubrious surrounding sprawl. *Superior US$280–600 dbl, all FB.*

Sunset Bay Hotel (32 rooms) m 0774 555555; e reservations@sunsetZanzibar.com, info@bluebayZanzibar.com; www.sunsetZanzibar.com. Rooms at this relatively small hotel (by north coast standards) are divided across 8 slightly crude, 2-storey buildings. Inside, they are spacious, if soulless, with en-suite shower room, separate dressing area & balcony, plus AC, TV, fan & mini fridge. For a sea view, request a room towards the front of the complex. It all feels a little stark, but a raised 'imported' beach above the cliff allows day-long sunbathing on the sand, & there's a lovely large swimming pool. The resort has a high number of Italian guests & staff, & some rather surly security staff on the gate. *US$205–270/300–416 sgl/dbl FB.*

Moderate

Mosquito Blue (50 rooms) e sales@ mosquitoblue.com; www.mosquitoblue.com. The African sibling of identically named hotels in Brazil & Mexico promises to bring the same chic style to this brand-new resort. The 2-storey, whitewashed accommodation blocks have a slightly Spanish feel & boast flat-screen TVs, Wi-Fi, AC & even 'waterfall' showerheads. Yet the facilities planned over the next year are designed to lure couples from their dens with a spa, gym, games room & sparkling pool. *US$240 dbl FB.*

Mnarani Beach Cottages (37 rooms) ☎ 024 224 0494; m 0777 415551/0713 334062; e mnarani@ zanlink.com; www.lighthousezanzibar.com. Close to the northernmost tip of the island, Mnarani overlooks a stunning stretch of beach, & is separated by dense vegetation from the lighthouse; unlike most other plots on this coast, it feels less boxed in by development. Some of its en-suite rooms have sea views; others are set in lush, tropical gardens close to the pool. There are also new self-catering cottages & flats. Kayaks, windsurfers & surfboards can be hired, & the lagoon in front of the hotel is a great place for kitesurfers. The bar has a cool, relaxed vibe, & the staff are some of the friendliest on the north coast. US$120–200 dbl HB.

⌂ **Flame Tree Cottages** (14 rooms) ✆ 024 224 0100; m 0777 479429/0713 262151; e etgl@zanlink.com; www.flametreecottages.com. On the edge of Nungwi village, these whitewashed bungalows & a new house are spread across extensive gardens, beside the beach. Immaculate en-suite rooms have shady verandas, AC & fans, & a shared or private kitchenette. Flame Tree also offers one of Nungwi's best dining experiences (think delicious fish goujons with tartare US$5.50, or steamed chilli crab claws US$9). There is a real feeling of space & peace that is increasingly difficult to find in Nungwi, & the staff are genuinely happy to help. Activities range from lemongrass oil massage to snorkelling trips aboard the owner's dhow. US$120 dbl.

⌂ **Golden Dragon** ✆ 024 550 0590; m 0777 413953; e goldendragonlodge@yahoo.com, info@goldendragonlodge.com; www.goldendragonlodge.com. The name & tasselled red lanterns may conjure images of a Chinese take-away, but the angular buildings are more Mediterranean in appearance – though set way back from the beach, facing the breeze-block wall of the neighbouring resort, rather than out to sea. Yet the rooms are spotless & spacious, well equipped & with wide verandas (book the 1st floor for better views). The food also is rumoured to be very good, with a Chinese chef rustling up some tasty stir-fries. US$120 dbl; 30% discount for advance booking.

⌂ **Game Fish Lodge** m 0753 451919; e gamefish@zanlink.com. This small South African-owned lodge specialises in fishing trips for fellow nationals. Renovated rooms sit in a terrace beside the road, with a cracking view downhill towards the sea. All have pine furniture, a fan, TV, CD & DVD player, & a small en-suite bathroom. Down the hill is an open-sided restaurant/bar, a good place to chill out. Most guests will be heading for the owners' boats, which are moored offshore & fully kitted out with the necessary rods & reels. US$108–122 dbl.

⌂ **Sazani Beach Hotel** (10 rooms) ✆ 024 224 0014; m 0713 324744; e sazanibeach@aol.com; www.sazanibeach.com. Adjacent to Ras Nungwi Beach Hotel, Sazani Beach opened in 1997 & retains its slightly off-beat, laid-back character. Set high up on coral rock, its rooms – some en suite – have 24hr electricity, mosquito nets, fans, hot water & a stunning sea view. Fish dinners are served by the

beach. The dive centre, Divemaxx, had no instructors when last visited, but the manager, Mike, is a divemaster & will rent out equipment & escort group trips for experienced divers. Sazani is also a hangout for kitesurfers keen to catch the shore trade winds (up to Force 6) in the clear lagoon in front of the hotel. Advice & backup can be sought from Chris, at the neighbouring Ras Nungwi Beach Hotel, even if the accommodation price there is over budget. Free internet is available for guests. US$105 dbl.

⌂ **Baobab Beach Bungalows** (120 rooms) ✆ 024 223 6315; m 0777 416964; e baobabnungwi@zanzinet.com, baobabnungwi@yahoo.com; www.baobabbeachbungalows.com. Currently the largest establishment on this stretch of coast, Baobab is now aimed primarily at the Italian market. Above the sandy cove is a raised 'beach', from where rooms of 5 categories stretch inland. All are spotlessly clean with en-suite bathrooms, hot water, fans, mosquito nets, electricity, & a private balcony. Unless you can't stretch to the extra US$20, go for the lodges & deluxe rooms which, although far from the water's edge, have a reasonable sea view & are close to the pool. The buffet-only restaurant serves passable Italian cuisine, & the diving operation (www.oceandiving.it) is open to non-residents. US$90–280 dbl HB.

⌂ **Smiles Beach Hotel** (16 rooms) ✆ 024 224 0472; m 0777 417676/444334; e infosmiles@zanzinet.com; www.smilesbeachhotel.com. One of the best-quality quiet options in Nungwi, Smiles is a firm favourite with overland groups & repeat visitors. Around a flower-filled, semicircular garden are 4 striking villas, resplendent in pale yellow & white paint, with pagoda-like roofs & exterior spiral staircases. High-quality en-suite rooms are Indian in flavour, & all are immaculate. Expect sliding mosquito nets, AC, a phone, safe, satellite TV & beach towels. For those who can drag themselves the few metres to the beach, there's an on-site restaurant (no alcohol) & regular beach BBQs. US$75–100 dbl.

⌂ **Langi Langi Beach Bungalows** (33 rooms) ✆ 024 224 0470; e langi_langi@hotmail.com. The hotel is divided by a footpath, with newer rooms on the seafront & the original ones by the pool in a lush garden on the other. Although all are en suite with AC & fans, the latter probably still get our vote as the rooms of choice. On the seafront, aim for rooms higher up for the best views. The reasonably good Marhaba Café is a popular hangout for visitors & expats, serving curries in particular; bring your own alcohol. The owners are friendly, employing only local staff, & are genuinely hospitable. US$60–150 dbl.

Budget

🏠 **Amaan Bungalows** (58 rooms) ☎ 024 224 0026/34; 📱 0777 417390; ✉ amaannungwi@yahoo.com; www.amaanbungalows.com. This sprawling complex is popular with a young, lively crowd. Of its deluxe, garden & sea-view rooms, the last — perched on a cliff above the sea — more than justify the higher cost, though all are clean & well cared for, with en-suite bathrooms, fans &, in deluxe & sea-view rooms, AC. A grocery shop, bureau de change & internet café add to the package. The affiliated Fat Fish Restaurant & Blue Sea, immediately opposite on the seafront, are good places to eat pizza & seafood & drink virtually anything all day (HB rates include meals at either place). *US$40–120 dbl.*

🏠 **Safina Bungalows** (30 rooms) 📱 0777 415726; ✉ newsafina@hotmail.com. Despite the lack of sea view, Safina is a comfortable & spotlessly clean retreat, & benefited enormously when the main road was diverted away from its garden. The staff remain as accommodating as ever & the flower-filled garden continues to flourish. All rooms have 24hr electricity, AC & hot water in en-suite bathrooms. If post-beach chilling on the veranda isn't enough, there is a massage room. *US$40–50.*

🏠 **Baraka Beach Bungalows** (10 rooms) ☎ 024 224 0412; 📱 0777 422910/415569; ✉ barakabungalow@hotmail.com; http://barakabungalow.atspace.com. In the shadow of Paradise Beach Bungalows, these bungalows surround a small garden. Simple, en-suite rooms are dark but fairly clean with fans, electricity & hot water. Proximity to West Beach is ideal for sun-worshippers, but music from Cholo's is likely to prevent any sleep before dawn. At the beachfront restaurant, the coconut curries (US$6–8) are good. Also check out the adjoining Baraka Spa. *US$45 dbl.*

Kendwa

Kendwa If you plan to walk along the beach, make sure you know the tide times before setting off, or you could be cut off. Note, too, that it's not advisable to walk alone between Baobab Beach Bungalows and La Gemma dell'Est, where there have been reports of robbery.

Upmarket

🏠 **La Gemma Dell'Est** (138 rooms) ☎ 024 224 0087; ✉ info.gemma@planhotel.com; www.planhotel.com. This stylish resort at the northern end of Kendwa Beach is one of Zanzibar's best choices for families. Comfortable but contemporary rooms, with all mod-cons, are designed to give each a sea-view veranda, while remaining fairly unobtrusive. Exotic plants characterise the sloping gardens, & the beach is backed by an enormous pool with a children's area, jacuzzi & swim-up bar. Guests have the choice of several bars & restaurants, serving anything from pizza to Mediterranean buffets — although the seafood restaurant is charged extra. Activities range from diving (run by Scuba Do) & other watersports to quizzes & Swahili BBQs. *US$336–696 dbl, all inclusive.*

🏠 **Kendwa Breezes Beach Lodge** (16 rooms) 📱 0777 703999; ✉ relax@kendwabreezes.com; www.kendwabreezes.com. Entirely unconnected with Breezes Beach Club on the east coast, this new hotel has rooms in staggered rows of whitewashed buildings, inspired by the Arab Fort. The design also guarantees everyone a sea view. A Zanzibari wooden door leads to spotless en-suite rooms, kitted out with 4-poster beds, mosquito nets, fans, AC, TV & safe. The thatched, open-sided restaurant specialises in seafood. Should the laminate tables & formal chairs not appeal, there's a beach bar (⊕ 10.00–18.00) for snacks & cocktails. *US$160–180 dbl.*

Moderate

🏠 **Duniani Lodge** (8 rooms) 📱 0754 578099; ✉ dunianilodgekendwa@gmail.com; http://dunianikendwa.com. Formerly Malaika Bungalows, Duniani is a neat cluster of bungalows on a rugged coral outcrop above an idyllic stretch of beach. Light, airy rooms are basic but clean, with Zanzibari dbl beds & mosquito net, plus electricity, fan & en-suite facilities. B/fast is served under the shady casuarinas on the beach. *US$60 dbl.*

🏠 **Kendwa Rocks Resort** (35 rooms) 📱 0777 415473/5; ✉ booking@kendwarocks.com; www.kendwarocks.com. Kendwa Rocks is totally chilled, so don't expect anything to happen fast. Its clifftop bungalows, beach bungalows, motel-style rooms & an 11-bed dormitory get booked up in that order. Bungalows are all en suite, with those on the beach having a particularly good location. There's a beach bar, a Finnish steam bath

(US$6.50/2 persons), & a huge, refurbished cargo ship (*www.jahazihouseboat.com*) which offers a seductive overnight trip for US$500. Every evening, a US$15 dhow cruise leaves for Tumbatu laden with island punch, & at full moon there's a lively beach party. *US$55–100.*

🏠 **Sunset Bungalows** (56 rooms) m 0777 413818/414647; e info@sunsetkendwa.com; www.sunsetkendwa.com. A faded surfboard in the sand marks Sunset Bungalows' location – & its bar, where US$6 lunches feature everything from fresh fish to egg & chips. Pleasant bungalows (some with AC) have been built on the beach behind, with en-suite bathrooms & a shady terrace. Other rooms (no AC) are in thatched cottages in a colourful garden, with the most recent housed in 4 huge buildings at the rear. If these have taken

away a lot of the beach retreat vibe, the Sunset remains a reliable choice & is remarkably convenient for divers using Scuba Do on the foreshore. *US$40–90 dbl.*

🏠 **White Sands Beach Hotel** (32 rooms) m 0777 480987. Since 2002, White Sands has been subject to fairly constant low-level renovation & rebuilding. Neatly planted gardens surround the accommodation, which ranges from cosy standard rooms, which are clean & functional, to spacious king-size rooms. All are en suite, but the cheaper rooms have no hot water & the newest, most expensive rooms, are without a sea view (though it's barely a stagger to the beach). A suspended oil drum on the beach announces the restaurant, a fun hangout with swings to rival bar stools & a comfy sunken central lounge. *US$35–70 dbl.*

Budget
🏠 **Les Toits de Palme** (10 rooms) m 0777 418548. Simple en-suite rooms are in bungalows above the beach, while *bandas* with woven palm sides share

facilities. It's all very simple, but there are flush toilets, hot water & generator electricity in the evenings. *US$20–40 dbl.*

✕ **WHERE TO EAT** Nearly all the hotels and guesthouses in Nungwi and Kendwa have attached restaurants, many of which are open to guests and non-guests alike. Others are stand-alone places, that tend to close and spring up again as if with the tide. A few stand out as worth investigating in their own right, as listed below, but do ask around for the current culinary hotspots.

✕ **Cholo's Bar** Tucked at the back of West Beach, this perennial favourite is well known for its 24hr pumping music, cool crowd, & free-flowing alcohol. Beach bonfires are a periodic evening attraction along with ad hoc BBQs & dining at upturned dhow tables. In the next few years, it's possible this long-standing bar will be taken over & given a facelift, but current plans will see its late-night opening & beach bar basics retained.

✕ **Fat Fish Restaurant & Bar** The expansive mangrove-pole terrace of this relaxed hangout is cantilevered over the beach, affording uninterrupted views out to sea & a welcome breeze. The local fishermen's catch determines the menu, & is served freshly grilled or in spicy curries. Sunset drinks are equally popular & there's a satellite sports TV.

✕ **Mangi's Bar & Restaurant** Sandwiched between the curio market & Z Hotel's pool, Mangi's overhangs the coral rock above South Beach. It's another relaxed hangout serving fresh juices, US$4 cocktails & snacks such as samosas & chapattis from US$4.50.

✕ **Marhaba Café & Restaurant** On Langi Langi's large seaside deck, this is a relaxed coffee shop by day, & a Swahili restaurant by night. It's a popular place & worth booking for dinner, inside or out. Alcohol is not sold, but bring your own & it'll be chilled & served.

✕ **Ombeliko del Mondo** This pleasant *cucina Italiana* is tucked behind Amaan Bungalows, with precious little view but a menu full of traditional Italian delicacies: seafood antipasti, pastas, risottos & tempting *dolcis*. Mains are US$5–10, & while reviews are consistently good, portions are on the small side.

✕ **Saruche Restaurant** The formal restaurant at Z Hotel, Saruche serves an à la carte menu of African–European fusion food with a heavy emphasis on seafood. Accompanied by an international wine list, ocean views & island antiques, it's one of the smartest options currently in Nungwi. There are traditional music & entertainment nights throughout the week.

11

SHOPPING There are several small shops in Nungwi village, where you'll find an array of cheap souvenirs, including carvings, paintings and jewellery, as well as

Temporary **henna tattoos** seem to be *de rigueur* in Nungwi. Painted on to your skin by friendly local ladies, as you lie under their makeshift palm shades on the beach, they seem to mark a rite of passage in the backpacker fraternity. But be warned: the henna can badly mark bed linen, and many hotel owners will charge for stains. For all-out African beach chic, **hair-braiding** services are also available from the same ladies, along with basic beach **massages**. For a less-public massage experience, try one of the following:

Baraka Spa In a small, immaculate room, adjoining Baraka's Restaurant on West Beach, 2 friendly, trained therapists offer excellent treatments, from deep muscle rubs to Indian head massage, foot treatments & facials — though this is not in any way a 'spa'. *Body treatment US$20/hr; manicure US$10.*

Peponi Spa Set in the tropical gardens of Ras Nungwi Hotel, this is the area's best spa by far. Run by internationally qualified therapists using natural oils & ingredients, treatments are carried out in calm, minimalist rooms with soothing music & intoxicating aromas. It's a wonderfully relaxing place to spend a few hours, & who could resist the hour-long Peponi Zanzibari Glow to bring out their holiday tan? *Body treatment US$50–120/40–80mins; manicure US$40/1hr; waxing & eyebrow tinting/threading US$10–35.*

Safina Massage On the first floor of Safina Bungalows' restaurant building, gentle Fatima offers massage & beauty therapy. In spite of limited facilities, she tries hard to ensure guests relax & enjoy their treatment, & her quiet, smiling manner goes a long way to achieving her aim. *Body treatment US$20/hr; manicure US$10.*

essential items. Head inland across the football pitch behind Cholo's, and you'll first come to a neat building on your right, one half of which is the Nungwi School computer room (see *Other practicalities*, opposite), while the other half is **Choices**, a souvenir shop which also sells swimwear. A few steps further on is a small parade of shops. Here, the Pink Rose Salon advertises 'we prepare hair', Jambo Brother Shopping Centre offers a mixed bag of goods, an anonymous cosmetic shop does limited trade, and the **Nungwi Supermarket** is a veritable Aladdin's den of imported luxuries, from toothpaste and toiletries to chocolate and Pringles.

Taking the road deeper into the village, there's another internet access point, the California Foto Store for film processing (we cannot vouch for the quality of your prints!), the New Nungwi Salon where the brave can have a bikini wax, and the local-style Jambo Mixed Shop, behind which is the Ahsanna Dispensary for villagers.

Amaan Bungalows Supermarket has a reasonable selection of knick-knacks and food/drink basics, whilst behind Paradise Beach Bungalows, Mr Alibaba and his sons sell everything from *kangas* to cold drinks, postcards and tours.

If you just need a few essentials and don't want to stray too far from sunbathing, there are a couple of places on South Beach: **Nungwi Inn Supermarket**, next to its namesake hotel, stocks a good selection of snacks, drinks, toiletries and beach requisites, while, between the curio market and North Coast Snorkelling, up some very steep steps, **New Worldwide Supermarket** sells a similar range of goods, though less well laid out. Alternatively, stay on the beach and wait for the beach traders with their boards covered in mirrored sunglasses, beaded jewellery and cold drinks.

For artwork and souvenirs, a fairly contained **curio market** is beginning to grow on the alley running perpendicular to South Beach, between Mangi's Bar and North Coast Snorkelling.

OTHER PRACTICALITIES Several of the larger hotels have **internet** facilities, and a reasonable number of the smaller backpacker places will let you use an office PC to quickly check email. Amaan Bungalows has three PCs available for general use, and there will shortly be a similar facility at Langi Langi. However, we would like to recommend the reliable Nungwi School IT centre as a first choice, as its income is used to reinvest in the school's excellent computer initiative.

Founded in 2002 by Bibi Biorg, a generous 75-year-old lady who first visited Nungwi as a tourist, **BBs Computer Room** (e *bbs@zanlink.com;* ⊕ *08.00–20.00 Mon–Fri, 08.30–19.30 holidays & w/ends; rates are very low at US$0.60/30min or US$1/hr*) was designed to offer computer lessons to all Nungwi School's pupils as well as IT training for local adults. Now the classroom has 15 computers and five Nungwi-resident teachers, who hold classes day and night to ensure all Form 1 and 2 pupils encounter computer technology. Adult classes are also offered to Zanzibari locals, helping to fund the centre's school activities. Four computers at the back of the class have WiFi internet access, and are available to paying customers, mostly tourists, during opening hours, regardless of whether classes are present. The centre is clearly signposted beside the football field, on the right as you approach the beach.

ACTIVITIES If you want peace, quiet and fewer people, you will probably need to head to a different corner of the island; if not, then here are details of the area's main activities:

Water sports On the west side of the peninsula, especially on South Beach, locals offer simple boat rides, Mnemba picnic excursions, sunset booze cruises and snorkelling trips. It's also possible to go sailing (m *0774 441234,* e *info@dive-n-sail.com/yachtjulia@hotmail.com; www.dive-n-sail.com*) or kitesurfing (*Ras Nungwi Beach Hotel;* ✆ *024 2240487/78;* m *0777 415660;* e *chris@kiteZanzibar.com; www.kiteZanzibar.com*). Prices are all very similar; quality is variable. Listen to other travellers' advice carefully when deciding who is currently offering the best trip.

⚓ **Adam's Canoe Rentals** m 0754 949578. On the coastal path between Union Bungalows & Flame Tree Cottages, this does exactly what you'd expect: rents canoes — in great condition. Either hire & paddle yourself, or have Adam guide you around the coast. *US$15 pp per half-day.*

🤿 **Captain Mau** m 0777 415496; e mauZanzibar@yahoo.com. Next to Bam Bam Bar on West Beach, Captain Mau hires out mask & fin sets (*US$5/half day; US$10/day*) & arranges water excursions in his small wooden boat, complete with shade cloth. He will take visitors to Mnemba, Tumbatu & Kendwa Reef for snorkelling, but if you opt to go to the further destinations, be aware that he has only 1 motor & it's a long paddle back if it breaks!

🤿 **Cholo Usi Snorkelling** Next to Adam's Canoe Rentals, this is one of many rent-a-mask outfits to have sprung up. At US$15/day for mask & fin hire, it's more expensive than other outfits & the quality is much the same, so try bargaining or head to North Coast Snorkelling Shop for a bigger range.

🤿 **North Coast Snorkelling Shop** ⊕ 06.00–18.00. This small shop hires out masks, snorkels, fins & fishing rods. The quality is variable but you can try things on & select the best for you, & there is a range of good brands available, as well as adult & child sizes. *Snorkel kit US$5/day; fishing rod US$10 /day. A half-day's fishing costs US$200.*

Diving Many of the hotels offer diving and dive courses, either on the local reef, or further afield. Each of the dive operators in Nungwi is very different in feel and ethos, so divers are advised to talk to the individual operators about safety and experience before signing up.

🤿 **Divemaxx** Sazani Beach Hotel; ✆ 024 2240014; m 0713 324744; e info@sazanibeach.com; www.sazanibeach.com. Divemaxx did not have a resident dive instructor when we visited in 2008, so

11

does not run courses, but the English lodge manager, Mike, is a divemaster & will rent out equipment & escort group trips for experienced divers. *Diving US$40–50; Mnemba snorkelling trip US$35.*

᳁ **East Africa Diving & Watersport Centre** m 0777 416425/420588; e EADC@zitec.org; www.diving-Zanzibar.com. The oldest dive centre on the north coast is an efficient PADI 5* Gold Palm Resort, offering very well-priced courses to divemaster & a host of scuba trips. Dive sites are reached by dhow or speedboat, & each boat has 2 experienced captains. Safety appears to be taken seriously & nitrox is available. *US$60/110/190/400 (plus US$30 to Mnemba Atoll) for 1/2/4/10 dives; Discover Scuba US$95; Open Water/Advanced US$380; Nitrox US$300.*

᳁ **Rising Sun Diving Centre** Royal Zanzibar Hotel; ᳁ 0777 440883–5/88; e bookings@risingsun-zanzibar.com; www.risingsun-zanzibar.com. This fully accredited PADI 5* Gold Palm Resort with National Geographic status offers diving & watersports to hotel guests, but only scuba courses & trips to non-residents. Safety is taken seriously. Mnemba dives are offered on request but the focus is on short transfers & maximum underwater time. *US$85/170/464/695 for 1/2/6/10 dives; Open Water US$672; equipment US$39/day; underwater camera (inc CD) US$46/day.*

᳁ **Sensation Divers** Bagamoyo Spice Villa; m 0746 442203; e sensationdivers@yahoo.com, info@sensationdivers.com; www.sensationdivers.com. The emphasis at this PADI & SSI centre is on some of the more adrenaline-influenced diving options, with a raft of underwater toys from DPV motorised scooters to underwater cameras & nitrox tanks. The company is also affiliated with the game-fishing boat, *Unreel* (see below). *US$45/130/270 (plus US$30 for Mnemba); for 1/4/10 dives; Discover Scuba US$90; Open Water US$360; nitrox US$200; 10% discount for divers with own equipment.*

᳁ **Spanish Dancer Dive Centre** ᳁ 024 2240091; m 0777 417717/430005; e spanishdancerznz@hotmail.com; www.spanishdancerdivers.com. Based on South Beach, Spanish Dancer is PADI accredited with good safety standards & 2 boats. Courses are taught in Spanish, Italian or English. There is a live-aboard option on their 23m sailing boat, MS *Jambo*. *US$132/226/320/475 (plus US$47 for Mnemba) for 2/4/6/10 dives; Discover Scuba US$117; Open Water US$585.*

᳁ **Zanzibar Watersports** ᳁ 024 2233309; m 0773 165862; e info@zanzibarwatersports.com; www.zanzibarwatersports.com. This PADI 5* Gold Palm Instructor Development Centre has 2 Nungwi outlets, at Ras Nungwi Beach Hotel for guests only, & within the central Paradise Beach Bungalows complex for all comers. Those who have not dived for 6 months must do a refresher course on arrival. Facilities at the Paradise Centre are less upmarket than at the hotel, but divers here benefit from a 12% rate reduction. Snorkelling trips & sunset dhow cruises are an option, & there are 1- & 2-person kayaks, waterskiing & wakeboarding equipment available for hire. *US$55/100/295/460 (plus US$65 for Mnemba) for 1/2/6/10 dives, exc equipment; Refresher US$30; Open Water US$550; Advanced US$440; equipment US$15; kayaks US$10pp/hr; waterskiing US$70/15min; windsurfing US$30/hr. Group deals available for 4+ persons.*

Fishing

Nungwi's proximity to some of Africa's best deep-sea fishing grounds – Leven Bank and the deep Pemba Channel – offers serious anglers outstanding fishing opportunities. In addition to the weather-beaten local dhows which plough the coastal waters, three operators currently offer game fishing in fully equipped, custom-built boats, seeking out black, blue & striped marlin, sailfish, yellowfin tuna, spearfish, dorado, trevally, king and queen mackerel, barracuda and wahoo.

᳁ **Fishing Zanzibar** e gerry@fishingZanzibar.com, info@fishingZanzibar.com; www.fishingZanzibar.com. Operated in conjunction with Sensation Divers, *Unreel* is a 30ft fly-bridge, sport-fishing boat based in Nungwi. It takes small charter groups (max 4 anglers) to Leven Bank & the Pemba Channel. Night fishing for broadbills is a further option. A catch-&-release approach to billfish & sharks is encouraged. *US$500 half day; US$800 full day, inc lunch; live-aboard US$1,000/day for 4 persons.*

᳁ **Game Fish Tours** Game Fish Lodge; m 0753 451919; e gamefish@zanlink.com. This South African operation runs half-day, night-fishing & 2-day Pemba tours for reef & bottom fishing. They have 2 boats: the 4.2m fibreglass *El Shaddai*, & the 25ft *Karambisi* with a harness chair for fighting fish & sleeping facilities. *US$220pp/6hr (max 2 persons) on El Shaddai; US$165pp/6hr (max 3–4 persons) on Karambisi; 2-day Pemba US$550pp.*

⚓ Zanzibar Big Game Fishing Ras Nungwi Beach Hotel; ☏ 024 2233767/2512; e info@ rasnungwi.com; www.rasnungwi.com. Arguably the best game-fishing operation on Zanzibar is extremely well kitted out for both professional fishermen & have-a-go holidaymakers, with 3 new professional sport-fishing boats, professional tackle & international safety equipment. Tag-&-release fishing is encouraged. Half-day (5hr) outings depart at 06.30 or 13.30; full days depart at 06.30. *US$385–609/520–900 half/full day, inc boat charter, skipper, bait, tackle equipment & lunch.*

WHAT TO SEE Most visitors come to this area to relax on the beach, swim in the sea and perhaps party at night. For local attractions, the small turtle sanctuary and terrific local coral reefs are still a draw. If you want a more cultural experience, head down the coast to the 16th-century Swahili ruins at Fukuchani and Mvuleni, the bustling, ramshackle market at Mkokotoni, or venture across the water to Tumbatu Island. Note that the lighthouse at Ras Nungwi is still in operation and, although it is not open to visitors, no photography is allowed.

Mnarani Natural Aquarium Hawksbill turtles have traditionally been hunted around Zanzibar for their attractive shells, and green turtles for their meat. In 1993, with encouragement and assistance from various conservation bodies and some dedicated marine biologists, the local community opened the Mnarani Natural Aquarium (⊕ *09.00–18.00 daily; admission US$3*).

In the shadow of the old lighthouse, at the northernmost tip of Zanzibar Island, the aquarium was created around a large, natural, tidal pool in the coral rock behind the beach. Originally set up to rehabilitate and study turtles that had been caught in fishing nets, the aquarium project expanded to ensure that local baby turtles were also protected.

Turtles frequently nest on Nungwi Beach, and village volunteers now mark and monitor new nests. The resulting hatchlings are carried to small plastic basins and concrete tanks at the aquarium where they remain for ten months. By this time, their chances of survival at sea are dramatically increased, and all bar one of these turtles are then released into the sea, along with the largest turtle from the aquarium pool. The remaining baby turtle is then added to the pool, ensuring a static population of 17 turtles. Currently, this equates to four hawksbills, identified by the jagged edge on their shell, sharper beak and sardine diet, and 13 seaweed-loving green turtles. In spite of the aquarium being little more than a glorified rock pool, it's fascinating to see the turtles at close quarters. Further, the money raised secures the project's future, and goes towards local community schemes – in a bid to demonstrate the tangible value of turtle conservation to the local population. With luck, this will lessen the trade in souvenir shell products and ensure the species' survival.

On a practical note, when timing your visit, the water is clearest about two hours before high tide.

Dhow-building and harbour activity Nungwi is also the centre of Zanzibar's traditional dhow-building industry, where generations of skilled craftsmen have worked on the beach outside the village, turning planks of wood into strong ocean-going vessels, using only the simplest of tools. It is a fascinating place to see dhows in various stages of construction, but do show respect for the builders, who are generally indifferent towards visitors, and keep out of the way. Most do not like having their photos taken (ask before you use your camera), although a few have realised that being photogenic has a value, and will reasonably ask for payment.

Fishing continues to employ many local men, who set out to sea in the late afternoon, returning at around 06.00 the following morning, taking their catch to the beach fish market. The spectacle is worth the early start, but if you don't make it, there's a smaller rerun at around 15.00 each day.

11

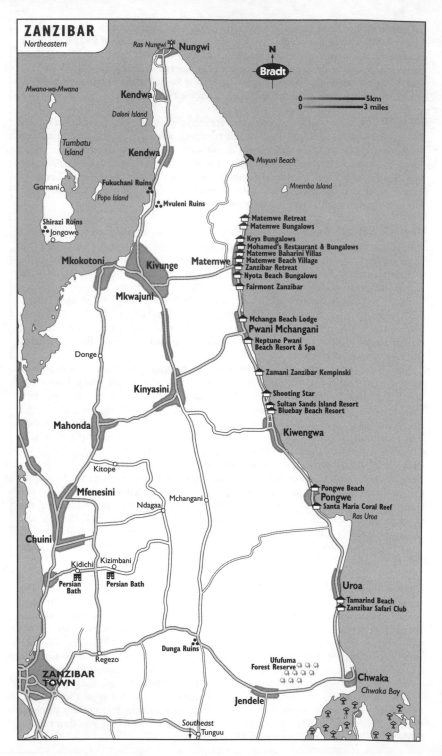

ZANZIBAR
Northeastern

Ras Nungwi Nungwi

N

Bradt

0 ————— 5km
0 ————— 3 miles

Mwana-wa-Mwana

Kendwa

Daloni Island

Muyuni Beach

Tumbatu
Island

Kendwa

Mnemba Island

Gomani

Fukuchani Ruins

Popo Island

Mvuleni Ruins

Shirazi Ruins
Jongowe

Matemwe Retreat
Matemwe Bungalows

Mkokotoni

Kivunge   Matemwe

Keys Bungalows
Mohamed's Restaurant & Bungalows
Matemwe Baharini Villas
Matemwe Beach Village
Zanzibar Retreat
Nyota Beach Bungalows
Fairmont Zanzibar

Mkwajuni

Mchanga Beach Lodge
Pwani Mchangani

Neptune Pwani
Beach Resort & Spa

Donge

Zamani Zanzibar Kempinski

Kinyasini

Shooting Star
Sultan Sands Island Resort
Bluebay Beach Resort

Mahonda

Kiwengwa

Kitope

Mfenesini

Pongwe Beach
Pongwe

Ndagaa   Mchangani

Santa Maria Coral Reef
Ras Uroa

Chuini

Kidichi Kizimbani

Persian
Bath   Persian Bath

Uroa

Tamarind Beach
Zanzibar Safari Club

Dunga Ruins

Regezo

Ufufuma
Forest Reserve

ZANZIBAR
TOWN

Chwaka
Chwaka Bay

Jendele

Southeast
Tunguu

As on the east coast, the other key marine industry here centres on seaweed. Local women tend this recently introduced crop on the flat area between the beach and the low-tide mark. The seaweed is harvested, dried in the sun and sent to Zanzibar Town for export.

Fukuchani Ruins The Fukuchani Ruins lie about 200m off the main road to Zanzibar Town, about 10km south of Nungwi. Also known as the Portuguese House, this well-preserved ruin dates from the 16th century and, while it may have been occupied and even extended by Portuguese settlers, it was probably built in the Shirazi era.

THE EAST COAST

The east coast of Zanzibar is where you will find the idyllic tropical beaches you dreamed about during those interminable bus rides on the mainland: clean white sand lined with palms, and lapped by the warm blue water of the Indian Ocean. Some travellers come here for a couple of days, just to relax after seeing the sights of Zanzibar Town, and end up staying for a couple of weeks. Visitors on tighter time restrictions always wish they could stay for longer.

The east coast is divided into two discrete stretches by Chwaka Bay, which lies at the same latitude as Zanzibar Town on the west coast. Traditionally, the most popular stretch of coast is to the south of this bay, between Bwejuu and Makunduchi, but recent years have seen an increasing number of developments further north, between Matemwe and Chwaka. Most hotels have restaurants, and you can usually buy fish and vegetables in the villages, but supplies are limited. If you are self-catering, stock up in Zanzibar Town.

GETTING THERE AND AWAY The east coast can easily be reached by bus or *dala-dala* from Zanzibar Town. North of Chwaka Bay, No 6 buses go to Chwaka (some continue to Uroa and Pongwe), No 13 to Uroa via Chwaka, No 15 to Kiwengwa and No 16 to Matemwe. South of the bay, No 9 goes to Paje (sometimes continuing to Bwejuu or Jambiani) and No 10 to Makunduchi. Chwaka Bay can sometimes be crossed by boat between Chwaka and Michamvi, with the help of local octopus fishermen. Most travellers prefer to use private transport to the east coast: several tour companies and some independent guides arrange minibuses (*US$5–8 pp each way*). Unless you specify where you want to stay, minibus drivers are likely to take you to a hotel that gives them commission.

NORTHEASTERN ZANZIBAR

Where to stay The roughly 40km of coastline north of Chwaka Bay is lined with numerous lovely beaches and punctuated by a number of small traditional fishing villages, the most important of which – running from north to south – are Matemwe, Pwani Mchangani, Kiwengwa, Uroa and Chwaka. Hotels along this stretch of coast mostly fall into the mid-range to upmarket bracket, though good budget accommodation is available at Kiwengwa.

Upmarket

⌂ **Matemwe Retreat** (3 rooms) m 0777 475788/0774 414834; e info@asilialodges.com, matemwebungalows@zanzinet.com; www.matemwe.com/www.asilialodges.com. Matemwe Bungalows' new sibling is one of Zanzibar's most impressive & exclusive places to stay, its exceptional

villas creatively designed with panoramic ocean views, an infinity plunge pool & a private, 2-tier roof terrace that catches the sunrise. A butler takes care of your every need & almost anything seasonally available is prepared on request & served where you like. There are no public areas, but

11

guests can use the facilities at Matemwe Bungalows. US$860–1,050 dbl, FB.

🏠 **Fairmont Zanzibar** (109 rooms) ➲ 024 224 0391; e zanzibar@fairmont.com, zan.reservations@fairmont.com; www.fairmont.com/zanzibar. At Matemwe, lush grounds, plenty of facilities & immaculate staff have quickly made this Zanzibar's premium family resort. Newly renovated rooms & suites, each with contemporary facilities & in a range of styles & sizes, are dotted around tropical gardens. Outside are 2 lovely pools & a super-soft sandy beach, as well as an on-site dive centre & a spa. Enjoy sundowners at the cocktail bar before dinner at the à la carte restaurant (southern African game meats & local seafood) or something more casual at Tradewinds buffet & pizza parlour. US$600–690 dbl, inc HB & activities.

🏠 **Matemwe Bungalows** (12 rooms) m 0777 414834; e info@asilialodges.com, matemwebungalows@zanzinet.com; www.matemwe.com, www.asilialodges.com; ☼ Jun–Mar. Smart yet informal, the quiet Matemwe Bungalows is popular with couples. Each of its thatched cottages is perched on the edge of a low coral cliff, with a superb view across to Mnemba Island. All have been upgraded into stylish suites, with mains electricity, mosquito nets, fan (on request), safe box, a day bed & an area to chill out as standard. Lush tropical gardens lead to the swimming pools, dining area & sandy beach. Activities include snorkelling & sailing in dhows, fishing, diving, & escorted reef walks. The lodge supports the local community through the provision of fresh water, a primary school, 2 deep-sea dhows for fishing, & teaching English. US$530–620 dbl, FB.

🏠 **Zamani Zanzibar Kempinski** (110 rooms) m 0777 444477; e sales.zanzibar@kempinski.com; www.kempinski.com. The most modern resort on the island is set in 12ha of landscaped gardens, & the quality of its rooms reflects its association with a serious hotel group – though the lack of a beach is a problem for some. As well as 2 restaurants – a Mediterranean buffet & a smart seafood grill overlooking the sea – drinks & snacks are on offer poolside. The spa is one of the island's best, while the active might prefer the large outdoor swimming pool, 23m lap pool & fully equipped fitness centre, as well as watersports from surfboarding to sailing; diving is easily arranged. US$400–600 dbl.

🏠 **Neptune Pwani Beach Resort & Spa** (154 rooms) ➲ 024 223 3449/1955; e neptunezanzibar@

zanzinet.com; www.neptunehotels.com. This arresting hotel extends from the beach up along the coral cliff behind. Striking 2-storey accommodation blocks with steep *makuti* thatch & external staircases are laid out in rows across lush lawns. Spacious bedrooms with locally crafted furniture & wide balconies have all the accoutrements of a 5-star hotel. An extensive network of pools incorporates a paddling section & swim-up *shisha* bar, with disco music throughout the day. Non-motorised watersports are available, but divers have to make arrangements with nearby centres. The autonomous Coconut Spa is a good place for guests & non-residents alike to take a break from the sun. US$300–680 dbl, all inclusive.

🏠 **Zanzibar Safari Club** (50 rooms) m 0777 844481; e reservations@zanzibarsafariclub.com; www.zanzibarsafariclub.com. South of Uroa village, this slightly kitsch resort run by efficient, if brusque, staff, has all the trappings of a large hotel but the feel of a hospitality training school. The large central pool is lovely, & there's an idyllic, palm-fringed beach. Mediocre buffets are served in the poolside restaurant, or there's Swahili cuisine at the Ocean View Restaurant beside the beach. At the end of the jetty, the Zinc Discotheque has state-of-the-art sound & light systems, a good Kenyan DJ, & a free pool table. No children under 12. US$260 dbl, HB; no credit cards.

🏠 **Bluebay Beach Resort** (112 rooms) ➲ 024 224 0240/2; e mail@bluebayzanzibar.com; www.bluebayzanzibar.com. Set on a lush, gently sloping site, rooms at the environmentally conscious Bluebay are in thatched, 2-storey villas or in the more exclusive Club 24, a superior hotel-within-a-hotel. All are en suite with plenty of mod-cons, & 2 rooms are kitted out for disabled visitors. Children are well catered for, with a children's pool & playground; there's also a large pool with jacuzzi, a floodlit tennis court, & a professional spa & fitness centre. There are restaurants at both sites, as well as a grill & pool bar. Activities range from canoeing, catamaran sailing & waterskiing to diving & snorkelling trips. US$240–580 dbl; Club 24 US$340–640 dbl; all FB.

🏠 **Shooting Star** (16 rooms) m 0777 414166; e star@zanzibar.org; www.zanzibar.org/star. Standing above Kiwengwa Beach, about 8km south of Matemwe, this is a delightfully social place, whose garden rooms, sea-view cottages & suites all feature Zanzibari beds & colourful Tingatinga pictures. A stunning infinity pool & sundeck afford views over the ocean, barrier reef & beach below. Dining is split across 3 shady areas, offering simple & filling meals, but it's the lively bar & relaxed lounge area that are the true heart of Shooting Star — & especially the lobster beach BBQ (extra US$45 pp). Diving, snorkelling & fishing trips can be organised. *US$215–610 dbl, all FB.*

⌂ **Sultan Sands Island Resort** (76 rooms) m 0777 422137. This Moorish hillside resort shares an activity centre & spa with the neighbouring Bluebay. Rooms are in planted terraces above the beach, but few have a sea view. In the reception, alongside the lounge & restaurant, arches, fountains & potted palms set the tone, while outside, water from the pool laps gently beside comfortable loungers. The lack of activities makes this a place to relax, although energetic guests can venture next door to Bluebay where facilities abound. *US$150–540 dbl.*

⌂ **Zanzibar Retreat** (7 rooms) m 0773 079344, 0753 452244; e info@zanzibarretreat.com, inforetreat@zanzinet.com; www.zanzibarretreat.com. Behind a wall of bougainvillea, this peaceful hotel is best suited to older couples. Bright & airy rooms

with AC & fans have timber floors, Zanzibari beds & dbl shower, as well as WiFi & satellite TV. There's a well-tended garden, & an attractive sea view best enjoyed from the restaurant. The large pool is an asset at low tide but for those keen to hit the ocean, activities, including diving, can be arranged with the nearby (10mins) Fairmont Zanzibar or at One Ocean in Matemwe Beach Village. *US$145 dbl.*

⌂ **Matemwe Baharini Villas** (16 rooms) m 0777 417768/429642; e info@matemwevillas.com, kibwenibeachvilla@zitec.org; www.matemwevillas.com. Benefiting from recent improvements, these villas & bungalows are clean & tidy, with electricity, hot water, fans, mosquito nets, & some with AC. Facilities are quite limited, but there is a beachfront restaurant, a pool, Scuba Libra dive centre (www.scubalibrezanzibar.com), Swahili massage, & local fishing excursions on request. For self-drivers, there is the advantage of secure parking. *US$50–70 dbl.*

Moderate

⌂ **Mchanga Beach Lodge** (8 rooms) m 0773 952399/569821; e tradewithzanzibar@zantel.com; www.mchangabeachlodge.com. Simple, stylish construction, high-quality interiors & a happy, efficient staff characterise Mchanga, & the location near Pwani Mchangani is stunning. Thatched rooms have a 4-poster bed, as well as a *baraza* alcove & small terrace. A thoughtful mix of wooden shutters, ceiling fans, AC & high-beamed ceilings ensure that rooms remain cool. Outside are a stunning swimming pool & open-sided bar & restaurant, serving a mix of Swahili specials. Diving can be arranged. *US$190–230 dbl.*

⌂ **Pongwe Beach Hotel** (16 rooms) m 0784 336181/0773 169096; e info@pongwe.com; www.pongwe.com. In its own quiet cove, in the shade of coconut palms, this simple lodge is well managed & good value. Airy bungalows have mosquito nets, an en-suite bathroom, & limited electricity, & there's a huge library of over 5,000 books. The barrier reef is only 15min offshore & the resort has its own dhow for sailing, snorkelling trips (US$15), & fishing. A large infinity pool has recently opened to the north of the beach. Pongwe serves tasty lunches from US$4 & varied set menus at dinner, including succulent spiced meats. With a little notice, children are welcome. *US$160 dbl.*

⌂ **Matemwe Beach Village** (22 rooms) ☎ 024 2238374; m 0777 417250; e matemwebeachvillage@zitec.org; www.matemwebeach.com; ⊕ Jun–Mar. Firmly a place

to relax, this simple, unassuming beach resort is popular with family groups & honeymooners. Simple but stylish en-suite rooms (2 with AC) are a mere hop, skip & a jump from the beach, while newer thatched suites, though very classy, are set well back with limited views. The resort's raised lounge area, overlooking the beach, encourages lazy afternoons & evenings, while the adjoining restaurant offers an à-la-carte menu. There's an attractive pool, although with no shade, & an on-site dive centre. *US$130–450 dbl FB.*

⌂ **Tamarind Beach Hotel** (16 rooms) m 0777 413709/411191; e tamarind@zanzinet.com; www.tamarind.nu. On a stunning stretch of beach, these semi-detached cottages house rooms with electricity, fans & mosquito nets, plus en-suite 'wet-room' style bathrooms. Lunch & dinner (US$12pp) are on offer in the restaurant, & the beach bar produces freshly squeezed juices. There's also a local TV room & a curio shop. Children are generally welcome, though activities are limited & the roof 'terrace' is not childproof. *US$80 dbl. Payment in local or major international currencies; VISA & MasterCard accepted without surcharge.*

⌂ **Nyota Beach Bungalows** (10 rooms) m 0777 484303/439059; e nyota@zanzinet.com; www.nyotabeachbungalows.com; ⊕ Jul–May. On a lovely stretch of beach, in the centre of Matemwe village, Nyota's stone-&-thatch cottages are colourful & well equipped, with fans/nets, electricity, & en-suite bathroom with hot water. There's a small lounge &

11

bar overlooking the sea, & the food is pretty good. Diving & snorkelling trips can be arranged. US$65–80 dbl.

🏠 **Keys Bungalows** (4 rooms) m 0777 411797. Keys is a very friendly beach bar with some surprisingly nice en-suite rooms in lush gardens, a good option for beach-focused backpackers. Fans,

mosquito nets, cold water & a small veranda are standard. A sociable crowd sets the vibe in the bar above the beach, where – from the comfort of a hammock or bar stool – it's possible to arrange snorkelling & boat trips. Meals are possible with some notice. US$60 dbl.

Budget

🏠 **Santa Maria Coral Reef** (7 rooms) m 0777 432655; e info@santamaria-zanzibar.com; www.santamaria-zanzibar.com. The only development along the beach at Pongwe is a delightful hideaway, set in a coconut grove. Both *bandas* & bungalows are

basic with solid wooden beds, coconut-rope & timber shelves & colourful mats. All are en suite with flush toilets & showers, & there is generator electricity 18.00–midnight. For lunch & dinner expect freshly cooked fish or chicken with rice (around US$6).

MANGROVE FOREST DEPLETION

Mangroves are salt-tolerant, resilient, evergreen trees, anchored by stilt-like roots in the inter-tidal zone (eg: *Rhizophora mucronata*) or simply growing in sandy muddy bottoms (eg: *Avicennia marina*), or even perched on fossil coral pockets with minimum soil. They are found in sheltered bays and river estuaries, where the waves have only low energy levels, and are vital components of the tropical marine environment. They ensure shoreline stability by protecting soft sediment from erosion, providing nutrients for sea organisms, and offering sanctuary to migratory birds, juvenile fish, shellfish and crustaceans.

Mangroves are nevertheless one of the most threatened habitats in the world. Environmental stress from changing tides and pollution takes its toll, but increasingly it's human interference that is the primary cause of irreparable damage. On Zanzibar, this is certainly the case: many people rely on the forests for fuel (firewood and charcoal), lime burning, boat repair and dugout manufacture, as well as material for house construction. Mangrove wood is dense and, because of its tannin content, is termite-resistant, making it preferable for house construction. Income is also generated from trading in cut wood, poles and charcoal. As the rural population continues to grow, so does the demand for this fragile resource. In order to have any chance of developing successful conservation initiatives, it is critical to fully understand and address the needs of the villagers.

Chwaka Bay is fringed by Unguja's largest area of mangrove forest, approximately 3,000ha and accounting for 5% of the island's total forest cover. Here, fairly dense stands of diverse mangrove species, zoned by their tolerance to water and salt levels, are drained by a number of lovely creeks. Over the last 60 years, assorted management plans have been drawn up with the communities bordering the forests, in a bid to control over-exploitation in the area. Yet each, from issuing permits to control harvesting, imposing mangrove taxes and limiting creek access, has successively failed to halt rapid deforestation. Ever-changing forestry policy, lack of serious patrolling, a decline in the authority of village elders, insufficient alternative income sources and minimal resources are all cited as reasons for the failure.

Conservation and development organisations continue to attempt to halt deforestation in the area, improve villager understanding of the forests' importance and lobby local and national government for support; but, without doubt, these valuable natural resources will be irretrievably ruined unless human activities are carefully controlled.

There's a simple thatched lounge/library area, & snorkelling trips can be arranged. *US$50 dbl.*

⌂ **Mohamed's Restaurant & Bungalows** (4 rooms) m 0777 431881. The beachfront location & budget continue to make this a great backpacker option.

Follow the sign from the main road & you'll find the cottages behind a high wall in the heart of Matemwe village. Rooms are basic but fairly clean & bed linen can usually be arranged. Simple meals can be organised with a day's notice. *US$40 dbl.*

Mnemba Island The tiny island of Mnemba, officially titled Mnemba Island Marine Conservation Area (MIMCA), lies some 2.5km off the northeastern coast of Zanzibar, and forms part of the much larger submerged Mnemba Atoll. It is now privately leased by &Beyond (formerly Conservation Corporation Africa, or CCAfrica) and has become one of Africa's ultimate beach retreats. It cannot be visited without a reservation.

The island itself boasts wide beaches of white coral sand, fine and cool underfoot, backed by patches of tangled coastal bush and a small forest of casuarina trees. The small reefs immediately offshore offer a great introduction to the fishes of the reef for snorkellers, while diving excursions further afield allow you to explore the 40m-deep coral cliffs, a good place to see larger fish including the whale shark, the world's largest fish. The bird checklist for the island, though short, includes several unusual waders and other marine birds.

⌂ *Where to stay*

⌂ **Mnemba Island Lodge** (10 *bandas*) ➣ South Africa +27 11 8094441; e reservations@ andbeyond.com; www.andbeyond.com; ⊕ Jun–Mar. The crème de la crème of &Beyond's impressive portfolio, Mnemba Island Lodge is the height of rustic exclusivity: a place where the term 'barefoot luxury' & eco-friendly policies are a reality. Overlooking the beach from the forest's edge, its secluded, split-level *bandas* are constructed entirely of local timber & hand-woven palm fronds. Large, airy & open-plan, each has a huge bed & solid wooden furniture, softened with natural-coloured fabrics. A 'butler' is assigned to each room to ensure that everyone is content. The cuisine is predictably excellent, with plenty of fresh seafood, fruit &

vegetables, though guests may choose what, when & where to eat. A number of superb dive sites are within 15min of the lodge, & during the trip sightings of dolphin are not uncommon, & even humpbacks in season. Up to 2 dives a day are included for qualified PADI divers, though courses are charged extra. There's also snorkelling, dbl kayaks, windsurfing, power-kiting, sailing, & fly or deep-sea fishing. Hot stone, aromatherapy, deep-tissue massage & reiki are all available, too. Mnemba is unquestionably expensive, but its flexibility & service levels are second to none, & its idyllic location & proximity to outstanding marine experiences are very hard to match. *US$1,250 pp/night, inc FB & activities.*

Ufufuma Forest Habitat The Ufufuma Forest conservation project, set up by the people of nearby Jendele village, aims to protect the forest habitat and to educate the villagers in sustainable use. The local volunteers, led by the dedicated and charismatic Mr Mustafa Makame, hope to make it a place for both locals and foreigners to visit, and to preserve the traditional worship of *shetani*, or spirits, which is performed here. Of the many underground caves hidden in the dense forest undergrowth, three are *shetani* caves being used by the local traditional healer (or 'witch-doctor'), which tourists may also visit. (A full ceremony lasts for about seven hours and must be prebooked.)

The forest area is at present only 1km², but the villagers are leaving the surrounding 4km² area uncultivated to allow the forest habitat to expand in size. A visit here is not a great wildlife experience, nor is it meant to be, although you might be fortunate enough to see skittish red colobus (apparently early morning is best), island birdlife, snakes and lizards. The villagers who act as guides are not wildlife specialists but they are trying to learn and, meanwhile, they are very enthusiastic about Ufufuma's cultural importance – which is the primary reason to visit.

11

Six villages in the vicinity already benefit from the forest income. All of the money goes directly to the community leaders, who assess their village's primary needs, and channel the money as appropriate. If more people visit the forest, accepting that it's not a slick tourism enterprise, the village coffers will slowly increase, and in turn the communities will begin to see the benefits of preserving rather than plundering their surroundings. We wish the Ufufuma Forest conservation project every success.

Arranging your visit To visit Ufufuma Forest, it is best to make contact in advance (*Mr Mustafa Makame Ali;* m *0777 491069;* e *himauje@yahoo.com*), to ensure that an English-speaking guide will be available. Costs are variable, but for a guided forest walk lasting a few hours, a visit to the caves, and usually a gift of fresh fruit or coconut refreshment, expect to pay US$5 per person per guide, and then volunteer to make a larger donation to the community fund. A full *shetani* ceremony, consisting of about seven hours of singing, dancing and assorted rituals, costs US$50 (1–2 people), and must be booked in advance for a time convenient to the local 'doctor'.

Getting there From Zanzibar Town, take the road west towards Chwaka: the forest is on the left, about 5km before Chwaka. If you have contacted the Ufufuma volunteers in advance, a welcoming party will likely be waiting for you, but if your visit isn't scheduled, stop at Jendele village and ask in the market area for an official forest guide. Take sturdy shoes and, in the hot season, plenty of water to drink.

To reach the forest on public transport, talk to the *dala-dala* drivers heading towards Chwaka (No 206 or 214), and ask to be dropped in Jendele village: be aware that this is a sprawling village with little tourism connection so it may not be an easy task.

SOUTHEASTERN ZANZIBAR The coastline south of Chwaka Bay caters better to budget travellers than the coast further north, though a few relatively upmarket hotels are also found in the area. Until a few years ago, the southeast stretch of coast had the most crowded beaches on Zanzibar, but these days the area is quieter than Nungwi on the north coast.

Coming from Zanzibar Town along the main road through Jozani Forest, the first coastal settlement you'll hit is Paje, a small fishing village situated at a junction, from where minor roads run north and south along the coast. The most important settlement north of Paje and south of Chwaka Bay is Bwejuu, a fishing village whose livelihood is linked to the gathering and production of seaweed. Several resorts catering to all budgets lie within a few kilometres' radius of Bwejuu. South of Paje, Jambiani is a substantial village that runs for several kilometres along the beach, while the more southerly town of Makunduchi, lacks any real tourist development.

BEACHED SEAWEED

From December to mid-February, some of the beaches on the east coast have large patches of brown seaweed washed ashore from the ocean by the wind. This can be quite a shock if you expect pristine, picture-postcard tropical beach conditions. The seaweed normally stays on the beaches until the start of the rainy season, when it is carried back out to sea. After March, and up until November, the beaches are mostly clear.

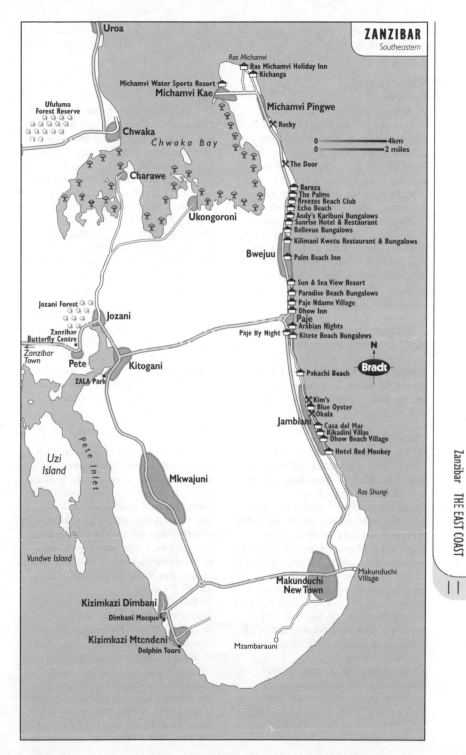

The Michamvi Peninsula which demarcates Chwaka Bay is very similar to the northeast of the island, with the same stunning powder-white beaches, barrier reef, palm trees and a significant tidal change.

⌂ Where to stay

Exclusive

⌂ **Baraza** (30 rooms) e info@ baraza-zanzibar.com; www.baraza-zanzibar.com. The youngest sibling of The Palms & Breezes, opened in mid 2008, Baraza offers an all-inclusive option at a similar high level to The Palms, but promises to be more child-friendly. With strong Omani influences in its architecture, ornate gardens & plunge pools in every room, it aims at affluent families who are not interested in the island's activity-focused mega-resorts. Villas, divided into categories based on their proximity to the sea & size, are spacious & well kitted out. Given the success of its sister hotels & the affiliation with the respected Rising Sun Dive Centre, we anticipate Baraza being a high-quality, slick operation. *US$730–790 FB.*

⌂ **The Palms** (6 villas) m 0774 440882; e info@palms-Zanzibar.com; www.palms-zanzibar.com. Adjacent to Breezes & owned by the same family, The Palms is small & stylish, with a colonial feel, attracting affluent honeymooners lured by image & intimacy. That said, the family-friendly Breezes shares the same beach, so romantic dinners for 2 on the sand may be subject to intrusion. In the colonnaded

Plantation House, housing a bar/lounge, dining room & mezzanine library, antique furniture rests on highly polished floors, while old-fashioned fans spin in the high *makuti* thatch. In the villas, huge rooms are classically elegant but with all mod-cons & a private outdoor plunge pool. They share a small swimming pool, & each has a private *banda* overlooking the beach. Most activities, take place at Breezes. *US$642–770pp dbl FB; min age 16.*

⌂ **Kikadini Villas** (5 villas) e reservations@ kikadinivillas.com; www.escape-zanzibar.com. On a large beachfront plot in the centre of Jambiani, the villas that make up Kikadini are unparalleled on the island. This is in essence a boutique hotel, with striking architecture, delicious food, attentive staff & tremendous individuality. Each of the beach-facing villas is architecturally different, while the interiors feature eclectic *objets d'art* & huge oil paintings. All have electricity, fans, small fridges & WiFi as standard. There are roof terraces for shady lunches & stargazing, & a swimming pool is planned. No children under 10 unless a villa is exclusively booked. *US$235–310 HB.*

Upmarket

⌂ **Echo Beach Hotel** (9 rooms) m 0773 593260/593286; e echobeachhotel@hotmail.com; www.echobeachhotel.com. Opened in Oct 2007, this small, friendly lodge with high aspirations is receiving admirable reviews. Arranged in a dbl arc behind the inviting swimming pool, the vast majority of its rooms have a sea view from a private terrace, with all enjoying a 4-poster dbl bed swathed in a mosquito net, polished floors, AC, ceiling fans & an open, en-suite bathroom with walk-in shower. The open-sided lounge/dining room, where the food is consistently very good, is a stone's throw from a lovely stretch of beach. For water-based activities, Breezes is a 10min beach walk away. Children are welcome at the discretion of the management. *US$250–300 dbl HB.*

⌂ **Breezes Beach Club** (70 rooms) m 0774 440883/5; e info@breezes-zanzibar.com; www.breezes-zanzibar.com. A perennial favourite with honeymooners & families, Breezes is a large, efficient, family-run beach resort. Comfortable rooms are set in whitewashed villas with all the amenities of a

good hotel. Facilities include large swimming pool & a great stretch of sandy beach, plus plenty of watersports, including a dive centre. For landlubbers, there's a modern spa, yoga studio, fitness centre & floodlit tennis court. Several restaurants & bars complete the package, including carved beach hut for dining *à deux* (but note that dinner at the smaller restaurants is not included in HB rates). Beach weddings, which must be arranged in advance, are increasingly popular here. *Standard US$240–594 dbl HB.*

⌂ **Kichanga** (23 rooms) m 0773 175124/193775; e info@athomehotels.com; www.athomehotels.com. At the tip of the Michamvi Peninsula, this attractive lodge above a sandy cove has rustic cottages with a mix of beach-facing & garden outlooks. If these are a little tired, they do benefit from large wooden terraces, as well as mosquito nets, fans, safes & en-suite bathrooms. Facilities include lounge bar, Italian-influenced buffet restaurant, swimming pool with bar, massage *banda* for local treatments (US$25/hr) & even a local tailor. Watersports are well catered for with a dive centre, organised snorkelling & boat trips, & canoe rental. The cove geography means that few non-residents come close to the beach, & children are pretty safe from wandering too far. The sand is at its best Aug–Dec; the beach gets progressively rockier as the *kaskazi* wind blows. *US$190–470 dbl HB.*

⌂ **Michamvi Water Sports Resort** (20 rooms) m 0777 878136 or 0784 758633; e michamvi@yahoo.com; www.michamvi.com. North of Michamvi Kae village, overlooking the mirror-like Chwaka Bay, this caters mainly to energetic holidaymakers seeking aquatic adventure, with virtually every watersport available (for a charge) on site. There are also sunset mangrove safaris (US$20), massage (US$25/hr) & henna tattoos (US$10/large). Rooms (half allocated to an Italian tour operator) are light & spacious, & each has

Moderate

⌂ **Arabian Nights** (11 rooms) 🕾 024 2240190; m 0777 854041; e anights@ zanzibararabiannights.com, anights-arabian@ hotmail.com; www.zanzibararabiannights.com. Tucked down a narrow alley to the beach beside Kitete Beach Bungalows is one of Paje's more sedate options. Rooms in thatched, coral-rock cottages surround the large pool & 2 suites with a private plunge pool face the beach. All have cool, spacious en-suite bedrooms, lockable wardrobes, TV & AC. The upstairs Swahili restaurant is open to all & there's an efficient PADI dive school, as well as a small shop & 2 PCs (no memory card downloading). *US$120–150 dbl.*

⌂ **Ras Michamvi Holiday Inn** (15 rooms) 🕾 024 2231081; e info@rasmichamvi.com; www.rasmichamvi.com. Opened in Jul 2007, this impressive & remote little resort sits high up on the very tip of the peninsula. Unless you have your own transport or enjoy extremely long walks it's unlikely to appeal. Walkways lead to en-suite rooms with tiled floors & quality Zanzibari beds. Though some are classed as 'disabled-friendly', with ramp entrances & walk-in showers, the beds are probably too high for those who are wheelchair-bound. From the restaurant, which offers fabulous panoramas, steps lead down the cliff to a small private cove, where the sand is at its best in Jun/Jul. *US$80 dbl.*

⌂ **Sunrise Hotel & Restaurant** (13 rooms) 🕾 024 2240270; m 0777 415240; e sunrise@ zanlink.com; www.sunrise-zanzibar.com; ⏰ Jun–Apr. Standards of service at this once-popular hangout have slipped, & reliable reports are increasingly less than glowing. Rooms (some with sea view) are not

either a private balcony or ground-floor terrace. In 2008, a fairly sizeable development was under construction immediately next door; if ever completed, this will impact on the beach dynamic. *US$140–220 dbl HB.*

⌂ **Dhow Inn** (5 rooms) m 0773 215929/0786 266941; e info@dhowinn.com; www.dhowinn.com. The newest of Paje's accommodation options, neighbouring Paje Ndame to the south, opened in Nov 2007, with plans to extend to 15 rooms in 2009. Set 40m back from the water's edge, the rooms – each with hot water, fans, mosquito nets & Wi-Fi – have no sea view but the 2-storey bar-restaurant does. There is a flexible dining programme with Full Moon pool parties & regular poolside BBQs. Non-guests can use the pool at US$4/day. *US$93–108 twin or dbl, US$116–132 trpl.*

fancy but they are clean, en-suite & reasonably priced, with AC, fans & nets, ensuring it retains a value-for-money feel. Food is tasty, & there's a sheltered pool, bikes to rent, local massage (US$10/hr) & internet access. Diving & snorkelling can be arranged. *US$75–90 dbl. Surcharge of 10% on credit cards; 5% on travellers' cheques.*

⌂ **Paje Ndame Village** (28 rooms) m 0777 865501; e booking@ndame.info; www.ndame.info. Set on a lovely long stretch of beach, Paje Ndame caters mainly to Scandinavian families so is busiest during the Nordic school holidays in Jul & Dec. Simple but bright & clean rooms have lino flooring, tiled en-suite bathrooms, mains electricity & fans, & either a shared balcony with a sea view or a garden terrace. Though activities are relatively limited, there's a pleasant seafront restaurant, a curio shop, a beach bar & a popular beach volleyball court. *US$75 dbl; child & student discounts available.*

⌂ **Paje By Night** or **PBN Bizzare Hotel** (23 rooms) m 0777 460710; e info@pajebynight.net; www.pajebynight.net. The row of hammocks at the entrance hints at the pervading mood of this unpretentious joint. Set 50m back from the beach, & without a sea view, the hub of PBN is the bar, with an adjoining TV lounge showing international news & sport virtually all day. The food is good with a definite Italian bent; seafood & Swahili BBQs are a weekly occurrence & the cocktail bar is open 24hr. Around the garden are spacious en-suite rooms, each with hot water, mains electricity & a fan, & rustic 2-storey 'jungle bungalows'. On a practical note, there's a curio shop, games area, free internet access, a safety deposit box, & night-time security.

US$60–75 dbl. Local & major currencies accepted; Visa, MasterCard & Amex subject to 5% surcharge.

🏠 **Palm Beach Inn** (14 rooms) 📞 024 2240221; m 0777 410070/411155/0773 414666; e mahfudh28@hotmail.com. In the heart of Bwejuu, Palm Beach Inn is a real hotch-potch of a place, rather cluttered & a little oppressive, but the management makes an admirable effort to employ Bwejuu residents, affording a distinctly local feel. En-suite rooms, in separate cottages as well as in a central building, have mains electricity, mosquito nets, fans, AC & a fridge. In the split-level restaurant, enclosed against the evening wind, basic meals include island staples (special fried prawns with rice & vegetables US$10), but order early, & accept that service is slow. The beach below the hotel (separated by a fence) suffers from sharp rocks, litter & a theft problem, while at night, motorbikes are known to take a short cut across the sands. US$60/70 dbl low/high season.

🏠 **Blue Oyster Hotel** (19 rooms) 📞 024 224 0163; m 0713 33312; e blueoysterhotel@gmx.de; www.zanzibar.de. In lovely gardens, Blue Oyster remains one of the friendliest, most cared for & best-value hotels in its range. Ground-floor rooms are around a palm courtyard & others in a trio of smaller 2-storey buildings, all with en-suite facilities & balconies. The wonderfully breezy 1st-floor restaurant, with a wide veranda overlooking the sea, offers snacks (around US$3), delicious salads (US$4) or pizzas & evening meals like coconut-infused octopus with rice (around US$5). In front of the hotel a raised stretch of sand is perfect for sunbathing, or for a coconut-oil massage (US$15). US$60–70 dbl.

🏠 **Andy's Karibuni Bungalows & Romantic Garden** (2 rooms) m 0784 430942; e romantic-garden@

Budget

🏠 **Kitete Beach Bungalows** (21 rooms) 📞 024 2240226; m 0773 444737/074373; e reservations@kitetebeach.com, kitetebeach@hotmail.com; www.kitetebeach.com. Kitete has moved on from being just an old villa offering basic rooms. Guests are still welcome at the original Kitete Cottage opposite Paje By Night, but a little further along the beach are the new, blush-pink villas, where immaculate rooms are cool, modern & offer much better facilities, including mains electricity, fans, mosquito nets, burglar bars & a small outside terrace/balcony. In a prime spot next to the beach, the funky restaurant has stunning views, & serves traditional Swahili dishes (US$5.50–12) alongside

web.de/nussera@web.de; www.eastzanzibar.com. Away from the village, this tranquil place has light, airy rooms with a spotless en-suite toilet & cold-water shower, & a small terrace overlooking shaded gardens to the beach. The casual restaurant offers local produce, cooked simply but well, & best ordered in advance. US$60 dbl; payment preferred in US$.

🏠 **Bellevue Bungalows** (6 rooms) m 0777 209576; e bellevuezanzibar@gmail.com; www.bellevuezanzibar.com. This relaxed, gentle place offers one of the best budget deals on the island & is a firm favourite. Under new management, the restaurant has been transformed, lounge & rooms decorated with vibrant colours & original solutions to storage & lighting implemented. Clean, spacious dbl rooms in 3 thatched bungalows have good en-suite bathrooms & a sunrise terrace, with coir dividers for privacy. The chef makes terrific tapas as well as a variety of European & Swahili cuisine (US$5–7). With a 5min walk to the beach & a kitesurfing school, the focus is on traditional seaside activities. US$60 dbl.

🏠 **Dhow Beach Village** (6 rooms) m 0777 417763; e dhowbeachvillage@yahoo.com, info@dhowbeachvillage.com; www.dhowbeachvillage.com. Set above the beach, this is a good option in this price range. The en-suite rooms are small but stylishly simple, each with a little outside terrace. The restaurant serves both Swahili & European cuisine favourites, & the bar on the beach is popular for 'cockatails' & also the focus for regular beach parties (18.00–06.00 in high season Sat & at full moon). Rates depend on room size, not location, with Room 3 on the beach being arguably the best but not the most expensive. US$50–55 dbl; up to 50% discount in low season.

specials such as lobster thermidor (US$30). Evening cocktails & shisha pipes are on offer, & a beach BBQ at full moon. US$60–90 dbl.

🏠 **Pakachi Beach Hotel** (8 rooms) m 0777 423331; e pakachi@hotmail.com; www.pakachi.com. Appropriately, pakachi means border, for this pleasant little hotel is situated roughly half way between Paje & Jambiani. It's a friendly, rustic haven, its simple thatched bungalows set amid flower-filled gardens. Spotlessly clean en-suite rooms have ceiling fans, & there's also a 2-bedroom family house. The bar/restaurant overlooks the sea, where a range of boats is available, though it's not ideal for swimming. The chef rustles up both local &

international dishes, with his pizzas recommended. *US$150 dbl; family house US$100.*

🏠 **Casa Del Mar** (12 rooms) m 0777 455446; e infocasa-delmar@hotmail.com; www.casa-delmar-zanzibar.com; lodge ⊕ Jun–Mar. Casa del Mar is run with impressive enthusiasm, skill & environmental awareness. Rooms are in thatched 2-storey houses, made almost entirely of organic material. The majority of the staff are Jambiani residents, & the school & clinic receive regular support. These credentials aside, the accommodation & friendly vibe are good reasons to stay too. En-suite rooms are either 1- or 2-storey, both with balconies & the latter with a galleried bedroom high in the thatch, & a lounge (or children's room). Good food is served in the cool, shady restaurant. There's a range of activities & excursions & the lodge has its own boat for snorkelling trips (US$15 pp/day). *US$50 dbl.*

🏠 **Sun & Sea View Resort** (10 rooms) m 0773 168839; e info@sunandseaviewresort.com; www.sunandseaviewresort.com. On a large, open plot by the beach, this is a relaxed place with cheerful African music playing at the bar. Large rondavels contain 2 independent rooms, each simple & clean with nets, mains electricity & fans. There's plenty of natural light, & a bath as well as a shower in the en-suite bathrooms. The hospitable owner is often around & his views on the island, its people & politics are enlightening; with time he can arrange village tours. There is no gate to the property, so self-drivers may prefer a more physically secure option, but otherwise this is a reasonable budget choice. *US$50 dbl.*

🏠 **Kilimani Kwetu Restaurant & Bungalows** (4 rooms) 📞 024 2240235; m 0777 465243/0777 214133; e info@kilimani.de; www.kilimani.de. A partnership between 5 Germans & the village of Bwejuu, Kilimani Kwetu is rooted in community development & has already financed the construction of an adult education centre & library. Built on a hill overlooking the sea by local people from local materials, this is a relaxed, hassle-free spot. Rooms in 2 white, thatched bungalows are basic if a little uninspiring, with a fan, & en-suite bathrooms (cold-water shower & squat, flush toilet). Fresh fish is served in the restaurant, & vegetarian dishes on request. Just 50m along a zigzag path leads to a private beach area & new beach bar. *US$45 dbl.*

🏠 **Paradise Beach Bungalows** (10 rooms) 📞 024 2231387; m 0777 414129; e paradisebb@zanlink.com, saori@cats-net.com; www.geocities.jp/paradisebeachbungalows. The track opposite Dreams Restaurant on the tar road leads to this long-standing budget favourite, under Japanese ownership. The new chalets, with European toilets & showers, are a better bet than the original, basic rooms, with their squat toilets & cold showers. Despite storm lanterns, frequent power cuts make a torch essential. Good-quality home-cooked food include fresh sushi & tempura, but supplies are limited so order well in advance. Paradise can get very busy, so advance booking is advisable. And be aware that there are a number of not-so-docile dogs around the gardens! *US$30–40/35–45 dbl low/high season. Local & major international currencies accepted. No credit cards; travellers' cheques 7% surcharge.*

🏠 **Hotel Red Monkey** (9 rooms) m 0777 497736; e soloman@sansibarulaub.de, marketing@rundfluege-online.de; www.rundfluege-online.de. The most southerly lodge in Jambiani lies about 2km from the centre along a bumpy track, & is named for the red colobus monkeys that live in the adjacent forest & pass through the grounds most days. Rooms, complete with timber beds, ceiling fan, mosquito nets & high-pressure en-suite showers, are extremely clean & represent one of the better budget deals in this part of Zanzibar. A skilful chef prepares fresh fish & other good meals (about US$4). There's a good view of the beach (which is reached by a short flight of steps), & the German Zanzibar staff are very friendly. *US$30 dbl.*

✕ Where to eat

✕ **Kim's Restaurant** This simple, shaded restaurant, the realisation of the owner's childhood dream, serves authentic Zanzibari cuisine for lunch & dinner (best ordered in advance), all freshly prepared by Kim & his mother. The spicy fish samosas (US$2.50), fish soup (US$2.50) & coconut-crusted fish with mango chutney (US$5) are particularly tasty. Located between Kipepeo Lodge & Blue Oyster Hotel, this is one of a few reliably good village dining options in Jambiani.

✕ **Okala Restaurant** m 0777 430519. In a small, unremarkable *makuti* building, just up from the beach (between the Rising Sun & Oasis Beach hotels), Okala's food far exceeds any expectations arising from its architecture! It's run by a small co-operative of Jambiani families, & the Zanzibari food is excellent by any standards. With some notice, the team can prepare a fabulous meze of Swahili curries, grilled seafood & tasty vegetable accompaniments. Filling up on fresh coconut rice,

11

wilted spinach with lime & rich tomato fish curry is a real Zanzibari treat. Individual dishes, such as grilled octopus or fish, are US$4–5, with special items, like the amazing (& enormous!) coconut-crusted jumbo prawns, at US$11. Short courses in Zanzibari cooking are also offered. The team here is closely involved with several community projects, so ask them if you're interested in what's happening, or arrange to end your Eco&Culture village tour (see below) with a satisfying lunch.

✗ **Rocky Restaurant** m 0777 840724/490681. Perched on top of a marooned, seriously undercut coral-rock outcrop, just off the shore of the Michamvi Peninsula, Rocky's is accessed by wandering across the sand at low tide, or by boat or breaststroke at high tide. It's a dilapidated building, basic, quirky & often empty, serving a

simple 'catch of the day' menu. The views are terrific, the staff friendly & the experience unique. Calling in advance is a good idea if you're coming from afar.

✗ **The Door** m 0777 414962; ⊕ lunch & dinner daily. Accessed from the beach, The Door is a sizeable shady restaurant on top of the coral cliff above the Rafiki shop; from the tar road, it's signed down a bumpy track. The staff are friendly, & there's a great outlook to the Blue Lagoon (the only place in this area where swimming is possible at low tide). After some fried squid with lemon rice (US$6.50) or a divine 2-person whole grilled lobster (US$40), leave your things behind the bar & take a cooling dip or snorkel. Book in advance for dinner.

What to see and do While most visitors are here for the beach and attendant watersports, two community projects in this area are well worth the support of visitors.

Eco&Culture Jambiani Cultural Tours Probably the island's best insight into genuine rural life is afforded by Eco&Culture's village tours (⤮ 024 223 3731; m 0777 410873; e ecoculturetours@gmail.com, hajihafidh@yahoo.co.uk, kassimmande@hotmail.com; www.ecoculture-zanzibar.org; see page 307). Meet in the small, signposted hut in the centre of the village (opposite the school), or be collected on foot from your hotel for these well-run, enlightening community-focused walks, organised & guided by resident Kassim Mande (m 0777 469118) and his colleagues. A percentage of your fee goes directly towards community development initiatives, a direct result of the organisation's original NGO status.

Depending on your enthusiasm and heat tolerance, tours last anything from a few hours to the best part of a day and take in many aspects of everyday life. Spend time helping the women make coconut paste, reciting the alphabet in unison at the efficient kindergarten and meeting the *mganga* (traditional healer). Kassim's presence, reputation within the community and ability to translate allow for genuine interaction with the Jambiani residents and a thoroughly engaging time. The trip can also be arranged in advance from Eco+Culture's Stone Town office on Hurumzi Street (see page 307).

Do be aware that of late there are a few villagers operating apparently copycat walks. It is well worth taking the time to seek out Kassim or the Eco+Culture office, not only for his knowledge & friendliness, but also to be sure that your money is directed back into vital village projects.

Jambiani Wellness Centre Opened in 2003 by a joint Canadian–Zanzibari NGO, Hands Across Borders, the Jambiani Wellness Centre (e habszanzibar@yahoo.ca; www.handsacrossborderssociety.org; ⊕ 09.00–14.00 Mon/Tue & Thu/Fri) primarily offers chiropractic treatment, homeopathic remedies & other therapy free of charge to the local community. Tourists are welcome to visit for massage, acupuncture, breema or homeopathic treatments. A donation of at least US$15 is asked in lieu of a fee. The charitable work of the group now extends well beyond the clinic boundaries, with current community projects including a vocational school to educate adults about tourism & starting up a business.

SOUTHWESTERN ZANZIBAR

For most overseas visitors, Zanzibar's southwest corner holds little more than day trip opportunities to see dolphins from Kizimkazi or troops of red colobus monkeys in Jozani Forest. As a result, few people stay in this area, with most opting instead for the endless beaches of the east coast or the buzz of Zanzibar Stone Town. Away from the main tourist attractions, the villagers in these parts rarely encounter visitors, and their welcome is one of genuine friendliness and interest. It's a refreshing contrast to the more crowded and visitor-centric feeling taking over significant parts of the island's north and east coasts.

WHERE TO STAY AND EAT
Upmarket

Unguja Lodge (10 rooms) m 0774 477477/ 857234; e info@ungujalodge.com; www.ungujaresort.com. Opened in Dec 2006, Unguja Lodge at Kizimkazi Mkunguni is already up with the best on the island, its style a mix of modern & traditional. Enormous rooms under steep *makuti* roofs are set in densely planted gardens. Inside each, sinuous walls enclose a lounge, shower room, mezzanine seating area & bedroom. 3 'baobab villas' each have a small plunge pool, whilst others have a sea view. For a cool dip, try the pool or make for the crushed-shell beach. There's a PADI dive centre, with shore diving & boat dives possible. Other activities include dhow cruises, dolphin viewing & a village tour. *US$350–510 dbl HB.*

Fumba Beach Lodge (26 rooms) m 0777 860504/878025; e info@fumbabeachlodge.co.tz; www.fumbabeachlodge.com. To the south of Zanzibar Town, & created in line with contemporary, upmarket safari camps, this is one of the islands' most stylish places to stay. Rooms & uber-luxurious suites have canopied beds, mains electricity, en-suite showers, fans & a sea view. A large infinity pool lies next to the lounge & a sophisticated, open-sided restaurant, specialising in seafood, while an ingenious open-air treehouse is home to a spa. There's an on-site dive centre & day trips around Menai Bay's islands make for one of Zanzibar's most beautiful & indulgent outings. *US$210–410 dbl.*

Moderate

Swahili Beach Resort (19 rooms) \ 024 2240491; e info@swahilibeachresort.com, annaswahilibeachresort@gmail.com; www.swahilibeachresort.com. At the far side of Kizimkazi Mkunguni, high gates guard this new property. From a castellated reception area, there are views over the swimming pool & to the sea beyond. Spacious en-suite rooms, most in single-storey bungalows, come in 3 categories, each with a fan, AC, mini fridge, TV & tiled terrace as standard. There is an on-site PADI dive centre (e kizimkazidivers@hotmail.com); kayaks can be hired, & island excursions organised. *US$160–210 dbl FB; high season supplement US$10–20.*

Karamba (14 rooms) m 0773 166406; e karamba@zanlink.com; www.karambaresort.com.

This appealing clifftop lodge at Kizimkazi Dimbani has smart, en-suite bungalows, each thoughtfully decorated & with a sea view. In the restaurant, try fresh sushi (US$20 sharing platter) & tapas dishes (US$3–6 each), or just a sunset cocktail overlooking the bustling dhow harbour below. *US$84–216 dbl.*

Dolphin View Village (9 rooms) m 0777 863421. The most southerly of Kizimkazi's accommodation options is under the careful management of a smart, imposing Maasai called Freddy. Neat semi-detached bungalows house simple & functional en-suite rooms with fans, *mkeke* mats & small terraces. These come in a variety of sizes so do see if there's a choice when you arrive. The staff are very friendly but the lodge's finest feature is its small secluded beach. *US$65 dbl.*

Budget

Kumi Na Mbili Centre (3 rooms) m 0777 841252; e info@d-t-p-ev.de; www.zanzibartourism.org. The neat white building of this village development centre at Kizimkazi Mkunguni has simple, clean en-suite rooms with fans & mosquito nets. There's an affiliated bakery & juice

bar, as well as an internet café & shop. Bicycles are available for rent & tours can be arranged. For US$3, you can plant a tree, for which a little KiSwahili helps: *Ningombu kupanda mnazi moja/tatu/kumi* means, 'I would like to plant 1/3/10 palm trees'. *US$30 dbl.*

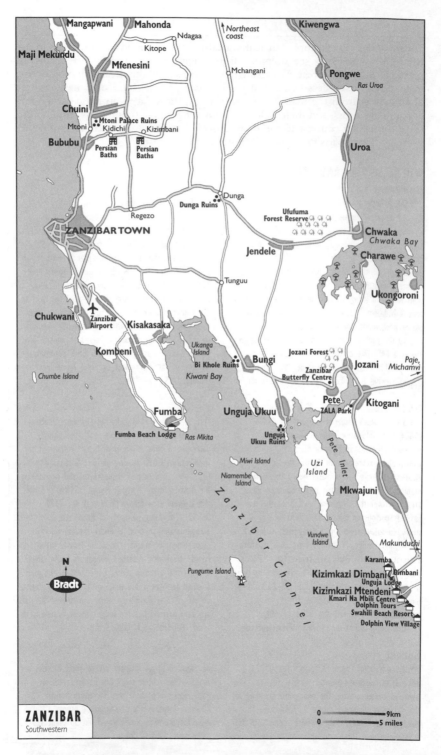

ZANZIBAR
Southwestern

KIRK'S RED COLOBUS

Kirk's red colobus (*Procolobus kirkii*) is named after Sir John Kirk, the 19th-century British consul-general in Zanzibar, who first identified these attractive island primates. They are endemic to the archipelago and one of Africa's rarest monkeys. Easily identified by their reddish coat, pale underside, small dark faces framed with tufts of long white hairs, and distinctive pink lips and nose, the monkeys are a wildlife highlight for many visitors to Zanzibar.

Kirk's red colobus live in gregarious troops of five to 50 individuals, headed by a dominant male and comprising his harem of loyal females and several young (single births occur year-round). They spend most of the day hanging out in the forest canopy, sunbathing, grooming and occasionally breaking away in small numbers to forage for tasty leaves, flowers and fruit. Their arboreal hideouts can make them hard to spot, but a roadside band at the entrance to Jozani–Chwaka Bay National Park allow for close observation and photography.

Timber felling, population expansion and a rise in agriculture have resulted in the rapid destruction of the tropical evergreen forests in which the Kirk's red colobus live, thus dramatically reducing population numbers. Researchers estimate that around 2,700 of these monkeys currently exist, a fact verified by their classification as 'endangered' on the IUCN Red List (2004) and their inclusion in Appendix II of the Convention on International Trade in Endangered Species of Wild Flora and Fauna (CITES).

Human behaviour has undoubtedly caused the decline in Kirk's red colobus population numbers, yet now tourism may help to save the species. With national park status now protecting their habitat in Jozani Forest, and visitor numbers increasing, the local communities are beginning to benefit from the tangible economic rewards that come from preserving these striking monkeys. If this continues, the future survival of the species should be secured.

JOZANI–CHWAKA BAY NATIONAL PARK This newly declared national park (⊕ 07.30–17.00 daily; admission US$8) incorporates **Jozani Forest**, protecting the last substantial remnant of the indigenous forest that once covered much of central Zanzibar. It stands on the isthmus of low-lying land which links the northern and southern parts of the island, to the south of Chwaka Bay. The water table is very high and the area is prone to flooding in the rainy season, giving rise to this unique 'swamp-forest' environment. The large moisture-loving trees, the stands of palm and fern, and the humid air give the forest a cool, 'tropical' feel.

Jozani's main attraction is Kirk's red colobus, a beautiful and cryptically coloured monkey with an outrageous pale tufted crown. Unique to Zanzibar, Kirk's red colobus was reduced to a population of around 1,500 individuals a few years back, but recent estimates now place it at around 2,500.

The forest used to be the main haunt of the Zanzibar leopard, a race that is found nowhere else, but which recent research suggests may well be extinct. The forest is also home to Ader's duiker, a small antelope that effectively may now be a Zanzibar endemic, as it is probably extinct and certainly very rare in Kenya's Sokoke Forest, the only other place where it has ever been recorded. Several other mammal species live in Jozani, and the forest is one of the best birding sites on the island, hosting a good range of coastal forest birds, including an endemic race of the lovely Fischer's turaco.

A network of nature trails has been established through the forest. The main one takes about an hour to follow at a leisurely pace, with numbered points of interest which relate to a well-written information sheet which you can buy for a nominal cost at the reception desk. There are also several shorter loops. As you walk around the nature trails, it's possible to see lots of birds and probably a few colobus and Sykes monkeys, but these animals are shy, and will leap through the trees as soon as they hear people approaching. On the south side of the main road live two groups of monkeys that are more used to humans and with a guide you can watch these at close quarters. This is ideal animal viewing – the monkeys are aware of your presence but not disturbed. Some visitors have been tempted to try to stroke the monkeys or give them sweets, which is not only bad for the monkeys, but can be bad for tourists too – several people have been given a nasty nip or scratch.

South of the forest, a long thin creek juts in from the sea, and is lined with mangrove trees.

A new development in the area, based in the village of Pete, 1km from the entrance to the forest, is a mangrove boardwalk, allowing visitors a rare view into the unique mangrove habitat.

When to visit Keen naturalists who want to watch wildlife undisturbed, or those who just like a bit of peace and quiet, should try to visit the reserve either very early or in the middle of the day, as most groups come at about 09.00–10.00 on their way to the coast, or 15.00–16.00 on their way back. The monkeys and birds seem subdued in the midday heat, so about 14.00–15.00 seems to be the best time for watching their behaviour.

Getting there and away The entrance to Jozani Forest is clearly signposted on the main road between Zanzibar Town and the southern part of the east coast, north of the village of Pete. You can visit at most times of the year, but in the rainy season the water table rises considerably and the forest paths can be under more than 1m of water. The entrance fee includes the services of a guide and the mangrove boardwalk.

Many tour companies include Jozani on their east-coast tours or dolphin tours, but you can easily get here by frequent public bus (routes 9, 10 or 13), *dala-dala* (nos 309, 310, 324 or 326), hired bike or car. Alternatively, take a tourist minibus heading for the east coast, and alight here. This road is well used by tourist minibuses and other traffic throughout the day, so after your visit to the forest you could flag something down and continue to the coast or return to Zanzibar Town.

AROUND JOZANI Also of interest in the Jozani area are ZALA Park, a small private zoo off the main east coast road, the Zanzibar Butterfly Centre, and the Bi Khole Ruins.

Zanzibar Land Animals Park The Zanzibar Land Animals Park (*ZALA*; m *0713 329357*; e *mohdayoub@hotmail.com*; ⊕ *08.00–17.30 daily; admission US$5 adults; children free*) is in the village of Muungoni, just south of Kitogani, where the main road from Zanzibar Town divides into roads towards Paje and Makunduchi.

At first glance it's just a zoo, with various pens and compounds to hold the animals (mostly reptiles). However, this private project, run by the tireless and enthusiastic Muhammad Ayoub, has a more important purpose. It's primarily an education centre for groups of Zanzibari schoolchildren to come and learn about their island's natural heritage.

For tourists this is one of the few places in Zanzibar where you can observe snakes and lizards at close quarters; the chameleons are particularly endearing. Also look out for the geometric tortoises which are not native, but were brought to the park by customs officials who confiscated them at the airport from a smuggler of exotic pets. There are a few other species on display, most notably the small group of tree hyrax who spend some time in their pen and some time in the nearby forest.

These part-time zoo animals come back mostly at feeding time, then seem quite content to rest or play in their pen before returning to the trees at nightfall.

ZALA Park is only about 3km down the road from Jozani Forest, and can be combined with a visit there. If you have an overwhelming interest in wildlife, conservation or education, it is sometimes possible to stay in the small one-roomed guesthouse, although this is often used by visiting volunteers. Muhammad plans a nature trail in the nearby forest and mangrove stands, and can organise guided walks if you are interested in seeing more of this area: ideally, this should be arranged in advance.

Zanzibar Butterfly Centre (*ZBC;* e *mail@zanzibarbutterflies.com; www.zanzibarbutterflies.com;* ☉ *09.00–17.00 daily; admission US$4 pp*) Opened in January 2008, the Zanzibar Butterfly Centre aims to show visitors the forest's fluttering friends close up as well as generating an income for local villagers and preserving the forest. Participants (currently 26 farmers) are taught to identify butterfly species, gently capture female butterflies, net small areas for breeding, harvest eggs, plant appropriate caterpillar fodder and ultimately collect the resulting pupae for breeding the next generation and sale back to the centre. The pupae are then sold on to overseas zoos and live exhibits, or displayed for visitors to the centre in the large, netted tropical garden. Here, 200–300 colourful butterflies can be seen in the enclosure, making for a fascinating diversion and one of Africa's largest butterfly exhibits. There are good guides and clear informative signs to explain the project and butterfly lifecycle, and experienced photographers can also get some wonderful shots. The income generated from visitors to ZBC is channeled back into further funding local conservation and poverty-alleviation projects, whilst the message is made clear to the communities that protecting the natural habitat of these insects provides much-needed income. The centre is a fun, worthwhile 30min stop, and its location, just outside Jozani Forest, makes it a convenient addition to a forest trip.

Bi Khole ruins The Bi Khole ruins are the remains of a large house dating from the 19th century. Khole was a daughter of Sultan Said (*Bi* is a title meaning 'lady') who came to Zanzibar in the 1840s, after Said moved his court and capital from Oman. With her sister, Salme (see box, page 326), she helped their brother, Barghash, escape after his plans to seize the throne from Majid were discovered. Khole had this house built for her to use as a private residence away from the town; she is recorded as being a keen hunter and a lover of beautiful things. The house had a Persian bath-house where she could relax after travelling or hunting, and was surrounded by a garden decorated with flowering trees and fountains. The house was used until the 1920s but is now ruined, with only the main walls standing.

The main front door has collapsed into a pile of rubble but this is still the way into the ruin. Directly in front of the door is a wide pillar, designed so that any visitor coming to the door would not be able to see into the inner courtyard, in case Khole or other ladies of the court were unveiled. In this room are alcoves and niches with arabesque arches, although the windows are rectangular. With some imagination, it's possible to see what an impressive house this once was.

The ruins lie a few kilometres to the west of the main road from Zanzibar Town to the southern part of the east coast, about 6km south of the village of Tunguu. The road passes down a splendid boulevard of gnarled old mango trees, supposed to have been planted for Khole (although they may date from before this period): about halfway along is the track to the ruins. If you're travelling on public transport, take any of the buses (routes 9, 10 or 13) or *dala-dalas* (No 309, 310, 324 or 326) heading southeast and ask the driver to tell you when to alight.

KIZIMKAZI The small town of Kizimkazi lies on the southwestern end of the island, and is best known to tourists as *the* place to see humpback and bottlenose dolphins, both of which are resident in the area. Most tourists visit Kizimkazi on an organised day tour out of Zanzibar Town, which costs US$25–100 per person, depending on group size, season and trip quality, including transport to/from Kizimkazi, the boat, all snorkelling gear and lunch. Alternatively, the town can be reached independently in a hired car, or with a No 326 *dala-dala* from Zanzibar Town.

Dolphin watching The best time of year to see the dolphins is between October and February. From June to September, the southerly winds can make the seas rough, while during the rainy season (March to May) conditions in the boat can be unpleasant. However, out at sea you're likely to get wet anyway. You should also protect yourself against the sun. Sightings used to be almost guaranteed, but it's not unusual now for groups to return without having seen a single dolphin. Sadly, as the disturbances from too many boats and people increasingly outweigh the benefits of food and shelter, this trend is likely to continue, with fewer and fewer dolphins appearing in Kizimkazi's waters in the future.

Never encourage your pilot to chase the dolphins or try to approach them too closely yourself. With up to 100 people visiting Kizimkazi daily in the high season, there is genuine cause to fear that tourism may be detrimental to the animals. If you do get close enough and you want to try your luck swimming with the dolphins, slip (rather than dive) into the water next to the boat, and try to excite their interest by diving frequently and holding your arms along your body to imitate their streamlined shape.

Kizimkazi Mosque Hidden behind its new plain walls and protective corrugated-iron roof, the mosque at Kizimkazi Dimbani is believed to be the oldest Islamic building on the East African coast. The floriate Kufic inscription to the left of the *mihrab* (the interior niche indicating the direction of Mecca) dates the original mosque construction to AD1107 and identifies it as the work of Persian settlers. The silver pillars on either side of the niche are decorated with pounded mullet shells from the island of Mafia, and the two decorative clocks, which show Swahili time (six hours different from European time), were presented by local dignitaries. However, though the fine-quality coral detailing and columns date from this time, most of the building actually dates from an 18th-century reconstruction. The more recent additions of electrical sockets and flex have not been installed with a comparable degree of style or decoration.

Outside the mosque are some old tombs, a few decorated with pillars and one covered by a small *makuti* roof. The pieces of cloth tied to the edge of the tomb are prayer flags. The raised aqueduct which carried water from the well to the basin where hands and feet were washed is no longer used: running water is piped straight into a more recently built ablution area at the back of the mosque.

Archaeological evidence suggests that when the mosque was built Kizimkazi was a large walled city. Tradition holds that it was founded and ruled by a king, Kizi, and that the architect of the mosque itself was called Kazi. Legend has it that when the city was once attacked by invaders, Kizi prayed for divine intervention and the enemies were driven away by a swarm of bees. Later the enemies returned, but this time Kizi evaded them by disappearing into a cave on the shore. The cave entrance closed behind him and the enemies were thwarted once again.

Today, very little of the old city remains, but non-Muslims, both men and women, are welcome to visit the mosque and its surrounding tombs. It's normally locked, and you'll probably have to find the caretaker with the key (he lives nearby, but is usually under the trees near the beach a few hundred metres further down the road). Show respect by removing your shoes and covering bare arms and legs (this part of the island is very traditional so, out of politeness, your arms and legs should be covered anyway). On leaving you'll be shown the collection box and be able to make a donation.

MENAI BAY EXCURSIONS The Menai Bay Conservation Area has a number of picturesque, uninhabited islands and sandbanks to explore, as well as some fascinating marine life. It's well worth taking a full-day excursion, either through Fumba Beach Lodge (see page 351), if you're a guest, or with one of the two operators running trips: Safari Blue or Eco&Culture. Take towels, and waterproof shoes for wading out to the boat across coral rock.

Eco&Culture \ 024 223 3731; m 0777 410873; e ecoculture@gmx.net; www.ecoculture-zanzibar.org. This full-day excursion on a traditional dhow departs from Unguja Ukuu, taking small groups (max 8 people) past mangrove forests to the pristine beaches of Miwi, Nianembe or Kwale islands & accessible sandbanks. Snorkelling kit is provided, & a BBQ lunch is prepared on the beach. An English-speaking guide with knowledge of the surroundings & local traditions is always on board. The company's policy of limiting numbers on their trips, & taking out a maximum of 2 boats at any time, makes this a firm favourite. Trips leave Stone Town at 08.00, returning at 17.00. US$50 pp for 4 people, or US$30 pp for groups of 8.

Safari Blue m 0777 423162; e adventure@zanlink.com; www.safariblue.net. Traditional sailing dhows kitted out with safety & comfort in mind offer time to explore some of the bay's islands & sandbanks, guided snorkelling trips & watching for humpback & bottlenose dolphins, as well as a tasty lunch on Kwale Island. It may also be possible to have a go at sailing a *ngalawa*, to swim in a mangrove lagoon, & to go for an island walk. Bear in mind that there are no changing facilities, & note that these popular excursions can get very busy. Boats leave from close to Fumba Beach at 09.00, returning about 18.00. US$45/22 adult/child 6–14; under 6 free. Stone Town transfer additional US$50/vehicle

PEMBA ISLAND

Lying to the northeast of the larger island of Zanzibar, directly east of the mainland port of Tanga, Pemba is visited by few travellers. While tourist facilities on Zanzibar have mushroomed in recent years, Pemba has changed little over the last decade, making it a particularly attractive destination for those seeking to 'get away from it all'.

Pemba has a more undulating landscape than Zanzibar, and is more densely vegetated with both natural forest and plantation. The main agricultural product is cloves, which Pemba produces in far greater abundance than Zanzibar, with the attendant heady aroma permeating much of the island.

There is nothing on Pemba to compare with Zanzibar's Stone Town, but it does boast a number of attractive beaches, as well as some absorbing ruins dating to the Shirazi era. During holidays, traditional bullfights are sometimes held, presumably introduced during the years of Portuguese occupation. The island is also a centre for traditional medicine and witchcraft, and it is said that people seeking cures for spiritual or physical afflictions come from as far away as Uganda and the Congo to see Pemba's doctors.

Accommodation is limited to just a handful of lodges, hotels and guesthouses. Most are geared to the diver in search of the island's renowned underwater attractions, including some exciting drift dives and the possibility of seeing some of the larger pelagics.

The island's largest town is Chake Chake. To the north lies the port of Wete, while to the southwest is the port of Mkoani, used by most passenger ferries. There are **banks** and **post offices** in Chake Chake, Wete and Mkoani, but only

11

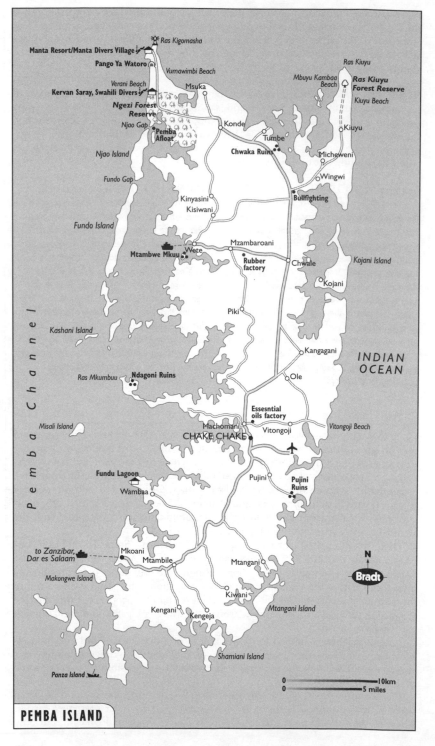

Manta Resort/Manta Divers Village
Pango Ya Watoro
Verani Beach
Kervan Saray, Swahili Divers
Ngezi Forest Reserve
Njao Gap
Pemba Afloat
Njao Island

Ras Kigomasha
Vumawimbi Beach
Msuka
Konde

Ras Kiuyu
Mbuyu Kambaa Beach
Ras Kiuyu Forest Reserve
Kiuyu Beach
Kiuyu

Tumbe
Micheweni
Chwaka Ruins
Wingwi
Bullfighting

Fundo Gap

Fundo Island

Kinyasini
Kisiwani

Mzambaroani
Mtambwe Mkuu
Were
Rubber factory
Chwale
Kojani Island
Kojani

Piki

Kashani Island

Ras Mkumbuu
Ndagoni Ruins

Kangagani

INDIAN OCEAN

Ole

Misali Island

Essesntial oils factory
Machomani
CHAKE CHAKE
Vitongoji
Vitongoji Beach

Fundu Lagoon
Wambaa

Pujini
Pujini Ruins

to Zanzibar, Dar es Salaam
Mkoani
Mtambile
Mtangani

Makongwe Island

Kiwani

Kengani
Kengeja
Mtangani Island

N
Bradt

Shamiani Island

Panza Island

0   10km
0   5 miles

PEMBA ISLAND

the Chake Chake bank can change travellers' cheques. The main **hospital** is in Chake Chake, where there is also a **ZTC** office, opposite the ZTC Hotel.

GETTING THERE AND AWAY

By air ZanAir operates two daily flights between Dar es Salaam and Pemba: 09.00 from Dar via Zanzibar, arriving Pemba at 10.15, and a direct service, departing Dar at 13.45 and arriving in Pemba at 14.30. Fares on this route are US$240 return, including tax. Coastal Aviation operates one daily flight from Dar to Pemba, which travels via Zanzibar, then onwards to Tanga on the Tanzanian mainland. Flights depart Dar at 14.00 and Zanzibar at 14.30, and arrive on Pemba at 15.05. The one-way fare from Dar is US$110 and from Zanzibar US$90. The onward 20-minute flight to Tanga leaves Pemba at 15.15, and costs US$70. For return journeys, the flight leaves Pemba at 16.35, arriving in Zanzibar at 17.05, and landing back in Dar at 17.35. Fares are the same as for the outbound trip.

By boat The main ferry port on Pemba is at Mkoani on the south end of the island.

MV Sepideh Operated by Mega Speed Liners, the *Sepideh* runs between Dar es Salaam & Zanzibar Island once a day, with a 2hr crossing to Pemba (Mkoani) Mon–Thu & Sat. On Mon, Thu & Sat, the ferry starts its circuit in Dar es Salaam at 07.15, arriving in Zanzibar around 09.00, before heading on to Pemba at 09.30. The boat then returns from Pemba to Zanzibar at 12.30, & back to Dar at 16.00. On Tue, Wed & Sun, it departs Dar for Zanzibar at 07.30 & returns at 16.00; Pemba boats depart Zanzibar at 10.00 & return at 12.30 on these days. *Pemba–Dar US$79 one way; Pemba–Zanzibar US$44.*

Aziza This leisurely weekly service connects Pemba (Wete) with Zanzibar Island & Tanga. It leaves Zanzibar on Fri at 22.00, arriving 06.00 in Wete; departs Wete for Tanga Sun 10.00, taking 4hr, returning Tue at 10.00 to arrive in Wete at 14.00, & leaves Wete for Zanzibar on Wed at 06.30, arriving 14.30. *US$20 one way, inc port tax.*

Mapinduzi This old government-run Zanzibar Shipping Corporation vessel plies between Zanzibar Town & Mkoani, carrying both cargo & passengers. Departs Zanzibar Island on Mon & Fri at 22.00, returning from Pemba on Tue & Sat at around 10.00, with the journey taking about 6hr. *Deck US$15; cabin bed US$20 – 25, both one way.*

Serengeti Much more reliable than the old ZSC vessel is the passenger ship *Serengeti*, operated by Azam Marine Ltd. The 6–8hr crossing between Zanzibar Town & Mkoani runs 3 times a week (currently Tue, Thu & Sat), returning the following day. *US$20 one way.*

Sea Express II This speedboat owned by Fast Ferries Ltd runs between Dar, Zanzibar & Mkoani on Pemba. Ferries depart Zanzibar at midday for the 3hr crossing to Pemba on Mon, Wed & Sat; for the return Pemba to Zanzibar boats depart at 08.30 on Thu. Journeys from Dar to Zanzibar depart 07.30 & 09.00, arriving 2–3hr later. *Non-residents Zanzibar–Pemba US$45 one way; Dar–Pemba US$65.*

GETTING AROUND A network of inexpensive *dala-dalas* connects most main points of interest on Pemba, starting up at 06.00 (or 04.00 during Ramadan), with the regularity of the service depending on the popularity of the route; one of the most frequent is the No 606, with several buses each day. Services to and from Mkoani are tied in closely with ship (especially the *Sepideh*) arrivals. Fares on the longer routes, such as Chake Chake to Mkoani, are around US$1 one way, with shorter trips about half that. The most useful routes are listed below (though note that *dala-dalas* will stop to collect or drop off passengers at any point along their route):

602	Chake Chake to Konde
603	Chake Chake to Mkoani
606	Chake Chake to Wete
305	Chake Chake to Wesha (Chake's port)
316	Chake Chake to Vitongoji (5km east of Chake Chake)

Other buses connect Chake Chake and, to a lesser extent, Wete with outlying villages; for details, check with the station manager at the bus depot in each town.

Most tour companies on the island can arrange car hire with a driver at around US$70 per day. Self-drive is less easy to set up, but would cost around Tsh45,000 per day. Recommended drivers include Said (m *0777 430201*) and Suleiman (m *0777 431793*). It's normally possible to arrange bicycle hire through your hotel reception at around US$4 per day, and motorbike hire at around US$22 per day.

CHAKE CHAKE This is the largest town on Pemba, and several centuries old, but it has never achieved a degree of importance comparable to Zanzibar Town. The busy market area and old port are pleasant to walk around, and seem very relaxed and untouristy after Zanzibar, but sightseeing is pretty much limited to the remains of an Omani fort near the modern hospital, part of which is now a good little museum.

Tour operators For tours, transport bookings and most other travel services, **Treasure Island Travel & Tours** (❏ *024 245 2278*), next to Le Tavern, has a range of tours and will help with ferry tickets.

Where to stay and eat Chake Chake's renowned Old Mission Lodge, for years the home of Swahili Divers, has closed its doors and the operation has moved north to Kervan Saray Beach (see page 363), leaving something of an

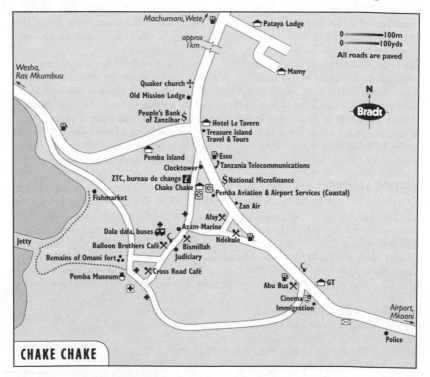

accommodation vacuum in the town. Fortunately there are a couple of decent and central alternatives:

Pemba Island Hotel (15 rooms) ☎ 024 245 2215; e islandhotelpembaevergreen@hotmail.com. Run by strict Muslims, this welcoming & pleasant place is in the centre of town, just down the hill from the People's Bank of Zanzibar. En-suite rooms have dbl beds with AC/fans, nets, TV & fridge. In keeping with the hotel's Muslim ethos, no alcohol is permitted on the premises, & a marriage certificate is required for a couple to share a room. There's a rooftop restaurant. *US$55 dbl.*

Hotel Le Tavern (9 rooms) ☎ 024 245 2660. On the main street, between the Chake Chake Hotel & the Old Mission Lodge, above a small row of shops, the Le (pronounced 'Lay') Tavern has clean, en-suite rooms with single beds, mosquito nets & fans; some have AC. Meals to order around US$5. *US$25–30 dbl.*

Chake Chake Hotel ☎ 024 245 4301. The government-run establishment may be cheaper, but the bathrooms don't look as though they've been touched for years. On the plus side, the bar is one of the few places on the island to serve alcohol. *US$15 dbl.*

To the north of the town, you could try one of the private guesthouses, reached by taking a No 606 *dala-dala* towards Wete:

Venus Lodge m 0777 475164. Just beyond the village of Machumani, about 3km north of Chake Chake, Venus Lodge is simple & reasonably clean, although when we visited there was no-one available to show us round. *US$25 dbl.*

Pataya Lodge (6 rooms) m 0777 852970. This simple place gives a feel of suburban living, Pemba-style. Rooms, 1 en suite, have mosquito nets & ceiling fans. To get there, head north out of town, then take the first major right turn you come to — look out for the big white wall with railings on the top. The lodge is signposted on your left, about 20m from the junction. *US$20 dbl.*

While each of the above serves meals to guests, usually with advance notice, there are also several simple places to eat in the narrow streets around Chake Chake's bus station.

What to see and do Chake Chake itself has a dusty charm that repays a walk through its small market and around its narrow streets and alleys crowded with shops selling a wide range of goods. Worth a visit is the **Pemba Museum** (⊕ *08.30–16.30 Mon–Fri, 09.00–16.00 Sat & Sun; admission US$2*). Located in part of the town's 18th-century Arab Fort, it retains the original wooden door, but other features were lost during restoration, and the cannons at the entrance came from Wete. Clearly laid out exhibits cover every aspect of Pemba's history, economy and culture. Of particular interest are the display on the ruins of Pemba, and the room on the island's maritime history and boatbuilding. In addition, several rooms are set out to represent the interior of a Swahili house, while related displays focus on individual aspects of Swahili culture, from initiation and burial rituals to the use of herbal plants and traditional musical instruments. Visitors are accompanied around the exhibitions by a guide.

MKOANI AND THE SOUTH The smallest of the three main towns on Pemba, Mkoani is also the busiest tourist centre, thanks to the boat services connecting it to Zanzibar and Dar es Salaam.

Where to stay and eat

Fundu Lagoon (16 rooms) Reservations ☎ 024 223 2926; hotel m 0777 438668; e info@ fundulagoon.com; www.fundulagoon.com. In the south of the island, this upmarket & romantic hideaway is accessed by boat from Mkoani, & is extremely popular with honeymooners. Tented rooms, with en-suite bathrooms & verandas overlooking the sea, nestle among the trees. Meals — varying in quality from mediocre to superb — are served in the restaurant or at the end of the jetty, with regular

11

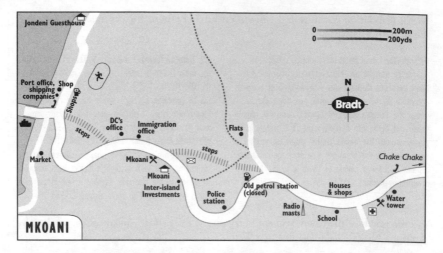

MKOANI

BBQ & Swahili nights. Snorkelling, kayaking & fishing are on offer, & there's a fully equipped dive centre; less strenuous are sunset dhow cruises, boat trips to Misali Island, & village excursions. There's also a treatment room, & a games room with satellite TV. *US$610–1,220 dbl.*

🏠 **Jondeni Guesthouse** (8 rooms) ☎ 024 245 6042; e pembablue@hotmail.com. To the north of town, a dusty 10–15min walk uphill from the port, this white-painted bungalow is set in lush gardens, & the friendly staff make staying here a pleasure. Clean, simple rooms – some en suite – have fans & mosquito nets. Drinks & meals (around US$5) are taken on the shady terrace overlooking the sea.

Snorkelling, sailing & fishing trips, & island tours can be arranged. *US$20–30 dbl.*

🏠 **Mkoani Hotel** This ZTC-run hotel is a clone of the ZTC Hotel in Chake Chake, with the same prices, & is equally uninspiring. *US$15 dbl.*

🏠 **Pemba Lodge** ☎ 024 224 0494; m 0777 415551/0713 334062; e mnarani@zanlink.com; www.pembalodge.com. Set to open towards the end of 2009 on Shamiani Island, off Pemba's southeastern tip, Pemba Lodge will focus on those seeking privacy & R&R. With one eye firmly on minimum environmental impact, its en-suite thatched bungalows along the beach will be designed to harness the sea breeze, obviating the necessity for energy-guzzling AC.

WETE AND THE NORTH The quiet and pleasant town of Wete, the second largest on the island, lies on a large inlet on the northwest coast.

🏠 **Where to stay and eat** Wete itself has several small guesthouses, as well as the run-down Wete Hotel, but most visitors head north to one of the beach lodges.

In town
🏠 **North Lodge** (4 rooms) ☎ 0747 427459. Not far from the ZTC hotel, this converted house has basic rooms of sometimes dubious cleanliness, with fans & nets; 2 are en suite. The owner is prepared to arrange tours, & cars or bikes for rent. Dinner on request. *US$20–25 dbl.*

🏠 **Sharook Guesthouse** (5 rooms) ☎ 024 245 4386. On a quiet street near the market & bus station, this small, clean, family-run place is peaceful

& friendly. There's constant running water & a functioning TV. Dinner, with local dishes, must be ordered in advance. Bike hire (US$5 per day) & tours can be arranged. Dinner US$5. *US$20–25 dbl.*

🏠 **Wete Government Hotel** (6 rooms) ☎ 024 245 4301. This is the third in the series of cloned ZTC-run hotels on Pemba, & its en-suite rooms afford no pleasant surprises. *US$15 dbl.*

The Sharook Guesthouse offers a fair range of **tours** at reasonable prices, and Bachaa Tours (m *0777 422639*) opposite the post office is also recommended for excursions around the island.

North of Wete

⌂ **The Manta Resort** (10 rooms)
www.themantaresort.com; ⊕ Aug–May. Overlooking
the northern end of Verani Beach, & newly
renovated, this caters to divers & landlubbers alike.
Large seafront chalets, each en-suite & with AC,
are built on stilts overlooking the Pemba Channel,
while behind are smaller garden rooms. From the
cavernous main building, housing the restaurant,
bar & lounge, steps lead down to the beach &
beach bar. Watersports are the main focus, but
walking & birding are additional options. There's
also a pool, a spa, & a small shop. *US$335–525
dbl FB.*

⌂ **The Manta Divers Village** (10 chalets)
www.themantaresort.com. Sister property to the

Manta Resort, this is cheaper & more low key in
feel, with en-suite rustic chalets dotted around the
gardens behind the resort. *US$255 dbl FB.*

⌂ **Kervan Saray Beach** m 0773 176737/8, 0784
394980; e resort@kayakpemba.com;
www.kervansaraybeach.com. Swahili Divers' new home
is a simple & unpretentious affair located in the far
northwest of the island. En-suite rooms have all the
essentials, including mosquito nets & solar-heated
outdoor shower, but don't come expecting luxuries.
This is a place for diving (the lodge has its own
dive operation), snorkelling, birdwatching & kayaking
– or just to chill out. *US$150/280 dbl low/high
season, FB; dorm/family room US$45 pp FB. 2 dives
inc equipment US$99/160 low/high season.*

EXCURSIONS FROM CHAKE CHAKE

Kidike Just 7km north of Chake Chake is Kidike (⊕ *08.00–18.00 daily; admission
US$3.50*), home to more than half of Pemba's flying foxes. Several tour operators
run trips here, and individual drivers charge around US$25 from Chake Chake,
including entrance. Alternatively you can take a *dala-dala* from Chake Chake, then
walk the 45 minutes or so along the 3.5km track to the reserve.

Misali Island This small island west of Chake Chake, an easy boat ride from the
main island, is surrounded by a coral reef. Its idyllic beach is good for swimming,

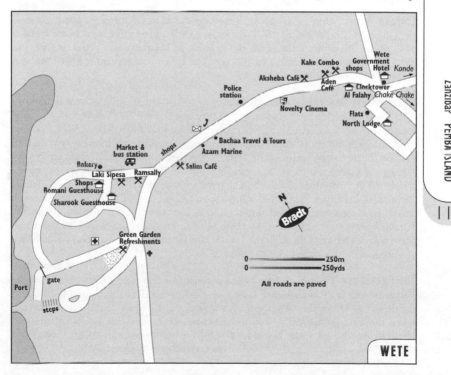

363

whether at high or low tide, and it's worth bringing a mask and snorkel for the excellent reef fish. The waters are also a favourite with divers.

The forested interior of the island, criss-crossed by a network of clear walking trails, harbours a rich variety of birds including the endemic Pemba white-eye and sunbird.

The notorious pirate Captain Kidd is reputed to have had a hideout here in the 17th century, but today the island and the surrounding reef are incorporated within the Misali Island Marine Conservation Area.

Ras Mkumbuu Ruins In the opposite direction, about 14km west of Chake Chake, these well-preserved ruins lie at the tip of a long peninsula. Thought to have been one of the largest towns on the coast during the 11th century, Ras Mkumbuu may also have been the site of the earlier port of Qanbalu. Today, the remains of a mosque are visible, albeit overgrown, along with several pillar tombs.

The most enjoyable way to reach Ras Mkumbuu is by boat, perhaps combined with a visit to Misali Island. While there is a road from Chake Chake, the final 5km is negotiable only on foot or by bike.

Pujini Ruins This site is about 10km southeast of Chake Chake. You can walk there and back in a day, but it is easier to travel by hired bike or car. The ruins are the remains of a 13th-century Swahili town, known locally as Mkame Ndume ('milker of men'), after a despotic king who forced the inhabitants to carry large stones for the town walls while shuffling on their buttocks. The overgrown remains of the walls and ditches can be seen, as can a walkway which joined the town to the shore, some wide stairways that presumably allowed access to the defensive ramparts, and the site of the town's well.

Chwaka Ruins More ruins can be found on the island's northeast coast, close to the village of Tumbe (whose fish market is worth a visit in itself). Dating from as early as the 9th century, the town of Chwaka, or Harouni, was active as a port in the 15th century. In addition to the ruins of two small mosques, there are also remains of houses and tombs.

Ngezi Forest Reserve This small reserve (⊕ 07.30–15.30 daily; admission short tour US$5 pp, longer tour or birdwatching US$10; transit fee US$2; night walks by prior arrangement) on the north of the island protects the last of the indigenous forest that used to cover much of the island. The forest supports an interesting range of vegetation, including the most substantial patch of tropical moist forest on Pemba. It is a good place for birders, who can seek out the Pemba white-eye, green pigeon, scops owl and sunbird, all of which are endemic to the island. Mammals include the endemic Pemba flying fox, Kirk's red colobus, vervet monkey, blue duiker, marsh mongoose and a feral population of European boars, introduced by the Portuguese and left untouched by their Muslim successors, who don't eat pork. A short nature trail runs through the forest. Not far from here, the open sandy beach at Vumawimbi is a great place to chill out.

The lighthouse The west of the Ngezi peninsula is flanked by the long expanse of Verani Beach, with a lighthouse (admission US$2 pp) at Ras Kigomasha marking its northern tip. At low tide, it's possible to walk along the beach to the lighthouse, but when the water is up you'll need to take the path across the fields. If you want to climb to the top, ask at the house nearby for the lighthouse keeper; the views from the top both out to sea and across Pemba certainly repay the effort.

Zanzibar PEMBA ISLAND

||

366

12

Mafia Archipelago

Chris and Susan McIntyre

While Zanzibar is entrenched as probably the most popular ocean resort in East Africa, the small archipelago around Mafia Island, 160km to its south, remains virtually unknown. Poor communications with the mainland and a rather unfortunate name have not served Mafia well, but a growing trickle of visitors over recent years has been unanimous in singing the island's praises. A few interesting Swahili ruins notwithstanding, Mafia lacks for an equivalent to Zanzibar's atmospheric Stone Town, so that it cannot be recommended as an alternative destination for those whose primary interest in Tanzania's islands is cultural or historical.

By contrast, the combination of a clutch of small, high-quality lodges, offshore diving and snorkelling that ranks with the very best in the Indian Ocean, and a conspicuous absence of hassle and crime, make it the ideal destination for those seeking an exclusive but low-key Indian Ocean retreat. Paradoxically, perhaps, Mafia also has considerable potential for budget travellers seeking a truly off-the-beaten-track and adventurous experience.

The Mafia Archipelago, which lies in the Indian Ocean some 20km east of the Rufiji River Delta in central Tanzania, probably became isolated from the mainland some 20,000 years ago. The archipelago consists of about 15 sandstone and coral-rag islands and numerous smaller atolls and sandbars, none of which reaches an elevation above 80m, and all but two of which are little more than 1km² in extent. The central island, known today as Mafia (though it seems that this name applied to the archipelago rather than any specific island prior to the 20th century), is by far the largest, approximately 50km long by 15km across. The second-largest island is Juani, about 8km long and up to 4km wide, which lies to the southeast of the main island and was the centre of local political activity in medieval times. Sandwiched between these two larger islands, the tiny Chole Island superseded Juani as the local centre of trade in the Omani era.

The archipelago's estimated population of nearly 41,000 lives in rustic fishing communities and farming villages dotted all over Mafia and the smaller islands, although many of the islands are theoretically uninhabited. The largest town and

WHAT'S IN A NAME?

There are a number of suggestions for the source of the archipelago's name, but it isn't derived from the Sicilian crime syndicate. It may have origins in the Arabic word *morfiyeh*, meaning 'group', describing the archipelago of Mafia, or be named after the Ma'afir, an Arab tribe from Merku (Mocha) in present-day Yemen. An unlikely suggestion is that the name derives from the Arabic *mafi* meaning 'waste' or 'rubbish', or perhaps from the Swahili *mahali pa afya* meaning 'a healthy place to live'. The authors would be grateful for any further suggestions!

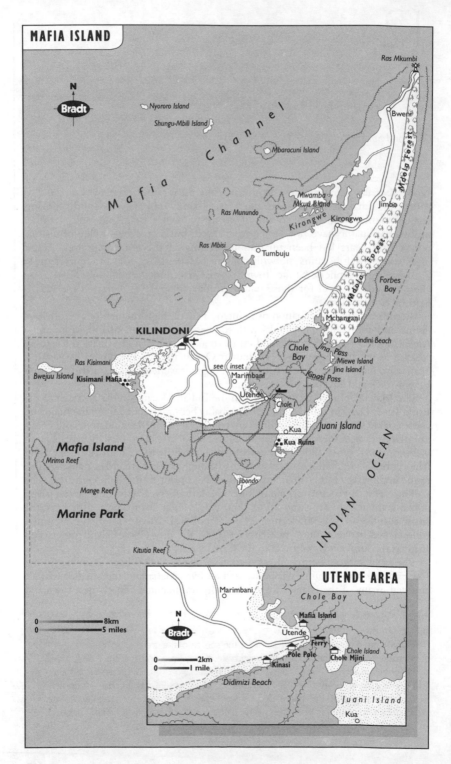

port on Mafia Island is Kilindoni in the southwest, the site of the airstrip and the main landing point for dhows from the mainland. Although several local guesthouses can be found in Kilindoni, the centre of upmarket tourist development is Chole Bay on the southeastern side of the island. Three established tourist lodges lie within 1km of each other near the village of Utende, roughly 10km from Kilindoni by road, with a fourth situated on Chole Island within the bay. Utende is the only area other than Kilindoni that has electricity.

CLIMATE

The Mafia Archipelago experiences a tropical climate tempered by ocean breezes. Rainfall averaging 2,000mm a year occurs mainly between April and May, although November can also be wet. February and March are hot and humid, while a strong southerly wind, the *kusi*, blows during July. The best holiday period is from June until mid-October, when the islands enjoy blue skies with temperatures kept pleasant by light coastal breezes. The water temperature varies from 24°C to 31°C; the air temperature rarely exceeds 33°C or drops below 20°C.

HISTORY

Little is known about the early history of the Mafia Archipelago, but presumably it has been settled for millennia, and it may well have participated in the ancient coastal trade with Arabia. The eminent archaeologist Neville Chittick regarded Mafia as a strong candidate for the 'low and wooded' island of Menouthesias, described in the 1st-century *Periplus of the Erythrian Sea* as being two days' sail or 300 *stadia* (roughly 50km) from the river port of Rhapta (which, according to this theory, was situated in the Rufiji Delta) Although the anonymous writer of the *Periplus* also mentions the sewn boats and hollowed-out tree canoes that are still used widely on Mafia today (as they are elsewhere on the coast), several other aspects of the description count against Mafia. Two days rather exaggerates the sailing distance from the island to the Rufiji Delta; furthermore, either the *Periplus* was mistaken in its assertion that there are 'no wild beasts except crocodiles' on Menouthesias, or the crocs have subsequently vanished and the island's few hippos are a later arrival.

The earliest known settlement on the archipelago, Kisimani Mafia, was situated at Ras Kisimani in the far southwest of the main island. Archaeological evidence suggests that this town, which covered about 1.2 hectares, was founded in the 11th century, possibly by a favoured son of the Sultan of Kilwa. Several coins minted at Kilwa have been unearthed at the site, as have coins from China, Mongolia, India and Arabia, all minted prior to 1340. A second important town, Kua, was probably founded in the 13th century, again as a dependency of Kilwa, and it must surely have usurped Kisimani as the islands' political and economic hub soon after that. In its prime, Kua was probably the second-largest city along what is now the southern coast of Tanzania, boasting seven mosques as well as a double-storey palace and numerous stone homesteads spread over an area of more than 12 hectares.

Following the Portuguese occupation of the coast, Kua was chosen as the site of a Portuguese trade agency in 1515, when a fortified blockhouse was built at the town. The name Mafia (more accurately Morfiyeh) was well established by this time, and the islands are marked as such on the earliest Portuguese naval charts. Several explanations have been put forward for the origin of this name (see box on page 367). Because the archipelago lies 20km offshore, Mafia attracted a large influx of refugees from the mainland during the cannibalistic Zimba raids that dealt the final deathblow to so many coastal settlements during the late 16th century.

Control of Mafia changed hands frequently in the 17th century as Portugal's fortunes declined. An Omani naval raid in 1670 effectively terminated the Portuguese presence on the Mafia islands, and by 1598 the entire East African coast north of modern-day Mozambique was under Omani control. Little is known about events on the islands over the next two centuries. In about 1829, however, the archipelago was attacked by the cannibalistic Sakalafa of Madagascar, who succeeded in wreaking havoc at Kua, one of the few coastal towns left untouched by their Zomba forbears 250 years earlier. Kisimani, though also attacked by the Malagasy, stumbled on into the 1870s, when a devastating cyclone dealt it a final deathblow, but Kua was abandoned to go to ruin.

One reason why Kua was not resettled after 1820 is that a new seat of the Sultanate of Zanzibar had been founded on the north end of Chole Island barely ten years earlier. Known as Chole Mjini (Chole Town), this settlement was also attacked by the Sakalafa, but it was soon rebuilt to emerge as the most important town on the islands. Chole became the established home of a number of wealthy Omani traders and slave owners, while the main island of Mafia, known at the time as Chole Shamba (Chole Farm), was occupied by newly established coconut plantations and the slaves who worked on them. Although Chole was not so directly involved in the slave trade as Pangani, Bagamoyo or Kilwa Kivinje, it was an important stopover for slave ships heading between Kilwa and Zanzibar, and the ruined mansions that survive today indicate that it was a very wealthy settlement indeed.

Mafia was part of the Zanzibar Sultanate throughout the Omani era, and it should have remained a part of Zanzibar in the colonial era, according to a treaty that placed it under British protectorateship along with Zanzibar and Pemba islands. However, in the complex Anglo-German treaty of 1890, Mafia was ceded to Germany in exchange for a part of what is now Malawi, and it has been administered as part of mainland Tanzania ever since. In 1892, Germany sent a local administrator to Chole, who constructed the two-storey Customs House that can still be seen on the beach today.

In 1913, Germany relocated its administration from Chole to the deeper harbour at Kilindoni on the main island. Two years later, Mafia was the first part of German East Africa to be captured by British forces. The island was subsequently used as the base for a series of aerial assaults on the German cruiser *Königsberg* which, having evaded capture in the Rufiji Delta, was finally sunk on 11 August 1915. A six-cent German Tanganyika Territory stamp overprinted 'Mafia' by the British and listed at £9,000 in the Stanley Gibbons catalogue makes philatelists one of the few groups of people aware of the existence of the islands.

ECONOMY

Coconuts were the main source of income for the islands until the 1970s, when the price of coconut products dropped, and the fishing industry grew in importance. Cultivated since the 19th century, coconuts remain a secure income source and, although the trees are still climbed by hand, some 30 tonnes are exported to Dar daily in dhows. Coconut products have a number of local uses: leaves are used for roofing, coconut coir makes doormats and ropes, and even the ribs are used to make fishing traps and brooms. The wood can also be used to make furniture.

Other produce grown on Mafia is used for subsistence farming, particularly the primary crop, cassava. Rice, sweet potato, maize, pumpkin, okra, banana, pineapple, lime, mango and tomato are also seen growing on the islands, some of which are exported to Dar. Cashew nuts are either sold locally or exported, and the cashew fruit is used to make local beer. At subsistence level, mushrooms, raffia fibre, medicinal plants and game (monkey, bush pig and duiker) play an important role. Mangrove trees provide many raw materials; their wood is used for building poles, and boatbuilding and repair. Dead mangrove branches are used for firewood; leaves, bark and fruit are all used for medicines and colour dyes. Firewood is collected to burn coral rag for lime, and also for charcoal, which is sold to locals, hotels, and at Kilindoni, as well as exported.

The sea is vital to the livelihood of many of Mafia's inhabitants. Seaweed farming exists on a small-scale basis, used for export and for processing food additives. It is grown on lines attached to wooden stakes across the seabed of shallow lagoons, and is dried on palm leaves. Traditionally the inter-tidal area has been the women's domain, where they fish for octopus at spring tide. In the 1990s, however, men too began collecting octopus on the inter-tidal flats, as fish catches were declining yet prices increasing. Now 60% of octopus is caught by men, often through free-diving. Sea cucumbers are harvested for export to Zanzibar or Dar, then out to the Far East. Fish is also exported. Chole and Jibonde were well known for their boatbuilding in the past, but this now is in decline. You can still see people working in the shipyards, but more of the work is now repairing smaller dhows rather than building large cargo-carrying boats.

RELIGION AND CULTURE

The majority of the islanders are Muslim, but there are also many Christians. Voodoo manifests itself in ritual dances linked to the lunar cycle. While traditionally reserved, the islanders are tolerant of visitors provided they dress discreetly and behave in a manner becoming to local customs. Mafia women wear the colourful patterned *kanga* of the Swahili coast, and on weekends and religious holidays men exchange Western dress for the long, white *kanzu*. Older folk who remember the British era can speak some English, as can staff working at the tourist lodges, but it can help to know a little Swahili when talking to other islanders.

A word of caution: Mafia is a conservative society, and the passing visitor is unlikely to be asked for handouts. Children who beg from tourists are quickly reprimanded by their elders. Please make sure that you, and your travelling companions, keep it this way.

NATURAL HISTORY

VEGETATION Natural vegetation on Mafia ranges from tidal mangrove thickets (eight species of mangrove grow here), marshland, heath and scrubby coastal moorlands to palm-wooded grassland and lowland rainforest, although the evergreen forest was cleared for coconut plantations in the 1980s. Baobabs are prominent along with the native Albizia. A patch of coastal high forest, the Chunguruma Forest, is a dense tree canopy interlaced with lianas and having an abundant floor covering of ferns.

WILDLIFE
Mammals A large, reed-lined lake in central Mafia, probably a relic lagoon dating from when the island was joined to the mainland, harbours about 20 hippo that were washed out to sea during flooding in the Rufiji River system. Unpopular with locals, they eat from the rice farms at night and can cause considerable damage, but are hard to see. Other island fauna includes a colony of flying foxes (the lesser Cormoran fruit bat), while bush pigs are found in Mdola Forest and Juani Island. The pigs eat the cassava from farms on Juani, so are a menace to farmers, who try to trap the pigs where possible.

Mdola Forest stretches along the east coast of Mafia Island for about 30km, from Bweni to Chole Bay, and has a high level of diversity, as well as a number of endemic species, such as the blue duiker, a subspecies endemic to Pemba and Mafia. Other fauna includes at least one bushbaby species, the genet, and the black-and-rufous elephant shrew. Monkeys (Sykes's and vervet) and squirrels were introduced for the pot by the Portuguese.

Reptiles and insects The leaf-litter toad has been recorded in Mdola Forest, and may be endemic to Mafia; the writhing gecko is found both in Mdola Forest and on the Tanzanian mainland. The monitor lizard is known locally as *kenge*. Butterflies (there are five endemics) are best in the wet season, particularly around Ras Mbizi and mangroves, which flower during the rains.

Birds More than 120 species of birds have been recorded on Mafia, including five different types of sunbird. The island is of particular interest for its concentrations of resident and migrant shorebirds, which have breeding grounds in northern Europe but come to Mafia from October to March for the nearby mangrove estuaries, where they feed on the mudflats. Waders include ringed plover, crab plover, grey plover, Mongolian plover, great sandplover, curlew, whimbrel and turnstone, and the island is also a nesting area for fish eagles and open-billed storks.

Marine life Of far greater ecological importance than Mafia's terrestrial habitats is the immensely rich marine environment, which provides some of the finest snorkelling and diving sites in the Indian Ocean. It may be surprising that the biodiversity of the Rufiji–Mafia complex has global significance, and of 21 sites in East Africa has been described as having 'one of the world's most interesting and diverse ecosystems'. The coral-reef habitats around Mafia have a diversity of species rivalled only by rainforests, with at least 380 species of fish and 48 of coral. The beds of seagrass (12 species of which are found here, the only flowering plants to have colonised the sea) and the deep open waters support some of the planet's most endangered marine life.

Four species of turtles live in Mafia's waters, and two of these use Mafia as a nesting ground. The hawksbill (*Cretmochelys imbricata*) lays eggs between December and January; the green turtle (*Chelonia mydas*) between April and June. The East African coast is one of the last strongholds for the critically endangered dugong (*Dugong dugon*), and during the 1960s and 1970s these gentle seacows were regularly caught in the shark nets of Mafia's fishermen. Despite two separate sightings in 1999, there are fears that the dugong may now be extinct from Mafia's waters.

The lowland coastal forest of the eastern seaboard has been 'recognised as a critical site for biodiversity', and the inter-tidal flats are important for octopus, while in the open sea marine mammals like the humpback whale give birth and nurse their young in East Africa's warm waters. Sadly the demand for shark-fin soup in the Far East is one contributor to diminished populations of shark along the coastline. The large pelagics such as marlin, billfish and tuna also inhabit the deeper sea.

Oceanographers often talk of the Rufiji River Delta–Mafia–Kilwa area being one extended ecosystem. It's particularly exciting that a coelacanth was caught here in 2003. Archaeologists have found fossils of this very rare, bony fish which date back to the era of the dinosaurs, and today's specimens are almost identical.

From October to April, whalesharks are seen in the area. Chole Mjini on Chole Island is the headquarters for the newly formed Mafia Island Whaleshark Conservation Project and during the season offers regular dhow excursions for guests to visit these gentle giants.

Over the past 2,000 years, turtle-shell, mangrove poles and seashells have been part of East Africa's trade to Arabia. By the 1960s, however, it had become clear that natural resources were not coping with human progress. In Tanzania, dried and salted fish, exported to the mainland, contributes more to the national protein consumption than meat and poultry combined. Dynamite fishing became very popular on Tanzania's coast, despite the destruction that it causes to fish populations and to coral. Small-mesh, beach-seine nets were catching all sizes of fish, again damaging populations. In some areas the only source of building materials has been coral, used as bricks and in the production of lime: this was the second-largest industry on Mafia at one time. Mangrove wood is very hard, insect-resistant, and makes excellent building material, so vast areas were cleared to provide timber, fuelwood, farmland and salt-pans for salt production.

In the 1970s, four islands were declared marine reserves to slow the damage, but in the absence of facilities to police the park, fishermen ignored the rules and continued as usual. By 1995, it was clear that conservation had become an urgent priority, so the following year a partnership of investors, communities and the government set up the Board of Trustees of Marine Parks and Reserves of Tanzania, and on 6 September 1996, an area of Mafia extending across 822km^2 was gazetted as Tanzania's first marine park, to protect the ecosystems as well as the future livelihood of coastal people. The park embraces most of the southern and eastern shore of Mafia, including Chole Bay and associated reefs, a number of isolated atolls to the south of the main island, and the reefs enclosing Juani, Jibondo and Bwejuu islands.

The marine park now owns six boats and has one full-time park warden. The park authorities are aiming to co-operate and collaborate with local residents, using community-based projects to dispel conflict between groups. If the islands are to be protected, the success of the marine park is imperative. Mangroves trap river sediments that would be otherwise washed out to sea and, along with coral reefs, protect the shoreline from the erosion of rising sea levels. The natural forest shields the island's crops from storm damage from the ocean, and a healthy ecosystem helps in the recovery from natural disasters such as cyclones, hurricanes and floods. Significantly, wetlands have also been shown to provide clean water, perhaps the most significant issue in terms of sustainable development of the islands.

For further details, contact the warden-in-charge, Mr George Msumi, Mafia Island Marine Park (✆ 023 2402690; e mimpMafia@raha.com).

GETTING THERE AND AWAY

BY AIR The most efficient way of getting to Mafia is by light aircraft (Cessna Caravan or Airvan) with either Tropical Air or Kinasi who jointly operate a morning service from Zanzibar via Dar es Salaam to Mafia, or with Coastal Travel who run two scheduled flights from Dar es Salaam every day, costing US$110 for a single flight: the first leaves at 15.00, arriving in Mafia at 15.30, and the second at 17.00, arriving at 17.30. This is perfectly timed so that the sun sets behind the Rufiji Delta as you fly in. If one of these flights is not running, you can sometimes persuade Coastal to fly by paying for a minimum of two passengers. Coastal also fly from Kilwa via Songo Songo to Mafia daily (departing 06.15; arriving 06.50) for US$110 one-way and Zanzibar to Mafia daily, usually via Dar (14.00–15.30), costing US$145 single.

If you are staying at Kinasi Lodge for three nights or more, ASF Kinasi can fly you one-way to/from Mafia from Dar for US$110, to/from Zanzibar to Mafia for

US$140 or to/from the Selous Game Reserve (see page 386) for US$190. They try to be as accommodating as possible for their guests, looking after bags etc, but these flights are ad hoc, and therefore not scheduled. If you're not staying at Kinasi, it's worth giving them a call anyway: it's the same rate for non-guests if there's space on a flight already running. It is possible that at the end of 2008, Kinasi will operate twice-daily flights from Dar to Mafia.

You can also charter planes to Mafia with a range of companies in Dar es Salaam and Zanzibar, with a flight in a small aircraft from Coastal, Tropical or Kinasi costing around US$500.

The flightpath to Mafia is within sight of the Rufiji River Delta, at 40km² the largest delta in East Africa, with the region's greatest concentration of mangroves. The dhows look tiny as they go about their fishing unfeasibly far from shore. With a new 1.9km runway too, arrival on Mafia is not the bumpy ride it once was.

Note that an airport departure tax of US$5 per person, which includes a US$1 'safety fee', is payable in cash on leaving Mafia.

Airline operators

✈ **Coastal Aviation** 107 Upanga Rd, Dar es Salaam, or Dar airport; ☏ 022 2117959 (HQ), 022 2842700/1 (Dar airport) or 024 2233112; m 0713 670815 (Zanzibar airport); e safari@coastal.cc; www.coastal.cc

✈ **Kinasi** m 0777 474911/0773 719719 (Dar airport); e kinasilodge@mafiaisland.com
✈ **Tropical Air** Zanzibar; ☏ 024 2232511 (HQ); m 0773 511679 (Zanzibar airport) or 0773 618367 (Dar airport); e reservations@tropicalair.co.tz; www.tropicalair.co.tz

Mafia Airport Mafia's small airport (⊕ around 08.00–18.30, unless there's an early-morning flight) is situated on the edge of the main town of Kilindoni, a 15km drive from Utende, where the tourist lodges are located. The airport is Mafia's centre of communication for visitors, and even if visitors arrive on Mafia by boat they tend to be directed the 1km from the harbour to the airport.

Currently, the airport has a simple waiting room with wooden benches and basic toilets but a new terminal is promised following the addition of a decent runway in 2007. At the Chole Interbureau Change (⊕ 08.00–17.00), you can change limited amounts of currency at market rates, as well as US dollar, euro and sterling travellers' cheques, but it's probably best not to rely on this tiny exchange for all your financial needs on Mafia. There is a branch of the National Microfinance Bank in Kilindoni and lodges will take credit cards, but it's still wise to bring an amount of cash with you.

Visitors holding a hotel reservation will be met at the airport for their transfer. If you don't have a reservation, most of the lodges have representatives who speak English, and can radio the lodges to organise your accommodation. They can also help individual travellers to find a Land Rover taxi, costing US$25 to Utende one-way; note that you'll cross the border into the marine park *en route*, so have the fee (US$10 per person per day) for the requisite number of days ready in US dollar cash, and remember to keep your receipt as proof of payment when you leave the island.

BY BOAT The options for budget travellers who wish to visit Mafia are limited to boats that connect Kilindoni to the mainland. Many of these dhows are uncomfortable and crowded and the trip can take anything from ten to 24 hours. The safety record is none too inspiring: sailing dhows have a reputation for hitting reefs, as these are very dangerous waters that require an experienced captain. If you want to take a boat, make sure you check that it's properly licensed to carry passengers or vehicles, and at least that it has a marine radio and life jackets.

For the incorrigible, a tide table is incorporated in the free booklet, the *Dar Guide*, available from bars and hotels in Dar es Salaam. This is invaluable when trying to organise a boat trip to Mafia, as the boats have to arrive at high tide, and often leave on a high tide, too. There are, though, plans to build a jetty in Kilindoni, which would mean that boats no longer have to restrict their arrival to high tide. This should lead to a much more regular service in the future.

The closest mainland port to Mafia is Kisiju, 30km from Dar and 45km southeast of Mkuranga on the Kilwa road. From the Kariakoo bus depot in Dar, you take a bus to Kisiju and then a dhow to Mafia. Another possibility from Dar es Salaam is via Kimbiji, easily reached by catching the motor ferry from the city centre to Kigomboni (boats leave every ten minutes or so and take five minutes), then a *dala-dala* direct to Kimbiji (about one hour). There are also dhows connecting Mafia to Kilwa Kivinje.

GETTING AROUND

The island infrastructure is basic. Hardly any villages are connected to mains water or electricity and at the time of writing there are no tarmac roads. Throughout the island the best you'll find is a bouncy sandy track. Vehicles are few, mainly Land Rover pick-ups and 4x4s belonging to the hotels and other organisations. Most local people use bicycles to get around, although this is quite hard work on the sandy roads. Bicycles can be rented by arrangement with the Hotel Lizu in Kilindoni, or from any of the lodges.

A minibus runs every three hours or so between Kilindoni and Utende charging around US$1 one-way. It seats a minimum of 12, and has no fixed timetable – it departs when it's full. There are also two *dala-dalas*, one at Kilindoni and one at Utende, and these pick people up along the way. They're not the most comfortable way of getting around, but are a good way of meeting local people and really getting to understand life on Mafia. Hitchhiking is an accepted means of getting about, but it usually entails a long wait. Islanders also use *jahazis* – widely referred to in English as dhows – to commute between Kilindoni and outlying villages on Mafia, and for inter-island travel.

Maps of Mafia can be obtained from Mafia Island Tours at Mafia Island Lodge for US$5.50.

WHERE TO STAY

Mafia isn't really the place for easy backpacking, but budget travellers who do come here may stop in Kilindoni itself. Meanwhile, the majority of Mafia's (very few) tourists head straight through town and over to one of three or four more upmarket small lodges on Chole Bay.

Camping There is a campsite at Mafia Pwani (see page 380). Otherwise, check with the marine park authorities before camping independently, as it's not legal to camp in Tanzania unless you're in a specified area. Don't take any chances.

ACTIVITIES

DIVING *With Jean de Villiers*
Many people visit Mafia purely for its diving, which is often considered the best anywhere in East Africa. It's easy to dive two sites outside the bay on a single outing; the trip out and back can also be great for fishing, sunbathing, sailing and dolphin-spotting. The marine park off Chole Bay is home to 48 species of coral,

12

including giant table corals, delicate sea fans, whip corals and huge stands of blue- and pink-tipped staghorn coral.

As well as the spectacular variety of reef fish there are turtles and large predatory fish such as grouper, Napoleon wrasse and barracuda. Manta rays and several species of shark are encountered in Kinasi Pass. November to January is best for black-tip and white-tip reef sharks. The corals of Chole Bay, in the heart of the marine park, have recovered dramatically from damage caused by El Niño (of 1997–98) and the destructive fishing practices used before the establishment of the park.

Almost all Mafia's best diving is in depths of less than 30m. Between June and September you can dive only within Chole Bay, albeit in almost any weather. For the more challenging dives outside the bay, you have to wait until the calmer conditions in mid-September. Outside the bay the average size of the fish is bigger, and you've a good chance of seeing a 2–3m grouper; these are friendly and let you come quite close. Visibility from June to September tends to be 10–15m, whereas in October to February it can be 25m. Mafia is good for beginner divers, as it's very safe inside the bay. However, diving outside the bay on an outgoing tide can be extremely dangerous, with strong currents that can sweep you out to sea: in this position, if you miss your rendezvous with a boat, the next stop is Mogadishu.

When diving in the open ocean, divers are advised always to carry two means of signalling: one audible (a whistle or air horn) and one visible (an inflatable surface marker, a flare, strobe light or mirror). In addition, always wear a full wetsuit as protection against exposure, and drink water before commencing a dive. Don't take any risks or push the safety boundary while diving here; it's a long way to the nearest decompression chamber in Nairobi. Note that you can't buy diving insurance in Tanzania – you must have this before you travel.

All of the lodges on Mafia offer diving excursions as well as full PADI courses. Chole Mjini, Pole Pole, Kinasi and Mafia Island lodges all offer specialist diving courses with every conceivable type of dive site – reefs and bommies, channels, walls, caves, drift, ocean and night dives. All these are accessible in a day, while diving safaris catering for 12 people can be arranged to destinations further afield such as Ras Mkumbi, Forbes Bay southeast of Mafia, and the spectacular reef complex around the Songo Songo Islands, which lie about 80km south of Mafia and about 50km north of Kilwa.

Diving and snorkelling sites in Mafia Marine Park There are at least half a dozen more scuba-diving sites in the park and numerous snorkelling sites. Wherever possible, names given are those used by local fishermen.

The first three sites are relatively close together and can be reached on a stronger drift dive starting near the Pinnacle in Kinasi Pass. These sites sometimes suffer from being in the mouth of a bay in that the visibility can be poor for a few days after stormy periods at sea and when tidal currents are very strong at full moon or new moon.

Kinasi Pass – South Wall (*Dive depth: max 27m. Recommended for experienced divers or beginners under professional supervision.*) Justifiably Mafia's most famous dive site, this has it all: wall with caverns, big critters & spectacular corals. At times huge volumes of water flow through the pass, creating an exhilarating drift dive, or dive at slack water to enjoy the 30m wall & its resident potato cod & giant grouper. Schools of snappers & sweetlips are often here, as are their predators: barracuda, giant trevally, jacks, cobia, wahoo & kingfish. Rays & morays are common, with whalesharks, eagle rays & manta rays seasonal visitors (late Dec–Mar is best). Finish the dive in a splendid coral garden, & maybe catch up with a Napoleon wrasse or a feeding turtle.

Utumbi (or Kinasi Wall) (*Dive depth: 5–25m. Recommended experience: all certified divers. (Outstanding snorkelling site nearby, mainly at low tide.*) If you don't tackle the pass right off then this is the must-do dive in Mafia. About 300m before the pass, inside the bay, is a truly gorgeous reef: the ease of access & safe, sheltered location & the obliging currents all add up to a world-class dive. The corals rapidly change from soft corals (gorgonians & whip corals at the pass end), to more & more hard corals, until finally you find yourself in shallow gardens of tabular & staghorn acropora & gold-hued fire coral. The fish fauna is mostly typical reef inhabitants, with a huge variety of multi-coloured wrasses, parrotfish, damsels, surgeons, triggerfish & anthiases. Big wahoo & barracuda cruise off reef, & 2–3ft greasy cod & malabar grouper are abundant.

Kinasi Pass – Pinnacle (*Dive depth: max 29m. Recommended for experienced divers or beginners under professional supervision.*) In the entrance of the bay, 50m north of Kinasi Wall, this pinnacle rises sharply to within 8m of the surface, usually surrounded by a school or two of sweetlips or trevally & their attendant predators. When the visibility is good, this is the most likely place within the bay to meet a bull shark (or zambezi). We also occasionally come across a 3m guitar fish (shark that is half ray, with a flat, triangular head) & a huge, mottled green-black giant grouper accompanied by a bevy of attendant yellow-and-black-striped pilotfish. It's an excellent site at slack water.

Dindini or Shangani Wall (*Dive depth: max 24m. Recommended for experienced divers only.*) Dindini is only accessible seasonally: It's directly in front of surf-pounded cliffs. There are a lot of fish: big fish, small fish, sharks, rays & also turtles. In periods of good visibility, usually Nov–Mar, this is one of the better places in Mafia to see sharks (usually reef sharks). It's also good for large groupers &, very occasionally, big-game fish like tuna, sailfish & marlin. The wall has many caverns & U-shaped tunnels, & some deep, unexplored caves: there is the occasional appearance of a big shark or other large creature. The dive ends on the top of the wall, with really spectacular powder blue, purple & pink alcyonaria soft corals teeming with fish, especially red-toothed triggerfish, & a variety of surgeons.

Mlila or Jina Wall (*Dive depth: max 24m. Recommended for experienced divers or beginners under professional supervision.*) Seasickness can be a problem. Less than a mile away, the wall has formed a slight fold close to the cliffs. It starts out quite mediocre but rapidly changes as you get where fishing boats seldom penetrate. In the pocket there are more grouper than you'll probably ever see. There are also lots of other fish around & this is likely to be your best chance of seeing big Napoleons or getting close to a feeding turtle. At the base of the wall is a lot of coral, with many holes to investigate; look out for lobster & small stingrays as well as giant & ribbon-tailed rays.

Milimani – 'mountain tops' in Swahili (*Dive depth: max 20m. Recommended experience: all skill levels; often used for courses & Discover Scuba experiences.*) The most often-requested repeat dive in the park. This is a long reef inside the bay, characterised by spectacular coral turrets rising above corals to form mini mountains & alleys. A gentle entrance in just 6m of water over pure white sand makes this the easiest dive in the park, & the diversity of the coral is phenomenal: the topology of the reef is stunning & it just goes on & on. As you explore the twisting, turning reef interspersed with mounds of coral teeming with fish you may become so absorbed that you suddenly find you're in 20m with a towering reef above. A small gap in the reef is an excellent place to view planktivores, usually swarms of counter-shaded fusiliers & schools of unicorns but occasionally (in the right season) a cruising manta, accompanied by a flotilla of remoras & pilotfish. You can end the dive by climbing over the reef crest to look for turtles or to join the millions of kasmira & blackspot snappers in the very shallow water among the magnificent fire corals.

Miewe Shoulder – the 'Washing Machine' (*Dive depth: max 25m. Recommended experience: in slack water possible for all levels.*) In deep water just outside the bay during spring tides, 2hr before high tide, this is almost white-water diving & only for experienced & advanced divers who can control their buoyancy instinctively & know how to surf currents without fear of injury. Outside the bay, this is a sloping fringing reef north of the pass, with a fabulous diversity of fish, corals & topology. The reef is teeming with fish but you can't stop because the relentless current drags you over the top. The trick is to then drop down into one of the many deeper pools that lie just behind the jagged reef crest for a 'rinse & spin' cycle & watch the fish rush in & out. When you have been thoroughly wrung out you leave this lunar landscape of craters & spires & head south, across the current as much as possible, & will soon drift along the drop-off through Kinasi Pass for a very satisfying & relaxed end to an awesome experience.

Mkadini (*Dive depth: max 25m. Recommended experience: all skill levels.*) Outside the bay, off Miewe Island, there is a short vertical step in shallow water (12–14m max). This flattens out into a deeper shallow-sloping reef. There are many alcyonaria soft corals & diverse hard corals, lots of turtles (green & hawksbill), diverse groupers (back-saddled, lyretail, greasy cod, potato cod), schools of batfish & a good chance to see white-tip reef sharks & dolphins.

Juani Reef (*Dive depth: max 30m. Recommended for experienced divers or beginners under professional supervision.*) Outside the bay, a sloping fringing reef south of the pass extends for 12km. This is a good place to see turtles (green & hawksbill), guitar fish & white-tips, as well as stunning alcyonaria soft corals.

Mange Reef (*Dive depth: max 24m. Recommended experience: all skill levels.*) 12 nautical miles south-south-east of Chole Island, this is another beautiful coral-encrusted sandbar, once feared by local fishermen because of the many sharks. There is a good variety of reef fish & this is easily combined with Kitutia (see below) for an excellent day trip.

Chole Wall (*Dive depth: max 16m. Recommended experience: all certified divers; good training site.*) Reef inside the bay; gentle slope. About 1km in length with lots of coral & reef fishes. A grand skin-diving site when the weather is calm.

Musambiji (*Dive depth: max 16m. Recommended experience: Open Water or equivalent; good training site.*) This is a submerged island inside the bay, with diverse walls & sloping fringing coral reefs. It would be better if it were deeper & didn't suffer from poor visibility so often; but it can be a great snorkelling site.

Kitutia (*Dive depth: max 20m. Recommended experience: all skill levels.*) Once a fantastic dive site, Kitutia was badly degraded by El Niño some years ago, although it's recovering rapidly & regaining much of its former glory. It is a spectacular sandbar encrusted with corals, ideal for a day of mellow dives, snorkelling & swimming. Combined with a picnic & a fabulous sail home, it's the perfect day.

Although Mafia is predominantly visited for its waters, many choose to explore the islands, and see some of Mafia beyond the marine park. It's easiest to arrange this through one of the lodges. For a good English-speaking guide, ask for either Moussa from Chole Mjini or Ali from Pole Pole. To go it alone, you could either hire a bike or negotiate a price with the 4x4 drivers parked in Kilindoni to take you on an excursion.

KILINDONI All arrivals on Mafia pass through Kilindoni, the main town as well as the island's airport and sea port, but few visitors venture into Kilindoni for any length of time. New by East African standards, the town was established by the Germans in 1913 on discovering that Chole Island lacked a deep-water anchorage. While it has none of the Arab architecture of Stone Town on Zanzibar, its coral and lime-mortar shop-houses with quaint signs and rusting corrugated-iron roofs exude an ambience of old Indian Ocean days.

At first, Kilindoni appears to have all the accoutrements of a small town: a district hospital, school (complete with science laboratories), police station, bank, post office, airport, mosque and churches. Then suddenly the sandy road opens into a square full of clothes for sale, music and activity. There are stands selling mobile phone chargers (continental two-pins), an unexpected but necessary slice of modern Africa.

Peaceful rather than bustling, the **market** is the centre of local life. Tomatoes, chillies, potatoes, onions, limes, dried prawns, bananas, cassava and whatever the trader can get his hands on are arranged in little piles. A large amount of food here is from Dar, grown elsewhere on the Tanzanian mainland. Spices are from Zanzibar, naturally, all wrapped up in little plastic packets. Baobab seeds for kids to chew are sold in piles and the fish stalls are pungently gathered together a little further off. Other stalls sell pottery, *kangas* and secondhand clothes, and if you're brave enough to buy a homemade snorkelling/diving mask, ingeniously made of pieces of metal stapled to thick black rubber, it'll set you back US$2.50.

A number of small **shops** are of interest to the visitor: the **Dubay Store**, next to Mapozi Haircutting Salon, sells cold Cokes and Fantas for US$0.50. For items such as sausage, orange juice, Sprite, water, chocolate, toilet paper, washing powder and toothpaste, try **Mwishehe Shopping Centre**. On the road to the harbour (Bandani Road), by the little roundabout, you'll find **WTC** selling drinks, ice cream and chocolate, chicken and chips. **Kisoma Store** sells basic stationery; its proudly advertised 'computer' doesn't have internet access, but you can print from it at Tsh800 per sheet. Make a right turn from the petrol and diesel pumps (opposite the 4x4 parking area), and you'll find **Fantastic Hair Cutting** which can cut different grades using a proper shaver for US$2 a haircut, and US$1 for a wet shave.

There are more stores on the road descending to the dhow landing. The **Market General Supply Store** and the **Peace and Love** sell soft drinks, and off the main square, Utende Road has the rather vulgar monument presented by the fish factory. On the left is a grey weather-beaten **mosque** and further along the Roman Catholic **church**, one of at least six churches.

The **landing** in Kilindoni usually has 15–20 *jahazis* moored on the beach. Whether unloading fish or mending their nets, the fishermen object strongly to being photographed, as do the people frying cassava chips and cooking octopus on small stoves under the trees.

Where to stay The guesthouses in town are all pretty basic, with little to draw travellers to them; even Mafia Pwani Camp has relatively little to recommend it.

🏠 **Mafia Pwani Camp aka Sunset Resort** (4 *bandas*, camping) ✆ 023 2402244; 📱 0755 696067; 📧 carpho2003@yahoo.co.uk. A 15min walk from the airport, in a beautiful area overlooking the sea, this relaxed camp is an excellent place for spotting the rufous elephant shrew, as well as vervet monkeys. To get there, turn right out of the airport, follow the road round to the right, & take the first left by the concrete wall. Individual *bandas* are sizeable & clean, with nets on windows & beds, 24hr electricity, & a laundry service. Buckets of water are provided in the shared bathroom, & can be heated on request. A steep pathway down to the beach leads to the campsite. There are plans to build a platform, bar & lounge area. *US$24 dbl; camping US$7 pp.*

🏠 **New Lizu Hotel** (5 rooms) Bookings c/o Post office, Mafia; ✆ 023 2402683. The most comfortable guesthouse in the centre of Kilindoni is a 1min walk from the market, & 10min from the dhow landing jetty. It's clean but very basic, with 24hr electricity, mosquito nets & fans. All but 1 room (a single) share washing facilities, with limited water; toilets are flushed with a bucket. There's a laundry service,

& a simple bar/restaurant serves rice & seafood. *Tsh10,000 twin; b/fast Tsh700–1,000.* Bike hire *Tsh3,000/day;* motorbike (with helmet) *Tsh20,000–30,000/day.*

🏠 **Harbour View Lodge** (10 rooms) 📱 0755 360314. Walk through the timber yard to get to this good, basic lodge, where tables outside the large bar & dancefloor have a view of the harbour. Rooms have fans or AC, nets on the windows (not on the beds), lockable cupboard & 24hr electricity; some are en suite, with hot water on request. There's also a small restaurant. *Tsh8,000–12,000 dbl.*

🏠 **Classic Visitor's House** (7 rooms) 📱 0746 749176. This very basic but pleasant guesthouse has mosquito nets on the windows & beds, & ceiling fans (24hr electricity). Existing rooms share 2 squat toilets with a tap & bucket, & 2 sporadically functioning showers; newer en-suite rooms are similarly basic. There is no restaurant but a laundry service is offered & the owner speaks English. To get here from the Sports Bar on your left, take the first right, then left – it's behind the white wall. From the mosque, take the first left at Sofia Soft Drinks, walk to the end of the road, then it's on your left.

✖ **Where to eat** With a burst of modernity, Kilindoni has recently gained the **Mafia Sports Bar**, complete with flat-screen TV and satellite. This big orange building is slap-bang in the middle of the town, providing a bar and restaurant for tourists and locals alike, and is part owned by Kinasi Lodge. A more African establishment, the tiny **Royal Pub Mafia**, may be rather surprised by visitors, but sells local beers: Kilimanjaro, Tusker, Serengeti, Bin Bingwa for US$1, and Konyagi (a local firewater with rather descriptive flames on the bottle) for US$2.50. This local bar also sells food: chips are US$0.50, egg and chips US$1, and a beef kebab US$1.50.

Other practicalities A bank and a post office are located on the airport road. The bank is the National Microfinance Bank (🕐 08.30–15.00 Mon–Fri, 08.30–12.30 Sat). The post office (🕐 08.00–13.00 & 14.00–16.30 Mon–Fri, closed Sat) is just past the bank, but be aware that your letter may take months to leave Mafia. A better option may be to ask your lodge to post your letters in Dar es Salaam.

NORTH OF KILINDONI One of the few places that travellers visit on Mafia is the lighthouse at Ras Mkumbi, via the charming village of Bweni. This is approximately 47km north of Kilindoni, and the drive there, over bouncy sand roads that follow or run parallel to the west coast of Mafia, takes about two hours direct, or all day if you want to include swimming and a picnic. Note, though, that while there are some stunning white-sand beaches along this coast, with excellent swimming opportunities, the sea on this side of the island is largely devoid of the underwater attractions around Chole Bay to the east. The excursion is best organised through one of the lodges; you'll find an English-speaking guide is invaluable. Alternatively, a full-day excursion to Ras Mkumbi with Mafia Island Tours costs US$50 per person. Bring everything you are likely to need from your hotel, not forgetting clothes to cover knees and shoulders, suncream, and insect repellent in case you return after dark.

Driving through Mafia is a good way of seeing the island, and finding out about everyday life here. As you drive through the villages, you'll see crops of mangoes, pineapples, bananas, cassava and cashew nuts, as well as sweet potatoes, which grow after the rainy season. About 8km from Kilindoni is a picturesque swamp covered in mauve lotus. Small tilapia and catfish dart among the reeds. Further on, the old agricultural village of **Kirongwe**, with a tradition of making clay pots, counts a score of houses, a handful of shops and a market selling the usual dried octopus, bananas and coconuts. Beyond here the countryside is intensively cultivated with beans, pigeon pea and cassava, and – rather less attractive – numerous indications of slash-and-burn agriculture. Sykes's and vervet monkeys raiding the crops flee at the sound of any vehicle.

The north of Mafia is markedly different from the wetter southern part of the island, which is dominated by vast coconut plantations. After **Jimbo**, where you may see local blacksmiths working by the side of the road, the landscape suddenly becomes more undulating open grassland with outcrops of mia'a or palm, and baobabs similar to those on the mainland coastal plain. Birdlife is plentiful with bee-eaters and lilac-breasted rollers flashing amongst the trees and large flocks of guinea fowl scuttling off the road. While only about 30m above sea level, it is noticeably cooler here than on the coast.

Bweni village, built behind 2km of glistening white-sand beach, seems a likely spot for future tourism development. Its traditional Swahili-style houses of coral and lime plaster are dotted among slender coconut palms. You need to stop to collect the lighthouse key from a keeper in the village, and will be soon surrounded by excited and curious children, delighted at the chance to shout *Mzungu!* at the unexpected visitor. Their behaviour is polite, however, and their fascination mixed with a fear of the unknown. Bweni women are experts at weaving striped prayer mats from the palms on the plateau, and you only need to show interest for items to be shyly produced. The larger mats are 2.5m by 1.5m, and cost around US$4; smaller oval mats go for US$3.

The **lighthouse** at **Ras Mkumbi** is a 3km drive on a good stretch of road from Bweni. Built on coral rag on the northern tip of Mafia, it is worth climbing the 15m up to the top of the red-and-white structure for a spectacular view of the Mafia Channel lying between the archipelago and the mainland. The stretch of deep-blue water is reputed to offer some of the best big-game fishing in East Africa. This working lighthouse also has concrete outbuildings, now owned by Pole Pole, who organise trips to the area. One of the buildings has basic rooms with mosquito nets around basic beds, and flushing toilets. At present it is used for overnight fishing trips but is being developed into a small guesthouse.

The grassy area in front of the lighthouse leads towards a rocky beach which repays half an hour or so of exploration at low tide. Black kites swoop low over the cliffs, while further out fishermen search for octopus in their race against the tide. It's possible to rent a bike from the village, or to go on a forest walk to see birds and monkeys. Snorkelling, fishing and diving trips can also be organised in this area.

KISIMANI MAFIA Kisimani (KiSwahili for 'the place of the well') lies on Ras Kisimani at the south end of the island, 30 minutes' drive from Kilindoni or a two-hour boat trip. The town was an important centre during the Shirazi domination of Kilwa between the 12th and 14th centuries. The hands of the sultan's chief mason were cut off after he built the palace, so that he could never repeat the task. The story goes on to claim that this was why a few months later Kisimani was inundated by the sea. There is little left of the submerged medieval settlement, but you can see the well for which it is named on the beach. Wandering about, you might find a few coins and pottery shards.

The shady coconut palms are a nice spot for a picnic, and there's a lovely white beach here with good birding and snorkelling, but bring everything you want to eat or drink.

UTENDE The three main tourist lodges on Mafia Island all lie along the beach below this small village, at the end of the 15km road west from Kilindoni. Many of Utende's inhabitants are Makonde people from the mainland, who keep their fishing boats in Chole Bay. One or two shop-houses sell strings of dried octopus and fish. Like everywhere else on Mafia, the village is quite safe to explore, being only ten minutes' walk from any of the hotels. The beach in front of Utende (close to Mafia Island Lodge) is where local dhows leave for Chole Island every 30 minutes or so, costing US$0.50 on a local ferry one-way. Alternatively, it'll cost around US$10 to hire a boat.

Schools here are developing with aid from the lodges. A new primary school is being built on the site of the old school, offering Standards 1–6, and nursery education for 31 pupils. Since 2000, this has been financed by Pole Pole. The government then helped them to build another school building for seven- to 14-year-olds. Utende also has a couple of small shops, and you'll notice a number of buildings made with cement blocks and corrugated iron. Although not as picturesque, cement blocks are relatively cheap and an easy material for building, while corrugated-iron roofs last longer than a palm-leaf roof, which has to be replaced every three years or so.

OTHER EXCURSIONS Most other villages on Mafia are inaccessible by road and, like the offshore islands, may be visited only by boat. Given advance warning, the lodges can usually arrange trips to visit them.

However, the most popular excursions are probably those to isolated sandbars. You'll sail to these from your lodge, and then the boat crew will set up some shade on the beach, and cook lunch over a barbecue. Meanwhile, you can relax, sunbathe, swim and snorkel with nothing around you except miles and miles of deep blue ocean. Trips like these are included by some of the lodges, while others will charge you extra, depending on the destination (US$40–60 per person per trip is typical).

Destinations for excursions include Chole, Juani and Jibondo islands, described in the following pages, and several smaller spots including:

Mchangani Village is the end of an interesting excursion winding for nearly 3km up a creek on the north side of Chole Bay. Sykes's monkeys can be seen in the mangrove forests and fish eagles are commonly observed. The village lies on the east bank of the creek, and takes about an hour to reach. Depart only on a high tide. If you would rather walk, it takes 90 minutes over sand and rock.

Dindini Beach is likewise accessible only at high tide. It faces the ocean from Mafia Island just north of Chole Bay, and from December to February can see big waves. Behind the beach is a large, sea-fed rock pool, which contains a variety of marine life. There are also low sand dunes and interesting vegetation on the coral rag.

Didimizi Beach is the lovely white-sand beach seen from Chole Bay, around 4km from the main tourist lodges, or a 45-minute walk. You could arrange for a vehicle going to Kilindoni to drop you at the turn-off and walk back, not forgetting to take refreshments and a hat. Alternatively a short trip by dhow brings you straight to the beach dotted with little pyramids of sand caused by the white ghost crabs that scuttle around – they'll be all you share the sandbar with.

Bwejuu Island, off Ras Kisimani to the west of Mafia, has its own small village and makes a good day trip. Located between the Rufjiji River Delta and Mafia's main island, it offers good snorkelling at Mange Reef, as well as diving and fishing.

You can also camp on Bwejuu Island for a few nights. Further afield, the Rufiji River is close enough for trips which can go all the way to the Selous Game Reserve.

Ras Mbisi, only 90 minutes by road from Kilindoni, has an ideal beach for picnics, swimming and snorkelling.

Mbaracuni Island, lying 12km northwest of Mafia, can be visited by arrangement. Uninhabited, quiet and said to be very beautiful, it is used by fishing dhows. This is a good place to see black kites and occasionally two or three fish eagles.

Miewe is another small, uninhabited island, used by fishermen to clean and dry fish, and can be visited for picnics, as can the sandbank of Marimbani. If you're interested in sailing a little further, and for a good chance of seeing dolphins, you can take a day excursion to the island of Kitutia. After a couple of hours under sail, you'll be rewarded by some stunning snorkelling on a reef which surrounds a pure-white sandbank. This is all covered by the sea at high tide, so the trip needs to be timed carefully.

CHOLE ISLAND

Chole is the lush, tropical island lying to the west of Kinasi Pass. With the adjacent islands of Juani and Jibondo, it forms a barrier between Mafia and the open ocean. The shallow reef in front is rich in soft corals, sea anemones and sponges, and,

---

RECOLLECTIONS OF CHOLE

Factual histories of the East African coast tend to focus on the activities of the ruling classes – whether indigenous, Arabic or European – largely because such accounts are drawn from historical sources written by the powerful, and archaeological excavations of their mosques and palaces. The following quotes provide a rather different perspective, though it should be borne in mind that they are not first-hand accounts, but traditions passed from one generation to the next.

The woman quoted is the late Bi Hadija Mahommedi Bacha of Chole Island, and her stories are reproduced from the *Chole Handbook* (available from any of the lodge gift shops on Mafia) with the kind permission of its editors, Chris Walley and Dudley Iles.

The wife of an Arab slave owner said, 'I don't understand how a child lies in the womb', so [her husband] cut open a pregnant slave woman to show his wife how the foetus lay inside. That young woman was cut open like a piece of dried fish so they could see how the child lay inside the womb of its mother ... Next the wife asks the slave master, 'When a monkey is shot what happens?' So a person is found to climb up a tree, like that baobab over there. He sends a gun over there, he shoots, Pow! Down falls a human being. That slave master was called Masinda; he was the owner of Kaziwa ... He was harsh! If you did anything at all, you would be made to climb a tree and shot – boom! – with a gun. You would fall down like an animal. You would already be dead and then you would be thrown away.

[Under the Germans,] if someone did something wrong, that person would be hanged at the Boma there on the beach, near the Casuarina tree at the spot along the beach where people today like to sit. It was an open spot and a box would be placed below and the person's neck would be placed in a rope. It was the Germans who arranged to use the place in this manner, and indeed they were the ones who did the hanging.

sloping to 15m, it is a good spot to practise drift diving. The bay itself is ideal for sailing and windsurfing. The town of Chole Mjini was the main urban centre on the archipelago for much of the 19th century, the home of wealthy merchants whose plantations lay on the main island of Mafia (see *History*, page 369, and box, *Recollections of Chole*, page 383). Ruins dating from this era include a reasonably preserved German customs house on the waterfront, and several more ruined mansions dating to the Omani era. A path behind the new market leading to the village brings you to a prison, whose broken cells are invaded by tangled tree roots. Farther along and also in ruins is a Hindu temple.

Hanging upside down in a nearby baobab is a colony of fruit bats of the same family as the Comoros Islands' lesser flying fox (*Pteropus seychellenis comorensis*), found in the Comoros, the Seychelles and Mafia, but nowhere on mainland Africa. Each evening the bats fly across Chole Bay to feed on the cashew-nut and mango trees of Mafia, as well as marula fruit, figs, and mangrove flowers. Like the Comoros bats they dip over the surface of the water – an action which scientists believe may be an attempt to rid themselves of parasites. A more enchanting local explanation claims 'they are washing before evening prayers'. Bats are nocturnal, so it's imperative for the continuation of the Chole colony that visitors allow them to sleep in the day, ensuring that neither they nor their guide throw stones at them, or shake their tree, just to wake them up and take photos of the bats in flight. Remember that it is a bat sanctuary.

Chole's population was estimated at 5,000 during the early years of German rule, but today it is no more than 1,000. The islanders cultivate smallholdings of cassava, beans, mangoes, paw-paw, citrus (including very sweet oranges) and passion fruit. Encouraged by the lodges, these smallholdings have flourished and produce is now exported to Mafia, with the oranges also making their way to the mainland. Most of the menfolk fish, while many of the women are engaged in catching octopus beyond the mangroves at low tide. Winding past traditional houses, the path brings you to a beach where fishermen can be seen mending nets, or making sails and coconut-coir ropes. Chole was once a centre of boatbuilding, and boats are still repaired and occasionally built on the island. The boatyard is indicated on the circular walk available from Chole Mjini, about half an hour from the lodge.

The Norwegian Women's Front and Chole Mjini Lodge have been instrumental in much of Chole's development. They have funded the building of a hospital and a free clinic for the under fives, a kindergarten, a market, and the Society for Women's Development (which runs savings and loan schemes). They have also helped to set up a school, so that children no longer have to walk across to Juani Island at low tide, and a learning centre to help educate adults.

GETTING THERE AND AWAY The lodges at Utende operate boat trips to Chole, or you can visit it independently from Mafia, or on a 'bat and village tour' with Mafia Island Tours (US$10). A dhow dubbed the 'Chole taxi' leaves the beach in front of Mafia Island Lodge throughout the day – last sailing at 16.00 – a crossing of 10–15 minutes depending on the wind and tide, for a cost of Tsh500 one-way. It is also possible to charter a local boat across for a fee of about US$10. If you plan to stay more than a few hours on the island it is advisable to bring a picnic and refreshments from your hotel, and note that you'll have to wade a short distance from the boat. Make sure that you're wearing shoes, as there are stingrays in this area.

There is no motorised transport on Chole Island. In the early 1990s there was only one bike, which now hangs from the rafters of Chole Mjini; today there are 150. Neither are there any budget hotels; the only place to stay is Chole Mjini Lodge, which does not cater to passing custom or serve meals to non-residents.

WHERE TO STAY Chole's three upmarket lodges – Pole Pole, Kinasi and Chole Mjini – are all totally different in style and approach, and each has its advocates claiming that it is 'the best'. The truth is that they're all very good, given their different styles – and all offer really very good value for money given their relative isolation, and the quality of the marine experience to be had here. The trick is to choose the one that's right for you.

Mafia Lodge doesn't reach the standards of the other three, but you won't find a better-value spot for a quiet retreat with access to great diving.

Chole Mjini Lodge (6 treehouses, 1 chalet) m 0784 520799; e 2chole@bushmail.net. This fabulous lodge, situated on Chole Island, is set amongst the crumbling 19th-century ruins of Chole Mjini. Large, treehouse-style rooms are perched high in the baobabs, while a chalet at ground level, & a converted wooden dhow offer appealing alternatives.The owners, Jean & Anne de Villiers, who live on site, stress that they are not catering to people seeking Sheraton-style luxury or a conventional beach retreat – there is no electricity for starters, & the waterfront in front of the lodge is overgrown with mangroves. Nevertheless this must rank as one of the most original & aesthetically pleasing lodges on the East African coast. It's also an atmospheric base for exploring Chole Island & the surrounding waters. Meals – a mixture of African & European styles – are served at group or individual tables, sometimes set among the ruins. The owners & their dive instructor have more than 50 years' experience of diving Mafia between them, & can instruct in English, Italian, French or German, making Chole Mjini an excellent lodge for divers at

all levels. There are also organised walks, snorkel trips & excursions to nearby sandbars – with 1 or 2 complimentary trips organised every day. US$720–1,080 dbl FB, inc village levy & daily activity. Mafia Airport transfer US$30/vehicle; diving US$40/dive; scuba equipment US$15/day. No children under 2.

Pole Pole (7 bungalows) 022 2601530; e info@polepole.com; www.polepole.com. The Italian-managed Pole Pole, meaning 'slowly, slowly' in Swahili, is the ultimate destination for relaxation. Smart without being pretentious, it is set in a garden of coconut palms with a small beach in front fringed by mangroves. Large en-suite bungalows, built almost entirely from organic materials, feature polished wooden floors, stylishly simple furniture, a ceiling fan & 24hr electricity, & each has a wide veranda overlooking the sea. Guests are requested to keep phones on silent mode & only make calls from within their rooms. Typical Italian 4-course dinners are served at private tables in the restaurant, with Swahili dinners once a week or on request. Service is attentive, & there are 2 good local masseuses. Excursions include snorkelling, diving & game fishing, & a complimentary dhow trip is normally offered every day. Between Oct & Mar the lodge operates trips to see (& on occasion swim with) migratory whalesharks. *US$440–500 dbl FB, inc airport transfers, laundry, tea, coffee & bottled water, snorkelling & excursions in Chole Bay; diving US$40/70 sgl/dbl; equipment US$20/day.*

⌂ **Kinasi Lodge** (14 bungalows) m 0747 418256, operations m 0713 242977; e kinasi@intafrica.com; www.mafiaisland.com; ☉ Jun–end Mar. A 5min walk along the beach from Pole Pole brings you to this more formal hideaway, set in landscaped grounds sloping down to a small sandy beach. A swimming pool, with poolside bar & grill, is surrounded by en-suite thatched bungalows with verandas, furnished with Zanzibar-style dbl beds enveloped in vast mosquito nets. In the dining area, adjacent to an open-sided bar & lounge, an eclectic fusion menu & themed dinners are served, & there's a separate grill & pizza kitchen for more casual dining. A fully equipped watersports & dive centre offers snorkelling trips, windsurfing, kayaking & game fishing, with further options including dhow trips, village visits, mountain biking, & 4x4 drives & birdwatching. The Isis Spa is open to guests from any of the Mafia lodges. *US$430–604 dbl FB; Mafia Airport transfer US$24 pp one-way.*

Moderate

⌂ **Mafia Island Lodge** (40 rooms) m 0786 303049; e info@mafialodge.com; www.mafialodge.com. This very simple lodge, situated on one of the island's few open, palm-lined beaches, is next to Pole Pole & about 10min walk from Kinasi Lodge. It's a reliable, functional place, with a mix of en-suite, box-like rooms that have recently undergone a much-needed refurbishment. There's AC & 24hr hot water. The bar/restaurant has a large airy terrace & serves a seafood-inspired menu. There's internet access (US$5/hr), a pool table & equipment for beach volleyball, & a small shop selling a few essentials. Mafia's only real tour company, Mafia Island Tours, is based here, & makes an obvious choice from which to book dives & excursions if you're not staying at one of the upmarket lodges. Options include a village tour on Chole Island, with a visit to the flying foxes (US$10 pp); a half-day trip to the Kua Ruins & Channel, or Jibondo Island (US$25 pp), a longer snorkelling trip with lunch to Marimbani or Kitutia (US$35/45 pp); & a full-day excursion to Ras Mkumbi or Bwejuu Island (US$50/60 pp). *US$140–180 dbl HB. Diving US$40/dive, equipment US$30/day.*

JUANI ISLAND

The boat trip from Mafia to Juani, site of the ruined city of Kua, takes about ten minutes longer than the one to Chole, but the island can be approached only at high tide. The landing, in a small bay sheltered by dense mangroves, is covered in thousands of opened oyster-shells, so remember to wear good shoes, as you'll have to wade to shore. Seafood is the staple diet on Juani, but, unlike Chole, Juani has no well water, and locals practise rain-dependent cultivation.

Beneath three big baobabs near the landing, your shoes crunch on the rocky paths of a buried civilisation. Bits of blue-and-white Shirazi pottery suggest trade links with China are embedded in the dirt. In the past, people from the mainland came to Juani to bathe in a seawater cave reputed to have curative properties for rheumatism. It is a long, difficult walk across to the ocean side, where there are also said to be three turtle-nesting beaches. The Kua Channel slices a tiny chunk off Juani as it opens into Chole Bay. It makes a superb picnic excursion with birdwatching and swimming. A friendly grouper lives in one of the rock pools at the southern end.

The ruined city of **Kua** (see *History*, pages 369–70), spread across 6 hectares on the west coast of Juani, was the Shirazi capital of Mafia. It was one of the few East African ports to be continuously inhabited from medieval times into the early 19th century, when it was sacked by raiders from Madagascar. A trail hacked out of the undergrowth leads up to a large building shedding masonry: the former palace, still revered locally as a 'spirit place' where offerings such as bits of glass are left. The ruins here have been defeated by the powerful strangler figs that dominate a number of the walls, and the tomb of the sultan himself has been destroyed by a tree growing in its centre. The path passes other ruined edifices, including two 14th-century mosques and a series of tombs. The buildings are made from coral rock and lime cement, which does not survive well in this sea air. Looking at cracks in the walls you wonder how long they will remain standing, with the occasional monkey as the only inhabitant. If you see the caretaker, he expects and deserves a small gratuity; ask him to show you the foundations of the house referred to in the box *Kua's revenge*, page 384.

You depart on a beautiful sail home between the islands, watched by the scores of ibis on the mangroves. There is a guide and map of the ruins, as well as the report on its archaeology, in the library at Kinasi Lodge.

JIBONDO ISLAND

Jibondo is a long, low-lying island another 20-minute sail from Juani. This traditional village community is rather different from the rest of Mafia, and the atmosphere is somehow more charged than in other villages. Coming ashore, a big jahazi dhow is one of the first things you see. Built 15 years ago, it has never been launched and is subsequently something of a museum piece, but the old men sitting under the quinine tree nearby have already learned its value to tourism, wanting to charge US$1 for a photo. Behind the boat is a rather plain white mosque, built in 1979.

Some of its furniture was taken from the queen's palace in the ruins at Kua, and it's worth wandering around the back to see the carved wooden door from Kua (by contrast, the window frames were made of wood from India). This is all set off by the pungent smell from the row of long-drop loos that literally drop into the sea. Jibondo does not have a fresh water supply, so the islanders depend on rain which is collected in a primitive concrete catchment area.

The rainwater lasts only three months after the rains; after this, the islanders have to go to Mafia with drums to collect water. Jibondo people are well known as shipbuilders and, as on Chole, use only traditional tools. Even the nails are handmade and the holes are plugged with local kapok and shark fat. Local women play a prominent role in trading as well as fishing. They also sail boats, which is unusual in African society, and are more affable and confident than women elsewhere. Jibondo people also collect and dry seaweed to export.

Another unusual aspect of Jibondo is that cultivation is carried out at one end of the island while the people live in an urban community at the other. The village, which consists of traditional Swahili-style houses with *makuti* roofs, is laid out in a grid pattern. As on Chole and Juani, there is no transport other than boats which shelter on the western side of the narrow neck of the island.

The island has one school, easily identified by the football field in front. If the tide is good for fishing, the children – encouraged by their parents – go straight out on the water, ignoring lessons. In a year, only one child is likely to leave the island and go to secondary school on Mafia. There are, however, three madrasas on the island, where there is a strong Muslim faith. There are no other social services, and only a basic shop. On the other side of the island is Flamingo Beach, which makes an interesting two-hour trek. The village trail and sailing dhow with Mafia Island Tours costs US$25.

12

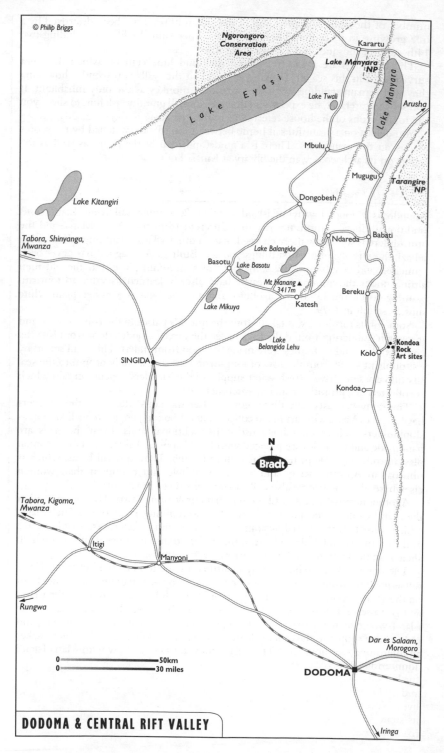

© Philip Briggs

Ngorongoro
Conservation
Area

Karartu

Lake Manyara
NP

Lake Eyasi

Lake Manyara

Lake Twali

Arusha

Mbulu

Mugugu

Tarangire
NP

Lake Kitangiri

Dongobesh

Tabora, Shinyanga,
Mwanza

Ndareda

Babati

Lake Balangida

Basotu

Lake Basotu

Mt Hanang ▲
3417m

Bereku

Lake Mikuya

Katesh

Lake
Belangida Lehu

Kondoa
Rock
Art sites

SINGIDA

Kolo

Kondoa

N

Bradt

Tabora, Kigoma,
Mwanza

Itigi

Manyoni

Rungwa

Dar es Salaam,
Morogoro

0 ————50km
0 ————30 miles

DODOMA ■

DODOMA & CENTRAL RIFT VALLEY

Iringa

13

Dodoma and the Central Rift Valley

Despite its status as national capital and its central location within Tanzania, the nascent city of Dodoma is of limited interest to travellers, and the same might safely be said for the vast and predominantly flat badlands that surround it. Far more worthwhile, though also visited by few tourists, the central Rift Valley to the north of Dodoma is studded with underrated attractions, most notably the Kondoa rock paintings, a UNESCO World Heritage Site since 2006, and the scenic and eminently climbable Mount Hanang.

The southern gateway to the Central Rift Valley, Dodoma is a major domestic route focus, connected to Dar es Salaam and Morogoro by a good surfaced road and reliable bus services, to Arusha and Iringa by rougher gravel roads, and to Tabora, Mwanza and Kigoma by rail. Most other sites covered in this chapter are accessible by dirt roads only, and a 4x4 or other vehicle with good clearance will be desirable. Climatically, the area can be classified as semi-arid, typified by hot but not humid days and pleasantly cool to chilly nights, and the low level of precipitation means that travel is usually as straightforward during the rains as in other months. Mount Hanang supports its own relatively moist microclimate, and the upper slopes are often cold at night.

DODOMA

The city of Dodoma, set at an elevation of 1,135m on the arid, windswept plains that characterise the central Tanzanian plateau, is the mildly improbable designate capital of Tanzania. It was proposed for this role in 1959, during the transitional period leading up to independence, on the equitable basis that it is the country's most centrally located large town. Nyerere formally earmarked Dodoma as national capital in 1974, and it was originally expected to be fully functional in this role before 1990. Lack of funding, an absence of decent roads in three directions – and quite possibly the sense of contrivance attached to the entire project – have conspired to ensure that this deadline was repeatedly set back. Parliament finally relocated to Dodoma in February 1996, but most government departments and embassies are still based out of Dar es Salaam, and this seems unlikely to change in the immediate future.

An important stopover on the 19th-century caravan route to Lake Tanganyika, Dodoma was made a regional administration centre after Germany built a railway station there in 1910, and was even mooted to replace Dar es Salaam as colonial capital prior to the intervention of World War I. The post-war British administration felt Dodoma had few advantages over Dar es Salaam, and was further dissuaded by the series of famines that afflicted the region between 1916 and 1920, cruelly capped by an influenza epidemic that claimed at least 30,000 lives. Nevertheless, Dodoma grew steadily between the wars, in large part due to its strategic location at the junction of the central railway and the trans-Tanzania road. Its strategic importance declined after an improved north–south road was constructed between Iringa and Morogoro, but Dodoma retained its role as the market centre for a vast but low-yielding agricultural region producing maize, beans, peanuts, grains and wine – as well as boasting several large cattle ranches.

As designate capital, Dodoma has experienced a high influx of people from surrounding rural areas and other parts of the country. The city's population has risen from 45,000 in 1978, when it was the 13th largest urban centre in the country, to an estimated 150,000, placing it 8th on that list in 2002. But whatever its past and future claims to importance (and we *are* talking about a town that served as a staging post on the renowned Cape-to-Cairo flights of the 1930s), Dodoma remains unremittingly small-town in atmosphere and of limited interest to tourists. True, there must be some travellers out there who collect capital cities as others collect passport stamps, in which case a foray into Dodoma might well be the highlight of a visit to Tanzania. Wine enthusiasts, too, might be tempted to visit Dodoma to taste the product of Tanzania's viniculture industry, founded by a priest in 1957, at source. The local wine and port can be tasted at the Tanganyika Vineyard Company on the outskirts of town, but it's really nothing special, and is just as readily available in Arusha and other tourist centres. Otherwise, you'd be

THE GOGO OF DODOMA

Dodoma is the principal town of the Gogo (referred to in Swahili as Wagogo) people, and its name – probably in use before any major settlement existed at the site – is derived from the local word *idodomya*, which means 'place of sinking'. The most widely accepted explanation for this name is that it was coined by a group of villagers who came down to a stream to collect water, to find an elephant stuck irretrievably in the muddy bank. Another version of events is that a local clan stole some cattle from a neighbouring settlement, slaughtered and ate the stolen beasts, then placed their dismembered tails in a patch of swamp. When a search party arrived, the thieves claimed that the lost animals had sunk in the mud (whether or not anybody actually believed this unlikely story goes unrecorded!).

One of the most populous of Tanzania's ethno-linguistic groups, the Gogo people are semi-pastoral Bantu-speakers, noted within Tanzania for their exceptional musicianship and basketwork. Their homeland around Dodoma is characterised by a low annual rainfall figure, and historically it has proved to be unusually prone to drought and crop failure. Gogo oral tradition recalls more than half a dozen serious famines in the 19th century. The first of these, and according to tradition the most severe, is remembered by the name *Mpingama* ('Hindrance'). The famine of 1870, referred to in the writings of Henry Stanley, is remembered as *Mamudemu* ('Burst Intestine'). A famine in 1881 is known as *Kubwa-Kidogo* (Big-Small), presumably because it was initiated by a plague of quelea – a sparrow-sized bird that sometimes flock in their tens of thousands to descend locust-like on grain fields.

The threat of famine has played a significant role in moulding the lifestyle and society of the Gogo, who traditionally live in small permanent villages of wood-and-clay huts, around which they practise low-yield subsistence agriculture. Herders would, however, move long distances to find grazing and water for their cattle, relying – particularly in years of low rainfall – on a co-operative social structure that allowed for the communal use of water sources and grazing within extended clans. The construction of several large dams within a 100km radius of Dodoma region notwithstanding, recurrent drought remains a feature of the region to this day. One of the most severe famines in living memory occurred in the early 1960s, when at least 600,000 people received emergency food rations.

unlikely to visit Dodoma from choice, and if for some reason you do wash adrift there, then it probably won't be long before you think about moving on.

GETTING THERE AND AWAY Most travellers who pass through Dodoma are on one of the trains crossing between Dar es Salaam and Kigoma or Mwanza. Coming from the west, should you want to take a proper look at Dodoma, there's nothing stopping you from buying a ticket as far as Dodoma and spending a night there before bussing on to Dar es Salaam the next day. Coming in the opposite direction, it's possible to buy a ticket out of Dodoma from the railway station in Dar es Salaam. Westbound trains pass through Dodoma between 08.00 and 10.00 the morning after they leave Dar es Salaam. For further details, see the box, *The Central Railway*, on page 393.

The 450km road between Dar es Salaam and Dodoma is surfaced in its entirety and shouldn't take longer than five or six hours to cover in a private vehicle. A fairly steady stream of buses runs between the past and designated capitals, generally leaving before midday and taking around seven hours. You can pick up these buses at Morogoro.

Dodoma is strategically positioned in the centre of Tanzania. As a consequence, many travellers are tempted to cut between other parts of the country through Dodoma, based solely on the impressions of distance gained from a map. It's emphatically worth stressing that most plans which hang on bussing through Dodoma as a 'short cut' should be nipped firmly in the bud, certainly if they involve using the direct road south to Iringa, north to Arusha or west to – well anywhere in the west really. Should you use one of these routes, buses generally leave in either direction in the early morning – you're advised to book a seat an afternoon in advance and to check the exact time of departure (bearing in mind you'll almost certainly be quoted Swahili time). Most buses depart from the main bus stop just behind the Oilcom petrol station on Dar es Salaam Avenue, while the Scandinavia Express terminal is 500m east of the roundabout.

Note that while it would be an act of masochism to bus along the 440km road between Dodoma and Arusha for the pleasure of it, there are a couple of spots along this road that really *are* worth making an effort to visit, as covered later in this chapter. A few days' exploration of the region between Dodoma and Arusha would allow you to break the unsurfaced 330km south of the Tarangire National Park junction into three discrete chunks, an altogether more manageable prospect than covering the road in one go.

WHERE TO STAY
Upmarket

New Dodoma Hotel [388 C6] (96 rooms)
\ 026 232 1641; e reservation_newdodomahotel@ yahoo.com. Formerly run by Tanzania Railways, this attractive building opposite the railway station has been extensively expanded & renovated since it was privatised, with the addition of facilities including

gym, swimming pool, health club, internet café & hair salon. It's one of the best places to eat in Dodoma, serving Indian, Chinese & continental meals in the Tsh5,000–10,000 bracket. *Tsh50,000/70,000 sgl/dbl B&B with fan; Tsh70,000/90,000 with AC & satellite TV.*

Moderate

Cana Lodge [388 A4] \ 026 232 1199. This well-maintained modern lodge, located on 9th St 5 blocks west of Kuu St, has spic-&-span en-suite dbls with fans, TV & telephone. There is a good restaurant & bar, & an internet café next door. *Tsh25,000 dbl.*

National Vocational Training Centre [388 D5] (40 rooms) \ 026 232 2181. About 2km from the town centre along the Morogoro Rd, this hotel training centre is good value, serves decent food in the Tsh4,000–5,000 range, & has a lively bar. *Tsh15,000/24,000 en-suite sgl/dbl with hot water, net & fan.*

13

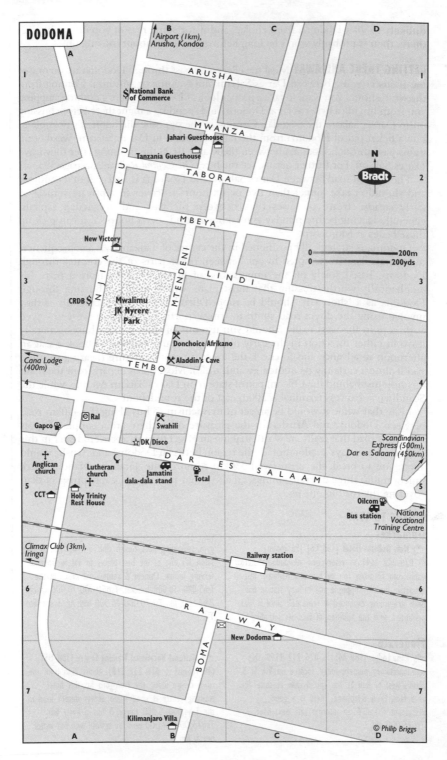

DODOMA

Airport (1km),
Arusha, Kondoa

ARUSHA

National Bank
of Commerce

MWANZA

Jahari Guesthouse
Tanzania Guesthouse

TABORA

N
Bradt

MBEYA

New Victory

0   200m
0   200yds

LINDI

CRDB
Mwalimu
JK Nyrere
Park

MTENDENI

Donchoice Afrikano

Cana Lodge
(400m)

Aladdin's Cave

TEMBO

Ral
Gapco

Swahili

DK Disco

DAR ES SALAAM

Scandinavian
Express (500m),
Dar es Salaam (450km)

Anglican
church

Lutheran
church

Jamatini
dala-dala stand

Total

Oilcom

CCT

Holy Trinity
Rest House

Bus station
National
Vocational
Training Centre

Climax Club (3km),
Iringa

Railway station

RAILWAY

New Dodoma

BOMA

Kilimanjaro Villa

© Philip Briggs

Budget

🏠 **Holy Trinity Rest House** [388 A5] (5 rooms)
📞 026 232 1190. Run by the Lutheran Church, this homely B&B, opposite the CCT Hostel, has clean no-frills en-suite rooms with net & fan. Meals can be arranged. *Tsh12,000 dbl.*

🏠 **Christian Council of Tanzania (CCT) Hostel**
[388 A5] 📞 026 232 1682. This long-serving hostel, 300m from the railway station next to the domed Anglican church, is probably the best budget option in the town centre. Food is available, but alcoholic drinks are banned. *Tsh7,000 dbl with common shower, Tsh8,000/12,000/14,000 en-suite sgl/dbl/trpl.*

THE CENTRAL RAILWAY

Between 1905 and 1914, Germany constructed a 1,238km railway line from Dar es Salaam to Kigoma, following a centuries-old caravan route through Dodoma and Tabora to Ujiji. A century later, the so-called Central Railway remains the best way for budget-conscious travellers to get between the coast and the west of Tanzania, cheaper than flying and more comfortable than bussing. There are two main lines from Dar es Salaam, one running to Mwanza and the other to Kigoma. Trains to both Mwanza and Kigoma stop at Morogoro and Dodoma, but the service splits at Tabora. A branch line running from Tabora to Mpanda is run as a separate service.

Passenger trains run twice weekly in either direction. Westbound trains leave Dar es Salaam at 17.00 on Tuesday and Friday, while trains out of Kigoma and Mwanza leave at 16.00 on Thursday and Sunday, usually. The trip is scheduled to take 40 hours, but frequent delays mean it's not unusual to pitch up ten hours late. On the Mpanda sideline, trains leave from Tabora at 21.00 on Monday and Friday and from Mpanda at 13.00 on Tuesday and Saturday, and the trip might last 10–15 hours. There are three classes. First class consists of two-berth compartments and second class consists of six-berth compartments, which may not be shared by men and women unless the compartment is booked as a whole. Each theoretically has a light, fan and running water, but it's rare that all three are operating. Third class consists of seated carriages with more passengers than seats, and is only worth thinking about if you value neither your comfort nor your possessions.

One-way tickets between Dar es Salaam and Kigoma or Mwanza cost around US$45/35/25 for first/second/third class. Tickets between Mpanda and Tabora cost US$16/11/6 for first/second/third class. Tickets on the main central line can only be booked in advance at Dar es Salaam, Kigoma, Tabora and Mwanza, and it's generally advisable to book as far in advance as possible (though odds of getting a ticket on the day aren't bad). Dining cars serve reasonably priced meat, fish and chicken meals, with beers and sodas also available, though not on the service to Mpanda. In addition, at most large and many small stations, vendors sell snacks, meals, sodas and bottled water. Theft from train windows is a regular problem, so close the windows securely at night (a block of wood is provided for this purpose) and don't leave loose objects lying around the compartment.

Historical the central line may be, but whether it would rank among the world's greatest rail journeys is debatable. Scenically, the trip is less than spectacular, with the stretch between Dodoma and Tabora passing through what is perhaps the most barren and monotonous part of Tanzania, a seemingly endless plain of baked red sand and sparse *brachystegia* woodland. The scenery is lusher closer to Kigoma, with patches of indigenous forest, swamp and dense *miombo* woodland along the line, while the stretch on the approach to Mwanza on Lake Victoria is memorable for the strange granite formations that break the monotony.

Shoestring There are at least ten basic resthouses clustered around the market and bus station. It's difficult to make any specific recommendations – for starters, half of them are likely to be full on any given day – but you should have no problem finding a room for around Tsh6,000. Most places have nets and common showers, so pass over a room that doesn't.

✖ WHERE TO EAT The **Ndigwa Restaurant** at the **New Dodoma Hotel** [388 C6] serves decent Indian and continental cuisine, while the same hotel's **China Garden** is one of the best Chinese restaurants in Tanzania, with dishes in the Tsh5,000–10,000 range. Closer into the centre, the long-standing **Swahili Restaurant** [388 B4] serves good local and Arabic food from around Tsh1,500.

Behind the Mwalimu JK Nyerere Park, **Aladdin's Cave** [388 B4] is a great spot for ice cream, yoghurt, juices and inexpensive snacks. Located nearby, **Donchoice Afrikano Restaurant** [388 B4] serves good and filling local dishes such as fried chicken, chips and *ugali* for around Tsh2,000–4,000. The **Climax Club** [388 A6], 2km west of the city centre, is a good place to meet expatriates, down a cold beer, eat, or swim in the pool. The indomitable **DK Disco** [388 B5], housed in a one-time cinema on Dar es Salaam Avenue, hosts regular discos and the odd live music show.

OTHER PRACTICALITIES

Foreign exchange The central National Bank of Commerce on Kuu Street [388 B1] has the best rates. Local currency can be drawn, against Visa cards only, at the ATM outside here, or at the CRDB Bank [388 A3].

Internet There are internet cafés at the New Dodoma Hotel [388 C6] and Cana Lodge [388 A4]. Less expensive and more central is RAL Internet [388 A4] (⊕ *08.00–20.00 daily; Tsh1,000/hr*), north of the main roundabout.

Swimming The Climax Club [388 A6] charges Tsh3,000 to use its small pool, while the New Dodoma [388 C6] charges Tsh3,500.

KONDOA

Kondoa, the principal town of the Irangi people, lies on the north bank of the small but perennial Kondoa River, roughly 160km north of Dodoma and some 4km west of the so-called Great North Road to Arusha. Comprised of a dust-blown grid of roads lined with low-rise shops and houses, Kondoa exudes something of a Wild West character, and it's a more than adequate place to break up the journey north from Dodoma. Nevertheless, a decided deficit of distinguishing features means that Kondoa would scarcely warrant a mention in a travel guide, were it not the most convenient base from which to explore the Kondoa rock art sites, covered later in this chapter. A recommended guide based in Kondoa is Moshi Changai (❧ *0784 948858;* e *moshi@tanzaniaculturaltours.com; www.tanzaniaculturaltours.com*).

GETTING THERE AND AWAY The 160km road south to Dodoma is in poor condition and occasionally becomes impassable after heavy rain. The trip will take the best part of four hours in a private vehicle, longer by bus. The 280km road north to Arusha is similar as far as the Tarangire National Park junction, from where the last 110km is surfaced and in good condition. In a private vehicle, the drive from Arusha should take up to six hours, but direct buses can take 12 hours, so it's advisable to break up the trip with a night at Babati or similar.

WHERE TO STAY AND EAT The **New Planet Hotel** (✆ *026 236 1957*), with the best restaurant in town, and **Sunset Beach Hotel** (m *0784 948858*) both charge around Tsh10,000–12,000 for a no-frills en-suite room with net, fan and running water. Cheaper options include the **Savannah Inn Guesthouse** and **New Splendid Guesthouse.** The **Just Imagine Bar** is a green outdoor drinking hole right opposite the New Splendid Guesthouse.

KONDOA ROCK ART SITES

Inscribed as a UNESCO World Heritage Site in 2006, the prehistoric rock art that adorns the Maasai Escarpment north of Kondoa is the most intriguing outdoor gallery of its sort in East Africa, and among the most ancient and stylistically varied anywhere on the continent. Although it extends over an area of 2,350km², the best-known panels are centred around Kolo, about 20km north of Kondoa and 50km south of Babati on the Great North Road. Kolo sits at the centre of an area once earmarked to become the Maasai Escarpment Rock Art Reserve (the first in East Africa to be dedicated to prehistoric art), but sadly this plan appears to be on permanent hold.

The rock art around Kolo and Kondoa is the most prolific in equatorial Africa. This is partly due to the lay of the land. Like the equally rich uKhahlamba-Drakensberg region in South Africa, Kondoa is endowed with numerous granite outcrops tailor-made for painting. The major rock art panels here are generally sited within small caves or beneath overhangs aligned to an east–west axis, a propensity that might reflect the preferences of the artists, or might have provided the most favourable conditions for preservation against the elements. The age of the paintings is tentatively placed at between 200 and 4,000 years, but their intent is a matter of speculation (see box, *But what does it mean?*, pages 398–9).

The pigments for the paintings were made with leaf extracts (yellow and green), powdered ochre and manganese (red and black), and possibly bird excrement (white), and were bound together by animal fat. Subjects and styles vary greatly. The most widely depicted animals are giraffe (26%) and eland (14%), which may have held mystical significance to the artists, or might simply have been their favoured prey. A large number of panels also contain human figures, generally highly stylised and often apparently engaged in ritual dances or ceremonies. At some sites, particularly those of the relatively recent and unformed 'late white' style, readily identifiable subjects are vastly outnumbered by abstract or geometric figures, the significance of which can only be guessed at. A common feature of the more elaborate panels is the jumbled superimposition of images, which is now widely thought to be a deliberate ploy to associate two or more significant images with each other.

The proposal to enshrine the Kondoa rock art as a UNESCO World Heritage Site stated that 'in terms of conservation, most of the sites are stable and relatively well preserved although there are a variety of problems including salt encrustation, erosion, water damage, and fading caused by sunlight'. Exposure to the elements notwithstanding, the rock art has been left undisturbed by locals in the past because it is regarded as sacred or taboo. In 1931, a government employee, AT Culwick, documented an example of one such taboo, so deeply ingrained that its source had evidently been forgotten. When Culwick needed to climb Ilongero Hill near Singida on official business, the chief of the village at the base warned him off, saying that the hill was inhabited by a demon. Culwick eventually persuaded the reluctant chief and entourage to accompany him on the ascent, where he discovered a large shelter covered with ancient rock art. The fear displayed by the villagers before climbing, combined with their startled reaction to the rock panel, left Culwick in no doubt that they had genuinely never suspected the existence of the paintings.

13

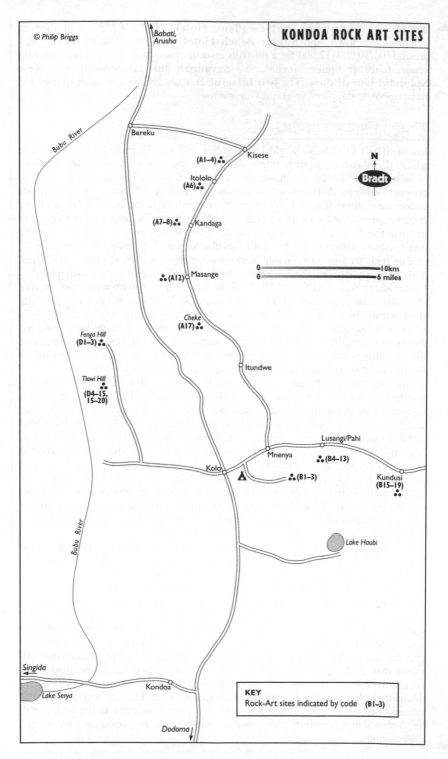

© Philip Briggs

Babati,
Arusha

KONDOA ROCK ART SITES

N

Bradt

Bubu River

Bereku

Kisese

(A1–4) ⦂

Itololo
(A6) ⦂

(A7–8) ⦂ Kandaga

⦂ (A12) Masange

0 ━━━━━━━━━━ 10km
0 ━━━━━━━━━━ 6 miles

Cheke
(A17) ⦂

Fenga Hill
(D1–3) ⦂

Itundwe

Tlawi Hill
(D4–15,
15–20) ⦂

Lusangi/Pahi

Mnenya   ⦂ (B4–13)

Kolo

⦂ (B1–3)   Kundusi
(B15–19)
⦂

Bubu River

Lake Haubi

Singida

Kondoa

Lake Serya

KEY
Rock-Art sites indicated by code   (B1–3)

Dodoma

The erosion of traditional beliefs in recent years places the art at greater threat of local interference. A few sites already have been partially defaced by graffiti or scratching. Tourist volumes may be low, but unofficial guides have been recorded splashing the paintings with water to bring out the colours for snap-happy visitors, and many tourists photograph the paintings using a flash, which can cause great damage to sensitive organic pigments over repeated exposure. More bizarrely, a local legend that the Germans buried a hoard of gold near one of the rock art sites during World War I has resulted in fortune-seekers manually excavating and dynamiting close to several rock sites. Under such circumstances, the formal inscription of the rock art as a UNESCO World Heritage Site is welcome indeed.

GETTING THERE AND AWAY It is forbidden to explore the rock art within the proposed reserve without an official guide, and even if this were not the case, most of the sites would be difficult to locate independently. For this reason, all prospective visitors must first report to the Department of Antiquities office on the main junction in Kolo, where they pay the entrance fee of US$2 and collect a guide. Kolo lies about 20km north of Kondoa and 50km south of Babati on the Great North Road, and any public transport heading between these two towns can drop you alongside the Department of Antiquities office.

Further details on reaching the individual sites are provided under the heading *Major rock art sites* below, but it is worth noting that, while distances between various sites are relatively short, the roads are very rough (4x4 only) and visiting most sites will entail some walking, often on steep slopes. For this reason, even motorised travellers will find it unrealistic to visit more than one cluster of sites in the space of one morning or afternoon, and a full three days would be required to explore the lot.

Travellers without private transport will find exploring the area more tricky. It is possible to undertake the round trip from Kolo to the famous Mungomi wa Kolo site on foot, but this would take the best part of a day, and you'd be expected to pay the guide a reasonable fee for walking out, which way exceeds the bounds of duty.

BACKGROUND TO THE ROCK ART OF KONDOA DISTRICT

Outside attention was first drawn to the rock art of Kondoa District in the 1920s, though it would be several decades before the full extent of its riches was grasped. In 1923, District Commissioner Bagshawe visited and described the two main shelters at Mungomi wa Kolo, and six years later several of the sites on and around Twali Hill were visited by Dr T Nash, who went on to describe them in the *Journal of the Royal Anthropological Institute* of 1929. In 1935, the eminent archaeologists Louis and Mary Leakey explored a handful of new sites, notably Cheke III, on which was based Louis Leakey's formative attempt at stylistic categorisation and relative chronology, published in his 1936 book, *Stone Age Africa*.

By the late 1940s, enthusiasts and archaeologists had located 75 sites in the Kondoa region, and their discoveries led to the publication in 1950 of a unique special edition of *Tanganyika Notes and Records* dedicated solely to the rock art. The first intensive survey of the region was undertaken in 1951 by Mary Leakey, who boosted the tally of known panels for A sector alone from 17 panels to 186, of which one-third were sufficiently well preserved to be studied. Leakey traced and redrew 1,600 figures and scenes, an undertaking that formed the basis of her 1983 book, *Africa's Vanishing Art: The Rock Paintings of Tanzania*. Leakey said of her time in the Kondoa region that: 'No amounts of stone and bone could yield the kinds of information that the paintings gave so freely... here were scenes of life, of men and women hunting, dancing, singing and playing music'.

There is a strangely eerie sensation attached to emerging from a remote and nondescript tract of bush to be confronted by an isolated panel of primitive paintings executed by an artist or artists unknown, hundreds or maybe thousands of years before the time of Christ. Faded as many of the panels are, and lacking the perspective to which modern eyes are accustomed, one can still hardly fail to be impressed by the fine detail of many of the animal portraits, or to wonder at the surrealistic distortion of form that characterises the human figures. And, almost invariably, first exposure to these charismatic works of ancient art prompts three questions: how old are they, who were the artists, and what was their intent?

When, who and why? The simple answers are that nobody really knows. The broadest time frame, induced from the absence of any representations of extinct species in the rock galleries of Kondoa, places the paintings at less than 20,000 years old. The absence of a plausible tradition of attribution among the existing inhabitants of the area – a Gogo claim that the paintings were the work of the Portuguese can safely be discounted – makes it unlikely that even the most modern paintings are less than 200 years old. Furthermore, experts have noted a clear progression from the simplest early styles to more complex, expressive works of art, and a subsequent regression to the clumsy graffiti-like finger painting of the 'late white' phase, indicating that the paintings were created over a substantial period of time.

Early attempts at dating the Kondoa rock art concentrated on categorising it chronologically based on the sequence of superimposition of different styles on busy panels. The results were inconclusive, even contradictory, probably because the superimposition of images was an integral part of the art, so that a foreground image might be roughly contemporaneous with an image underneath it. It is also difficult to know the extent to which regional style, or even individual style, might be of greater significance than chronological variation. The most useful clue to the age of the paintings is the stratified organic debris deposited alongside red ochre 'pencils' at several sites. Carbon dating of a handful of sites where such deposits have been found suggests that the artists were most active about 3,000 years ago, though many individual paintings are undoubtedly much older. The crude 'late white' paintings, on the other hand, are widely agreed to be hundreds rather than thousands of years old, and there is evidence to suggest that some underwent ritual restoration by local people who held them sacred into historical times.

The identity of the artists is another imponderable. In the first half of the 20th century, the rock art of southern Africa was solely attributed to 'bushmen' hunter-gatherers, a people whose click-based Khoisan tongue is unrelated to Bantu and who are of vastly different ethnic stock to any Bantu speakers. True, the bushmen are the only people who practised the craft in historical times, but much of the rock art of southern Africa (like that of eastern Africa) dates back thousands of years. Coincidentally, two of East Africa's few remaining click-tongued hunter-gatherers, the Sandawe and the Hadza, both live in close proximity to the main concentration of Tanzanian rock art, but neither has a tradition relating to the paintings.

Given that the archaeological record indicates east-southern Africa was populated entirely by hunter-gatherers when the paintings were probably executed, furthermore that a succession of human migrations have subsequently passed through the region, postulating an

More accessible are Lusangi and Pahi, which are connected to Kolo by a few *dala-dalas* daily passing through Mnenya (Pahi also has a guesthouse). A few *dala-dalas* run daily between Kolo and Kisese via Mnenya. In both cases, however, you'd still need to cover the costs of a guide, and offer him a fair fee for his efforts. Another option would be to hire a vehicle for the day in Kondoa – since the distances ancestral link between the artists of Kondoa and modern hunter-gatherers would be tenuous in the extreme. If anything, the probable chronology of the rock art points in the opposite direction. Assuming that creative activity peaked some 3,000 years ago, it preceded the single most important known migration into East Africa, the mass invasion of the Bantu-speakers who today comprise the vast majority of Tanzania's population. Most probable, then, that a Bantu- or perhaps Nilotic-speaking group, or another group forced to migrate locally as a ripple effect of the Bantu invasion, moved into the Kondoa region and conquered or assimilated the culture responsible for the rock art, resulting in the gradual stylistic regression noted by archaeologists. All that can be said about the artists with reasonable certainty is they were hunter gatherers whose culture would have vanished without trace, were it not for the painted testament left behind on the granite faces of Kondoa.

The most haunting of the questions surrounding the rock art of Kondoa is the intent of their creators. In determining the answer to this, one obstacle is that nobody knows just how representative the surviving legacy might be. Most extant rock art in Kondoa is located in caves or overhangs, but the small number of faded paintings that survive on more open sites must be a random subset of similarly exposed panels that have been wiped clean by the elements. We have no record, either, of whether the artists dabbled on canvases less durable than rock, but unless one assumes that posterity was a conscious goal, it seems wholly presumptuous to think otherwise. The long and short of it, then, is that the extant galleries might indeed represent a sufficiently complete record to form a reliable basis for any hypothesis, but they might just as easily represent a fraction of a percentage of the art executed at the time. Furthermore, there is no way of telling whether rocks were only painted in specific circumstances – it is conceivable that the rock art would maker greater sense viewed in conjunction with other types of painting that have not survived.

Two broad schools of thought surround the interpretation of Africa's ancient rock art. The first has it that the paintings were essentially recreational, documentary and/or expressive in intent – art for art's sake if you like – while the second regards them to be mystical works of ritual significance. It is quite possible that the truth of the matter lies between these poles of opinion. A striking feature of the rock art of Kondoa is the almost uniform discrepancy in the styles used to depict human and non-human subjects. Animals are sometimes painted in stencil form, sometimes filled with bold white or red paint, but – allowing for varying degrees of artistic competence – the presentation is always naturalistic. The people, by contrast, are almost invariably heavily stylised in form, with elongated stick-like bodies and disproportionately round heads topped by a forest of unkempt hair. Some such paintings are so downright bizarre that they might more reasonably be described as humanoid than human (a phenomenon that has not gone unnoticed by UFO theorists searching for prehistoric evidence of extraterrestrial visits).

The discrepancy between the naturalistic style favoured for animals and highly stylised presentation of humans has attracted numerous theoretical explanations. Most crumble under detailed examination of the evidence, but all incline towards supporting the mystical or ritualistic school of interpretation. Ultimately, however, for every tentative answer we can provide, these enigmatic ancient works pose a dozen more questions. It is an integral part of their charisma that we can speculate to our heart's content, but will never know the whole truth!

involved would be relatively short, no more than 100km in all, this shouldn't be too costly.

Although few people do so, it is perfectly feasible to tag a trip to the proposed reserve on to a standard northern circuit safari. Some safari companies will visit the rock art sites as a day trip from Tarangire National Park, a slightly pressured but by no means impossible foray. Equally, you could spend a night in the region, either camping at the Department of Antiquities site outside Kolo or sleeping in one of Kondoa's guesthouses. The advantage of a day trip for travellers for whom comfort is a high priority is that it will allow you to make use of one of the commodious lodges in Tarangire rather than roughing it at Kolo or Kondoa. For more adventurous or budget-conscious travellers, a night in the area will save on wasted national park entrance fees as well as allowing you to see a greater variety of sites.

WHERE TO STAY Accommodation options in the immediate vicinity of Kolo are somewhat restricted, for which reason travellers using private transport are advised to overnight in Kondoa, which boasts a fair selection of budget lodgings (see *Kondoa* above). Otherwise, the Department of Antiquities in Kolo runs an attractive campsite on the banks of the seasonal Kolo River about 3km east of town, along the road towards Mungomi wa Kolo site and Mnenya. Water and toilet facilities are available at the campsite, which costs US$2 per person, but food and other drinks must be brought from Kolo. There is no accommodation in Kolo, but basic local guesthouses can be found in Pahi and Masange, both of which lie below the Maasai Escarpment within walking distance of several good sites.

MAJOR ROCK ART SITES

Mungomi wa Kolo Most visitors with limited time are taken to the region's recognised showpiece, a cluster of ten sites scattered across the craggy upper slopes of Ichoi Hill about 10km from Kolo by road. Prosaically labelled B1–3, more evocatively known as Mungomi wa Kolo (The Dancers of Kolo), the three finest panels here provide a good overview of the region's rock art, and – aside from the last, very steep, foot ascent to the actual panels – it is easily reached in a 4x4 vehicle. To get there from Kolo, you need to follow the Mnenya road west for about 4km, crossing the normally dry Kolo River on the way, before turning right on to a rough 4x4 track that reaches the base of the hill after about 6km.

Probably the most intriguing of the panels is B2, which lies in a tall overhang right at the top of the hill. This panel includes more than 150 figures, including several fine, but very faded, paintings of animals (giraffe, leopard, zebra and rhino), as well as some abstract designs and numerous humanoid forms. Richard Leakey regarded this site as representing a particularly wide variety of superimposed styles and periods, and it must surely have been worked over hundreds if not thousands of years. One striking scene, which Mary Leakey dubbed 'The Abduction', depicts five rather ant-like humanoid forms with stick bodies, spindly limbs and distended heads. The two figures on the right have elongated heads, while the two on the left have round heads, as does the central figure, which also appears to have breasts and whose arms are being held by the flanking figures. Leakey interpreted the painting as a depiction of an attempted abduction, with the central female figure being tugged at by two masked people on the right, while friends or family try to hold on to her from the left. Of course, a scene such as this is open to numerous interpretations, and it could as easily depict a ritual dance as an abduction. And why stop there? I recently stumbled across a web page that makes an oddly compelling case for this haunting scene, and other paintings in Kondoa, providing evidence of extraterrestrial visits to Kondoa region in the distant past. If this sort of speculation tickles you, the long-snouted figures to the right, according to this interpretation, are alien abductors, while a separate scene to the right shows another alien standing in a hot air balloon!

Panel B1, also in an overhang, is even larger and more elaborate, though most of the paintings have been partially obliterated by termite activity. Prominent among several animal portraits are those of elephants and various antelope. The most striking scene consists of three reposed humanoid figures with what appear to be wild, frizzy hairstyles (some form of headdress?) and hands clutching a vertical bar. A small cave in front of the panel is used for ceremonial purposes by local rainmakers, and sacrifices are still sometimes left outside the shelter. Finally, near the base of the mountain, the most accessible of the three main panels, B3 depicts the animated humanoids that gave rise to the local name, along with a few faded animal figures, including a cheetah and buffalo.

Pahi–Lusangi and Kinyasi Panels B4–13 all lie close to the base of the escarpment near the twin villages of Lusangi and Pahi about 12km from Kolo. To reach them from Kolo, follow the same road you would to get to Mungomi wa Kolo, but instead of turning right after crossing the river, keep straight on the main road, passing through Mnenya, until you reach Lusangi. This site is normally accessible in any vehicle, though 4x4 may be useful after rain. Lusangi can be reached by *dala-dala* from Kolo, and there is a guesthouse about 1km away in Pahi. A 1km piste leads from the main road to the base of the escarpment, from where a flat 100m footpath leads to three shelters about 20m apart.

The art at Lusangi is not as impressive as that at Mungomi wa Kolo, but it is probably a more suitable goal for those unwilling or unable to climb steep footpaths. Several figures do stand out, however, the most notable being a 70cm high outlined giraffe superimposed on a very old painting of a rhino. Below this, a red and yellow figure of an eland-like antelope with a disproportionately small head is regarded by archaeologists as one of the very oldest paintings known in Kondoa region. Only a couple of clear humanoid figures are found across these sites, and several of the panels are dominated by bold, childlike patterns in the 'late white' style, often superimposed over older and more finely executed portraits. From Pahi it is possible to drive another 12km to Kinyasi, where sites B14–19 are situated in a valley below the 1,000m high Kome Mountain. The most interesting of these sites is a 1m² panel of small, finely executed antelopes, which also includes one of the few known examples of a painting depicting a homestead.

Mnenya to Kisese Sites A1–18 all lie along the stretch of the Maasai Escarpment that runs immediately east of the reasonable dirt road connecting Mnenya to Kisese. This road itself runs roughly parallel to and about10km east of the Great North Road, and is connected to it by a roughly 8km road between Kolo and Mnenya in the south and a roughly 15km road between Bereko and Kisese in the north. In theory, travellers driving southwards from Babati or Arusha along the Great North Road would ideally explore sites A1–18 by turning on to the Kisese road at Bereko, then following the Mnenya road south and returning to the Great North Road at Kolo. Unfortunately, however, it is mandatory to pass through Kolo first to pay fees and collect a guide, which will enforce quite a bit of backtracking for southbound travellers (but makes no real difference to travellers driving north from Kondoa). There isn't much public transport on the Mnenya–Kisese road, but a few *dala-dalas* run along it daily, and there is basic accommodation in Masange.

Running northwards from Mnenya, the direction in which regulations practically enforce one to travel, the first major site is A17 or Cheke III, which lies about 5km along the Kisese road. This extensive, intricate panel contains at least 330 figures and is rich in superimposition, and studded with various animals as well as surreal humanoids with circular heads and pincer legs and a couple of unusually robust human figures seemingly draped in robes. The shelter is dominated by the so-called Dance of the Elephant, a red painting of a solitary elephant surrounded by perhaps a dozen people – who might as easily be

13

worshipping or hunting the elephant as dancing around it. Getting to Cheke III involves following a 2km motorable track west of the main road, followed by a short but steep ascent to the actual panel.

About 5km further along the road, you arrive at Masange village, from where a roughly 1km-long side road leads to the base of the escarpment, and another 5–10 minutes' climb brings you to sites A12–14. The most compelling panel in this cluster is A13, another elaborately decorated overhang with numerous superimposed paintings, but A14 is of interest for its solitary painting of ten faded human figures in a row. Most of the sites between Masange and Kisese lie some distance from the main road, but site A9 or Kandaga III, 6km past Masange, consisting of a series of geometric representations in the 'late white' style first described in 1931 by Julian Huxley, is particularly recommended to serious enthusiasts. The excellent and well preserved site dubbed Kisese II or A4 lies another 8km past Kandaga on a tall rock no more than ten minutes' walk from the road.

Bubu River Sites Unlike the other rock art sites within the proposed reserve, this cluster lies to the west of the Great North Road, overlooking the Bubu River about 12km from Kolo. Short of walking there and back from Kolo, this is the one cluster that cannot easily be reached without private transport, ideally a 4x4. It is, nevertheless, perhaps the best cluster of them all, with several panels in close proximity and in a particularly good state of preservation.

Of the three panels D1–3 situated on Fenga Hill, the most worthwhile is D3, sometimes referred to as the Trapped Elephants. Covered in a jumble of superimposed red features, including several slim humanoid figures with distended heads and headdresses, this panel is named for the central painting of

KAHEMBE TREKKING

Based in Babati, this highly commendable set-up (m *0784 397477; e kahembeculture@yahoo.com; www.kahembeculturalsafaris.com*) started life in the mid 1990s as a private ecotourism concern and is now an official cultural tourist project catering to the significant proportion of travellers who want to see more of Tanzania than the 'Big Five' and beaches. It remains under the management of founder Jaos Kahembe, an excellent contact for those who want to explore a little-known part of Tanzania in an organised manner, but without paying through the nose.

Kahembe arranges a variety of local tours, including three-day and two-day Hanang climbs out of Babati, respectively using the Gendabi and Jorodom routes (fixed departures Tuesday, Wednesday and Friday). Other local trips range from a three-day Barabaig walking safari to seven- or eight-day walking itineraries visiting local *bomas* and the game-rich verges of Lake Manyara and Tarangire national parks. A two-week 'African rural life adventure' includes overnight stays with a number of different ethnic groups, an ascent of Mount Hanang, and game walks around lakes Burungi and Manyara. Day trips on Lake Babati and to local villages are also arranged, and special interests can be catered for with advance notice.

These overnight trips are not luxurious by any standard, but they are well organised and informative, and offer interested travellers an unforgettable glimpse into an ancient way of life that has vanished in most other parts of Africa. They are also reasonably priced, at less than US$100 per person per day inclusive of local transport, accommodation and meals in local guesthouses or villages, and local guide and village fees. It is not mandatory to book ahead, but it's advisable for those operating to a tight time frame.

two elephants surrounded by a stencilled oblong line. Some experts believe that this depicts an elephant trap, a theory supported by three fronds below the elephants that might well represent branches used to camouflage a pit. Others believe that it might have a more mystical purpose, placing the elephants in a kind of magic circle. A trickle of circles dripping from the left base of the picture could be blood, or the elephants' spoor.

About 3km south of Fenga Hill, the immediate vicinity around Twali Hill hosts at least ten panels, numbered D4–5 and D15–22. A dedicated enthusiast could easily devote half a day to this cluster of very different sites. Panel D19 is notable for an almost life-size and unusually naturalistic attempt to paint a human figure in a crouched or seated position, and it also contains some finely executed paintings of animals, including a buffalo head and a giraffe leaning forward. Directly opposite this panel, site D20 depicts several seated human figures, while 500m further away site D22 is also known as the Red Lion for the striking painting of a lion, with a stencilled black outline and red fill, that dominates the shelter.

Five minutes' walk along the same ridge towards the Bubu River brings you to a pair of shelters called D17 or The Hunter, for a rare action painting of a hunter killing a large antelope – presumably an eland – with his bow and arrow. Several other interesting human figures are found on these twin shelters. Another 10–20 minutes' walk downhill towards the river stand two large rock faces, D4 and D5, respectively known as The Rhino and The Prancing Giraffe. The former is named for the 60cm-long portrait of a rhino, with rather narrow head, and it also depicts what appears to be a herd of antelope fleeing from human pursuers. The nominated painting at site D5 is a strikingly lifelike depiction of a giraffe with its front legs raised as if cantering or rearing, but no less interesting is a tall pair of very detailed, shaggy-headed human figures sometimes referred to as The Dancers.

BABATI

Set below the forested 2,415m peak of Mount Karwaa, this small but bustling market town straddles the Great North Road near the junction with the road west to Katesh and Singida, some 70km north of Kondoa. It's a useful place to break up long bus journeys, and the best springboard for travel west to Hanang. Further justification for stopping over in Babati, the eponymous lake on its outskirts, is easily reached by walking along the Kondoa road for about ten minutes. The papyrus-fringed stretch of shore alongside the road supports a good selection of waterbirds – egrets, waders and storks – while flotillas of pelican sail pompously across the open water. Several pods of hippo are resident, and it's easy enough to negotiate with a local fisherman to take you out in search of them. Kahembe's Trekking & Cultural Tours, based in Babati, is a useful contact for arranging local excursions and Hanang climbs (see box, opposite).

GETTING THERE AND AWAY Babati lies 172km south of Arusha. The road is surfaced for the first 110km out of Arusha, after which it deteriorates rather abruptly, but it shouldn't take longer than three hours to cover the full distance in a private vehicle. Buses in either direction between Arusha and Babati leave throughout the day, starting at 07.30 and taking three to four hours. There are also several buses daily to Katesh and Singida in the west, as well as to Kondoa via Kolo in the south. The driving distance from Babati to Kondoa in a private vehicle is about 90 minutes (an hour to Kolo). The drive to Katesh is similar in duration.

WHERE TO STAY
Moderate
🏠 **Royal Beach Hotel** m 0784 395814;
e meshakingomuo@yahoo.com. Boasting an idyllic situation on a small peninsula that juts out into Lake Babati, this newly opened hotel is the most upmarket option in the Central Rift Valley. It forms an ideal base for visiting the Kondoa Rock Art, trekking Mount Hanang or cruising Lake Babati, activities that can all be arranged through the enthusiastic management. Accommodation is in comfortable concrete buildings with large beds, net, TV & en-suite toilet & shower. The restaurant is good & has lots of outdoor seating overlooking Lake Babati. *Tsh 30,000 dbl.*

Budget
🏠 **Kahembe's Guesthouse** (8 rooms) m 0784 397477; e kahembeculture@yahoo.com; www.kahembeculturalsafaris.com. This pleasant guesthouse is less than 500m from the bus station, next door to the office of the affiliated Kahembe Trekking (see box page 402). It has recently been upgraded to offer good quality en-suite accommodation, & a restaurant serving continental dishes is attached. *US$12/20 sgl/dbl.*

Shoestring
🏠 **Motel Paapaa** \ 027 253 1111. This decent if slightly run-down hotel is about the smartest in town, & conveniently situated next to the bus stop. The restaurant serves large portions of reasonable food. *En-suite dbls with cold running water US$4; rooms with common shower US$2.50.*

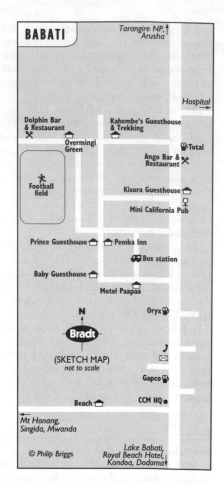

BABATI (SKETCH MAP) not to scale
© Philip Briggs

✗ WHERE TO EAT Aside from the good restaurant at the **Motel Paapaa**, the **Dolphin** and **Ango** restaurants are decent and affordable local eateries, the latter with a pleasant outdoor sitting area.

MOUNT HANANG AND KATESH

Mount Hanang is Tanzania's fourth-highest mountain after Kilimanjaro, Meru and Lolomalasin in the Crater Highlands. Volcanic in origin, it is a product of the same geological process that sculpted the Rift Valley, and it is the only one of these mountains to actually stand within the rift. The dormant caldera towers to an elevation of 3,418m above the low-lying plains, and is visible from hundreds of kilometres away on a clear day. Not surprisingly, this imposing free-standing mountain is revered by the Barabaig who inhabit its lower slopes, and it features prominently in their myths. Hanang supports its own distinct microclimate and forms an important local watershed. Most of the rain falls on the northern and eastern slopes, where extensive forests still support elusive populations of bushbuck, duiker and various monkeys, as well as a wide range of forest birds.

Seldom visited by tourists, Hanang lies outside the national park system and forms a very affordable alternative montane hike to Kilimanjaro or Meru. The slopes support the usual range of montane forest and grassland habitats, and offer excellent views over a stretch of the Rift Valley studded with smaller volcanic cones and shallow lakes. The normal springboard for climbing Hanang is Katesh, which lies at its southern base 75km west of Babati. Further details of routes and costs are provided under the heading *Climbing Mount Hanang*, but travellers broadly have two options: placing themselves in the experienced hands of the cultural tourism programme in Babati, or making their own arrangements out of Katesh.

The attractions of the Hanang area are not restricted to the mountain. On the contrary, the primal scenery of the surrounding plains is enhanced by the colourful presence of traditional pastoralists such as the Barabaig, people who have consciously retained their traditional way of life. Several substantial lakes also lie in the vicinity of Katesh, including the shallow and highly saline Lake Balangida, which is set at the base of the Rift Valley scarp immediately north of Mount Hanang. Finally, Katesh forms the starting point for an obscure but not unrewarding back route to Karatu and the Ngorongoro Crater Highlands via Basotu, Dongobesh and Mbulu. All these options are detailed on our website, http://bradttanzania.wordpress.com.

GETTING THERE AND AWAY Katesh lies 250km from Arusha and 75km west of Babati. In a private vehicle, the drive from Arusha – surfaced for the first 110km – will take less than five hours, and the drive from Babati about 90 minutes. For those travellers dependent on public transport, buses run between Babati and Singida via Katesh throughout the day, taking two to three hours in either direction between Babati and Katesh. Several buses travel between Arusha and Singida via Katesh; the thrice-daily service operated by Mtei Express Coaches is recommended, and takes about six hours.

WHERE TO STAY AND EAT The pick is the **Colt Guesthouse** (\ *027 253 0030*), which lies near the main market and charges around Tsh8,000 for a clean and spacious en-suite double with hot running water. Cheaper options include the **Hanang View Guesthouse** and nearby **Matunda Guesthouse**. All things being relative, the best place to eat is **Mama Kaborge's Restaurant**, a cramped but homely *hoteli* situated a couple of blocks from the Colt Guesthouse.

CLIMBING MOUNT HANANG Although several routes can be used to ascend Hanang, only two are recommended for first-time hikers. These are the Jorodom and Giting routes, which start from the villages of the same names, the former on the southern slopes of the mountain some 2km from Katesh and the latter on the eastern slopes about 10km out of town. The Jorodom Route – also sometimes referred to as the Katesh Route – is marginally the easier of the two, and the more accessible, making it a clear first choice for travellers making their own arrangements out of Katesh. The Giting Route ascends the side of the mountain that receives more rain, which means it is far more densely forested, but also that it is likely to be more slippery underfoot during the rainy season.

The most straightforward way of arranging a climb is through the cultural tourism programme in Babati, which charges a pretty reasonable US$40 per person per day for one or two people, or US$30 per person per day for a larger group. The obvious advantages of working through the cultural tourism programme are that they have plenty of experience on the mountain, will provide an English-speaking guide and food, and will make sure that you carry enough

The Barabaig are the most populous of a dozen closely related tribes, the Datoga or Tatoga. At around 100,000, the Datoga are one of Tanzania's smaller ethno-linguistic groupings, but their territory, centred on Mount Hanang, extends into large semi-arid tracts within Arusha, Dodoma and Singida.

Superficially similar to, and frequently confused with, their Maasai neighbours by outsiders, the Barabaig are dedicated cattle-herders, speaking a Nilotic tongue, who have steadfastly resisted external pressure to forsake their semi-nomadic pastoralist ways. Unlike the Maasai, however, the Barabaig are representatives of the earliest known Nilotic migration into East Africa from southwest Ethiopia. Their forebears probably settled in western Kenya during the middle of the first millennium AD, splitting into two groups. One, the Kalenjin, stayed put. The other, the proto-Datoga, migrated south of Lake Natron 500 to 1,000 years ago to the highlands of Ngorongoro and Mbulu, and the Rift Valley plains south towards Dodoma.

Datoga territory was greatest before 1600, thereafter being eroded by migrations of various Bantu-speaking peoples into northern and central Tanzania. The most significant incursion came in the early 19th century with the arrival of the Maasai. Oral traditions indicate that several fierce territorial battles were fought between the two pastoralist groups, resulting in the Maasai taking over the Crater Highlands and Serengeti Plains, and the Datoga retreating to their modern homeland near Mount Hanang. The Lerai Forest in Ngorongoro Crater is said to mark the grave of a Datoga leader who fell in battle in about 1840, and the site is still visited by Datoga elders from the Lake Eyasi area. The Maasai call the Barabaig the *Mangati* ('Feared Enemies'), and the Barabaig territory around Mount Hanang is sometimes referred to as the Mangati Plains.

The Barabaig used to move around the plains according to the feeding and watering requirements of their herds. They tend a variety of livestock, including goats, donkeys and chickens, but their culture and economy revolves around cattle, which are seen as a measure of wealth and prestige, and every part and product of the animal, including the dung, is ingested, or worn, or used in rituals. In recent years, agriculture has played an increasingly significant support role in the subsistence of the Barabaig, which together with increased population pressures has more or less put paid to the nomadic lifestyle.

Barabaig territory receives an average annual rainfall of less than 500mm, which means that water is often in short supply. Although the area is dotted with numerous lakes, most are brackish and unsuitable to drink. Barabaig women often walk miles every day to collect gourds of drinking water, much of which comes from boreholes dug with foreign aid. The cattle cannot drink from the lakes directly when water levels are low and salinity is high, but the Barabaig get around this by digging wells on the lakes' edges and allowing the water to filter through the soil. Even so, the herders won't let their cattle drink from these wells on successive days for fear that it will make them ill.

Barabaig social structure is not dissimilar to that of the Maasai, although it lacks the rigid division into hierarchical age-sets pivotal to Maasai and other East African pastoralist societies. The Barabaig do not recognise one centralised leader, but are divided into several hereditary clans, each answering to a chosen elder who sits on a tribal council. The central unit of society is the family homestead or *gheida*, dwelt in by one man, his

water and whatever else is necessary. For more details, see the box, *Kahembe Trekking*, page 402. You could cut at least 50% off the cost were you to arrange your own climb, but should bear in mind that this will involve arranging your own food and water, and working with guides and porters who may not speak a word of English between them.

wives and their unwed offspring. This homestead consists of a tall outer protective wall, built of thorny acacia branches and shaped like a figure eight, with one outer gate entered through a narrow passage. Within this wall stand several small rectangular houses – low, thick-roofed constructions of wooden poles plastered with mud – and the all-important cattle stockade. Different huts are reserved for young men, young women, wives and elders. A number of *gheida* may be grouped together to create an informal community, and decisions are made communally rather than by a chief.

Patrilineal polygamy is actively encouraged. Elders accumulate four or more wives, up to three of which might share one hut, but marriage within any given clan is regarded as incestuous. The concept of divorce is not recognised, but a woman may separate from her husband and return to her parent's home under some circumstances. The Barabaig openly regard extramarital sex to be normal, even desirable, although a great many taboos and conventions dictate just who may have intercourse with whom, and where they can perform the act. Traditionally, should a married woman bear a child whose biological father is other than her husband, the child remains the property of the husband – even when husband and wife are separated.

The appearance of the Barabaig is striking. The women wear heavy ochre-dyed goatskin or cowhide dresses, tasselled below the waist, and decorated with colourful yellow and orange beads. They adorn themselves with brass bracelets and neck-coils, and tattoo circular patterns around their eyes, and some practice facial scarification. Men are less ornate, with a dyed cotton cloth draped over the shoulders and another around the waist. Traditionally, young men would prove themselves by killing a person (other than a Datoga) or an elephant, lion or buffalo, which might be used as the base of a ceremonial headdress along with the pelts of other animals they had killed.

The Barabaig are monotheists who believe in a universal creator whom they call Aseeta. The sun – which they give the same name – is the all-seeing eye of Aseeta, who lives far away and has little involvement in their lives. Barabaig legend has it that they are descended from Aseeta's brother Salohog, whose eldest son Gumbandaing was the first true Datoga. Traditionally, most Barabaig elders can trace their lineage back over tens of generations to this founding father, and ancestral worship plays a greater role in their spiritual life than direct worship of God. Oddly, given the arid nature of their homeland, the Barabaig have a reputation as powerful rainmakers. It is said that only 1% of the Barabaig have abandoned their traditional beliefs in favour of exotic religions – a scenario which, judging by the number of internet sites devoted to the state of the Barabaig's souls, has spun quite a few evangelical types into a giddy froth.

The above statistic is indicative of the Barabaig's stubborn adherence to a traditional way of life. In the colonial era, the Barabaig refused to be co-opted into the migrant labour system, on the not unreasonable basis that they could sell one good bullock for more than the typical labourer would earn in a year. Other Tanzanians tend to view the Barabaig as embarrassingly primitive and ignorant – when the Nyerere government outlawed the wearing of traditional togas in favour of Westernised clothing, the Barabaig resolutely ignored them. Even today, few have much formal education nor speak a word of English – it would, for that matter, be pretty unusual to meet a Barabaig who could hold a sustained conversation in Swahili.

In theory, Hanang can be climbed as a full-day round trip out of Katesh, but this will reduce the hike to something of an endurance test, with little opportunity to enjoy the scenery. What's more, while a very fit hiker could complete the full ascent and descent in a tight 12 hours, less fit hikers may struggle to do it all within one day. It is therefore recommended that you overnight on the mountain: there

Brian Doench

The Barabaig are enthusiastic beekeepers, and their unique wine, *Gesuda*, is made from honey, together with a rare local root that is gathered on the upper slopes of Mount Hanang and said to lend the drink a medicinal property. *Gesuda* is fermented in huge gourds, the size of a half keg, and it takes a week to reach perfection, during which period entry to the room in which it is being made is restricted to the brewers. Reserved for special occasions, the drinking of *Gesuda* is governed by a complex and rigid set of rules and procedures. The wine is traditionally drunk from hollowed cow horns, and since the drinking rules revolve around age and rank, the most important people are served in the biggest horns. The man who supplied the honey for any given batch of *Gesuda* will monitor the drinking, and one needs his invitation – or to be a member of his family – to join a drinking party. A close friend or brother of the host will be designated the wine pourer, in charge of keeping the guests' horns filled, and of refusing to refill the horn of any man who is obnoxious or drinking irresponsibly. Any outsider who is offered the drink should regard it as a great honour

are several good places to pitch a tent, or you can sleep in the caves on the Giting Route (checking in advance that your guide knows their location). Either way, the upper slopes of Hanang get very chilly at night, so you'll need a good sleeping bag or thick blanket, and enough warm clothes.

Climbers intending to use the Jorodom Route will need to walk the 2km from Katesh to Jorodom village, where they must check in at the village office (*Ofisi ya Kijiji*). Here, you can arrange for a guide (US$5 per party) and porters (US$2 each). It is recommended that you take two porters per climber, one to carry the luggage and the other the water. From Jorodom, the hike to a good campsite on the lower ridge takes about six hours. The upper ridge looks deceptively close at this point, but is in fact at least four hours distant. It is thus advisable to camp at the top of the lower ridge, then to tackle the final ascent and full descent the next day.

To climb via the Giting Route, you must first follow the Babati road out of Katesh for 5km to Nangwa. Here, turn left on to a side road and continue for another 4km to the village of Giting. The main office of the Hanang Forestry Department, where you can arrange a guide and porters at the same rate charged in Jorodom, is on the outskirts of Giting. There is no accommodation in Giting, but you can camp in the grounds of the Forestry Department Office.

Please note that there is no permanent standing or running water on the mountain. Climbers must bring with them all the drinking water they will require. Bottled mineral water is available in Katesh, but not in Giting or Jorodom. An *absolute* minimum of 4l per climber per day (more during the hot, dry season) is essential, and better to overestimate your requirements than run out of water *en route*.

SINGIDA

Some 80km west of Katesh, this modestly sized town is most often visited by travellers bussing or driving to the Lake Victoria region via Shinyanga. Set at an elevation of 1,500m, it is most notable for the pair of Rift Valley lakes on its outskirts, in particular the shallow and hypersaline Lake Singida, a surreal apparition whose eerie green waters are offset by a shimmering white salt-encrusted shore and weird rock formations. Only 15 minutes' walk from the town centre, Lake Singida (together with the more distant Lake Kindai) is listed as an

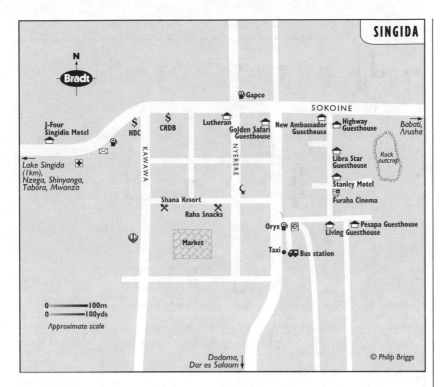

SINGIDA

SOKOINE

J-Four Singida Motel

NDC

CRDB

Lutheran Guesthouse

Golden Safari Guesthouse

New Ambassador Guesthouse

Highway Guesthouse

Babati, Arusha

Rock outcrop

Lake Singida (1km), Nzega, Shinyanga, Tabora, Mwanza

KAWAWA

NYERERE

Libra Star Guesthouse

Stanley Motel

Furaha Cinema

Shana Resort

Raha Snacks

Oryx

Pesapa Guesthouse

Living Guesthouse

Market

Taxi Bus station

0 ——— 100m
0 ——— 100yds
Approximate scale

Dodoma, Dar es Salaam

© Philip Briggs

Important Bird Area, attracting thousands of lesser flamingo when the water level is suitable. There's also a small regional museum (out past the J-Four Motel) and facilities include a good internet café close to the bus station, and a couple of banks.

GETTING THERE AND AWAY Coming from the east, Singida lies 350km from Arusha, a day's drive assuming you've no interest in stopping along the way. The thrice-daily nine-hour Mtei Express Coach between Arusha and Singida via Katesh and Babati is recommended, but other buses also cover the route in full or in hops.

🏠 WHERE TO STAY AND EAT

🏠 **J-Four Singida Motel** 📞 026 250 2193. This rustic lodge lies 500m from the bus station on the road to Lake Singida. It has a slightly down-at-heel feel & the green grounds don't really compensate. *Tsh20,000 en-suite dbl with hot water, net, fan & TV.*
🏠 **Stanley Motel** 📞 026 250 2351; f 026 250 2285. Set at the base of the large rock outcrop that overlooks the town centre, this reliable stalwart has

a good restaurant, en-suite rooms with net, fan, hot water & TV, as well as rooms using common showers. *Tsh7,000/10,000 sgl/dbl, Tsh16,000 en-suite.*
🏠 **Lutheran Guesthouse** 📞 026 250 2013. Clean accommodation with common showers. *Tsh5,000 dbl.*
✗ **Shana Resort** Prominently & promisingly signposted all over town, this small restaurant serves *chipsi mayai* & other cheap local favourites.

SHINYANGA

Set on the dusty plains that slope towards Lake Victoria, Shinyanga is a large yet oddly unmemorable town whose post-World War II economic heyday was founded on a cotton boom and on the local gold and diamond mining industry. Diamonds are still mined at Mwadui, 40km further north, and several small dealerships are scattered around town, but that aside Shinyanga now has a rather subdued aura –

13

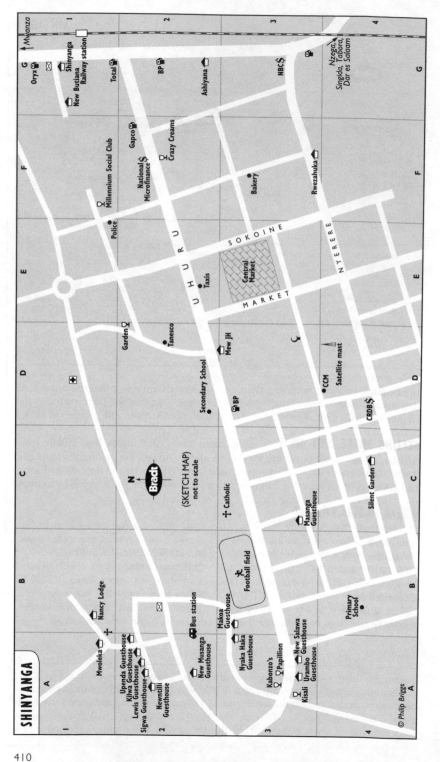

SHINYANGA

Mwanza

G
Oryx
Shinyanga
New Butiana
Railway station
Total
BP
Ashiyana
NBC
Nzega,
Singida, Tabora,
Dar es Salaam

F
Millennium Social Club
Gapco
Crazy Creams
National
Microfinance
Bakery
Rwezahuka

E
Police
U H U R U
Taxis
S O K O I N E
Central
Market
M A R K E T
N Y E R E R E

D
Garden
Tanesco
Mew JH
Secondary School
BP
CCM
Satellite mast
CRDB
Silent Garden

C
N
Bradt
(SKETCH MAP)
not to scale
† Catholic
Masanga
Guesthouse

B
Nancy Lodge
Football field
Primary
School

A
Mwoleka
Upenda Guesthouse
Kilwa Guesthouse
Lewis Guesthouse
Sigwa Guesthouse
Newntili
Guesthouse
Bus station
Makoa
Guesthouse
New Musanga
Guesthouse
Nyaka Haka
Guesthouse
Kabonzo's
Papillion
Kisali
Urambo
Guesthouse
New Salawa
Guesthouse

© Philip Briggs

Two of Tanzania's Important Bird Areas, both part of the Wembere River System associated with Lake Eyasi, are accessible from the road between Singida and Shinyanga. **Lake Kitangiri**, which lies about 20km north of the main road, close to Sekenke, is a shallow and moderately saline Rift Valley lake set below a 500m-high scarp at the western base of the Mbulu Highlands. The reed-lined shore and mudflats harbour a wide variety of waders and waterfowl, but the main attraction is sporadic concentrations of up to 500,000 flamingo.

West of the turn-off to Lake Kitangiri, the road crosses the **Wembere Steppe**, one of the largest seasonal wetlands in Tanzania, extending over 1,000km^2 and more than 30km wide in parts. This is an important breeding ground for waterbirds, including reed cormorant, yellow-billed stork and glossy ibis. The site is particularly rich in herons and relatives, including relatively scarce and elusive species such as the black egret, white-backed and black-capped night herons, purple and Goliath herons, and dwarf and little bitterns. The patches of acacia woodland also support a diversity of birds, including four species endemic to the Serengeti biome: Fischer's lovebird, rufous-tailed weaver, Karamoja apalis and grey-throated spurfowl.

Nzega, the largest town along this road, 77km south of Shinyanga, has an assortment of places to bed down for the night. The pick of these is the Forest Inn Hotel (✆ 062 269 2555), which lies in green gardens about 1km west of the town centre and charges Tsh12,000 for a neat, clean en-suite double with netting, fan and TV. Cheaper central options include Fourways Executive Lodging (✆ 062 669 2535) and Nzega Hotel (✆ 062 669 2534).

here, every day really is like Sunday – and there's not much in the way of local sightseeing. Its dusty Wild West aura is enhanced by the fabulous granite outcrops that dot the surrounding landscape, and run-down colonial buildings that serve as an anachronistic memento of headier days.

GETTING THERE AND AWAY Shinyanga lies 165km south of Mwanza by road, and roughly 320km northwest of Singida, along roads that are greatly improved of late. There are good bus services in both directions: Mwanza to Shinyanga takes four to five hours and Singida to Shinyanga the best part of a full day. Shinyanga lies on the central railway line between Dar es Salaam and Mwanza, and all trains stop here, but seldom at convenient times.

⌂ WHERE TO STAY AND EAT

⌂ **Shinyanga Hotel** [410 G1] ✆ 028 276 2369/2458. This dazzling orange 3-storey hotel opposite the railway station is easily the best in town, offering a variety of large clean en-suite dbls with fan, TV, hot water & balcony. The garden bar faces the railway station, & it has a good restaurant. *Tsh25,000/30,000 without/with AC.*

⌂ **Mwoleka Hotel** [410 A1] ✆ 028 276 2250; f 028 276 3540. Around the corner from the bus station, this is of a similar standard to the Shinyanga but pricier & not such good value.
⌂ **Silent Garden Motel** [410 C4] ✆ 028 277 2368. There's no garden, of course, & it's not as silent as it might be, but still it's one of the better cheapies scattered around town. *Tsh7,000 twin or dbl with common shower.*

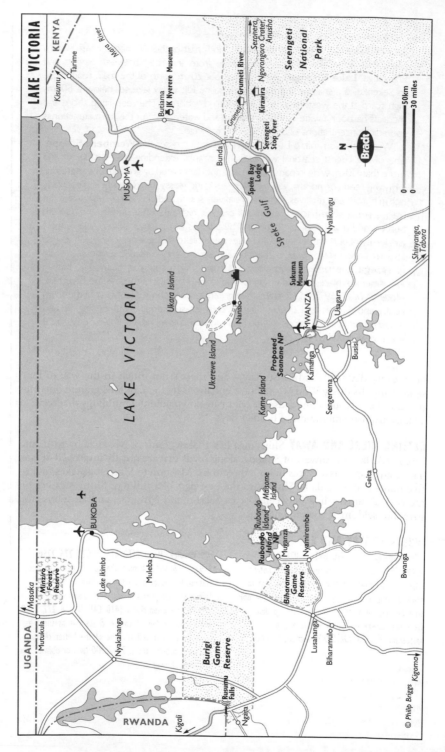

LAKE VICTORIA

KENYA

Kisumu

Tarime

Mara River

Butiama

JK Nyerere Museum

Bunda

Grumeti

Grumeti River

Kirawira

Serengeti Stop Over

Serengeti National Park

Serengeti, Ngorongoro Crater, Arusha

MUSOMA

Speke Bay Lodge

Speke Gulf

Nyalikungu

N

Bradt

50km

30 miles

Shinyanga, Tabora

Ukara Island

Nansio

Sukuma Museum

Ukerewe Island

MWANZA

Usagara

LAKE VICTORIA

Kome Island

Proposed Saanane NP

Kamanga

Busisi

Sengerema

Geita

Rubondo Island

Mdisome Island

Rubondo Island NP

Muganza

Nyamirembe

Bwanga

BUKOBA

Minziro Forest Reserve

Masaka

Lake Ikimba

Muleba

Biharamulo Game Reserve

Lusahanga

Biharamulo

UGANDA

Mutukula

Nyakahanga

Burigi Game Reserve

Rusumu Falls

Kigoma

RWANDA

Kigali

Ngara

© Philip Briggs

412

Lake Victoria

Straddling the borders with Kenya and Uganda, Lake Victoria extends over almost 70,000km² – an area comparable to Ireland – making it the second-largest freshwater body in the world after North America's Lake Superior. Some 51% of the lake's surface area falls within Tanzania, and the largest ports on the Tanzanian part of the lake are Mwanza, Musoma and Bukoba. Other important ports include Kisumu in Kenya, and Port Bell, Entebbe and Jinja in Uganda. Some 30 million people across the three counties are dependent on Lake Victoria as a primary source of water and/or food.

Lake Victoria fills an elevated depression between the two major forks of the Rift Valley. Nowhere more than 75m deep, it's very shallow by comparison with lakes Tanganyika and Nyasa, both of which hold a greater volume of water. Much of the shoreline is shallow and marshy, while the open water laps four of the world's 20 largest freshwater islands (including Ukerewe and Rubondo). The water level has fluctuated little in historical times, but the lake dried up entirely some 10,000–15,000 years ago. The Kagera River, rising in the highlands of Rwanda and emptying into Lake Victoria near Bukoba, is the most remote source of the Nile, the world's longest river, which exits the lake near Jinja in Uganda.

Lake Victoria practically borders the Western Serengeti but it has never featured prominently on Tanzania's tourist circuit. The one nascent upmarket tourist attraction in the region is the pedestrian-friendly Rubondo Island National Park. Mwanza, the largest Tanzanian port on the lake, is the main regional route focus and public transport hub, while other significant ports include Musoma, Bukoba and Muleba. Away from these towns, most of the people who live around Lake Victoria are fishermen, whose livelihood is increasingly threatened by the recent proliferation of introduced Nile perch and other ecological threats mentioned in greater detail in the box, *A Dying Lake*, on pages 432–3.

MWANZA

Once the second-largest city on mainland Tanzania, Mwanza now ranks fourth on that list, with a population of around 220,000. It sprawls across the undulating and rocky southwest shore of Lake Victoria, below the small hill where Speke reputedly arrived in 1858. The name Mwanza is a bastardisation of the Sukuma word *nyanza*, which simply means lake, and there's no reason to suppose that any settlement of significance existed on the site of the modern town prior to 1890, when the modern town was founded as a German administrative outpost and the surrounding area was developed for cotton production.

Captured by Britain in July 1916, Mwanza received two economic boosts in the 1920s. The first was the discovery of significant gold deposits in Mwanza and Musoma districts. The second was the completion of the railway line from Dar es Salaam in 1928, which liberated Mwanza from dependence on the coastal rail link from Kisumu on the Kenyan shore of Lake Victoria. By the late 1930s, gold mined in the Lake Victoria region had become Tanganyika's second most profitable export after sisal. Production dried up in the post-independence era – a mere 84 ounces of gold was sold in 1975 – largely due to the depletion of established mines. The Mwanza area remains rich in minerals, however, and several gold veins discovered in the 1990s are currently being mined, notably at Geita. In addition, the cotton and textile industries remain important economic mainstays for the Mwanza region.

Mwanza's main significance to travellers today is as a transport hub, it being the most important air, rail, road and lake terminal in northwest Tanzania. The city centre, with its recent rash of new modern buildings standing jarringly alongside decaying colonial-era buildings, is nothing very special, but it does have a likeable and quite lively atmosphere – and travellers arriving from the sticks will doubtless enjoy the proliferation of reasonably priced lodgings, restaurants, bars and internet facilities. The best-known local landmark is Bismarck Rock, a precariously balanced granite formation that lies within the main harbour, but several similarly impressive outcrops can be seen by wandering along Station Road on the peninsula to the south of the city centre. For a good view over the lake from the city centre, clamber up the rocky green hills above Station Road – the rocks are crawling with colourful agama lizards, and surprisingly, given the urban location, the trees still harbour a small troop of vervet monkeys. Further afield, worthwhile day or overnight trips from Mwanza include the Sukuma Museum at Bajoro, the proposed Saanane National Park, and Ukerewe Island in the heart of the lake.

GETTING THERE AND AWAY Mwanza is the main transport hub on Lake Victoria, and likely to be passed through at some point by any traveller exploring the northwest of Tanzania, or travelling between Tanzania and Uganda or Rwanda.

LAKE VICTORIA FERRIES

The Tanzania Railway Corporation (TRC; ℡ 022 211 7833; e ccm_cserv@ trctz.com; www.trctz.com) runs ferries out of Mwanza to Bukoba and Ukerewe Island. The boats are in good condition, and first- and second-class cabins offer a level of comfort matched in East Africa only by the train between Nairobi and Mombasa in Kenya, though third class tends to be overcrowded and there is a real risk of theft. The restaurants serve good, inexpensive meals and chilled beers and sodas. Timetables change regularly, since one or the other boat is almost always in dry-dock, but current schedules and fares are listed below. In addition to these fares, a port tax of US$5 must be paid in hard currency upon leaving any Tanzanian port.

MWANZA TO BUKOBA There is one overnight ferry in each direction on three days each week, with duties split between MV *Serengeti* and the larger MV *Victoria*. Ferries leave Mwanza at 18.00 on Tuesday, Thursday and Sunday, and Bukoba at 18.00 on Monday, Wednesday and Friday. The trip takes around 12 hours one-way. One-way fares are Tsh35,000/25,000 for first-/second-class cabins, or Tsh22,000/20,000 for second-/third-class sitting.

MWANZA TO NANSIO (UKEREWE ISLAND) MV *Clarias* and MV *Butiama* set sail on alternate days to Nansio on Ukerewe Island. Services depart Mwanza at 09.00 and 14.00 on weekdays, and at 16.00 on Saturday and 14.00 on Sunday. The trip takes about three hours and costs Tsh6,500 second-class sitting or Tsh4,500 third class.

Many travellers arrive in Mwanza from Uganda or Rwanda wanting to cross directly to Arusha. Unless you are prepared to fly, this is a problematic route, and there is no quick and cheap way of doing it. If time is a greater factor than money, best to cross through the Serengeti, though this does entail paying US$100 in entrance fees for Serengeti National Park and Ngorongoro Conservation Area over and above the bus fare – a waste of money if you already plan to go on safari. On the other hand, for those who can't afford a proper safari, it's a cheap way of seeing the Serengeti, as the road passes through the heart of the reserve and game viewing is excellent, particularly from December to May. At least three buses do this trip weekly, as do a number of private Land Rover *dala-dalas*.

The cheap and nasty way of getting between Mwanza and Arusha is to use one of the buses which cross south of the Serengeti through Singida and Shinyanga. While this route has noticeably improved with the paving of the section between Nzega and Singida, it is still a hellish ride, taking around 36 hours and passing through a dry, unattractive part of the country where stops are most likely to be dictated by breakdowns and flat tyres. Looking on the bright side, you could break up this route with a few stops at places discussed more fully in *Chapter 13, Dodoma and the Central Rift Valley* (and on our website, http://bradttanzania.wordpress.com).

By train The most normal way to get between Lake Victoria and the coast is by train. The railway station lies at the southern end of the town centre [416 C5]; details of the twice-weekly services to and from Dar es Salaam via Tabora are included in the box *The Central Railway* on page 393. Note that no direct train service runs between Mwanza and Kigoma (on Lake Tanganyika), so travellers covering this route will need to change trains at Tabora – a relatively minor inconvenience when the only affordable alternative is bussing along some truly appalling roads!

By ferry For current details of ferries out of Mwanza see the box *Lake Victoria Ferries* opposite.

For anyone driving westwards to Geita, the most direct route is via the northern ferry crossing between Kamanga and Mwanza. The MV *Nansio* and MV *Orion*, operated by Kamanga Ferry Ltd [416 B2] (✆ 0784 626337; www.kamangaferry.com), depart every hour or so from the southern port just off Nasser Road with the 30-minute ride costing Tsh800 per person and Tsh3,000 per vehicle. Other details for travelling west to Geita, Biharamulo and the Rwanda border are included on our website, http://bradttanzania.wordpress.com.

By air Mwanza airport is situated on the lakeshore about 12km north of the city centre. Precision Air (✆ 028 250 0046; www.precisionairtz.com) runs daily flights to Mwanza from Dar es Salaam, with some services stopping via Musoma and Shinyanga. Coastal Aviation (m 0784 520949; www.coastal.cc) flies daily between Arusha and Mwanza with some flights connecting via Grumeti in the western Serengeti as well as occasional services to Rubondo Island National Park. The taxis that hang around in the airport parking lot generally ask around Tsh10,000 for a ride to the town centre, but regular minibuses to town leave from along the main road, about 500m from the airport.

By car Roads out of Mwanza are generally in poor condition. The most obvious exception to this is the surfaced road running east of the lake, via the turn-off to

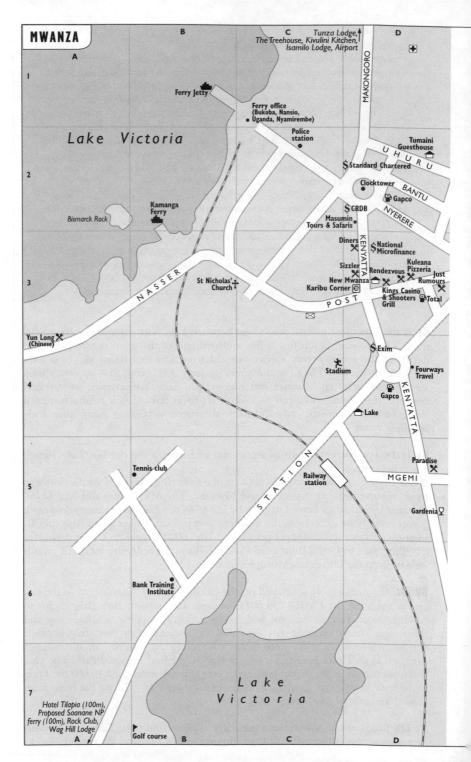

MWANZA

A

B

C Tunza Lodge,
The Treehouse, Kivulini Kitchen,
Isamilo Lodge, Airport

D

Ferry Jetty

Ferry office
(Bukoba, Nansio,
Uganda, Nyamirembe)

Police
station

Lake Victoria

Tumaini
Guesthouse

U H U R U

Standard Chartered

Clocktower

B A N T U

Gapco

CRDB

N Y E R E R E

Kamanga
Ferry

Bismarck Rock

Masumin
Tours & Safaris

Diners

National
Microfinance

K E N Y A T T A

Sizzler

Kuleana
Pizzeria

Rendezvous

Just

New Mwanza

Rumours

N A S S E R

St Nicholas'
Church

Karibu Corner

Kings Casino
& Shooters
Grill

P O S T

Total

Yun Long
(Chinese)

Exim

Stadium

Fourways
Travel

K E N Y A T T A

Gapco

Lake

Paradise

Tennis club

S T A T I O N

Railway
station

M G E M I

Gardenia

Bank Training
Institute

*Lake
Victoria*

Hotel Tilapia (100m),
Proposed Saanane NP
ferry (100m), Rock Club,
Wag Hill Lodge

Golf course

A

B

C

D

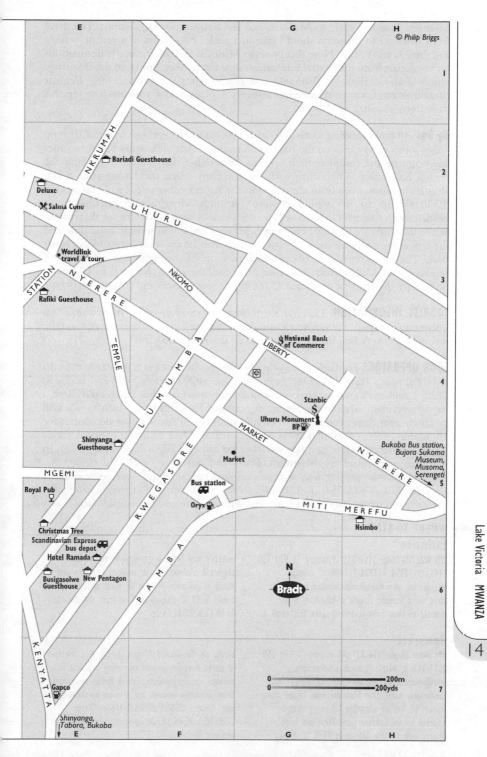

© Philip Briggs

Bariadi Guesthouse

NKRUMAH

Deluxe

Salma Cone

UHURU

NKOMO

Worldlink
travel & tours

STATION

NYERERE

Rafiki Guesthouse

TEMPLE

National Bank
of Commerce

LIBERTY

LUMUMBA

Stanbic

Uhuru Monument
BP

Shinyanga
Guesthouse

RWEGASORE

MARKET

Market

MGEMI

Royal Pub

Bus station

Oryx

Bukoba Bus station,
Bujora Sukoma
Museum,
Musoma,
Serengeti

NYERERE

MITI MEREFU

Christmas Tree

Scandinavian Express
bus depot

Hotel Ramada

PAMBA

Nsimbo

N

Bradt

Busigasolwe
Guesthouse

New Pentagon

KENYATTA

Gapco

0 ————————— 200m
0 ————————— 200yds

Shinyanga,
Tabora, Bukoba

Serengeti National Park, to Musoma and the Kenyan port of Kisumu. The drive from Mwanza to Musoma should take just under two hours in a private vehicle and three hours by bus. Note that buses to Musoma and other easterly destinations do not depart from the central bus station near the market, but from the Buzuruga terminal about 5km – a Tsh5,000 taxi ride – from the town centre. Regular minibuses run between the two bus stations. Muhammad Trans runs four services daily from Mwanza to Musoma.

By bus All buses heading south now depart from the Nyegezi bus terminal, around 10km south of Mwanza on the road to Shinyanga. That said, many bus companies still originate and complete their services from either their offices in town or the central bus station, so confirm with the company when purchasing your ticket. Regular minibuses run from the centre to the station; otherwise it will cost around Tsh10,000 by taxi. We would, however, strongly advise against catching buses headed south towards Dodoma or Dar es Salaam, or west to Kigoma for that matter. While the roads are steadily being upgraded they are still in terrible condition, and the trip is normally measured in days rather than hours – far better to catch the train! The one exception is Tabora which now only has roughly around 150km of unpaved road. Muhammad Trans runs two buses daily from Mwanza to Tabora via Shinyanga, departing at 06.00 and 13.00, taking seven hours and costing Tsh14,000.

TOURIST INFORMATION There is no tourist information office in Mwanza. An informative website, www.mwanza-guide.com, is well worth checking out and the webmaster is very helpful when it comes to answering queries.

TOUR OPERATORS For flights and other bookings, the best bet is generally thought to be Fourways Travel [416 D4] (*main roundabout on Station Rd;* \ *028 250 2273/250 2620;* e *fourways@fourwaystravel.net; www.fourwaystravel.net*). For budget travellers, a day or overnight safari to the Serengeti National Park from the Mwanza side will be far cheaper than a full northern circuit safari out of Arusha. A good contact for affordable Serengeti excursions is Serengeti Stop Over near the national park's Ndaraka Entrance Gate (see *Between Mwanza and the Kenyan Border,* page 423). In Mwanza, you could try Masumin Tours and Safaris (\ *028 250 0192/3292;* e *info@masumintours.com; www.masumintours.com*) or Serengeti Services and Tours (\ *028 250 0061/0754;* f *028 250 0446;* e *reservations@serengetiservices.com; www.serengetiservices.com*) which both deal with car hire and Serengeti safaris.

WHERE TO STAY
Exclusive
Wag Hill Lodge [416 A7] (3 rooms) \ 028 250 2445; m 0754 917974/777086; e info@waghill.com; www.waghill.com. Situated on a 17ha stand on a forested stretch of lakeshore a few minutes by boat from central Mwanza, this small & exclusive new lodge is particularly suited to keen anglers & birdwatchers, or anybody else who just wants to get away from it all. Rates include meals, drinks & 10.00 pick-up by boat from the Mwanza Yacht Club. *US$275 pp*

Upmarket
Hotel Tilapia [416 A7] (40 rooms) \ 028 250 0517/617; e tilapia@mwanza-online.com, info@tilapiahotel.com; www.hoteltilapia.com. This comfortable hotel, 1km from the town centre along Station Rd, has an attractive lakeshore position adjacent to the Saanane jetty. There are large chalets with satellite flat-screen TV & AC, luxury berths on the docked *African Queen,* & a selection of suites. Facilities include swimming pool, car hire, business centre, Japanese, Thai & Indian restaurants, & an attractive wooden bar & patio overlooking the lake. Chalets *US$85 dbl B&B; African Queen US$110; suites US$120 upwards; substantial resident discounts.*

Isamilo Lodge [416 D1] (25 rooms) ☎ 028 254 1627/8; e isamilolodge@isamilo.com; www.isamilo-lodge.com. Carved into the hillside overlooking the city, this impressive new lodge is reputedly located in the exact spot where Speke first saw Lake Victoria. Catering mostly to local business travellers, its 25 rooms – found up & down a confusing maze of stairways – all have AC, wireless internet, satellite TV, phone & tiled en-suite. 2 good restaurants serve continental, Indian & Asian dishes, & there's a very pleasant terrace bar with fabulous panoramic lake views. It's in the Isamilo area, 3km from the city centre & 8km from the airport (the junction is signposted on the left as you enter Mwanza from the airport). *US$60/70/80 std en-suite sgl/dbl/twin; suites from US$120.*

Tunza Lodge [416 D1] (12 rooms) ☎ 028 256 2215; www.tunzalodge.com. The closest thing to a genuine beach resort anywhere on the Tanzanian portion of Lake Victoria is the lusciously laid-back Tunza Lodge, in the village of Ilemela around 8km from the centre of town. The green gardens verge on a small private swimming beach with a volleyball court, where a weekly yoga class is offered as the sun sets over the lake. Fishing trips with rod, tackle & boat supplied can be arranged at US$150 for 1 or 2 people, or US$50 pp for larger groups. A good open-sided thatch bar & restaurant serves a variety of grills & fish meals for around US$5. The clearly signposted junction is just off the main airport road, 2km from the airport; from here it's another 2km along a dusty dirt road to the lake. *Clean, simply furnished en-suite chalets US$45/60 sgl/dbl B&B.*

New Mwanza Hotel [416 D3] (55 rooms) ☎ 028 250 1070/1; m 0754 487396; e nmh@raha.com, nmh@mwanza-online.com. This renovated former government hotel on Post Rd is similar in standard to the Tilapia, with the advantages of a more central location & cheaper rates, & disadvantages of a blander atmosphere & the absence of a lake view. A business centre, coffee shop, restaurant, casino & shopping arcade are within the hotel building. *US$45/55 sgl/dbl B&B with AC & satellite TV; US$50/60 deluxe with 24hr internet connection; US$85–150 suites.*

Moderate

The Treehouse [416 D1] (5 rooms) ☎ 028 254 1160; e treehouse@streetwise-africa.org; www.streetwise-africa.org. This great homely B&B, located around 600m from Isamilo Lodge, is perfect for travellers interested in contributing to the community. Run by the charity group Stwise Africa, all profits help to fund programmes supporting street kids in Mwanza. All rooms have 24hr internet access & include delicious homemade b/fast.

Budget

Christmas Tree Hotel [417 E5] ☎ 028 250 2001. This likeable high-rise hotel lies a short distance from the bus station, within 5min walk of better restaurants & shops in the town centre. Clean en-suite rooms come with large dbl bed, net, fan, satellite TV & running hot water. Good value. *Tsh16,000 dbl, inc full b/fast for 1 person.*

Lake Hotel [416 D4] ☎ 028 254 2030. The long-serving Lake Hotel is conveniently situated off Kenyatta Rd between the railway station & town centre, & despite looking a bit run-down it remains a reliable fallback in the budget range. Large en-

Discounts available for backpackers & volunteers. 2 comfy sgls with shared bath US$30, 2 en-suite dbls US$45/50 sgl/dbl, family banda US$70.

New Pentagon Hotel [417 E6] (19 rooms) ☎ 028 254 1950. This smart, new hotel, next door to Hotel Ramada, is conveniently located near the central bus station. Clean, serviceable rooms with tiled en-suite, TV & AC. *Tsh25,000/30,000 sgl/dbl, Tsh20,000 en-suite sgl with fan.*

suite rooms have hot water, net & fan. The restaurant closed years ago, but the outdoor bar remains a pleasant drinking hole. *Tsh15,000/20,000 sgl/dbl, inc derisory b/fast.*

Hotel Ramada [417 E6] ☎ 028 254 0223. This bland multi-storey budget hotel on Rwegasore Rd lies close to the central bus station & next to the Scandinavia Express depot. Clean en-suite rooms, with fan & hot water, aren't bad value, but unfortunately they are very cramped & – a serious omission in this neck of Tanzania – they lack mosquito nets. *Tsh14,000/16,000 sgl/dbl.*

Shoestring

Nsimbo Hotel [417 H5] ☎ 028 40948. On Miti Meferu Rd near the bus station, the Nsimbo Hotel is looking a bit run-down, but at the price, it's difficult to take issue with the large & reasonably clean en-suite dbls with fan, net & running water. *Tsh7,000 dbl.*

Deluxe Hotel [417 E2] Like the costlier Lake Hotel, the Deluxe on Uhuru Rd has been justifiably popular with travellers for years, & remains a good compromise between comfort & price. The clean but rather worn en-suite rooms with nets & running water are good value. A restaurant & 2 bars are on the ground floor, along with a noisy disco over w/ends. *Tsh5,000 dbl.*

✕ WHERE TO EAT AND DRINK

✕ **Deluxe Hotel** [417 E2] The ground floor restaurant at this hotel looks rather seedy, but the food is pretty good — mostly Asian & African dishes — & very reasonably priced at around Tsh3,000 for a heaped plate!

✕ **Diners** [416 D3] Situated roughly opposite the New Mwanza Hotel, this serves a huge variety of Indian & Chinese dishes for around Tsh6,000 with rice or *naan* bread. You won't find a better Indian restaurant anywhere in Tanzania, & it's definitely the first choice in Mwanza if price isn't an issue.

✕ **Hotel Tilapia** [416 A7] With 4 themed restaurants including Teppanyaki, Mwanza's only Japanese restaurant, where you can cook your own dishes on an iron griddle in the middle of your table, & Domo Domo which offers a selection of continental, Indian & Thai cuisine, the Talipa offers plenty of choice. Meals Tsh7,000–15,000.

✕ **Just Rumours** [416 D3] This 'sports bar' set-up, opposite the New Mwanza Hotel, serves (pricey) draught beer & a good range of cocktails & bar grub, accompanied by loud MTV or (sometimes &) stereo. The w/end disco is the most popular in town.

✕ **Kivulini Kitchen** [416 D1] m 0784 558869; ⏱ 09.00–22.00 daily. Run by a local women's empowerment group, this small restaurant alongside the Treehouse serves a variety of local & continental dishes for around Tsh5,000.

✕ **Kuleana Pizzeria** [416 D3] ✆ 028 256 0566; ⏱ 08.30–17.00. Run by a charity for street children, this popular pizzeria serves good pizzas & a selection of other snacks & sandwiches. Prices are in the Tsh2,500–4,000 range. Fresh brown bread is usually available to take away.

✕ **New Mwanza Hotel** [416 D3] This hotel restaurant is a good central option serving pizzas, pasta dishes, Indian food & light grills in the Tsh5,000–7,000 range.

✕ **Salma Cone** [417 E2] Great ice cream sundaes & fresh popcorn at reasonable prices.

✕ **Shooters Grill** [416 D3] Next to the New Mwanza Hotel, this popular chain restaurant serves a decent range of grills, including delicious T-Bone steaks, from around Tsh5,000. The attached Kings Casino hums from noon until around midnight daily.

✕ **Sizzler Restaurant** [416 D3] ⏱ lunch & dinner daily. A couple of doors down from Diners (see below), & not quite in the same class, the Sizzler is nevertheless a very Indian restaurant, & meals are about half the price. In the evenings, an outdoor barbecue does *mishkaki*, chicken tikka & fresh chapatis & roti bread. No alcohol.

✕ **Yun Long Chinese Restaurant** [416 A4] m 0784 821723; ⏱ lunch & dinner daily. About 5min walk from the town centre, this lovely outdoor bar & restaurant is pretty much unique for Mwanza in that it actually has a view over the lake & Bismarck Rock. It's a great spot for sundowners, but the restaurant also serves excellent, though pricey, Chinese food as well as a few continental dishes for Tsh6,000–15,000.

OTHER PRACTICALITIES

Foreign exchange All the main banks are represented, and have foreign exchange facilities, with the National Bank of Commerce [417 G4] usually offering the best rates and fastest service. The ATM outside this bank allows you to draw local currency against Visa cards, as does the one at the Standard Chartered Bank [416 D2], while the Exim Bank on Kenyatta Road [416 D2] accepts both Visa and MasterCard. The banks are mostly clustered close to the roundabout at the junction of Makongoro and Nyerere roads, or in the vicinity of the clocktower at the other end of Nyerere Road. The best place to change cash and travellers' cheques is at the Bureau de Change at Serengeti Services & Tours on Post Street.

Internet There's no shortage of internet cafés dotted around Mwanza city centre (see map), charging a fairly uniform rate of Tsh800 per 30 minutes. The best and most central is Karibu Corner Café [416 D3] (opposite the New Mwanza Hotel). It charges Tsh1,500 per hour and is open from 08.00 Monday to Saturday and from 09.00 Sunday.

Swimming There is no public swimming pool in Mwanza. Swimming in the lake around town is emphatically not recommended due to the high risk of contracting bilharzia.

EXCURSIONS FROM MWANZA

Saanane Proposed National Park This small, rocky island in Lake Victoria, likely to be gazetted as a national park during the lifespan of this edition, makes for a worthwhile and straightforward day trip out of Mwanza. For many years, it was essentially a glorified zoo, established in 1961 as an interim home to various captive large mammals prior to their release on to Rubondo Island. Today, thankfully, all the listless captive animals have been relocated elsewhere, and the depressingly cramped cages stand empty. Free-ranging animals include the herd of re-introduced impala that grazes the grassy shore.

A variety of smaller animals inhabit the island naturally. Gaudily coloured agama lizards bask on the rocks, while water monitors (the largest African lizard) crash gracelessly through the undergrowth. Birdlife is profuse, with fish eagle, pied kingfisher and white-bellied cormorant common near the shore, and more localised species such as swamp flycatcher, yellow-throated leaflove, grey kestrel and slender-billed weaver present in the forest. The rock hyrax is the most visible naturally occurring mammal.

Saanane lies about five minutes from the mainland using the motorboat service that leaves from the jetty next to the Tilapia Hotel, ten minutes' walk from Mwanza town centre along Station Road. The boat departs for the island every two hours between 11.00 and 17.00 and does the return trip every two hours from 12.00 to 18.00. The daily entrance fee, inclusive of the boat ride, is a very reasonable Tsh1,000, but this could increase dramatically should the island acquire full National Park status. You can spend as long as you like on the island provided that you take the last boat back to town.

Bujora Sukuma Museum The excellent Sukuma Museum (*www.sukumamuseum.org; entrance Tsh8,000 pp*), situated within the Bujora parish grounds about 20km east of Mwanza, is dedicated to the culture and history of the Sukuma, Tanzania's most populous tribe (see box, *The dancers of Usukuma*, pages 422–3). The museum was established in the 1950s by Father David Clement (whose local nickname *Fumbuka* means 'Unexpected'), and designed in collaboration with a local Sukuma committee with the primary intent of preserving this culture for local Sukuma visitors.

The museum consists of five discrete pavilions or buildings, each devoted to a particular aspect of Sukuma culture. First up is the Sukuma homestead, which contains traditional household effects such as cooking utensils, religious objects and agricultural tools. The blacksmith's house is a low circular thatched hut containing cowhide bellows and other implements used to forge metal, as well as metal tools and spearheads made by the blacksmith. The concrete house of the *Iduku* (traditional healer) contains medicinal calabashes, divination tools, various charms and other traditional medical paraphernalia. The Dance Society Pavilion concentrates on the history and costumes of the Bagika and Bagalu, the competing dance societies of the Sukuma. Most impressive of all is the Royal Pavilion, a two-storey building designed in the shape of a royal throne. This section houses a vast collection of royal Sukuma thrones and crowns, while a wall display delineates the area and name of each of the 52 Sukuma chiefdoms, as well as lineages for the more important ones. The second storey of the pavilion houses royal drums donated by some local chiefs. The colourful Bujora Church, on a hilltop overlooking the museum, is also worth a look around, since it incorporates large elements of Sukuma royal symbolism into its design, for instance an altar shaped like a traditional throne.

Usukuma – literally 'Northern Land' – lies to the immediate south and east of Lake Victoria, and is home to the Bantu-speaking Sukuma, the largest tribe in Tanzania, comprising approximately 13% of the national population. The Sukuma are thought to have migrated into their present homeland prior to the 17th century, possibly from elsewhere in the Lake Victoria hinterland. Pre-colonial Usukuma differed from the centralised states that characterised areas to the north and west of the lake in that it was comprised of about 50 affiliated but autonomous local chieftaincies. Historically, culturally and linguistically, the Sukuma are strongly affiliated to the Nyamwezi of the Tabora area. It may well be that no marked division between the local chieftaincies of the two groups existed until the latter half of the 19th century, when the militant aspirations of Mirambo, who forged the more centralised Nyamwezi state, would have enforced a greater degree of political unity among the Sukuma.

The traditional political structure of Usukuma is typical of the *ntemi* chieftaincies of central Tanzania. Chiefs are part of a royal line, and are invested with mystical and religious qualities as well as political power. However, any autocratic tendencies are curbed by the necessity for a chief to be elected by a committee of princes and elders, which also has the ability to remove any chief whose actions are unpopular or inappropriate. The chief is thought to be mystically linked to the supreme being, who is regarded by the Sukuma as having many of the attributes of the sun. Ancestor worship plays as important a role in Sukuma religion as direct worship of the creator, since the spirits of the dead are seen to occupy a realm close to God. Although most Sukuma today are practising Christians or Muslims, many adhere concurrently to the traditional religion, and particularly in rural areas it is normal to leave offerings to the ancestors in the hope that they will bring rain, health and prosperity.

The Sukuma have the reputation within Tanzania of being snake charmers, and are also known for their varied and spectacular traditional dances, disciplines which combine in a ritual dance called the Bugobogobo. The dancers coil a live python around their body, then writhe to a frenetic drumbeat, alternately pretending to embrace the gigantic snake and to fight with it. The dance becomes more frenzied as the drumbeat speeds up and the snake becomes increasingly excited or agitated, often causing the audience to scatter in all directions. Bugobogobo dances are sometimes held at the Bujora Sukuma Museum (see page 421) on Saturday afternoons.

The Sukuma Museum lies a short walk from Kissesa on the Mwanza–Musoma road. Any bus to Musoma can drop you off there at the junction. The best day to visit is Saturday, when the Sukuma Snake Dance is sometimes performed in tandem with a live python. Traditional performances can be arranged for Tsh60,000 per person. An inexpensive campsite and a few rooms are available for travellers who want to stay the night.

Ukerewe Island The 530km² Ukerewe Island is the largest island in Lake Victoria – actually, trivia lovers, the sixth-largest lake-bound landmass in the world! It is also the most accessible substantial island on the Tanzanian part of the lake. The principal town and port, Nansio, takes two to three hours to reach using the daily ferry service from Mwanza (see *Lake Victoria Ferries* box, page 414, for details), and it is also connected to Bunda on the main Mwanza–Musoma road by a causeway and occasional *dala-dalas*. The ferry trip to Nansio is a good way to see some of Africa's largest lake, and if Nansio itself is a rather scruffy little place, the island is very pretty, boasting some attractive, sandy (and reputedly bilharzia-free) beaches and plenty of possibilities for casual rambling.

Traditionally, most Sukuma people under the age of 30 will belong to one of several dance societies, of which the largest and oldest are the Bagika and Bagalu. According to oral tradition, the two societies were respectively founded about 150 years ago by Ngika and Gumha, rival dancers and traditional healers who held regular competitions to determine which had the most potent medicine. The two would dance alongside each other, using magic charms to attract spectators and induce errors in their rival's routine, and the winner was the one who eventually attracted the largest crowd.

A similar format is followed in modern dance competitions held by the rival societies, with the two troupes dancing concurrently and attempting to outdo each other in order to attract the greater number of spectators. The dancers mostly base their performances around traditional routines, but innovative and outrageous stunts – masks, props, costumes or fresh steps – are encouraged, and may well be decisive in attracting the crowd required in order to win the competition.

Until recent times, the dancing societies of Sukuma were important spiritual entities with somewhat Masonic overtones. Members of any given society would wear a distinctive tattoo. The Bagika favour a diagonal double incision running from one shoulder to the opposite side of the waist, and sometimes a series of arrow-shaped incisions on one cheek. The Bagalu used circular rather than linear incisions, sometimes around the left eye or breast, sometimes around the torso. Today, the dance competitions are held mainly as entertainment, but a large element of mysticism is still attached to the societies. The leader of a troupe will consult traditional spiritual leaders prior to the competition, and cover his body in a paste made from a powdered dance medicine called samba when dancing. Some dancers even build ancestral shrines on the dance ground!

Dance competitions take place throughout Usukuma after the end of the harvest season, starting in June and running through to August, with particularly impressive festivals likely to be held on the public holidays of 7 July and 8 August. If you're in the area at the time, ask around about where competitions are being held. For more information about the Sukuma dancers and other aspects of Sukuma culture, take a look at Sukuma Museum's website, www.sukumamuseum.org, which covers most aspects of Sukuma culture and history.

If you visit the island as a day trip out of Mwanza, you'll only have an hour or so to explore, so it's worth dedicating a night to the visit. The best place to stay is the **Monarch Motel** (m *0784 682488;* e *uktoas@yahoo.com; Tsh15,000/25,000 sgl/dbl en-suite with nets; cheaper rooms with common shower*), previously the Gallu Beach Hotel, set in a former District Commissioner's residence on the lakeshore about 500m from Nansio Port. A restaurant and bar are attached, but the food is much better at the nearby **Umjamii Hostel**. If the Monarch is too expensive, there are several local guesthouses in Nansio, of which the **Umjamii** and **Island Inn** are about the best.

BETWEEN MWANZA AND THE KENYAN BORDER

The 240km road between Mwanza and the Kenyan border is of interest primarily as a through route to Kenya, and because it skirts the western edge of the Serengeti National Park. Except for the first 30km out of Mwanza, the road is in good condition, and plenty of public transport runs along it. The roadside scenery is quite attractive, too, as you pass through dry, flat country dotted with small granite outcrops and rustic Sukuma homesteads, with regular glimpses of Lake Victoria to

14

The first European to see Lake Victoria was John Hanning Speke, who marched from Tabora to the site of present-day Mwanza in 1858 following his joint 'discovery' of Lake Tanganyika with Richard Burton the previous year. Speke named the lake for Queen Victoria, but prior to that Arab slave traders called it Ukerewe (still the name of its largest island). It is unclear what name was in local use, since the only one used by Speke is Nyanza, which simply means lake.

A major goal of the Burton–Speke expedition had been to solve the great geographical enigma of the age, the source of the White Nile. Speke, based on his brief glimpse of the southeast corner of Lake Victoria, somewhat whimsically proclaimed his 'discovery' to be the answer to that riddle. Burton, with a comparable lack of compelling evidence, was convinced that the great river flowed out of Lake Tanganyika. The dispute between the former travelling companions erupted bitterly on their return to Britain, where Burton – the more persuasive writer and respected traveller – gained the backing of the scientific establishment.

Over 1862–63, Speke and Captain James Grant returned to Lake Victoria, hoping to prove Speke's theory correct. They looped inland around the western shore of the lake, arriving at the court of King Mutesa of Buganda, then continued east to the site of present-day Jinja, where a substantial river flowed out of the lake after tumbling over the cataract that Speke named Ripon Falls. From here, the two explorers headed north, sporadically crossing paths with the river throughout what is today Uganda, before following the Nile to Khartoum and Cairo.

Speke's declaration that 'The Nile is settled' met with mixed support back home. Burton and other sceptics pointed out that Speke had bypassed the entire western shore of his purported great lake, had visited only a couple of points on the northern shore, and had not attempted to explore the east. Nor, for that matter, had he followed the course of the Nile in its entirety. Speke, claimed his detractors, had seen several different lakes and different stretches of river, connected only in Speke's deluded mind. The sceptics had a point, but Speke had nevertheless gathered sufficient geographical evidence to render his claim highly plausible, and his notion of one great lake, far from being mere whimsy, was backed by anecdotal information gathered from local sources along the way.

Matters were scheduled to reach a head on 16 September 1864, when an eagerly awaited debate between Burton and Speke – in the words of the former, 'what silly tongues called the "Nile Duel"' – was due to take place at the Royal Geographic Society (RGS). And reach a head they did, but in circumstances more tragic than anybody could have anticipated. On the afternoon of the debate, Speke went out shooting with a cousin, only to stumble while crossing a wall, in the process discharging a barrel of his shotgun into his heart. The subsequent inquest recorded a verdict of accidental death, but it has often been suggested – purely on the basis of the curious timing – that Speke deliberately took his life rather than face up to Burton in public. Burton, who had seen Speke less than three hours earlier, was by all accounts deeply troubled by Speke's death, and years later he was quoted as stating 'the uncharitable [say] that I shot him' – an accusation that seems to have been aired only in Burton's imagination.

Speke was dead, but the 'Nile debate' would keep kicking for several years. In 1864, Sir Stanley and Lady Baker were the first Europeans to reach Lake Albert and nearby

the west. Before reaching Bunda, herds of zebra and wildebeest are likely to be seen along the eastern side of the road.

The largest town in this part of Tanzania is Musoma, a substantial port and regional administrative centre situated on the lakeshore 18km west of the main

Murchison Falls in present-day Uganda. The Bakers, much to the delight of the anti-Speke lobby, were convinced that this newly named lake was a source of the Nile, though they openly admitted it might not be the only one. Following the Bakers' announcement, Burton put forward a revised theory, namely that the most remote source of the Nile was the Rusizi River, which he believed flowed out of the northern head of Lake Tanganyika and emptied into Lake Albert.

In 1865, the RGS followed up on Burton's theory by sending Dr David Livingstone to Lake Tanganyika. Livingstone, however, was of the opinion that the Nile's source lay further south than Burton supposed, and so he struck out towards the lake along a previously unexplored route. Leaving from Mikindani in the far south of present-day Tanzania, Livingstone followed the Rovuma River inland, continuing westward to the southern tip of Lake Tanganyika. From there, he ranged southward into present day Zambia, where he came across a new candidate for the source of the Nile, the swampy Lake Bangweulu and its major outlet, the Lualaba River. It was only after his famous meeting with Henry Stanley at Ujiji, in November 1871, that Livingstone (in the company of Stanley) visited the north of Lake Tanganyika and Burton's cherished Rusizi River, which, it transpired, flowed *into* the lake. Burton, nevertheless, still regarded Lake Tanganyika to be the most likely source of the Nile, while Livingstone was convinced that the answer lay with the Lualaba River. In August 1872, Livingstone headed back to the Lake Bangweulu region, where he fell ill and died six months later, the great question still unanswered.

In August 1874, ten years after Speke's death, Stanley embarked on a three-year expedition every bit as remarkable and arduous as those undertaken by his predecessors, yet one whose significance is often overlooked. Partly, this is because Stanley cuts such an unsympathetic figure, the grim caricature of the murderous pre-colonial White Man blasting and blustering his way through territories where Burton, Speke and Livingstone had relied largely on diplomacy. It is also the case, however, that Stanley set out with no intention of seeking out headline-making fresh discoveries. Instead, he determined to test out the various theories that had been advocated by Speke, Burton and Livingstone about the Nile's source. First, Stanley sailed around the circumference of Lake Victoria, establishing that it was indeed as vast as Speke had claimed. Stanley's next step was to circumnavigate Lake Tanganyika, which, contrary to Burton's long-held theories, clearly boasted no outlet sufficiently large to be the source of the Nile. Finally, and most remarkably, Stanley took a boat along Livingstone's Lualaba River to its confluence with an even larger river, which he followed for months with no idea as to where he might end up.

When, exactly 999 days after he left Zanzibar, Stanley emerged at the Congo mouth, the shortlist of plausible theories relating to the source of the Nile had been reduced to one. Clearly, the Nile did flow out of Lake Victoria at Ripon Falls, before entering and exiting Lake Albert at its northern tip to start its long course through the sands of the Sahara. Stanley's achievement in putting to rest decades of speculation about how the main rivers and lakes of East Africa linked together is estimable indeed. He was nevertheless generous enough to concede that: 'Speke now has the full glory of having discovered the largest inland sea on the continent of Africa, also its principal affluent as well as its outlet. I must also give him credit for having understood the geography of the countries we travelled through far better than any of us who so persistently opposed his hypothesis.'

14

road to the border and 180km from Mwanza, and covered under a separate heading below. Other significant towns, situated along the main road, are Bunda, which lies close to the Serengeti about 70km south of Musoma, and Tarime, 20km south of the border. The smaller town of Butiama, which lies about 30km east of the main road, is of note as the birth and burial place of former President Nyerere, and for a small museum dedicated to his memory.

⌂ WHERE TO STAY

⌂ **Speke Bay Lodge** (8 bungalows, 12 standing tents) ☎ 028 262 1236; e spekebay@ africaonline.co.tz; www.spekebay.com. About 1km from the main Musoma road, 125km from Mwanza & 15km south of the Ndaraka Gate to Serengeti NP, this attractive & moderately priced lakeshore lodge is a good spot for birdwatching on the lake & game fishing by boat. *En-suite thatched bungalow US$105/132 sgl/dbl B&B or US$144/210 FB; standing safari tent with common showers & toilets US$42/60 B&B or US$81/138 FB.*

⌂ **Serengeti Stop Over** (10 rooms) ☎ 028 262 273; m 0784 406996/422359; e info@ serengetistopover.com; www.serengetistopover.com. This excellent budget lodge lies along the eastern side of the main Mwanza–Musoma road, in an area where quite a bit of game can be present, about 1km

south of the Ndaraka Entrance Gate to Serengeti NP & 18km south of Bunda. The lodge consists of 10 bandas & a campsite with hot showers & cooking shades. A great advantage of staying here for motorised travellers coming from Kenya or Mwanza is that park fees are only payable once you enter the park. The lodge can arrange safaris to Serengeti NP, which work out more cheaply than a safari out of Arusha, if only because the lodge is a mere 1km from the entrance gate & 135km from Seronera, so an overnight or day trip is a realistic possibility. A vehicle for 5 for a day trip into the park is US$130. Other activities include a walking safari to Lake Victoria at US$18 pp, traditional & game fishing trips, a visit to the Nyerere Museum, & dancing & other cultural activities. *US$30/55 sgl/dbl B&B; camping US$5 pp plus US$10 tent hire.*

BUTIAMA This otherwise undistinguished small town is of note as the birthplace of former President Julius Nyerere, and it is also where he is buried. The **Mwalimu Julius K Nyerere Memorial Museum** (☎ *028 262 1338;* e *mwljknyereremus@ juasun.net; www.museum.or.tz/nyerere.asp;* ⊕ *09.30–18.00 daily; entrance US$5 pp*) was officially opened here in July 1999, and contains a variety of exhibits about Tanzania's first president, including various personal possessions and gifts presented to him on his inauguration and retirement, as well as about the local Zanaki culture. Nyerere's grave and those of his parents can also be visited. Butiama lies off the main road along a 30–40km side road branching from Bunda. The drive from Bunda takes less than an hour in a private vehicle, and there is some public transport.

MUSOMA

Situated on the eastern shores of Lake Victoria, Musoma is the administrative centre of Mara Region, and a reasonably substantial town, with a population estimated at just over 100,000 in 2002. The compact town centre shares with Mwanza and Bukoba a likeable combination of run-down colonial architecture – the old Boma on Mkendo Hill dates to the German period – and friendly African bustle. And its setting, on a narrow, rocky peninsula, is the equal of any port on Lake Victoria, terminating in an impressive granite outcrop covered in clucking cormorants and offering an almost 360° vantage point for sunsets over the lake. Unfortunately, however, because it is tucked up so close to the Kenyan border, Musoma is something of a dead end in terms of travel within Tanzania, and it would be difficult to justify a special diversion there. For travellers headed between Mwanza and the Kenyan port of Kisumu, however, this remote but hospitable port is likely to prove a more than agreeable place to break up the trip. Two possible water excursions from Musoma are to Lukuba Island, known for its impressive breeding bird colonies, and to the crocodile-infested Mara River mouth – Mara Riverboat Safaris (m *0786 900316/0787 948463; www.marariverairboatsafari-ltd.com*) runs daily airboat tours to the wetlands starting at US$75 per person for a 45 minute round-trip. The Nyerere Museum in Butiama also makes for an easy day trip out of Musoma.

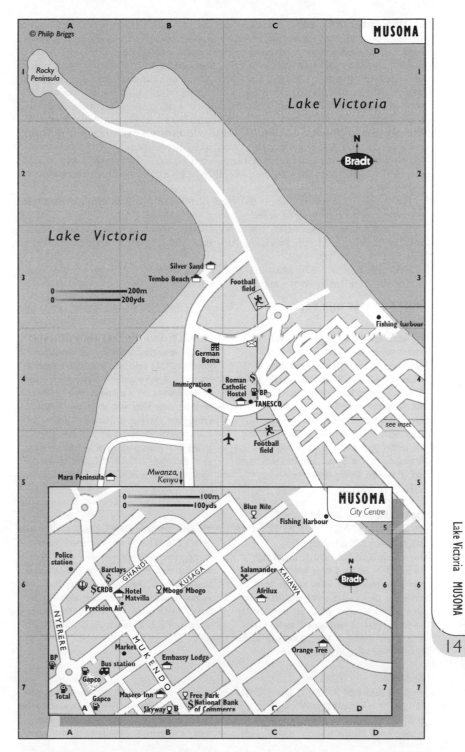

A   B   C   D

© Philip Briggs

Rocky
Peninsula

Lake Victoria

N

Bradt

Lake Victoria

0 ▬▬▬ 200m
0 ▬▬▬ 200yds

Silver Sand
Tembo Beach

Football
field

Fishing harbour

German
Boma

Immigration

Roman
Catholic
Hostel
BP
TANESCO

see inset

Football
field

Mara Peninsula

Mwanza,
Kenya

Blue Nile

MUSOMA
City Centre

Fishing Harbour

0 ▬▬▬ 100m
0 ▬▬▬ 100yds

Police
station

Barclays

GHANDI

KUSAGA

Salamander

KAHAWA

N

Bradt

CRDB

Precision Air

Hotel
Matvilla

Mbogo Mbogo

Afrilux

NYERERE

MUKENDO

Market

Bus station

Gapco

Embassy Lodge

Orange Tree

BP

Total

Gapco

Masero Inn

Skyway

Free Park
National Bank
of Commerce

A   B   C   D

Lake Victoria MUSOMA

14

GETTING THERE AND AWAY Musoma lies about 180km from Mwanza along an 18km-long side road branching west from the main road towards the Kenya border. The road between Mwanza and Musoma is surfaced and in pretty good nick for most of its length, the major exception being the very bumpy 30km stretch immediately outside Mwanza. The drive takes around two hours in a private vehicle. Regular buses run along the road, taking about four hours one-way; the most reliable is Muhammed Trans which runs three services daily, departing Musoma at 06.00, 09.00 and 13.30. Small and very regular minibuses cover the stretch between Musoma and Bunda, but don't seem to operate any further south towards Mwanza. Coming from the Kenya side, direct buses between Kisumu and Mwanza run past the junction to Musoma, but generally bypass the town itself. If you need to get out at the junction, you'll have no difficulty finding transport on to Musoma.

For details of stopovers along the road north and south of Musoma, see the preceding section, *Between Mwanza and the Kenyan border*.

An airstrip lies on the outskirts of central Musoma between the Catholic Hostel and the Peninsula Hotel. Precision Air runs four flights a week from Dar es Salaam.

However you arrive in Musoma, should you want to stay at one of the beach hotels, the standard fare for a taxi is around Tsh1,000–2,000.

WHERE TO STAY AND EAT
Upmarket

Lukuba Island Lodge (5 rooms) ☎ 027 254 8840; e lukubaisland@habari.co.tz; www.lukubaisland.com. Set on a small island a 45min boat ride from Musoma, this peaceful retreat is ideally suited to keen birdwatchers, with more than 70 species recorded, & it's also home to spotted-necked otters, vervet monkeys & agama lizards, while anglers have the prospect of hooking Nile perches that clock in at up to 80kg. Accommodation is in 5 stone bungalows with thatch roofs & verandas offering idyllic lake views. *US$288/520 sgl/dbl FB.*

Mara Peninsula Hotel [427 A5] ☎ 028 264 2526; e marapeninsula@yahoo.com. The former government Lake Hotel, now privatised, revamped & renamed, is a well-maintained & atmospheric wood & whitewash set-up on a somewhat sterile stretch of lakeshore about 500m west of the town centre. Coming from elsewhere in Tanzania, it seems a little pricey, however. The open-sided restaurant on the ground floor serves a variety of western & Indian dishes for around Tsh5,000. *US$58/66 en-suite sgl/dbl with satellite TV, AC, fridge & hot bath; US$83–116 suites.*

Moderate

Afrilux Hotel [427 C6] ☎ 028 262 0031; f 028 262 0534; e info@afriluxhotel.net; www.afriluxhotel.net. This smart & perhaps slightly self-consciously modern 4-storey hotel is situated right in the town centre, 500m from the bus station. The clean en-suite rooms with satellite TV, fan & running hot water are all you could possibly ask for the price. The restaurant & garden bar serves decent continental & Indian meals for around Tsh4,000. *Tsh25,000/30,000 sgl/dbl.*

Hotel Matvilla [427 A6] (24 rooms) ☎ 028 262 2445; f 028 262 2294. This new central hotel, located above the Precision Air office, offers clean, if somewhat small, en-suite rooms with stylish modern furnishings (a real treat in these parts!). The attached open-air garden restaurant serves regular themed buffets for around Tsh12,000. The entrance to the hotel is on Ghandi St. *Tsh20,000/30,000 sgl/dbl.*

Budget

Tembo Beach Hotel [427 B3] (7 rooms) ☎ 028 262 2887; e tembobeach@yahoo.com. Set on a small strip of beach around 500m from the centre of town, Tembo Beach is a popular stop-off on the

overland route. The rooms, with their fabulous retro 70s ski lodge appeal – loads of wood panelling; some with loft beds – seem optimistically priced. There's a campsite, & a friendly bar & restaurant serves meals for around US$3–6. Bike hire is also available & boat trips on the Mara River can be arranged. *US$30 B&B en-suite dbl with fan; camping US$8 pp.*

Shoestring

⌂ **Silver Sand Hotel** [427 B3] ✆ 028 262 2740. About 1km out of town, within a wooded compound that would overlook the beach were it not enclosed by tall stone walls, this has definitely seen better days, but it's a friendly & affordable set-up all the same. Faintly musty en-suite rooms have netting but no fan, & a functional shower. Meals by prior arrangement only. *Tsh6,000/10,000 sgl/dbl.*

⌂ **Orange Tree Hotel** [427 C7] ✆ 028 262 2353. This long-established budget hotel has possibly seen better days, but it remains a friendly, sensibly priced option. *Tsh10,000/15,000 clean en-suite sgl/dbl.*

⌂ **Roman Catholic Conference Centre & Hostel** [427 C4] ✆ 028 262 0168. This is the best budget option in town, about 200m from the bus station along the road towards the airport, & consisting of 30 clean dbls with netting (but no fan). A canteen serves inexpensive local meals. *Tsh8,000 dbl.*

RUBONDO ISLAND NATIONAL PARK

The only bona fide tourist attraction on Lake Victoria, Rubondo Island National Park, gazetted in 1977, lies in its far southwest corner, some 200km west of the Serengeti as the crow flies, where it forms a potentially very different extension to a standard northern Tanzania safari package. That so few tourists do actually make it to Rubondo is in some part because the island's attractions are more low-key and esoteric than those of Tanzania's high-profile savannah reserves. But a greater factor in Rubondo's obscurity is quite simply that the park long lacked for the sort of tourist infrastructure and ease of access that would have made it a realistic goal for any but the most intrepid or wealthy of travellers.

All this has changed, at least in theory, following the construction of the indisputably lovely Rubondo Island Camp, and the more recent introduction of scheduled flights to Rubondo from the Serengeti and Mwanza. In practice, however, Rubondo remains among the most underrated and least visited of all Tanzania's national parks. This is a real shame, because it is a lovely retreat, offering the combination of a near-perfect climate, atmospheric jungle-fringed beaches, some unusual wildlife viewing, and the opportunity to explore it all on foot or by boat. Rubondo may not be to everybody's taste, but the island can be recommended without reservation to anybody with a strong interest in birds, walking or game fishing – or simply a yen to escape to an uncrowded and blissfully peaceful tropical paradise!

Rubondo has a remarkably pleasant climate all year through, with temperatures rarely falling outside a range of 20–25°C by day or by night. The average annual rainfall is around 1,200mm, with the driest months being June to September, and January and February. These dry months are the perfect time to visit Rubondo, but the park and lodge are open all year round, and there is no serious obstacle to visiting during the rains. The entrance fee of US$20 per 24 hours must be paid in hard currency. A national park fishing licence valid for three days costs US$50.

GEOGRAPHY AND VEGETATION The 457km² national park is dominated by the green and undulating 240km² island for which it is named, but it does protect another 11 islets, none much larger than 2km², and there is talk of extending the boundary eastward to incorporate the forested west of Maisome Island. Rubondo Island itself essentially consists of a partially submerged rift of four volcanically formed hills, linked by three flatter isthmuses. It measures 28km from north to south but is nowhere more than 10km wide. The highest point on Rubondo is the Msasa Hills in the far south, which reaches an elevation of 1,486m (350m above the level of the lake). The park headquarters, airstrip and various

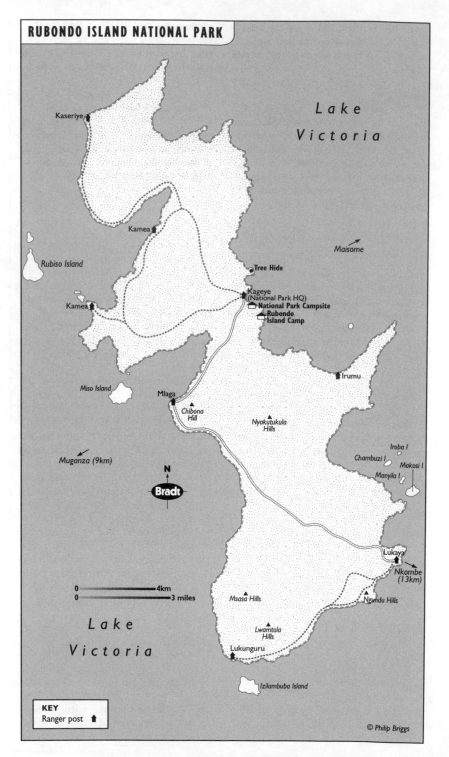

RUBONDO ISLAND NATIONAL PARK

Kaseriye

Lake Victoria

Kamea

Maisome

Rubiso Island

Tree Hide

Kamea

Kageye
(National Park HQ)
National Park Campsite
Rubondo
Island Camp

Irumu

Miso Island

Mlaga

Chibona Hill

Nyakutukula Hills

Muganza (9km)

N

Bradt

Iroba I

Chambuzi I

Makosi I

Manyila I

Lukaya

Nkombe
(13km)

0 ──────── 4km
0 ──────── 3 miles

Msasa Hills

Ngundu Hills

Lake Victoria

Lwamtola Hills

Lukunguru

Izilambuba Island

KEY
Ranger post

© *Philip Briggs*

accommodation facilities lie within 2km of one another at Kageye, on the central isthmus, about 10km from the northern tip at the narrowest part of the island.

The dominant vegetation type is closed-canopy lowland forest, which covers about 80% of the island's surface area. This is interspersed with patches of open grassland and, all but restricted to the Lukaya area, acacia woodland. The eastern lakeshore is characterised by rocky areas and sandy beaches (such as those in front of the lodge and camp), while the western shore supports extensive papyrus swamps, often lined with wild date palms. Between December and March, an estimated 40 terrestrial and epiphytic orchid species come into bloom, as do gloriosa and fireball lilies. The red coral tree, which flowers almost all year round, is also a spectacular sight.

WILDLIFE Rubondo's wildlife doesn't offer the easy thrills of many savannah reserves, but many large mammals are present, most alluring perhaps the introduced populations of chimpanzee and elephant (see box, *The floating zoo*, pages 434–5). However, the presence of these glamour boys shouldn't shift the focus away from the island's interesting assemblage of naturally occurring residents, including the aquatic sitatunga antelope, hippopotamus, crocodile and water monitor.

Vervet monkeys are numerous and easily seen all over Rubondo, but no other primate species occurs there naturally. This is difficult to explain, given the variety of primates that are present in similar island habitats on the Ugandan part of the lake, and given that the lake dried up fully in the biologically recent past, which would have allowed a free flow of species between the island and mainland forests.

There is no better place in Africa to observe the spot-necked otter, a widespread but elusive diurnal predator that feeds mainly on fish and frogs. A few pairs of otter are resident in the rocky bay around the lodge and camp – they regularly swim past camp, and the den can sometimes be seen through binoculars during the breeding season. The only terrestrial predators that occur on the island are the marsh mongoose and large-spotted genet, the latter regularly coming to feed around the lodge at dinnertime.

Birds With its combination of aquatic and forested habitats, Rubondo Island makes for an alluring destination for birdwatchers, especially as it can so easily

STALKING THE SITATUNGA

Two closely related antelope species occur naturally on the Rubondo Island, the swamp-dwelling sitatunga and forest-dwelling bushbuck. Of these, the more interesting is the sitatunga – a widespread but localised species with uniquely splayed hooves that allow it to manoeuvre through swampy habitats – since Rubondo is one of only two East African parks where it is easily observed. The males of both these antelopes are very handsome, with large spiralled horns, but the sitatunga is larger, shaggier in appearance, and grey where the bushbuck is chestnut brown. The females of both species are smaller and less striking, but easily distinguished from one another, since the bushbuck is striped on its sides, whereas the sitatunga is unmarked.

Rubondo's sitatunga population probably exceeds ten individuals per km2, and is not so habitat-specific as elsewhere, apparently – and unexpectedly – outnumbering bushbuck even in the forest. Researchers have noted that the sitatunga of Rubondo's forests are more diurnal than is normally the case, and have less-splayed feet and darker coats than those resident in the swamps – whether this is genetically influenced, or a function of wear and sun bleaching, is difficult to say. A possible explanation for this anomalous situation is that sitatunga colonised the island and expanded into forested habitats before there were any bushbuck around.

14

Lake Victoria has been afflicted by a series of manmade ecological disasters over the past century. The degradation started in the early colonial era, with the clearing of large tracts of indigenous vegetation and drainage of natural swamps to make way for plantations of tea, coffee and sugar. One result of this was an increase in the amount of topsoil washed into the lake, so that the water became progressively muddier and murkier during the 20th century. More serious was the wash-off of toxic pesticides and other agricultural chemicals, which in addition to polluting the water contain nutrients that promote algae growth, in turn tending to decrease oxygenation levels. The foundation of several large lakeshore cities and plantations attracted migrant labourers from around the region, many of whom settled at the lake, leading to a disproportionate population increase and – exacerbated by more sophisticated trapping tools introduced by the colonials – heavy overfishing.

By the early 1950s, the above factors had conspired to create a noticeable drop in yields of popular indigenous fish, in particular the Lake Victoria tilapia (ngege), which had been fished close to extinction. The colonial authorities introduced the similar Nile tilapia, which restored the diminishing yield without seriously affecting the ecological balance of the lake. More disastrous, however, was the gradual infiltration of the Nile perch, a voracious predator that feeds almost exclusively on smaller fish, and frequently reaches a length of 2m and a weight exceeding 100kg. How the perch initially ended up in Lake Victoria is a matter of conjecture – game fishermen might have introduced some perch, while others possibly swam downriver from Uganda's Lake Kyoga, where they had been introduced in the mid 1950s. But, however they first arrived in Lake Victoria, Nile perch regularly turned up in fishermen's nets from the late 1950s. The authorities, who favoured large eating fish over the smaller tilapia and cichlids, decided to ensure the survival of the alien predators with an active programme of introductions in the early 1960s.

It would be 20 years before the full impact of this misguided policy hit home. In a UN survey undertaken in 1971, the indigenous haplochromine cichlids still constituted their traditional 80% percentage of the lake's fish biomass, while the introduced perch and tilapia had effectively displaced the indigenous tilapia without otherwise altering the ecology of the lake. A similar survey undertaken ten years later revealed that the perch population had exploded to constitute 80% of the lake's fish biomass, while the haplochromine cichlids – the favoured prey of the perch – now accounted for a mere 1%. Lake Victoria's estimated 150–300 endemic cichlid species, all of which have evolved from a mere five ancestral species since the lake dried out 10,000–15,000 years ago, are regarded as representing the most recent comparable explosion of vertebrate adaptive radiation in the world. Ironically, these fish also are currently undergoing what Boston University's Les Kauffman has described as 'the greatest vertebrate mass extinction in recorded history'.

For all this, the introduction of perch could be considered a superficial success within its own terms. The perch now form the basis of the lake's thriving fishing industry, with up to 500 tonnes of fish meat being exported from the lake annually, at a value of more than US$300 million, by commercial fishing concerns in the three lakeshore countries. The tanned perch hide is used as a substitute for leather to make shoes, belts, and purses,

be explored on foot. Oddly, the park's avifauna has never been properly studied, with the result that the only checklist, compiled from reported sightings by the Frankfurt Zoological Society and available at the Rubondo Island Camp, tallies up at a relatively low 225 species. It is likely that a substantial number of forest species that are resident on the island, or regular visitors, have thus far gone unrecorded.

and the dried swim bladders, used to filter beer and make fish stock, are exported at a rate of around US$10 per kg. The flip side of this is that as fish exports increase, local fishing communities are forced to compete against large commercial companies with better equipment and more economic clout. Furthermore, since the perch is too large to roast on a fire and too fatty to dry in the sun, it does not really meet local needs.

The introduction of perch is not the only damaging factor to have affected Lake Victoria's ecology. It is estimated that the amount of agricultural chemicals being washed into the lake has more than doubled since the 1950s. Tanzania alone is currently pumping two million litres of untreated sewage and industrial waste into the lake daily, and while legal controls on industrial dumping are tighter in Kenya and Uganda, they are not effectively enforced. The agricultural wash-off and industrial dumping has led to a further increase in the volume of chemical nutrients in the lake, promoting the growth of plankton and algae. At the same time, the cichlids that once fed on these microscopic organisms have been severely depleted in number by the predatorial perch.

The lake's algae levels have increased fivefold in the last four decades, with a corresponding decrease in oxygen levels. The lower level of the lake now consists of dead water – lacking any oxygenation or fish activity below about 30m – and the quality of the water closer to the surface has deteriorated markedly since the 1960s. Long-term residents of the Mwanza area say that the water was once so clear that you could see the lake floor; from the surface to depths of 6m or more; today visibility near the surface is more like 1m.

A clear indicator of this deterioration has been the rapid spread of water hyacinth, which thrives in polluted conditions, leading to high phosphate and nitrogen levels, and then tends to further deplete oxygen levels by forming an impenetrable mat over the water's surface. An exotic South American species, the water hyacinth was introduced to East Africa by expatriates in Rwanda, and made its way down to Lake Victoria via the Kagera River. Unknown on the lake prior to 1989, it has subsequently colonised vast tracts of the lake surface, and clogged up several harbours, where it is barely kept under control by constant harvesting. To complete this grim vicious circle, Nile perch, arguably the main cause of the problem, are known to be vulnerable to the conditions created by hyacinth matting, high algae levels and decreased oxygenation in the water.

As is so often the case with ecological issues, what might at first be dismissed by some as an esoteric concern for bunny-huggers in fact has wider implications for the estimated 20–30 million people resident in the Lake Victoria basin. The infestation of hyacinth and rapid decrease in indigenous snail-eating fish has led to a rapid growth in the number of bilharzia-carrying snails. The deterioration in water quality, exacerbated by the pumping of sewage, has increased the risk of sanitary-related diseases such as cholera spreading around the lake. The change in the fish biomass has encouraged commercial fishing for export outside of the region, in the process depressing the local semi-subsistence fishing economy, leading to an increase in unemployment and in protein deficiency. And there is an ever-growing risk that Africa's largest lake will eventually be reduced to a vast expanse of dead water, with no fish in it at all – with ecological, economic and humanitarian ramifications that scarcely bear thinking about.

The main avian attraction for casual visitors will be the concentrations of large waterbirds that occur along the island's swampy shores. Rubondo hosts Lake Victoria's densest fish eagle population – 638 individuals were recorded in a 1995 census – as well as large numbers of open-billed and yellow-billed storks. An excellent spot for varied waterbirds (as well as aquatic mammals and reptiles) is Mlaga Bay on the western side of the island, where some of the more prominent species are Goliath, purple and squacco heron, long-toed plover, blue-headed coucal, swamp flycatcher and various weavers. Of interest less for their variety than for their volume of birds are the so-called Bird Islands, a pair of tiny rocky islets that lie about 1km off the southeast shore of Rubondo, and support breeding colonies of various cormorants, egrets and ibises.

Dedicated birders are likely to be more interested in the forest and other terrestrial species. Two common birds on the island – Vieillot's black weaver and black-and-white casqued hornbill – are Guinea–Congo biome species with a very limited range in Tanzania. The lodge grounds and adjacent road and forest loop – where it is permitted to walk unguided – is as good a place as any to seek out other forest birds. Among the more interesting species recorded in this area are the blue-breasted kingfisher, grey-winged akalat, snowy-headed robin-chat, paradise flycatcher, common wattle-eye and green twinspot. The area around the lodge is also the main stomping – and screeching – ground for the recently introduced flock of African grey parrots.

GETTING THERE AND AWAY The only simple way to get to Rubondo is by air. Coastal Travel has recently implemented a daily scheduled service connecting Rubondo to Geita, Mwanza and Grumeti in the Western Corridor of Serengeti National Park. For travellers appending a visit to Rubondo to a standard northern circuit safari, the easiest option would be to fly directly from Grumeti. For those trying to keep costs to a minimum, the best bet would be to bus from Mwanza to

THE FLOATING ZOO

Rubondo Island is unique among Tanzania's national parks not only in its aquatic location, but also in that it was conceived less as a game reserve than as a sort of 'floating zoo'. Proclaimed a forest reserve in German times, the island was upgraded to a game reserve in 1966, at the behest of Professor Bernhard Grzimek of the Frankfurt Zoological Society. Grzimek, best known for his tireless efforts to protect the Serengeti, believed that the forested island would make an ideal sanctuary for the breeding and protection of introduced populations of endangered Congolese rainforest species such as golden cat, okapi, bongo and lowland gorilla.

This plan never quite attained fruition, even though several chimpanzees were introduced to the island along with small numbers of elephant, giraffe, roan antelope, suni, black-and-white colobus monkey and black rhinoceros – most of which would not normally be regarded as forest-specific species. This arbitrary introduction programme was abandoned in 1973, only to be resurrected briefly in July 2000, when a flock of 37 grey parrots – captured in Cameroon for sale in Asia and confiscated in transit at Nairobi – were released on to the island.

Not all of the mammal re-introductions were a success. The 16 black rhinoceros that were relocated from the Serengeti in 1965 were poached in the 1970s, while the five roan antelope introduced in 1967 evidently died of natural causes before producing any offspring. By contrast, the six sub-adult elephants that were released on to the island over 1972–73 have bred up to a population of 30–40, with the larger herds concentrated in the south and lone bulls ranging all over the island – they are quite regularly seen around the park headquarters and lodge. Some concern has been expressed that an overpopulation of elephants could lead to the destruction of the natural forest, but the herd would probably need to grow to 200 before this became a real threat, and contraception can be used to keep numbers in check.

The introduced black-and-white colobus also occasionally roam close to the lodge, but the main population of about 30 is concentrated in the far south of the island, and

Geita and pick up the flight in Geita. For travellers coming from elsewhere in the country, it is easiest to fly to Mwanza (direct flights from Dar es Salaam and Kilimanjaro International Airport, connecting to Zanzibar) and hop on a Rubondo-bound flight there. At the time of writing, daily departures are guaranteed, with the provision that a minimum of three passengers is booked on to the flight.

🏠 WHERE TO STAY
Upmarket

🏠 **Rubondo Island Camp** (10 rooms) 🕿 027 250 8790; m 0784 327234; f 027 250 8896; e info@africanconservancycompany.com; www.rubondoislandcamp.com. This attractive & immensely tranquil tented lodge consists of 10 luxury self-contained *bandas*, each with private veranda. It has a truly fabulous location, with a tall forest gallery rising high behind the tents, & a sandy palm-lined beach fringed by rocky outcrops directly in front. The open-sided communal areas stand on one of the rocky outcrops, offering a pretty view over the lake. This leads down to a secluded beachfront platform where a variety of large waterbirds have taken up more or less permanent residence. Pied & malachite kingfishers hawk for food, paradise flycatchers flutter in the trees — & the occasional pair of otters swims past. The swimming pool is built in a natural rock outcrop. A good selection of boat & foot excursions can be arranged, as can fishing trips. A stay of at least 3 nights is recommended to make the most of Rubondo, & the lodge offers a variety of attractively priced fly-in packages ranging from 3 to 7 nights. *US$450/770 sgl/dbl FB inc park fees, drinks, laundry & all activities except fishing.*

their normal territory can be reached by boat or car, followed by a ten-minute walk. The giraffe herd is most likely to be encountered in the restricted area of acacia woodland around Lukaya, some distance south of the lodge and park headquarters. The suni are the most elusive of the introduced species, because they are so small, and secretive by nature.

Between 1966 and 1969, eight male and nine female chimpanzees were released on to the island, all of them born wild in the Guinean rainforest belt but captured when young to be taken to European zoos and circuses. Some had been held in good zoos where they had the company of other chimpanzees, while others were caged inadequately or in solitary confinement. Several individuals were regarded as troublesome and had regularly attacked or bitten their keepers, and two of the males were shot after their release because they had attacked people living on the island. The others appeared to settle down quickly. Two newborn chimps were observed in 1968, and it is now estimated that the total community numbers at least 30, most of them second or third generation, but it is possible that a couple of the original individuals survive. The chimps are normally resident in the central and northern parts of the island, near the Kamea and Irumu ranger posts, which respectively lie about 5km northwest and a similar distance southeast of the park headquarters at Kageye.

In 1996, the Frankfurt Zoological Society and Tanzania National Parks initiated a joint project with the dual purpose of monitoring chimpanzee numbers and behaviour, and habituating a community for tourist visits. Chimpanzee tracking is now offered to visitors, but with so few chimps ranging over such a large area, the odds of an encounter are far smaller than in the parks of Lake Tanganyika. At this stage, it is most sensible to view the excursion as a forest walk with a chance of seeing chimpanzees. However, a new research project, recently implemented, may hasten the habituation process as well as improving the day to day information regarding the exact whereabouts of the chimps.

14

Budget

National Park Campsite & bandas The national park banda & camping site lies on a lovely forest-fringed beach about 1km north of Rubondo Island Camp, & a similar distance from park headquarters. No meals are available, & it's advisable to bring most of what you will need with you, but a shop in the park headquarters does sell a few basic foodstuffs (essentially what the national park staff would eat), as well as warm beers & sodas. A cook can be arranged on request. Travellers staying at the bandas are welcome to visit Rubondo Island Camp for a chilled drink or a meal – it's fine to walk along the footpath or road between the banda site & camp unaccompanied, but the camp would need a bit of advance warning to prepare meals – US$8 b/fast, US$12 lunch, US$15 dinner. Rather grotty chalets with common showers US$20 pp, smarter self-contained chalets US$50 pp; camping US$20 pp.

WHAT TO SEE A wide variety of activities can be arranged either through Rubondo Island Camp or through the National Park headquarters. A good, inexpensive introduction to the park, taking two to four hours depending on how often you stop, is the guided trail to Pongo Viewpoint and Nhoze Hide, the latter a good place to see sitatunga, a variety of birds and – very occasionally – elephant. Another popular activity is chimpanzee tracking from either Kamea or Irumu ranger posts (ask at headquarters which of the two currently offers the better chance). This generally takes about six hours, with a 50–60% chance of encountering chimps at present, and it costs US$25 per person inclusive of a guide and transport to the ranger post. Other options include boat trips to the swampy Mlaga Bay or Bird Island, fishing expeditions (the record catch is a 108kg Nile perch), and walks on more remote parts of the island to look for colobus monkeys or giraffes.

As for unguided activities, quite a bit of wildlife and lots of birds can be seen in the grounds of Rubondo Island Camp and the national park campsite, while the roughly 1km footpath and road between the two can be walked unaccompanied as a loop. Swimming is reputedly safe, at least at the beaches in front of the lodge and camp. The lake water is regularly tested for bilharzia, thus far always with a negative result, and – bearing in mind that human beings form an integral part of the bacteria's life cycle – all residents of the island take the bilharzia cure as a precautionary routine every six months. Do be aware that crocs occasionally swim past the beaches, so far without incident – still, you might want to look before you leap in!

BUKOBA Updated with assistance from Kiroyera Tours

Founded as a German administrative centre by the Emin Pasha in 1890, Bukoba is today the regional headquarters of the Kagera Region, and the second most important port on the Tanzanian part of Lake Victoria, though its population of around 60,000 is far smaller than that of Musoma. Bukoba is situated about 50km south of the Uganda border on a lush, moist and hilly stretch of lakeshore that supports a thriving coffee industry as well as recently discovered deposits of nickel and cobalt that are likely to be exploited in the near future. The main food crop and dietary staple of the Bukoba area, as in Uganda, is batoke (or matoke), a large green banana that is roasted or steamed, and eaten in much the same manner as ugali elsewhere in Tanzania.

Bukoba's flat, compact town centre is dominated by several mid-20th-century Asian buildings – most in a poor state of repair – and lies about 1km inland of the lakeshore, to which it is connected by the leafy Jamhuri Avenue. At the lake end of Jamhuri Road, near the Lake View Hotel, stands a cluster of old German buildings, including the old Boma and Magistrate's Court, the original post office, the German cemetery, and the first general store, known locally as duka kubwa ('big shop'). The main port and ferry terminal is situated on a separate part of the

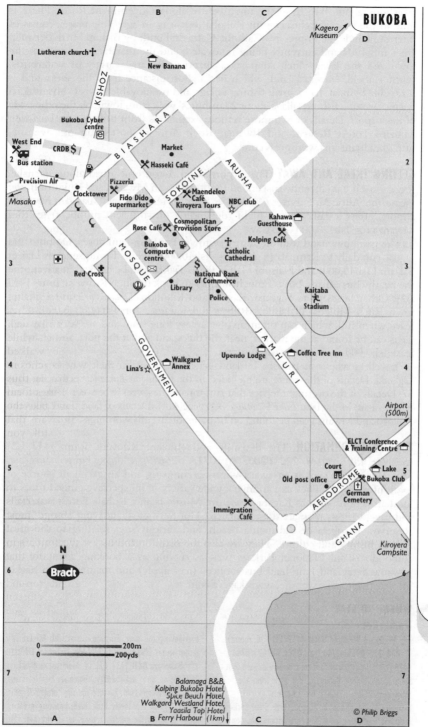

BUKOBA

Kagera Museum

Lutheran church ✝

New Banana

KISHOZ

BIASHARA

Bukoba Cyber centre

West End
CRDB $
Bus station

Precision Air

Masaka

Market

Hasseki Café

SOKOINE

ARUSHA

Clocktower

Pizzeria

Fido Dido supermarket

Maendeleo Café

Kiroyera Tours

NBC club

Kahawa Guesthouse

MOSQUE

Rose Café

Cosmopolitan Provision Store

Kolping Café

Bukoba Computer centre

Catholic Cathedral

Red Cross

Library

National Bank of Commerce

Police

Kaitaba Stadium

GOVERNMENT

JAMHURI

Walkgard Annex

Lina's

Upendo Lodge

Coffee Tree Inn

Airport (500m)

ELCT Conference & Training Centre

Court

Old post office

AERODROME

Lake Bukoba Club

German Cemetery

Immigration Café

CHANA

Kiroyera Campsite

N

Bradt

0   200m
0   200yds

Balamaga B&B,
Kolping Bukoba Hotel,
Spice Beach Hotel,
Walkgard Westland Hotel,
Yaasila Top Hotel
Ferry Harbour (1km)

© Philip Briggs

Lake Victoria BUKOBA

14

lakeshore, about 3km from the town centre along Government Road. There is little in the way of sightseeing in Bukoba, but it is an agreeable place. Points of interest include the impressive Catholic Cathedral built by Bishop Hirth between 1893 and 1904 and currently being renovated, and the marshy area between the town and the lake, which supports a surprisingly large variety of waterbirds. Further afield, Musira Island, which lies a short distance from the shore and is accessible by boat, has a small fishing village and is enjoyable to visit. Nyamukazi is a picturesque fishing village about 20 minutes' walk from town, on the other side of the airport. Details of two more remote excursions from Bukoba, the bird-rich Minziro Forest Reserve and Bwanjai Rock Art, are posted on our website, http://bradttanzania.wordpress.com.

GETTING THERE AND AWAY The airport is on Aerodrome Road along the lake. Precision Air has currently suspended flights between Mwanza and Bukoba. In the meantime, Auric Air Services (❧ *028 256 1286; www.auricair.com*), based at Mwanza airport, offers a daily charter flight (depending on sufficient numbers) to/from Mwanza for Tsh120,000 one-way.

The main bus stand is in the centre of town. For long-haul buses, Dolphin and Jaguar run daily to Kampala (5–6 hours, Tsh10,000), while Tawfiq services Dar es Salaam (Tsh45,000) and Nairobi (Tsh28,000). Tickets can be booked in advance at the nearby bus offices, but it's much simpler to book through Kiroyera Tours [437 B2]. Other buses go to Kigoma, Kasulu and Kibondo. *Dala-dalas* run to smaller towns such Muleba, Nshamba, Rubya and Karagwe for Tsh4,000–5,000. They leave when full, which can often involve a very long wait, and are very crowded. Taxis can be found at the market, near the bus stand and at the port, and charge at least Tsh3,000 for a charter trip in town.

Travellers who visit Bukoba by land generally do so on their way to or from Uganda. Details of this route are included in the *Getting to Tanzania* section on page 57. Details of the overnight ferries that run three times weekly between Bukoba and Mwanza are in the box, *Lake Victoria ferries*, page 414). Details of land travel between Bukoba and Mwanza can be found on http://bradttanzania.wordpress.com.

TOURIST INFORMATION The dynamic and efficient Kiroyera Tours [437 B2] (*Sokoine Rd;* ❧ *028 222 0203;* m *0713 526649;* e *info@kiroyeratours.com; www.kiroyeratours.com*) is an award-winning company and an excellent source of local information. They can arrange a wide variety of inexpensive guided tours to local attractions such as Kagera Museum, Musila Island, Rubale Forest waterfalls and cave, various rock art sites, Mutagata Hot Springs, Ibanda and Burigi Game Reserves, Karobela or Kabaranda beach, and various sites relating to the local Bahaya history and culture. They are also the main organisers for short safaris to Rubondo Island National Park as well as serving as a booking agent for the Mwanza ferry and long-haul bus services (fees apply) and maintaining a highly informative tourist website, www.kagera.com.

⌂ WHERE TO STAY
Upmarket
⌂ **Walkgard Westland Hotel** [437 C7] (30 rooms) ❧ 028 222 0935/42/46; m 0713 482423/0784 407841; e info@walkgard.com; www.walkgard.com. Situated on breezy Balamaga Hill 3km from the town centre, this is easily the smartest accommodation option in Kigoma, with good facilities including swimming pool, & a grandstand position

overlooking the port. *En-suite rooms with AC, DSTV & hot water US$40/50 sgl/dbl HB, suites US$80.*
⌂ **Balamaga B&B** [437 C7] (4 rooms) m 0787 757289; e bbb_bukoba@yahoo.co.uk; www.balamagabb.com. Further up the same hill as the Walkgard, this lovely little B&B, boasting great views & an idyllic garden setting, is a refreshing

alternative to the bland, run-of-the-mill hotel rooms offered elsewhere in Bukoba. Accommodation in 4 bright, airy rooms – 2 with dbl bed & en-suite, 2 with twin beds & shared bathroom – & satellite TV. Meals are also available. *Tsh40,000/60,000 sgl/dbl.*

Moderate

🏠 **Kolping Bukoba Hotel** [437 C7] ✆ 028 222 0199. Also on Balamaga Hill, this church-run hotel next to the Walkgard has clean en-suite rooms, & is good value if you don't mind the institutional atmosphere. *US$30/50 sgl/dbl.*

🏠 **Walkgard Annex Hotel** [437 B4] (30 rooms) ✆ 028 222 0626; www.walkgard.com. Formerly the Eden Hotel, this smart 2-storey hotel near the Red Cross is an amenable choice. En-suite rooms have TV, phone & hot water. *US$20/35 sgl/dbl HB.*

🏠 **Yaasila Top Hotel** [437 C7] ✆ 028 222 1251. This evergreen hotel has a nice location near to the port, budget rooms using common showers & larger en-suite rooms with king size bed, lake-facing balcony, fridge, TV, AC & telephone. It's a good place to eat or drink while you wait to board the ferry. *US$7/10 sgl/dbl with common showers; US$20/30 en-suite.*

Budget

🏠 **Upendo Lodge** [437 C4] (16 rooms) ✆ 028 222 0620; f 028 222 1285. Near the police station on Rwaijumba St, this lies halfway between the town centre & the airport, & 500m from the lakeshore. It has en-suite rooms with hot water, DSTV & large beds, a well-stocked bar, & a modern restaurant with Tanzanian & European dishes. *US$15 dbl.*

🏠 **ELCT Conference & Training Centre** [437 D5] (22 rooms) ✆ 028 222 0027, e elct-nwd@ africaonline.com. Situated close to the Lake Hotel & within walking distance of the airport, this efficient church-run hostel has comfortable clean AC rooms, a small restaurant serving the usual fried fish, chicken & rice fare for around Tsh4,000–5,000, & a curio shop, internet café & communal TV room. No alcohol. *US$12/18 sgl/dbl with shared bath; US$16/30 sgl/dbl en-suite.*

🏠 **Spice Beach Motel** [437 C7] ✆ 028 222 0142. This pleasant beach hotel near the ferry jetty has en-suite rooms with TV, hot water & AC. *Tsh15,000 dbl.*

🏠 **Lake Hotel** [437 D5] (14 rooms) Boasting a scenic location at the lakeshore end of Jamhuri Av & overhung with an aura of fading colonial charm, this rambling old hotel has drab but spacious en-suite dbls with TV, fan & net. There's a lovely outdoor garden & restaurant. *Tsh10,000–15,000 dbl, depending on size.*

Shoestring

🛆 **Kiroyera Campsite** [437 D6] (5 *bandas*) ✆ 028 222 0203; e info@kiroyeratours.com; www.kiroyeratours.com. Right on the beach overlooking Lake Victoria & only a few min walk from the centre of town, this perfectly positioned new campsite operated by Kiroyera Tours is a great choice for budget travellers. There are clean facilities, hammocks to laze in & a volleyball court if you're feeling active, as well as a lively beach bar & restaurant serving tasty pizzas & large plates of fish, chicken & chips. *Traditional banda US$10 pp; camping US$4 pp (own tent) or US$5 pp to rent a tent.*

✖ WHERE TO EAT AND DRINK Recommended for cheap lunches and snacks is the **Rose Café** [437 B3], which serves matoke, beans, samosas, fruit juice etc, and is popular with volunteers working in and around Bukoba. The **Pizzeria** [437 B2] near the market serves chicken, vegetarian and meat pizzas, as well as sausages and chips, but is open in the mornings only. The **Kolping Café** [437 C3] opposite the Kahawa Guest House near the cathedral dishes up inexpensive fish, meat, rice and matoke and has a TV. The **Hasseki Café** [437 B2] near the market dishes up similar fare, while **Maendeleo Café** [437 B2], next to Kiroyera Tours, serves up large helpings of *Nyama choma* and other local standards daily at lunch.

For evening meals, the **Lake Hotel** [437 D5] is recommended for its view of the lake and good variety of food and drink. The satellite TV and outdoor beer garden makes it a popular mazungu hangout, particularly on Friday nights. Also recommended is the restaurant at the **Yaasila Top Hotel** [437 C7], which serves a good variety of food and has a nice location, with two pool tables, darts and TV.

Cheaper options include the lakeshore **Bukoba Club** (opposite the Lake Hotel) [437 D5] and **Spice Beach Hotel** [437 C7],and the more central **West End Restaurant** [437 A2] near the bus stand and **NBC Club** [437 C2] near the National Bank of Commerce.

If you're self-catering, or want to stock up on packaged goods before visiting Minziro Forest or catching the ferry, the **Fido Dido Supermarket** [437 B2] and **Cosmopolitan Provision Store** [437 B3] stock packaged and refrigerated imported goods, including bread and many types of biscuits and drinks.

The top spot in town for after hours entertainment is the effervescent **Lina's Nightclub** [437 B4] which is open 24 hours, while discos often take place on Friday, Saturday and Sunday nights at **Red Cross** [437 A3] (near the government hospital) and the **NBC Club** [437 C2] (near the NBC bank).

OTHER PRACTICALITIES

Foreign exchange The National Bank of Commerce (NBC) near the Catholic Cathedral [437 B3] has foreign exchange facilities, but travellers coming from Uganda should note that it doesn't exchange Ugandan Shillings – you're best off trading any excess Ugandan money for Tanzanian currency at the border post. An ATM outside the NBC [437 C2] accepts international Visa cards for cash withdrawals.

Internet The best options are the Bukoba Cyber Centre [437 A2] (e *bcc@ bukobaonline.com* or *bcyberc@yahoo.com*) near the CRDB, and the Post Office Internet Café [437 B3]. Both stay open until 20.00 except on Sunday, and charge around Tsh500 per 30 minutes. There is also a reliable internet café at the ELCT Conference & Training Centre [437 D5].

Swimming There is no swimming pool in town, but you can swim at the Walkgard Westland Hotel [437 C7] for Tsh2,500 per day. A number of nearby beaches are worth a visit, including Bunena beach, within easy walking distance of town. The lake is infested with bilharzia, so swimming anywhere carries an element of risk.

Sporting facilities The Bukoba Club [437 D5] has tennis, snooker, table tennis and darts. The Kaitaba Stadium [437 C4] hosts football matches and other events including concerts and the annual celebration of Farmers Day on 8 August. The Red Cross [437 A3] has a basketball court and volleyball net.

WHAT TO SEE

Kagera Museum [437 D1] (✆ *028 222 0203;* f *028 222 0009;* e *kmuseum@ kiroyeratours.com;* ⊕ *09.30–18.00 daily; entrance US$2 pp*) This small museum houses a superb collection of wildlife photographs taken by Danish wildlife photographer Dick Persson, whose work is also displayed at the National Museum in Dar es Salaam, as well as a small exhibit of traditional tools and artefacts. The quickest way to get there is to walk east along the lakeshore past the airstrip, then turn left and follow the signs. While this is the route promoted by the museum, it cannot be recommended as you're not in fact allowed to walk over the airstrip. The longer route follows Sokoine Street northeast as it rambles its way around the top end of the airstrip, from where the museum is again signed. Alternatively, you can arrange a guided walking tour with Kiroyera Tours which cost US$3 per person excluding entrance fee.

15

Lake Tanganyika and the Western Safari Circuit

Following the contours of the Rift Valley along the border between Tanzania and the Congo, Lake Tanganyika is something of a statistician's dream, measuring 675km from north to south, an average of 50km wide, and reaching a depth of up to 1,435m. Tanganyika holds a volume of water seven times greater than that of Lake Victoria (the largest lake on the continent), and it is the longest freshwater body in the world, as well as the second deepest after Lake Baikal in Russia. It is also a very beautiful lake, hemmed in by the verdant hills on either side of the Rift Valley, and boasting crystal clear water that adds credence to its reputation for having the lowest pollution levels of any lake in the world. Lying at a relatively low elevation of 730m, the lake and its hinterland can be quite hot and sticky, but the climate is generally drier and cooler than anywhere along the coast.

Lake Tanganyika is at least three million years old, and although it is fed by more than 50 rivers and streams, its sole outlet is the Lukuga River, into which it overflows only in years of exceptionally high rainfall. Due to its great age and isolation from any similar habitat, Lake Tanganyika forms one of the most biologically rich aquatic habitats in the world, supporting more than 500 fish species of which the vast majority is comprised of endemic cichlids (see box, *Cichlids of the great lakes*, pages 464–5). The most important fish economically is the dagaa, a tiny plankton-cater that lives in large shoals and is sun-dried on the lakeshore for sale throughout western Tanzania. One of the most characteristic sights along any inhabited part of the lakeshore is the nocturnal spectacle of hundreds of small fishing boats lit by small lamps and bobbing in the waves like a low-lying swarm of fireflies.

The only substantial town on the Tanzanian lakeshore, and the normal entry point to the region, is Kigoma. This attractively sleepy port was founded under German rule 6km away from Ujiji, the 19th-century Arab trading post where Burton and Speke first reached the lakeshore in 1858, and where the historic meeting between Livingstone and Stanley took place in 1872. The main tourist attraction of the region is the two national parks that fringe the lake shore, Gombe and Mahale Mountains, which are best known for their habituated chimp communities, the most approachable wild chimp populations anywhere in Africa. Some distance east of the lake, the little-known and underrated Katavi National Park protects a range of plains animals similar to more accessible southern reserves such as Ruaha and Selous. Very few fly-in tourists ever get close to Lake Tanganyika, but the area does attract an erratic trickle of backpackers, for whom the weekly lake ferry service ranks as one of East Africa's most compelling public transport rides.

TABORA

All roads – and, perhaps more to the point, all railway lines – through central Tanzania lead to Tabora, a substantial town of around 130,000 people, and the

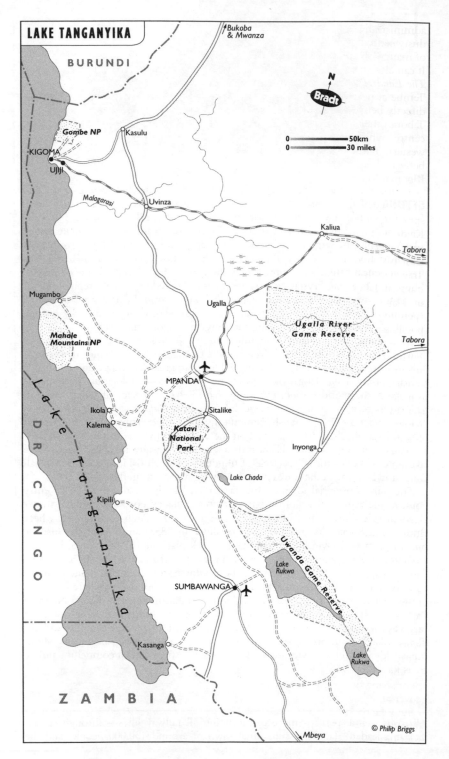

administrative centre of the eponymous region. Located in the heart of the hot, dusty central plateau, Tabora is a friendly and relaxed place, and the spacious layout of mango-shaded avenues goes some way to blunting the seasonally torrid climate. It can also stake claim to being the oldest urban settlement in the interior (see box, *The Land of the Moon*, page 446–7), though with the exception of Livingstone's Tembe at nearby Kwihara, there's little evidence of this today. Travellers chugging directly between the coast and Lake Tanganyika or Lake Victoria will see little of Tabora other than the rather chaotic railway station to the northeast of the town centre, which is no great loss. But those who travel more extensively around western Tanzania are likely to end up in Tabora at some point, be it to overnight between long drives, to change buses or to switch between trains heading to or from Kigoma, Mwanza or Mpanda.

GETTING THERE AND AWAY Tabora is where the railway line from Dar es Salaam splits into a northern branch heading to Mwanza and a western branch heading to Kigoma. It is also the terminal of the railway line south to Mpanda. The trains that run between Dar es Salaam and Kigoma or Mwanza generally stop in Tabora for at least two hours for shunting, but there is no need for passengers to disembark. Travellers heading between Mwanza and Kigoma, however, will need to change trains at Tabora, as will travellers heading between Mpanda and Kigoma, Mwanza or Dar es Salaam. Under normal circumstances, changing trains will involve spending a full day in Tabora, and possibly an overnight stay. Frustratingly, it is not possible to book a train ticket out of Tabora from anywhere else, which means that travellers intending to change trains will have to pitch up and hope for the best. Fortunately, the first- and second-class carriages between Tabora and Mpanda are seldom fully booked, while on the main Central Railway line at least one carriage in each class is normally set aside for passengers embarking at Tabora, so obtaining a ticket on the day is normally straightforward. If you have to spend a full day in Tabora between trains, and want somewhere to leave luggage and have a shower, your best bet is to take one of the cheaper (Tsh4,000) rooms at the nearby Aposele Inn & Guesthouse [444 D3] (see *Where to stay*).

Details of train schedules out of Dar es Salaam, Kigoma and Mwanza are included in the box, *The Central Railway*, in *Chapter 13*, page 393. At the time of writing the scheduled thrice-weekly services on the Central Line had been reduced to two services a week. Travellers crossing between Kigoma and Mwanza via Tabora can expect trains from either port to arrive in Tabora about 12–14 hours after departure, in other words at around breakfast time on Friday and Monday. Trains to Kigoma or Mwanza typically pass through Tabora around 26 hours after they leave Dar es Salaam, in other words shortly after sunset on Wednesday and Saturday. On the Mpanda sideline, trains leave from Tabora on Monday and Friday at 21.00 and from Mpanda on Tuesday and Saturday at 13.00, with the trip taking anything from 10 to 15 hours. Delays are increasingly frequent on the main Central Railway, which can be frustrating when waiting for trains heading to Kigoma or Mwanza, as a long delay *en route* from Dar es Salaam will leave you hanging around the station into the wee hours of the morning. The railway station workers normally have a pretty good idea of how far the train is running behind schedule, so keep checking the current situation with them.

The roads between Tabora and Dodoma, Kigoma, Mbeya and Mpanda are in poor shape, and can only realistically be covered in a good 4x4 vehicle. Buses do cover all of these roads, but they are generally very slow and overcrowded, and cannot be recommended, especially when trains also cover most of these routes. The two exceptions are: the road between Tabora and Mwanza, which is covered four times daily by the Muhammad Trans bus service, taking around seven hours

15

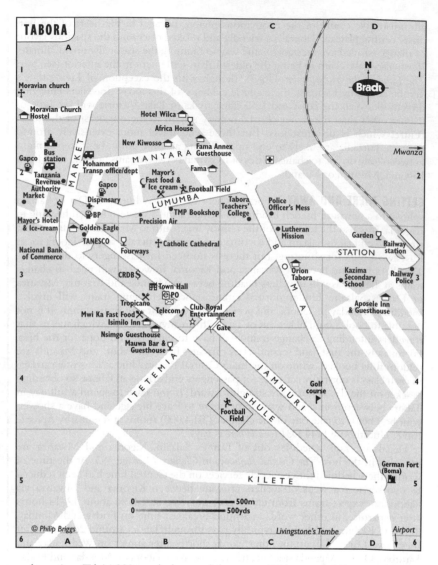

TABORA

Moravian church

Moravian Church Hostel

Gapco

Bus station

Tanzania Revenue Authority Market

Mayor's Hotel & Ice-cream

National Bank of Commerce

MARKET

Mohammed Transp office/dept

Gapco

Dispensary

BP

TANESCO

Golden Eagle

Fourways

CRDB

Tropicano

Mwi Ka Fast Food

Isimilo Inn

Nsimgo Guesthouse

Mauwa Bar & Guesthouse

ITETEMIA

Hotel Wilca

Africa House

New Kiwosso

MANYARA

Mayor's Fast food & Ice cream

LUMUMBA

Precision Air

Town Hall

PO

Telecom

Club Royal Entertainment

Gate

SHULE

Fama Annex Guesthouse

Fama

Football Field

TMP Bookshop

Catholic Cathedral

Tabora Teachers' College

JAMHURI

Football Field

KILETE

Police Officer's Mess

Lutheran Mission

STATION

Orion Tabora

BOMA

Garden

Railway station

Kazima Secondary School

Railway Police

Aposele Inn & Guesthouse

Golf course

German Fort (Boma)

Mwanza

N

Bradt

Livingstone's Tembe

Airport

0 ————— 500m
0 ————— 500yds

© Philip Briggs

and costing Tsh14,000, and the road between Tabora and Mbeya, which is covered by a twice-weekly bus service that takes at least 20 hours. Anybody driving between Tabora and Kigoma should be aware that several incidents of banditry have been reported in the vicinity of Uvinza, so do ask around before heading out this way.

Given that Tabora is of interest to travellers primarily as a rail junction, few will specifically want to fly to the town. Should you be in that minority, however, Precision Air runs a scheduled daily flight between Dar es Salaam and Kigoma, stopping at Tabora. The airport is around 5km south of the centre of town.

Tabora sprawls between the bus and railway stations, which lie a good 2km apart, both some distance from all but a couple of accommodation options. Charter taxis can easily be found outside either of the public transport terminals, and generally charge around Tsh2,000 for a lift within the town centre.

GETTING AROUND Plenty of charter taxis can be found around the bus station [444 A2], and also at the railway station [444 D3] whenever trains arrive. Expect to pay less than Tsh2,000 for a charter within the town centre, or Tsh6,000–10,000 for a charter to Livingstone's Tembe at Kwihara.

WHERE TO STAY
Moderate

🏠 **Orion Tabora Hotel** [444 C3] (35 rooms) 📞 026 260 4369. Formerly the Railway Hotel but thoroughly renovated under new private management, this was originally built as a colonial hunting lodge, & it retains some period character with its wide shady balconies & whitewashed exterior. Conveniently located near the railway station, it's far & away the best place to stay, & there's an excellent indoor/outdoor restaurant as well as a lively terrace bar & disco. *Tsh45,000/60,000 B&B en-suite sgl/dbl with net, fan & DSTV.*

Budget

🏠 **Hotel Wilca** [444 B1] (10 rooms) 📞 026 260 5397. This long-serving & very pleasant budget hotel lies 500m east of the town centre on Boma Rd. The en-suite rooms with hot water, net & fan are centred on a green courtyard. Meals at the garden bar & restaurant cost around Tsh4,000 & are a very decent second to the Orion. Facilities include pool table, table tennis & satellite TV. The hotel isn't signposted but can be recognised by its white outer wall about 50m past Africa House. *Tsh20,000/25,000 sgl/dbl.*

🏠 **New Kiwosso Hotel** [444 B2] 📞 026 260 0515. Located in a quiet dusty back street just off Manyara St south of Africa House, this amenable hotel has decent no-frills rooms with fan, net & en-suite. A friendly bar & restaurant is attached. *Tsh13,000 dbl.*

🏠 **Fama Hotel** [444 B2] 📞 026 260 4657. Similar in standard to Aposele Inn, but older & more expensive, this is a clean, friendly & reasonably central guesthouse whose en-suite rooms have fan & net. *Tsh10,000 dbl.*

🏠 **Golden Eagle Hotel** [444 A3] (13 rooms) 📞 026 260 4623; e goldeneagleflies@yahoo.com. This centrally located hotel may not look much from the outside, but is in fact a pleasant surprise. Recently spruced up, it is a convenient option for travellers arriving or departing by bus. Facilities include spacious common room with pool table & dartboard as well as a good Indian restaurant & sunny rooftop terrace bar. Plans were afoot for a mini-theatre & internet café. *Tsh10,000 dbl with fan, net & common shower; Tsh20,000 en-suite.*

Shoestring

🏠 **Aposele Inn & Guesthouse** [444 D3] 📞 026 260 4510. This popular guesthouse, though looking a little worn, is still one of the best cheapies, & the closest to the railway station. The large en-suite rooms come with two three-quarter beds, fan, net & cold shower. The garden bar serves the usual chilled drinks, plus snacks such as *chipsi mayai* & *mishkaki* kebabs. Excellent value. *Tsh4,000/6,000 dbl without/with en-suite shower.*

🏠 **Moravian Church Hostel** [444 A1] (10 rooms) 📞 026 260 4710. This long-serving hostel is easily the best shoestring option in Tabora. It's behind the bus station, but not madly convenient for travellers arriving & leaving by train. *Tsh3,000–8,000 dbl with netting (but no fan) with clean common showers & toilets.*

WHERE TO EAT

🍷 **Africa House** [444 B2] This quiet little bar on Boma Rd comes to life on Wed & Sat nights with live music & the odd disco. Grilled meats & other dishes are available.

❌ **Golden Eagle** [444 A3] Attached to the eponymous hotel, this airy restaurant serves tasty Indian dishes including vegetarian meals & meat curries in the Tsh4,000–5,000 range. There's a good outdoor bar & pool table.

❌ **Hotel Wilca** [444 B1] The restaurant here serves good stews & curries for around Tsh3,500.

❌ **Mayor's Hotel & Ice Cream** [444 A2] This long-standing favourite, behind the NBC bank, serves a wide range of Indian snacks, light meals such as grilled chicken & chips, & excellent ice cream & pineapple juice. There's a 2nd outlet on Lumumha St opposite the TMP Bookshop.

15

✕ **Orion Tabora Hotel** [444 C3] ⊕ b/fast, lunch & dinner daily. The Orion has by far the best restaurant, serving a mix of Asian & African dishes for around Tsh5,000–7,000. You can eat indoors or on the large shaded terrace bar. On w/ends there is live music on the terrace as well as a regular weekly disco.

✕ **Tropicano** [444 B3] Similar to Mayor's but seedier, Tropicano dishes up cheap curries & other local meals as well as snacks, juice & tea.

THE LAND OF THE MOON

Beyond Ugogo undulated the Land of the Moon, or Unyamwezi, inhabited by a turbulent and combative race, who are as ready to work for those who can afford to pay as they are ready to fight those they consider unduly aggressive. Towards the middle of this land, we came to a colony of Arab settlers and traders. Some of these had built excellent and spacious houses of sun-dried brick, and cultivated extensive gardens. The Arabs located here were great travellers. Every region round about the colony had been diligently searched by them for ivory. If Livingstone was anywhere within reach, some of these people ought surely to have known.

From the autobiography of Henry Stanley, describing his arrival in Tabora, where he would be stalled for three months in 1871 before continuing to Ujiji and his legendary meeting with Livingstone.

The Nyamwezi are Tanzania's second most numerous tribe after the Sukuma, whose territory borders theirs to the north. Prior to the early 19th century, however, Nyamwezi–Sukuma was a more or less homogenous cultural entity, comprised of at least 200 autonomous *ntemi* chieftaincies. This decentralised society would later polarise into two distinct (and occasionally antagonistic) political units, which evidently referred to each other as Usukuma and Utakama – simply meaning the lands to the north and to the south. When and how Utakama became Unyamwezi – and its Nyamwezi inhabitants acquired the lunar association – goes unrecorded. But, since these names stem from the Swahili word *mwezi* (moon), an external origin seems likely. Coincidence or not, the Arab colony in Unyamwezi was, at least in the eyes of a succession of Victorian explorers, the last 'civilised' port of call en *route* to the terra incognito in which it was assumed lay the fabled source of the Nile: Ptolemy's mysterious Mountains of the Moon.

The foundation of the Arab colony, referred to by Stanley, on the site of present-day Tabora *circa* 1800 was almost certainly the catalyst for the rift between Usukuma and Unyamwezi. Described by Speke as 'the great central slave and ivory merchants' depot', this settlement lay where the three most important caravan routes out of Bagamoyo diverged, one leading to Ujiji on Lake Tanganyika, another to Lake Victoria, and the third to the south of Lake Tanganyika. The Arabs, and the European explorers, generally referred to the Arab colony as Kazeh, and most modern sources follow suit, implying that Tabora is a newer name, but as early as 1861 Speke unambiguously wrote of Kazeh as 'the name of a well in the village of Tbora'.

The local *ntemi* chiefs became increasingly involved in the ivory and slave trade at Tabora. Initially, their role was peripheral, providing porters and fresh produce to the caravans that rolled in from the coast, but eventually they would come to control the trade at its source, launching slave raids into neighbouring territories and exchanging the captives for imported goods, most significantly guns and ammunition. The ensuing local power struggle led to the collapse of the *ntemi* chiefdoms and the formation of a more centralised local polity – essentially Unyamwezi – under chief Fundi Kira, who ensured Arab support by allowing free trade within his territory. By contrast, Usukuma, which was further removed from the main caravan routes, still adhered to the *ntemi* system of old, and its villages became one of the prime targets of Nyamwezi slave raids.

In 1858, when Burton and Speke rested up at Tabora before marching westward to Lake Tanganyika, the town supported about 25 Arab merchants, including a

SHOPPING

Books TMP Bookshop [444 B2] (✆ *026 260 5097;* e *tmpbookdept@yahoo.com;* ⊕ *08.30–17.00 Mon–Fri, 08.30–13.00 Sat*) stocks a good selection of local maps and English language books including Swahili/English dictionaries and second-hand guidebooks.

governor appointed by the Sultan of Zanzibar. Every merchant had his own *tembe*, a house built with local material but to palatial proportions, centred on a large courtyard, with separate quarters for his slaves and his harem. Speke returned to Tabora in 1861, and wrote that: 'Instead of the Arabs appearing merchants, as they did formerly, they looked more like great farmers, with huge stalls of cattle attached to their houses.' Speke's arrival at Tabora in 1861 coincided with a period of great instability. King Manua Sera, the successor of Fundi Kira, had imposed a tax on all goods entering his territory, and the Arabs responded by driving him from Tabora and installing a puppet king on his throne. Manua Sera blockaded the main caravan routes and launched a series of successful attacks on pursuant Arab troops, and although he never regained the throne, he was still leading the Arabs a merry dance when Speke left Tabora.

This civil war paved the way for the emergence of King Mirambo, a Nyamwezi of noble birth who grew up among Ngoni refugees from Zululand, and adopted their brutally effective military tactics to capture the Uyowa chiefdom in 1860. Over the next decade, Mirambo's army conquered one chiefdom after the next, installing a puppet leader of local nobility, to build an empire extending to Sumbwa in the north, Sukuma in the east, Nyaturu in the south and Tongwe in the west. Mirambo was able to demand large taxes – preferably exacted in the form of firearms – from caravans passing through to Tabora. The Arab merchants were less than enthralled by the growing power wielded by this hostile local leader. By 1871 the rival forces were engaged in what would today be described as guerrilla warfare.

It was the inevitable showdown between the Arabs and Mirambo that caused Stanley's search for Livingstone to be stalled by three months at Kwihara, 6km from Tabora. In August 1871, according to Stanley, a 2,000-strong Arab force 'waving banners denoting the various commanders, with booming horns, and the roar of fifty brass drums left' to hunt down Mirambo. When the attack was launched, Mirambo's army appeared to retreat, but in fact they circled behind the Arab forces and ambushed them on their way home. Mirambo followed up this victory by capturing and razing Tabora itself. Having established a stronghold at Tabora, Mirambo became the main supplier of slaves to the Arab traders, and his superior military strength convinced the Arabs is was worth paying him taxes to maintain the peace.

The former warmonger clearly recognised that diplomacy had its place. Aware of the growing British influence at Zanzibar, Mirambo attempted to woo the British Consul John Kirk by inviting the British to establish missions and trade outposts within Unyamwezi. In his letter to Kirk, Mirambo stated that 'the country is a hundred times more prosperous, tenfold more peaceful and a thousandfold safer than it was before I became chief. I wish to open it up, to learn about Europeans, to trade honestly with all, and to cultivate peaceful friendships.' Mirambo died in 1884, but his defiant pride lived on in his successor Isike, who resisted German colonisation by blockading the caravan routes and successfully ambushing any German troops sent to the region. In January 1893, the Germans led a large surprise attack on Tabora. Isike, realising he didn't stand a chance and unwilling to be captured, blew up his fort, in the process taking his own life.

15

OTHER PRACTICALITIES

Foreign exchange The central National Bank of Commerce [444 A2] (☉ *08.30–15.00 Mon–Fri, 08.30–12.30 Sat*) exchanges cash and travellers' cheques at the usual rates and has an ATM (it takes Visa only). There is no private foreign exchange bureau.

Internet The Post Office Internet Café on Jamhuri Street [444 B3] charges Tsh1,000 per hour for access, but the connection is slow and unpredictable. The Orion Tabora Hotel [444 C3] is more reliable but out of the way and very expensive. The Golden Eagle [444 A3] plans to open an internet café that will most likely be available to casual visitors.

LIVINGSTONE'S TEMBE [444 D6] Preserved as a museum (☉ *08.00–17.00 daily; entrance Tsh2,000 pp*) by the Department of Antiquities, the *tembe* – Arab house – where Livingstone resided during his sojourn in Tabora in 1872 is about 6km from the town centre at the otherwise defunct settlement of Kwihara. Despite the Livingstone association, the house was in fact the residence of one of the Arabs resident at Tabora in the mid to late 19th century. An information sheet at the museum indicates that the *tembe* belonged to the notorious slave trader Tippu Tip. The contemporary journals of Stanley and Livingstone, as well as other external sources, state that it actually belonged to Said bin Salim, the local governor appointed by the Sultan of Zanzibar. Originally, the *tembe* at Kwihara – which means 'in the open' in the Nyamwezi tongue – must have served as an out-of-town governor's residence, but after Mirambo captured Tabora in 1871 Kwihara became the main local Arab settlement in the area for a brief period.

Livingstone's Tembe is a typical Arab merchant's house of the period, an attractive red clay quadrangle of large rooms built around a central courtyard and set beneath tall shady mango trees, said to date to before Livingstone's time. In 1871, Henry Stanley resided for a full three months in the house – which he described as a 'most comfortable place' – while waiting for the war between the Arabs and King Mirambo to subside, so that he could head towards Lake Tanganyika to seek the lost Doctor Livingstone. Stanley's travel companion, John William Shaw, stayed with him at Kwihara, and set off alongside him towards Lake Tanganyika, but was forced to turn back through illness. Shaw died at Kwihara and is buried in a marked grave in a field next to the *tembe*.

Following their famous meeting at Ujiji in November 1871, Stanley and Livingstone returned to Kwihara and the *tembe* on 18 February 1872. A month later, Stanley set back off to the coast, promising to send Livingstone a caravan of fresh supplies as soon as he arrived. Livingstone spent 189 days 'wearily waiting' at Said bin Salim's residence before the provisions finally arrived, and he was free to embark upon what would prove to be his final, fatal expedition south to Lake Bangweulu. In August 1873, Cameron, Dillon and Murphy, members of a Royal Geographic Society expedition sent out to assist Livingstone, arrived at Kwihara in poor health and spent several months recuperating at the *tembe*. Before the ailing trio was fully recovered, however, Livingstone's porters Chuma and Sisi arrived at Kwihara carrying their leader's sun-dried remains. Today, the main rooms in the front of the house exhibit several old documents (including contemporary newspaper reports) and fading photographs relating to Livingstone and his discovery by Stanley.

To get to the restored *tembe* from Tabora, follow Boma Road out of town past the traffic circle in front of the Old Boma. About 50m past this traffic circle, follow the right fork, signposted for the Huima Training and Conference Centre. You pass the Wasichama Secondary School after about 1km, then after another

2km you must turn right along a side road marked with a fading blue signpost reading 'Livingstone's Tembe'. The *tembe* lies about 2km along this road in a grove of mango trees. The road is flat enough that you could easily walk out over about an hour, bearing in mind that the area gets very hot in the middle of the day. A taxi from the town centre will charge Tsh6,000–10,000 for the round trip. Alternatively, occasional *dala-dala* to the small village of Kipalapala can drop you at the turn-off 2km from the *tembe*.

KIGOMA

The largest port and most important transport hub on the eastern shores of Lake Tanganyika, Kigoma sprawls attractively across hilly, green slopes rising from Kigoma Bay, a deep natural harbour protected to the south by the narrow Bangwe Peninsula. Although this superb bay has presumably been inhabited for millennia, Kigoma owes its modern significance to the German colonials, who favoured it as a regional administration centre over the more established 19th-century Arab slave trading centre at Ujiji, only 6km to the southeast. The ascendancy of Kigoma over Ujiji was sealed in February 1914, when the railway line from the coast finally reached the nascent German port, almost ten years after the first tracks had been laid at the coast, and mere months before the outbreak of Work War I.

Kigoma is definitely one of the more characterful towns in the East African interior: an almost archetypal tropical African port whose cinematic sense of place is enhanced by a conspicuously easygoing mood and captivating setting alongside the crystal clear waters of Lake Tanganyika. Given its relatively remote location, Kigoma also has a surprisingly cosmopolitan flavour, at times positively crawling with independent travellers waiting for various transport connections, not to mention African cross-border businessmen taking advantage of Lake Tanganyika's status as an international free trade zone. Following the turmoil in the neighbouring states of Rwanda, Burundi and the DRC during the 1990s, Kigoma became the focal point for UN and other international aid organisations involved with a number of refugee camps. While most refuges have since returned home, many of the foreign agencies still remain in the area.

Kigoma's compact town centre is dominated by a long mango-lined avenue, which snakes uphill from the lakeshore railway station and harbour to the market and bus station. Sightseeing in the town centre is pretty much restricted to the railway station itself [452 B2] – a fine example of German colonial architecture – and the so-called Kaiser House which is reputedly linked to the railway station by a subterranean escape tunnel excavated during World War I. There is, however, plenty to see in the immediate vicinity. The mango-lined avenue described above continues running southeast out of town, passing after about 2km through the small but bustling suburb of Mwanga, before arriving after another 4km at the historic port of Ujiji. To the south of the town centre, a dirt road runs out of town, past the prison and upmarket Kigoma Hilltop Hotel, to the fishing village of Katonga, Zungu Beach and the now closed Kitwe Point Chimpanzee Sanctuary. Another road running north from the town centre leads past a series of tall fuel storage towers – the contents of which are mostly exported to neighbouring countries – to the fishing village of Kibirizi, where local boats leave daily for Gombe National Park.

In addition to some worthwhile local sightseeing, Kigoma is the obvious springboard from which to undertake a tourist activity which, given Tanzania's high profile as a safari destination, has to rank as the most inexplicably under-subscribed in the country. In a 1943 *Tanganyika Notes and Records* article about the

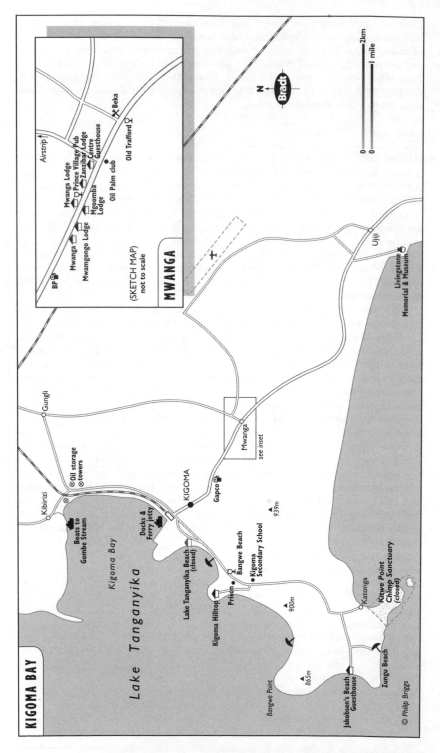

KIGOMA BAY

MWANGA

(SKETCH MAP)
not to scale

Airstrip

BP

Mwanga
Mwamgongo Lodge

Mwanga Lodge
Prince Village Pub
Mgoomba
Lodge
Zanzibar Lodge
Centre
Guesthouse
Oil Palm club

Beka

Old Trafford

N

Bradt

0   2km
0   1 mile

Gungli

Mwanga

see inset

Kibirizi
⊗ Oil storage
⊗ towers

Boats to
Gombe Stream

Docks &
Ferry jetty

Kigoma Bay

KIGOMA

Gapco

939m

Lake Tanganyika Beach
(closed)

Bangwe Beach

Kigoma
Secondary School

Kigoma Hilltop

Prison

Lake Tanganyika

900m

Katonga

Kitwe Point
Chimp Sanctuary
(closed)

Ujiji

Livingstone
Memorial & Museum

Bangwe Point

865m

Jakobsen's Beach
Guesthouse

Zungu Beach

© Philip Briggs

distribution of chimpanzees in mainland Tanzania, the former District Officer of Kigoma, Captain Grant, recalled that 'it was a rare but occasional sight to see a family party on the lakeshore inside Kigoma Bay opposite the township'. You'd have to imbibe some seriously heavy stuff to be treated to such an apparition from Kigoma today, but the nearby Gombe and Mahale Mountains national parks vie with each other as *the* best place in Africa to see habituated wild chimps in their natural habitat. If you're in the area, and can afford the time and expense, the chimpanzee tracking at Gombe or Mahale is simply not to be missed.

GETTING THERE AND AWAY The only realistic ways to get to Kigoma are by air, rail or water. Precision Air flies daily from Dar es Salaam to Kigoma via Tabora, leaving Dar es Salaam at 09.15 and Kigoma at 12.20. The airport is located about 5km southeast of the town centre. A taxi to the airport costs around Tsh5,000.

The railway is covered in the box, *The Central Railway*, in *Chapter 13*, page 393, and the ferry in the box, *MV Liemba*, on page 456. You could come to Kigoma by road from Mwanza, but you would be measuring the journey in days.

WHERE TO STAY
Upmarket

Kigoma Hilltop Hotel [452 A7] (30 rooms) 028 280 44357; m 0732 984090; e kht@raha.com; www.mbalimbali.com. Perched dramatically on a cliff overlooking Kigoma Bay, roughly 2km south of the town centre, this is easily the best in Kigoma, with large swimming pool, watersports equipment, fishing, snorkelling, various indoor games, gymnasium, secretarial services, generator & private beach. Accommodation is in en-suite, AC chalets (with satellite TV, hot water & fridge) lining a large central garden inhabited by a small, friendly herd of zebra. The attached restaurant serves good Indian & western dishes in the US$5+ range. Alcohol is not sold on the premises, but guests are permitted to bring their own. This is a

good contact for tours to the western national parks, since the management owns a private motorboat & runs tented camps at Mahale & Gombe. US$70/90 sgl/dbl B&B, US$110–150 suites.

Gibbs Resort [452 D1] (6 rooms) 028 280 4272. Located up the hill from the post office in the Kiyeza area of town, this intimate new resort with its attractive lake views is a good alternative to the Hilltop Hotel. Clean, spacious en-suite rooms have AC, TV & fridge. A good restaurant serves a variety of pizzas for around Tsh4,500–7,000 as well as a selection of continental & Indian dishes. Good value. Tsh50,000/60,000 sgl/dbl, Tsh60,000/70,000 suite.

Moderate

Jakobsen's Beach Guest House (4 rooms) 028 280 3409; e info@kigomabeach.com; www.kigomabeach.com. Set on an attractive swimming beach signposted off the road towards Katonga about 3km past the Kigoma Hilltop Hotel, this homely guesthouse consists of just 4 bedrooms sleeping up to 14, using 2 shared bathrooms. No food is available but facilities include an observation deck with barbecue area & picnic table, & fully equipped self-catering kitchen. A one-off monthly

membership fee of Tsh10,000 is levied. Tsh40,000/55,000 dbl/trpl. Camping Tsh3,000/6,000 pp members/non-members.

Magorofan Lodge [452 D6] (10 rooms) 028 280 4626. An annexe of Gibbs Resort, this newish lodge is located at the southern end of Lumumba St. While the rooms are clean & perfectly serviceable they seem a little overpriced. Tsh30,000/35,000 en-suite sgl/dbl B&B with fan.

Budget

Kigoma Hotel [452 C3] (9 rooms) m 0764 484448. Opposite the Lake View Hotel, this once popular budget place seems to be experiencing a little bit of a revival. While it's still a little scruffy

around the edges, it is very central. Fair value. Tsh12,000/14,000 sgl/dbl.

Zanzibar Lodge 028 280 3306. In Mwanga, on the Ujiji road 2km from the town centre, this clean

15

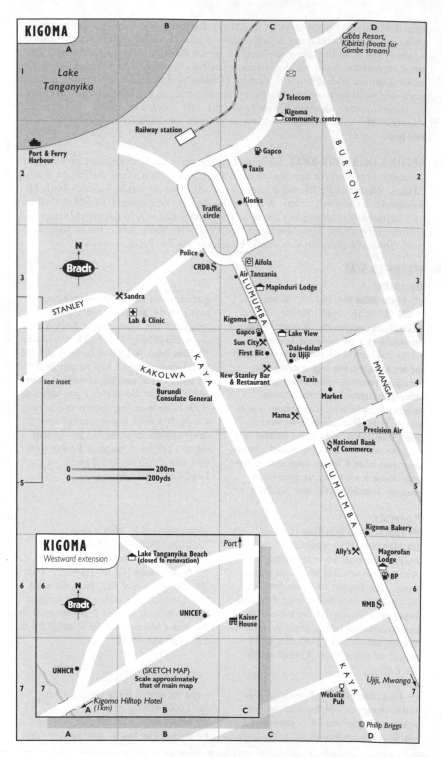

KIGOMA

A

Lake Tanganyika

Gibbs Resort, Kibirizi (boats for Gombe stream)

BURTON

Telecom

Kigoma community centre

Railway station

Port & Ferry Harbour

Gapco

Taxis

Kiosks

Traffic circle

N

Bradt

Police

Aifola

CRDB

Air Tanzania

Mapinduri Lodge

LUMUMBA

Sandra

STANLEY

Lab & Clinic

Kigoma

Gapco

Lake View

Sun City

'Dala-dalas' to Ujiji

First Bit

KAKOLWA

KAYA

New Stanley Bar & Restaurant

Taxis

MWANGA

see inset

Burundi Consulate General

Market

Mama

Precision Air

National Bank of Commerce

0   200m
0   200yds

LUMUMBA

Kigoma Bakery

KIGOMA

Westward extension

Port

Lake Tanganyika Beach (closed fo renovation)

Ally's

Magorofan Lodge

N

Bradt

BP

UNICEF

Kaiser House

NMB

UNHCR

(SKETCH MAP) Scale approximately that of main map

KAYA

Ujiji, Mwanga

Website Pub

Kigoma Hilltop Hotel A (1km)

A   B   C   D

© Philip Briggs

smart double-storey lodge is built around a central courtyard, with a decent restaurant attached. The one drawback is the distance from the town centre, though regular *dala-dalas* to Ujiji run right past. Excellent value. *Tsh8,000 en-suite dbl or twin with net & fan;Tsh4,000 with common showers.*

🏠 Lake Tanganyika Beach Hotel [452 B6] ↖ 028 280 2694. Formerly the Railway Hotel, this now-privatised hotel has a perfect location, right on the lakeshore & only a short walk from the town centre. It was closed for renovations at the time of research, but should reopen in 2009.

Shoestring

🏠 Kigoma Community Centre [452 C1] ↖ 028 280 2520. Conveniently located along the short road between the railway station & the post office, this church-run hostel is rather run-down but not unreasonably priced. *Tsh2,500/Tsh3,000 sgl/dbl with shared facilities.*

✖ **WHERE TO EAT AND DRINK** The restaurants at the **Kigoma Hilltop** [452 A7] and **Gibbs Resort** [452 D1] can both be recommended for Western and Indian meals, with Gibbs sporting a more extensive and marginally cheaper menu featuring tasty pizzas and pasta dishes. On the downside though, both are a little off the beaten path for anyone without transportation.

The pick of the eateries in the town centre, is the colourful **Sun City** [452 C4] which serves a variety of inexpensive local dishes such as *ugali* with chicken or fish for Tsh1,500 as well as a variety of other light snacks and juices. Its outdoor balcony is a perfect place to watch the passing parade of people along the main street. Otherwise, **Ally's Restaurant** [452 D6] serves a wide variety of inexpensive meals and snacks as does **Sandra Restaurant** [452 B3] which is well-located nearby both the port and train station.

The dozy **New Stanley Bar & Restaurant** [452 C4] serves a decent selection of grills and other dishes for Tsh2,500–3,500 throughout the day, but comes to life at nights with a regular and rowdy disco. The **Bangwe Beach Bar** on the road to Kigoma Hilltop Hotel is a friendly spot to stop for a few drinks near the lake side, while the most popular watering hole is the open-air **Website Pub** [452 D7], located off Lumumba Street about one block back from the NMB bank, which draws huge crowds with its satellite TV showing all the latest football matches.

If you're stocking up on food before heading to Gombe or Mahale Mountain, the central **market** [452 D4] and the shops immediately around it are very well stocked with fresh fruit and vegetables and imported tinned and other packaged goods. The **Kigoma Bakery** [452 D5] roughly opposite Ally's Restaurant bakes fresh bread every morning.

OTHER PRACTICALITIES

Foreign exchange The National Bank of Commerce [452 D5], opposite the market, exchanges travellers' cheques and cash at the usual rates. It also has an ATM which accepts Visa only, as does the CRDB Bank [452 B3] on the roundabout near the train station. There is no private bureau de change in Kigoma.

Internet The only internet café in town is the Aifola Internet Café [452 C3], opposite the CRDB Bank, but thanks to frequent power cuts connection is erratic at best.

Swimming The swimming pool at the Kigoma Hilltop Hotel [452 A7] is open to non-residents for a small fee. Local people swim with apparent impunity at the sandy beach bar next to the prison, but that doesn't necessarily mean it is free of bilharzia. The best bathing spot in the Kigoma area is Zungu Beach, near the village of Katonga, some 5km south of Kigoma. Regular *dala-dalas* between Kigoma and Katonga can drop you at the start of the 2km turn-off to the beach.

In March 1866, Dr David Livingstone, the most famous and arguably the greatest explorer of his – or perhaps any – era, set off from the coastal port of Mikindani with the aim of resolving the whereabouts of the source of the Nile. Almost nothing concrete was heard of Livingstone over the next few years, and rumours of his death vied with equally difficult-to-substantiate rumours of his imminent return to the coast. So it was that in 1869, the American journalist Henry Morton Stanley, then on assignment in Spain, received a telegram from his editor at the New York Herald bearing a simple command that would take him two wearisome years to fulfil: Find Livingstone! The rest, as they say, is history.

In his autobiography, published in 1909, Stanley recalled the momentous day:

'We slept at a chief's village in Ukaranga, with only one more march of six hours, it was said, intervening between us and the Arab settlement of Ujiji, in which native rumour located an old, grey-bearded, white man, who had but newly arrived from a distant western country. It was now 235 days since I had left the Indian Ocean and 50 days since I had departed from [Tabora]… At cockcrow…we strengthened ourselves with a substantial meal, and, as the sun rose in the east, we turned our backs to it, and the caravan was soon on full swing on the march… About eight o'clock we were climbing the side of a steep and wooded hill, and [from] the very crest… I saw, as in a painted picture, a vast lake in the distance below, with its face luminous as a mirror, set in a frame of dimly blue mountains… For hours I strode nervously on… brushing past the bush on the hill-slopes and crests, flinging gay remarks to the wondering villagers who looked on… in mute surprise, until near noon, when, having crossed the last valley and climbed up to the summit of the last hill: Lo! Lake Tanganyika was distant from us but half a mile…

'Hard by the lake shore, embowered in palms, on this hot noon, the village of Ujiji broods drowsily. No living thing can be seen moving to break the still aspect of the outer lines of the town and its deep shades… I rested awhile, breathless from my exertions; and, as the stragglers were many, I halted to reunite and reform for an imposing entry. Meantime, my people improved their personal appearance; they clothed themselves in clean dresses, and snowy cloths were folded round their heads. When the laggards had all been gathered, the guns were loaded to rouse up the sleeping town. It is an immemorial custom, for a caravan creeps not up into a friendly town like a thief. Our braves knew the custom well; they therefore volleyed and thundered their salutes as they went marching down the hill slowly, and with much self-contained dignity. Presently, there is a tumultuous stir visible on the outer edge of the town. Groups of men in white dresses, with arms in their hands, burst from the shades, and seem to hesitate a moment, as if in doubt; they then come rushing up to meet us, pursued by hundreds of people, who shout joyfully, while yet afar, their noisy welcomes.

'The foremost… cried out: "why, we took you for Mirambo and his bandits, when we heard the booming of the guns. It is an age since a caravan has come to Ujiji. Which way did you come? Ah! You have got a white man with you! Is this his caravan?" Being told it was a white man's caravan by the guides in front, the boisterous multitude pressed up to

AROUND KIGOMA

Ujiji The small but sprawling lakeshore port of Ujiji, dwarfed today by the nearby and more modern town of Kigoma, is best known as the place where the immortal enquiry 'Doctor Livingstone, I presume?' was made by Stanley on 10 November 1871 (see boxed text, above). Ujiji's historical significance does, however, extend beyond the utterance of one Victorian banality. For centuries, it was the main port from which the salt mined at nearby Uvinza was transported across the lake to the present-day eastern Congo. In about 1800, Ujiji was settled by Arab traders from the coast, and began its rise to prominence as the lakeshore me, greeted me with salaams, and bowed their salutes. Hundreds of them jostled and trod upon one another's heels... when a tall black man, in long white shirt, burst impulsively through the crowd on my right, and bending low, said "Good morning, sir," in clear, intelligent English.

'"Hello!" I said, "Who in the mischief are you?"

'"I am Susi, sir, the servant of Dr. Livingstone."

'"What! Is Dr. Livingstone here in this town?"

'"Yes, sir."

'"But, are you sure; sure that it is Dr. Livingstone?"

'"Why, I leave him just now, sir."

'"Well, now that we have met, one of you had better run ahead, and tell the Doctor of my coming."

'The same idea striking Susi's mind, he undertook in his impulsive manner to inform the Doctor, and I saw him racing headlong, with his white dress streaming behind him like a wind-whipped pennant. The column continued on its way, beset on either flank by a vehemently enthusiastic and noisily rejoicing mob, which bawled a jangling chorus of "Jambo" to every mother's son of us, and maintained an inharmonious orchestral music of drums and horns. I was indebted for this loud ovation to the cheerful relief the people felt that we were not Mirambo's bandits, and to their joy at the happy rupture of the long silence that had perforce existed between the two trading colonies of [Tabora] and Ujiji.

'After a few minutes we came to a halt. The guides in the van had reached the marketplace, which was the central point of interest. For there the great Arabs, chiefs and respectabilities of Ujiji had gathered in a group to await events; thither also they had brought with them the venerable European traveller who was at that time resting among them. The caravan pressed up to them, divided itself into two lines on either side of the road, and, as it did so, disclosed to me the prominent figure of an elderly white man clad in a red flannel blouse, grey trousers, and a blue cloth, gold-banded cap.

'Up to this moment my mind had verged upon non-belief in his existence, and now a nagging doubt intruded itself into my mind that this white man could not be the object of my quest, or if he were, he would somehow contrive to disappear before my eyes... "It may not be Livingstone after all," doubt suggested. If this is he, what shall I say to him? My imagination had not taken this question into consideration before. All around me was the immense crowd, hushed and expectant, and wondering how the scene would develop itself.

'Under all these circumstances I could do no more than exercise some restraint and reserve, so I walked up to him, and, doffing my helmet, bowed and said in an inquiring tone:

'"Dr. Livingstone, I presume?"

'Smiling cordially, he lifted his cap, and answered briefly:

'"Yes."'

terminal of the most important ivory and slave caravan route to Bagamoyo, eventually to be governed by an agent of the Sultan of Zanzibar. Ujiji is also where, in 1858, the exhausted Burton and Speke – the former with an ulcerated jaw and practically paralysed below the waist, the latter partially blind and driven close to dementia by an insect that had burrowed into his ear canal – arrived on the shore of the 'Sea of Ujiji'.

For all its historical associations, Ujiji today is something of a backwater, and although it displays some Swahili influences one wouldn't normally associate with this part of the country, anybody who visits the small port expecting to find a

This 800-ton steamer, the main ferry service on Lake Tanganyika, undertakes a weekly circuit from Kigoma to Mpulungu (Zambia) and Bujumbura (Burundi). Originally called the Graf van Goetzen, this historic ship was railed in pieces from Dar es Salaam to Kigoma shortly before World War I. It was assembled at Kigoma, then embarked on an aborted maiden voyage to Kasanga carrying 700 soldiers, after which the Germans sank it in the Malagarasi River mouth rather than letting it fall into enemy hands. In 1927, Britain and Belgium undertook the costly task of rescuing the Graf van Goetzen from its watery grave, and renamed it *Liemba* (according to Livingstone, the local name for Lake Tanganyika). It has subsequently steamed up and down the lake almost continually, though the oft-repeated story that it features in the movie *The African Queen* is a myth (the film was shot on Lake Albert in Uganda).

In theory, the *Liemba* does a round trip every week between Kigoma, Bujumbura and Mpulungu, stopping at several small ports on the lakeshore south of Kigoma. It departs from Kigoma at 16.00 Wednesday and arrives in Mpulungu at 10.00 Friday. It then turns back at 16.00 Friday and arrives in Kigoma at 10.00 Sunday. It leaves Kigoma at 16.00 Sunday and arrives in Bujumbura at 10.00 Monday. The return trip from Bujumbura departs at 16.00 Monday and arrives back in Kigoma at 10.00 Tuesday. However, sanctions against Burundi mean that the Bujumbura leg of this voyage hasn't been running for many years. Although departures are reasonably punctual, protracted delays for loading at the smaller ports can cause it to gradually fall behind schedule by up to ten hours.

All non-residents *must* pay for tickets in US dollar cash – local currency and travellers' cheques are not accepted. The full one-way trip from Kigoma to Mpulungu costs US$55/45/40 first/second/third class. Tickets from Kigoma to Lugosa or Kasanga respectively cost US$50/45/35 or US$25/20/15 first/second/third class. All fares include the US$5 port tax. First-class berths consist of clean, comfortable and lockable two-berth cabins, while second class consists of scruffier but perfectly adequate lockable four-bed cabins. Third class is deck only, which – since the deck is far from being crowded – is fine for shorter hops, but risky for luggage on overnight trips. A restaurant/bar serves decent meals for US$1.50, as well as cold beers, sodas and imported wines and spirits.

The ferry stops at numerous lakeshore villages, of which the most significant to travellers are Lugosa (for Mahale Mountains National Park) and Kasanga (the last port before the Zambian border, with a few basic guesthouses and road transport to Sumbawanga and on to Mbeya). There is nowhere for ships to dock at most of these villages, so the ferry is greeted by a floating market selling dried fish and other foodstuffs, while passengers are ferried to and from the shore on rickety fishing boats. Viewed from the upper decks this is a richly comic sight. If you are disembarking, however, it is a rather nightmarish experience, the hold seething with passengers climbing over each other, the ticket officer frantically trying to identify and extract fares from the newcomers, and small boats at the exit gate ramming each other trying to get the best position.

Information about minor ports on the southern lakeshore is included on our website, http://bradttanzania.wordpress.com.

thriving market town will be disappointed. Most travellers passing through Kigoma do nevertheless make the short trip to Ujiji, primarily for the monument and museum dedicated to Livingstone and Stanley's meeting at the port in 1871. Decorated with an engraved outline of Africa, the stone monument stands under a shady mango tree, and bears a brass plaque reading 'Under the mango tree which then stood here Stanley met Livingstone 10th November 1871'. A smaller monument dedicated to Burton and Speke stands alongside it.

The Livingstone Museum, adjacent to the monument, consists of several large and virtually empty rooms, one of which contains a few ineptly executed and comically captioned paintings of the great explorer, as well as life-size papier mâché statues of Stanley and Livingstone doffing their caps in greeting. Attempts to maintain a straight face in this mildly surreal scenario will be further subverted by the caretaker, who treats visitors to an informative lecture about Livingstone, delivered in a rising monotone suggestive of a church sermon. Entrance to both the monument and museum is free, though the caretaker will expect a donation of around Tsh2,000.

The Livingstone Museum is also a good place to see traditional Ha dancing, since the Washirika Dance Troupe – complete with traditional dresses made from the bark of the Marimba tree – practices in its grounds from 17.00 to 18.00 every Wednesday, Friday and Sunday. Watching the rehearsals is free – though a small donation will almost certainly be asked for – but you'll need to negotiate with the caretaker if you want to take photographs or arrange a special performance outside of practice hours. Outside of dancing hours, having dutifully snapped a picture of yourself and a pal shaking hands in front of the Livingstone Monument, the most interesting aspects of Ujiji is the traditional harbour, where you can watch local fishermen and boatbuilders ply their respective trades.

A good surfaced road covers the 6km between Ujiji and Kigoma. A regular *dala-dala* service runs back and forth between the two ports, charging Tsh200 per person, and leaving Kigoma from next to the market every five minutes or so. Assuming you're mainly interested in the Livingstone Museum and Monument, the signposted junction lies on the outskirts of central Ujiji – the conductor will drop you off there if you ask for 'Livingstone'. From the junction, it's a walk of about five minutes to the monument and museum, along a straight road populated by some of the most vociferous children in Tanzania (Stanley's description of arriving in Ujiji to a mob that 'bawled a jangling chorus of "Jambo"' still rings true today!). When you're ready to return to Kigoma, walk back to the junction, and any passing *dala-dala* will pick you up.

GOMBE NATIONAL PARK

Gazetted as a game reserve in 1943 and made a national park in 1965, Gombe – also known as Gombe Stream – is one of a handful of African national parks that could reasonably claim to be a household name in the west. It is best known for its chimpanzees, or more accurately perhaps for the research into their behaviour undertaken by the groundbreaking primatologist Jane Goodall. Yet, surprisingly, it remains a rather low-key and little-visited reserve, moreover one whose profile has shrunk – along with its annual tally of tourist visits – over a 20-year period during which Tanzania as a whole has attracted a consistent growth in tourist numbers. The reasons for this decline are manifold. Gombe's relatively remote location has always been, and remains, a dissuasive factor for short-stay visitors to Tanzania. Meanwhile, backpacker traffic, once the mainstay of the park, has abated due to the unusually high fee structure, the introduction of cheap chimp tracking in several Ugandan reserves, and the eastward shift of popular overland routes following the succession of civil wars in Rwanda, Burundi and the DRC.

Travel patterns may change, but Gombe remains a thoroughly worthwhile destination. True, the more southerly Mahale Mountain National Park is much larger, and correspondingly wilder in atmosphere, but Gombe is the more

Almost certainly, you'll hear them before you see them: from somewhere deep in the forest, an excited hooting, just one voice at first, then several, rising in volume and tempo and pitch to a frenzied unified crescendo, before stopping abruptly or fading away. Jane Goodall called it the 'pant-hoot' call, a kind of bonding ritual that allows any chimpanzees within earshot of one another to identify exactly who is around through each individual's unique vocal stylisation. To the human listener, this eruptive crescendo is one of the most spine-chilling and exciting sounds of the rainforest, and an almost certain indicator that visual contact with man's closest genetic relative is imminent.

It is, in large part, our close evolutionary kinship with chimpanzees that makes these sociable black-coated apes of the forest so enduringly fascinating. Humans, chimpanzees and bonobos (also known as pygmy chimpanzees) share more than 98% of their genetic code, and the three species are far more closely related to each other than they are to any other living creature, even gorillas. Superficial differences notwithstanding, the similarities between humans and chimps are consistently striking, not only in the skeletal structure and skull, but also in the nervous system, the immune system, and in many behavioural aspects – bonobos, for instance, are the only animals other than humans to copulate in the missionary position.

Unlike most other primates, chimpanzees don't live in troops, but instead form extended communities of up to 100 individuals, which roam the forest in small socially mobile subgroups that often revolve around a few close family members such as brothers or a mother and daughter. Male chimps normally spend their entire life within the community into which they were born, whereas females are likely to migrate into a neighbouring community at some point after reaching adolescence. A highly ranking male will occasionally attempt to monopolise a female in oestrus, but the more normal state of sexual affairs in chimp society is non-hierarchical promiscuity. A young female in oestrus will generally mate with any male that takes her fancy, while older females tend to form close bonds with a few specific males, sometimes allowing themselves to be monopolised by a favoured suitor for a period, but never pairing off exclusively in the long term.

Within each community, one alpha male is normally recognised – though coalitions between two males, often a dominant and a submissive sibling, have been recorded. The role of the alpha male, not fully understood, is evidently quite benevolent – chairman of the board rather than crusty tyrant. This is probably influenced by the alpha male's relatively limited reproductive advantages over his potential rivals, most of whom he will have known for his entire life. Other males in the community are generally supportive rather than competitive towards the alpha male, except when a rival consciously contests the alpha position, which is far from being an everyday occurrence. In Mahale's Mimikere Community, for instance, an alpha male called Ntologi retained his status from 1979 to 1995, interrupted for about a year towards the end of that period.

Prior to the 1960s, it was always assumed that chimps were strict vegetarians. This notion was rocked when Jane Goodall witnessed a group of chimps hunting down a red colobus monkey, something that has since been discovered to be common behaviour, particularly during the dry season when other food sources are depleted. Over

accessible goal for independent travellers. Furthermore, and disregarding financial considerations, you could go chimp tracking a dozen times practically anywhere else in Africa, and still not be adequately prepared for the in-your-face encounters with wild chimpanzees that characterise either of the two national parks on Lake Tanganyika. Whether you visit Gombe or Mahale, you will, with a modicum of luck, be treated to one of most extraordinary and memorable wildlife experiences our planet has to offer!

subsequent years, an average of 20 kills has been recorded in Gombe annually, with red colobus being the prey on more than half of these occasions, though young bushbuck, young bushpig and even infant chimps have also been victimised and eaten. In the dry season, visitors are quite likely to see an attempted hunt at Gombe, though a successful kill is less commonplace. The normal modus operandi is for four or five adult chimps to slowly encircle a colobus troop, then for another chimp to act as a decoy, creating deliberate confusion in the hope that it will drive the monkeys into the trap, or cause a mother to drop her baby.

Although chimp communities appear, by and large, to be stable and peaceful entities, intensive warfare has been known to erupt once each within the habituated communities of Mahale and Gombe. In Mahale, one of the two communities originally habituated by researchers in 1967 had exterminated the other by 1982. A similar thing happened in Gombe in the 1970s, when the Kasekela community as originally habituated by Goodall divided into two discrete communities. The Kasekela and breakaway Kahama community coexisted alongside each other for some years. Then in 1974, Goodall returned to Gombe after a break to discover that the Kasekela males were methodically persecuting their former community mates, isolating the Kahama males one by one, and tearing into them until they were dead or terminally wounded. By 1977, the Kahama community had vanished entirely.

Chimpanzees are essentially inhabitants of the west and central African rainforests, and the Tanzania population of perhaps 2,000 individuals represents less than 1% of the continental total. Somewhat paradoxically, however, much of what is known about wild chimpanzee society and behaviour stems from the ongoing research projects that were initiated in Gombe and Mahale Mountain national parks back in the 1960s. One of the most interesting patterns to emerge from the parallel research projects in these nearby reserves is a large number of social and behavioural differences in the two populations that can only be described as cultural.

One striking difference between the two populations is their apparently inexplicable food preferences. Of the various plants that occur in both national parks, as many as 40% that are used as a food source by one community are left untouched by the other. In Gombe, for instance, you'll often see chimps in the vicinity of palm trees, and the palm nut seems to be considered to be something of a delicacy. Exactly the same palms are found at Mahale, but the chimps have yet to be recorded eating from them. Likewise, the 'termite-fishing' behaviour that was first recorded by Jane Goodall at Gombe in the 1960s has a parallel in Mahale, where the chimps are often seen 'fishing' for carpenter ants in the trees. But the Mahale chimps have never been recorded fishing for termites, while the Gombe chimps are not known to fish for carpenter ants. At Mahale, you're bound to come across chimps grooming each other with one hand while holding each other's other hand above their heads – once again, behaviour that has never been noted at Gombe. More than any structural similarity, more even than any single quirk of chimpanzee behaviour, such striking cultural differences – the influence of nurture over nature if you like – bring home our close genetic kinship with chimpanzees.

Gombe's chimpanzee research project, the longest-running study of an individual wild animal population in the world, was initiated by Jane Goodall in 1960 and sponsored by Louis Leakey, who felt that his protégé's lack of scientific training would allow her to observe chimpanzee behaviour without preconceptions. After initial difficulties trying to locate her subjects, Goodall overcame the chimps' shyness through the combination of a banana-feeding machine and sheer persistence. Since the late 1960s Goodall's work has achieved both popular and scientific recognition. Her painstaking studies of individual chimps and the day-to-day social behaviour of troops have been supplemented by a series of observations confronting conventional scientific wisdom. Observations that initially caused controversy – tool-making, inter-troop warfare and even cannibalism – have since been widely accepted. Much of Goodall's work is described in her books *In the Shadow of Man* and *Through a Window*, which are highly recommended to interested readers. Fifi, a three-year old when Goodall first arrived at Gombe in 1960, was regularly seen by tourists until shortly before her death in 2004.

The park's population of roughly 100 chimpanzees is divided across three communities. The habituated Kasekela community studied by Jane Goodall is the largest of the three, numbering about 45 individuals, and its territory lies in the central part of the park, around the Kasekela research centre, rest camp and river. To see the chimpanzees, however, you will need to go on a guided walk from the research centre, which costs US$20 per party. A few years ago, it was normally very easy to locate chimps, because they still made routine visits to the feeding station established by Goodall above the research centre. The practice of feeding chimps was discontinued in 1995, however, so chimp tracking now normally involves some fairly strenuous walking on steep slopes. The best time to track the chimps is shortly after sunrise, because the guides normally know where they nested the previous night, and are thus likely to find them quite easily. During the dry season, when the chimps tend to forage on the lower slopes of the escarpment, it often takes less than an hour to locate a group. In the wet season, when the chimps forage higher and walking conditions are tougher, it could take three or four hours.

Because chimpanzees are so genetically close to humans, they are susceptible to many of the same diseases. If you are unwell, do not visit the park. Even a common cold has the potential to kill a chimpanzee, which may not share your immunity.

PARK FEES The entrance fee of US$100 per 24 hours, the highest for any Tanzanian National Park, is applicable only to time spent in the forest, not to time spent in the rest camp. To independent travellers, for whom a two-night stay is enforced by the lake-taxi schedules, this means that you need only pay US$100 in entrance fees to track chimps at Gombe. In addition, you need to pay US$10 per person per night for the most basic accommodation, and a daily guide fee of US$20 per group. Add on transport, food and drink costs, and a two-night stay for two people will work out at around US$150 per person. Fees must be paid in hard currency, ideally US dollars. Change may not be available, so make sure you have the right denomination banknotes.

FLORA AND FAUNA Gombe extends over 52km^2 of hilly terrain climbing from the lakeshore, at an elevation of 773m, to above 1,500m at the top of the rift escarpment. At no point measuring more than 3.5km from east to west, the narrow national park is bisected by 13 streams which carve steep valleys into the rift escarpment before flowing into the lake. This rugged topography is covered not in the rainforest one might expect of a reserve whose best-known inhabitants are chimpanzees, but rather in thick *brachystegia* woodland that gives way to narrow belts of lush riparian forest along the rivercourses.

Although chimpanzees hog the limelight, Gombe harbours a surprisingly varied fauna for a park of its small size. Fascinating in their own right are the olive baboons that beachcomb in front of the rest camp. These have been the subject of ongoing research since 1967, and – like their larger and more celebrated cousins – they are apparently oblivious to the presence of humans, without showing any of the aggression one normally associates with baboons that forage close to habitations. Other common primates in Gombe are vervet, blue, red-tailed and red colobus monkeys, the latter frequently seen while searching for chimps.

Most of the other mammals found here are secretive or nocturnal, and are seldom seen by visitors. The only part of the park where you may walk unguided is along the lakeshore and in the immediate vicinity of the rest camp, which is a good place to seek out some of the 200 bird species recorded in the park. Of particular note are the palmnut vultures and fish eagles that perch on palms and other trees along the lakeshore, and the gem-like Peter's twinspot, a normally elusive forest bird that is tame and easily spotted within the rest camp.

GETTING THERE AND AWAY

Organised tours Most safari operators based outside of Kigoma can arrange Gombe safaris, but they will generally be working with a local operator. The best place locally to arrange organised trips to Gombe is the Kigoma Hilltop Hotel, which offers a variety of package excursions for one to 12 people using their own motorboat, a trip of 25 minutes in either direction. The packages range from three to eight days in duration (with the first and/or last night being spent at their hotel in Kigoma) and vary greatly in price depending on duration and number of passengers, but include national park fees, guide fees, all meals, boat transfers, collection from the airport, and accommodation in Kigoma and Gombe Forest Lodge. They also organise combined packages to Gombe and Mahale Mountains, lasting from six to ten days in total; again prices depend on duration and group size. The contact details and website for the Kigoma Hilltop Hotel are listed in Kigoma's *Where to stay* section, page 451.

Independent visits The southern boundary of Gombe National Park lies 16km north of Kigoma, and the Kasekela Research Station and Rest Camp is situated on the lakeshore about 8km further north. Although there is no road into Gombe, this is one of the few national parks in East Africa that is easily accessed on public transport and can only be explored on foot, making it an excellent goal for independent travellers.

The cheapest way to get to Kasekela is with one of the lake-taxis that run between the beach at Kibirizi village, 3km north of Kigoma, and a village called Mwamgongo on the northern boundary of the national park. These lake-taxis stop by request at all lakeshore settlements on the way, Kasekela Rest Camp included. At least two boats ply the route daily, generally leaving from Kibirizi between 13.00 and 14.00 and taking two to four hours to get to Kasekela, depending on the number and duration of stops. On the return trip, the lake-taxis generally pass Kasekela between 07.00 and 08.00 and arrive at Kibirizi two to three hours later. The fare in either direction is Tsh2,000 per person.

Several practical issues relate to the lake-taxis. First, there is no public transport along the 3km road between Kigoma and Kibirizi, which means that you must walk or use a charter taxi, costing around Tsh3,000. Second, the lake-taxis are not covered, and can become uncomfortably hot in the sun, so if you have an umbrella take it along, otherwise bring a hat and sunscreen – as well as a bottle of water to drink on the way. Finally, the timing of the lake-taxis effectively enforces a two-night stay in Gombe. Should you need to visit the park as a day excursion or one-night trip, for instance because you need to catch a ferry or train elsewhere, a private boat charter at Kibirizi costs around Tsh80,000. More efficiently, the Hilltop Kigoma Hotel will rent out its 12-seater at a flat fee of US$500 per party for the round trip, plus US$50 for every night spent in the park.

⌂ WHERE TO STAY

Exclusive

⌂ **Gombe Forest Lodge** (6 tents) ✆ 028 280 4437; f 028 280 4434; e kht@raha.com or info@mbalimbali.com; www.mbalimbali.com. This luxury tented camp, on Mitumba Beach at the northern end of the park & operated by Mbali Mbali Lodges & Camps, which also owns the Kigoma Hilltop Hotel, opened in late 2003. The camp consists of 6 standing dbl tents on raised wooden platforms spaced out along the lakeshore. *US$400 pp all-inclusive.*

Budget

⌂ **Kasekela Research Station & Rest Camp** The smarter accommodation here is in the resthouse, which contains 2 twin rooms with nets but no fan, as well as a screened porch, & costs US$20 pp. There is also a hostel with smaller, scruffier rooms that lack for nets, but cost US$10 pp. Camping is permitted, too, but since it costs US$20 pp, there's no advantage in pitching a tent. In theory the accommodation is self-catering, but in practice there aren't formal facilities available for cooking, & you'll end up spending hours arranging to have pots, crockery, cutlery, charcoal etc brought to you. If you do bring food, a local cook is available to put a meal together, but you should be prepared to give him a reasonable tip. Alternatively, one of the ladies in the staff village will gladly prepare a simple meal – fish, beans, rice, chapatis & tea – at a very reasonable price. A staff shop sells biscuits & a few other basic foodstuffs, & visitors are welcome to visit the staff bar, which is stocked with beer & sodas. It might nevertheless be a good idea to bring mineral water & some fruit with you – though do be warned that the baboons are likely to attack anybody who carries food outdoors. If you do camp, don't leave any food in your tent, or the baboons are likely to knock it down. All food must be brought from Kigoma.

MAHALE MOUNTAINS NATIONAL PARK

Like a grand-scale version of Gombe, Mahale Mountains is one of the most beautiful national parks anywhere in Africa, and also ranks among the top destinations for chimpanzee tracking. The crystal clear waters and deserted sandy beaches that characterise this part of Lake Tanganyika would be alluring even without the forested peaks that rise high above them. As it is, the setting is scenically reminiscent of a volcanic island beach resort somewhere deep in the Indian Ocean – with the added bonus that these forests are inhabited by the greatest number of primate species of any Tanzanian national park, including an estimated 700–1,000 chimpanzees divided across a dozen communities.

Gazetted in 1985, the park is 30 times larger than Gombe at 1,613km². Set on a mountainous knuckle that juts into Lake Tanganyika some 150km south of Kigoma, the park is dominated topographically by the Mahale Range. This is a part of the Rift Valley escarpment that rises sharply from the lakeshore to the 2,462m Nkungwe Peak – which can be climbed as a very long and tiring day hike from the lakeshore camps – and six other peaks that exceed 2,000m in elevation. It is awe-inspiring to swim off one of the (reputedly bilharzia-free) beaches of Mahale, look up at the mountains and recognise that you are roughly midway in elevation between the highest peak in the range and the deepest point on the floor of the lake that surrounds you!

A common misconception about Mahale is that its habituated chimps are less approachable than their counterparts at Gombe. This is far from being the case – indeed, it is quite remarkable to find oneself in the midst of a group as it moves along a forest trail, and have a full-grown male chimpanzee brush past you casually as if you were just another tree in his way. What is true, however, is that the habituated community at Mahale occupies a far larger territory, which means that locating chimps can entail far more walking, with a higher risk than at Gombe of missing out altogether. As a rule, the odds of finding the chimps easily improves

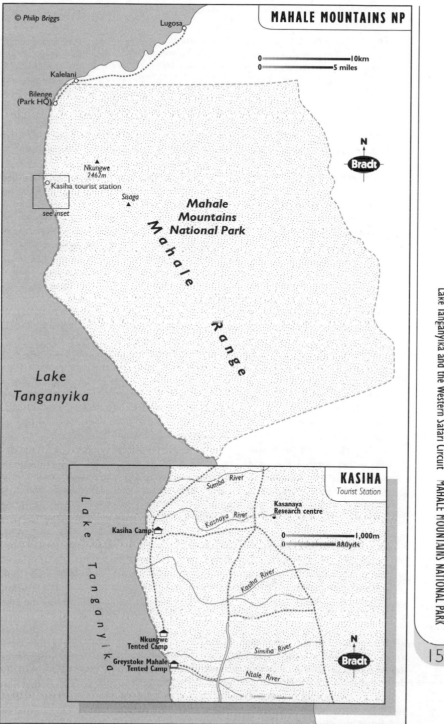

© Philip Briggs

Lugosa

MAHALE MOUNTAINS NP

0 ▬▬▬▬▬▬10km
0 ▬▬▬▬▬▬5 miles

Kalelani

Bilenge
(Park HQ)

N

Bradt

▲ Nkungwe
2462m

○ Kasiha tourist station

▲ *Sisaga*

*Mahale
Mountains
National Park*

Mahale

Range

see inset

*Lake
Tanganyika*

KASIHA
Tourist Station

L a k e   T a n g a n y i k a

Sumba River

Kasnaya River

Kasanaya ■
Research centre

Kasiha Camp ▢

0 ▬▬▬▬▬▬1,000m
0 ▬▬▬▬▬▬880yds

Kasiha River

Nkungwe
Tented Camp ▢

Simsiha River

Greystoke Mahale
Tented Camp ▢

Ntale River

N

Bradt

15

The staggering diversity of Tanzania's terrestrial fauna is old news, but few people are aware that Tanzania also probably harbours the greatest freshwater fish diversity of any country in the world. Significant portions of all of Africa's three great freshwater bodies – Lakes Victoria, Tanganyika and Nyasa–Malawi – lie within the borders of Tanzania, and each one of them harbours a greater number of fish species than any other lake in the world bar the other two. Which of the three lakes supports the greatest fish diversity is an open question, since new species are regularly discovered and large parts of the lakes remain practically unexplored by ichthyologists. Lake Victoria almost certainly takes the wooden spoon, because it is relatively young, but the most conservative estimates for Lakes Nyasa–Malawi and Tanganyika are around 500 species apiece – a greater number of freshwater species than are found in Europe and North America combined. The actual tally may well be closer to 1,000 species in each lake, of which more than 90% are endemic to that particular lake.

All well and good to trot out the boring statistics, but the greater significance of the great lakes' fish diversity is that it is the product of the most dramatic incidence of explosive speciation known to evolutionists. The majority of these fish species are cichlids – pronounced 'sicklids' – members of a perch-like family of freshwater fishes called cichlidae that ranges through Middle East, Madagascar, Asia and South and Central America. It is in Africa's three largest lakes, however, that this widespread family has undergone an unprecedented explosion of evolutionarily recent speciation that has resulted in it constituting an estimated 5% of the world's vertebrate species!

The cichlids of Africa's great lakes are generally divided into a few major groupings, often referred to by scientists by their local Malawian names, such as the small plankton-eating *utaka*, the large, pike-like and generally predatory *ncheni*, the bottom-feeding *chisawasawa*, and the algae-eating *mbuna*. People who have travelled in any part of Africa close to a lake will almost certainly have dined on one or other of the *tilapia* (or closely related *oreochromis*) cichlids, large *ncheni* that make excellent eating and are known in Malawi as *chambo*. To aquarium keepers, snorkellers and scuba divers, however, the most noteworthy African cichlids are the *mbuna*, a spectacularly colourful group of small fish of which some 300 species are known from Lake Nyasa–Malawi alone.

The *mbuna* of Lake Nyasa–Malawi first attracted scientific interest in the 1950s, when they formed the subject of Dr Geoffrey Fryer's classic study of adaptive radiation. This term is used to describe the explosion of a single stock species into a variety of closely related forms, each of which evolves specialised modifications that allow it to exploit an ecological niche quite different to that exploited by the common ancestral stock. This phenomenon is most likely to occur when an adaptable species colonises an environment where several food sources are going unused, for instance on a newly formed volcanic island or lake. The most celebrated incidence of adaptive radiation – the one that led Charles Darwin to propose the theory of evolution through natural selection – occurred on the Galápogos Islands, where a variety of finch species evolved from one common seed-eating ancestor to fill several very different ecological niches.

towards the end of the dry season, from July to October, when they tend to stick to the lower slopes of the mountain, sometimes even walking through the various tourist lodgings on the lakeshore. During the rainy season of November to April, the forest trails are tougher underfoot, and the chimps are often more difficult to locate, so a flying visit might well result in disappointment. But at any time of year, you'd be extremely unfortunate to spend two or three days in the park and not encounter any chimps at all.

The explosive speciation that has occurred among Africa's cichlids is like Darwin's finches amplified a hundredfold. The 500 or more cichlid species present in each of Lake Tanganyika and Lake Nyasa–Malawi are evolved from a handful of river cichlids that entered the lakes when they formed about 2–3 million years ago. More remarkable still is that the 200 or so cichlids in Lake Victoria – many of which are now extinct or heading that way (see box, A Dying Lake, pages 432–3) – have all evolved from a few common ancestors over the 10,000–15,000 years since the lake last dried up. In all three lakes, specialised cichlid species have evolved to exploit practically every conceivable food source: algae, plankton, insects, fish, molluscs and other fishes. Somewhat macabrely, the so-called kiss-of-death cichlids feed by sucking eggs and hatchlings from the mouths of mouth-brooding cichlids! No less striking is the diverse array in size, coloration and mating behaviour displayed across different species. In addition to being a case study in adaptive radiation, the cichlids of the great lakes are routinely cited as a classic example of parallel evolution – in other words, many similar adaptations appear to have occurred independently in all three lakes.

Not only have cichlids undergone several independent radial explosions in all three of Africa's great lakes, but the same thing has happened in microcosm in many smaller lakes throughout the continent. Uganda's Lake Nabugabo, for instance, harbours five endemic cichlid species, all of which must have evolved since the lake was separated from Lake Victoria by a sandbar less than 4,000 years ago.

Why cichlids and not any of several other fish families is a question that is likely to keep ichthyologists occupied for decades to come. One factor is that cichlids are exceptionally quick to mature, and are thus characterised by a very rapid turnover of generations. They also appear to have an unusually genetically malleable anatomy, with skull, body, tooth and gut structures readily modifying over a relatively small number of generations. Their capacity to colonise new freshwater habitats is boosted by a degree of parental care rare in other fish – the mouth-brooders, which include all but one of the cichlid species of Lake Nyasa–Malawi, hold their eggs and fry in their mouth until they are large enough to fend for themselves. Most fascinating, bearing in mind that the separation of breeding populations lies at the core of speciation, there is mounting evidence to suggest that cichlids have a unique capacity to erect non-physical barriers between emergent species possibly linked to a correlation between colour morphs and food preferences in diverging populations.

Tanzania's lake cichlids are never likely to rival the country's terrestrial wildlife as a tourist attraction. All the same, it is mildly astonishing that, at the time of writing, virtually no snorkelling or diving facilities exist for tourists visiting the Tanzanian shores of any of the three great lakes. Lake Tanganyika, in particular, already lies at the core of a nascent tourist circuit incorporating the game-rich plains of Katavi National Park and chimp-tracking in the lakeshore forests of Gombe and Mahale Mountains. What more logical extension to this circuit than snorkelling and diving excursions – already offered by lodges on the small Zambian stretch of lake frontage – in a lake that has justifiably been described as a 'unique evolutionary showcase'?

The entrance fee is US$80 per 24 hours, an additional guide fee of US$20 per party must be paid for all chimp walks, and the cheapest accommodation costs US$20 per person. Mahale National Park is the subject of a beautifully produced coffee table book entitled *Mahale: A Photographic Encounter with Chimpanzees*, by Angelika Hofer, Michael Huffman and Gunter Ziesler (Sterling Publishing, New York, 2000). The park's website (*www.mahalepark.org*) also contains some very useful information on the chimpanzees, birds and other wildlife in the park.

HISTORY The Mahale Mountains were one of the last parts of East Africa to be explored by outsiders. The British naval officer Verney Lovett Cameron passed below the mountains in 1873 on his way to becoming the first European to cross equatorial Africa from the Indian to the Atlantic coastline, and gave brief mention to them in *Across Africa*, the book he published in 1877. Aside from sporadic visits to the lower slopes by the White Fathers based at Kalema between 1911 and 1916, however, the area was ignored until 1935, when Dollman exhibited a chimpanzee skull found at Mahale to the Linnaean society of London. No European is known to have ascended the highest peak in the range before 1940, and it was only in 1958 that a team of Oxford scientists started serious scientific exploration of the area.

In 1961, the future national park was one of several areas visited by a team of primatologists from the University of Kyoto in Japan looking for a suitable site to study chimpanzees. The expedition agreed that Mahale was the most promising site, and in 1965 a permanent research centre was established at Kasoge, about 1km inland of the lakeshore, close to the present-day tourist camp at Kasiha. Over the course of the next five years, the two communities whose territories lay closest to the camp were habituated, using a feeding system similar to that pioneered by Jane Goodall further north along the lake.

Over the next 15 years, the Japanese scientists documented a fascinating series of developments in the local chimpanzee population. In 1967, the habituated Mimikere and Kajabala communities were comprised of about 100 and 27 individuals respectively, with territories that bordered each other. During the early years of the study, however, the smaller community gradually shrank in number, partially through the migration of females to the neighbouring territory, partially due to a protracted inter-community war that resulted in several fatalities, including the killing of two successive alpha males in the Kajabala Community. By 1982, no adult males were left in the Kajabala Community, and the surviving females and youngsters were integrated into the Mimikere community, which was free to occupy its former rival's territory. As with the chimp research project at Gombe, the Kyoto University project at Mahale Mountains continues to this day, with the Mimikere community – now numbering about 80 individuals – being the main subject of study, as well as of tourist visits.

FLORA AND FAUNA The elevation range of Mahale is reflected in its wide variety of habitats, with a floral composition that reflects a unique combination of influences associated with the eastern savannah, western rainforest and southern *miombo* woodland biomes. Altogether, some 15 different plant communities are recognised, but in simplistic terms there are four main vegetation zones. The foothills of the western slopes and most of the eastern slopes support a cover of open canopied woodland of various types, dominated by *brachystegia* woodland, which probably accounts for about 60–70% of the park's area. Although small in area, the closed-canopy riparian woodland that follows watercourses through the western foothills are of great ecological significance, as they provide refuge to species more normally associated with rainforest habitats. At higher elevations, particularly on the moister western slopes, which receive an average annual rainfall of 2,000mm, Afro-montane forest predominates, interspersed with patches of bamboo forest and containing some species more typical of the western lowland forests. Towards the peaks, the forest gives way to montane grassland and patches of heather studded with proteas and other flowering plants.

Chimps aside, eight other primate species have been recorded in Mahale Mountains, and at least five are likely to be encountered on the lakeshore and nearby *brachystegia* woodland. These are yellow baboon, red colobus, blue monkey, red-tailed monkey and vervet monkey. An endemic race of Angola black-and-white colobus is more or less confined to the montane forest of the higher slopes, while the lesser galago and thick-tailed greater galago are nocturnal and more likely to be heard than seen. Other lowland forest species are similar to those found at Gombe, but supplemented by isolated populations of west African species such as brush-tailed porcupine and giant forest squirrel. The eastern slopes of Mahale support savannah and woodland species such as elephant, lion, African hunting dog, roan antelope, buffalo and giraffe, but the only such creature that is frequently seen by tourists is the warthog. Lions, however, have killed several chimps in the forest, and African hunting dogs were once recorded on the beach!

No proper study of Mahale's birdlife has yet been undertaken, but at least 230 species have been recorded. Among the more colourful and interesting species likely to be seen close to the tourist lodges are crowned eagle, scaly francolin, crested guinea-fowl, Ross's turaco, giant kingfisher, blue-cheeked bee-eater, trumpeter hornbill, crested malimbe and Viellot's black weaver. The forests of Mahale are the only place in Tanzania where the rare bamboo warbler and Stuhlman's starling have been recorded, and they support an endemic race of the globally threatened Kungwe apalis.

GETTING THERE AND AWAY

Organised tours The main local specialists in trips to Mahale are the two companies that have permanent tented camps in the park (for contact details see *Where to stay* below). As with their respective tented camps, Nomad Tanzania arranges very exclusive visits at the top end of the safari price bracket, generally involving charter flights and tied in with a stay at their tented camp in Katavi National Park. The Kigoma Hilltop Hotel can arrange a wide variety of all-inclusive packages for one to 12 people, using their private motorboat to transfer between Kigoma and the national park, as well as cheaper packages using the MV *Liemba*. For independent travellers, this cost could be shaved further by arranging your own accommodation in Kigoma and your own ferry ticket, and arranging the local boat transfer and accommodation through the Kigoma Hilltop Hotel.

Independent visits Mahale Mountains is neither as quick nor as straightforward on public transport as Gombe, but it can be done by anybody who is prepared to put in a bit of legwork. There are several options, so read through the following carefully to decide which option best suits your comfort level and budget.

Four local landmarks are of significance in the trip. Two are villages outside the park boundaries. Lugosa (also known as Magambo or Buhingu) lies 15km north of the park and is the closest port serviced by the MV *Liemba*. Kalelani lies almost immediately outside the northern boundary. Within the park, the headquarters at Bilenge, only 1km south of Kalelani, are where all park fees must be paid. The tourist camp at Kasiha about 10km further south is the site of the national park's Mango Tree Rest Camp and the starting point for chimp tracking and other forest walks.

The most reliable and comfortable way to get within striking distance of Mahale Mountains is to board the lake ferry MV *Liemba* to Lugosa. If you are visiting the park as a round trip from Kigoma, the MV *Liemba* is scheduled to depart on its southern leg on Wednesdays at 16.00, and it generally arrives at Lugosa between midnight and 02.00 on Thursdays. For the return trip, the *Liemba* passes Lugosa at any time between 21.00 on Saturday and 06.00 on Sunday, arriving in Kigoma about 10–12 hours later. It is possible to visit the park by ferry *en route* between Kigoma and a more southerly port such as Ikola, Kasanga or Mpulungu, but since the ferry only runs once per week in either direction, this would enforce a stay of a full week in the vicinity of Mahale. Tickets between Kigoma and Lugosa cost US$25/20/15 first/second/third class, inclusive of port tax. If you're looking to cut costs, third class is fine for this relatively short hop.

Travellers who want to spend the full three days in the national park can arrange in advance for the park's motorised boat to meet the ferry at Lugosa and transport them directly to the park headquarters (to sort out fees) and then on to the rest camp at Kasiha. The transfer costs US$50 per party one-way and the boat should easily accommodate up to a dozen people. Advance arrangements can be made with the captain of the *Liemba*, who maintains radio contact with the park headquarters before arriving there, or through the Kigoma Hilltop Hotel in Kigoma.

The cheaper but more adventurous option is to disembark from the *Liemba* at Lugosa, where several local boats meet the ferry to transport passengers to the shore for Tsh200. There's a basic guesthouse in Lugosa where you can overnight, otherwise camping – or kipping out on the beach – is considered perfectly safe. From Lugosa, you can easily arrange a boat transfer on to Kalelani or Bilenge with a local fisherman, for which you should expect to pay up to US$10 per party. Another possibility would be to wait for the daily lake-taxi between Kigoma and Kalelani, which charges US$1 per person for the stretch between Lugosa and Kalelani. Cheaper still – and less dependent on the vagaries of local transport – would be to walk along a flat 15km footpath that more or less follows the lakeshore from Lugosa to Bilenge via Kalelani. If you want to tie this in with the ferry timetable, you'd need to walk south on Thursday, spend Friday tracking chimps, and then walk back north to Lugosa on Saturday to meet the ferry which heads to Kigoma on Saturday night.

Suitable only for the truly intrepid or masochistic, a local lake-taxi service runs between Ujiji and Kalelani daily except Sundays, in theory leaving from Ujiji at 18.00 and from Kalelani at 06.00. Be warned, however, that the lake-taxis are crowded, unsafe, uncovered, and can take up to 24 hours to cover the distance. It is also worth noting that, while no scheduled transport other than the MV *Liemba* heads south from Lugosa or Kalelani, you can usually expect one or two lake-taxis per week to run between one of the ports and Kalema or Ikola to the south.

However you get to Kalelani, there is no accommodation, but camping on the beach is considered safe, and will allow you to visit the park as a day trip, thus paying only one day's park entrance fees. Alternatively, you could sleep at the national park resthouse at Bilenge or the tourist camp at Kasiha (see *Where to stay* below), bearing in mind that spending the nights either side of your chimp walk at the resthouse would mean paying two day's park entrance fees. All fees must be paid and chimp walks arranged at Bilenge, from where you will be transferred by boat to Kasiha. No formal charge is levied for the transfer from Bilenge to Kasiha (at least not for visitors who are going on a chimp walk or staying at Mango Tree Rest Camp), but you may be asked to cover fuel (around US$20 per party for the round trip).

⌂ WHERE TO STAY
Exclusive

⌂ **Greystoke Mahale** (6 tents) ⤳ 022 286 5156; f 022 286 5731; e info@nomad.co.tz; www.nomad-tanzania.com. Set on a sandy private beach 3km south of Kasiha tourist camp, this Nomad Tanzania camp is in the classic old-style safari camp mould. The dbl tents, spaced out along the woodland that verges the beach, combine a high level of comfort with a winning rusticity epitomised by the open-air long-drop toilet & shower attached to each tent. The common dining & reception area is a stylish 2-storey wood, thatch & canvas construction with a good library of reference books. In addition to chimp tracking & other walks, visitors can snorkel in the lake from a large sailing dhow, the only one of its sort in this part of Tanzania. The understated bush chic does, however, come at a price, & most people will visit as part of a fly-in package. *US$1,000/1,500 sgl/dbl inc meals, drinks, national park fees & all activities.*

Upmarket

🏠 **Nkungwe Camp** ⟍ 028 280 4437; f 028 280 4434; e kht@raha.com or info@mbalimbali.com; www.mbalimbali.com. Affiliated to the Kigoma Hilltop Hotel, this reasonably priced tented camp stands on a secluded sandy beach near the Sisimba River mouth about halfway between Greystoke & Kasiha. The furnished standing tents each have large dbl bed & en-suite flush toilet & shower, while the dining & lounge area consists of a large raised wooden construction on the beach. No alcohol is sold, but you can bring your own from Kigoma, or the staff can arrange beers from the park headquarters. Open Mar–Nov only. *US$400 pp all-inclusive.*

Budget

🏠 **Kasiha Camp** (9 rooms) e sokwe@mahale.org. The main national park rest camp at Kasiha is situated in a glade of mango trees about 100m inland of the lakeshore, 10km south of the park headquarters. All rooms are clean & brightly painted, have 2 beds with netting; some are en-suite while others use common showers. There is no electricity or running water, but kerosene lamps & bucket showers are available, or you can swim in the lake. No food is available, so you'll need to bring everything with you from Kigoma, whether you want to self-cater or arrange a local cook. Beers & other drinks can be bought at the park headquarters, which you will need to visit in order to pay park fees before coming to the rest camp. Camping is not permitted. *US$20 pp.*

🏠 **Bilenge Welfare Club & Resthouse** (5 rooms) e sokwe@mahale.org. 2 types of accommodation are available at the park headquarters at Bilenge, both primarily aimed at visiting park officials but also open to tourists. The improbably named Welfare Club is essentially a staff bar, complete with satellite TV, & with 3 small twin rooms attached. The resthouse, which has a pretty, isolated location above the lakeshore about 300m from the main headquarters buildings, consists of 2 twin bedrooms, a lounge & an equipped kitchen. They cost the same, so the choice rests mainly on whether you want to socialise with the rangers or chill out in the bush. Drinks are available at the bar, & basic local meals can easily be arranged with the staff at the headquarters, though it might still be a good idea to bring a supply of tinned & packaged food. Note that although all park fees must be paid at Bilenge, all chimp-tracking excursions leave from Kasiha, for the simple reason that it lies within the territory of the habituated chimp communities. *US$20 pp.*

KATAVI NATIONAL PARK

In the 1980s, when Tanzania's elephant and rhino poaching crisis had reached its calamitous peak, Nicholas Gordon, author of *Ivory Knights*, described Katavi National Park as 'isolated and unloved, and in need of support'. Since then, the original 2,250km² has been extended southeast to cover more than 4,500km², making it the country's third-biggest national park, and the solitary concrete bunker that once formed the only tourist accommodation has been supplemented by several top-notch seasonal tented camps. Even so, Katavi remains probably the most obscure and least visited of Tanzania's major savannah reserves, making it the perfect goal for those seeking a true wilderness experience.

Katavi lies within the so-called Rukwa Rift, a shallow easterly extension of the main Western Rift Valley that culminates in the extensive Lake Rukwa basin to the east of the national park. The dense cover of dry *brachystegia* woodland that characterises Katavi is transected by the Katuma and Kapapa Rivers, which converge to become the Kavu River, a major effluent of Lake Rukwa. Because they are highly seasonal in the volume of water they carry, all the rivers are flanked by open floodplains throughout their courses. In three places, however, the rivers run through large, shallow depressions, depicted in bright blue on most maps, but

15

actually open expanses of tall, yellow grass and fine alluvial dust which are transformed into lush marshes or shallow lakes during the height of the rainy season. These are Lake Katavi on the Katuma River about 2km west of the main Mpanda–Sumbawanga road, the Chemchem Springs to the west of the Usevia road, and Lake Chada at the confluence of the Katuma and Kapapa Rivers about 3km east of the Usevia road. The name Katavi, incidentally, is said locally to derive from Katabi, a deified traditional healer who lived close to the eponymous lake.

Katavi is a classic dry-season reserve. During the rains, from late November to April, the wildlife disperses far and wide into the woodland, game viewing is by all accounts erratic, and the sweltering heat and humidity, combined with hordes of mosquitoes and other insects, makes for a highly uncomfortable safari prospect. After the last rains fall, however, the Katuma is reduced to a sluggish, muddy stream, in parts little more than a metre wide, yet the only source of fresh water for miles in any direction. It is then that the park comes into its own, with the three main floodplains attracting copious concentrations of wildlife, particularly between August and early November.

If ever a national park warranted that well-worn accolade of 'Africa's best-kept game viewing secret', it is surely Katavi in the dry season. Among the more prominent large mammals on the floodplains are elephant (over 4,000 are resident in the area), zebra, giraffe, hartebeest, topi, impala, reedbuck and Defassa waterbuck. Lions are abundant, with several different prides' territories converging on each of the so-called lakes. Spotted hyenas are regularly sighted in the early morning, while leopards are common but elusive in the fringing woodland. A notable feature of the park is its thousand-strong buffalo herds – at least three or four such herds roam along the river and associated floodplains. The woodland is less rewarding for game, at least in terms of volume, but it is where you are most likely to encounter eland, sable and roan antelope, which are drawn to the open grassland only at the very end of the dry season.

Most remarkable of all, perhaps, are the spectacular numbers of hippos that converge on any stretch of the river sufficiently deep to wallow in during the dry season. There are several pools where hundreds of hippo can reliably be seen, flopped all over each other like seals at a breeding colony. These huddled concentrations consist of several different pods that would not normally associate with each other during the rains (when they are able to disperse more widely into the seasonal marshes and lakes) and as a result the territorial competition between rival males is fierce. Bloody fights are an everyday occurrence, with dominance over any given hippo pool often passing from one bull to another several times in the course of a season, and the rejected behemoths being forced to spend their days foraging on the plains alongside the buffalo and zebra. We've not encountered anything like this anywhere else in Africa – the hippo density per kilometre of riverfront must be comparable to that of the Rufiji River or the Victoria Nile, except that instead of occupying a wide, deep river the hippos are squeezed into a shallow, muddy stream!

The rivers also harbour some impressively proportioned crocodiles, as well as concentrations of water-associated birds such as yellow-billed, open-billed and saddle-billed stork, pink-backed pelican, Africa spoonbill, and numerous herons, egrets and plovers. Raptors are well represented, with fish eagle, bateleur and white-backed vulture prominent. The acacia grove around Katavi Tented Camp is a particularly rewarding spot for woodland birds such as little bee-eater, red-billed hornbill, lilac-breasted roller, sulphur-breasted bush shrike, black cuckoo-shrike, African golden oriole, paradise flycatcher and crested barbet. A characteristic sound of the floodplain is the gurgling chuckle of yellow-throated sandgrouse, which flock along the river to drink about two hours after sunrise and shortly before sunset.

Less endearing altogether are Katavi's notorious tsetse flies, whose unusually vicious bites often result in painful swelling. Fortunately, the tsetse flies are more or less restricted to thickets and woodland away from the main game viewing circuits on the floodplains. Self-drive visitors should be alert to the elephants, which (presumably an aftermath of the poaching that subsided a decade back) are among the most aggressive in Africa and should definitely be given the right of way. It is also worth noting that the roads in the park are mostly in poor condition, and signposts are non-existent, which – given that the game tends to be concentrated in a few specific areas – makes it well worth hiring a guide from the park headquarters. Finally, you should take local advice before exploring the park beyond the main roads during the rainy season (November to March) – game viewing is poor at this time of year, and if the mosquitoes don't get you, the inundated black cotton soil along the seasonal tracks almost certainly will.

Such minor inconveniences are part and parcel of experiencing a tract of practically untrammelled bush that offers the alluring combination of tiny tourist volumes and superlative game viewing. Put it this way: in which other African national park are you likely to see more lions that you are other people? This impression is reinforced by several comments in the tented camps' visitors' books, many written by East African residents: 'Africa as it must have been 200 years ago', 'the best park in East Africa', 'safaris like they were 30 years ago'… Katavi does, however, seem to be generating a high degree of interest among safari operators elsewhere in Tanzania and, while the remote location alone makes package tourism somewhat improbable in the foreseeable future, a gradual increase in visitor numbers seems inevitable over the next few years. For the sake of the future conservation of this underrated park, an increase in tourist revenue can only be a good thing. Nevertheless, adventurous readers – whether they take an upmarket safari or travel independently – are unlikely to regret visiting Katavi before its remarkable wilderness character is diluted by the greater recognition it undoubtedly warrants.

FEES The entrance fee is US$20 per 24 hours. For travellers who are simply passing through, no entrance fee is charged for driving or using public transport along the two public roads that pass through the park, ie: the road between Mpanda and Sumbawanga and the road that branches southeast from Sitalike to Usevia. It is, however, illegal to deviate from these roads on to side roads, or into the bush, without having paid park fees. Park fees can only be paid at the headquarters near Sitalike, so people who are driving up from Sumbawanga and want to explore beyond the main roads must first report to the park headquarters. The park's well-maintained website (*www.katavipark.org*) is loaded with useful information.

GETTING THERE AND AWAY

By air The most normal way to reach Katavi is by charter flight to either the Sitalike or Ikuu airstrip. All three lodges operate charter flights.

Independent visits Remote and seldom visited it may be, but paradoxically Katavi is actually one of the more accessible national parks for independent travellers, since the main road between Mpanda and Sumbawanga runs right through it. The main entrance gate and park headquarters are situated alongside this road at the northern extreme of the park, about 1km south of the village of Sitalike, 200km north of Sumbawanga and 35km south of Mpanda. The main road between these towns is not in the greatest nick, and can be particularly bad after rain, so in a private vehicle you should probably expect the drive from Mpanda to take 45 minutes to one hour, and from Sumbawanga about 4–5 hours. Make sure you carry enough fuel, since there is nowhere to fill up between Mpanda and Sumbawanga.

Using public transport, several trucks and *dala-dalas* run between Mpanda and Sitalike daily, leaving Mpanda from in front of the Super City Hotel complex, taking about an hour in either direction, and charging Tsh1,500 per person. From Sitalike you can walk to the park headquarters in about 15 minutes, crossing a river *en route* where a pod of hippos is resident. Accommodation is available at the park headquarters, and 4x4 vehicles can be hired for US$100 per 100km per party inclusive of fuel, which is cheaper than a day on safari in the northern circuit for two or more people. Alternatively, you could try setting up a day or overnight safari out of Mpanda with one of the 4x4s that serve as *dala-dalas* along the local roads; it's bound to be cheaper than hiring a national park vehicle.

For people driving themselves, the excellent game viewing circuit around the Chada floodplain is most easily reached by following the public road that branches to the southeast at Sitalike, heading towards the small town of Usevia outside the southern boundary of the park. Initially, this road isn't very promising, passing through dense *brachystegia* woodland that is sparsely populated with game. After about 40–50km, however, you reach a bridge across the Katuma River – look out for the concentrations of hippo below it – and about 1km further a track to the left runs towards the Chada floodplain. A few *dala-dalas* run daily from Mpanda to Usevia, where there are a couple of basic guesthouses.

If you need to overnight in Mpanda, the best option is the affordable Super City Hotel (✆ *028 282 0459*). The best options in Sumbawanga are the Mbizi Forest Hotel (✆ *025 280 2746*) and Moravian Conference Centre (✆ *025 280 2853*; e *confcen@twiga.com*). For more details on Sumbawanga and Mpanda, see our website, http://bradttanzania.wordpress.com.

⌂ WHERE TO STAY
Exclusive

⌂ **Chada Katavi Camp** ✆ 022 286 5156; f 022 286 5731; e info@nomad.co.tz; www.nomad.co.tz. This superb wilderness lodge is set in a glade of tall acacia trees overlooking the seasonal Lake Chada flood plain. It consists of half a dozen standing dbl tents, each with private open-air hot shower & long-drop toilet. It is broken down entirely every Nov & reconstructed in May, so there are no concrete or stone structures, no neat footpaths, no lawns, no fences – just a few tents in a patch of pristine woodland regularly traversed by elephants, lions & other large mammals. It is precisely this air of uncluttered rusticity that lends Chada Tented Camp its exclusivity, offering a raw bush experience harking back to safaris as they must have been in the days of Karen Blixen & Denis Finch-Hatton. & this compelling wilderness atmosphere takes on a heightened immediacy at night, when it's not unusual to hear several prides of lion & numerous hyenas calling at the same time, while elephants & hippos crash through the surrounding bush. Not for the faint of heart, perhaps, but in its own understated way arguably the finest & most exciting upmarket camp in Tanzania. The management also arranges fly-camp safaris & game drives into the new park extension towards Lake Rukwa & the Rungwa River, as well as game walks on to the game-rich floodplain & drives in open-topped Land Rovers. US$770/1040 sgl/dbl, inc all meals, drinks, park fees & activities.

⌂ **Palahala Luxury Tented Camp** (6 tents) ✆ 027 250 8773; e info@firelightexpeditions.com; www.firelightexpeditions.com. This seasonal tented camp comes with all the lux trimmings – king-size beds, goose-down bedding, en-suite with hot water, gourmet meals – not to mention an idyllic riverside setting. There's also a spacious dining tent with lounge, bar & library. *All-inclusive fly-in rates from US$645 pp.*

⌂ **Katavi Wildlife Camp** ✆ UK 01452 862288; ✆/f 022 286 2357; m 0754 237422; e fox@ safaricamps.info; www.tanzaniasafaris.info. Owned by Foxes Safaris, which runs a string of camp sites in Tanzania's southern national parks, this reasonably priced tented camp is well-sited near the Ikuu ranger post. With each of the raised en-suited tents hidden away under a canopy of trees overlooking a flood plain, you're afforded exceptional game viewing right from your tent. *Fly-in rates US$475/750 sgl/dbl inc all meals & activities.*

Moderate

🏠 **Park Headquarters Resthouse** e katavinp@ yahoo.com. A well-equipped resthouse (with satellite TV!) aimed primarily at visiting Tanapa officials but also open to tourists is at the park headquarters about 500m from the main road to Sumbawanga & 1km south of Sitalike. Basic meals are available, & beers & sodas are served at the staff bar. *US$30 pp.*

🏠 **Katavi Hippo Garden Hotel** (12 *bandas*) ☎ 025 282 0393/023 262 0461; e info@ genesismotel.com; www.genesismotel.com. Affiliated to the Genesis Motel in Mikumi, this comfortable hotel in Sitalike, 1km from Katavi park headquarters, is a good option for anyone wanting to save costs on park entrance fees. Its en-suite *bandas* do feel a little overpriced, but they overlook the river & its resident pod of hippos. 4x4 safaris can be arranged. *US$30 pp; camping US$5 pp.*

Budget

🏠 **Lake Katavi Rest House** e katavinp@yahoo.com. The unfurnished 2-room concrete bunker that overlooks the Katavi floodplain, 15km south of the entrance gate & about 1km west of the main Sumbawanga road, is extortionately poor value, but it does boast a stunning situation, & there is excellent game viewing from the balcony. No mattresses or bedding are available, so you will need your own sleeping bag. Firewood is available, but drinking water must be brought from a spring near the entrance gate. The rangers will fill up a jerry can on request. Bring all provisions from Mpanda or Sumbawanga. *US$20 pp.*

Camping For budget travellers, your best bet is to pitch a tent in the grounds of the **Katavi Hippo Garden Hotel** in Sitalike, which costs US$5 per person. Self-sufficient travellers with private transport may camp at a number of places in the park, including outside the hut at the Katavi Floodplain. The best site is at Lake Chada. Campsites are basic, with firewood but no drinking water.

15

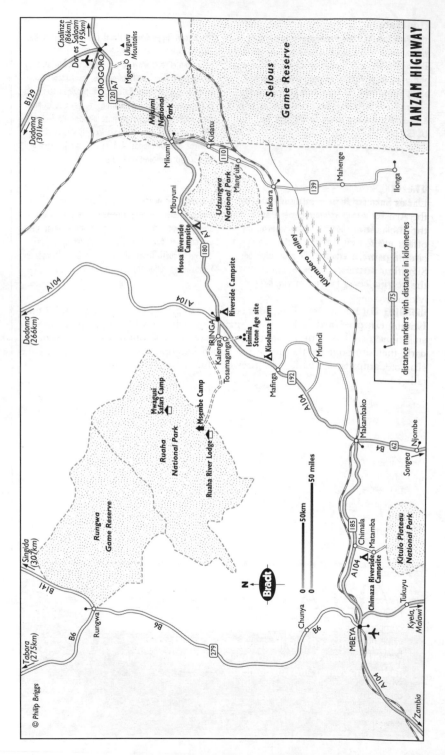

TANZAM HIGHWAY

© Philip Briggs

474

16

The Tanzam Highway and Southern Safari Circuit

The 1,000km Tanzam Highway, the main road through southern Tanzania, links Dar es Salaam to the Tunduma border post with Zambia. Forking southwest from the Arusha road at Chalinze, 100km west of Dar es Salaam, the highway bypasses the substantial but rather humdrum towns of Morogoro, Iringa and Mbeya, and offers access to the five major parks and reserves that comprise the southern safari circuit, namely Selous, Ruaha, Mikumi, Udzungwa Mountains and Kitulo Plateau. Significant natural landmarks include the Uluguru Mountains near Morogoro and the Rufiji River, Tanzania's largest waterway. The road is most scenic between Morogoro and Iringa, passing first through Mikumi National Park, then following the Great Ruaha River, a tributary of the Rufiji, as it flows through the baobab-clad Udzungwa foothills.

In pure game viewing terms, the southern safari circuit doesn't quite compare with the Serengeti and Ngorongoro – what could? – but its untrammelled character arguably makes for a more holistic bush experience. Tourist densities are rather low, and camps cater more to upmarket fly-in packages than the mid-range

THE TAZARA RAILWAY

Built in the 1970s with Chinese assistance, the **Tazara Railway** (↘ 022 262 191; f 022 262 474; www.tazara.co.tz) connects Dar es Salaam to Kapiri Mposhi in Zambia via Mbeya. Three passenger trains run weekly in either direction, though only two continue past Mbeya to Kapiri Mposhi. The two express trains leave from Dar es Salaam on Tuesday and Friday at 15.50, and from Kapiri Mposhi on the same days at 13.00, taking around 36 hours each way and stopping at Ifakara, Makamako, Mbeya and Tunduma. One additional slow train runs every week from Dar es Salaam to Mbeya, leaving Dar es Salaam on Monday at 09.00 and Mbeya at 15.00 Tuesday. Slow trains are scheduled to pass through Selous Game Reserve during daylight hours, and there is usually plenty of game to be seen. It is advisable to book tickets a few days in advance.

Fares between Dar es Salaam and Mbeya are around US$25/20/15 first/second/third class, payable in local currency. First-class compartments have two berths and second-class have six, and both are single-sex unless the whole compartment is booked by one party. Third class is worth thinking about only if you value neither your comfort nor your possessions. All trains have dining cars, and beers and sodas are normally available.

Theft from train windows at night is not unusual, so close the windows securely when you turn the light off. A block of wood is provided for this purpose; if you cannot find one in your compartment speak to the steward. Don't leave loose objects lying around the compartment; keep your luggage under the bunks. If you leave the compartment, take all valuables with you.

16

4x4 safaris that dominate in the north. The most popular regional safari destination is the immense Selous Game Reserve, which extends over a vast area of *miombo* woodland east of the Tanzam Highway, but game viewing here is matched and arguably surpassed by Ruaha National Park, which lies to the west of the highway near Iringa. There's also plenty of big game in Mikumi National Park, which is bisected by the Tanzam Highway, while the more recently gazetted Udzungwa Mountains and Kitulo Plateau national parks cater mainly to hikers, wildflower enthusiasts and birdwatchers.

MOROGORO

Situated at an elevation of 500m, some 200km inland of Dar es Salaam by road, Morogoro is an unusually attractive town, with an orderly layout below the Uluguru Mountains (which tower to 2,635m on the southern horizon) and a healthy, lively atmosphere. It is a fast-growing town, with an estimated population of 210,000 (the country's fifth-largest) and its bustling fruit and vegetable market is an important supplier of fresh produce for Dar es Salaam. There are few tourist attractions in the immediate vicinity of Morogoro. The most noteworthy architectural landmarks are the Old German Boma [477 C4], 1km from the town centre along Boma Road, and the German-era railway station in the town centre [477 F1]. A worthwhile short walk leads uphill past the Morogoro Hotel to the Rock Garden Resort [477 E4], a small indigenous botanical garden on the lower slopes of the Ulugurus. For travel possibilities deeper into in the Uluguru Mountains, see our website, http://bradttanzania.wordpress.com.

GETTING THERE AND AWAY Buses between Dar es Salaam and Morogoro leave hourly, cost Tsh6,000 and take about three hours. The main bus station is in Msamvu, 2km out of town on the Dar es Salaam road, and a taxi there from the town centre costs around Tsh2,000. Scandinavia Express, Hood and Sumry High Class all run regular buses from Dar es Salaam through Morogoro to Mikumi, Iringa and Mbeya. There is also regular public transport from Morogoro to Ifakara and Dodoma.

TOURIST INFORMATION AND TOURS The new community-based Chilunga Cultural Tourism Programme [477 E3] (m *0754 477582/0713 663993;* e *chilungamg@yahoo.co.uk; www.chilunga.8m.net*) is based in the YWCA opposite the hospital on the road towards the Morogoro Hotel. It offers a selection of day and overnight hikes into the Uluguru Mountains, ranging from a two-hour round trip to Kigurunyembe ('Keep on Walking' in the Luguru language), where a forested stream next to a venerable teachers college built by the White Fathers harbours a variety of birds and monkeys, to the ascent of Lupanga Peak, at 2,150m the highest in the vicinity of town. 4x4 rental for visits to Mikumi National Park works out at around US$360 per vehicle per day, including guide and park entrance fees.

   Uluguru Mountains Biodiversity and Conservation Project (❨ *023 260 3122;* e *uluguru@morogoro.net; www.africanconservation.com/uluguru*) Details about hiking routes, camping and local guides for the Uluguru Mountains can be obtained from this **Wildlife Conservation Society** office on the top floor of **Pamba House**, opposite the post office [477 D3].

🏠 **WHERE TO STAY**
Upmarket
🏠 **New Acropol Hotel** [477 F2] (5 rooms) ❨ 023 260 3403; m 0754 309410; e newacropol@   morogoro.net; www.newacropolhotel.biz. This small Canadian-owned hotel, with bright airy rooms &

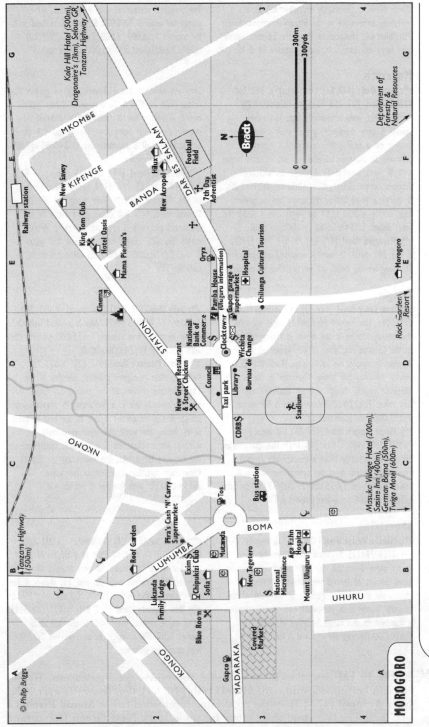

MOROGORO

Labels on map:

KONGO

KINGO

Tanzam Highway (500m)

Roof Garden

Pira's Cash 'N' Carry Supermarket

Lukanda Family Lodge

Blue Room

Chipukizi Club

Sofia

Exim

Muzanda

LUMUMBA

BOMA

New Tegetero

Aga Kahn Hospital

National Microfinance

Mount Uluguru

Gapco

MADARAKA

Covered Market

UHURU

Tos

Bus station

Masuka Village Hotel (200m), Sosine Inn (400m), German Boma (500m), Twiga Motel (600m)

NKOMO

New Green Restaurant & Street Chicken

National Bank of Commerce

Council

Taxi park

Library

Clock tower

Wichita

Bureau de Change

CDRB

Stadium

STATION

Cinema

Mama Pierina's

King Tom Club

Hotel Oasis

New Savoy

KIPENGE

MKOMBE

Railway station

Kola Hill Hotel (500m); Dragonaire's (3km); Selous GR; Tanzam Highway

BANDA ES SALAAM

DAR ES SALAAM

Hilux

New Acropol

7th Day Adventist

Football Field

Pamba House (Uluguru information)

Gapco garage & supermarket

Oryx

Hospital

Chilunga Cultural Tourism

Rock Garden Resort

Morogoro

Department of Forestry & Natural Resources

N

300m
300yds

© Philip Briggs

The Tanzam Highway and Southern Safari Circuit MOROGORO

16

stylish décor, is thoroughly recommended as a refreshing alternative to the blandly functional hotels that otherwise characterise Morogoro. En-suite rooms have large dbl bed, sofa, fridge, satellite TV & AC.

Moderate

⌂ **Hotel Oasis** [477 E1] (35 rooms) ☎ 023 260 4178/3535; f 023 260 4830; e hoteloasistz@ morogoro.net; www.hoteloasistz.com. This smart, central & very reasonably priced multi-storey hotel is centred on a neat green courtyard & caters primarily to business travellers. It has en-suite rooms with AC, nets, satellite TV & fridge. An attached business centre charges US$1.50/hr for internet use, & there's a good Indian restaurant on the ground floor asking around US$4 for vegetarian & US$5 for meat dishes. *US$45/50/60 sgl/dbl/suite B&B.*

⌂ **Morogoro Hotel** [477 E4] ☎ 023 261 3270/2; f 023 261 4001; e morogorohotel@morogoro.net. This long-serving hotel, set on the Uluguru footslopes

Budget

⌂ **New Savoy Hotel** [477 F1] (15 rooms) ☎ 023 260 3041. This former government hotel opposite the railway station is the oldest in Morogoro, dating to the German era, when it was known as the Barnhof (renamed the Savoy after World War I). It retains an attractive period character, & the large timeworn rooms, though scarcely luxurious, aren't bad value. *Tsh22,500 dbl with nets & hot water; Tsh30,000 mini-suite with TV.*

⌂ **Mount Uluguru Hotel** [477 B3] (58 rooms) ☎ 023 260 3489; f 023 260 4079. This characterless but reliable 5-storey hotel is conveniently located around the corner from the central bus station, & reasonably priced. *Tsh15,000/29,000/39,000 en-suite sgl/dbl/suite with hot water, fan, net & TV*

Shoestring

⌂ **Masuka Village Hotel** [477 C4] (30 rooms) m 0754 280223. A 10min walk from the town centre along Boma Rd, this appealingly idiosyncratic hotel consists of several semi-detached circular chalets set in flowering gardens at the base of the Uluguru. Rooms look somewhat worn, but it remains a standout in this range in terms of value. *Tsh10,000 en-suite dbl with net & hot showers.*

The attached restaurant, also very stylish, serves pizzas for around Tsh4,000 & steak & seafood grills for around Tsh6,000–7,000. *Tsh50,000/60,000 sgl/dbl B&B; Tsh60,000/80,000 sgl/dbl suite.*

2km out of town, has a flowering green garden that rattles with birdlife & borders on a 9-hole golf course. A decent bar & restaurant is attached. The revamped en-suite bungalows, though quiet & clean, are rather small & characterless. *US$40/60 sgl/dbl with AC & hot shower.*

⌂ **Kola Hill Hotel** [477 G1] (32 rooms) ☎ 023 260 3707; f 023 260 4394. Set in bare gardens in the Uluguru foothills 3km along the old Dar es Salaam road, Kola Hill offers good views to the mountain peaks & a restaurant serving decent meals. En-suite rooms have dbl bed, hot water, net & fan. *Tsh20,000/35,000 dbl without/with AC & satellite TV.*

⌂ **Sofia Hotel** [477 B2] (20 rooms) ☎ 023 260 4847/8; m 0713 334421. This is a clean well-run set-up near the bus station. *Tsh15,000 en-suite dbl with fan & TV; Tsh24,000 with AC.*

⌂ **Mama Pierina's Hotel** [477 E2] ☎ 023 260 4640. Another Morogoro stalwart, founded in the 1960s by the mother of the present-day Greek owner-manager, this is a welcoming & unpretentious set-up, & the restaurant is one of the best in town, quiet during the week but often very lively at w/ends, when volunteers & expatriates congregate on the veranda for drinks. The rooms are starting to show their age, but they remain fair value. *Tsh15,000 dbl with fan, net & hot shower.*

⌂ **Sasine Inn** [477 C4] (10 rooms) ☎ 023 260 0220; m 0754 683040. Part of a cluster of small new hotels on Saba Saba Rd near Masuka Village, its compact tiled rooms with dbl bed, hot shower & fan seem pretty good value. *Tsh10,000 dbl.*

⌂ **New Tegetero Hotel** [477 B3] ☎ 023 260 3398. Good value central hotel with scruffy but clean rooms. *Tsh7,000 en-suite dbl with balcony; Tsh6,000 with common showers.*

✘ **WHERE TO EAT** Several of the hotels listed above have good restaurants. Try the efficient Indian restaurant at the **Hotel Oasis** [477 E1], the classy restaurant at the **New Acropol** [477 F2], or the good value continental fare at **Mama Pierina's** [477 E2]. The best stand-alone eatery for some years, **New Green Restaurant**

[477 D2] (✆ *023 261 4021*) serves good Indian and Portuguese dishes for Tsh5,000–8,000 range. In the evenings, a popular **street chicken** vendor sets up just outside the restaurant selling delicious and cheap *mishkaki*, chicken and chips.

A favourite with local *wazungu*, **Dragonaire's** [477 G1], 3km from town off the old Dar es Salaam road, has a lovely outdoor setting, scrumptious Pizzas (*w/ends only; Tsh3,000–6,000*) and a selection of Chinese and continental dishes. There's a children's playground, satellite TV and Karaoke on Friday and Saturday nights. Another family friendly option is the **King Tom Club** [477 E1] outdoor bar and grill next to the Oasis Hotel. It's open for lunch and dinner with meals costing around Tsh3,500–5,000. For local Tanzanian fare, the **Blue Room** [477 B2], across the road from the Chipukizi Club, is a reliable choice serving up large helpings of chicken, *ugali*, rice and beans for around Tsh2,000.

If you need to stock up before heading off to the southern parks, **Pira's Cash and Carry** [477 B2] stocks a wide variety of packaged and canned food items, as does the **Gapco Supermarket** [477 D3] above the Gapco petrol station, while the **market** [477 A3] is the best place for fresh produce.

OTHER PRACTICALITIES

Foreign exchange The National Bank of Commerce on the old Dar es Salaam road [477 D3] exchanges foreign currency travellers' cheques and cash during normal banking hours. There is also a private bureau de change next to the post office.

Internet Several internet cafés are dotted around town, with two of the best situated opposite and next to the Sofia Hotel [477 B2]. Rates are Tsh500–1,000 per hour, but cafés tend to close at around 18.00.

Swimming There's no public pool in Morogoro, but if you fancy a dip the Oasis Hotel [477 E1] has a pool and charges a daily entry fee of Tsh3,000 per person.

SELOUS GAME RESERVE

The 45,000km² Selous Game Reserve is Africa's most extensive such entity, three times larger than Serengeti National Park, more than double the size of South Africa's Kruger National Park, and roughly 50% bigger than either Belgium or Swaziland. Selous also forms the core of the 155,000km² greater Selous–Niassa ecosystem, the largest chunk of comparatively untrammelled bush left in Africa, incorporating several other reserves including Mikumi and Udzungwa National Parks, the swampy Kilombero Game Protected Area, and the 23,400km² Niassa Game Reserve in northern Mozambique. Here live some of Africa's most prodigious large mammal populations. An elephant herd of around 70,000 is the largest of any modern ecosystem, representing 5–10% of the continental total. The Selous also harbours an estimated 100,000 wildebeest, 35,000 zebra, 25,000 impala and significant herds of greater kudu, hartebeest and eland. The buffalo population of 120,000–150,000 is probably the largest in Africa, and tallies of 40,000 hippo and 4,000 lion must also be there or thereabouts.

That the Selous is one of Africa's most alluring and satisfying safari destinations is not in dispute. However, given that much of the publicity surrounding the Selous focuses on its vast area, prospective visitors should be aware that in practice this is something of a red herring. The Selous is divided into two uneven parts by the Rufiji and Great Rauaha rivers. Roughly 90% of the Selous lies to the south of these rivers, and is cut up into privately leased hunting concessions, and much of the northern sector is also set aside for hunting. As a result, the public part of the

16

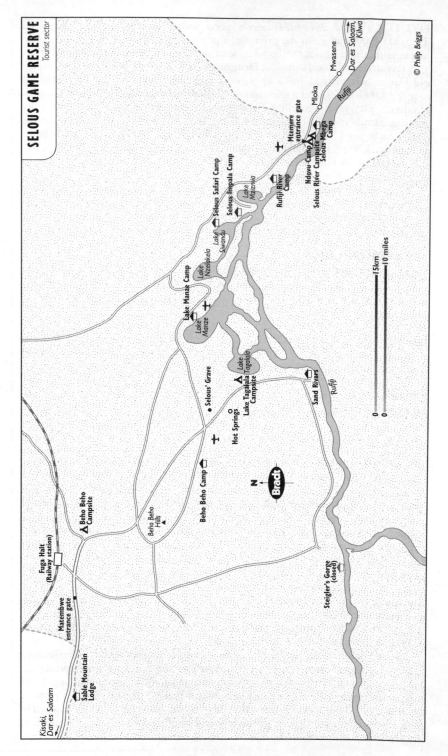

SELOUS GAME RESERVE
Tourist sector

© Philip Briggs

Dar es Salaam, Kilwa

Mwasene

Rufiji

Mloka

Mtemere entrance gate

Ndovu Camp
Selous River Campsite
Selous Mbega Camp

Rufiji River Camp

Lake Mzizimia

Selous Safari Camp

Selous Impala Camp

Lake Siwandu

Lake Nzelekela

Lake Manze Camp

Lake Manze

15km

10 miles

0

0

Selous' Grave

Lake Tagalala

Lake Tagalala Campsite

Sand Rivers

Rufiji

Hot Springs

N

Bradt

Beho Beho Camp

Beho Beho Hills

Steigler's Gorge (closed)

Beho Beho Campsite

Fuga Halt (Railway station)

Matembwe entrance gate

Kisaki, Dar es Salaam

Sable Mountain Lodge

480

reserve accounts for just 5% of the total surface area, and the main tourist camps are all concentrated within an area of 1,000km² immediately north of the Rufiji.

While the marketing line of 'only five small camps in a 50,000km² wilderness' does rather overstate the exclusivity of the Selous experience, it is true that a mere 5,000 foreigners annually – about 1% of tourist arrivals to Tanzania – ever make it to this excellent reserve. Particularly if one is based at one of the western lodges – Beho Beho, Sand Rivers and Sable Mountain – it is still possible to undertake a game drive in the Selous without coming across another vehicle. Whereas the northern circuit is dominated by large impersonal hotels that evidently aim to shut out the bush the moment you enter them, the Selous boasts a select handful of low-key, eco-friendly, thatch and canvas lodges whose combined bed capacity amounts to little more than 100 clients.

What's more, the public part of the Selous is wonderfully atmospheric, a dense tract of *miombo* wilderness abutting the meandering Rufiji River, and an associated labyrinth of five pretty lakes connected to each other and the river by numerous narrow streams. Arriving by light aircraft, as most visitors do, it is exhilarating to sweep above the palm-fringed channels teeming with hippos and waterfowl, the swampy islets where immense herds of elephant and giraffe graze alongside each other, and exposed sandbanks where antelope drink and all manner of shorebirds scurry about. An indisputably great feature of the Selous is that it is not subject to the regulations that govern national parks, which means that game drives can be supplemented by guided walks and boat trips, creating a more primal and integrated bush experience than the usual repetitive regime of one game drive after another.

Roads within the Selous become impassable after heavy rain. As a consequence, most camps close towards the end of the wet season, in April, and reopen in July. An entrance fee of US$50 per person per day is charged.

HISTORY In 1859, Burton and Speke passed through what would later become the Selous Game Reserve, noting that the area lacked for any significant human settlements. This uninhabited state is partly explained by a profusion of tsetse flies (which carry livestock diseases) and the limited amount of permanent water south of the Rufiji River. Another factor, doubtless, would have been regular slave raids associated with the Arab trading post of Kisaki, today an overgrown village set on the northern boundary of the game reserve, but in the 19th century the junction of two main caravan routes into the interior. In 1905, the region was further depopulated when the German colonial authorities undertook a brutal series of raids in retaliation for the Maji Maji uprising. The section of the present-day Selous Game Reserve lying to the north of the Rufiji River was gazetted in the same year, as a gift from Kaiser Wilhelm to his wife, earning it the local nickname Shamba la Bibi (The Woman's Field).

Selous (pronounced 'Seloo') is named in honour of Frederick Courtney Selous, who left England for Africa in 1871 as an athletic 18 year old – his school pals called him The Mighty Nimrod – and spent the next four decades acquiring a reputation as perhaps the most accomplished hunter of his age. Selous served as Great White Hunter to the likes of Theodore Roosevelt, and was renowned as a writer of rollicking African hunting yarns, notably *A Hunter's Wanderings in Africa*. A staunch patriot, Selous was right-hand man to Cecil John Rhodes's campaign to annex present-day Zimbabwe to the British Empire, though he also achieved brief notoriety in 1899 for speaking out against England's war on the Boer Republics of South Africa.

In 1914, when war broke out between Britain and Germany, Selous was more than 60 years old, yet he unhesitatingly volunteered and was made Captain of the

16

The most endangered of Africa's large carnivores, after the very localised Ethiopian wolf, is almost certainly the **African wild dog**, and the Selous's importance as a sanctuary for this fascinating pack animal is difficult to overstate. Recent surveys indicate that every part of the Selous falls within the home range of at least one pack of wild dogs. The reserve's total population of around 1,300 individuals is twice that of any other African country, let alone any individual game reserve, representing 20–30% of the global free-ranging population. Quite why the Selous has been unaffected by the precipitous decline that has characterised wild dog populations practically everywhere else in Africa is an open question. Perhaps it is because the surrounding area is so thinly inhabited, minimising the wild dog's exposure to canid-borne disease and vengeful stock farmers. Perhaps, as suggested by biologists Scott and Nancy Creel, who spent the best part of a decade studying several packs of wild dogs in the Selous, it is because the wild dogs in Selous face less competition from other large predators than they do in many other reserves. Quite possibly, it is simply a matter of good luck. Whatever the reason, Selous is probably the best place in Africa to see free-ranging wild dogs, with three separate packs, collectively totalling about 60 individuals, living to the north of the Rufiji River. Wild dogs are highly mobile and wide ranging creatures, but it's unusual for more than a few days to pass without one or another pack showing up somewhere around the lakes of the tourist circuit, and once sighted the pack is normally easy to locate until it moves off again. The one time when wild dog sightings are practically guaranteed is the denning season from June to August.

Less glamorously, the greater Selous–Niassa ecosystem is of particular significance to two antelope species classified as Low Risk Conservation Dependent by the IUCN. The 8,000 **sable antelope** that migrate through the area constitute by far the largest wild population anywhere in Africa. In 1998, DNA testing placed the Selous's sable in the race *Hippotragus niger roosevelti*, formerly thought to be endangered, since the only confirmed population was a herd of 120 protected within Kenya's Shimba Hills National Reserve. The estimated 50,000 **puku antelope** resident within the greater ecosystem represent about 75% of the global population of this localised wetland species. Although a small proportion of the puku's range lies within the western boundaries of the Selous Game Reserve, the bulk is accorded a far lower level of protection within the adjacent Kilombero Game Controlled Area (see page 25). Unfortunately, neither of the above antelope species is seen with any frequency in the main tourist circuit.

In common with several other East Africa conservation areas, the Selous Game Reserve suffered greatly from commercial ivory poaching during the 1980s, its vulnerability exacerbated by its proximity to the then war-torn Mozambique. In 1976, Selous's **elephant** population stood at around 110,000, which was probably an artificial high, arguably related to the fact that the protected area formed a relatively safe refuge for herds that might formerly have ranged more widely. The 1981 census indicated a relatively small numerical drop, possibly seasonal, to 100,000, but the next ten years saw elephants being poached at an alarming rate of roughly 20 per day, with the estimated population dropping to 55,000 in 1986 and 25,000 in 1989.

In 1988, fearing that the Selous's elephants might be eliminated entirely, the Tanzania government launched the Selous Conservation Programme with support from several

25th Royal Fusiliers, winning a DSO in 1916. With his intimate knowledge of the bush, Selous was the automatic choice to head up the chase after the ragtag German guerrilla army that Colonel Von Lettow led through southern Tanzania for longer than a year, consistently evading or defeating the British troops. On New Year's Day 1917, the opposing troops converged on each other close to the banks of the Beho Beho River, and Selous was shot dead by a sniper. The most international conservation agencies such as the Frankfurt Zoological Society, the African Wildlife Foundation and the World Wide Fund for Nature. This programme aimed to involve bordering communities in conservation activities, as well as raising funds for better policing of the reserve. Aided by the controversial CITES ban on ivory in the early 1990s, poaching was brought under control. By 1994, the Selous's elephant population had climbed back above 30,000. The most recent aerial survey in 1998 placed the population at 55,000–60,000, and today the population of the greater ecosystem probably stands at a healthy 70,000.

In 1980, Selous's estimated herd of 3,000 **black rhinoceros** was the largest to be confined within any one East African conservation area. It still is, come to think of it, but with the critical difference that the most optimistic estimates place the current population at fewer than 150. The only viable rhino herd that is resident to the north of the Rufiji consists of about ten individuals resident in the Kidai sector and Beho Beho Hills of the northwest. The Sand Rivers Selous Rhino Project – established by the lodge of the same name in 1995 – has been largely responsible for funding a 12-ranger anti-poaching unit that closely monitors this group of rhinos, and has recently extended its attention to elsewhere in the reserve with a patrol plane. Given the limited gene pool from which southern Africa's large black rhino population derives, the survival of the genetically distinct Selous population, together with that of the so-called desert rhinos of Namibia, is not merely of local significance.

Paradoxically, a significant factor in stemming the poaching within Selous has been the utilisation of almost 90% of the reserve for low-volume trophy hunting. Whatever one might feel about the sort of individual who is prepared to pay vast sums of money to blow the brains out of a lion or elephant or kudu in the prime of its life, the hunting concessions are by all accounts well monitored, and their benefits are clear. First, the lessors have a strong interest in driving poachers off their concessions, and thus play an important role in policing remote parts of the reserve. Second, the revenue derived from the hunting concessions and their patrons – four times the sum raised by less pugnacious forms of tourism – form an important source of funding for anti-poaching patrols and reserve management.

Setting aside ethical issues, the low-volume hunting does have several negative effects. The large tuskers that once characterised the region are today conspicuously absent, and although the commercial poaching of the 1980s is primarily to blame for this, trophy hunting – which targets the most physically impressive specimens of most species – does not help the situation. It is also noticeable how skittish much of the Selous's wildlife is – proof, say those who subscribe to the Selous myth machine, that the animals here are 'wilder' than in other reserves. A far more plausible explanation, given that the Selous is not that lightly trafficked, is that many of its animals regularly cross between the sanctuary of the tourist sector and neighbouring hunting concessions. For the time being, the hunting concessions form an integral part of the management strategy for Africa's largest game reserve, but it is to be hoped that the day will come when a greater volume of non-hunting tourists will justify allocating a larger portion of the Selous to conventional safaris.

famous casualty of East Africa's so-called 'Battle of the Bundu', Selous was held in such universal esteem that Colonel Von Lettow, upon hearing of his death, described the old hunter as having been 'well known among the Germans, on account of his charming manner and exciting stories'.

Less than two years later, P H Lamb trekked to the site of the simple wooden cross that marked the spot where the septuagenarian Selous had fallen and was buried. 'It is', Lamb reported, 'a wild inhospitable district, the haunt of a great variety of big game, including elephants, giraffes and rhinos. Not more than four miles away is a warm salt spring running down into a salt lake, where hippos, wild ducks, egrets and numerous other wild fowls abound. But despite these alleviations it can hardly be called a fascinating part of the world, and the object of most people who have seen it will be to avoid it carefully in the future.'

While the opening sentences of Lamb's report could have been written yesterday, hindsight does lend a certain irony to his final prediction. Five years after Selous's death, the plains of the Shamba la Bibi were greatly extended by the British colonists to incorporate a number of existing game reserves south of the river, and the whole was named in honour of the hero buried within the reserve. The Selous Game Reserve reached its present size and shape in the 1940s, when the colonial government moved the remaining tribes out of the area to combat a sleeping sickness epidemic. It was inscribed as a UNESCO World Heritage Site in 1982, and far from being carefully avoided, the site of Selous's Grave lies within 15km of two of the most exclusive safari lodges in Tanzania!

GETTING THERE AND AWAY

Package safaris Most safari companies in Tanzania (especially those based in Dar es Salaam) offer fly-down packages to the Selous, anything from two to seven nights in duration, and optionally combined with Ruaha National Park. Most packages use one of a few scheduled daily flights connecting to Dar es Salaam, Zanzibar and Ruaha, which can land at any of the camps' airstrips by arrangement. Game drives and other activities are usually provided by the individual camp as part of the package. Some companies also offer drive-down safaris from Dar es Salaam, but be warned that the road trip can be uncomfortable, and consumes the best part of a day in each direction. Fly or drive, the price of the safari will vary greatly depending on which camp you stay at, your length of stay, how you travel to the reserve, and the size of your group.

Independent visits With a private 4x4, there are two possible routes from Dar es Salaam. Best for stand-alone visits is the 240km easterly route via Kibiti and Mloka to Mtemere Gate, which typically takes about six hours. This route is also viable for backpackers, as there are buses from Dar es Salaam to Mloka, and the nearby Selous River Camp and Mbega Camp can pick you up from the bus station by prior arrangement (phone or email the camps for further details).

More suitable for linking up with the other southern reserves is the 330km route that involves following the surfaced Tanzam Highway to Morogoro, from where the 140km long Matombo road leads southwards via Kisaki to Matembwe Gate on the northwest border of Selous. If you use this road, look out for the interesting roadside quartzite formations about 50–60km south out of Morogoro just after the small town of Mkuyuni, and for the forest-fringed Ruvu River (plenty of monkeys) between Mgazi and Kisaki.

⌂ WHERE TO STAY
Exclusive

⌂ **Beho Beho Camp** (8 units) ☏ 022 260 0353; e reservations@behobeho.com; www.behobeho.com. The most luxurious lodge in the Selous offers large attractively decorated en-suite stone cottages that blend harmoniously into their setting on the footslopes of the westerly Beho Beho Hills. The dining area & swimming pool offer a fabulous view over the plains to Lake Tagalala. Although Beho Beho is the only lodge within Selous set away from the river, a permanent pool supports hippos & attracts other passing wildlife. The relatively remote location means few tourist vehicles are found in the vicinity, & excellent game viewing can be had at nearby lakes Tagalala & Manze. Game walks are offered, as are boat trips on Lake Tagalala, which reputedly has one of the Africa's highest crocodile populations. Nearby sites of interest include Selous's Grave & a group of hot springs set in a patch of riparian woodland. US$700 pp FB inc activities.

🏠 **Sand Rivers** (8 rooms) 🕿 022 286 5156; e info@nomad.co.tz; www.nomad-tanzania.com. Set above a wide, sandy bend in the Rufiji River, this rivals Beho Beho in terms of luxury, & is the most isolated lodge in Selous, situated in the wild southwest of the public part of the reserve, an area that is infrequently visited by vehicles from the other lodges. The en-suite stone & makuti units are airy & elegant, & each has a large dbl bed & private balcony overlooking the river. There is a swimming pool. The emphasis is on walking safaris, & guiding standards are exceptionally high. Game drives are also offered, with nearby Lake Tagalala being one obvious goal. It is the only lodge that offers boat trips through Stiegler's Gorge, the most reliable place in the reserve for sightings of leopard & black-&-white colobus monkey. Plenty of animals come down to the river to drink, & black rhino are resident in the surrounding dense bush, though seldom seen. US$700/1,000 sgl/dbl FB inc activities.

Upmarket

🏠 **Lake Manze Camp** (12 units) 🕿 022 245 2005/6; e reservations@adventurecamps.co.tz; www.adventurecamps.co.tz. Opened in mid 2007, this lovely tented camp, also operated by Coastal Aviation, lies on the palm-fringed shores of Lake Manze, an area rich in wildlife & especially good for elephant & wild dog. Accommodation is in smart stilted en-suite standing tents with a private balcony, & there's a large thatched lounge with a library & views to the hippo- & croc-infested lake. US$395/670 sgl/dbl inc activities; US$365/610 low season.

🏠 **Sable Mountain Lodge** (12 rooms) 🕿 022 211 0507; e info@selouslodge.com; www.selouslodge.com. This sensibly priced lodge lies in a patch of small hills 1km outside the western park boundary near Matembwe Gate. It consists of 8 cottages & 4 tented bandas, all with en-suite hot shower & toilet & 24hr electricity, set spaciously across the hillside. A treehouse on one of the slopes offers a grandstand view over a waterhole regularly visited by buffalo & elephant. The surrounding woodland is very thick, & guided walks offer the opportunity to see forest-associated species such as blue monkey, black-&-white colobus & the amazing chequered elephant shrew, as well as a host of forest birds including the exquisite

🏠 **Selous Safari Camp** (13 rooms) 🕿 022 212 8485; m 0784 953551; f 022 211 2794; e info@selous.com; www.selous.com. This plush camp on the shores of Lake Siwando is divided into a 9-unit main camp & a 4-unit private camp. Both provide accommodation in spacious stilted en-suite tents, which are set far apart from one another & have fans, open-air showers & private decks. The common lounge & dining area is a fabulous stilted treehouse lit at night by dozens of gas lamps. There is a swimming pool. Game drives, boat trips, guided walks & fly-camping are all offered. US$830/1,100 sgl/dbl FB inc activities.

🏠 **Selous Impala Camp** (7 units) 🕿 022 245 2005/6; e reservations@adventurecamps.co.tz; www.adventurecamps.co.tz. Operated by Coastal Aviation, this unpretentiously tasteful camp boasts a magnificent location on a wooded stretch of the Rufiji & offers accommodation in stilted en-suite standing tents with a private balcony. The thatched lounge & communal deck overlooks the river, which is regularly visited by elephants & other wildlife. Amenities include swimming pool. US$600/1,000 sgl/dbl inc activities; US$465/790 low season.

Livingstone's turaco, a variety of hornbills & the vociferous forest weaver. Between Dec & May, sable antelope move into the area. Game drives concentrate on the plains north of the main cluster of lodges, which can be very worthwhile seasonally, with very few other vehicles around. Fly-camping is also available, as are river trips during the wet season on the lushly forested Mbega River. US$200/290 sgl/dbl FB, US$330/550 inc activities; tented bandas US$260/350 FB, US$390/610 inc activities.

🏠 **Rufiji River Camp** (20 rooms) 🕿 UK 01452 862288; 🕿/f 022 286 2357; m 0754 231422; e fox@tanzaniasafaris.info; www.tanzaniasafaris.info. The first lodge to be established in the Selous, the ever-popular Rufiji River Camp is situated at the eastern extremity of the tourist sector overlooking an atmospheric stretch of the Rufiji River alive with hippos & crocs, & regularly visited by elephants. Recently acquired by Foxes (which also runs well-established lodges in Ruaha & Mikumi), the camp currently consists of 20 en-suite standing tents, spaced along the river in a lush stretch of woodland populated by monkeys & numerous birds, but it will be split into 2 smaller camps – one with 6 units & one with 14 – over the course of 2009. It offers an excellent range of boat & foot activities, as well as half-day game drives encompassing the 3 nearby lakes, full-day excursions further afield & overnight

Moderate

🏠 **Selous Mbega Camp** (13 rooms) ➲ 022 265 0250; m 0784 624664; e info@selous-mbega-camp.com; www.selous-mbega-camp.com. This small German-owned camp lies on the banks of the Rufiji immediately east of the park boundary some 5.5km from Mtemere Gate. Most of the en-suite tents are set in riparian woodland overlooking the river, but 2

fly-camping. There's a swimming pool too. Expect rates to compare with Lake Manze.

stand alongside a small waterhole. Affordable game drives, guided walks, & boat trips are offered. Substantial discounts are offered by prior arrangement to backpackers who bus from Dar es Salaam to Mloka (from where a free transfer is provided). *US$135/190 sgl/dbl FB.*

Budget and camping

🏠 **Ndovu Campsite** (6 units) m 0744 782378; e hkibola@yahoo.co.uk. This pleasant budget camp between Mbega Camp & the Mtemere Gate has 6 twin standing tents with thatched roofs & tiled en-suite showers. There is also a campsite with common toilets & showers. The restaurant & bar form part of a 3-storey wood & *makuti* structure offering great views into the bush. The camp caters primarily to self-drive visitors, but boat trips are offered. *US$25 pp standing tents (bed only); US$10 pp camping; meals by prior arrangement US$10–15.*

⚑ **Selous River Campsite** m 0784 237525/0763 757395; e enquiries@selousrivercamp.com; www.selousrivercamp.com. Owner-managed by a

friendly young Tanzanian–English couple, this inexpensive campsite is outside the reserve boundaries between Mbega Camp & the Mtemere Gate. You can pitch your own tent, or arrange to have them set up a medium-sized tent with bedding. Independent travellers are advised to make contact in advance (SMS is more reliable than phone or email), & the management will collect you from the bus to Mloka by prior arrangement. Guided walks US$15 pp, boat trips US$35 pp, & game drives into the park can usually be arranged. There is a bar, & you can either self-cater or arrange to have a local chef prepare food. *US$10 pp camping; US$40 dbl tent with bedding.*

WHAT TO SEE AND DO The **game drives** along the network of rough roads to the north of the Rufiji are reliably rewarding, especially towards the end of the dry season, when large mammals concentrate around the five lakes. More frequently seen ungulates include impala, common waterbuck, bushbuck, white-bearded wildebeest, eland, greater kudu, buffalo and common zebra. The northern sector of the park has been dubbed Giraffic Park, with some justification, as herds exceeding 50 individuals come down to drink in the heat of the afternoon. Oddly, giraffe are entirely absent south of the Rufiji, which also forms a natural barrier between the ranges of the distinctive white-bearded and Niassa races of wildebeest.

The endangered African wild dog is commonly observed on game drives north of the Rufiji, as is the spotted hyena, while leopards are common but elusive. Cheetah, by contrast, have not been recorded in this part of the reserve for about 20 years. Much in evidence, with two or three different pridal territories converging on each of the five large lakes, are Selous's lions, which typically have darker coats and less hirsute manes than their counterparts elsewhere in East Africa. During the dry season, the lions of Selous evidently rely on an unusual opportunistic diurnal hunting strategy, rarely straying far from the lakes, where they rest up in the shade to wait for whatever ungulate happens to venture within pouncing distance on its way to drink. As a result, the Selous probably offers a better chance of seeing a lion kill than almost any reserve in Africa.

Another popular activity, **boat excursions** along the Rufiji River, generally culminate with a brilliant red sun setting behind the tall borassus palms and baobabs that line the wide sandy watercourse. Gulp-inducing dentist-eye views of the Selous's trademark gigantic crocs can pretty much be guaranteed from the boat, as can conferences of grunting, harrumphing hippos – and you'd be unlucky not to be entertained by herds of elephant, buffalo or giraffe shuffling down to drink.

The most memorable aspect of the boat trips, however, is the profuse **birdlife**. Characteristic waterbirds along this stretch of the Rufiji include yellow-billed stork, white-crowned and spur-winged plovers, various small waders, pied and malachite kingfishers, and African skimmer. Pairs of fish eagle and palmnut vulture perch high on the borassus palms, seasonal breeding colonies of carmine and white-throated bee-eater swirl around the mud cliffs that hem in some stretches of the river, and pairs of trumpeter hornbill and purple-crested turaco flap between the riparian trees. Worth looking out for among a catalogue of egrets and herons is the Malagasy squacco heron, a regular winter visitor, while the elusive Pel's fishing owl often emerges at dusk to hawk above the water.

Walking within the Selous is permitted in the company of an armed ranger, and all the camps offer **guided game walks** for their clients. These come with a real likelihood of encountering elephant or buffalo – even lion – on foot, and also offer a good chance to enjoy the reserve's wealth of woodland birds and invertebrates. Better still are the overnight **fly-camping** excursions offered by most camps, which entail sleeping beneath a glorified mosquito net on the shore of a lake teeming with hippos and crocs – thrilling stuff!

MIKUMI

This small town extends untidily along the Tanzam Highway immediately outside the southern border of the eponymous national park. Founded in 1914 by Chief Kikiwi of the Wavindunda tribe, it is named for the borassus palms that once flourished there. It is now the main service town to the adjacent national park, and the junction town for the B127 to Udzungwa. Though nothing much to look at, Mikumi is an organised little town, with a clutch of decent hotels and restaurants, and internet access at the Vocational Education & Training Authority campus.

GETTING THERE AND AWAY Mikumi straddles the Tanzam Highway 120km southwest of Morogoro and 200km northeast of Iringa, and it's a straightforward drive in either direction. The 50km stretch of road through the national park immediately east of town is punctuated by regular speed bumps, and worth taking slowly to look for wildlife. There is regular bus transport along the Tanzam Highway with Scandinavia Express, Hood and Sumry High Class all passing through en route to/from Dar es Salaam to Iringa, while several buses daily run southward along the Ifakara road, passing the entrance to Udzungwa National Park.

⌂ WHERE TO STAY AND EAT

🏠 **Tan-Swiss Inn** (5 rooms) m 0755 191827/0784 246322; e zillern@vtxmail.ch. This bright little lodge on the Dar es Salaam side of town has emerged from recent fire damage better than ever. Its 5 spacious en-suite rooms with hot water, fan & DSTV are great value, & 5 family-sized bandas are also planned. Management can arrange half-/full-day game drives into the park for US$100/150. There's an excellent restaurant & bar offering a good selection of tasty Chinese, Indian & pasta dishes in the US$5–6 range. US$40/53 dbl/trpl B&B; US$70–80 for planned family bandas; US$3 pp camping.

🏠 **Mikumi Genesis Motel** (23 rooms) ☎ 023 262 0461; e info@genesismotel.com; www.genesismotel.com. Situated alongside the main road, this pleasant but overpriced hotel is the established choice of budget tour operators & researchers. Adequate but gloomy en-suite bandas have net, fan & hot water. The attached snake park is quite interesting, with Gabon viper, green mamba & rock python among the more intimidating species present, but the US$5 entrance fee seems over the top. The bar is well stocked & the restaurant has a varied menu, including game meat & pizzas, with most dishes US$6–7. US$20 pp B&B; US$35/50 pp suite HB/FB.

16

Kilimanjaro Village Inn ℡ 023 262 0429. This acceptable budget hotel on the Morogoro side of town near the railway crossing is popular with tour drivers & recommended to budget travellers. A variety of rooms, all with fan, are available, a decent bar & somnambulant restaurant are attached, & several other bars & eateries are dotted around. *Tsh10,000/15,000 sgl/dbl with common shower; Tsh20,000 en-suite dbl.*

Mikumi Health Guesthouse St Kizito (2 bungalows) ℡ 023 262 0421; e mikumi@ raha.com. This tranquil guesthouse in the shaded grounds of the Mikumi Health Centre consists of 2 cottages, each with 2 bedrooms (one with single & dbl bed, the other with 2 single beds) with fans & nets, a well-equipped kitchen (with complimentary tea, coffee, bread & jam), a bathroom with hot shower & a common covered outdoor entertainment area. Meals can be arranged. It's signposted on the south side of the main road around 500m from the Kilimanjaro Village Inn just before the Ifakara junction. Great value. *Tsh7,000 pp; camping Tsh4,000 pp.*

MIKUMI NATIONAL PARK

The 3,230km² Mikumi National Park, the fourth-largest in Tanzania, protects a combination of flat open grassland and wooded hills flanked by the Uluguru Mountains to the north and the Udzungwa to the south. Named after the town on its southern border, the national park was gazetted in 1964 following the construction of the Tanzam Highway between Morogoro and Iringa, which opened up this formerly remote area to poachers. The park boundary was extended in 1975 to share a border with the Selous Game Reserve, which means that Mikumi is now officially an extension of that vast reserve, though in reality there has always been a degree of local game migration between the two.

The 80% of Mikumi southeast of the Tanzam Highway is more or less inaccessible to tourists, though this may change if a new road is constructed through the southern hills to connect with Selous. For the time being, the park's centrepiece is the extensive Mkata River floodplain northwest of the main road. Comprised of open grassland interspersed with patches of acacia woodland and the occasional baobab, the floodplain is the closest thing on the southern safari circuit to the Serengeti, and while the game might not be quite so prodigious, it is certainly impressive. It can be explored over five to six hours by following a 60km loop of game viewing roads that starts at the main entrance gate and terminates at Mwanambogo Dam in the north.

Characteristic of the grasslands of Mikumi are large herds of zebra, wildebeest, buffalo and impala, as well as smaller parties of warthog, waterbuck and Bohor reedbuck, and troops of vervet monkey and yellow baboon. Giraffe and elephant are common on the main road loop, especially in the vicinity of acacia trees. Lion and spotted hyena are around in reasonable numbers, and if you don't see them by day you'll certainly hear them at night. Of the rarer antelope, the Mkata Plain is reliable for good sightings of the outsized eland, while the *brachystegia* woodland to the southeast of the main road harbours substantial populations of the impressive greater kudu and sable antelope. More than 400 bird species have been recorded in the park, though generally speaking the less visited woodland hosts a greater variety of birds than the grassland. Common birds on the floodplain include bateleur eagle, black-bellied bustard, lilac-breasted roller, ground hornbill, yellow-throated longclaw and long-tailed fiscal, while Mwanambogo Dam is a good place to see fish eagle and water-associated birds such as white-faced duck and African spoonbill.

Mikumi, despite its accessibility, has never featured prominently on safari itineraries. The major reason for this is probably the demystifying presence of the Tanzam Highway, which is made doubly intrusive by lying within earshot of most of the camps. But Mikumi is emphatically worth a night or two on any road safari through southern Tanzania. It also makes for an excellent one- or two-night safari destination out of Dar es Salaam (the majority of visitors are in fact expatriate

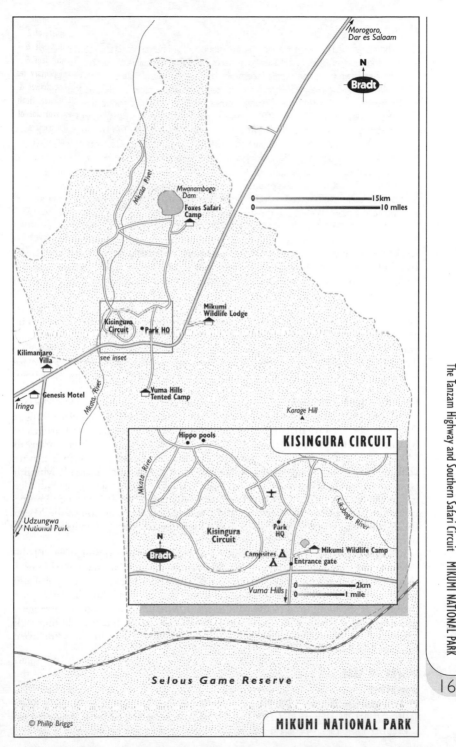

Morogoro,
Dar es Salaam

N

Bradt

15km
10 miles

Mwanambogo
Dam

Mkata River

Foxes Safari
Camp

Kisingura
Circuit

Mikumi
Wildlife Lodge

Park HQ

Kilimanjaro
Villa

see inset

Genesis Motel

Iringa

Mkata River

Vuma Hills
Tented Camp

Karage Hill

Hippo pools

KISINGURA CIRCUIT

Mkata River

Kikaboga River

Udzungwa
National Park

Kisingura
Circuit

N

Bradt

Park
HQ

Mikumi Wildlife Camp

Campsites

Entrance gate

Vuma Hills

2km
1 mile

Selous Game Reserve

16

© Philip Briggs

MIKUMI NATIONAL PARK

weekenders), and the camps remain extremely affordable by national standards. Ironically, once you're away from the main road, tourist traffic is very low by comparison to anywhere in northern Tanzania or even the main road loop through the Selous.

The park entrance fee of US$20 per person per 24 hours must be paid in hard currency. Two guided walking trails have recently been opened in Mikumi. The shorter trail passes through the Vuma Hills, and takes about five hours to complete, while the longer trail passes through the Ngotikwe Hills and takes about eight hours. The hikes cost US$20 per person and can be arranged at the main entrance gate close to Kikoboga Lodge. An early start is recommended to avoid the heat of the afternoon.

GETTING THERE AND AWAY During high season, Safari Air Link (✆ 022 550 4384; e flights@safariaviation.info; www.safariaviation.info) runs a daily shared charter flight (US$160 per person) that departs from Dar es Salaam at 10.30 and arrives at Mikumi at 12.00, stopping at Selous Game Reserve on the way. Road safaris to Mikumi also run from Dar es Salaam, which is four hours away in a private vehicle. The park can be visited as a stand-alone trip, but more normally Mikumi is combined with a longer road safari to Selous, Ruaha or Udzungwa. The entrance gate is always accessible, even in an ordinary saloon car, but 4x4 may be required inside the park. Between November and April, the black cotton soil of the Mkata floodplain often becomes waterlogged, placing the main game-viewing circuit out of bounds, so check road conditions in advance.

Mikumi is perhaps the only Tanzanian reserve to offer the combination of large numbers of plains animals and easy access from a reasonably substantial town on a major thoroughfare. Travellers using public transport between Morogoro and Mikumi town should see plenty of game from the main road, but this isn't quite the same as spending time in the park itself. In Mikumi town, you can arrange a game drive of the park with Tan-Swiss (US$100/150 half/full day, excluding park entrance fees) while Chilunga Cultural Tours in Morogoro runs fully inclusive full-day drives for US$360.

WHERE TO STAY
Upmarket

🏠 **Foxes Safari Camp** (8 tents) ✆ (UK) 01452 862288; ✆/f 022 286 2357; m 0754 237422; e fox@tanzaniasafaris.info; www.tanzaniasafaris.info.

This archetypal bush lodge is the only one in Mikumi to lie far enough from the Tanzam Highway that the tranquillity of the bush isn't interrupted by the occasional rumble of passing trucks. Situated on a rocky hillside, it provides accommodation in en-suite tents raised on wooden platforms, with a small swimming pool & thatched restaurant/bar perched on the top of the hill, offering superb views in all directions. There's plenty of game to be seen from the camp, & game drives are usually rewarding as it lies in the middle of the excellent Mkata Plains road circuit. Day trips to Udzungwa NP are arranged by request. It suffered extensive fire damage in late 2008 but should be up & running by 2009. *US$255/350 sgl/dbl FB, US$335/510 full game package.*

Vuma Hills Tented Camp (16 tents) ☎ (UK) 01452 862288; ☎/f 022 286 2357; m 0754 237422; e fox@tanzaniasafaris.info; www.tanzaniasafaris.info. Under the same ownership as Foxes, this popular camp, set amongst the thick brachystegia woodland of the Vuma Hills southeast of the Tanzam Highway, has deservedly acquired a reputation as a 1st-class w/end retreat among expatriates working in Dar es Salaam, & also makes for a useful stopover between the coast & destinations further south. Classic safari accommodation in large standing tents perched on stilted wooden platforms that offer a fabulous view over the wooded plains below. The food is excellent, made largely with fresh produce sourced from the nearby highlands, & there is a small swimming pool. Vuma Hills is probably the most atmospheric & aesthetically pleasing lodge in Mikumi, with traffic from the main road only faintly audible, but its one drawback is that there isn't a great deal of game visible from the camp or on the roads immediately around it. *US$255/350 sgl/dbl FB, US$335/510 full game package.*

Moderate

Mikumi Wildlife Camp (12 rooms) ☎ 022 260 0352/4; f 022 260 0347; e mikumiwildlifecamp@africa-reps.co.uk. This underrated & reasonably priced lodge lies 1km from the Tanzam Highway inside the main park entrance gate, the start of the park's best game-viewing circuit. Large & well appointed en-suite stone cottages each have large dbl bed, netting & private patio. A pair of waterholes situated right in front of the dining area & cottages attracts a steady stream of zebras, giraffes & elephants, sometimes a passing lion or hyena, as well as a resident flock of very habituated marabou storks. The elephants are also rather partial to sipping the water in the small swimming pool! Casual visitors are welcome to drop in for a snack (mostly in the US$4–5 range). The one drawback of this lodge is its proximity to the main road, which means that the rumble of passing trucks vies with the nocturnal howling of the hyenas. Good value. *US$126/144 sgl/dbl FB.*

Camping

National Park Campsites ☎ 023 262 0487. There are 3 campsites near the main gate, with long-drop toilets & firewood but no water, but they cannot be classed as great value for money at US$30 pp. Special campsites within the park cost US$50 pp.

UDZUNGWA MOUNTAINS NATIONAL PARK

Formally opened in October 1992 by Prince Bernhard of the Netherlands, this 1,900km² national park protects a northeasterly block of the Udzungwa Range, less than one-fifth of the total area of what is the most extensive mountain range in Tanzania. In common with the other mountains of the Eastern Arc (see box, *An African Galápagos?*, in *Chapter 8*, pages 234–5), Udzungwa is an ancient crystalline structure that rose above the surrounding plains at least 100 million years ago, due to upward faulting in the earth's crust. Despite subsequent erosion, the modern massif has a wide elevation range, rising from around 250m to the 2,576m Luhomero Peak. The name Udzungwa means Land of the Dzungwa, a subgroup of the Hehe who are said to have settled on the western slopes of the range after being driven away from the Iringa area during the internecine battles that accompanied the rise of Chiefs Munyigumba and Mkwawa.

The eastern escarpment of the Udzungwa supports sub-montane rainforest with a canopy reaching to 50m tall in some areas. Central and southern parts of the plateau consist of rolling hilly country covered in grassland, *miombo* woodland and scattered patches of Afro-montane forest. Elevation decreases gradually to the west where there is arid woodland, and semi-desert conditions in the rain shadow of the mountains. Three-quarters of the forest cover has disappeared over the last 2,000 years as a direct result of human activity, but the 2,000km² of extant forest protected within the national park and a number of smaller forest reserves are the most substantial tract found on any of the Eastern Arc ranges. Udzungwa is also unique within East Africa in that it boasts an unbroken cover of closed-canopy forest spanning the full transition from lowland forest communities at 250m above sea level, through to montane forest communities at above 2,000m.

This variety of habitats makes Udzungwa a strong contender for the accolade of Tanzania's most important terrestrial biodiversity hotspot. More than 25% of the plant species recorded in Udzungwa are endemic, ranging from a recently described violet species of the genus *Saintpaulia* to a number of trees standing 30m tall or higher. The level of endemism among the Udzungwa fauna is the highest of any East African range, with several species of reptile, amphibian and particularly invertebrates being unique to the range. The most celebrated of the forest residents are a trio of endemic primates, namely Uhehe red colobus, Sanje crested mangabey and Matunda galago. What is remarkable about the first two of these endemics is their geographical isolation from other closely allied species. Aside from one population on the Tana River in Kenya, the mangabey group of monkeys is essentially restricted to the Congolese and Guinean rainforests thousands of kilometres to the west. Red colobus, too, are absent from most of eastern Tanzania,

UDZUNGWA ON FOOT

There are no motorable tracks into the national park, but several walking and hiking trails have been cut through the forested eastern slopes, most of them leaving from the main entrance gate at Mang'ula. There is an office at the entrance gate where you must pay the park entrance fee of US$20 per person per 24 hours, as well as the daily guide fee of US$10 per party. For longer hikes, you will also need to be accompanied by an armed ranger, which costs US$20 per party. The office can also arrange porters, who will carry up to 20kg apiece at a charge of US$5–10 per porter depending on which trail you are hiking. Outside the national park, the main road through Mang'ula makes for pleasant walking, since it follows a stream for quite some distance, and you'll see plenty of birds and possibly baboons, but probably not any arboreal monkeys.

The short and flat **Prince Bernhard Waterfall Trail**, which leads to a small but pretty waterfall no more than 1km from the entrance gate, offers an excellent introduction to the park's wildlife. No guide is needed to walk this trail, which not only means it is effectively free once you've paid the park entrance fee, but also allows serious wildlife enthusiasts to explore it slowly, quietly and repeatedly without being frog-marched by the guide or expected to make idle chit-chat. And, taken slowly, the trail can be remarkably rewarding. Blue monkey and the endemic red colobus (actually grey and white with a bright orange fringe) are common in the area and likely to be seen. Look out, too, for the shy red duiker, which often emerges on to the trail in the early morning and towards dusk, and for the bizarre chequered elephant shrew with its tan striped flanks and habit of crashing noisily through the litter. Birding is erratic and can be quite frustrating, but you can be reasonably sure of seeing the outsized trumpeter and crowned hornbill, the lovely green-headed oriole (listen for its repetitive four-note song in the canopy) and the brightly coloured forest weaver, whose gentle fluting call is all around. If you sit quietly at the waterfall in the early morning or evening, you might see monkeys come to drink at the pool below it.

though another isolated population occurs on Zanzibar Island, and they range through the Lake Tanganyika region southeast to the Ufipa Plateau near Sumbawanga. See also the box, *Secrets of the Forest*, on pages 496–7.

Numerous other large mammals are present in the mountains. Primate species include yellow baboon, blue monkey, vervet monkey, Angola colobus, and mountain dwarf galago. The forests of the Udzungwa almost certainly harbour the largest single population of the rare Abbott's duiker, a Tanzania endemic, as well as red duiker, blue duiker and bushbuck. The peculiar chequered elephant shrew is the most striking of the smaller forest mammals. Because Udzungwa is part of the Mikumi–Selous ecosystem, a number of typical savannah and woodland species are resident in the higher plateaux of the range or pass through the park on a regular basis, including lion, elephant, leopard, buffalo and sable antelope.

Despite its ecological significance, Udzungwa Mountains National Park remains a somewhat esoteric destination, though interest has definitely picked up over the last few years, and we saw a couple of tour groups hanging around when we last visited the park. For tourists exploring the southern safari circuit by road, the park makes for a straightforward day trip or overnight excursion from Mikumi, and there are now a couple of low-key but affordable hotels situated close to the park entrance. The eastern footslopes can easily be explored using a limited network of guided and unguided day trails (see box, *Udzungwa on foot*, below), with a good chance of encountering the endemic red colobus. Disappointingly, however, the higher slopes can only be reached along more

The most popular guided hike is the **Sanje Waterfall Trail**, a round trip of at least four hours' duration leading to the Sanje Waterfall, in fact a series of falls that plunge more than 300m down over three separate stages, with a pool at the base where swimming is permitted. This trail offers excellent forest birding, and you can be practically sure of seeing the endemic red colobus as well as black-and-white colobus. The Sanje crested mangabey was first heard by researchers in the vicinity of the waterfall, but it is not normally resident in the area, and is unlikely to be seen by casual visitors. The area around the waterfall is legendarily rich in butterflies, including several endemic taxa, with activity typically peaking from mid morning to mid afternoon. Visitors with a vehicle have the option of using a shorter trail, by driving back along the Mikumi road towards the Sanje ranger post, which lies a couple of hundred metres below the base of the waterfall. Alternatively, if the above trail seems too daunting, the shorter **Sonjo Trail** is about half the length, and usually takes around three hours to cover, and it passes two smaller waterfalls.

The longest existing hike is the **Mwanihana Trail**, a 38km circuit to Mwanihana Peak, at 2,150m the second highest point in the range, that normally takes three days to complete with two nights spent camping on the mountain. This is the only trail that exposes visitors to the closed-canopy montane forest and grassland habitats of the range's higher slopes. As such, it provides the best chance within the national park of encountering the endemic mangabey, the rare Abbott's duiker, larger mammals such as buffalo and elephant, as well as some of the more interesting birds. Prospective hikers will need to have their own camping gear, and to carry all the food they will need. An armed ranger is mandatory, due to the presence of potentially dangerous animals, and a porter is recommended if you want to make the most of the hike.

The park headquarters can also arrange visits to a traditional healer for US$5 per party, and are in the process of opening up several new trails to various traditional shrines, caves and other sites of interest in the national park.

16

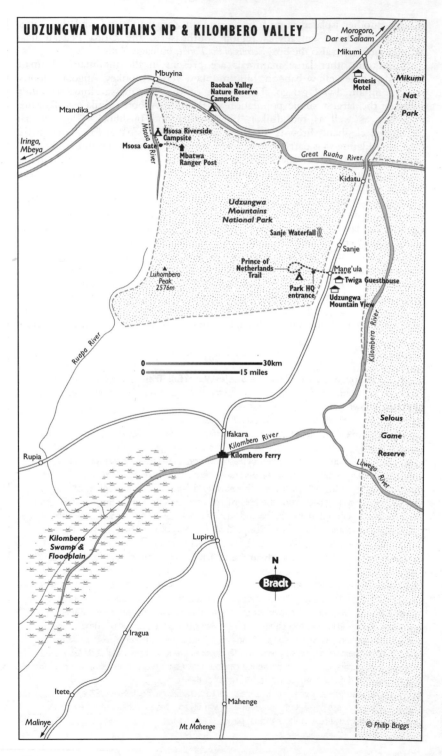

UDZUNGWA MOUNTAINS NP & KILOMBERO VALLEY

Morogoro,
Dar es Salaam

Mikumi

Mikumi

Nat

Park

Mbuyina

**Baobab Valley
Nature Reserve
Campsite**

**Genesis
Motel**

Mtandika

Msoso River

**Msosa Riverside
Campsite**

Msosa Gate

**Mbatwa
Ranger Post**

*Iringa,
Mbeya*

Great Ruaha River

Kidatu

*Udzungwa
Mountains
National Park*

Sanje Waterfall

Sanje

**Prince of
Netherlands
Trail**

**Luhombero
Peak
2576m**

Mang'ula

**Park HQ
entrance**

Twiga Guesthouse

**Udzungwa
Mountain View**

Ruapa River

Kilombero River

0 ⎯⎯⎯⎯⎯⎯⎯⎯⎯⎯ 30km
0 ⎯⎯⎯⎯⎯⎯⎯⎯⎯⎯ 15 miles

Selous

Game

Reserve

Ifakara

Kilombero River

Rupia

Kilombero Ferry

Lweyo River

*Kilombero
Swamp &
Floodplain*

Lupiro

N

Bradt

Iragua

Itete

Mahenge

Malinye

Mt Mahenge

© Philip Briggs

494

arduous overnight trails, and there is no accommodation set within the forest (aside from the national park campsites). For these logistical reasons, we would have to recommend Amani Nature Reserve (which has accommodation in the thick of the Eastern Usambara forest and boasts a far superior network of trails) over Udzungwa to first-time visitors to Tanzania seeking an introduction to the Eastern Arc Forests.

The Udzungwa Mountains are particularly alluring to birdwatchers, with more than 400 species recorded in the national park and/or the various forest reserves, including at least 25 of the 32 species unique to the Tanzania-Malawi Endemic Bird Area. Tanzanian endemics and species that generate a high degree of interest among visiting birdwatchers are the Nduk eagle-owl, dappled mountain robin, spot-throat, Swynnerton's robin, white-chested alethe, white-winged apalis, Chapin's apalis, banded green sunbird, Usambara weaver and Kipengere seedeater. Three bird species, the Iringa akalat, rufous-winged sunbird and Udzungwa forest partridge, are often cited as endemic to the Udzungwa Mountains. The akalat has in fact been recorded in a handful of other forests and the partridge was recently discovered in the remote Rubeho Mountains, but Udzungwa is certainly the main stronghold for all three species. It should be noted that several of the more interesting birds of Udzungwa are more or less absent from the eastern foot slopes as passed through by the day trails out of the park headquarters. Dedicated birdwatchers are advised to skip the national park in favour of the forest reserves on the western side of the mountains for a realistic chance of seeing the Udzungwa specials; see the box, *Birding the western Udzungwa*, on page 498 for details.

An entrance fee of US$20 per person per 24 hours must be paid in hard currency at the park headquarters (↘ *023 262 0224;* f *023 262 0293;* e *udzungwa@ gmail.com; www.udzungwa.org*).

GETTING THERE AND AWAY The access road to Udzungwa National Park is the B127, which connects the town of Mikumi on the Tanzam Highway to Ifakara on the Tazara railway over a distance of roughly 100km. The park can be approached either by road or by rail. Backpackers who are visiting the park as a round trip out of Dar es Salaam might think about arriving by rail and returning by road. The slow train from Dar to Ifakara passes through the Selous Game Reserve in daylight, and returning by road you will pass through Mikumi National Park. The train station is about a 30-minute walk from the park's main entrance, with the journey from Dar es Salaam costing Tsh10,000/6,700/4,900 first/second/third class.

In a private vehicle, the drive from Mikumi town to the park entrance gate at Mang'ula shouldn't take much longer than an hour (so it's easy to visit Udzungwa as a day trip from Mikumi National Park). Clearly signposted out of Mikumi town, the road is surfaced as far as Kidatu, 37km south of Mikumi. South of Kidatu, it passes through Sanje village after 13km, then about 2km further it passes the Sanje Ranger Post, the starting point for the short route to Sanje Waterfall. After another 10km or so, the road reaches Mang'ula, site of the main entrance gate and the park headquarters (signposted to the right) as well as two of the hotels listed below.

As many as a dozen buses run between Mikumi and Ifakara daily, all passing the park entrance gate at Mang'ula. Many of these buses continue to (or come from) Morogoro or Dar es Salaam, but if you don't use a direct bus from one of these towns, the best place to pick up Ifakara-bound transport is at the junction in Mikumi town. The two-hour bus ride costs around Tsh3,500. For details of Ifakara and surrounds, see our website, http://bradttanzania.wordpress.com.

16

Until recently, the Udzungwa Mountains and environs were poorly known to scientists, certainly by comparison to the more accessible Usambara or Uluguru ranges. The main reason for this is that early biological exploration in the Udzungwa concentrated on more developed and easily accessible parts of the central and southern plateau. Forests visited were mostly secondary with widespread Afro-montane species. Only in more recent times have researchers visited the primary forests along the eastern escarpment, resulting in a flurry of new discoveries.

The endemic **rufous-winged sunbird**, for instance, was first described in 1984, while the **Udzungwa forest partridge** was discovered as recently as 1991. The story behind the discovery of the partridge is that two Danish biologists working in the mountains noticed an unusual pair of feet swimming in a chicken stew that had been prepared for them by a local cook. The next day, a local guide snared them another 'wild chicken', and it turned out to be an unknown fowl more closely related to the forest partridges of Asia than to any African bird. Placed in its own genus, the Udzungwa forest partridge is now recognised as the sole representative of an otherwise extinct lineage that dates back more than 15 million years, when the forests of East Africa and Asia were probably linked to each other via the Middle Eastern coast.

The endemic **Sanje crested mangabey** was unknown to western science in 1979, and the circumstance of its discovery by the ecologists Katherine Homewood and Alan Rodgers illustrates just how little attention the area had previously received from biologists. Homewood, studying the red colobus at Sanje waterfall while suffering from a fever, heard a distinctly mangabey-like whooping call. At first she thought she was hallucinating with fever or that Rodgers was somewhere nearby playing a recording of a mangabey call as a joke. But Homewood's guide Langson recognised the call as that of a monkey, known locally as *n'golaga*, and different to a baboon or red colobus. The next day, Langson led the researchers to a troop of monkeys sitting high in the canopy, and their suspicion was confirmed: these were definitely a type of mangabey, furthermore one significantly different in appearance to the closest population, which lives about 1,000km further north on Kenya's Tana River. Langson, incredulous that this large monkey, with its loud and distinctive call, could have been overlooked by other *wazungu*, casually mentioned that an orphaned *n'golaga* was resident in Sanje village on the main Ifakara–Mikumi road. The excited researchers rushed to the village, and there they were able to photograph the tame young mangabey, which clearly belonged to an undescribed race or species. Twenty years after it was discovered, the Sanje crested mangabey had the dubious distinction of

WHERE TO STAY
Moderate

🏠 **Udzungwa Mountain View Hotel** 📞 023 262 0218; f 023 262 0443; e info@genesismotel.com; www.genesismotel.com. Affiliated with the Genesis Motel in Mikumi, & very similar in standard, this comfortable small hotel lies on the Ifakara road a 10 min walk from Mang'ula & the Udzungwa park

headquarters. The restaurant has a varied menu, with most dishes costing around US$5. The management can organise day trips & hikes into the adjacent national park. *US$30 pp en-suite dbl with full English b/fast; US$5 pp camping.*

Shoestring There is no shoestring accommodation in the immediate vicinity of the park entrance gate, but numerous cheap local lodges can be found in Kidatu. The best of these is the **Lobore Guesthouse**, which charges Tsh5,000 for an en-suite double and Tsh2,000/4,000 for a single/double with common showers. Similarly priced alternatives include **Riverside Guesthouse**, **Rose Guesthouse** and **Muna Annex Guesthouse**.

being the solitary East African species included on a list of the world's 25 most threatened primate taxa compiled by the IUCN Primate Specialist Group.

While the endemic birds and mammals tend to receive the greatest attention, the abrupt recent decline in the population of an amphibian endemic to the Udzungwa illustrates how precarious the situation of a range restricted species can be. One of seven species in a genus of toads endemic to Tanzania, the yellow-streaked **Kihansi spray toad** is so tiny that an adult can fit on a human fingernail, and unusual among amphibians in that it does not lay eggs, but rather gives birth to a brood of live miniatures. The extremely localised range of the Kihansi spray toad is a unique 20,000m² ferny habitat – which also contains three plant species found nowhere else – sustained by the spray from a single waterfall on the Kihansi River. When the toad was first discovered in 1996, the population was estimated at more than 10,000. Subsequently, something like 90% of the river's water has been diverted to feed a government hydro-electric dam that generates a third of the nation's electricity supply, and the formerly substantial waterfall has been reduced to a quiet trickle. As a result, the toad's unique habitat has been reduced to less than 1,000m², and by March 2001 the toad population had declined to an estimated 100 individuals. In the *East African* of 20–26 August 2001, environmental writer Ann Outwater reported that the Tanzanian government responded to the toad's decline by supplementing the spray with piped sprinklers. It has also reputedly instituted a study to determine the toad's breeding and feeding requirements, with a long-term view to regulating the water flow into the hydro-electric scheme accordingly. Failing that, the only chance for the Kihansi spray toad would be to close the dam, a solution that can scarcely be considered viable given the importance of the hydro-electric scheme and the huge investment made in it.

On a more positive note, the list of Udzungwa endemics grows with practically every passing year, a prominent recent discovery being the **Matunda dwarf galago** *Galagoides udzungwensis* in 1996. Furthermore, three endemic species of bird have been discovered in the Kilombero Valley immediately southwest of Udzungwa, and it has been noted that several Eastern Arc specials likely to occur within the Udzungwa Mountains National Park have yet to be actually recorded there. In more recent times, scientists were excited by the discovery of the world's largest species of elephant shrew *Rhynchocyon udzungwensis*, first photographed in 2005 and described in 2008. One can only guess at how many birds and other creatures endemic to the Udzungwa still await scientific discovery.

Camping

⚐ National Park Campsites ☎ 023 262 0224; e udzungwa@gmail.com; www.udzungwa.org. A series of campsites has been cut into the forest along the stream immediately uphill of the park headquarters at Mang'ula. The campsites are very atmospheric, but as usual they lack any facilities other than a dirty long-drop toilet. Given the affordability of hotel rooms in Mang'ula, they are unlikely to attract any but the most dedicated campers. *US$30 pp.*

⚐ Msosa Riverside Campsite m 0787 111663/0755 033024; **e** riversidecampsitetz@hotmail.com; www.riversidecampsite-tanzania.com. This rustic new campsite, under the same management as Riverside Campsite near Iringa, lies on the bank of the Msosa River on the western edge of the park. It's a good base for anyone interested in exploring the untrammelled west of the park, with access via Msoma gate. Several trails follow the river outside the park, where it's possible to see dik-dik, bushbuck & other wildlife. There's a communal shower/toilet, but no restaurant, so stock up on food in advance. Take the turn-off from the main highway 100km before Iringa (signposted for Udzungwa National Park), then follow the signs to the park for around 10km, & turn right into the camp after crossing a bridge over the Msosa River. *US$6 pp camping; US$15 pp tent hire.*

A reasonable assumption made by many birders visiting Tanzania is that the place to seek out the Udzungwa Mountains' endemics and near-endemics is in the national park. This is not the case. Although birding in the eastern forests of the national park is very rewarding, and key species such as rufous-winged sunbird and Swynnerton's robin might be seen above Sanje waterfall, the most alluring endemic – Udzungwa partridge – has yet to be recorded in this area. The best chance for seeing that species, and other specialities, is in the forests on Luhombero Mountain (the tallest point in the national park) and Ndundulu Ridge and Nyumbanitu Mountain in the adjacent West Kilombero Forest Reserve, all of which lie in the western part of the range and are not realistically approached from Mang'ula.

The gateway to the western forests is Udekwa, which lies three hours from Iringa by road. To get to Udekwa, follow the Tanzam Highway out of Iringa towards Mikumi for 45km to Ilula. Ask there for the turn-off to Udekwa. The best time to go looking for forest birds is from September to early December. Before visiting, a permit must be obtained from the Catchment Forestry Office in Iringa or directly from the village government at Udekwa.

On reaching Udekwa, report to the village government office near the primary school. After introductions are complete and fees or permits presented, ask the village chairman or secretary to assist with the selection of porters. Never select porters on your own! If anything goes wrong, you are less likely to receive help from the village government. Make an agreement with the porters to come to Chui Campsite (7km into the forest reserve at the end of the motorable track) very early the next morning and start the expedition from there. This may no longer be necessary once a planned village campsite – to ensure that the villagers get some revenue from tourist visits – is built near the Tanzania National Parks ranger post 4km from Udekwa.

From Udekwa or Chui, you can go to one of two campsites. The most accessible is in Luala Valley, a grassy glade in the forest on the Ndundulu ridge. Luala is at an elevation of 1,900m and it can be very cold at night, especially from June to August. Take good raingear as it can rain during any month up there. Luala is a five- to six-hour walk from Chui Campsite, very steep and tiring in places. After about 1.5 hours, you enter the forest and head up the ridge along a path that offers good birding. From Luala, the forest trails to the northeast toward Luhombero Mountain are a good place to find Udzungwa partridge and rufous-winged sunbird.

Alternatively, you can go to Mufu Camp, where the partridge was originally discovered. This is about a six-hour walk from Chui, also quite steep. The Mufu camp is right in the middle of the forest and dappled mountain robin, Iringa akalat, Swynnerton's robin, Nduk eagle owl and Udzungwa partridge may be seen around the camp.

Organised birding safaris to the Western Udzungwa can be arranged through Masumbo Ltd (m *0786 446 665;* e *masumbo@masumbo.co.tz*).

IRINGA

Perched at an elevation of around 1,500m on a small plateau above a steep escarpment rising to the north of the Tanzam Highway, Iringa is an important regional administrative centre with a population of around 150,000, making it the third-largest town in southern Tanzania after Morogoro and Mbeya. While it could scarcely be described as exciting, Iringa is an agreeable and interesting place to spend a couple of days in transit between Dar es Salaam and Mbeya.

In addition to offering great views over the Ruaha Valley, the compact town centre is studded with old German and Asian buildings centred around the old market, an excellent place to buy the rugs and baskets for which the region is famed. Majumba Street, the main trading road, is also very colourful and lively. Rather more sombre is the German War Cemetery down the road from the Iringa Hotel.

Iringa is the principal town of the Hehe people, who provided perhaps the most sustained resistance of any local tribe to the German colonisation of the Tanzania interior (see box, *Chief Mkwawa and Uhehe*, pages 504–5). The town's name is a corruption of the Hehe word *lilinga*, a reference to the large fort built by the Hehe Chief Mkwawa at Kalenga to the southwest of the modern town.

Several interesting sites related to Mkwawa can be visited from Iringa, of which the closest, about 2km from the town centre past the Lutheran Centre, is Gangilonga – 'Talking Rock' – where the chief used to meditate and hold conferences. Further afield, the Isimila Stone Age Site is not only of archaeological interest, but also lies close to some bizarre sandstone formations. Iringa is best known to tourists as the springboard for road safaris into the Ruaha National Park.

GETTING THERE AND AWAY Iringa town centre lies about 2km north of the Tanzam Highway along a steep ascent road 310km southwest of Morogoro and 390km northeast of Mbeya – in a private vehicle allow four to five hours for either drive. On public transport, you can get to Iringa very easily from anywhere on the Tanzam Highway. When you are ready to leave Iringa, regular minibuses leave from the central bus station [500 C2] in most directions. Buses running along the Tanzam Highway more often start their journey at Ipigogo bus station [500 F4], which lies alongside the Mbeya road about 3km from the town centre and can be reached by a steady stream of *dala-dalas* from the central bus station. A taxi to Ipigogo station from the centre of town should cost around Tsh2,000.

The best bus service along this road is Scandinavia Express [500 C2] (❨ *026 270 2308*), whose daily services from Dar es Salaam to Kyela and Songea both stop at Iringa. Tickets for Scandinavia Express are sold at the booking office around the corner from the central bus station, but the buses leave from in front of their office in the Ipigogo bus station. The fare from Iringa to Mbeya, Kyela or Songea is Tsh14,000 and to Dar es Salaam about Tsh15,000.

The bus services operated by Sumry High Class and Hood are similarly priced. Other less reputable bus companies and minibuses charge about two-thirds that price.

TOURIST INFORMATION AND TOURS Run by the friendly folk from Riverside Campsite, **Iringa Info** [500 D2] (❨ *026 270 1988;* m *0786 921281;* e *riversidecampsitetz@hotmail.com;* ⊕ *09.00–17.00 Mon–Fri & 09.00–15.00 Sat)* is a great source of information on the region. It arranges safaris to Ruaha at around US$225 per party per day inclusive of driver and fuel, as well as car hire and other local excursions.

🏠 WHERE TO STAY
Moderate

🏠 **Lutheran Centre Guesthouse** [500 F1] ❨ 026 270 2286. This recently revamped church hostel is one of the best options in Iringa. It doesn't quite meet international standards, but it's a far cry from the backpacker haunt it once was. Located a 10min walk from the bus station, it has clean, comfortable en-suite rooms with AC & TV, set in quiet gardens. *US$30/50 sgl/dbl B&B.*

🏠 **New Ruaha International Lodge** [500 F1] ❨ 026 270 0641/2. This garish new lodge next to the Lutheran Centre is another good & reasonably priced option. The spacious en-suite modern rooms all have

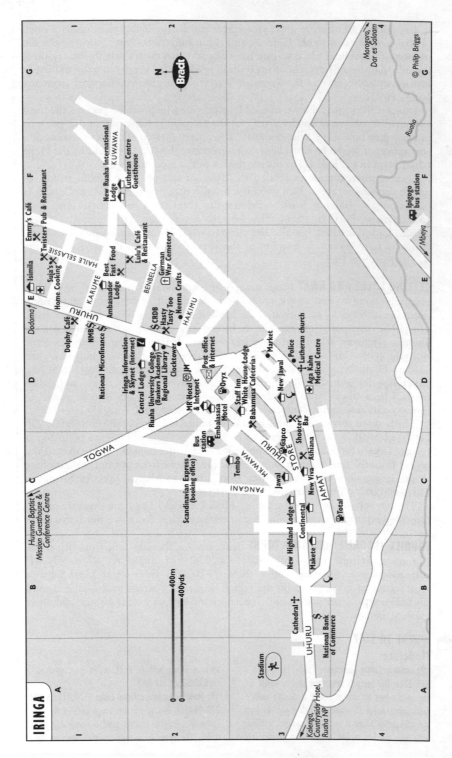

IRINGA

N

Bradt

0 ____ 400m
0 ____ 400yds

Huruma Baptist
Mission Guesthouse &
Conference Centre

New Ruaha International
Lodge KUWAWA

Lutheran Centre
Guesthouse

Emmy's Café

Suja's
Twisters Pub & Restaurant

Isimila

Home Cooking

HAILE SELASSIE

Best
Fast Food

Lulu's Café
& Restaurant

German
War Cemetery

Dodoma

UHURU

Dolphy Café

KARUME

Ambassador
Lodge

BENBELLA

Neema Crafts

HAKIMU

NMB

National Microfinance

CRDB

Hasty
Tasty Too

Iringa Information
& Skynet (Internet)

Ruaha University College
(Bankers Academy)
Regional Library

Clocktower

Central Lodge

MR Hotel
& Internet

Oryx

Post office
& Internet

Market

Police

Lutheran church

New Jawal

Aga Kahn
Medical Centre

Staff Inn
White House Lodge
Babamusa Cafeteria

Embalasasa
Hotel

Bus
station

TOGWA

Scandinavian Express
(booking office)

Shooter's
Bar

Gapco

STORE

New Viva
Ashiana

Tembo

MKWAWA

UHURU

PANGANI

Jawal

JAMAT

New Highland Lodge

Continental

Makete

Total

Cathedral

UHURU

National Bank
of Commerce

Stadium

Kalenga,
Countryside Hotel,
Ruaha NP

Morogoro,
Dar es Salaam

Ruaha

Ipigogo
bus station

Mbeya

© Philip Briggs

500

AC & TV. *US$35/45 sgl/dbl B&B; US$20 sgl with shared shower.*

⌂ **MR Hotel** [500 D2] (17 rooms) ☎ 026 270 2006/2779; ▫ 0754 696056; ℮ info@ mrhotels.co.tz; www.mrhotel.co.tz. This multi-storey place has let standards slip in recent years, & the

Budget

⌂ **Isimila Hotel** [500 E1] (48 rooms) ☎ 026 270 2605. On the Dodoma Rd a 10min walk from the bus station, this clean, comfortable multi-storey hotel is excellent value for money, provided you get a room with netting (the mosquitoes can be vicious). The 2nd-floor restaurant serves good Indian & other dishes for Tsh2,000–5,000, & there are several other good eateries nearby. *Tsh16,000/20,000 en-suite dbl/twin with hot water.*

⌂ **Central Lodge** [500 D2] ▫ 0786 126888. Despite its rather ramshackle approach, this quiet little guesthouse, tucked away behind the Iringa Info office, is a very pleasant surprise. Located in a converted old hospital building, it has cosy en-suite rooms with TV, fan & nets. *Tsh15,000/20,000 sgl/dbl B&B.*

⌂ **Emblasasa Motel** [500 D2] (6 rooms) This fairly smart hotel, on the main road around the corner

Shoestring

⌂ **Countryside Hotel** [500 A3] ▫ 0773 134777. Situated in a green compound 500m from the Tanzam Hwy, along a signposted turn-off about 1km towards Mbeya, this small hotel is only convenient for travellers with their own transport. It's probably better value than anything in town, though contrary to what the signpost reads, camping is not available. *Tsh7,000/8,000 en-suite sgl/dbl.*

Out of town

⌂ **Riverside Campsite** (12 rooms) ▫ 0787 111663/0755 033024; ℮ riversidecampsitetz@ hotmail.com; www.riversidecampsite-tanzania.com. This attractively rustic camp on the Little Ruaha River, 1.5km from the Tanzam Highway, is clearly signposted 13km northeast of Iringa. More than 300 bird species have been recorded, with the elusive African finfoot & Pel's fishing owl both resident on the river. Guided bird walks, horseback excursions &

✗ WHERE TO EAT

✗ **Hasty Tasty Too** [500 D2] ☎ 026 270 2061; ◷ early–20.00 Mon–Sat, 10.00–14.00 Sun. This long-serving eatery serves a variety of tasty & inexpensive stews, juices, & Indian snacks, as well as good b/fasts.

shabby en-suite rooms with TV & fan feel decidedly overpriced. On the plus side, it's centrally located, around the corner from the bus station, & a decent restaurant serves international cuisine. *US$35/45 sgl/dbl.*

from the bus station, feels a touch overpriced, but is probably the most comfortable central option in this range. *US$14/18 en-suite sgl/dbl with fan & net.*

⌂ **Staff Inn White House Lodge** [500 D3] The best of several cheapies dotted around the bus station, this has clean single rooms with common shower. *Tsh15,000 pp.*

⌂ **Huruma Baptist Mission Guesthouse & Conference Centre** [500 C1] ☎ 026 270 0184; ℮ hbcc@ maf.org.tz. Set in large green grounds on Togwa Rd 2.5km from the town centre, this place is popular with self-drive visitors, but less convenient for those using public transport. Large en-suite rooms have hot water & seem reasonable value. Rooms with 3–5 beds are available. Decent local meals cost around US$3. No alcohol, no smoking. *US$8/12 sgl/dbl B&B.*

⌂ **Ruaha University College** [500 D2] ☎ 026 270 2407. Located in the Bankers Academy Building just down from Iringa Info, this university-run place is now filling the backpacker void vacated by the Lutheran Centre. It's a little institutional but conveniently located, & the range of options suits most budgets. *Tsh4,000 sgl with shared facilities; Tsh12,000 en-suite sgl; Tsh18,000 dbl suite with sitting room, TV & tub.*

mountain bike hire are on offer, as is 4x4 rental for Ruaha. There are en-suite wood chalets & simple tented *bandas* using common showers, or you can pitch your own tent. There is a bar on site, & firewood is available, but simple meals can also be provided with notice. A Swahili School offers day- to month-long courses including FB accommodation. *US$20 pp chalet; US$15 pp tented banda; US$6 pp camping.*

✗ **Lulu's Café & Restaurant** [500 E2] ☎ 026 270 2122; ◷ 08.30–15.00 & 18.30–21.00 Mon–Sat. This pleasant café in the back streets off Uhuru Rd is recommended for snacks, light meals & ice cream, eaten indoors or on the garden patio.

✕ **Neema Crafts Café** [500 E2] Attached to the eponymous workshop, this café is a favourite with aid workers & expatriates, who have been known to travel for miles to stock up on Neema's famous homemade cookies & fudge. The extensive menu features Italian paninis, fresh ground coffee & delicious real cream ice cream. Staffed by deaf people from the workshop, they've created an ingenious ordering system whereby you write down what you'd like & then turn on a flashing light to let them know you've ordered.

✕ **Shooters Bar** [500 D3] This lively first-floor bar on Store Rd boasts satellite TV, pool table & a good stock of alcoholic drinks. The restaurant, in a separate room, has an extensive menu of Indian, Chinese & other dishes in the US$4–5 range. The service isn't the quickest, but the food is pretty good.

✕ **Suja's Home Cooking** [500 B1] ⊕ 07.00–23.00 daily. Next door to Twisters, this family-run restaurant offers a similar range of dishes at cheaper prices, though the quieter & more homely atmosphere is undermined by a blaring TV.

✕ **Twisters Pub & Restaurant** [500 B1] Also situated a block off Uhuru Rd, this justifiably popular bar & eatery specialises in Indian dishes (great chicken tikka) but it also serves a good range of other dishes in the US$4–5 range.

OTHER PRACTICALITIES

Foreign exchange Cash and travellers' cheques can be converted to local currency at the National Bank of Commerce on Uhuru Road [500 B3] during normal banking hours. It also has an ATM which accepts Visa only, as does the CRDB Bank further down the road [500 E2]. No private foreign exchange facilities exist in Iringa.

Internet Numerous internet cafés charge the usual Tsh500 per 30 minutes. Try Skynet Internet Cafe in the same building as Iringa Info [500 D2], MR Internet next to the eponymous hotel [500 D2], or the internet café at the post office [500 D2].

Neema Crafts Workshop Newly relocated to much larger premises in Hakimu Street, this admirable vocational workshop for deaf and disabled youngsters [500 E2] (e neemacrafts@gmail.com; www.neemacrafts.com) produces a variety of handmade paper products (from material as varied as pineapple leaves and elephant dung), as well as Maasai-influenced beadwork, patchwork quilts and rugs for sale to visitors. Free guided tours of the workshop are available, after which you can pop upstairs for a coffee at the attached café. The centre also has plans to open an internet café as well as a mini theatre for movie nights and live performances featuring their in-house dance and drum group.

EXCURSIONS FROM IRINGA

Kalenga This small village on the banks of the Ruaha was the site of Mkwawa's fortified capital before it was destroyed by German cannon fire in 1894. A small site museum in the village houses several of Mkwawa's personal effects, including some of his clubs, spears and guns. Outside the museum stand the tombs of Mkwawa's son and grandson, Chief Sapi Mkwawa and Adam Sapi Mkwawa, the latter famous in his own right as the first Speaker of Parliament in independent Tanzania. About 500m from the museum is the tomb of the German Commander Erich Maas, who died in the battle of Kalenga.

The museum caretaker will happily take you around the village, which seems pretty unremarkable to the untrained eye, but is in fact dotted with relics of Mkwawa's capital: the remains of fortified walls, the mound used by the chief to address his people, and the foundations of his home. The caretaker will also point out the ridge from where the Germans unleashed the barrage of cannon fire that destroyed the capital. This hill has since become known as Tosamaganga (throwing stones), and is now the site of a quaint 1930s Italian mission.

Pick-up trucks to Tosamaganga and Kalenga leave Iringa every hour or so. They wait for passengers at the end of the surfaced road 200m past Samora Stadium. At Kalenga you will be dropped off next to the market; it is a five-minute meander through the village from there to the museum. Keep asking for directions. If your Swahili is limited, asking for Mkwawa will get you further than asking for a museum.

Isimila Stone Age Site South of Iringa off the Tanzam Highway, the seasonal Isimila watercourse, which only flows after very heavy rain, has yielded one of the richest assemblages of Stone Age tools known from anywhere in the world. The significance of the site was first recognised in 1951 by a local schoolboy who collected two rucksacks full of stone implements, amongst them a 40cm-long axe weighing 4kg. Formal excavations by American universities took place over 1957–58 and 1969–70.

The watercourse at Isimila has yielded its wealth of ancient tools because it cuts through a series of sediment layers deposited on the bed of a shallow lake that flourished for a few thousand years before drying out 60,000 years ago. The tools mostly date from when the lakeshore was inhabited by Stone Age hunter-gatherers, and though they aren't the oldest unearthed in East Africa – similar implements of half a million years old are known from Olduvai Gorge and other sites – they do form an unusually varied and numerous showcase of late Acheulean workmanship. The site museum houses a selection of these tools, including several pear-shaped hand-axes, as well as picks, cleavers, hammers and cutting stones.

The site has also thrown up the fossilised bones of several large mammals, giving a good impression of what the area's large fauna must have looked like at the time. These include several extinct pig species, including a giant variety far larger than any that survives today, one extinct antelope, and a giraffe-like ungulate with large antlers and a relatively short neck. The fossilised bones and teeth of the extinct *Hippopotamus gorgops* – another extinct species with telescoped projecting eyes – are protected in a shelter on site. Ten minutes' walk from the Stone Age Site, a scenic gully studded with 10m-high sandstone pillars carved by the extinct river looks like the set of a Lilliputian cowboy movie.

Isimila lies about 2km from the Tanzam Highway along a turn-off signposted about 20km from Iringa in the direction of Mbeya. If you don't have private transport, you could hire a taxi from Iringa (expect to pay around Tsh15,000 for the round trip), or ask any southbound bus to stop at the junction, from where it's a 20-minute walk to the archaeological site. Entrance is Tsh3,000. Drinks are available, and an informative booklet written by Neville Chittick in 1972 is on sale.

Kisolanza Farm This 1,000ha farm (m *0754 306144;* e *info@kisolanza.com; www.kisolanza.com*), which lies alongside the Tanzam Highway some 50km southwest of Iringa and 20km before Mafinga, is one of the most attractive places to break up the long road trip between Morogoro and Mbeya. Owned by the same family for over 60 years, Kisolanza is divided more or less evenly between cultivation and natural vegetation, and its atmosphere and climate fall midway between the English countryside and the African bush. Guests can walk freely around the farm roads, from where an impressive checklist of 250 bird species has been recorded.

All accommodation is located about 1km from the main house. The smartest and most luxurious are two large en-suite farm cottages, set in a lushly flowering private garden, which cost US$100/150 single/double inclusive of a home-cooked dinner and large breakfast served in the Kihehe Hut restaurant. At the main campsite there are three smaller cottages each sleeping one to four people which vary in price from US$55 to US$85, excluding meals. Also available are four wood-and-thatch chalets, which cost US$25, and five double rooms in a stable

The area around Iringa is known as Uhehe: homeland of the Hehe, the dominant regional military force during the late 19th century (the name Hehe derives from the warriors' feared *hee-hee* battle cry) and the most successful in initially resisting German colonisation. The Hehe Empire took shape *circa* 1850 under Chief Munyigumba, who asserted control over about 100 *ntemi* chieftaincies to forge a centralised polity ruled from Lungemba, 10–15km south of modern-day Iringa. The formation of Uhehe coincided with a trend towards centralisation in the Tanzanian interior, a phenomenon attributed to the threat posed by militant Ngoni warriors coming from the south, and the economic opportunities created by coastal slave caravans.

In 1879, Munyigumba died (the tree under which he was reputedly buried can still be seen at Lungemba), prompting a violent secession dispute. Tradition has it that Munyigumba had appointed his younger brother Muhalwike as his successor, or failing that had asked that the empire be divided between his two eldest sons. Instead, his son-in-law Mwamubambe seized the throne by force, and had Muhalwike and one of the chosen royal sons killed. The other son, only 21 years old at the time, was forced into exile. But Mwamubambe lacked for popular support, and the Hehe elders conspired with the exiled heir to overthrow him. Mwamubambe and 1,000 of his warriors were killed in battle at a place now known as Lundamatwe – 'where skulls are heaped'.

Munyigumba's only surviving heir was appointed Chief of the Hehe, and he took on (or subsequently acquired) the throne name Mkwawa, a diminutive form of Mukwavinyika – 'conqueror of lands'. Mkwawa established a capital at Kalenga, 15km west of present-day Iringa, and embarked on a series of military campaigns to expand his empire into other territories traversed by the coastal trade caravans. Mkwawa demanded substantial levies from the passing slavers, and he also sold them any enemies captured in battle by the Hehe. By the mid 1880s, the military prowess of the Hehe and tactical skills of Mkwawa were legendary among follower and foe alike.

In 1888, as Mkwawa continued to expand his territory ever coastward, Germany secured its first permanent foothold on the East African mainland at Bagamoyo. Initially, the Germans were preoccupied with asserting their legitimacy at the coast. By 1891, however, Germany had not only quelled a series of coastal rebellions, but it had also gained nominal custody over the interior of modern-day Tanzania by treaty with Britain. In response to these ominous developments, Mkwawa mobilised his army, announcing that Uhehe would remain an independent state irrespective of the lines drawn on maps in Europe. Germany, meanwhile, recognised that Mkwawa, more even than Chief Mirambo of Nyamwezi, was likely to prove the most formidable obstacle to realising its nominal rule over the interior.

In July 1891, the German Commissioner Emil von Zelewski led a formidably armed expedition of 13 German officers and 570 African troops and porters into Uhehe, razing several villages on the way, then shooting dead the trio of envoys sent by Mkwawa to open negotiations. Mkwawa interpreted this as an open declaration of war, and – quietly

bunkhouse which cost US$22, while camping costs US$4 per person. A second campsite aimed at overland trucks is located around 400m away. Meals are available from the restaurant and there's also an on-site bar. Campers and self-caterers can buy a variety of fresh farm produce – meat, eggs, vegetables but no dairy products – at the kiosk at the main gate. A picnic site has been set up for passing day visitors.

Kisolanza Farm and The Old Farm House are clearly signposted along the Tanzam Highway, to the left coming from Iringa. The Scandinavia Express bus service between Dar es Salaam and Mbeya will drop and collect visitors at the gate.

keeping tabs on the German progress – he set a trap for the invaders at a rocky gorge on the Little Ruaha River near Lugalo, 15km east of Iringa. On 17 August, as Zelewski and his troops set up camp, some 3,000 Hehe warriors armed with spears and a few guns surged across the shallow river, closing in on the German troops to enforce hand-to-hand combat. Within 15 minutes, Zelewski and all but three of the German officers, and 140 of the Africans under his command, lay dead. Mkwawa boosted his armoury by making off with hundreds of rifles and many rounds of ammunition. A monument to Zelewski and the other slain officers still stands at Lugalo today.

Following this victory, Mkwawa fortified Kalenga, raising a 4m-high stone enclosure around the royal village, and surrounding that with a deep trench. He also tormented the Germans by launching surprise attacks on their positions, on one occasion wiping out an entire garrison at Kondoa. The Germans lusted for revenge but bade their time, gradually isolating Uhehe by forging alliances with neighbouring chiefs unsympathetic to Mkwawa. On 28 October 1894, the Germans set a row of cannons high on a hill above Kalenga, and bombarded the fortified capital for two days, before descending to the fort to pit their bayonets against the Hehe spears in hand-to-hand combat. The Germans easily took possession of the fort, then destroyed the ammunition store, and confiscated the chief's stockpiles of ivory and guns.

Mkwawa proved to be more elusive. Having fled Kalenga when defeat became inevitable, he spent the next four years roaming through Uhehe, inflicting occasional guerrilla attacks on German garrisons. His success in evading the Germans can be attributed to the loyalty of his subjects, who refused to give away his position. No German knew what Mkwawa looked like, and even when the German Governor offered a reward of 5,000 rupees for Mkwawa's head, it was to no avail. The chief's luck eventually ran out on 19 June 1898, while encamped at Mlambalasi, 50km west of Iringa. A German garrison surrounded the camp, and Mkwawa, facing certain defeat, shot himself rather than being taken captive.

The German sergeant who arrived at the fatal scene cut off Mkwawa's head and took it to Iringa. Mkwawa's decapitated corpse was buried at Mlambalasi, but his skull was taken to the Bremen Anthropological Museum in Germany. There it would remain until 1954, when – 56 years to the day after Mkwawa's death – Sir Edward Twining handed it over to Mkwawa's grandson, Chief Adam Sapi Mkwawa. The skull was displayed unceremoniously at the Mkwawa Museum in Kalenga until 1998, the centenary of Mkwawa's death, when it was finally interred alongside the chief's body at Mlambalasi. A memorial to Mkwawa, still widely revered in Tanzania for his resistance to colonisation, was unveiled at the same time – it can be reached along an 11km road signposted to the right 40km out of Iringa en route to Ruaha National Park.

For further information, check out the website www.mkwawa.com, which describes several sites associated with Chief Mkwawa and includes several photos.

Mufindi This highland area to the south of Iringa, known for its tea production, is the site of **Mufindi Highland Lodge** (\ (UK) 01452 862288; \f 022 286 2357; m 0754 237422; e fox@tanzaniasafaris.info; www.tanzaniasafaris.info; US$220/280 single/double FB including activities; low season discount of 10%.). Lying at an elevation of over 2,000m, this homely lodge consists of eight log cabins and a two-storey stone and wood fishing lodge with a ground floor restaurant and upstairs bar and snooker room. The walls are covered with carved replicas of record rainbow trout caught in the area through most of the last century, surrounding an enormous stone fireplace with a roaring fire that is lit all year round. There is excellent walking in the surrounding montane forest, which harbours similar species to those found in Udzungwa National Park minus the endemics, as well as some good drives and mountain biking opportunities. The lodge lies some 45km to east of the Tanzam Highway, and can be reached from Iringa by following the Tanzam Highway towards Mbeya for 70km, then turning left at Mafinga. Transport can be arranged from Iringa or Mafinga for people without vehicles. Activities include guided forest walks, mountain biking, boating and swimming in lakes, horseriding and fishing for rainbow trout.

RUAHA NATIONAL PARK

Protecting a tract of wooded hills and open plains to the west of Iringa, Ruaha is now Tanzania's largest national park, having been extended to cover 20,300km², and it lies at the core of a twice larger ecosystem embracing several other contiguous game reserves. Ruaha is widely regarded by the cognoscenti to vie with Katavi as the country's best-kept game viewing secret, and it has retained a compelling wilderness character that is increasingly savoury in this day of package safaris and hundred-room game lodges. The dominant geographical feature is the Great Ruaha River, which follows the southeast boundary for 160km, and is known to the local Hehe people as Lyambangori (Ruaha being a corruption of *luhava*, which simply means 'river').

Ruaha has a hot, dry climate; the annual rainfall, averaging 500mm, falls almost exclusively between October and May, peaking in February and March. Daytime temperatures in excess of 40°C are regularly recorded, particularly over October and November before the rains break, but very low humidity makes this less noticeable than might be expected, and it cools down reliably at night. The best game viewing is generally from May to November, but the bush is greener and prettier from January to June, and birding peaks during the European winter months of December to April. The vegetation of Ruaha is transitional to southern *miombo* and eastern savannah biomes, and a wide variety of habitats are protected within the park, including riparian forest along the watercourses, swamps, grassland and acacia woodland. The dominant vegetation type is *brachystegia* woodland. Several areas of the park support an impressive number of large baobab trees, and much of the scenery is strongly reminiscent of Tarangire National Park on the northern circuit.

The floral variety of Ruaha is mirrored by the variety of wildlife likely to be seen over the course of a few days on safari. The most common ungulates, not unusually, are the widespread impala, waterbuck, bushbuck, buffalo, zebra and giraffe, all of which are likely to be encountered several times on any given game drive. The park lies at the most southerly extent of the range of several East African ungulate species, including lesser kudu and Grant's gazelle. Yet it also harbours a number of antelope that are rare or absent in northern Tanzania, most visibly the splendid greater kudu – some of the most handsomely horned males you'll come across anywhere in Africa – but also the more elusive roan and sable antelope. The elephant population is the largest of any Tanzanian national park, despite heavy losses due to poaching in the 1980s, with some 12,000 elephants migrating through the greater Ruaha ecosystem. The most impressive pair of tusks weighed in the 20th century – combined weight 201kg – were from an individual shot in Ruaha in the 1970s, but the poaching of the recent past means you're unlikely to see anything comparable these days.

Ruaha is an excellent park for predators. Lions are not only numerous and very habituated to vehicles, but the prides tend to be unusually large, often numbering more than 20 individuals. The park also boasts a justified reputation for good leopard sightings, and while it's not as reliable as the Seronera Valley in the Serengeti, leopard are usually seen every few days and they are less skittish than in

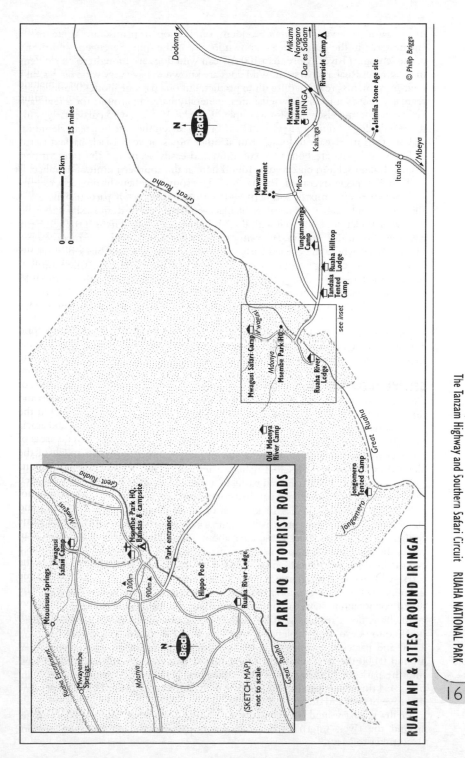

© Philip Briggs

RUAHA NP & SITES AROUND IRINGA

PARK HQ & TOURIST ROADS

(SKETCH MAP)
not to scale

16

many game reserves. Cheetah, resident on the open plains, are quite often encountered in the Lundu area – known locally as the mini-Serengeti – northeast of the Mwagusi River. More than 100 African wild dogs are thought to be resident in the greater Ruaha ecosystem. Wild dogs are known to have very wide ranges, and their movements are often difficult to predict, but one pack of about 40 individuals regularly moves into the Mwagusi area, generally hanging around for a few days before wandering elsewhere for a couple of weeks. Visitors who particularly want to see wild dogs should try to visit in June or July, when they are normally denning, and are thus more easy to locate than at other times of year. Black-backed jackal and spotted hyena are both very common and easily seen, and the rarer striped hyena, though seldom observed, is found here at the southern limit of its range.

With 450 species recorded, Ruaha also offers some excellent birding, once again with an interesting mix of southern and northern species. Of particular note are substantial and visible populations of black-collared lovebird and ashy starlings, Tanzanian endemics associated with the Maasai Steppes found here at the southern extreme of their distribution. By contrast, this is perhaps the only savannah reserve in East Africa where the crested barbet – a colourful yellow and black bird whose loud sustained trilling is a characteristic sound of the southern African bush – replaces the red-and-yellow barbet. Raptors are well represented, with bateleur and fish eagle probably the most visible large birds of prey, and the localised Eleonora's falcon quite common in December and January. The watercourses support the usual waterbirds.

An entrance fee of US$20 per 24 hours must be paid in hard currency. The Selous Safari Company, which operates Jongomero Tented Camp, maintains a highly informative website on Ruaha (*www.ruaha.com*).

GETTING THERE AND AWAY The most straightforward way to reach Ruaha is by air. Coastal Aviation flies daily from Dar es Salaam and Selous, while Safari Air Link offers a daily shared air charter service from Dar es Salaam to Ruaha via Mikumi and Selous in the high season. Fly-in packages, often combined with a visit to Selous, can be arranged directly through the lodges listed below, or through any other safari operator, and a minimum stay of three nights is recommended. Stand-alone drive-down packages to Ruaha are less attractive, because of the driving distance involved, but Ruaha can easily be visited by road as part of a safari taking in some of the other southern national parks and reserves.

The park entrance gate lies 100km west of Iringa along a fair dirt road that takes about three hours to cover and usually requires 4x4. The road passes through Kalenga, former capital of Chief Mkwawa, after about 15km, and another 25km further it passes the signposted side road north to Mlambalasi, site of the Mkwawa Memorial erected in 1998. Another 20km or so closer to Ruaha, the road branches into two forks, which converge shortly before the entrance gate. There is no substantial difference between the two forks in terms of distance or quality, but you need the left fork if you intend to stay at accommodation along the Tungamalenga road.

Ruaha is not a realistic goal for budget-conscious independent travellers. It is possible to get to Tungamalenga Campsite using a daily bus that leaves Iringa at 13.00 and passes the campsite at 18.00, coming past again on the return trip at around 04.00 the next morning. The campsite can arrange full-day game drives into the park for US$200 per vehicle excluding park fees. Alternatively you can hire a 4x4 through Iringa Info in Iringa, which should cost around US$225 per day inclusive of fuel and driver.

Ruaha is best visited between July and November, when animals concentrate around the river. Internal roads may be impassable during the rainy season (December to May).

WHERE TO STAY
Exclusive

⌂ **Jongomero Tented Camp** (8 tents) ☎ 022 212 8485; m 0784 953551; e reservations@selous.com; www.selous.com. The most overtly luxurious lodge in Ruaha & the only one with a swimming pool, Jongomero offers spacious standing tents with private balconies carved into the dense woodland bordering the eponymous seasonal river 500m upstream of its confluence with the Ruaha, where a semi-permanent pool hosts a resident hippo pod. Situated 60km southwest of the entrance gate, the camp has an isolated feel, & the little-used road running to the entrance gate often yields good elephant & buffalo sightings. The area south of camp functions much as a private game reserve, because so few other vehicles head this way, but wildlife tends to be rather skittish. The birdlife within camp can be excellent, with Livingstone's turaco topping the gaudiness stakes, while the localised Bohm's spinetail can be distinguished from other swifts & swallows by its distinctive bat-like fluttering. *US$830/1,100 sgl/dbl FB inc activities but not drinks.*
⌂ **Mwagusi Safari Camp** (10 tents) ☎/f (UK) 144 75 2517 0940; e oeas.co@btinternet.com. This

small & exclusive owner-managed tented camp, on the north bank of the seasonal Mwagusi River, is one of the most alluring in East Africa, immensely comfortable yet with a real bush atmosphere. The spacious walk-in tents, strung along the riparian woodland fringing the river, are enclosed in a wood, thatch & reed shelter, each with a vast shower & toilet area, & a private balcony. Service is top-notch & includes some great touches — most memorably, starlit bush dinners around a campfire in a clearing above the camp or in the riverbed. Game viewing is superb, with elephant & greater kudu regularly putting in an appearance, & plenty of birds hopping around the trees. Wild dog are regularly sighted in the area, several lion prides are resident, & it's far enough from any other lodge that you feel you have the park to yourself. Game walks with an armed ranger come with a good chance of encountering elephants & other large animals. *The fly-in rates, inc meals & activities, fall between those of Jongomero & Ruaha River Lodge, but drive-in rates (exclusive of activities) are comparable to the latter.*

Upmarket

⌂ **Old Mdonya River Camp** (10 tents) ☎ 022 245 2005/6; e reservations@adventurecamps.co.tz; www.adventurecamps.co.tz. Operated by Coastal Aviation, this camp lies on the wooded banks of the 'old' Mdonya River, which has not flowed in earnest since the river changed course a couple of decades ago. Comfortable rather than luxurious, the en-suite standing tents all have private balcony, while the culinary emphasis is on tasty home-style cooking, eaten beneath the stars. The camp offers good access to the Mwagusi River game-viewing circuit. The old riverbed is an important wildlife passage, & plenty of animals pass through camp daily, most profusely impala, warthog & giraffe, but also the occasional lion or elephant, & nocturnal visitors such as honey badger, genet & bushpig. Birding is superb, with the likes of purple-crested turaco, bearded woodpecker, crested barbet, black-necked weaver, orange-breasted bush-shrike & green-winged pytilia among the colourful & conspicuous residents. *US$390/650 sgl/dbl FB; US$450/760 full game package.*
⌂ **Ruaha River Lodge** (28 rooms) ☎ (UK) 01452 862288; ☎/f 022 286 2357; m 0754 237422; e fox@tanzaniasafaris.info; www.tanzaniasafaris.info. This scenic & comfortable camp is the oldest in Ruaha, situated on a rocky hillside above a set of

rapids 15km from the entrance gate. Game viewing is excellent, with rock hyrax scuttling everywhere, hippos resident on the river, elephant passing through regularly, & many other animals coming down to drink. Accommodation is in unpretentious stone cottages, some of which lie directly along the river for game viewing. It is divided into 2 camps of 14 rooms, each camp with its own restaurant & bar. *US$270/380 sgl/dbl FB, US$375/590 full game package.*
⌂ **Tandala Tented Camp** (10 units) m 0784 355023; e reservations@tandalatentedcamp.com; www.tandalatentedcamp.com. Situated 13km outside the entrance gate along the Tungamalenga Rd, this tented camp overlooks a seasonal river in a private conservancy buffering the national park. The no-frills but comfortable en-suite tents stand on stilted wooden bases, while facilities include attractive *makuti* restaurant & bar area alongside a small swimming pool. The greater kudu for which the camp is named is evidently quite common in the surrounding woodland, while a waterhole attracts a steady stream of wildlife in the dry season, including elephants on most days. Because it lies outside the national park, activities such as night drives, guided game walks & fly-camping are offered. Game drives into the park cost US$60/80 pp half/full day. *US$175/350 sgl/dbl FB.*

The Tanzam Highway and Southern Safari Circuit **RUAHA NATIONAL PARK**

16

Moderate

🏠 **Ruaha Hilltop Lodge** (8 rooms) ☎ 026 270 1806; m 0784 726709; e ruahahilltoplodge@yahoo.com; www.ruahahilltoplodge.com. Situated on a steep hillside 20km from the park entrance gate along the Tungamalenga road, this small lodge has simple en-suite thatched *bandas* with hot water, solar power & a private balcony. There's a great view from the restaurant/bar area, & the management can arrange transfers from Iringa as well as game drives into the park by prior arrangement. Good value. *US$80 pp FB.*

Budget and camping

🏠 **Tungamalenga Camp** ☎ 026 782196; m 0784 707287; e tungcamp@yahoo.com; www.ruahatungacamp.com. This well-run camp & curio shop is situated in the eponymous village about 27km before the park entrance gate. The small en-suite *bandas*, each with 2 beds & netting, would seem rather overpriced were it not for their proximity to the park. Camping, with access to a clean shower & toilet & a self-catering area, is permitted too. There is a good restaurant & staff can organise game drives into the park for US$200/vehicle excluding park fees. *US$40 pp B&B, US$60 FB; camping US$10 pp.*

🏠 **Msembe Camp** (11 rooms) This national park camp near the headquarters lies close to the river & some extensive open plains teeming with game. The accommodation isn't up to much – prefabricated en-suite dbl & family *bandas* that look like they must get seriously hot during the middle of the day – but it's the cheapest on offer within the park. Bedding, firewood & water are provided, & drinks can be bought at the nearby staff bar, but all food must be brought with you. *Camping US$30 pp.*

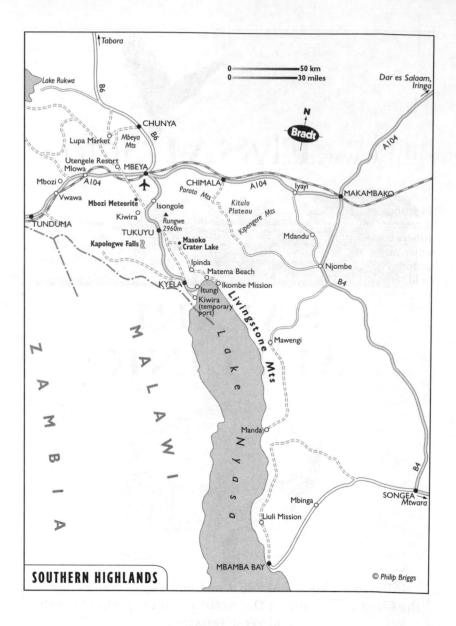

SOUTHERN HIGHLANDS

↑ Tabora

Lake Rukwa

B6

0 ——— 50 km
0 ——— 30 miles

N

Bradt

Dar es Salaam,
Iringa

CHUNYA

Lupa Market

Mbeya
Mts

B6

A104

Utengele Resort
Mlowa

MBEYA

Mbozi

A104

Vwawa

Mbozi Meteorite

Kiwira

Isongole

TUNDUMA

TUKUYU

Rungwe
2960m

Kapologwe Falls

Masoko
Crater Lake

Ipinda

Matema Beach

KYELA

Itungi

Ikombe Mission

Kiwira
(temporary
port)

CHIMALA

Poroto Mts

A104

Kitulo
Plateau

Kipengere Mts

Iyayi

MAKAMBAKO

Mdandu

Njombe

B4

Mawengi

Manda

Mbinga

Liuli Mission

MBAMBA BAY

SONGEA
Mtwara

B4

Z A M B I A

M A L A W I

L a k e   N y a s a

Livingstone Mts

© Philip Briggs

17

The Southern Highlands and Lake Nyasa

Snuggled up to the borders with Zambia, Malawi and Mozambique, the southern highlands of Tanzania, though exceptionally pretty and reasonably cheap and accessible, are seldom explored by travellers. The main town and route focus Mbeya is well connected to Dar es Salaam and other towns by road and rail, while other major towns include Tukuyu and Kyela. Scenic highlights are many, and include Ngosi Crater Lake, Mount Rungwe and Kitulo National Park, all of which hold some allure to hikers. Oddly enough, the most significant physical feature in the midst of these highlands is the vast but low-lying Lake Nyasa–Malawi, whose lush beaches are enclosed by the dramatic Poroto, Kipengere and Livingstone ranges on the Rift Valley escarpment.

GEOLOGY OF THE SOUTHERN HIGHLANDS

Tanzania's southern highlands, centred around Mbeya, are often perceived to form a practically contiguous extension of the Eastern Arc Mountains to their north, and the two biomes do indeed share some strong biological affinities. The geology of the southern highlands and affiliated ranges in bordering parts of Mozambique, Malawi and Zambia, which together form the Southern Rift Montane Eco-region, is, however, quite unique, representing some of the most ancient and the most modern rock formations on the Africa continent.

Underlying most of the southern highlands are the Pre-Cambrian Ubendian sediments, named after a locale close to Lake Tanganyika, and comprised of quartzite and other crystalline rocks that formed at least two billion years ago when two tectonic plates drifted into each other. The vast, high mountain range created by this collision, comparable perhaps to the modern Himalayas, has subsequently been eroded to comparative insignificance, while in lower-lying areas the original crystalline rocks have been overlaid by other sediments during periods when they lay underwater. The Mbeya Range, which rises above Mbeya, is probably the most substantial single relic of this ancient geological activity.

A more recent factor in shaping the topography around Mbeya has been the tectonic drift responsible for the formation of the Great Rift Valley. The southern highlands lie at the juncture of two separate rifts – the main eastern rift and smaller Rukwa branch – resulting in a high level of volcanic activity, particularly over the last four million years. The volcanic landscape east of Mbeya is dominated by Mount Rungwe, which last erupted about 200 years ago, as well as several extinct or dormant volcanoes and crater lakes, most notably Ngosi. Solidified lava flows are in strong evidence throughout this region, most strikingly at Daraja la Mungu, a natural bridge of basaltic lava rock that spans a gorge comprised of almost two-million-year-old crystalline rock. Then, of course, there is the 585km-long, 700m-deep Lake Nyasa, set at an elevation of around 500m on the Rift Valley floor below an escarpment rising to almost 2,500m.

With elevations ranging from below 478m to 2,901m, this region has a varied climate. Lake Nyasa is hot and humid, but other areas are more temperate, with Tukuyu boasting the highest rainfall in Tanzania, and visitors to the highlands will appreciate some reasonably warm clothing at night. For hikers, the dry season (May to October) might seem promising, but the scenery is far less interesting and you'll miss out on the flower displays that form one of the regional highlights.

MBEYA

Perched at an elevation of 1,737m in a valley below the extensive Mbeya Range, Mbeya was established in 1927 to service the Lupa gold fields near Chunya. Although the mining ceased in the 1950s, Mbeya has continued to prosper thanks to the rich agricultural land that surrounds it, and its strategic position along the Tanzam Highway and Tazara Railway. With a population of around 230,000, it is today the third-largest town in Tanzania. Mbeya is an appealing town, with a skyline dominated by the impressive – and climbable – Mbeya and Loleza peaks. It also has an unusually Westernised, bustling feel and shows few of the signs of neglect that characterise many other Tanzanian towns. Mbeya is mainly visited by travellers as a stop-off point on the way to Zambia or Malawi, but it is a good base for exploring the southern highlands.

HIGHLAND FLORA AND FAUNA

The indigenous vegetation of the southern highlands shares several superficial similarities with that of the Eastern Arc Mountains. In other respects, it is very different. This is because the geologically and climatically stable Eastern Arc has experienced an ecological continuity unparalleled in East Africa over the last 30 million years, while the southern highlands have undergone large scale climatic change and topographic transformation.

The varied vegetation of the southern highlands is shaped by wide contrasts in elevation and climate, with annual rainfall figures that vary from 800mm on the Ufipa Plateau to almost 3,000mm in the Livingstone and Poroto Mountains. The typical vegetation type below 1,800m is savannah or thick *miombo* woodland, dominated by trees in the genera *Brachystegia, Isoberlinia*, and *Julbernardia*. Closed-canopy montane rainforest generally blankets the slopes between 1,800m and 2,300m, often interspersed with stands of tall bamboo *(Sinarundinaria alpina)* forest. Higher elevations are dominated by open montane grassland, dotted with seasonal marshes and in some areas divided from the forest zone by a belt of heather and moorland.

The woodland and forest zones of the Southern Rift Montane Eco-region are characterised by a significantly lower floral and faunal diversity than the more ancient forests of the Eastern Arc, and also harbour far fewer endemic species. Not so, however, the grassland and heath communities, which support possibly the richest variety of flowering plants of any East African eco-region, particularly on Malawi's Nyika Plateau and the Kitulo Plateau east of Mbeya. Orchids are particularly well represented – some 300 species, the highest total anywhere in the world, have been identified on the Nyika Plateau alone – as are proteas, aloes, fireball lilies and various smaller and less distinctive colourful flowers. The wet season floral displays on the Kitulo Plateau are arguably the most underrated natural spectacle anywhere in Tanzania.

The southern highlands are of great interest to ornithologists. Three Tanzanian endemics are represented in the area, namely Uhehe fiscal, Iringa akalat and Kipengere seedeater. Grassland species whose range is centred on the Southern Rift Montane Eco-region include the spectacular buff-shouldered widowbird and somewhat duller yellow-browed seedeater and churring cisticola. The montane forests are especially rewarding,

GETTING THERE AND AWAY Many people travel between Mbeya and Dar es Salaam by the Tazara Railway (see the box, *The Tazara Railway*, in *Chapter 16*, page 475). Tazara railway station is 4km out of town on the Tanzam Highway towards Zambia [516 A5]; a taxi there will cost around Tsh3,000. The booking office is at the station and there is also an office in town, although it's not always open. Your best bet is either to get a taxi or take a bus towards the Zambian border and ask to be dropped off.

There are also regular buses between Dar es Salaam and Mbeya, an 893km trip that takes up to 20 hours in local buses and about 12 hours on Scandinavia Express, which operates three buses daily and charges Tsh25,000 one-way. It is possible to break up the trip at Morogoro, Mikumi or Iringa.

From western Tanzania, the most comfortable option would be to get to Dar es Salaam by train and proceed to Mbeya from there. A more adventurous route goes via Mpanda and Sumbawanga; see *Chapter 15*. At least three buses every week run during the dry season along the little-used road connecting Tabora to Mbeya, passing through one of the most remote parts of Tanzania. This trip will take at least 20 hours.

Buses to local destinations such as Kyela, Tukuyu, Njombe and Tunduma leave regularly from the central bus station [516 A6] on a fill-up-and-go basis. There are also several buses daily to Iringa, Songea and Sumbawanga, but these should be booked in advance. *Dala-dalas* to most of the above destinations leave from Mwanjelwa station, which lies on the Tanzam Highway about 1km back towards

with widespread gems such as bar-tailed trogon, starred robin-chat and paradise flycatcher occurring alongside several skulkers endemic to the Eastern Arc and Southern Rift Mountains, notably Fuelleborn's black boubou, Sharpe's akalat, spot-throat and long-billed tailorbird. By comparison, large mammals are poorly represented, though most forests harbour populations of Angola black-and-white colobus (an endemic southern highlands race *Colobus angolensis sharpei*), vervet and blue monkey. Also present are the elusive bushpig, bushbuck, suni, Harvey's duiker, bush duiker and (on Rungwe only) the rare Abbott's duiker, a Tanzania endemic. Smaller mammals include endemic semi-melanistic races of Tanganyika mountain squirrel and chequered elephant shrew, while endemic reptiles include three species each of chameleon, snake and amphibian.

With the notable exception of Malawi's Nyika National Park, the Southern Rift Mountains are accorded a relatively low conservation status, and not protected at all within Zambia or Mozambique. Tanzania has 28 demarcated forest reserves within the region, only a handful of which cover more than 100km², and another 20 or so are possibly to be gazetted in the foreseeable future. The most important of these reserves in terms of area and environmental integrity are on the Chimala Scarp (below the Kitulo Plateau), the Livingstone Mountains, the Mbeya Range, the Poroto Ridge (around Mount Ngosi) and Mount Rungwe. While most of these large reserves still contain substantial tracts of indigenous forest, grassland and heath, several smaller reserves have been seriously compromised through a combination of subsistence wood collection, charcoal making, grazing, bush fires, clearing for cultivation, and pit sawing.

The conservation profile of the region has been raised following the recent establishment of the Southern Highlands Conservation Programme (*SHCP*; e enquiries@ southernhighlandstz.org; www.southernhighlandstz.org), a Wildlife Conservation Society (WCS) funded project based in Mbeya and dedicated to the study and conservation of the highland habitats and species of southern Tanzania. Two significant recent developments in the southern highlands are the upgrading and creation of the new Kitulo National Park and the discovery of a monkey species previously unknown to western science (see box, *Kipunji!*, page 524).

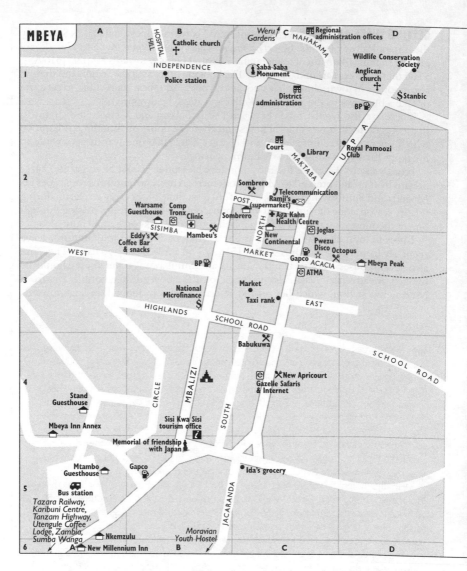

MBEYA

A | B | C | D

HOSPITAL HILL

Catholic church

INDEPENDENCE

Police station

Weru Gardens

MAHAKAMA

Saba-Saba Monument

Regional administration offices

Wildlife Conservation Society

Anglican church

Stanbic

District administration

BP

Court

Library

MAKTABA

LUPA

Royal Pamoozi Club

Sombrero

Telecommunication

Ramji's

POST

(supermarket)

Warsame Guesthouse

Comp Tronx

Clinic

SISIMBA

Sombrero

Eddy's Coffee Bar & snacks

Mambeu's

NORTH

Aga Kahn Health Centre

New Continental

Joglas

Pwezu Disco

Octopus

WEST

BP

MARKET

Gapco

ACACIA

ATMA

Mbeya Peak

National Microfinance

HIGHLANDS

Market

Taxi rank

EAST

SCHOOL ROAD

SCHOOL ROAD

Babukuwa

CIRCLE

MBALIZI

New Apricourt

Gazelle Safaris & Internet

Stand Guesthouse

Mbeya Inn Annex

SOUTH

Sisi Kwa Sisi tourism office

Memorial of friendship with Japan

Mtambo Guesthouse

Gapco

Ida's grocery

Bus station

Tazara Railway, Karibuni Centre, Tanzam Highway, Utengule Coffee Lodge, Zambia, Sumba Wanga

JACARANDA

Nkemzulu

New Millennium Inn

Moravian Youth Hostel

Dar es Salaam and is connected to the town centre by regular minibuses that run along Karime Avenue past the NBC and Rift Valley Hotel.

TOURIST INFORMATION Gazelle Safaris [516 C4] (\/f *025 250 2482;* m *0764 293553;* e *info.sales@gazellesafaris.com; www.gazellesafaris.com;* ☉ *08.30–17.30 daily*), opposite the New Apricourt Restaurant, is the best source for all local travel information. This dynamic new outfit can arrange guides and transport for excursions around the Mbeya area, as well as car hire and safaris to all game parks. The **Sisi Kwa Sisi Tourism Office** [516 B4] (*cnr School St & Mbalizi Rd;* m *0754 463471,* e *sisikwasisitours@hotmail.com*), opposite the Memorial of Friendship with Japan, charges around US$10 per person for guided day trips to most reasonably accessible sites of interest covered in this chapter, though these do receive mixed reports. The office is theoretically open from 08.00 to 16.00 Monday to Saturday,

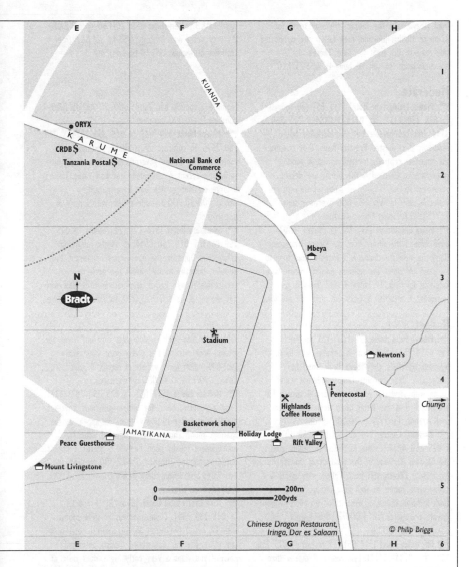

but you may need to pop past a few times before you find anybody at home! A lot of flycatchers hang around the bus station claiming to be from Sisi Kwa Sisi (which means 'People to People' or 'Pull Together'), so best visit the office yourself.

WHERE TO STAY
Upmarket

Utengule Coffee Lodge [516 A5] (16 rooms, 8 bungalows) m 0753 020901/0786 481902; e utengule@iwayafrica.com; www.riftvalley-zanzibar.com. The most attractive option in or around Mbeya, Utengule lies on a 500-acre coffee estate near Luiji, a 30min drive from the town centre. The surrounding forested slopes harbour a variety of birds & small mammals, & form a useful base for hikes in the Mbeya Range. Facilities include large swimming pool, tennis & squash courts, mini-golf, pool table & helicopter pad. The lodge manager is very knowledgeable about excursions further afield in the southern highlands. The restaurant is widely regarded as the best in the region. To get there

The Southern Highlands and Lake Nyasa MBEYA / 17

from Mbeya, take the Tanzam Highway south for 12km to Mbalizi junction, then follow the signposted side road to the right for 8km. There's accommodation to suit all budgets. *US$75/110*

Moderate
🏠 **Mount Livingstone Hotel** [517 E5] (40 rooms) 📞 025 250 3332; m 0713 350484; f 025 250 3334. This comfortable but unremarkable hotel reputedly once hosted Princess Anne, & it remains the smartest centrally located option. A good restaurant is attached & the rooms are decent value. *Tsh35,000/55,000 en-suite sgl/dbl with hot water & satellite TV; Tsh65,000 executive suite; Tsh75,000 Princess Anne's room.*

🏠 **Peace Guesthouse** [517 E5] (5 rooms) 📞 025 250 0498. Around the corner from the Mount Livingstone Hotel, this new guesthouse is a friendly alternative to the staid old hotel. The spacious en-suite rooms have king-size dbl beds, TV, fridge & tiled floors. A good restaurant is attached & plans are afoot for additional

Budget
🏠 **Mbeya Peak Hotel** [516 D3] (25 rooms) m 0754 756101. Central & popular with local business travellers, the Mbeya Peak Hotel has respectably clean en-suite rooms with hot water (some with views). A good restaurant & garden bar are attached, & the latter often hosts live music over w/ends. *Tsh17,500/20,000 sgl/dbl.*

🏠 **Karibuni Centre** [516 A5] 📞 025 250 3035; f 025 250 4178; e mec@maf.or.tz. 500m from the Tanzam Highway in the grounds of the Mbalizi Evangelical Church, this hostel offers very clean & comfortable rooms as well as camping. The out-of-town location counts against it for travellers without private transport. *Tsh15,000/20,000 sgl/dbl; camping Tsh3,000 pp.*

🏠 **Rift Valley Hotel** [517 G5] (39 rooms) 📞 025 250 2004; m 0784 355141. Less central & quieter than the above, but otherwise similar in standard, the Rift

Shoestring
🏠 **Moravian Youth Hostel** [516 B5] This long-established backpackers' haunt lies a few mins' walk out of town along Jacaranda Rd, & offers clean, secure accommodation. Aside from the somewhat institutional character of the set-up, the main disadvantage of staying here, assuming that you intend to eat or drink in the town centre, is that the road out to the hostel has a reputation for nocturnal muggings. *Tsh7,000 dbl.*

sgl/dbl B&B std en-suite; US$120/160 sgl/dbl B&B 2-storey suites with balcony; US$45 dbl B&B free-standing bungalow; US$10 pp camping.

rooms & a rooftop bar. *Tsh45,000–50,000 dbl B&B; camping Tsh20,000 per tent.*

🏠 **Mbeya Hotel** [517 G3] 📞 025 250 2224; f 025 250 2575. In contrast to its shabby exterior, the rooms at this former government Railway Hotel are surprising decent & altogether not bad value. There's a large outdoor garden bar & restaurant. *Tsh35,000/50,000 en-suite sgl/dbl with fan, TV & hot water.*

🏠 **Sombrero Hotel** [516 C2] (22 rooms) 📞 025 250 0663; f 025 250 0544; e sombrerohotel@ yahoo.com. Opposite the eponymous restaurant, this popular, centrally located hotel has perfectly serviceable though rather cramped en-suite dbls with hot shower & DSTV. *Tsh25,000 dbl, Tsh45,000 suite.*

Valley Hotel has good en-suite dbls with hot water. The ground floor restaurant is pretty good value, charging Tsh3,000–4,000 for a variety of curries & grills. *Tsh12,000/15,000/48,000 sgl/dbl/suite.*

🏠 **Holiday Lodge** [517 G5] 📞 025 250 2821/3375. Long a popular choice for budget-conscious travellers, the Holiday Lodge is slowly losing its appeal as the spacious rooms show growing signs of wear. The management speaks good English, & there's a decent bar & restaurant attached. *Tsh12,000 en-suite dbl with large bed, writing desk & hot shower; Tsh4,000 with common shower.*

🏠 **New Continental Hotel** [516 C2] (6 rooms) 📞 025 250 2511. Clean, spacious en-suite rooms with TV, net & hot water at this central hotel seem fair value. The bar downstairs, though potentially noisy if you want a very early night, does close at 23.00. *Tsh8,000/12,000 sgl/dbl.*

🏠 **New Millennium Inn** [516 A6] 📞 025 250 0599. This clean lodge opposite the bus station is excellent value; all rooms are 'singles' with a dbl bed. *Tsh6,000 common shower; Tsh7,000–10,000 en-suite with satellite TV.*

🏠 **Warsame Guesthouse** [516 B2] m 0713 298395. Basic but adequately clean local guesthouse that seems far more inviting than anything in the cluster of cheapies scattered around the bus station. Rooms use a common shower. *Tsh3,000/5,000 sgl/dbl.*

✖ WHERE TO EAT The upmarket and moderate hotels listed above all boast adequate to good restaurants. The pick is the **Utengule Coffee Lodge** [516 A5] whose daily set menu features fine French-inspired cuisine with main meals around Tsh7,000. There's also a lengthy coffee menu as well as an excellent wine list and on Sundays at lunch wood-fired pizzas are served on the lawn. Bookings are advised. The restaurants at the **Rift Valley Hotel** [517 G5] and **Mount Livingstone Hotel** [517 E5] are also good and reasonably priced.

In the centre of town, **Babukuwa Restaurant** [516 C4] is a local favourite, serving seafood, poultry and meat dishes with an Indian flavour in the Tsh5,000 range. Also recommended is the café-style **Sombrero Restaurant** [516 C2], which has an extensive menu of grills, curries and pasta dishes for around Tsh5,000.

Away from the town centre, along the road connecting the Rift Valley Hotel to the Tanzam Highway, the new **Chinese Dragon Restaurant** [517 G5] serves good Chinese food in the Tsh4,000–5,000 range. For cheaper local food, **Mambeu's Restaurant** [516 B3] (*Sisimba Rd*) and the **New Apricourt Restaurant** [516 C4] (*Lupa Rd*) are recommended. The **Weru Gardens** [516 C1] (*Commissioner Rd, Uzunguni*), ten minutes' walk up from the post office, is the best and most popular bar in town, set in extensive gardens and serving all types of drinks as well as chicken, *nyama choma*, chips and local dishes.

SHOPPING Mbeya is the place to stock up if you are planning a few days' hiking or camping in the area. The supermarkets on Market Square sell a fair variety of imported goods. Fruit and vegetables are best bought at the **market** [516 C3]. Plenty of small *dukas* (stalls or small shops) surround the market. For ice cream and packaged food items, try **Ramji's Supermarket** [516 C2] in the THB Building near the post office – it's also a good place to pick up recent international newspapers and magazines.

OTHER PRACTICALITIES

Internet The best internet café is **Gazelle Safaris Internet Cafe**, in Gazelle Safaris' office on Jacaranda Street [516 C4], which charges Tsh1,000 per hour. There are several other cafés dotted around town if this one is busy.

Foreign exchange The National Bank of Commerce [517 F2] (*Karume Av*) offers foreign exchange facilities for travellers' cheques and cash as well as an ATM accepting Visa only. The Stanbic Bank at the top of town [516 D1] also changes cash at a reasonable rate and has an ATM accepting both Visa and MasterCard. There are no private bureaux de change in Mbeya, which could be problematic for travellers arriving from Malawi or Zambia outside of normal banking hours. If you are likely to be in this position, try to change enough cash at the border to see you through the next working day.

EXCURSIONS FROM MBEYA This section covers places of interest that lie along, or are most easily accessed from, the Tanzam Highway, as well as those to the west of Mbeya town. The numerous scenic sites around Tukuyu (on the road towards Lake Nyasa and the Malawi border) are covered separately later in this chapter, under the heading *Excursions from Tukuyu*. Most of the places of interest around Tukuyu could be visited as a day trip out of Mbeya, whether independently or with a guide from either Gazelle Safaris or the Sisi Kwa Sisi tourism office in Mbeya.

The Mbeya Range The gneiss mountain range for which Mbeya town is named is about 25km long and forms an important watershed for both the Lake Nyasa and Lake Rukwa drainage systems. It has three major peaks, of which the central

17

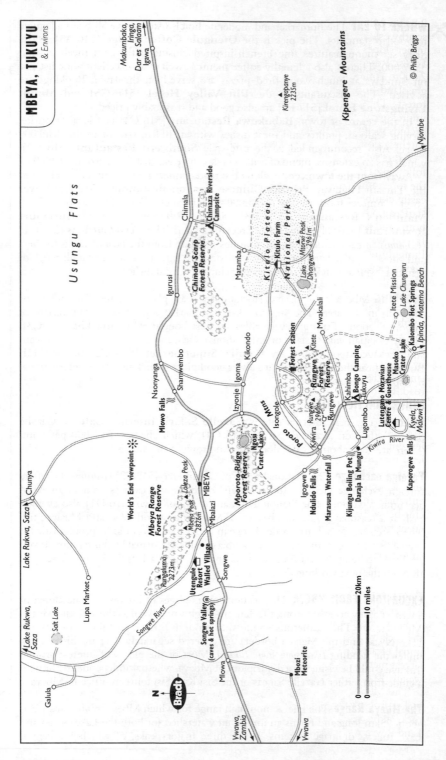

MBEYA, TUKUYU
& Environs

© Philip Briggs

Kipengere Mountains

Usungu Flats

Makumbako, Iringa, Dar es Salaam, Igawa

Kirengepanye 2235m

Njombe

Chimala

Chimala Scarp Forest Reserve

Chimaza Riverside Campsite

Kitulo Plateau National Park

Kitulo Farm

Mtorwi Peak 2961 m

Matamba

Lake Dhangwe

Igurusi

Kikondo

Itete Mission

Lake Chungruru

Kalombo Hot Springs

Ipinda, Matema Beach

Mwakalali

Forest station

Kitete

Shamwembo

Nsonyanga

Mlowo Falls

Izyonje

Igoma

Rungwe Forest Reserve

Rungwe 2960m

Rungwe

Kahimba

Bongo Camping

Masoko Crater Lake

Lutengano Moravian Centre & Guesthouse

Kyela, Malawi

Isongole

Kiwira

Tukuyu

Lugombo

Kaporogwe Falls

Kiwira River

Chunya

Lake Rukwa, Saza

World's End viewpoint

Mbeya Range Forest Reserve

Loleza Peak

Mbeya Peak 2826m

MBEYA

Mbalazi

Mporoto Ridge Forest Reserve

Ngosi Crater Lake

Poroto Mtns

Igogwe

Nduildo Falls

Marasusa Waterfall

Kijungu Boiling Pot Daraja la Mungu

Rungaluma 2273m

Utengule Resort

Walled Village

Songwe

Songwe River

Lupa Market

Lake Rukwa, Saza

Salt Lake

Galula

Mlowa

Mbozi Meteorite

Songwe Valley (caves & hot springs)

Vwawa, Zambia

Vwawa

N

Bradt

0   20km

0   10 miles

520

2,835m Mbeya Peak is the tallest, flanked by the 2,273m Pungulumo Peak to the southwest, and the 2,656m Loleza or Kaluwe Peak to the northwest. In 1957, the upper slopes of the mountains were gazetted as the roughly 160km² Mbeya Range Forest Reserve, most of which still supports indigenous vegetation. Below the 2,000m contour, this is mainly open-canopy *brachystegia* woodland. Higher, open grassland and heath predominate, interspersed with strips of riparian *Hagenia* forest. The grassland receives a mean annual rainfall of 1,750mm and hosts impressive wildflower displays during the rainy season, with proteas and terrestrial orchids well represented. Blue and velvet monkeys are thinly distributed in forest patches, along with dik-dik, bushpig and a wide variety of birds.

From Mbeya town, Loleza Peak can be ascended in about two hours, by following Hospital Hill Road to the hospital, then climbing a footpath through the forest immediately before the electricity lines. The higher Mbeya Peak is most easily climbed from Utengule Coffee Lodge; several routes are possible and the staff can advise you about current conditions. The round hike takes about six hours and is steep in parts, so it should only be attempted if you are reasonably fit. If you want to do a longer hike, you can cross from Mbeya Peak west to Pungulumo Peak. The footpaths are indistinct in places, and mist is a risk at higher elevations, so best to arrange a guide from Gazelle Safaris, Sisi Kwa Sisi or Utengule Coffee Lodge.

Songwe Valley Caves and Hot Springs Straddling the Tanzam Highway 25km south of Mbeya, Songwe is the site of a large factory that produces cement from the surrounding limestone sediments. Of greater interest to tourists, however, are the nearby caves and hot springs in the Songwe River Valley, which can be reached by following the Tanzam Highway for 3km south of Songwe town and crossing a small bridge, then almost immediately turning right on to an unsignposted dirt road. Follow this track for 2km, and you'll reach a quarry and group of limestone kilns; here you must turn left on to a smaller track and follow it for about 8km to a pink marble quarry.

From the marble quarry, anybody will be able to direct you to the caves, only a few minutes' walk away. The caves are eroded into a limestone cliff and have at least two entrances, which you can walk between with a decent torch, though it would be dangerous to go too far in. They offer an attractive view over the river, and seasonal bat colonies comprising six different species stream out of the entrances at dusk to spectacular effect. Some small hot springs lie at the base of the cliff below the caves. Larger and more beautiful are the springs and geysers that erupt from the ground about one to two hours' walk away at Malonde.

If you want to stay overnight in Songwe, the Songwe Hotel has affordable en-suite rooms. Note that the village at the Malawi border post near Kyela is also called Songwe, because it also lies on the Songwe River.

Mbozi meteorite This substantial meteorite lies on the slopes of Merengi Hill near Mbozi Mission, 70km southwest of Mbeya. The meteorite was first reported in 1930 by a South African land surveyor, W H Nott, whose attention was drawn to the rock by a local assistant who feared its legendary supernatural powers. Nott's initial measurements created a real stir among mineralogists, indicating it was the largest meteorite on the earth's surface, weighing more than 70 tonnes. In fact it weighs 12 tonnes, the eighth-largest in the world.

The Mbozi meteorite is classified as a siderite, comprised almost entirely of nickel–iron alloy (extremely rare on the earth's surface) as opposed to igneous rock, and it is the only one known in Africa. Although the rock is smaller than a Land Rover, it is composed of 90.45% iron and 8.69% nickel, with traces of copper, sulphur and phosphorus. The outer crust of the meteorite is darkened by metal fusion caused by the scorching heat that was generated when it fell through the earth's atmosphere – essentially a shooting star so large that it reached the planetary surface before it burned out.

With a private vehicle, Mbozi can easily be visited from Mbeya in conjunction with the bat caves at Songwe. Follow the Tanzam Highway for 30km south of Songwe until you see the dirt road to Mbozi signposted to your left. The meteorite lies 13km along this road, just past Ndolezi village. No entrance fee is charged, but a caretaker is present. There is no formal accommodation in the immediate vicinity, but Sisi Kwa Sisi in Mbeya can arrange a village stay nearby. There is no public transport between the Tanzam Highway and the meteorite.

Chunya, Lake Rukwa and surrounds The intriguing small town of Chunya, 50km northwest of Mbeya as the crow flies, was the site of a local gold rush in the 1920s and 1930s. Mining activity ceased in the 1950s because it was no longer profitable, but Chunya subsequently enjoyed a short-lived tobacco boom before degenerating into something approaching a ghost town. Many of its grander buildings are boarded up, and there's a general air of faded prosperity. Local gold prospectors still pan the river that runs through town, and there is talk of reworking the gold using modern methods.

The most direct route to Chunya leaves from central Mbeya roughly opposite the Rift Valley Hotel. This scenic 72km road takes two to three hours by 4x4 in dry weather, but it might take longer – or be practically impassable – after rain. A worthwhile diversion, assuming you're driving yourself, World's End Viewpoint lies near the Chunya road 22km from Mbeya and offers excellent views to the Usunga Flats. Using local transport, a few pick-up trucks ply the road from Mbeya to Chunya daily, and you should be able to get there and back within a day. There are a couple of guesthouses in Chunya should you opt – or be forced – to stay the night.

In a private 4x4 vehicle, it would be possible to return from Chunya using a second, longer and more southerly route through Makongolosi, Saza, Kanga, Utengule Coffee Lodge and Mbalizi. A couple of points of interest lie within striking distance of this route. The first, 5km east of the road at Kanga, is Magadi soda lake, which often supports flocks of flamingo between July and October. Second is the century-old White Fathers Mission at Galula, notable for its large 1920s wooden church, which lies 4km from the road along a westerly turn-off some 8km past Kanga in the direction of Mbeya.

Mlowo Falls This waterfall lies alongside the Tanzam Highway towards Iringa, some 33km from Mbeya town. It is a very scenic spot, with the Mlowo River tumbling over a 15m-high basaltic cliff into a large pool, before flowing through a steep, narrow gorge lined with euphorbia shrubs. The waterfall itself faces away from the main road, and is therefore not visible from it. If, however, you park (or disembark from a bus) next to the bridge across the Mlowo River (no more than 1km before Shamwembo village), a short footpath leads to a good viewpoint over the waterfall, and a bridge over the gorge.

KITULO NATIONAL PARK

Based primarily on information supplied by Tim Davenport of the Southern Highlands Conservation Programme (see box, Highland flora and fauna, *pages 514–15, for further details of this organisation).*

Known locally as *Bustani ya Mungu* (God's Garden) and elsewhere as the *Serengeti of Flowers*, the unique Kitulo Plateau – formerly known as the Elton

Plateau after the British explorer who first traversed it in 1873 – is one of Tanzania's most neglected biological gems. Perched above 2,600m between the Kipengere Range and the Poroto and Livingstone Mountains, the plateau is comprised of 273km² of Afro-montane and Afro-alpine grassland, representing the largest and most important plateau grassland community in Tanzania. The newest of Tanzania's national parks, the 13,500ha Kitulo Plateau is the first such entity in tropical Africa to be gazetted primarily for its floristic significance.

Kitulo has long been heralded as a botanists' paradise, boasting a rich floral diversity influenced by its fertile volcanic soils and an average annual rainfall of 1,400mm. The 350 species of vascular plants documented to date include 45 species of terrestrial orchid, as well as the yellow and orange red-hot poker *Kniphofia kirkii* (a southern highland endemic), aloes, proteas, geraniums, giant lobelias, lilies and aster daisies. Many of the species are of restricted distribution: 31 are Tanzanian endemics, 16 are endemic to Kitulo/Kipengere, ten are restricted to Kitulo/Poroto, and at least three are endemic to the plateau itself and two more known only from the plateau and adjoining forests. Trees are relatively sparse on the plateau, except along the streams, though the Ndumbi Gap below Mount Mtorwi supports a patch of juniper trees some of which stand 50m high – reputedly the tallest junipers in the world. It is, however, the abundance of flowering plants in the wet season, starting in November and running through to April, that immediately impresses. The phenomenon has been described as one of the great floral spectacles of the world.

The plateau is also home to important animal species including some national and regional endemics. Breeding colonies of blue swallow and Denham's bustard, as well as species such as lesser kestrel, pallid harrier, mountain marsh widow, Njombe cisticola and Kipengere seedeater, contribute to the plateau being listed as an Important Bird Area. The satyrid butterfly *Neocoenyra petersi* is endemic to Kitulo, and southern highland endemic chameleons, lizards and frogs are also found. Two of the highest peaks in the southern highlands rise from the plateau: the 2,961m Mount Mtorwi and the 2,929m Chaluhangi Dome.

FEES AND FURTHER INFORMATION The park's infrastructure is still only in the early stages. Until completed, park entrance fees of US$15 per person are to be paid at TANAPA's temporary head office in Matamba village. Walking safaris cost US$20 and guides can be arranged for US$10. Pick up a copy of Liz de Leyser's *Guide to the Southern Highlands of Tanzania*, published in 2003 (US$5) here.

GETTING THERE AND AWAY Although Kitulo can be approached from a signposted side road leading northward from near Uyole on the Mbeya–Tukuyu road, the more conventional point of access road is Chimala on the Tanzam Highway 78km east of Mbeya. Chimala is readily accessible on public transport from Iringa or Mbeya, and boasts the usual motley collection of local guesthouses, of which the Sun Valley, Miami and Lutheran Guesthouses are relatively good. From Chimala, a spectacular road called *Hamsini na Saba* ('57' – a reference to the number of hairpin bends along its length) leads to the small town of Matamba. This drive takes up to two hours in a private vehicle, and it is covered by a couple of 4x4 *dala-dalas* daily. From Matamba, it's a one-hour drive or three-hour walk – no public transport – to the edge of the plateau.

WHERE TO STAY

Kitulo Farm m 0754 362683; e kitulonp@ tanzaniaparks.com. The only accommodation on the plateau is this very inexpensive & reasonably comfortable state-owned resthouse, which would take the best part of a day to reach on foot from Matamba, but is only a couple of hours away by road. Otherwise, there are a couple of quite decent local guesthouses in Matamba.

It was while interviewing Nyakyusa subsistence hunters in early 2003 that biologists Tim Davenport and Noah Mpunga of the WCS Southern Highlands Conservation Programme were first alerted to the possible existence of an unusual monkey on the forested slopes of Mount Rungwe. Initially, the researchers assumed that this creature, known locally as *kipunji*, was a form of blue monkey, or possibly even one of the many spirit animals integral to Nyakyusa culture. However, along with colleagues Sophy Machaga and Daniela De Luca, they investigated the forest further, obtaining the first of several fleetingly inconclusive sightings in May 2003.

Unfortunately, the combination of steep terrain, thick undergrowth and the animal's shy nature meant that several months would pass before the semi-contiguous Livingstone Forest (now part of Kitulo National Park) rewarded the WCS team with a clear sighting of a *kipunji*. And when it did, in December 2003, it provided confirmation of their growing suspicion that this elusive canopy-dweller, with its unique 'honk-bark' alarm call, was a previously undescribed species – the first such monkey to be discovered in Africa in more than two decades.

Somewhat unromantically named the highland mangabey (the original Nyakyusa name is preserved in the Latin binomial *Lophocebus kipunji*), this almost exclusively arboreal monkey has an unusually shaggy coat, presumably an adaptation to the chilly nocturnal temperatures that characterise the upper slopes of Rungwe and Kitulo. Almost 1m long, it is grey-brown in colour, with a long crest standing erect on its head, elongated cheek whiskers, and an off-white belly and tail. It lives in medium-sized troops that forage in the safety of the canopy (up to 50m high), and is thus most likely to be located by its distinctive call.

Given that Tanzania is among the most biologically well-known of African countries, it is remarkable that this distinctive large mammal managed to elude scientists into the 21st century. But more bizarre still is that having remained invisible for so long, the highland mangabey was effectively discovered twice by independent research teams working at sites more than 350km apart. Just months after Davenport's still unannounced discovery, in May 2004, Caroline Ehardt and Trevor Jones identified what was clearly an undescribed mangabey in the remote Ndundulu Forest Reserve in the Udzungwa Mountains. And as chance would have it, one of the first confidantes to whom Ehardt divulged her exciting secret – over a sociable beer in a Dar es Salaam bar – was none other than a rather astounded Davenport. Having recovered from the mutual shock of their joint discovery, the two teams subsequently prepared a joint paper describing the new species for the May 2005 edition of *Science* magazine.

Although it is conceivable that further populations await discovery, the known range of the highland mangabey is restricted to three sites – the semi-contiguous Rungwe and Livingstone forests as well as isolated Ndundulu – with a total extent of less than 75km². It must tentatively be regarded as extremely rare and critically endangered, with an estimated total population of between 500 and 1,000 animals, and it is particularly vulnerable to subsistence hunting, illegal logging and other unmanaged resource extraction in its main stronghold, the Rungwe–Livingstone forests. Encouragingly, a large portion of this forest has been incorporated into the new Kitulo National Park, and there is also a possibility that Udzungwa National Park will be increased in extent to include Ndundulu. For further details, log on to www.wcs.org/international/Africa/Tanzania/highlandmangabey.

Chimaza Riverside Campsite m 0787 111663/ 0755 033024; e riversidecampsitetz@hotmail.com; www.riversidecampsite-tanzania.com. A good option is this well-run new campsite, which is located just off the dirt road to Kitulo near Mfumbi Village, & under the same ownership as Iringa's Riverside Campsite. The staff are very knowledgeable & will happily arrange guided hikes into the park. There are permanent safari-style tents using shared shower, or you can pitch your own tent. There's a small shop in the village where you can stock up on basic provisions. The campsite is 3km from Chimala & signposted off the main highway. *Standing tent US$15 pp; camping US$6 pp.*

TUKUYU

This amorphous small town, set at an elevation of 1,650m in the Poroto Mountains 70km south of Mbeya by road, is salvaged from anonymity by its setting at the base of Mount Rungwe, the second-highest peak in the southern highlands (Mtorwi on the Kitulo Plateau pips it by a metre). Originally called Neu Langenburg, the town was founded as a German administrative centre in the late 19th century after its namesake near Ikombe Mission on Lake Nyasa was abandoned due to the high incidence of malaria. The modern name of Tukuyu derives from the extinct volcanic hill called Ntukuyu across which the town sprawls. Pretty setting aside, Tukuyu is of interest primarily as a base from which to explore the surrounding mountains, which are studded with waterfalls, crater lakes and forest patches – all capped by stirring views to Lake Nyasa more than 1,000m below.

GETTING THERE AND AWAY Tukuyu lies along the surfaced road between Mbeya and Kyela, about 70km or an hour's drive from either town. Regular buses run in both directions on a fill-up-and-go basis, taking about two hours to either Mbeya or Kyela. Public transport is more erratic on by-roads leading east and west from the main surfaced road, but there is a fair amount of private traffic along most roads, and vehicles will generally take passengers for a fee, so exploring the area over a few days from one base is possible.

TOURIST INFORMATION AND TOURS The very helpful Rungwe Tea & Tours (^ 025 255 2489; m 0784 293042; www.rungweteatours.com; ⊕ 08.00–18.00 daily), a small community-based tourism project initiated by the local tea farmers' association, is located next to the post office. Staff can organise a number of tours including tea tours of nearby estates (Tsh12,000 per person) as well as half-/full-day hikes (Tsh10,000/15,000 per person) to Kaporogwe Falls, the Bridge of God and Kyela Mountain. They can also arrange transport to Kyela and Matema Beach.

WHERE TO STAY AND EAT
Moderate
Landmark Hotel (27 rooms) \/f 025 255 2400; e landmahotel@yahoo.co.uk. This smart & centrally located 3-storey hotel is the most comfortable base for exploring the Tukuyu area. A good, though very slow, restaurant is attached. Spacious en-suite rooms with modern décor are tiled & have DSTV, balcony & hot water. *Tsh20,000/25,000/55,000 sgl/dbl/suite B&B; Tsh5,000 pp camping.*

Budget
Laxmi Guesthouse (16 rooms) \ 025 255 2191. Next to the Landmark Hotel, this likeable guesthouse has clean & tidy no-frills en-suite dbls, & sgl rooms with shared facilities. *Tsh10,000/15,000 sgl/dbl.*
DM Motel (10 rooms) \ 025 255 2332; m 0754 410275. Run by the benevolent Mama Florence, this friendly local guesthouse with its marvellous view of Mount Rungwe is an amenable budget option. The rooms are clean & comfortable, with the option of using a hot common shower or en-suite. There is a bar & restaurant (meals must be ordered in advance). Located off the main road just before the turn-off into Tukuyu. *Tsh10,000 dbl with common shower; Tsh15,000 en-suite.*

17

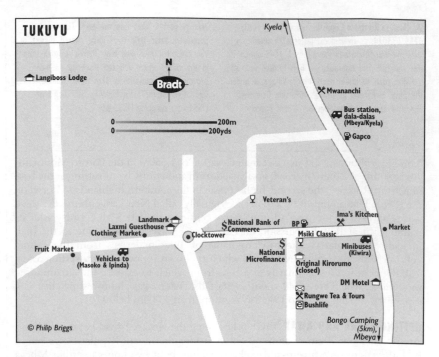

© Philip Briggs

Camping

⚑ Bongo Camping e bongocamping@gmail.com;
www.bongocamping.com. An excellent base for
motorised travellers, this popular new campsite is set
in large green grounds around 5km from Tukuyu in
the village of Kibisi. The non-profit campsite organises
tours around the area as well as regular performances
by a local theatre group. Basic meals are available at
the attached restaurant. It is signposted off the main
road to the left just before Tukuyu. *Tsh6,000 pp
basic standing tent; Tsh4,000 pp camping.*

✗ WHERE TO EAT The restaurant in the **Landmark Hotel** serves a good variety of
continental dishes in the Tsh5,000–7,000 range, but the service is excruciatingly
slow – we waited almost three hours for our meals! Better service and better
value can be found down the road at **Ima's Kitchen**, which dishes up huge
helpings of local favourites such as *ugali*, beans and chicken for around
Tsh1,000–2,000.

EXCURSIONS FROM TUKUYU This area is ideal for casual rambling. Wander along
any of its winding dirt roads and you will be rewarded with lovely views and
scenery, varied birdlife and vegetation, and regular glimpses into rural African life.
The following section runs more or less from north to south, describing some of
the more accessible spots, most of which are easily visited as a day trip from
Tukuyu. With time, initiative and 1:50,000 maps, you can explore further. The
booklet *Welcome to Mbeya* has plenty of useful walking information, assuming that
you can locate a copy.

Ngosi Crater Lake The single most alluring natural attraction anywhere in the
southern highlands, this beautiful body of emerald green water is nestled within
the 300m-high walls of the collapsed caldera of Ngosi, an extinct volcano which
last erupted at least two million years ago. The peak of Ngosi – 'Big One' in the
local Safwa language – is at 2,620m the highest point within the 90km² Poroto

Ridge Forest Reserve, and its upper slopes protect what is probably the largest extant patch of ecologically intact montane vegetation in the mountain range after those on Mount Rungwe. The eastern slopes of Ngosi support extensive stands of bamboo forest, standing up to 15m high. The other slopes are covered in montane forest, as is an area of 20km² within the caldera, and three small islands in the northern part of the lake.

The slightly brackish waters of the 4km², 75m-deep crater lake are too sulphurous to support any fish naturally – locals have tried to stock it but not surprisingly the fish keep dying. According to local legend, however, the lake does harbour a large snakelike monster with supernatural powers. The Lake Ngosi Monster reputedly has the power not only to change colour to blend with that of the lake, but also to change the lake's colour when it elects to reveal itself. Local people won't swim or fish in the lake, and tend to blame local disasters on the monster's anger, which they appease by sacrificing a black goat, sheep or chicken.

UNYAKYUSA

The fertile slopes between Mbeya and Lake Nyasa are referred to as Unyakyusa – the home of the Nyakyusa, a group of around one million people whose territory crosses over into neighbouring Malawi, where they are known as the Ngonde. Blessed with rich volcanic soil and an annual rainfall exceeding 1,500mm, the verdant mountains of Unyakyusa are dotted with small subsistence farms growing bananas, mangoes, grains, tea and coffee, set around the neatly painted Nyakyusa homesteads that led the explorer Joseph Thomson to describe Unyakyusa as 'perfect Arcadia'. The origin of the Nyakyusa has been a source of some speculation, for their Bantu language has a vocabulary significantly different to that of any neighbouring tongue, and it is one of the few Bantu languages that does not make significant use of tones.

Nyakyusa society, before it was undermined by the Ngoni wars, and the missionary and colonial influence, had a uniquely egalitarian structure based around so-called 'age villages'. When a set of adolescents reached puberty, they would all leave their villages of birth to found a new community at an uninhabited site. This new village would function rather like a commune, as an economically self-sufficient unit in which work was divided equally between men and women, crop and land rotation were practised, and cattle were distributed between the wealthier members of the community and their poorer age peers. The village would be abandoned once the last of the founding age set had died, possibly to be re-inhabited a couple of generations later.

Traditional Nyakyusa society has several unusual customs relating to death. At a funeral, the mourners indulge in an elaborate ritual dance which, as might be expected, expresses their anger and loss, but also involves the ritualised mocking of the dead, often resulting in violent quarrels and sometimes murder. Corpses, instead of being buried, were left out in the open at a sacred grove called an Itago, which literally means 'place of casting away', and is the source of local place names such as Itaga and Itagata. The geographer Kerr-Cross, who visited Unyakyusa in 1893, documented how 'on the crests of rounded mounds of considerable size are to be seen clumps of thick forest... the burial-places of their ancestors'. In 1925, McKenzie described how: 'In the long past, when a man was dying, and all hope of recovery had been abandoned, he was carried to the Itago, placed in a sitting position, and left to die. After death, the flesh was devoured by birds or beasts.' McKenzie noted that 'nowhere, as far as I have discovered, is this repulsive practice now followed'.

Lake Ngosi is also said to be the home of powerful ancestral spirits, which lend a special potency to any medicinal plants collected in the surrounding forest.

If the monster doesn't reveal itself, the dense forest along the footpath to the crater rim harbours readily observed troops of black-and-white colobus monkey, as well as a host of secretive forest birds characteristic of the southern highlands. The endemic Ngosi Volcano (or Poroto three-horned) chameleon *Chameleo fuelleborni*, a little-known species first described in 1900, is more or less restricted to the forested slopes of Ngosi. The male of this chameleon measures up to 20cm long, is mostly brown and green in colour (though it may go partially red, white and black) and has two small, lightly coloured pre-ocular horns and one rostral horn. The female is smaller and has less developed horns.

The turn-off to Ngosi Crater Lake is marked by a signpost on the surfaced road between Mbeya and Tukuyu, about 2km east of Isongole village and 35km from Mbeya. Follow this turn-off for about 3km through cultivated fields until you arrive at a sharp leftward fork, where you need to turn to the right, heading into the forest. After another 2km, a left turn takes you to a forest clearing where there is room to park a car. The footpath to the crater rim runs from close to the parking area, and the 5km ascent shouldn't take longer than two hours. Travellers without a vehicle will have no problem finding a *dala-dala* to drop them off at the junction, but will need to walk from there, adding another hour to the hike in each direction. Most visitors are content to enjoy the view from the rim, but there is a steep and rather treacherous footpath to the base of the caldera and the lakeshore. If you still have the energy on the way back from Ngosi, a 1km footpath to the left, about 1km after leaving the forest (2km before returning to the main Mbeya–Tukuyu road), leads to the 60m-deep Isungunia Explosion Crater, which hosts a rainy-season lake.

It is advisable to organise a guide to visit the lake, since the footpath is very indistinct in places. This is best done through Rungwe Tea & Tours in Tukuyu, though informal guides can also be found around Isongole and the junction. During the rainy season, ask about the condition of the footpath in advance, as it is sometimes too muddy to be a realistic prospect.

Mount Rungwe Dominating Tukuyu's northern skyline, the 2,960m Mount Rungwe is a dormant volcano studded with more than ten different calderas. The mountain formed about 2.5 million years ago and has experienced considerable activity in the last million years – ossified lava flows are clearly visible throughout the surrounding region. Several of the volcano's subsidiary calderas now harbour attractive crater lakes, while the explosion crater of the uppermost caldera is clearly visible from the peak – which also offers expansive views to Lake Nyasa, Lake Rukwa and the Kitulo Plateau. Rungwe is last thought to have erupted between 200 and 400 years ago, but a series of tremors over the cusp of 2000 and 2001 generated some concern locally that another eruption might be in store. The worst of these tremors measured 4.0 on the Richter scale, not cause for serious alarm to travellers but sufficient to destroy 400 houses, leaving more than 5,000 people homeless.

The wild, uninhabited upper slopes of the mountain are protected within the 135km² Rungwe Forest Reserve, originally gazetted by the German colonial administration in 1902. Extensive indigenous montane forests are to be found within the forest reserve, particularly on the moister southern slopes, which receive up to 2,000mm of rainfall annually. Above the 2,500m contour, the dominant vegetation is montane grassland, separated from the forest in the southwest by a belt of heath moorland dotted with protea scrubs, terrestrial orchids and other wildflowers. The most visible forest mammals are black-and-white colobus and blue monkey, but the forest also forms an important refuge for the rare

Abbott's duiker (see box, *Abbott's duiker*, in *Chapter* 7, page 219). The prolific birdlife is characteristic of southern highland forests.

The easiest and most popular ascent route of Rungwe starts at the Kagera Estate Timber Camp, which lies on the northeast foot slopes of the mountain 18km from the surfaced Mbeya–Tukuyu road. To get there, follow a dirt side road that branches south from the main road at Isongole, turning sharply to the right at an intersection near the forestry office after 11km. The ascent to the rim from the timber camp takes about two hours, and it will take at least another hour to reach the peak. An alternative route, passing through the extensive montane forest on the western slopes and taking about six hours, leads from the Rungwe Moravian Mission, which lies about 7km from the main Mbeya–Kyela road along a turn-off close to Kiwira. It is possible to ascend the mountain using one route and to descend via the other.

Reasonably fit travellers should be able to ascend the mountain and return to the base within a day, at least during the dry months of June to November. Alternatively, with a tent and adequate preparation, one could spend a couple of days exploring the slopes. Either way, the combination of poorly marked, criss-crossing footpaths and occasional mist make it strongly advisable to climb with a local guide. This can be arranged locally, or through Rungwe Tea & Tours in Tukuyu. The 1:50,000 map of Rungwe is sometimes available from the Department of Lands and Surveys in Dar es Salaam.

Ndulido and Marasusa waterfalls The Ndulido and Marasusa waterfalls lie within easy walking distance of the village of Kiwira on the main Mbeya–Tukuyu road, making them attractive goals to travellers dependent on public transport, especially as there is a guesthouse in Kiwira.

The Ndulido Falls lie on the Igogwe River about 5km northeast of Kiwira village. Although the waterfall is quite small, there's an interesting sinkhole alongside it, full of bats, but safe to walk through. To get there, follow the Igogwe road east out of Kiwira village for about 5km, with the river visible to your left most of the way, until you reach the Igogwe Hospital, from where it's ten minutes' walk to the waterfall.

The Marasusa Waterfall on the Kiwira River plunges over a large solidified lava flow, and there is a footpath to its base. To reach it, you also need to leave Kiwira along the Igogwe road, but after about 1km, having crossed the bridge across the Kiwira River, you need to turn left on to a side road that crosses the Igogwe River shortly before it's confluence with the Kiwira River. The waterfall lies to the left about 4km along this side road.

Daraja la Mungu One of the easier sites in the Poroto region to visit using public transport, Daraja la Mungu – The Bridge of God – is a spectacular natural rock bridge spanning the Kiwira River. It was reputedly formed less than a thousand years ago by a water-cooled lava flow from Mount Rungwe. To get there from Tukuyu, follow the Mbeya road out of town for about 6km to Kyimo (also known as KK), and then take a left turn along a good dirt road signposted for the Prison Officers College. After 8km, this road passes through the village of Lugombo, connected to Kyimo by reasonably regular transport, especially on the busy market day of Monday.

Continuing through Lugombo, the road descends into the Kiwira Valley, reaching a large intersection after about 2km. Turn to the left here, along a road following the course of the Kiwira River, and after about 500m a large artificial bridge offers an excellent view over its natural counterpart. About 200m past the artificial bridge, you'll reach a complex of buildings – trainee prison officers' dwellings – where a clear footpath to the left leads across the natural bridge, and another one leads to the riverbank below the bridge. Note that photography of the natural bridge is forbidden without permission from the Prison Officers College, easy enough to obtain if you have sufficient time and patience.

Little more than 2km from the natural bridge, situated within the Prison Officers College compound, the Kijungu Boiling Pot consists of a small waterfall on the Kiwira River that tumbles into a circular pot-hole before flowing under a much smaller natural bridge. To reach Kijungu from Daraja la Mungu, walk back to the intersection 500m from the artificial bridge, and then turn left (in the opposite direction to Lugombo). After another 500m or so, you'll cross a bridge above a small waterfall (clearly visible from the intersection), immediately after which you need to turn right towards the college gates. The wardens will ask you to fill in the visitor book and show your passport before guiding you to Kijungu, which lies about 1km past the gates.

Masoko Crater Lake The main attraction along the 45km back road that connects Tukuyu to Ipinda (the closest town to Matema Beach on Lake Nyasa) is the attractive Masoko Crater Lake. As implied by its name – *masoko* means 'markets' – a small market village lies adjacent to the lake, which, although not as spectacular as Ngosi Crater Lake, is far easier to visit by either public or private transport.

Masoko has some interesting historical associations. The solid stone building on the crater rim was constructed in 1912 to house the German Fifth Field Garrison, and it was the base from which Germany fought British troops in the neighbouring Nyasaland Protectorate. The stone building housed British troops between the wars, and it now serves as a courthouse. It is rumoured that towards the end of World War I, the Germans dumped a fortune in gold bars, money and military vehicles into the lake to avoid their falling into British hands – believable enough when you consider that the same thing happened to the *Liemba* on Lake Tanganyika. Difficult to say whether there's anything to be read into the fact that the occasional German coin is washed up on the shore of the lake.

Masoko lies 19km from Tukuyu along the Ipinda–Matema road. A fair amount of traffic heads this way, predominantly overcrowded pick-up trucks. You may prefer to walk out: it's gently downhill most of the way, and very pretty with intimate, cultivated slopes occasionally giving way to magnificent vistas to Lake Nyasa. With an early start, you'll have no problem getting a lift back. There is no accommodation at the lake, but the GNG Guesthouse, a kilometre or two further along the Ipinda road, has basic single rooms.

If you are driving on south from Masoko towards Ipinda and Matema Beach, an easy and worthwhile diversion is to the old Itete Lutheran Mission and Hospital, which is built on an ancient volcanic plug overlooking the attractive Chungruru Crater Lake, home to the endemic Chungruru tilapia. To get there, follow the Ipinda road south from Masoko for about 5km, then, after crossing the bridge over the Mbaka River, turn left on to the Lwangwa road. About 10km along this road, a signposted right turn-off leads to the mission after 5km.

Kaporogwe Waterfall The impressive Kaporogwe or Makete Waterfall plunges roughly 20m over a large basaltic ledge into the Kiwira Gorge about 15km downriver of Daraja la Mungu. An interesting feature of the waterfall is that it is possible to follow a footpath into a cave below the ledge, so that you can view it from behind. A second footpath leads to the base of the falls. A Tsh500 entrance fee is charged. According to the guides, a rope bridge across the Kiwira River lies about one hour's walk from the waterfall.

To reach Kaporogwe Waterfall, follow the Kyela road south from Tukuyu for about 5km, then turn right along a side road signposted for the Lutengano

Moravian Centre. After 7km, you'll reach the Moravian Centre, which offers good-value accommodation and camping (see *Where to stay* above). About 2km past the centre, turn left along a road signposted for Ilulwe School, passing the Katumba Dispensary after about 1km, then after another 500m you'll reach the school, where the road forks two ways. Take the right fork, then after another 1km a left fork, from where it's about 8km to the parking area above the waterfall. The footpath from the parking lot to the cave behind the waterfall takes about five minutes to walk.

LAKE NYASA

Split between Malawi, Mozambique and Tanzania, this 585km-long Rift Valley lake, enclosed by tall mountains, is arguably the most scenic body of water in Africa. Although the Malawian part of the lake is more popular with travellers, the Tanzanian portion is perhaps more attractive, particularly Matema Beach on the northeast tip of the lake, where the combination of a stunning location and affordable accommodation more than justify the relatively minor effort required to get there. Unfortunately, the rest of the Tanzanian part of the lake – with the exception of the workmanlike Itungi Port – is relatively inaccessible. The only accessible place on the eastern lakeshore is Mbamba Bay, a lovely village that is linked to Songea by road and to Itungi Port on the western shore by ferry. Lake Nyasa boasts little in the way of terrestrial wildlife – vervet monkeys are common in some areas – but it does support a wide variety of birds, most conspicuously the vociferous fish eagle. The lake is also known for its great variety of fish and in particular its colourful cichlids (see box, *Cichlids of the great lakes*, in *Chapter 15*, pages 464–5).

Lake Nyasa is most often referred to today as Lake Malawi, a name which, despite its widespread international usage, has no historical veracity. During the colonial era, and in recorded descriptions predating colonialism, the lake was universally referred to as Nyasa. The appellation Malawi came into use as recently as 1964, when the first post-independence government of the former Nyasaland Protectorate renamed both country and lake in order to nurture popular mystical associations between the new leadership and the legendary mediaeval Maravi Empire. Understandably, the neighbouring states were not particularly inclined to be influenced by this act of political expediency, and today the same body of water is known officially and colloquially as Lake Malawi in Malawi, Lake Nyasa in Tanzania and Lago Niassa in Mozambique.

Climatically, arriving at the lakeshore might take some adjustment if you are coming from the cool highlands around Tukuyu. Less than 500m above sea level, Lake Nyasa can be swelteringly hot, though the breeze – sometimes a howling wind – that comes off the lake generally cools things down at night. Lake Nyasa has a bad reputation for cerebral malaria, so take your pills, continue to take them for four weeks after you leave the area, and get to a doctor quickly if you display malarial symptoms during that period.

KYELA Kyela, the gateway town to the Tanzania part of Lake Nyasa, comes as something of an anticlimax after the breathtaking 1,000m ascent from Tukuyu – with tantalising glimpses through the lush montane escarpment to the blue waters of the lake far below. Scruffy, sweaty and scenically unmemorable, Kyela is stranded some 10km inland of the lakeshore port of Itungi, and possesses all the oppressive attributes of the tropical lakeshore climate, bar the all-redeeming waterside breeze. It is also one of those irritating towns, so rare in Tanzania, whose more youthful residents are evidently unable to conquer the impulse to yell

'*Mzungu!*' at any passing European. With Matema Beach beckoning to the north, you'd be unlikely to stay in Kyela out of choice, though you may need to should you intend to catch a ferry. Fortunately, should you sleep over, Kyela's long-standing collection of tawdry shoestring guesthouses has of late been supplemented by a smattering of decent budget hotels.

LAKE NYASA FERRIES

Due to the formidable natural obstacle formed by the Livingstone Mountains and associated ranges along the northeast of Lake Nyasa, no roads worth talking about connect the ports on the eastern and western shores. The best – indeed the only – way travellers can take a look at the more remote parts of Lake Nyasa, or get between the eastern and western shores, is the erratic ferry service that connects Itungi Port to Mbamba Bay. It's a wonderfully scenic trip, with the Livingstone Mountains rising sharply above the clear blue waters of the lake, and visits a number of ports that are otherwise practically cut off from the outside world. Luxurious, however, the boats are not. Facilities are very basic third-class only, and schedules somewhat whimsical, as the ferry stops interminably at one fishing village after the next, to be greeted by a flotilla of local dugouts whose occupants thrust fish, fruit and other goods at the passengers in the hope of a sale.

All going well, two Tanzanian ferries ply the Nyasa lakeshore, though it is often the case that one or the other boat – very occasionally both – is in dry-dock for repairs. Following flooding and the build-up of a sandbar blocking the Itungi Port, in mid 2008 ferry services were diverted to a temporary port in Kiwira around 5km further south along the lakeshore from Itungi. The Itungi Port is expected to be dredged in 2009; until that time all services will continue to depart from Kiwira.

In theory, the MV *Songea* leaves Itungi at around 07.00 on Monday and Thursday and arrives at Mbamba Bay at midnight the same day, after stopping at Lupingu, Manda, Lundu, Nindai and Liuli. After arriving at Mbamba Bay, the Monday ferry turns around more or less immediately, to arrive back at Itungi at 17.00 the next day. The Thursday ferry continues travelling on to Nkhata Bay in Malawi, arriving some time on Friday, before starting the return voyage to Itungi. The smaller MV *Iringa* leaves Itungi at 07.00 on Tuesday and arrives back on Wednesday afternoon. This stops at most lakeside villages, including Matema, but doesn't go as far as Mbamba Bay. The above timings are *very* approximate. Due to the unpredictable nature of the service you are best advised to check the current schedule with the TRC office just outside of Kyela. Tickets cost US$10/4 first/second class. Meals are available on board, as are sodas and beers.

More comfortable than either of the above boats is the Malawian MV *Ilala*, which normally crosses between Nkhata Bay and Mbamba Bay and back once weekly. In theory, it leaves Nkhata Bay at 01.00 on Tuesday morning, arrives at Mbamba Bay three to four hours later, and then starts the return trip at 07.30. In practice, the MV *Ilala* is just about always six to twelve hours behind schedule, and when it falls too far behind, the crossing to Mbamba Bay is omitted from its weekly voyage.

There is no accommodation in Itungi or Kiwira. You will have to spend the night in Kyela and get a vehicle to the port at around 05.30 on the morning of departure. Vehicles leave from in front of the TRC office, 1km out of town. There is a booking office at the TRC building, but as the ticket officer travels with the ferry it serves no practical function. You can buy a ticket while you wait for the ferry to be loaded up. If you go all the way to Mbamba Bay there is a fair selection of accommodation there, as well as transport on to Makambako (on the Tanzam Highway) via Mbinga, Songea and Njombe, all of which boast several guesthouses. See our website, http://bradttanzania.wordpress.com, for more details of this route.

Getting there and away The normal approach route to Kyela is the 140km road from Mbeya, which passes through Tukuyu at the midway point and is surfaced except for the last 5km stretch between the junction to Songwe (on the Malawi border) and Kyela itself. In a private vehicle, this road can be covered in two-and-a-bit hours without stops, while regular buses from Mbeya take about four hours, stopping at Tukuyu on the way. This is one of the most scenic roads in Tanzania, so be sure to get a window seat. Regular minibuses run between Kyela and Tukuyu, taking one hour to make the journey, and Mbeya taking around three hours.

Buses from Mbeya all stop at the junction for the Songwe border post, 5km before the road from Mbeya enters Kyela, from where it is normally easy enough to catch a lift to the border post, though bicycle taxis are also available. Be warned that if you are intending to travel through to Kyela, local bus conductors are used to foreign travellers disembarking at this junction, and it may require some convincing before they accept that you know what you are doing! Arriving at the border in the late afternoon used to be unwise, because there was no accommodation, and transport on to Karonga in northern Malawi was thin on the ground. These days, however, there is an excellent guesthouse at the border (see *Where to stay* below) and there is also plenty of onward transport.

The ferries on Lake Nyasa normally leave from Itungi Port 10km from Kyela. At the time of writing, however, Itungi Port was closed, with services departing from the makeshift Kiwira Port 16km from Kyela. Itungi Port is reached via a tar road from Kyela, while a clearly signposted dirt road branches off this road to Kiwira. There is a ferry office about 1km out of town towards Itungi where departure times should be confirmed in advance. For further details, see the box, *Lake Nyasa Ferries*, opposite.

Where to stay
Moderate
Kyela Resort 025 254 0158;
e kyelaresort@yahoo.com. Arguably better than anything in town, this pleasant new lodge 1.5km from town just off the road to Tukuyu offers quiet, clean en-suite rooms with fans, mosquito nets & hot water. There's also a decent garden restaurant. *Tsh25,000/35,000 sgl/dbl.*

Matema Beach Hotel (30 rooms) \/f 025 254 0158; e matemabeach2002@yahoo.com. This

confusingly named hotel (it's nowhere near the beach & certainly not in Matema!) 500m before the turn-off to Kyela is another well-priced new option just out of town. The attached restaurant serves meals in the Tsh1,000–3,000 range. *Tsh20,000/25,000 spacious en-suite sgl/dbl with AC & TV;Tsh30,000 executive suite with computer & internet, sitting room & balcony.*

Budget
The Oberoi Park (8 rooms) 025 254 0395. This smart hotel 200m from the bus station has spotless en-suite rooms with dbl bed, fan & running water. It's easily the best place in the centre, though the lack of mosquito netting in this climate is a serious oversight. *Tsh10,000 dbl.*

MSM Lodge This agreeable lodge is situated in Songwe about 1km before the border post with Malawi. All rooms have fans, netting & running water. There is a beer garden & snack bar in the green grounds. *Tsh7,000/8,000 sgl/dbl banda with common showers;Tsh9,000/10,000 en-suite.*

Shoestring
Pattaya Hotel 025 254 0015. Also quite close to the bus station, this is an above average guesthouse & the rooms are clean & have fans, but once again no mosquito netting! *Tsh7,000/8,000 en-suite dbl/twin.*

Makete Half London Guesthouse (7 rooms) Situated right opposite the bus station & market, this has rather gloomy though reasonably clean en-suite rooms with fan & mosquito netting. *Tsh7,000 dbl.*

✕ Where to eat The **New Steak Inn Restaurant**, opposite the market, is clean and comfortable, and while the tantalisingly elaborate menu rather overstates the culinary options, it does serve a decent plate of chicken and chips for Tsh1,500.

MATEMA BEACH The long sandy tropical beach at Matema is perhaps the most beautiful anywhere on Lake Nyasa–Malawi. Situated on the lake's northern tip, Matema lies in the shadow of the Livingstone Mountains, which rise sharply to an elevation of nearly 2,500m within 4km of the lakeshore, with the Poroto Mountains set further back on the western horizon. Matema Beach is relatively undeveloped for tourism, certainly by comparison with such legendary Malawian backpacker hangouts as Nkhata Bay or Cape Maclear – which has its pros and cons. On the minus side are the facilities, which might politely be described as unexciting: a couple of decent if decidedly institutional church-run lodges that serve basic meals of the fish-and-*ugali* ilk and operate a no-alcohol

KISI POTTERY

The small Kisi tribe, which lives in a series of villages along the northwest shore of Lake Nyasa, is renowned throughout Tanzania and northern Malawi for the high-quality and distinctively pale pottery it produces. The pots are made exclusively by women – Kisi men, like their peers elsewhere along the lake, are dedicated fishermen – and were originally made for home use and to trade with neighbouring tribes for agricultural produce. These days, however, Kisi pottery has been transformed into a lucrative cottage industry, the product of which is sold in bulk to traders at the Saturday market at Lyulilo near Matema, for distribution to larger markets in Kyela, Mbeya, Dar es Salaam, Karonga (in northern Malawi) and further afield.

About a dozen types of pot are made by Kisi women, each with a specific purpose. The largest pots, with a capacity of about 25 litres, are called *ngumbe* and used to store various grains. The smallest *tukalango* pots, by contrast, are about the size of a moderate saucepan and used exclusively for cooking. Younger women customarily learn their craft by making *tukalango*, graduating stage by stage to crafting *ngumbe* as they grow in age and skill.

The technique used by the potters is unique within Tanzania. First, a ball of unmoulded clay is placed on a circular plate and hollowed out with two hands to form a rudimentary bowl. The potter will then rotate the plate manually with one hand, while refining and evening the pot with the other. A white clay finish is then applied to the outside of the completed pot using a maize cob or a smooth pebble. The unfired pot will then be left out to sun-dry for a few days, before being decorated in geometric patterns using an ochre paste. Finally, once a sufficient number of pots are ready, they will be fired using a method similar to the one used by traditional brick-makers throughout rural Africa. A layer of banana leaves and firewood is placed in a depression, the pots are arranged on top of this, and then smothered with a thick cover of grass, to be left for about two hours in the smouldering fire.

Although the main Kisi pottery market is within easy walking distance of Matema, the bulk of the pottery sold there is produced at the village of Ikombe, which is situated close to a feldspar outcrop that gives the Kisi clay its attractive creamy white coloration. Ikombe lies only 30 minutes from Matema by local canoe, and visitors are welcome. If you are interested in a souvenir, the pots are very affordable, particularly if bought locally, where they sell for about a quarter of the price asked in Dar es Salaam.

policy. The flip side of the coin is that Matema, unlike the more popular and buzzing Malawian beach hangouts, doesn't yet come across as a budding resort whose soul is gradually being eroded in order to accommodate the requirements of international travellers. Refreshingly rustic and uncompromisingly African, Matema is the kind of place you could settle into for a while: swimming in the deliciously warm (and reputedly bilharzia-free) water, chatting to the local fishermen, undertaking local excursions, or just waiting for the sun to set behind the Poroto.

Getting there and away The two main roads to Matema converge at the small junction town of Ipinda, about 10km inland of the lake as the crow flies and 27km from Matema by road. Coming from Mbeya or Kyela, the normal route to Matema leads from the surfaced road between these two towns about 3km north of Kyela, from where it's a straightforward 14km run to Ipinda. Coming from Mbeya, a rougher but shorter 46km back route to Ipinda, via Masoko Crater Lake, runs from Tukuyu, where you need to turn left at the main intersection on the Kyela road, passing Langboss Lodge to your left after about 1km.

Direct public transport to Matema is restricted to a daily bus to and from Mbeya, passing through Tukuyu, Kyela and Ipinda, but since this bus arrives at Matema after dark and leaves again at 05.00, it's not all that convenient. It is easier to get to Matema using light vehicles. If you can't find a pick-up truck running directly between Kyela and Matema, you should find one from Kyela to Ipinda. There is also the odd pick-up truck running between Tukuyu and Ipinda via Masoko Crater Lake. The daily bus aside, there is normally some private transport between Ipinda and Matema, especially on Saturdays, and most vehicles will stop to pick up passengers for a small fee. Should you need to spend the night in Ipinda, there is a basic but adequate guesthouse behind the bank. It is also possible to walk between Ipinda and Matema in two to three hours, following the Lufirio River to its mouth 3km west of the mission. On the day before you plan to leave Matema, it's worth asking the mission whether any of their vehicles are heading to Ipinda the next morning.

The ferry that leaves Kiwira/Itungi at 07.00 Wednesday arrives at Matema an hour later. It also stops at Matema on Thursday afternoon on its way back to Kiwira/Itungi. Ferries to Mbamba Bay *do not* stop at Matema. The Lutheran Guesthouse in Matema can arrange for a local canoe to take you to Itungi Port for Tsh2,000, and it should presumably be possible to make a similar arrangement privately for a transfer in the opposite direction.

Where to stay
Moderate
⌂ **Matema Lake Shore Resort** (8 rooms) ゝ/f 025 250 4178; e mec@maf.org.tz. This smart resort, which lies on an attractive stretch of beach on the western fringe of Matema village, is popular with expatriate families. Accommodation consists of a row of comfortable en-suite double-storey beachfront chalets with private verandas. A restaurant serves decent meals & chilled soft drinks, but no alcohol. *Tsh20,000/30/60,000 for a 2/3/5-bed unit.*

Budget and camping
⌂ **Lutheran Guest House** ゝ 025 255 2598. This well established guesthouse, immediately below the main roundabout in the village, consists of numerous small *bandas*, each with 2–4 comfortable beds & mosquito nets, clustered above the beach. Several of the rooms are starting to look decidedly mildewed & scruffy. A beach kiosk sells cold sodas & coffee/tea, & a canteen serves substantial but uninteresting set meals, which must be ordered in advance & cost around Tsh3,000 pp. Although no alcohol is served, a small kiosk on the roundabout above the hostel sells lukewarm beers. *Tsh15,000/25,000 dbl/quad en-suite; Tsh10,000 dbl with common showers.*

The penultimate stop on the southbound ferry trip from Itungi to Mbamba Bay is Liuli, whose attractive natural harbour is looked over by the sphinx-like rock formation referred to by its German name, Sphinxhafen. Liuli hosts the largest mission in this part of Tanzania, and it's the burial place of William Johnson, the Anglican missionary who co-founded the Likoma Mission on the eponymous island in Malawi. Johnson is one of the most fondly remembered missionaries who worked in the Lake Nyasa area; for 46 years he preached all around the lake, despite being practically blind and well into his 70s when he died in 1928. His grave at Liuli was for several decades a pilgrimage site for Malawian Christians.

Somewhat improbably, Liuli witnessed the first naval encounter of World War I, an incident trumpeted by *The Times* in London as 'Naval Victory on Lake Nyasa' and by a participant, Mr G M Sanderson, as 'pure comedy'. Shortly after the outbreak of war, the British Commissioner of Nyasaland dispatched the protectorate's only ship, the *Gwendolyn*, to destroy its German counterpart, the *Hermann Von Wessman*. The *Gwendolyn's* captain, Commander Rhoades, was informed at Nkhata Bay that the *Wessman* was docked for repairs at Sphinxhafen. He sailed into the harbour in the cover of dawn with a somewhat nervous crew. The only gunner was a Scots storeman who had trained several years previously as a seaman-gunner and who freely admitted that he remembered little of his training. After several misfires, caused by a combination of dud ammunition and rusty aiming, a shell finally connected with the German boat.

'Immediately afterwards,' wrote Sanderson several years later, 'a small white dinghy put off from shore, in which was a European clad in a singlet and a pair of shorts pulling furiously for the *Gwen*. Rhoades ordered "Cease fire" and blessed silence fell. It was his drinking pal [Captain Berndt], the skipper of the *Wessman*, with whom every meeting was a drinking party. The dinghy came alongside and its furious occupant leaped to his feet and, shaking both fists above his head, exclaimed "Gott for dam, Rrroades, vos you drunk?"' It transpired that news of the war had not yet reached sleepy Sphinxhafen, and when Rhoades informed his old friend that he was now a prisoner of war, Sanderson wrote that 'one could see his anger turn to horror as he realised his fatal mistake.'

Excursions from Matema Beach In the stifling heat of the lakeshore even the shortest stroll can feel like a major excursion, for which reason the best time to explore is the early morning. One pleasant 15-minute stroll leads along the beach east of Matema to the small fishing village of **Lyulilo**, renowned locally for its Saturday **pottery market** (see box, *Kisi pottery*, page 534). If you walk out there along the beach, you might want to return by a rough dirt road that runs a short distance inland, passing through lush tropical vegetation – plenty of birdlife – and neat traditional Nyakyusa homesteads.

Close to the lakeshore, about 500m past Lyulilo, **Pango Cave** (also known as Likyala Cave) was an important Nyakyusa sacrificial site in times of drought, before missionaries arrived in the area and forbade the practice. The cave harbours a significant bat colony, and a small waterfall close by tumbles into a cool, clear pool. The rocky lakeshore between Lyulilo and the cave hosts a large variety of colourful cichlids, and makes for excellent snorkelling, but you'll need your own gear to explore it. If you don't feel like walking, the Lutheran Mission can arrange a local boat to take you to the market or cave for around Tsh1,000 per person.

Although the main regional pottery market is held at Lyulilo, the pots are mostly crafted at the village of **Ikombe**, which is the place to visit if you want to see potters at work or buy pottery on days other than Saturday. Ikombe can be reached on foot by following a rough footpath along the lakeshore past Lyulilo. Better, however, to travel there by canoe, which takes about 30 minutes in each direction, and costs Tsh1,500 for the round trip if organised through the Lutheran Mission in Matema.

In the opposite direction, heading along the beach for about 3km west of Matema, the extensive papyrus beds at the **Lufirio River mouth** offer excellent birding as well as a chance of seeing crocodiles. Hippos are resident a short distance upriver. Once again, you have the option of walking from Matema or of arranging a local canoe at the Lutheran Mission, which costs Tsh2,000 per person for the round trip.

A one-hour walk inland of the beach leads to the **Mwalalo Waterfall** – or more accurately a series of waterfalls formed by the Mwalalo River as it tumbles down the escarpment of the Livingstone Mountains. The Mwalalo River is the sole source of fresh water for the village and mission, who are concerned that travellers visiting without a guide might pollute it. For this reason, you need permission from the village council and a local guide to visit the waterfall, all of which can be easily arranged through the mission for Tsh2,000 per person. More energetically, the mission can also arrange guided day walks up the **Livingstone Mountains**.

One warning: crocodiles are not resident on Matema Beach, but they are common on rockier and shallower stretches of the lakeshore and at river outlets, where they kill villagers with a frequency that suggests you should definitely ask local advice before swimming, except on the main beach. Best, too, to avoid swimming anywhere after dark – crocs have been known to travel long distances at night.

The Southern Highlands and Lake Nyasa **LAKE NYASA**

17

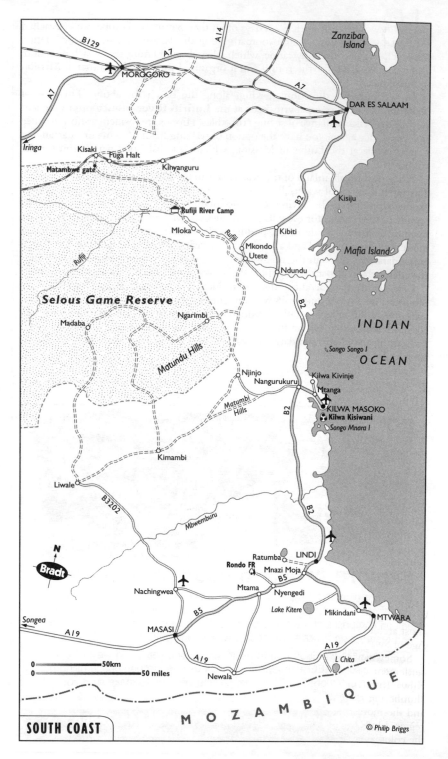

18

The South Coast

The 600km coastline that stretches south from Dar es Salaam to the Rovuma River on the Mozambican border is one of the least touristed corners of East Africa. The region is not quite so remote as it was a few years back, thanks to the recent upgrading of the main road between Dar es Salaam and Mtwara, and the advent of modest tourist-class accommodation in the main centres of Kilwa Masoko, Lindi, Mikindani and Mtwara. Nevertheless, it is unlikely to hold much appeal to travellers who place a high priority on creature comforts.

Low-key facilities aside, the south coast is a fascinating, thought-provoking and often enchanting area, endlessly rewarding to those with a sense of adventure and curiosity. Older towns such as Kilwa Kivinje, Lindi and Mikindani are steeped in coastal history, their roads lined with crumbling German and Arab buildings, a time-warped architectural milieu underscored by the gracious pace of life enjoyed by their Swahili inhabitants.

Scenically, the south coast is all you might expect: stunning palm-lined beaches, thick mangrove swamps, with baobab-studded acacia scrub stretching inland. And, while there is an element of travel for its own sake attached to exploring this region, it does boast one genuine travel highlight in the form of Kilwa Kisiwani and Songo Mnara, inscribed as a UNESCO World Heritage Site in 1981 in recognition of their status as the most impressive and historically significant of the ruined medieval cities that line Africa's Indian Ocean coast.

KILWA

Halfway between Dar es Salaam and the Mozambican border, the 20km² island of Kilwa – 'Place of Fish' – is separated from the mainland by a palm-fringed channel no more than 2km wide. Today, the small island supports a fishing community of around 300 people, but in medieval times it housed the most important settlement on the east coast of Africa, the hub of a thriving international trade dominated by gold mined in the distant highlands of present-day Zimbabwe, immortalised as Quiloa in Milton's Paradise Lost and once thought to be the site of King Solomon's mythical mines. And what does survive of the abandoned city – the haunted mosques, derelict palaces and lonely tombs – stands today as the most architecturally impressive and expansive testament to the so-called Golden Age of Swahili.

Somewhat confusingly, the name Kilwa now applies to three neighbouring settlements: the island-bound ruined city and adjacent fishing village is called Kilwa Kisiwani (Kilwa on the Island), while the facing mainland hosts the slumbering 19th-century settlement of Kilwa Kivinje (Kilwa of the Casuarinas) and the more modern town of Kilwa Masoko (Kilwa of the Market), the main regional hub of commerce, administration, transport and accommodation since the colonial era.

For visitors, the main point of interest here is history and architecture – Kilwa Kisiwani and Kivinje are possibly unique in containing well-preserved buildings that represent virtually every era over the past millennium of coastal history. But Kilwa is also a good place to immerse yourself in a traditional Swahili port-cum-fishing-village culture, and the surrounding coast is very attractive, with good angling and diving possibilities for those who can afford them.

HISTORY Neglected by Tanzania's safari-based tourist industry and universally ignored in modern school curricula, Kilwa, in its medieval pomp, was the most important settlement in subequatorial Africa. For more than 300 years it was the commercial pivot of a gold trading network that linked the interior of present-day Zimbabwe to Arabia, China and India. The most widely travelled man of the age, Ibn Battuta, ranked it as 'one of the most beautiful and well-constructed cities in the world'. And the city's finest buildings – the Great Mosque and the Sultan's Palace or Husuni Kubwa – formed the undisputed apex of Swahili architectural aspirations. Fortunately, while many details of Kilwa past are open to conjecture, the combination of archaeological excavations, a few surviving contemporary descriptions and two known versions of the *Kilwa Chronicle* (written in 1520 under the supervision of the then-exiled sultan) means that the history of Kilwa is better understood than that of most medieval Swahili settlements.

Early settlement Kilwa Kisiwani was occupied by the Shirazi precursors of the Swahili in about AD800, though little is known about this early period. In 1150, the island was settled by Ali bin Al-Hasan, whose father, according to the *Kilwa Chronicle*, had a dream in Shiraz in which 'he saw a rat with an iron snout gnawing holes in the town wall … a prophecy of the ruin of their country'. The father and his six sons set sail for East Africa, where they disembarked at seven different ports. According to this tradition, Ali was known locally as Nguo Myingi ('many clothes') after having traded Kilwa Kisiwani with the 'infidel king' of the facing mainland, in exchange for a quantity of cloth, 'some white, some black, and every other colour besides' sufficient to 'encircle the island'.

Tradition has it that Ali bin Al-Hasan ruled over Kilwa for 40 years, and his importance can be gauged by the fact that coins bearing his name – probably minted long after his death – have been found as far afield as Pemba and Mafia islands. The dynasty he founded endured for 150 years, and is widely credited with having established Kilwa as a significant trade centre, whose sphere of influence stretched at least as far as Mafia and quite possibly beyond it. The earliest surviving reference to Kilwa is in an Arabic document written in 1222, and while it is less than illuminating ('a town in the country of the Zanj', if you really want to know), it does confirm that Kilwa was by then a trade centre of significance.

Another Arabic document, written a few years later, goes further in describing Kilwa as the principal port between Mogadishu and Madagascar, confirming that the island port flourished under Ali bin Al-Hasan and his successors. Kilwa does, however, seem to have entered a period of political (though perhaps not economic) turmoil in the late 13th century, initiated by repeated conflicts with the indigenous Shanga Kingdom of the nearby island of Sanje ya Kati. According to the *Kilwa Chronicle*, the Sultan of Kilwa was during this period twice overthrown by the Shanga, who installed their leader in his place, though in both instances the upstart ruler was soon deposed by the islanders and a sultan of the Al-Hasan dynasty reinstalled. This instability in turn seems to have prompted a series of internal coups, culminating in 1300 with the ascent of Sultan Al-Hasan Mahdali, founder of the Mahdali dynasty.

Kilwa's pre-eminence during the early 14th century is linked to broader patterns associated with the medieval gold trade out of Africa. The inland source of this gold was long shrouded in mystery, and gave rise to such myths as King Solomon's Mines. However, we now know that the gold was mined in the vicinity of Great Zimbabwe, the fabulous stone ruin for which the country Zimbabwe is named.

The exact mechanism of trade between Great Zimbabwe and the coast remains a matter of conjecture. It seems likely that the gold was carried by foot along the Zambezi Valley to the coastal port of Sofala (near modern-day Beira in Mozambique). It is assumed that, prior to the mid 13th century, local middlemen transported it northward along the coast from Sofala to Mogadishu (in present-day Somalia), which was then the most important trade centre on the Swahili Coast – presumably reflecting the inability of contemporary Arab vessels to sail much further south within the annual monsoon cycle.

As the volume of coastal trade increased, however, improvements in Arab navigation and ship design allowed them to penetrate steadily further south. But Sofala would have been beyond their reach whatever they did, since the winds south of Kilwa are notoriously fickle. Nevertheless, it would have suited the merchants of Sofala to bring the centre of trade closer to home. And Kilwa would have been the ideal compromise: much closer to Sofala than Mogadishu or Mombasa, but still within reach of the Arab vessels. By the early 14th century, Sofala and Kilwa had assumed joint control of the gold trade, and it is often suggested that the Mahdali dynasty of Kilwa had its roots in Sofala.

That Kilwa and Great Zimbabwe were the most important subequatorial African cities of their age is beyond question. And clearly the prosperity of either city was dependent on that of the other. Yet the only surviving physical evidence of this link is a solitary Kilwa-minted coin that was unearthed at Great Zimbabwe a few decades back. Cultural and architectural parallels between the two cities are non-existent – indeed, no evidence exists to suggest that the coastal traders ever visited, or indeed knew of, Great Zimbabwe.

The Golden Age Al-Hasan Mahdali's was a short reign, as was that of his son and successor Sulaiman, who was killed by followers of the old sultan. Stability was finally restored during the reign of Sultan Al-Hasan bin Sulaiman (1310–32), a highly respected scholar who had studied in Aden and made the pilgrimage to Mecca, and it was maintained during that of his brother Daud bin Sulaiman (1332–56). These two brothers presided over what was almost certainly Kilwa's peak in international prominence and commercial prosperity. Al-Hasan is generally credited with the reconstruction of the Great Mosque and the domed extension to that building, and it was also he who built the splendid out-of-town palace now known as the Husuni Kubwa.

Kilwa at this time was the dominant town on the coast, with a population exceeding 10,000, the first coin mint in sub-Saharan Africa, and an extensive system of wells (the last still in use today). The Friday Mosque and Husuni Kubwa, the most impressive buildings on the island, if not the entire coast, date to this period. In addition to gold, Kilwa exported ivory and ebony, and imported such fineries as Eastern cloth and Chinese porcelain. The wealthy traders lived in houses of coral and some had small private mosques. Ordinary townsmen lived in mud-and-wattle huts. Even though some Arab traders settled on Kilwa, the vast majority of its occupants were local Swahili. The island was too small to be self-sufficient in food, so had extensive agricultural interests on the mainland. The only

18

surviving description of Kilwa in this era, penned by Ibn Battuta, the greatest globetrotter of his era, is reproduced in the box, *Kilwa in 1331*, page 547.

Towards the end of Sultan Duad's rule, the maritime gold trade through Kilwa slowed almost to a standstill. The cause of this unexpected slump must have baffled the islanders, but almost certainly it was linked to the King of Timbuktu's trans-Saharan trek to the Mediterranean a few years earlier. Timbuktu, at this time, was the Sahelian equivalent of Kilwa, the trade funnel for gold mined in the rainforests of west Africa, and when its king arrived in Cairo, he carried such an abundance of golden gifts that the gold market temporarily collapsed. The long voyage south to Kilwa must suddenly have looked financially unattractive to Arabian merchants who could as easily pick up other popular trade items, such as ivory and tortoiseshell, further north. The loss of trade, possibly exacerbated by the Black Death that struck much of Europe and Arabia over 1346–49, caused a serious economic slump in Kilwa, presumably the reason why the Husuni Kubwa was abandoned after the death of Sultan Daud. For the next 50 years, Kilwa was almost forgotten by the outside world.

Revival and decline In the early 15th century, a sudden increase in the demand for gold across Europe and Arabia sparked a reversal in Kilwa's fortunes. The Arabian ships started to arrive as regularly as they had in the commercial heyday of the 1330s, and although the Husuni Kubwa remained in disuse, the town centre experienced a huge influx of wealth and a corresponding construction boom. The Great Mosque was fully renovated, several ornate smaller mosques were built, and Makutani Palace was erected to house the incumbent Sultan Muhammad bin Sulaiman (1412–21) and his son and successor Al Malik bin Muhammad (1421–41), the latter regarded as one of the island's greatest leaders.

For reasons that are unclear, Kilwa seems to have slid backwards economically after Al Malik's death – a protracted succession dispute described in somewhat confusing terms in the *Kilwa Chronicle* might have been a factor in this. Kilwa remained an important trade centre, but Mombasa was steadily in the ascendant from 1450 onwards, and it had probably become the dominant coastal trade centre well before the end of the 15th century.

In 1498, the Portuguese explorer Vasco Da Gama rounded the Cape and sailed up the east coast on his way to establishing trade links with India. He described Kilwa in detail, but as he was not allowed to go near the island, his report is probably pure fabrication. Da Gama received an equally hostile reception in Mombasa, but did meet with the sultan there, who may have exaggerated the declining Kilwa's strength to frighten the Portuguese away from the coast. Da Gama's description of Kilwa might explain why the island was so heavily targeted when the Portuguese took over the coast in 1505. Three-quarters of Kilwa's residents were killed or forced to flee. A Portuguese fort was built, the gold trade moved to Mozambique and the sultan exiled to the mainland.

Little is known of events on and around Kilwa over the next 250 years. The Portuguese fort that would later form the foundation of the Omani Gereza was abandoned in 1512, when most of the garrison succumbed to malaria. In 1587, the island's 3,000 remaining residents were rounded up and imprisoned, to become rations for the cannibalistic Zimba. An Omani settlement reported to be on the island in 1712 had vanished by 1719.

The rise of Kilwa Kivinje The first indication of Kilwa's re-emergence as a trade centre, and of the nature of its future trade, came in 1776 when the Sultan of Kilwa – presumably of Shirazi or indigenous descent – signed a contract to provide a French merchant from Mauritius with 1,000 slaves annually. That treaty fell through in 1784 when Kilwa was attacked by, and made subject to, the Sultan of Oman. The island was reoccupied by Omani agents, who left their mark in the form of the large fort (Gereza) on the waterfront, and minor restoration work to the Great Mosque and Makutani Palace.

In 1812, when HMS *Nisus* anchored off Kilwa, James Prior noted that the Gereza was still in use as the Omani governor's residence, but was unimpressed by the scattering of thatch huts that comprised the town, 'if town it should be called'. Within a few years, the Omani settlers evacuated the island to establish the mainland town of Kilwa Kivinje. Kilwa Kisiwani went into terminal decline thereafter – the last Sultan of Kilwa, interviewed by Lieutenant Christopher of the *Tigris* in 1846, was captured by the Sultan of Zanzibar and sent into exile before 1856.

Within years of its establishment, Kilwa Kivinje had become the centre of the southern slave trade. By the mid 19th century it was a very wealthy town, with up to 20,000 slaves passing through annually. Although the Sultan of Zanzibar outlawed the slave trade in 1873, it persisted out of Kilwa for longer than anywhere else, but had been stopped almost entirely by 1880. Many of Kilwa's slave traders established rubber plantations, and business continued to prosper. In 1886, Kilwa Kivinje became a German administrative centre, and it remained a town of regional importance during the first half of the 20th century. Since the end of World War II it has gradually been reduced to backwater status, with the more modern town of Kilwa Masoko serving as the regional headquarters.

GETTING THERE AND AWAY

By air Coastal Aviation (m *0784 875762; www.coastal.cc*) runs a daily return flight between Dar es Salaam and Kilwa Masoko, stopping at Mafia Island or continuing on to Zanzibar by request. It costs US$130 one-way, takes one hour, and leaves Dar at 17.00 and Kilwa at 18.15. The airstrip lies about 500m from the town centre.

By road Kilwa is about 300km south of Dar es Salaam along a vastly improved road – all but 50km is surfaced – and the drive should take four to five hours in a private vehicle. At least one bus daily for Kilwa (Tsh8,000) leaves Dar es Salaam at 06.00 from the obscurely located Ubungo terminal; ideally, book your ticket a day in advance and arrange to be collected by a taxi on the morning of departure. The return service leaves Kilwa Masoko at around 05.30 and passes through Kilwa Kivinje 30 minutes later to pick up passengers departing from there. Kilwa Masoko and Kilwa Kivinje aren't on the main coastal road but lie 12km east of the small junction town of Nangurukuru. There is plenty of public transport between the three towns.

KILWA MASOKO This friendly modern town is the most useful base in the Kilwa area, though it's of less inherent interest than its more antiquated namesakes. The nominal town centre, a small grid of dirt roads emanating from a central market, lies about 1km inland of the harbour, to which it is connected by a tar road. All the cheaper accommodation is in the town centre near the market, while most government buildings and banks are found along the main tar road towards the harbour. The smarter lodges lie along an attractively sandy baobab-lined beach a few hundred metres east of the main tar road (to get there, turn left at the CCM buildings, near the statue of a man running).

Where to stay and eat

Upmarket

Kilwa Ruins Lodge [544 C4] (14 rooms)
0024 906775, e info@kllwaruinslodge.com; www.kilwaruinslodge.com. Catering first & foremost to anglers, this new lodge on the beach outside Kilwa Masoko has charter boats available as well as other fishing & watersport equipment. Facilities include a

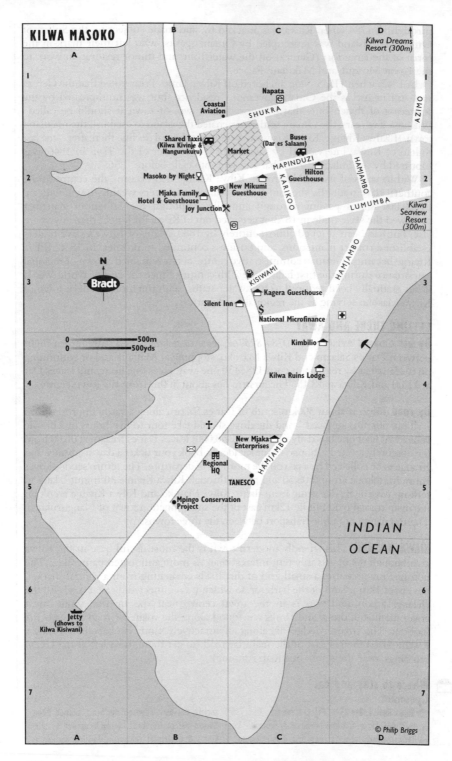

KILWA MASOKO

Kilwa Dreams
Resort (300m)

A

SHUKRA

Napata

Coastal
Aviation

Shared Taxis
(Kilwa Kivinje &
Nangurukuru)

Market

Buses
(Dar es Salaam)

MAPINDUZI

Hilton
Guesthouse

Masoko by Night

BP

New Mikumi
Guesthouse

Mjaka Family
Hotel & Guesthouse

Joy Junction

KARIKOO

LUMUMBA

HAMJAMBO

AZIMO

Kilwa
Seaview
Resort
(300m)

KISIWAMI

Kagera Guesthouse

Silent Inn

National Microfinance

HAMJAMBO

Kimbilio

Kilwa Ruins Lodge

N

Bradt

0 — 500m
0 — 500yds

New Mjaka
Enterprises

Regional
HQ

HAMJAMBO

TANESCO

Mpingo Conservation
Project

INDIAN
OCEAN

Jetty
(dhows to
Kilwa Kisiwani)

© Philip Briggs

544

good restaurant, satellite TV, pool table & swimming pool, all set on a lovely tropical beach. 3 types of en-suite accommodation are available: mahogany-clad dbl bungalows with sea-facing verandas, beach bungalows with 2 dbl rooms & AC, & deluxe 6-person beach chalets with AC. *US$120–175pp FB depending on room type.*

⌂ **Kimbilio Hotel** [544 C4] (6 rooms) m 0787 034021/211201; e info@kimbiliolodges.com;

Moderate

⌂ **Kilwa Seaview Resort** [544 D2] (12 rooms) \ 022 265 0250; e info@kilwa.net; www.kilwa.net. This attractive beachfront lodge on the fringe of Kilwa Masoko is under the same German management as Selous Mbega Lodge & equally good value. Accommodation is in comfortable & spacious en-suite bungalows with tall *makuti* roofs, & there's a good restaurant (superb 3-course seafood dinners for Tsh8,000) & swimming pool (empty of water on the most recent inspection). The beach is a few paces from the rooms, & excursions

Budget and shoestring

⌂ **New Mjaka Enterprises Hotel** [544 B2 & 544 C5] \ 023 201 3071. The dominant force in Kilwa's local accommodation scene since the 1st edition of this book was published, the Mjaka family now operates a veritable chain of inexpensive hotels &

www.kimbiliolodges.com. Opened in 2008, this latest addition to Kilwa's burgeoning beach resort scene offers comfortable accommodation in cool *makuti* beachfront huts with dbl or twin beds, nets & effective natural ventilation. Fishing trips & excursions to the ruins are offered, & it's the site of the only diving operation in Kilwa. The Italian manager is a chef & promises excellent seafood & pasta dishes. *US$70/120 sgl/dbl B&B, US$120/180 FB.*

to Kilwa Kisiwani & Songo Mnara are offered. *US$80/90 B&B sgl/dbl; camping US$5 pp.*

⌂ **Kilwa Dreams** [544 D1] (7 rooms) m 0784 585330; e info@kilwadreams.com; www.kilwadreams.com. Situated on Pwani Beach about 3km (well signposted) from the town centre, this small owner-managed lodge caters mainly to anglers & offers accommodation in a string of airy, gaudy blue cottages literally 10m from the sea. There's a good seafood restaurant with DSTV, & a very peaceful isolated atmosphere. *US$60 dbl B&B.*

guesthouses, 3 of which are clustered around the main junction a block from the market, while the 4th is at the beach near Kimbilio. *From Tsh5,000 sgl with common shower to Tsh25,000 en-suite cottage.*

What to see Kilwa Masoko forms a base for several day trips. The main point of local interest is the ruins on the facing island of Kilwa Kisiwani, but nearby Kilwa Kivinje is also easily visited and worthwhile in its own right. Further afield, there are more ruins at Songo Mnara, but these are relatively costly to visit. The more remote Matumbi Caves of the interior form part of the online content on our website, http://bradttanzania.wordpress.com.

Other activities arranged by most of the lodges listed in the upmarket and moderate categories include boat trips to a nearby creek inhabited by hippos and crocs, and angling expeditions into the Kilwa Channel, which supports large numbers of giant marlin, yellowfin, dorodo and kingfish, with the best months being from August to April. The offshore reefs and islands are rich in diving possibilities: the only dive operator in Kilwa runs out of the Kimbilio Hotel [544 C4] (see contact details above) and charges US$60/100 per person for a single/double dive.

KILWA KISIWANI The half-day round excursion to the ruins on Kilwa Kisiwani can be arranged through any lodge in Kilwa Masoko for around Tsh20,000 per person, or for about half that price if you make your own arrangements, and for next to nothing if you use public transport. Permits (Tsh1,500) are issued without fuss from the Department of Antiquities in the District Commissioner's Office on the main road near the harbour (⊙ *07.30–15.00 Mon–Fri*). Most travellers visit Kilwa Kisiwani as a day trip, but you could ask here about staying in the Department of Antiquities' resthouse on the island – a cheap, basic and

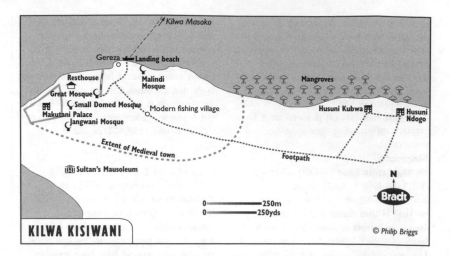

KILWA KISIWANI

somewhat bat-ridden set-up that nevertheless offers the rather wonderful opportunity to be among these atmospheric ruins after dark, and to explore them in the gorgeous dawn and dusk light.

The office can also help organise a fishing dhow charter (around Tsh10,000 per party for the round trip) or you can just head down to the dhow harbour, pay the statutory Tsh200 harbour tax, and wait for the next public dhow to cross (Tsh200pp). The trip usually takes 15–30 minutes each way, though in becalmed conditions it's been known to take an hour. Upon reaching the island, you'll be met by one of the two caretaker/guides, who speak little English and are less than fully conversant with the island's history, but are otherwise very helpful.

The partially collapsed quadrangular building that first draws the eye when you sail across to the island is called the **Gereza**. This Swahili word, meaning prison, is derived from a Portuguese word meaning church, but the Gereza on Kilwa is actually a fort built by Omani Arabs in about 1800. It has thick coral walls and an impressive arched door, and incorporates the walls of a smaller Portuguese fort built in 1505.

Uphill from the Gereza, you pass through the small modern village before arriving in the **medieval city centre**. It is difficult to gain much of a feel for the layout of the original town, since many of the smaller stone buildings have vanished without trace, largely through the removal of rubble as building material. But the most important structures – the mosques and palaces – have been left untouched, largely because they are still sanctified by locals.

The **Great Mosque**, which would have been the focal point of spiritual life in medieval Kilwa, is the largest coastal mosque of its period, with 30 bays covering about 100m², and the best preserved and most aesthetically satisfying of all extant Shirazi buildings. The original mosque, erected *circa* 1050 under Ali bin Al-Hasan, was more modest in ambition than the present structure, and reputedly collapsed in the late 13th century. It was rebuilt in about 1320 under Sultan al-Hasan bin Sulaiman, who elaborated on the original design by adding an imposing wing of 16 domed ceiling cupolas supported by rows of tall arches – unquestionably the mosque's distinguishing architectural features. These ostentatious flourishes, intended to show off the contemporary wealth and sophistication of Kilwa, may also reflect architectural influences absorbed during the sultan's pilgrimage to Mecca as a teenager. It is to the immense credit of the masons involved that their handiwork remains in such fine shape almost 700 years later.

Close to the Great Mosque, the so-called **Small Domed Mosque** dates to the 15th century and is also built over an older structure. This mosque has three bays, three aisles and seven ceiling domes, some still intact, but its fine decorations have been removed by modern visitors. Closer to the Gereza, the **Malindi Mosque** is a 15th-century construction associated with settlers from Malindi (Kenya), and was extensively renovated during the late 18th-century Omani occupation. **Jangwani Mosque**, a similar structure to the Small Domed Mosque, is now all but collapsed.

West of the mosques, the tall triangular **Makutani Palace** is still very well preserved. The palace was built and fortified in the 15th century after the Husuni Kubwa fell into disuse (see below), and it is enclosed by a low, crumbling 18th-century wall built by the Omani. Also of interest, a few hundred metres south of the Great Mosque, the **Sultan's Mausoleum** houses the tombs of many of Kilwa's most important sultans. All around town you'll see traces of the **ancient well system**, which is still used by the villagers today.

The eminent archaeologist Neville Chittick, who carried out excavations on Kilwa from 1958, regarded the **Husuni Kubwa**, perched on a low seafront cliff 1km east of the main ruins, as 'the only attempt to go beyond the merely practical and approach the grand'. Oddly, locals refer to the Husuni Kubwa as Sao Jago, reflecting a widespread local belief that it is of Portuguese origin (even the Department of Antiquities guides, who should know better, call it the Portuguese House). Persistent as this Portuguese association might be locally, it lacks for any historical foundation.

KILWA IN 1331

The first detailed eye-witness account of Kilwa was written by Ibn Battuta, a young Arabian lawyer and inveterate globetrotter who is estimated to have covered something like 120,000km (more than Marco Polo) in his thirst for fresh sights. Ibn Battuta arrived in Kilwa in 1331, when the port was at its commercial peak, possibly at the invitation of Sultan Al-Hasan bin Sulaiman, with whom he might well have crossed paths in Mecca.

We ... set sail for Kilwa, the principal town on the coast, the greater part of whose inhabitants are Zanj of very black complexion. Kilwa is one of the most beautiful and well-constructed towns in the world. The whole of it is elegantly built. The roofs are built with mangrove poles. The people are engaged in a holy war, for their country lies beside that of Pagan Zanj. The chief qualities are devotion and piety ... The sultan ... [is nicknamed] Abu Al-Mawahib (Giver of Gifts) ... He frequently makes raids into the Zanj country, attacks them, and carries off booty, of which he reserves a fifth, using it in the manner prescribed by the Koran ...

The sultan is very humble: he sits and eats with beggars, and venerates holy men and the descendants of the prophets ... One Friday as he was coming away from prayer ... a faqir from Yemen stopped him and said 'O Abu Al-Mawahib'. He replied: 'Here I am, O beggar! What do you want?' 'Give me the clothes you are wearing!' And [the sultan] said: 'Certainly you can have them.' 'At once?' [the beggar] asked. 'Yes, immediately!'

When this virtuous and liberal sultan died ... his brother Daud became ruler, and acted in the opposite manner. If a poor man came to him, he said: 'The giver of gifts is dead, and has nothing left to give.' Visitors stayed at his court a great number of months, and only then did he give them something, so much that eventually no-one came to visit him.

18

With grim irony, the most detailed eyewitness account of Kilwa in its prime is included in *The Sack of Kilwa and Mombasa*, penned by Francisco de Almeida after he led the Portuguese attack on the island in 1505, and is interspersed with comments relating to the sacking:

> In Kilwa there are many strong houses several storeys high. They are built of stone and mortar and plastered with various designs ... As soon as the town had been taken ... they went to the palace and there the cross was put down. Then everyone started to plunder the town of all its merchandise and provisions.
>
> The island and town have a population of 4,000 people. It is very fertile and produces maize ... butter, honey and wax. On the trees hang beehives like jars of three almudes' capacity, each closed with woven palm leaves ... There are many trees and palms on the mainland, some of them different to those of Portugal ... There are sweet oranges, lemons, vegetables, small onions, and aromatic herbs. They are grown in gardens and watered with water from the wells.
>
> Here also grows betel that has leaves like ivy and is grown like peas with sticks at the root for support. Wealthy Arabs chew the leaf, together with specially prepared limes that look like an ointment. They keep the leaves as if they were to be put on wounds. These leaves make the mouth and teeth very red, but are said to be most refreshing.
>
> There are more black slaves than white moors here: they are engaged on farms growing maize and other things ... The soil is red, the top layer being sandy; the grass is always green. There are many fat beasts, oxen, cows, sheep and goats and also plenty of fish; there are also whales which swim around the ships. There is no running drinking water on this island. Near the island there are other small inhabited islands. There are many boats as large as a caravel of 50 ton and other smaller ones... They sail from here to Sofala, 255 leagues away.
>
> People here sleep raised above the ground in hammocks made of palm leaves, in which only one person can lie. Flasks of very good perfume are exported from here and a large

Most likely the Husuni Kubwa was constructed by Al-Hasan ibn Sulaiman as a palace and storehouse *circa* 1320 (almost two centuries before the Portuguese arrived) and was abandoned after two generations as too costly to maintain. In some aspects – its geometrical design, for instance – the clifftop palace is a typical Swahili building, but its scale and complexity are unprecedented, and it boasts many unique features. The building incorporates extensive domestic quarters, an audience court, several large ornamental balconies, a stairwell to the beach, and even a swimming pool. Few walls are still left standing after six centuries of disuse, but the ground plan is still clearly discernible.

Not far from the Husuni Kubwa, **Husuni Ndogo** superficially resembles a fort, but its purpose is a mystery. There is no comparable building elsewhere in East Africa, and it has variously and inconclusively been cited as a mosque, a storehouse, a minor residence and a fortified marketplace.

KILWA KIVINJE This run-down town, though less frequently visited than Kilwa Kisiwani, is no less absorbing in its own way. A living memorial to a more prosperous past, the broad impression is of a once grand town returning to its fishing village roots – much of the main street consists of boarded-up shops, while mud huts are built on to the still-standing walls of old Omani dwellings and fortifications, many in good enough condition to allow you to imagine what they must have looked like 150 years ago.

quantity of glass of all types and all kinds of cotton piece goods, incense, resin, gold, silver and pearls. The Grand Captain ordered the loot to be deposited under seal in a house. The fortress of Kilwa was built out of the best house there was. All the other houses were pulled down. It was fortified and guns were set in place.

Cotton is found in abundance. It is of good quality ... The slaves wear a cotton cloth around the waist and down to the knees; the rest of the body is naked. The white Arabs and slave owners wear two pieces of cotton cloth, one around the waist down to the feet, and the other over the shoulders and reaching down to the first cloth. There are copper coins [but] no gold coin. The Grand Captain ... saw 25 gazelle which had been let loose on the island ... There are many vaulted mosques, one of which is like that of Cordova. All the upper-class Moors carry a rosary.

The contrast between the above and James Prior's 1812 description of the island during the brief Omani re-occupation is striking:

The present town, if town it should be called, consists merely of a number of huts, scattered from the margin of the sea to a mile from its shore; the glittering white of only two stone houses enlivens and embellishes the cocoa-thatched metropolic ... Quiloa seems to offer only ivory and tortoiseshell for commerce ... The number of slaves formerly exported used to be many thousands, but at present the demand is confined to the Arabs, who do not take many. The articles principally in request here are arms, ammunition, dollars, tobacco, coarse cloths, and hardware. Refreshments ... seem scarce, and the natives poor ... The [Arab] people are generally good figures ... they domineer over the Negro nations within their reach [and] sometimes make war to get more slaves, but more generally get them in traffic with people that come from a considerable distance in the interior. The common dress is a piece of cotton cloth wrapped around the middle, and extending to the knee, and another thrown loosely over the shoulders ... They profess Muhammadism, but do not very strictly adhere to it.

The waterfront German Boma, the town's largest building, served as an administrative centre into the 1950s; these days it looks just one powerful gust away from total collapse. A cannon, presumably dating to World War I, stands on the common (complete with park benches) between the Boma and a stone seawall. Behind the Boma a small monument commemorates two Germans who died in 1888. Another relic of the German era is the covered central market. The roads radiating out from the market offer glimpses of Kilwa Kivinje in the 1940s and 1950s: double-storey buildings with ornate balconies, small homes with Zanzibar-style doors, and a few steel advertising boards that must date to the 1950s.

KILWA KIVINJE IN 1859

In February 1859, on their return trip from 'discovering' Lake Tanganyika, Burton and Speke diverted to Kilwa Kivinje to fulfil a promise made by Burton prior to starting the expedition. The town was, at the time, in the grip of a terrible cholera epidemic, and Burton wrote of how 'corpses lay in the ravines and dead Negroes rested against the walls of the Customs House. The poorer victims were dragged by the leg along the sand to be thrown into the ebbing water of the bay; those better off were sewn up in matting. Limbs were scattered in all directions and heads lay like pebbles on the beach.' They did not stay in Kilwa Kivinje long.

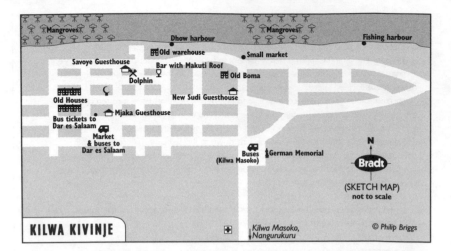

KILWA KIVINJE

Historical interest aside, Kilwa Kivinje lies on an attractive beach surrounded by an extensive mangrove swamp, where odd little mud-skippers scuttle across the sand, and pairs of the beautiful mangrove kingfisher emit their high descending call from bare branches. It's also a very traditional Muslim town, marked by the characteristic Swahili reserve – though tourists remain a rare enough sight that you'll find no shortage of people wanting to practise their English on you. It's fascinating to watch the local fishermen at work along the beach to the south of the Boma, or youngsters preparing to smoke the day's catch in the back streets.

Accommodation options in Kilwa Kivinje are uniformly cheap and dire: try the New Sudi Guesthouse or Mjaka Guesthouse. Two bars serve lukewarm beer and *chipsi mayai*, to a rather limited clientele; otherwise eating-out options in Kilwa Kivinje are limited to a couple of basic *hotelis* near the market.

SONGO MNARA ISLAND Some 10km south of Kilwa, Songo Mnara is the site of a second ruined town contemporaneous with medieval Kilwa. Little is known

THE SONGO ARCHIPELAGO

Kilwa Kisiwani, Songo Songo and Songo Mnara all form part of the Songo Archipelago, a 50km-long conglomeration of islands and atolls formed many thousands of years ago when an estuary system flooded. Several other islands in the archipelago – most notably Songo Mnara – were settled in medieval times and today host extensive stone ruins. The surrounding seas reputedly harbour the world's densest population of dugong – a large and peculiar marine mammal, believed to have been the origin of the mermaid myth, and now IUCN listed as Vulnerable – but you would be extraordinarily fortunate to encounter one.

The Songo Archipelago also incorporates perhaps the most extensive of Tanzania's unprotected reef systems, comprising roughly 80km of coastal reef and 40 smaller patch reefs (until recently, few facilities existed for snorkelling or diving, but both activities can now be arranged through Kimbilio Lodge in Kilwa Masoko). In common with other offshore reefs in Tanzania, those around Kilwa have suffered some damage as a result of coral mining and dynamite fishing, but the deeper reefs are considered to be in pristine condition, and there is some talk of gazetting the entire archipelago as a marine park.

Captain Philip Beaver of HMS *Nisus*, the first British ship to enter Kilwa harbour, explored the ruins at Songo Mnara with the ship's surgeon James Prior. The notes made by Prior indicate that the Omani had recently abandoned the city they briefly re-occupied. Some extracts follow, with original imperial measurements converted to metric:

We discovered a large well ... about 6m in depth [and] hollowed out of calcareous rock ... formerly enclosed by a wall, part of which is still standing. Further on, towards Pagoda Point, appeared several decayed huts, tenanted by bats and reptiles ... The first object [after this] was a small cemetery, about 12m square, enclosed with stone and raised less than 1m above the ground; the graves were convexly raised ... with stones at the head and feet ... but no trace could we find of inscriptions ... Attached [were] the remains of ... a place of worship, above 7x4m. The walls remaining seemed about 5m high, built of stone, cemented by mortar formed by the bastard coral ... in which were wedged many pieces of coconut shell, that seemed of no other use than of emblems ... An arched door in front, and two in rear, formed the entrances, and a circular white stone raised above the ground may, perhaps, have received the inclined knee of many a humble supplicant for divine mercy ... Two or three hundred metres from this spot lie the ruins of a stone building, larger than any at present possessed by the Quiloans, except the residence of the Sultan. Its apartments have been numerous ... the walls are broad ... and their height must have been considerable. Captain Beaver thought he could distinguish the remains of Saxon arches; but this resemblance is probably accidental.

about the origin and history of this town, but it was allegedly built by Ali Hussein, the founder of Kilwa, and the layout indicates that it was founded as a fortified outpost to defend the sea route into the harbour against naval attacks. Most constructions on Songo Mnara date from the 15th century or earlier, but – like Kilwa Kisiwani – the old town was re-occupied by the Omani in the late 18th century, and some renovation and new building occurred during this period.

The ruins on Songo Mnara lack the impact of those on Kilwa Kisiwani, but they have also suffered less damage through removal of building material, so they give a clearer idea of the layout of the ordinary houses and the town as a whole. The name Songo is ancient, but Mnara is a relatively modern appellation meaning 'tower', and refers to the tall but collapsed minaret of the main 15th-century mosque. A second large labyrinthine building with beautiful arched doors is generally referred to as the Sultan's Palace, but since the island had no sultan, it was probably the secondary residence of the Sultan of Kilwa.

A daily passenger boat connects Kilwa Masoko and Songo Mnara, weather permitting. You can also arrange private transport in a local fishing dhow, while the various lodges in Kilwa Masoko can arrange combined sightseeing and snorkelling day trips to the island. For those with a serious interest in coastal archaeology, it would be possible, over the course of a day, to combine a visit to Songo Mnara with two other islands that contain substantial ruins. The first of these is the ruined town on **Sanje Mjoma**, which lies about 3km from Songo Mnara, and is noted for several large coral houses enclosed in courtyards with tall arched entrances. The second is **Sanje Ya Kati**, the capital of the Shanga people, a local tribe who resisted the rule of the Shirazi at Kilwa into the 13th century.

SONGO SONGO ISLAND The 3km² coral island of Songo Songo is the most northerly in the Kilwa archipelago, lying about 40km north of Kilwa itself. It has recently grabbed a few headlines as the site of the long-mooted Songas Project, which received full funding in late 2001 and has been operational since 2003. The natural gas from two onshore and three offshore gas wells, discovered in 1974, is extracted and processed on site, then piped to Dar es Salaam to fuel Ebbing Electric Generator, which has a capacity of greater than 100MW and was previously fuelled by expensive imported oil.

Of greater interest to travellers is Songo Songo's attractive sandy beach, and a vast coral cave haunted by a profusion of bats, reached via a concrete staircase built during World War I when the cave served as a German ammunition dump. Songo Songo makes for an easy day trip from Kilwa Kivinje. Passenger dhows do the return trip most days, taking about three hours in either direction, and charging a fare of around Tsh1,500 per person.

LINDI

This compact, somewhat decrepit port on the western bank of the Lukuledi Estuary is the most substantial coastal town between Dar es Salaam and Mtwara, with a population of around 30,000. It is also the administrative capital of the vast but thinly populated Lindi region, which at 66,000km² is about the same size as the Republic of Ireland. For all that, Lindi comes across as something of a backwater: a pleasant enough place to hang out, but also a vivid reminder of what much of Tanzania was like in the economically deprived 1980s.

The one part of town to escape the general air of torpor is the busy bus station [553 B4], which rings late into the night with stuttering *bongo flava* (Swahili hip-hop) and bass-heavy reggae. Here the town's unemployed youth and orphaned children hang around all day, breaking into unselfconscious dances, while vendors scrape a living selling fried chicken, dried fish, melting sweets and single cigarettes to passing bus passengers.

From Lindi's central jetty, regular motorised ferries cross the Lukuledi Estuary, taking about five minutes in either direction. The ferries land at **Kitunda**, a small village where the people spend their time drinking local beer and farming their *shamba*s. There is little to do in Kitunda, but there is a fantastic view if you walk a little way up the hill. A 90-minute walk, starting by heading uphill from Kitunda, takes you to a quiet, thickly vegetated and very beautiful beach. The Lukuledi Estuary can be explored more thoroughly by hiring a local boat at a negotiable price – crocodiles can reportedly be seen 10–12km upstream. It is also possible to hire a boat in the bay, to do some snorkelling or to visit the large colony of fruit bats resident on Kisiwa Cha Popo (Island of Bats).

A number of excellent beaches are scattered around Lindi Bay. The largest, on the northern edge of town, is white and sandy with hardly any rocks; a few small wooden fishing boats lie on the shore and children play football throughout the day. On the western side of the bay are several more secluded beaches – including Ras Bora, Mitema (the biggest and best) and Mitwero.

Further afield, details of the lakes around Rutamba and Rondo areas inland of Lindi are among the supplementary sites detailed in our website, http://bradttanzania.wordpress.com.

HISTORY It seems more than probable that Lukuledi Estuary has long been the site of a fishing village, but Lindi in its present incarnation most probably started life as an Omani port in the late 18th century, though oral traditions suggest it may have existed for a century or so before that (see box, *The Ancient History of Lindi*, pages

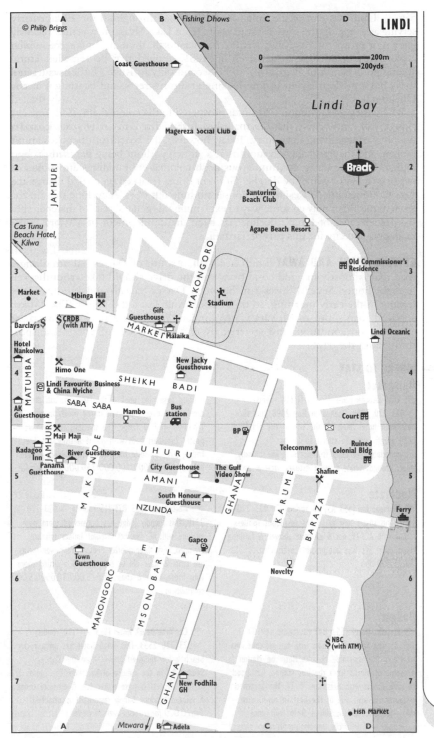

© Philip Briggs

LINDI

Fishing Dhows

Coast Guesthouse

Lindi Bay

Magereza Social Club

N

Bradt

Santorino Beach Club

Cas Tunu Beach Hotel, Kilwa

Agape Beach Resort

Old Commissioner's Residence

Market

Mbinga Hill

CRDB (with ATM)

MAKONGORO

Stadium

Barclays

Gift Guesthouse

Hotel Nankolwa

MARKET

Malaika

Lindi Oceanic

Himo One

MATUMBA

SHEIKH   BADI

New Jacky Guesthouse

Lindi Favourite Business & China Nyiche

AK Guesthouse

SABA SABA

Mambo

Bus station

Court

Maji Maji

JAMHURI

Kadagoo Inn

River Guesthouse

MAKONDE

UHURU

BP

Panama Guesthouse

City Guesthouse

The Gulf Video Show

Shafine

AMANI

KARUME

Telecomms

Ruined Colonial Bldg

South Honour Guesthouse

GHANA

NZUNDA

BARAZA

Ferry

Gapco

Town Guesthouse

MAKONGORO

EILAT

MSONOBARI

Novelty

NBC (with ATM)

GHANA

New Fodhila GH

Mtwara

Adela

Fish Market

556–7). Lindi was part of the Sultanate of Zanzibar throughout the 19th century, serving as a stop on the slave caravan route from Lake Nyasa. It was never as well known or prosperous as Kilwa Kivinje further north, though Captain Foot, who explored the south coast extensively in 1881, implied that he regarded Lindi, among ports 'south of Bagamoyo' to be second only to Kilwa. Either way, Lindi today has a modern layout of interlocking gridiron streets, and boasts few if any Omani relics.

There is every indication that Lindi prospered in the colonial era. With one eye closed, you can imagine that the main beach served as a resort of sorts, possibly used by farmers living upcountry. Today, however, the beachfront benches are all broken, and they probably go months at a stretch without being perched on by a tourist. In the town centre, numerous posh colonial-era buildings are ruined or heading that way, while the derelict German Boma (marked on a 1970 map as the Area Commissioner's Residence) houses nothing but trees. A cyclone that hit the town in the 1950s may go some way to explaining this general state of disrepair, but the deeper cause of Lindi's decline has been the development of Mtwara as the main port and city for this part of Tanzania.

GETTING THERE AND AWAY Lindi lies 470km south of Dar es Salaam along a road that is mostly in good condition, and the drive should take around seven to eight hours. Several buses run between Dar es Salaam and Lindi, mostly leaving in the early morning, so try to book your seat a day ahead. The 110km surfaced road south to Mtwara via Mikindani and 165km road to Masasi are also in good condition, and covered by a steady stream of public transport throughout the day.

WHERE TO STAY
Upmarket
Lindi Oceanic Hotel [553 D4] (14 rooms) 023 220 2880. Opened in May 2008, this slick beachfront hotel (built on the site of the old Lindi Club) greatly ups the stakes so far as accommodation in Lindi is concerned. The blandly smart grounds boast a great estuary view & an inviting swimming pool, & the large *makuti* dining area serves decent but uninspired meals in the Tsh8,000–10,000 range. The spacious rooms have 4-poster Zanzibari beds with frame netting, satellite TV, fridge, large en-suite bathroom with tub, & private balcony. *Tsh75,000/100,000/150,000 sgl/dbl/suite.*

Moderate
Kadagoo Inn [553 A5] (6 rooms) 023 220 2507. This smart new place has small but spotless rooms with AC, TV, net & en-suite shower & flushing squat toilet. It's fine but possibly overpriced. *Tsh35,000 dbl.*

Adela Hotel [553 B7] (15 rooms) 023 220 2310. This friendly lodge has 2 types of room, both en-suite with AC, fan, net & chair. Indoor sgls are cramped, with three-quarter beds, while newer rooms are airier & have dbl or twin beds & a sitting room with fridge, table & chairs. *Tsh15,000/30,000/45,000 sgl/dbl/twin.*

Budget
Malaika Hotel [553 B4] (8 rooms) m 0713 263335. The favourite option with budget-conscious travellers, the venerable Malaika Hotel on Market St, a couple of blocks from the bus station, has good en-suite rooms with nets, fans & TV. The attached restaurant is also one of the best in town, with meals for around Tsh2,500 & fresh fruit juice. *Tsh13,000–15,000 dbl, depending on room size.*

Cas Tunu Beach Hotel [553 A3] (10 rooms) 023 220 2553. This small hotel lies on a rocky beach a few hundred metres from the Dar es Salaam Rd in the suburb of Kariakoo. The rooms are in little chalets & have a net, fan, & en-suite toilet. A relaxed outdoor bar & restaurant is attached. *Tsh10,000 for a room with ¾ beds.*

🏠 **Coast Guesthouse** [553 B1] (17 rooms) m 0754 628150. This revamped stalwart has a wonderful location on the palm-lined beach immediately north of the town centre, a 10–15min walk from the bus station. The en-suite rooms are now very pleasant, with tiled floors, king-size beds with netting, TV & fan, & there are also a few cheaper sgls with common showers. *Tsh5,000/10,000 sgl/dbl.*

Shoestring

🏠 **South Honour Guesthouse** [553 B5] Around the corner from the bus station, this is one of the best of several cheap guesthouses in this part of town (others are shown on the map). *Tsh4,000/5,000 sgl/dbl with net, fan & common bucket shower.*

✘ WHERE TO EAT AND DRINK The restaurant at the **Lindi Oceanic Hotel** [553 D4] stands out for quality and ambience, but it's about four times the price of the **Malaika Hotel** [553 B4], which serves decent local food for Tsh2,500 per portion. **Mbinga Hill** [553 A3] is another decent local eatery serving *mishkaki*, fish, chicken with chips and various other staples for around Tsh2,000 per plate. **Himo One** [553 A4] serves barbecued chicken tikka and *mishkaki* for a similar price, and has indoor or outdoor seating. Large prawns and other fresh seafood can be bought at the **fish market** [553 D7] south of the main boat jetty, ideally in the afternoon before 16.30. The quality is excellent, the price is good, and it shouldn't be a problem to arrange for somebody to cook for you. For a beachfront beer, the **Santorino Beach Club** [553 C2] and **Agape Beach Resort** [553 C3] are both recommended, and they also serve *nyama choma* and snacks.

OTHER PRACTICALITIES The **football stadium** [553 C3] is sporadic host to large crowds, as Lindi's football team – somewhat improbably – regularly battles it out in Tanzania's First Division. The **Gulf Video Show** [553 C5] opposite the South Honour Guesthouse is the best place to watch live transmissions of English Premiership and international football matches. The **National Bank of Commerce** [553 D7] has foreign exchange facilities and both it and the **CRDB Bank** [553 A3] have ATMs where local currency can be drawn with a Visa card. Internet access is available at **Lindi Favourite Business** [553 A4] and **China Nyiche Internet** [553 A4], both on Jamhuri Street (Tsh1,000 per 30 minutes).

MIKINDANI

This small port 10km north of Mtwara, with its sleepy old Swahili town of narrow alleys, balconied double-storey homesteads and carved Zanzibar doors, is of far greater historical significance than its upstart neighbour. Indeed, for much of the 19th century, Mikindani was the most important port south of Kilwa Kivinje, and it is from here that Livingstone launched his last fatal expedition into the interior. Today, Mikindani is overshadowed by Mtwara in most respects, but it does make the more appealing base for travellers, largely thanks to the efforts of two under-publicised tourist organisations based here.

The first of these is the British non-profit organisation Trade Aid, which funds community projects and provides local employment and educational opportunities through sustainable ecotourism. The pivot of this project is the restored German Boma, which now provides the best upmarket accommodation anywhere along the south coast. Other ventures include an organic market garden, a tree nursery, and a small restaurant called Samaki to serve the local people.

A newer development is the establishment of eco2 (m 0746 855833; e martin@ eco2.com; www.eco2.com), a diving, marine research and education centre whose waterfront office stands alongside the affiliated Ten Degrees South. Owned by a qualified marine biologist and PADI instructor with ten years' experience in the region, the centre offers diving and snorkelling expeditions outside Mikindani Bay and in Mnazi Bay–Ruvuma Estuary Marine Park, the latter possibly the best diving site in East Africa. Eco2 is an active participant in reef protection projects and its community development fund gets a dollar from every dive.

HISTORY Named for the palms (*mikinda*) that flourish in the vicinity, Mikindani town is not so antiquated as its timeworn façade might suggest. A late 19th-century settlement, it peaked commercially as an exporter of rubber and agricultural produce during the years that divided the abolition of the slave trade from German colonisation. It remained an important administrative centre until the end of World War II; the time-warped aura that envelops Mikindani today is attributable to lack of urban development after 1947, when it was abandoned as a regional centre in favour of Mtwara.

Early years Human habitation of Mikindani Bay, the arc of small harbours and inlets on which both Mikindani and Mtwara are sited, stretches back for millennia. The proto-Makonde had arrived on the bay by the 9th century, and Shirazi traders may have settled there at about the same time, though no ruins survive to confirm this probability. The first known reference to Mikindani Bay (under a different name) is on a 1796 map drawn by Alexander Dalyrimple.

The oldest first-hand account of the area was penned by Lieutenant Boteler of the HMS *Barracouta*, which anchored at the bay in 1824. The major settlement at this time was Pemba, on the northern entrance of the harbour on which Mikindani stands today. Boteler describes Pemba as being dominated by a 'fine castellated

THE ANCIENT HISTORY OF LINDI

This is the title of an intriguing but somewhat effusive history of Lindi transcribed from local oral sources in the 1890s by a German scholar named Velton. Lindi, according to this document, was established by a Makonde leader called Kitenga, and its name refers to a large pit latrine on the town's outskirts. The date of foundation is not specified, but subsequent events related by the document, which can be dated in conjunction with references to three different sultans of Zanzibar, indicate that it must surely have been before 1750.

After some years in power, Kitenga agreed to 'sell' his town to a Makua leader called Mtukura. In exchange, Kitenga was given all of Mtukura's worldly goods: 'a female slave, a powder mortar for grinding snuff a cubit long, lengths of American cloth, and the head and liver of a wild pig'! Mtukura evidently assumed the title of Sultan and founded a dynasty that appears to have ruled for three or four generations, all the time producing copious numbers of children. Many of the children were apparently married into wealthy Arabic families, a common brand of upward mobility along the coast, where a Shirazi or Omani pedigree stood one in high social and commercial stead. Unfortunately, it was such a liaison – the marriage of two of the sultan's daughters to a pair of prominent merchant brothers from Zanzibar in 1830 or thereabouts – that led directly to Lindi being co-opted into the Omani Sultanate of Zanzibar.

The newlywed brothers evidently went behind the back of their father-in-law to usurp control of Lindi. They sailed to Zanzibar to make Sultan Seyyid Said an offer no acquisitive megalomaniac could refuse: 'We have built a fort at Lindi: now give us your authority to judge the [local people], and all taxes we collect will be for you.' So it was that Nasoro bin Isa, the elder brother, became *ipso facto* Sultan of Lindi, instituting a regime characterised by the oral traditions as 'evil'. Nasoro and his brother building of the old Portuguese ... on the side of a steep hill ... neatly whitewashed [and] most likely garrisoned'. Boteler also noted that the bay was 'inhabited by Arabs, probably under the Sultan of Muscat'. It is known that Pemba was then a major supplier of slaves to Reunion, Seychelles and Comoros: the Arabic inhabitants mentioned by Boteler were almost certainly Omani slave traders, and it would have been they, rather than the Portuguese, who constructed the castellated hillside fortification.

Livingstone in Mikindani The explorer David Livingstone arrived at Mikindani on 24 March 1866, rented a house in the nearby village of Pemba, and rested up for two weeks before embarking on his final expedition into the African interior. Livingstone cited Mikindani as 'the finest port on the coast', but was unimpressed by its Arabic inhabitants, whom he characterised as 'a wretched lot physically, thin, washed out creatures – many with bleary eyes'. Nor were they particularly devout: 'many of them came and begged brandy, and laughed when they remarked that they could drink it in secret, but not openly'.

Upon enquiring about the settlers' history, Livingstone was told they had 'not been here long' but noted that 'a ruin on the northern peninsula ... built of stone and lime Arab fashion, and others on the northwest, show that the place has been known and used of old'. The fort described by Boteler was evidently disused by then, perhaps due to a slump in the slave trade, and the sense of economic decline is reinforced by Livingstone's reference to the 'agent of the Zanzibar customs house [who] presides over the customs, which are very small'. Eight years later, Vice Consul Elton reported that the district had 'been subjected to attacks from the inland and neighbouring tribes, who have burnt the houses [and] lifted the cattle

Muhammad 'killed their relatives and sold them into slavery', whilst Sultan Said 'knew nothing of how for five years his subjects suffered oppression'. The situation deteriorated when 'the Almighty God sent ... a very great famine that lasted seven years ... caused by locusts [that] did not leave a single [crop] living, but ate everything'.

Nasoro, who did not survive the famine, was succeeded first by his brother Muhammad 'who remained in power for a long time', and then by his son Hemedi bin Nasoro. After the death of Sultan Said of Zanzibar in 1854 (at around the same time Hemedi assumed power), his successor Majid sent a military expedition to Lindi to capture the fort and install direct Zanzibari rule. This event precipitated decades of hostility and sporadic wars between the coastal people of Lindi, who accepted the new order, and their upcountry neighbours and kin, who did not. This tradition is largely substantiated by references in Vice Consul Elton's 1874 report on visiting Mikindani. The squabbling factions 'never agreed until the Germans came', one reason perhaps why Lindi never acquired the political or commercial status of Kilwa Kivinje.

A report from the Deputy Commissioner of German East Africa, dated September 1890, states that 'In Lindi also, lately, caravan trade has considerably increased. A caravan that arrived not long ago counted 1,200 heads and brought 340 tusks; the entire arrival of the last six weeks is estimated to be at least 700 tusks.' The so-called *Ancient History*, too, suggests that the arrival of the Germans fostered renewed trade activity and harmony in Lindi. This is probably because the withdrawal of Zanzibar allowed Rashid bin Shabawa, the leading light of the popular dynasty that had been displaced in the 1830s, to regain his rightful position as Sultan of Lindi – albeit within the constraints of colonial rule.

18

... It is proposed to desert Mikindani and make a stand at Lindi. Trade is at stand still.'

Boom years By 1880, when Vice Consul Holmwood undertook an extensive tour of the south coast, Mikindani was entrenched as the main urban centre on the eponymous bay, with a rapidly growing population 'both Arabs and natives ... Banyans and Hindi'. Its fortunes, too, had undergone a dramatic upswing. Holmwood noted that 'Mikindani had prospered immensely since Livingstone had visited it', and felt that the recently established rubber plantations had resulted in 'a complete revolution [with] all classes deriving their income from it or through it'. He remarked on the 'large number of goats and cattle', and on how 'trade had increased exceedingly [with] almost all the produce of the Rovuma region finding its way there'. Holmwood ended his glowing appraisal by stating that 'South of Bagamoyo, Mikindani will now rank in importance next after Kilwa and Lindi'.

Prosperous Mikindani formed the obvious choice for Germany's southeast regional headquarters, and it was settled as such in 1890. Mikindani remained the most important settlement on the bay, and the administrative centre for Rovuma region, until the late 1940s, when the colonial government relocated to Mtwara to develop its harbour to service the infamous post-war groundnut scheme (see *History* under *Mtwara*, page 561).

GETTING THERE AND AWAY Mtwara Airport is only 15km distant, and road transfers can be arranged in advance through the Old Boma. In addition, taxis wait at the airport for all incoming flights. Mikindani straddles the main surfaced road towards Lindi some 10km north of Mtwara, making it highly accessible whether by public transport or in a private vehicle. All buses heading between Lindi and Mtwara will stop at Mikindani on request. Regular light buses ply the road between Mtwara and Mikindani all day through.

WHERE TO STAY
Upmarket

The Old Boma (8 rooms) m 0784 360110; e oldboma@mikindani.com; www.mikindani.com. Dominating the Mikindani skyline, the former German Boma, built in 1895, lies on the slopes of Bismarck Hill about 300m from the main road. It served as the regional administrative headquarters in 1947, then as a police station, but had fallen into an advanced state of disrepair when it was taken over by Trade Aid in 1998. Now immaculately restored to its former whitewashed pomp, the Old Boma is arguably the nicest hotel on the south coast, with airy en-suite dbls with netting, fan, hot bath & Swahili furnishings, & wooded grounds containing a swimming pool & excellent restaurant. It has the only internet access in town. *US$105–165 dbl B&B depending on room size.*

Moderate/budget

Ten Degrees South (10 rooms) m 0746 855833; e info@tendegreessouth.com; www.tendegreessouth.com. Affiliated with eco2, this friendly English-owned lodge on the waterfront has pleasant rooms with dbl bed, netting & fan with common showers, & a new wing of en-suite rooms, with further accommodation planned in the form of self-catering cottages on a new hilltop plot with wonderful views over the bay. The outdoor restaurant has a varied menu, with seafood something of a speciality. The satellite TV in the bar shows important sport events, & the music selection is unusually eclectic. *US$20 dbl with common showers; USD$60 en-suite dbl.*

WHERE TO EAT The **Old Boma** serves the best and most imaginative food in town, with most meals in the Tsh8,000–12,000 range. **Ten Degrees South** has a varied seafood-dominated menu with main courses at Tsh5,000–8,000. Several cheaper places are scattered around town, the best being **Ismaili's Corner Bar** in the Old

Slave Market, and the greener **Muku's Bar** next to the main *dala-dala* stop, both of which serve chilled beers and sodas, along with seafood and chicken dishes for around Tsh5,000–6,000.

WHAT TO SEE The alleys of Mikindani have an absorbing time-warped mood that makes the town more than the sum of its architectural landmarks. Nevertheless, a short stroll around reveals a wealth of buildings dating from the late Omani and German colonial periods. The most distinguished of these, built in 1895, is the **Old Boma** which combines elements of German and Arabic architecture and was recently restored as a hotel.

Below the Old Boma is the so-called **Old Slave Market**, a German building that actually post-dates the slave trade by two decades, though it is reputedly constructed over a former Omani slave market – which, some claim, previously served as a Portuguese ivory store. Whatever the truth of this story, the misconceived 'restoration' of the old market has forsaken much of its architectural integrity by bricking in the old arches and slapping lavish paint all over the stone exterior. Historical continuity, at least, is maintained by the clutch of – very good – local craft shops and eateries that trade out of the restored market.

Opposite the old market, a commemorative plaque celebrating 'the reputed dwelling place of **David Livingstone**' is posted with palpable disingenuity on the wall of a two-storey balconied building on the corner of the waterfront road. Livingstone almost certainly resided in a nearby village called Pemba, and his 'reputed dwelling place' is nothing more or less than one of several fading early to mid-20th-century homesteads built by Arab or Indian merchants. Several other such homesteads, many with wooden first-floor balconies, can be seen alongside the alleys that lead inland from this corner.

Of a similar vintage to the Old Boma, the ruined **German Customs House**, which stands on the waterfront next to the bus station and was possibly expanded from an Omani or Portuguese slave prison, was damaged during a British naval raid in 1916. The nearby **Aga Kahn Building**, also on the waterfront, is probably the oldest in town; built in the mid 19th century by a wealthy Arab trader and distinguished by its unusual staircase, it now serves as an Islamic preschool. Several old **Arab graves** can be seen around town; it was customary in Mikindani to mark the tomb of a sultan with a baobab tree at each end, so the two would eventually intertwine.

The Old Boma acts as a tourist information centre and local tour operator. Several day excursions are on offer. These include guided walks through Mikindani, dhow trips, snorkelling and fishing motorboat trips, and a visit to Lake Chidya and the Rovuma River. Overnight excursions include a snorkelling trip to Msimbati in the Mnazi Bay Marine Reserve, a round excursion to the Rondo Plateau and a two-night safari to the wild Lukwika Lumesule Game Reserve. Meanwhile, eco2, with a waterfront office next to Ten Degrees South, is the place to organise diving and snorkelling excursions in Mikindani Bay and further afield.

MTWARA

Something of a dead end in terms of Tanzanian travel, Mtwara is the springboard for travellers crossing into neighbouring Mozambique. Supporting a population of 80,000, it is the largest town on the south coast, with a disjointed and unfocused layout that reflects an ambitious but as yet unfulfilled development plan initiated by the colonial government after World War II. The nominal town centre, set about

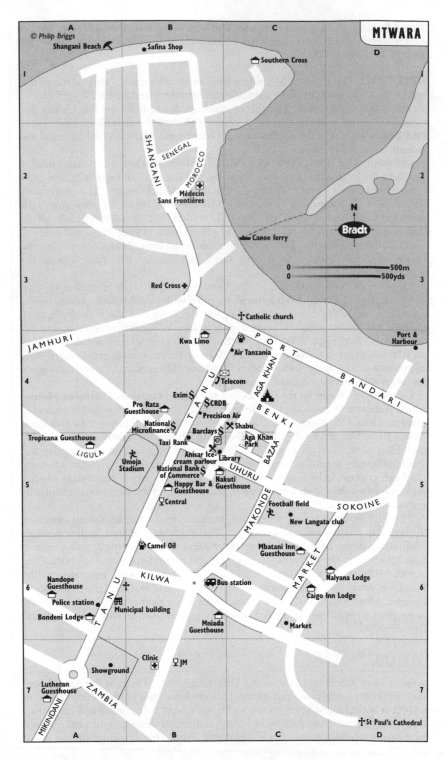

MTWARA

© Philip Briggs

Shangani Beach
Safina Shop
Southern Cross

SHANGANI
SENEGAL
MOROCCO
Médecin
Sans Frontières

N

Canoe ferry

Bradt

0 _____ 500m
0 _____ 500yds

Red Cross

Catholic church

JAMHURI

Kwa Limo
Air Tanzania

PORT

Port &
Harbour

BANDARI

Telecom

Exim
CRDB
Precision Air

Pro Rata
Guesthouse

National
Microfinance
Taxi Rank

Barclays
Shabu

AGA KHAN
BENKI

BAZAA

Aga Khan
Park

Tropicana Guesthouse

LIGULA

Umoja
Stadium

Anisar Ice-
cream parlour
Library

National Bank
of Commerce

Happy Bar &
Guesthouse

Nakuti
Guesthouse

UHURU

Central

MAKONDE

Football field

SOKOINE

New Langata club

Camel Oil

Mbatani Inn
Guesthouse

MARKET

Nalyana Lodge

Nandope
Guesthouse

KILWA

Bus station

Caigo Inn Lodge

TANU

Police station

Municipal building

Bondeni Lodge

Mniada
Guesthouse

Market

Clinic

JM

Lutheran
Guesthouse

Showground

ZAMBIA

MIKINDANI

St Paul's Cathedral

560

1km inland of the modern harbour, is a small, sleepy grid of roads framing tiny Aga Khan Park. A more convincing hub of commercial activity is the Chiko Ngola area, around the main market and bus station, 1km south of the town centre, while the beach and smarter residential area of Shangani lie about 2km to the north.

Mtwara is a pleasant enough town without offering much in the way of sightseeing. The market is worth a look, while the multi-storey Indian houses and shops in the town centre, most dating to the 1950s, are slowly acquiring an endearingly time-warped atmosphere. One worthwhile goal, depending on your interest in modern ecclesiastical art, is the Benedictine Church of St Paul, which lies in Majengo, ten minutes' walk southeast of the market, and is elaborately decorated with paintings executed over a two-year period by the German priest Polycarp Uehlien.

At Shangani, to the north of the town centre, there is a good swimming beach surrounded by coral flats, the latter interesting for the rock pools that form on them and the wading birds that visit. A better beach, at Msangamkuu on the opposite side of the bay, can be reached inexpensively using the dhow-taxis that leave from a conspicuous launching site on the road to Shangani. There's brilliant snorkelling at low tide, but beware of jellyfish and the rather evil sea urchins with long black spikes and a shiny orange eye.

HISTORY Prior to 1947, Mtwara was but a village compared with nearby Mikindani; indeed its one pre-World War II claim to posterity was as the location for the 1928 silent film *The Blue Lagoon*. After the war, the British administration relocated their regional administrative capital from Mikindani to Mtwara and started to develop its harbour as the main port to service a groundnut scheme that was expected to rejuvenate the economy of southeast Tanzania. Some 30 million pounds were spent creating the required infrastructure before it was realised that the local soil was unsuitable to grow groundnuts, and the area received insufficient rainfall anyway. This expensive failure caused more suffering than it ever alleviated, by coercing local farmers into replacing subsistence crops with groundnuts. And Mtwara's costly harbour remains to this day something of a white elephant, though activity has picked up slightly in recent years thanks to increased trade through Mozambique.

GETTING THERE AND AWAY Mtwara Airport, 4km from the town centre, is serviced by regular Precision Air and Air Tanzania flights from Dar es Salaam, costing about US$140 one-way or US$220 return. Taxis are available to meet all incoming flights. Current flight details can be found on the website www.mikindani.com.

Several buses daily run between Dar es Salaam and Mtwara, leaving from the main bus station [560 B6] at around 05.30–06.30. The trip should take about eight to ten hours in the dry season but may take a bit longer during the rains. Several buses daily run between Mtwara, Masasi and Lindi. These leave when full, and take a few hours only.

🏠 **WHERE TO STAY**
Moderate

🏠 **Southern Cross Hotel** [560 C1] (9 rooms) 📞 023 233 3206; 📱 0786 678283; e msemo@ makondenet.com. Rather confusingly signposted from town as the Msemo Hotel, this is easily the nicest place to stay in Mtwara, set on a rocky peninsula at the end of Shangani Beach about 2km from the town centre. In addition to stunning views across the bay, the hotel has a good restaurant serving grills & stews for around Tsh10,000, & large en-suite rooms with wood ceilings, terracotta tiled floors, king-size 4-poster bed with nets, TV, AC, hot water & private sea-facing balcony or lounge. *Tsh35,000/55,000 sgl/dbl B&B.*

Budget

🏠 **Caigo Inn Lodge** [560 C6] ☎ 023 233 4155. Situated near the bus station, this new lodge has smart en-suite rooms with AC, TV, fan, dbl bed with net, & hot water. *Tsh20,000 dbl.*

🏠 **Nalyana Lodge** [560 D6] Also near the bus station, this has spacious & clean en-suite rooms with tiled floor, TV, fan, dbl bed with net, & hot water. *Tsh15,000 dbl.*

🏠 **Kwa Limo Hotel** [560 B4] 📱 0712 329014. This small, reasonably central hotel lies a short

distance from the main road towards Shangani. The open-air bar & restaurant is on the opposite side of the road. Adequate en-suite rooms with dbl bed, net, TV & fan. *Tsh12,000 dbl.*

🏠 **Bondeni Lodge** [560 A6] ☎ 023 233 3769. This small quiet lodge lies alongside the main road from Mikindani about 1km from the town centre. A pleasant garden bar serves chilled drinks & good meals, though the latter take some time to prepare. En-suite rooms with net, fan & TV are good value. *Tsh10,000 dbl.*

Shoestring

🏠 **Pro Rata Guesthouse** [560 B4] Central & very clean, this small local hotel near the stadium is fair value & there's a lively garden bar & restaurant in

front of the hotel. *Tsh5,000 sgl (small bed) with net, fan & common shower.*

✗ **WHERE TO EAT** The best place to eat is the **Southern Cross Hotel** [560 C1], which charges around Tsh8,000–10,000 for a substantial main course. The Indian-run **Shabu Restaurant** [560 C4] in the old town centre serves simple Swahili and Indian dishes. **Anisar Ice Cream Parlour** [560 B5] at the market is the best place in town for ice creams, milkshakes and the like. Otherwise the choice is surprisingly limited; you might even think about catching a *dala-dala* to Mikindani and eating at one of the far nicer options there.

OTHER PRACTICALITIES There is no private forex bureau in Mtwara, but several banks will change US dollar travellers' cheques and cash. The ATM at the National Bank of Commerce (NBC) [560 B5] accepts Visa and the one at the Exim Bank [560 B4] takes MasterCard.

The best internet café is on Uhuru St opposite the NBC [560 B5], but there are several others, most relatively cheap and surprisingly fast.

A feature of Mtwara are the old ship containers that have been converted to shops, many selling luxury items such as baked beans, chocolate, shampoo, Pringles and bug spray. Another good shop in the town centre is the Mini Market which sells most imported items, albeit at a price higher than any other shop in town. IkoIko, a booze warehouse at the top end of the straight road in this part of town, sells the cheapest spirits and wine in Mtwara and has a good choice. The Tingatinga stall at the Southern Cross Hotel [560 C1] sells good quality work. For day tours and other information, the best places are the Old Boma and eco2 in Mikindani.

EXCURSIONS FROM MTWARA AND MIKINDANI

Msimbati Beach Guarding the open sea entrance to Mikindani Bay, idyllic Msimbati Beach stretches for miles between the Ras Msimbati and Ras Ruwura peninsulas, 25km east of Mtwara as the crow flies. It is a very beautiful spot, totally unspoilt and lined with broad palm trees, with a steep shelf and non-tidal reef that means swimming is good 24 hours a day, and a rare western orientation offering spectacular sunsets. The beach overlooks Mnazi Bay, part of Mnazi Bay–Rovuma Marine Park, a multi-use conservancy running from Mtwara to the Mozambique border. The park is an important turtle breeding site, and an extensive reef system offers great snorkelling and diving. The shallow bay is listed as an Important Bird Area, primarily for its large concentrations of crab plover and sand plover. For independent travellers, a few trucks head from Mtwara to Msimbati daily, taking about an hour in either direction, while diving and snorkelling excursions can be organised through eco2 in Mikindani (see page 555).

Lake Kitere Some 3km² in extent, this lake lies on the Mambi River 20km east of the main road between Lindi and Mikindani. It's a pretty spot, primarily of interest for its prolific pelicans and other waterbirds. To reach the lake, head northwest from Mikindani along the surfaced Lindi road for about 25km to Mpapura. Shortly after passing through Mpapura, take a turn-off to your left, and follow it for about 20km to Kitere village on the lakeshore. A limited amount of public transport runs to Kitere from Mpapura, but there is no accommodation.

Lake Chidya This remote 10km² lake lies on the Mozambique border about 40km inland of the Rovuma River mouth. It supports large numbers of crocodile, hippo and waterfowl, and elephants are quite frequently seen in the area. Access is from the small town of Kitaya, site of a memorial dedicated to the crew of a Tanzanian plane shot down during a conflict with Mozambican guerrillas in the 1970s. To get there, follow the Newala road out of Mtwara for about 35km to Nanguruwe, then turn left and drive for another two hours to Kitaya, where you can hire a local boat to take you 5km downstream to the lake.

Newala This isolated, friendly town lies inland of Mtwara on the Makonde Plateau, home to East Africa's most renowned craftsmen, the Makonde carvers. The main attractions here are the unexpectedly bracing climate – a refreshing contrast to the sticky coast – and the legendary Shimu ya Mungu viewpoint, which looks over a vast sheer escarpment to the Rovuma Valley and the mountains beyond (it's opposite the secondary school about 200m north of Plateau Lodge). More ambitiously, you could cycle to the Rovuma River as a day trip (bikes can easily be hired so long as you leave a deposit) following the central road downhill through town. The most distinguished building here is the old German Boma, which is now a prison and closed to casual visitors.

Direct buses leave for Newala from the main bus stand in Mtwara every 30 minutes or so throughout the day, and take about four to five hours. There is also plenty of transport on to Masasi, which is connected by a tar road to Lindi and Mtwara. As for accommodation, two places stand out. The first choice, about 500m along the road to Masasi, is the **Country Lodge** (☏ 023 241 0355) which has comfortable en-suite rooms with net, fan and TV for Tsh25,000/30,000 single/double and a great *makuti* restaurant/bar serving grills, stews and seafood in the Tsh5,000–7,000 range. The cheaper **Plateau Lodge**, between Shimu ya

Mungu and the old German Boma, has comfortable en-suite rooms in the Tsh8,000–12,00 range.

OVERLAND FROM MTWARA TO THE SOUTHERN HIGHLANDS

One of the most rugged, remote and little-used routes in Tanzania connects the south coast to the southern highlands and Lake Nyasa region via the towns of Masasi, Tunduru and Songea. You'd want at least two days to cover this route in a private vehicle, and should bank on three or four using public transport. Travel conditions are highly variable: an excellent surfaced road and numerous buses connects Lindi and Mtwara to Masasi, but things deteriorate quickly after that, both in terms of road surfaces and regularity and quality of public transport. Accommodation tends to be rather basic throughout.

MASASI Situated at the base of the Makonde Plateau, Masasi was founded as a Universities Mission to Central Africa (UMCA) refuge for freed slaves in 1875. Best known today as the birthplace of former president Benjamin Mkapa, it has since grown to be a rather bustling and prosperous small town, though its coastal nickname *Kama Ulaya* ('Like Europe') flatters to deceive. Sprawling untidily along one long main strip of asphalt, it is surrounded by a striking cluster of granite outcrops that tower to an elevation of 951m above the plains. If you want to explore these hills or nearly Makonde Plateau with a guide, talk to the Masasi Association of Geography and Antiquity office (\ *023 251 0267*) close to the Holiday Motel.

Practicalities The surfaced 125km road that connects Masasi to Mnazi Moja on the main Lindi–Mtwara route is in good condition, and regular buses cover it in around three hours coming from Lindi or five hours from Mtwara. Masasi has more than its fair share of indifferent local guesthouses. The Holiday Motel (\ *023 251 0108*) diagonally opposite the bus station is as good as any, charging Tsh8,000 for an en-suite double with net, fan and TV; or you could try the nearby and somewhat smarter Masasi Inn (\ *023 251 0055*), which has en-suite rooms with AC, net, hot water and TV for Tsh30,000 and a decent restaurant serving Indian and continental dishes for Tsh4,000–8,000. There are plenty of local eateries to choose from.

TUNDURU About 200km west of Masasi, Tunduru can be reached either by the daily bus (departs 09.00 and takes around eight hours) or 4x4 *dala-dala*, with the latter being faster and more reliable, especially after rain. It's a rough sandy road through a thinly inhabited area, but at most villages you find hawkers selling water, chicken, cashew nuts etc. An old mining town, Tunduru enjoyed some notoriety in the late 1980s, when almost 50 people were killed by man-eating lions before they were shot.

Practicalities There are a few basic accommodation options, of which Naweka and Yakati guesthouses are worth a try.

Travel-wise, the 273km road from Tunduru to Songea is more of the same, serviced by one daily bus (seven to nine hours, departing 06.00; book in advance) and a few slightly faster 4x4 dala-dalas. The trip passes through many uninhabited areas, though some refreshments are available *en route* at Namtumbo.

SONGEA Songea is a route focus of sorts, sitting at the three-way junction of the dirt road from Tunduru, a surfaced road to Makambako (on the Tanzam Highway between Iringa and Mbeya) and a rougher road down the Rift Valley escarpment to Mbamba Bay on Lake Nyasa. The town's busy market and general state of good repair reflect its status as the fastest growing town in Tanzania and an important centre of gemstone trade (sapphires and rubies are both found here). Of historical

MAKONDE CARVINGS

The Makonde are widely considered the finest sculptors in East Africa. Oral tradition suggests that the males of this matrilineal society have been carving to woo their women for 300 years, when the first person on earth, not yet male or female, sculpted a piece of wood into the shape of a human figure. The carver left his creation outside his home before he retired for the night, and awoke to find it had been transformed into a living woman. Twice the woman conceived, but both times the child died after three days. Each time, the pair moved higher on to the plateau, believing this would bring them luck. The third child lived, and became the first true Makonde. The mother is considered the spiritual ancestor of all the Makonde, and the legend is sometimes said to be a parable for the difficulty of creation and the necessity to discard unsatisfactory carvings.

In their purest form, the intricate, stylised carvings of the Makonde relate to this ancestral cult of womanhood, and are carried only by men, as a good-luck charm. Traditional carvings almost always depict a female figure, sometimes surrounded by children, and the style was practically unknown outside of Tanzania until a carving workshop was established at Mwenge in suburban Dar es Salaam during the 1950s. Subsequently, like any dynamic art form, Makonde sculpture has been responsive to external influences and subject to changes in fashion, with new styles becoming increasingly abstract and incorporating wider moral and social themes.

The most rustic of the new styles is the Binadamu sculpture, which depicts traditional scenes such as old men smoking pipes or women fetching water in a relatively naturalistic manner. Altogether more eerie and evocative is the Shetani style, in which grotesquely stylised human forms, sometimes with animal-like features, represent the impish and sometimes evil spirits for which the style is named. Many Makonde and other East Africans leave offerings for Shetani sculptures, believing them to be possessed by ancestral spirits. Most elaborate of all are the naturalistic Ujamaa sculptures, which depict many interlocking figures and relate to the collective social policy of Ujamaa fostered by the late President Nyerere. Also known as People Poles or Trees of Life, these statues sometimes incorporate several generations of the carver's family, rising in circular tiers to be up to 2m high. A newer style called Mawingu – the Swahili word for clouds – combines human figures with abstract shapes to represent intellectual or philosophical themes. Today, the finest examples of the genre fetch thousands of US dollars from international collectors

The Makonde traditionally shape their creations exclusively from *Dalbergia melanoxylon*, a hardwood tree known locally as *mpingo* and in English as African Blackwood or (misleadingly) African Ebony. The carver – always male – will first saw a block of wood to the required size, then create a rough outline by hacking away excess wood with an adze. The carving is all done freehand, with hammers, chisels and rasps used to carve the fine detail, before the final sculpture is sanded and brushed for smoothness. A large Ujamaa sculpture can take several months to complete, with some of the carving – appropriately – being undertaken communally. Traditionally, the craft was more or less hereditary, with sons being apprenticed by their fathers from a young age, and different families tending to work specific subjects related to their own traditions.

18

THE NGONI

The Ngoni of Songea are an offshoot of the Nguni of South Africa. Originally known as the Ndwandwe, the proto-Ngoni, led by Chief Zwangendaba, crossed the Limpopo in the early 1820s to flee the warmongering associated with the creation of the Zulu Kingdom by the iconic King Shaka. The Ndwandwe, inspired by the military innovations and militancy that had served Shaka so well, cut a bloody swathe through present-day Zimbabwe, Mozambique, Zambia and Malawi, raiding local communities for cattle, crops and women until the plundered resources were depleted, before pushing on to Ufipa, to the east of Lake Tanganyika, in 1845.

Zwangendaba died in 1848, leading to a heated secession battle that split the Ngoni into several factions. As a result, a large splinter group led by the former royal advisor Chief Mbonani fled in the direction of Lake Nyasa and settled there for several years. In the 1860s, the Ngoni expanded coastward, launching merciless attacks on smaller tribes who were then co-opted into the kingdom under the local leadership of trusted generals – the most famous of whom, incidentally, was Songea, whose camp lay about 2km from the modern town that bears his name.

The Ngoni Empire peaked in influence during the 1880s, when it controlled most of the interior between the coast and Lake Nyasa. It had by this time forged a strong trade relationship with the Arab merchants of Kilwa and Mikindani; indeed it was brutal Ngoni slave raids that provided most of the human booty sold at these coastal ports. The indigenous tribes of the region – or at least those who had survived the slave raids – were fully integrated into the Ngoni Kingdom, and comprised the bulk of the royal army. Nevertheless, a rigid social distinction existed between 'true' Ngoni descendants of the Ndwandwe, and newer recruits, with all leadership roles reserved exclusively for the former.

In 1897, the Germans established a military base at Gumbiro, 70km north of modern-day Songea. The Ngoni offered little initial resistance to the colonists, hoping to forge a similar trade relationship to the one they had enjoyed with the Arab merchants. However, Germany rapidly demonstrated that it would support only those Ngoni chiefs and generals who subordinated themselves to the colonial authorities. In September 1905, spurred by news of the Maji Maji Rebellion elsewhere in the territory, King Chabruma launched an unsuccessful attack on the Gumbiro garrison and razed the Benedictine Mission at Maposeni. Following this, the Ngoni army was soundly defeated by the Germans in a bloody battle.

Not content with this decisive victory, the Germans launched a series of arbitrary punitive raids, razing crops, destroying homes and executing villagers at whim. Chabruma fled, to die in exile in Mozambique. Other chiefs and military leaders were hanged by the Germans, robbing the Ngoni of legitimate leadership from grassroots up. By the end of the decade, the Ngoni Kingdom, born of violence only 50 years earlier, was essentially an entity of the past – destroyed by a similarly ruthless but better armed conquering power.

interest is the Maji Maji Museum and Monument (⊕ *08.00–16.00 Mon–Fri*) next to the tree where the German colonisers hanged several Ngoni chiefs involved in the Maji Maji rebellion in 1907.

Practicalities For those with private transport, the best place to stay is the White House Hotel (☏ *025 260 0892*), which lies 2km out of town along the Njombe Road, charges around Tsh15,000 for an en-suite double, and serves reasonable food. More central budget options include the Africa House Executive Lodge (☏ *025 260 2921*) and Yulander Holiday Lodge.

The uncomplicated onward option from Songea is the 300km surfaced road to Makambako, which takes three to four hours in a private vehicle, and a bit longer by bus (services include a daily Scandinavia Coach on to Dar es Salaam). The main urban punctuation along this road is **Njombe**, a quiet highland town with a surprisingly chaotic bus station and several overnight options including the pleasant Chani and Milimani motels, both with en-suite rooms, and the more basic Lutheran Centre Hostel. Alternatively, at **Makambako**, the junction town on the Tanzam Highway, the unexpectedly good Uplands Hotel (↘ *025 273 0201*) and Jay Jay Highlands Hotel (↘ *026 273 0475; www.jayjay.highlandshotel.4t.com*), both charge around Tsh15,000 for an en-suite double with hot water.

The more adventurous gateway out of Songea is the Lake Nyasa port of **Mbamba Bay**, a small port of clay-brick, thatched houses set on a pretty coconut-lined beach whose western orientation offers good sunsets. Mbamba Bay is connected to Itungi Port (near Kyela) on the western lakeshore by a thrice-weekly domestic ferry link. A rough but spectacular 170km road leads down the Rift Valley escarpment from Songea to Mbamba Bay via **Mbinga**. There are buses as far as Mbinga, but the last 65km between here and Mbamba Bay are covered by 4x4 *dala-dalas* only, and can be hair-raisingly slippery. The pick of the hotels in Mbamba Bay are the laboriously named Neema Beach Guest Garden Hotel Bar and Pharmacy and more succinct Nyasa View Lodge, both of which charge around Tsh10,000 for a double and have bar/restaurants.

18

Appendix I

LANGUAGE

SWAHILI Swahili, the official language of Tanzania, is a Bantu language which developed on the East African coast about 1,000 years ago and has since adopted several words from Arabic, Portuguese, Indian, German and English. It spread into the Tanzanian interior along with the 19th-century slave caravans and is now the *lingua franca* in Tanzania and Kenya, and is also spoken in parts of Uganda, Malawi, Rwanda, Burundi, Congo, Zambia and Mozambique.

Even if you are sticking to tourist areas, it is polite and can be useful to know a bit of Swahili. In Dar es Salaam, Zanzibar, Arusha, Moshi and the northern game reserves, you can get by with English well enough. If you travel in other parts of the country, you will need to understand some Swahili.

There are numerous Swahili–English dictionaries on the market, as well as phrasebooks and grammars. A useful dictionary for travellers is Daba Malaika's *Friendly Modern Swahili–English Dictionary* (MSO Training Centre for Development Co-operation, PO Box 254, Arusha, second edition 1994; ISBN 8770 28742 2), which costs around US$25. Better still, though probably too heavyweight for most travellers, is the *TUKI English–Swahili Dictionary* (University of Dar es Salaam, 1996; ISBN 9976 91129 7), which costs around US$16. Peter Wilson's *Simplified Swahili* (Longman) used to be regarded as the best book for teaching yourself Swahili, but it has probably been superseded by Joan Russell's *Teach Yourself Swahili* (Hodder and Stoughton, 1996; ISBN 0340 62094 3), which comes complete with a cassette and costs around US$15. Of the phrasebooks, Lonely Planet's and Rough Guides' *Swahili* are both good. It is best to buy a Swahili book before you arrive in Tanzania as they are difficult to get hold of once you are there.

For short-stay visitors, all these books have practical limitations. Wading through a phrasebook to find the expression you want can take ages, while trying to piece together a sentence from a dictionary is virtually impossible. In addition, most books available are in Kenyan Swahili, which often differs greatly from the purer version spoken in Tanzania.

The following introduction is not a substitute for a dictionary or phrasebook. It is not so much an introduction to Swahili as an introduction to communicating with Swahili-speakers. Before researching this guide, my East African travels had mainly been in Kenya, Uganda and parts of Tanzania where English is relatively widely spoken. We learnt the hard way how little English is spoken in most of Tanzania. I hope this section will help anyone in a similar position to get around a great deal more easily than we did at first.

Pronunciation Vowel sounds are pronounced as follows:

a   like the a in *father*
e   like the e in *wet*
i   like the ee in *free*, but less drawn-out
o   somewhere between the o in *no* and the word *awe*
u   similar to the oo in *food*

The double vowel in words like *choo* or *saa* is pronounced like the single vowel, but drawn out for longer. Consonants are in general pronounced as they are in English. *L* and *r* are often interchangeable, so that *Kalema* is just as often spelt or pronounced *Karema*. The same is true of *b* and *v*.

You will be better understood if you speak slowly and thus avoid the common English-speaking habit of clipping vowel sounds – listen to how Swahili-speakers pronounce their vowels. In most Swahili words there is a slight emphasis on the second-last syllable.

Basic grammar Swahili is a simple language in so far as most words are built from a root word using prefixes. To go into all of the prefixes here would probably confuse people new to Swahili – and it would certainly stretch my knowledge of the language. They are covered in depth in most Swahili grammars and dictionaries. The following are some of the most important:

Pronouns

ni	me	*wa*	they
u	you	*a*	he or she
tu	us		

Tenses

na	present
ta	future
li	past
ku	infinitive

Tenses (negative)

si	present
sita	future
siku	past
haku	negative, infinitive

From a root word such as *taka* (want) you might build the following phrases:

Unataka soda	You want a soda
Tutataka soda	We will want a soda
Alitaka soda	He/she wanted a soda

In practice, *ni* and *tu* are often dropped from simple statements. It would be more normal to say *nataka soda* than *ninataka soda*.

In many situations there is no interrogative mode in Swahili; the difference between a question and a statement lies in the intonation.

Greetings There are several common greetings in Swahili. Although allowances are made for tourists, it is rude to start talking to someone without first using one or another formal greeting. The first greeting you will hear is *Jambo*. This is reserved for tourists, and a perfectly adequate greeting, but it is never used between Tanzanians (the more correct *Hujambo*, to which the reply is *Sijambo*, is used in some areas).

The most widely used greeting is *Habari?*, which more or less means *What news?*. The normal reply is *Nzuri* (good). *Habari* is rarely used by Tanzanians on its own; you might well be asked *Habari ya safari?*, *Habari yako?* or *Habari gani?* (very loosely, *How is your journey?*, *How are you?* and *How are things?* respectively). *Nzuri* is the polite reply to any such request.

A more fashionable greeting among younger people is *Mambo*, especially on the coast and in large towns. Few tourists recognise this greeting; reply *Safi* or *Poa* and you've made a friend.

In Tanzanian society it is polite to greet elders with the expression *Shikamu*. To the best of my knowledge this means *I hold your feet*. In many parts of rural Tanzania, children will greet you in this way, often with their heads bowed and so quietly it sounds like *Sh..oo*. Don't misinterpret this by European standards (or other parts of Africa where *Mzungu give me shilling* is the phrase most likely to be offered up by children); most Tanzanian children are far too polite to swear at you. The polite answer is *Marahaba* (I'm delighted).

Another word often used in greeting is *Salama*, which means peace. When you enter a shop or hotel reception, you will often be greeted by a friendly *Karibu*, which means *Welcome*. *Asante sana* (thank you very much) seems an appropriate response.

If you want to enter someone's house, shout *Hodi!*. It basically means *Can I come in?* but would be used in the same situation as *Anyone home?* would in English. The normal response will be *Karibu* or *Hodi*.

It is respectful to address an old man as *Mzee*. *Bwana*, which means *Mister*, might be used as a polite form of address to a male who is equal or senior to you in age or rank, but who is not a *Mzee*. Older women can be addressed as *Mama*.

The following phrases will come in handy for small talk:

Where have you just come from?	*(U)natoka wapi?*
I have come from Moshi	*(Ni)natoka Moshi*
Where are you going?	*(U)nakwenda wapi?*
We are going to Arusha	*(Tu)nakwenda Arusha*
What is your name?	*Jina lako nani?*
My name is Philip	*Jina langu ni Philip*
Do you speak English?	*Unasema KiIngereze?*
I speak a little Swahili	*Ninasema KiSwahili kidigo*
Sleep peacefully	*Lala salama*
Bye for now	*Kwaheri sasa*
Have a safe journey	*Safari njema*
Come again (welcome again)	*Karibu tena*
I don't understand	*Sielewi*
Say that again	*Sema tena*

Numbers

1	*moja*	30	*thelathini*
2	*mbili*	40	*arobaini*
3	*tatu*	50	*hamsini*
4	*nne*	60	*sitini*
5	*tano*	70	*sabini*
6	*sita*	80	*themanini*
7	*saba*	90	*tisini*
8	*nane*	100	*mia (moja)*
9	*tisa*	150	*mia moja na hamsini*
10	*kumi*	155	*mia moja hamsini na tano*
11	*kumi na moja*	200	*mia mbili*
20	*ishirini*	1,000	*elfu (moja)* or *mia kumi*

Swahili time Many travellers to Tanzania fail to come to grips with Swahili time. It is essential to be aware of it, especially if you are catching buses in remote areas. The Swahili clock starts at the equivalent of 06.00, so that *saa moja asubuhi* (hour one in the morning) is 07.00; *saa mbili jioni* (hour two in the evening) is 20.00 etc. To ask the time in Swahili, say *Saa ngapi?*

Always check whether times are standard or Swahili. If you are told a bus leaves at nine, ask whether the person means *saa tatu* or *saa tisa*. Some English-speakers will convert to standard time, others won't. This does not apply so much where people are used to tourists, but it's advisable to get in the habit of checking.

Day-to-day queries The following covers such activities as shopping, finding a room etc. It's worth remembering most Swahili words for modern objects, or things for which there would not have been a pre-colonial word, are often similar to the English. Examples are *resiti* (receipt), *gari* (car), *polisi* (police), *posta* (post office) and – my favourite – *stesheni masta* (station master). In desperation, it's always worth trying the English word with an *ee* sound on the end.

Shopping The normal way of asking for something is *Ipo* or *Zipo?*, which roughly means *Is there?*, so if you want a cold drink you would ask *Soda baridi zipo?* The response will normally be *Ipo* or *Kuna* (there is) or *Hamna* or *Hakuna* (there isn't). Once you've established that the shop has what you want, you might say *Nataka koka mbili* (I want two Cokes). To check the price, ask *Shillingi ngape?* It may be simpler to ask for a brand name: *Omo* (washing powder) or *Blue Band* (margarine), for instance.

Accommodation The Swahili for guesthouse is *nyumba ya wageni*. In my experience *gesti* works as well, if not better. If you are looking for something a bit more upmarket, bear in mind *hoteli* means restaurant. We found self-contained (*self-contendi*) to be a good key-word in communicating this need. To find out whether there is a vacant room, ask *Nafasi zipo?*

Getting around The following expressions are useful for getting around:

Where is there a guesthouse?	*Ipo wapi gesti?*
Is there a bus to Moshi?	*Ipo basi kwenda Moshi?*
When does the bus depart?	*Basi itaondoka saa ngapi?*
When will the vehicle arrive?	*Gari litafika saa ngapi?*
How far is it?	*Bale gani?*
I want to pay now	*Ninataka kulipa sasa*

Foodstuffs

avocado	*parachichi*	food	*chakula*
bananas	*ndizi*	fruit(s)	*(ma)tunda*
bananas (cooked)	*matoke/batoke*	goat	*(nyama ya) mbuzi*
beef	*(Nyama ya) ngombe*	mango(es)	*(ma)embe*
bread (loaf)	*mkate*	maize porridge	
bread (slice)	*tosti*	(thin, eaten at	
coconuts	*nazi*	breakfast)	*uji*
coffee	*kahawa*	maize porridge	
chicken	*kuku*	(thick, eaten as	
egg(s)	*(ma)yai*	staple with	
fish	*samaki*	relish)	*ugali*
meat	*nyama*	rice	*pilau*
milk	*maziwa*	salt	*chumvi*
onions	*vitungu*	sauce	*mchuzi/supu*
orange(s)	*(ma)chungwa*	sugar	*sukari*
pawpaw	*papai*	tea	*chai*
pineapple	*nanasi*	(black/milky)	*(ya rangi/maziwa)*
potatoes	*viazi*	vegetable	*mboga*
rice (cooked plain)	*wali*	water	*maji*
rice (uncooked)	*mchele*		

Days of the week

Monday	*Jumatatu*	Friday	*Ijumaa*
Tuesday	*Jumanne*	Saturday	*Jumamosi*
Wednesday	*Jumatano*	Sunday	*Jumapili*
Thursday	*Alhamisi*		

Family

family	*familia*	granddad	*babu*
father	*baba*	grandmother	*bibi*
mother	*mama*	brother	*kaka*
sister	*dada*	fiancée	*mchumba*
uncle	*mjomba*	child	*mtoto*
aunt	*shangazi*	kids	*watoto*
cousin	*binamu*	parents	*wazazi*
friend (s)	*rafiki (zungu)*	grandchildren	*wujukuu*

Livestock

cat	*paka*	duck	*bata*
chicken	*kuku*	goat	*mbuzi*
cow	*ng'ombe*	rabbit	*sungura*
dog	*mbwa*	sheep	*kondoo*

Health

flu	*mafua*	recover	*pona*
fever	*homa*	treatment	*tiba*
malaria	*malaria*	cure	*ponyesha*
cough	*kikohozi*	injection	*sindano*
vomit	*kutapika*	bone	*mfupa*
swollen	*uvimbe*	death	*mauti*
injure	*jeruha*	to examine	*vipimo*
weak	*dhaifu*	to fall down	*kuanguka*
pain	*maumizu*	to bleed	*kutokwa na damu*

Other useful words and phrases

afternoon	*alasiri*	me	*mimi*
again	*tena*	money	*pesa/shillingi*
and	*na*	more	*ingine/tena*
ask (I am	*omba (ninaomba …)*	morning	*asubuhi*
asking for …)		nearby	*karibu/mbal kidogoe*
big	*kubwa*	night	*usiku*
boat	*meli*	no	*hapana*
bus	*basi*	no problem	*hakuna matata*
car (or any		now	*sasa*
vehicle)	*gari*	only	*tu*
cold	*baridi*	OK or fine	*sawa*
come here	*njo*	passenger	*abiria*
excuse me	*samahanio*	pay	*kulipa*
European(s)	*mzungu (wazungu)*	please	*tafadhali*
evening	*jioni*	person (people)	*mtu (watu)*
far away	*mbale kubwa*	road/street	*barabara/mtaa*
friend	*rafiki*	shop	*duka*
good (very good)	*mzuri (mzuri sana)*	sleep	*kulala*
goodbye	*kwaheri*	slowly	*polepole*
here	*hapa*	small	*kidogo*
hot	*moto*	soon	*bado kidogo*
later	*bado*	sorry	*polepole*
like	*penda*	station	*stesheni*
(I would like...)	*(ninapenda...)*	stop	*simama*
many	*sana*	straight or direct	*moja kwa moja*

thank you	*asante*	toilet	*choo*
very much	*(sana)*	tomorrow	*kesho*
there is	*iko/kuna*	want (I want...)	*taka (ninataka...)*
there is not	*hamna/hakuna*	where	*(iko) wapi*
thief (thieves)	*mwizi (wawizi)*	yes	*ndiyo*
time	*saa*	yesterday	*jana*
today	*leo*	you	*wewe*

Useful prepositions include *ya* (of) and *kwa* (to or by). Many expressions are created using these; for instance *stesheni ya basi* is a bus station and *barabara kwa Mbale* is the road to Mbale.

MAA *Emma Thomson*

Maa is the language of the Maasai. It does not exist in written form, so the spellings below are approximate.

Greetings

Father/Elderly man, I greet you	*Papa ... supai*
Warrior/middle-aged man, I greet you	*Apaayia ... supai*
Young woman, I greet you	*Siangiki ... supai*
Boy, I greet you	*Ero ... supai*
Girl, I greet you	*Nairo ... supai*
Mother/ middle-aged woman, I greet you	*Yeyio ... takwenya*
Grandmother/elder woman	*Koko ... takwenya*
How are you?	*Koree indae?*
Are you fine/healthy?	*Kira sedan/kira biot?*
My name is ...	*Aji ...*
What is your name?	*Kekijaa enkarna?*
I come from ...	*Aingwaa ...*
Where do you come from?	*Kaingwaa?*
Goodbye	*Serae*

Numbers

1	*nabo*	13	*tomon ok ooni*
2	*are*	14	*tomon o ongwan*
3	*ooni*	15	*tomon o imiet*
4	*ongwan*	16	*tomon o ille*
5	*imiet*	17	*tomon o opishana*
6	*ille*	18	*tomon o isiet*
7	*naapishana*	19	*tomon o odo*
8	*isiet*	20	*tikitam*
9	*naudo*	100	*iip nabo*
10	*tomon*	1,000	*enchata nabo*
11	*tomon o obo*	2,000	*inkeek are*
12	*tomon o are*	3,000	*inkeek ooni*

Shopping

How much does it cost?	*Empesai aja?*
I want/need it	*Ayieu*
I don't want/need it today	*Mayieu taata*
I will buy this one	*Ainyang ena*
I will buy these	*Ainyang kuna*
I won't buy anything today	*Mainyang onyo taata*
I haven't got any money	*Maata empesai*

EATING THE NEWS

Emma Thomson

In the same way that it is rude not to greet a Tanzanian with the standard *HuJambo* or *Mambo*, no Maasai will encounter another without going through the amusing paces of a ritual known as 'eating the news'. It is basically a quick catch-up on the health of the family, state of the livestock, etc. The aim is to race through these formalities as fast as possible so you can continue with the rest of the conversation. Bizarrely, even if you are on your deathbed, you must reply that all is well to maintain the front of warrior strength integral to Maasai psychology. Give it a go and they will be bowled over!

Man:	*Yeyio...*	Mother...
Woman:	*Eeu...*	Yes...
Man:	*Takwenya!*	I greet you!
Woman:	*Iko! Apaayia...*	Hello! Warrior...
Man:	*Ooe...*	Yes...
Woman:	*Supai!*	I greet you!
Man:	*Epa!*	Hello!
Woman:	*Ayia, koree indae?*	Ok, how are you?
Man:	*Kitii...*	We are around...
Woman:	*Ee*	Uh-huh
Man:	*Kira sedan*	We are fine
Woman:	*Ee*	Uh-huh
Man:	*Kira biot*	We are healthy
Woman:	*Ee*	Uh-huh
Man:	*Supat inkera*	The children are well
Woman:	*Ee*	Uh-huh
Man:	*Biot inkishu*	The cattle are healthy
Woman:	*Ee*	Uh-huh
Man:	*Metii endoki torono*	There are no problems
Woman:	*Ayia*	OK
Woman:	*Kira siyook...*	As for us...
Man:	*Ee*	Uh-huh
Woman:	*Mekimweyaa*	We are not sick
Man:	*Ee*	Uh-huh
Woman:	*Biot inkera*	The children are healthy
Man:	*Ee*	Uh-huh
Woman:	*Supat indare*	The goats are well
Man:	*Ee*	Uh-huh
Woman:	*Ayia*	OK
Man:	*Ayia, enda serian*	OK, that's good news

Useful words and phrases

Thank you	*Ashe*
Thank you very much	*Ashe naleng*
Take it (used when giving a gift)	*Ngo*
I receive it (used when accepting a gift)	*Au*
Leave me/it alone (to children)	*Tapala*
Go outside (to children)	*Shomo boo*
Expression of sympathy (like 'pole' in Swahili)	*Kwa adei*
May I take a picture?	*Aosh empicha?*
Yes	*Ee*

OK	*Ayia*
No, I don't want you to	*A-a, mayieu*
Stop it	*Tapala*

AFRICAN ENGLISH Although many Tanzanians speak a little English, not all speak it fluently. Africans who speak English tend to structure their sentences in a similar way to how they would in their own language: they speak English with Bantu grammar.

For a traveller, knowing how to communicate in African English is just as important as speaking a bit of Swahili, if not more so. It is noticeable that travellers who speak English as a second language often communicate with Africans more easily than first-language English-speakers.

The following ground rules should prove useful when you speak English to Africans:

- *Unasema KiEngereze?* (Do you speak English?). This small but important question may seem obvious. It isn't.
- Greet in Swahili then ask in English. It is advisable to go through the Swahili greetings (even *Jambo* will do) before you plough ahead and ask a question. First, it is rude to do otherwise; second, most Westerners feel uncomfortable asking a stranger a straight question. If you have already greeted the person, you'll feel less need to preface a question with phrases like 'I'm terribly sorry' and 'Would you mind telling me' which will confuse someone who speaks limited English.
- Speak slowly and clearly. There is no need, as some travellers do, to speak as if you are talking to a three year old, just speak naturally.
- Phrase questions simply and with Swahili inflections. 'This bus goes to Dodoma?' is better than 'Could you tell me whether this bus is going to Dodoma?'; 'You have a room?' is better than 'Is there a vacant room?' If you are not understood, don't keep repeating the same question; find a different way of phrasing it.
- Listen to how people talk to you, and not only for their inflections. Some English words are in wide use; others are not. For instance, 'lodging' is more likely to be understood than 'accommodation'.
- Make sure the person you are talking to understands you. Try to avoid asking questions that can be answered with a yes or no. People may well agree with you simply to be polite.
- Keep calm. No-one is at their best when they arrive at a crowded bus station after an all-day bus ride; it is easy to be short tempered when someone cannot understand you. Be patient and polite; it's you who don't speak the language.

Appendix 2

GLOSSARY

Acacia woodland	type of woodland dominated by thorny, thin-leafed trees of the genus *Acacia*
banda	a hut, often used to refer to hutted accommodation at hotels and lodges
boma	traditional enclosure or homestead; administration building of the colonial era
bui-bui	black cloth worn veil-like by women, mainly in Islamic parts of the coast
Brachystegia woodland	type of woodland dominated by broad-leaved trees of the genus *Brachystegia*
Chama Cha Mapinduzi (CCM)	ruling party of Tanzania since independence
cichlid	family of colourful fish found in the Rift Valley lakes
closed-canopy forest	true forest in which the trees have an interlocking canopy
dala-dala	light vehicle, especially minibus, serving as public transport
dhow	traditional wooden seafaring vessel
duka	kiosk
endemic	unique to a specific country or biome
exotic	not indigenous, for instance plantation trees such as pines and eucalyptus
forex bureau	bureau de change
fly camping	temporary private camp set up remotely from a permanent lodge
guesthouse	cheap local hotel
hoteli	local restaurant
indigenous	naturally occurring
kanga	colourful printed cloth worn by most Tanzanian women
kitenge (pl *vitenge*)	similar to kanga
koppie (or *kopje*)	Afrikaans word used to refer to a small hill such as those on the Serengeti
mandazi	deep fried doughball, essentially the local variant on a doughnut
miombo	synonym for Brachystegia woodland
mishkaki	meat (usually beef) kebab
mzungu (pl *wazungu*)	white person
ngoma	Swahili dance
Omani era	period when the coast was ruled by the Sultan of Oman, especially 19th century
self-contained room	room with en-suite shower and toilet
savannah	grassland studded with trees
Shirazi era	medieval period during which settlers from Shiraz dominated coastal trade

taarab	Swahili music and dance form associated particularly with Zanzibar
TANAPA	Tanzania National Parks
ugali	stodgy porridge like staple made with ground maize meal
wazungu	white people
woodland	area of trees lacking a closed canopy

Appendix 3

FURTHER INFORMATION

HISTORY AND BIOGRAPHY

A limited number of single-volume histories covering East Africa and/or Tanzania are in print, but most are rather textbook-like in tone, and I've yet to come across one that is likely to hold much appeal for the casual reader. About the best bet is Iliffe's *Modern History of Tanganyika* (Cambridge, 1979). For a more general perspective, Oliver and Fage's *Short History of Africa* (Penguin, sixth edition, 1988) is rated as providing the best concise overview of African history, but it's too curt, dry, wide-ranging and dated to make for a satisfying read.

If I were to recommend one historical volume to a visitor to Tanzania, it would have to be Richard Hall's *Empires of the Monsoon: A History of the Indian Ocean and its Invaders* (HarperCollins, 1996). This highly focused and reasonably concise book will convey a strong historical perspective to the general reader, as a result of the author's storytelling touch and his largely successful attempt to place the last 1,000 years of east and southern African history in an international framework.

Considerably more bulky, and working on an even broader canvas, John Reader's *Africa: A Biography of the Continent* (Penguin, 1997) has met with universal praise as perhaps the most readable and accurate attempt yet to capture the sweep of African history for the general reader.

Several books document specific periods and/or regions in African history. Good coverage of the coastal Swahili, who facilitated the medieval trade between the gold fields of Zimbabwe and the Arab world, is provided in J de Vere Allen's *Swahili Origins* (James Currey, 1992). Among the better popular works on the early era of European exploration are Hibbert's *Africa Explored: Europeans in the Dark Continent* (Penguin, 1982) and Alan Moorehead's peerless classics of the genre history-as-adventure-yarn, *The White Nile* and *The Blue Nile*, published in 1960 and 1962 respectively and available in Penguin paperback. An excellent biography pertaining to this era is Tim Jeal's *Livingstone* (Heinemann, 1973, recently reprinted). For an erudite, compelling and panoramic account of the decade that turned Africa on its head, Thomas Pakenham's gripping 600 page tome *The Scramble for Africa* was aptly described by one reviewer as '*Heart of Darkness* with the lights switched on'. For a glimpse into the colonial era itself, just about everybody who sets foot in East Africa ends up reading Karen Blixen's autobiographical *Out of Africa* (Penguin, 1937).

Freeman-Grenville G S P (ed) *The East African Coast: Selected Documents from the First to the Nineteenth Century* Oxford, Clarendon Press, 1962

Piggott, D W I *History of Mafia*, 1941. Good historical overview.

Walley, Chris *Chole History and Mafia in General* 1997. A report based on anthropological field study conducted on Chole Island between August 1994 and November 1996: a fascinating read to help understand the people of Mafia.

FIELD GUIDES AND NAURAL HISTORY

General *East African Wildlife* by Philip Briggs (Bradt, 2008) is a handy and lavishly illustrated one-stop handbook to the fauna of East Africa, with detailed sections on the region's main habitats, varied mammals, birds, reptiles and insects. It's the ideal companion for first time visitors whose interest in wildlife extends beyond the Big Five but who don't want to carry a library of reference books.

Mammals Dorst and Dandelot's *Field Guide to the Larger Mammals of Africa* (Collins) and Haltennorth's *Field Guide to the Mammals of Africa (including Madagascar)* (Collins) were the standard mammal field guides for years, but have been rendered obsolete by several newer and better books. The pick of these, especially if your interest extends to bats and other small mammals, is Jonathan Kingdon's *Field Guide to African Mammals* (Christopher Helm, 2003), which also contains a goldmine of information about the evolutionary relationships of modern species. The same author's *Pocket Guide to African Mammals* (Christopher Helm, 2004) is a more compact, inexpensive title that will meet the requirements of all but the most dedicated wildlife enthusiasts. Chris and Tilde Stuart's *Field Guide to the Larger Mammals of Africa* (Struik Publishers, 1997) is another good option for space-conscious travellers who are serious about putting a name to all the large mammals they see. For backpackers, the same authors' *Southern, Eastern and Central African Mammals: A Photographic Guide* (Struik Publishers, 1993) is far lighter and still gives adequate detail for 152 mammal species.

Not a field guide in the conventional sense so much as a guide to mammalian behaviour, Richard Estes' superb *The Safari Companion* (Green Books UK, Chelsea Green USA, Russell Friedman Books South Africa, 1992) is well organised and informative but rather bulky for casual safari-goers.

Birds Zimmerman, Turner, Pearson, Willet and Pratt's *Birds of Kenya and Northern Tanzania* (Christopher Helm, 1996) is a contender for the best single-volume field guide available to any African country or region. I would recommend it to any serious birder sticking to northern Tanzania, since it provides complete coverage for the northern safari circuit, the Usambara and Pare mountains and Pemba Island, and although it stops short of Dar es Salaam and Zanzibar, this wouldn't be a major limitation. The gaps in its coverage would, however, limit its usefulness south of Dar es Salaam or in the Lake Victoria and Lake Tanganyika regions. The original hardback edition is too bulky, heavy and expensive to be of interest to any but the most bird-obsessed of backpackers, but a condensed paperback version, also entitled *Birds of Kenya and Northern Tanzania* (Helm Field Guides, 2005) is now available.

For any birding itinerary extending to parts of Tanzania west of the Serengeti or south of the Usambara, the best option is the *Field Guide to the Birds of East Africa* by Williamson and Fanshawe. Published by Christopher Helm in early 2002, this field guide provides comprehensive coverage for the whole of Tanzania, as well as Kenya, Rwanda and Burundi, with accurate plates, good distribution maps and adequately detailed text descriptions.

Ber Van Perlo's *Illustrated Checklist to the Birds of Eastern Africa* (Collins, 1995) is a useful, relatively inexpensive and admirably compact identification manual describing and illustrating all 1,488 bird species recorded in Eritrea, Ethiopia, Kenya, Uganda and Tanzania. Unfortunately, however, the distribution maps and colour plates are often misleading, and the compact format means that descriptions are too terse and pictures too massed up to allow identification of more difficult genera. It is, however, far more useful than John Williams's pioneering but now obsolete *Field Guide to the Birds of East Africa*, also published by Collins and still referred to in many brochures and guides.

Birdwatchers whose African travels are likely to extend beyond the area covered by the above books are pointed to Ian Sinclair and Peter Ryan's superb *Birds of Africa South of the Sahara* (Struik Publishers, 2003). The first complete field guide to this vast region, it covers all 2,100-plus species recorded in sub-Saharan Africa in a remarkably compact 700-odd pages, with accurate illustrations supported by reliable text and good distribution maps.

Other field guides The past few years have seen the publication of a spate of high-quality field guides to other more specialised aspects of East Africa's fauna and flora. Among the more interesting of these titles are Najma Dharani's *Field Guide to Common Trees and Shrubs of East Africa* (Struik, 2002) and a simply magnificent *Field Guide to the Reptiles of East Africa* by Stephen Spawls, Kim Howell, Robert Drewes and James Ashe (A & C Black, 2004). Alan Channing and Kim Howell's *Amphibians of East Africa* (Comstock Books in Herpetology, 2006) is also highly worthwhile. Matt Richmond and Irene Kamau's East African Marine Ecoregion (Worldwide Fund for Nature USA, 2005) examines the whole of the East African coast.

Wildlife studies Those with an interest in ape behaviour would do well to read Jane Goodall's books about chimpanzee behaviour, *In the Shadow of Man* (Collins, 1971) and *Through a Window* (Weidenfeld & Nicolson, 1990), based on her acclaimed research in Tanzania's Gombe Stream National Park. Also available is Nishida's *Chimpanzees of Mahale* (University of Tokyo, 1990), based on the similarly long-standing research project in Mahale Mountains National Park. A more visually attractive alternative is the coffee-table book *Mahale: A Photographic Encounter with Chimpanzees*, by Angelika Hofer, Michael Huffman and Gunter Ziesler (Sterling Publishing, New York, 2000).

Bernhard Grzimek's renowned book *Serengeti Shall Not Die* (Collins, 1959) remains a classic evocation of the magic of the Serengeti, and its original publication was instrumental in making this reserve better known to the outside world. Ian Douglas-Hamilton's *Amongst the Elephants* (Penguin, 1978) did much the same for publicising Lake Manyara National Park, though the vast herds of elephants it describes have since been greatly reduced by poaching.

National parks A series of excellent booklets was published in the early 1990s in association with TANAPA, covering most of the national parks in Tanzania. These are widely available in Arusha, and will cost US$5 at a reputable bookshop and considerably more when bought from a street vendor. The African Publishing House has recently published another similar series of glossier booklets, also in association with TANAPA and also widely available within Tanzania.

TRAVEL GUIDES Bradt also publishes Philip Briggs's *Northern Tanzania: The Bradt Safari Guide*, aimed at those who want to explore the northern safari circuit in more depth, while *Zanzibar, Pemba & Mafia: The Bradt Travel Guide* by Chris and Susan McIntyre is the most useful book for those visiting the islands in isolation. Travellers with limited mobility may also be interested in Bradt's *Access Africa: Safaris for People with Limited Mobility* by Gordon Rattray. For people combining a visit to Tanzania with one or other of its neighbours, there are also detailed Bradt guides available to Kenya, Ethiopia, Uganda, Zambia, Congo, Mozambique, Malawi and Rwanda.

COFFEE-TABLE BOOKS The best book of this sort to cover Tanzania as a whole is Paul Joynson-Hicks's *Tanzania: Portrait of a Nation* (Quiller Press, 2001), which contains some great down-to-earth cultural photography and lively anecdotal captions. Also recommended is *Journey through Tanzania*, photographed by the late Mohamid Amin and Duncan Willets and published by Camerapix in Kenya. Both of the above books are stronger on cultural, landmark and scenic photography than on wildlife photography, for which M Iwago's superb *Serengeti* (Thames and Hudson, 1987) has few peers. Also worth a look is John Reader's definitive *Kilimanjaro* (Elm Tree Books, 1982). Javed Jafferji's atmospheric photographs are highlighted in *Images of Zanzibar*, while *Zanzibar – Romance of the Ages* makes extensive use of archive photographs dating to before the turn of the century. Both were published by HSP Publications in 1996, and are readily available on the island. For more wide-ranging pictorial coverage of Africa, look no further than the comprehensive *Africa: Continent of Contrasts*, with text by Philip Briggs and photography by Martin Harvey and Ariadne Van Zandbergen (Struik Publishers, 2005).

TRAVEL MAGAZINES The TTB produces a quarterly magazine called *Tantravel*, which normally includes a few gushing but interesting articles as well as plenty of ads, and can normally be picked up at Air Tanzania and tourist board offices. Far better is the quarterly magazine *Kakakuona: African Wildlife*, which is produced by the Tanzania Wildlife Protection Fund, and frequently includes several good articles about conservation in Tanzania (e *kakakuona@africaonline.co.tz*).

For readers with a broad interest in Africa, an excellent magazine dedicated to tourism throughout Africa is *Travel Africa*, which can be visited online at www.travelafricamag.com. Recommended for their broad-ranging editorial content and the coffee-table standard photography and reproduction, the award-winning magazines *Africa Geographic* (formerly *Africa Environment and Wildlife* and *Africa Birds and Birding*) can be checked out at the website www.africa-geographic.co.za. Another South African magazine devoted to African travel is *Getaway*, though this tends to devote the bulk of its coverage to southern Africa.

HEALTH Self-prescribing has its hazards so if you are going anywhere very remote consider taking a health book. For adults there is *Bugs, Bites & Bowels: The Cadogan Guide to Healthy Travel* by Jane Wilson-Howarth (2006); if travelling with the family look at *Your Child Abroad: A Travel Health Guide* by Dr Jane Wilson-Howarth and Dr Matthew Ellis, published by Bradt Travel Guides in 2005.

MAPS A number of road maps covering Tanzania are available, the best of which is the very accurate 1:1,400,000 *Tanzania Travel Map* published in 2004 by Harms Verlag (*www.harms-ic-verlag.de*). For most tourists, the map of Tanzania produced by the TTB and given away free at their offices in Arusha or Dar will be adequate.

A series of excellent maps by Giovanni Tombazzi covers most of the northern reserves, as well as Kilimanjaro, Mount Meru and Zanzibar. Colourful, lively and accurate, these maps are widely available throughout northern Tanzania, or they can be ordered directly from the co-publisher Hoopoe Adventure Tours (for contact details, see *Safari operators*, pages 128–9).

Town plans and 1:50,000 maps covering most parts of the country can be bought from the Department of Lands and Surveys map sales office on Kivukoni Front in Dar es Salaam.

FICTION Surprisingly few novels have been written by Tanzanians or about Tanzania, though it's worth trying to locate English translations of Swahili poets such as *The Poetry of Shabaan Robert* (translated by Clement Ndulute and published by the Dar es Salaam University Press). An excellent novel set in World War I Tanzania is William Boyd's *An Ice cream War*, while the same author's *Brazzaville Beach*, though not overtly set in Tanzania, devotes attention to aspects of chimpanzee behaviour first noted at Gombe Stream.

A Tanzanian of Asian extraction now living in Canada, M G Vassanji, is the author of at least one novel set in Tanzania and the Kenyan border area, the prize-winning *Book of Secrets* (Macmillan, 1994). This is an atmospheric tale, with much interesting period detail, revolving around a diary written by a British administrator in pre-war Kenya and discovered in a flat in Dar es Salaam in the 1980s. Vassanji is also the author of *Uhuru Street*, a collection of short stories set in Dar es Salaam.

WEBSITES The following offer information on Tanzania and Zanzibar:

www.ntz.info
www.intotanzania.com
www.allaboutzanzibar.com
www.africatravelresources.com

Adventure in Selous

Imagine...

we give you a car, a driver/guide

and a tent,

the Selous is yours!

And it REALLY is affordable.

Bradt Travel Guides

www.bradtguides.com

Africa

Africa Overland	£15.99
Algeria	£15.99
Benin	£14.99
Botswana: Okavango, Chobe, Northern Kalahari	£15.99
Burkina Faso	£14.99
Cameroon	£15.99
Cape Verde Islands	£14.99
Congo	£15.99
Eritrea	£15.99
Ethiopia	£15.99
Gambia, The	£13.99
Ghana	£15.99
Johannesburg	£6.99
Madagascar	£15.99
Malawi	£13.99
Mali	£13.95
Mauritius, Rodrigues & Réunion	£13.99
Mozambique	£13.99
Namibia	£15.99
Niger	£14.99
Nigeria	£17.99
North Africa: Roman Coast	£15.99
Rwanda	£14.99
São Tomé & Principe	£14.99
Seychelles	£14.99
Sierra Leone	£16.99
Sudan	£13.95
Tanzania, Northern	£13.99
Tanzania	£16.99
Uganda	£15.99
Zambia	£17.99
Zanzibar	£14.99

Britain and Europe

Albania	£15.99
Armenia, Nagorno Karabagh	£14.99
Azores	£13.99
Baltic Cities	£14.99
Belarus	£14.99
Belgrade	£6.99
Bosnia & Herzegovina	£13.99
Bratislava	£9.99
Budapest	£9.99
Bulgaria	£13.99
Cork	£6.99
Croatia	£13.99
Cyprus see North Cyprus	
Czech Republic	£13.99
Dresden	£7.99
Dubrovnik	£6.99

Estonia	£13.99
Faroe Islands	£15.99
Georgia	£14.99
Helsinki	£7.99
Hungary	£14.99
Iceland	£14.99
Kosovo	£14.99
Lapland	£13.99
Latvia	£13.99
Lille	£6.99
Lithuania	£14.99
Ljubljana	£7.99
Luxembourg	£13.99
Macedonia	£14.99
Montenegro	£14.99
North Cyprus	£12.99
Paris, Lille & Brussels	£11.95
Riga	£6.99
Serbia	£14.99
Slovakia	£14.99
Slovenia	£13.99
Spitsbergen	£14.99
Switzerland Without a Car	£14.99
Tallinn	£6.99
Transylvania	£14.99
Ukraine	£14.99
Vilnius	£6.99
Zagreb	£6.99

Middle East, Asia and Australasia

China: Yunnan Province	£13.99
Great Wall of China	£13.99
Iran	£14.99
Iraq: Then & Now	£15.99
Israel	£15.99
Kazakhstan	£15.99
Kyrgyzstan	£15.99
Maldives	£15.99
Mongolia	£16.99
North Korea	£14.99
Oman	£13.99
Shangri-La: A Travel Guide to the Himalayan Dream	£14.99
Sri Lanka	£15.99
Syria	£14.99
Tibet	£13.99
Turkmenistan	£14.99
Yemen	£14.99

The Americas and the Caribbean

Amazon, The	£14.99
Argentina	£15.99

Bolivia	£14.99
Cayman Islands	£14.99
Chile	£16.95
Colombia	£16.99
Costa Rica	£13.99
Dominica	£14.99
Falkland Islands	£13.95
Grenada, Carriacou & Petite Martinique	£14.99
Guyana	£14.99
Panama	£13.95
Peru & Bolivia: The Bradt Trekking Guide	£12.95
St Helena	£14.99
Turks & Caicos Islands	£14.99
USA by Rail	£14.99

Wildlife

100 Animals to See Before They Die	£16.99
Antarctica: Guide to the Wildlife	£15.99
Arctic: Guide to the Wildlife	£15.99
Central & Eastern European Wildlife	£15.99
Chinese Wildlife	£16.99
East African Wildlife	£19.99
Galápagos Wildlife	£15.99
Madagascar Wildlife	£16.99
New Zealand Wildlife	£14.99
North Atlantic Wildlife	£16.99
Peruvian Wildlife	£15.99
Southern African Wildlife	£18.95
Sri Lankan Wildlife	£15.99
Wildlife and Conservation Volunteering: The Complete Guide	£13.99

Eccentric Guides

Eccentric Australia	£12.99
Eccentric Britain	£13.99
Eccentric California	£13.99
Eccentric Cambridge	£6.99
Eccentric Edinburgh	£5.95
Eccentric France	£12.95
Eccentric London	£13.99

Others

Your Child Abroad: A Travel Health Guide	£10.95
Something Different for the Weekend	£9.99
Britain from the Rails	£17.99

WIN £100 CASH!
READER QUESTIONNAIRE

**Send in your completed questionnaire for the chance to win
£100 cash in our regular draw**

All respondents may order a Bradt guide at half the UK retail price – please
complete the order form overleaf.
(Entries may be posted or faxed to us, or scanned and emailed.)

We are interested in getting feedback from our readers to help us plan future Bradt
guides. Please answer ALL the questions below and return the form to us in order
to qualify for an entry in our regular draw.

Have you used any other Bradt guides? If so, which titles? . . . .

. . . .

What other publishers' travel guides do you use regularly? . . . .

. . . .

Where did you buy this guidebook? . . . .

What was the main purpose of your trip to Tanzania (or for what other reason did
you read our guide)? eg: holiday/business/charity etc. . . . .

. . . .

What other destinations would you like to see covered by a Bradt guide?

. . . .

Would you like to receive our catalogue/newsletters?

YES / NO (If yes, please complete details on reverse)

If yes – by post or email? . . . .

Age (circle relevant category) 16–25   26–45   46–60   60+

Male/Female (delete as appropriate)

Home country . . . .

Please send us any comments about our guide to Tanzania or other Bradt Travel
Guides. . . . .

. . . .

. . . .

. . . .

Bradt Travel Guides
23 High Street, Chalfont St Peter, Bucks SL9 9QE, UK
+44 (0)1753 893444 f +44 (0)1753 892333
e info@bradtguides.com
www.bradtguides.com

CLAIM YOUR HALF-PRICE BRADT GUIDE!

Order Form

To order your half-price copy of a Bradt guide, and to enter our prize draw to win £100 (see overleaf), please fill in the order form below, complete the questionnaire overleaf, and send it to Bradt Travel Guides by post, fax or email.

Please send me one copy of the following guide at half the UK retail price

Title		Retail price	Half price
...	....	....	....

Please send the following additional guides at full UK retail price

No	Title		Retail price	Total
...	....		....	....
...	....		....	....
...	....		....	....

Sub total ......
Post & packing ......
(£2 per book UK; £4 per book Europe; £6 per book rest of world)
Total ......

Name . . . .

Address. . . . .

Tel . . . .   Email . . . .

☐ I enclose a cheque for £. . . . . made payable to Bradt Travel Guides Ltd

☐ I would like to pay by credit card. Number: . . . .

    Expiry date: . . . / . . .   3-digit security code (on reverse of card) . . . . .

    Issue no (debit cards only) . . . . .

☐ Please add my name to your catalogue mailing list.

☐ I would be happy for you to use my name and comments in Bradt marketing material.

Send your order on this form, with the completed questionnaire, to:

Bradt Travel Guides TAN6
23 High Street, Chalfont St Peter, Bucks SL9 9QE
☎ +44 (0)1753 893444   f +44 (0)1753 892333
e info@bradtguides.com   www.bradtguides.com

NOTES

Index

Entries in **bold** indicate main entries, those in *italics* indicate maps